American Writers
Before 1800

AMERICAN WRITERS BEFORE 1800

A Biographical and Critical Dictionary

A–F

EDITED BY James A. Levernier AND Douglas R. Wilmes

GREENWOOD PRESS
WESTPORT, CONNECTICUT
LONDON, ENGLAND

Library of Congress Cataloging in Publication Data
Main entry under title:

American writers before 1800.

Bibliography: p.
Includes index.
1. American literature—Colonial period, ca. 1600-
1775—History and criticism. 2. American literature—
Revolutionary period, 1775-1783—History and criticism.
3. American literature—1783-1850—History and criticism.
4. American literature—Colonial period, ca. 1600-1775—
Bio-bibliography. 5. Authors, American—18th century—
Biography. 6. Authors, American—To 1700—Biography.
I. Levernier, James A. II. Wilmes, Douglas R.
PS185.A4   810′.9′001   82-933
ISBN 0-313-23476-0 (lib. bdg. : v. 1)   AACR2

Library of Congress Catalog Card Number: 82-933
ISBN 0-313-22229-0 (set)
          0-313-23476-0 (vol. 1)
          0-313-23477-9 (vol. 2)
          0-313-24096-5 (vol. 3)

First published in 1983

Greenwood Press
A division of Congressional Information Service, Inc.
88 Post Road West
Westport, Connecticut 06881

Printed in the United States of America

10 9 8 7 6 5 4 3 2 1

In Memory of
Theodore Hornberger

Contents

Preface

This book is designed to provide a convenient source of information about the lives and works of a large number (786) of early American writers. Each writer is discussed in an individual entry that includes primary and secondary bibliographical references, a brief biography, and a critical appraisal of the writer's works and significance. The entries are arranged alphabetically and are followed by appendixes (classifying the writers by date of birth, place of birth, and principal place of residence and presenting a chronology of important events from 1492 to 1800) and by a general index.

A noteworthy feature of this reference tool is its wide scope and broad principles of inclusion, enabling us to include entries on a variety of minor writers. Although we have also provided entries on the major writers of the period, which should prove useful and informative in their own right, we have recognized that treatments of authors such as William Bradford, Benjamin Franklin, Cotton Mather, and Edward Taylor are available in a variety of readily accessible reference formats. However, convenient accessibility of information does not prevail when one turns to the study of the many early American writers who are not well-known or highly valued in strictly literary terms but who are nevertheless worthy of our attention. As microform reproductions of practically all texts published in colonial and early national America are now available, the need for widely inclusive reference tools is all the more apparent. In an effort to meet this need, we have included entries on a large number of lesser-known writers, many of whom are discussed and evaluated here in some detail for the first time.

Students of early American culture will be aware of the vitality and scope of current scholarly interest in early American writing. It would be impossible to summarize briefly and fairly the development of this body of scholarship; a thorough survey would note the many biographies and works of criticism focusing on major writers, but it would also note the appearance of a number of anthologies and histories or interpretations founded in wide-ranging appreciations of the pluralism and multiplicity of early American writing. Works such as

The New England Mind by Perry Miller, the anthology of Puritan writing edited by Miller and Thomas H. Johnson, the anthologies of early American poetry edited by Harrison T. Meserole and Kenneth Silverman, the writings of Sacvan Bercovitch and Richard Beale Davis, and many other distinguished contributions have immeasurably broadened and deepened our knowledge of the substance and import of the lesser-known voices of early American culture.

In fact, our early literature has always—by its nature—demanded of its students an acquaintance with minor voices. In 1878, when Moses Coit Tyler wrote the preface to his pioneering literary history of the colonial period, he was careful to define his subject broadly, as inclusive of those "early authors whose writings, whether many or few, have any appreciable merit, or throw any helpful light upon the evolution of thought and of style in America, during those flourishing and indispensable days." The history of twentieth-century scholarship in early American studies has validated Tyler's approach, and this reference work is based upon a similar reluctance to define narrowly the matter of early American literature.

A reference tool's success is measured by its practical, utilitarian ability to perform the task for which it is designed. We have kept this principle firmly in mind when preparing these volumes, and it has informed two areas of our responsibility that merit particular explanation. These areas are the method by which we selected writers for inclusion and the format of the entries.

SELECTION OF ENTRIES

The writers included in *American Writers Before 1800* are not necessarily the 786 "best" writers of the period. We have not, in other words, selected writers by applying any original definition of literary quality. Such a methodology would have presupposed an ability to form a widely useful and acceptable objective definition of literary quality, which has important subjective components. Moreover, to apply such a definition to a project of this size would require encyclopedic knowledge, and the book would become in part an argument for the validity of the definition and for the accuracy of its application.

Therefore, the selection of writers for this volume was not based upon our individual and personal judgments of their merit. Rather, we have worked inductively from the evidence of a selection of anthologies, literary and cultural histories, and bibliographies of the period. In the first instance, writers have been included in these volumes by virtue of their appearance in secondary works likely to be read or used by scholars and students of early American literature. This array of writers—which we believe includes most writers of works with clearly significant literary merit—forms the backbone of the book. It has been expanded upon in two additional ways. First, in some areas we included some very minor figures in order to provide a representative coverage of certain subgenres, such as the Puritan elegy or early nature reportage. Second, we have sought the advice of experts in certain specialized fields, such as Quaker writing, German pietism, and black literature, to ascertain whether we had included significant and representative writers from those fields.

In examining the results of this process of selection, other scholars will undoubtedly discover sins of omission and commission. As a matter of individual judgment, one might wish for an entry on one writer at the expense of another. Stepping beyond the limits of this equation, we would regard the sin of omission as the more serious and the more to be regretted but also as an inevitable result of limitations of space and human fallibility. There are certainly many more early writers who deserve at least the kind of preliminary and limited discussion and evaluation that our format allows. On the other hand, we are not persuaded that we have included writers who are not worth even the brief discussion they have received in these volumes.

In every regard, our selection is founded upon a considered estimation of the practical uses to which this reference book may be put. We hope, for example, to have met the needs of readers of anthologies, histories, or critical analyses of early American literature who discover passing references to minor writers and want to obtain a sense of who those writers were and what they wrote. Our method of selection should ensure that these volumes will meet such needs in many cases. Furthermore, although the book has a literary bias, its scope is broad enough to accommodate the needs of many constituencies within the field of early American studies. Finally, practical considerations have led us to avoid any prescriptive limitation that might make the book less useful. We have not, for example, interpreted the meaning of "American writers" narrowly. The world of early America obviously had important transatlantic dimensions, and we have therefore included entries on a number of temporary residents or visitors to America who could not themselves be considered "American." In a few instances, we have included entries on writers who themselves never visited America but whose writings concern America and influenced, in some significant way, the development of an American literary heritage and cultural self-identity. In every case, we have asked whether or not the entry would benefit the student of early American culture; we have allowed no consideration to outweigh this central concern.

ENTRY FORMAT

In keeping with our intention to provide information on a variety of lesser-known writers, we have not scaled the length of the entries in proportion to the importance of the writer being discussed in a given entry. Although in some cases minor writers have received a relatively shorter treatment and major writers a relatively longer treatment, in general we have tried to maintain a fairly constant length. Thus a minor writer will often receive more attention than that writer might otherwise have gained, and a major writer less attention, on the principle that the reader may easily obtain further information and critical analyses of the major figures in early American literature. First references within each entry to other writers included in the book are indicated by cross-references (q.v.).

Each entry has been divided into four sections, which organize the content in a predictable and convenient manner:

Works: Each writer's major publications are listed in chronological order. Works are listed by short title, and each title is followed by the date of publication. Significant delays between composition and publication have been indicated when possible. Unpublished material is included where appropriate. In general, we have excluded writers whose work exists only in manuscript, but we have made a few exceptions to this rule where future publication of such material is expected. Although the focus of this book is not primarily bibliographical, we have attempted to ensure that these primary bibliographies are as complete and accurate as possible. In a very few instances, a complete listing of the writer's major publications has not been practicable; in these instances, the reader is directed to appropriate bibliographies or sources. Both American and European imprints are listed; in most cases, the titles will have been published in America, and texts may be obtained by using Charles Evans's *American Bibliography* or the *National Index of American Imprints Through 1800: The Short-Title Evans* (1969), by Clifford K. Shipton and James E. Mooney. Texts listed in these bibliographies may be read in microprint in the Early American Imprints Series. Further references to modern printings or reprintings are included in the "Works" or "Suggested Readings" sections of the entry as appropriate.

Biography: A brief summary of the salient features of the writer's life is included in the second section. In some instances, very little is known about the writer's biography, but in every instance, the entry provides an overview of the writer's life and social context within the limitations of present knowledge.

Critical Appraisal: The third section of the entry is devoted to a summary of the writer's work and a critical estimation of its value. Depending on the nature of the writing, the appraisal may place the writer's work into the context of intellectual, religious, social, or political history. This section of the entry is judgmental and offers opinions; however, an attempt has been made to present each writer in a positive light, without being misleadingly uncritical. Since a vast variety of writing is discussed in these volumes, the kinds of analyses made in the critical appraisals will necessarily vary. But in each case, the appraisal supplies a critical introduction to the writer and serves as a guide to further readings in the original texts.

Suggested Readings: The final section of each entry is devoted to a secondary bibliography. References to standard sources (such as the *Dictionary of American Biography* [DAB] and the *Dictionary of National Biography* [DNB]) are listed first in abbreviated form, followed by fuller references to other sources.

These suggested readings do not in any way pretend to be inclusive or exhaustive, and in the cases of major writers, they are highly selective. Their purpose is solely to direct the reader to sources that the authors of entries in these volumes found particularly useful or informative when they wrote their essays.

The entries in this book have been contributed by some 250 scholars of early American culture and literature. These volumes are thus a collective effort and do contain many voices and many points of view. The format has been designed to maintain a productive tension between the consistency of form required in a reference tool and the variety of content implicit in the individuality of the writers selected for inclusion and of the scholars who have interpreted and judged them.

James A. Levernier
Douglas R. Wilmes

Acknowledgments

In organizing and undertaking this project, we have incurred professional debts far too numerous to list in these acknowledgments. For their invaluable assistance in helping us review the entries to be included in these volumes and/or seek appropriate contributors, we are especially indebted to Ronald Bosco of the State University of New York at Albany; Hennig Cohen of the University of Pennsylvania; Michael Lofaro of the University of Tennessee; Pattie Cowell of Colorado State University; David S. Wilson of the University of California at Davis; Sacvan Bercovitch of Columbia University; Richard Beale Davis, late of the University of Tennessee; and Philip Barbour, late of the Early American Institute in Williamsburg, Virginia.

In addition, we wish to acknowledge a special debt of gratitude to the following individuals for their willingness to assume responsibilities well above and beyond the call of duty for entries that we requested them to research and write: Douglas M. Arnold of Yale University; Dorothy and Edmund Berkeley of Charlottesville, Virginia; Steven Kagle of Illinois State University; Daniel F. Littlefield, Jr., of Little Rock, Arkansas; Julian Mason of the University of North Carolina at Charlotte; David Minter of Emory University; Irving N. Rothman of the University of Houston; John Shields of Illinois State University; Frank Shuffelton of the University of Rochester; James Stephens of Marquette University; and Marion Barber Stowell of Milledgeville, Georgia.

We wish also to thank the editorial staff at Greenwood Press, particularly Cynthia Harris, Anne Kugielsky, Maureen Melino, Mildred Vasan, and James T. Sabin, for their strong commitment to this project, from its inception through to its publication, and for their patient and always helpful advice, commentary, and attention. In this capacity, we likewise wish to thank Mary DeVries for the painstaking attention she gave to copy-editing the completed manuscript. Our thanks also go to the many friends and colleagues, especially David Jauss, Mary De Jong, Frank Parks, Julian Wasserman, and Bruce Weigl, who gave us their tireless encouragement and support. To these individuals we owe an immeasurable debt; without their assistance and confidence we could not have completed this project.

In addition, we wish to thank the following institutions and their staffs for allowing us access to their resource materials and holdings: The Boston Public Library, The Newberry Library, and the libraries at Alliance College, Harvard University, Northwestern University, the Pennsylvania State University, Rice University, the University of Arkansas at Fayetteville, the University of Arkansas at Little Rock, the University of Connecticut, the University of Pennsylvania, Wesleyan University, Westminster College (New Wilmington, Pennsylvania), Yale University, and Youngstown State University. In this capacity, we wish to express particular gratitude to Shirley A. Snyder, librarian, and Eric R. Birdsall, associate director for academic affairs, both of the Pennsylvania State University, the Shenango Valley Campus.

Finally, we wish to thank the Donaghey Foundation and the faculty research committee at the University of Arkansas at Little Rock for a grant that helped defray expenses related to this project, and we wish to thank all of our contributors for their patience, cooperation, and support.

J.A.L. and D.R.W.

Abbreviations

STANDARD REFERENCE SOURCES

BDAS
: Clark A. Elliott, *Biographical Dictionary of American Science: The Seventeenth Through the Nineteenth Centuries* (Westport, Conn., 1979).

CCMC
: Frederick Lewis Weis, *The Colonial Churches and the Colonial Clergy of the Middle and Southern Colonies, 1607-1776* (Lancaster, Mass., 1938).

CCMDG
: Frederick Lewis Weis, *The Colonial Clergy of Maryland, Delaware and Georgia* (Lancaster, Mass., 1950).

CCNE
: Frederick Lewis Weis, *The Colonial Clergy and the Colonial Churches of New England* (Lancaster, Mass., 1936).

CCV
: Frederick Lewis Weis, *The Colonial Clergy of Virginia, North Carolina and South Carolina* (Boston, Mass., 1955).

DAB
: *Dictionary of American Biography*, ed. Allen Johnson and Dumas Malone, 20 vols. (New York, 1928-37; Seven Supplements, 1944-1965).

DARB
: Henry Warner Bowden, *Dictionary of American Religious Biography* (Westport, Conn., 1977).

Dexter
: Franklin Bowditch Dexter, *Biographical Sketches of the Graduates of Yale College*, 6 vols. (New York, 1885-1912).

DNB
: *The Dictionary of National Biography*, ed. Leslie Stephen and Sidney Lee, 21 vols. and 1 supplement (London, 1882-1900; Six Supplements, 1901-1950).

FCNEV
: Harold S. Jantz, *The First Century of New England Verse* (Worcester, Mass., 1944; 1962; 1974).

LHUS	*Literary History of the United States*, ed. Robert E. Spiller et al., 2 vols. (New York, 1948; 4th ed., 1974).
NAW	*Notable American Women, 1607-1950: A Biographical Dictionary*, ed. Edward T. James et al., 3 vols. (1971-1980).
P	*Princetonians: A Biographical Dictionary* (Vol. 1: *1748-1768*, ed. James McLachlan; Vol. 2: *1769-1775* and Vol. 3: *1776-1783*, ed. Richard A. Harrison, Princeton, N.J.).
Sibley-Shipton	John L. Sibley and Clifford K. Shipton, *Biographical Sketches of Those Who Attended Harvard College* (Vols. 1-3: 1642-1689, Boston, Mass., 1873; Vols. 4-17: 1690-1771, Boston, Mass., 1933-1975).
Sprague	*Annals of the American Pulpit*, ed. William B. Sprague, 9 vols. (New York, 1857-1869; 1969).
T_1	Moses Coit Tyler, *A History of American Literature During the Colonial Period, 1607-1765*, 2 vols. (New York, 1878; 1897; 1898).
T_2	Moses Coit Tyler, *The Literary History of the American Revolution, 1763-1783*, 2 vols. (New York, 1897).

JOURNALS AND PERIODICALS

AC	*American Collector*
AEST	*American Ethnological Society Transactions*
AGR	*American German Review*
AH	*American Heritage*
AHAAR	*American Historical Association Annual Report*
AHR	*American Historical Review*
AJHQ	*American Jewish Historical Quarterly*
AJP	*American Journal of Physics*
AL	*American Literature*
AM	*Atlantic Monthly*
AMH	*Annals of Medical History*
AmR	*American Review*
APSR	*American Political Science Review*
AQ	*American Quarterly*
AS	*American Speech*
ASJ	*Alchemical Society Journal*
BB	*Bulletin of Bibliography*
BC	*Baptist Courier*
BEM	*Blackwood's Edinburgh Magazine*
BFHA	*Bulletin of the Friends' Historical Association*
BHM	*Bulletin of the History of Medicine*
BHSP	*Bulletin of the Historical Society of Pennsylvania*

Biblioteca	*Biblioteca Sacra*
BJHH	*Bulletin of the Johns Hopkins Hospital*
BNYPL	*Bulletin of the New York Public Library*
Bookman	*The Bookman*
BPLQ	*Boston Public Library Quarterly*
BQ	*Baptist Quarterly*
BrHP	*Branch Historical Papers*
BRPR	*Biblical Repertory and Princeton Review*
BSMHC	*Bulletin of the Society of Medical History of Chicago*
BSP	*Bostonian Society Publications*
BSPNEA	*Bulletin of the Society for the Preservation of New England Antiquities*
CanHR	*Canadian Historical Review*
CanL	*Canadian Literature*
CGHS	*Collections of the Georgia Historical Society*
CH	*Church History*
CHer	*Choir Herald*
CHR	*Catholic Historical Review*
CHSB	*Connecticut Historical Society Bulletin*
CHSC	*Connecticut Historical Society Collections*
CJ	*Classical Journal*
CLAJ	*College Language Association Journal*
CM	*The Connecticut Magazine*
CMaineHS	*Collections of the Maine Historical Society*
CMHS	*Collections of the Massachusetts Historical Society*
CNHamHS	*Collections of the New Hampshire Historical Society*
CNYHS	*Collections of the New York Historical Society*
CR	*Church Review*
CRevAS	*Canadian Review of American Studies*
CS	*Christian Spectator*
CUQ	*Columbia University Quarterly*
DAI	*Dissertation Abstracts International*
DalR	*Dalhousie Review*
DBR	*De Bow's Review*
DedHR	*Dedham Historical Review*
DiaN	*Dialect Notes*
DN	*Delaware Notes*
EAL	*Early American Literature*
ECS	*Eighteenth-Century Studies*
EIHC	*Essex Institute Historical Collections*
EN	*Essex Naturalist*
ES	*Economic Studies*
ESQ	*Emerson Society Quarterly*
ESRS	*Emporia State Research Studies*

EUQ	*Emory University Quarterly*
GHQ	*Georgia Historical Quarterly*
GHR	*Georgia Historical Review*
HER	*Harvard Educational Review*
HGM	*Harvard Graduates' Magazine*
Historian	*The Historian*
HL	*Historica Linguistica*
HLB	*Harvard Library Bulletin*
HLQ	*Huntington Library Quarterly*
HM	*The Historical Magazine*
HMagPEC	*Historical Magazine of the Protestant Episcopal Church*
HTR	*Harvard Theological Review*
HTS	*Harvard Theological Studies*
HudR	*Hudson Review*
HumLov	*Humanistica Lovaniensia: Journal of Neo-Latin Studies* (Louvain, Belgium)
IHSP	*Ipswich Historical Society Publications*
IUS	*Indiana University Studies*
JA	*Jahrbuch für Ameríkastudien*
JAH	*Journal of American History*
JAmS	*Journal of American Studies*
JD	*Journal of Documentation*
JHI	*Journal of the History of Ideas*
JHS	*Johns Hopkins University Studies in History and Political Science*
JLH	*Journal of Library History*
JNH	*Journal of Negro History*
JPH	*Journal of Presbyterian History*
JPHS	*Journal of the Presbyterian Historical Society*
JQ	*Journalism Quarterly*
JR	*Journal of Religion*
JRUL	*Journal of the Rutgers University Library*
JSAH	*Journal of the Society of Architectural Historians*
JSBNH	*Journal of the Society for the Bibliography of Natural History*
JSCBHS	*Journal of the South Carolina Baptist Historical Society*
JSH	*Journal of Southern History*
JSR	*Jackson State Review* (Mississippi)
Judaism	*Judaism: A Quarterly Journal of Jewish Life and Thought*
LCR	*Lutheran Church Review*
MagA	*The Magazine of Art*
MagH	*Magazine of History*
MdHM	*Maryland Historical Magazine*
MH	*Methodist History*
MHSP	*Memoirs of the Historical Society of Pennsylvania*

MichH	*Michigan History*
MiH	*Minnesota History*
MLN	*Modern Language Notes*
MQ	*Mississippi Quarterly*
MR	*Massachusetts Review*
MusQ	*Musical Quarterly*
MVHR	*Mississippi Valley Historical Review*
Nation	*The Nation*
NCarF	*North Carolina Folklore*
NCF	*Nineteenth-Century Fiction*
NCHR	*North Carolina Historical Review*
NEG	*New England Galaxy*
NEHGR	*New England Historical and Genealogical Review*
NEM	*New England Magazine*
NEQ	*New England Quarterly*
NHB	*Negro History Bulletin*
NHR	*Narragansett Historical Review*
NJHSC	*New Jersey Historical Society Collections*
NJHSP	*New Jersey Historical Society Proceedings*
N&Q	*Notes and Queries*
NYGBR	*New York Genealogical and Biographical Review*
NYH	*New York History*
NYHSQ	*New York Historical Society Quarterly*
NYTBR	*New York Times Book Review*
OC	*Open Court*
OCHSC	*Old Colony Historical Society Collections*
OHSQ	*Oregon Historical Society Quarterly*
OntHSPR	*Ontario Historical Society Papers and Records*
PAAS	*Proceedings of the American Antiquarian Society*
PAH	*Perspectives in American History*
PAHS	*Papers of the Albemarle Historical Society*
PAJHS	*Publications of the American Jewish Historical Society*
PAPS	*Proceedings of the American Philosophical Society*
PBosS	*Proceedings of the Bostonian Society*
PBSA	*Papers of the Bibliographical Society of America*
PCSM	*Publications of the Colonial Society of Massachusetts*
PennH	*Pennsylvania History*
Phaedrus	*Phaedrus: An International Journal of Children's Literature Research*
Phylon	*Phylon: The Atlanta University Review of Race and Culture*
PIHS	*Publications of the Ipswich Historical Society*
PM	*Presbyterian Magazine*
PMHB	*Pennsylvania Magazine of History and Biography*
PMHS	*Proceedings of the Massachusetts Historical Society*

PMichA	*Papers of the Michigan Academy of Sciences, Arts, and Letters*
PMLA	*PMLA: Publications of the Modern Language Association of America*
PMPJ	*Philadelphia Medical and Physical Journal*
PNHCHS	*Papers of the New Haven Colony Historical Society*
PNYHS	*Proceedings of the New York Historical Society*
PQ	*Philological Quarterly*
PRev	*Princeton Review*
PSR	*Political Science Review*
PULC	*Princeton University Library Chronicle*
PWASA	*Proceedings of the Wisconsin Academy of Sciences and Arts*
PWHS	*Proceedings of the Wesley Historical Society*
QH	*Quaker History*
QMIMS	*Quarterly Magazine of the International Musical Society*
QQ	*Queen's Quarterly*
RACHSP	*Records of the American Catholic Historical Society of Philadelphia*
RALS	*Resources for American Literary Study*
RIH	*Rhode Island History*
RIHSC	*Rhode Island Historical Society Collections*
RP	*Register of Pennsylvania*
RS	*Research Studies* (Pullman, Washington)
RSCHS	*Records of the Scottish Church History Society*
SAQ	*South Atlantic Quarterly*
SatR	*Saturday Review*
SB	*Studies in Bibliography: Papers of the Bibliographical Society of the University of Virginia*
SCBHSP	*South Central Baptist Historical Society Proceedings*
SCHM	*South Carolina Historical Magazine*
SChR	*Scottish Church Review*
SCLR	*South Carolina Law Review*
SCM	*South Carolina Magazine*
SCN	*Seventeenth-Century Notes*
SEJ	*Southern Economic Journal*
Serif	*The Serif* (Kent, Ohio)
SF	*Social Forces*
Signs	*Signs: Journal of Women in Culture and Society*
SLitI	*Studies in the Literary Imagination*
SLJ	*Southern Literary Journal*
SLL	*Studies in Language and Literature*
SoPR	*Southern Presbyterian Review*
SP	*Studies in Philology*
SRC	*Studies in Religion and Culture*
SS	*Scandinavian Studies*

SSS	*Studies in the Social Sciences*
TA	*Theatre Annual*
TAAS	*Transactions of the American Antiquarian Society*
TAPS	*Transactions of the American Philosophical Society*
TCSM	*Transactions of the Colonial Society of Massachusetts*
TennSL	*Tennessee Studies in Literature*
ThS	*Theatre Survey*
TMHS	*Transactions of the Moravian Historical Society*
TQHGM	*Tyler's Quarterly Historical and Genealogical Magazine*
TR	*Texas Review*
TRSC	*Transactions of the Royal Society of Canada*
UCC	*University of California Chronicles*
UMS	*University of Missouri Studies*
USCHM	*United States Catholic Historical Magazine*
VC	*Virginia Cavalcade*
VELM	*Virginia Evangelical and Literary Magazine*
VMHB	*Virginia Magazine of History and Biography*
VMM	*Virginia Medical Monthly*
WHQ	*Western Historical Quarterly*
WL	*Woodstock Letters*
WMH	*Wisconsin Magazine of History*
WMQ	*William and Mary Quarterly*
WPHM	*Western Pennsylvania Historical Magazine*
YR	*Yale Review*
YULG	*Yale University Library Gazette*

Biographical and
Critical Dictionary

JAMES ADAIR (c. 1709-c. 1783)

Works: *History of the American Indians* (1775).

Biography: Little is known about James Adair's life before or after his sojourn of thirty-five years among the southeastern Indians. He was born probably in Antrim County, Ire., was apparently well educated, and was living in S.C. by 1735. From then until 1744, he traded among the Catawbas and Cherokees; from 1744 to 1750, among the Chickasaws; from 1751 to 1759, among the Cherokees; and from 1761 to 1768, among the Chickasaws once more. During this time, he often went on the warpath with the Chickasaws against their Indian enemies and worked hard to thwart the designs of the French among the Indians and to keep the tribes aligned with the British. Meanwhile, he wrote his *History* and in 1769 went to N.Y. to seek from Sir William Johnson and others an endorsement and subscriptions for its publication. For some unknown reason, however, the work was not published until 1775. After 1769 Adair's movements are obscure. Whether he married is not established, but he is thought to have resettled in N.C. The exact year of his death is uncertain.

Critical Appraisal: Nearly one-half of Adair's *History* is devoted to establishing the theory that the American Indians descended from the Lost Tribe of Israel. Although the modern reader may grow tired of Adair's numerous comparisons between the Indians and the Hebrews, it should be remembered that during the eighteenth century, this theory was popular. Before Adair, the Spanish writers Garcia, Bartolomé de Las Casas, and Antonio Montesinos had advanced the theory as had the American colonial writers John Eliot (q.v.), Cotton Mather (q.v.), Roger Williams (q.v.), and William Penn (q.v.), and the English writer Thomas Thorowgood. After Adair, a number of writers embraced the theory, including Elias Boudinot and Edward King, the viscount of Kingsborough, who reprinted the first part of Adair's work in his *Antiquities of Mexico* (1848).

Despite the dearth of biographical information concerning Adair, his name appears in all of the major biographical dictionaries. He earned his place there by his work. The reader who looks beyond the overriding thesis of Adair's book will find much that is interesting and useful. In fact, Adair's work has outlived his theory because of the vast amounts of rich information concerning the culture of the southeastern tribes that he gave while trying to prove his theory. As a result, his work is a valuable source for modern ethnologists on matters such as language, dress, agriculture, social organization, warfare, and religion among those tribes. Historians, too, turn to Adair as a source on tribal rivalries, trader influence, and international intrigue on the frontier during the middle decades of the eighteenth century. Adair's temperament as a man of strong opinion lends vitality to the prose, which is liberally sprinkled with humor and sarcasm, especially in his treatment of certain Carolina officials, the French, and the Choctaws.

In general, the *History* was well received by Adair's contemporaries. It was among the works that Jonathan Carver (q.v.) plagiarized in his *Travels*, and nineteenth-century writers such as William Gilmore Simms were familiar with his work. The *History* was translated into German in 1782, and it has been reprinted several times in the twentieth century.

Suggested Readings: DAB; LHUS; T$_2$. *See also Appleton's Cyclopaedia of American Biography*, I, 10; John Thomas Lee, "James Adair's 'History of the American Indians,' " *The Nation*, Aug. 27, 1914; John Henry Logan, *A History of the Upper Country of South Carolina* (1859), pp. 345-371; Samuel Cole Williams, ed., Introduction, *Adair's History of the American Indians* rep. (1973).

Daniel F. Littlefield, Jr.
Little Rock, Arkansas

ABIGAIL ADAMS (1744-1818)

Works: *Letters of Mrs. Adams, the Wife of John Adams* (1840-1848); *Familiar Letters of John Adams and His Wife, Abigail Adams, During the Revolution* (1876); *New Letters of Abigail Adams, 1788-1801* (1947); *The Adams-Jefferson Letters* (1959); *Adams Family Correspondence* (1963-1973); *The Book of Abigail and John: Selected Letters of the Adams Family, 1762-1784* (1975).

Biography: Abigail (Smith) Adams was born on Nov. 22, 1744, the daughter of Elizabeth (Quincy) Smith and Rev. William Smith, minister of the Congregational Church at Weymouth, Mass. The family's social prominence was secured not only by the Rev. Smith's clerical position but also through Mrs. Smith's family, which traced its American origins to three exalted members among the first generation of Puritan ministers. Presumably because of her delicate health, Abigail never went to school. Her education came from access to family libraries and from her eager participation in the activities of the many branches of her family. A statement from one of her letters, written when she was an adult, expresses her lifelong indignation over the restrictions that denied her any formal learning: "Every assistance and advantage which can be procured is afforded to the Sons, whilst the daughters are wholly neglected in point of Literature."

On Oct. 25, 1764, Abigail Smith married John Adams (q.v.), a promising young lawyer. For the next ten years, they lived an ordinary life either on their farm at Braintree or in Boston, as Adams's law practice dictated. Because her husband was frequently absent from home while fulfilling his circuit duties, Abigail oversaw the upbringing of their daughter and three sons, as well as the management of their farm and business affairs.

In 1774 John Adams began his public service as a delegate to the First Continental Congress. For the next twenty-seven years, John and Abigail were frequently separated because of his succession of government appointments and election as the first vice-president and second president of the U.S. In his memoir, their grandson Charles Francis Adams summed up his grandmother's duties in her husband's absence by calling her "a farmer cultivating the land...; a merchant reporting prices...; a politician speculating upon the probabilities of peace or war; and a mother writing the most exalted sentiments."

During periods of her husband's service, Abigail and the family often traveled with him. They lived in Fr. in 1784 and then for three years in Eng. while John served as the colonies' first ambassador at the Court of St. James. Always eager for new experiences, Abigail relished her life abroad. She developed a particular fondness for Eng. despite the coolness of the British Court toward the emissaries from their former colony. From 1789 to 1801, during John's terms as vice-president and president, the Adamses followed the removals of the U.S. government from New York City to Philadelphia and then to Washington, D.C. Stimulated by the political atmosphere, Abigail followed events closely, fulfilling her own duties in ways supportive to her husband and the new nation. In 1801, when John retired from public service, he and Abigail settled once again on their farm at Braintree. Abigail Adams died on Oct. 28, 1818.

Critical Appraisal: In 1840, twenty-two years after Abigail Adams's death, her grandson Charles Francis Adams resolved to publish a collection of his grandmother's letters. Recognizing that America had collected an abundance of "materials for a history of action," he deplored the absence of materials for a history of "feeling." By this statement he meant "the private, familiar sentiments that run into the texture of the social system, without remark or the hope of observation." Noting that the sentiments of women, in particular, had been neglected, he focused on his grandmother's generation: "The heroism of the females of the Revolution has gone from memory with the generation that witnessed it, and nothing, absolutely nothing, remains upon the ear of the young of the present day, but the faint echo of an expiring general tradition."

Letters of Mrs. Adams, the Wife of John Adams remedies this deficiency. Between 1840 and 1848, four editions were published, all prepared by Charles Francis Adams. Each includes his introduction titled "A Memoir of Mrs. Adams." The 1st and 2nd editions (the 2nd published only six weeks after the 1st), contain 114 letters written between 1761 and 1814. The 3rd, published in 1841, has some new letters by Abigail and some letters by John Adams to his wife, which Charles Francis thought were necessary "to explain many allusions...which have heretofore appeared obscure, as well as to give completeness to a correspondence of the revolutionary period believed in some respects to be unique." Among other inclusions in this 3rd edition are 14 letters that Abigail wrote to Thomas Jefferson (q.v.) in 1804, which served to break the silence between Jefferson and her husband that was a consequence of their political differences. The 4th edition, published in 1848, is revised and enlarged, including an appendix of letters John Quincy Adams sent his son on the study of the Bible. The "Memoir" includes a section explaining the addition of still more letters to Jefferson and the relationship between Jefferson and the Adams family.

Abigail's letters reveal a woman devoted to husband, family, and country. They show that she possessed all of the appropriate womanly virtues for her time and yet had a strongly independent nature. Indicative of this fact is a passage from a letter to John that she wrote in Mar. 1776:

> And by the way in the new Code of Laws which I suppose it will be necessary for you to make I desire you would Remember the Ladies, and be more generous and favourable to them than your ancestors. Do not put such unlimited power into the hands of the Husbands. Remember all Men would be tyrants if they could. If particular care and attention is not paid to the Ladies we are determined to foment a Rebellion, and will not hold ourselves bound by any Laws in which we have no voice, or Representation.

When the documents drawn up by the Continental Congress did not show this "care and attention," she wrote to her husband: "I can not say that I think you very generous to the Ladies, for whilst you are proclaiming peace and good will to Men, Emancipating all Nations, you insist upon retaining an absolute power over Wives. But you must remember that Arbitrary power is like most other things which are very hard, very liable to be broken."

In 1876 Charles Francis Adams published the *Familiar Letters*, which contains 235 letters, some previously unpublished, that the couple wrote to each other during the Revolution. This collection quickly became a valuable source for historians, since it provided a uniquely personal view of the war period. *The Adams Family Correspondence* was sponsored by the Massachusetts Historical Society, which has custody of the family's personal and public papers. The editors exposed the extent to which Charles Francis Adams followed the taste of his day, leaving out passages he regarded as too intimate or revealing, such as those in which Abigail reported the progress of a pregnancy, discussed disease or business interests, and became frank in comments about acquaintances. He also revised spelling, grammar, and punctuation to meet the standards of his time. By removing archaisms and country idioms, he robbed the letters of much of their precision and personal flavor. *The Adams Family Correspondence* gives complete texts in their original form.

New Letters of Abigail Adams contains 141 previously unpublished letters that Abigail wrote to her sister Mary Cranch, most of them during the period of her husband's vice-presidency and presidency. Printed as she wrote them, they are significant for their candor, especially in reference to politics. Abigail said about herself: "My pen is always freer than my tongue. I have written many things to you that I suppose I never could have talked." *The Adams-Jefferson Letters* contains the complete correspondence between Jefferson and Abigail and between Jefferson and John. *The Book of Abigail and John* is a Bicentennial publication, intended to update Charles Francis Adams's centennial contribution of the *Familiar Letters*. It contains what the editors considered the best letters the couple exchanged from their courtship in 1762 to their reunion in Europe in 1784. Also included are some letters to other persons and some of John's diary and autobiographical material. Once again the editors' intention is to reveal much of the personal information, and hence the character of these two individuals, that Charles Francis Adams suppressed.

The correspondence of Abigail Adams constitutes an extremely valuable historical source, providing a rare, highly personal view of eighteenth-century colonial society, the Revolution, and the establishment of the new government. It also introduces a woman, extraordinary in her time, whose courage and strength sustained her and her husband during times of personal trial and historical significance.

Suggested Readings: DAB; NAW; T_2. *See also* Charles W. Akers, *Abigail Adams: An American Woman* (1980), Ralph Ketcham, "The Puritan Ethic in the Revolutionary Era: Abigail Adams and Thomas Jefferson" in *"Remember the Ladies": New Perspectives on Women in American History*, ed. Carol V. R. George (1975); Meade Minnigerode, *Some American Ladies: Seven Informal Biographies* (1926); Janet Whitney, *Abigail Adams* (1947).

Rosemary Whitaker
Myra Jo Moon
Colorado State University

AMOS ADAMS (1728-1775)

Works: *The Character of a Christian's Life* (1756); *The Expediency and Utility of War* (1759); *Songs of Victory* (1759); *A Sermon Preached at the Ordination of. . .Samuel Kingsbury* (1762); *A Sermon Preached at the Ordination of. . .John Wyeth* (1766); *The Only Hope and Refuge of Sinners* (1767); *The Pleasures Peculiar to the Ministerial Life* (1768); *Religious Liberty* (1768); *A Concise, Historical View of New England* (1769); *Ministerial Affection* (1769).

Biography: Born in Medfield, Mass., on Sept. 1, 1728, Amos Adams was to become the seventh minister of the First Congregational Church of Roxbury. During his fifth year at Harvard, Adams accepted the call of the Roxbury parish and was ordained in 1753. In the same year, he married Elizabeth Prentice of Cambridge and took up residence in the Oliver Peabody (q.v.) house in Eliot Square. A prominent minister of New Eng., Adams was a trustee of the Bell

Endowment for the Roxbury Free School and a member of the Massachusetts Society for the Propagation of Christian Knowledge among the Indians of North America. In addition, he was active as an overseer of Harvard College and was a trustee of the famous Dudleian Lectures.

A liberal in matters of politics and religion, Adams used his influential position in Roxbury to impress his liberal views on the townspeople. He publicly opposed orthodoxy tests for ministers and championed the Tate and Brady Psalm Book over its more traditional New Eng. rival. Although Adams's egalitarian views rejected the Calvinistic belief in the "elect" on which the Whigs based their defense after the Stamp Act, he began, in 1767, a series of lectures and sermons, sympathetic to the Whigs, in which he reinterpreted the history of religious and political liberty in Eng. and the colonies to denounce former orthodox church and government leaders in Eng. and disclaim "all authority, in matters of worship." These declarations, together with others like them, helped flame the fires of the coming Revolution. Near the onset of the Revolution, Adams preached to companies of minutemen in Roxbury and Boston, and at the outbreak of hostilities, he served as chaplain to Col. David Brewer's Ninth Continental Regiment in Roxbury. He died in Dorchester on Oct. 5, 1775, and was buried in the Roxbury Parish tomb.

Critical Appraisal: The writings of Amos Adams epitomize the thought and role of the Congregational Church in Mass. at the time of the American Revolution. Stressing the importance, for all men, of spiritual and religious liberty, they call for independence on the part of Americans from the Church of England as a prerequisite for the freedom gained through a personal acceptance of Christ. Hence they contributed to the growing body of eighteenth-century American literature on the subject of independence.

Like many documents of the time, the sermons and discourses of Adams wed reason with a faith in traditional Calvinism. For Adams, the role of the preacher was less to interpret scripture than to present it in a way that was clearly understandable. Well read in both secular and ecclesiastical literature, Adams, like Jonathan Edwards (q.v.), used the writings of Enlightenment thinkers like John Locke to reinforce a belief in the supremacy of faith over reason. According to Adams, "Neither law of nature... nor yet all the boasted improvements of reason and philosophy" give the understanding derived from Christ. This reason, typical of much eighteenth-century New Eng. pulpit rhetoric and characteristic of Adams's writing generally, prepares the audience for an exhortation designed to "prick the consciences of sinners." For purposes of rhetorical effect, Adams fused vivid images of the fate of the "unblessed" with the calmer, less emotional, language of reason. He also used temporal images familiar to his congregation, and he frequently employed rhetorical devices of interrogation, exclamation, and extended parallelism for maximum rhetorical effect. As a result, the sinner hearing a sermon by Adams found himself cleverly condemned to "weeping and wailing and gnashing of teeth" in a "fire that shall never be quenched."

Because Adams saw the forms and conventions of ecclesiastic orthodoxy as barriers dividing the individual from his faith, liberation from the dictates of a centralized church body is the subject of two of his most significant works. In *Religious Liberty*, Adams traced the history of the reform movement in the Church of England from the time of Wycliffe, using the events of history to emphasize that Christ is "the sole head, king, and lawgiver" in any church and to denounce all forms of idolatry, councils, and systems to select ministers outside the congregation. In *A Concise, Historical View of New England*, Adams traced the history of the struggle for liberty from the first pilgrims who underwent "perils and hardships" in the name of freedom to more recent struggles for independence on the American shores. Anticipating later theories of Manifest Destiny, the sermon also acknowledged the mercy of God and the "intervention of divine providence" as a means of explaining the successful growth of the colonies. Praised by his contemporaries for writing some of "the best publications produced in North America" and for his refusal to relinquish personal liberty to "the dread of an ecclesiastical power, armed with state authority," Amos Adams provided a link worth noting in the chain of events that joined the American clergy and the patriots of 1776.

Suggested Readings: CCNE; Sibley-Shipton (XIII, 178-186); T$_2$. *See also* Gaius Glenn Atkins and Frederick L. Fagley, *History of American Congregationalism* (1942), pp. 1-132; Walter E. Thwing, *History of the First Church in Roxbury, Massachusetts, 1630-1904* (1908), pp. 175-177.

William B. Pettit
University of Houston

ELIPHALET ADAMS (1677-1753)

Works: *A Discourse Putting Christians in Mind to Be Ready to Every Good Work* (1706); *The Necessity of Judgment* (1710); *A Discourse Occasioned by the Late Distressing Storm (1717)*; *Eminently Good and Useful Men* (1720); *A Sermon Preached at Windham* (1721); *A Funeral Discourse* (1724); *The Works of Ministers* (1725); *Ministers Must Take Heed* (1726); *A Brief Discourse* (1727); *The Gracious Presence* (1730); *A Discourse Delivered at Colchester* (1734); *A Discourse Shewing* (1734); *God Sometimes Answers* (1735); *A Sermon Preached on Katherine Garrett* (1738); *A Short Discourse* (1749); *Two Funeral Discourses* (1749).

Biography: Eliphalet Adams was born in Dedham, Mass., on Mar. 26, 1677, into the family of the Rev. William (q.v.) and Mrs. Mary Manning Adams. Adams graduated from Harvard in 1694 and in the late 1690s was a missionary to the Pequot, Mohegan, and Niantic Indians. From 1701 to 1703, he assisted the Rev. Benjamin Colman (q.v.) at Boston's Brattle Street Church and in 1709 was ordained and succeeded Governor Gurdon Saltonstall (q.v.) at the New London church, where he became a leader in the Congregational Church and remained until 1752. From 1720 to 1738, Adams was a trustee of Yale College, and in 1723 he declined an offer of its rectorship. Throughout his career, he continued preaching to the Indians, and he often prepared young men for the ministry in his home.

The father of six children, Adams was twice married: to Lydia Pygan in 1709 and to Elizabeth Wass in 1751. He died in New London on Oct. 4, 1753.

Critical Appraisal: Any consideration of Eliphalet Adams must begin with the man and his learning, judgment, character, and moral qualities. Adams held a distinguished position among New Eng.'s Congregational clergy of the mideighteenth century. He served on numerous ecclesiastical councils, and other churches often turned to him for advice during times of crisis. Similarly, in 1723, a troubled year for Yale College, the trustees offered him its rectorship. Unsure whether to accept the position, he placed the question before a town meeting, and his fellow New Londoners refused to give him up. This incident suggests that the affection in which he was held in his own church was comparable to the high esteem in which he was held by his fellow clergymen.

During his prime, Adams's own church went through a "stormy period." The Baptists established their first society in New London; the New Lights were causing unrest; and an Anglican Church was created out of Adams's own congregation. But Adams, employing his strengths as a minister and, doubtless, the force of his character, led the New London church safely through the storm.

The Rev. John Barnard (q.v.) described Adams as a "man of excellent talents. . . and no inconsiderable degree of eminence as a preacher," whose "published sermons are characterized by vigorous thought, and direct, earnest, and often eloquent appeals." Adams's persuasive powers indeed seem to have been great, for despite a rigid method of building his sermons that included tediously stating his topics and subheads and repetitiously introducing paragraphs with the same phrase or clause, he was much sought after as a speaker at ordinations and funerals of other divines. In addition, Adams was chosen to deliver the funeral discourse of Governor Gurdon Saltonstall (whom Adams succeeded at New London), to preach at Windham upon an occasion of thanksgiving, to address societies of young men, and, on at least one occasion, to deliver the Election Day sermon before the General Assembly.

As a preacher and writer, Adams possessed an appealing, effective style. His verbal skills were considerable, and he was especially adept in using figures of speech:

> Unless our Sins are repented of and reformed, we may expect that they will bring upon us yet more temporal Evils. The Lord's Quiver is not yet Emptyed, nor his Arrows spent when he hath sent a few Judgments, though heavy ones[,] upon a Sinful people[.] He hath more and more terrible Ones in store for their Punishment and Destruction[,] and so they shall find before he hath done with them.

In fact, Adams was among the most earnest of preachers, continually exhorting laymen and clergymen alike to self-examination and diligence in their Christian lives. In 1710, long before the Great Awakening, he denounced religious zeal that "shroud[s] Unrighteousness and Uncharitable practices Underneath." In his election sermon, *The Necessity of Judgment*, he voiced concern about the future of the Americans, enjoining the General Assembly "to Intercede that this Vineyard of the Lord be not destroyed." In addressing a society of young men, he postulated that "the Ways of Young Persons need Cleansing, that they have already taken many wrong steps," reasoning that "All Persons are Polluted by Nature and altogether Born in Sin." In his sermon on the occasion of the execution of Katherine Garrett, an Indian servant who had murdered her illegitimate infant, he warned everyone to "take heed and beware of loose living," disobedience to one's parents, Sabbath-breaking, "misspence of precious Time, and such like Evils."

Lest it seem that Adams's view of humanity, and of God, be too bleak, however, it should be noted that everyone found him a loving man and that his sermons reveal a tender concern for the welfare of others—even Katherine Garrett —and his land. It was out of this concern, evidently, that at the conclusion of his daughter's funeral sermon, he abjured the mourners to "Live as those that stand upon the Borders of Eternity[.] Put not off a Preparation for Death from Day to Day."

Suggested Readings: CCNE; DAB; Sibley-Shipton (IV, 189-198); Sprague (I, 233-236). *See also* Francis M. Caulkins, *History of New London* (1852); W. H. Starr, *A Centennial Sketch of New London* (1876).

Joseph H. Harkey
Virginia Wesleyan College

HANNAH ADAMS (1755-1831)

Works: *An Alphabetical Compendium of the Various Sects* (1784), with rev. 2nd and 3rd eds. (1791 and 1801) published as *A View of Religions* and rev. 4th ed. (1817) titled *A Dictionary of All Religions; A Summary History of New-England* (1799); *An Abridgement of the History of New-England* (1801); *The Truth and Excellence of the Christian Religion* (1804); *The History of the Jews from the Destruction of Jerusalem to the Nineteenth Century* (1812); *A Narrative of the Controversy Between the Rev. Jedidiah Morse, D.D. and the Author* (1814); *A Concise Account of the London Society for Promoting Christianity Amongst the Jews* (1816); *Letters on the Gospels* (1824); *A Memoir of Miss Hannah Adams* (1832).

Biography: Hannah Adams was born and brought up in Medfield, Mass., without the advantages of money, connections, or formal schooling. Her father was an unsuccessful storekeeper and bookseller. Raised among books, she educated herself, beginning with novels, moving on to languages and, eventually, religious controversy. Her interest in the latter led her to assemble the first American dictionary of world religions, which she published, with much trouble and little profit, in 1784. Although plagued by poverty, poor health, and failing eyesight, she persevered as a compiler, popularizer, and writer of textbooks, becoming the first woman in America to make a living by her writing. Most of her books sold well, going through numerous printings, and her life was generally calm and uneventful. A ten-year dispute with Jedidiah Morse (q.v.), for instance, over the publication of one of her books was more than offset by a series of intellectual friendships with men such as Josiah Quincy (q.v.) and, most importantly, Joseph Buckminster. Hannah Adams died in 1831 and was the first person buried in the new garden cemetery at Mt. Auburn in Cambridge. Chester Harding's portrait of her in her later years, now hanging in the Boston Athenaeum, shows a scholarly woman, living from within, in quiet illusionless endurance.

Critical Appraisal: Hannah Adams's *Memoir* emphasizes her education and her career as a writer, concentrating heavily on the difficulties she faced in both. She is generous in her acknowledgment of help from friends and family, but her narrative is too general, too little detailed to be a fully effective piece of writing. Gently but firmly feminist, it is valuable as a testimony to the problems faced by a woman trying to make a place for herself as a literary professional during the early years of the Republic.

Her major works, *The History of the Jews*, the *History of New-England*, and the *Dictionary of Religions*, resulted from her finding no adequate general, unbiased account of a subject of major contemporaneous interest. Although on occasion she worked from original sources, the value of her work is less in its original scholarship than in her lucid and organized presentation of large and confusing subjects. Not only is her *History of the Jews* the first American general treatment of the subject, it is also notable for its strongly sympathetic viewpoint. Deeply impressed by "the singular phenomenon of a nation subsisting for ages without its civil and religious polity, and thus surviving its political existence," she cited a series of writers, including David Hartley, Joseph Priestley, and G. S. Faber, who "have written in defence to the restoration of the Jews to their native country."

The book variously titled *An Alphabetical Compendium, View of Religions*, and *A Dictionary of All Religions* is Hannah Adams's most important work. Disgusted with the partiality of Thomas Broughton's then standard *Historical Dictionary of Religions* (1742) and other such books "in giving the most unfavorable descriptions of the denominations they disliked, and applying to them the names of heretics, fanatics, enthusiasts, &," she struggled to produce a reference book on modern religions that would "avoid giving the least preference of any denomination above another." Although her work cannot, of course, be said to be wholly objective, she sought objectivity, and the four editions of the work are therefore of great interest as a reflection of the evolving religious situation in America between 1784 and 1817. The 1st edition, for example, gives Congregationalism nine lines, Shakers four pages, Presbyterians three-fourths of a page, Unitarians six lines, Universalists seven pages, and Calvinists four and a half pages. Appendixes deal briefly with "Pagans, Mahometans, Jews and Deists" and with "Religions of America," beginning with American Indian religions. In the 2nd edition (1791), the article on Calvinism is unchanged, the Methodist entry is longer, a nine-page entry on Unitarianism appears for the first time, and the Millenarian entry is much expanded. For the 3rd edition (1801), three introductory chapters on religion and philosophy at the start of the Christian era were added as a result of her reading Jacob Bryant's *A New System*, Sir William Jones's "On the Gods of Greece, Italy and India," Priestley, Jean-Jacques Barthélémy, and others. Her viewpoint expanded with her learning, and both reflect the expansion of Western knowledge about religions other than Christianity. The 4th edition (1817) is largely, but not entirely, a rearrangement of the 3rd. Because the various editions of this work appeared at crucial points during an era of rapid religious change, Hannah Adams's work is now an indispensable aid in assessing American self-awareness of those changes and in assessing the extent to which Americans of this period were aware of the relations between their own evolving beliefs and the larger context of world religions.

Suggested Readings: DAB; NAW. *See also* S. T. Armstrong, *Remarks on the Controversy Between Dr. Morse and Miss Adams* (1814); J. Morse, *Appeal to the Public on the Controversy Respecting Harvard College by the Complaints of Miss Adams* (1814).

Robert D. Richardson, Jr.
University of Denver

JOHN ADAMS (1705-1740)

Works: "To a Gentleman on the Sight of Some of His Poems" (1727); *Jesus Christ, an Example to His Ministers* (1728); "An Epistle to the Rev. Turell, Occasioned by the Death of His Late Virtuous Consort" (1735); *Poems on Several Occasions* (1745).

Biography: John Adams, minister and poet, was born in Boston, Mass., on Mar. 26, 1705, the youngest of five children of John and Hannah Adams. Although his family eventually moved to Annapolis Royal, Nova Scotia, young John returned to take a degree at Harvard, where he graduated in 1721 in the same class as Ebenezer Turell (q.v.). A year later, while returning to visit his family in Nova Scotia, Adams was almost killed by Indians. In the fall of 1727, he received an invitation to serve as assistant pastor to the Rev. Nathaniel Clap of Newport, R.I. Several months later, however, Clap, apparently having become displeased with Adams, refused to allow the younger man to continue as his colleague. Clap showed his disapproval by occupying the pulpit during both of the church's two Sunday services. About half of the congregation, finding Clap's behavior unacceptable, separated from Clap and established what became known as the Second Congregational Church of Newport, with John Adams as pastor. Adams was ordained in this position on Apr. 11, 1728, the occasion of his only printed sermon, *Jesus Christ, an Example to His Ministers*.

Despite the efforts of Adams's followers, he was dismissed in 1730 from his post and returned to Harvard, where he remained for the following four years, probably serving as tutor. In 1735 Adams was appointed assistant pastor to Jedidiah Andrews of the Presbyterian Church in Philadelphia, but he was soon back in Boston preaching at an almshouse. In 1740, after a second brief tenure in Philadelphia, Adams came down with a feverish delirium and removed from Boston to Cambridge, where he soon died. At the time of his death, Adams's reputation as a learned scholar was widespread. His library was described as "massive and scholarly," and his uncle, Matthew Adams, wrote of him: "He was Master of Nine Languages, and had read all the most famous Greek Lattin Italian French and Spanish Authors."

Critical Appraisal: What little we know about the preaching of John Adams we learn primarily from his only published sermon, *Jesus Christ, an Example to His Ministers*, delivered in 1728 on the occasion of his ordination. Written in clear, effective prose with a syntax designed for immediate and logical communication, this sermon, although an imitation of Christ, shows the unmistakable influence of Classical theories, an achievement for which Adams is remembered. At one crucial point in the sermon, for example, Adams daringly refers to Platonism: "For it is a Maxim in Philosophy, That the first and most perfect of its kind, should be the Standard of everything else of the same Sort. According to this, the Rule of Living must be that Being who possesses Life after the highest and most perfect Manner. Now this is God Himself."

This same debt to Classicism and to Plato's theory of ideal forms also characterizes Adams's poetry, especially poems like "The Perfection of Beauty," published in *Poems on Several Occasions*. A paraphrase of Canticles 5:9, this poem presents a Platonic treatment of traditional Christianity. *Poems on Several Occasions* also contains other biblical paraphrases, not the least of which is a paraphrase of the entire book of Revelation; some devotional pieces such as "On Contentment" and "On Joy"; verses of belles lettres on melancholy and society; occasional verse; several elegies; and translations of six of Horace's odes.

Strikingly daring for its time, a predominant theme of many poems by Adams is that of poetic inspiration. *Poems* opens, for example, with an "Address to the Supreme Being, For His Assistance in My Poetical Composition," in which the poet ignores the pagan muses and calls unabashedly upon God himself to "lift my humble strains / My verse inspire." An elegy on the death of the poet Jane (Colman) Turell (q.v.), wife of Adams's Harvard classmate Ebenezer Turell, celebrates her inspired lines. In this poem, Adams observed that God "smoth'd her strains, and tun'd her sacred Lyre, / And breath'd within her Soul Seraphic Fire." This poem was written in 1735, the year of its subject's death, and appeared in her 1741 *Memoirs*, published by her husband. "To a Gentleman on the Sight of Some of His Poems," a piece that appeared in the *New England Weekly Journal* (Oct. 9, 1727), shows even greater poetic fervor: "But tho' the subject [poetic excellence] tow'rs above my sight, / I'll stretch my wings, and dare the wondrous height." According to C. Lennart Carlson, the gentleman of this piece is Mather Byles (q.v.), an incorrigible prankster and exhorter of aspiring young poets whose own example in verse apparently provoked Adams to write couplets that sound distinctly Romantic in their portrait of the poet's world wholly removed from the less satisfactory, real world: "Lost in a pleasing maze [of poetic rapture] I wandering rove, / Here crop a rose, and there a tulip prove, / Nor ever fix'd my wanton footsteps stray, / But o'er the beauteous field take an unbounded play."

The success, however modest, Adams achieved in these lines confirms the nineteenth-century observation of the Duyckinck brothers that Adams's later verse "does not deserve the neglect into which it has fallen." One touchstone, for example, of Adams's achievement as a poet is his successful use of Classicism for purely aesthetic effect. No longer thinking of Classical deities as devils, as did Edward Taylor (q.v.) and Cotton Mather (q.v.), Adams described, for example, the moon's movement across the evening sky in terms of a Classical paraphrase of Revelation: "Fair Cynthia plies / Her Silver Circle thro' the gleeming skies." But Adams displayed his Classicism to best advantage in his superior translations of Horace's odes. To be sure, any translation can be construed as an interpretation, but Adams's translations, hardly transliterations, are closer to alternate versions than to translations and equal if not superior to their originals in imagination and power. In the first of his six versions, Adams chose, appropriately, the first ode of Book I, Horace's obligatory plea to Maecenas, his patron, that he praise the Roman poet's efforts. Horace concluded his ode with this exaggerated request-pledge: "*quodsi me lyricus vatibus inseres,* / *sublimi feriam sidera vertice*" (but if you enroll me among the lyric poets, I will achieve the highest fame [lit: I will carry the stars to the highest summer]; my trans.). While matching the Roman's hyperbole, Adams distended the Latin into graceful couplets of iambic tetrameter: "If you the deathless Bays bestow, / And by Applauses make them grow, / Toward the Stars, my winged Fame / Shall fly, and strike the heavenly Frame." In another ode, when discussing how the promise of spring causes one to forget death's certainty, Horace observed that winter's end has arrived when "*nec prata canis albicant pruinis*" (neither are the fields made white with white front; my trans.). From this same Latin line, Adams created a strikingly beautiful pastoral image: "And now the Fields, in native Beauty drest, / Are by the Arms of Frost no more carest."

If Adams's poetry gives pleasure, there is yet another reason why his poems should find a place in anthologies of early American poetry. His liberal attitude toward the Classics indicates an unmistakable shift in the aesthetic theories of colonial America. Along with poets such as Mather Byles and Joseph Green (q.v.), Adams was a pioneer of American belletristic writing; that is, he and others who shared his view of literature were among the first Americans to depart from the belief that all literature should be subservient to religious convictions. Although much of Adams's poetry is biblical paraphrase and devotional verse, clearly not all of it may be so classified; he contributed many poems that display a purely aesthetic concern, and his achievement is well worth noting.

Suggested Readings: CCNE; Sibley-Shipton (VI, 424-427); Sprague (I, 350); T_1. *See also* C. Lennart Carlson, Introduction, *Poems on Several Occasions by Mather Byles* (1940), pp. xxv-xxix; *A Collection of Poems by Several Hands* (1744)—for the text of "To a Gentleman on the Sight of Some of His Poems"; Evert and George Duyckinck, *Cyclopaedia of American Literature* (1875), I, 143-145.

John C. Shields
Illinois State University

JOHN ADAMS (1735-1826)

Works: *Essay on Canon and Feudal Law* (1765, 1768); *Novanglus, and Massachusettensis* (1774-1775, 1819); *Thoughts on Government* (1776); *A Defence of the Constitutions of Government of the United States of America* (1787-1788); *Discourses on Davila* (1790, 1805); *Correspondence of the Late President Adams* (1809).

Collections: Charles Francis Adams, ed., *The Works of John Adams*, 10 vols. (1850-1856); Lester J. Cappon, ed., *The Adams-Jefferson Letters*; *The Complete Correspondence Between Thomas Jefferson and Abigail and John Adams*, 2 vols. (1959); Lyman H. Butterfield et al., eds., *The Adams Papers* (1961-).

Biography: From Oct. 19, 1735, when he was born, until his death in 1826, John Adams maintained virtually unbroken residence in Braintree (later Quincy), Mass. He left home to study at Harvard (1751-1755), to study law in Worcester, Mass. (1756-1758), and, after his marriage to Abigail (Smith) Adams (q.v.) in 1764, to live in Boston for periods of a year or two when his legal work drew him there. He was resident in the city when the Boston Massacre took place and immediately, in a gesture of principled independence typical of his life and works, agreed to defend the soldiers who had fired into the crowd.

From 1774 to 1777, Adams was in Philadelphia for the sessions of the Continental Congress, during which time he served on the committee to frame a declaration of independence and afterwards on the Board of War. He was sent to Fr. by the Congress in 1778-1779, returning in time to draft a new constitution for Mass. He then served in Europe from 1779 until 1788 as minister empowered to negotiate treaties of peace and commerce with G.B., minister to negotiate with the Neth. (1780), and, finally, first American minister to the Court of St. James (1785).

On his return home, he was soon called away from Braintree to serve as vice-president under Washington (1789-1797) and then as president of the U. S. (1797-1801). Thereafter, Adams returned home and never traveled more than a few miles from his birthplace, where he died Jul. 4, 1826, the fiftieth anniversary of independence. Adams is remembered not so much for any particular act or writing, although preventing war with Fr. stands out in his presidency, as for the long years of selfless devotion that he gave to the American Revolution and the new national government.

Critical Appraisal: Although Adams produced at least as many pages of prose as any of his contemporaries, he was not a writer of books. The *Defence of the Constitutions* was the only work that he conceived of and completed as a whole, and even there the three volumes that he rushed to compose in 1786 and 1787— two of which were commentaries on medieval Italian history—display the organizational defects common to his other writings. Everything else printed under his name is some kind of collection, usually assembled without his participation.

During his lifetime, Adams's printed works were overwhelmingly political and were not thought of by himself or others as having literary interest. Yet in his youth, Adams would have attempted to become a man of letters if only he had had the means to support a gentleman's life of leisure. In retrospect, his essays under the pseudonym "Novanglus," in which he opposed the Loyalist arguments of Daniel Leonard (q.v.) writing as "Massachusettensis," stand out for their energy and their vividness of expression, although not for systematic thought. Adams's later writings are commonly regarded as more conservative politically than those written through 1776, although his increasingly expressed pessimism about human nature appears in virtually everything he wrote.

Influenced by his legal training, Adams wrote as a disputant and commentator on documents and arguments set forth by others, never as an original thinker. As a consequence, his marginalia, some of which were collected by Zoltán Haraszti, hold as much interest as his formal writings. As he would have been surprised to learn, his literary monuments are his personal letters and diary. His general correspondence contains the best account of Adams's political ideas and actions, and his letters to his wife trace the evolution of a married relationship unmatched in its time for both passional and intellectual intimacy.

Adams kept his diary on and off for some forty years, from the 1750s when he was at college, into the 1790s, and up to the time when he was nominated for the presidency. Its pages have served as a mine of information on politics, domestic life, and local color. But above all, they trace the development of a personality. The diarist's aspirations, doubts, weaknesses, idealism, and merciless self-criticism produce as intimate a literary portrait as any in the eighteenth century, not excluding Rousseau's.

In his twenty-six-year retirement, Adams wrote at length on his life but never completed an autobiography. Starting in 1802 he traced his youth and early career through the Continental Congresses and part of his diplomatic service. In this fragmentary autobiography, Adams intermittently expressed disappointment, disillusionment, and personal failure, thereby anticipating the tone of his great-grandson's *The Education of Henry Adams*. Adams abandoned his autobiography to write a self-justifying account of his early Revolutionary services in a series of letters to his former friend and historian of the Revolution, Mercy Otis Warren (q.v.). Finally, he detailed later parts of his career in a series of letters to the Boston *Patriot*, some of which were printed in 1809. In each case, the spirit of controversy that had served him well during his active years continued to prevent him from expressing himself in a completed, literary form.

Instead, starting in 1812, Adams resumed a correspondence with Thomas Jefferson (q.v.) that had begun in the 1780s but had been broken off when the two became political rivals during the 1790s. Here was rekindled the enlightened broadness of culture and humaneness of outlook on man, politics, and religion typical of his aspiring early years. These wide-ranging letters, written in Adams's enthusiastic, argumentative prose, together with Jefferson's, stand as a monument to the founding generation of the American Revolution and as a distinctive contribution to American literature.

Suggested Readings: DAB; LHUS; T₂. *See also* Howard F. Bremer, ed., *John Adams, 1735-1826: Chronology, Documents, Bibliographical Aids* (1967); Zoltán Haraszti, *John Adams and the Prophets of Progress* (1952); John R. Howe, Jr., *The Changing Political Thought of John Adams* (1966); Stephen Kurtz, *The Presidency of John Adams; the Collapse of Federalism, 1795-1890* (1957); Peter Shaw, *The Character of John Adams* (1976); Page Smith, *John Adams*, 2 vols. (1962).

Peter Shaw
New York, New York

SAMUEL ADAMS (1722-1803)

Works: *An Appeal to the World* (1769); Harry A. Cushing, ed., *The Writings of Samuel Adams*, 4 vols. (1904-1908; rep., 1968).

Biography: Samuel Adams was born Sept. 16, 1722, in Boston, one of twelve children of Samuel and Mary (Fifield) Adams. The elder Samuel was a prosperous brewer and deacon in the Old South Church. Adams attended Boston Latin School and graduated from Harvard in 1740. Three years later, he received an M.A., arguing the affirmative of the proposition "Whether it be lawful to resist the Supreme Magistrate, if the Commonwealth cannot be otherwise preserved." Adams studied law briefly, was unsuccessful in a business of his own, and then joined his father in the brewery. He married Elizabeth Checkley in 1749; she died in 1757, leaving two children. In 1764 he married Elizabeth Wells.

Adams followed his father's example in his active participation in local Boston politics. By 1764, when he drafted the instructions to Boston's representatives to the General Court, his influence had become considerable, and the following year he was elected to the Mass. House of Representatives. Acknowledged the leader of the radical party, which controlled the General Court from 1766 on, Adams led the opposition to the Townshend Acts and was the chief leader and agitator of the Sons of Liberty. He contributed numerous unsigned articles to the *Boston Gazette* and other newspapers and kept up a steady correspondence with influential persons in the colonies and in Eng. When the anti-British sentiment of his fellow Bostonians began to cool, Adams kept the flame alive by denouncing

British officials and by warning the colonists of the imminent danger to their liberties. Most important, he was the prime initiator of the Committees of Correspondence, which helped bind the colonies together.

Adams's firm belief in the premises upon which the Declaration of Independence is based was expressed as early as 1765. As a representative to the First and Second Continental Congresses, he was an early supporter of the Declaration. He served as a member of the Mass. Constitutional Convention and was later elected lieutenant governor under John Hancock. Upon Hancock's death in 1793, Adams became governor of Mass. and was elected to that office in 1794. He died Oct. 2, 1803.

Critical Appraisal: Almost all of Adams's published writings were political, but few were signed with his own name. His writings included resolutions and instructions of the town of Boston, official letters and appeals of the Mass. House of Representatives, circular letters to Committees of Correspondence, and articles in the Boston newspapers under as many as twenty-five pseudonyms. In addition, he kept up a steady correspondence with political leaders in Eng. and America.

One of the first official pieces Adams had a hand in writing was the instructions of the town of Boston to its representatives in the General Court, written in 1764. There the emphasis was upon the necessity of the legislature's independence of the executive branch; the representatives were urged to have a law passed vacating the seat of any representative who accepted a crown appointment. They were also instructed to protest parliamentary taxes on trade as being against their rights as British citizens, reducing them "to the miserable state of tributary slaves." This latter theme was repeated many times in Adams's writings, although at the same time he insisted that, because of distance, it would be impossible for the colonies to send representatives to Parliament; thus only the colonial legislatures could tax the colonists.

A letter to Christopher Gadsden (q.v.) of S. C. (Dec. 1766) is typical of Adams's warnings of the ever-present and imminent danger of British tyranny. After expressing satisfaction and relief at the repeal of the Stamp Act, he asked:

> But is there no reason to fear the liberties of the colonies may be infringed in a less observable manner? The Stamp Act was like a sword that Nero wished for, to have decollated the Roman people at a stroke, or like Job's sea monster.... The sight of such an enemy at a distance is formidable, while the lurking serpent lies concealed, and not noticed by the unwary passenger, darts its fatal venom. It is necessary then that each colony should be awake and upon its guard.

One of the surest ways of arousing New Englanders was to play upon their aversion to Roman Catholicism. Accordingly, in 1768 Adams published a series of articles in the *Boston Gazette*, under the signature "A Puritan," in which he declared that popery was rampant and more to be dreaded than taxes or Stamp

Acts. He accused representatives who supported the governor of being papists; only those who supported the Boston Whigs were "sound Protestants."

One issue to which Adams devoted much attention was the presence of British troops in Mass. Hoping to enlist the support of every colony in demanding the withdrawal of the troops, Adams sent to sympathetic printers throughout the colonies a "Journal" recounting innumerable British "atrocities": soldiers beating small boys, harassing merchants, violating the Sabbath, and raping Boston women. By fanning Bostonians' hatred of the British troops with his imaginative descriptions of riots, rapes, and insults, Adams probably contributed to the very real tragedy of 1770 known as the "Boston Massacre." Yet following the trial of the soldiers involved in that incident, he continued to agitate, writing a series of articles for the *Boston Gazette*, signed "Vindex," attempting to prove the guilt of the soldiers, and attributing their acquittal to the shortcomings of the jury. Adams painted the scene in lurid colors, accusing the soldiers of "savage barbarity" and describing bayonets five inches deep in innocent civilian blood. As he continued to agitate against the British troops and against the royal government, he filled the pages of the *Boston Gazette* not only with his own writing but also with items from other papers, official documents, and extracts from correspondence.

One significant official document in which Adams had a major voice was the "State of the Right of the Colonists" adopted by the Boston Town Meeting on Nov. 20, 1772. Clearly stated there is the Lockeian principle that all civil rights are firmly rooted in natural law: "All men have a right to remain in a state of nature as long as they please: and in case of intolerable oppression, civil or religious, to leave the society they belong to, and enter into another." As the actual war progressed, Adams produced less public propaganda, not writing for publication for years at a time. In the 1780s he wrote an occasional admonishment to the public concerning the desirable characteristics of officeholders and the responsibilities of citizens. In 1794, having assumed the governorship of Mass., he publicly reaffirmed his strong belief in the Lockeian principles of natural law and natural rights and the compact theory of government.

Educated in theology, the ancient Classics, and the law, Samuel Adams employed all of his knowledge and talent not for self-gain but for what he saw as the public good. His writings, along with his other activities, were unquestionably a major propaganda force in the pre-Revolutionary period.

Suggested Readings: DAB; LHUS; T₂. *See also* Philip Davidson, *Propaganda and the American Revolution* (1941); R. V. Harlow, *Samuel Adams* (1923); John C. Miller, *Sam Adams, Pioneer in Propaganda* (1936).

Elaine K. Ginsberg
West Virginia University

WILLIAM ADAMS (1650-1685)

Works: *Diary* (w. 1670-1681; pub. 1852); "An Elegie Upon . . . Seth Flint" (frag.: w. 1673; pub. 1944); *God's Eye on the Contrite* (1685); *The Necessity* (w. 1678; pub. 1679).

Biography: William Adams was born in New London, Conn., on May 27, 1650. Orphaned at 9, he nonetheless remained devoted to Congregationalism. With the assistance of two uncles, he attended Harvard College where he graduated in 1671 in the company of noted classmates such as Edward Taylor (q.v.), Samuel Sewall (q.v.), and John Norton II (q.v.). In his *Diary*, Adams noted that he visited Samuel Sewall in Ipswich in Mar. of the year they graduated. Shortly after his graduation, members of the church at Dedham began to solicit Adams for their church. In 1672 Adams wrote in his *Diary* that he refused the call, "neither finding my mind inclined to take upon me at present that work nor seeing the providence of God clearly directing me thereto." It was during this period that Adams made the acquaintance of the Revs. Samuel Torrey (q.v.) and Josiah Flint, who "were urgent with me," apparently in regard to his ministerial calling. Finally, in the latter part of May 1673, young William "removed from Cambridge to Dedham to the solemn undertaking of the ministry there on triall for future settlement."

In Dec. 1673 Adams was ordained pastor of the Church of Christ in Dedham, and the following Oct. he married his first wife, Mary Manning, with whom he had three children. After Mary's death in 1679, Adams again married, this time to Alice Bradford, with whom he fathered four more children. One of Adams's sons, Eliphalet Adams (q.v.), graduated from Harvard College in 1694 and eventually became a missionary to the Indians, preaching to them in their own language. William Adams died in 1685 while still young. Of his short career, Torrey and Flint have left this memorial: the young Rev. Adams "hath had a more early call into that work wherein he hath been more happy than most of his fellow Servants."

Critical Appraisal: Although the brevity of Adams's career allowed him to leave behind only a slender canon, what he did manage to produce shows great promise. His *Diary*, for example, is rich with personal anecdotes about the harshness of the times. Twice he barely escaped freezing to death from a winter fall into a river, once while "abroad" with his close friend Hezekiah Willet and again with a Mrs. Ruth Flint (not Josiah's wife, whose name was Esther, but probably a member of the larger Flint family). In an Oct. 1671 entry, he described "the strange effects of a violent hurricane" that ripped through a forest for some fifteen miles, "tearing up by the roots, or breaking the bodyes of almost all trees within its compasse." Among the many occasions on which he attended funerals, only once did Adams describe the event. Francis Willoughby, a former magistrate of Massachusetts Bay, was "solemnly interred" to the accompaniment of the "doleful noise of trumpets and drums," joined by "3 thundering volleys of shot...answered with the loud roaring of great guns, rending the heavens with noise at the losse of so great a man." Having been the witness or the unwitting victim of such vicissitudes, Adams understandably recorded in his *Diary*, "if these be but preliminaria, well may I tremble to think what the penetralia will be."

Despite these harsh realities, Adams found the people of his congregation to be filled with pride and with the certainty that, since they were a covenant people, they would be thrust into heavenly reward. Both of his extant sermons address this issue. The earlier sermon, *The Necessity of the Pouring Out of the Spirit...Upon a Sining Apostatizing People*, is academic and pedantic, laborious and tedious, and reads more like a meditation than a public exhortation—of which the later sermon is indeed a forceful example. *God's Eye on the Contrite* opened by citing the prideful notion of the Israelites who thought they could confine God in an elaborately adorned temple. He then moved by an intricately wrought logical process into a consideration that his congregation should "be poor, contrite in spirit and tremble at" God's word, and he even went so far as to attribute the sufferings of his congregation to God's displeasure, caused by its glorying in the notion that too many members claimed to be "saints." Such pride had brought upon his church all manner of fears, storms, floods, droughts, sickness, pestilence, and fires. The minister pictured these mishaps and disasters in vivid language; of storms he observed, "God hath drawn out His sword against us, and hath given it a charge to devour round about our Coasts, and many have fallen down slain by it." He then concluded, "Now all these things God hath done to humble us; for we are His covenant People: we have not been therefore humble enough." At a later point, he maintained that "Pride is an enemy to profiting," and shortly thereafter he observed, "There must be an awful, sanctifying, reverential, fiducial fear in all our Transactions with God." The use of the words *profiting* and *transactions*, from the rhetoric of economics, suggests the incipient economic flourishing of the colony and a mutual (spiritual-temporal) assent to it. The politically loaded word *fiducial* used within this same context, even though said of man's relation to God, points directly to Adams's conclusion, in which he urged application of his doctrine. Addressing all classes within his congregation, he first called upon "Rulers," to whom he made the statement that: "If God continue: You that are *from among ourselves* in this Trust: Your faithful endeavors in this matter will be expected." Here he seems to imply that the crown may be taking over the rule of the colony and consequently threatening its economic freedom. In fact, Charles II had revoked the colony's independent charter in 1684.

Perhaps it was Adams's implication that the crown's assumption of authority over the colony threatened its economic future and not merely the fact that he and Adams had been Harvard classmates that provoked Samuel Sewall, one of Massachusetts Bay's most successful businessmen, to request the printing of this sermon shortly after Adams's death. At any rate, Adams provided historical commentary beyond merely instructing his congregation in spiritual matters. The Dedham minister's surviving verse fragment again reflects ministerial intention: spiritual instruction. Regarding the life of Seth Flint, younger brother of Josiah, Adams characteristically observed, "the tender love of God reveald / In Christ constraine[d] him forcing him to give / Himselfe." Although the literary merit of his extant works is not extensive, certainly the historical significance of Adams's *Diary* and *God's Eye on the Contrite* makes fascinating and informative reading. In fact, all of Adams's productions reveal an intelligent devotion, regrettably cut short at the moment of maturity.

Suggested Readings: CCNE; FCNEV; Sibley-Shipton (II, 380-387); Sprague (I, 181-183). *See also* Frances M. Caulkins, "Memoir of the Rev. William Adams" (with his *Diary*), CMHS, 4th. ser., 1 (1852), 5-51; Perry Miller and Thomas H. Johnson, *The Puritans: A Sourcebook of Their Writings* (1963), I, 9; Samuel Eliot Morison, *Harvard College in the Seventeenth Century* (1936), I, 81, 84, 111-112; II, 393.

John C. Shields
Illinois State University

ZABDIEL ADAMS (1739-1801)

Works: *The Nature, Pleasure, and Advantages of Church-Musick* (1771); *The Happiness and Pleasure of Unity* (1772); *An Answer to a Pamphlet Lately Published* (1773); *Brotherly Love* (1775); *The Grounds of Confidence* (1775); *The Bishop's Office a Good Work* (1782); *A Sermon on the Duty and Importance of Making the Scriptures the Rule and Standard of Preaching* (1782); *A Sermon Preached Before His Excellency John Hancock* (1782); *The Evil Designs of Men* (1783); *The Duty and Necessity of People's Praying for Their Ministers* (1788); *Our Lapse in Adam* (1791); *The Duty of Ministers Giving Themselves Wholly to Their Work* (1792).

Biography: Cousin to John Adams (q.v.), Zabdiel Adams was born in Braintree, Mass., on Nov. 5, 1739. He attended Harvard College, graduating in 1759 with a B.A. In Sept. 1764 Adams was ordained a Congregationalist minister and accepted a call to the church in Lunenburg, Mass., where he spent the remainder of his life. In his theology, Adams was an Arminian, but he apparently got along well with his more orthodox parishioners, for he acquired an admirable reputation as a preacher and orator and was judged a remarkably able extemporaneous speaker. In 1782 Adams was chosen to deliver the Mass. election sermon and in 1794 the Dudleian Lecture at Harvard, where he preached on the validity of Presbyterian ordination and where his lecture was considered one of the best in the series. At his church in Lunenburg, Adams introduced hymn singing to replace psalm chanting and published a sermon justifying the change. He was appointed one of the trustees of Groton Academy in 1793. While he was a Federalist in the 1790s, Adams generally avoided introducing politics into his pulpit. He died in Lunenburg on Mar. 1, 1801.

Critical Appraisal: With one exception, all of Zabdiel Adams's published works were sermons, many of them very conventional. He delivered and published three ordination sermons, plus three additional sermons devoted to the improvement of public morals. Adams's most significant publications were his sermon in 1771 on the subject of hymn singing, his 1782 election sermon, and his sermon in 1783 marking the eighth anniversary of the Battle of Lexington, which he developed into a general survey of the progress of the American Revolution.

Adams's *Nature, Pleasure, and Advantages of Church Musick* was preached to justify his introduction of instruments and conducting into the liturgy of his Lunenburg church; like other ministers who were attempting to introduce hymn singing and instruments into the Congregational service, Adams had encountered opposition from some traditionalists who argued that the new practices smacked of "popery." Adams responded that such innovations were fully supported by scripture and doctrine. He conceded that church music would not make a person religious, but he countered that "it will do much toward polishing his manners." In the end, his parishioners accepted the musical innovations.

In his 1782 election sermon, Adams invoked the usual themes of obedience to authority, the need for public virtue, and the necessity of religion to national happiness—themes common to New Eng. sermons of the time. Indeed, his election sermon was noteworthy chiefly because of his spirited account of the progress to date of the American Revolution. He told the assembled Mass. magistrates that "so wonderful were the interpositions of God's providence" in the course of the Revolution "that we may, without presumption, adopt the words of the Psalmist and say, *the Lord of hosts is with us, the God of Jacob is our refuge.*" He urged his audience to "anticipate the rising glory of America," to consider the day when "this your native country will become the permanent seat of Liberty, the retreat of philosophers, the asylum of the oppressed, the umpire of contending nations."

Adams continued this approach in his 1783 Lexington anniversary sermon. After the Revolutionary War had broken out, Adams intoned, "the *king* of *Britain* meant one thing, but the KING of HEAVEN another." According to Adams, the Lord was manifestly supporting the American cause and would make the Americans "a great and numerous people, the depositories of that liberty which has forsaken the greater part of the world, flown over the *Atlantic*, and now *domesticates* itself with us."

Adams's significance lies in his musical innovations and particularly in his preaching, which combined religion and nationalism during the period of the American Revolution. Most of the themes of the emerging American civil religion found expression in his public sermons.

Suggested Readings: CCNE; Sibley-Shipton (XIV, 377-383); T$_2$. *See also* Kenneth Silverman, *A Cultural History of the American Revolution* (1976), pp. 196-197.

John F. Berens
Northern Michigan University

FRANCIS ALISON (1705-1779)

Works: *Peace and Union* (1758); *An Address of Thanks to the Wardens of Christ-Church* (with John Ewing; 1764).

Biography: Francis Alison was born in 1705, in the parish of Lock (or Lac), in County Donegal, Ire. His attendance at the Royal School at Raphoe, then under the inspection of the Anglican bishop of Raphoe, suggests that he was raised an Anglican. Alison received an M.A. from the University of Edinburgh in 1732; there is evidence to suggest that he also studied at the University of Glasgow. In 1735 the Presbytery of Letterkenny, Ire., granted Alison a license to preach, and in the fall of 1735, he immigrated to America, where on May 25, 1737, hc was installed pastor of the Presbyterian Church at New London, Pa. There he married Hannah Armitage, of New Castle, Del. The couple had six children.

During the Great Awakening, Alison opposed the "Enthusiasm & wild disorders," which he believed were "like to destroy religion, & ruin our Churches," but even though he belonged to the Old Side (antirevivalist) faction, hc was somewhat of a moderate. When, for example, the New Side (prorevivalist) faction was expelled from a meeting of the Synod of Philadelphia in May 1741, thus plunging American Presbyterians into a schism that continued for seventeen years, Alison did not endorse the action and sought for conciliation. In 1743 Alison founded an Old Side Academy at New London (later the Univ. of Del.), where he taught until 1752, when he was appointed rector of the academy and copastor of the First Presbyterian Church in Philadelphia. In 1755, when a college (later the Univ. of Penn.) was added to the academy, Alison was appointed its vice-provost and a professor of classics and metaphysics. For the remainder of his life, he served simultaneously at the college and at First Church.

In 1756 Alison received an honorary D.D. degree from the University of Glasgow, the first honorary degree ever awarded by a European university to a Presbyterian clergyman in America. In addition, Alison received honorary M.A. degrees from Yale (1755) and the College of New Jersey (1756). During this period, Alison also founded the first life insurance company in America. Now called the Presbyterian Ministers' Fund, it is the oldest surviving life insurance company in the world. In 1766 Alison was the Old Side candidate for the presidency of the College of New Jersey but lost when the New Side trustees chose John Witherspoon (q.v.). Opposed to Anglican efforts to dominate the College of Philadelphia, where the first provost, William Smith (q.v.), was an Anglican, Alison participated in the joint conventions of Presbyterians and Conn. Congregationalists that were held, starting in 1766, to form a united front against pressures to introduce Anglican bishops in America. Alison died in Philadelphia on Nov. 28, 1779.

Critical Appraisal: Benjamin Franklin (q.v.) described Alison as "a Person of great Ingenuity & Learning, a catholic Divine, & what is more an *Honest Man*...one of *God's Nobility*." Jacob Duché (q.v.) listed Alison among "the first that introduced science into this heretofore untutored wilderness." Ezra Stiles (q.v.) wrote that Alison was "the greatest classical scholar in America" and "a great literary character," and Alison's former student, Episcopal Bishop William White, looked back on him as "a man...of real and rational piety, of a liberal mind;—his failing was proneness to anger; but it was forgotten,—for he was placable and affable."

Alison's major published work, *Peace and Union*, was preached in May 1758 to a Presbyterian audience finally reunited after the schism of 1741. Replete with Classical allusions and quotations, Alison's sermon illustrates why he must have been an effective preacher and leader. Although he said comparatively little about the specific subject of Presbyterian reunion, thus avoiding the possibility of reawakening controversy among the members of his audience, Alison addressed the problem of schism in general terms that might just as easily be addressed to Protestants in general, saving any direct references to Presbyterian reunion for his concluding "Application." He cited various indications, for example, that the pagan Greeks and Romans, living by purely human wisdom, recognized the value of unity and forebearance, and he drew from this fact the lesson that there is even more reason for Christians to do so under the light of the Gospel. Emphasizing the positive rather than the negative, Alison approached the Presbyterian schism by paying tribute to the eight great peacemakers, living and dead, who worked to bring about a reunion of factions. Included on this list is the name of Gilbert Tennent (q.v.), whose abusive sermon, *The Danger of an Unconverted Ministry* (1740), had previously been a major factor in precipitating the schism of 1741 in the first place.

Alison's other published work, *An Address of Thanks* (for letting Presbyterians gather in Anglican churches in 1764), coauthored with John Ewing, is a broadside, ironical in tone, stemming from the period when the Presbyterians and Anglicans of Pa., during and after the French and Indian War, cooperated closely in common opposition to the pacifistic Quakers. Presbyterian alarms over proposals for sending Anglican bishops to America, however, soon brought this cooperation to an end.

Ultimately, it is disappointing that someone with Alison's multifaceted mind and profound scholarship published so little. His former student Matthew Wilson attributed this lack of productivity to Alison's "great aversion to appearing in print." Church historians have tended to overlook Alison's significant contributions to the history of Presbyterianism in early America, possibly because the Old Side to which he belonged was dwarfed in numbers and influence by the more rapidly growing New Side. Perhaps Alison's greatest importance, however, was as an educator, and his influence upon his students, many of whom became prominent in American public life, was a factor in fostering the ideal of American independence in the middle colonies. If for no other reason, the fruits of Alison's labors live after him today in the continuing vitality of the two universities and the life insurance company he founded.

Suggested Readings: CCMC; DAB; Sprague (III, 73-76). *See also* Alan Heimert, *Religion and the American Mind* (1966), pp. 169, 172, 185, 187, 360, 365-366, 370, 376-378, 389; James L. McAllister, Jr., "Francis Alison and John Witherspoon: Political Philosophers and Revolutions," JPH, 54 (1976), 33-60; Alexander Mackie, *Facile Princeps* (1956); Thomas Harrison Montgomery, *A History of the University of Pennsylvania* (1900), pp. 163-166; Thomas Clinton Pears, Jr., "Francis Alison, Colonial Educator," DN, 17 (1944), 9-22; idem, "Francis Alison," JPHS, 29 (1951), 213-235; idem, "Presbyterians and American Freedom," JPHS, 29 (1951), 77-95; Jonathan Powell, "Presbyterian

Loyalists: A Chain of Interest in Philadelphia," JPH, 57 (1979), 135-160; Douglas Sloan, ed., *The Great Awakening and American Education* (1973), pp. 169-177; idem, *The Scottish Enlightenment and the American College Ideal* (1971), pp. 73-102.

Richard Frothingham
University of Arkansas at Little Rock

ETHAN ALLEN (1738-1789)

Works: *A Brief Narrative of the Proceedings of the Government of New York* (1774); *An Animadversary Address to the Inhabitants of the State of Vermont* (1778); *A Narrative of Colonel Ethan Allen's Captivity* (1779); *A Vindication of the Opposition of the Inhabitants of Vermont* (1779); *A Concise Refutation of the Claims of New Hampshire and Massachusetts Bay to the Territory of Vermont* (1780); *The Present State of the Controversy* (1782); *Reason the Only Oracle of Man* (1784); *An Essay on the Universal Plenitude of Being* (w. 1788; pub. 1873).

Biography: Born in Litchfield, Conn., on Jan. 21, 1738, Ethan Allen was the oldest of eight children whose ancestors ranked among the earliest settlers of the Massachusetts Bay Colony. Despite the hardships of pioneer life, education was prized by Allen's parents who provided their children with a rudimentary knowledge of language, the Scriptures, and numbers. Except for a brief period when he was tutored in preparation for admission to Yale College, formal instruction was unknown to Allen. The death of his father, however, demanded Allen's return to the family farm and dashed his hopes for a college education. At home on the edge of civilization, Allen continued to instruct himself and became a rough-hewn intellectual, thinking and writing about revolutionary ideas in religion and politics and often signing his letters as "The Philosopher."

Although he never completely abandoned his "youthful disposition to contemplation," by 1770 Allen began to assume the flamboyant public character that history and legend have assigned to him. At this time, he was chosen to represent a group of pioneer settlers who, embroiled in land title disputes with the province of N.Y., were threatened with eviction from the N.H. Grants, now the state of Vt. Following an unfavorable legal judgement, the Grants settlers elected to defend their holdings with force and formed a volunteer militia known as the Green Mountain Boys, headquartered at the Catamount Tavern in Bennington and led by "Colonel Commandant" Ethan Allen.

At the time of the outbreak of hostilities between G.B. and its American colonies, Allen's rag-tag insurgents were in a position to capture Ticonderoga, Britain's mighty fortress guarding Can.'s main water route to N.Y. Although situated upon one of the most strategic positions in North America, the fort was poorly maintained and understaffed. It was with ease, therefore, that on May 10, 1775, Allen and his Green Mountain Boys surprised a sleepy contingent of

British regulars and demanded the surrender of the fort "In the name of the Great Jehovah and the Continental Congress."

The taking of Ticonderoga was a bold stroke that had enormous consequences for the outcome of the war. As a military maneuver, however, it demanded more pluck than strategy and was followed by a pair of humiliating defeats for Allen, first at St. Johns and later at Montreal, where he was taken captive. In 1778, after nearly thirty-two months as a prisoner of war, Allen was exchanged for a British officer. Following his release, the Continental Congress awarded Allen a commission, but his abrasive and at times undisciplined personality won him the displeasure of America's political and military leaders, who never called him into active service.

Although Allen's leadership talents were not employed by the Continental Army, they proved valuable to the state of Vt., which had declared itself a republic during his captivity. Congress, however, was reluctant to recognize Vt. as an independent state. Consequently, Allen engaged in clandestine negotiations with G.B. to return Vt. to the fold of the British Empire, but the war ended before such a reunion could have become a reality. The case against Allen was never proven during his lifetime, but scholarship has shown that he was indeed guilty of collaboration with the British. Although he was motivated in large part by self-interest, it is also likely that Allen acted out of sincere regard for his vision of the future of Vt. He spent his final years more or less tranquilly on his farm in Burlington, Vt., where he died on Feb. 12, 1789.

Critical Appraisal: Ethan Allen always had a cause to champion, and most of the time he was successful. With or without a weapon, he was a fearsome opponent no less intimidating in the halls of government than on horseback dressing down a "Yorker" partisan. Moreover, Allen was master of the pen as well as the sword, and he effectively enlisted the written word in defense of the land rights of the Grants settlers. Most of Allen's political pamphlets and essays dealt with this highly specific topic and have limited interest to contemporary readers, but his *Brief Narrative of the Proceedings of the Government of New York* is significant for the way in which he represented the case of the Grants settlers. His argument did not recognize property ownership as deriving from the fine points of legal doctrine. Rather, Allen established his case upon the notion—articulated in John Locke's *Second Treatise of Government*—that a man has a natural right to the property he acquires through his labor.

Allen's most popular work, however, was *A Narrative of Colonel Ethan Allen's Captivity*. Ostensibly an account of the privations Allen saw and experienced during his thirty-two months as a British prisoner of war, the *Narrative* was "interspersed with some Political Observations" and served as a much-needed morale boost for the embattled American forces. It was a paean—at times fanciful, always lively—to the survival and ultimate victory of the underdog, and as such, it struck heartening chords among the Americans who were desperate for a success story. Published in 1779 after one of the darkest periods of the Revolution, the *Narrative* was an immediate best-seller and went through nineteen editions during the next seventy-five years.

In his final years, Allen assumed a far less active role in public affairs and devoted himself to what he called "matters of the mind." During this time, he resumed working on a book that he had begun in collaboration with a scholarly physician, Dr. Thomas Young, nearly two decades earlier. The result was published in 1785 under Allen's own name as *Reason the Only Oracle of Man*. Familiarly known as *The Oracles of Reason* or *Allen's Bible*, the work is considered to be the first major attack on the Christian religion to be published in the Western Hemisphere, for in it Allen proposed no less than the dissolution of the fundamentals of conventional Christianity. The Scriptures, revelation, clergy, and prayer, for example, were to be discarded. In their stead, Allen proposed a "compenduous system of natural religion" based on an assortment of principles derived from nature and discovered by reason. Should reason fail, intuition could be called upon as a reliable guide. For his efforts, Allen was denounced by Christian clergymen who branded him an atheist. But his work, although uneven and at times inconsistent, is important for the way it expressed the Deism of one century while anticipating the Transcendentalism of the next.

Suggested Readings: DAB; DARB; LHUS; T_2. *See also* George P. Anderson, "Who Wrote Ethan Allen's 'Bible?' " NEQ, 10 (1937), 685-696; John Ditsky, "The Yankee Insolence of Ethan Allen," CRevAS, 1 (1970), 32-38; Dana Doten, "Ethan Allen's 'Original Something,' " NEQ, 11 (1938), 361-366; Clarence Gohdes, "Ethan Allen and His *Magnum Opus*," OC, 43 (1929), 129-151; Edwin P. Hoyt, *The Damndest Yankees: Ethan Allen & His Clan* (1976); Charles A. Jellison, *Ethan Allen: Frontier Rebel* (1969); John Pell, *Ethan Allen* (1929); B. T. Schantz, "Ethan Allen's Religious Ideas," JR, 18 (1938), 183-217.

Carmine Andrew Prioli
North Carolina State University

JAMES ALLEN (1632-1710)

Works: *New-England's Choicest Blessing* (1679); *Serious Advice* (1679); *Neglect of Supporting and Maintaining the Pure Worship of God* (1687); *Man's Self-Reflection* (1699).

Biography: James Allen (*also spelled* Allin), born in Hampshire, Eng., in 1632, and trained for the ministry at Oxford, found it necessary to leave Eng. in 1662, when the Act of Uniformity forced Puritan clergymen from their pulpits. Arriving in Boston, Mass., he was invited to preach at Boston's First Church, and some years later, in 1668, he was installed there as teacher. From that time until his death in 1710, Allen served as one of the pillars of Puritan orthodoxy in the town of Boston, which had seven churches (four were Puritan/Congregational) and 7,000 people at the beginning of the eighteenth century. Although Allen published little and remained largely passive in the religious controversies of his time, he had a handsome personal fortune, and "his wealth gave him the power, which he used, as a good bishop, to be kind and hospitable."

Critical Appraisal: Although James Allen held one of the most prestigious pulpits in Boston, he published only four sermons during his lifetime.
Harold Jantz, in *The First Century of New England Verse*, cited one poem, "A
Funerall Elegie upon the Lamented Death of Mr. Danielle Russell. . ." (1678),
by Allen, and noted that the only extant copy is in private hands. Allen's literary
contribution seems slight, indeed, when set beside those of his contemporaries,
Increase Mather (q.v.) of Boston's Second Church, and Samuel Willard (q.v.) of
the Old South Church. These two published sixty and forty sermons respectively, not including their other religious works. James Allen prefaced two of his
publications with self-deprecatory remarks, and his modesty was not unwarranted. His sermons follow the form of the Puritan "plain style," but the prose is
devoid of imagery or metaphor, and the tone is relentlessly hortatory. All four
sermons are variations on the same theme: God is remote and reproving, and man
is weak and sinful. Allen's election sermon, *New England's Choicest Blessing*
(1679), is a call to other-worldliness in affairs of state and an exhortation to
elected officials and voters to meditate often upon the presence of God, which is,
above all material considerations, the government's "choicest blessing."

It should be noted that *Two Practical Discourses* (1727), a work attributed to
James Allen in William Buell Sprague, *Annals of the American Pulpit* (I, 164);
Samuel Allibone, *Critical Dictionary of English Literature* (I, 52); and Joseph
Sabin, *Dictionary of Books Relating to America* (I, 103), where it is cited as *Two
Discourses on Providence*, is actually the work of James Allin (1692-1747), the
pastor of the church at Brookline, Mass. Even though Allen died seventeen years
before the date of publication, some confusion arises from the vagaries of
seventeenth- and eighteenth-century typography and spelling, in which *Allen* and
Allin were often interchanged. Furthermore, the style and imagery of *Two Practical Discourses* are unmistakably those of James Allin. Although Clifford K.
Shipton and James E. Mooney, in *The Short-Title Evans*, spelled Allen's name
Allin, his colleague Benjamin Wadsworth (q.v.) spelled it *Allen* in his funeral
sermon, and so did Cotton Mather (q.v.) in his *Magnalia Christi Americana* (I,
187).

Suggested Readings: CCNE; FCNEV; Sprague (I, 163-164). *See also* John
Eliot, *Eliot's Biographical Dictionary* (1809), pp. 21-22; *Records of the First Church in
Boston*, PCSM, 39 (1961), xxxii-xxxvi.

Virginia Bernhard
University of St. Thomas

JAMES ALLEN (1739-1808)

Works: *Poem* (1772); "The Recollection" [pub. in *Boston Magazine*, 2
(1785), 471-472; 3 (1786), 35-37; 3 (1786), 132-135]; "An Intended Inscription
for the Monument on Beacon-Hill" and "On Washington's Visit to Boston,

1789" [pub. in Samuel Kettell, ed., *Specimens of American Poetry* (1829), I, 170-173].

Biography: The profligate son of a prosperous merchant, James Allen (not to be confused with others of the same name), was born in Boston, Mass., on July 24, 1739. Although his father went to great efforts to educate him, from an early age on Allen showed little inclination toward industry or scholarship. After three years at Harvard, Allen discontinued his education without receiving a degree. According to a nineteenth-century source, his "inattention to his books, and his free notions upon religion, hindered his attaining to the honors of the University."

Remaining in Boston, Allen continued to prefer leisure to work. He refused to take up a steady trade and was known throughout the literary circles of Boston as an occasional author and poet whose life was characterized by "considerable whim and eccentricity." According to William Dunlap (q.v.), Allen sometimes slept in a coffin which he kept as a bed; and, according to another source, he dressed in "ragged and slovenly" clothes and wrote best when under the influence of "West Indian Muses, sugar, rum, and lemon juice." Nonetheless, Allen was evidently an entertaining companion and host. Although he never married, he had numerous friends and was something of a legend to those who knew him. James Allen died in Boston sometime in 1808.

Critical Appraisal: Although James Allen never seems to have taken anything in his life, including his writing, very seriously, he is remembered today as the author of *The Poem Which the Committee of the Town of Boston Had Voted Unanimously to Be Published*. About this poem there exists considerable mystery, much of which will probably never be explained. As well as can be determined, Allen seems to have written his *Poem* at the request of Dr. Joseph Warren (q.v.), who apparently wished to append a poem on the Boston Massacre to a pamphlet he was writing on the same subject. Delivered in Boston along with the Warren oration, Allen's *Poem* was initially well received, and a committee of patriots subsequently decided to have both works published. When it was rumored, however, that Allen was secretly a Loyalist, the committee quickly reversed its decision and decided instead to suppress Allen's work.

As Lewis Leary aptly explained in a study of Allen and his verse, although Allen may very well have been sympathetic with the Loyalist position, his poem is nonetheless a thoroughly patriotic endorsement of American "virtue" and a biting indictment of British tyranny: "If then our lives thy lawless sword invade, / Think'st thou, enslaved, we'd kiss the pointed blade?" Angered by the committee's decision, Allen's friends had his *Poem* published themselves, appending to it selections from another of Allen's poems titled "The Retrospect." Unlike the *Poem* on the Massacre, "The Retrospect" was indeed Loyalist in its sentiments: "Her hallow'd courts no vulgar trophy soils, / No rapined gold, nor unillustrious spoils; / . . . Britain gives the weary world repose." Printed along with both poems was a statement by Allen's "Friends" that the author was a Tory and that the committee's earlier decision to publish the *Poem* was clear evidence that the patriots were not infallible in their reasoning. The joke, according to Allen's friends, was on the patriots for paying more attention to rhetoric than to truth.

According to Lewis Leary, the publication of Allen's "*Poem* and its antithetical counterpart seems to have been one among many minor skirmishes in the verbal battles between Tories and Patriots on the eve of the Revolution, in which skirmish Allen seems to have been more pawn than participant." "What evidence is available suggests," writes Leary, "that James Allen as a younger man, like many colonials, had been enthusiastically a loyal British subject, grateful for Britain's protection of her colonies, but that after the horror of the massacre in Boston on March 5, 1770, had become at thirty-six a patriot who could bitterly challenge the British."

In the end, however, it is Allen's reputation as a poet that suffers; and this is unfortunate, for the extant examples of his verse stand up well to the test of time. Had Allen indeed succeeded in duping Boston's patriot leaders, his verse, like that of his Boston contemporaries Mather Byles (q.v.) and Joseph Green (q.v.), would be acclaimed for its cleverly disguised satire. Had his verse been read literally, his patriotic poems, several of which were reprinted during the nineteenth century, would probably stand alongside the lesser verses of such poets as Philip Freneau (q.v.) and Francis Hopkinson (q.v.). Regrettably, Allen's natural inclination toward laziness and cynicism seems to have hindered his publishing more frequently. Although Sarah Wentworth Morton (q.v.) claimed that Allen had written a celebrated epic poem on the Battle of Bunker's Hill, this work has now been lost, and unless it should one day come to light, Allen's reputation as a poet will most likely rest on his *Poem* and the controversy surrounding it.

Suggested Readings: William Dunlap, *The Diary of William Dunlap* (1930), I, 177; Evert A. and George L. Duyckinck, *Cyclopaedia of American Literature* (1856), I, 245-246; Samuel Kettell, ed., *Specimens of American Poetry* (1829), I, 160-173; Lewis Leary, "The 'Friends' of James Allen, or, How Partial Truth Is No Truth at All," EAL, 15 (1980), 165-171; Sarah Wentworth Morton, *Beacon Hill* (1797), pp. 17, 53.

James A. Levernier
University of Arkansas at Little Rock

JOHN ALLEN (fl. 1764-1788)

Works: *The Ends of Providence* (1741); *The Spiritual Magazine*, 3 vols. (1752); *A Compendious Descant* (1762); *A Chain of Truths* (1764); *The Beauties of Truth Vindicated* (1765); *A Spiritual Exposition of the Old and New Testament* (1765); *The Christian Pilgrim* (1766); *The Spirit of Liberty: Junius's Loyal Address* (c. 1770); *The American Alarm* (1773); *An Oration, Upon the Beauties of Liberty* (1773); *The Watchman's Alarm* (1774); *A Concise Discant* (1786); *A Morning Thought* and *Christ the Christian's Hope in His Last Hours* (1788); *The Door of Knowledge Opened* (1800).

Biography: Little is known of Allen's life before he was ordained as pastor of the Baptist church in Petticoat Lane, near Spitalfields, London, on Jan. 8, 1764, other than that he had been a preacher and had written *The Spiritual Magazine: or the Christian's Grand Treasure*. While pastor at Petticoat Lane, Allen published several theological works. He was dismissed from his pastorate after some legal and financial difficulties and later was tried for forgery. About 1770 he published *The Spirit of Liberty: Junius's Loyal Address*, a work that discussed both political and religious issues. He appeared in Boston in Nov. 1772 to preach at the Second Baptist Church. Although he was not called to the pastorate, he continued to preach and write. His *Oration*, delivered on the annual Thanksgiving Day, became a best-seller. *The American Alarm* (1773) and *The Watchman's Alarm* (1774) enhanced his reputation as a polemicist. The remainder of Allen's career is obscure. Several later pamphlets attributed to a "John Allen, V.D.M." seem to bear the stamp of his style and subject matter. If two N.H. publications, *A Morning Thought* and *Christ the Christian's Hope in His Last Hours*, poems recording some of the author's dying thoughts, are Allen's work, then his death probably occurred in 1788.

Critical Appraisal: John Allen's early works, published in Eng., are with one exception theological and express his dissenting views. His 1770 work, *The Spirit of Liberty: Junius's Loyal Address*, opens with a plea to the king to restore John Wilkes to his seat in Parliament. This statement is then followed by an essay, "Upon the Rights of the People." His "political tale," as he called it, took the form of a dialogue between Theophilus and Philagathus on politics, especially on an unfaithful ministry. He then moved from civil liberty to religious liberty, defending the beliefs of the Baptists.

An Oration, Upon the Beauties of Liberty, written shortly after his arrival in Boston, and signed "A British Bostonian," was the sixth bestselling pamphlet published in the colonies before the Declaration of Independence, reprinted seven times in four cities between 1773 and 1775. Delivered originally on Dec. 3, 1772, on the occasion of the annual Thanksgiving Day, it is, like Allen's other Revolutionary pamphlets, an eloquent and fiery defense of liberty and the rights of the American people. Unlike the majority of the patriot pamphlets—lengthy philosophical arguments buttressed by references to and quotations from Classical antiquity, British common law, and Enlightenment writers—Allen's pamphlet is remarkable for its uncluttered simplicity, a quality that may have had as much to do with its popularity as the arguments themselves. Allen declared as simple fact what Americans had been arguing for years: "The Parliament of England cannot justly make any laws to tax the Americans; for they are not the Representatives of America, and therefore they are no legislative power of America." Allen resorted to no lengthy constitutional or historical arguments but rather, in the language of the common people, insisted upon the legislative and judicial autonomy of the colonies. Furthermore, he averred "that king is not worthy to reign, that does not make the RIGHTS of his people the rule of all his actions...the king is no more than the servant of his people."

In his three Revolutionary writings, Allen's appeals are general and emotional. He exhorted the American people to defend those rights for which their ancestors suffered and died, demanded that they "stand alarmed," and insisted that the defense of liberty is not rebellion. His third Mass. pamphlet, *The Watchman's Alarm*, written in response to the order closing the port of Boston in 1774, is the most poetic and sermonlike of his pamphlets. He defined political liberty but also poetically defined "liberty of the mind" as "the free thought that expands, ruminates from sea to sea, and from rivers to the end of the earth." He worked throughout with the figure of a watchman overlooking the city. Taken from Isaiah 21, the repeated refrain "watchman what of the night?" lends poetic unity to his exhortation. For most of the essay, "night" suggests sorrow, loss of rights, loss of liberty, and suffering under tyrannical rulers. The "watchman" closes, however, with the assurance that the dark night will end and the "morning of hope, the morning of help, the morning of mercies" will come.

Several works by an author identified as John Allen, V.D.M., were published in the 1780s. They somewhat resemble the earlier work of the "British Bostonian" in subject and style. *A Concise Discant, Upon the Majesty, Excellency, and Preciousness of the Scriptures*, first published in Philadelphia in 1786, is a theological work. *A Morning Thought* and *Christ the Christian's Hope In His Last Hours*, two poems, supposedly written by the author shortly before his death, were first published in N.H. in 1788 at the request of his son. They record the dying thoughts of the poet.

Although the reasons why John Allen and his writings were largely unacknowledged and unpraised by the patriot leaders of Mass. are unknown, he was undoubtedly an eloquent and effective spokesman for the Revolutionary generation, despite the fact that he, like Thomas Paine (q.v.), was a recent immigrant to America.

Suggested Readings: Thomas R. Adams, *American Independence, the Growth of an Idea: A Bibliographical Study of the American Political Pamphlets Printed between 1764 and 1776* (1965), passim; Bernard Bailyn, *Ideological Origins of the American Revolution* (1967), pp. 18, passim; John M. Bumsted and Charles E. Clark, "New England's Tom Paine: John Allen and the Spirit of Liberty," WMQ, 3rd ser., 21 (1964), 561-570; Walter Wilson, *The History and Antiquities of Dissenting Churches and Meeting Houses* (1814), IV, 426-428.

Elaine K. Ginsberg
West Virginia University

PAUL ALLEN (1775-1826)

Works: *An Oration on the Death of Roger Williams Howell* (1792); *An Oration Delivered in the Benevolent Congregational Meeting House* (1796); *An Oration on the Necessity of Political Union* (1797); *An Oration Delivered in the*

Benevolent Congregational Meeting House (1798); *An Oration Delivered in the Benevolent Congregational Meeting House* (1799); *An Oration on the Principles of Taste* (1800); *Original Poems, Serious and Entertaining* (1801); *History of the Expedition Under the Command of Captains Lewis and Clark* (editor; 1814); *The Life of Charles Brockden Brown,* 2 vols. (1815); *History of the American Revolution,* 2 vols. (1819); *Noah* (1821).

Biography: Paul Allen—journalist, editor, eccentric, and minor poet—was born in Providence, R.I., in 1775, to Paul Allen and Polly (Cooke) Allen. His mother was the daughter of Nicholas Cooke, governor of R.I. in the late 1770s. Before graduating from Rhode Island College (now Brown Univ.) in 1793, Allen had established a collegewide reputation as an orator. At least six of his early orations are extant. Although Allen went on to study for the bar, his irresolute and highly credulous nature made him temperamentally unfit to practice law. According to John Neal, Allen was "plain looking... with a character of sluggishness, slovenly inaptitude, and moroseness, all about him."

After moving to Philadelphia, Allen soon became known as a magazine contributor. He published frequently in Joseph Dennie (q.v.) and Nicholas Biddle's *Port Folio*, supervising the printing of the first history of the Lewis and Clark expedition. Soon after, he moved to Baltimore, where he spent the remaining twelve years of his life, contributing frequently to the *Portico* and acting for a time as editor of the *Federal Republican and Baltimore Telegraph*. Following a quarrel with his associates, he resigned this latter position. During a subsequent period of poverty, Allen was at one point imprisoned for a debt of thirty dollars but was soon rescued by friends and fellow members of the Delphian Club. To give Allen an editorial position and financial security, this group started the *Journal of the Times*. Eventually, Allen became editor of the *Morning Chronicle*, retaining this position from 1818 until 1824. From 1824 until his death in 1826, Allen edited the *Saturday Evening Herald*, and he functioned, as well, as publisher of the *Morning Post*. He also planned an ambitious *History of the American Revolution*, most of which was actually written by his friend John Neal and published in 1819. In 1821 Allen published his most ambitious poem, *Noah*, in five cantos. He never married.

Critical Appraisal: Paul Allen was better known to his friends and contemporaries as an editor and journalist rather than a poet. In his mid-20s, he collected his scattered lyrics and published them under the title of *Original Poems, Serious and Entertaining* in 1801. Graceful and not untypical productions of their time and clearly patterned after English models, they show little originality.

The 1st edition of the journals of the Lewis and Clark expedition was published in 1814 under Allen's editorship. However, most of the work of compilation was performed by Allen's friend Nicholas Biddle who worked directly from the manuscripts of the journals that had been turned over to him by Clark following the death of his partner. *The Life of Charles Brockden Brown* was published in the following year (1815) in two volumes at Philadelphia. This work, which is an original source of information on its subject, was begun by Allen and completed by Brown's friend William Dunlap (q.v.). This *Life* was published under Dunlap's name, but the title page fails to acknowledge Allen's contribution. Although the work is frequently inaccurate, it has often been followed by subsequent writers and critics. A one-volume abridgement was issued in London in 1822 as *Memoirs of Charles Brockden Brown*.

Although Allen had long meditated writing a history of the American Revolution, very little of the two-volume work published in 1819 as *History of the American Revolution* is actually his. Most of the actual writing was performed by his friend John Neal. Another long-meditated work on American history, a projected life of Washington (q.v.), finally reached print in two volumes in 1821. Although this work appeared under the name of Allen, it was in actuality written by Neal and Tobias Watkins, with Allen contributing only a page or two of the preface. The serviceable Neal also proved instrumental in readying his friend's ambitious and prolix narrative poem *Noah* for the press: he reduced it to one-fifth its original length, securing its publication in five cantos in 1821. As with Allen's earlier poetic productions, the highly explicit, frequently diffuse and derivative verses cannot be said to manifest any particularly original poetic distinction.

Suggested Readings: DAB; LHUS. *See also* John Neal, *Randolph* (1823), I, 135-137; II, 181, 227; J. T. Scharf, *History of Baltimore City and County* (1881).

Robert Colbert
Louisiana State University in Shreveport

RICHARD ALLEN (1760-1831)

Works: *The Life, Experience, and Gospel Labors of. . .Richard Allen* (1793); *A Narrative of the Proceedings of the Black People, During the Late Awful Calamity in Philadelphia* (Absalom Jones, coauthor; 1794); *Spiritual Song* (c. 1800); *Confession of John Joyce* (1808); *The Doctrine and Discipline of the African Methodist Episcopal Church* (Jacob Tapisco, coauthor; 1813); *The African Methodist Pocket Hymn Book* (compiler; 1818); *The Life, Experience, and Gospel Labors. . .to Which Is Annexed the Rise and Progress of the African Methodist Episcopal Church* (1833).

Biography: Richard Allen was born a slave in Philadelphia, Pa., on Feb. 14, 1760. When he was young, he and his family were sold to a farmer near Dover, Del. As a young man, he became religious and began to conduct services under the influence of Methodism. He educated himself and was allowed to hire himself out sawing wood, making bricks, and hauling by wagon. After the Revolution, Allen traveled extensively in the Mid. Atl. states, preaching to both blacks and whites. At the first conference of American Methodism, in Baltimore in Dec. 1784, Allen was accepted as a minister and was invited to travel with

Bishop Francis Asbury (q.v.). He continued to preach, while also providing for himself.

Having purchased his freedom, he returned in 1786 to Philadelphia, where he met Absalom Jones (q.v.). The two would collaborate as leaders in various projects for over three decades, usually for justice and equality for blacks in Philadelphia in religion and society or for the community's general welfare. In 1787 they organized the Free African Society in Philadelphia. After having been made unwelcome in the Methodist Church they attended, they moved to form a separate church for blacks, the African Church in Philadelphia, in 1791. In 1794 Allen led in forming the Bethel Church (Methodist) for blacks, in which he served as minister for the rest of his life. In 1795 he added a school. His church was a primary influence in the spread of Methodism among blacks in Philadelphia and elsewhere, and in 1816 sixteen congregations joined to found the African Methodist Episcopal (AME) Church, with Allen as its bishop. He was outspoken against the African colonization movement, calling America "our mother country." However, he accepted as not inappropriate a Canadian colonization plan for blacks. He also was outspoken for God and against slavery and was a leader in founding the Free Negro Convention movement in 1830. Allen became wealthy from real estate and a shoe business. By the end of his life, the AME Church was well established and well on its way to becoming a strong national force. He served as its bishop until his death in Philadelphia on Mar. 26, 1831.

Critical Appraisal: Of Allen's writings, his 1793 biography and the twenty-eight-page yellow fever pamphlet he coauthored with Jones in 1794 have received the most attention and deservedly so. The full title of the latter was *A Narrative of the Proceedings of the Black People, During the Late Awful Calamity in Philadelphia in 1793: And a Refutation of Some Censures, Thrown Upon Them in Some Late Publications*, which reflects the primarily defensive origins of the work. Responding to requests that blacks help the sick and the dead in the yellow fever epidemic, Allen and Jones organized admirable and invaluable assistance at great cost and danger to the black participants. After the sickness abated, Mathew Carey (q.v.) published derogatory remarks about the black community's involvement. *A Narrative* strongly, but with reason and restraint, successfully refutes and rebuts the unwarranted accusations; and this problem consumes the first twenty pages of the pamphlet, including various vivid details of the sickness and related conditions confronted by those helping the victims. One interesting account is almost a parallel to the Good Samaritan parable, with a black in the caring role. The other eight pages contain a letter to Mayor Clarkson; his favorable response; "An Address to Those Who Keep Slaves. . ." (pointing out the evils to all of slavery and how God abhors it); an address "To the People of Colour" reminding them to conduct themselves (even in slavery) as those whom God has not forgotten and whom he expects to help themselves in whatever state; thanks to those who help blacks; and finally a hymn. The style of Allen is more evident in this writing than is that of Jones. It was reprinted in

London the same year, and a Philadelphia 1808 reprint added a "Thanksgiving Sermon." (It might be noted that in 1814 Jones and Allen again were called upon to organize the black community to help in a crisis, responding with 2,500 black citizens to assist in defending Philadelphia against the British.) Since the 1793 brief biography of course omits almost the last four decades, the crowning ones, of his life, its contents are in various ways like those of other slave narratives. It focuses on his life as a slave and both the overcoming of that through religion and finally freedom from bondage, followed by finding a firm place for himself as a free man in the North, in this case with growing involvement and success as a religious leader, including the beginnings of separate churches for blacks in Philadelphia. It also very much reflects Allen's worldly theology of love, faith, and responsibility. It was republished in 1833 and 1887, each time without extension of the biography per se, but with important addenda. The corpus of Allen's works is not large, but they are interesting historical records of important aspects of early black accomplishments in the life of Philadelphia and in organized religion for blacks in America, as well as of the life of an outstanding man and leader. Allen's verse is undistinguished, but his prose is strong, straightforward, and honest, even though artistically unexceptional and at times a bit pious. Everything he published reflects his ministerial role and his firm belief in both his race and his God.

Suggested Readings: DAB; DARB. *See also Afro-American Encyclopedia* (1974), I, 117-120; Philip S. Foner, *History of Black Americans from Africa to the . . . Cotton Kingdom* (1975), pp. 540-541, 550-552, 557-558; Carol V. R. George, *Segregated Sabbaths: Richard Allen and . . . Independent Black Churches, 1760-1840* (1973); Sidney Kaplan, *The Black Presence in the Era of the American Revolution, 1770-1800* (1973), pp. 81-94; Vernon Loggins, *The Negro Author* (1931), pp. 56-61, passim; Marcia M. Mathews, *Richard Allen* (1963); Dorothy Porter, ed., *Early Negro Writing, 1760-1837* (1971), pp. 414-426, 559-561; Theresa G. Rush et al., *Black American Writers Past and Present* (1975), I, 25-26; Milton C. Sernett, *Black Religion and American Evangelism* (1975), passim; "Some Letters of Richard Allen and Absalom Jones to Dorothy Ripley," JNH, 1 (1916), 436-443; Charles H. Wesley, *Richard Allen* (1935); Jerome H. Wood, Jr., "Richard Allen," *Encyclopedia of American Biography* (1974), pp. 29-30; Henry J. Young, *Major Black Religious Leaders, 1755-1940* (1977), pp. 25-40.

Julian Mason
University of North Carolina at Charlotte

THOMAS ALLEN (1743-1810)

Works: "The Petition Remonstrance and Address of the Town of Pittsfield to the Honorable Board of Councellors and House of Representatives of the Province of the Massachusetts Bay" (w. 1775; pub. in Oscar and Mary Handlin, eds., *The Popular Sources of Political Authority* (1966), pp. 61-64); "A Vindication of the County of Birkshire" (w. 1778; pub. in WMQ, 3d ser., 33 (1976),

518-527); *Benefits of Affliction* (1798); *An Historical Sketch of the County of Berkshire* (1808); *A Sermon Preached Before...James Sullivan, Esq., Governor* (1808).

Biography: Thomas Allen was born and spent his early years in Jonathan Edwards's (q.v.) Northampton, Mass. After graduation from Harvard in 1762, he was called to the pulpit of the recently incorporated town of Pittsfield in westernmost Mass., where he served a long and sometimes stormy pastorate. In his last years, his outspoken support of Thomas Jefferson (q.v.) led to a schism in the church. But Allen is best remembered for his activities during the Revolutionary War. Intimately involved in the military, political, and ideological aspects of the struggle, Allen helped plan the movement of cannon from Fort Ticonderoga to Dorchester Heights, served as an army chaplain at White Plains, and saw action as a militia private at Bennington, where he reportedly killed several British soldiers. In addition, Allen was an important elucidator of the Revolutionary ideology and the leader of the Berkshire "Constitutionalists," a group that, in the midst of war, shut down the county courts to dramatize its demand for a new state constitution.

Critical Appraisal: Thomas Allen published only two short works in his lifetime—one election sermon and one brief historical sketch of Berkshire County. But these works are relatively insignificant. Allen's Revolutionary writings, largely petitions and pamphlets, some of which have been published only recently in anthologies of documents and scholarly journals, are of immeasurably greater importance. These writings are neither lengthy, numerous, nor presently well known, but they place Allen at the forefront of American Revolutionary theorists and are noteworthy primarily for their forceful, reasoned, and eloquent assertion of what the quarrel and ultimate break with Britain meant for Americans and their new indigenous governments.

The best example of Allen's argument for independence is his "Vindication of the County of Birkshire." Written in the autumn of 1778, this document stands as a clear and cogent summary of the position of the Constitutionalist movement in New England. It maintained that the existing state government of Mass. lacked legitimate foundation and that the people of Berkshire were therefore justified in refusing to admit the courts of that government. The Declaration of Independence, Allen asserted, had thrown the states into a "perfect state of nature." In this situation, only a "fundamental constitution," approved by the people, could properly reestablish social "compact" and legitimate government in Mass.

Allen was concerned not only with the mode of adoption of a constitution but also with its content and effect. According to Allen, a constitution must, as nearly as possible, eliminate the possibility of corruption and function as "a Sacred Barrier against Tyranny and Despotism" by clearly enumerating the rights of the people and carefully circumscribing the power of officials. Although his emphasis on corruption and tyranny strongly resembles the "opposition ideology" of eighteenth-century Anglo-American politics, Allen and the Constitutionalists pioneered a constructive phase in the development of the Revolutionary ideology and Revolutionary politics in which, as Bernard Bailyn has suggested, "the ideas, fears and hopes that had first become decisive in the attacks on the British government were turned to positive uses in the framing of the first state constitutions."

Significantly, Allen and his Berkshire followers were among the first to insist on an "Essential Distinction. . .Between the fundamental Constitution and the Power of legislation." In fact, their opposition—based on that insistence—to existing state government was a major factor in the decision of Mass. to call a special constitutional convention and thus become the first state to develop a separate and distinct mode of framing and ratifying a constitution. This action established a precedent for the procedures used in 1787-1788 for the state to ratify a national constitution.

In short, Thomas Allen developed and elucidated, with brilliance and with homespun common sense, several doctrines central to the American Revolution and to the American concept of government in general: the notion of popular sovereignty, the idea that a popularly approved constitution must be the foundation for all government, and the concept that a constitution should protect the liberties of the people from governmental abuse.

Suggested Readings: CCNE; Sprague (I, 607-612). *See also* Richard D. Birdsall, "Reverend Thomas Allen: Jeffersonian Calvinist," NEQ, 30 (1957), 147-165; Samuel Burnham, *Reverend Thomas Allen* (1869); J.E.A. Smith, *The History of Pittsfield, Massachusetts*, 2 vols. (1869); Theodore M. Hammett, "The Revolutionary Ideology in Its Social Context: Berkshire County, Massachusetts, 1725-1785" (Unpublished Ph.D. diss., Brandeis University, 1976); George D. Langdon, Jr., "The Reverend Thomas Allen of Pittsfield" (M.A. thesis, Amherst College, 1957).

Theodore M. Hammett
Abt Associates Inc.
Cambridge, Massachusetts

JAMES ALLIN (1692-1747)

Works: *What Shall I Render!* (1722); *Two Practical Discourses* (1727); *Thunder and Earthquake* (1727); *Evangelical Obedience* (1731); *The Eternity of God* (1732); *Magistracy an Institution* (1744).

Biography: James Allin (also spelled *Allen*) was born in Roxbury, Mass., in 1692. He graduated from Harvard College in 1710 and prepared for a career in the ministry. In 1718 the tiny Puritan community of Brookline, which had been incorporated as a town of thirty-two families in 1705, chose Allin as minister. In Nov. 1718 he married Mehitabel Shepard, daughter of the Rev. Jeremiah Shepard (q.v.) of Lynn, Mass., whose half-brother was the famous Puritan divine, Thomas Shepard (q.v.). Little is known of Allin's ministry, but he apparently avoided the controversies over salaries, meeting house locations, and doctrine that often beset his colleagues in other eighteenth-century Puritan New Eng. pulpits. There is evidence that some of his congregation left the church during the 1740s when he turned against the emotionalism of the religious revival known as the Great Awakening, but the town continued to show its approval of his ministry in the 1730s and 1740s by paying him from forty to eighty pounds "over and above his Stated psallery." He died at age 56 in 1747, having served his congregation for "28 years, 3 months and 13 days."

Critical Appraisal: Although James Allin's audience was small—the town of Brookline had 338 people in 1765—and his reputation modest, his surviving sermons are not without literary merit. In content, all of his sermons progress with inexorable logic toward the traditional Puritan ideas that God is omnipotent and that man is helpless to effect his own salvation. Although Allin's works are composed in the Puritan "plain style" that eschewed high-flown rhetoric and followed its own carefully prescribed form, they nonetheless abound in vivid imagery and graceful cadences, which make them well worth considering.

Allin's longest published work, *Two Practical Discourses* (1727), for example, defends Puritan orthodoxy against the heretical belief that merit and good works were themselves capable of earning salvation but does so in a style that makes tradition more appealing than it might otherwise have been. In the first of the two sermons, "The Wheels of the World Govern'd," Allin argued for an unseen harmony in a universe where sinful man perceives only chaos. God's providence orders all: life and death, calamity and good fortune, revolution, and the rise and fall of kingdoms. God, said Allin, is all-knowing and all-powerful, and "The loftiest angel and the meanest worm are equally under him." The second sermon, "The Doctrine of MERIT Exploded," is a powerful statement of divine omnipotence and human insignificance in which Allin reminded his audience that "we contribute no more to his nature and beatitude, than the light of a candle, or the dim shining of a gloworm [sic] in the hedge, doth [to] the lustre of the sun in the heavens."

The only one of Allin's sermons known to have survived in more than one edition was *Thunder and Earthquake* (1727), a jeremiad on the tremor that shook New Eng. on Oct. 29, 1727. The sermon was preached on Nov. 1. This sermon began with a vivid description of the earthquake's effects on the citizens of Brookline: "Our Faces were pale as Ashes, our Lips quivered, our Speech faultred, and our Knees smote together, and there was no strength left in us." After a detailed discussion of the scientific theory of earthquakes, supported by a careful annotation of severe thunderstorms in the vicinity in the months preceding the earthquake, Allin reminded his audience that God causes all natural phenomena, and that lightning is "the *Fire of Heaven* [that] may in a moment dispatch you to the *Flames of Hell*."

This sermon, with its dramatic call to repentance and reformation, foreshadows the evangelical fervor of the Great Awakening and shows that Allin was capable, when the occasion demanded, of writing in the spirited style that came to characterize preachers like Jonathan Edwards (q.v.). Allin, who had used the expression "born again" as early as 1722, initially welcomed the revival movement and wrote an enthusiastic "Brief Account" of its work at Brookline for his friend Thomas Prince's (q.v.) *Christian History*, published weekly from 1743 to 1745. Later in life, like most of his contemporaries, Allin criticized the emotional excesses and the uneducated preaching generated by the Awakening and returned to the more orthodox Puritan tenets he had always favored. It should be noted that *A Letter to a Friend in the Country* (1740), which is attributed to Allin in Charles Evans's *American Bibliography* (4467) was written by a Boston merchant, James Allen (1697-1755), the grandson of the Rev. James Allen (q.v.). The error in attribution is discussed in *Sibley's Harvard Graduates*, (VI, 164).

Suggested Readings: CCNE; Sibley-Shipton (V, 506-510). *See also* William D. Andrews, "The Literature of the 1727 New England Earthquake," EAL, 7 (1973), 281-294; John Pierce, *Reminiscences of Forty Years* (1837), pp. 27-30; idem, *Muddy River and Brookline Records, 1634-1838* (1875), pp. 107-162, passim; William T. Youngs, Jr., *God's Messengers: Religious Leadership in Colonial New England, 1700-1750* (1976).

Virginia Bernhard
University of St. Thomas

HENRY ALLINE (1748-1784)

Works: *Two Mites* (1781); *Hymns and Spiritual Songs* [I] (1782); *A Sermon on a Day of Thanksgiving* (1782); *A Sermon Preached to a Religious Society of Young Men* (1782); *The Anti-Traditionalist* (1783); *A Sermon, Preached at Fort Medway* (1783); *Hymns and Spiritual Songs [II] (1786); A Gospel Call to Sinners* (rep. of Fort Medway Sermon; 1795); *Life and Journals* (1806).

Biography: Henry Alline was born in Newport, R.I., on Jan. 14, 1748. In the autumn of 1760, his family immigrated to Falmouth, Nova Scotia, as part of the resettlement of Acadian land in the Annapolis Valley by New Englanders in the wake of the expulsion of the Acadians. Life in Nova Scotia was difficult; yet in spite of the utilitarian demands of frontier life, Alline was attracted to spiritual concerns and found widespread sympathy for his religious interests. In 1776 he dedicated himself to preaching the Gospel full time, and almost single-handedly precipitated a revival of faith among the people of Maritime Can. His followers were called New Lights.

Although best remembered as a charismatic preacher, Alline sought to broaden his influence through the written word. He published sermons and theological works, and at the time of his death at North-Hampton, N.H., on Jan. 28, 1784, he was journeying to Boston to publish his hymns and possibly to begin preaching in New Eng. But he had been seriously ill throughout the spring and summer of 1783, and such an arduous journey late in autumn was foolhardy. Driven by religious zeal, Alline literally burned himself out between 1776 and 1784.

Critical Appraisal: Alline's theological works have not worn well. His ideas are not particularly original nor is his theological position clearly, coherently, and systematically articulated in his writings. He appears to have been influenced strongly by William Law, the English theologian. He responded to the pietistical character of Law's writings and found Law's mysticism and asceticism very attractive. But Alline's works also proclaimed the need for enthusiastic evangelism, demanding a strong commitment to spreading the Gospel message. Moreover, his evangelical spirit was characterized by its anti-Calvinism: his view of spiritual grace was essentially Universalist and Arminian. He believed that any Christian truly touched by Christ could not help but proclaim the gift of Free Grace to the rest of mankind.

His attraction to both asceticism and evangelism created an inconsistency and a tension in this theological position that he never fully resolved in his prose writings. He was torn between focusing on the inner life of the spirit and focusing on the necessary proclamation of the knowledge of the spirit, between seeing the light and spreading the light. The theological inconsistencies arising from this blurred focus were attacked in his own day from several points of view, most notably by the Calvinist preacher Jonathan Scott, a Congregationalist minister at Yarmouth, Nova Scotia, who published a detailed refutation of Alline's *Two Mites* in his book, *A Brief View of the Religious Tenets and Sentiments...of Mr. Henry Alline* (1784). John Wesley was equally unimpressed by Alline's theology when it was brought to his attention by a Methodist preacher in Nova Scotia. Today, Alline's theological works hold little intellectual interest, although occasionally one is impressed with the force of his descriptive powers when articulating certain aspects of religious experience.

But the inconsistencies that mar his theological works become an important source of the vitality and energy in his hymns and spiritual verses, found principally in *Hymns and Spiritual Songs* [II]. Emotionally, Alline was able to accept and absorb the apparent tension between his inclination to turn inward and the evangelical urge to reach outward to others by viewing the characteristic condition of human religious experience in terms of polarities that were apparently irreconcilable in this life. From Alline's point of view, the life of the Christian was composed of both intense agony and extreme ecstasy, of fear and hope, a profound awareness of terrifying damnation and exhilarating salvation. The dichotomous nature of religious experience created a dramatic tension that expressed itself internally in an awareness of the interrelationship between good and evil in individual lives and externally in a recognition of the struggle between good and evil in the relationship between God and man. The Christian, then, was caught between preoccupation with his inner conflicts and his responsibility to further the cause of good in the world.

In his poetry, Alline treated both of these struggles again and again. In many ways, the verse in *Hymns and Spiritual Songs* [II], most of which was probably written during his last illness in the spring and summer of 1783, amounts to a form of spiritual autobiography. Because he used relatively simple hymn verse-forms, he was able to focus on the various aspects of the ups and downs of religious experience (internal and external) with clarity, candour, and precision. But what makes his poetry inspirational and not simply analytical, theologically and psychologically, is Alline's resolution of all levels of Christian struggle in an intensely intimate awareness of the person of Christ.

Just as it lay at the heart of his religious faith, Alline's vision of Christ lies at the heart of his poetry. His success in articulating that vision in verse ultimately overrides the sense of struggle in which most of his poetry begins and is certainly much more effective than all of his theological efforts put together. In placing Christ at the heart of his poetry, Alline is following in the path of Isaac Watts and shares a common concern with his great contemporary Charles Wesley. But where Watts, like other seventeenth-century poets, saw Christ and the redemptive act of the Crucifixion in the broad context of the historical evolution of man's relationship to God, Alline and Wesley approached Christ as an intimate in whom they could simply place their trust and faith. For Alline, even more so than Wesley, there appeared to be no need to go beyond the knowledge of Christ. In Christ lies the resolution of inner struggle and of the cosmic struggle between good and evil. In Christ lies the emotional and spiritual peace that all men seek in a world torn by a myriad of conflicts (not the least of which was the American Rebellion).

In his simple descriptions of struggle and of peace-in-Christ, Alline placed the fundamental elements of his religious vision within the imaginative grasp of even his most unsophisticated followers. Moreover, by using his own inner religious experience as an instrument of outreach to others, he imaginatively bridged in poetry the apparent dichotomy between personal illumination and evangelical responsibility.

The influence of Alline's works is difficult to assess. His followers in Nova Scotia were largely nonliterate although a few imitated his hymns. In New England, he had a posthumous influence on Benjamin Randall, leader of the Free Will Baptists in New Hampshire and Maine. Between 1795 and 1804, Randall had most of Alline's prose reprinted as well as three editions of his *Hymns and Spiritual Songs*. However, there was never broad interest in Alline's theology or his verse. His great flaw as a poet is the sheer quantity of his verse: more than 500 hymns. He overwhelmed the reader and was often repetitious, obscuring the coherence of his religious vision. Although he clearly attempted to shape his principal volume of verse, his instincts were more those of a preacher providing a selection of hymns for his followers than those of a poet creating a cohesive body of verse. As a poet, he was strong in his vision but weak in his sense of structure.

Suggested Readings: DAB. *See also* Maurice W. Armstrong, *The Great Awakening in Nova Scotia* (1948), pp. 61-107; J. M. Bumstead, *Henry Alline* (1971); G. Stewart and G. Rawlyk, *A People Highly Favoured of God* (1972); T. B. Vincent, "Alline and Bailey," CanL, 68-69 (1976), 124-133.

Thomas B. Vincent
Royal Military College of Canada

GEORGE ALSOP (c. 1636-c. 1673)

Works: *A Character of the Province of Maryland (1666).*

Biography: The elder of two sons in the family of Rose and Peter Alsop of London, George Alsop was baptized in Eng. at St. Martin-in-the-Fields on Jun. 19, 1636. Peter was a tailor, and we can infer from that fact and other facts in George's life that the Alsop family must have been in humble circumstances. No information exists concerning George's early education; the *Character*, however, indicates wide reading and knowledge of French and Greek. At the age of 18, George Alsop began a two-year apprenticeship in an unspecified craft. A Royalist supporter, Alsop, however, was sufficiently intimidated by the Cromwell regime to seek his fortune elsewhere than in his native country.

After indenturing himself to one Thomas Stockett for four years in return for passage to Md., Alsop arrived in Md. in Dec. 1658 or early Jan. 1659. On a farm in Baltimore County, near the present site of Havre de Grace, Alsop spent four years of servitude, experiencing kind treatment but falling severely ill near the end of his period of indenture. Although Alsop evidently admired "Mary-Land" and was enthusiastic about that colony's attributes, upon recovery from his illness and after a brief period working possibly as an Indian trader, he returned to Eng.

Arriving in London in 1663, Alsop joined the host of celebrators still penning encomia at the Restoration of Charles II. In addition to writing loyal verse, Alsop wrote the *Character* in 1665 and published this promotional tract in 1666. After the publication of the *Character*, "George Alsop was appointed rector of Chipping Ongar, Essex" and gained some notoriety from his attempt to "read divine service in the Quakers' meeting house in Gracechurch Street" and suffering an attack on his person by the angry mob of "Friends" (Lemay). He was succeeded in his post at Chipping Ongar on May 7, 1673. Lemay pointed out that after "a few glimpses of the later life of George Alsop, he drops out of sight."

Critical Appraisal: The subject of much passing commentary and historical analysis, Alsop's *A Character of the Province of Maryland* has elicited little unanimity from its critics. Assessments of Alsop's writing have ranged from Clayton Hall's statement that the "author had in some way acquired a quantity of ill-assorted information, and also an extensive vocabulary, but was without sufficient education to enable him to make proper use of either" and that "his style is therefore extravagant, inflated, and grandiloquent" to Louis B. Wright's assertion that "Alsop's descriptions, written in colorful and idiomatic prose, have the rhythms of the Elizabethans and their zest for the world around them." "With a boisterous humor that is sometimes coarse but never dull," stated Wright, Alsop told "about the country and its customs." Furthermore, according to Wright, Alsop's *Character* is "the most vigorous and original work of the middle decades of the seventeenth century."

The most ground-breaking and enlightened analysis of Alsop's *Character*, however, comes from J. A. Lemay, who concluded that "Erudite and slangy, reverent to king and God while scurrilous and scatalogical to men and manners, poetry mixed with prose, humorous literary allusions (mainly biblical and classical), an extraordinary delight in assonance and consonance, and a plenitude of rhetorical devices—all characterize Alsop's Menippean satire." According to Lemay, *A Character of the Province of Mary-Land* is a jewel in the genre of promotion literature. No one can be certain of the literary influence of George Alsop, but this tract is the earliest of a long line of distinguished southern works in baroque prose."

Certainly, as the reader plows through the copious prefatory matter (including a dedication to Lord Baltimore), Alsop's enthusiastic chapters, including sections on Maryland flora and fauna, the inhabitants, its government, the state of servitude, the importance of trade, and the Susquehanna Indians; the amateurish poems that celebrate even more profusely the province's attributes; and the dated letters to friends and relatives that terminate the volume and that supposedly lend credence to the points made, he senses, as Lemay put it, that Alsop is "chafing against the restrictive form and content of the typical promotion tract."

Capable of approaching the fatuousness that characterizes many early promotional tracts, Alsop could in fact sound very much like a Crèvecoeure when he apostrophized the homogenizing influences of the wilderness: "Here the Roman Catholick, and the Protestant Episcopal . . . contrarywise concur in an unanimous parallel of friendship." But when he espoused the concept of subordination, so warmly stating "that there must be Servants as well as Masters," and when he talked of the Indians sacrificing their young to the devil, the reader perceives an elaborate spoof. Regardless of interpretation, however, Alsop's *Character* stands out as one of the most interesting and valuable works of its kind, as well as a work of light, pleasing jocularity.

Suggested Readings: DAB; LHUS; T₁. *See also* Robert A. Bain, ed., Introduction, *A Character of the Province of Mary-Land* (1972), pp. v-xix; Clayton Colman Hall, Introduction, *Narratives of Early Maryland* (1910), pp. 337-339; Jay B. Hubbell, *The South in American Literature* (1954), pp. 61-62; J. A. Leo Lemay, *Men of Letters in Colonial Maryland* (1972), pp. 48-69; Harrison T. Meserole et al., eds., *American Literature: Tradition and Innovation* (1969), I, 27-28; Montrose Moses, *The Literature of the South* (1910), pp. 41-44; Leslie A. Wardenaar, "Humor in the Colonial Promotional Tract: Topics and Techniques," EAL, 9 (1975), 286-300.

A. Franklin Parks
Frostburg State College

RICHARD ALSOP (1761-1815)

Works: *A Second Address to the Freemen* (1790); *To the Freemen of the State of Connecticut* (1790) *Addressed by the Boy Who Carries the American Mercury* (1793); *Aristocracy* (1795); *The Lovers of La Vendee* (translator; 1799);

The Political Green-House (contributor/editor; 1799); *A Poem Sacred to the Memory of George Washington* (1800); *To the Freemen* (1803); *The Enchanted Lake* (1806); *The Echo* (1807); *The Geographical, Natural, and Civil History of Chile* (1808); *The Universal Receipt Book* (1814); *A Narrative of the Adventures...of John R. Jewitt* (1815); *The Charms of Fancy* (w. 1788; pub. 1856).

Biography: Richard Alsop was by birth the wealthiest of the Conn. Wits and the only one not to pursue a nonliterary profession. He was also evidently the most amiable member of the group. His family wealth derived from commerce, but although he did on occasion involve himself in the affairs of the family business in Middletown, Alsop did not multiply his portion. He was, his sister reported, "much attached to books." He entered Yale in 1776, but he did not graduate. (He was awarded an honorary M.A. in 1798.) Alsop developed an interest in natural history and became proficient in the art of taxidermy. Around 1800 he began to associate himself with Isaac Riley, his brother-in-law and a New York City publisher. He himself served for a time as a bookseller and publisher in Hartford. Alsop divided his last years between Hartford and N.Y. (Flatbush). He died and was buried in the latter location, survived by his wife and children.

Critical Appraisal: Elihu Hubbard Smith (q.v.) described Alsop's place among the Wits as "the moon shining among lesser lights." The metaphor has an unintended accuracy: much of Alsop's most interesting work is essentially derivative. His greatest successes were in the areas of translation, editing, and burlesque.

His most ambitious original effort, *The Charms of Fancy*, unfortunately illustrates this point. It consists of more than 200 pages of couplets and notes arranged in four books, and it comprises a survey of the world as revealed to Alsop's imagination by his library. An extract from the Argument to the Third Book suggests the extent to which he, in the words of his editor, Theodore Dwight (q.v.), "selected, compounded and used" fragments from his reading: "The Bohon Upas Tree. Borneo. The Ourang Outang. Celebes. The Opium Tree. Character of the Macassars. Molucca Islands...Imperial Palace at Delhi. Magnificence of the Court. Reflections on its empty pomp and ostentatious parade." The poem combines a delight in details of geography and history with a conventionally melancholic view of the vanity of human wishes. The most interesting moments occur when Alsop considers the American scene: his celebrations of American culture—in the persons of Benjamin Trumbull (q.v.), Joel Barlow (q.v.), and Timothy Dwight (q.v.)—and American patriotism—George Washington (q.v.)—and his inclusion of the New World in the general prospect of degeneration: "Yon cities, too, in infant pride that rise, / And shine, Columbia! mid thy favor'd skies, / Some future day may see in dust o'erthron."

Alsop was apparently the prime mover behind the important Wit satire, *The Echo*—in collaboration with Mason Fitch Cogswell (q.v.), Theodore Dwight, Lemuel Hopkins (q.v.), and Elihu Smith. The initial conceit—a series of verse parodies ("echoes") of the rhetoric of editors and politicians—was certainly suited to Alsop's abilities. The later numbers tended to choose objects of derision more for their political error than for their rhetorical excesses. Alsop, as a matter of course, subscribed to the Federalist dogmas of his fellow Wits. He joined Hopkins and Dwight to write *The Political Green-House* (published separately and later included in *The Echo*), a typical assault on Thomas Jefferson (q.v.) and the Democrats and on Fr. and the Jacobins.

Modern critics have preferred Alsop's shorter, more lyric poems—"Ode to Sheerwater," "A Song. From the Italian," and "Inscription for a Family Tomb" —but in his own time, his most popular works were "A Poem Sacred to the Memory of George Washington" and *Narrative of the Adventures and Sufferings of John R. Jewitt*. The former is a long, unexceptional elegy; the latter is a genuinely attractive production. It represents a significant expansion of Jewitt's previously printed journal describing his two-year captivity among the Indians of Vancouver Island's Nootka Sound. Alsop's prose style was unobtrusive and effective, and he retold the adventure with a close attention to anthropological detail.

Alsop's easy prose also proved useful in his translations of Giovanni Molina's account of Chile and Étienne Gosse's novel of revolutionary France (*La Vendee*). He also undertook several verse translations, his largest effort being *The Enchanted Lake*, a selection from Francesco Berni's *Orlando Innamorato*. His interest in translating Scandinavian poetry—"Runic Poetry: Twilight of the Gods," "Extract from *The Conquest of Scandinavia*," "Versification of . . . Ossian's *Temora*"—shows Alsop to be an early experimenter in the new mode of the Gothic. Not the most original poet of the Wits, Alsop made a virtue of imitation and exercised his not inconsiderable literary talents to their best advantage.

Suggested Readings: DAB; LHUS. *See also* Adolph Benson, "Scandinavian Influences," SS, 9 (1927); Benjamin Franklin V, ed., *The Poetry of the Minor Connecticut Wits* (1970); idem, *The Prose of the Minor Connecticut Wits* (1974); idem, "The Published Commentary on the Minor Connecticut Wits," RALS, 8 (1978); Karl P. Harrington, *Richard Alsop* (1939); Vernon Louis Parrington, *The Connecticut Wits* (1926, 1969).

J. Kenneth Van Dover
Lincoln University

NATHANIEL AMES II (1708-1764)

Works: *The Astronomical Diary and Almanack* for 1726-1764 (1725-1763).

Biography: Nathaniel Ames II—physician, almanac maker, tavernkeeper, and part-time attorney—was born in Bridgewater, Mass., the son of Nathaniel Ames, an astronomer. He was descended from John Ames of Bruton, Somerset, Eng., whose son William (great-grandfather of Nathaniel Ames II) immigrated to Mass. and settled at age 35 in Braintree about 1640. William's son John moved to West Bridgewater about 1672, where the first Nathaniel Ames was born in 1677. Capt. Nathaniel Ames married Susannah Howard, Dec. 2, 1702, and had six children, the eldest of whom was Nathaniel II, who became a physician through self-study and probably an apprenticeship. In 1730 Nathaniel

II settled in Dedham and in 1735 married Mary Fisher, daughter of Capt. Josiah Fisher; her widowed mother's tavern-residence became their home, and Ames added tavernkeeping to his full-time professions of almanac maker and physician. Mary died on Nov. 11, 1737, shortly after the birth of their son Fisher, who survived his mother only until Sept. 17, 1738. These circumstances were important in Ames's eventually winning a famous lawsuit that established a precedent in Mass. inheritance cases. After the widow Fisher died, Ames claimed the property under province law against the in-laws and other family members who claimed inheritance under English common law. In his 1751 almanac, Ames announced victoriously that he was the owner of the Sun Tavern.

In 1740 Ames married Deborah Fisher, Mary's cousin and daughter of Jeremiah Fisher. They had five children: Nathaniel III, who continued the almanac series for ten years after his father's death; Seth, a physician and surgeon in the American army; Fisher, who became a famous Federalist pamphleteer, essayist, and orator and helped draft the Constitution; Deborah, married to Rev. William Shuttleworth; and William, lost at sea in 1778.

Ames's legal involvements were notorious; he was personally involved as plaintiff in at least forty- eight cases between 1740 and 1757. Although a member of the First Church of Christ of Dedham, he did not attend church. Cantankerous by nature, he was a clever eccentric, a versatile intellectual, and a sometime annoyance in the Dedham community.

Critical Appraisal: Nathaniel Ames's most lasting accomplishment was an annual series of almanacs, spanning thirty-eight consecutive years. Beginning in 1725 (for 1726), the series predated James Franklin's (q.v.) *Rhode-Island Almanack* (by Poor Robin) by three years and Benjamin Franklin's (q.v.) *Poor Richard* by eight years. Ames's *Astronomical Diary* sold as many as 60,000 copies a year, and Moses Coit Tyler rated it higher in quality than *Poor Richard*, which resembled Ames's almanac in content and format more than it resembled any other contemporary almanac. This series is of value to both literary and social historians in that these almanacs influenced literary tastes and also reflected current customs and attitudes. Ames not only calculated the almanac but also filled its pages with essays, verse, and phrases of wit and wisdom.

Ames's specialty was the essay, chiefly on the subjects of health or astronomy. As an educator, Ames excelled in disseminating the "new science" (Copernican and Newtonian) in an entertaining and understandable form to the masses. In 1743 Ames defended the Copernican hypothesis against scriptural objections. Other Ames essays during this period were "Astro-Theology, or a Demonstration of the Being and Attribute of God from a Survey of the Heavens" (1735), a biological essay on the generation of "Animalcula" (1736), the probability of habitation on other planets and descriptions of the inhabitants (1736, 1737, and 1759), a summary of the progress in astronomy (1739), an explanation of "Newton's Law of Gravitational Attraction" (1740), "Comets, or Blazing Stars" (1743), "On Conjuration and Witchcraft" (1747), a description of the planetary systems of Kepler and Newton (1750), on medical theory (1752), "On Regimen," emphasizing temperance (1754), and on national progress (1758). Ames's reputation as a physician doubtless enhanced almanac sales. His advice on health was usually given in his essay-prefaces rather than in the usual "receipts" for cures.

Satire, although occasionally found in his essays, appeared more often in his verse and in scattered phrases on the calendar pages in the blank spaces. The subject matter was varied. As Ames related his satiric concerns to his personal life and to public events and affairs, he naturally sustained reader interest. Employing the stylistic devices used traditionally by satirists, he sometimes attacked two or three professions simultaneously, jeering at lawyers most of all. Burlesque and innuendo were particularly effective weapons. He ridiculed lawyers, physicians, clergymen, politicians, astrological predictions, women's foibles and frivolities, the male-female relationship, and the petty vices of men and women.

Ames, an astronomer as well as an astrologer, had a high regard for conscientious astronomers. He printed the Man of Signs (familiar to almanac readers today) for the first time in 1729 but ceased to include it after 1734. Satirizing prognostications was uncommon in America, and most almanac makers used the Man of Signs. Apparently assured of his reading public, Ames was one of the few almanac makers who could afford to ignore these conventions without losing sales.

Ames's patterns were mainly those of the English satirists: Dryden, Pope, Addison, Swift, and Butler. Although Ames borrowed verse frequently, most of it was his own. His borrowed verse was primarily from Pope, apparently his favorite. At his best, Ames wrote poetry as good as Pope's worst; Ames, at his own worst, descended into doggerel. His verse, inconsistent in quality, still surpassed that of his competitors. Two rhymes on intolerance (Mar. 1744) and intemperance (Sept. 1756) were superior in wit and style. The use of dialect in almanac writings was rare. Yet Ames used it in 1742 in a political satire featuring a rustic and again in 1746 in a dialogue between a rustic "clown" and a scholar in which the rustic had the clever lines while the scholar taught astronomy.

Ames influenced his contemporaries and his successors. Many of his rivals scanned his pages for ideas; and his son Nathaniel III continued his father's successful format and style until 1775. Nathaniel Ames's *Astronomical Diary* actually set the standards for its competitors; it is doubtful that any almanac other than Benjamin Franklin's ever surpassed it or that any other almanac, either before or after Ames, ever equalled it in quality and popularity.

Suggested Readings: DAB; T_1. *See also* Azel Ames, M.D., "Next of Kin to Fisher," NEM (Sept.1897), pp. 57-69; Samuel Briggs, *Essays, Humor, and Poems of Nathaniel Ames, Father and Son...1726-1775* (1891); Robert Brand Hanson, *History of Dedham, Massachusetts: 1635-1890* (1976), pp. 120-128; Samuel Eliot Morison, "Squire Ames and Doctor Ames," NEQ, 1 (1928), 5-31; EIHC; Matthew A. Stickney, "Almanacs and Their Authors," EIHC, 14 (1877), 81-82; Marion Barber Stowell, *Early American Almanacs* (1977), pp. 72-75.

Marion Barber Stowell
Milledgeville, Georgia

EDWARD ANTILL (1701-1770)

Works: "An Essay on the Cultivation of the Vine, and the Making and Preserving of Wine, Suited to the Different Climates in North-America," "The Method of Curing Figs," and "Observations on the Raising and Dressing of Hemp," American Philosophical Society *Transactions* (1771).

Biography: Born in 1701 to Edward (fl. 1659-1704) and Sarah Antill in New York City, Edward Antill II moved in 1722 onto lands at Raritan Landing, N.J., across from New Brunswick, left him by his godfather and "quondam alleged pirate," Giles Shelley, whom his father had once bailed out of trouble. Young Antill's first wife, Catherine, died, and he married Anne Morris, daughter of Governor Lewis Morris (q.v.), in 1739. The next decade became one of honor and advancement for Antill; he was elected to the Provincial Assembly in 1738, then appointed a judge in 1739 and to Council in 1741, and eventually commissioned justice of the peace in one county after another from 1744 to 1750. He farmed extensively, raising trees and apples, and prospered sufficiently to be able to give 1,800 pounds in 1754 toward the founding of Columbia College, then called King's. He became interested in agricultural improvement, proposing better ways to raise and fatten hogs, raise black cattle without milk, increase milk production, and feed oxen and sheep by the use of boiled potatoes. In addition, he became interested in the medicinal properties of rhubarb and in the possibility of raising olives in the South.

His greatest achievements and honor, however, derived from his interest in growing grapes and making wine, his turning of that interest into projects for the good of America and "mankind," and his publication of his thoughts on culture and viticulture in the American Philosophical Society's first volume of *Transactions* (1771). The Royal Society of Arts, in its project to patronize colonial viticulture and oenology, offered a number of premiums. Antill won the largest individual one ever awarded to an American, a first premium of 200 pounds. What he had accomplished in only three years (1764-1767) he believed others could also achieve, and he urged the society to underwrite the planting and management of a model, experimental vineyard. In these same years, he began his "treatise" on the planting of vineyards, cultivation of grapes, and making of wine. Eventually running to eighty pages and published posthumously in the American Philosophical Society *Transactions*, it became the first American publication on the subject and remained the authoritative work for more than fifty years.

Critical Appraisal: As "how-to" pieces, Antill's several essays rate both our appreciation and critical attention. He wrote authoritatively and in clear, pleasant prose, framing his observations with the lore of locals and the learning of the ancients. He systematically laid out the steps a young vigneron must follow, year-by-year, or a drier of figs or raiser and processor of flax must take, step-by-step, if their projects are to succeed. In his "Essay" he reported his own experiences with grapes but also drew freely on the wisdom of others, a distinct service to readers in the days when most libraries were private and sketchy. Critics have sometimes cast this conventional "borrowing" of matter from other authors as dependency or even plagiarism. However, although Antill made use of Hermann Boerhaave, Philip Miller, Cicero, and Columella, he chiefly conveyed his own experience and wisdom about matter-of-fact things like planting, pruning, and manuring and protecting his grapes from birds and wasps, his vines from rot, and his wine from spoiling.

Antill achieved certain aesthetic effects, especially in the longer "Essay" about viticulture, which lead one to read his prose as literature, spying out figures and appreciating texture. Portions of his prose work well on two levels of meaning at once. He found native species of vine, for example, "much more untractable than those of Europe" and predicted that "they will undergo a hard struggle indeed, before they will submit to a low and humble state, a state of abject slavery." Since self-regulation and tyranny were becoming lively topics in the colonies during the 1760s when he composed his piece, Antill's figurative speech enlivened both his viticultural manifesto and the public dialogue about larger, civil matters. Antill linked vineyard planting with the progress of civilization and supposed that "America should give the finishing stroke" to this ancient art. His respect for good discipline in the vineyards and his identification of viticulture with classical culture make his "Essay" a more complex piece of writing than the *Transactions* context prepares the reader to expect. One bridge between the import of viticulture and its everyday practice is the metaphorical nomenclature generally applied to vines: "eyes" for buds, "blood" for sap, "mother" for stock vines, "suckers" for offshoots, and the like. Occasionally, Antill handled conventional figures in a way that produces surprising effects. About pruning too early, he stated, for instance, that "the parent suffers by her fresh wounds, . . . grows faint and exhausted by excess of bleeding, and her eyes are drowned in her own blood." Perhaps as evocative as these metaphysical flourishes but of an entirely different texture and tenor are passages where, in giving out particular, concrete instructions, he so catalogued the stuff of everyday life as to recreate its domestic economy. In recommending ways to build a manure compost heap, for example, he told us to throw in "soap sups, chamberlye, the blood of beasts, pork and beef pickle, cyder and beer emptyings, and greasy dish-water, the water that salt meat has been boiled in."

Although Antill's piece on figs amounts to no more than a paragraph of directions on drying, his "Observations" presents in miniature the same patriotism, paternalism, and practicality that appeared in the essay on wine. Hemp production, he assured, is good for colony and crown and "worthy of the serious attention" of legislatures and of every man "who truly loves his country." He went on to "Instruct the honest husbandman in a few easy rules" and to reassure females and farmers prejudiced against cloth made from hemp: "And let [the farmer] not be disgusted and think that I am about to persuade him, his wife and daughters to wear ozenbrigs, for I can assure him that I have seen dowlass, which is made of hemp, worth five and six shillings the yard, which no farmer need be ashamed to wear."

Suggested Readings: Brooke Hindle, *The Pursuit of Science in Revolutionary America, 1735-1789* (1956), p. 198; R. P. McCormick, "The Royal Society, the Grape, and New Jersey," NJHSP, 81 (1963), 75-84; William Nelson, "Edward Antill and Some of His Descendants," NJHSP, 3d ser., 2 (1897), 25-56; David Scofield Wilson, *In the Presence of Nature* (1978), pp. 30-32, 206n20.

David Scofield Wilson
University of California, Davis

NATHANIEL APPLETON (1693-1784)

Works: *A Great Man Fallen in Israel* (1724); *Isaiah's Mission Consider'd* (1728); *Righteousness and Uprightness* (1728); *The Wisdom of God* (1728); *The Origin of War Examin'd* (1733); *Gospel Ministers* (1735); *The Christian Glorying in Tribulation* (1736); *Comfortable Reflections* (1737); *Superiour Skill* (1737); *Evangelical and Saving Repentance* (1741); *God, and Not Ministers* (1741); *A Discourse on the Nature and Excellency of Saving Faith* (1742); *The Great Blessing* (1742); *The Clearest and Surest Marks...Several Discourses from Romans VIII* (1743); *Faithful Ministers* (1743); *The Christian's Daily Practice of Piety* (1744); *The Usefulness and Necessity of Gifts* (1746); *The Cry of Oppression* (1748); *The Difference Between a Legal and an Evangelical Justification* (1749); *The Great Apostle Paul* (1751); *The Servant's Actual Readiness* (1752); *How God Wills the Salvation of All Men* (1753); *A Funeral Sermon: Occasion'd by the Death of the Honourable Spencer Phips* (1757); *The Blessedness of a Fixed Heart* (1760); *A Sermon...Occasioned by the Surrender of Montreal* (1760); *Some Unregenerate Persons* (1763); *A Faithful and Wise Servant* (1765); *A Plain and Faithful Testimony Against...Profane Swearing* (1765); *A Thanksgiving Sermon on the Total Repeal of the Stamp-Act* (1766); *The Crown of Eternal Life* (1769); *The Right Method* (1770).

Biography: Nathaniel Appleton, minister of the church in Cambridge, trustee of the Hopkins Foundation, charter member of the Massachusetts Society for Propagating Christian Knowledge Among the Indians of North America, extraordinary supporter of Harvard College, and Puritan-turned-patriot at the time of the American Revolution, was born at Ipswich, Mass., on Dec. 9, 1693. His father was the Honorable John Appleton, judge of the Court of Probate and member of the Royal Council, and his mother was Elizabeth (Rogers) Appleton, daughter of Harvard's President John Rogers (q.v.). Appleton, who received an A.B. from Harvard in 1712 and an A.M. in 1715, remained at the college after completing his education, becoming Scholar of the House in Apr. 1716. When the pulpit of the Cambridge church became vacant upon the death of William Brattle (q.v.), Harvard's President John Leverett, Appleton's uncle, pressed for the young minister's candidacy. On Apr. 19, 1717, Appleton was elected pastor of the church; he accepted on Jun. 10 and was ordained there on Oct. 9, 1717, in a grand ceremony during which Increase Mather (q.v.) preached and gave the charge and Cotton Mather (q.v.) gave the right hand of fellowship. Shortly before his ordination, Appleton succeeded Brattle in the Harvard Corporation, thus beginning a career of service to Harvard that would last an unprecedented sixty-one years. As the pastor of the church in Cambridge, Appleton early established a pattern for conduct that he followed throughout his career: he made it clear that although he was intellectually and temperamentally liberal, he was not so liberal as to give up an affection for the past or an awareness of the importance of religion in New Eng. affairs. At the same time, he developed a reputation for tolerance and fair-mindedness in religious and doctrinal matters. For instance, when one of his parishioners joined a Baptist church, Appleton saw no reason to disenfranchise him from the Cambridge church. By the 1730s Appleton had become a leading minister and preacher known throughout Mass., and his popularity was repeatedly noticed by invitations to preach at ordinations, church councils, and the funerals of influential citizens, ministers, and civil leaders. For instance, he preached ordination sermons for Oliver Peabody (q.v.) and Stephen Badger (q.v.) and funeral sermons on John Leverett, Benjamin Wadsworth (q.v.), John Hancock (q.v.), Edward Wigglesworth (q.v.), and Edward Holyoke. He preached the artillery election sermon for 1733, the Mass. election sermon for 1742, and the sermon at the annual convention of New Eng. ministers in 1743. Appleton seemed initially to favor the New Light position during the Great Awakening, and he was among the principal ministers who welcomed George Whitefield (q.v.) to Cambridge and Boston in 1740. However, when the Cambridge association of ministers balked at the prospect of another visit by Whitefield in 1745, Appleton sided with the majority so that Whitefield, according to one account, "preach'd on the Common. . .not only without the Consent, but contrary to the Mind of the Rev. Mr. Appleton."

Appleton thereafter kept to a middle course, holding to neither the Old Light nor the New Light position exclusively. He again shunned Whitefield when the revivalist returned to Cambridge in 1754, but during his last visit in 1770, Appleton offered Whitefield the use of his pulpit. In an unusual departure from his practice of peacekeeping, Appleton refused to join the majority of his colleagues in the censure of the heretical Jonathan Mayhew (q.v.), but that did not undermine his popularity. In 1758 he was given the honor of presenting the Dudleian Lecture; in 1771 the Harvard Corporation, recognizing that Appleton had "been long an ornament to the pastoral character and eminently distinguished for his knowledge Wisdom Sanctity of manners and usefulness to the Churches— and having for more than fifty Years exerted himself in promoting the Interests of Piety & learning in this Society," bestowed upon him the degree of doctor of divinity. Before Appleton, only Increase Mather had been given that honor.

At the time of the American Revolution, like many of his ministerial colleagues, Appleton found himself in the curious position of supporting the patriot cause at the same time as he exercised the ideals of Christian charity toward his Tory friends and parishioners. Declining health forced him to accept Timothy Hilliard as a colleague in 1782. Married in 1719 to Margaret Gibbs, who was the daughter of the Reverend Henry Gibbs (q.v.) of Watertown and who died in 1771, Appleton died on Feb. 9, 1784, survived by several sons and daughters. A notice of Appleton published in a history of Cambridge some years after his death offers an apt summary of his personality and character:

> Dr. Appleton, if venerable for age, was more venerable for his piety. His religion, like his whole character, was patriarchal. Born in the last [17th] century, and living till near the close of this . . . he brought down with him the habits of other times. In his dress . . . manners . . . conversation . . . [and] ministry, he may be classed with the Puritan ministers, of revered memory, who first came to New England. . . . . Early consecrated to God, and having a fixed predilection for the ministry, he was happily formed, by a union of good sense with deep seriousness, of enlightened zeal with consummate prudence, for the pastoral office.

Critical Appraisal: Although Appleton's career spanned the greater part of the eighteenth century and although the preacher was party to most of the affairs that had a significant impact upon the New Eng. consciousness as New Englanders changed from Puritan colonials to cosmopolitan republicans, in many respects Appleton was a preacher of the old school, liberal, to be sure, but careful not to allow liberal attitudes to compromise the integrity of his orthodox beliefs or of his pulpit manners. In this respect, it is not surprising to find that a colleague of his in the Cambridge pulpit wrote of Appleton that

> He preached the Gospel, with great plainness of speech, and with primitive simplicity. Less concerned to please than to instruct and edify . . . he frequently borrowed similitudes from familiar, sometimes from vulgar, objects; but his application of them was so pertinent, and his utterance and his air was so solemn, as to suppress levity and silence criticism.

Noticing too that Appleton subscribed to the metaphysics and cosmology of the seventeenth century rather than to the new science of the eighteenth, this same colleague wrote.

> He carefully availed himself of special occurrences, whether prosperous or adverse . . . to obtain a serious attention to the truths and duties of religion- . . . . Vigilantly attentive to the state of religion . . . he marked prevailing errors and sins, and pointed his admonitions and cautions against them, both in public and private, with conscientious . . . fidelity.

This appraisal of Appleton is easily substantiated by a review of his printed works. There we learn that the preacher's early openness to different ideas likely did much to help his popularity and that at the same time his preaching technique probably did much to placate those who might resent his occasional departure from the straight-and-narrow principles of the past. To Appleton's credit as a preacher and writer is the fact that several of his works, among them *The Christian's Daily Practice of Piety* (1744), *The Cry of Oppression* (1748), and *The Servant's Actual Readiness* (1752), went through more than one edition, and others, notably *Gospel Ministers* (1735), *The Christian Glorying in Tribulation* (1736), and *Evangelical and Saving Repentance* (1741), were reprinted in foreign editions or collected as part of a volume of sermons by an impartial hand.

Among the features of Appleton's ministry that deserve particular attention are his views on religious toleration and his doctrinal open-mindedness. Although these features may strike the contemporary reader as compromises between Appleton's liberalism and his orthodoxy, they never appeared to Appleton that way. It has been said that he was a fit successor to Brattle for their shared opinions on toleration. Repeatedly during his career—in the many ordination sermons he preached and published; in *The Great Blessing*, the election sermon he preached in 1742; and in *Faithful Ministers*, the convention sermon he preached in 1743—Appleton spoke for and acted upon the principle of toleration. He explained the source of his "catholick temper" in a series of sermons that he preached at the Thursday lecture in 1743. In *The Clearest and Surest Marks* (1743), the title under which those lecture sermons were collected, Appleton argued, "Surely we ought to be very cautious in judging and censuring those who in some Points do differ from us," and he said that the "Points" could be "either...doctrinal or practical."

In addition to toleration as a practical point upon which Appleton differed from the opinion of many of his colleagues, there is the matter of his doctrinal open-mindedness. Although he may be classed with the Puritan ministers "of revered memory," Appleton was not a Puritan to the extent that the term implied that he was a Calvinist. This point was made clear in 1753, when Appleton preached *How God Wills the Salvation of All Men* at the ordination of Stephen Badger (q.v.). In the sermon, he measured the seventeenth-century Puritans' God, who was born of Calvin's thought-supported theories such as predestination, against the eighteenth-century cosmopolitans' God, who was born of "brotherly love," and he decided that each figure and the attributes each was said to have possessed had merit. "It rather becomes us," he said, "with humble Reverence to receive them both...than to deny either, or too curiously to pry into them." As it happens, the sermon made clear that the God of Appleton's choice is the more modern of the two: the one who would exercise his will and thus interfere in the affairs of man only to assure the salvation of all.

Like many of his fellow clergymen whose careers spanned the period from the decline of Puritanism to the rise of an independent America, Appleton shared in the political and social discussions of the 1760s and 1770s, siding always with the patriot cause. Although few of his sermons from this period were printed, in *A Thanksgiving Sermon on the Total Repeal of the Stamp-Act* (1766) and in *The Right Method*, a collection of fast and prayer day sermons preached in 1770, there is sufficient evidence to rank Appleton among those outspoken Congregational ministers whose hostility toward sin and declension during the 1730s and

1740s and whose language used to decry the same were transformed by 1770 into strongly stated hostility against both Eng. and the oppressive rule of royal appointees in the colonies. In light of this feature of his ministry and for the privileged position he held in New Eng. for more than a half-century, Appleton deserves more critical recognition than scholars have thus far given him.

Suggested Readings: CCNE; Sibley-Shipton (V, 599-609); Sprague (I, 301-304).

Ronald A. Bosco
State University of New York at Albany

EAST APTHORP (1733-1816)

Works: *The Constitution of a Christian Church* (1761); *Considerations on the Society for the Propagation of the Gospel in Foreign Parts* (1763); *The Felicity of the Times* (1763); *The Character and Example of a Christian Woman* (1764); *Of Sacred Poetry and Music* (1764); *A Review of Dr. Mayhew's Remarks on the Answer to His Observations* (1765); *Conspectus Nova Editiones Historicorum* (1770); *A Sermon Preached at Guildhall Chapel, London* (1770); *A Sermon on the General Fast* (1776); *A Fast Sermon on the Unhappy Differences Between This Country and Her American Colonies* (1777); *The Excellence of the Liturgy* (1778); *Letters on the Prevalence of Christianity Before Its Civil Establishment* (1778); *A Sermon Before the Lord Mayor and the Governors of the Several Hospitals* (1780); *A Sermon on the Annual Commemoration of the Fire of London* (1780); *A Sermon Preached in Lambeth Palace* (1781); *Select Devotions* (1785); *Discourses on Prophecy*, 2 vols. (1786).

Biography: East Apthorp was born in Boston in 1733, the son of Charles Apthorp, one of Boston's wealthiest merchants and a prominent Anglican. An exceptional student, Apthorp received a B.A from Jesus College, Cambridge, in 1755 and an M.A. in 1758. In 1760 he returned to Cambridge, Mass., to fill the newly created missionary post of the Society for the Propagation of the Gospel (SPG). His specific charge for the position was to counteract the "Socinianism, Deism, and other bad principles" emanating from Harvard. In 1761 Apthorp married Elizabeth Hutchinson, niece of Thomas Hutchinson (q.v.) and granddaughter of Governor William Shirley (q.v.). The young couple moved into a mansion near Harvard Yard, quickly dubbed the "Bishop's Palace" because of its elegance.

Although Apthorp seemed destined for high position, (he had turned down Samuel Johnson's [q.v.] offer of the presidency of King's College [Columbia] and was generally considered the likely first bishop if an American episcopate were established), he became embroiled in the American episcopate controversy, asked the SPG for a leave of absence, and sailed to Eng., never to return to America.

In Eng. Apthorp devoted himself to preaching and writing. Archbishop Thomas

Secker appointed him to the vicarage of Croydon in 1765, and in 1780 he received the degree of doctor of divinity and the rectorship of Bowchurch in London. In 1790 Apthorp declined an offer of the bishopric of Kildare. In 1793 he received the valuable Prebend of Finsbury, attached to St. Paul's Cathedral, for which he relinquished all of his other preferments. He spent his last years in retirement in Cambridge, where he died and was buried in 1816 at the age of 83.

Critical Appraisal: Although he spent but a few years of his adult life in America, East Apthorp is deserving of recognition as a minor American writer because of his participation in the phase of the American episcopate controversy that bears his name. Indeed, all of Apthorp's writings demonstrate his firm commitment to the Church of England. *The Constitution of a Christian Church*, for example, preached at the opening of Christ Church in Cambridge, provided the occasion for Apthorp to reexamine "the nature and genius of the Christian religion" and to emphasize the importance among religious groups of Christian tolerance. Of course, roles in Puritan Cambridge, where Apthorp's Episcopal congregation were the nonconformists, were the opposite of Anglican Eng., and Apthorp's sermon pleads the cause of the Anglican minority.

To the Puritans of Mass., however, Apthorp and the Anglican invasion of the citadel of Congregationalism were threatening in the extreme, and Apthorp quickly became the center of a significant controversy, primarily through his publication in 1763 of *Considerations on the Institution and Conduct of the Society for the Propagation of the Gospel in Foreign Parts*, written in response to a satirical obituary of a fellow SPG missionary, Dr. Ebenezer Miller of Braintree, which appeared in the *Boston Gazette* in Feb. 1763. The anonymous author of the obituary, known only as "T.L.," charged that the SPG had violated its charter by sending missionaries to convert dissenters rather than Indians and Negroes. In his controversial response, Apthorp defended the society on the grounds that its principal function was to further the cause of religion among Englishmen in the colonies, with evangelization of Indians and slaves as a subordinate objective.

The newspapers and press were soon filled with responses to Apthorp's pamphlet, among them Jonathan Mayhew's (q.v.) *Observations on the Charter and Conduct of the Society for the Propagation of the Gospel in Foreign Parts*, a frontal attack on the SPG as well as a critique of East Apthorp's version of history and his personal life-style. Mayhew criticized Apthorp and the society for setting up "altar against altar," for criticizing the severity of New Eng.'s "Forefathers," and for building a mansion, "designed for the *Palace* of one of the *humble successors* of the apostles." As the quotation suggests, a central issue in Mayhew's pamphlet, as well as in the whole newspaper and pamphlet warfare known as the Apthorp-Mayhew Controversy, was the possible establishment of an American episcopate. Even young John Adams (q.v.) entered the fray with his "Humphrey Ploughjogger" letters, mimicking the prominent issues in the conflict. Unlike many of his colleagues and antagonists, however, Apthorp did not relish controversy, and although the controversy bears his name, he penned only a small portion of its voluminous newspaper and pamphlet literature. In fact, he refused to answer Mayhew until after he returned to Eng., where, in a calmer atmosphere, he devoted himself to study, preaching, and writing.

In Eng. most of Apthorp's writings were well received and noncontroversial. In 1770 he proposed a large and comprehensive scheme of publishing ancient historians, but he found insufficient support for the project. In 1778 he published an attack on the work of Edward Gibbon, the historian, but Gibbon responded politely and good-humoredly. Apthorp was also invited to deliver the Boyle and Warburton lectures, and he was generally recognized as a learned cleric.

Suggested Readings: CCNE; Sprague (V, 174-180); T$_2$. *See also* Charles Akers, *Called unto Liberty: A Life of Jonathan Mayhew, 1720-1760* (1964), pp. 180-197; Bernard Bailyn, *Pamphlets of the American Revolution, 1750-1776* (1965), vol. I; Carl Bridenbaugh, *Mitre and Sceptre: Transatlantic Faiths, Ideas, Personalities, and Politics, 1689-1775* (1962); Arthur L. Cross, *The Anglican Episcopate and the American Colonies* (1902), pp. 140-159; Wendell D. Garrett, *Apthorp House, 1760-1960* (1960); Don Gerlach, "Champions of an American Episcopate: Thomas Secker of Canterbury and Samuel Johnson of Connecticut," HMagPEC, 41 (1972), 381-414; Richard J. Hooker, "The Mayhew Controversy," CH, 5 (1936), 239-255; Lorenzo Sabine, *Biographical Sketches of Loyalists of the American Revolution with an Historical Essay*, 2 vols. (1864), I, 170.

Mary F. Quinlivan
University of Texas of the Permian Basin

GABRIEL ARCHER (1575-1610)

Works: "The Relation of Captain Gosnold's Voyage to the North Part of Virginia" (1602), first printed in *Purchas His Pilgrimes* (1625), rep. in *Collections of the Massachusetts Historical Society*, 8, 3d ser. (1843), 72-81; "Letter Touching the Voyage of the Fleet of Ships Which Arrived at Virginia, Without Sir Thomas Gates and Sir George Summers, 1609," first printed in *Purchas His Pilgrimes* (with omissions and marginalia), rep. in Alexander Brown, *The Genesis of the United States*, 1 (1964), 327-332. Works usually attributed to Archer also include three companion pieces on Jamestown: *A Relatyon of the Discovery of Our River* (1607); "The Description of the Now-Discovered River and Country of Virginia" (1606); and *A Brief Description of the People* (1606); all rep. in Philip L. Barbour, ed., *The Jamestown Voyages under the First Charter: 1606-1609* (1969), I, 80 ff.

Biography: Gabriel Archer's origins are obscure. He is best known for accompanying his friend Captain Bartholomew Gosnold on the historic voyage to New Eng. in 1602 and for the colorful, accurate "Relation" of their experiences, which was written the same year, passed on to Richard Hakluyt and then to Samuel Purchas (q.v.), and finally published in Purchas's *Pilgrimes* in 1625. Archer has also become notorious for his battles with Captain John Smith (q.v.)

in early Jamestown and is a subject for much disagreement among historians of the period.

Although he may have been one of the Essex Archers (also spelled *Auchers*) and certainly studied at one of the Inns of Court, Archer's life began to be documented thoroughly only when he took an official position in Jamestown. Among the first settlers in Va., Archer was the official recorder, or secretary, for "His Majesties Counsel in Virginia." Educated at Cambridge and Gray's Inn, he had a gift of description and, from most contemporary accounts, argument as well. By 1608, when he returned, perhaps under duress, to Eng., Archer was a vocal opponent of John Smith and his government of the settlement. Just before his departure, one of American history's best-known and most confusing series of events had occurred. Smith and several of his men were taken prisoner by Indians late in 1606. After nearly three weeks as a captive, Smith was returned to Jamestown by an Indian friend who had saved him; there the Council, with Archer as a new and outspoken member, condemned Smith to death by hanging. This harsh sentence was handed down because Smith had deserted his fellow captives, leaving at least two to die. Although many accounts of this episode are extant, neither Archer's nor that of George Percy (q.v.), his supporter, has been found. Thus Smith's was the accepted version of events at least until Alexander Brown examined them closely and published a vigorous defense of Archer in his *Genesis of the United States* (1890). More recent scholarship has conclusively shown only that Smith was spared by the fortuitous arrival of Capt. Newport, who brought supplies to the tense settlement and put a temporary end to the political squabbling. Archer, it appears, was then asked to return to Eng., which he had requested and had been forbidden to do, several times before.

In 1609, however, Archer returned to the colony and very quickly became active in the renewed campaign to depose Smith, whose authority as governor had expired. Sir Thomas Gates, the newly appointed governor, had not arrived in Va., though, and the anti-Smith faction was forced to seek official approval for the appointment of Thomas West, Baron de la Warr (q.v.). Archer's "Letter" was clearly written to suggest and justify this course of action. Although Samuel Purchas printed some of the "Letter" in his *Pilgrimes* (1625), most of the complaints against Smith were suppressed as unpatriotic cavilling by a malcontent. Archer, who had always suffered physically in Va. and who twice was wounded by Indians, died during the miserable winter of 1609-1610.

Considering his importance and contributions to the new colony, it is odd that Archer's reputation should depend so heavily on that of John Smith. Although Alexander Brown extolled Archer as an unsung hero, a man who "has the honor of having been much abused by Captain John Smith," other historians took at face value the contemporary complaints against the man. Edward Maria Wingfield (q.v.), a man continually at odds with Archer, for example, spoke in his *Discourse* (1608) of Archer's political chicanery and the papers, or articles of complaint, that he was often pulling "out of his bosome." John Smith's charges are even sharper and lengthier, particularly in *A Map of Virginia*. Yet some historians dismiss most of Smith's writings as mere fables with himself as hero. Brown's version of the captain is that of a vain, unjust man, whose accounts of Va. distort history and amount to no more than a "mere eulogy of this adventurer, and a disparagement of others." Philip A. Barbour has defended Smith by describing Archer as a "self-assertive" troublemaker. We must conclude, then, that Archer's written contributions, including fine descriptions of Va. and the Maine coast, and a rough-draft dictionary of Indian place names, are enough to certify his significance in American history. As Brown said, "he gave his life to the enterprise, and no one could do more."

Critical Appraisal: Archer excelled at the construction of lively narrative. His accounts of both Capt. Gosnold's and the Va. fleets' voyages are vivid and readable. The *Relatyon of the Discovery of Our River* and the two other documents narrating Capt. Christopher Newport's exploratory trips around Jamestown are among the few truly literary products of the early years of the Va. colony. Archer's straightforward style is enlivened by humor, a flair for concrete imagery, and, above all, directness and honesty.

The *Relation of Captain Gosnold's Voyage* (1602) serves as a valuable supplement to John Brereton's (q.v.) *Briefe and True Relation* (1602) of the same journey. It tells the exciting tale of the first trip by settlers to New Eng. The thirty-two sailors were thrilled by the new birds and fish they saw; they took time to give names (some humorous) to many landmarks, including Cape Cod and Martha's Vineyard; and they recorded in detail the variety of fruits and vegetables they discovered both on the islands and on the mainland. Archer provided a diarylike, personal account of each day's work and accomplishments. Of great interest are the affectionate records of contacts with the "savages" in residence. After much negotiating and socializing, the travelers became fast friends with the natives. They were on such good terms, in fact, that a small joke could be played: mustard was fed to the Indians and its "nipping them in the noses they could not endure: it was a sport to behold their faces."

Archer's *Letter* (1609) is more somber. Written to an unknown English friend, it is among the more important documents handed on by Richard Hakluyt to Samuel Purchas, the great botcher of manuscripts. Purchas censored the *Letter*, because it is a political piece, designed both to set the record straight on Va.'s real condition (which was miserable) and to garner support for the appointment of Baron de la Warr as governor. Purchas's marginal notes tell us that this is the work of a malcontent who, by mysteriously supplanting Smith for reasons of his own, raised "stirs" and brought "miseries" to Va., in which "this author with almost the whole Colony perished." In truth, the *Letter* is a moving account of the rampant illness, the forty-hour "huracano" that split up the fleet, and the unpleasant reception Archer's ship met with when it finally arrived in Va. Although he refused to be political, preferring to focus on food and survival, Archer did express outrage at the glowing reports of Va. being sent home by Newport and others. In particular, he resented the description of "such plenty of victuall," when supplies were slow to arrive and most of the colonists existed on a diet of oysters. As the other ships in the ill-fated fleet arrived, the dramatic power of the narrative intensified. Their masts were broken; their vessels leaked in a dozen places; their sailors were nearly all ill; and their reception from Capt. John Smith was decidedly hostile. Nearly all of the gentlemen in the colony, especially the new arrivals, then combined to depose Smith, refusing "to be governed by the President that now is." This document, expurgated by Purchas, remains a strong corrective to Smith's and others' reports on the same unhappy period in Jamestown.

Archer's putative writings include the *Relatyon* (1607) and two useful descriptions of Va.'s terrain and its people (1606), which Capt. Newport took to Eng. in 1607. The expedition described in the *Relatyon* was the first trip inland from Jamestown. Archer's diary covers each day's discoveries and contains pleasant descriptions of various islands and the surrounding flora. The liveliest parts of the work describe the Indians, "a most kind and loving people," and one of their rulers, Queen Apumatec, a "fatt lustie manly woman" dressed magnificently in copper and deerskins. The king, on the other hand, "striving to be stately," seemed a fool. This passage is among those cited by Howard Mumford Jones in *The Literature of Virginia in the 17th Century* as a "delectable" example of the colonial literary cargo being shipped to Eng. Archer's affection for and gratitude to the Indians is striking, since most writers of the time were contemptuous of the natives and sought only to exploit and convert them. Taken together, Archer's works entitle him to a secure place among early America's writers.

Suggested Readings: Philip L. Barbour, *The Three Worlds of Captain John Smith* (1964); idem, *The Jamestown Voyages under the First Charter: 1606-1609* (1969); Alexander Brown, *The Genesis of the United States*, 2 vols. (1890; rep., 1964); Philip A. Bruce, *The Virginia Plutarch* (1929); Warner F. Gookin and Philip L. Barbour, *Bartholomew Gosnold: Discoverer and Planter* (1963); Howard Mumford Jones, *The Literature of Virginia in the 17th Century* (1968), p. 20; idem, *O Strange New World: American Culture: Its Formative Years* (1964), pp. 114-161; H. C. Porter, *The Inconstant Savage: England and the North American Indian* (1979); Captain John Smith, "A Map of Virginia" in *The Jamestown Voyages*, ed. Philip L. Barbour (1969); William Stith, *The History of the First Discovery and Settlement of Virginia* (1865); Lyon G. Tyler, *England in America: 1580-1652* (1904), pp. 45-65.

James Stephens
Marquette University

BENEDICT ARNOLD (1741-1801)

Works: *Col. Arnold's Journal of His Expedition to Canada* (w. 1775; pub. 1903, 1938); *Col. Arnold's Letters Written during the Expedition to Quebec* (w. 1775-1776; pub. 1831, 1938); *By Brigadier-General Arnold, A Proclamation* (1780); *To the Inhabitants of America* (1780); *Thoughts on the American War* (w. 1782; pub. 1880).

Biography: Benedict Arnold was born at Norwich, Conn., on Jan. 14, 1741. Raised in a strict home, he ran away at the age of 14 to join the army in the French and Indian War, but he later deserted to return home. Arnold eventually became a druggist and bookseller in New Haven and made successful investments in the West Indies. Enlisting as a captain in the Conn. militia, Arnold took his troops to Cambridge when word arrived of the battle at Lexington. His outstanding service to the rebel cause began when, with Ethan Allan (q.v.), he took Fort Ticonderoga on May 10, 1775. Basing his plan on a map by British engineer John Montrésor (q.v.), Arnold convinced Gen. George Washington (q.v.) of the merits of invading Quebec via the Kennebec and Chaudier rivers. His expedition, which left Newburyport on Sept. 19, 1775, and climaxed in an unsuccessful assault on Quebec in a howling blizzard on the night of Dec. 31, was one of the most heroic yet tragic episodes in American history.

In Oct. 1776 Brigadier-General Arnold hindered Carleton's invasion of N.Y. from the north. Bypassed when Congress made promotions in Feb. 1777, Arnold nonetheless turned back the British in Conn. Finally promoted to major-general, he resigned his commission following an investigation and only withdrew his resignation at the personal request of Gen. Washington, after which he went on to defeat Burgoyne's army in the crucial battle at Saratoga, where he was wounded. With Washington at Valley Forge in May 1778, Arnold was named military commander of Philadelphia. There he met and married Margaret Shippen, but his lavish life-style rapidly led him into heavy debt, a court martial, and a reprimand.

In the spring of 1779, Arnold began treasonously sending military secrets to the British through Sir Henry Clinton, and in the summer of 1780, given command of West Point by Washington, he plotted to turn it over to the British for a price. The plan was thwarted when on Sept. 23 Arnold's British contact, Maj. John André, was captured while carrying incriminating evidence. Arnold fled, was named a brigadier-general by the British, and earned intense hatred in America by leading raids into Va. (Dec. 1780) and Conn. (Sept. 1781). In Dec. 1781 Arnold sailed to Eng., where suspicion left him unable to secure further army service. Despite a grant of 13,400 acres in Canada, Arnold did not flourish, and after unsuccessfully attempting to obtain a military appointment in the Napoleonic Wars, he died in London on Jun. 14, 1801, of "dropsy and a disease of the lungs."

Critical Appraisal: America's most notorious traitor, Benedict Arnold was once a skilled and courageous leader in the Continental Army. Among the most interesting of Arnold's papers are the journal and letters he wrote during the expedition to Quebec. These documents were collected by Kenneth Roberts in *March to Quebec* (1938), along with other sources Roberts used during the writing of his historical novel *Arundel* (1930), which portrays Arnold sympathetically. The journal begins on Sept. 15, 1775, at Cambridge and was transcribed in the handwriting of Arnold's secretary, Capt. Eleazer Oswald. A vigorous account of troop movements and individual officers, a ledger of distances and directions, and a stirring picture of terrible hardships, the *Journal* contains verbatim portions of the journal kept by British officer John Montrésor during a similar expedition in the summer of 1761, proving that Arnold used the Montrésor account as a guide. But neither Montrésor's journal nor his map could prevent the early winter storms and flooding, damaged provisions, and smashed batteaux that plagued Arnold's march, and the extant journal ends abruptly on Oct. 30.

Although Arnold's letters deal primarily with personnel, provisions, enemy intelligence, and troop movements, they also reveal a gracious and dynamic personality, whose intense determination and self-confidence, although enabling him to persevere in the face of great odds, perhaps also kept him from accurately assessing not only the strength of his adversaries but his own limitations as well. Especially revealing are letters to Gen. Washington, in which he admitted surprise at "a thousand difficulties" on the march, and the letter to Gen. Montgomery, who was marching from Montreal to join forces with Arnold for the assault. Repeatedly, Arnold described Quebec as "in great confusion" and "short of provisions," and he was highly optimistic despite the American illnesses and desertions and the increasing shortages of clothing, cash, and sound ammunition. Although in a Dec. 31 letter to Gen. Wooster, he recounted the tragic failure of the attack on Quebec and the death of Montgomery, Arnold was still insisting to Washington and the Continental Congress that 5,000 more men and a good general could take and hold Quebec, because "the overruling hand of Providence" is with the Americans. Dauntlessness and overconfidence mark the enigma of Benedict Arnold, and these characteristics are beguilingly revealed in his correspondence.

Arnold wrote two broadsides after his defection to G.B. In *To the Inhabitants of America*, dated Oct. 7, 1780, he explained "the motives which have induced me to join the King's arms." Originally, he declared, "A redress of grievances was my only object and aim"; and he maintained that Britain's offer to meet this concern undercut any rationale for the Declaration of Independence. Arnold openly charged American leaders with "impolicy, tyranny and injustice," and exploiting the popular fear of Catholicism, he also argued that America should not feel bound by the alliance with the "feeble" and antidemocratic monarchy of Fr. G.B., he declared, intends "not only to leave the rights and privileges of the Colonies unimpaired, together with their perpetual exemption from taxation, but to superadd such further benefits as may consist with the common prosperity of the empire." In the broadside *By Brigadier-General Arnold, A Proclamation*, dated Oct. 20, 1780, he challenged the officers and soldiers of the Continental Army to avoid the duplicity of the Congress and Fr. and join "His Majesty's Arms." More inflammatory than in his first broadside, Arnold used the same appeals. He played on the plight of the soldiers, blaming their sufferings on "the neglect, contempt, and corruption of Congress" and on the "tyranny" of their leaders. Again tapping anti-Catholic sentiment, he proclaimed his intention to rescue "our native country from the grasping hand of *France*," and to men tired of strife, he held out the comforting image of a magnanimous Britain restoring the colonies' rights and offering "protection" from internal corruption and external threats.

At the request of King George III, Arnold wrote *Thoughts on the American War* in 1782, outlining a plan for reconciling Britain and the colonies. According to this document, Britain grossly underestimated the loyalty of "a great Majority of the Americans," he declared; the colonies were weary of conflict and the abuses of the "minority" of "Zealots"; and "the Friends of the Restoration are most numerous." Loyalists would respond, Arnold suggested, if the crown would "set up the *Civil* Authority" in the colonies. The inept Congress was "Bankrupt" and incapable of maintaining a sound army. G.B. could hold her empire, he argued, if in a spirit of conciliation she initiated "*a new Peace Commission.*" A shrewd analysis, *Thoughts on the American War* is also pathetic and ironic, reflecting Arnold's habitual wishful thinking only months before the colonies he had betrayed won their independence.

Suggested Readings: DAB; DNB; T₂. *See also* Isaac N. Arnold, *The Life of Benedict Arnold* (1880); Mark Mayo Boatner III, *Encyclopedia of the American Revolution* (1974); James Thomas Flexner, *The Traitor and the Spy: Benedict Arnold and John André* (1953); Kenneth Roberts, comp., *March to Quebec* (1938), pp. 41-123 (prints the journal and letters written by Arnold during the expedition to Quebec); Charles Coleman Sellers, *Benedict Arnold: The Proud Warrior* (1930); Justin H. Smith, *Arnold's March from Cambridge to Quebec* (1903); idem, *Our Struggle for the Fourteenth Colony*, 2 vols. (1907); Jared Sparks, *The Life and Treason of Benedict Arnold* (1835); Carl Van Doren, *Secret History of the American Revolution* (1941); Willard M. Wallace, *Traitorous Hero: The Life and Fortunes of Benedict Arnold* (1954).

Wesley T. Mott
University of Wisconsin at Madison

SAMUEL ARNOLD (1622-1693)

Works: *David Serving His Generation* (1674); Letter to the General Court at Plymouth (with John Cotton; 1676); "Mr. Samuel Arnold...His Last Farewell to the World" (1693).

Biography: Born in Eng. in 1622, Samuel Arnold spent his early years as a fisherman. Cotton Mather (q.v.) listed him as part of a group of young scholars who came to New Eng. to finish their education at the new Harvard College, but there is no evidence to prove that he ever attended that institution. In 1653 Arnold was admitted as a freeman of the colony of New Plymouth, and after living in Yarmouth and possibly Sandwich, he became in 1658 the third pastor of the Church of Marshfield. Arnold died in 1693. Shortly after his death, a broadside was circulated containing his own poem and an elegy and an anagram by Ichabod Wis[h]wall (q.v.), "Upon the Death of Mr. Samuel Arnold" and "Leave Old Arm's." In these poems, Wiswall praised Arnold as a "Text-Man large and ready" and as a fisherman like Peter and John who stopped the mouths of Quakers and whose passing has made the "Pulpit groan and drop a Tear."

Critical Appraisal: Only three published works bear Samuel Arnold's name: a poem on his own death published posthumously in which he praised God for drawing him to New Eng.; a letter written with John Cotton (q.v.) to the General Court at Plymouth arguing children's responsibility for the crimes of their parents; and an election sermon preached in 1674, *David Serving His Generation*. The sermon is a typical call for communal responsibility and the suppression of self-love and personal ambition, couched in a typological description of men's place in the divine order. In the sermon, Arnold also identified the good of individuals with that of the generation of which they are a part, and he concluded with a caution to the people to exercise their vote wisely and with a plea to ministers for a true unity that can fortify the hypocritical faith of the times. Neither the format nor the tone of this sermon is unusual, although the series of metaphors by which Arnold established the importance of the election in the conclusion does demonstrate his competence with some of the more common rhetorical techniques available to the Puritan preacher. Unfortunately, that competence did not extend to poetry. The poem Arnold wrote just before his death is listed in Harold Jantz's bibliography (FCNEV), but its conventional meditative posture and the forced iambic pentameter are more representative of the casual verse of the period than remarkable for any poetic merit. Despite its clumsy appearance, however, the poem does convey the obvious sincerity of Arnold's gratitude for his salvation and the deep concern behind his prayer that his family and flock might find their own place in the Lord's sight. Through this combination of humble manner and enduring commitment, Arnold's poem remains a vivid example of the qualities that made him one of the most respected ministers of his day.

Suggested Readings: CCNE; FCNEV. *See also* Cotton Mather, *Magnalia Christi Americana* (1702; rep., 1855), III, intro., p. 237; Increase Mather, *An Earnest Exhortation to the Inhabitants of New England* (1676), p. 10; NEHGR, 7 (1853), 277; Charles M. Segal and David C. Stineback, *Puritans, Indians, and Manifest Destiny* (1977).

Michael P. Clark
University of Michigan

FRANCIS ASBURY (1745-1816)

Works: *A Form of Discipline* (1787); *To the Friends and Benefactors of Cokesbury College* (1789); *The Causes, Evils, and Cures, of Heart and Church Division* (1792); *An Extract from the Journal* (1792); *An Extract from the Journal* (1802); *The Journal and Letters* (w. 1771-1816; pub. 1958).

Biography: Born in Handsworth near Birmingham, Eng., Francis Asbury was greatly influenced by the character of his parents. While his father's improvidence placed Asbury in servitude by age 12 and into apprenticeship to a black-smith by age 14, the piety of his mother inspired him to read the entire Bible by the age of 6 and earned from his childhood playmates the nickname "Methodist parson." By the time he was 16, Asbury's religious preoccupations reached the point where he began preaching as many as five times weekly, and in 1767 Asbury forsook his trade to devote himself fully to the mission of itinerant preaching. From that time on, in both principle and practice, Asbury never swerved from a belief in the spiritual need for an itinerant clergy. In 1771 this belief led Asbury to immigrate to the American colonies where he remained until his death on March 31, 1816. During these years, "The Father of American Methodism" traveled more than 300,000 miles on horseback, crisscrossing the American seaboard from N.H. to Ga., delivering some 17,000 sermons, ordaining more than 4,000 preachers, and nurturing congregations wherever he went.

In 1775 Asbury assumed the leadership of American Methodism after John Wesley denounced the revolutionary fervor of the colonists. Although Wesley urged the return of all itinerant preachers to Eng., Asbury stayed, and the Methodist Episcopal Church became the first religious body to ally itself to the new government of the United States. During the Revolutionary War, the independence of the American church increased, until in 1784, at the "Christmas Conference" in Baltimore, Francis Asbury (along with Thomas Coke) was elected bishop. By electing Asbury, the American branch of the Methodist Church effectively superseded Wesley's previous appointment of him to the same post and thereby established the autonomy of the American church. Called "The Bishop on Horseback," Asbury continued his indefatigable labors until his death, never finding time to marry or make a home for himself, though Baltimore was his center of operations. Sometimes accused of being dictatorial, Asbury jealously guarded his authority to appoint preachers to congregations, but his life-long effort to abolish slavery among Methodists failed. Establishing a church on an undeveloped continent took all of Asbury's life. He died at the plantation of George Arnold in Va. en route to a church conference in Baltimore. He is buried at the Eutaw Methodist Episcopal Church, Baltimore, Md.

Critical Appraisal: The most widely known of Asbury's writings is *A Form of Discipline, for the Ministers, Preachers, and Members . . . of the Methodist Episcopal Church*. Originally little more than an American edition of Wesley's work by the same name, *The Discipline* came to assume the character of both its author-editor and the unique American church he founded. Posing and answering eighty-one questions dealing with such varied topics as administrative duties, theological issues, clerical conduct, and slave emancipation, an updated version of *The Discipline* is still in use today, and its original publication helped found the Methodist Publishing House, one of the world's largest religious publishers. This same publishing concern printed Asbury's extracts from Baxter and Burroughs, titled *The Causes, Evils, and Cures, of Heart and Church Division*. Like *The Discipline*, this pamphlet sought to provide cohesiveness and coherence to the new church in America.

Were Asbury to have published no more than *The Discipline*, his place in American letters would be assured. But inspired by John Wesley's example, the young missionary began a journal as he sailed to America in 1771. This journal was to become a travelogue of unparalleled scope. Spanning forty-four years and filling nearly 1,600 printed pages, the journal is the history of a man, a nation, a continent, and a religion. It contains a wealth of primary source material for a host of scholarly disciplines. In the *Journal*, for example, Asbury recorded his own theological and spiritual growth at the same time that he recorded the birth and growth of a major religious denomination with its concomitant saints and sinners, love feasts and quarrels, dogmas and heresies. The *Journal* also provided information about early American settlements, families, businesses, finances, customs, climate, diet, indigenous populations, and religious beliefs. It offered a view of the American Revolution from the perspective of an uninvolved citizen, and it documented the conquering of a new continent by brave and sometimes foolish individuals.

Aware of its significance, Asbury wrote his *Journal* meticulously and filled it with detailed and extensive descriptions. In 1792 and 1802, he published pertinent extracts from the *Journal* and began taking pains to ensure posthumous publication for the whole work. In 1821 the *Journal* was first published in its entirety, and even though the original manuscripts were destroyed by fire in 1836, in 1958 the Methodist Episcopal Church authorized the publication of a new, definitive edition. While recent studies corroborate the continued cultural, religious, and historical importance of the *Journal*, it has just come to light that the 1821 edition expurgated Asbury's criticisms of slavery and that these omissions also occurred in the 1958 edition. The letters of Asbury that are published with the *Journal* in 1958 are equally inaccurate. Most of these letters are housed in the Drew University Library, and the cause of the inaccurate transcriptions is unknown.

Suggested Readings: CCMC; CCMDG; DAB; DARB; DNB; Sprague (VII, 13-28). *See also* Frank Baker, *From Wesley to Asbury: Studies in Early American Methodism* (1976); Frederick E. Maser, "Discovery," MH, 9 (1971), 34-43; L. C. Rudolph, *Francis Asbury* (1966); Ezra Squier Tipple, *Francis Asbury, The Prophet of the Long Road* (1916).

John F. Schell
University of Arkansas at Little Rock

ELIZABETH ASHBRIDGE (1713-1755)

Works: *Some Account of the Fore-Part of the Life of Elizabeth Ashbridge* (1774).

Biography: Elizabeth Ashbridge was born in Middlewich, Cheshire, Eng., in 1713, the only child of Thomas and Mary Sampson, who had two children by a previous marriage. At age 14, Ashbridge eloped with a stocking weaver. When her husband died five months later, her father refused to support her, and she spent the next three years with maternal relatives in Ire., where she was attracted for a time to the Catholic faith. Intrigued by the New World, and having relatives in Pa., Ashbridge immigrated to N.Y., where she was forced to serve as an indentured servant, having been coerced into signing indenture papers by an unscrupulous ship's captain, even though she had saved him from mutiny during the voyage to America.

After serving three years under a master whose harsh treatment brought her to the brink of suicide, Ashbridge succeeded in buying the remainder of her debt and five months later married Sullivan, an itinerant schoolmaster, whom, from her own account, she grew to love only after several years of marriage. As a result of her husband's occupation, Ashbridge traveled extensively in R.I., Long Island, N.Y., and N.J., during which time she became involved with Seventh-Day Baptists, Presbyterians, and Anglicans. On a visit to Quaker relations in Pa., she became interested in Quakers, and despite her husband's active disapproval, she became a Quaker and eventually a Quaker preacher. In 1740 Sullivan impulsively enlisted in the British army and died after being punished and disciplined for refusing to fight in Cuba. Left with a large debt, Ashbridge reimbursed her creditors by teaching school and doing needlework, although she also spent much time traveling in the ministry. In 1746 she married Aaron Ashbridge, a Quaker from Goshen, Pa., and in 1753 the Society of Friends granted her permission to travel in Eng. and Ire., where she died on May 16, 1755, and was buried.

Critical Appraisal: Elizabeth Ashbridge's sole work is the journal she wrote during her second widowhood about her spiritual growth from youth through the death of her second husband. As was customary for the time, Ashbridge's account was not published until after her death.

Like most eighteenth-century Quaker journals, Ashbridge's work was written "to make some remarks on the dealings of Divine goodness with me." Accordingly she delineated, in a conventional way, the afflictions that transformed her from a British Anglican who loved dancing to a devout Pa. Quaker who traveled widely and suffered in the name of her faith. What distinguishes Ashbridge's journal from numerous others of its day and has probably led to its frequent reprinting is the dramatic way her physical and spiritual wanderings parallel each other and give her work more narrative unity than is usual in Quaker journals, a fact that has helped provoke comparison between her journal and the "injured female" biographies and novels that were so popular during the eighteenth century. Whether by accident or design, Ashbridge enhanced the narrative and dramatic unity by concentrating on her suffering and her wanderings and by minimizing or omitting what most Quaker journalists considered spiritual milestones: speaking out in meeting for the first time, being approved to travel in the ministry, and the formal and often empty lists of meetings attended and families visited during such travel. The result is a readable narrative that moves swiftly and without disruption.

Finally, Ashbridge wrote with a human compassion that greatly enhances the appeal of her narrative. In describing her second husband and the unhappiness he caused her, for instance, she did not portray him as a beast but sympathized with his anguish at seeing his wife undergo a steady and undesired transformation from a lively young woman into a Quaker preacher. As such, Ashbridge's account is one of the most readable and satisfying of eighteenth-century American Quaker journals, and it shows that although eighteenth-century Americans often decried forms of entertainment such as the novel and the stage, the literary imagination was nonetheless alive and well, finding its expression in "acceptable" forms of writing such as journals, diaries, and autobiographies.

Suggested Readings: Howard H. Brinton, *Quaker Journals, Varieties of Religious Experience Among Friends* (1972); Daniel B. Shea, Jr., *Spiritual Autobiography in Early America* (1968), pp. 30-39; Luella M. Wright, *The Literary Life of the Early Friends, 1650-1725* (1932), pp. 155-197.

John Stratton
University of Arkansas at Little Rock

THOMAS ASHE (fl. 1680-1682)

Works: *Carolina; or a Description of the Present State of the Country* (1682).

Biography: Scholars generally believe that the "T.A. Gent., clerk on board his majesty's ship the Richmond" referred to in the title page of *Carolina* was Thomas Ashe. If they are correct, all that is known of him relates to the gathering of information for that tract. In 1680, the H.M.S. *Richmond* left Eng. for a tour of duty in the waters off Britain's colonies in the New World. Its orders included the transportation of forty-five French Protestants to Carolina who were expected to establish the production of silk and the examination of the health and progress of the new colony of Carolina. The silk worms died en route, but Ashe carried out the second set of instructions. While the *Richmond* continued on to the Caribbean, he stayed behind, and over the next two years, this gentleman, who was obviously well educated, especially in natural history, talked to local planters and gathered his own personal observations. In 1682 the *Richmond* picked Ashe up, and during the passage home, he wrote *Carolina*, which was subsequently published in London. Ashe, however, disappeared from the historical record.

Critical Appraisal: *Carolina* was written to extoll the virtues of the new colony and entice settlers to relocate there. Thomas Ashe, therefore, described the climate, soil, crops, products, flora, and fauna of the region and then offered his assessment of the opportunities awaiting the enterprising colonist in the unexploited industries of silk production, shell fishing, wine making, and naval store production and the harvesting of lumber.

The obvious historical value of the tract lies in its description of Carolina's environment at an early stage in European colonization. Ashe's work has been assessed as a "glowing, but not exaggerated" account, but he did omit some detrimental information, especially concerning early complaints that some planters were monopolizing the fur trade. But Ashe's optimism tended to color only his assessment of future possibilities; his analysis of the flora and fauna generally concurs—although vastly more detailed—with other contemporary accounts. *Carolina* is particularly valuable in this regard, because Ashe's keen observations note the introduction of Old World cultigens and herbivores as part of the process recently labeled the "Columbian Exchange."

What makes *Carolina* doubly valuable is its significance as an example of seventeenth-century propaganda and an articulation of myths about America that have formed a significant strand of American literature since the seventeenth century. Ashe's organization appears to be principally topical, but the pamphlet attempts to persuade at a more sophisticated level by emphasizing two myths common in discovery literature: the New World as garden and the New World as capable of being reshaped in a European image.

Like Capt. John Smith's (q.v.) Va. and George Alsop's (q.v.) Md., Ashe's New World poses few dangers. There might be frost on a few mornings in Dec, and Jan., but it soon evaporates, with "Snow," he asserted, "having been seen but twice in ten Years." "Agues and Fevers" come in the summer but are not violent; there are "no Distempers either Epidemical or Mortal." The Indians are primitive but friendly and willing to help; they may paint their faces, but Ashe implied that they are not terrifying for he could not discern whether they did it for war or adornment. Wild animals might harass the settler's herds, but the cattle would "fend" them off; most beasts were simply described in the context of being resources, that is, furs. Even alligators were not a problem; they were dangerous in the water, but Ashe insisted that unless caught by surprise they would not attack a man on land. His description, however, tends to focus attention on far more passive fauna: manatees, sea turtles, hummingbirds, parakeets, and fireflies. Throughout, Ashe never let the reader forget that this idyllic "garden" contained untold riches that were easily harvested. The forests teemed with game and fowl. Even the seas yielded their wealth: ambergris often washed up on the shore; sponges could be gathered by hand; prawns were twice the size of those in Eng.; and oysters were "inexhaustible; a man may easily gather more in a day than he can well eat in a year."

Ashe's second theme, that this land could be remade in an English mold, also extended throughout the pamphlet. Cattle herds often constituted "many thousand head," and sheep and pigs multiplied in similar abundance. Fruit trees were abundant and varied: apple, pear, plum, cherry, quince, peach, and chestnut. "Their [the colonists] Gardens begin," Ashe noted, "to be supplied with such European Plants and Herbs as are necessary for the Kitchen, viz., Potatoes, Lettice, Coleworts, Parsnips, Turnip, Carrot and Reddish." Flowers, too, had been brought in: "Rose, Tulip, Carnation and Lilly." Wheat, pease, and beans were being cultivated; even barley had received some experimentation, in order Ashe averred, "to make Malt for brewing English Beer and Ale, having all Utensils and Conveniences for it."

It is not known what influence Ashe's small tract had in luring prospective settlers to Carolina, but the result is a highly readable and extremely valuable description, not only of early Carolina in a period of rapid environmental change, but of the complex images Europeans, especially Englishmen, entertained of the New World.

Suggested Readings: LHUS. *See also* Alexander S. Salley, Jr., ed., *Narratives of Early Carolina, 1650-1708* (1911), pp. 135-159; Bartholomew R. Carroll, ed., *Historical Collections of South Carolina*, 2 vols. (1836), pp. 59-84.

Richard L. Haan
Hartwick College

JONATHAN ASHLEY (1712-1780)

Works: *The Great Duty of Charity* (1742); *The United Endeavours* (1742); *The Great Concern of Christ* (1743); *A Letter from the Reverend Mr. Jonathan Ashley* (1743); *Ministers and People* (1749); *An Humble Attempt* (1753).

Biography: Born in Westfield, Mass., Nov. 11, 1712, Jonathan Ashley was a member of a prominent frontier family and was allied, through marriage, with the influential Rev. William Williams (q.v.) of Hatfield, Mass. After graduation from Yale College in 1730, Ashley was ordained as second pastor of the Congregational Church in Deerfield, Mass., Nov. 8, 1732. The Rev. William Williams delivered the ordination sermon, and in 1736 Ashley married Williams's daughter Dorothy.

The two great public events of Ashley's lifetime were the Great Awakening and the American Revolution—both of which Ashley opposed. In the former case, particularly, he was an active opponent, preaching against revivals and ultimately attacking the Rev. Jonathan Edwards (q.v.) of Northampton (his wife's cousin) during the 1750 controversy over qualifications for communion that culminated in Edwards's dismissal. Later, in 1780, Ashley was himself the center of congregational controversy, largely because of his Toryism, but he died before any action was taken. An intelligent and learned man with a lively imagination, Ashley was considered to be a forceful preacher in an era of polemical divinity.

Critical Appraisal: "Ministers of *Christ* should be Men of *Reason*, for they are to preach *a most reasonable Gospel*." Thus Jonathan Ashley identified himself, in *The Great Concern of Christ*, with the Stoddardean intellectualists and with the broader currents of eighteenth-century liberal Christianity. One who found valid sanctions in tradition and convention and who saw radical innovation, whether in church or state, as disorder, Ashley asserted the preeminence of order: "Authority is as necessary in a Church as in a Kingdom: and the more this sinks, the more will Religion die with it" (*The United Endeavours. . .to Promote the great Design of the Ministry*). To accommodate the uncertainties and sheer messiness of institutional life, Ashley insisted that neither ministers nor church members need be truly converted to fulfill their respective roles in the church. As long as all strive to gain faith in Christ and realize its chief fruit, Christian love, it is neither necessary nor wise to look too closely into one another's inner states. Most important is that ministers labor to instruct and exhort their people, and the people loyally support their designated ministers.

Perhaps Ashley's most notable publication is *The Great Duty of Charity*, preached at the Brattle Street Church in Boston, Nov. 28, 1742. A critique of the Great Awakening, this sermon defined the upheaval by comparing it with the disorders in the church at Corinth. However, the seminal ideas of the revivalists pertaining to conviction, religious affections, and the necessity of strict examination are all peremptorily dismissed, and an occasional phrase, such as "vagrant preacher," reveals the claw beneath his floss. Ironically, Ashley was not preaching in his own pulpit, and he had the effrontery to publish the sermon against the wishes of his host, the Rev. William Cooper (q.v.), causing a published exchange between the two men. Comparable in several respects to this sermon is *An Humble Attempt*, "Two Sermons" preached in Deerfield on Jun. 24, 1753, according to the title page, although the preface reveals that the work was originally preached Feb. 10, 1751, in Northampton. While preaching from Edwards's recently vacated pulpit, Ashley attempted to demolish the position of Jonathan Edwards respecting qualifications for communion. Insisting the entire issue was a mere quibbling over terminology respecting the historical meaning of "saint," Ashley argued that the church consisted only of professors whose inner state must remain mysterious in this life and that the idea of a restricted communion originated in the doctrine of Transubstantiation, a hard blow in Protestant New Eng.

In the sermons of Jonathan Ashley, learning and elegant exposition mediate an uncommon intensity of intellect and spirit rarely encountered. However, his religion is clearly not pietistic, and his view of the church in history would seem hardly to differentiate it from secular institutions: in the end, it is the ordered procession of civilized society that best embodies true religion.

Suggested Readings: CCNE; Dexter (I, 406-408); Sprague (I, 20). *See also* Edwards A. Park, "Memoir" in *The Works of Samuel Hopkins, D.D.* (1852), I, 228; Lorenzo Sabine, *Biographical Sketches of Loyalists of the American Revolution*, 2nd ed. (1864), I, 184-186; George Sheldon, *A History of Deerfield, Massachusetts*, 2 vols. (1896), I, 470-471, 535-539; II, 901-903; Joseph Tracy, *The Great Awakening* (1842), pp. 334-335; G. A. Ward, ed., *The Journal and Letters of Samuel Curwen*, 4th ed. (1864), p. 497.

Wilson H. Kimnach
University of Bridgeport

ANTHONY ASTON (fl. 1682-1747)

Works: *The Coy Shepherdess* (1709); also published as *Pastora* (1712); *The Fool's Opera* (1731); *Tony Aston's Petition and Speech* (1735); *A Brief Supplement to Colley Cibber, Esq.* (1742); "A New South Sea Ballad Made and Sung by Mr. Anthony Aston in the Magician or Harlequin Director" (unknown).

Biography: The facts about Anthony Aston's life are fragmentary, and much that is known is contained in his autobiographical "Sketch of the Life...of Anthony Aston," which he appended to *The Fool's Opera*. Although he did not provide the date of his birth, Aston mentioned that his father, Richard Aston, Esq., was a lawyer who lived in Brooke's Market and was a "Principal of Furnivals-Inn," and his mother was the "daughter of Col. Cope of Drumully Castle" in County Armagh, Ire. Aston was educated in Staffordshire and served as an "unworthy, idle clerk" to two masters, spending his time writing verse, reading plays, and acquiring "a Taste of the Girls."

His various occupations and adventures read like those of a classic picaro: "Gentleman, Lawyer, Poet, Actor, Soldier, Sailor, Exciseman, Publican, in England, Scotland, Ireland, New-York, East and West Jersey, Maryland (Virginia on both sides Cheesapeek), North and South Carolina, South Florida, Bahamas, Jamaica, Hispaniola." Although his account of these adventures is rambling and often confusing, Aston apparently reached Charleston, S.C., in 1703, where he became a poet and actor and "wrote one Play on the subject of the Country"; there is, however, no record of publication or any extant copies of the play. Regarded as the first professional actor in America, Aston undertook a series of voyages through Va. and N.Y., during which he frequently became a castaway.

In 1704 he sailed from Va. back to London, toured Eng., Scot., and Ire. as an actor, and appeared before the House of Commons in 1735. His *Supplement* to Colley Cibber's *Lives* details his association with many of the Drury Lane actors of his day, and throughout the vicissitudes of his life, Aston encouraged himself and his audiences to accept their fortunes with a smile and laugh.

Although Aston's contribution to American drama is slight, he is significant as a harbinger of those English actors who toured the early colonies in companies headed by Walter Murray and Thomas Kean, David Douglass, and Lewis Hallam in the 1750s. It is not surprising that Aston and these actors chose Charleston as a location for their productions. Unlike Puritan New Eng. and Quaker Pa., the southern colonies were far more tolerant of diversions such as balls, cotillions, and plays and generally encouraged various forms of entertainment.

Critical Appraisal: Anthony Aston's most important works are his two plays, each of which displays a sharp wit and buoyant vision of life. *The Coy Shepherdess* is a twenty-page pastoral written in rhyming couplets, involving the humorous activities of three sets of lovers. Similar in length, *The Fool's Opera* is written as a parody of John Gay's *The Beggar's Opera*, and its action involves the adventures of a Fool and Poet, each trying to embarrass and shame the other. The play ends with a ballad that mocks Gay and is followed by Aston's sketch of his life.

Aston's *Supplement* to Cibber's *Lives* has little intrinsic literary worth, but it does provide a number of interesting portraits of his colleagues. In a similar way, his *Petition and Speech* before the House of Commons is important not so much for its style as for the glimpse it provides of a lively orator who managed to convince the House to defeat the Playhouse Bill of 1734, which would have suppressed unlicensed theatres. Aston is an engaging writer, possessing a puckish sense of humor that reveals itself in continual pleas at the ends of each of his works for money.

Suggested Readings: DNB. *See also* Kent G. Gallagher, *The Foreigner in Early American Drama* (1966); Robert W. Lowe, ed., *Apology for the Life of Colley Cibber* (contains Aston's *Supplement*; 1966), pp. 297-318; Walter J. Meserve, *An Emerging Entertainment: The Drama of the American People to 1828* (1977), pp. 24, 37-38; Watson Nicholson, *Anthony Aston, Stroller and Adventurer* (1920); Sybil Rosenfeld, *Strolling Players & Drama in the Provinces, 1660-1765* (1939), pp. 6-7, 43, 52, 169; Henry W. Wells, *Three Centuries of Drama, 1500-1830* (contains Aston's two plays; 1952-1956).

David W. Madden
University of California, Davis

JOSIAH ATKINS (fl. 1781)

Works: *Diary of Josiah Atkins* (w. c. 1781; pub. 1975).

Biography: Little is known of Josiah Atkins's life before Jan. 1781, when he enlisted in the Fifth Connecticut Regiment of the Continental Army, except that he had lived and worked in Waterbury (probably as a merchant and metalsmith) and was an active member of his church. An ardent supporter of the American cause, Atkins had an aversion to killing and delayed enlisting until the final year of the war. In the diary that he kept regularly after leaving home on Apr. 5, he indicated that he felt less concern about the dangers of war than enforced absence from regular religious services. After an initial period of training, Atkins was sent south to join Lafayette's army in Va., which at the time was shadowing a larger British force under Cornwallis. Atkins was only involved in one major engagement, the Battle of Green Spring (Jul. 6, 1781), before he became ill and was sent to a hospital near Hanover Court House, Va. After recovering, Atkins was asked to continue at the hospital as a doctor's mate. He had been in that post only two months when he became sick and died. According to his earnest request, his diary was returned home to the "dear wife" he had "left at home to moan my misfortune."

Critical Appraisal: Atkins's diary is one of the finest written by an

American soldier during the Revolution; however, although the work describes and is limited to Atkins's period of military service, its artistic unity lies elsewhere. The force behind the work is spiritual rather than martial. Like so many others in the history of New Eng., Atkins saw religious and political goals as linked. He only reluctantly embarked on a course that would force him to use the "cruel and unwelcome instruments of war" and become a "stranger in a strange land" isolated not only from family and friends but also from regular participation in the church. He was able to make this sacrifice, because he believed that the American cause was a divinely ordained quest. However, when early in the diary he saw slaves on George Washington's (q.v.) Va. plantation, he began to question his decision. The diary gives an excellent portrait of Atkins's anguish at finding out that "persons who pretend to stand for *the rights of mankind* for the *liberties of society*, can delight in oppression, & that even of the worst kind!" Such incidents focus the reader's attention on the personal tension that animates the diary. Atkins was finally able to resolve this tension by taking a position in a military hospital. There he faced greater dangers from disease than those he faced in the infantry; yet he termed this noncombatant role evidence of divine favor. In the few months covered by the diary, Atkins effectively described a wide range of experiences, but it is the resolution of the internal conflict that provided the artistic unity that makes the work notable.

Suggested Readings: Joseph Anderson, *The Town and City of Waterbury Connecticut* (1896), I, 472-480; Steven E. Kagle, *American Diary Literature* (1979), pp. 127-130.

Steven E. Kagle
Illinois State University

PETER ATTWOOD, S.J. (1682-1734)

Works: *Liberty and Property or the Beauty of Maryland Displayed. Being a Brief and Candid Search and Inquiry into Her Charter, Fundamental Laws and Constitution. By a Lover of His Country* (1718).

Biography: Peter Attwood was born in Worcestershire, Eng., on Oct. 18, 1682, entered the Society of Jesus (Jesuits) in 1703, was ordained a priest, and came to Md. in 1711. In 1728 he became the superior of the Maryland Mission of the English Province of the Jesuits, a post he held until his death in 1734. The Md. Jesuits were in an unusual position. With the exception of two English secular priests in the 1640s and a few Franciscans from 1672 to 1720, they were the only Catholic clergy in the English-speaking colonies. Arriving with the first settlers in 1634, the Jesuits had taken up land like the other colonists. By making the clergy self-supporting and having no established church, Cecil Calvert, the second Lord Baltimore, had intended to provide complete religious liberty in his colony—all of the colonists, clergy or lay of any denomination, were to enjoy that freedom which was derived from ownership of property. The challenge to this tradition led to Attwood's sole contribution to colonial literature, the first "history" of Catholicism in Md.

Critical Appraisal: Ten of Attwood's sermons, preserved at Georgetown University, give no indication of the political struggles of Md. Catholics, but his tract "On Liberty and Property" was his response to the Md. Assembly's effort in 1718 to impose English penal laws against Catholics by repealing the 1704 "Act to Prevent the Growth of Popery." That act was part of the anti-Catholic legislation that began with the Glorious Revolution, as a result of which Md. became a royal colony and the Church of England was established. In Sept. 1704 the Assembly had prohibited Catholic priests from celebrating Mass. For a first offense, a priest was to be fined fifty pounds and sentenced to six months in jail; for a second offense, he was to be deported to Eng., where he would be subject to life imprisonment, included in the penal laws passed under William III. In Dec. 1704, however, the Assembly suspended these penalties, provided that priests said Mass in private homes. Queen Anne approved this suspension clause in 1706. In 1713 Md. reverted to the Calvert family, which had become Anglican, but John Hart, the former royal governor, retained his post. He persuaded the Assembly that the 1704 act was unnecessary, since the statutes of William III provided adequate safeguards against Catholics by prohibiting them from voting, purchasing or inheriting property, and receiving an education. The Assembly thus implied that Md. was subject to parliamentary statutes. Attwood sought to address these issues.

Attwood narrated the history of Md. under the Catholic Calverts, when "a general liberty in the enjoyment of each one's religion and property was a great encouragement to the first adventures"; to curtail that liberty would depopulate the colony. Gov. Hart had also argued that neither Charles I in 1633 nor any subsequent monarch could have granted Catholics rights in Md. that they did not enjoy in Eng. Against this situation, Attwood argued that the freedom in Md. was much publicized throughout Eng. and that, despite this public knowledge, no English authority, even Oliver Cromwell, had ever sought to countermand it. It was, moreover, publicly known that all of the colonists, even priests, had taken up land and had the right to buy, sell, bequest, or inherit it. This right to property, he said, was premised on "a fundamental and perpetual law" of religion, according to which no one was to be deprived of any right because of religion, but such deprivation would result from the imposition of the penal laws of William III.

Attwood then turned to the right to vote and the right of the Md. Assembly to enact its own laws. It was unjust, he stated, that "neither Quakers [who were ultimately not disenfranchised in the act] nor Roman Catholics are allowed to have a vote in the making of any law, tho' they and their late posterity must be bound by the same." For him, laws were to be made with the consent of the governed. In regard to whether the Assembly had the right to pass its own laws, Attwood addressed his plea to all of his fellow "Marylandians," both Catholic and Protestant. He warned them that by declaring parliamentary statutes to be binding in Md., the Assembly was denying the right, recognized since the colony's beginning, of being an independent legislative body. Marylanders, he asserted, had brought with them English laws of privilege but not statutes. As proof for this, he argued from the 1704 act and its subsequent suspension clause that if the royal governor and the Assembly at that time had believed parliamentary statutes to be binding in Md., they would not have passed the act.

Regardless of Attwood's arguments—and Charles Carroll the attorney, the grandfather of Charles Carroll of Carrollton (q.v.) made remonstrations in Eng. against the governor—the Assembly passed the act repealing the 1704 act. Whether Lord Baltimore approved it, however, remains uncertain. Except for the right to vote, hold office, and receive an education, the penal laws against Catholics were not enforced. Only in the 1750s did the question again arise, and then it was addressed in terms similar to Attwood's by George Hunter, S.J. (q.v.). Attwood's tract is not a work of literary style, but it is of interest to the political, cultural, and religious historian for the insight it provides into Md.'s colonial Catholic community and for its arguments that property was the basis of civil rights, that the publicity given Md.'s freedom constituted a custom with the force of law, and that the Assembly had the right to enact its own laws independent of Parliament.

Suggested Readings: CCMDG. *See also* Peter Attwood, "Liberty and Property or the Beauty of Maryland Displayed," USCHM, 3 (1889-1890), 237-263; James Hennesey, S.J., "Roman Catholicism: The Maryland Tradition," *Thought*, 51 (1976), 282-295.

Gerald P. Fogarty, S.J.
University of Virginia

SAMUEL AUCHMUTY (1722-1777)

Works: *A Sermon Preached at the Opening of St. Paul's Chapel* (1766); *A Sermon Preached Before the Corporation for the Relief of the Widows and Children of Clergymen* (1771); *Letter to Capt. Montrésor* (1775).

Biography: Samuel Auchmuty was born in Boston in 1722, the son of Robert Auchmuty, a judge of the Admiralty Court and a vestryman of King's Chapel. Although he did not complete his studies at Harvard, Samuel Auchmuty was later granted the degree with his classmates of 1742. In 1747 he was admitted to holy orders by the bishop of London. The Society for the Propagation of the Gospel in Foreign Parts (SPG) appointed him to the post of catechist of the Negro school in New York City and assistant at Trinity Church. He was energetic and successful in both positions. In 1764 Auchmuty became rector of Trinity Church. Under his direction, St. Paul's Chapel was completed and opened in 1766. Auchmuty received the doctoral degree from Oxford in 1766 and from King's College (Columbia) in 1767. Dr. Auchmuty was influential in the denial of incorporation to the Presbyterian Church and in keeping Presbyterians from service on the governor's Council. He was also closely involved in the attempts by the northern Anglican clergy to obtain the American Episcopate, but he was more moderate than such "firebrands" as Thomas Bradbury Chandler (q.v.). As the American Revolution approached, Auchmuty's position as a staunch Loyalist became well known. In September 1776, while he and his family were in Brunswick, N. J., a great fire destroyed Trinity Church as well as Auchmuty's home. He did not long survive this disaster and died in N. Y. in March 1777. He was buried in St. Paul's chancel. His three sons graduated from King's College and served in the British army during the American Revolution. The eldest son, Samuel, remained in the army, became a general, and was knighted for the capture of Java in 1811.

Critical Appraisal: Although he published only two sermons and no books or pamphlets, Samuel Auchmuty has a place among the writers of early America. He carried on a voluminous correspondence with the SPG, governmental officials, and fellow American clerics, wrote on controversial topics in colonial newspapers, and was an articulate participant in important humanitarian, ecclesiastical, and political activities in N. Y. in the quarter-century before the Revolution. The principal themes in his writing are High Church Anglicanism, humanitarianism, and, finally, unbending Loyalism.

The two published sermons by Dr. Auchmuty demonstrate in turn his High Church stance and his humanitarian concerns. In 1766 he presided over a spectacular affair, the consecration of St. Paul's Chapel. In his sermon on this occasion, he used examples from Scripture, the early church fathers, and even "heathens" to develop the thesis that God is "eminently present" in one place more than another and that since churches dedicated to God are such places, reverent and devout behavior is obligatory. In his other published sermon, preached to the Corporation for the Relief of Widows and Children of Clergy, he described the plight of a widow of a clergyman dramatically and emotionally. Auchmuty had been instrumental in the formation of the corporation to provide relief.

Auchmuty's humanitarian concerns reached beyond his race and church to the plight of blacks and Indians. His letters to the SPG are an important source of scholarly information about the development of Negro schools in the colonies. Auchmuty also corresponded with Sir William Johnson, superintendent of Indian affairs, concerning the education of Indians. In his concern for the Indians, Auchmuty's staunch Anglicanism was as prominent as his humanitarianism. He had nothing but contempt for the schemes of the Congregational minister Eleazar Wheelock (q.v.) for educating Indians: "Wheelock and his associates will engross the Indian Country, and lay the seeds of Schism so deep that it will hereafter be impossible to eradicate them."

During the 1760s, much of Auchmuty's energy and correspondence was devoted to his great dream of the appointment of an Anglican bishop for America. To this end, he worked closely with fellow clerics in America and gave his friends in Eng. no peace. He was more moderate in tactics and less sanguine about the likelihood of success in the endeavor than were many of his fellow leaders in the movement.

The high Toryism that Dr. Auchmuty displayed as the American Revolution approached was part of his birthright. The bit of writing for which he became most widely known was something he had not intended for publication. On Apr. 19, 1775, he wrote to his stepdaughter's husband, Capt. John Montrésor (q.v.), an engineer with the British army. The letter fell into patriot hands and was published as a broadside and in the *Massachusetts Spy* and the *New England Chronicle*. In it he wrote: "I must own I was born among the saints and rebels, but it was my misfortune. Where are your Congresses now? What say [John] Hancock, [John] Adams [q.v.], and all their rebellious followers? Are they still bold? I trow not." A reply to Auchmuty's letter—from a man who identified himself as an Anglican and signed himself "C.J."—was hawked about N. Y. The author accused Dr. Auchmuty of inflicting upon the church a "mortal wound" by his letter to Capt. Montrésor. The letter had, C.J. averred, not only brought "a most hearty contempt" upon Auchmuty but had also strengthened the idea that the Church of England, because of its close connection with the state, was inimical to liberty in America. After this unfortunate incident, Dr. Auchmuty announced that he had ceased writing letters.

Suggested Readings: CCMC; DAB; Sibley-Shipton (XI, 115-127); Sprague (V, 127-129). *See also* Carl Bridenbaugh, *Mitre and Sceptre: Transatlantic Faiths, Ideas, Personalities, and Politics, 1689-1775* (1962), pp. 226-267, passim; William W. Kemp, *The Support of Schools in Colonial New York by the Society for the Propagation of the Gospel in Foreign Parts* (1913), pp. 256-261; Frank J. Klingberg, *Anglican Humanitarianism in Colonial New York* (1940), pp. 95-114, 147-152; Lorenzo Sabine, *Biographical Sketches of Loyalists of the American Revolution*, 2 vols. (1864), I, 194-195; Clifford K. Shipton, *New England Life in the 18th Century: Representative Biographies from Sibley's Harvard Graduates* (1963), pp. 469-482.

Mary E. Quinlivan
University of Texas of the Permian Basin

_B_

BENJAMIN FRANKLIN BACHE (1769-1798)

Works: Philadelphia _General Advertiser_ (publisher and editor; 1790-1794); Philadelphia _Aurora_ (publisher and editor; 1794-1798); _Proposals for Publishing...The Daily Advertiser_ (1790); _A Specimen of Printing Types_ (1790); _Remarks Occasioned by the Late Conduct of Mr. Washington_ (1797); _Truth Will Out_! (1798).

Biography: Benjamin Franklin Bache was born in Philadelphia, the son of Richard Bache and his wife Sarah, the daughter of Benjamin Franklin (q.v.). In 1776 Bache accompanied Franklin to Europe, where he attended school in Paris and Geneva and learned the basics of the printing trade. After he returned to America in 1785, he completed his education at the College of Philadelphia (Univ. of Pa.). In 1790 he started the _General Advertiser_ (later renamed the _Aurora_), which became one of the leading political journals of its day. Bache gave his support to the Democratic-Republican party and attacked the Federalist administrations of George Washington (q.v.) and John Adams (q.v.). He was arrested for libel in 1798, shortly before he died of yellow fever.

Critical Appraisal: Benjamin Franklin Bache was one of the most innovative, influential, and notorious political journalists of the 1790s. After the demise of Philip Freneau's (q.v.) _National Gazette_ in 1793, the _General Advertiser_ and the _Aurora_ were the leading Democratic-Republican newspapers in the U.S. In fact, the _Aurora_ even maintained this position after Bache's death under the direction of his widow (Margaret) and his associate William Duane (q.v.). Bache enjoyed the support of Thomas Jefferson (q.v.) and printed pieces by James Madison (q.v.) and other opposition leaders; he also published pamphlets by Jeffersonian spokesmen. Bache's editorial comments and exposés did much to heighten the political controversies of the decade, including the disputes over the activities of the French diplomat Edmond Genêt, the Jay Treaty, and the "XYZ Affair." In the columns of his papers, he and his contributors publicized the basic Republican arguments: that the Federalists were a moneyed aristocracy; that they sought to betray popular government; and that they were intent on making America subservient to G.B. while repudiating Fr., America's ally in the War of Independence.

As a journalist, Bache pioneered several techniques. Although the editors of the Revolutionary era had also focused on politics, Bache was among the first to be unabashedly partisan, using brief editorial notes to express his own opinions. He was also one of the first to provide extensive reports of congressional debates. The thoroughness of his coverage made his papers a source upon which editors across the country depended for political news.

Most of Bache's writings are found in his newspapers—as editorial comments or disguised as letters from readers. His only independent publication was *Remarks Occasioned by the Late Conduct of Mr. Washington. Truth Will Out*! was simply a compilation of materials from the *Aurora*, documenting and defending his role in the XYZ controversy. The *Remarks* is a good example of how far his partisanship could go. Like most Jeffersonians, Bache believed that the Washington administration had pursued many unfortunate policies. But although many Republicans stopped short of criticizing the president himself, Bache put the blame directly on Washington—or, as he called him, "the *George* of America." Mincing no words, Bache set out "to prove the want of claim in Mr. Washington either to the gratitude or confidence of his country," arguing that the president, despite his admirable qualities, had promoted a disposition toward monarchy by his haughty behavior. In addition, Bache contended that Washington had actively supported a pro-British policy and betrayed the French and that he had also helped to establish a self-serving party, the Federalists, at the heart of government. Throughout, Bache asserted his faith in the French Republic and called for constitutional changes that would curb the powers of the president and make the central government less aristocratic.

The 1790s were a decade of intense political controversy, and both Bache and his Federalist adversaries were carried to argumentative excesses by the passions of the time. Bache's fiery style earned him the nickname of "Lightning Rod, Junior" and the contempt of the Federalists, who accused him of "Jacobinism," subservience to Fr., anti-Americanism, and outright lying. They made several attempts to drive him from business, resorting on occasion to physical violence. Bache matched their invectives with accusations of "monarchism" and corruption that now seem equally exaggerated. Whatever the truth of the charges and countercharges, Bache must be recognized as one of the key organizers of an effective opposition press and a staunch defender of journalistic freedom: "A free press," he wrote, "is a most formidable engine to tyrants of every description."

Suggested Readings: DAB. *See also* Bernard Fay, *The Two Franklins: Fathers of American Democracy* (1933); Claude-Anne Lopez and Eugenia Herbert, *The Private Franklin: The Man and His Family* (1975), pp. 304-312; Marshall Smelser, "The Federalist Period as an Age of Passion," AQ, 10 (1958), 391-419; Donald H. Stewart, *The Opposition Press of the Federalist Period* (1969), pp. 9-10, 24-25, 27, 609-613; James D. Tagg, "Benjamin Franklin Bache and the Philadelphia *Aurora*" (Ph.D. diss., Wayne State University, 1973).

Douglas M. Arnold
Yale University

CHARLES BACKUS (1749-1803)

Works: *A Discourse Delivered at the Funeral of Mr. John Howard* (1785); *A Sermon Preached in Long-Meadow* (1788); *Faithful Ministers of Jesus Christ* (1792); *A Sermon Preached at Enfield* (1792); *Afflictions Improved* (1793); *A Sermon Preached...on the Day of the Anniversary Election* (1793); *Man's Mortality Illustrated* (1794); *Qualifications and Duties of the Christian Pastor* (1795); *The Folly of Man's Choosing* (1796); *Ministers Serving God* (1796); *A Sermon Delivered at Tolland...Before the Uriel Lodge of Free Masons* (1796); *Five Discourses on the Truth and Inspiration of the Bible* (1797); *The Benevolent Spirit of Christianity* (1798); *The Principle Causes of the Opposition* (1798); *The True Christian* (1798); *The High Importance of Love* (1799); *The Living Warned* (1799); *A Sermon Preached...at the Funeral of Mrs. Agnes Prudden* (1799); *The Scripture Doctrine of Regeneration* (1800); *The Faithful Ministers of Jesus Christ Thankful to Him* (1801); *A Sermon...Containing a Brief Review of Some Distinguishing Events of the Eighteenth Century* (1801).

Biography: Born in 1749 at Norwich, Conn., Charles Backus received a B.A. (1769) and an M.A. (1772) from Yale. Orphaned in early childhood, he subsidized his education through the charity of friends and relatives who recognized the potential of his intellectual abilities. During college, he reconciled doubts concerning divine grace and came to accept the Calvinistic doctrine of total depravity that characterized his theology throughout his later career. After graduation from college, Backus prepared for the ministry under the tutelage of the Rev. Dr. Hart of Preston, Conn. He began preaching in 1773, and in 1774 he was ordained as minister to the congregation at Somers, Conn. The following year he married Bethiah Hill of Cambridge, Mass., but their only son, Jabez, died suddenly while a student at Yale. This tragic loss, undoubtedly associated in Backus's mind with the early death of his parents, sombered his outlook on life and gave him an unhealthy obsession with death. Along with fits of depression, he was also subject to outbursts of anger, but his ministerial duties, particularly the training of young ministers was therapeutic enough for him to lead a productive existence.

According to contemporary accounts, Backus preached with power and conviction. As a mentor to the students who boarded in his household, he was exacting but fair. In theological arenas, Backus was a follower of Dr. Samuel Hopkins's (q.v.) traditional Calvinistic theories. Backus died in 1803, after having served some twenty-nine years in the ministry.

Critical Appraisal: Charles Backus's sensitivity to the political events of his day, coupled with his ambivalence in regard to the new American nation and complete distrust of the French, makes him an interesting example of the general attitude among New Eng. Calvinists during the late eighteenth century. As an educator of some fifty ministerial candidates, he is also important for his diffusion of Hopkinsian ideas, thus assuring the continuity of strict Calvinism even in the face of the strengthening liberal challenge of the times.

Following the Hopkinsian school of Calvinism, Backus considered regeneration "an instantaneous change," arguing that a belief in "progressive regeneration" (preparation) was "built on principles which deny the full extent of man's depravity." The work of divine grace in conversion was thus explicated in his *Scripture Doctrine of Regeneration Considered*, wherein he argued that "disinterested benevolence" (a Hopkinsian term) not only determined the nature of regenerate individuals but also of society. For Backus, progress belonged to the realm of sanctification consequent upon the imperceptible moment of regeneration. Thus a moral society, for him, was based on divine love rather than on principles of benevolent self-interest or duty, as many Enlightenment thinkers would have it. In his *Sermon. . .Before the Uriel Lodge of Free Masons*, Backus declared that tyranny could not be combated by the application of political checks and balances alone, but only by the law of God "governing the hearts of both rulers and subjects." Despite all advances in learning, invention, and discovery acknowledged in his *Brief Review of the Distinguishing Events of the Eighteenth Century*, Backus believed the commencement of the new century was to be a "day of trouble" portended by a decline in piety, an increase in atheism, and the bloodiness of the recent French Revolution. He did, however, note that "within three years past" the revival of piety in New Eng. indicated some slight hope for the future.

Suggested Readings: Dexter (III, 310-316); Sprague (II, 61-68). *See also* Timothy Dwight, *Travels in New England and New York*, 4 vols., ed. Barbara M. Solomon and Patricia M. King (1969), I, 409; II, 182, 188-191, 396.

Barbara Ritter Dailey
Boston University

ISAAC BACKUS (1724-1806)

Works: *All True Ministers* (1754); *A Short Description* (1756); *Spiritual Ignorance* (1763); *A Letter to the Reverend Mr. Benjamin Lord* (1764); *Family Prayer* (1766); *A Fish Caught in His Own Net* (1768); *Gospel Comfort* (1769); *A Short Description of the Difference* (1770); *The Doctrine of the Sovereign Grace* (1771); *A Letter to a Gentleman* (1771); *Evangelical Ministers* (1772); *A Reply to a Piece Wrote Last Year* (1772); *An Appeal to the Public for Religious Liberty* (1773); *A Discourse Concerning the Materials. . .of the Church* (1773); *The Sovereign Decrees of God* (1773); *A Church History of New England*, I (1777), II (1784), III (1796); *Government and Liberty* (1778); *Policy as Well as Honesty* (1779); *The Substance of an Address* (1779); *An Appeal to the People at Massachusetts* (1780); *Truth Is Great* (1781); *The Doctrine of Universal Salvation* (1782); *A Door Opened for Equal Christian Liberty* (1783); *Godliness Excludes Slavery* (1785); *The Testimony of the Two Witnesses* (1786); *An Address to the Inhabitants of New England* (1787); *An Address to the Second Baptist Church*

(1787); *The Atonement of Christ* (1787); *True Faith* (1787); *The Doctrine of the Particular Election* (1789); *The Liberal Support of Gospel Ministers* (1790); *An Answer to Mr. Wesley* (1791); *The Infinite Importance* (1791); *The Kingdom of God* (1792); *The Nature and Necessity* (1792).

Biography: Isaac Backus was born into a well-to-do family of Norwich, Conn. After a youth spent working on the family farm and attending local schools, he experienced a New Light conversion in 1741 during the Great Awakening. Along with other members of his family, Backus withdrew from the Norwich Congregational Church and formed a Separate congregation. In 1747 Backus felt a call to preach, and the following year he became the pastor of a Separatist church in Titicut, Mass. Two years later, he married the former Susanna Moore, who eventually bore them eight children. Backus became a Baptist in 1751 and helped to form the First Baptist Church of Middleborough, Mass., which he served for the rest of his life.

Despite the fact that Baptists could exempt themselves from religious taxation in colonial Mass., they resented the existence of the Congregational State Church. Backus became the leading Baptist spokesperson on this issue, and he was one of three delegates from the Warren Baptist Association who confronted John Adams (q.v.) and other Mass. delegates to the First Continental Congress on the issue of religious liberty. He later fought against the general assessment for religion that was part of the Mass. Constitution of 1780. As a result of his activities, Backus is recognized as a leading figure in the struggle for freedom of religion in the U.S., and was a defender of Baptist principles in general. Despite his extensive writing, Backus was an active minister. Between 1747 and 1806, he traveled more than 1,000 miles a year and delivered nearly 200 sermons annually.

Critical Appraisal: Isaac Backus stood as a living contradiction to those who associated the Great Awakening with anti-intellectualism. Beginning his career as a lay exhorter without a college education, he wrote a history of the Baptists in New Eng. that is still an important source, and he published more than thirty pamphlets on the pressing religious and political issues of his day.

Backus is best known for his tracts dealing with religious liberty. Among the most important was *An Appeal to the Public for Religious Liberty*, which stated the Baptist case against the established Congregational Church of colonial Mass. Backus disagreed with the state religion because it baptized infants, required that clergymen be college educated, and supported parish ministers with public taxes. For none of these practices could he find Gospel support. More important, Backus believed that civil and ecclesiastical governments were separate spheres and that religion was corrupted by involvement with the state. For him, "the law of Christ...required [every man] to judge for himself concerning the circumstantials as well as the essentials of religion." After independence, in *Government and Liberty Described*, he quoted from the writings of Congregationalist Charles Chauncy (q.v.) against the Anglican episcopate and claimed that the Baptists wanted the same liberty as did Chauncy. His *Truth Is Great and Will Prevail* expressed the opposition of the Baptists to the general assessment for religion and their determination to resist, despite the fact that the law would provide some public funds for their church. *A Door Opened* rejoiced at the Balkcom decision that seemed to exempt Baptists from the assessment—a ruling later overturned. Backus did not live to see in Mass. the full separation of church and state that he sought, but no one did more to make it possible.

While he fought for religious liberty, Backus also helped to define the Baptist faith and defend it from rival creeds. In *A Short Description*, published in 1756, he explained his newly found belief in adult baptism by using the concept of two covenants: according to Backus the New Testament covenant of faith superceded the Old Testament covenant of works and with it the Hebrew tribalism that allowed infants to enter the church. In a number of sermons, Backus defended his own view of Calvinism from stricter versions and from the growing Arminianism of his time. William McLoughlin, his biographer, testified to the breadth of his contribution to the intellectual life of the Baptist Church: "Backus also wrote tracts emphasizing the importance of baptism by immersion, the internal call to preach, the liberal support of gospel ministers, family prayer, congregational autonomy, and strict discipline for the maintenance of a pure church of gathered saints."

Backus's style was marked by an unaffected clarity, aptly illustrated, for example, in his third-person account of his own conversion:

> As he was alone in the field, it was demonstrated to his mind and conscience, that he had done his utmost to make himself better, without obtaining any such thing; but that he was a guilty sinner in the hands of a holy God, who had a right to do with him as seemed good in God's sight.... And soon upon this a way of relief was opened to his soul, ... wherein truth and justice shine with lustre, in the bestowment of free mercy and salvation upon objects who have nothing in themselves but badness.

Backus could also be artful. In his influential pamphlet *Government and Liberty*, he suggested that the various Christian denominations were like "streams and rivers" whose cumulative effect was beneficial to mankind and whose running waters ought not be obstructed by the coercive hand of the state.

A logical mind, lucid style, and balanced judgment made Isaac Backus one of the more effective publicists of his time. Attacking religious establishments in *An Appeal to the Public*, he wrote that the "true liberty of man" was "to know and enjoy his Creator, and to do all the good unto, and enjoy all the happiness with and in his fellow creatures that he is capable of." One has the sense that, in his own terms, Isaac Backus was truly free.

Suggested Readings: CCNE; DAB; DARB; T_2. *See also* Edwin Scott Gaustad, *The Great Awakening in New England* (1968), pp. 115-116, 121-122; C. C. Goen, *Revivalism and Separatism in New England, 1740-1800, Strict Congregationalism and Separate Baptists in the Great Awakening* (1969); Alan E. Heimert, *Religion and the American Mind, from the Great Awakening to the Revolution* (1966); Alvah Hovey, *A Memoir of the Life and Times of the Rev. Isaac Backus, A.M.* (1859); Thomas B. Maston, *Isaac Backus, Pioneer of Religious Liberty* (1962); William G. McLoughlin, *Isaac Backus* *and the American Pietistic Tradition* (1967); Anson Phelps Stokes, *Church and State in the United States*, 3 vols. (1950), I, 306-310.

Sidney Charles Bolton
University of Arkansas at Little Rock

NATHANIEL BACON (1647-1676)

Works: "The Humble Appeale of the Voluntiers to All Well-Minded and Charitable People" (w. 1676; unpub.); "The Virginians' Plea for Opposing the Indians Without the Governor's Order" (w. 1676; unpub.); *Manifesto Concerning the Present Troubles in Virginia* (w. 1676; pub. 1893); *The Declaration of the People* (w. 1676; pub. 1893); *Appeale to the People of Accomack* (w. 1676; pub. 1893).

Biography: Born into a landed Suffolk family in 1647, Nathaniel Bacon entered St. Catherine's Hall, Cambridge, at the age of 18. After two years, he was withdrawn by his father for having "broken into some extravagances" and sent with a tutor on an extended grand tour of the Continent from which he did not return until 1666, when he reentered Cambridge. He received an M.A. and had embarked on a course of study at Gray's Inn before going home in 1670 to marry Elizabeth Duke much against her father's wishes. Somewhat under a cloud, Bacon left Eng. for Va. in 1674 with his family and a substantial sum of money from his father. Once arrived, he bought two plantations on the James and, through the influence of an elder cousin and namesake, was appointed to Governor Sir William Berkeley's (q.v.) Council, but he sided with dissidents in the colony who charged Berkeley with corruption and a negligent attitude toward intensifying Indian raids on the frontier (in which Bacon himself had lost an overseer and substantial property). When he assumed command of an unauthorized body of troops in the spring of 1676, Berkeley declared him a rebel, and the situation gradually flared up into a full-scale mutiny under Bacon's leadership. The governor, soundly defeated on the mainland, was driven into exile on the Eastern Shore and was able to regain control of the colony only after the destruction of Jamestown and, on Oct. 26, 1676, Bacon's succumbing to the "bloody flux" (dysentery).

Critical Appraisal: Although it cannot be proven that Nathaniel Bacon himself was the author of the various public papers issued by his faction, his education and unquestioned gifts as a galvanizing orator supply a firm basis for the belief that he was. The position in which he found himself demanded that he justify his actions both to the crown and to the Va. populace if he hoped to avoid personal and collective disaster, and his earliest efforts show him trying to soothe concerns on both sides of the Atlantic. "The Virginians' Plea" is directed toward London, calmly assuring Charles II that no treason lurks in the planters' disobedience to Berkeley but growing to a calculated shrillness as it describes their plight under a governor apparently indifferent to the suffering of menaced women and children. On the other hand, his "Humble Appeale" addresses the colonials themselves and undertakes in the sanest of tones to demonstrate the logic of using Bacon's irregulars against the Indians rather than levying additional taxes for defense, as Berkeley proposed to do. But the deepening of the schism throughout the summer of 1676 is traceable in the increasingly bitter domestic pronouncements made by the chief mutineer against his enemies. The *Manifesto* ironically pleaded the Baconians culpable, "If vertue be a sin, if Piety be guilt," but it also called upon the public to take a hard look at the men of "vile extraction" who have attained unmerited and cruelly abused power under Berkeley's regime. In *The Declaration of the People*, Bacon recalled his legal training and drew up a formal indictment of the Loyalists, complete with a bill of particulars not unlike Thomas Jefferson's (q.v.) impeachments of George III. The *Appeale to the People of Accomack*, an attempt to move Berkeley's protectors on the Eastern Shore to deliver him up to the rebels, forwarded a cunning, if specious, argument that the governor's signing of Bacon's commission and then revoking it proved him either a liar or unfit to hold office and undeserving of support in either case.

Like many documents revered as sacred texts in intellectual and political history, Bacon's communications to the world were pure propaganda and ad hoc self-justifications at the time when they first appeared. That the passage of time has made them something different is neither surprising nor necessarily wrong. In the centuries since the establishment of American independence, they have become a part of the legend of Bacon himself, the "Torchbearer of the Revolution" whose assault on British authority foreshadowed the events of 1776 by exactly 100 years.

Contemporary accounts of Bacon's Rebellion, such as those by John Cotton of Queen's Creek (q.v.) and Thomas Mayhew (q.v.), provided authors on both sides of the Atlantic with material to turn the uprising into a subject for poetry, drama, and fiction. Its literary treatments include Aphra Behn's *The Widow Ranter* (w. c. 1688), a long hudibrastic satire by Ebenezer Cooke (q.v.), and numerous nineteenth- and twentieth-century romantic novels.

Suggested Readings: DAB; DNB; LHUS; T₁. *See also*, for purported texts and summaries of Bacon's speeches, the "True Narrative" of the rebellion by Sir John Berry and Francis Moryson in *Narratives of the Insurrections, 1675-1690* by Charles M. Andrews (1915), pp. 105-141; "Proclamations of Nathaniel Bacon," VMHB, 1 (1893), 55-63; Wilcomb E. Washburn, *The Governor and the Rebel* (1957); Thomas Jefferson Wertenbaker, *Torchbearer of the Revolution* (1940).

W. H. Ward
Appalachian State University

THOMAS BACON (c. 1700-1768)

Works: *A Compleat System of the Revenue of Ireland* (1737); *Two Sermons, Preached to a Congregation of Black Slaves* (1749); *Four Sermons Upon the*

*Great and Indispensible Duty of All Christian Masters and Mistresses to Bring
Up Their Negro Slaves in the Knowledge and Fear of God* (1750); *A Sermon
Preached at the Parish Church of St. Peter's, in Talbot County, Maryland*
(1751); *A Sermon Preached at Annapolis. . .Before a Society of Free and Accepted Masons* (1753); *Laws of Maryland at Large* (1765).

Biography: Thomas Bacon was born near the turn of the eighteenth century, perhaps on the Isle of Man and perhaps in Whitehaven on the northwest
English coast. The earliest solid information about his life concerns Dublin,
where he followed a series of occupations, including keeping a coffeehouse,
serving as a customs agent, and publishing newspapers (the *Dublin Mercury* and
the *Dublin Gazette*). Three months after his Anglican ordination in 1745, Bacon
came to Md., where his brother Anthony had been engaged in business for
several years. Received as curate of St. Peter's Parish, Talbot County, the Rev.
Bacon shortly became a prominent member of the colony's society and an
honorary member of Dr. Alexander Hamilton's (q.v.) Tuesday Club, owing
partly to his gift for music. He was evidently an extraordinary performer on
stringed instruments and wrote a number of original pieces under the playful *nom
de plume* "Signior Lardini."

In public life, Bacon was most visible as an advocate of progressive educational projects and a loyal supporter of the proprietary Calvert family against
popularly minded factions. The esteem he enjoyed led in 1758 to his appointment
to the colony's most remunerative parish, All Saints, in Frederick. Somewhat
ironically, however, he is best remembered for his compilation of Md. law—"a
dry sort of Stuff," he complained, "and sometimes apt to stick in the Throat."
Bacon died in 1768 during a visit to Warm Springs, Va., one week following his
election to the American Philosophical Society.

Critical Appraisal: Thomas Bacon's place in the intellectual history of
eighteenth-century Md. is attributable less to any remarkable powers as a writer
than to his active involvement in social, religious, and political issues of the day.
As liberal in his views on education as he was conservative in his Anglicanism
and his fealty to the proprietary party, he dedicated himself to the establishment
of a "charity working school" for both male and female students in St. Peter's
Parish; although not an abolitionist, he asserted the humanity of black slaves and
insisted on the propriety of catechizing them.

The picture of Bacon that emerges from his extant writings presents a man
who relished audiences and whose protean personality could alter itself to suit
them. Preaching to a congregation of slaves, he chided and comforted by turns,
warning his listeners against letting the privileges of religion make them "proud
and saucy," yet assuring them that "God is no respecter of persons." Before a
body of their owners, he was precise and firm in his repeated applications of the
injunction of St. Paul that masters give their servants "that which is just and
equal." To his brother Masons in Annapolis, his sermon counseled fraternal love
and caution in avoiding the moral pitfalls of so worldly a capital. The surviving
homily on the topic of his school for indigent children becomes at points an
exalted anatomy of the idea and claims of charity, bearing at least thematic

resemblance to John Winthrop's (q.v.) *A Model of Christian Charity*. In con-
claves with his fellow ministers, however, he could be a fearsome adversary if
we can believe his 1753 account of the "Proceedings of the Parochial Clergy"
(first printed by the *Maryland Historical Magazine* in 1908).

His private letters reveal still other sides of Bacon. His dinner invitations to his
good friend Henry Callister sparkle with the anticipation of "demolishing" a
sirloin and passing a jovial evening at cards or music. Wholly different are his
complaints back to Eng. about the "wild and savage" state of religion in Md. and
his sardonic observation that Deism is no stronger there than it is only because
the colonials are mostly incapable of grasping its arguments. Nothing better
illustrates the improbable mixture of elements in Bacon than his reaction to the
appearance of two rivals in the task of collecting and publishing the Md. statutes,
a development that might have been expected to call forth from him a formal
declaration of prior intent. The Rev. Bacon's only known response was to send
his friend Callister a rather scurrilous hudibrastic poem about his competitors
titled "A Letter. Originally Wrote Three Thousand Years Ago."

Although Bacon's school proved ephemeral, in his gathering of the colony's
laws and his sermons on slaves, masters, and public charity, he produced volumes that succeeding generations apparently found useful or edifying enough to
reprint occasionally. Taken as a whole, his American career is characteristic of
the attempts of a host of learned immigrants to transplant British civilization and
sensibilities to the New World.

Suggested Readings: CCMDG; DAB; Sprague (V, 117-121). *See also* Ethan
Allen, "Rev. Thomas Bacon, 1745-1768, Incumbent of St. Peter's Talbot Co., and All
Saints, Frederick Co., Maryland," *Church Review*, 17 (1865), 430-451; Richard Beale
Davis, *Intellectual Life in the Colonial South* (1978), pp. 745-747, 1425-1426, passim;
J. A. Leo Lemay, *Men of Letters in Colonial Maryland* (1972), pp. 313-342 (see pp.
382-386 for a checklist of works written by Bacon or ascribed to him).

W. H. Ward
Appalachian State University

STEPHEN BADGER (1726-1803)

Works: *The Nature and Effects of Drunkenness* (1774); *Address of a Minister to the Church under His Pastoral Care* (1784); "Historical and Characteristic
Traits of the American Indians in General, and Those of Natick in Particular"
(1798).

Biography: Missionary to the Indians at Natick, Mass., and precursor of
Unitarianism, Stephen Badger was born at Charlestown in 1726. Son of a potter,
he studied at Harvard as a charity student, receiving a B.A. in 1747 and an M.A.
in 1750. In 1753 he accepted ordination to minister to the Indians and to the

whites who worshipped with them at Natick. Adversity, however, dogged Badger's long pastorate. By the 1760s, disease had reduced the Indians to a handful. In addition, a faction of whites abused the missionary because he opposed their plans to relocate the meetinghouse and because he questioned original sin and predestination. The Revolutionary War cut off mission funds from Eng.; the town often disputed paying his salary; and in 1797 his parish broke up when, against his will, the town finally succeeded in moving the meetinghouse. Badger died in Natick in 1803, survived by his second wife and two of six children. Harriet Beecher Stowe modeled the character of Parson Lathrop in *Old Town Folks* after memories of this dignified, if short-tempered, divine.

Critical Appraisal: In reaction to the uncompromising Calvinism of Jonathan Edwards (q.v.), whose works he had read closely, Stephen Badger adopted liberal views both in doctrine and in pastoral practice. His rational disposition shows up in his preaching. His sermons, which he read without oratorical flourish, pressed Christian ethics with pragmatic considerations such as the detrimental consequences of sin and the benefits of virtue for success in life. His *Nature and Effects of Drunkenness* describes the self-destruction brought about by excessive use of the creature comforts God provides for man's enjoyment, health, and strength. By having his hearers draw upon their own experience for examples, Badger made his lessons immediate and relevant. He repeatedly asked, "how many are there within the compass of our own knowledge" who, through intemperance, have ruined their business, reputation, health, or souls and rendered themselves unfit for service to society as well as for Christian fellowship? One brief passage, in which he described a drunken mother, "her Children around her without Direction, without Instruction, and calling upon her in vain for the Supplies of daily food," is the sole intimation of the pathos that would characterize much of the temperance literature of the next century, including such works as Walt Whitman's *Franklin Evans; or The Inebriates* (1842) and T. S. Arthur's *Temperance Tales* (1843) and *Ten Nights in a Barroom* (1854). Badger's suggestion that habitual drunkards be treated as incompetent and set to labor is indicative of his desire to be useful to the public.

In an effort to be useful to the church, Badger advocated the relaxation of membership practices. He feared that requirements in the New Eng. churches, unwarranted by reason or Scripture, were keeping diffident persons, otherwise properly qualified, from seeking admission. Under his predecessor, Oliver Peabody (q.v.), the church at Natick had waived the formal relation of experience of grace. Badger wanted to go further and allow the profession of faith to be made in private to the pastor or at least before the church alone, and not before the entire congregation. In his *Address of a Minister to the Church under his Pastoral Care*, he took arms against another requirement, confession of particular sins before making the profession of faith. His chief legalistic argument is that the church has no right to judge those outside it, and that before profession of faith, the individual is outside the church. His most persuasive argument is compassion for the timid whose sincerity is evident. The example of

Jesus's refusal to judge the woman caught in adultery effectively concludes the piece.

Badger wrote "Historical and Characteristic Traits of the American Indians," essentially an analysis of the disintegration of the Christian Indian community at Natick, in response to queries from the Massachusetts Historical Society about the mission. At the beginning of the eighteenth century, some 200 Indians lived at Natick, owned all of the land, and elected the town officials. Writing in 1797, Badger supposed there were then fewer than 20 pure-blooded Natick Indians. During the intervening century, whites had moved in, bought land, joined the church, and finally taken complete control of civil affairs from the Indians, who had become the object of contempt. "This sinks and cramps their spirits," Badger observed, "and prevents those manly exertions which an equal rank with others has a tendency to call forth." The whites encouraged indolence and debt among the Indians so they could get their land. Dispirited, the Indians took to vagabondage and drink, which made them susceptible to tuberculosis. The men, easily enticed into military service, brought contagious diseases back to their families. Badger suggested that the shock of too rapid acculturation destroyed the Christian Indians. They were urged to replace the set of customs and manners to which centuries had habituated them with a set totally foreign and, in some cases, directly opposite. In particular, they were asked to forsake venerated religious rituals and to exchange indolence and improvidence for industry and self-denial. The radical transition injured their health and shortened their lives. Badger recognized powerful connections among tradition, self-perception, self-respect, and survival. Although colored by condescension towards native Americans and their culture, his essay contains significant insights into the nearly total failure of eighteenth-century North American missions.

Direct, clear, and thoughtful, Badger's writings demonstrate, without pedantry, why his contemporaries enjoyed his conversation and admired his memory, reasoning, and knowledge.

Suggested Readings: CCNE; Sibley-Shipton (XII, 104-108). *See also* Michael J. Crawford, "Indians, Yankees, and the Meetinghouse Dispute of Natick, Massachusetts, 1743-1800," NEHGR, 133 (1978), 278-292; "Historical and Characteristic Traits" was printed in CMHS 1st ser., 5 (1798), 32-45.

Michael J. Crawford
Naval Historical Center, Research Branch

JACOB BAILEY (1731-1808)

Works: *A Little Book for Children* (1758). Principal poems: "Farewell to Kennebec" (1779); "Character of a Trimmer" (1779-1780); "America" (1780-1784); "The Adventures of Jack Ramble, the Methodist Preacher" (c. 1790). Principal fiction: "The Flower of the Wilderness, or The History of Miss Ann Rosedale"

(c. 1770); "Serena" (c. 1780). Principal expository prose: "A Description and Natural History of the New Entered Province Between New Hampshire and Nova Scotia" (1773); "Description of Various Journeys Through Nova Scotia" (c. 1784). Bailey's journals were edited and published by William S. Bartlet in *The Frontier Missionary, a Memoir. . .of Jacob Bailey* (1853).

Biography: Jacob Bailey was born in Rowley, Mass., on Apr. 16, 1731. His exceptional intelligence attracted the attention of the local Congregationalist minister, who prepared him for Harvard: A.B., 1755; M.A., 1758. He subsequently taught school and served briefly as a Congregationalist minister, but converted to the new mission-parish at Pawnalborough (now West Dresden, Maine). At Pawnalborough, the state-supported Church of New England (and Bailey) were resented by the predominantly Congregationalist community. This resentment sharpened as America slipped into open rebellion; from 1774 on, Bailey was frequently harassed and assaulted. In 1779 he and his family were finally permitted to leave for the loyal province of Nova Scotia.

In Nova Scotia he served as parish priest at Cornwallis (1779-1782) and Annapolis Royal (1782-1808). These parishes were large and sprawling, and after 1784 his responsibilities became even more demanding with the influx of hundreds of Loyalist refugees, fleeing the new U.S. After years of faithful service, Bailey died at Annapolis Royal on Jul. 26, 1808.

Critical Appraisal: Jacob Bailey appears to have had virtually an obsession with the written word. Even the type of writing one would expect from a man in his position—correspondence, journals, sermons, and moral commentaries—is voluminous. Although he published only a few of his works (anonymously in newspapers), Bailey was a prolific writer of poetry, fiction, and expository prose, and his important works were circulated in manuscript form, mainly among close friends. The sum of his expository prose, fiction, and poetry makes him remarkable.

Most of Bailey's expository prose falls into two categories: sermons and geographical "descriptions." His sermons have been missing since the mid-nineteenth century, making it impossible to judge their merit. But we know Bailey came close to publishing a small collection in London in the early 1780s, suggesting they may have been of some interest. Of the extant prose, his two chief works present "descriptions" of two frontier areas of eighteenth-century northeastern America: Maine in the 1760s and Nova Scotia in the 1780s. In both cases, Bailey's approach is to present an overview of his subject by describing various aspects of the area and its inhabitants under what amounts to subject headings. Even when he uses a journey motif, his logic is categorical, developing as comprehensive a view as possible of the geography, ecology, society, and history of the area in question. The scholarly comprehensiveness of his writings distinguishes them from the more blatantly propagandistic "descriptions" of the nineteenth century, which seem so consciously designed to attract settlers to a given area rather than simply to impart knowledge.

Bailey's fiction is interesting because it comes at such an early stage in the history of the American novel. Although none of it was ever published (indeed, both his major works were left incomplete and are fragmented as well), his efforts reflect interesting attempts to integrate form and intention. He appears to have worked on "The Flower of the Wilderness" during the 1770s, perhaps even as early as the 1760s. The form is a mixture of narrative, letter, and dialogue and involves the travels of Mr. Thomas Watkins in rural New Eng. and the romantic involvements of Miss Ann Rosedale, with frequent digressions into moral and philosophical topics. The novel is structurally weak; even if it were not incomplete and fragmented, it would be something of a shambles. "Serena," the story of a Loyalist girl captured and carried back to New Eng. from Nova Scotia by privateers, is a later (c. 1786-1790) and more coherent work. Bailey focuses clearly on a central character (Serena) and on a central action (her trials), using an epistolary format to good effect. Unfortunately, this work was also left incomplete; the primary action is never resolved.

It was in poetry that Bailey produced his best literary works. In spite of a weak sense of structure and a propensity never to complete longer poems, he wrote verse as a serious amateur from his college days on. His early style was lyric and sentimental, which became somewhat melodramatic in the late 1770s as he turned to more serious subjects in poems dramatizing the suffering of innocent noncombatants in the American Rebellion. The best of these, "Farewell to Kennebec," expressed his regret and personal sense of loss at having to leave his home and parish in Maine for exile in Nova Scotia. The poem is reasonably well crafted, but Bailey's excessive reliance on pathos for poetic effect undermines the intensity of the emotions he wishes to express and blurs the moral focus of the poem.

In Nova Scotia, influenced by Samuel Butler's *Hudibras*, Bailey turned his pen to writing political satire, vigorously and savagely attacking the American rebels and their aims. Between 1779 and 1784, he produced many satires, usually in hudibrastic verse form, the most interesting of which were "The Character of a Trimmer" and "America." "Trimmer" is a 304-line attack on political fence-sitters and on Rebel Committees of Correspondence. It is early in Bailey's satiric career (1779-1780), and its dual focus ultimately works against the sharpness and effectiveness of his attack. Nevertheless, it is the poem in which Bailey first explores the tonal flexibility and the range of emotional expression permitted by hudibrastic verse. In Bailey's hands, hudibrastic verse became a trenchant and incisive instrument for clarifying and articulating his fears, frustrations, and moral indignation. He used it to admirable effect in "America," a satire designed to demonstrate the insidious madness and immoral folly of the Revolutionary cause and to link it to the destructive and diabolical effects of the English Civil War of the seventeenth century. The poem begins with the illegitimate offspring of Hudibras immigrating to America and planting the seeds of rebellion there. It proceeds to castigate Dr. Faustus (Benjamin Franklin [q.v.]) and the leaders of incipient revolution at Boston. But at this point (after more than 4,100 lines), the poem ends, left incomplete by Bailey at the Peace of 1784. It was simply no longer relevant, politically or poetically.

Bailey's longest (9,200 lines extant) and most ambitious poem was "The Adventures of Jack Ramble, the Methodist Preacher." It was written in response to the inroads that evangelical itinerant preachers were making into Bailey's congregation at Annapolis Royal. In the poem, Bailey retained the vigor and sharpness of his political satire, but his perspective broadened to encompass the religious and social realities of his time. He focused on evangelical religious beliefs and activities, attacking them as the primary vehicle for promoting irrationality and immorality in man and for disseminating disrespect for order, all of which point inevitably to social and political chaos. Bailey's attacks were vicious and often unfair, probably because the issue was so central to his world view. Perhaps, too, in spite of his unwavering commitment to the rectitude of his position, he sensed the world as he knew it slipping away as the eighteenth century drew to a close.

Suggested Readings: CCNE; DAB; Sprague (I, 200-204). *See also* B. I. Granger, *Political Satire in the American Revolution* (1960); Ray Palmer Baker, "The Poetry of Jacob Bailey, Loyalist," NEQ, 2 (1929), 58-92; T. B. Vincent, "Bailey and Alline," CanL, 68-69 (1976), 124-133; idem, "Keeping the Faith: the Poetic Development of Jacob Bailey," EAL, 14 (1979), 3-14; idem, *Narrative Verse Satire in Maritime Canada, 1779-1814* (1978).

Thomas B. Vincent
Royal Military College of Canada

BENJAMIN BANNEKER (1731-1806)

Works: *Benjamin Banneker's Pennsylvania, Delaware, Maryland and Virginia Almanack* for 1792-1795 (1791-1794); *Banneker's Almanack* for 1793-1795 (1792-1794); *Copy of a Letter. . .to the Secretary of State* (1792); *The Virginia Almanack* for 1794 (1793); *Bannaker's New-Jersey, Pennsylvania, Delaware, Maryland and Virginia Almanac* for 1795 (1794); *Bannaker's Wilmington Almanac* for 1795 (1794); *The New Jersey & Pennsylvania Almanac for 1795 (1794); Bannaker's Maryland, Pennsylvania, Delaware, Virginia, Kentucky, and North-Carolina Almanac* for 1796 (1795); *Bannaker's Maryland and Virginia Almanack* for 1797 (1796); *Bannaker's Virginia and North Carolina Almanack* for 1797 (1796); *Bannaker's Virginia, Pennsylvania, Delaware, Maryland and Kentucky Almanack* for 1797 (1796).

Biography: Benjamin Banneker, almanac maker, was the grandson of Molly Welsh, an English serving girl who chose transportation to Md. in 1683 rather than imprisonment in Eng. for the alleged theft of a pail of milk. After serving her term of indenture, she bought a farm and two African slaves. She eventually freed her slaves and married one of them, Bannaka (spellings vary), who claimed to be an African prince. Mary, the eldest of their four daughters, married Robert, a freed slave who adopted his wife's surname. In 1737 Robert Banneker purchased a 120-acre farm near Baltimore, which his oldest son, Benjamin, inherited. Although he briefly attended a local school where a few white and black children received instruction together, Benjamin Banneker was primarily self-taught. At age 22, with only a borrowed pocket watch as a model, he constructed a wooden clock that chimed the hours. Considered a remarkably versatile and gifted black man for his time, he could also play the flute and the violin.

Through his business dealings with the Ellicotts, he became their friend and protege. In his 50s he studied mathematics, astronomy, and celestial mechanics, borrowing books from George Ellicott, who had recognized Banneker's unusual computational ability. Andrew Ellicott— astronomer, almanac calculator, and surveyor—requested that Banneker be appointed in 1791 to survey the Federal Territory (District of Columbia). Banneker never married. He sold his farm to the Ellicotts, thereby setting up a fifteen-year annuity for himself. Miscalculating, he lived twenty-three years longer, supported for eight years by the Ellicotts, to whom he willed his papers.

Critical Appraisal: Benjamin Banneker deserves a prominent place in the history of the American almanac, because he is the only black who ever calculated almanacs. For seven years (1792-1797) Banneker's almanacs were printed in many editions, in varying versions with varying titles within the same year and from year to year, and by various printers and publishers in Philadelphia, Baltimore, Wilmington, and Trenton. These almanacs were among the most successful of the period, a distinction perhaps attributable to miscellaneous selections by his editors and to the promotional efforts of his influential friends. One of his publishers, for example, was Joseph Crukshank in Philadelphia, a founding member of the Pennsylvania Society for the Abolition of Slavery and a Quaker. The Ellicotts, proprietors of the flour mills of Ellicott City and Banneker's chief patrons, were members of the Society of Friends (the Quakers) and the Maryland Society for the Abolition of Slavery. From the outset, the Maryland Society for the Abolition of Slavery determined, to a great extent, Banneker's success. To launch the almanac, a brief sketch of Banneker's life was prepared in the form of a letter to the printers signed by a zealous society member—Dr. James McHenry, military surgeon and politician, who became secretary of war under George Washington (q.v.) and John Adams (q.v.).

Elias Ellicott and James Pemberton (another member of the society) prepared a "certificate" signed by eleven men, seven of whom were members of the Ellicott family and the other five their friends, to certify that Banneker was indeed the author of the almanac. The almanac was sent to David Rittenhouse, America's foremost astronomer and also a calculator of almanacs. Rittenhouse replied, "I have no doubt that the Calculations are sufficiently accurate for the purposes of a common Almanac." Other testimonials were obtained. Meanwhile, Banneker sent a copy of his 1792 manuscript, accompanied by a letter, to Thomas Jefferson (q.v.). The Goddard and Angell edition contained the manuscript and the letter, as well as Jefferson's reply. The letter to Jefferson seems to have been the most popular and effective protest against slavery composed by a Negro in the eighteenth century. Jefferson's response was sympathetic and encouraging. Privately, however, Jefferson wrote to Joel Barlow (q.v.) on Oct. 8, 1809:

We know he had spherical trigonometry enough to make almanacs, but not without the suspicion of aid from Ellicot, who was his neighbor and friend, and never missed an opportunity of puffing him. I have a long letter from Banneker, which shows him to have had a mind of very common stature indeed.

We probably shall never know the extent of Banneker's authorship. Several works attributed to Banneker were not his; for example, the "Plan of *Peace-Office*, for the United States," published in the Crukshank edition of the 1793 almanac, was written by Dr. Benjamin Rush (q.v.). Because the fable "The Two Bees" (1792) is not enclosed in quotation marks, it may be the work of Banneker, who was a skilled beekeeper and who left in his journal an account of some bees robbing another hive. The appearance of the "Epitaph on a Watch-Maker" in all four versions in 1797 indicated that Banneker may have written this epitaph, but many other selections were exactly the same in all four almanacs. Banneker was interested in timepieces and had a little literary ability, but this work exists in Devonshire, Eng. as an actual epitaph on the tomb of George Routleigh. The evidence for Banneker's authorship of this pleasantry, as well as for other works, is slender.

A rhymed puzzle (which may have been original) that Banneker gave to George Ellicott was written with wit and style. Evidence of Banneker's literary attempts can be found in accounts of dreams found among his personal papers: the search for Rosannah Crandolph's soul, an encounter with "the Infernal Spirit," an incident involving sympathy for a white fawn, and an incident expressing compassion for a child with a peculiar hole in its head. Banneker also signed his name to one antislavery poem, the only evidence besides the letter to Jefferson that he was ever actively involved in the antislavery cause.

Banneker's character remains elusive. If a personality is at all manifested, it is that of a modest, retiring man of exceptional ability who enjoyed studying mathematics and astronomy and applying his skill to calculating almanacs. Banneker was neither professional astronomer, mathematician, nor surveyor; but he had learned enough celestial mechanics to make adequate almanac calculations. He lived in the relatively liberal Md. society, where he attended school with white children, was a free man and a voting citizen, and was encouraged by leading abolitionists. (The voting law was changed in Md. in 1802.) We know very little about his actual mathematical and literary capabilities and still less about his personal views on race and slavery. It is true that Banneker acquired considerable computational skill late in life. He was an extraordinarily able, self-taught amateur astronomer and almanac calculator.

Biographies and appraisals of Banneker have been so full of errors and prejudice that students should choose their sources with extreme caution. Before 1972 almost everything written about him was based on the sketch by James McHenry that appeared in Banneker's 1792 almanac, two publications by Mrs. Tyson (a member of the Ellicott family) in 1854 and 1884, a paper by Jno. H. B. Latrobe read before the Historical Society of Maryland in 1845, and partial examination of Banneker's almanac series. Mrs. Tyson's observations appear to be fairly accurate, but many others of her time and later have been unduly creative. For almost a century, most writers on Banneker have reiterated the errors in this early material or have invented something new. Silvio Bedini's biography (1972) has separated fact from legend and is, in fact, the only complete and accurate source.

Suggested Readings: BDAS. *See also Banneker, The Afric-American Astronomer. From the Posthumous Papers of Martha E. Tyson. Edited by Her Daughter* (1884); Silvio A. Bedini, *The Life of Benjamin Banneker* (1972); Benjamin Brawley, *Early Negro American Writers* (1935); Paul Leicester Ford, ed., *The Works of Thomas Jefferson* (1904), XI, 261; Marion Barber Stowell, *Early American Almanacs* (1977), pp. 102-111; Martha E. Tyson, "A Sketch of the Life of Benjamin Banneker; From Notes Taken in 1836," read by J. Norris at Maryland Historical Society (Oct. 1854).

Marion Barber Stowell
Milledgeville, Georgia

MARK BANNERMAN (d. 1727)

Works: Congratulatory verse to Allan Ramsay, quoted (perhaps in part) by Ramsay in the preface to the 5th edition of *The Tea-Table Miscellany*, 5th ed., (1730).

Biography: If it were not for the civil and church records of Middlesex County, Va., Allan Ramsay's preface to *The Tea-Table Miscellany*, and a will recorded in 1727, no trace of Mark Bannerman's sojourn in this world would have survived. But on Apr. 3, 1722, Bannerman sued Colonel William Fleet for reasons now unknown, and although Bannerman lost the suit, the case entered him into the records of Urbanna, Va., and likewise into the history of colonial America. Although nothing of his birth and formal education is known, he probably attended medical school in Scot. sometime before 1720-1721, for it is certain that Bannerman had medical credentials in hand when he immigrated to the Va. colony. The Vestry Book of Christ Church Parish, for example, shows Bannerman to have ministered to the poor, and in Oct. 1724 he was granted an allowance of 3,000 pounds of tobacco for the treatment of Mary Cosley and Mary Robinson's "girl." In addition, there were two later allowances, one in 1726 and the other in 1728.

If medicine was Bannerman's vocation, litigation was apparently his avocation. In 1723, Bannerman sued a Col. John Turpeley. Turpeley countersued, and both cases were eventually dismissed. In 1725 a Hugh Roach sued Bannerman for assault and battery. On this occasion, the doctor won, but he and Roach were in court again later in the same year in a case that shows no recorded resolution. During this period, Bannerman retained strong connections with Scot. His will speaks of several men (all with Scottish names—Hamilton, Gordon, and Fraser) with whom he shared fellowship and fraternity. Of the fifty-three books in his possession, one was certainly Ramsay's collection of ballads. This miscellany inspired Bannerman's only surviving poem, and the epigram attests to the doctor's pleasure that Scottish songs had invigorated the literary life of the Va. colony. Clearly, Ramsay valued Bannerman's praise, because he introduced the verse sent by "My worthy friend Dr. *Bannerman*. . .from *America*." Bannerman may have been led into similar creative work either from other readings or literary associations, but like other southern writers of the period, he would have been thwarted by the absence of printing in Va. before 1730.

Despite a nostalgic attachment to his native soil, Bannerman prospered in the New World. On Aug. 12, 1724, he married Catherine Barker of St. Mary's Chapel Parish, by whom he had a daughter, Margaret. He purchased plantation land called "Nehocknay" in Essex County; the property, in excess of 200 and perhaps as large as 1,000 acres, had buildings and livestock. In a will dated Jul. 4, 1727, Bannerman stated the likelihood that his widow would bear him a son posthumously, that she would remarry, and that his friend Gilbert Hamilton would return safely from Scotland. These sentiments suggest that Bannerman believed his death to be imminent, and his diagnosis was correct. Within a few short months, on Oct. 3, 1727, the widow Bannerman was in court to enter into the record her husband's last testament to a brief but productive life in colonial Va.

Critical Appraisal: In the eight-line verse that Ramsay quoted in the preface to *The Tea-Table Miscellany*, Mark Bannerman perhaps overstated the Scotsman's reputation in America, but he accurately anticipated the renaissance of highlands balladry and rural sentiment that culminates in the poetry of Burns, Goldsmith, Percy, and other late eighteenth-century men of letters who prepared the way for Wordsworth's *Lyrical Ballads* in 1798. Contrasting Ramsay's native songs to the artificial parlor pastorals of Milton and Pope, Bannerman referred specifically to "The last time I came o'er the Moor," "Mary Scot," "Mary Gray" ("Bessy Bell and Mary Gray"), and "Tweed-side" ("We'll a'to Kelso go"). These love songs convey the zest and ardor with which lads and lassies seek one another over the heaths and through the burn-brakes of the Scottish countryside. Given Bannerman's love of his homeland, his youth, his joy in a new family and a growing medical practice, and the vitality he must have felt from the thriving Va. seaport to which he now belonged, his enthusiasm for Ramsay's ballads is certainly understandable. Ironically, in his own verse, Bannerman used the very style he declared passé. His poem is in heroic couplets that are pseudo-Miltonic and neo-Classical. Of course, Bannerman was writing in an established genre, the congratulatory epigram; thus it would violate decorum for him to have chosen a form and manner that was untraditional. Not the least constrained by the narrow limits of the genre, Bannerman successfully conveyed the pleasures of Ramsay's "new" style. In the 1720s he thus became an early admirer of a literary form (the ballad) that his adopted countrymen would make their own as they moved westward over the mountains and prairies of the New World.

Suggested Readings: Dr. Gordon W. Jones, "Ramsay the Poet Immortalizes a Virginia Physician," VMM, 87 (1960), 642-646; Allan Ramsay, *The Tea-Table Miscellany: A Collection of Choice Songs* (1871).

Roslyn L. Knutson
University of Arkansas at Little Rock

JOEL BARLOW (1754-1812)

Works: *The Prospect of Peace* (1778); *An Elegy on the Late Honorable Titus Hosmer* (1780); *A Poem Spoken at the Public Commencement at Yale College* (1781); *The Carrier of the American Mercury Wishes His Customers a Happy New-Year* (1785); *Doctor Watt's Imitation of the Psalms...Corrected* (1785); *A Translation of Sundry Psalms* (1785); *The Anarchiad: A Poem* (1786); *An Oration Delivered at the North Church* (1787); *The Vision of Columbus* (1787); *Advice to the Privileged Orders* (Pt. I, 1792; Pt. II, 1794); *A Letter to the National Convention of France* (1793); *The Conspiracy of Kings* (1794); *A Letter Addressed to the People of Piedmont* (1795); *The Hasty Pudding* (1796); *The Political Writings of Joel Barlow* (1796); *Strictures on Bishop Watson's "Apologies for the Bible"* (1796); *Psalms Carefully Suited to the Christian Worship in the United States* (1797); *Barlow's Letter from the Connecticut Courant* (1798); *Letters from Paris to the Citizens of the United States of America* (1800); *Prospectus of a National Institution* (1806); *The Columbiad* (1807); *Letter to Henry Gergoire* (1809); *Oration Delivered at Washington, July Fourth, 1809* (1809); *A Review of Robert Smith's Address* (1811); "Advice to a Raven in Russia" (1812).

Biography: Born Mar. 24, 1754, in Redding, Conn., Joel Barlow— schoolteacher, army chaplain, publisher, and ambassador—graduated from Yale in 1778 and is best known for his association with the Connecticut Wits, a group of young Yale poets, and with his lifelong ambition to write the great American epic poem. In 1787, six years after he married Ruth Baldwin, he published *The Vision of Columbus*, which he later revised and published as *The Columbiad*. Barlow spent seventeen years in Europe, where his interest in liberal Democratic politics surfaced and resulted in the publication of several political tracts inspired by his friend Thomas Paine (q.v.). In 1795 Barlow was appointed consul to Algiers. Ten years later, he returned to America and continued his career as scholar. In 1812, a year after he had been sent to Fr. as minister by President James Madison (q.v.), Barlow died in Pol. after unsuccessfully chasing Napoleon across Europe in an attempt to consummate a treaty.

Critical Appraisal: Despite his attempts at writing the great American epic, *The Hasty Pudding* remains Joel Barlow's most popular and frequently anthologized poem. Written on a "virgin theme, unconscious of the Muse, / But fruitful, rich, well suited to inspire / The purest frenzy of poetic fire," the poem is a mock epic composed in three cantos of heroic couplets, celebrating the creation of boiled Indian meal as a distinctive American dish. In exaggerated fashion, Barlow described the origin of the dish, the steps necessary for preparation, and the proper mode of consuming it. Unlike his ongoing epic poem, the success of *The Hasty Pudding* results from Barlow's use of a distinctive portion of American folklore treated in a light fashion to appeal to an American audience. Void of any attempt at chronicling world history and of unfamiliar exempla to illustrate the way to glory and greatness, *The Hasty Pudding* is distinctly American verse, and it is as the poet of cornmeal mush that Barlow's popularity rests.

But popularity is different from importance, and his epic poems remain Barlow's most important contribution to the democratic fervor present at the turn of the eighteenth century. Before he wrote *The Vision of Columbus* and revised it as *The Columbiad* twenty years later, Barlow had prepared his audience with a series of poems singing a hymn to America's struggle for independence. On his graduation day at Yale in 1778, Barlow read his class's commencement poem, *The Prospect of Peace*. Drafted in heroic couplets like others of its genre, *The Prospect* was patriotic in tone and predicted the achievement of American science, philosophy, and poetry. Barlow's verse announced what appeared to be a tremendous opportunity for the inhabitants of the new American Republic. Three years later, as a speaker at another Yale commencement, Barlow repeated his performance by reading *A Poem*. At this time, Barlow revealed that his theme was taken from a larger work in progress— *The Vision of Columbus*—and that his newest commencement poem reflected the "affairs of America at large, and the future progress of Society." Much of what Barlow said in his commencement poems formed the basis for *The Vision of Columbus*. Inspired by his friends Timothy Dwight (q.v.), John Trumbull (q.v.), and David Humphreys (q.v.), Barlow completed *The Vision* and published it in 1787. The poem was a bestseller and provided the very tonic needed in the colonies for establishing a sense of national pride and unity.

The plan for *The Vision* was ambitious but simple: the history of America, past, present, and future—and to inculcate, as his preface stated, "the love of national liberty." *The Vision* began with Columbus, then an old man dying in prison, traveling with a "radiant seraph" who hoped to assuage Columbus's fears with a prospect of the future glories of America. Barlow traced their voyage across the ocean and described the landscape, settlement of America, history of the Inca empire, colonization of America from the French and Indian War through the Revolution, accomplishments of Americans in the arts and sciences, and vision of what America could and should become. If only because they more closely align themselves with Barlow's talent at the time, the narrative sections in the poem are better than the philosophical portions. But even they lack originality and vitality. Despite these problems, the critical reception in America was largely favorable. With his revision of *The Vision* over the next two decades and with the publication of *The Columbiad*, Barlow's epic vision was complete.

Barlow's interest in democratic ideas found more effective shape, however, in his essays. The best of his essays treat a variety of issues important to his prospect of the world at the turn of the century: the value of revolution (*Advice to the Privileged Orders*); advice to the leaders of Europe (*A Letter Addressed to the Piedmont*) and America (*Two Letters*); and the importance of a national university (*Prospectus*). Of these essays, *Advice to the Privileged Orders* is probably his best. In this essay, Barlow argued that the French Revolution was both necessary and desirable. Barlow was convinced that tyranny was destructive and that it not only violated the equal rights of every man but also prevented him from taking part in his own government and determining his own future happiness. Taking a page or two from *The Vision of Columbus*, Barlow advocated, in strong and forceful language, that the "example of America would have had great weight in producing this conviction." He believed that when Europeans recognized this fact, authoritarianism would be eliminated, and man would become free.

Freedom, of course, was on Joel Barlow's mind in 1812, when he wrote his finest piece of satire, "Advice to a Raven in Russia." This poem is a bitter invective against Napoleon's destructive and wasteful European campaign. Barlow's description of the frozen corpses left behind in the madness of Napoleon's march—"Mere trunks of ice, tho limb'd like human frames" who "cannot taint the air, the world impest"—paints a bleak portrait of the world in 1812. No longer a naive singer of hymns to the freedom he had found in the ideas of the French Revolution, Barlow now vehemently condemned what that Revolution and its precepts had produced.

Since his death, readers have recognized Barlow's limitations as a poet, but his influence and role in American letters are important. At a time when America was in search of its identity, Barlow's contributions to the vision of America as vital, and his additions to our national literary and cultural tradition are significant.

Suggested Readings: DAB; Dexter (IV, 3-16); LHUS; T_2. *See also* Robert Arner, "The Connecticut Wits" in *American Literature, 1764-1789, The Revolutionary Years*, ed. Everett Emerson (1977), pp. 233-252; Kenneth R. Ball, "Joel Barlow's 'Canal' and Natural Religion" in ECS, 2 (1969), 225-239; William Bottorff and Arthur Ford, eds., *The Works of Joel Barlow*, 2 vols. (1970); Arthur L. Ford, *Joel Barlow* (1971); John Griffith, "*The Columbiad* and *Greenfield Hill*: History, Poetry, and Ideology in the Late Eighteenth-Century," EAL, 10 (1975), 235-250; Leon Howard, *The Connecticut Wits* (1943); Christine M. Lizanich, " 'The March of This Government': Joel Barlow's Unwritten History of the United States," WMQ, 33 (1976), 315-330; Mason Lowance, *The Language of Canaan* (1980), pp. 208-246; Roy Harvey Pearce, "Toward an American Epic," HudR, 12 (1959), 362-377; Robert D. Richardson, Jr., "The Enlightenment View of Myth and Joel Barlow's *Vision of Columbus*," EAL, 13 (1978), 34-44; Cecelia Tichi, *New World, New Earth* (1979), pp. 114-150; Charles B. Todd, *Life and Letters of Joel Barlow* (1886); James Woodress, *A Yankee's Odyssey: The Life of Joel Barlow* (1958); Theodore Zunder, *The Early Days of Joel Barlow* (1934).

Jeffrey Walker
Oklahoma State University

JOHN BARNARD (1681-1770)

Works: *The Hazard of Losing a Soul* (1712); *The Christian's Behavior* (1714); *The Fatal Consequences of a People's Persisting in Sin* (1714); *The Peaceful End of the Peaceful and Upright Man* (1714); *Nature and Manner of Man's Blessing God* (1717); *Elijah's Mantle* (1724); *Ashton's Memorial* (1725); *Earthquakes Under Divine Government* (1727); *Sermons on Several Subjects* (1727); *Two Discourses Addressed to Young Persons* (1727);*Worship of God* (1729); *Birth of Our Lord* (1731); *The Throne Established* (1734); *A Call to Parents* (1737); *The Lord Jesus Christ* (1738); *Zeal for Good Works* (1742); *Imperfection of the Creature* (1747); *Janua Coelestis* (1750); *A New Version of the Psalms* (1752); *A Proof of Jesus Christ* (1756); *True Divinity of Christ* (1761).

Biography: John Barnard was born in Boston, Mass., on Nov. 6, 1681. His education was totally directed toward service in the ministry. At an early age, Barnard entered Harvard, graduating in 1700. Although during his last years of college and those immediately following Barnard devoted himself to serious study of mathematics, Hebrew, and divinity, Jonathan Edwards's (q.v.) *Autobiography*, where Barnard is mentioned, reveals that he was far from the traditionally restrained candidate for the ministry and that he cultivated a zest for livelier diversions than the study of theology.

In 1704 Barnard preached on an irregular basis at Yarmouth, Mass., turning down a permanent offer for the pulpit because of the limited salary it offered. In 1707 he was appointed chaplain to the Port Royal Expedition and in 1709 sailed to the Barbados and London as chaplain on the *Lusitania*. He returned to America in 1710, and after preaching in the churches of Boston, he accepted a position at the First Congregational Church at Marblehead, where he was ordained on Jul. 18, 1716. Barnard apparently served his congregation well, and his moderation is credited with saving it from the general disruptions of the Great Awakening. After some fifty years in the ministry, Barnard died at Marblehead in 1770.

Critical Appraisal: John Barnard is best remembered for his role during the Great Awakening and for his anticipation of Enlightenment political theory. Although other ministers often succumbed to the pressures of the period, Barnard acted with discretion. However, even though he was not among the more militant antirevivalists of the mideighteenth century, he is listed among those New Englanders who opposed the revival. If the characteristic that most distinguished the controversy was the distinction between preachers who appealed to emotions and those who appealed to reason, John Barnard was most assuredly on the side of reason.

A persistent thread running through Barnard's sermons stressed the need for the application of wisdom and moderation in matters of religion and politics.

This element appeared, for example, as early as 1712 in works like *The Hazard of Losing a Soul*, a sermon preached before the representatives of Massachusetts Bay on the day when the governor was elected. In this work, Barnard claimed that although government might come from God, the form of government was the choice of man and should be determined by reason and understanding. According to Barnard, knowledge applied with prudence had much greater efficacy in the affairs of men than did excessive zeal. In the series of nine sermons published under the general heading of *The Imperfections of the Creature*, Barnard repeated the idea that men are rational agents and that as rational agents they are instrumental in governing themselves and their fellow creatures. As such, Barnard anticipated by some forty years the political and religious theories of thinkers like Thomas Jefferson (q.v.), Thomas Paine (q.v.), and John Adams (q.v.). The twenty-two sermons of *Janua Coelestis*, for example, are replete with direct references to God's view of man as a rational creature and man's need to view himself as rational. Although the references that occur throughout the sermons do not include a direct criticism of the revivalists, the ideas of Barnard are clearly opposed to the major emphasis of that group, and even appear in four sermons included in *A Call to Parents*, about parental responsibility toward the religious and worldly well-being of their children. According to Barnard, reason, knowledge, and prudence were the guiding principles for bringing children to the worship of God and for providing prudent government in their lives.

Although Barnard has been justly acclaimed for his contribution to the rising eighteenth-century vision of America's future greatness and destiny, he should also be remembered for his skills as a stylist. Described by contemporaries as simple, logical, emotional, and extemporaneous, Barnard's style of preaching was intellectual yet robust and virile, mathematical and logical yet ample and glowing. Admittedly, although every sermon by Barnard is not distinguished by this impressive catalog of virtues, he was markedly more eloquent and effective than many of his contemporaries. His language and tone were, according to contemporary accounts, consistently moderate and polished. Unlike much eighteenth-century pulpit oratory, his sermons were never garrulous or offensive and were considered in their time to be models of a logical and reasonable theology, much welcome in an era of divisive and sometimes destructive religious tensions.

Suggested Readings: CCNE; DAB; Sibley-Shipton (IV, 501-514); Sprague (I, 252-255); T_1. *See also* Sacvan Bercovitch, *The American Jeremiad* (1978); Joseph J. Ellis, *The New England Mind in Transition* (1973); Edwin Scott Gaustad, *The Great Awakening in New England* (1957); Alan Heimert, *Religion and the American Mind* (1966); Perry Miller, ed., *The American Puritans* (1956); idem, *Jonathan Edwards* (1949); idem, *The New England Mind* (1967).

George Craig
Edinboro State College

THOMAS BARNARD (1716-1776)

Works: *Answer to Mr. Joseph Adams' Letter to the Rev. Mr. Thomas Barnard* (1742); *Tyranny and Slavery in Matters of Religion Caution'd Against* (1743); *The Christian Salvation* (1757); *A Sermon Preached to the Ancient and Honorable Artillery Company* (1758); *A Sermon Preached. . .Before the Society for Encouraging Industry and Employing the Poor* (1758); *A Sermon Preached Before His Excellency Francis Bernard, Esq.* (1763); *A Sermon Preached at the Ordination of the Rev. William Whitwell* (1763); *The Future Inheritance* (1768); *The Power of God* (1768).

Biography: Thomas Barnard, the son of the Rev. John Barnard (q.v.) and Sarah (Martyn) Barnard, was born in Andover, Mass., on Aug. 17, 1716. John Barnard noted the birth in his diary and added, "I pray God the Child may live, and live to God." After graduating from Harvard in 1732, Barnard became a schoolteacher in Hampton, Mass. In 1735 he returned to Harvard for an M.A., and in 1737 he was appointed a Hopkins Fellow, remaining in residence at Harvard for one year, after which he became pastor of the First Congregational Church of West Newbury, Mass., where he was ordained on Jan. 31, 1739. On Apr. 9, 1741, Barnard married Mary Woodbridge of Newbury. The couple had eight children, four of whom died in infancy.

Theologically liberal for his time, Barnard did not believe in predestination or infant damnation and abhorred the excesses of religious revivals. These beliefs made him a favorite target of the New Lights and created a controversy in his church. When in 1750 New Light members of his congregation refused to attend Barnard's services, he resigned from the pulpit and began studying law. A successful lawyer, he was elected to the House of Representatives of Mass. in 1755. Nonetheless, when the first church of Salem called him to be its minister, Barnard resigned from the House of Representatives and was installed on Sept. 17, 1755, serving there for the rest of his life, except for a four-year hiatus because of ill health. On Mar. 24, 1770, Barnard suffered a stroke, which affected his speech. His son Thomas Barnard, Jr., assumed his father's pulpit until 1774, when Barnard was sufficiently recovered to resume preaching. Barnard died in Salem on Aug. 5, 1776.

Critical Appraisal: John Eliot, author of the *Biographical Dictionary* (1809), and son of Barnard's closest friend, Andrew Eliot (q.v.), described Barnard's preaching as rather dull: "He had not sufficient animation in his delivery. . . .It was observed also by men of good sense, that Mr. Barnard's preaching was not the most perspicuous." However dull his delivery may have been, his ideas are more acceptable to a modern reader than they were to Barnard's own congregation, influenced as it was by George Whitefield (q.v.) and the Great Awakening.

Unlike the revivalists of his day, Barnard preached a God of universal salvation, "not a stern, inexorable being, ready to catch hold of the smallest slip of his creatures for their condemnation, but the Fountain of Love, who delights in the happiness of all his creatures and promotes it, unless they obstinately reject it." According to Barnard, Christ died for all repentant sinners. His sacrifice was not a bloody atonement but an occasion of joy. His crucifixion is less important than his resurrection, which is "proof and pledge of ours." A good minister, according to Barnard, should teach the simple message of God's love and redemption and "not engage in petty points to perplex the simple." The revealed word needs no metaphysical or theological embellishments: "Refiners are apt not to leave off where God had thought proper to stop, but would be wise above what is written." In his ordination sermon for the Rev. Josiah Bayley, for example, he urged the new minister to avoid "the ministry of Condemnation" and "the maze of metaphysics." Instead, he exhorted the Rev. Bayley to preach "the Gospel of Peace" and to let "integrity and good sense," rather than "Plato or Cato" be his guide.

In fact, integrity and good sense are the guiding spirits of all of Barnard's sermons. He repeatedly said that faith and Scripture are the best paths to knowledge. According to Barnard, Christianity should be plain and intelligible to even the simplest mind. While the good minister will avoid overintellectualizing his message, he will also avoid overemotionalizing it. Addressing himself very sharply to Joseph Adams, a revivalist who had condemned his refusal to participate in "inspired" religion, Barnard said he would not turn his church into "a Dancing Room for Satyrs...full of ignorance and wild Imagination which you call Inspiration." Preaching at the ordination of Rev. William Whitwell, Barnard acknowledged his failings as an orator and explained that a plain, distinct, calm tone gives the listener's mind a chance to remain free and to receive and weigh the preacher's message without bias, but a more fiery, "pungent" expression might sway him for the wrong reasons, causing him to exchange "the real edification of the mind for the pleasures of the eye and ear."

When preaching before men in public office, Barnard showed himself liberal and tolerant in politics as well as in religion, and the distant rumblings of the American Revolution can even be heard in some of his phrases. "The doctrines of slavery, political or theological, are not the maxims of Reason, Prudence, or Revelation," he told the governor of Mass. in an election sermon in 1763. In that same sermon, he refuted the divine right of kings, saying that hereditary rule in a certain family may be accepted only "so long as the succession in it consists with the well-being of Society." He praised Eng. for its dedication to freedom and civil and religious rights: "Even the conquering Normans became Patrons of Liberty in English air," he said. He saw America as a transplanted Eng., "the seat of Peace and Freedom," where arts, sciences, and "uncorrupted Faith, the Pure Worship of God in its primitive Simplicity" would flourish.

Suggested Readings: CCNE; Sibley-Shipton (IX, 120-129). *See also* John Eliot, *Biographical Dictionary* (1809), p. 46; *Historical Collections Relating to the American Colonial Church* (1873), III, 507; *National Cyclopaedia of American Biography* (1887), VII, 163.

Zohara Boyd
Appalachian State University

BENJAMIN SMITH BARTON (1766-1815)

Works: *An Inquiry into . . . the Apis Mellifica* (1783); *Proposals for Printing by Subscription* (1789); *An Account of the . . . Means of Preventing . . . the Consequences of the Bite of the Rattlesnake* (1792); *Memoir Concerning . . . the Rattlesnake and Other American Serpents* (1796); *New Views of the Origin of the Tribes and Nations of America* (1797); *Collections for an Essay Toward a Materia Medica of the United States* (Pt. I, 1798; Pt. II, 1804); *Fragments of the Natural History of Pennsylvania* (1799); *Supplement to a Memoir* (1800); *Elements of Botany* (1803).

Biography: Benjamin Smith Barton was born in 1766 in Lancaster, Pa., where his father was the Episcopalian rector. Both parents died before Barton was 15, and he subsequently took up residence with an older brother in Philadelphia, where he attended classes at the College of Philadelphia and at 18 began to study medicine. During this period, he participated in a survey party that defined the western boundary of Pa.; from this early experience, he acquired his lifelong interest in the history and customs of the American Indian.

In 1786 Barton went to Edinburgh to continue his medical studies. There he became a member of the Royal Medical Society and won the Harveian Prize for his dissertation on the *Hyoscyamus Niger*. From Scot. he went to Gottingen, Ger., where he received his medical diploma, returning to Philadelphia in 1789 to begin medical practice. In 1790 the College of Philadelphia (later the Univ. of Pa.) appointed Barton, then only 24, professor of natural history and botany. He afterwards succeeded Dr. Griffiths as professor of materia medica, and in 1813 he succeeded Dr. Benjamin Rush (q.v.) as professor of the theory and practice of medicine. Barton suffered from poor health during much of his adult life, and in 1815, at the age of 49, he died of pulmonary tuberculosis.

Critical Appraisal: Among Benjamin Smith Barton's many professional distinctions is the fact that he was the first instructor of natural history in Philadelphia, if not the first in any American college. What is generally regarded as the first botanical textbook in the U.S. is Barton's *Elements of Botany* (1803). In addition, his college lectures on the subject did much to diffuse a taste for this branch of science. Barton's chief medical work is his *Collection for an Essay Towards a Materia Medica of the United States* (1798). This work is a systematic treatise on the medicinal plants of the country, containing lists and descriptions of the various indigenous plants; much of this material is based on first-hand research. Barton was founder and editor of the *Philadelphia Medical and Physical Journal* (1805-1808). His writings for this publication attest to the wide scope of his interests; he wrote, for example, on diverse topics such as anthropology of the North American Indians, North American alligators, earthquakes, and hummingbirds.

Although Barton's botanical writings are not extensive, he was an industrious collector and a tireless proselytizer for medical and botanical investigation. It has been said that he planned more than he was ever able to achieve, but his strategic position in Philadelphia, which allowed not only for his close contact with important contemporary scientists but also with President Thomas Jefferson (q.v.), enabled him to promote the growth of American botanical science. He was the teacher of William Baldwin, William Darlington, Eli Ives, and Thomas Horsfield, and he played a decisive role in the lives of William Bartram (q.v.), Frederick Pursh, and Thomas Nuttall. His style is generally casual rather than studied, making it apparent that at most points in his work, it was content, rather than style, that claimed his foremost attention. Contemporary reports indicate that his lectures, too, were noted for their content and decidedly not for their style of delivery.

   Suggested Readings: BDAS; DAB; T₂. *See also* Joseph Ewan, ed., *A Short History of Botany in the United States* (1969), pp. 37-38, 40, 47, 48, 115, 148; John W. Harshberger, *The Botanists of Philadelphia and Their Work* (1899); Harry Baker Humphrey, *Makers of North American Botany* (1961), pp. 21-23; Howard A. Kelly, *Some American Medical Botanists* (1914), pp. 88-96; F. W. Pennell, "Benjamin Smith Barton," *Bartonia* 9 (1926), 17-34.

Robert Colbert
Louisiana State University in Shreveport

THOMAS BARTON (1730-1780)

   Works: *Unanimity and Public Spirit* (1755); *The Conduct of the Paxton-Men* (1764); *The Family Prayer-Book* (1767).

   Biography: Thomas Barton was born to Anglo-Irish parents of modest means in County Monaghan, Ire., in 1730. After completing his education at Trinity College, Dublin, he immigrated to Pa., apparently in search of economic opportunities. In 1753 he obtained a position as assistant tutor in the Academy of Philadelphia. Two years later, he sailed to Eng., where he was ordained an Anglican minister. Returning to Pa. in Apr. 1755, he assumed the duties of "itinerant missionary" to the counties of York, Huntingdon, and Carlisle. His reappearance in the colony coincided with the defeat of General Edward Braddock in the early stages of the French and Indian War, and Barton took a part in organizing the backcountry for military resistance. In 1758 he served as chaplain to the successful expedition under General James Forbes to reduce Fort Duquesne. He never lost his interest in military affairs, and at one point even considered (then reconsidered) a change of career.

   Some years earlier, Barton had struck up an acquaintance with the scientist David Rittenhouse. Through this friendship came an introduction to Rittenhouse's sister Esther, to whom Barton was married in 1753. Their union produced eight children. The heavy financial burden of supporting such a large family on a minister's salary was relieved somewhat in 1769, when patrons arranged for

Barton's occupation of an income-producing farm, Conestoga Manor, on the outskirts of Lancaster. Still, Barton yearned to be part of a less isolated society, and he participated wholeheartedly in efforts to transform Lancaster into a more bustling, intellectually alive community. His most successful effort was the creation of the Juliana Library Company. Barton's activities as an amateur scientist eventually earned him membership in the American Philosophical Society. He also took seriously his charge to Christianize the Indians. Joining with Indian Superintendent Sir William Johnson, he developed a network of Indian schools and personally tutored Johnson's Indian son.

The American Revolution closed this chapter of Barton's life and opened a new, less happy one. Although Barton attempted to remain neutral, suspicion of his activities grew so intense that he was first confined to his home and then, in 1778, forced to escape to a Loyalist enclave in N.Y., where he died two years later.

Critical Appraisal: Thomas Barton published three short works. The first, *Unanimity and Public Spirit*, came in the wake of the Braddock disaster and was a call for an end to the political and religious divisions that were, in the author's opinion, laying Pa. open to French and Indian depredations and ultimately to a Roman Catholic takeover. This war sermon is distinguishable from others of the genre chiefly by the intensity of its concentration upon the theme of anti-Catholicism. In 1767 Barton was prompted by his concern about the neglect of family worship to prepare *The Family Prayer-Book*, containing prayers appropriate for children, youths, parents, and servants. It was bound with a set of instructions for proper worship (not by Barton) and a catechism.

Barton's major literary effort, however, was his anonymous contribution to the "pamphlet war" that followed the Paxton Riots in colonial Pa. during the winter of 1763-1764 and that eventually involved leaders such as Benjamin Franklin (q.v.), Joseph Galloway (q.v.), and Hugh Williamson. For decades, people living beyond the orbit of Philadelphia had resented what they perceived to be a studied lack of concern about backcountry problems. When provincial officials attempted to apprehend those persons responsible for murdering a group of Indians living under the protection of the government (at Conestoga Manor, Barton's future home), this discontent flared into a march on the capital city by a small army of frontiersmen. The threat of civil war soon evaporated, but the march produced a long and bitter public debate. As a resident of Lancaster, Barton was in complete sympathy with the marchers, and his pamphlet *The Conduct of the Paxton-Men* emerged as the most vigorous defense of their activities.

His format was that of a letter from a backcountry gentleman to a friend in Philadelphia. His technique, noteworthy for its audacity if not for its strict adherence to facts, was to indict the victims of the massacre and the government that had attempted to protect them. The only crime to be laid at the door of the Paxton-Men, he argued, was that of performing a duty (ridding the province of hostile Indians) more properly than that of legally constituted authority. As evidence, he produced affidavits presumably establishing the guilt of the Indians. He further argued that the Society of Friends, long the dominant force in Pa. politics (the sect had recently renounced such involvement, but a "Quaker" party remained, and Barton saw no signs of a decline in influence), had created the possibility of such incidents by encouraging Indians to press their claims against whites.

The significance of the pamphlet lies not in the argumentation of the author, which at times is strained in the extreme, even granting it the latitude properly due a polemic. Rather, it is important because of the context out of which it came. Most colonial literature, understandably, has an urban perspective; less common, but perhaps more illuminating, is colonial life as it was confronted by the vast majority. Barton, to be sure, remained to offer this perception only because his constant pleas for transfer to a more cosmopolitan atmosphere were repeatedly denied. Nevertheless, his enforced stay on the frontier produced a voice that could speak with the authority of experience about matters such as the emotions generated by Indian-white tensions. For this reason, his pamphlet, however biased it may be in its distribution of guilt and responsibility, is of great value for the indirect insights it provides on the realities of the nonurban colonial environment.

Suggested Readings: CCMC; CCMDG; DNB; Sprague (V, 168-201). *See also* Brooke Hindle, "The March of the Paxton Boys," WMQ, 3rd ser., 3 (1946), 461-486; Marvin F. Russell, "Thomas Barton and Pennsylvania's Colonial Frontier," PennH, 46 (1979), 313-334; A. H. Young, "Thomas Barton: A Pennsylvania Loyalist," OntHSPR, 30 (1934), 33-42.

David Sloan
University of Arkansas at Fayetteville

JOHN BARTRAM (1699-1777)

Works: *Observations. . .Made in Travels from Pensilvania to Onondago, Oswego, and the Lake Ontario in Canada* (1751); Preface and appendix to the 3rd ed. of William Short's *Medicina Britannica* (1751); *An Account of East Florida* (with William Stork; 1766); "Diary of a Journey Through the Carolinas, Georgia and Florida, 1765-1766," annotated by Francis Harper, TAPS, n.s., 33, pt. I (Dec. 1942), 1-120; nine extracts of his letters to Peter Collinson and one to Benjamin Franklin, published in the *Philosophical Transactions* of the Royal Society of London, two in the *Gentleman's Magazine*, and four in the *Medical and Physical Journal* (Philadelphia); letters to and from Bartram in William Darlington, ed., *Memorials of John Bartram and Humphry Marshall* (1849), pp. 38-465.

Biography: John Bartram, son of William and Elizah Hunt Bartram, was born at Darby, Pa. William and his parents had been among the many members of the Society of Friends who fled from persecution in Eng. to Pa. in the early 1680s. Elizah died in 1701, and William was killed by Indians in N.C. in 1711. John received a sound elementary education at the Friends' school at Darby but was otherwise self-educated. He was twice married and the father of eleven children, of whom the best known was his son William Bartram (q.v.). Throughout his life, John was a very successful farmer at Kingsessing, Pa. It was, however, for his plant collecting and his botanic garden that he achieved fame. Plants and seeds collected by him from northern N.Y. to Fla. enriched the gardens of Eng. and other European countries for many years. His scientific interests were broad, including geology and zoology as well as botany, and he corresponded with many of the better known American and European naturalists of his day. He first conceived of an American Philosophical Society and, with his friend Benjamin Franklin (q.v.), became one of its founders.

Critical Appraisal: Most of Bartram's published writing consists of descriptions of observations he had made on his many horseback collecting trips through the eastern and southern colonies or at his farm or botanic garden. Although the published accounts listed above are familiar to many, more may know him through William Darlington's *Memorials*. In 1849 Darlington edited and published a large number of the letters exchanged between Bartram and Peter Collinson, Mark Catesby (q.v.), John Clayton (q.v.), Cadwallader Colden (q.v.), Johann Jacob Dillenius, John Fothergill, Benjamin Franklin, Alexander Garden (q.v.), John Frederick Gronovius, Carolus Linnaeus, Philip Miller, John Mitchell (q.v.), Hans Sloane, and others with scientific interests. These letters give perhaps the best single picture of eighteenth-century American science and its relation to that of Europe.

It is customary to think of Bartram as a botanist, and certainly botany was his first love. Yet his observations and writings dealt with diverse subjects such as detailed life histories of insects, migration of birds, hibernation of bears, ecological influences on both plants and animals, the formation of the earth and its evolution, the formation of fossils, the existence of mountains under the seas, the origins and customs of American Indians, and a wide variety of medical matters. As a botanist, he was by no means a mere collector and describer of plants. He was deeply interested in aspects of botany such as ecology, physiology, plant geography, pollination and its influence on inheritance, and soil composition and its influence on plant growth.

Bartram had a gift for detailed and accurate observation of natural phenomena, coupled with the scientist's curiosity and demand for more rational explanations of what he observed. A surprising array of more highly educated men in America and Europe, including many members of the Royal Society of London, valued both his observations and his explanations of them. He corresponded with a number of them for many years.

Bartram often wrote in haste, by candlelight, at the end of a strenuous day. Not surprisingly, his spelling and use of grammar were sometimes rough and ready. He was well aware of this fact and once replied to some "remarks on my deficiencies" made by Peter Collinson: "Good grammar and good spelling, may please those that are more taken with a fine superficial flourish than real truth." Nevertheless, his descriptions were often vivid. Thus he wrote of his first night in the council house of the Indians at Onondago:

> Soon after we were laid down to sleep and our fire almost burned out, we were entertained by a comical fellow, disguised in as odd a dress as *Indian* folly could invent. He had on a clumsy vizard of wood colour'd black, with a nose 4 or 5 inches long, a grinning mouth set awry, furnished with long teeth, round the eyes circles of bright brass, surrounded by a larger circle of white paint.

He was capable of a very eloquent and poetic use of language in describing the beautiful works of the Creator, as when he wrote to Alexander Garden of the beauty of flowers: "What charming colours appear in the various tribes, in the regular succession of the vernal and autumnal flowers—these so nobly bold— those so delicately languid! What a glow is enkindled in some, what a gloss shines in others! With what a masterly skill is every one of the varying tints disposed!" In this respect, he had a profound influence on the writing of his son William who in turn is believed to have influenced writers such as Coleridge and Wordsworth.

Suggested Readings: BDAS; DAB; LHUS; T_1; T_2. *See also* John Hundley Barnhart, "Bartram Bibliography," *Bartonia*, Supplement to no. 12 (Dec. 31, 1931), 51-67; Edmund Berkeley and Dorothy Smith Berkeley, *From Lake Ontario to the River St. John; The Life and Travels of John Bartram* (1981); Emily Read Cheston, *John Bartram, 1699-1777; His Garden and His House* (1953); Ernest Earnest, *John and William Bartram, Botanists and Explorers* (1940); Raymond Phineas Stearns, *Science in the British Colonies of America* (1970), pp. 575-593.

Dorothy Smith Berkeley
Edmund Berkeley
Charlottesville, Virginia

WILLIAM BARTRAM (1739-1823)

Works: *Travels* (1791); "Account of the Species, Hybrids, and Other Varieties of the Vine of North-America," *Medical Repository*, hexade 2, 1 (1) (1803), 19-24; "Some Account of the Late Mr. John Bartram, of Pennsylvania," *Philadelphia Medical and Physical Journal*, 1, pt. 1 (1804), 115-124; "Anecdotes of an American Crow," *Philadelphia Medical and Physical Journal*, 1, pt. 2 (1805), 89-95; "Description of an American Species of Certhia, or Creeper," PMPJ, 1, pt. 2 (1805), 103-106; Witmer Stone, ed., "Bird Migration Records of William Bartram," *Auk*, 30 (1913), 325-358; "Travels in Georgia and Florida, 1773-74"; Francis Harper, ed., "A Report to Dr. John Fothergill," TAPS, 33, pt. ii (1943),

121-242; Joseph Ewan, ed., *William Bartram, Botanical & Zoological Drawings, 1756-1780*, American Philosophical Society *Memoirs*, 74 (1968).

Biography: William Bartram, son of John Bartram (q.v.) and Ann (Mendenhall) Bartram, was born at Kingsessing, Pa. His early life was spent at the family farm and botanic garden and on collecting trips with his father. Greatly influenced by the latter, he showed an early enthusiasm for botany and a talent for drawing. Recognizing his potential, his father sent this son only to the academy in Philadelphia. Following an apprenticeship to a Philadelphia merchant, he became a trader at Cape Fear, N.C. In 1765 he joined his "king's botanist" father in exploring the St. John's River in Fla. Having tried, unsuccessfully, to become a planter in Fla., he returned to Philadelphia, where he again undertook merchandising and continued his drawing. Peter Collinson, of London, impressed by his artistic talent, obtained commissions for him from the Duchess of Portland and Dr. John Fothergill. Having fled to N.C. to avoid creditors, Bartram, in 1773, persuaded Fothergill to give financial support to his collecting of seeds and plants in the southeastern U.S. During the next four years he traveled as far west as the Mississippi River, including the territories of the Cherokee and Creek Indians. In 1777 (not 1778 as often stated) he returned to Philadelphia. There he spent the next forty-six years assisting in the care of the botanic garden and farm, drawing, writing, and studying birds. He refused to leave this sanctuary to become professor of botany at the University of Pennsylvania, or to accompany an expedition to the Red River with Thomas Freeman, or even to attend a meeting of the American Philosophical Society to which he had been elected. There were, however, many visitors to the botanic garden, attracted by his father's reputation and his own. He was generous in helping those naturalists who sought his assistance. Among them were William Baldwin, Dr. Benjamin Smith Barton (q.v.), William P. C. Barton, Zaccheus Collins, André Michaux, Francois André Michaux, Henry Melchior Muhlenberg (q.v.), Thomas Nuttall, George Ord, and Alexander Wilson.

Critical Appraisal: William Bartram's reputation as an eighteenth-century writer of importance has been based primarily on a single work, his *Travels*. This account of the four years during which he wandered through the southeastern U.S. collecting seeds and specimens for Dr. Fothergill and recording his observations of plants and animals in rough field journals and sketches, was not published until fourteen years after his return home to Kingsessing. It is not surprising though, that publication was delayed. During the Revolution, communication with Fothergill was difficult. Bartram had prepared reports for him before his return, during temporary interruptions of his travel, and no doubt thought that the doctor would publish them as Peter Collinson had published his father's accounts of travels. Fothergill did not do so, however; following his death in 1780, the manuscripts passed to others, eventually finding a home at the British Museum (Natural History), and not until 1943 did they see print, with annotation by Francis Harper.

Bartram at length realized that there would be no English publication of his

Fla. travels and prepared his own manuscript from his field journals. In 1786 a broadside was published by Enoch Storey, Jr., a job printer in Strawberry Alley. It sought subscriptions for Bartram's *Travels*, which he proposed to print and would be dedicated to Benjamin Franklin (q.v.) and illustrated with Bartram's sketches. For some reason, perhaps insufficient subscriptions, Storey abandoned his proposal. A young Philadelphia medical student, Benjamin Smith Barton, who was studying at the University of Edinburgh, volunteered to have Bartram's manuscript printed in Ger. at his own expense, but Bartram declined the offer. Finally, in 1791 the Philadelphia firm of James and Johnson published the *Travels*, dedicated to Thomas Mifflin, governor of Pa. and father of one of Bartram's academy classmates.

Undoubtedly, the recognition of Bartram's scientific contributions was greatly diminished by the delay in publication. Many of the new species he had found were described in the publications of others during the interim. The effect of the delay on his literary reputation is more debatable. Writing at greater leisure, he had more opportunity to polish his writing. Yet Harper, who annotated the earlier reports, found the manuscript "a far fresher document than the *Travels*." Bartram's literary debt to his father is very apparent. Although the latter's published descriptions tended to be formal, personal letters to friends frequently exhibited the dramatic, colorful, and poetic descriptions so often employed by his son. William's writing evidenced the same sensitive feelings, the same unconstrained admiration for the works of the Creator, and the same complete conviction of the goodness of God.

Contemporary reaction to the *Travels* differed greatly between North America and Europe. The romantic, poetic style of his accounts met with a cool reception at home but delighted many Europeans. So great was the demand abroad that during the next few years nine pirated editions were published in London, Dublin, Haarlem, Berlin, and Paris. The 2nd American edition, however, did not appear for 136 years, in part, no doubt, because Bartram's accounts of the beauties of nature seemed to embarrass American reviewers. One of them thought that Bartram's "rhapsodical effusions" might well have been omitted. Another thought his descriptions "too luxuriant and florid." There was some comparable criticism by reviewers abroad but, on the whole, Bartram's style was appreciated there.

The *Travels* definitely influenced several nineteenth-century writers. Samuel Taylor Coleridge made a great many notes from it, particularly on alligators, and critics have traced passages in "Kubla Khan" and "The Ancient Mariner" to the *Travels*. Its influence on William Wordsworth is also apparent in Wordsworth's "Ruth" and in certain writings by Chateaubriand. Perhaps Coleridge's description of the book is the most fitting: that it was not a travel book "but a series of poems."

There was, of course, much interest at home and abroad in Bartram's descriptions of new plants and animals and in his accounts of Indian life, which have been important in ethnological studies. Because of his dramatic, poetic style, many were skeptical during his lifetime and later about the accuracy of his accounts. Gradually, he has been, to a great extent, vindicated by the observations of others, but this is not to say that Bartram was not occasionally careless and inaccurate, particularly with regard to dates. Such problems confused many readers of the *Travels*, and the chronology was established only after a great deal of dedicated labor by Francis Harper. A number of competent biologists have traveled parts of Bartram's routes and found his descriptions to be correct. John Eatton LeConte, who was skeptical when he first read the *Travels* and thought that it had been written from memory, later conceded that he had been wrong. Much the same was true of John James Audubon. Harper, who traveled 10,000 miles in retracing the routes traveled by the two Bartrams, concluded that "There can be no question of Bartram's fundamental integrity as a naturalist."

Bartram's reputation as a naturalist rests not only on his writing but also upon his magnificent drawings of plants and animals. Some of the earliest of them, when he was only 16, were compared favorably, by Peter Collinson in London, with those of the great George Ehret. Later Collinson found it difficult to distinguish his drawing from an engraving. When Benjamin Smith Barton published the first American botany text book in 1803, the majority of the copper plate illustrations were done by Bartram.

Suggested Readings: BDAS; DAB; LHUS. *See also* Edmund Berkeley and Dorothy Smith Berkeley, *The Life and Travels of John Bartram* (1981); Emily Read Cheston, *John Bartram, 1699-1777; His Garden and His House* (1953); G. Chinard, *L'Exotisme American dans l'Oeuvre de Chateaubriand* (1918); William Darlington, *Memorials of John Bartram and Humphry Marshall* (1849); Ernest Earnest, *John and William Bartram: Botanists and Explorers* (1940); N. Bryllion Fagin, *William Bartram, Interpreter of the American Landscape* (1933); Joseph Kastner, *A Species of Eternity* (1977), pp. 79-112; Livingston Lowes, *The Road to Xanadu* (1927); George Ord, "Biographical Sketch of William Bartram," *Cabinet of Natural History and American Rural Sports* 2 (1832), i-vii.

Dorothy Smith Berkeley
Edmund Berkeley
Charlottesville, Virginia

JOHN BASS (1717-1762)

Works: *A True Narrative (1751); A Letter to the Rev. Mr. Niles* (1753).

Biography: Born in Braintree, Mass., on Mar. 26, 1717, John Bass, the brilliant son of a small farmer also named John, worked his way through Harvard College while achieving the highest academic honors. After graduation, Bass was called to serve as the second minister to the First Congregational Church in Ashford, Conn., and was installed there Sept. 7, 1743. From the first, some members of the congregation had opposed his installation because of questions respecting his orthodoxy, but serious opposition did not erupt until 1750, when members of Bass's congregation accused him of abandoning the essential Calvinist doctrines—particularly those of election and original sin—which he had promised to uphold.

Rather than take a stiffly autocratic stance, Bass attempted to plead his position before the church but did not disguise his modified views. After a period of debate and review involving an ecclesiastical council of the Windham County Consociation, Bass was dismissed on Jun. 4, 1751. In 1752 the tarnished clergyman was installed over the small and obscure First Congregational Church of Providence, R.I., where he supplemented his income first through acquiring an interest in a distillery and later through opening an apothecary shop and practicing medicine. In 1758 he served as both chaplain and surgeon's mate in a regiment raised for a summer campaign. John Bass died after several years of failing health on Oct. 24, 1762, leaving a personal library remarkably strong in medicine and English literature.

Critical Appraisal: John Bass never published a sermon, and his only literary achievement attended his professional defeat. His two publications are a documentary narrative of his expulsion from the pastorate of Ashford for Arminian heresy and a published epistle to the Rev. Mr. Samuel Niles (q.v) in which he defended his admitted Arminianism and protested the harshness of language used about him. The remarkable thing about these publications is not the thought or technical style but rather the character they reveal. Bass appears as courageous as any martyr who refused to recant or conform; moreover, as one who saw his case as ultimately just, he did not fear allowing the facts to speak for themselves. Thus his narrative is a collage of full documents and carefully reported oral exchanges that together preserve the issues and much of the dynamics of the proceedings. In fact, there are few documents of the ecclesiastical struggles attending the Great Awakening as comprehensive, succinct, and accurate even to nuance as Bass's twenty-eight-page account. His position was clear, and his defense was refreshingly naive as he related how he lost commitment to cardinal Calvinist points such as the doctrines of election and original sin, was discovered by members of the church, and was forced to resign his pastorate upon the vote of the church membership and the advice of a consociation meeting. Bass was clearly angry and thought that his freedom of speech had been denied, but his *True Narrative* bares the conflict ingenuously.

The final statement of Bass on the issue of repression by the Calvinist majority is his public letter to the Rev. Mr. Samuel Niles. Niles's *Vindication* (1752), to which Bass responded, had actually attacked Lemuel Briant's (q.v.) *Absurdity and Blasphemy* and had devoted only a few of its 120 pages to Bass; however, although Bass was not confuted, he was held up as an example of corrupt clergy. Bass, already defeated, responded with vigor and disciplined rhetoric: "'Tis evident that I deny some of the fundamental Doctrines of *Calvinism*, but it remains to be proved, that I have fallen from and deny some of the most important Doctrines contained and taught in the Gospel." Evidently choosing to forget that the great Anglican preachers did not necessarily influence New Eng.

Calvinists, Bass argued that not only his theological inspiration, John Taylor's *The Scripture-Doctrine of Original Sin Proposed to Free and Candid Examination*, questioned basic Calvinistic doctrines, but so did John Tillotson, Isaac Barrow, and others of the great English preachers.

The voice of John Bass is a mincr note in the history of New Eng., but his simple, vigorous, and occasionally elegant statements enhance the literature of the controversial pamphlet in America, and his *True Narrative* participates in the tradition of autobiographical literature written in Puritan New Eng. during the seventeenth and eighteenth centuries.

Suggested Readings: CCNE; Sibley-Shipton (X, 114-120). *See also* Edward B. Hall, *Discourse Comprising a History of the First Congregational Church in Providence* (1836); Alan Heimert and Perry Miller, eds., *The Great Awakening* (1967), pp. 465-479; Conrad Wright, *The Beginnings of Unitarianism in America* (1955).

Wilson H. Kimnach
University of Bridgeport

JOHN BEACH (1700-1782)

Works: *A Vindication of the Worship of God* (1736); *An Appeal to the Unprejudiced* (1737); *The Duty of Loving Our Enemies* (1739); *A Sermon Shewing That Eternal Life Is God's Free Gift* (1745); *God's Sovereignty* (1747); *An Attempt to Prove* (1748); *A Second Vindication* (1748); *A Calm and Dispassionate Vindication* (1749); *A Continuation of the Calm and Dispassionate Vindication* (1751); *A Modest Enquiry* (1755); *An Attempt to Vindicate Scripture Mysteries* (1760); *A Friendly Expostulation* (1763); *A Familiar Conference* (1764); *A Second Familiar Conference* (1765); *A Defense of the Second Conference* (1766); *Three Discourses* (1768); *A Funeral Sermon upon. . .Samuel Johnson* (1772).

Biography: John Beach, son of Isaac Beach, a tailor, was born in Stratford, Conn., in 1700. Encouraged by Timothy Cutler, pastor of the Congregational Church that the Beach family attended and later rector of Yale College, he graduated from Yale in 1721 and then studied theology until he was invited to settle as minister at Newtown, Conn. During his eight years as the Congregational minister at Newtown, Beach maintained close contact with Samuel Johnson (q.v.), his former Yale tutor and an active missionary of the Church of England.

Eventually, Beach's growing doubts about the validity of his ordination led him to refuse to administer the sacraments, whereupon an ecclesiastical council deposed him in Feb. 1732. Two months later, he sailed to Eng. for ordination in the Church of England, and the Society for the Propagation of the Gospel named him missionary to Newtown (where he had earlier served as Congregational minister) and Redding, Conn. In this capacity, Beach served faithfully, and under his leadership, the Anglican groups in Newtown and Redding grew steadily, and neighboring congregations were created. Clearly the most successful Anglican priest in Conn., Beach also defended the church during any controversies that arose. As the American Revolution approached, Beach's Tory leanings involved him in the anti-Congress movement, and he alone among Conn.'s Anglican priests maintained prayer book worship throughout the Revolution, defying rebels with prayers for the king. Beach died at Newtown in 1782 at the age of 81.

Critical Appraisal: Most of John Beach's published writings were polemical exchanges with notable Congregational and Presbyterian clergymen such as Jonathan Dickinson and Noah Hobart (q.v.) on subjects such as liturgy, history, church polity, and theology. To defend his position, Beach employed a variety of literary techniques and drew on numerous sources. As a result, he is considered one of the ablest defenders of the Anglican Church in Conn., Samuel Johnson excluded.

Beach's earliest theological exchange occurred with Jonathan Dickinson, Puritan author of *The Vanity of Human Institutions in the Worship of God* (1736), which condemned the usages of the Church of England. In response to Dickinson, Beach wrote *A Vindication of the Worship of God according to the Church of England*, in which he detailed the lack of substance and numerous misrepresentations he found in Dickinson's work. The controversy continued for more than a decade, ending only with Dickinson's death in 1748, and even then Beach had the last word in *A Second Vindication* (1748), a final assault on the thinking of his antagonist.

Dickinson's death, however, did not leave Beach bereft of antagonists. In 1749 he published *A Calm and Dispassionate Vindication* to counteract the "falacious argumentations" of Noah Hobart concerning the validity of Presbyterian ordination, and although Beach won the controversy, his writings against Hobart have been characterized as "ill-tempered" pieces, void of "anything new, calm, or dispassionate."

Although John Beach resembled many SPG missionaries in his willingness to engage in controversy with Congregationalists and Presbyterians, he was unique in delivering and publishing a sermon that led to his being disciplined for heresy. In 1755, in the midst of illness and personal loss, Beach published *A Modest Enquiry into the State of the Dead*, which challenged traditional Protestant belief toward death, judgment, and the resurrection. A Congregational ministerial association brought Beach's sermon to the attention of the SPG and asked that the society act to "discountenance such dangerous principles," and the bishops to whom the SPG referred the matter declared Beach's thesis heretical and recommended that the missionaries "contradict & confute" it. After the SPG had admonished Beach by letter, a formal conference was held between Beach and eight of his fellow missionaries, where Samuel Seabury (q.v.) preached a sermon on traditional theories of resurrection, with Beach then issuing an apology.

But John Beach's brush with heresy did not mark the end of his controversies with non-Anglican clergy. In 1762 Noah Welles (q.v.)—masquerading as an

Anglican clergyman—anonymously published a cutting satire, *The Real Advantages Which Ministers and People May Enjoy Especially in the Colonies, by Conforming to the Church of England*, which lampooned the social distinctions of Anglicans. Beach answered the unknown attacker (whom he thought was probably Hobart) with *A Friendly Expostulation*, and during the 1760s Beach was once again the church's watchman against the errors of the time when he published several tracts against Antinomianism in a Yale thesis. In these as in all of the controversies in which Beach engaged, neither side exercised particular courtesy or restraint, but as pastor and polemicist, John Beach made noteworthy contributions to the religious history and literature of eighteenth-century America.

Suggested Readings: CCNE; Dexter (I, 239-243); Sprague (V, 82-85). *See also* James B. Bell, "Anglican Quill-Drivers in Eighteenth Century America," HMagPEC, 44 (1975), 23-45; Carl Bridenbaugh, *Mitre and Sceptre: Transatlantic Faiths, Ideas, Personalities, and Politics, 1689-1775* (1962), pp. 88-89; Nelson R. Burr, *The Story of the Diocese of Connecticut: A New Branch of the Vine* (1962), pp. 98-101; Francis L. Hawks and William S. Perry, *Documentary History of the Protestant Episcopal Church in Connecticut, 1704-1789*, 2 vols. (1863); Marc Mappen, "Anglican Heresy in the Eighteenth Century: The Disciplining of John Beach," HMagPEC, 48 (1979), 465-472; Lorenzo Sabine, *Biographical Sketches of Loyalists of the American Revolution with an Historical Essay*, 2 vols. (1864), I, 219-222; Herbert and Carol Schneider, eds., *Samuel Johnson, President of King's College: His Career and Writings*, 4 vols. (1929); Bruce Steiner, *Connecticut Anglicans in the Revolutionary Era* (1978), pp. 41-62; idem, *Samuel Seabury, 1729-1796: A Study in the High Church Tradition* (1971), pp. 95-99, 184-189.

Mary E. Quinlivan
University of Texas of the Permian Basin

CHARLES CLINTON BEATTY (c. 1715-1772)

Works: *A Sermon Preached in Woodbury* (1752); *Double Honour Due to the Laborious Gospel Minister* (1757); "Journal of Beatty's Trip to the British Isles in 1762" (w. 1762, pub. 1962); "Journal of Beatty's Trip to the Ohio Country in 1766" (w. 1766, pub. 1962); *The Journal of a Two Months Tour...to Which Are Added, Remarks on the Language and Customs of Some Particular Tribes Among the Indians, with a Brief Account of the Various Attempts That Have Been Made to Civilize and Convert Them* (published version of the Ohio Country manuscript journal; 1768); "Journal of Beatty's Visit to England in 1769" (w. 1769, pub. 1962).

Biography: Charles Beatty—Presbyterian minister, missionary, and trustee for the College of New Jersey—was born in County Antrim, Ire., sometime around 1715. His father died when he was young, in 1729, and at age 14 he immigrated to America with his mother and uncle. Although Beatty had received a Classical and religious education in Ire., the family's poverty sent him traveling as a backwoods peddler. On one of his trips, he called at the Log

College in Neshaminy, Pa., where the headmaster, William Tennent (I), per-suaded him to stay and prepare for the ministry. Licensed in 1742 and ordained the following year, Beatty succeeded Tennent to the pastorate of the church at Neshaminy. Already sympathetic to schemes for converting the Indians, Beatty quickly became enthusiastic about such projects when the great frontier mission-ary David Brainerd (q.v.) visited his church in 1745.

In 1746 Beatty was chosen moderator of the Synod, and in 1754 he was commissioned to undertake a missionary trip through Va. and N.C. Two years later he served as chaplain to the Pa. troops who, under Benjamin Franklin (q.v.), were sent in defense of the colony's northwestern borders. In 1759 Beatty was appointed to the Corporation for the Relief of Poor and Distressed Presbyte-rian Ministers, and of the Poor and Distressed Widows and Children of Presbyte-rian Ministers, organized to aid frontier clergy during the French and Indian Wars. Three years later, he undertook a fund-raising voyage to Eng. on behalf of the corporation, producing a manuscript journal account of the mission. In 1766 Beatty was sent, with fellow minister George Duffield (q.v.), into the Ohio country to gather first-hand information on "poor and distressed" frontier Presby-terians and to bring the Gospel to the Indians. This expedition produced another manuscript journal, which Beatty reworked and published in 1768.

In 1767, a year after his Ohio country expedition, Beatty sailed to Eng. seeking a cure for his wife, who was then suffering from cancer and who died shortly after arriving in Eng. Before returning to America in 1769, Beatty spent a year soliciting more money for the corporation and writing yet another manu-script journal. A trustee of the College of New Jersey since 1763, Beatty was sent by that institution in 1772 to solicit funds in the W. Ind. Soon after reaching Barbados, he died of yellow fever.

Critical Appraisal: A popular preacher, Charles Beatty published just one sermon, *Double Honour Due to the Laborious Gospel Minister* (1756), written for the ordination of William Ramsay and conventional for such an occasion. His fund-raising efforts for frontier relief and missionary work pro-duced the two manuscript accounts of visits to G.B. mentioned above. Flat chronicles recording contributors and contributions and usually lacking complete sentences, these works are of historical, literary, and cultural interest. His loglike descriptions of treacherous Atlantic crossings, for example, because of their very matter-of-factness, are effective narrative.

Beatty's most significant literary contribution, however, is the *Journal* of his 1766 trip into the Ohio country. The author's own description of the work, a "plain, artless narrative of matters of fact," is accurate. Lacking the acute obser-vation and self-dramatization of the Anglican Charles Woodmason's (q.v.) Car-olina missionary journal of 1766-1768 or the detailed eloquence of David Brainerd's *Mirabilia Dei Inter Indicos* (1746), Beatty's more laconic account is nevertheless a valuable frontier document, containing, among other things, significant notes on life among the Delaware Indians, including their religious customs. The speech of a Delaware king on the evils of rum and prostitution, for example, is a poignant comment on Indian-white relations of the period, and the sketch of an Indian named Neolin, a touchingly misinformed would-be Christian, is a brief glimpse of a spontaneous grass-roots evangelist. In addition, Beatty's letter to Rev. John Erskine of Edinburgh, included with the published *Journal*, develops the intriguing theory, later popularized by James Adair (q.v.), that the Indians are related to the Ten Tribes of Israel.

Nor is the *Journal* entirely devoid of more strictly literary interest. Although Beatty rarely sketches scenes, a quick look, for example, at frontier worship deftly conveys its vicissitudes: "in time of sermon a Ratle Snake creep in the house which alarmed the people but was hapily Discovered and killed before it did any damage." In the published version, the English is normalized, and Beatty shows himself not entirely "artless" when he interprets the incident as a remarkable manifestation of Providence "in preserving us from the venom of the creature."

In its overall leanness, austerity of scene, and understatement, the *Journal* is also an unintentional testament to the character of Charles Beatty. Drenched, cold, and generally miserable after days of unrelenting rain, Beatty, on the verge of a racking ague, allowed only that "our Condition [was] not very comfortable."

Suggested Readings: CCMC; DAB; P; Sprague (III, 119-125). *See also* Guy Soulliard Klett, ed., *Journals of Charles Beatty, 1762-1769* (transcribes the manuscript journals and provides valuable biographical and background information; 1962); *Record of the Family of Charles Beatty Who Emigrated from Ireland to America in 1729* (1873); *Records of the Presbyterian Church in the United States* (1904), passim; William W. Sweet, *Religion on the American Frontier: 1783-1840* (1964), II, 24-25; David Wynbeek, *David Brainerd: Beloved Yankee* (1961), pp. 129-132.

Alan Axelrod
Furman University

JOHN JAMES BECKLEY (1757-1807)

Works: "Mercator" essays in *National Gazette* (1792); essays signed "A Calm Observer" and "Timon" in *National Gazette* (1793); *An Examination of the Late Proceedings in Congress Respecting the Official Conduct of the Secretary of the Treasury* (with James Monroe; 1793); "Calm Observer" essays in *American Minerva* (1793 and 1795); "Calm Observer" essays in *Aurora* (1795 and 1799); *Address to the People of the United States*, signed "Americanus" (1800); *An Epitome of the Life and Character of Thomas Jefferson* (1800); "Senex" essays in the *Aurora* (1800); *Oration Delivered. . .in the German Reformed Church in Philadelphia* (1801); *An Oration Delivered at Philadelphia the Fourth of July* (1801); "Andrew Marvel" essays in *Aurora* (1802).

Biography: Born in or near London, Eng., on Aug. 4, 1757, John Beckley came to Va. in 1769 as an indentured scribe for John Clayton (q.v.), clerk of court for Gloucester County and a noted botanist. Following Clayton's death in

1774, Beckley served as clerk for a wide variety of committees and studied law. Eventually, Beckley became clerk of the Va. Senate, succeeded Edmund Randolph (q.v.) as clerk of the Va. House of Delegates, took over Randolph's law practice during the latter's absence from Williamsburg, and became a member and early secretary of the original Phi Beta Kappa Society, helping to prepare charters for additional chapters at Harvard and Yale. When the General Assembly moved to Richmond, Beckley continued as its clerk. He also practiced law in Richmond and became active in city government, serving as the city's first alderman and its second mayor, to which office he was three times elected. In early April of 1787, Beckley accompanied Randolph, then governor, to the Constitutional Convention at Philadelphia and was later elected secretary of the state convention that ratified it. In 1802 Beckley was appointed by Thomas Jefferson (q.v.) as the first librarian of Congress, and he continued to serve in that post until his death in 1807. He was also elected the first clerk of the U.S. House of Representatives, serving in that capacity from 1789 to 1797 and again from 1801 until 1807. Beckley acquired large tracts of land in what is now W. Va., and his son, Gen. Alfred Beckley, founded and named the town of Beckley after his father.

  Critical Appraisal: John Beckley's writing was almost entirely political. An extremely ardent Republican, Beckley was a leader among the anti-Federalists and helped to develop a political philosophy attractive to the ordinary voters—workers and farmers as opposed to those with financial interests. As a result, he has been called the first party manager or party chairman. Beckley's early years in Va. had brought him into close association with Jefferson, James Madison (q.v.), James Monroe, Randolph, and others who played important early roles in the federal government. His position as clerk of the House kept him at the seat of government even when Congress was not in session, and he kept up an extensive correspondence with absent members. His early experience in city government at Richmond gave him a good background for subsequent political activity at city, state, and national levels. Beckley early recognized the importance of political writing in the public press, and he worked closely with Philip Freneau (q.v.), Benjamin Franklin Bache (q.v.), Mathew Carey (q.v.), William Duane (q.v.), and others, publishing numerous articles under a variety of pseudonyms, among them "Mercator," "Timon," "Senex," "Americanus," and "Andrew Marvel." A gifted political writer capable of adopting a variety of styles, developing arguments logically and forcefully, and carefully documenting his statements, Beckley was unusually adept at drawing political opponents into public controversies that they wished to avoid and at attracting wide attention while keeping his adversaries on the defensive.

  In fact, Beckley's strongly partisan activity so annoyed the Federalists that in 1797 they adopted devious methods to oust him from office as clerk. Earlier, the Federalists had similarly treated Randolph and Monroe, whom Beckley avenged by persuading James Thomson Callender to edit for publication papers relating to the alleged affair of Alexander Hamilton (q.v.) with Mrs. Reynolds. This evidence, plus Hamilton's unwise explanation of the matter, significantly undermined the future of his political career.

Beckley was an ardent admirer of Jefferson, and his writings and political activities on Jefferson's behalf played an important part in Jefferson's elections. An orator as well as a writer, "the Ciceronian Beckley," as he was sometimes called, was chosen to be the orator at the victory celebration at Philadelphia when Jefferson was elected president in 1800. Indeed, no one was more responsible than Beckley for the overthrow of the Federalists and the long succession of Va. Republicans that followed, all of whom were his friends and associates.

Suggested Readings: Edmund Berkeley and Dorothy Smith Berkeley, " 'The Ablest Clerk in the U.S.,' John James Beckley," VMHB, 70 (1962), 434-446; idem, "The First Librarian of Congress, John Beckley," *Librarians of Congress, 1802-1974*, ed. Daniel J. Boorstin (1977), pp. 2-37; idem, *John Beckley, Zealous Partisan in a Nation Divided* (1973); idem, " 'The Piece Left Behind,' Monroe's Authorship of a Political Pamphlet Revealed," VMHB, 75 (1957), 174-180; Joseph Charles, *The Origins of the American Party System: Three Essays* (1956); Noble E. Cunningham, Jr., *The Jeffersonian Republicans, the Formation of Party Organization, 1789-1801* (1957); idem, *The Jeffersonian Republicans in Power* (1963); idem, "John Beckley, An Early American Party Manager," WMQ, 3rd ser., 13 (1956), 40-52; Philip M. Marsh, "John Beckley Mystery Man of the Early Jeffersonians," PMHB, 62 (1948), 54 63; David C. Mearns, *The Story Up to Now* (1947).

Dorothy Smith Berkeley
Edmund Berkeley
Charlottesville, Virginia

GEORGE BECKWITH (1703-1794)

Works: *Adam's Losing* (1735); *Whatsoever God Doeth* (1739); *Christ the Alone Pattern* (1742); *Two Sermons at Lyme* (Spiritual Judgments) (1744); *Ministers of the Gospel* (1752); *That People* (1756); *The Invalidity or Unwarrantableness of Lay Ordination* (1763); *Second Letter on the Subject of Lay Ordination* (1766); *Visible Saints* (1769); *The Infant Seed* (1770); *An Attempt to Shew* (1783).

Biography: Born in Lyme, Conn., the son of Matthew Beckwith, Jr., George Beckwith received a bachelor's degree from Yale College and a master's in divinity in 1728. Shortly thereafter, he married Sarah Brown of Middletown, Conn. They had two sons, George and Nathaniel, who also graduated from Yale. Beckwith was an orthodox Congregationalist minister, ordained in Lyme on Jan. 22, 1730, and pastor of its North Society Church. According to Ezra Stiles (q.v.), between a quarter and a third of Beckwith's parish were Separatists, but unlike others in Lyme, his church remained Congregational. During the French and Indian Wars, Beckwith was, by direct appointment of Governor Fitch in 1755, chaplain to the First Regiment of Connecticut Men. Recorded are dates of service of Mar. 27-Nov. 1, 1758; Mar. 1759; Mar. 24-Oct. 17, 1760; Apr.

1-Nov. 20, 1761; and Mar. 1775. A member of the Corporation of Yale College from Jun. 1763 to Sept. 1777, Beckwith resigned because of infirmity. He died on Dec. 26, 1794. His wife survived him by two years.

Critical Appraisal: Despite his numerous publications, all dealing with religious issues, George Beckwith made little lasting impression upon the religious scene of his day. In conventional sermonic form, his writings express orthodox viewpoints on the two issues in which he became a participant: the ordination of lay ministers and infant baptism. On the issue of lay ministers, Beckwith argued that since Jesus Christ had not committed his believers to ordination of lay ministers, such ordination was unacceptable. Israel Holly, pastor of the Congregational Church in Suffield, Conn., answered Beckwith's first letter (1763) with *A Word in Zion's Behalf* (c. 1765), and his second (1766) with *A Letter Occasioned by Mr. Beckwith's Second Letter upon the Subject of Lay-Ordination* (1767). Beckwith's point of view did not prevail, and his arguments, couched in fairly standard biblical allusions and interpretation, had little effect. Regarding the Sacraments, which had for the past century been reduced to baptism and the Lord's Supper, Beckwith felt that children of those who were visible saints in the Congregational Church had the right to be baptized. This view challenged the practice that only visible saints (thus adults) should be baptized. Beckwith's *Visible Saints* (1769), a reaction to a sermon on the subject of adult baptism by Jacob Green (q.v.) at Hanover, N.J., on Nov. 4, 1764, provoked Green's *A Reply...Entitled, Christian Baptism* (c. 1769).

Beckwith continued the disagreement with *The Infant Seed* (1770). The controversy was old and continuing, involving the separation of the Particular Baptists, who first came to New Eng., from the established church. The argument for adult baptism was based on the Calvinistic doctrine of individual atonement rather than general atonement through Christ; individual atonement was possible only after personal confession, that is, only after an age of accountability. The important Half-Way Covenant drafted by Richard Mather (q.v.) in 1662 argued that children of those who had a personal experience of conversion were to share church privileges, including baptism and excluding only the Lord's Supper, although not church membership. Solomon Stoddard (q.v.) favored the convenant, ultimately moving to "Stoddardism," which was rejected by his grandson Jonathan Edwards (q.v.), who deplored its extension of communion and full church membership to those merely professing repentance and faith.

In all, Beckwith's writings and historical presence represent the numerous ministers of the day whose names are not remembered, and he may be said to typify the ministers whose reactionary and conservative concepts existed in opposition to some of the religious trends reported in modern-day discussions.

Suggested Readings: Dexter (I, 366-368).

John T. Shawcross
University of Kentucky

JOHN BEETE (fl. 1795-1797)

Works: *The Man of the Times; Or, A Scarcity of Cash* (1797).

Biography: Very little is known about John Beete. A minor English actor, he seems to have begun his career in America with Thomas Wignell's troupe in Baltimore during the autumn of 1795 and then returned to Philadelphia with the troupe. From Dec. 14, 1795, through Jul. 1, 1796, he was a member of the company at the New Theatre in Philadelphia where he appeared fifty-five times in almost as many roles. He was a "comedian," as he identified himself on the title page of his published play, and acted parts such as Careless in *The School for Scandal*, Milford in *The Road to Ruin*, and Captain Dudley in *The West Indian*. The following season he was a member of John Solee's company at the Church Street Theatre in Charleston, S.C., where on Apr. 14, 1797, his original work, *The Man of the Times; Or, A Scarcity of Cash*, was played for his benefit.

Beete acted in other American cities, but that is the extent of factual information historians have seen fit to record. Some conclusions, however, might be drawn from his play. Beete was, apparently, anti-British, pro-Ire., against corrupt business practices everywhere, and a strong supporter of America. It is worth recording, too, that his statement "to the Public" included a plea for "native dramatic literature, so that our stage may not always exhibit foreign productions." Whatever the particulars of his life, Beete considered himself an American.

Critical Appraisal: After the Revolutionary War when the theatres were once again opened, there was an obvious demand for performers and plays. As America could provide neither in adequate numbers, theatre managers such as Thomas Wignell made regular trips to Eng. for actors who, to help supply the demands of the growing theatre in America, occasionally wrote plays. John Hodgkinson (q.v.) wrote *The Man of Fortitude: Or, A Knight's Adventure*; J. Robinson (q.v.), comedian, wrote *The Yorker's Strategem; Or, Banana's Wedding*; both William Milns and James Fennell wrote plays. John Beete belongs in the company of these actor-playwrights, and his single known work was the first original play produced in Charleston that has survived in print.

The Man of the Times, the "maiden piece" of "Mr. Beete, Comedian," is a two-act farce that satirizes the greedy, speculating, expedient man of the times. In structure and in theme, the play is much like other such slight plays of the time. Were it not for its place in history as one of a few extant plays, it would not be considered worthy of serious dramatic criticism. It is not a carefully constructed play, nor can it be said that its theme boasts imaginative embellishment. During the first half of the play, the heavy-handed pro-American sentiments and anti-British statements obscure the humor that good farce should generate. The object of the satire, "the man of the times," is the comically corrupt American businessman, Old Screwpenny (the part Beete acted), who sends his son to Eng.

to learn corrupt business practices, scoffs at honor, and brags of his manipulation of congressmen. His obligatory defeat and subsequent absence from the final scenes of the play, however, only reveal that the play focuses on love, not corruption. It is Screwpenny's son Charles who dominates and determines the action of the play. Falling in love with the daughter of Major Upright, Charles thwarts his father at every turn and brings the play to its proper conclusion.

In a superficial and farcical way, Beete interprets a picture of his times. That he could see the "man of the times" as not only a businessman but a corrupt businessman whom he could sweepingly condemn shows both insight and strength of purpose. Although structurally weak, the play has interesting ideas for the social historian. If the playwright lacked great talent, he was not worse than many of his contemporaries and carried the advantage of admirably nationalistic motives. With a tired plot, stereotyped characters, and a moral adapted to the tastes of conservative Americans, Beete added his undistinguished work to the history of American drama.

Suggested Readings: Walter J. Meserve, *An Emerging Entertainment: The Drama of the American People to 1828* (1977), pp. 128-129; Thomas Clark Pollock, *The Philadelphia Theatre in the Eighteenth Century Together with the "Day Book" of the Same Period* (1933, 1968), pp. 268-305; Charles S. Watson, *Antebellum Charleston Dramatists* (1976), pp. 28-29; Eola Willis, *The Charleston Stage in the XVIII Century with Social Settings of the Time* (1924), p. 351.

Walter J. Meserve
Indiana University

JOHANN CONRAD BEISSEL (1690-1768)

Works: *Mystyrion Anomias* (1728), English version, *The Mystery of Lawlessness* (by Michael Wohlfaht; 1729); *Mystische Und Sehr Geheyme Sprueche* (1730), English version, *99 Mystical Proverbs* (by Peter Miller; n.d.); *Die Ehe das Zuchthaus Fleischlicher Menschen* (1730); *Urständliche und Erfahrungsvolle Hohe Zeugnüsse (Deliciae Ephratenses, Pars II)* (1745); *Eine Sehr Deutliche Beschreiburg Wie Sich Dieses Hoche u. Wichtige Werck Dieser Unserer Göttlichen Sing Arbeit erboren* (ms. 1746); *Das Gesang Der Einsamen Und Verlassenen Turtel-Taube* (1747); "Letter Book" (ms., c. 1751-c. 1756); *Theosophische Gedichte (Theosophische Lectionen)* (c. 1752), pp. 396-431; *Paradisisches Wunder-Spiel*, hymns 1-296 (1766); *Deliciae Ephratenses, Pars I* (1773); *Gottliche Wunderschrift* (1789), English version, *A Dissertation on Man's Fall* (by Peter Miller; 1765); *Geistliche Briefe Eines Friedamen Pilgers, Welche Er Von 1721. Bis an Seine 1768. Darauf Erfolgte, Entbindung Geschrieben* (1794).

Biography: Johann Conrad Beissel was born in Eberbach in the Palatinate (Modern Ger.) in Apr. 1690. His father, a baker by profession and a drunkard by avocation, died two months before his son's birth, and his mother died when he was 8. Apprenticed to a baker and working when he could as a journeyman baker, Beissel quite early demonstrated pietistic interests and ultimately achieved conversion in 1717. His outspoken religious views, however, eventually led to his banishment from the Palatinate. At the urging of friends, he fled Europe and subsequently arrived in America in 1720, settling first in Germantown (now part of Philadelphia). He soon retreated to live the solitary life of a hermit in Muehlbach in Lebanon County. Charismatic, he attracted people, and the strict seventh day baptism he espoused became the basis for "Economy" at Ephrata in Lancaster County, a religious communal society established in 1732. The "Ephrata Cloister," as it has been known, commonly consisted of three orders: celibate sisters, celibate brothers, and married householders. Although Beissel maintained that God had "preserved him from the allurements of the female sex," hints and accusations of sexual scandal were rife. Under Biessel and his disciple Peter Miller, the order grew to encompass several hundred largely self-sufficient brethren including, for a brief period, Conrad Weiser. The Ephrata community achieved fame as a printing center and for its distinctive music and calligraphy. Beissel himself is said to have composed more than 1,000 hymns. The surviving buildings his followers constructed are the most significant Germanic Gothic structures in America. The colony's decline began with his death on Jul. 6, 1768, but small numbers of followers at both Ephrata and its offshoot, Snowhill Monastery in Franklin County, maintained their distinctive life-style well into the nineteenth century.

Critical Appraisal: Most of Conrad Beissel's work is theological in basis and pietistic in flavor. In his lifetime, his works were very influential within the large German-speaking population of Pa. However, as Walter C. Klein, Beissel's principal biographer, ultimately concluded: "Intellectually, Beissel was largely an echo. Spiritually, he bears the impress of Pietism and presents nothing startlingly distinctive." The Vorsteher's most interesting and original feature was his bizarre temperament. Although several of Beissel's works were translated into English (primarily as missionary devices), his literary works were essentially unknown to the English-speaking world. His first major work, *Mystyrion Anomias* (1729), sets forth the philosophic basis for his sectarian beliefs. The materials set forth in *Mystische Und Sehr Geheyme Sprueche* (1730) were used as guidance for the later life-style of the Ephrata community. Many of the subsequent writings from the 1740s on attempt to answer criticism and solidify his position as absolute spiritual leader of his movement. Those of his hymns published, *Paradisisches Wunder-Spiel* (1766), were meant for community use. From a literary vantage point, Beissel's most important contribution was not as an author but as the moving force behind the Ephrata Press, among whose many titles was the *Mennonite Book of Martyrs*, the largest book published in North America in the eighteenth century.

Suggested Readings: CCMC; DAB; DARB; LHUS. *See also* James Emanuel Ernst, *Ephrata; A History*, posthumously edited by J. J. Stout; (1963); J. M. Hark, trans., *Chronicon Ephratense*, compiled by Brothers Lamech and Agrippa (1889); Walter C.

Klein, *Johann Conrad Beissel: Mystic and Martinet, 1690-1768* (1972); Julius F. Sachse, *History of the Church of the Brethern of the Eastern District of Pennsylvania* (1915).

Irwin Richman
The Pennsylvania State University

SAMUEL BELCHER (c. 1640-1715)

Works: *Concio ad Magistratum* (1707); *An Essay Tending to Promote the Kingdom of Our Lord Jesus Christ* (1707).

Biography: Samuel Belcher, the son of Jeremy Belcher, who came to New Eng. aboard the *Susan and Ellen* in 1635, was born at Ipswich, Mass., sometime around 1640. Probably prepared for college by Ezekiel Cheever (q.v.) at the Ipswich Grammar School, Belcher attended Harvard from 1655 to 1659. About 1660 he succeeded the Rev. John Brock as pastor of the church at Isles of Shoals, N.H., and he remained there until the mid-1670s, when, according to one account, he "was so impair'd in his Health that He was forc'd to leave the Shoals." Except that he resided in and around Portsmouth, N.H., little is known of Belcher between the mid-1670s and the mid-1690s. Sometime between 1692 and 1696, Belcher and his family moved to West Newbury, Mass., where he was eventually called to be minister of the First Church (known then as the Second Church of Newbury) and ordained there on Nov. 10, 1698. Forced by poor health to relinquish his position in 1711, he returned to his native Ipswich, where he died on Mar. 10, 1715. Married twice, first to Mary Cobbett of Lynn, who died in 1679, then to Mercy Wigglesworth, oldest daughter of Michael Wigglesworth (q.v.), Belcher was survived by Mercy and a son, Jeremy.

Critical Appraisal: According to an account published after Belcher's death, the minister's

> Religion was Pure & Undefiled; His Divinity Sound and Orthodox, his Conversation very chearfull & agreeable, yet grave withall, But that which highly Distinguished him in his order was his Excellent Gift in Preaching, nothing being more accurate and entertaining than his ordinary Sermons; Like a well instructed Scribe...he always brought forth things New and Old, Profitable and Pleasant.

Unfortunately, only two examples of Belcher's preaching survive in print. *Concio ad Magistratum* is an assize sermon preached before the Mass. Superior Court of Judicature on May 21, 1702. In 1707 it was printed together with *An Essay Tending to Promote the Kingdom of Our Lord Jesus Christ*, which was the Mass. election sermon for that year.

Preached on May 28, 1707, *An Essay* is the more noteworthy of the two sermons for both its occasion and its subject matter. Since, traditionally, only ministers of considerable reputation as preachers were invited to speak before the governor and other officials on Election Day, Belcher most likely deserved the high praise the occasion customarily bestowed. The purity of his religion and the orthodoxy of his divinity (and politics) are apparent throughout *An Essay*, as subjects that had informed the attitudes and rhetoric of election preachers during the last decades of the seventeenth century are developed in earnest. Belcher argued that with the clergy and the people of New Eng., his audience must endeavor to bring about "the happy Symptoms [of]. . . the flourishing State of the Kingdom of Christ." Assuming a calm, fatherly tone toward his audience, Belcher urged that among other "Symptoms," an increase in the number of conversions, rigorous observance of the Sabbath, and zeal for discipline and reform in church government be sought after in the community. Like election preachers of the 1670s and 1680s in whose sermons such subjects repeatedly appeared, he developed the example of the Puritans' "errand into the wilderness" as a reminder of the original purpose for New Eng.'s settlement and to inspire all for the work they have to accomplish. He said of the founders that "[they] came not hither, for the sake of Dominion...[and] not to Inrich themselves.... [Their] Design it was to Exalt our Lord. . . [and] to lay the Foundations of his Kingdom in the Remote Parts of the Earth. . . that this part. . . might be leaven'd with the favour of the Gospel." The founders' "design" for New Eng., Belcher made clear, remains as the responsibility of the "Generation. . . Risen up in their places," and, he asserted, it must "stir up all of Us, in our several Stations and Capacities to promote the Interest of CHRIST's Kingdom in Our Selves and Others."

If the content and style of *An Essay* are typical of that of his "ordinary sermons," Belcher was well entrenched in the intellectual and oratorical mainstream of Puritan New Eng. That would indicate how this "well-instructed scribe" would have had appeal to audiences of the late-seventeenth and early-eighteenth centuries. In effect, the "profitable and pleasant" lessons that Belcher derived from his subjects were the very staples out of which the New Eng. "community of saints" routinely considered itself and its mission.

Suggested Readings: CCNE; Sibley-Shipton (II, 42-45).

Ronald A. Bosco
State University of New York at Albany

JEREMY BELKNAP (1744-1798)

Works: *An Eclogue Occasioned by the Death of. . .Alexander Cumming* (1763); *A Plain and Earnest Address from a Minister* (1771); *A Sermon on Military Duty* (1773); *Jesus Christ, the Only Foundation* (1779); *The History of New-Hampshire*, 3 vols. (1784, 1791, 1792); *An Election Sermon* (1785); *A Sermon Preached at the Installation of. . .Jedidiah Morse* (1789); *Proposal for Printing by Subscription* (1790); *The Subscriber* (1790); *The Foresters* (1792); *Memoirs of the Lives, Characters and Writings of. . .Watts and. . .Doddridge*

(1793); *Dissertations on...Jesus Christ* (1795); *Queries Respecting...Slavery in Massachusetts* (1795); *Sacred Poetry* (1795); *A Sermon Delivered Before the Convention* (1796); *A Sermon Delivered on the 9th of May* (1798).

Biography: Jeremy Belknap was born in Boston, Mass., on Jun. 4, 1744. After graduation from Harvard, Belknap served as assistant pastor and later as pastor of the Congregational Church in Dover, N.H. In 1787 he became pastor of the Federal Street Church in Boston, where he remained as minister for the duration of his life and developed his capacities as historian, novelist, pamphleteer, and writer. In Jul. 1775 Belknap agreed to the request of the committee of safety of N.H. to serve as chaplain to its troops at Cambridge, and his journal provides an account of the military preparations for the Continental defense of Cambridge, Roxbury, and Charlestown. Belknap also contributed to the *Columbian Magazine*, where he addressed an array of theological and political issues. A vocal antislavery crusader, Belknap was a member of the committee for the abolition of the slave trade in R.I. With a keen sense of detail, he recorded the proceedings of the Mass. Constitutional Convention whose meetings he attended in 1788, and it was largely due to Belknap's concern for the preservation of the legal and documentary materials for the writing of future histories of America that the Massachusetts Historical Society was founded in 1791. Until his death on Jun. 20, 1798, Belknap contributed to the growth of the society's membership and physical facilities, and apart from his own achievements as a historian and writer, the Massachusetts Historical Society remains his most significant legacy.

Critical Appraisal: Alexis de Tocqueville asserted that "the reader will find more strength of thought in Belknap than in any other American historian." The breadth of scope and the meticulous sense of detail found throughout Belknap's *The History of New-Hampshire* underscore the aptness of de Tocqueville's remark. The history traces the course of northerly coastal settlement from Plymouth, Mass., to Dover and Portsmouth, N.H., and of inland settlement from Haverhill, Mass., northward. Belknap's narrative pattern is artfully concentric: we observe the way in which events in Boston and the larger centers generate their ramifications in remote settlements. His account, for example, of the excesses of Sir Edmund Andros in 1686-1687 is particularly well detailed and probably furnished Nathaniel Hawthorne with some of the material for his fictional treatment of these events in "The Gray Champion."

With the completion of the history's third and final volume, Belknap turned his hand to the writing of satirical history. *The Foresters* is a satirical novel written in the spirit of Swift's *Gulliver's Travels*. Although it stands outside the "realistic" tradition of Defoe and Fielding, *The Foresters* nevertheless contributes to an American tradition of fantasy narrative that may be said to begin with Joseph Morgan's (q.v.) *The History of the Kingdom of Basaruah*, and that points toward the "fantastical history" of Hawthorne's "The Earth's Holocaust" and "The Celestial Railroad."

Suggested Readings: CCNE; DAB; Sprague (VIII, 73-83). *See also* Alice M. Baldwin, *The New England Clergy and the American Revolution* (1958); John Spencer

Bassett, *The Middle Group of American Historians* (1917); Michael D. Bell, *Hawthorne and the Historical Romance of New England* (1971); Sidney Kaplan, *"The History of New Hampshire:* Jeremy Belknap as Literary Craftsman," WMQ, 21 (1964), 18-39; George B. Kirsch, *Jeremy Belknap: A Biography* (1982); Jane Belknap Marcou, *Life of Jeremy Belknap* (1847).

Lewis A. Turlish
Bates College

JOSEPH BELLAMY (1719-1790)

Works: *Early Piety Recommended* (1748); *True Religion Delineated* (1750); *The Great Evil of Sin* (1753); *The Law, Our School-Master* (c. 1756); *A Letter to the Reverend Author of the Winter Evening Conversation* (1758); *Sermons upon . . . the Divinity of Christ, the Millennium, the Wisdom of God in the Permission of Sin* (1758); *Theron, Paulinus, and Aspasio* (1759); *A Letter to Scripturista* (1760); *The Wisdom of God* (1760); *An Essay on the Nature and Glory of the Gospel* (1762); *Sermon Delivered Before the General Assembly* (1762); *A Blow at the Root of the Refined Antinomianism* (1763); *Remarks on the Rev'd Mr. Croswell's Letter to the Rev. Mr. Cumming* (1763); *The Half-Way Covenant: A Dialogue* (1769); *The Inconsistence of Renouncing the Half-Way Covenant* (1769); *That There Is but One Covenant* (1769); *A Careful and Strict Examination of the External Covenant* (1770); *The Sacramental Controversy* (1770); *Family Religion* (n.d.).

Biography: Born in Cheshire, Conn., in 1719, Joseph Bellamy graduated from Yale in 1735. Shortly thereafter, he experienced conversion and began studying for the Congregational ministry. In 1736 he made a pilgrimage to the new spiritual hub of New Eng., Northampton, Mass., where he boarded with Jonathan Edwards's (q.v.) family and studied theology under the leader of the "frontier revival" of the mid-1730s. His residency in Northampton, although lasting only several months, inspired his later efforts as an Edwardsian theologian, teacher, and revivalist. Licensed to preach in 1737, Bellamy was called to Bethlehem, Conn., the following year and permanently installed as minister in 1740. During the Great Awakening, Bellamy became a successful itinerant revivalist who, with important theological publications in the 1750s, achieved widespread recognition as a leading disciple of Jonathan Edwards. As a result, clerical aspirants began to make their way to Bellamy's western Conn. manse, and in the second half of the eighteenth century, Bellamy trained approximately sixty ministers, a record unsurpassed during that period. Bellamy remained with his Bethlehem Church until his death in 1790. During his fifty-year pastorate, he came to be known as the "pope of Litchfield County."

Critical Appraisal: Although not a highly original thinker, Joseph Bellamy was a leader of the New Divinity, the school of theology that grew from the teachings of Jonathan Edwards. Bellamy's writings were part of the "pamphlet warfare" that resulted from the religious controversies of the Great Awakening. In his published treatises, essays, sermons, and dialogues, Bellamy upheld but also modified and popularized Edwards's thought.

Bellamy's most important work, *True Religion Delineated*, was the first major theological volume published by a follower of Edwards. Although it drew heavily on Edwards's comprehensive work on *Religious Affections* (1744), *True Religion* was written "not for the learned and polite but for the common people." Moreover, Bellamy's work altered Edwards's thought in important ways. Specifically, he portrayed God as a benevolent moral governor, not as the wrathful, arbitrary Deity of traditional Calvinism. Furthermore, Bellamy compromised the Calvinist idea of a limited atonement, arguing that the Moral Governor of the universe was too benevolent to restrict salvation to a small portion of the human race.

In a *Sermon on the Millennium* (1758), Bellamy developed his belief that the benefits of Christ's sacrificial death were far from limited to a small group of elect saints. Like so many of his contemporaries, Bellamy was fascinated by population growth, particularly the high rate of increase in mideighteenth-century New Eng. Assuming that the rate of growth would continue through the millennium, the 1,000-year reign of Christ on earth, which he believed imminent, Bellamy provided a chart intended to illustrate that most of the world's population was yet to be born. Bellamy granted, for the sake of argument, that even if all members of the human race who lived before the millennium suffered damnation, population growth during the 1,000-year earthly reign of Christ would still ensure a general atonement: "That is, above 17,000 would be saved, to one lost; which was the point to be proved. Therefore, nothing hinders, but that the greatest part of mankind may yet be saved, if God so pleases."

Bellamy's thought in the 1750s expresses the kind of millennial optimism that the Great Awakening stimulated a decade earlier. *True Religion Delineated*, *Sermon on the Millennium*, and other Bellamy works from this period also disclose the beginnings of the liberalization of Edwardsianism—what has been described as the New Divinity movement's incorporation of eighteenth-century rationalism and humanism into Edwards's thought, foreshadowing the watered-down Calvinism of the nineteenth century.

In addition to his important alterations of Edwards's thought and to his success as a teacher of clerical aspirants, Bellamy made other contributions to New Eng. Congregationalism in general and the New Divinity movement in particular. He was one of the outstanding evangelical preachers of mideighteenth-century New Eng. and was frequently compared with Edwards and even with the famous English revivalist George Whitefield (q.v.). Bellamy was also a leading advocate of church reform. Between 1769 and 1770, he published a series of dialogues and essays urging the abandonment of the Half-Way Covenant, the practice of offering baptism and partial church membership to individuals who had not experienced conversion. Bellamy's *Dialogues on the Half-Way Covenant* are especially noteworthy, for they conveyed Edwards's ecclesiastical ideas in a popular literary form—as a debate between a minister and a parishioner.

Theologian, church reformer, teacher, and revivalist, Bellamy stands as one of the clerical luminaries of eighteenth-century New Eng. His writings contributed to a shift away from Edwards's God-centered Calvinism toward the more humanistic Calvinism that came to dominate nineteenth-century America.

Suggested Readings: CCNE; DAB; Dexter (I, 523-529); Sprague (I, 404-412); T₂. *See also* Glenn P. Anderson, "Joseph Bellamy: The Man and His Work" (Ph.D. diss., Boston University, 1971); Tyron Edwards, "Memoir of His Life and Character" in *The Works of Joseph Bellamy*, 2 vols. (1850), I, iii-lxv; Percy Coe Eggleston, *A Man of Bethlehem: Joseph Bellamy, D.D., and His Divinity School* (1908); Joseph Haroutunian, *Piety Versus Moralism: The Passing of the New England Theology* (1932).

Joseph Conforti
Rhode Island College

JOSEPH GROVE JOHN BEND (c. 1762-1812)

Works: *A Discourse Delivered in Christ-Church, Baltimore* (1798).

Biography: A Christian concern for souls and apprehension over the welfare of others drove Bend at what must have been a furious pace, cutting his life short but giving us ample testimony of the extent of his duties as organizer, editor, writer, preacher, and pastor. According to an 1852 issue of *Church Times*, Bend had left New York City, where he was born sometime around 1762, for a Classical and business education in the Barbados. After completing his education, Bend returned to New York City as minister of the united parish of St. Peter's and Christ Church. In 1791 Bend took a position as minister at St. Paul's in Baltimore, where he served until 1807. Among the works by Bend on deposit in the Maryland Historical Society are some 472 sermons, written over a reported period of twenty-one years, and hundreds of letters.

Like Thomas Chase (q.v.) of St. Paul's, Bend was jealous of his liberties of doctrine and of form. In a letter dated Feb. 28, 1809, for example, he feared the massacre of family and congregation by rival parties; yet through all of his stressful career, he taught that Christianity was always the "spring of spiritual joy." The father of two sons and a daughter, Bend was twice married. He died in 1812, at the age of 50.

Critical Appraisal: According to one biographer, the Rev. Joseph Bend "set a standard of worship" and of "liturgical pattern" that was maintained by successive rectors at St. Paul's. As a result of Bend's example, said F. W. Kates, the rectors at St. Paul's have believed "both in the frequency of services" and in the "dignity, beauty, and reverence" of their performance. Certainly, it may be said that in the writing of his sermons, Bend exhibited qualities of beauty, dignity, and reverence, qualities evident in the portrait of Bend printed on page seventy-three of the Maryland Historical Society's *Four Generations of Commis-sions*, where the controlled stress in the character of the Rev. Joseph Bend attracts the viewer to the visionary intentness of his eyes and to mouth and chin, moderately rugged, with lips pursed in Stoic apprehension and Christian con-cern. A fine literary craftsman, Bend knew well how to put the thoughts and feelings of doctrine into appealing forms.

Bend's *Discourse Delivered in Christ-Church, Baltimore*, about a month after the death by drowning of its subject, Charles H. Wilmans, is one of the few published works by Bend, but when compared with his many unpublished ser-mons, it is seen as an epitome of a substantial talent that regularly applies good homiletic strategy through the traditional framework of text with exposition, doctrine, and applications. Bend's basic technique takes the listener through the fear of death in David (I Samuel 20:3), to the fearful unexpectedness of death in life generally, to the particular death occasioning the text, and to the doctrine of the hope of heaven through good works motivated by a faith in the Lord, "the first-born." Throughout the *Discourse*, Bend skillfully uses metaphor and rhythm, seldom falling into a harsh note or cliché.

Suggested Readings: Sprague (V, 353-355). *See also* Rev. Ethan Allen, *Clergy in Maryland of the Protestant Episcopal Church* (1860), p. 20; Francis F. Beirne, *St. Paul's Parish Baltimore: A Chronicle of the Mother Church* (1967), pp. 57-58; "Joseph Bend" [*Church Times*, c. Oct. 31] 1852 (article attributed either to Hugh Davey Evans or to Rev. Ethan Allen); F. W. Kates, *Bridge Across Four Centuries: The Clergy of St. Paul's* (1957), pp. 14-15, 21-23.

Fred R. MacFadden
Coppin State College

ANTHONY BENEZET (1713-1784)

Works: *An Epistle of Caution and Advice* (1754); *Observations on...In-slaving* (1759); *Extract of the Memorial* (1760); *Short Account of That Part of Africa* (1762); *Caution and Warning* (1766); *Thoughts on the Nature of War* (1766); *Serious Considerations* (1769); *Some Serious and Awful Considerations* (1769); *Some Historical Account of Guinea* (1771); *Collection of Religious Tracts* (1773); *Extract of a Letter Wrote by a Pious Person* (1773); *Mighty Destroyer Displayed* (1774); *Extract of a Letter Wrote by the Earl of Essex* (1775); *Remarks on...Bad Effects of Spirituous Liquors* (1775); *Serious Reflections* (1775); *Penn-sylvania Spelling Book* (1776); *A First Book for Children* (1778); *Some General Maxims* (1778); *Some Necessary Remarks* (1778); *Some Observations Relating* (1778); *Essay Towards the Most Easy Introduction to...Grammar* (1779); *Ex-tract from a Treatise* (1780); *Extracts from Different Authors* (1780); *Plain Path* (1780); *Short Account of the People Called Quakers* (1780); *Notes on the Slave Trade* (1781); *Short Observations on Slavery* (1781); *Plainness and Innocent*

Simplicity (1782); *Branntewein* (1783); *Case of Our Fellow Creatures* (1783); *Serious Address* (1783); *In the Life of the Lady Elizabeth Hastings* (1784); *Letter* (to Raynal; 1785); *Mite Cast* (1785); *Some Observations on the. . .Indian Natives* (1784).

Biography: Anthony Benezet, the son of Jean Étienne and Judith Benezet, was born into a family of French Huguenots at St. Quentin, Picardy, on Jan. 31, 1713. Fleeing religious persecution, the Benezets left Fr. for Hol. when Anthony was 2. They soon immigrated to Eng., however, and in 1731 the large family removed to Philadelphia, where the young man, with little formal schooling, was expected to join his father and three brothers in a mercantile career. At an early age, he joined the Society of Friends, and on May 13, 1736, Benezet married a Quaker, Joyce Marriot of Burlington, N.J. He abandoned business in 1739, became a schoolmaster at Germantown, and three years later accepted a position at the Friends' William Penn Charter School, Philadelphia. Except for a short period in the 1750s, when he managed the Pennsylvania Hospital, Benezet spent the remainder of his life as a Quaker teacher. In 1750 he founded a school for poor blacks in his home, and between 1754 and 1782, he also operated a school for girls.

In 1766 bad health forced Benezet into temporary retirement at Burlington, N.J., where he hoped to write for some of his numerous causes: the abolition of slavery, educational reform, pacifism, the relief of Nova Scotia Acadians exiled in Philadelphia, temperance, justice for Indians, and Christianity. But the next year he was back at his girls' school. Charitable activities, pamphleteering, a lending library at his home, and a heavy correspondence with other colonies and Europe permitted him no leisure. In 1775 he founded America's first antislavery society, and he had already taken on the duties of a Quaker elder. He resigned from the girls' school in 1782 to teach full time at his school for Negroes, which he moved to his house on Chestnut Street. Benezet died there, childless, on May 3, 1784, leaving nearly all he had, upon his widow's death, for the education of blacks and Indians.

Critical Appraisal: "Who could have lived a month in Philadelphia without knowing Anthony Benezet!" wrote Barbé Marbois, a French diplomat during the American Revolution. Marbois added that this Quaker "carries his love of humanity to the point of madness." For more than forty years, Benezet was the conscience of America, and his tracts, letters, and pamphlets addressed to various injustices were distributed even to its remote villages. A friend and companion of John Woolman (q.v.), one of the first Quakers to declare war on slavery, Benezet joined him in his mission in 1750 and carried on alone when the younger man died. His first antislavery tract, *An Epistle of Caution and Advice* (1750), was prepared to influence the yearly meeting of the Society of Friends, for his duty then, as he saw it, was to convince the society to repudiate the practice, which they did in 1758.

Benezet's best-known pamphlet is *A Caution and a Warning to Great Britain on the Calamitous State of the Enslaved Negroes* (1766), which the Quakers sent to London in 2,000 copies and distributed throughout America. In this work, as in those that followed, Benezet wrote with sorrow and disbelief but seldom in anger, for he did not wish to antagonize his readers. The subject hinted at in the title was the danger for whites (and the opportunity for blacks) that lay in a slave rebellion, but Benezet did not emphasize this possibility. His goals were to show that blacks were "industrious, humane, sociable people" who did not deserve their brutal treatment and that the slave trade to the Western Hemisphere should be stopped immediately as a first step towards eradicating the evil itself.

In 1771 Benezet published a second important and pathfinding work on slavery. Titled *Some Historical Account of Guinea*, the book-length pamphlet describes the civilization that existed in Africa and contains a wealth of documented detail on the horrors of the slave trade. In his *Short Observations on Slavery* (1781), Benezet could say with pride, backed by years of experience at his school for poor Negroes, that "the notion entertained by some, that the Blacks are inferior to the whites in their capacities is a vulgar prejudice" designed to relieve the consciences of those who owned or trafficked in human bodies. Between 1754 and his death, Benezet published more than ten pamphlets and tracts on slavery. His continuing influence on the legislatures of various colonies, including Pa., was considerable, and his appeal through petitions, tracts, letters, pamphlets, and books was equally strong in Europe. For example, he influenced the barrister Granville Sharp, who argued the famous *Somerset* case (1772), which put an end to slavery in Eng. He also influenced Thomas Clarkson, who worked successfully with others for the suppression of the slave trade in the British Empire (1807). Benezet helped persuade the Methodist leader John Wesley and also Benjamin Rush (q.v.) of Philadelphia to write in his cause.

Because one of Benezet's first concerns was the abolition of slavery, his writings in other areas are not as well known. In the field of education, his life's career, he prepared several innovative primers, spelling books, and a simplified grammar (1779) that proceeded on the novel assumption that English could be taught successfully without Latin as a base. In the 1770s he also prepared three tracts against the use of alcohol, the most important being *The Mighty Destroyer Displayed* (1774). This work stimulated his friend Benjamin Rush to initiate his own campaign against the immoderate use of spirits. During both the French and Indian War and the American Revolution, Benezet published pacifist pamphlets that were received in good humor by friends who opposed his views. Benezet also wrote a sympathetic essay on the plight of the Indians of western Pa., whom he had championed since 1755. *Some Observations on the Situation, Disposition and Character of the Indian Natives of This Continent* (1784) sought to do for the Indians what he tried to do for blacks: to humanize them, to show that they originally possessed a culture and a way of life that was valuable. As always, Benezet appealed basically to the reader's sense of shame and religious principles.

Benezet's character and piety are best displayed in his religious tracts, the most informative being *A Short Account of the People Called Quakers: Their Rise, Religious Principles and Settlement in America* (1780). In 1778 he described himself as "small, old and ugly," but when this gentle man died in 1784 the city of Philadelphia turned out for the largest funeral it had ever seen.

Suggested Readings: DAB; DARB; DNB; LHUS. *See also* Wilson Armistead, *Memoirs of Anthony Benezet* (rev. 1859); George S. Brookes, *Friend Anthony Benezet* (1937); Amelia M. Gummere, ed., Introduction, *The Journals and Essays of John Woolman* (1922); Marquis de Chastellux, *Travels in North-America* (1787), pp. 278 ff.; Roberts Vaux, *Memoirs of the Life of Anthony Benezet* (1817); Arthur Zilversmit, *The First Emancipation* (1967), pp. 74-75, 85-93.

A. R. Riggs
McGill University

GEORGE BERKELEY (1685-1753)

Works: *Description of the Cave of Dunmore* (w. 1706; pub. 1871); *Arithmetica* (1707); *Of Infinities* (w. 1707; pub. 1901); *Miscellanea Mathematica* (1707); *Philosophical Commentaries* (w. 1707-1708; pub. 1871); *On Revelation* (w. 1708; pub. 1871); *Essay Towards a New Theory of Vision* (1709); *Let Your Zeal Be According to Knowledge* (w. c. 1710; pub. 1932); *Treatise Concerning the Principles of Human Knowledge* (1710); *Passive Obedience* (1712); *Dialogues Between Hylas and Philonous* (1713); Essays in *Guardian* (1713); *On Charity* (w. 1714; pub. 1871); *On the Mission of Christ* (w. 1714; pub. 1871); *Advice to the Tories* (1715); *Journals of Travels in Italy* (w. 1717-1718; pub. 1871); *Observations on Eruptions from Mount Vesuvio* (1717); *De Motu* (1721); *Essay Toward Preventing the Ruin of Great Britain* (1721); *Proposal for Churches in Our Foreign Plantations* (1724); *On the Mystery of Godliness* (w. c. 1729-1731; pub. 1936); *Alciphron: the Minute Philosopher* (1732); *On Eternal Life* (w. c. 1732; pub. 1871); *Sermon Before Society for Propagation of the Gospel* (1732); *The Theory of Vision* (1733); *The Analyst* (1734); *A Defence of Free-Thinking in Mathematics* (1735); *The Querist* (1735-1737); *Reasons for Not Replying to Mr. Walton* (1735); *On Confirmation* (w. c. 1737; pub. 1871); *Letter on a National Bank* (1737); *Primary Visitation Charge* (w. c. 1737; pub. 1871); *A Discourse Addressed to Magistrates* (1738); *The Irish Patriot* (c. 1738); *Directions for Making and Using Tar-Water* (1744); *Further Directions for Making and Using Tar-Water* (1744); *Siris: Concerning the Virtues of Tar-Water* (1744); *On "SIRIS" and Its Enemies* (1744); *To T. P., Esq.* (1744); *An Abstract from Dr. Berkeley's Treatise on Tar-Water* (1745); *The Bishop of Cloyne's Letter to His Clergy* (1745); *The Bishop of Cloyne's Letter to the Roman Catholics* (1745); *Letters on the Militia* (1745-1746); *On the Disputes about Tar-Water* (1746); *A Second Letter to Thomas Prior on Tar-Water* (1746); *A Letter on the Petrifactions of Lough Neagh* (1747); *Letter to Thomas Prior Concerning Usefulness of Tar-Water in the Plague* (1747); *Two Letters on the Benefit of Tar-Water in Fevers* (1747); *A Word to the Wise* (1749); *Maxims Concerning Patriotism* (1750);

Observations Concerning Earthquakes (1750); *Sermon: Thy Will Be Done* (w. 1751; pub. 1931); *Miscellany* (1752); A. Luce and T. Jessop, eds., *Works* (1948-1957).

Biography: George Berkeley was born at Kilkenny, Ire., in 1685. After attendance at Kilkenny College, he entered Trinity College, Dublin, where, after graduating in 1704, he stayed on as lecturer and later dean. The publication of his *Essay Towards a New Theory of Vision* (1707) and *Treatise Concerning the Principles of Human Knowledge* (1710) established his reputation as an original philosophical thinker, and his responses to critics (e.g., *Dialogues Between Hylas and Philonous*, 1713) revealed his skills as a controversialist. In 1713 he visited London, where he became friends with Swift, Steele, Pope, Addison, and Arbuthnot, and in the ensuing eight years he traveled extensively, both in G.B. and on the Continent. In 1721 he returned to Ire., where, after receiving his divinity degree from Trinity, he became dean of Dromore (1721) and then dean of Derry (1724).

About this period, Berkeley conceived of the idea of establishing a college in Bermuda to train clergy and scholars. By 1728 the proposed college (with Berkeley as its president) had been granted a charter, and he set out for the New World. While waiting for Parliament to vote financial backing, Berkeley came to Providence, R.I. There he spent almost three years, writing (most notably *Alciphron*), preaching, and waiting for the needed funds. In 1731 it became clear that they would not be forthcoming, so Berkeley gave up his dream of a college and returned to London. In 1734, after his appointment as bishop of Cloyne, he busied himself not only with episcopal duties, but with numerous writings on philosophy, Irish public affairs, and questions of health and hygiene. In this latter connection, his private experiments in America had convinced him of tar-water's medicinal efficacy, and beginning with *Siris* (1744), he published a series of tracts arguing its virtues and answering skeptics. By 1752 age and infirmities led Berkeley to retire. While visiting his son at Oxford in 1753, he died.

Critical Appraisal: Berkeley stands forth as one of the most important of British and American philosophers. His theory of vision, his immaterialism, and his philosophies of metaphysics, nature, and mathematics were all influential, both in adherents they won and the opposition positions they helped to inspire. Building upon elements in Descartes, Spinoza, Locke, Malebranche, and Bayle, Berkeley discarded traditional ideas of material substance and promulgated a view in which the objects perceived by the mind do not represent a reality outside the mind, but rather a reality that exists entirely in the mind itself. In general, Berkeley's thought is built upon a bedrock of piety: by coming to terms with the new philosophy that was outmoding traditional scholasticism, he sought to combat what he considered the pernicious doctrines of skepticism, Deism, and atheism that had become intellectually fashionable in his day. Although he was accused by his opponents of arguing that objects of sense have only an intermittent existence, coming into being only when perceived, he specifically denied such opinions. He saw himself as a philosophical empiricist and exponent of common sense—hence his rejection of the doctrine of abstract ideas, a rejection embraced by the empirical school of English philosophers, one of whose leaders, John Stuart Mill, acknowledged the centrality to his own thought of Berkeley's "first-rate philosophical discoveries."

Beyond his stature as a philosopher, Berkeley must be counted as a courageous pioneer of social concern in Ire., particularly after his installation there as bishop of Cloyne. In his numerous writings on Irish questions, Berkeley addressed himself not only, as one might expect from a clergyman, to the moral and ethical welfare of the nation, but likewise to its citizens' material well-being. Like his friend Swift, he was an active pamphleteer for economic and monetary reforms to alleviate Irish poverty. Even his latter-day enthusiasm for tar-water as a panacea, however medically dubious it seems today, derived from the same humanitarian solicitude that led him to work so hard on behalf of relief for his suffering countrymen.

In literary terms, Berkeley belongs in the front rank of the great prose stylists of the Augustan Age. As a philosopher and writer on ecclesiastical doctrine, he frequently dealt with subjects of an abstruse and difficult nature, but his prose—straightforward, concrete, and expressive is a model of expository grace and clarity. This is particularly true in such works as the *Dialogues Between Hylas and Philonous* and *Alciphron*, where the informality of the dialogue form gives Berkeley the perfect vehicle for the conversational grace and argumentative resourcefulness that characterize his best work.

Berkeley's sojourn in America came when his powers and reputation were at their height. His well-known "Verses on the Prospect of Planting Arts and Learning in America" reveal his clear conviction that the New World would be the site of a new cultural golden age. In furtherance of that conviction, he made Whitehall (his house in R.I.) something of an intellectual gathering place for the clergymen, scholars, and writers of R.I. and Conn. He likewise helped to found a philosophical society in Newport, and he was active in preaching to various congregations in the area. Although his dreams of a missionary college in Bermuda never came to pass, he made a significant contribution to higher education in the New World. While in residence at Newport, he became close friends with Samuel Johnson (q.v.) who subscribed to much of Berkeley's immaterialist philosophy and who helped disseminate his ideas in the colonies. To such intellectual bequests should be added the more tangible gifts Berkeley made to American colleges, especially Yale, to which he signed over his house and ninety-six-acre farm, as well as a collection of books numbering close to 1,000. He also donated a sizeable collection of books to Harvard, where he preached his final sermon before embarking on his return trip to London.

Suggested Readings: CCNE; DNB; Sprague (V, 63-69); T$_2$. *See also* D. Armstrong, *Berkeley's Theory of Vision* (1960); H. Bracken, *The Early Reception of Berkeley's Immaterialism* (1959); A. Brayton, *George Berkeley in Newport* (1954); Edwin Gaustad, *George Berkeley in America* (1979); G. Hicks, *Berkeley* (1932); G. Johnston,

The Development of Berkeley's Philosophy (1923); A. Luce, *Berkeley's Immaterialism* (1945); idem, *Berkeley and Malebranche* (1934); idem, *The Life of George Berkeley* (1948); S. Pepper, K. Aschenbrenner, and B. Mates, eds., *George Berkeley* (1957); B. Rand, *Berkeley's American Sojourn* (1932); A. Ritchie, *George Berkeley: A Reappraisal* (1967); E. Sillem, *George Berkeley and the Proofs for the Existence of God* (1957); W. Steinkraus, ed., *New Studies in Berkeley's Philosophy* (1966); I. Tipton, *Berkeley: The Philosophy of Immaterialism* (1974); G. Warnock, *Berkeley* (1953); J. Wild, *George Berkeley: A Study of His Life and Philosophy* (1936); J. Wisdom, *The Unconscious Origin of Berkeley's Philosophy* (1953).

Richard I. Cook
Kent State University

SIR WILLIAM BERKELEY (c. 1608-1677)

Works: *The Lost Lady* (1637); *Cornelia* (1662); *A Discourse and View of Virginia* (1663).

Biography: Sir William Berkeley, born sometime around 1608 into a distinguished and influential family, established himself early as knowledgeable and dynamic. In 1629, not long after receiving an M.A. at Oxford, he was appointed one of the royal commissioners for Can., where he earned repute for his capabilities and courtly polish. Returning to Eng., he wrote his first play *The Lost Lady*, which had several productions, including one at court, before it was published in 1637. He was appointed governor of Va. in 1642, a post he honored and retained, except for one intermission, for the rest of his life.

In his first decade as governor, he was in high esteem, a wise administrator with an ardent vision of making Va. a microcosm of Eng. at its best, a vision he turned into action on his own estate, Green Springs. There Berkeley, although long a bachelor, entertained with grace and generosity, and he set a laudable example for other landowners in diversifying the crops he cultivated, perceiving early that tobacco as the single-grown crop would limit the colony's potentials. In 1644 he courageously led the routing of Indian savages after the massacre of white settlers, and he established a peace treaty that under his firm leadership lasted more years than most. Perhaps his most far-reaching accomplishment, however, was his persuasive offer of Va. as a haven for "cavaliers" fleeing Cromwell. Families like the Lees (Arthur, Charles, Henry, and Richard Henry Lee [q.v.]), Carters (Landon Carter [q.v.]), Randolphs (Edmund Randolph [q.v.]), Masons (George Mason [q.v.]), and later the Byrds (William Byrd of Westover [q.v.]), warmly encouraged by Berkeley, settled into their dynasties and engendered a culture that would strongly influence American history.

In 1652, when Cromwell wrested control of Va., Berkeley was deposed, but his petition to remain in Va. was granted. Eight years later, with the restoration of Charles II, Berkeley was once again appointed Va.'s governor. In this second term, Berkeley's strengths became edged with hardness, and the more he was blamed for the colony's problems, over many of which, like the plagues, the Dutch War, and the avarice of the king, he had no control, the more he turned in his advancing age into "William the Testy."

History has not been kind to Berkeley, remembering him for his excesses but seldom balancing them with his staunch leadership. One of these excesses is his unfortunate—and inaccurate—letter "thanking God" there was no free education in Va. Yet Berkeley's letter probably has done more to stimulate research establishing the creditable literacy of the colony and its active concern for learning than a more tempered writing might have done. Later, in references to the 1676 episode known as Bacon's Rebellion, historians tended to romanticize Nathaniel Bacon (q.v.) as a folk hero sowing seeds of democracy, but they cast Berkeley in the role of demagogue. When the facts are weighed, both views need adjustment. After his excessive revenge following the rebellion, Berkeley was called to Eng. to appear before the king. Sir William Berkeley set sail in May 1677, became very ill upon landing in Eng., and died in early Jul. before his audience was granted.

Critical Appraisal: Vigorous and dramatic in his actions, these characteristics also permeate the writings of Sir William Berkeley. His first published writing is a play written in 1637, *The Lost Lady*, a tragicomedy in five acts. Throughout the play, there is stately cadence to the blank verse, with a frequent heightening in dramatic intensity, as when the protagonist exclaims: "What furies govern man! we hazard all / Our lives and fortune to gain hated memories; / And in the search of virtue tremble at shadows." Dramatic, too, are the contrasts in characters and moods, with some scenes of worldly wit regarding the differing ways of a man with a wife or a wench. The play returned to the stage after the Restoration, joined for a time in 1662 by Berkeley's second play *Cornelia*, which is thought to be the first American play produced in London. It is interesting to speculate that Berkeley wrote *Cornelia* during his "internment" at Green Springs and that he took the play with him when he went to London in 1661 as a colonial agent for Va. There he vigorously defended Va.'s rights to free trade and extolled the colony's many advantages.

His major Va. writing, *A Discourse and View of Virginia* (1663), is a polished and eloquent treatise. He praised Va.'s many "natural helps" that make it a "glorious and flourishing country" and presented in well-ordered sequence its many natural resources and potentials. He ardently pleaded the case for many commodities capable of being reaped, such as flax, cotton oats, and all sorts of fruits that "taste of a perfection above English varieties." Boldly, then, he bared his abiding concern for Va.'s being caught in the king's greed. "The vicious, ruinous plant of Tobacco I would not name but that it brings more money to the Crown than all the Islands in America." The *Discourse* is climaxed by a spirited call to embark on an adventure of high worth in Va. "A younger brother [can] erect a flourishing family in a new world; and adde strength, wealth, and honour to his native country."

Berkeley's writing style bespeaks his colorful personality even in official documents. Concerning his struggle over a treaty with Lord Baltimore, he related that in a perilous hurricane "in the depth of winter. . .to the very great hazard" of his health he did "perform" the journey for negotiation. Later, writing of the injustices to Va. of the Navigation Act, he asserted that "we should not repine" if the act really served Eng. but "on my soul, it is contrary to the interests of his Majesty as well as to the welfare of his subjects of Virginia." The dramatic vigour of Berkeley's language carries its pungency even in the official report concerning Bacon's Rebellion. To cite only one instance, Berkeley "bared his breast and cried to Bacon: 'Here, shoot me, fore God fair mark.' "

A well-educated aristocrat, Sir William Berkeley was also a playwright, a writer of polished grace with a creditable dramatic skill, and a royal governor. He was an often vigorous, frequently eloquent, and always literate writer.

Suggested Readings: DAB; DNB; LHUS; T_1. *See also* Richard Beale Davis, *Intellectual Life in the Colonial South, 1585-1763*, vol. III (1978); Howard Mumford Jones, *The Literature of Virginia in the Seventeenth Century*, 2nd ed. (1968); Richard Lee Morton, *Colonial Virginia*, vol. I (1960); Thomas Stewart, ed., Introduction, *A Discourse and View of Virginia* by Sir William Berkeley (1914). For Berkeley's *The Lost Lady*, see W. Carew Hazlitt, ed., *Old English Plays*, vol. 12, 4th ed. (1875), pp. 537-627.

Leota Harris Hirsch
Rosary College

JOHN BEVERIDGE (1703-1767)

Works: *In Obitum Magnae Spei Juvenis* (1757); *Epistolae Familiares* (1765).

Biography: John Beveridge was born in Scot. in 1703. He taught Latin in Edinburgh, where his pupils included the blind poet Thomas Blacklock. Between 1739 (by which time he had married and fathered two children) and 1752, he composed many of the Latin verse letters to friends and patrons later included in his collection. In 1752 Beveridge immigrated to Casco Bay, Me., where he remained for five years, but Indian attacks and the harsh climate eventually drove him to Hartford, Conn., where he successfully conducted a Latin grammar school. In 1758 the trustees of the College of Philadelphia appointed Beveridge master of Latin and professor of languages, and although his duties as schoolmaster allowed him little time for writing, in 1762 he did prepare a new edition of *Whittenhall's Latin Grammar* (memorable for its many errors—151 in 137 pages—and for the prose satire by Francis Hopkinson [q.v.] occasioned by these mistakes). Although Beveridge attempted to win the favor of John Penn and the aid of Benjamin Franklin (q.v.) in promoting his book, he was unsuccessful. As Deborah Franklin noted in a letter to her husband, "the good Mr. Beverridg" died on Jun. 26, 1767.

Critical Appraisal: John Beveridge's main claim to literary eminence was his position as the author of the last pre-Revolutionary War miscellany in

Philadelphia and as Philadelphia's most prominent eighteenth-century Latin poet. The introduction to *Epistolae Familiares*, Beveridge's collection of verse, for example, praises him as one who may "Contend with Flaccus on the Roman lyre." Early commentators, although not always sharing this enthusiasm, generally agreed that he was Pa.'s leading Classical poet. That Beveridge knew the language and Latin verse forms seems indisputable. Included in his forty verses are letters in Alcaic and Sapphic stanza, dactylic hexameter, elegiac meter, and First Archilochian, and Beveridge has repeatedly been praised for his "remarkably easy and lively" lines that "imitate the verse of the first of Latin poets in pureness of language and variety of versification."

Nonetheless, Beveridge's poetic achievements are not without their faults and their detractors. Francis Hopkinson, for example, a student of Beveridge's, thought that the poems "bray'd Abuse, foul language & false Grammar." (Beveridge, it should be noted, in turn, answered Hopkinson with a similarly phrased Latin rebuttal to that "dull ass"), and yet another of Beveridge's pupils, Alexander Graydon (q.v.), admitted that his teacher's works were pure and correct but added: "I should doubt their possessing much of the soul of poetry.... 'Tis perhaps too much to expect from a modern, good Latin, good poetry, and good sense all at the same time." Nearly every reader of Beveridge's poetry has expressed reservations about the extravagance of his poetical appeals for favor, in particular his plea to John Penn for a comfortable home and stipend.

The account in the *Pennsylvania Gazette* of Jul. 2, 1767, of Beveridge's funeral service provides a fitting summary of his achievements: he was "justly esteemed by Men of Learning in both Countries for his critical, profound Knowledge, as well as elegant Composition in the Latin Tongue. His Death is a considerable Loss to the Republic of Letters, and a very particular one to the Seminary whereof he was a member."

Suggested Readings: Joshua Fisher, "Some Account of the Early Poets and Poetry of Pennsylvania," *Memoirs of the Historical Society of Pennsylvania*, 2 (1830), 80-81; Alexander Graydon, *Memoirs of a Life Chiefly Passed in Pennsylvania* (1811; rep., 1822), pp. 25-32; Thomas P. Haviland, "Francis Hopkinson and the Grammarians," PMHB, 76 (1952), 63-70; Leo M. Kaiser, "John Beveridge: Latin Poet of Two Worlds," CJ, 58 (1963), 215-223; Francis H. Williams, "Pennsylvania Poets of the Provincial Period," PMHB, 17 (1893), 27.

Timothy K. Conley
Bradley University

ROBERT BEVERLEY (c. 1673-1722)

Works: *A Ballad Address'd to the Reverend Members of the Convocation* (1704); *The History and Present State of Virginia* (1705, rev. ed. 1722); *An Abridgement of the Public Laws of Virginia* (1722).

Biography: The first native American to write a significant account of a whole colony, Robert Beverley was born about 1673, the son of Maj. Robert Beverley of Middlesex County, Va. An obstreperous, wealthy planter who had come to Va. in 1663 from Yorkshire, Robert Beverley the elder led a turbulent career as a supporter of Governor William Berkeley (q.v.) during Bacon's Rebellion and as the recognized leader of the opposition party to several governors subsequent to Berkeley's administration. After an education in Eng., possibly at Beverley Grammar School in Yorkshire, Robert Beverley the younger served in several clerkships, including clerk of King and Queen County. In 1697 he married the 16-year-old Ursula Byrd, daughter of William Byrd I and sister of William Byrd II of Westover (q.v.). She died giving birth to a son less than a year later and Beverley never remarried.

While in Eng. in 1703, he sent letters home attacking Governor Francis Nicholson and Robert Quarry, surveyor of customs, for what Beverley considered their plans to subvert the liberties of Virginians. This indiscretion provoked Beverley's dismissal from his clerkship in King and Queen County and kept him from obtaining future appointments. With the exception of a term in the Va. House of Burgesses in 1706, Beverley spent the remainder of his life at his family seat of Beverley Park in the frontier region of King and Queen County. A strong believer in moderation and self-sufficiency and a confirmed iconoclast, Beverley purposely lived a simple life with an individualistic disregard for trends and fashions. Through his astute business acumen and voracious appetite for land, Beverley left at his death on Apr. 21, 1722, one of the largest estates in Va.

Critical Appraisal: Robert Beverley's generally accepted literary canon includes only four titles: *A Ballad Address'd to the Reverend Members of the Convocation* (1704), *The History and Present State of Virginia* (1705, 1722), "Mr. Beverley's Acct of Lamhatty" (w. 1707), and *An Abridgement of the Public Laws of Virginia* (1722). The anonymous *Ballad*, printed in London during Beverley's stay there, lampoons seventeen of Governor Francis Nicholson's friends among the Va. clergy who had met in Williamsburg to sign an affidavit against Anglican Commissary the Rev. James Blair (q.v.) during his famous quarrel with Nicholson. Beverley's "Acct of Lamhatty" is a manuscript note on a map drawn by a Creek Indian named Lamhatty describing a journey from Va.'s Blue Ridge Mountains to the Gulf after having escaped from the Shawnees. During the last years of his life, Beverley worked on *An Abridgement of the Public Laws of Virginia* and dedicated the work to Governor Alexander Spotswood (q.v.), the one governor who won Beverley's friendship. Spotswood is praised for preserving the liberties of Virginians, reviving William and Mary College, and extending frontier settlements. The *Abridgement* is a useful, workmanlike manual that appears in many subsequent book inventories of Va. gentlemen. Louis B. Wright edited and suggested Beverley as the author of *An Essay Upon the Government of the English Plantations on the Continent of America* (1701), but subsequent scholarship has ascribed authorship to either Ralph Wormeley or Benjamin Harrison III.

Beverley's significant place in the development of American literature rests upon his *History*, one of the major works of colonial historiography. It is especially valuable as history because of the thoroughness of its first-hand observations, and it has real worth as literature because of its individual and effective plain style. Although his works reveal him to be widely read, Beverley's dedication to simplicity led him deliberately to avoid pedantic displays and to adopt a plain style suited to his material. He stated in his preface to the *History* that "I am an Indian" in the use of language. Indeed, the *History* is more original than anything previously written in Va. and is significant in the development of American ideas, because it is one of the earliest literary works that is self-consciously American in a secular and realistic sense in which the works of Beverley's New Eng. contemporaries never were meant to be. In fact, the predominant quality throughout Beverley's life and his *History* is his patriotic devotion to "my country" Va.

It was in London in 1703 that Beverley's loyalty to Va. prompted him to write the *History* in response to the errors and distortions he found in the manuscript's Va. section intended for John Oldmixon's *The British Empire in America*. Beverley organized his work into four books: Book I, the history of the colony from the first settlers to his own time; Book II, the natural history of the region; Book III, an account of the Indians; Book IV, the present state of the province in government polity and improvement of the land. In its organization, the *History* is reminiscent of earlier promotion tracts and general histories, and the work is an important part of the present-state essay tradition that culminated in Thomas Jefferson's (q.v.) *Notes on the State of Virginia*, a work that was also written in defense of America against European distortions.

The first book of the *History* is the least valuable, for the narrative is sketchy and condensed to an extreme. Beverley does weigh his material, however, and frequently comments on his disagreements with his sources. He is sympathetic with Governor Sir William Berkeley, to whom Robert Beverley the elder had been loyal; however, subsequent governors, especially Thomas Lord Culpepper and Francis Nicholson, received scathing attacks for what Beverley considered their greed and their attempts to subvert the liberties of Virginians. Beverley deleted these attacks in the 1722 edition.

In the second book, based mostly on his own observations, Beverley presented the natural environment of Va. in its "Unimprov'd State, before the English went thither." Here the author exhibited a genuine love of nature, a scientific attitude toward his observations, and a patience in studying animals that make his observations extremely valuable to students of the colonial South. He is, for example, the only colonial Va. historian before Jefferson who devoted considerable attention to animal life. Beverley's treatment of nature places him within the mainstream of southern literature in its expression of joy in the natural world. Unlike his New Eng. counterparts, the southern author focused his attention in a secular way upon his environment as a natural paradise and upon its future potential.

Nowhere in the *History* are Beverley's intellectual curiosity and skills as an observer more evident than in Book III where he described Indian life. He presented an urbane, critical portrait of the Indian based primarily upon careful observation, but with some material borrowed from such previous authors as John Smith (q.v.), Father Louis Hennipen, Louis Armand, and Baron de Lahontan. Beverley not only acknowledged his sources with quotations, but he also pointed out the contradictions between what they said and what he had observed first-hand. Unlike most observers of his day, Beverley portrayed Indians as a people with a culture that has something to offer whites. He, like John Lawson (q.v.) and William Byrd II, supported intermarriage between whites and Indians as a means of ending hostilities, and he commented on the evil effects of European civilization on the primitive Indian. His intellectual curiosity was strong enough that he examined the inside of an Indian house of worship at the risk of his life. He also plied an Indian with hard cider to elicit perhaps the most revealing explanation of aboriginal religion any colonial ever received. Moreover, he soundly criticized slothful colonial whites for wasting and spoiling the natural plenty that the Indians used wisely. All in all, Beverley's accomplishments as an ethnologist have proved invaluable to subsequent scholarship.

The fourth and last book of the *History* treats in two parts the government of the colony and its husbandry and improvements. The first part is a succinct discussion of civil government, religion, the college, and the courts and laws. Chapter XII of the first part, along with all of the second part, may also be taken as colonization propaganda. In this chapter, Beverley painted an attractive picture of the welcome that refugees received in Va., illustrating the welcome by citing William Byrd I's many kindnesses to French Huguenots. In fact, a great deal of the work may be seen as promotional literature, and three editions of the *History* were published in French between 1707 and 1712.

Suggested Readings: DAB; LHUS. *See also* Richard Beale Davis, *Intellectual Life in the Colonial South, 1585-1763*, 3 vols. (1978); Fairfax Harrison, "Robert Beverley, the Historian of Virginia," VMHB, 36 (1928), 333-344; Wilbur R. Jacobs, *Dispossessing the American Indian* (1972), pp. 114, 116-118, 125; Leo Marx, *The Machine in the Garden* (1964) pp. 75-88; W. G. Stanard, "Major Robert Beverley and His Descendents," VMHB, 2 (1894-1895), 405-413; 3 (1895-1896), 47-52, 169-176, 261-271, 383-392; Louis B. Wright, "Beverley's *History . . . of Virginia* (1705), a Neglected Classic," WMQ, 3rd ser., 1 (1944), 49-64; idem, *First Gentlemen of Virginia* (1964), pp. 286-311; idem, Introduction, *The History and Present State of Virginia*, by Robert Beverley (1705).

Homer D. Kemp
Tennessee Technological University

BARNABAS BIDWELL (1763-1833)

Works: *The Mercenary Match, A Tragedy* (1734); *An Oration on the Death of Roger Newton* (Sept. 2, 1789); *An Oration, Delivered at the Celebration of American Independence, in Stockbridge, July, 1795* (1795); *The Susquehannah*

Title Stated and Examined (1796); *An Address to the People of Massachusetts* (1804); *An Address to the People of Massachusetts* (1805); *A Summary, Historical and Political Review of the Revolution, the Constitution and Government of the United States: An Oration, Delivered at Sheffield, July 4th, 1805* (1806); *Commonwealth of Massachusetts—The Attorney General's Report Respecting Claims for Confiscated Debts* (1808); contributed eleven sketches to *Statistical Account of Upper Canada* (by Robert Gourlay; 1822).

Biography: The son of the Rev. Adonijah Bidwell and Jemima Devotion, Barnabas Bidwell was born in Tyringham, Mass., on Aug. 23, 1763. After receiving an A.B. from Yale College in 1785, Bidwell held a position as tutor at Yale from the fall of 1887 until 1890. His next twenty years were a period of achievement. He married, had two children, opened a law practice in Stockbridge, and gained prominence as an orator and public servant. In elected offices, he served as treasurer of Berkshire County (1791-1810) and in both the Mass. Senate (1801-1805) and the congressional House of Representatives (1805-1807). In Jun. 1807 he was appointed attorney general for the state of Mass. Then as President James Madison (q.v.) was considering him for the U.S. Supreme Court, his life changed abruptly.

In Jun. 1810 a private investigation of his accounts as county treasurer disclosed falsified records for his personal gain to the amount, including due interest, of $10,000. To avoid prosecution for embezzlement, Bidwell fled with his family to Bath, a village north of Lake Ontario in Can., moving to Kingston in about 1820. Unable as an alien to practice law or accept political office, he remained active in public affairs until his death in 1833—a man of culture, agreeable manners, and legal acumen.

Critical Appraisal: As a writer, Bidwell's reputation rests upon several political orations, some sketches, and a play written and published during his senior year at Yale College. Given his success in political life, his powers of oratory must have been effective, and his orations, both in tone and content, seem eternally characteristic of American politics: "The political heresy, that a national debt is a public blessing, is now so effectively exploded that its former believers are disposed to disavow this creed" (*An Address to the People of Massachusetts*, Feb. 1805).

In the annals of American literature, Bidwell is remembered mainly as the author of two dramatic pieces: a dialogue called *The Modern Mistake*, which was given at a meeting on Apr. 3, 1884, of the Brothers of Unity, a Yale debating society of which Bidwell was a member; and *The Mercenary Match, a Tragedy*, written, acted, and published during Bidwell's senior year. Unfortunately, this play has been treated to a certain amount of unwarranted abuse through the frequently quoted comments of William Dunlap who "vividly recollected" the "very pleasant and laugh-provoking tragedy." Although the play does not deserve enthusiastic critical praise, neither does Dunlap's sarcasm provide a fair assessment of it.

A critical appraisal of this play would reflect the usual comments made on the youthful efforts of any dramatist. First, it is basically derivative. Indebtedness to Shakespeare's *The Taming of the Shrew, Macbeth,* and *Julius Caesar* is clear along with suggestions of Aeschylus's *Agamemnon* and George Lilly's adaptation of *Arden of Feresham.* Characteristic of the times, the structure of the play shows the influence of neo-Classical attention to the unities of time, place, and action. There are also the hackneyed sentiments, the stereotyped characters, and the absence of motivated action that haunts most amateur playwrights. That Bidwell realized his limitations is made clear in his epilogue where he admitted that his plot contained "faults of almost every name, / That candour can forgive, or censure blame."

In certain ways, however, Bidwell was too severe. His model was clearly the domestic bourgeois tragedy that enthralled eighteenth-century Europeans and provided them with appropriate moral guidance. Whatever its structural weaknesses, Bidwell's play was the first example of this form in America. The tale of the woman, forced to marry a man she did not love, and then seduced by a villain, strikes a weary note with modern audiences, but with countless variations, it was a popular theme in the theatre throughout the eighteenth and nineteenth centuries. Bidwell also remained consistent with his time by employing a rhetorical and declamatory style. He was a far-from-finished playwright; however, some of his major problems as a playwright appeared in the final act where he destroyed any sympathy he had created for his heroine as well as any perverse admiration one might have felt for the villain. Thus "the miseries of a man and wife, / A simple circumstance of modern life," as he described his work in his prologue, became a melodramatic tangle of improbable actions. Yet many of the poetic lines read smoothly, and there is a forcefulness in his dramatized action. It is unfortunate that extant examples of such early American drama came from the pens of college students, amateur playwrights, and actors trying to produce vehicles for their talents, but the truth is there, and *The Mercenary Match* has more value for the literary historian than for the dramatic critic.

Suggested Readings: DAB; Dexter (IV, 387-390). *See also* Edwin M. Bidwell, *Genealogy of the First Seven Generations of the Bidwell Family in America* (1884); Oral Summer Coad, "An Old American College Play," MLN, 37 (1922), 157-163; William Dunlap, *History of the American Theatre* (1832; rep., 1963), p. 136; Walter J. Meserve, *An Emerging Entertainment: The Drama of the American People to 1828* (1977), pp. 128-129.

Walter J. Meserve
Indiana University

WILLIAM BILLINGS (1746-1800)

Works: *New-England Psalm-Singer* (1770); *Singing Master's Assistant* (1778); *Psalm-Singer's Amusement* (1781); *Peace, an Anthem* (c. 1783); *The American*

Bloody Register (1784); *The Porcupine, Alias the Hedge-Hog: Or, Fox Turned Preacher* (1784); *Suffolk Harmony* (1786); *The Bird and the Lark* (1790); *Anthem for Thanksgiving* (1793); *Continental Harmony* (1794); *Easter Anthem* (1795); *A Vision Experienced by Miss Eliza Thomas* (1800).

Biography: William Billings, born in Boston to William and Elizabeth (Clark) Billings, had little formal education. He conducted singing schools in Boston and nearby communities and supplemented his income through work as a tanner after establishing himself as a compiler, composer, and author. The first American author to apply for a copyright, Billings was also the first, and one of the few, American psalmodists to write original texts. During the 1780s his compositions enjoyed considerable popular and critical esteem. Familiar to southerners and frontiersmen as well as to New Englanders, his works were performed in concert in Boston and Philadelphia and were included in collections by other compilers. In addition, Billings edited the first issue of the *Boston Magazine*, transcribed narratives by two condemned criminals and one religious enthusiast, and is credited with having written a satirical pamphlet. In financial difficulty during the late 1780s, Billings accepted various municipal appointments in Boston. Called by the Rev. William Bentley of Salem "the father of our New England music," Billings died in poverty and was buried in an unmarked grave.

Critical Appraisal: Renowned as one of the first Americans to compose and publish his own music, William Billings was also a compiler and author. Except the textless *Music in Miniature* (1779), his tunebooks are collections of eighteenth-century religious verse, primarily by British poets such as Isaac Watts, Nahum Tate, and Nicholas Brady. A few texts by Americans, among them Mather Byles (q.v.) and Perez Morton (q.v.), also appear in Billings's collections.

As a writer of hymn texts, Billings is noted for the variety of sources, meters, and rhyme patterns he used. In composing texts for anthems, he synthesized passages from the Bible, Anglican prayer book, and work of other poets, skillfully repeating, altering, and adding words and phrases to achieve rhyme, emphasis, and coordination of text and musical setting. Some of his texts are at once religious and nationalistic. "Chester," for example, published as a quatrain in his first book and in a five-stanza version in his second, became a popular rallying song, as did Francis Hopkinson's (q.v.) "Battle of the Kegs," during the Revolution and remained popular throughout the nineteenth century. Another patriotic anthem, "Lamentation over Boston," published in the *Singing Master's Assistant* and perhaps written in collaboration with Samuel Adams (q.v.), opens with a clever paraphrase of Psalm 137 that emphasizes the American response to the British occupation of Boston in 1775-1776: "By the Rivers of Watertown we sat down & wept when we remember'd thee O Boston. . . . Forbid it Lord God that those who have sucked Bostonian Breasts should thirst for American Blood." Similar works in the *Singing Master's Assistant* are "Retrospect," "Columbia," and "Independence," an exuberant development of the theme that "the States" have no "rightful King" but God. "Retrospect," a celebration of the patriots' cause, urged Americans to fight, grieved over their suffering, and closed with a vision of universal peace under God's reign. "Shiloh" dramatized the angels' proclamation of Christ's nativity, and despite its erudition has its homely touches: the shepherds are called "rural swains." Billings's verse, a hybrid of temporal and timeless concerns, elevated and earthy diction, remains accessible and even appealing.

As a prosewriter, Billings is distinguished for his lively and inventive wit. His most ambitious prose work, *The Porcupine, Alias the Hedge-Hog: Or, Fox Turned Preacher* (1784), described by its author as "a burlesque upon them that burlesque the scriptures" and attributed to Billings by nineteenth-century music scholar Alexander Wheelock Thayer, satirized not only hypocritical clergymen but also a number of other offenders, including misers, papists, Calvinists, astrologers, and "Chesterfieldians." The fox's diffuse sermons set vices and follies of Old Testament times cheek by jowl with those of the eighteenth century. Far from subtle, the author's treatment of the misconstruction and translation (read "alteration") of scripture to suit one's purposes is effective and sometimes even amusing.

As an editor of the *Boston Magazine*, Billings offered not only the standard fare of poems, humorous and informative essays, and political news but also an essay titled "On the Seduction of Young Women," a satirical "proof" of transmigration, and "The Life of Sawney Beane," an explicit account of barbaric murders and executions. Apparently disconcerted by Billings's lack of refinement, his publishers dispensed with his services after the first issue, but this setback only encouraged Billings's interest in popular literature. His transcription of the confessions of two condemned criminals appeared as *The American Bloody Register* (1784), and he was one of two men to have "received. . .from Miss Thomas's own mouth" a narrative published as *A Vision. . .Experienced by Miss Eliza Thomas* (1800).

Innocent of the canons of literary decorum, Billings, who once called literature "the Spring and Security of human Happiness," has rarely been celebrated as an author, but his belief that nature and genius take precedence over art and rules has been regarded as the American artist's declaration of independence from British tradition, and his originality, vitality, and delight in words more than merit the serious attention of literary historians.

Suggested Readings: DAB. *See also* J. Murray Barbour, *The Church Music of William Billings* (1960); David P. McKay and Richard Crawford, *William Billings of Boston: Eighteenth-Century Composer* (1975); Hans Nathan, *William Billings: Data and Documents* (1976).

Mary De Jong
The Pennsylvania State University

ARTHUR BLACKAMORE (c. 1679-c. 1723)

Works: *The Perfidious Brethren, or The Religious Triumvirate. Display'd in Three Ecclesiastical Novels. I. Heathen Priestcraft; Or, The Female Bigot. II.*

Presbyterian Piety; Or, The Way to get a Fortune. III. The Cloven-Hoof: Or, The Anabaptist Teacher Detected (1720); *Luck at Last; Or, The Happy Unfortunate* (1723; rep. as *The Distress'd Fair, or Happy Unfortunate*, 1737); Earl G. Swem, ed. (1960), *Arthur Blackamore's Expeditio Ultramontana* [w. 1716], from text in *Maryland Gazette*, Jun. 24, 1729, trans. from Latin by George Seagood; *A Summary of Christian Antiquities*, 2 vols. (1722).

Biography: A relative of the poet-physician Sir Richard Blackmore, Arthur Blackamore was probably born in London in 1679. He matriculated at Christ Church College, Oxford, at age 16 in 1695. In Sept. 1707 Blackamore was sent to Va. as a schoolmaster and shortly became master of the Grammar School of the College of William and Mary and also perhaps "professor of divinity" in the college. Soon becoming or already a confirmed alcoholic, he still had influential close friends in Governor Alexander Spotswood (q.v.) and William Byrd of Westover (q.v.) in whose diary he appears. In 1716 he returned to Eng., after having accompanied Spotswood and his Knights of the Golden Horseshoe on their journey across the Blue Ridge into the western country. He wrote his quasi epic on the expedition as one of the two annual literary "tributes" the college paid to the governor. In 1717, about the same time, Commissary James Blair (q.v.) wrote to the bishop of London a long account of Blackamore's misdemeanors and of the latter's intention to enter holy orders. Whether he actually took holy orders remains unknown, but in Eng. he espoused the cause of the colonial clergy and governor against Commissary Blair in 1720 in his curious little book *The Perfidious Brethren*, dedicated to Spotswood and concerning itself with examples of the perfidy of priests. In 1722 he published a two-volume condensation of an eight-volume collection of Christian laws and antiquities, and in 1723 he returned to the novel form in *Luck at Last; Or, The Happy Unfortunate*. Thereafter he disappeared from view.

Critical Appraisal: One would like to know more about Arthur Blackamore's long Latin poem on the expedition to the west. As his friend Seagood translated it, it remains a fairly effective course-of-empire piece with frequent local allusions to rivers, plantations, ethnic groups, rattlesnakes, and vegetation sometimes suggestive of the better verse of slightly later Marylander Richard Lewis (q.v.). That Seagood closely followed the original is indicated by a fragment of another contemporary translation by Godfrey Pole (printed in the *Southern Literary Messenger* in Mar. 1836), which is similar in phrase and meter.

The two novels, novelettes, or groups of novels are, however, of greater interest. *The Perfidious Brethren, or, The Religious Triumvirate. Display'd in Three Ecclesiastical Novels*, a staunch Anglican's attack on Presbyterians and Anabaptists, among other dissenters, employs well-worn plots of seduction, corrupt clerics, and pious ladies who are being persecuted. There are unmistakable references to the "false priest" James Blair, a Scot of Presbyterian background and perhaps ordination, who bedeviled the wise and benevolent Spotswood and his government. As a work of literature, the book is miserable stuff, but the flavor of Blackamore's prose is piquant.

Luck at Last; Or, The Happy Unfortunate is another matter. Borrowing its plot from a posthumous piece of Mrs. Aphra Behn, the little novel is at once a sermon or exemplum on virtue and patience rewarded and something of a sentimental novel of character. The editor of a recent edition of this little fiction indicated that its "pervasive sense of realism" and other qualities, such as "a mild touch of bawdy" and some real beggar's idiom, with its sentimental characters and virtue-rewarded plot suggest that it is an immediate and obvious forerunner of Samuel Richardson's *Pamela*. The air of realism is achieved in large part by the Va. references. Its dedication is to "Mr. David Bray of Virginia," refers to Bray's mother and father and their son, and avers that "the Lady Gratiana" is modeled on the young man's own mother. This female character also quite definitely suggests the plantation mistress of the nineteenth-century plantation novel. As Blackamore described him, another character shows qualities of physique and mind of young Bray himself. The rural scenes in which all of the action takes place fit the James River plantation country as well as eighteenth-century Eng. (one recalls that the author was almost entirely city born and bred).

Thus a poet and novelist who spent ten years of his troubled life in Va. drew from his experiences in America in writing in two literary forms. If it were possible to prove that either of or both his novels were written in the Chesapeake Bay country, the date of the first American novel could be moved up at least a half century. His poem is American in both theme and place of writing. His fiction seems in large part so.

Suggested Readings: CCV. *See also* Robert Bain et al., eds., *Southern Writers: A Biographical Dictionary* (1980); Louis D. Rubin, ed., *A Bibliographical Guide to the Study of Southern Literature* (1969), p. 338; R. B. Davis, "Arthur Blackamore: The Virginia Colony and the Early English Novel," VMHB, 75 (1967), 22-34; idem, *Intellectual Life in the Colonial South, 1585-1763* (1978), I, 330, 346, 348; III, 1458-1487; W. H. McBurney, ed., *Four Before Richardson: Selected English Novels, 1720-1727* (1963), pp. xvi-xix, 1-81.

Richard Beale Davis
University of Tennessee, Knoxville

JAMES BLAIR (c. 1655-1743)

Works: *Our Saviour's Divine Sermon on the Mount...Explain'd...in Diverse Sermons and Discourses*, 5 vols. (1722).

Biography: James Blair was born in the parish of Alvah in Baffshire, Scot., in the latter part of 1655 or the first part of 1656. Apparently encouraged in his education by his father, a clergyman in the Church of Scotland, Blair won a scholarship to Marischal College when he was 12 and went on to Edinburgh University, where he received an M.A. in 1679 and remained for theological studies. Eventually ordained into the Scottish church, he served the parish of

Cranston for three years before he was dismissed for refusing to take an oath making James II the head of the Church of Scotland. After this incident, Blair immigrated to London, where he came under the influence of the bishop of London, Henry Compton, who in 1685 sent him to Henrico Parish in Va.

Blair served as a Va. clergyman for fifty-eight years, and for most of that period, he was one of the most powerful political figures in the colony. Soon after arriving in Va., Blair married Sally Harrison, a member of a very prominent family, and in 1689 Bishop Compton made him the ecclesiastical commissary of Va. Using that position, Blair proposed the founding of a college, was sent to Eng. to further the cause, and returned with a charter for William and Mary College and with public and private endowments to inaugurate the project. In 1694 Blair joined the governor's council. Combative by nature and skilled in political intrigue, he feuded with successive governors and eventually used his English connections to bring about the dismissal of Edmund Andros, Francis Nicholson, and Alexander Spotswood (q.v.). Blair supported the college and usually sided with the Va. elite against the imperial authority of Eng., but personal power was always an important factor in his political quarrels.

Blair's political activity detracted from his effectiveness as a commissary, and a majority of Va. clergymen usually sided with his enemies. He was, however, a faithful parish clergyman. Diverse economic activities made him a wealthy man long before he died at 88 years of age. William and Mary College, which he also served as president, was his enduring monument.

Critical Appraisal: James Blair's significance as a writer rests on a series of sermons he began in 1707 based on the Sermon on the Mount. One hundred seventeen of these sermons were published in London in 1722. Titled *Our Saviour's Divine Sermon on the Mount*, this work was reprinted in 1740 and was translated into Danish and published in Copenhagen in 1761. Emphasizing behavior rather than doctrine, Blair's sermons were practical guides meant to improve the spiritual condition of laymen unversed in complex theological issues. These sermons were based on their author's knowledge of language and theology and his experience with men and society, and they reflect his conservative belief in traditional authority in both church and state.

The first sermon in the series, for example, illustrates Blair's virtues and defects as a writer and theologian. The text is Matthew 5:1-3: "And Seeing the Multitudes, he went up into a Mountain." After admitting that many commentators ignore these verses because of their introductory character, Blair argued that by "seeing" Matthew meant that Jesus assessed as well as observed the character and the mood of the people and that Christ was aware that the crowd considered him an earthly messiah who would improve their temporal conditions. Thus Christ's audience had "minds full of Covetousness, Ambition, Oppression, Luxury, Lust, Cruelty, Desire of Conquest, and Revenge; all which wicked Inclinations and Disposition they were in Hopes to gratify to the utmost, from the Victories and Prosperity they expected in that new State of Things, under the Messiah." According to Blair, Christ's response to their iniquities was the Beatitudes, which depicted his kingdom differently than they had imagined it.

Blair closed his sermon with practical lessons, not unlike those in Cotton Mather's (q.v.) *Bonifacius*, for both pastors and congregations: the former should imitate Jesus and preach a message appropriate for the audience and the latter were to accept "useful Truths" from the pulpit without taking offense. An intelligent sermon, it made important points, but the style, like that in Blair's other sermons, is sometimes tedious: the commissary's audience must have sighed, or perhaps smiled, when he indicated that he would pass over without exegesis the phrase *"opening his mouth."*

Although Blair's sermons have been characterized as devoid of any "sense of humor" and "neither brilliant nor very readable," they are, however, a testament to the industry of a remarkable man.

Suggested Readings: CCV; DAB; DARB; DNB; LHUS; Sprague (V, 7-9); T₂. *See also* Richard Beale Davis, *Intellectual Life in the Colonial South, 1585-1763* (1978), II, 731-736; Glenn Patton, "The College of William and Mary, Williamsburg, and the Enlightenment," JSAH, 29 (1970), 24-32; Parke Rouse, *James Blair of Virginia* (1971).

Sidney Charles Bolton
University of Arkansas at Little Rock

JOHN DURBARROW BLAIR (1759-1823)

Works: *A Sermon on the Death of. . .George Washington* (1800); *A Sermon on the Impetuosity and Bad Effects of Passion and the Most Likely Means of Subduing It* (1809); *Sermons Collected from the Manuscripts of the Late Rev. John D. Blair* (1825).

Biography: John Durbarrow Blair was born on Oct. 15, 1759, probably at Fagg's Manor, Pa. His early education was at the hands of his father, John Blair, who was later professor of theology at Princeton. The younger Blair graduated from Princeton in 1775 at the age of 16. After serving in the American Revolution, he moved to Hanover County, Va., where in 1780 he became president of Washington-Henry Academy and, later, the pastor of Pole Green Church. In 1790 Blair resigned these positions and moved to Richmond, Va., where he began his own school and became the first established Presbyterian clergyman in the city, sharing his pulpit at St. John's Episcopal Church with the Rev. John Buchanan, with each man preaching on alternate Sundays, until the latter's death in 1821. In 1796 Blair refused the presidency of Hampden-Sydney College, preferring to stay with his parishioners. Shortly after the completion of the Presbyterian Church on Shockoe Hill in Richmond, Blair became too ill to continue preaching. He died Jan. 10, 1823.

Critical Appraisal: John Durbarrow Blair's best-known and most important work is *A Sermon on the Death of Lieutenant-General George Washington*.

Much like a poetic elegy, the sermon compares Washington (q.v.) to other great historical leaders, elevating him above the rest for his lack of personal ambition and for his fidelity to God and country. The sermon reflects the post-Revolution optimism about America common in Blair's day, implying that Washington served God by serving America, the hope of the future. In addition, Blair's frequent quotations from the Bible, contemporary accounts of Washington's character, and literary sources show his breadth of knowledge and reading.

The only other Blair sermon published during his lifetime is *A Sermon on the Impetuosity and Bad Effects of Passion and the Most Likely Means of Subduing It*. The title, however, is somewhat misleading. The subject of the sermon is the effects and control of anger, which Blair viewed as the result of hasty action and lack of self-control. After citing some examples of the effects of anger, Blair presented five means of controlling it: cultivating humility, frequently meditating on the bad effects of anger, resolving "that we will not be under its controul," seeing insults as results of human frailty rather than as results of malign intent, and looking to more temperate people for examples. The sermon also contained a lengthy and informative digression on dueling, which Blair saw as the result of a mistaken code of ethics. This sermon was reprinted in vol. I of *The Virginia Evangelical and Literary Magazine* in 1818, and both of these sermons are included in *Sermons Collected from the Manuscripts of the Late Rev. John D. Blair* (1825), the latter under the more appropriate title of "On Anger." This book was published by Blair's friends and relatives after his death and includes sermons on a variety of theological subjects.

Blair's works reflect an optimism about his faith, his country, and his fellow man. Like other Presbyterian writers, such as Francis Makemie (q.v.), Blair placed a heavy emphasis on the power of the human mind as the means of man's self-improvement. His sermons are written in a rational manner, and his frequent quotations lend a literary style to his works.

Suggested Readings: P. *See also* Louisa Coleman Gordon Blair, *Blairs of Richmond, Virginia* (1933); William Henry Foote, *Sketches of Virginia: Historical and Biographical* (1850-1855), II, 112-113.

Frank Crotzer
University of Delaware

SAMUEL BLAIR (1712-1751)

Works: *The Gospel-Method of Salvation* (1737); *A Sermon on 2 Corinthians, III.18* (1739); *A Particular Consideration of a Piece, Entitled, The Querists* (1741); *The Doctrine of Predestination* (1742); *A Persuasive to Repentance* (1743); *A Short and Faithful Narrative of the Late Remarkable Revival of Religion* (1744); *A Vindication of the Brethren* (1744); *A Sermon Preached at George's Town* (c. 1746); *Animadversions on the Reasons of Mr. Alex. Creaghead's Receding* (1747); *The Works of the Rev. Mr. Samuel Blair* (1754).

Biography: Samuel Blair was born in Northern Ire. on Jun. 14, 1712. His family emigrated to America when he was young, and he studied at the famous "Log College" in Neshaminy, Pa., under William Tennent I. This school was a training ground for many of the evangelical ministers who led the Great Awakening in the Presbyterian Church. Blair was licensed to preach in 1733 and during the next few years served as pastor of several congregations in N.J. In 1739 he became minister of the church at New Londonderry, Pa. (also known as Fagg's Manor), where he led a major religious revival. He was one of the leaders of the "New Side" of the Presbyterian Church and devoted much of his time as a pastor, schoolmaster, and writer to the evangelical cause. He died in Fagg's Manor, Pa., Jul. 5, 1751.

Critical Appraisal: Samuel Blair's vigorous writings in support of the Great Awakening complemented his efforts as a pastor. Called "the most gifted among the Presbyterian partisans of the revival," he published, in a brief ten-year period, a series of influential sermons and tracts to propagate and defend the revival of religion.

Blair's theological tracts are among the most lucid expositions of evangelical Calvinism produced by a Presbyterian minister. He upheld the fundamental doctrines of original sin and limited salvation while linking them with the need for a direct personal experience of God's grace; like other evangelicals, he was intolerant of religion that is merely institutional. In *A Particular Consideration*, he lashed out against those ministers who had criticized the revival, particularly against the missionary work of George Whitefield (q.v.): they are "Dead secure Formalists" who are more concerned with the church as an organization than with the direct experience of saving grace; they are probably unregenerate themselves. For all of Blair's intellectual rigor, he is best understood as an active partisan of the revival. Even in a severely theological work like *The Doctrine of Predestination*, he made it clear that his exposition would best serve its purpose if it became "a comfortable Support to exercised Christians . . . at the Day, when there is such fierce Opposition made against the Revival of Religion."

Blair's *Short and Faithful Narrative* is among the best contemporary descriptions of an actual revival. Eloquent in its language and simple in its organization, it is an account of his work with the Fagg's Manor congregation in 1740. Blair described the previous state of religion, outlined the social composition of the church, discussed his own evangelical strategies, detailed the experiences of individual converts, and assessed the results. His frank description of his methods and his careful categorization of the types of religious experience he observed in his congregation provide insights into the mentality of a leading evangelist. The *Narrative* also illuminates a tension in the revival movement. Blair advised his flock to open themselves to the direct action of God's grace, but he also cautioned them "to moderate and bound their Passions." The question of how to maintain the centrality of individual experience while avoiding the behavioral excesses of some revivals was fundamental to the Great Awakening. Blair's *Narrative* is an excellent illustration of some of the practical quandaries that developed.

Blair's conclusions about the Fagg's Manor revival are modest: there is evidence of a thorough and saving conversion among many, but there has been backsliding in recent years. The *Faithful Narrative* is thus not only a testimony to the original spirit of the revivals of the early 1740s, it also illustrates the reaction of an insightful clergyman to the inevitable waning of enthusiasm.

Suggested Readings: CCMC; DAB; Sprague (III, 62-66). *See also* A. Alexander, *Biographical Sketches of the Founder, and Principal Alumni, of the Log College* (1845), pp. 254-292; Alan Heimert and Perry Miller, eds., *The Great Awakening: Documents Illustrating the Crisis and Its Consequences* (1967), pp. 127-128; Guy S. Klett, *Presbyterianism in Colonial Pennsylvania* (1937), pp. 146-159, 204, 207; Charles H. Maxson, *The Great Awakening in the Middle Colonies* (1920); Leonard J. Trinterud, *A Bibliography of American Presbyterianism* (1968), items 19-29, 1054-1055; idem, *The Forming of an American Tradition: A Re-examination of Colonial Presbyterianism* (1949), pp. 77-80, 96.

Douglas M. Arnold
Yale University

EDWARD BLAND (d. 1653)

Works: *The Discovery of New Brittaine* (1651).

Biography: An English merchant educated at London's Westminster School, Edward Bland was dispatched to the Va. colony by his brother, a member of the Old Virginia Company. While managing the family holdings in the colony, Bland was authorized by Governor William Berkeley (q.v.) to explore the interior of Va. Accompanied by Capt. Abraham Wood—Indian trader and militia captain of Fort Henry—four other colonists, and two native guides, Bland left Fort Henry at the falls of the Appomattox River on Aug. 27, 1650, and journeyed south and southwest through the piedmont country to the falls of the Roanoke River, near the present-day site of Clarksville. Discovering that a village of Occaneechee Indians blocked further progress, and fearing the treachery of the Indian tribes they had encountered, Bland and his group terminated their four-day journey and returned to Fort Henry by a modified route. Upon his return, Bland petitioned the Va. Assembly for permission to make another exploration in order to settle the area and to search for minerals and furs. The petition was granted with the stipulation that Bland recruit 100 men to join him, but in 1653, before the new expedition could begin, Bland died in Eng. after sailing there to attract settlers for his venture.

Critical Appraisal: Written as a promotional pamphlet to attract prospective settlers to "New Brittaine," Edward Bland's *Discovery of New Brittaine* reveals one more instance of European captivity to the dream of an earthly paradise in the New World Eden. After opening with an appeal to those readers who both "desirest the Advancement of God's glory by conversion of the Indians" and by "the Augmentation of the English Common-wealth," Bland quoted the passage from Sir Walter Raleigh's *The Marrow of History*, which argued that Eden was located at 35° north latitude. Bland's "New Brittaine," so-called because he thought his travels took him beyond the boundaries of the Va. colony, is located between 35° and 37° north latitude. With the title page declaring "New Brittaine" to be "(a pleasant Country,) of temperate Ayre, and fertile Soyle," few readers could mistake Bland's purpose in writing the daily entries of his travels.

If Bland's initial appeal to his audience's religious and political ideals was less than persuasive, he took care in the account of his eight-day journey to emphasize the landscape's susceptibility to cultivation and colonization. Because he believed that "New Brittaine" would be "a place so easily to be settled in," Bland suggested that the soil would support two crops of corn a year, extensive tobacco and sugar cane farming, and numerous hogs or cattle. Besides these economic opportunities, Bland also suggested that the land must contain deposits of silver or copper, because he noticed how the Indian pipes were tipped with these metals. The two major obstacles to any prospective settlement in the area—the rivers and the Indians—Bland sublimated in his narrative with varying degrees of success. The several waterways the group traversed in their journey were rendered safe for fording on horse or on foot. However, although Bland's relationships with the Indians were cordial—the only gunfire in the narrative occurred when the colonists displayed their marksmanship before an awed Indian tribe—the rumors of ambush and possible captivity intruded upon his idealized landscape portraits and thus created an interesting tension between Bland's future dreams and his present situation. One entire day's entry on the return journey, for instance, was devoted to the discovery that native runners were spreading malicious rumors about the travelers' intentions.

Bland's presentation of his dream of an economic utopia in this "very much rich, red, fat, marle land" is most tiresome when his wandering eye blatantly transforms the landscape into economic value. He observed, for example, a large rock and immediately perceived a millstone for the settlers' uses. Although one wishes that Bland had elaborated on the Meherrin ceremonial dances he observed, his narrative is at its most effective when his spare prose presents tribal lore learned from native guides, such as an interesting tale of murder and kidnapping involving Powhatan and the Tuscarora Indians he related one day while the group was resting on the trail. Such tales do not densely populate the pages of *The Discovery of New Brittaine*, but Bland's narrative—although neither as sustained as Captain John Smith's (q.v.) accounts of discovery nor as inventive as Robert Beverley's (q.v.) *History of the Present State of Virginia* (1705)—is of historical importance as one of our earliest narratives of interior land exploration at a time when the lure of riches was competing with the lure of religious salvation.

Suggested Readings: Clarence W. Alvord and Lee Bidgood, *The First Explorations of the Trans-Allegheny Region by the Virginians, 1650-1674* (1912), pp. 47-51; Howard M. Jones, *The Literature of Virginia in the Seventeenth Century* (1968), p. 71;

Howard H. Peckham, Introduction, *The Discovery of New Britain* (1954); John E. Pomfret, *Founding of the American Colonies, 1583-1660* (1970), p. 64; Alexander S. Salley, ed., *Narratives of Early Carolina, 1650-1708* (1911), pp. 3-19; John Seelye, *Prophetic Waters* (1977), p. 358; Louis B. Wright, *The Dream of Prosperity in Colonial America* (1965), pp. 80-81; Louis B. Wright and Elaine W. Fowler, *The Moving Frontier* (1972), pp. 62, 64.

Stephen Tatum
University of Utah

RICHARD BLAND (1710-1776)

Works: *A Modest and True State of the Case* (1753); *A Letter to the Clergy of Virginia* (1760); *The Colonel Dismounted* (1764); *An Inquiry into the Rights of the British Colonies* (1766).

Biography: Richard Bland was born May 6, 1710, the son of Richard Bland of Berkeley and Jordan's Point, Va., and his second wife, Elizabeth Randolph of Turkey Island. A scion of two successful and prominent Va. families, he attended William and Mary College and was admitted to the practice of law in 1746. Described by John Adams (q.v.) as "a learned and bookish man" and by George Washington (q.v.) as "a man of erudition and intelligence," Bland was a fine Classical scholar and an authority on the history of the colony of Va.

From 1742 to 1775, Bland represented Prince George's County in the House of Burgesses. One of the most active members, he was especially in demand as a committee chairman and drafter of bills, working on important and diverse issues such as taxation, the proceedings of county courts, estate probate, and currency adjustment. As a politician, Bland ardently defended the rights of the assembly and the people, especially on matters of taxation. During the Pistole Fee controversy (1753-1755), for example, he argued for the inseparability of taxation and representation, and during the Two-Penny Act controversy (1758-1764), he was the chief pamphleteer against the clergy. A colonel in the militia and an active member of the Va. Committee of Correspondence, Bland was elected delegate to the First and Second Continental Congresses, declining a third term because of ill health. Despite advanced age and illness, he served on the committee that drew up the Declaration of Rights and the first constitution of Va. Bland was married three times and fathered twelve children. He died Oct. 26, 1776.

Critical Appraisal: In addition to his separately published works, Bland wrote letters to the *Virginia Gazette*, laws, resolves, petitions, and addresses for the House of Burgesses. His writings demonstrate his knowledge of Classical and British authors—including Thucydides, Cicero, Locke, Shaftesbury, Bacon, Milton, Swift, and Pope—and his extensive knowledge of Va. history. Bland's 1760 pamphlet, *A Letter to the Clergy of Virginia*, vindicated the conduct of the General Assembly and answered the bishop of London's accusation that the

Assembly had attempted to diminish the power of the king by changing an existing law setting the salaries of the clergy. The bishop's letter, he wrote, was "an evidence of the imbecility of the human mind and a demonstration that at certain periods of life, the most learned and pious men are subject to the impositions of the crafty and malevolent." Bland turned the bishop's own words back upon him, arguing their untruth and using them to ridicule their author. He argued that "*Salus populi est suprema lex*" and threatened that the doctrines espoused by the clergy, if followed, would reduce the people "to a state scarce superior to that of galley-slaves in Turkey, or Israelites under an Egyptian bondage."

The Colonel Dismounted: Or, The Rector Vindicated (1764) represents a continuation of the dispute that prompted *A Letter to the Clergy*. To follow the history of the dispute, one should first read the three appendixes in the order they were written (III, I, II). A rather ingenious example of satire, *The Colonel Dismounted* employs an intricate literary conceit, a mock inversion of roles. Bland wrote as a defender of his antagonist, the Reverend John Camm (q.v.). The Rector's "defender" mocked Camm with his ridiculously effusive praise: "Wonderful genius! who with infinite wit and humor can transfer the *unripe crab*, the *mouth-distorting persimmon*, the most arrant *trash* into delicious fruit." He then reported a public debate between himself and the colonel in which the latter forcefully repeated Bland's arguments against the clergy and in defense of the Assembly's actions. The "defender," meanwhile, answered weakly or not at all, and Camm's own words were used to condemn him. The heart of the pamphlet is an attempt to explain the workings of the British constitution in America: in external matters, the colonies are subject to the authority of Parliament; internal matters are the sphere of the colonial legislatures. Any internal tax imposed by Parliament therefore deprives the colonists of their rights as citizens and may be opposed.

In an age of anonymous pamphleteering, *An Inquiry into the Rights of the British Colonies* (1766) was unique in that the author's name was on the title page. Although it was largely ignored by colonial newspapers and never republished, the pamphlet expressed ideas that were to be repeated many times in subsequent years. Thomas Jefferson (q.v.) said of this work that "there was more sound matter in [Bland's] pamphlet than in the celebrated Farmer's Letters, which were really but an *ignis fatuus*, misleading us from true principles." Bland's prose is clear and direct, and there is no mistaking his message: "If a man invades my property, he becomes an aggressor, and puts himself into a state of war with me: I have a right to oppose this invader; if I have not strength to repel him, I must submit, but he acquires no right to my estate which he has usurped."

Although not as radical as Patrick Henry and his followers, Bland exemplifies the spirit of eighteenth-century Va., and his writings are an accurate reflection of the dominant political and constitutional thought of his day.

Suggested Readings: CCV; DAB; T$_2$. *See also* Bernard Bailyn, *Ideological Origins of the American Revolution* (1967), passim; idem, *Pamphlets of the American*

Revolution, (1965) I, 292-354; Richard B. Davis, *Intellectual Life in the Colonial South, 1585-1763*, 3 vols. (1978) passim; Merrill Jensen, ed., *Tracts of the American Revolution* (1967) pp. 108-126; Clinton Rossiter, *Seedtime of the Republic* (1953), pp. 247-280, passim.

Elaine K. Ginsberg
West Virginia University

THEODORICK BLAND (1742-1790)

Works: Charles Campbell, ed., *The Bland Papers: Being a Selection from the Manuscripts of Colonel Theodorick Bland, Jr.*, 2 vols. (1761-1784; pub. 1840).

Biography: Theodorick Bland, Jr., was born in Prince George County, Va., in 1742, the son of Theodorick Bland of Cawsons. His father served in local politics and in the House of Burgesses, and his uncle, Richard Bland (q.v.), was an important leader of the Burgesses in pre-Revolutionary decades. At the age of ll, Theodorick Bland, Jr., began studying in Eng. and Scot., and in 1763 he received an M.D. from the University of Edinburgh. He practiced medicine in Va. from 1764 until the rigors of country practice forced him to retire in 1771. Bland became active in patriot politics and was one of the group of twenty-four who removed arms from Governor Dunmore's palace in Jun. 1775. The following year he was appointed captain of the first troop of Va. cavalry, and as colonel of the First Continental Dragoons, he commanded mounted troops in N.J. and Pa. and was partially responsible for the faulty intelligence that caused the American defeat at Brandywine in Sept. 1777. After retiring from military duty in Nov. 1779, Bland devoted the remainder of his life to politics. From 1780 to 1783, he was a delegate to Congress; and from 1786 to 1788, a member of the Va. House of Delegates. In 1788, as a member of the Va. convention, he voted against ratification of a federal constitution. Nevertheless, he was elected to the first House of Representatives, where he served until his death on Jun. 1, 1790, at the age of 48.

Critical Appraisal: Theodorick Bland's contribution to early American literature was primarily as a writer of letters, most of which were not intended for publication. His skill as a correspondent was suggested in 1898 by a reviewer of Moses Coit Tyler's *The Literary History of the American Revolution*, who regretted Tyler's decision not to include extended treatment of correspondence in his treatise. The reviewer asked: "What, for instance, can be more delightful than some of the letters of Theodorick Bland, Jr.?"

Although many of Bland's letters can be found in the published papers of Revolutionary figures such as George Washington (q.v.), Thomas Jefferson (q.v.), James Madison (q.v.), and Alexander Hamilton (q.v.), students are indebted primarily to Charles Campbell, the nineteenth-century historian, editor, and antiquarian, for the preservation and publication of the majority of Bland's papers. In his introduction to *The Bland Papers*, Campbell related the saga of his involvement with the papers, which he had found "mouse-nibbled, rat-eaten, stained, torn and faded." Bland's celebrated nephew, John Randolph of Roanoke, had earlier attempted unsuccessfully to obtain them from their disinterested and negligent owner. Campbell organized the papers, including letters to and from family members and acquaintances, in roughly chronological order and prepared a biographical sketch on Bland. In 1846 Campbell informed a colleague that although *The Bland Papers* had been received "with indifference" he hoped that "the future historian of Virginia will give me credit for having preserved some original materials." The preservation of these materials was important not only because of Bland's skill as correspondent but also because of the variety of activities in his career as physician, planter, revolutionary, military leader, and statesman.

Unfortunately, few documents have survived from Bland's early career as physician. While at Edinburgh, Bland was instrumental in organizing a club composed of Virginians who aspired to be physicians. His professional dedication was manifested also in the petition he prepared for the Council and House of Burgesses protesting the "unguarded state" of the practice of medicine in Va. By 1771, however, at the age of 29 and after only seven years as a physician, he wrote to his father: "I fear that . . . one or two years more would put a period to my existence were I to continue the practice." The tantalizing bits of information that have survived suggest that the collection of fees was more wearing on the young doctor than the dispensation of medical advice and treatment.

It was as a patriot that Theodorick Bland prepared the few materials he intended for publication. Late in 1775 the *Virginia Gazette* published several letters to Governor Dunmore written by Bland under the pseudonym "Cassius." In dramatic prose, he spoke of Dunmore's "evil genius" and asked him: "Is the heart of Pharaoh yet harden'd, and will nothing less than conversion of rivers into blood, convince your lordship of your error?"

In the various political offices he held from 1780 to 1790, Bland devoted himself to committee work, prepared and revised drafts of bills and resolutions, and corresponded with colleagues and constituents. Not only was he an active and dedicated member, he was also one whose views frequently differed from those of his fellow representatives. So greatly did he differ with James Madison, with whom he served as a delegate to Congress from 1780 to 1783 and in the House of Representatives in 1789 and 1790, that a recent biographer of Madison referred to Bland as Madison's "ancient antagonist." Bland's papers indicate controversies over numerous issues; they do not, however, contain personal vituperation.

Although Bland at times wrote turgid, occasionally clumsy prose—one scholar noted "a single sentence several hundred words long, containing twenty-seven verb forms"—most of his writing displayed what James Monroe characterized as Bland's "usual fire and elegance." Theodorick Bland is thus deserving of recognition in the literary history of Revolutionary America.

Suggested Readings: DAB. *See also* Irving Brant, *James Madison: The Nationalist, 1780-1787* (1948), pp. 50-57; 65-69; 83-98; 192-203; 226-243; William C. Bruce, *John Randolph of Roanoke, 1773-1833* (1922), I, 23-28; Charles Campbell, ed., *The Bland Papers*, 2 vols. (1840).

Mary E. Quinlivan
University of Texas of the Permian Basin

ANNE ELIZA BLEECKER (1752-1783)

Works: *The Posthumous Works of Ann Eliza Bleecker in Prose and Verse* (1793).

Biography: Anne Eliza Bleecker was born in Oct. 1752, in New York City, the daughter of the aristocratic Brandt Schuyler. She had no formal education, but she read assiduously. On Mar. 29, 1769, she married John J. Bleecker of New Rochelle, and in 1771 they moved to Tomhanick, where her husband owned property. Some of Bleecker's verses from this period, reflecting her happiness, were published in the *New-York Magazine*. In 1777, as Burgoyne's army approached, John Bleecker went to Albany to prepare for his family's removal. In his absence, Anne Eliza Bleecker, alarmed by news of an impending Indian attack, fled the house with her small children and joined other refugees in walking to safety in Stony–Arabia. Her husband found her the next day, took the family to Albany and then down the Hudson to Red Hook, where her mother awaited them. The Bleeckers' baby died on this journey. After Burgoyne's surrender, the family returned to Albany and then to Tomhanick. During the next few years, Bleecker spent her time reading the Classics and writing letters and poetry. In 1779 she again saved her life by flight and again returned to Tomhanick. In 1781 her husband was captured by Tories. Although he was rescued after six days, Anne Eliza Bleecker's emotional reaction to this incident induced an illness, and she died Nov. 23, 1783.

Critical Appraisal: The primary work for which Bleecker is known is "The History of Maria Kittle," a tale of Indian attack and capture during the French and Indian War. One of the earliest instances of the Indian in American fiction, the story borrows both from the captivity narrative and from Gothic fiction to tell an epistolary, sentimental tale, creating an interesting combination of horror and gruesome detail with extravagant sensibility. The Indians are not individualized and are portrayed as inhuman savages, and the other characters are flat and undeveloped. Their heavily emotional language contrasts sharply with the restraint of the captivity narrative of Mary Rowlandson (q.v.). The story reflects Bleecker's vivid imagination and creative elaboration on her own experiences.

In addition to poetry and letters, *The Posthumous Works* includes "The Story of Henry and Anne," unusual as an early fictionalized account of a German immigrant family who come to N. Y. to escape misfortune and poverty in their native country. The ending of the story was completed after Bleecker's death by her daughter, Margaret Faugeres (q.v.), an author in her own right.

Suggested Readings: DAB; NAW; T₂. *See also* Louise K. Barnett, *The Ignoble Savage. American Literary Racism, 1790-1890* (1975); Margaret Faugeres, "Memoir of Ann Eliza Bleecker" in *Posthumous Works of Ann Eliza Bleecker* (1793); George W. Schuyler, *Colonial New York*, vol. II (1885).

Patricia L. Parker
Salem State College

JOHN PHILIP BOEHM (1683-1749)

Works: *Getreuer Warnungs* (1742); *Abermahlige Treue Warnung* (1743); William J. Hinke, trans. and ed., *Life and Letters of the Reverend John Philip Boehm* (1916), pp. 155-480; James I. Good and William J. Hinke, trans. and eds., *Minutes and Letters of the Coetus of the German Reformed Congregations in Pennsylvania, 1747-1792, Together with Three Preliminary Reports of Rev. John Philip Boehm, 1734-1744* (1903), pp.1-31.

Biography: John Philip Boehm was born on Oct. 26, 1683, into the family of the Reformed minister at Hochstadt, located in the province of Hesse-Cassel, which later became part of Ger. His father's self-confessed "slippery tongue" caused difficulties with officials of his congregations and led to frequent moves. Surviving records do not describe his childhood or indicate where he obtained his education. By 1708 he had become a master in Reformed Church schools, serving at Worms from 1708 until 1715 and for the next five years at Lambsheim.

In 1720 Boehm emigrated to America, settling on a farm in southeastern Pa. Boehm's German Reformed neighbors quickly recognized his religious inclinations. In the absence of ordained clergymen of their faith, they asked him to conduct services for them. At first he consented to serve only as lay reader, but in 1725 he agreed to assume all ministerial responsibilities. Four years later, he was ordained by officials of the Dutch Reformed Church in N.Y.

For nearly a quarter-century, from 1725 until 1749, Boehm almost singlehandedly served the tens of thousands of immigrants of German Reformed background who settled in Pa. He organized at least twelve congregations and served another time as many. He taught them the doctrines expressed in the German Reformed Palatinate Liturgy. Boehm died on Apr. 29, 1749, while returning from administering the sacrament of the Lord's Supper to a distant congregation. He is buried beneath the altar of the church in Whitpain Township that still bears his name.

Critical Appraisal: John Philip Boehm's significance as a writer is that he described religious conditions among the German settlers in Pa. His two publications, as well as his letters and reports to Dutch churchmen, emphasize the prevalent ecclesiastical pluralism and reveal the characteristics of many little-known sects. They also contain information about German Reformed settlers and congregations that is not available elsewhere. In fact, the discovery and publication of these documents in the late nineteenth century led to the revision of much of the early history of the church in this country. They indicate not only that congregations emerged earlier than previously supposed but also that Boehm and not later leaders founded and maintained many of them. They also demonstrate the great extent to which Boehm and other settlers of German Reformed background depended on officials of the Dutch church for advice and support.

It was they who encouraged Boehm to write and publish in the German language two books against the Church of the Unitas Fratrum, members of which were known popularly as Moravians. Boehm was a staunch churchman who considered the Moravians' ecumenism and evangelism doctrinally unsound, insincere, and a threat to his church. Consequently, he published his first book titled *Faithful Letter of Warning Addressed to the High German Evangelical Reformed Congregations and All Their Members in Pennsylvania* in 1742, shortly after the Moravians' leader Count Nicolas Von Zinzendorf (q.v.) had arrived in Pa. In the first portion, Boehm relied heavily on two volumes that Dutch officials had sent him in an attempt to expose what he considered the differences between Reformed and Moravian beliefs. In the latter passages, he presented his interpretation of controversies between the two groups, including the Moravians' use of the Reformed and Lutheran place of worship in Philadelphia, the Moravians' ecumenical synods, and the Moravians' publication of a catechism for use by members of the Reformed Church. Because Boehm concluded that too few people had purchased his lengthy treatise, he brought out in 1743 a shorter and less expensive *Second Faithful Warning*. In this tract, Boehm condemned those Reformed churchmen who had gone over to the Moravians and urged others to remain faithful to their own doctrines and to "our devout Church Fathers."

It is impossible to determine precisely how efficacious Boehm's warnings were. Count Zinzendorf's rebuttal indicates that Boehm at least attracted his attention. Certainly, Boehm's publications alone did not prevent all but a few Reformed settlers from joining the Moravians and cause the Moravians within a decade to discontinue their efforts to join colonists of diverse religious backgrounds in their "Congregation of God in the Spirit." Regardless of what else Boehm may have accomplished by publishing these works, he provided additional evidence of the ecclesiastical warfare that occurred in Pa. during the second quarter of the eighteenth century.

Suggested Readings: CCMC; DAB; DARB; *See also* Clara Beck, "An Honest Effort to Save Pennsylvania from the Moravians," TMHS, 11 (1936), 189-198; Joseph Henry Dubbs, *The Reformed Church in Pennsylvania* (1902), pp. 79-90, 134-136; Charles H. Glatfelter, *Pastors and People: German Lutheran and Reformed Churches in the Pennsylvania Field, 1717-1793* (1980), pp. 21-31; James I. Good, *The History of the Reformed Church in the United States, 1725-1792* (1899), pp. 89-107, 120-133, 265, 278; William J. Hinke, *Life and Letters of the Rev. John Philip Boehm: Founder of the Reformed Church in Pennsylvania, 1683-1749* (1916), pp. 1-480; idem, *Ministers of the*

German Reformed Congregations in Pennsylvania and Other Colonies in the Eighteenth Century, ed. George W. Richards (1951), pp. 1-13.

John B. Frantz
The Pennsylvania State University

ROBERT BOLLING (1738-1775)

Works: "Complaint" (1761); "Daphne's *Speech* to Sylvia, in Tasso's Arminta" (1761); "On Matrimony, from the French of M. De Voltaire" (1761); "A Song" (1761); "To Miss Patty Dangerfield" (1761); "An Epitaph for a Lady" (1762); "O, if I Cou'd" (1762); "To a Turtle Dove" (1762); "The Art of Printing" (1764); "A Canzonet of Chiabura" (1764); "The Choice" (1764); "The Flamers" (1764); "Madrigal" (1764); "To My Flute" (1764); "To My Wife" (1764); "A Pathetic Soliloquoy" (1764); "Time's Address to the Ladies. This Imitation of Tasso" (1764); "Dignity Displayed" (1766); "The Gentleman" (1766); "A Key to the Virginia Gazettes" (1767); "Madrigal on the Death of an Infant" (1767); "A Satire on the Times" (1767); "A Memoir of the Bolling Family" (1868).

Biography: A descendant of an English immigrant who came to Va. in 1660 and the son of Col. John Bolling and Elizabeth Blair, Robert Bolling of Chellowe, Buckingham County, Va., was born in 1738 and was related to Pocahontas and many Va. aristocrats, including John Randolph of Roanoke and John Durburrow Blair (q.v.). Educated in a Yorkshire grammar school, Bolling studied law in Williamsburg after a brief stay in the Inner Temple in 1755. He was twice married: to Mary Burton in 1763 and, after her death, to Susan Watson.

A planter by occupation, Bolling was active in public affairs and served in the House of Burgesses from 1761 to 1765. Although a part of the Va. establishment, he often warred with its conservative wing, most notably in the affair of Col. John Chiswell, who was granted bail while under indictment for murder. William Byrd III sued Bolling over pieces he published in the *Virginia Gazette* about the affair, but Bolling was acquitted in a verdict credited with ending the "supervised press" in Va. Bolling, who was often referred to as "junior" or "colonel," died in 1775 on the eve of the Revolutionary War.

Critical Appraisal: Although Robert Bolling is usually remembered for his genealogical piece, *A Memoir of a Portion of the Bolling Family*, which traces his lineage to fifteenth-century Yorkshire, he was in fact a prolific and accomplished poet—perhaps the best of his time in Va. Although a final judgment must be withheld until a collected edition of Bolling's works is available, the numerous poems that Bolling published in Eng. and America reveal his poetic versatility and masterful craftsmanship. Writing at times under his own name and at other times under his initials or pseudonyms like "Prometheus," Bolling composed numerous lyrics, elegies, and satirical poems published in

America in periodicals such as the *Virginia Gazette, American Museum*, and *Columbian Magazine* and in Eng. the *Imperial, London*, and *Universal* magazines. These poems include translations of Voltaire and Tasso and illustrate a familiarity with writers like Ariosto. In fact, the strength of Bolling's poetry, both light and serious, seems to derive from his ability to read and write other languages. Because of his knowledge of French, Italian, Latin, and, evidently, Greek, he had available to him models that most American writers had to deal with in translation. He enjoyed writing in French and Italian and wrote his famous *Memoir* in French.

Although many of Bolling's lyrics are conventional, the range of their mood is impressive: from the ironic and witty to the sentimental and romantic. "Time's Addresses to the Ladies," an imitation of Tasso, has a carpe diem theme; "A Canzonet of Chiabura," addressed to a Nancy Blair, imitates Horace; and "A Song," written in four quatrains, begins with the earnest lines: "Oh! wou'dst those know what secret charm / Will thy Myrtilla's hate disarm; / Leave all those little trifling arts, / Which only please more trifling hearts." "Madrigal," a poem in memory of Bolling's dead wife, and "An Epitaph for a Lady" have an elegiac tone; yet the latter begins like a comical tombstone epitaph: "Here lies beneath this heap of stones / What once were lov'd Amanda's bones."

Two of Bolling's political satires, "A Key to the Virginia Gazettes" and "A Satire on the Times," are masculine, pungent, and allusive and test not only a reader's knowledge of literature but also his knowledge of the political controversies of Va. in the 1760s. In the "Satire," for example, Bolling recounted the events of John Chiswell's bailment and his own difficulties with Byrd. In one passage, Bolling accused John Wayles of turning Bolling's cousin Richard Randolph of Culres (Collin) against him and goading Byrd as Tamerlaine goaded Bajazet. The "Key" demonstrates Bolling's ability to impale a political adversary. Writing of Landon Carter (q.v.), who Bolling said "wrote like an ill natured Madman who in lucid Intervals...knew how to curb his Rancour," Bowling sounds almost Swiftian: "Methinks (the vast machine, behind) / I see him swell the bag, with wind,— / Then voiding blasts sonorous; / 'Til (wrapt to th'ideot's paradise) / Exulting———DEAR OURSELVES (he cries) / *Unstunn'd, none stand before us*." Just how much political satire Bolling wrote is uncertain, in part because some issues of the *Virginia Gazette* that carried his verse have been lost. But his surviving poems reveal an ability to write acidly and yet maintain a grace that ranks him with the better political satirists of the colonial and Revolutionary periods.

When Bolling died, an article in the *Columbian Magazine*, signed "Observator," called him "one of the greatest poetical geniuses that ever existed." Although this praise must be discounted somewhat, it reveals the prominent literary standing Bolling held among pre-Revolutionary War American poets. Had he published all of the manuscripts currently coming to light, he would certainly occupy a much higher place in American letters than has been given him.

Suggested Readings: Richard Beale Davis, *Intellectual Life in the Colonial South,*

1585-1763 (1978), III, 1380-1417, 1472, 1477-1479, passim; J. A. Leo Lemay, *A Calendar of American Poetry...through 1765* (1970); idem, "Robert Bolling and the Bailment of Colonel Chiswell," EAL, 6 (1971), 99-142; T. H. Wynne, ed., *A Memoir of a Portion of the Bolling Family*, by Robert Bolling (1868; 1964). Robert Arner is editing the Bolling manuscripts.

Joseph H. Harkey
Virginia Wesleyan College

JOHN BEALE BORDLEY (1727-1804)

Works: *Necessaries* (1776); *Summary View of the Courses of Crops* (1784); *On Monies* (1789); *Purport of a Letter on Sheep* (1789); *National Credit* (1790); *Supplement to the Essay on Monies* (1790); *Sketches on Rotation* (1792); *Intimations on Manufactures* (1794); *Outlines of a Plan* (1794); *Yellow Fever* (1794); *Intending to Retire* (1797); *Queries Selected* (1797); *Country Habitations* (1798); *On Pasturing Cattle* (1798); *Essays and Notes* (1799); *Hemp* (1799); *Husbandry Dependent on Livestock* (1800); *Epitome of Forsyth* (1803); *Gleanings From... Books on Husbandry* (1803).

Biography: John Beale Bordley was the posthumous son of a substantial Md. planter. After studying law with his brother, he established himself as a jurist through a series of appointments: clerk of Baltimore County (1753), judge of the Provincial Court (1766), judge of the Admiralty Court (1767). He also served on the Governor's Council, but his political sympathies began to conflict with his duties. He resigned the clerkship rather than enforce the Stamp Act. In 1770 he purchased a 1,600 acre estate on Wye Island and began to shift his activities from public affairs to agriculture. He undertook to make his farm self-sufficient in all matters; he read English publications conscientiously; and he corresponded with American planters, including George Washington (q.v.). His first wife died in 1773; his second wife, a Philadelphia widow, moved his attention to that city. Bordley worked actively to found and to maintain the Philadelphia Society for Promoting Agriculture. In 1791 Bordley removed his household to Philadelphia, but he continued to supervise the operation of his farms and to maintain his practical and theoretical interests in American agriculture.

Critical Appraisal: John Beale Bordley was an accidental author. As he read, experimented, and speculated on his various farms, he felt compelled to share his observations with his neighbors. He began by circulating manuscript notes. They led to handbills and then to pamphlets. Most of his publications fall into this last category: brief communications (four to twenty-five pages) addressing a particular problem. The prose is simple and direct; he usually omitted the formalities of introduction or conclusion. Notes from his library were verified by evidence from his fields. His primary written sources were the works of his great English contemporary Arthur Young, whose "Norfolk system" of farming Bordley believed best suited to conditions in Md. and Pa., but he obviously read broadly in the current literature. *Sketches on Rotation*, his largest pamphlet (rep., 1796, 1797), acknowledged his debt to Young and to Jethro Tull. Occasionally, Bordley published on nonagricultural affairs. *On Monies, Coins, Weights, and Measures*, for example, presented the case for the new nation adopting the decimal system and advocated, as a "new thing," the striking of a copper penny.

It is, however, as an agricultural writer that Bordley is most important. At the end of his life, he produced several large handbooks, derived primarily from his readings (*Epitome, Gleanings*), but his masterwork is *Essays and Notes*. This 591-page compendium reprints several of his pamphlets as well as a number of new essays. He drew upon his own experiences as well as upon his books, and again the reader is impressed with the simple straightforwardness of Bordley's approach. The text of the manual is accompanied by clear line drawings. It is recognized as the second major American book on agriculture (after *American Husbandry*, 1775) and is taken as a reliable source on the practices of the period. A 3rd edition was called for in 1826: Bordley's writings were useful in advancing the understandings and practices of his fellow American farmers, and this was his only purpose in publishing them.

Suggested Readings: DAB. *See also* Elizabeth G. Gibson, *Biographical Sketches* (1865); Lewis Cecil Gray, *History of Agriculture in the Southern United States* (1933).

Kenneth Van Dover
Lincoln University

BENJAMIN BOSWORTH (c. 1612-1700)

Works: *A Caution to Prevent Scandal* (1693); *Signs of Apostacy Lamented* (1693).

Biography: Born in Coventry, Eng., c. 1612, Benjamin Bosworth immigrated to New Eng. when he was 22 and by 1635 had established himself as a planter in Higham, Mass. A restless man, Bosworth moved to Hull in 1665, to Stow in 1682, and eventually to Boston, where he spent his last years in comfort, having devised an old-age security plan for himself and his wife, Beatrice. Although Bosworth did not publish until he was 81, he apparently cultivated literary connections throughout his life. His son, also called Benjamin, married a daughter of Secretary Nathaniel Morton (q.v.), author of *New-Englands Memoriall* (1699), and Bosworth was himself a close acquaintance of Samuel Sewall (q.v.). In fact, Sewall was probably responsible for getting Bosworth's poems into print. Sewall frequently encouraged his friends to write verse that he then had printed in small leaflets like *Signs of Apostacy*, Bosworth's only surviving work. Moreover, Sewall shared Bosworth's hatred of periwigs, considering them a "sign of apostacy." Benjamin Bosworth died in 1700; his wife, visited by Sewall during her remaining years, survived her husband by about twelve years.

Critical Appraisal: Benjamin Bosworth belongs to a fairly distinct group of seventeenth-century American verse writers, a group known as the "young immigrants of the founding years" who occupy a transitional place in American literary history between the early verse of poets like Michael Wigglesworth (q.v.) and the later verse of the eighteenth century. Although they were born in Eng., these writers emigrated to New Eng. in their 20s—too soon to be truly English—too late to be thoroughly American. This group of immigrants, most of whom lacked extensive formal education, nonetheless possessed a vivid sense of the ideals that formed American Puritanism. Most of the verse writers of this group lived to be old (many surviving well into their 80s and 90s), and in the later years of their lives, they saw themselves as instrumental in preserving those ideals from which the younger generations seemed to be falling away. Benjamin Bosworth, in many respects a typical member of this group, waited until old age to write poetry, and his verse contrasts the original religious ideals of early seventeenth-century New Eng. with what he perceived to be the increasing materialism of late seventeenth-century society.

Bosworth's two surviving poems, "Signs of Apostacy Lamented" and "A Caution to Prevent Scandal," published together in a four-page leaflet in 1693, resemble the broadside verse popular at the time, with the exception that they are not printed in the regular single-page format. Such verse formed a distinct class of seventeenth-century broadside literature, poetry marked by threats of fire and brimstone or the gentler tones of fervent pleas to abandon the wiles of Satan.

Bosworth's longest poem, "Signs of Apostacy Lamented," warns against the evils of "Perriwigs" and "Hairy Top-knots" and exhorts the reader to cast off the garb of "Pride." Contrasting such "foolish Fancies" with the mark of salvation described in the Book of Revelations, Bosworth noted that the mark is obscured by these vanities so that "it hardly will be own'd at the last Day." According to Bosworth, periwigs are an abomination, because they are the visible signs of the people's abandonment of God's covenant. In this poem, Bosworth lamented that New Eng., once a "land of Pray'r," had become a land of "Pray'r turned out of doors by Sin." The fashionable periwig thus becomes a perversion of the sign of salvation, and the poem becomes a jeremiad reinforcing the views of contemporaries like Increase Mather (q.v.) and Cotton Mather (q.v.), who shared many of Bosworth's views on the "dangers of apostacy." According to Bosworth, so-called Christians defile their hands with "the filthy *Hair* / Of some vile Wretch, by foul Disease that fell, / Whose Soul perhaps is burning now in Hell." Like his contemporaries in the pulpit, the poet admonished his readers to forego their backward ways and to guard against all sin "in *outward* Man as well as Heart within," echoing a continual theme of the poem—that physical appearance mirrors the state of the soul. In closing the poem, Bosworth turned from addressing the reader to praying earnestly for strength "to mind our way," so that Christians might reaffirm their faith with renewed vigor.

"A Caution to Prevent Scandal" is considerably shorter than "Signs of Apostacy Lamented," but it bears the same intense sincerity and fervor that characterizes the longer work and was written for many of the same reasons. Like the first poem, it is written in rhymed couplets, although by reason of its brevity (sixteen lines), it is not broken into stanzas. In the poem, Bosworth exhorted his audience to refrain from "a False Report against thy Brother," and he cleverly used an old image to warn of the consequences of defamation: "GOD is a just Revenger of such Wrong. / And will *again* them pay in their own Coin, / Who *thus* their Brothers Credit do purloin." As did "Signs of Apostacy," this poem emphasizes outward appearance as a reliable indicator of the inward state, and it closes with a prayer for an increase of love as a way of preparing for death, instead of fearing it.

At first glance, Bosworth's subjects—periwigs and scandal—may seem slight ones for poetry. But Bosworth was a product of the times, and for him they take on serious symbolic significance as external signs of a spiritual failure within the community. Benjamin Bosworth's poetry, brief as it is, reflects the concerns of a religious-minded man: it indicates a definite shift in the goals of the Mass. colony, and it adds to our insight about the origins of American poetic theory and practice.

Suggested Readings: FCNEV. *See also* Worthington Chauncey Ford, *Broadsides, Ballads, Etc. Printed in Massachusetts, 1639-1800*, CMHS, 75 (1922), v-xiv, 28; Ola Elizabeth Winslow, *American Broadside Verse* (1930), pp. xvii-xxvi.

Judith E. Funston
Michigan State University

JONATHAN BOUCHER (1738-1804)

Works: *A Letter from a Virginian to the Members of Congress* (1774); *Reminiscences of an American Loyalist* (1789); *A View of the Causes and Consequences of the American Revolution* (1797).

Biography: Jonathan Boucher was born in Blencogo, a village in Cumberland County, Eng., on Mar. 12, 1738. Previously wealthy, his family had suffered financial reverses for siding with the Puritans during the English Civil War, and Boucher grew up in near poverty. Determined to improve his financial condition, he taught himself to read, became a schoolmaster and an usher at a private school, and at the age of 21 went to Va. as a tutor. Offered the rectorship of Hanover Parish, he returned to Eng. and was ordained in the Church of England. In Va., Boucher prospered as both a clergyman and a planter, and he ran a boarding school attended by George Washington's (q.v.) stepson. In 1770 Boucher left Va. for a more lucrative parish in Md., where he became involved in politics. Although he had opposed the Stamp Act, Boucher joined the conservatives in Md. when they attempted to lower the salary of Anglican ministers and questioned the legal basis of the established church itself. Preaching Tory doctrines in his sermons and attacking Revolutionary politics and politicians, Boucher became one of the best-known Loyalists in Md. The reign of patriot committees, however, soon made it impossible for him to remain in the colony, and in Sept. 1775 he fled to Eng. In exile Boucher found employment as a clergyman and a teacher and also became a well-known writer. His first wife, Eleanor Addison of Md., died in 1784, his second in 1787, and his third, Elizabeth James, the widow of a close friend, bore three boys and five girls. Boucher died on Apr. 27, 1804.

Critical Appraisal: Jonathan Boucher combined an aptitude for written expression with an interest in public affairs and an aggressive personality. While in Va. and Md., he published several newspaper pieces and a pamphlet, most of them dealing with current political controversies. His literary reputation, however, rests on two works written in Eng.: *A View of the Causes and Consequences of the American Revolution* and *Reminiscences of an American Loyalist*.

A View of the Causes and Consequences of the American Revolution consists of thirteen sermons, allegedly delivered in the colonies, on unpopular Loyalist topics. Deeply traditional, Boucher believed in a hierarchical political system based on the premise that humans were born unequal and needed an aristocratic system of government. According to Boucher, "civil liberty" or "good government" existed "when the great body of the people are trained and led habitually to submit to and acquiesce in some fixed and steady principles of conduct." Religion and education, his own vocational fields, taught him that duty and self-interest lay in obedience to established authority. Boucher believed that Americans were too harsh in their judgment of British policy, but he had an even greater concern that by criticizing imperial government Americans were calling all institutions into question and threatening social order in general and were hence ushering into the world a period of destructive and unmitigated anarchy.

Most Tories accepted the political ideas of John Locke but rejected the way they were used by the patriots. Boucher attacked, however, the entire Lockean system. According to Boucher, men had never lived freely in a state of nature, had not created government by contract, and were not justified in resisting an abusive state. A follower of Robert Filmer, Boucher believed that the power of the state was an extension of the patriarchal authority given by divine ordination and exercised by fathers within the family. Boucher's criticism of Locke was sometimes penetrating: "A right of resistance . . . for which Mr. Locke contends, is incompatible with the duty of submitting to the determination of 'the majority': for which he also contends."

Boucher's sermons are carefully written, and they offer valuable insight into the politics and political ideology of the American Revolution. Like those of many colonial American preachers, Boucher's published sermons were probably different from the way they were originally delivered. Most, if not all, of Boucher's sermons were lost when he fled to Eng., and they were rewritten while the author was looking for employment and hoping for a pension from the British government and when his politics had become markedly more conservative. The published sermons reflect Boucher's knowledge of events after the original delivery, and his alteration of circumstance and of opinion probably also distorts the original content.

Written in 1789, *Reminiscences of an American Loyalist* is Boucher's autobiography. It reflects his material aspirations and interest in upward mobility and is a valuable source of information on the religious and political controversy in Va. and Md. that preceded the American Revolution. Throughout *Reminiscences*, Boucher blasted American patriots and offered memorable anecdotes. On one occasion, for example, he was forced to preach with loaded pistols in order to protect himself from a patriot mob, and on another occasion, he described a toast that "Americans all hang together in accord and concord," to which he allegedly responded, "In any cord...so it be but a strong cord."

Suggested Readings: CCMDG; CCV; DAB; DNB; LHUS; Sprague (V, 211-214). *See also* Michael D. Clark, "Jonathan Boucher: The Mirror of Reaction," HLQ, 33 (1969), 19-32; idem, "Jonathan Boucher and the Toleration of Roman Catholics in Maryland," MdHM, 71 (1976), 194-204; Philip Evanson, "Jonathan Boucher: The Mind of an American Loyalist," MdHM, 58 (1963), 123-136; Ralph Emmett Fall, "The Rev. Jonathan Boucher, Turbulent Tory (1738-1804)," HMagPEC, 36 (1937), 323-356; Anne Y. Zimmer, *Jonathan Boucher, Loyalist in Exile* (1978); Anne Young Zimmer and Alfred H. Kelley, "Jonathan Boucher: Constitutional Conservative," JAH, 58 (1972), 897-922.

Sidney Charles Bolton
University of Arkansas at Little Rock

JAMES BOWDOIN (1726-1790)

Works: *A Paraphrase...of the Oeconomy of Human Life* (1759); *Additional Observations to a Short Narrative* (1770); *A Short Narrative of the Horrid Massacre* (1770); *A Philosophical Discourse* (1780); *A Philosophical Discourse* (1786).

Biography: James Bowdoin was born in Boston, Mass., on Aug. 7, 1726, the grandson of a Huguenot immigrant. His father, James Bowdoin, Sr., was a wealthy merchant and a prominent political figure. Young Bowdoin was afforded the best education Mass. could offer, Master Lovell's Boston Latin School and Harvard College (1745). Caring little for mercantile pursuits, Bowdoin was interested throughout his life mainly in political economy and natural science. In 1753 he was elected to the Mass. House of Representatives and in 1757 to the Council, where he sat (except for one year) until 1774. At first Bowdoin supported the royal prerogative, but in the decade before the Revolution, he consistently opposed royal Governors Francis Bernard and Thomas Hutchinson (q.v.). He was the leader of a faction in the Council that cooperated with the Sons of Liberty in the House of Representatives in reducing British authority in Mass. Most of the strongest Council documents attacking royal policy were written by James Bowdoin.

During the Revolution, Bowdoin was chosen a member of the Provincial Congress, and for several years he was president of this governing body. In 1780 he was president of the Mass. Constitution Convention and was chairman of the committee that drafted the constitution. Later, amidst much social unrest in the state, Bowdoin was elected governor. When debtor agitators, suffering from severe economic distress, rose in arms against the government, Governor Bowdoin rallied forces and effectively suppressed Shays's Rebellion. Shortly thereafter he was working for the adoption of the U.S. Constitution.

Bowdoin's interest in scientific affairs led to an extensive correspondence with Benjamin Franklin (q.v.), the writing of a number of scientific papers, election to the Royal Society of London, and the founding of the American Academy of Arts and Sciences.

Critical Appraisal: James Bowdoin's numerous official political papers (some published) reveal a clear, direct, forceful, and uncluttered literary style, especially for that period. His point of view was that of a very intelligent, refined, wealthy person, and in his writing, he was incisively logical. In no sense a democrat, he saw the advantage of joining forces with Samuel Adams (q.v.) and his friends in the struggle against G.B. That he was capable of very effective propaganda can be seen in his *Short Narrative* of the Boston Massacre, one of the most inflammatory pieces of the period. Once independence was won, Bowdoin worked consistently for the creation of stable government in both Mass. and the nation. Only a portion of the large body of Bowdoin papers in the Massachusetts Historical Society has been published.

Suggested Readings: DAB; Sibley-Shipton (II; 514-550); T_2. *See also* Bowdoin and Temple Papers, Massachusetts Historical Society; F. G. Walett, "James Bowdoin, Patriot Propagandist," NEQ, 23 (1950), 320-338; idem, "The Massachusetts Council, 1766-1774," WMQ, 3rd ser., 6 (1949); R. C. Winthrop, *Life and Services of James Bowdoin* (1876).

Francis G. Walett
Worcester State College

BATHSHEBA BOWERS (c. 1672-1718)

Works: *An Alarm Sounded to Prepare the Inhabitants* (1709).

Biography: Bathsheba Bowers was born sometime around 1672 in Charlestown, Mass. Her parents, Benanuel and Elizabeth (Dunster) Bowers, and two older sisters were disciplined as Quakers by Puritan magistrates. As a result, Bathsheba and her three sisters were sent to Philadelphia. At the corner of Little Dock and Second Streets, Bowers built a small house (later known as "Bathsheba's Bower") and furnished it with books, a table, and a cup. Bowers never married, and she lived in seclusion, tending her garden, reading, and writing. According to Ann Bolton, who lived with her, Bathsheba Bowers was "very religious yet very whimsical"; she read her Bible closely, but "sometimes to no better purpose than to afford matter for dispute." Bolton also observed that Bowers owned a number of books "wrote by a female hand filled with dreams and visions and a thousand Romantic Notions of her seeing Various sorts of Beasts and Bulls in the Heavens." Some time after 1709, Bowers became a Quaker preacher and moved to S.C., where she died in 1718.

Critical Appraisal: Bathsheba Bowers called *An Alarm*, her only surviving work, an account of the "Dealings of God with [her] Soul." Echoing *Lam*. 3:12, she reflected on her troubled life: "Why it pleased the Almighty to bend his Bow and set me as a Mark for his Arrow, not only from my Youth, but even from my very Infancy up, I know not but even so it has been." At times she wept and cried out, seeking to understand her affliction. Because she had mortified her pride, her conscience acquitted her of disobedience; she, like Job, had received "Wounds without a cause." Citing Scripture, Bowers argued that God acts "for Reasons known to himself." The carnal mind cannot interpret afflictions as punishment for sin; man can only accept God's will. *An Alarm*, a demonstration of this principle, is intended to "be of Service" to the reader.

Like many writers of spiritual autobiography, Bowers portrayed her life as a "spiritual Warfair." She was seized at the age of 6 or 7 with a horror of death and damnation. In her teens, pride became "a very potent Enemy," leading her to esteem luxury, read romances, and enjoy "decking up and receiving and giving Visits," all the while fearing judgment. Conversion occurred at age 19 after a long illness when she was suddenly "overcome with a divine Sweetness." In these respects, Bowers's story resembles the spiritual autobiographies and journals of many seventeenth- and eighteenth-century Protestants. Unlike many Protestants of the time, however, Bowers became conscious of an "Inner Light"—"a strong Injunction" to abandon her frivolities and "take up the much despised saying *Thee* and *Thou* to a single Person."

Called to become a Quaker, Bowers "submitted, tho' it was not without Tears." She retired from the world, fasted, meditated, prayed, and attended meeting; she relinquished, as she put it, "all things which by Nature's Charter I might claim a title to"; yet she was rarely at peace. Often she longed for death, and she sometimes "received secret Whispers, That [she] must come to further Sufferings, to have the root or original of sin wrought out, to be made perfect." The "old Accuser and Troubler" tormented her with her obligation to obey the "Light within," even if it required that she go naked. (Some early Quakers "went naked for a sign" of the world's spiritual nakedness.) An "Infernal Pack" of tempters urged her to despair and die. Pride made her fear the world's scorn and ridicule; hence she dreaded being called to preach, terrified that she would refuse and be cast into hell. After experiencing a vision of hell and then being carried to "an exceeding high Mountain," where God assured her of his guidance, her fears were relieved; she believed that she would be rewarded.

At the end of her autobiography, dated Jul. 17, 1709, Bowers stated that she still experienced tranquility and misery by turns but that her periods of torment were "shorter and seldomer" than before. She anticipated further trials, for earthly life is a "long and tedious Travail," but she offered "evidence of the total overthrow" of Pride: she was content with her humble life. Furthermore, as she stated in the preface, her publishing this account without worrying about her literary reputation proved that she had succeeded in taming her "potent Enemy" —ambition.

In typical Quaker fashion, the central characters in Bowers's testimony are herself and God. She personified her soul's allies and foes but named no human beings, no external events. Attempting to recreate anguish and exaltation, she wrote of deserts, abysses, and mountains. Like other Quakers, she used an unadorned style, often incorporating biblical metaphors, allusions, paraphrases, and quotations. Although an acquaintance of Bowers remarked that her insatiable "thirst for knowledge" made her an avid reader, she did not display her learning. In the manner traditional among Friends, she used "first Day" and "fifth Moneth" rather than names derived from pagan sources. Her Quaker background is also evident in her mysticism, perfectionism, belief that the convert must deny his will, and conviction that God reveals himself through voices, visions, and dreams. *An Alarm*, then, epitomizes an experience common to the "Children of Light."

But Bowers was nothing if not unconventional. For all of her talk of submission, she sometimes sounded like an individual confident of her worth and her right to be heard, whatever others might think. In the preface she spoke of "meeting with Repulses in [her] proceeding to Print" and her hesitance in "bringing any of [her] Works to view." This reluctance is partly explained by the "Scorn and Ridicule" that unpopular ideas receive. (This fact she no doubt learned from personal experience as well as from the history of her family and her sect.) Although Bowers did not say who had "repulsed" her writings, fellow Quakers may have done so. A committee of Friends customarily examined any work that a brother or sister intended to publish. By the testimony of her own spiritual narrative, Bowers rarely knew the serenity that was supposed to follow the submission of a Quaker's will to God's. According to Ann Bolton, she called herself a Quaker but was "so Wild in her Notions it was hard to find out of what religion she really was of." At any rate, her autobiography was printed in New York City, not Philadelphia, probably by William Bradford (q.v.). If the world slumbered on after Bowers's "alarm" had been sounded, her work is nonetheless a poignant record of a strong-willed individual's struggle to find and follow the "Light within" and an excellent, if not typical, example of the eighteenth-century Quaker spiritual autobiography.

Suggested Readings: Pattie Cowell, "Bathsheba Bowers" in *American Women Writers: A Critical Reference Guide, from Colonial Times to the Present*, 4 vols., ed. Lina Mainiero (1979-), I, 204-205; Lucius R. Paige, *History of Cambridge, Massachusetts, 1630-1877* (1877), pp. 346-352, 493-494; William J. Potts, "Bathsheba Bowers," PMHB, 3 (1879), 110-113; Daniel P. Shea, *Spiritual Autobiography in Early America* (1968), pp. 3-44; Owen C. Watkins, *The Puritan Experience: Studies in Spiritual Autobiography* (1972), pp. 160-207; Luella M. Wright, *The Literary Life of the Early Friends, 1650-1725* (1932; rep., 1966), pp. 57-59, 155-238.

Mary De Jong
The Pennsylvania State University

ZABDIEL BOYLSTON (1679-1766)

Works: *Some Account of What Is Said of Inoculating* (1721); *An Historical Account of the Smallpox Inoculated in New England* (1726).

Biography: Born in Brookline, Mass., in 1679, Zabdiel Boylston was the grandson of Thomas Boylston, esq. (emigrant from Eng. in 1635) and son of Mary Gardner and Dr. Thomas Boylston (earliest physician of Muddy River, now known as Brookline). Boylston received his medical training from his father and Dr. John Cutler of Boston. Although he never received a medical degree, Boylston quickly attained the reputation of a very skilled and humane physician. For his pioneering effort in smallpox inoculation during the Boston epidemic of 1721, Boylston achieved worldwide fame, including an invitation in 1724 to lecture before the Royal Society, which elected him a fellow in 1726. After several years of experimenting on cures for rattlesnake bite and with cedar balsam, Boylston retired from practice in 1740 and died in 1766 on his Brookline farm. For his important contributions to preventive medicine, Boylston was honored with academic foundations at Harvard Medical School by his grand-nephew Ward Nicholas Boylston.

Critical Appraisal: In Apr. 1721 smallpox appeared in Boston, and by May it had reached epidemic proportions. At the urging of Cotton Mather (q.v.), Dr. Boylston courageously began scientific experiments in smallpox inoculation on his own son and two slaves. Battle immediately broke out against the practice of inoculation, taking form in pamphlet wars and in James Franklin's (q.v.) *New England Courant*, spearheaded chiefly by the pen of another Boston physician, Dr. William Douglass (q.v.). Enflamed mobs charged Mather and Boylston with murder, leading Boylston to fear for his safety and Mather to dodge a grenade hurled through his window. The mob objected to inoculation on religious grounds, seeing the practice as interference with the will of God, who they believed had sent the epidemic as punishment for sin. Evidence suggests, however, that Douglass probably led the attack simply to thwart Mather's attempted control of community affairs.

Zabdiel Boylston, however, was undoubtedly the hero of the epidemic, meeting the opposition's charges with carefully prepared scientific data supporting inoculation. In Sept. 1721, after three times being called to account by the selectmen of Boston, Boylston and Mather brought out *Some Account of What Is Said of Inoculating*, which summarized the accounts of smallpox inoculation in Turkey published in *Philosophical Transactions of the Royal Society* in 1717. To answer the erroneous testimony of a Dr. Dalhonde concerning the dangers of inoculation before the Boston selectmen and to assuage the fears of the people, Boylston and Mather showed that experiment must be the final criterion for judgment in medical practice. Although recent studies claim that Mather wrote much of the pamphlet, the introduction and accounts of experiences with patients were most certainly the work of Boylston.

In contrast to the 844 deaths among the 5,757 Bostonians who contracted smallpox in the natural way, Boylston lost only 6 of the 244 patients he inoculated. Boylston's *Historical Account* (1726) shows that he kept careful medical records that were clearly tabulated and logically set forth, and this masterly clinical presentation was the first of its kind from an American physician. In the account, Boylston narrated the history of his experiments with smallpox inoculation, giving careful details of the method of inoculation and the course of illness of those inoculated and contrasting this milder form of the disease with the more serious effects of natural smallpox. Most remarkable is Boylston's pioneering use of medical statistics.

Boylston's masterly clinical observations in the *Historical Account* were well received by the Royal Society and the Royal College of Physicians in London. The Boston experiment was influential in sustaining and extending the practice of inoculation in Eng. and in the other colonies. In medical literature, the account was often cited as evidence in support of the practice. As a scientist prevailing against the voices of dogma, superstition, and ignorance, Boylston performed one of the earliest important experiments in preventive medicine; he will take his place among the physicians who contributed to the birth of modern medicine.

Suggested Readings: BDAS; DAB. *See also* John B. Blake, "The Inoculation Controversy in Boston: 1721-22," NEQ, 25 (1952), 489-506; Samuel Gardner Drake, *The History and Antiquities of Boston* (1856); pp. 561-563; Reginal Fitz, "Zabdiel Boylston, Inoculator, and the Epidemic of Smallpox in Boston in 1721," BJHH, 22 (1911), 315-327; G. L. Kittredge, "Lost Works of Cotton Mather," PMHS, 44 (1912), 418-479; Arnold C. Klebs, "The Historic Evolution of Variolation," BJHH, 24 (1913), 69-83; R. P. Stearns, *Science in the British Colonies of America* (1970), pp. 411, 418-423, 436-442, 467, 472, 479-480, 679; G. B. Warden, *Boston, 1689-1776* (1970), pp. 86-87.

Linda Neal Bates
University of California, Davis

HUGH HENRY BRACKENRIDGE (1748-1816)

Works: *Father Bombo's Pilgrimage to Mecca in Arabia*, vol. II (1770); *Satires Against the Tories* (with Philip Freneau and James Madison; 1770); *The Rising Glory of America* (with Philip Freneau; 1771); *A Poem on Divine Revelation* (1774); *The Death of General Montgomery* (1777); *Six Political Discourses Founded on the Scriptures* (1778); *An Eulogium of the Brave Men* (1779); *The United States Magazine* (1779); *Narratives of a Late Expedition Against the Indians* (1783); *A Masque, Written at the Warm Springs in Virginia* (1784); "The Lone Indian" (1785); "The Trial of Mamachtage" (1785); "On the Running Away of the Nineteen Members of the Assembly, A Hudibrastic" (1787); "Oration on the Federal Constitution" (1788); *Modern Chivalry*, vols. I and II (1792), vol. III (1793), vol. IV (1797), (Pt. II, 1804), rev. (1815); *Incidents of the*

Insurrection in Western Pennsylvania (1795); *Scottish Poems* (1796, 1801); *An Ode in Honor of the Pennsylvania Militia* (1800); *Beauties of American Newspapers for 1805* (1806); *Gazette Publications* (1806); *An Epistle to Walter Scott* (1811); *Law Miscellanies* (1814).

Biography: In 1753, at age 5, Hugh Henry Brackenridge immigrated with his parents from Kintyre, Scot., to the "Barrens" of York County, Pa. There he helped clear the land and experienced the Indian terrors following Gen. Braddock's defeat. A prodigious reader by age 15, he entered Princeton, earning his way mostly by teaching and achieving enough stature to write, in collaboration with Philip Freneau (q.v.), the commencement poem *The Rising Glory of America*. He responded to the Revolution with two dramas commemorating Bunkers Hill and Gen. Montgomery's death and soon after was delivering fiery sermons against the British as an army chaplain. In 1779 he left the army to advance the national cause culturally by establishing *The United States Magazine*. Within a year of its failure, Brackenridge achieved a law degree and seeing no chance for advancement in Philadelphia headed for the frontier settlement of Pittsburgh, where he applied himself "to advance the country and thereby myself." For one term, he became a state assemblyman and established roads, a church, an academy, a newspaper, and a library. This trained Classicist, insisting on ideas of democratic citizenship, clashed with the boisterous frontier realities and temporarily withdrew from public life, a withdrawal that led to the writing of his satire *Modern Chivalry* and his reluctant involvement as moderator in the Whiskey Insurrection, for which he was castigated by both sides. At the end of the century, he established *The Tree of Liberty*, a Jeffersonian newspaper to rival the *Gazette* (now *Federalist*) that he had also established. For leading Thomas Jefferson's (q.v.) campaign in Western Pa., Brackenridge was appointed a Supreme Court justice of the state and retired to Carlisle in the East but continued to visit as a circuit rider, a role in which he acted with such eccentricity that the name of Judge Brackenridge became fixed in the legends with those of Mike Fink and Simon Girty.

Critical Appraisal: Brackenridge's writings span the last years of colonial America, the Revolution, and the incubation of democracy on the frontier. The portraits he drew of the burgeoning democracy on the early frontier and back East are most significant. In *Modern Chivalry* he borrowed Cervantes's picaresque structure to satirize the foibles and follies of frontier life as well as those of effete easterners. His criticism shows the new publicans their shortcomings—namely, their need for education, refinements, and self-knowledge. Ambition and ignorance are the targets. Success of the democratic experiment depends upon the people learning their lessons.

Captain John Farrago, a gentleman at leisure whose ideas are "drawn from the old school," the Greeks and Romans, administers the lessons while his servant Teague O'Regan, the unlikely student, bogtrots behind him. As they travel the breadth of the United States—Pittsburgh to Philadelphia and back—the characters, events, and customs they encounter stimulate the bogtrotter's ambition to rise in the new democracy although he cannot read or write. The captain's rhetoric is taxed again and again to dampen Teague's ambition to become a legislator, member of Dr. Benjamin Franklin's (q.v.) Philosophical Society, clergyman, actor, lawyer, professor, and even fake chief of the Kickapoos. It is as lover, however, after he has inspired "a kind of Teagueomania among the females of Philadelphia," that the captain finds him most irrepressible.

There is some development through the picaresque episodes. By the end of the second volume, Farrago is no longer able to hold against the popular demand for his ignorant servant; so he attempts to mitigate what he cannot prevent by educating Teague for a government position through the niceties of the French language and the dance, which implies the author's view of government officials. Given the position of exciseman in the western country, Teague is soon humbled by the tar and feathers of the insurgents and shipped to a French zoo as an American species by the same Philosophical Society that had invited him to membership in another guise.

In the second part, the action is suffocated in Brackenridge's attacks and strictures on American journalism and the judiciary. Even in the first part, the narrative action is too often subordinated to expository lessons on democracy. Although the narrative portions themselves are obviously exaggerated, they render likely portraits of the cultured and ignorant, the rich and poor, in the commonplaces of their daily lives. The reader sees the politicians, the lawyers, the clergy, the Philadelphia belles, and frontier gamecocks and responds to the election stupidity, demagogues, hypocrisy, the meaningless speeches of Congress, trials by ignorant juries, misappropriations by government, the snobbishness and artificiality of the East, and the westerner's ignorant resentment of law and learning.

In essence, *Modern Chivalry* is an essay illustrating social habits, abuses, and absurdities; it shows the substance of early democratic life in order to define its problems. The larger-than-life size characters and the attitudes it parodies are also woven into *Incidents of the Insurrection*. But here the author's intention was no longer instructional, and his method was no longer satirical. The reportorial realism of this narrative is drawn in an atmosphere of epic event and heroic posture. Still working within the framework of his early epic, *The Rising Glory of America*, Brackenridge associated the glorious past with the rebellious events of the moment. Warriors were characterized through their histories. They contested oratorically to build courage for the battle. Disasters were prophesied through omens. Even the similes were heroic. There is humor and sentiment also, but they are perceived in the scene being reported, not imagined. Like his "Trial of Mamachtaga," written ten years earlier, *Incidents* is a true narrative that seeks an artistic effect through the selection and dramatic arrangement of observations.

Among all of the characters—insurgent and patriot—only Attorney Brackenridge seems to understand the consequence of the struggle known as the Whiskey Rebellion. He equated his own destruction at the hands of the rebels with disruption of the Union, and the consequence is war between East and West. Yet he vacillated between government loyalty, community loyalty, and personal loyalty. He appeared to be a Federalist in the eyes of the insurgents and an insurgent in the eyes of the Federalists. As the thrust of events amplified, he contemplated immigration to the East, and when his efforts at reconciliation made him a symbol of rebellion, he weighed the possibility of warring against the government with the aid of the Indians. Finally, as the government troops advanced, he feared assassination and contemplated a run to the woods and a life among the people he had referred to as "animals vulgarly called Indians." The ultimate violence was avoided through amnesty, but this ideal victory brought personal defeat. Although he was not assassinated, he was humiliated as "A most artful fellow." The naked view of man's responsibility to himself is uncovered at the heart of the story, but it is too base a view for a man of ideals and ambitions. Consequently, the momentary glimpse of the naked self passed with the dangers that unveiled it. On a more obvious level, the narrative elements combine into a story of the individual will exerted upon social forces in tumult. On the level of the author's overt intention, it comprises a report of a man's conduct in the frontier turmoil.

The work of Brackenridge fuses the literary modes beginning in the eighteenth-century tradition of epic and mock-heroic; they travel the avenues of sensibility and realism, Practical and idealistic at once, Brackenridge directed his criticism at the abuses of the democracy he found in action. If his satire chastised the electorate, his realistic narrative spoke to the individual. The *Incidents* showed in actuality what *Modern Chivalry* had satirized, that the new democratic experiment could not flourish without a wise and sensitive citizenry, "the first springs of happiness in a republic."

Suggested Readings: CCMC; DAB; LHUS; P; T$_2$. *See also* Alexander Cowie, *The Rise of the American Novel* (1948); Neville B. Craig, *Exposure of a Few of the Many Misstatements in H. H. Brackenridge's History of the Whiskey Insurrection* (1859); John D. Dickenson, "The Influence of *Don Quixote* on *Modern Chivalry*" (Ph.d. diss., Florida State Univ., 1959); Michael T. Gilmore, "Eighteenth Century Oppositional Ideology and Hugh Henry Brackenridge's *Modern Chivalry*," EAL, 13 (1978), 181-192; Lynn Haims, "Of Indians and Irishmen: A Note on Brackenridge's Sources for Satire in *Modern Chivalry*," EAL, 10 (1975), 88-92; Thomas P. Haviland, "Hugh Henry Brackenridge and Milton's 'Piedmontese' Sonnet," N&Q, 176 (1939), 243-244; idem, "The Miltonic Quality of Brackenridge's 'Poem on Divine Revelation,' " PMLA, 56 (1941), 588-592; Daniel Marder, *Hugh Henry Brackenridge* (1967); Wendy Martin, "On the Road with the Philosopher and Profiteer: A Study of Hugh Henry Brackenridge's *Modern Chivalry*," ECS, 4 (1971), 241-246; William M. Nance, "Satiric Elements in *Modern Chivalry*," SLL, 9 (1967), 381-389; Claude M. Newlin, *The Life and Writings of Hugh Henry Brackenridge* (1932).

Daniel Marder
University of Tulsa

ANDREW BRADFORD (1686-1742)

Works: *The American Weekly Mercury* (editor and principal writer; 1719-1742); *Some Remedies Proposed* (1722); commentary on Massachusetts' persecution of

James Franklin (1723); *Some Necessary Precautions* (1727); prospectus for *American Magazine* (1740); *The American Magazine* (printer and coprincipal writer; 1741).

Biography: Andrew Bradford, remembered as the printer who established Pa.'s first newspaper in 1719, was born in or near Philadelphia in 1686. The son of William Bradford (q.v.), the colony's pioneer printer, he moved to N.Y. with his parents in 1693 and apprenticed under his father, listing himself as "printer" as early as 1709. He returned to Philadelphia three years later and was that colony's only printer until 1723. During this decade, he published more than seventy-five items, including an excellent volume of the laws of Pa. (still known in legal circles as "Bradford's Laws of 1714") and many tracts for the Quakers. In addition, Bradford established a bookstore and bindery; served as postmaster for the colony from 1728 to 1737; fought authorities over the still-severe attempts to restrict and control printing in the city; shared with his business rival Benjamin Franklin (q.v.) a deep involvement in city and colony policies and legislation; and was a city councilman and respected vestryman of Christ Church. But it was as a printer that he made his greatest contribution to the colonial era, establishing the *American Weekly Mercury* on Dec. 11, 1719 (Pa.'s first newspaper and third in the colonies, only one day after the *Boston Gazette* became the second), editing it until his death; and launching the *American Magazine* in 1741, three days ahead of Franklin's *General Magazine* and thus the first magazine in the colonies. He died and was buried in Christ Churchyard in 1742, victim of a lingering illness that had limited his activities to the editing of the *Mercury* for several months.

Critical Appraisal: Journalist-historians and Andrew Bradford's biographers agree that the *American Weekly Mercury* was the equal of any other of the early colonial efforts and was especially noteworthy for its literary content, its local coverage and commentary (when such were still alien to most colonial journals), and its innovative advertising typography. To be credited, as Bradford was, by Isaiah Thomas (q.v.) for having printed "early accurate reports of the proceedings of the colonial Assembly" was high praise indeed, particularly in a colony where there still was strong executive feeling against such publication. On at least two occasions, Bradford was brought before the courts and on one occasion was jailed. Nonetheless, he continued to chip away at Philadelphia's reactionary attitude toward freedom of expression in much the way his father had done in the 1690s. Some of his better essays and pamphlets (a few of which appeared first in the *Mercury*) seemed deliberately to provoke the authorities. *The American Magazine*, however, appearing nine years after Edward Cave's much-copied *Gentleman's Magazine* in London, was a poor effort—as were most of its colonial contemporaries. But it again illustrates Bradford's often-neglected role as innovator and risk taker.

As a book importer (and reviewer), Andrew Bradford contributed greatly to his city's reputation for enlightenment and for familiarity with the best in European thought. This same influx of European books, too, was reflected in the literary tone of the *Mercury*, giving it a flavor at times superior to Franklin's better-known *Gazette*.

Suggested Readings: DAB; LHUS. *See also* Henry Lewis Bullen, "The Bradford Family of Printers," *The American(a) Collector*, 1 (1926), 148-156, 164-170; Henry Darrach, *Bradford Family, 1600-1906* (1906); Anna Janney DeArmond, *Andrew Bradford, Colonial Journalist* (1949); Horatio Gates Jones, *Andrew Bradford* (1869; rep., 1970); Isaiah Thomas, *The History of Printing in America* (1870), pp. 356, 359-362, 364-365, 458-459.

Donovan H. Bond
West Virginia University

EBENEZER BRADFORD (1746-1801)

Works: *Preaching the Unsearchable Riches* (1785); *The Depravity of Human Nature* (1791); *A Discourse Delivered at the Ordination of. . .Nathaniel Howe* (1791); *The Faithfulness of a Minister* (1791); *The Qualifications, Commissions, and Works of an Ambassador* (1791); *Strictures on the Remarks of Dr. Samuel Langdon on. . .the Rev. Dr. Hopkins' System of Doctrines* (1794); *The Art of Courting* (1795); *Christ's Presence with His Ministers* (1795); *A Dialogue Between Philagathus. . .and Pamela* (1795); *The Duty of a Minister* (1795); *Mr. Thomas Paine's Trial* (1795); *The Nature of Humiliation* (1795); *The Nature and Manner of Giving Thanks to God* (1795).

Biography: Born in Canterbury, Conn., in 1746, Ebenezer Bradford received a B.A. from the College of New Jersey in 1773 and was appointed pastor of the Church of South Hanover, N.J., by the Presbytery of New York on Jul. 13, 1775. Bradford and his wife, Elizabeth Green, who were married on Apr. 4, 1776, had nine children. After a dispute over the independence of the local church and "notions of Presbyterial powers," he and several other clergymen, including his father-in-law, Jacob Green (q.v.), formed their own Presbytery of Morris County, N.J. Bradford served as pastor of the First Church in Danbury, Conn., between Apr. 9, 1777, and Nov. 22, 1779. After preaching at various churches, Bradford was invited to Rowley, Mass., where he was pastor of the Congregational Church from Aug. 4, 1782, until his death on Jan. 3, 1801. During that time the church doubled in size to 167 members. In addition to an M.A. from the College of New Jersey (1786), Bradford was awarded honorary M.A.s from Dartmouth (1785) and Brown (1800).

Critical Appraisal: Ebenezer Bradford's best-known work, *The Art of Courting*, is a rough-hewn novel about seven courtships and employs several techniques typical of early American fiction: the epistolary technique, the pretense to historical truth and factual verifiability, the authorial guise of mere editor, and the condemnation of novels—in this case described as suitable only for those "determined to live a vicious and irreligious life." But largely uninterested in novelistic possibilities, Bradford does not take advantage of the potential either for specific description or for heightened effect. His emphasis is squarely placed on the didactic content of the letters themselves, not on the potential of the epistolary framework, and, as such, *The Art of Courting* more closely resembles a sermon than a novel. The first chapter editorializes on marriage and courtship and the following seven chapters provide illustrations of its moral lessons. With only minor variations, all of the model courtships progress through four stages: mutual friendship, profession of love by the man, the testing of that affection by the woman, and her acknowledgment of love for and subsequent engagement to him. In each case, the lovers' foremost concern is the spiritual and intellectual welfare of the beloved. One character perhaps best summarizes the message of the book: religion is *"the one thing needful"* for a good marriage.

Many of Bradford's published works are ordination sermons that adhere to the rigid pattern associated with the form. In most of his sermons, a biblical passage introduces a theme that is applied to the spiritual and practical duties of ministerial office. Arguments are numerically listed and presented, the sermons concluding with a series of remarks addressed specifically to fellow ministers, the new minister, members of the congregation, and finally to all of those in attendance. More controversial are Bradford's political sermons, *The Nature and Manner of Giving Thanks to God* and *The Nature of Humiliation*. An early and outspoken anti-Federalist, Bradford described President George Washington (q.v.) as *"but a man* subject to like imperfections with his fellow-men," while defending Governor Samuel Adams (q.v.) as "a man and a true democrat." Called by one scholar "the almost sole representative of democratic sentiments" among the Congregational clergy, Bradford publicly disputed with David Osgood and David Tappan, which led to his nickname the "Vandal of Rowley" and to his ostracism by fellow clergymen in Essex County. With equal vigor, Bradford defended democratic societies and liberty for Fr. and attacked "the baneful influence of British politics, spoilation, and injustice" on national and international affairs. Bradford was more orthodox in matters of doctrine, and his defense of Dr. Hopkins (q.v.), for example, recommended "Dr. Watts on Ontology, Mr. Locke on Human Understanding, [and] Bailey and Sheridan on the signification of the word Metaphysics." *Mr. Thomas Paine's Trial*, Bradford's longest tract, attacked Deism by employing both vituperative broadsides and appeals to traditional Calvinistic theology. Bradford's voice was an important, if not major, part of the religious and political debates of the late eighteenth century, and he contributed an early example of the epistolary novel in America.

Suggested Readings: CCNE; P. *See also* Herbert Ross Brown, *The Sentimental Novel in America: 1789-1860* (1940), pp. 11, 53-54, 108; William De Loss Love, Jr., *The Fast and Thanksgiving Days of New England* (1895), pp. 370-373; Tremaine McDowell, "Sensibility in the Eighteenth Century Novel," SP, 24 (1927), 383-402; Jacob C. Meyer, *Church and State in Massachusetts, 1740-1833* (1930), pp. 138-142; Anson Ely Morse, *The Federalist Party in Massachusetts to the Year 1800* (1909), pp. 131-134; Henri Petter, *The Early American Novel* (1971), pp. 70-71.

Randall Craig
State University of New York at Albany

WILLIAM BRADFORD (1590-1657)

Works: *A Relation or Journall of the Beginning and Proceedings of the English Plantation setled at Plimoth in New England* (with Edward Winslow et al., 1622), commonly known as *Mourt's Relation; Governour Bradford's Letter Book* (pub. in CMHS; 1794); *A Dialogue or the Sume of a Conference Between Som Younge Men Borne in New England and Sundery Ancient Men That Came out of Holland and Old England* (w. 1648; pub. in Alexander Young, ed., *Chronicles of the Pilgrim Fathers*; 1841); *Of Plimmoth Plantation* (w. 1630-1650; pub. as *The History of Plymouth Plantation*; 1856); *A Dialogue; Or, •3d• Conference Betweene Some Yonge-Men Borne in New-England and Some Ancient-Men* (w. 1652; pub. in PMHS, 1st ser., 3 [1871]).

Biography: The son of a prosperous farmer, William Bradford was born in 1590 in Austerfield, Yorkshire, Eng. Since both of his parents died during his early childhood, he was brought up mainly by his grandfather and uncles. When he was only 12 years old, he began attending Separatist meetings for worship in nearby villages, eventually becoming a member of the congregation in Scrooby, Nottinghamshire. There he came under the influence of William Brewster, for merly a student at Cambridge University, who aided him in his efforts at self-education and remained his lifelong friend and adviser. Bradford accompanied the Scrooby congregation in its flight to Holland in 1608, finding employment there in the cloth trade. In 1611 he bought a house in Leyden and soon thereafter married Dorothy May, a daughter of a Separatist elder residing in Amsterdam. In 1620 he sailed on the *Mayflower* for New Eng. and was one of the signers of the "*Mayflower* Compact." In Provincetown Harbor, the *Mayflower's* first landfall, Bradford's wife was drowned either by jumping or falling overboard. At Plymouth, following the death of the first governor, John Carver, Bradford was elected governor, a position that he held for all but five years of the remainder of his life. In 1623 he married the widow Alice Southworth, sister-in-law of George Morton (q.v.). Bradford's leadership contributed enormously if not decisively to the success of the Pilgrim venture. Yet he found time and energy to continue his self-education (for example, he learned Hebrew in his old age) a well as to write his famous history of the colony and a number of poems and religious tracts.

Critical Appraisal: William Bradford's earliest writing—and the only specimen of it to be published during his lifetime—was his contribution to *A Relation or Journall of the Beginning and Proceedings of the English Plantation Setled at Plimoth in New England*, commonly referred to as *Mourt's Relation*, to which the other major contributor was Edward Winslow (q.v.). It is generally supposed that Bradford wrote the long first section that describes the Pilgrims' arrival at Cape Cod, their explorations there, and their landing and first winter at Plymouth. Lively and highly informative, this work reveals Bradford's flair for narration.

Bradford's literary reputation, however, rests on his *Of Plimmoth Plantation*. Described by one scholar as "the outstanding piece of historical writing produced in America before Francis Parkman," this work is indeed outstanding, not only as a unique and invaluable historical record but also for its literary qualities. Bradford divided *Of Plimmoth Plantation* into two books. The first book traces the origins of the Separatist movement in Eng., provides an account of the formation of his own congregation in Scrooby and its exile in Holland, and gives details of the Pilgrims' voyage to New Eng. and their first months there. The second book is written in the form of annals covering the years 1620-1646. But Bradford's writing was not spread out over these twenty-six years. In his own words, he "begane these scribled writings...about the year 1630," and "peeced [them] up at times of leasure afterward." Internal evidence indicates that all of Book I was written in a rather short period after 1630 and that Book II, the annals, was probably written in its present form between 1644 and 1650.

In composing the annals, Bradford made use of his *Letter Book*, part of it extant, containing letters by him and others relating to colony affairs. Very likely he also drew from personal notes and diaries, but his intention seems to have been to produce a more orderly and unified account than such records alone would provide. As one critic stated, Bradford had "a strong sense of literary responsibility which animates and controls" his narrative. Furthermore, the quality of Bradford's prose indicates conscious literary effort. In his preface to Book I, Bradford himself assured the reader that he would "endevor to manefest in a plaine stile" the "occasion and Indusments" that lay behind the planting of Plymouth Colony. Thus he carefully avoided the flowery rhetorical complexities so popular among Renaissance writers. The chief influence on his writing, both in content and in style, was of course the Bible—mainly the Geneva version— which he quoted or paraphrased on almost every page and which served as a source of images and tropes. In general, his prose is characterized by the concrete, predominantly Anglo-Saxon diction and the simple but balanced sentence structure of the English Bible. Yet in keeping with the "simplified" religion and unpretentious ways of the people he represented, his writing is sprinkled with the homely and colloquial phrases that inevitably creep into uninhibited discourse. The result is a freshness, a rapid movement, at times a humor and lightness of touch, that contribute much to the book's readability.

Bradford's purpose in writing *Of Plimmoth Plantation* was to demonstrate that the Separatist Church and its colonization of Plymouth was a divinely decreed manifestation of the Protestant Reformation in Europe. Throughout Book I, he emphasized this aspect of Separatism. Indeed, the compelling impulse for his spurt of writing around 1630 may well have resulted from his joy at the rapid growth and firm establishment of Congregational Church polity—essentially that of the Separatists—in the Massachusetts Bay Colony at that time. Likewise, the later stint of writing in the 1640s may have resulted from his elation at the news of Puritan successes in Eng. during that decade. The return to true Christianity— that is, the Christianity of prepapal times—seemed now assured; and the English immigrants to the New World, Bradford was convinced, were playing a major role in the process. Thus Bradford discerned parallels between the Pilgrims' voyage to New Eng. and the journey of the Israelites, under Moses's leadership, to the Promised Land. Like most Protestant writers of the time, he believed that God in his direction of current history was repeating biblical history. Yet despite much cause for optimism, Bradford was troubled during the 1640s by a marked falling off of piety and an alarming decline in morals in his own beloved Plymouth. A second impulse, then, for the writing of Book II was to remind the colonists of the divinely ordained nature of their mission and to warn them of God's wrath if they failed to measure up to the piety and dedication of the first settlers.

Bradford's alarm at the decline in morals and religious zeal among the Pilgrims found further expression in a number of poems and in several *Dialogues* that he composed during these years. The poems, totally lacking in literary merit, are mainly railings against the degeneracy of the present and prophecies of terrible retribution from on high unless the people mend their ways. Of similar purport, although less jeremianic in tone, are two *Dialogues* (a third one has been lost) supposedly "between som younge men borne in New England and sundery Ancient men that came out of holland and old England," as explained in the title of the first *Dialogue*. These "Conferences," as they were also called, were designed to kindle in an apparently apathetic younger generation some of the fire that had burned in their elders. It is doubtful that the "Conferences," if they ever actually occurred, accomplished much. The arguments of the elders are verbose, heavy-handed, and repetitive—and in general dull, even in their scurrilous attacks on the Anglican bishops and the Church of Rome.

Bradford's importance, both as a historian and a man of letters, rests entirely on *Of Plimmoth Plantation*. Like most of his lesser writings, this eminently publishable work did not appear in print until the nineteenth century. Yet it had long exerted an influence, for it was used as a source of information and inspiration by many colonial New Eng. historians, including Cotton Mather (q.v.) and Thomas Prince (q.v.). During the Revolution, it was carried away from Boston by soldiers of the retreating British army and was not discovered until some seventy-five years later in the library of the bishop of London. Eventually, it was returned to America and is now deposited in the Massachusetts State Library.

Suggested Readings: DAB; DNB; FCNEV; LHUS; T$_1$. *See also* E. F. Bradford, "Conscious Art in Bradford's *History of Plymouth Plantation*," NEQ, 1 (1928), 133-157; Robert Daly, "William Bradford's Vision of History," AL, 44 (1973), 557-569; Norman Grabo, "William Bradford: *Of Plymouth Plantation*" in *Landmarks of American Literature*, ed. Hennig Cohen (1969), pp. 3-19; Samuel Eliot Morison, ed., Introduction, *Of Plymouth Plantation, 1620-1647* (1952); Bradford Smith, *Bradford of Plymouth* (1951); Perry D. Westbrook, *William Bradford* (1978); George F. Willison, *Saints and Strangers* (1945), passim.

Perry D. Westbrook
State University of New York at Albany

WILLIAM BRADFORD (1663-1752)

Works: *A Secretary's Guide* (1698); *New York Gazette* (editor and principal writer, 1725-1742; coauthor of numerous almanacs and pamphlets, 1685-1744).

Biography: William Bradford, America's fourth printer, was born in Barwell, Eng., in 1663. He apprenticed under Daniel Sowle, a noted Quaker printer, and came to Pa. in 1682 along with his bride, Sowle's daughter, and some of the colony's earliest Quaker emigrants. His first imprint appeared in 1785, probably from a press he operated in Burlington, N.J. He was Philadelphia's sole printer until 1692, when he became embroiled in the Quaker schism that saw George Keith (q.v.) attempting to succeed George Fox as leader of the sect. Bradford sided with Keith, and the output of his presses until he ceased activity in 1744 was dominated by his opposition to Quaker conservatism and orthodoxy. Imprisoned for his forthright pamphlets in 1692, he later moved to N.Y., where he was named official printer to the colony, a post he held for fifty years, longer than any other colonial. During the 1720s, with a press at Perth Amboy, Bradford also served as N.J.'s official printer, and he began printing the *New York Gazette* on Nov. 8, 1725, the colony's first newspaper. His son Andrew Bradford (q.v.) continued the family business in Philadelphia and founded Pa.'s first newspaper, the *American Weekly Mercury*, in 1719, and his grandson was William Bradford "the third" (q.v.), who achieved fame as the "patriot printer of 1776." Bradford died in N.J. on May 23, 1752.

Critical Appraisal: Remembered chiefly for bringing printing to the middle colonies, William Bradford has more "firsts" to his credit than any other colonial printer, Benjamin Franklin (q.v.) not excluded. He was praised on the 200th anniversary of his birth at an extraordinary celebration by the New York Historical Society for his pioneering efforts in helping to establish the colonies' first paper mill (1690) and for printing the first legislative proceedings on the American continent (1698), the first paper money in N.Y. (1709), America's first *Book of Common Prayer* (1710), the first American-written drama (1714), the first *Indian Prayer Book* (1715), and the first history of the colony of N.Y. (1727).

His early works included a pioneering but ineffective book on spelling, grammar, and writing, and he became so intrigued with the idea of consistency in spelling and writing that he wrote his own best-known volume, *The Secretary's Guide*, which first appeared in 1698. Thirty years later, he wrote, "It is now above thirty years since I first compiled this short manual, during which time several impressions have been sold off."

Perhaps his greatest contribution to America's saga, however, was his successful flight in 1692-1693 to escape an indictment for seditious libel. Caught up in the toils of bitter internecine Quaker politics, he argued that the jury had the right to determine both the law and the fact in a libel proceeding, a principle not generally associated with colonial press law until the much better-known *John Peter Zenger* (q.v.) case of 1735. A score or more of his broadsides and pamphlets survive, but as is all too often the case with publications of his time, his authorship and his editorship are blurred. The climate in both Philadelphia and New York City was not conducive to bold critical writing, and anything that strayed from the accepted norm—political or religious—was carefully offered as anonymous. Except for Franklin and a few of his contemporaries, the calculating of almanacs was seldom done by the publisher, and when the printer did the work himself, it was seldom evident.

Suggested Readings: DAB; DNB; LHUS; T₁. *See also* Carl Bridenbaugh, "The Press and the Book in Eighteenth-Century Philadelphia," PMHB, 65 (1941), 1-30; William Brotherhead, *Forty Years Among the Old Booksellers of Philadelphia* (1972), pp. 103-115; Charles R. Hildeburn, *A Century of Printing: Issues of the Press in Philadelphia, 1685-1784* (1885-1886), pp. 1ff.; idem, *Sketches of Printers and Printing in Colonial New York* (1895); D. C. McMurtrie, *A History of Printing in the United States* (1936), pp. 1-9, 38, 135-137; Isaiah Thomas, *The History of Printing in America* (1870), pp. 22-23, 340-355, 375, 389; A. J. Wall, Jr., "William Bradford, Colonial Printer," PAAS, 78 (1963), 361-384; John William Wallace, *An Address Delivered on the Two Hundredth Birth Day of Mr. William Bradford* (1863).

Donovan H. Bond
West Virginia University

WILLIAM BRADFORD "THE THIRD" (1722-1791)

Works: *Pennsylvania Journal and Weekly Advertiser* (editor and principal writer, 1742-1778; coauthor of numerous pamphlets and almanacs, 1742-1778).

Biography: Known as "William the third" among a half-dozen prominent early Bradfords who were authors and printers, William was born in 1722, the son of William Bradford Jr., and the nephew of Andrew Bradford (q.v.), who had established Pa.'s first newspaper in 1719, and the grandson of William Bradford (q.v.), who had pioneered printing in the middle colonies. He apprenticed under Andrew and underwent additional training in Eng. before returning to his native Philadelphia in 1742. In that year, he established the paper that after several minor name changes became known as the *Pennsylvania Journal and Weekly Advertiser*—or more commonly as the *Pennsylvania Journal*. His newspaper carried the most dramatic of all protests against the Stamp Act on Oct. 31, 1765, its front page resembling a tombstone, the spot reserved for the tax stamp occupied by a death's head, and the nameplate emblazoned, "Expiring: In Hopes of a Resurrection to Life Again." From this point on, the *Journal* was the local focus of patriotic extremism and Bradford's "London Coffee House" the rallying point for the Sons of Liberty. Although past the normal age for military service, he helped to organize a militia company, served with distinction at Trenton, and was promoted to a colonelcy after the Battle of Princeton. His paper, carrying the familiar serpent and "Unite or Die" slogan, continuously trumpeting the patriot theme, suspended publication in Nov. 1776 and again from late 1777 until Dec. 1778; British proximity and / or occupation posed more than a mild threat to the man who was the official military commander of Philadelphia and who was known as the "patriot printer." When the *Journal* reappeared in late 1778,

William's son Thomas had succeeded him as editor and continued to serve as such until 1814. Another son, William the fourth, was George Washington's (q.v.) second attorney general. William "the third" died on Sept. 25, 1791.

Critical Appraisal: The Stamp Act crisis is generally credited with having united the colonial press for the first time, which in turn marked the beginning of a common public resistance to British rule that culminated in independence. Hence William Bradford's eloquent protest in 1765 had earned him a high place in the American heritage even if he had never published another thing. Although not a single issue of any colonial paper was ever printed on stamped paper, it was the *Journal*'s dramatic tombstoned front page that was—and still is—thought of whenever the Stamp Act resistance is mentioned.

As was the case in most of the patriot centers, much of the propaganda of Philadelphia's Sons of Liberty was intentionally anonymous. The *Journal*, however, along with perhaps three New Eng. journals, conspicuously printed the most extreme anti-crown letters and commentaries, and Bradford reprinted them as broadsides and pamphlets. Even his almanacs carried the message that helped to determine the course of Pa. politics. He was the first to recognize the value of and to publish Thomas Paine's (q.v.) *Crisis* essays, thus stimulating their later phenomenal sales in pamphlet form. How much of the patriot pamphlet flood in Philadelphia came from William's pen as well as from his press will never be known. But editors in the other colonies frequently introduced articles reprinted from the *Journal* as "the work of William Bradford, the Printer."

Suggested Readings: DAB. *See also* Charles R. Hildeburn, *A Century of Printing: Issues of the Press in Philadelphia, 1685-1784* (1885-1886), I, 175 ff.; Edmund S. Morgan and Helen M. Morgan, *The Stamp Act Crisis* (1953), pp. 182, 249, 251, 254; Arthur M. Schlesinger, *Prelude to Independence* (1957), pp. 74-78, 176, 186; Isaiah Thomas, *The History of Printing in America* (1870 ed.), pp. 374-377, 385, 386.

Donovan H. Bond
West Virginia University

ANNE BRADSTREET (c. 1612-1672)

Works: *The Tenth Muse Lately Sprung Up in America* (1650); *Several Poems Compiled with Great Variety of Wit and Learning* (1678); *The Works of Anne Bradstreet in Prose and Verse* (1867).

Biography: Born in 1612 or 1613 in Northamptonshire, Eng., Anne Dudley was the daughter of well-born parents, claiming descent on her father's side from the aristocratic Sutton-Dudleys who were also among the ancestors of Sir Philip Sidney. As a child, Anne had ready access to the library of the fourth earl of Lincoln at Sempringham where her father Thomas Dudley (q.v.) served as a steward, and the evidence of her early poems suggests that she made excellent use of this opportunity to acquire a respectable if informal education in Classic and some contemporary literature. Here also she first met Simon Bradstreet, whom she was to marry sometime around 1628 and accompany to America in 1630 with the first wave of Puritan immigrants. Settling originally in Boston, where she joined the church, she and her family moved to Newtown (now Cambridge) in 1631, then to Ipswich (around 1635), and once more to Andover (1645), where she lived until her death in 1672. Her first book of poems, *The Tenth Muse*, is the only one she saw in print, but it is generally agreed that most of her best work appears in the posthumous editions prepared by her nephew-in-law John Rogers (q.v.) and by the nineteenth-century editor John Harvard Ellis.

Critical Appraisal: Central to any understanding of Anne Bradstreet's poetry, as nearly every commentator has noticed, are the various tensions between her public and her private selves, between the head and the heart, and between Puritan doctrine and dogma on the one hand and domesticity and maternity on the other. Typically, Bradstreet's most successful poems express an intensely passionate love for her husband or a deep love for her family, framed, however, by reminders, often unconvincing, of the otherworldliness she is supposed to cultivate as a good Puritan. Like Emily Dickinson, whom she foreshadows in a variety of ways, Bradstreet is a poet of hesitancy and doubt rather than of direct and unequivocal statement, although it also seems fair to say that she is, first and last, far more firmly settled in her faith than ever Dickinson was.

Less frequently commented upon in criticism although surely just as central to Bradstreet's poetry as the other tensions noted above is the tension between the rich humanistic traditions of literature and learning in which Bradstreet appears to have immersed herself in the earl of Lincoln's library and the more restrictive tradition of Christian authority. Elements derived from both traditions are present in most of her poems, both early and late, and affect both theme and style. In "The Prologue" to *The Tenth Muse*, for example, she opposed the liberal view held toward women by the "antique Greeks," who accorded women the status of muses, and the narrow doctrines derived from the teachings of St. Paul, which would limit women to dull domestic entertainments and hold them in contempt for even attempting to write poetry. Similarly, in "The Four Monarchies," which surely has an abundance of other flaws, the major conceptual flaw is Bradstreet's failure to accommodate a Classical Plutarchan vision of history, the main symbol of which is the revolving Wheel of Fortune and all that such a wheel implies about history as a series of repetitive cycles, and the Christian vision of history as a record of progress toward Armaggedon and the Second Coming. Even in entirely personal poems, as in "To My Dear and Loving Husband," Bradstreet's imagery of desire—thirst and wealth—is derived from Canticles, and the rhetorical structure of individual lines and, above all, the concluding couplet—"Then while we live, in love let's so persevere / That when we live no more, we may live ever"—stylistically belongs to a Classical epigrammatic tradition and philosophically to the best traditions of Renaissance humanism: it makes the same claim for the primacy, not to say the eternity, of passion that, in far larger script, Shakespeare makes for the doomed lovers Antony and Cleopatra.

Despite the fact that it may seem merely fashionable to say so, it seems clear that Anne Bradstreet's reputation over the centuries has suffered because she was a woman, a writer whose best poems—"Contemplations" is usually taken as the exception that proves the rule—lack philosophical density and import. Once one has moved beyond her contemporaries' and the nineteenth century's wonder that a mere woman wrote poetry at all, there has not seemed much to say about a writer whose mature work stresses her love for her husband and children. Even in emphasizing the tension between her public and private selves, or her dogmatic self and her emotional self, it may be that criticism has unintentionally been damning her with faint praise—as much as to say that she is only another woman who cannot make up her mind. It appears, however, that a proper emphasis on the humanistic versus the Christian elements in her poetry may provide the best indication of the range of her thought and of her familiarity with participation in the broad intellectual and philosophical movement of her own time. She is a far richer writer than has yet been acknowledged even in the best of studies about her.

Suggested Readings: DAB; DNB; FCNEV; LHUS; NAW; T_1. *See also* Josephine Piercy, *Anne Bradstreet* (1965); Alvin Rosenfeld, "Anne Bradstreet's 'Contemplations': Pattern of Form and Meaning," NEQ, 43 (1970), 79-96; Anne Stanford, *Anne Bradstreet: The Worldly Puritan* (1974); Jennifer R. Waller, " 'My Hand a Needle Better Fits': Anne Bradstreet and Women Poets in the Renaissance," DalR, 54 (1974), 436-450; Elizabeth Wade White, *Anne Bradstreet: "The Tenth Muse"* (1971).

Robert D. Arner
University of Cincinnati

SAMUEL BRADSTREET (c. 1633-1682)

Works: "Aspice Venturo Latentur ut Omnia Seclo" and "The Saucy Ram 'gins Doss at Titans Mace" (pub. in *An Almanack for . . .1657*; 1657).

Biography: The eldest son of Governor Simon Bradstreet and the poet Anne [Dudley] Bradstreet (q.v.), Samuel Bradstreet was born sometime around 1633, probably in Newtown (Cambridge), Mass. Graduated from Harvard in 1653, Bradstreet was declared a freeman in 1656 and in Aug. of that year was installed as a fellow at the college. Two of his mother's poems—"Upon My Son Samuel His Going for England, Nov. 6, 1657" and "On My Son's Return out of England, July 17, 1661"—establish the duration of his stay abroad, probably studying medicine, the profession he practiced for several years in Boston after his return. Sometime after 1670, when he served as Andover's representative to the General Court, Bradstreet moved to Jamaica in the W. Ind., where in Aug. 1682 he died, survived by his second wife and four of his eight children.

Critical Appraisal: It would appear that Samuel ("The son of prayers, of vows, of tears, / The child I stayed for many years") was the only one of her children to inherit Anne Bradstreet's poetic inclinations. Even so, a spare forty lines of almanac verse is all that can, with assurance, be attributed to him. His poetry, however, is for the most part highly stylized and conventional. Replete with heavy alliteration ("fleet-fire-foaming-steeds from farre appear") and stilted Elizabethanisms ("hies apace," "Eftsoones," "anon"), it shows little of the genuinely personal poetic quality characteristic of his mother's best work. "Aspice Venturo," for example, relates the courtship and marriage of Tellus and Apollo in the most traditional of terms. In the gloom of early morning, the dreaming fertility goddess sees Apollo approach to drive away her "Lethargee." Awakening, she spies Apollo's herald, who bids her to be happy, for the sun god now draws near. Tellus adorns herself, the "burning Carre" arrives, and the lovers embrace and receive Hymen's blessing. Apollo presents his bride with a special garland, which she dons, "And buds that erst were green / Now sucklings at her milkey papps they been." Nonetheless, Bradstreet's verse, despite its conventionality, holds its own among almanac verse of his day when originality of style or subject was rarely attempted.

Suggested Readings: FCNEV; Sibley-Shipton (I, 360-361).

Cheryl Z. Oreovicz
Purdue University

DAVID BRAINERD (1718-1747)

Works: *Mirabilia Del Inter Indicos* (1746); Preface, *Meditations and Spiritual Experiences of Mr. Thomas Shepard* in Thomas Prince, ed., *Three Valuable Pieces* (1747); Jonathan Edwards, ed., *An Account of the Life of the Late Reverend Mr. David Brainerd* (1749); *To the Foregoing Testimonies of. . .Happiness* (1774).

Biography: Born on Apr. 20, 1718, in Haddam, Conn., David Brainerd was orphaned at the age of 14. In 1739, after a period of religious searching, he entered Yale College to study for the ministry, but in 1742 he was expelled for disrespect of authority and possibly for supporting the New Light party of the Great Awakening. After some months of private study, Brainerd was licensed to preach and late in 1742 was commissioned as a missionary to the Indians by the Correspondents of the Society in Scotland for the Propagation of Christian Knowledge (SPCK). Despite periods of incapacitating illness, including a confinement of four months beginning late in 1746, Brainerd traveled extensively during his years as a missionary. From 1743 until 1746, Brainerd preached among the native populations at Kaunaumeek in N.Y., at the forks of the Del. in Pa., and at Crossweeksung and Cranberry in N.J., and in Jun. 1744 he was ordained into the ministry at Newark. In 1747 Brainerd's rapidly failing health forced him to return to New Eng., where he was cared for in the home of Jonathan Edwards (q.v.) in Northampton and where he died on Oct. 9. Edwards preached his funeral sermon, and his brother John Brainerd continued his work among the Indians.

Critical Appraisal: Although tireless in his missionary efforts, Brainerd's success among the Indians was modest. His reputation is therefore less a product of his accomplishments among the Indians than the result of the publication of the diary he kept during those years about his travels, ministerial activities, and fluctuations of spirit. Portions of this diary were first published in two parts in 1746 at the direction of the Correspondents of the SPCK under the title *Mirabilia Dei Inter Indicos*, with a second title page midway through this document bearing the heading *Divine Grace Display'd*. These works describe Brainerd's activities from Jun. 1745 to Jun. 1746; the remainder of his diary was edited and published in 1749 by Jonathan Edwards as *The Life of the Late Rev. Mr. David Brainerd*.

Although Brainerd's writings record surprisingly little about Indians, they shed considerable light upon the network of evangelicals in New Eng. and the middle colonies, their religious perspective, and their desire to convert the natives. The diary reveals more about the texts Brainerd used for preaching than about the context of those whom he was addressing. Perhaps the reason for so little information about the life and religious practices of the Indians was his view that conversion to Christianity required acceptance of the language, values, and customs of Europeans.

The journals substantiate that Brainerd experienced periods of depression and melancholy punctuated by intermittent moments of spiritual exuberance. Numerous passages reveal him mining his soul for evidences of grace, meditating on his own unworthiness, and yearning for union with God. Others capture his delight with the doctrine of election, his satisfaction with suffering "for the sake of the Gospel," and his pleasure in contemplating the spread of the church. At times Brainerd dipped to the apparent nadir of human emotions; at other times he soared to the highest heavens in his thoughts. His theology was compatible with these radical variations in his state of mind. An evangelical Calvinist who affirmed the necessity of a new birth, the sufficiency of God in salvation, and the total unworthiness of an unregenerate individual, Brainerd believed that a Christian, once reborn, should submit to God's will, trust in providential care, use the ordinances, and work to spread true religion.

Acclaimed by one nineteenth-century evangelical as "probably the best manual of Christian experience, ever yet published," Brainerd's personal writings have gone through numerous editions in America and abroad and have often been abridged, extracted, or reissued. John Wesley, for example, published a version in 1768, and the American Tract Society printed segments for widespread distribution. Consequently, Brainerd was often regarded as a model for self-denial and trust in God and as an inspiration for self-effacing piety, selfless ministry, and energetic missionary activity.

The diary stands in a long tradition of spiritual autobiography written ostensibly for private reflection but often with an eye to a potentially wider audience.

Like Puritan diarists before him, among them Samuel Sewall (q.v.) and Cotton Mather (q.v.), Brainerd revelled in inner turmoil and spiritual distress, seeing them as prerequisites for saving grace, and he employed conventional rhetorical devices, including extreme melancholic introspection and self-vilification. Thus it was fitting that he wrote a preface for a section of Thomas Shepard's (q.v.) journal, a task he undertook in the last months of his life. On this occasion, Brainerd distinguished true religion from various forms of mistaken religious confidence that, in his judgment, had developed among enthusiasts of the Great Awakening. Not even during the weeks when he faced his own death—a painful inevitability he welcomed with disarming calm—did he allow himself any measure of self-esteem. As a result, Brainerd's writings have created a heroic, if somewhat pathetic, image of an evangelical divine caught up in the religious tensions of the times, whose works are examples of a long tradition of New Eng. autobiographical literature.

Suggested Readings: CCMC; DAB; DARB; Sprague (III, 113-117). *See also* Sereno E. Dwight, *Memoirs of the Rev. David Brainerd* (1822); Jonathan Edwards, *True Saints When Absent from the Body Are Present with the Lord* (1747); Philip Greven, *The Protestant Temperament* (1977), pp. 19-148; Alan Heimert, *Religion and the American Mind* (1966), pp. 312-314; Ebenezer Pemberton, *A Sermon Preach'd in New-Ark, June 12, 1744* (1744); Daniel D. Shea, Jr., *Spiritual Autobiography in Early America* (1968), pp. 182-233.

Stephen J. Stein
Indiana University

THOMAS BRANAGAN (1774-1843)

Works: *A Preliminary Essay on the Oppression of the Exiled Sons of Africa* (1804); *Avenia* (1805); *The Flowers of Literature* (1806); *Disquisitions on the Signs of the Times* (1807); *The Excellency of Female Virtue* (1807); *The Penitential Tyrant* (1807); *The Beauties of Philanthropy* (1808); *The Intellectual Telescope* (1809); *A Concise View of the Religious Denominations of the United States* (1811); *A Poetical Apotheosis of General George Washington* (1811); *The Charms of Benevolence* (1813); *A Beam of Celestial Light* (1814); *The Pride of Britannia Humbled* (1815); *A Glimpse of the Beauties of Eternal Truth* (1817); *The Pleasures of Contemplation* (1817); *The Pleasures of Paradise* (1832); *The Guardian Genius of the Federal Union* (1839; 1840).

Biography: Born in Dublin, Ire., of a respectable and reasonably well-to-do Roman Catholic family on Dec. 28, 1774, Thomas Branagan at 14 went to sea, for several years, on merchant vessels and slave ships, settling probably in the 1790s in Antigua as overseer on a sugar plantation. Converted, it is supposed by Moravian missionaries, to Protestantism and recognition of the evils of slavery, Branagan came to Philadelphia in 1799, where he became active as an itinerant preacher. Six years later, he began to break into print with a series of tracts on social and moral reform. In a *Preliminary Essay*, he bore testimony to his own former dealings in the slave trade, at the same time announcing that "because many will read a performance in poetry, who will not be induced to peruse the same materials. . . in prose," he would present a "tragical poem" over which he had worked for many years. *Avenia* was that poem, followed by *The Penitential Tyrant*, lavishly confessional. But most of Branagan's writing was in polemical prose, although scattered among it were several short poems on female virtue, the disgraceful condition of almshouses and jails, and, most often, the evils of slavery. His only other attempt in long verse was *The Poetical Apotheosis of General George Washington*, written to persuade citizens of Philadelphia to erect a statue to honor the father of their country. Branagan continued to write and preach throughout much of the rest of his life. The records of Saint George's Methodicy Episcopal Church in Philadelphia record his death in that city on Jun. 12, 1843.

Critical Appraisal: Thomas Branagan was less a talented than a dedicated writer. His verse is imitative and his prose doggedly repetitive. His main claim to literary fame may rest in *Avenia*, written in Popean couplets, setting forth the history of a beautiful dusky girl who shortly after her marriage to a handsome young husband is seized in Africa by slave traders and sold to captivity on the W. Ind. plantation, where to escape the lecherous advances of her white master she jumps to her death from a high rock overlooking the sea. *The Penitential Tyrant*, "a pathetic poem, in four cantos," is filled with horror as blood streams from lacerated backs, with heartache as slave families are torn apart, and with penitence also, as Branagan confesses his former part in such cruelties. He is confessedly no poet, only a person who wrote to persuade. Yet in him and his attitudes it may be possible to glimpse something of what later generations were to call Romanticism. He had little patience with rules; he looked into his own heart, his own experience, and wrote; he was fond of the first-person confessional; he celebrated the lives of primitive people and advocated unsophisticated, simple, but pervasive ideas; the far away and the horrible were favorite themes; he melted at the suffering of the poor; he yearned toward a good that transcended sense; he mixed rudely as a reformer into other people's business; he was concerned with the education of children, women, and the underprivileged; and he did his best to write in simple language that people could understand. He had every good qualification for a writer except effective talent.

Suggested Reading: Lewis Leary, "Thomas Branagan, Republican Rhetoric, and Romanticism in America" in *Soundings: Some Early American Writers* (1975), pp. 229-252.

Lewis Leary
University of North Carolina at Chapel Hill

THOMAS BRATTLE (1658-1713)

Works: *An Almanac of Celestial Motions* (1678); *A Full and Candid Account of the Delusion Called Witchcraft* (w. 1692; pub. in CMHS, 1st ser., 5 [1978], 61-80).

Biography: Thomas Brattle was born in Boston, Mass., in 1658 into one of New Eng.'s wealthiest families, and upon that foundation, he built his considerable power. A graduate of Harvard and its treasurer for twenty years, Brattle kept the accounts with what has been called "great minuteness and beauty," laboring over "elaborate acknowledgments" even for single books donated to the library. But during a trip to Eng. taken as a young man in the company of Samuel Sewall (q.v.), Brattle had developed a taste for Anglican worship and Old World style— both unknown in the Harvard of Increase Mather (q.v.) and Cotton Mather (q.v.). Like many of his fellow colonials, Brattle was thrilled by English approbation, especially when Isaac Newton himself acknowledged his sighting of the 1680 comet. "I took," Brattle wrote, "no small comfort...that I was none of the last of all the Lags."

More and more feeling "the great need...of another meeting-house in the town," Brattle joined in 1698 with other prominent merchants to build a new church on part of his Boston property where "the relations should be laid aside, and the Holy Scriptures publicly read." The Mathers were enraged. This was another blow to their efforts at holding the line against ecclesiastical innovation, too soon after Solomon Stoddard's (q.v.) insolence at Northampton, where the whole town was now admitted to communion. So the treasurer's name disappeared for a time from the proposed Harvard College charters. But Brattle's plans went ahead. He invited Benjamin Colman (q.v.), who was sojourning in Eng., to become the first minister of the candidly named Brattle Street Church, and it was arranged that Colman be ordained while still in London, thus avoiding trouble from the Mathers at home and defying the basic New Eng. tenet of congregational authority in the ordination of ministers.

Perhaps Brattle's secret hope for the church founded in his name is revealed in his bequest of a pair of organs to complete the repudiation of Puritan practice. Even for his like-minded colleagues, this act was too much. "With all possible respect to the memory of our devoted friend and benefactor," they voted to refuse the gift. There is no precise record of how gracious was the reception of another of Brattle's bequests: that "a half-crown Bill [be given] to each of the students of Harvard College that shall come to my funeral."

Critical Appraisal: Addressed to an unidentified English recipient, Thomas Brattle's letter of Oct. 1692 on "the delusion called witchcraft" may have circulated in manuscript but was not published until 1798. If not quite the "milestone" it has been acclaimed to be, this document is a notable expression of alarm (but with more than a hint of satisfaction) by an urbane New Englander watching the intellectual and moral collapse of the colonial leadership. Although it begins with an obsequious flourish—"I would sooner bite my fingers' ends than willingly cast dirt on authority"—it shortly becomes clear that the Salem judges have turned their titles of authority into marks of embarrassment rather than respect, and that this is a shift that Brattle does not convincingly deplore. His letter has a double thrust. First, it ridicules the judges for their handling of witnesses and evidence, calling the quality of their minds into question in terms that are roundly condescending. Second, it raises the whole issue of the meaning of repentance, an act of absolute centrality in the Puritan concept of covenant obligation.

It was an inescapable dilemma, one to which Joseph Heller has since given a permanent name, "Catch-22," and about which Arthur Miller has made the stuff of tragedy. If a man falsely repents, he is saved (on the presumption of a new conviction of sin), but if he honorably maintains his innocence, he is condemned (on the presumption that Satan has taken command of the guilty soul). Brattle saw this paradox clearly, and there are moments in his letter that dramatically evoke the pain of good men caught by the unyielding idea that repentance means hope and perseverance means damnation. For decades, New Englanders listened to this idea in the droning jeremiads through which their ministers beseeched the community to repent. Brattle's letter marks the decline, if not the death, of a formative conception in the intellect of New Eng., although he does not make explicit its obsolescence, and the covenant theme, as has been observed, is startling by its absence from his prose.

But more than reflecting the lost prestige of an idea, the letter makes its own contribution to the dismantling of the Puritan past. "The reasonable part of the world," Brattle declared, pointedly excluding New Eng., "will laugh" at the means by which the "Salem gentlemen" (as he mockingly called the judges) have "proven" the identity of their witches. A witch's spell, they say, is communicated through the eyes to the victim. By the simple test of fixing the witch's hand upon the victim's body, the spell—the victim's "fit"—will be relieved. This is because the "effluvia" can now travel a completed circuit, flowing out of the possessed back into the sorcerer. Brattle paused, then exulted: "A touch of any hand, and process of time, will work the cure . . . as experience teaches." Experience, not belief, should be the guide. The "superstitious" judges and their clerical allies are hopelessly deluded by an imperfect understanding of the new experimental method. Announcing himself "no small admirer" of Descartes, Brattle echoed the master's assault on "experiments insufficiently understood." The Puritan judges need to have their minds illuminated by Cartesian light but have instead been confused into imagining cause and effect where there is only deception.

Almost an Enlightenment treatise, Brattle's letter is proud and unimpeachable in its choice of loyalties. But one suspects that it is also an occasion for venting spleen. For in a curious way, it betrays a lower estimate of human motivation than do the wild acts of the judges. Through Brattle's scornful prose, we see that the distinction that had once been attempted between conviction and dissembling—

through, most notably, the conversion relations that the Brattle Street Church abandoned—is utterly lost. Brattle's picture of the New Englanders' mutual dealings is one of unrelieved duplicity: victims, confessors, justices, all feeding on the gullibility of an entire people. His is the voice of sophistication—knowing, satiric, and ultimately speaking the language of triumph as it chronicles a culture in the act of self-destruction.

Suggested Readings: BDAS; DAB; Sibley-Shipton (II, 489-498). *See also* the letter of invitation to Colman in S. K. Lothrop, *A History of the Church in Brattle Street* (1851), pp. 45-47; The *Full and Candid Account of the Delusion called Witchcraft* is in CMHS, 1st ser. 5 (1978), 61-80. A portion is reprinted in Perry Miller and Thomas H. Johnson, eds., *The Puritans* (1963), II, 758-762. Perry Miller, *The New England Mind: From Colony to Province* (1953), pp. 196-198, 240-242; S. E. Morison, *Harvard College in the Seventeenth Century* (1936), I, 220-222; II, 544-545.

Andrew Delbanco
Harvard University

WILLIAM BRATTLE (1662-1717)

Works: *An Ephemeris of Celestial Motions* (1682); *An Almanac of the Celestial Motion* (1694); *Sundry Rules and Regulations for Drawing up a Regiment* (1733); *Compendium Logicae Secundum Principia D. Renati Cartesii* (1735).

Biography: William Brattle was graduated with the Harvard class of 1680 and became a less public man than his brother Thomas Brattle (q.v.). "Secret and Silent in the Good he did," according to Benjamin Colman (q.v.), he nevertheless spoke too plainly for the taste of Cotton Mather (q.v.) and Increase Mather (q.v.), and so his name—together with his brother's and John Leverett's—was expunged from the Harvard charters during the last years of the Mather reign. Ordained a minister at Cambridge in 1696, Brattle shifted the base of his influence from college to church. He declined the laying on of hands at his installation ceremony—a harbinger of further deviations from traditional practice. The most important change, anticipating the same decision at the Brattle Street Church, was to allow private examination of candidates for church membership rather than demanding public relations. Increase Mather, perhaps uncharitably, commended Brattle above all for his humility and conceded that he was an able and diligent man but was pleased "to see his Character... published... without any Hyperbolizing." More popular with the students than with the president, Brattle tended sick undergraduates during the smallpox outbreak of 1691, almost succumbing himself. The grateful students dubbed him "Father of the College," which he and Leverett virtually ruled during Mather's long absence in Eng. on diplomatic business. Several months after his brother Thomas's death, William was elected to membership in the Royal Society. This appointment, however, may have been less a response to his erudition than a ploy by the society to acquire Thomas's "manuscripts relating to Astronomy, Musick, and other parts of the Mathematicks." "I have been thinking," wrote one New Englander involved in the negotiations, "that the Request will go with the better Grace if the Society be pleas'd to choose his Learned Brother William as a Fellow." William also stepped into his brother's shoes and discharged the duties of Harvard treasurer upon Thomas's death. He was indeed a large benefactor to Harvard, helping to usher in both the budget and the tone of the eighteenth-century university. "Temperate in all things," according to Colman, he "lov'd good Hours and good Order," and "his Dying Testimony" was against "Excess."

Critical Appraisal: William Brattle's published work is not substantial, but it offers a small window on his place and time. His *Ephemeris of Celestial Motions*, composed as a very young man, has almost an air of frolic.To relieve the dull prognostication of eclipses and full moons, for example, it includes twelve relatively lively sets of couplets corresponding to the months. They do not always cleave to monotonous dignity. Here is the wisdom for April:

> The Rusticks now the Flesh to satisfie
> Will not obscene, and dirty acts defie;
> With sweat they toil in th' earth, and do expect
> Seed by their Mother (Tellus) to erect
> But, if the heavens do from sweat abstain
> The Rusticks sweat will wholly be in vain.

The search for style, even for pomp, hinted at in the construction of this little book is made manifest in Brattle's *Sundry Rules for Drawing up a Regiment*. The concern here is much more with parades than with battles, and the book is tinged with regret that some of the more elaborate patterns of military choreography cannot be fully performed in America since we "have not [all] the before mentioned officers and men...in New England." In the provinces when "the compliment is to be paid" by a full-dress platoon, colonels may have to substitute for generals.

Brattle's most enduring work in print was his Cartesian logic. Published in Latin in 1735, it went through several editions and remained a Harvard textbook until 1765. It treated the mind as a potential thinking machine. Following the model of Descartes, it proclaimed the importance of clearing away the rubbish of received opinion and boiling down propositions to their simplest components. It banished the uncertain from the province of reason. "Nihil admittendum esse pro veritate quod aliquid dubitationis includit." This is the characteristic Brattle demand, put forth impressively by his brother Thomas at the time of the Salem executions. It is, among other things, an expression of impatience with the tremendous weight of ancestral precedent, an especially sensitive matter in Puritan New Eng. Even as early as the *Ephemeris*, Brattle's taste for modernity is frankly stated:

Seeing that [many men] are arrived at a Port, so near to that of Rationality, as that they are potentially . . . there, I think it could not be amisse, if everyone would endeavor . . . in turning this *potentia* in *actum*; Having respect to the verity of that philosophical axiome, *Frustra est potentia quae non traducitur in actum.*

Frustration with a laggard culture, one surmises, was not unknown to William Brattle as it was not to his brother, for neither man conceded that in the inevitable transition from the potential to the actual there may be loss as well as gain.

Suggested Readings: CCNE; DAB; FCNEV; Sibley-Shipton (II, 200-209); Sprague (I, 236-238). *See also* Benjamin Colman, *A Sermon at the Lecture in Boston after the Funerals of Those Excellent and Learned Divines . . . the Reverend, Mr. William Brattle . . . and the Reverend Mr. Ebenezer Pemberton* (1717); Allyn B. Forbes, "William Brattle and John Leverett, F.R.S.," PCSM, 28 (1935), 222-224.

Andrew Delbanco
Harvard University

THOMAS BRAY (c. 1658-1730)

Works: *Catechetical Lectures* (1696); *Bibliotheca Parochialis* (1697; 2nd ed., 1707); *An Essay Towards Promoting All Necessary and Useful Knowledge* (1697); *Apostolick Charity* (1699); *The Acts of Dr. Bray's Visitation* (1700); *A Letter from Dr. Bray* (c. 1700); *The Necessity of an Early Religion* (1700); *The Present State of Religion on the Continent of North America* (1700); *For God or for Satan* (1708); *The Good Fight of Faith* (1709); *Directorium Missionarium* (1726); *Primordia Bibliothecaria* (1726); *Missionalia* (1727).

Biography: Born in Eng. at Marton, Shropshire, sometime around 1658, Thomas Bray—churchman, missionary, and librarian—significantly influenced eighteenth-century American religious and cultural life. Born poor, Bray prospered through a series of benefactors, from a local clergyman to the bishop of London, who recognized his intelligence and vigor. Bray worked his way through Oxford as a *puer pauper*, receiving a B.A. in 1678. Further study brought an M.A. in 1693, and a doctor of divinity in 1696. Starting his religious career in 1681, Bray served the Anglican Church as deacon and priest in Warwickshire, but his fame began with his *Catechetical Lectures* in 1696, which called for improving the catechizing of the young. Bray continued to preach and to publish. His *Essay Towards Promoting All Necessary and Useful Knowledge* (1697) and *Apostolick Charity* (1699) established him as a leader in religious education, in missionary work, and in establishing libraries on a grand scale both at home and abroad. Appointed commissary to Md. in 1696, Bray visited the colony for a short time in 1699-1700. That year Bray founded two missionary societies, one of which—the Society for the Promotion of Christian Knowledge, or the SPCK—

still continues. In 1700 Bray's *Necessity of an Early Religion* became the first American sermon published in the new century. Returning to Eng. in 1700, Bray continued writing about missionaries and libraries, and by 1709 he had established more than fifty libraries in the colonies. In 1723, due to his illness, Bray's friends founded the Associates of Dr. Bray to continue his work in the educating and converting of slaves, Indians, and the poor. Benjamin Franklin (q.v.) was a member. The organization continued its philanthropic work after Thomas Bray's death at St. Botolph's in 1730.

Critical Appraisal: For a cleric who spent only six months in America, from 1699 to 1700, Thomas Bray had a pervasive influence on cultural and religious life of eighteenth-century America. Several of Bray's sermons are models of that sharply reasoned eloquence that distinguishes the craft of the Anglican divine. Yet, for the most part, Bray's primary contribution was disseminating learning and literature through a network of libraries. Bray's interests in catechizing the young, educating the disadvantaged of his time, spreading the gospel to the colonies—all of these things were served by his zeal for libraries.

Bray was a kind of bibliophic Johnny Appleseed sowing seeds of libraries in the colonies and in Eng. By 1709 he had established fifty libraries, some with 1,000 volumes or more, in places such as Boston, Philadelphia, Charleston, New York City, and Newport. The most extensive library was in Annapolis, Md., the colony to which Bray was appointed commissary of the Anglican Church in 1696. In all of his schemes for promoting his faith and ideas, Bray thought on a large scale. "I am called a *Projector*," he told a friend, "upon the account of these *Designs* I am continually forming."

Bray was a prolific and popular writer. His *Catechetical Lectures* sold 3,000 copies and earned him 700 pounds; and his sermon *Apostolick Charity* provides the cultural historian with a general view of life in the English colonies. Bray appealed for parochial education as the best defense of Anglicans against other orthodoxies or secularism and for libraries to aid education.

Bray made a similar point in a more artful sermon, *An Essay Towards Promoting All Necessary and Useful Knowledge Both Divine and Human* (1697). "Only Knowledge," contended Bray, "can conduct us through the Mazes and Labyrinths of the World." The knowledge to which Bray referred is both theological and practical; both are necessary for Christians to survive and to prosper in the colonies. Although the catalog of books that Bray proposed is heavily tilted toward theology, it contains secular and practical works. Bray himself plotted the logistics of developing and supporting such libraries. His *Bibliotheca Parochialis*, revised extensively to over 400 pages in 1709, is Bray's final statement about his library schemes.

Bray's most famous lecture, the first published in the American colonies in the eighteenth century, is *The Necessity of an Early Religion,* given before the Md. Assembly in 1700. Full of intriguing reference and lush metaphor, the sermon reflects Bray's lifelong concern with educating the young, especially against the proselytizing of Quakers and Catholics in the colonies. Bray's faith in the rational capacities of his fellow Anglicans speaks to his own enlightenment and the need for schools and libraries to develop that capacity of intellect—of course, with a scriptural guidance that teaches the fear of God and love of duty.

Although the two men never met, Bray's life and character suggest intriguing comparisons with those of Benjamin Franklin. Bray's decent but humble background; his rise to fame and position (although in service to a church that Franklin did not follow); his interest in lending libraries; his passion for educating the young, the poor, the Negro, and the Indian; his efforts at philanthropy and doing good; his practical mindedness in getting that good done—these qualities are reminiscent of Franklin's. Indeed, in 1760 Franklin became a member in the Associates of Dr. Bray, the organization that carried on Bray's religious and philanthropic work.

Suggested Readings: CCV; DAB; DARB; DNB; LHUS. *See also* Richard Beale Davis, *Intellectual Life in the Colonial South, 1585-1763* (1979), pp. 722-724, 782-783; Charles T. Laugher, *Thomas Bray's Grand Design: Libraries of the Church of England in America, 1695-1785* (1973); Bernard S. Steiner, ed., *Rev. Thomas Bray: His Life and Selected Works Relating to Maryland* (1901; rep., 1972); H. P. Thompson, *Thomas Bray* (1954).

Leonard Abram
Philadelphia, Pennsylvania

JOSEPH BREINTNALL (d. 1746)

Works: *The Busy Body Papers* (with Benjamin Franklin; 1729); "A Plain Description of One Single Street in This City" (1729); "A Letter from Mr. J. Breintnal to Mr. Peter Collison, F.R.S." (1746); "Verses to the Author of Batchelors-Hall" (n.d.).

Biography: We know very little of Joseph Breintnall's life. Most reports tell us that he was a scrivener by trade, but Breintnall was also an avid botanist and scientist, active merchant, sheriff of Philadelphia County, and first secretary of the Library Company.

We have no record of his early life, although in 1717 he did apply to the Philadelphia Monthly Meeting of the Society of Friends for a certificate of good standing. Six years later, Breintnall and Esther Parker were married according to Quaker custom. Some questions remain, however, whether he maintained such standing. Breintnall, who was the oldest member of Benjamin Franklin's (q.v.) Junto, was greatly influenced by current Deism and quite possibly in later life he became a freethinker. In 1746 Breintnall died, perhaps by suicide.

Critical Appraisal: In "The Wits and Poets of Pennsylvania" (1731), a contemporary literary critic singled out Breintnall for careful praise: "For choise of Diction, I would B—nt-al—choose, / For just conceptions, and a ready Muse." "Yet," continued the author, "is that Muse too labour'd and prolix / And seldom, on the Wing, knows where to fix." Lines from the "Verses to the Author of Batchelors-Hall" seem to bear out this judgment: "Censorious tongues, which nimbly move, / Each virtuous name to persecute, / Thy muse has taught the truth to prove, / And be to base conjecture mute." Breintnall's insistent metrics and rhymes here and elsewhere (as in "July 1740 On the Lately Discover'd Wild Raspberries," in which he comes upon "The Dunbrown Stalk no pointed Prickly wears; / A long stem'd Leaf, at every Curve, it bears"), suggest that the criticism is accurate and that we must look elsewhere for the source of Breintnall's historical importance.

With Franklin, Breintnall shared an interest in scientific observation and natural philosophy. In 1730 he conducted experiments to prove that the sun's rays penetrate colored material more readily than they do white. Later that decade, he also studied the seasonal difference in the sun's warmth, plant grafting, and leaf impressions. Breintnall also contributed two papers to the Royal Society of London: the first in 1738 on the Aurora Borealis and the second in 1746 on the effects and treatment of a rattlesnake bite.

Breintnall's connection with the Royal Society began in the 1730s as he corresponded with Peter Collinson, the noted English naturalist. Collinson served as the London agent of the Library Company of Philadelphia, organized in 1731 by Franklin and served by Breintnall as secretary from 1731 to 1746.

Two years before the founding of the Library Company, Breintnall and Franklin collaborated on a somewhat less charitable project—*The Busy Body Papers*, essays loaded with some wit and much invective and aimed at the hot-tempered Samuel Keimer (q.v.). Keimer had attempted a number of rather questionable schemes, and his effort to undercut Franklin's newspaper with his own *Universal Instructor* prompted the attacks by Franklin and Breintnall. Most of the thirty-two papers were written by Breintnall, who left little to the imagination in his comments on Keimer. Although he tried mightily to respond, Keimer proved unequal to the combined wit of Franklin and Breintnall, and the contest soon ended.

Breintnall's role in *The Busy Body Papers* has remained his best-known literary work. He was foremost a merchant and amateur scientist, not a poet. As is the case with many of his contemporaries, Breintnall remains in our minds as Franklin described him in the Autobiography: "A Copyer of Deeds for the Scriveners; a good-natur'd friendly middle-ag'd Man, a great Lover of Poetry, reading all he could meet with, and writing some that was tolerable; very ingenious in many little Nicknackeries, and of sensible Conversation."

Suggested Readings: Stephen Bloore, "Joseph Breintnall, First Secretary of the Library Company," PMHB, 59 (1935); J. Philip Goldberg, "Joseph Breintnall and a Poem in Praise of Jacob Taylor," PMHB, 86 (1962), 207-209; Frederick B. Tolles, "A Note on Joseph Breintnall," PQ, 21 (1942), 247-249.

Timothy K. Conley
Bradley University

JOHN BRERETON (fl. 1590-1602)

Works: *A Briefe and True Relation of the Discoverie of the North Part of Virginia* (1602).

Biography: John Brereton may have been any of the various Briertons, Brittons, Brettons, or Breretons who made small names for themselves in the late sixteenth and early seventeenth centuries. Most sources agree, however, that he was a British rector who was inspired by acquaintance with the family of Capt. Bartholomew Gosnold to join the first voyage to the New Eng. coast. He probably went to Cambridge, taking a B.A. in 1593, and was apparently a curate at Lawshall, Suffolk, where he met the Gosnolds. In May 1602 he sailed on the *Concord* from Falmouth. After about three weeks, exploring the coast of Maine, he and the rest returned to Eng. with tales of a new paradise.

Brereton's *Relation* is considered now, as then, to be the standard account of Gosnold's famous voyage. A full picture of what was seen and experienced, however, can be drawn only by integrating the *Relation* with Gabriel Archer's (q.v.) far less polemical "Relation of Captain Gosnold's Voyage to the North Part of Virginia" (1602). Since Archer was a lawyer, not a curate bent on establishing a Protestant outpost in America, his account of the voyage differs greatly in tone and selection of detail. Moreover, Archer often did not join the party on its explorations of Cuttyhunk Island and thus had other experiences to relate. Since Archer's *Relation* was not published until 1625, however, it was Brereton's work that inspired so many adventurers to follow Gosnold's lead. Capt. John Smith (q.v.), to name but one major figure, spoke of Brereton in his *Adventures and Discourses* as the primary influence on his determination to explore America for himself. Two editions of Brereton's *Relation* were published in 1602. The 1st edition included a short piece on Sir Walter Raleigh's efforts to locate the Lost Colony and Edward Hayes's *Treatise* on planting in the New World. The 2nd edition included an additional twenty-four pages consisting of notes and "briefe testimonies" concerning other voyages to America; they were probably written, or at least heavily edited, by Richard Hakluyt. There can be no doubt that John Brereton was the chief propagandist for British expansionism during Queen Elizabeth's time.

Critical Appraisal: *A Briefe Relation* is cast in the form of a letter to Sir Walter Raleigh, who may well have regarded Gosnold's voyage as an infringement on his own patented rights. It is a work of advertising, designed to "sell" America to wealthy or adventurous Englishmen. It succeeded primarily because of its beauty of description and hyperbolical richness of praise. Brereton was particularly good at describing the terrain of the New Eng. coastal areas he visited and on the profusion of exotic vegetation discovered there. The sailors were "ravished at the beauty and delicacy of this sweet soil" and made many planting experiments. They also collected a great haul of sassafras, later sold in

Eng. for 382 pounds per ton. Brereton excelled in his passages on the splendid variety of fish to be found in New Eng. waters but forgot to tell us that the best fishing ground of all was aptly named Cape Cod by the sailors. The climate was extolled as well; not one of the thirty-two adventurers fell ill during their three weeks in America.

Although the *Relation* purported to be a work of simple narration and description, its subtext argued powerfully that the New World is in every respect superior to Eng. No man of imagination and good sense, it was implied, could resist the opportunity to invest in a settlement there. In comparison with New Eng., for example, "the most fertile part of England is (of itself) but barren." Further enticements included the extreme friendliness of the native Indians, whose only fault was a forgivable tendency to petty theft. Brereton praised the charming and clever inhabitants as men of courage, courtesy, and physical beauty. Their wives, although shy, were "fat and very well-favored." Prospective settlers would find the Indians more adept at languages and generally wittier and more intelligent than their compatriots. In short, God and nature had combined to produce a congenial land for Englishmen to inhabit and exploit.

Brereton's *Relation* is a polished and subtle document. Its wealth of detail makes it a primary source for historians, and its impact on Raleigh, Smith, Hakluyt, and others assures its place in any account of America's formative years.

Suggested Readings: DAB; DNB; LHUS. *See also* George Bancroft, *History of the United States* (1888), I, 79-82; Philip L. Barbour, "A Biographical Directory," *The Complete Works of Captain John Smith* (forthcoming, by the University of North Carolina Press for the Institute of Early American History and Culture, Williamsburg, Va.); Alexander Brown, *The Genesis of the United States* (1890; rep., 1964), II, 832-34; Henry S. Burrage, ed., *Early English and French Voyages* (1906), pp. 325-340; Warner F. Gookin and Philip L. Barbour, *Bartholomew Gosnold: Discoverer and Planter* (1963); George Bruner Parks, *Richard Hakluyt and the English Voyages* (1930); David Beers Quinn, *England and the Discovery of America: 1481-1620* (1974); Louis B. Wright, ed., *The Elizabethans' America* (1965), pp. 26-44.

James Stephens
Marquette University

MARTHA WADSWORTH BREWSTER (fl. 1725-1757)

Works: *Poems on Divers Subjects* (1757).

Biography: Martha Brewster lived in Lebanon, Conn. Her date of birth is unknown but her parents were Joseph (d. Jan. 15, 1743) and Lydia (Brown) Wadsworth (d. 1759). In addition, we know that she had one sister, Mary. Around 1732 she married Oliver Brewster. The couple had two children: Ruby (b. 1732) and Wadsworth (b. 1737).

According to Lebanon town records, Martha Brewster bought and sold land, both with her husband and in her own name, during the years after her marriage. All of her family members, including her husband and children, are mentioned in Brewster's poetry. Brewster's one volume of poetry, *Poems on Divers Subjects*, was published in two editions, the first in 1757 in New London, Conn., and the second a year later in Boston. In the preface to her book, Brewster mentioned that public opinion frowned upon her aesthetic aspirations. In fact, when her book first appeared, the public doubted that she was its author, and she was forced to prove both her authorship and her ability to write by publicly paraphrasing a psalm into verse. The year of Brewster's death and the place of her burial are unknown.

Critical Appraisal: As one of only four volumes of poetry published by colonial American women, Brewster's *Poems on Divers Subjects*, containing seventeen poems and two acrostics, merits literary and historical attention, both for its intrinsic quality and for the fact that its author overcame the many difficulties a woman writer faced in eighteenth-century America. Hindered not only by a general lack of intellectual freedom, the women writers of eighteenth-century New Eng. were further limited by theological strictures against the writing of poetry and especially by the fact that society rigidly demanded the subjection of a wife to the will of her husband, an idea Brewster echoed in a poem to her husband's engaged sister. Furthermore, illiteracy among eighteenth-century American women was common, and life in general was taxing. Subject to frequent pregnancies and the dangers attendant upon them, the average colonial woman inhabited a one-room cottage, had several children who needed her almost constant attention, and subsequently had neither the means nor the wherewithal to pursue what little intellectual betterment was available, including, of course, the reading and writing of poetry.

In some respects, particularly with regard to her reliance on heroic couplets, Brewster's verse resembles Anne Bradstreet's (q.v.) and may even have been influenced by it. Her poetry also shows some indebtedness to British models. Nonetheless, Brewster ultimately wrote in an independent poetic style and did not hesitate to experiment with lines and ideas. This attempt is exemplified by her opening line eulogizing Nathanael Burt: "Oh - - he - - is - - gone." Although Brewster chose primarily religious topics and forms such as Bible versification, elegies, and lyrics containing religious counsel for family members and friends, she was not necessarily limited to conventional Puritan concerns. In poems such as "To the Memory of That Worthy Man Lieut. Nathanael Burt of Springfield" and "Braddock's Defeat, July 9, 1755," for example, Brewster departed from convention by writing on topics such as warfare and violence, hitherto covered only in literature written by men. Likewise, in a poem like "To the Subjects of the Special Grace of God and Its Oppressors Compos'd August 1741," she captured the stirrings of social change associated with the Great Awakening. Thus, although Brewster's *Poems* may not rival in quality the poetry of Anne Bradstreet or Edward Taylor (q.v.), her work is a noteworthy stepping stone in the emergence of a verse tradition among New World women writers.

Suggested Readings: Lina Mainiero, ed., *American Women Writers* (1979), I, 231-232; Emily Stipes Watts, *The Poetry of American Women from 1632 to 1945* (1977), pp. 20-22, 25-27.

Mindy Janak
Maurice Duke
Virginia Commonwealth University

LEMUEL BRIANT (1722-1754)

Works: *The Absurdity and Blasphemy* (1749); *Some Friendly Remarks* (1750); *Some More Friendly Remarks* (1751).

Biography: Born to Thomas and Mary Briant of Scituate, Mass., Lemuel Briant was baptized on Feb. 25, 1722. A graduate of Harvard College (1739), Briant made a career of the ministry, serving as pastor of the First Congregational Society of Quincy, Mass., from 1745 until 1753. Although his people supported him until failing health forced his resignation, Briant was a controversial figure in the disputes between the Calvinist and Arminian wings of the New Eng. clergy. When at the time of the Great Awakening the New Light preachers condemned man's self-reliance, Briant preached and published in open opposition to this position, though it had always been one of the essential points of Calvinist doctrine. He emerged as a voice of the liberal left in theological matters (though, in accord with a paradox of the times, on the *ecclesiastical* right) and was engaged in hot controversy with orthodox Calvinists while being supported by Jonathan Mayhew (q.v.). At the same time, his wife left him, charging him with "several scandalous Sins," and even some of his friends and supporters, such as John Adams (q.v.), admitted that his character, even as far back as his college days, revealed a temper too frivolous for the clerical office. Subsequently, he has been credited with being an early Unitarian, but the facts do not indicate that he had a program even anticipatory of that movement. Briant died on Oct. 1, 1754, nearly a year after his failing health had forced him to resign his ministerial position in Quincy.

Critical Appraisal: Lemuel Briant's entire career as an author derives primarily from a single publication, his sermon titled *The Absurdity and Blasphemy of Depretiating Moral Virtue*. In this sermon, Briant expressed the theory that most preachers distorted the word of God, resulting in a "bare jingle of words, without attending to the general Drift and Design of the Author":

> Hence it has come to pass that when men read of God's choosing whole Nations to certain Privileges (and those in this life only) they have rashly concluded that *particular persons* are *unconditionally* chosen to eternal Life hereafter.-- That when they have laid before them the character of a very loose and abandoned People, who by their *own* long practiced Wickedness, have rendered themselves the Children of Wrath, and fitted them-

selves for Destruction, they are induced to vilify humane Nature itself with the same vicious Character.-- That when they hear of our being *saved by Grace*, they conceive of it so as to destroy all moral Agency, and set themselves down with this vain Thought, that nothing on their part is necessary to Salvation, but if they are designed for it, they shall *irresistably* be driven into Heaven, whether they will or not.-- And if they are not, no Prayers, nor Endeavours will avail.-- And finally; when they meditate on the constant unchangeable Affection God bears to *good Men*, they make this groundless Inferrence from his Unchangeableness, that they are unchangeable also.

The interpretations Briant saw as distorted are none other than the cardinal points of election, natural depravity, irresistibility of grace, and the perseverance of the saints—elements of the Assembly's catechism that had for years constituted the very framework of New Eng. orthodoxy. This attack may have been provoked by the extremism attendant upon the Great Awakening and its aftermath, but in rejecting these essential doctrines and in insisting that Christ was essentially a moral teacher, Briant was hardly returning to a traditional theology.

Attacked by John Porter and others, Briant twice defended himself in published epistolary essays titled *Friendly Remarks*. In these essays, Briant insisted that he was the true Calvinist and his critics were Antinomians, that personal righteousness is by no means utterly worthless in the scheme of salvation, and that Christ saves only those who *obey* Him. His arguments were enlivened by sharp, witty jabs, but the tone was frequently vicious, particularly in the footnotes to his second defense of 1751, which are largely devoted to raillery, and in a final assault on Porter's alleged plagiarisms from the sermons of Tillotson. The final broadside in this exchange was fired by Samuel Niles (q.v.) in his *Vindication* of 1752, a substantial doctrinal polemic of 120 pages that Briant chose not to answer.

The style of Briant is lively; indeed, as the title of *Absurdity and Blasphemy* suggests, he was prone to irregular jets of rhetorical heat that tend to destroy what might have been much more elegant and persuasive arguments. The result is that his writings leave an impression more negative than positive, both with respect to his subject and himself, but his works nonetheless provide insight into the theological controversies raging in New Eng. during the early eighteenth century.

Suggested Readings: CCNE; Sibley-Shipton (X, 341-348). *See also* Edwin S. Gaustad, *The Great Awakening in New England* (1957), pp. 130-132; Alan Heimert and Perry Miller, eds., *The Great Awakening* (1967), pp. 540-550; Conrad Wright, *The Beginnings of Unitarianism in America* (1955).

Wilson H. Kimnach
University of Bridgeport

JOHN BRICKELL (c. 1710-c. 1745)

Works: *The Natural History of North-Carolina* (1737); *Catalogue of American Trees and Plants Which Will Bear the Climate of England* (1739).

Biography: A native of Ire., John Brickell was a physician and scientist with an eager but uncritical enthusiasm for medicine, botany, and zoology. Biographical information on him is sketchy and much of it unreliable. It is definitely known, however, that he arrived in N.C. in 1729 and visited the coastal towns of Beaufort, Bath, and Edenton. In 1730-1731 he was practicing his profession in Edenton, where among his patients were members of the household of Governor Sir Richard Everard. When George Burrington succeeded Everard in 1731, the loss of patronage evidently prompted Brickell to return soon thereafter to Ire. The first of his two books was printed "For the Author" in Dublin, the second in London. Nothing about his subsequent career has survived in the records.

Critical Appraisal: The general pattern of Brickell's *Natural History* is similar to that of colonial promotional tracts. The first pages provide a precise geographical description of inlets, capes, rivers, and towns. The history and government of the colony are then presented, along with the religion and national origin of the inhabitants, their dwellings, and their domestic animals. Most of the book, of course, deals with the produce and "beasts" of the land. Every tree has its paragraph, as does every bush, vine, grain, animal, reptile, insect, worm, bird, and fish. So determined was Brickell to mention each natural feature of the colony in its appropriate section that when one of them seemed to overlap two categories, he repeated what he had previously written. In truth, the *History* is poorly organized. The last section, over one-fourth of Brickell's 408 pages, is "An Account of the Indians of North Carolina."

Brickell clearly was a man with little sense of personal integrity. The "M.D." following his by-line on the title page seems to be a fabrication. Worse are his plagiarisms from John Lawson's (q.v.) *A New Voyage to Carolina* (1709). Percy G. Adams maintains that only two sections of any length—some sixty pages covering social conditions and insects—were original. Although borrowing by one travel writer from another was at that time common practice, Brickell's thefts were both blatant and excessive. About six-sevenths of his text, according to Percy G. Adams, was rearranged, expanded, paraphrased, and often even quoted verbatim from Lawson, who is never mentioned as a source. An account of a trip into the Indian backcountry tells of incidents experienced by Lawson that are now passed off as though Brickell were the adventurer, when it is doubtful that the doctor ever left the N.C. coastal area. Adams admonishes scholars to take care lest they credit Brickell with what is Lawson's.

But *The Natural History*, with its four plates and folding map, is nevertheless an attractive and sprightly document. Besides amusing comments about the settlers, Brickell inserted abundant listings of folk medicines and cures, often shocking and ridiculous, but always entertaining. He wrote that among the inhabitants "There are some *Christians* so charitable as to have the *Negroes* born in the Country, baptized and instructed in the *Christian Faith*," the planters calling them "by any whimsical Name their Fancy suggests, as *Jupiter, Mars, Venus, Diana, Strawberry, Violet, Drunkard, Readdy Money, Piper, Fidler, &c.*" One of the local wild animals is the valued possum, whose "Testicles given with Honey stir up Lust and cause Conception." As a cure-all, "The Fruit of the *Black Cherry* is good in *Epilepsies, Convulsions, Apoplexies, Palsies*, and many other Disorders." Even more versatile is the "Oil or Grease" from wild geese, which "cures Baldness, helps Deafness, pain and noise in the Ears, is good against Palsies, Lameness, Numbness, Cramps, pains, and contractions of the Sinews, and many other Disorders. The Dung is used with success in the Jaundice, Scurvy, and Gout. The green Dung gathered in the *Spring*, and gently dried, is best." Regrettably, though, no copy of *American Trees and Plants* is extant.

Suggested Readings: T$_1$. *See also* Percy G. Adams, "John Lawson's Alter-Ego—Dr. John Brickell," NCHR, 34 (1957), 313-326; Joseph D. Clark, "Folk Medicine in Colonial North Carolina as Found in Dr. John Brickell's *Natural History*," NCarF, 17 (1969), 100-124; Thomas C. Parramore, in *Dictionary of North Carolina Biography*, I (1979), 221-222; *National Cyclopaedia of American Biography*, VII (1897), 278.

Richard Walser
North Carolina State University, Raleigh

ZECHARIAH BRIGDEN (1639-1662)

Works: *An Almanack of the Coelestial Motions for This Present Year of the Christian Aera, 1659* (1659).

Biography: Born in Charlestown, Mass., in 1639, Zechariah (or *Zachary*) Brigden was the son of Thomas Brigden (also spelled *Bridgen*), from Faversham in Kent. The elder Brigden had sailed for New Eng. in the *Hercules* four years previously with his wife, Thomasin, and their two children and made their residence in Boston. At a relatively early age, Brigden matriculated at Harvard, where he studied for the ministry, graduating in 1657. While at Harvard, Brigden compiled *An Almanack of the Coelestial* (sic) *Motions for This Present Year*. According to Benjamin Trumbull (q.v.), Brigden "Officiated about three years" as a preacher at Stonington, Conn. (then in the jurisdiction of Mass.), before his untimely death on Apr. 24, 1662.

Critical Appraisal: The almanacs of colonial New Eng. were often compiled by young Harvard graduates serving as tutors at the college. Writing in 1658, the young Zechariah Brigden very much partook of this tradition when he both compiled and wrote his 1659 almanac. He departed significantly from tradition, however, in presenting to his New Eng. readers what is, in effect, the first recorded exposition in America of the Copernican, heliocentric view of the solar system in his "Breif [sic] Explication and Proof of the Philolaick Systeme." In calculating his almanac, Brigden drew heavily from *Astronomia Instaurata* (1656) by the English writer Vincent Wing, an amateur astronomer and almanac maker, for his own presentation. Wing was the first writer to popularize in English the new astronomical discoveries of Copernicus and Galileo. Significantly, Brigden's popular, brief exposition of the Copernican system did not receive any significant contradiction from the New Eng. clergy. Indeed, it would appear that the Harvard faculty and administration encouraged the almanac editors in their new, heliocentric interpretations and that by and large the New Eng. clergy actually promoted the new findings in an attempt to keep their theology abreast with advances in science.

Suggested Readings: CCNE; FCNEV; Sibley-Shipton (I, 494-495). *See also* Leo M. Kaiser, "Six Notes," EAL, 13 (1979), 294; Rose Lockwood, "The Scientific Revolution in Seventeenth-Century New England," NEQ, 52 (1980), 76-95; Samuel Eliot Morison, "The Harvard School of Astronomy in the Seventeenth Century," NEQ, 7 (1934), 3-24.

Robert Colbert
Louisiana State University in Shreveport

THOMAS BROCKWAY (c. 1744-1807)

Works: *America Saved* (1784); *The European Traveller in America* (1785); *Virtue Its Own Rewarder* (1794); *The Gospel Tragedy: An Epic Poem* (1795); *A Sermon Delivered at the Ordination of the Rev. Bezaleel Pinneo* (1796).

Biography: Born in Lyme, Conn., around 1744, Thomas Brockway attended Yale College and graduated with a B.A. in 1768. After graduation, he was ordained a Congregationalist minister and in Jun. 1772 was chosen pastor of the Second Society in Lebanon, Conn., where he remained until his death in Jul. 1807. In Dec. 1772 Brockway married Eunice Lathrop; the couple had thirteen children. Two of Brockway's sons followed him into the ministry. During the American Revolution, Brockway was known for his support of the patriot cause, and although that support was usually given through his preaching, he also helped to repel the British under Benedict Arnold (q.v.) when they raided New London, Conn., in Sept. 1781.

Critical Appraisal: Of Thomas Brockway's five published works, three are general: a thanksgiving sermon celebrating the end of the Revolutionary War, a fast sermon, and an ordination sermon. These sermons illustrate the intensity of Brockway's patriotism and the enthusiasm of his preaching. In his thanksgiving sermon, for instance, Brockway told his parishioners that George Washington (q.v.) had been "raised up" by Divine Providence to secure American victory, and he claimed that in America the Lord was "erecting a stage, on which to exhibit the great things of his kingdom"—a stage where "God's greatest works" would be enacted.

Brockway's main claim to literary fame rests with two works he published anonymously: *The European Traveller in America* and *The Gospel Tragedy*. The first consists of three letters to a British friend supposedly written by an English visitor to America. These letters reflect Brockway's nationalist fervor and give his views of American politics during the so-called "Critical Period" before the ratification of the Federal Constitution, and they comprise as good a specimen as any of the patriotism stimulated by the American Revolution. In these letters, the writer assured his friend that the new states would have no difficulty paying off debts contracted during the Revolutionary War and that there would be no impediments to state cooperation. In addition, he urged that the Continental Congress be strengthened to deal with foreign affairs and internal matters of commerce and manufacturing. In *The European Traveller*, Brockway also hinted that the millennium would commence in America, a sentiment many ministers shared after the successful rebellion and that foreshadowed the later theory of Manifest Destiny.

The work that Brockway certainly considered his most mature writing was *The Gospel Tragedy*. A long religious epic also published anonymously, the poem is a direct imitation of Milton's *Paradise Lost* and tells the story of Christ's ministry, death, and triumph. In Book I, Satan and his followers rebel against Christ and plan his fall through temptation; in Book II, Christ is tempted in the wilderness. Book III chronicles Christ's ministry up to his entry into Jerusalem, and Book IV deals with his death, resurrection, and ascension. Although certainly an ambitious undertaking, the poem is unfortunately dull and lacking in originality, and it suffers from comparison with contemporary epics like Timothy Dwight's (q.v.) *The Conquest of Canaan* (1785) or Joel Barlow's (q.v.) *The Vision of Columbus* (1787). Although there is little evidence that contemporaries ranked *The Gospel Tragedy* as a significant work and although no lasting fame certainly attached itself to the author, the poem is evidence of the literary activity spawned by the American Revolution, is at least as good as most of the religious poetry published in America in the last two decades of the eighteenth century, and is particularly noteworthy because of its theme and ambition.

Suggested Readings: CCNE; Dexter (II, 270-272); Sprague (I, 605-606). *See also* William Bradley Otis, *American Verse, 1625-1807: A History* (1909), pp. 79-80.

John F. Berens
Northern Michigan University

HENRY BROOKE (1678-1735)

Works: "Discourse Concerning Jests" (c. 1705). Charles Keith noted that this work is published "in one of the volumes of *Hazard's Register*." Rufus Griswold reprinted a selection in *The Poets and Poetry of America*. Neither

Charles Evans, Charles Hildeburn, nor Joseph Sabin recorded the separate publication of the poem.

Biography: Henry Brooke was born in Eng. in 1678. Little is known of his early years, except that his grandfather was Sir Henry Brooke of Norton in Cheshire. In 1702 Brooke arrived in Pa. to assume the office of collector of customs at Lewes (now Del.), where he earned the friendship and regard of James Logan (q.v.), who described him as "a young man of most polite education," and where he acquired an extensive library. In 1721 Brooke joined the Provincial Council, and six years later he was appointed one of six judges of the Supreme Court of the Lower Counties, where he simultaneously served as speaker of the Assembly. Brooke died in Philadelphia on Feb. 6, 1735, and was eulogized in *The General Magazine* (Feb. 1741) as one of America's finest poets.

Critical Appraisal: Henry Brooke's output as a poet was by no means large, but the quality of his verse was the occasion of much praise during the eighteenth and nineteenth centuries. In 1731 a rather caustic poem titled "The Wits and Poets of Pennsylvania" appeared in the *American Weekly*, which lambasted most of Philadelphia's literati, including Joseph Breintnall (q.v.), Jacob Taylor (q.v.), and George Webb (q.v.). Henry Brooke, however, escaped the author's censure and was instead praised for his "poignant wit" and elegant lines. Later commentators spoke equally well of Brooke's "elegance," "sprightliness," "refined taste," and considerable "social grace." In fact, to many early Pennsylvanians, Brooke epitomized the neo-Classical man of letters—witty and learned, yet nonetheless "sprightly."

In addition, Brooke was noted for his ability to imitate successful neo-Classical models, a trait much admired during the eighteenth century. Reprinted in Rufus Griswold's *The Poets and Poetry of America*, his most famous poem, titled "Discourse Concerning Jests," was written in decasyllabic couplets and betrays obvious indebtedness, both in sentiment and poetic idiom, to British neo-Classical poets like Pope and Dryden: "But for a man in 's wits, unpoisoned with the juice / To indulge so wilfully in empty prate, / And sell rich time at such an under-rate, / This hath no show nor colour of defence, / And wants so much of wit, it fails of common sense." In fact, if the anonymous eulogy in *The General Magazine* correctly dates the poem as 1705, it anticipates Pope's *Essay on Man* and Dryden's *The Dunciad*. In any event, Brooke deserves recognition as one of America's earliest neo-Classical poets, predating John Trumbull (q.v.), Joel Barlow (q.v.), and the Connecticut Wits by more than a half-century.

Regrettably, however, Brooke's poetic canon is meagre, and although he showed promise as a poet and social critic, he concentrated primarily on politics and only dabbled in poetry. As one contemporary admirer of Brooke put it: "Oh! would He oftener write."

Suggested Readings: T₁. *See also* Joshua Fisher, "Some Account of the Early Poets and Poetry of Pennsylvania," MHSP, 2 (1830), 71-72; Charles P. Keith, *The Provincial Councillors of Pennsylvania* (1883), pp. 155-156; Nancy McCreary, "Pennsylvania Literature of the Colonial Period," PMHB, 52 (1928), 289-316.

Timothy K. Conley
Bradley University

CHARLES BROCKDEN BROWN (1771-1810)

Works: *Alcuin* (1798); *Wieland* (1798); *Arthur Mervyn* (1799); *Edgar Huntly* (1799); *Ormond* (1799); *Arthur Mervyn. . .Second Part* (1800); *Clara Howard* (1801); *Jane Talbot* (1801); *An Address to the Government of the United States* (1803); *Monroe's Embassy* (1803); *The British Treaty* (1807); *An Address to the Congress of the United States* (1809); uncollected works in William Dunlap, ed., *Life of Charles Brockden Brown* (1815), and Harry R. Warfel, ed., *The Rhapsodist* (1943).

Biography: Born in Philadelphia, Pa., on Jan. 17, 1771, Charles Brockden Brown was educated at the Friends' Latin School and studied for the bar in the office of Alexander Wilcocks. He soon abandoned the legal profession, however, to pursue a career as a writer. Between 1796 and 1800, the period of his greatest literary activity, he lived from time to time in both Philadelphia and New York City. During these years, he published his four major novels and edited the New York *Monthly Magazine* (1799-1800). Among his friends were Elihu Hubbard Smith (q.v.), a medical doctor who encouraged his writing, William Dunlap (q.v.), the dramatist and painter, and other members of the New York Friendly Club. Late in 1800, Brown settled in Philadelphia and, until 1806, was associated with a mercantile business run by his brothers. He published two sentimental novels, wrote a number of political pamphlets, and edited two periodicals, *The Literary Magazine* (1803-1806) and *The American Register* (1807-1810). On Nov. 19, 1804, Brown married Elizabeth Linn, by whom he had four children. Never robust in health, Brown succumbed to tuberculosis on Feb. 21, 1810.

Critical Appraisal: Charles Brockden Brown has long been recognized as a significant American writer. In the early years of the nineteenth century, his novels caught the attention of important English writers such as John Keats, who was much impressed with *Wieland*; Percy and Mary Shelley, who both came under his influence; and William Godwin, who acknowledged his debt to *Wieland* in the preface to *Mandeville* (1817). In America, William Dunlap, E. T. Channing, John Neal, and Richard Henry Dana, Sr., were early admirers of Brown's fiction; James Fenimore Cooper, Edgar Allan Poe, and Nathaniel Hawthorne mention his work with respect; and Poe even borrowed from *Edgar Huntly* for two of his tales. Brown's novels have long appealed to intelligent and discriminating readers.

Part of the reason is the intellectual quality Brown instilled in his fiction. Although his education was limited by the usual Quaker distrust of advanced schooling, Brown grew up in a family where current books were read, even those by such radical writers as Mary Wollstonecraft, Robert Bage, and especially William Godwin, whose *Political Justice* and *Caleb Williams* exerted a strong influence on the young Philadelphian just as he was beginning to write. As a result, many advanced ideas are reflected in his work. *Alcuin*, for example, discussed the rights of women, a topic much in vogue in the 1790s, and *Ormond* can only be called a feminist book. Constantia Dudley, the well-educated hero-ine, not only makes her way successfully through a world filled with physical, intellectual, and moral difficulties, but she also defends herself against the mach-inations of Ormond, a member of a secret utopian society, who, with his sister, Martinette de Beauvais, espouses the most radical concepts of the time.

Brown, however, was not himself a proponent of such ideas. He included them in his work not to support them but to test their validity. Apart from *Alcuin*, which treats its subject in dialogue form, Brown's novels probe ideas through their actions. In *Wieland*, for example, Brown examined the sensationalist psy-chology of his day by confronting his characters with the problem of drawing just inferences from sensory data. Their task is made difficult, of course, by the voices that Carwin, a ventriloquist, projects, but the main point is clear. None of the major characters is able to interpret correctly the phenomena they perceive. Theodore Wieland goes mad and obeys the command of imaginary voices to kill his family; his sister Clara becomes increasingly disturbed by the strange phe-nomena she experiences; and their rational friend Henry Pleyel draws incorrect inferences from what he observes. The external world, Brown seems to con-clude, is not so easy to understand as rationalist theory might suggest.

Edgar Huntly and *Arthur Mervyn* probe equally interesting questions. In both books, the protagonists are young men eager to make their way in the world, but they come to different ends. Like the characters in *Wieland*, Edgar Huntly misinterprets the world he perceives and in his treatment of the mad Clithero Edny tries to live by the benevolist principles current in that day. He succeeds only in bringing disaster on himself and on Sarsefield, his mentor. In the process, however, he acquires a degree of self-knowledge that the more successful Arthur Mervyn never attains. A country boy who goes to Philadelphia to seek his fortune, Mervyn attaches himself to a series of men—and women—who can help him rise in the world. His face is so open and innocent, and the tale he tells so plausible, that most of those he meets believe in his essential goodness; yet everything Mervyn does leads to his personal advancement. Although perhaps not consciously a sharper—he insists that his motives are pure—he nonetheless benefits from every move he makes.

In depicting the experience of his characters, Brown touched on themes that resonate in later American thought. The epistemological problem faced by the Wielands, Pleyel, and Edgar Huntly became a topic of major concern to subse-quent writers, among them Nathaniel Hawthorne, Herman Melville, and Henry James, all of whom explored it in major works of fiction; and Arthur Mervyn's journey from the agrarian hinterland to find success in the city reflects a major theme in American literature. Mervyn himself is a kind of archetypal character who, as has been pointed out, represents an American moral type, the man of convenient virtue who fails to see the disparity between his professedly pure motives and his fundamentally selfish acts.

In form and technique, Brown's novels foreshadow two major types of Ameri-can fiction. The plague scenes in *Ormond* and *Arthur Mervyn* are early examples of literary realism, and the latter book anticipates in important ways the novelistic strain in American fiction. *Wieland* and *Edgar Huntly*, on the other hand, are Gothic romances that explore through symbols of enclosure the dark side of the human psyche. They are, like the tales of Edgar Allan Poe, told by distraught narrators who are deeply disturbed by the strange phenomena they perceive. These Gothic romances are perhaps the most important of Brown's works, for they set the tone for some of the most significant fiction of the succeeding century.

No one of Brown's books is completely successful. All are marred by flaws in structure and language, for Brown wrote rapidly and did not revise. The best of them remain important, however, both for the themes they develop and for their mode of expression. Charles Brockden Brown was a talented writer who could generate such interest in his novels that, despite their flaws, they remain absorbing reading even today.

Suggested Readings: DAB; LHUS. *See also* W. B. Berthoff, " 'A Lesson on Concealment': Brockden Brown's Method in Fiction," PQ, 37 (1958), 45-57; David Lee Clark, *Charles Brockden Brown: Pioneer Voice of America* (1952); Arthur Kimball, *Rational Fictions: A Study of Charles Brockden Brown* (1968); Donald A. Ringe, *Charles Brockden Brown* (1966); idem, "Charles Brockden Brown," *Major Writers of Early American Literature*, ed. Everett Emerson (1972), pp. 273-294; Harry R. Warfel, *Charles Brockden Brown: American Gothic Novelist* (1949); Larzer Ziff, "A Reading of Wieland," PMLA, 77 (1962), 51-57.

Donald A. Ringe
University of Kentucky

WILLIAM HILL BROWN (1765-1793)

Works: *The Better Sort* (1789); *The Power of Sympathy* (1789); "Harriot" and fourteen "Reformer" essays (signed Q. S.), *Massachusetts Magazine* (1789); twenty-two "Yankee" essays, *Columbian Centinel* (1790); "The Lion and the Tarapen" (1793); *West Point Preserved* (1797); twenty-four verse fables (signed "Pollio"), *Boston Magazine* and *Emerald* (1805-1807); *Ira and Isabella* (1807); *Penelope* (d. unknown).

Biography: America's first novelist, William Hill Brown, was born in Boston, Mass., in 1765, the son of Gawen Brown, a celebrated clockmaker, and his third wife, Elizabeth Hill Brown. Of Gawen Brown's fourteen children, two—William and his sister Elizabeth (Eliza)—were born during his marriage to Elizabeth Hill. Brown grew up and attended school in Boston. His interest in literature developed while he was young and was nurtured by his "aunt" Catherine Byles (actually, the half-sister of his father's second wife, Elizabeth Byles Brown), who seems to have encouraged Brown's imitations of the verse and prose forms of British writers. As a young man, Brown was associated with a fashionable set of young men, which included poet and essayist Robert Treat Paine (q.v.)—who would later write "Monody on the Death of William Hill Brown."

The Power of Sympathy, generally recognized as America's first novel, was published anonymously in Jan. 1789, when Brown was but 23. When it first appeared, the novel was noted for its thinly disguised retelling of a contemporary scandal, the illicit relationship of Fanny Apthorp and her sister's husband, Perez Morton (q.v.), and Fanny's resultant suicide. Although several sources report that Perez Morton denounced the novel and that it was suppressed shortly after publication, there is little evidence to support these claims. For many years, the novel was attributed to poetess Sara Wentworth (Apthorp) Morton (q.v.), apparently on the assumption that Mrs. Morton was most familiar with the scandal surrounding her sister Fanny's death. Brown's niece, Rebecca Volentine Thomson, raised Brown's claim to authorship after William Brayley reprinted the novel in the *Bostonian* (1894), attributing it to Mrs. Morton.

In 1792 Brown journeyed to Murfreesborough, N.C., to join his sister Eliza, who had married John Hinchborne. While in North Carolina, Brown began to study law with Gen. William Richardson Davie. He continued to write and publish as well, including his 100-line verse fable "The Lion and the Tarapen," which appeared in the Halifax *Journal*. After falling victim to a local fever epidemic, William Hill Brown died in Murfreesborough on Sept. 2, 1793.

Critical Appraisal: William Hill Brown—poet, essayist, and dramatist, as well as novelist—is primarily known for *The Power of Sympathy* (1789), a work generally acknowledged as America's first novel. Although there are other claimants to this distinction, most notably Charlotte Ramsay Lennox's *The Life of Harriot Stuart* (1751) and Thomas Atwood Digges's (q.v.) *The Adventures of Alonso* (1775), only *The Power of Sympathy* has all of the generally agreed upon requirements: an American plot and setting, composition and publication in America, and, perhaps most importantly, an explicit acknowledgment of its status as novel—not simply a use of fictional techniques for didactic purposes.

The Power of Sympathy is a novel of sensibility, in which Brown borrowed from Samuel Richardson's *Pamela* and *Clarissa*, Johann Wolfgang von Goethe's *The Sorrows of Werther*, and Laurence Sterne's *A Sentimental Journey*. From Richardson, Brown took the epistolary method, the theme of seduction, and the stock characters of the seduction plot; from Goethe, a model for his hero (who commits suicide with a copy of *The Sorrows of Werther* open by his side); and from Sterne, an extravagant style and a defense for sentimentality itself. Even though Brown embraced the sentimental method, he was troubled by the morality of feeling that underlies the sentimentalists' art. Brown's discomfort resulted in a split between the novel's thematic structure and its action. Brown's two spokesmen—Mrs. Holmes, the "serious sentimentalist," and Mr. Worthy, the voice of reasoned sensibility—convey the thematic norms of the novel. In addition to supplying commentary for the theme that Brown announced in the preface, exposing "the fatal *CONSEQUENCE* of *SEDUCTION*," Holmes and Worthy define the limits of sensibility and emotion as guides to conduct. Mrs. Holmes describes the principle of action as *"that conduct which will bear the test of reflection."* By tempering sensibility with reason, Brown intended *The Power of Sympathy* to be appropriately edifying and instructional for its young female audience.

In the Harrington-Harriot story, Brown examined the sensations that Holmes and Worthy criticize. Although the novel begins conventionally with a love that "softens and refines manners," this harmonious love changes when it is revealed that Harriot and Harrington are sister and brother. Because the lovers can never fully renounce their erotic feelings for one another, their relationship might best be described by Leslie Fiedler's phrase "unconsummated incest." In the words of Harriot, "I become lost in a wilderness and still I travel on, and find myself no nearer an escape. I cherish the idea of a lover—I see the danger and do not wish to shun it, because, to avoid it, is to forget it." The novel reinforces the lovers' refusal to deny their feelings, inviting the reader to share their sensations, and has as its resolution Harrington's self-proclaimed epitaph: "Here lies Harrington and his Harriot—in their lives they loved, but were unhappy—in death they sleep undivided." The tension between the insistent eroticism of Harrington's and Harriot's incestuous love and Holmes's and Worthy's reasoned sentimentalism is never explored—only terminated by the lovers' deaths. The "unbroken circuit" of American fiction that Richard Chase described with its contradictions and disharmonies exists even in its beginnings.

Brown's second novel, *Ira and Isabella* (1807), closely parallels the plot and themes of *The Power of Sympathy* but uses the incest motif satirically rather than seriously. Again the lovers discover that they are brother and sister, but fortunately, through a further plot reversal, Ira, the hero, discovers that his father is not really his father at all. Here illegitimacy is rewarded—and the lovers' "natural" feelings can be consummated. Brown's change of tenor is announced by his title page and preface: the claim "founded on fact" becomes "founded on fiction," and the didacticism of the earlier preface gives way to Brown's discussion of the novelist's art. Describing his artistic intentions, Brown said that he would "content" himself with "a moderate excursion into style," "finding it inexpedient to soar on pinions of invention."

Ira and Isabella is a more consciously crafted novel, in which Brown parodied the conventions of sentimental fiction. He experimented with dramatically heightening action for comic effects. For instance, Isabella's pose, while admonishing Ira to control his feelings, parodies the sentimental heroine's rectitude: "her posture was firm, and her eye fixed upon her brother, her right hand placed upon her breast, and her left pointing toward heaven." He also reversed the story of the sentimental ingenue so that Lucinda, the hero's mother, seduces a succession of men and is rewarded for her prowess with "a good and honest husband" (and without the pains of repentance). Because the target of Brown's satire so often seems to be his first novel rather than sentimental tradition itself, the main interest of *Ira and Isabella* is the perspective it affords on its more famous predecessor.

Brown's other literary work, although revealing the breadth of his readings, is for the most part highly imitative. *The Better Sort*, an "operatical...farce," is a typical comic melodrama with a tyrannical father who wants to marry off his daughter for money rather than for love. The characters, Mrs. Sententious and Yorick, for example, call attention to their literary ancestors. Brown's other two plays, *West Point Preserved* and *Penelope*, have been lost, although it is known that in Apr. 1797 the former had four performances at the Haymarket Theater in Boston. In his poetry, Brown imitated the themes and verse forms of his British contemporaries and displayed a particular fondness for the verse fable (twenty-four of which appeared in the *Boston Magazine* and the *Emerald* [1805-1807]). The most noteworthy of Brown's essays are the "Reformer" essays, which appeared in the *Massachusetts Magazine*, and the twenty-two "Yankee" essays, which appeared in the *Columbian Centinel*. Such diversity of work in addition to his two novels indicates that Brown was a prolific if untutored talent.

William Hill Brown's novels frequently are underestimated. Although the flaws of his work are obvious—thin characterization, hyperbolic style, and faulty plotting—Brown was a serious writer concerned with his craft. In exploring the ambiguities of sensibility and the reality of feeling, Brown anticipated the psychological capacities of the novelist's art that Hawthorne and Melville explored. If *The Power of Sympathy* and *Ira and Isabella* are more interesting for their promise than for their fulfillment, they do credit to a writer who died at 28.

Suggested Readings: DAB; LHUS. *See also* Herbert Ross Brown, *The Sentimental Novel in America: 1789-1860* (1940); Milton Ellis, "The Author of the First American Novel," AL, 4 (1937), 356-368; Leslie Fiedler, *Love and Death in the American Novel* (1960); William S. Kable, ed., Introduction, *The Power of Sympathy* (1969); Henri Petter, *The Early American Novel* (1971); Richard Walser, "The North Carolina Sojourn of the First American Novelist," NCHR, 28 (1951), 138-155.

David M. Craig
Clarkson College

DAVID BRUCE (c. 1760-1830)

Works: *Poems Chiefly in the Scottish Dialect* (1801).

Biography: David Bruce's printer and editor stated that the poet was born in Scot., but in his poems, Bruce claimed Ire. for his homeland. Nothing is known of Bruce's education, but his writings show that he was well read, especially in seventeenth- and eighteenth-century British authors. In 1784 he left Caithness for America, settling for a time near Bladensburgh in Prince Georges County, Md., and then moving to Pa., where he kept a store in Bavington. In 1795 Bruce purchased property in Burgettstown, Pa., and there the lifelong bachelor set up another store, acquired more property, and wrote poetry. From 1822 to 1830, Bruce served as postmaster for the community where he lived. He died in Sept. 1830 and was buried in Burgettstown's United Presbyterian Cemetery.

Critical Appraisal: David Bruce's poems were published during the 1790s in the Federalist *Western Telegraphe and Washington Advertiser*, William Cobbett's (q.v.) *Porcupine's Gazette*, and the *Pittsburgh Gazette*. Later, John Colerick, a founder of the *Telegraphe*, collected and printed forty-three of Bruce's poems along with two others by Hugh Henry Brackenridge (q.v.).

Bruce wrote fables, elegies, songs, verse epistles, and descriptive poems, and he employed various forms including the ballad stanza, Hudibrastic couplets, blank verse, and the six-line stanza popularized by Robert Burns, but although his forms were European, his themes—about frontier life, American politicians and voters, and French influence—were American. Many of Bruce's poems deal with political events of the middle and late 1790s. He criticized, for example, the activities and personalities of Brackenridge, Tench Coxe (q.v.), Albert Gallatin (q.v.), and several other prominent Pennsylvanians, summarizing his case in "A Review o' the Worthies," a comical but unsparing catalog of politicians and their offenses.

Like Richard Alsop (q.v.), Theodore Dwight (q.v.), and other conservative satirists of the time, Bruce considered the masses ignorant and credulous, representing them as cattle, horses, "witless Sheep," and even, in "The Democratic Office-Hunter," as vermin. Living in an area dominated by anti-Federalist sympathies, Bruce attacked what he called the "factious, jacobinic spirit" and urged men of reason and property to support a strong, stable government. He believed that at best democracy rewarded mediocrity and at worst led to demagoguery, violence, and tyranny. His horror of licentiousness is perhaps most forcefully expressed in "Paddy's Advice: A New Irish Song," which ironically extols "the dear French" for showing the "Liberty-Boys" how to overthrow leaders and strip aristocrats of their property. "To Albert Gallatin," another assault on revolutionary principles, portrays *"la Liberte"* as a whore fathered by Voltaire, "fondled" by Rousseau, and sported with by Lafayette. Rejected by Washington, she then seduces Gallatin. In response to the Whiskey Insurrection often attributed to the Scots-Irish of western Pa., Bruce wrote "To Whiskey," considered by some to be the finest of a series of eighteenth-century American poems praising liquor's power to inspire work, play, and poetry. In "To My Friends," Bruce justified his simple, solitary existence: if he had a bustling wife and noisy children, his dreams would not be occupied, as they were, with the muses.

Despite his jocular themes, however, Bruce took the writing of poetry seriously. At times he deprecated himself as an obscure, unambitious poet who used old-fashioned language, but he explained to "Peter Porcupine" (Cobbett) that he wrote in dialect because he was true to himself and his muse, and in "To My Musie," the poet playfully reproved the "wanton, hum'rous witch" who has kept him poor, when he might have been a preacher, lawyer, legislator, or even a family man. When his muse replied that she has given him wit, pleasure, and fame, he declared that he preferred his lot to any other. Nonetheless, the preface to Bruce's *Poems* expresses the hope that his verses, and the men and vices he satirized, would "*sink down together into oblivion.*" For the most part, his wish has come true, but his topical poems still interest students of political satire and Pa. history, and his analyses of the relations between the sexes, the origin of poetic inspiration, and the Scots-Irish experience on the frontier remain highly readable.

Suggested Readings: Boyd Crumrine, *History of Washington County* (1882), pp. 917-918; Wayland F. Dunaway, *The Scotch-Irish of Colonial Pennsylvania* (1944), pp. 82, 138-139, 174, 197-198; Alston G. Field, "The Press in Western Pennsylvania to 1812," WPHM, 20 (1973), 231-264; Abe C. Ravitz, "The Hudibrastic Attack on Western Pennsylvania Politicians, 1798-1804," WPHM, 37 (1954), 83-90; George L. Roth, "Verse Satire on 'Faction,' 1790-1815," WMQ, 17 (1960), 473-485; Harry R. Warfel, "David Bruce, Federalist Poet of Western Pennsylvania," WPHM, 8 (1925), 175-189, 215-234.

Mary De Jong
The Pennsylvania State University

THOMAS BUCKINGHAM (1671-1731)

Works: *Moses and Aaron* (1729); *The Private Journals Kept by Rev. John [Thomas] Buckingham of the Expedition Against Canada,* in *Journals of Madam Knight, and Rev. Mr. Buckingham* (1825).

Biography: Thomas Buckingham, minister of the Second Church in Hartford, chaplain on the Port Royal expedition of 1710 and the Crown Point expedition of 1711, and trustee of Yale College, was born at Milford, Conn., on Mar. 1, 1671. The oldest son of Elder Daniel Buckingham and his second wife, Alice Newton, Buckingham was probably fitted for college at the Hopkins Grammar School in New Haven. He attended Harvard College, receiving an A.B. in 1690 and an A.M. in 1725, the year that his classmate Benjamin Wadsworth (q.v.) became president of the College.

After a college career marked by an unusual number of fines, Buckingham settled in Hartford, becoming minister of the Second Church in 1694. His reputation as a preacher apparently developed and spread rapidly, for in 1705 Governor Fitz John Winthrop invited him to preach the annual election sermon, an invitation that Buckingham declined. Except for his tour as military chaplain in 1710-1711, Buckingham spent the next ten years serving his congregation and the yet-young Hartford community. About 1715 he was elected trustee of the Collegiate School of Connecticut, and along with Timothy Woodbridge, minister of the First Church of Hartford, he tried to secure the permanent location of the college at Wethersfield or Hartford. Failing in that effort, he resigned his position as trustee but resumed it in later years. In 1719 he and Woodbridge were elected the two Hartford deputies to the General Assembly.

A staunch Congregationalist, Buckingham fought the Episcopal incursion into Yale and Conn. politics, charging his colleagues in *Moses and Aaron* not to "put their necks under a Yoke which their fathers could not bear." His reputation well-established, he accepted the Assembly's invitation to preach the election sermon in 1728. He died on Nov. 19, 1731. Married in 1699 to Ann Foster, the only daughter of Isaac Foster, minister then of the First Church of Hartford, Buckingham was survived by Ann and two sons, Isaac and Joseph.

Critical Appraisal: As is true of many men who during this period combined ministerial careers with careers in public service, Thomas Buckingham enjoys a reputation that rests more on his accomplishments within the community than on his literary or oratorical talent. Although the invitations to preach at the 1705 and 1728 elections suggest that Buckingham's pulpit gifts were well known and respected, the only printed evidence that this was the case is the sermon *Moses and Aaron*.

Preached on May 9, 1728, at the Conn. election, *Moses and Aaron* develops a theme popular among New Eng. election preachers: "God's Favour to His Chosen People, in Leading them by the Ministry of Civil & Ecclesiastical Rulers." The theme indicates Buckingham's traditionalism and orthodoxy, a bias particularly apparent when he reminded the auditors on election day that although they were descendants of a chosen people ("a People [taken by God] from the midst of a People...[and led] into a Wilderness to Serve him"), they had lost their fathers' sense of "errand." Assuming the tone associated with preachers of the jeremiad, Buckingham stated that "the Inhabitants of this Land [have] reason to look back with Blushing & Shame on [the] ways wherein [they] have wandered from, and walked contrary to the LORD." Through events, God has sent "many...Appearances of his Anger." Buckingham cited the 1727 earthquake as one sign of divine wrath, "the more Ominous," he said, "for the great Security in which it found and is to be feared *left* the Generality of us." "Let us consider our ways, Confess our Sins, Judge ourselves, Reform our Manners, and...return to the Lord," Buckingham concluded. To assist His people in that work, God offers the ministry of their rulers, a ministry full of responsibility, oppression, and difficulty for those in power, but one as necessary as that of Moses and Aaron to bring about God's purpose. Noteworthy for its lucid style, the power of its argument, and its restatement of essential Puritan sermonic themes, *Moses and Aaron* is a sermon of literary and historic worth.

Although they are not equal in literary merit to the journals of Sarah Kemble Knight (q.v.) with which they were printed, Buckingham's *Private Journals* are of significance to the historian and antiquarian. Both will appreciate, for instance, Buckingham's full account in them of the rigors of the two campaigns in which he served as chaplain. At the same time, both will wonder, perhaps, at the curious incongruity between those rigors and the portrait of the gentleman-parson who carried into battle shoes with silver buckles, bottles of mint water and rum-and-clove water, pots filled with essence of roses, a Bible, a Psalm book, and a copy of Milton's *Comus*.

Suggested Readings: CCNE; Sibley-Shipton (IV, 30-33). *See also* Richard L. Bushman, *From Puritan to Yankee: Character and the Social Order in Connecticut, 1690-1765* (1967).

Ronald A. Bosco
State University of New York at Albany

THOMAS BUDD (fl. 1678-1698)

Works: *Good Order Established in Pensilvania & New Jersey in America* (1685); *A Brief Answer to Two Papers Procured from Friends in Maryland* (1692); *An Expostulation with Thomas Lloyd* (1692); *False Judgments Reprehended: And A Just Reproff to Tho. Everdon* (with George Keith; 1692); *A Just Rebuke to Several Calumnies, Lyes & Slanders Reported Against Thomas Budd* (1692); *The Plea of the Innocent Against the False Judgment of the Guilty* (with George Keith; 1692).

Biography: The son of a Somersetshire clergyman who died while imprisoned for refusing the oath of conformity, Thomas Budd immigrated in 1678 to N.J., where he became a Quaker and, as a member of the Colonial Council and a commissioner for the purchasing of land, took an active part in the economic and political life of the colony. In Philadelphia after 1685, Budd became embroiled in a bitter religious controversy, taking the side of George Keith (q.v.), leader of the "Keithian" or so-called "Christian Quakers" against the more orthodox Friends of Pennsylvania. Little else of Budd's origins or his activities in the period is known. He died in Philadelphia in 1698.

Critical Appraisal: A man of action as well as ideas, Thomas Budd wrote unadorned but vigorous prose. His most famous work, *Good Order Established in Pensilvania & New Jersey*, is a promotion tract, designed to encourage European settlement of Pa., which gives evidence of his natural energy, foresight, and enthusiasm for social projects. Among the "Improvements" advocated by Budd were public education, a public bank, and community-owned and operated granaries. "All which," he said, "is laid down very plain, in this small Treatise; it being easie to be understood by any ordinary Capacity." If Budd's style lacks the natural charm of writers such as Gabriel Thomas (q.v.), whose better known *Account of Pensilvania* appeared a dozen years later, the earnestness of his writing, which is evident in the dedication of his book to "those that have generous Spirits, whose desires and Endeavours are to bring the Creation into Order," more than compensates for what the work may lack in charm. Although his efforts to minimize the hazards of settlement led to certain unconscious ironies—he said, for example, that the Indians "are but few in Number, and have been very serviceable to us"—he was more direct in admitting minor irritants, noting that "on the River and Cricks are great quantities of rich fat Marsh Land, which causeth those parts, to some fresh People, to be somewhat unhealthful in the latter part of the Summer, at which time some of them have *Agues*." Budd knew his audience well, and he understood the kind of opportunities that, well described, would appeal to that mixture of purpose—both economic and ideal—that moved men and women to immigrate to early Pa., "out of that Slavery and Poverty they groan under."

Budd's later religious tracts are lagely polemical and distinguishable only for the rancor that attended the Keithian controversy.

Suggested Readings: LHUS; T$_1$. *See also* M. Katherine Jackson, *Outlines of the Literary History of Colonial Pennsylvania* (1907; 1966); Frederick J. Shepard, ed., *Good Order Established in Pensilvania & New Jersey* (1902).

Donald P. Wharton
Castleton State College

SAMUEL BUELL (1716-1798)

Works: *Christ the Grand Subject of Gospel Preaching* (1754); *The Divine Agency Acknowledged in the Death of Our Dearest Friends* (1757); *The Happiness of the Blessed Heaven* (1760); *The Saving Knowledge of the Lord Jesus Christ* (1761); *Useful Instructions and Evangelical Consolations for Mourners* (1763); *A Copy of a Letter from the Rev. Mr. Buell, of East Hampton, on Long Island, to the Rev. Mr. Barber* (1764); *An Account of the Late Success of the Gospel* (1765); *A Faithful Narrative of the Remarkable Revival of Religion* (1766); *A Faithful Narrative of the Remarkable Revival of Religion with Some Remarks* (1768); *Intricate and Mysterious Events of Providence* (1770); *A Spiritual Knowledge of God in Christ* (1771); *A Faithful Narrative of the Remarkable Revival of Religion...Aberdeen* (1773); *The Best New Year's Gift for Young People* (1775); *Useful Instructions and Evangelical Consolations for Mourners* (1783); *Divine Support and Comfort* (1787); *A Sermon Delivered at the Ordination of the Rev. Aaron Woolworth* (1788); *The Import of the Saint's Confession* (1792); *The Life of Christ as Lord and Redeemer* (c. 1794); *A Sermon Delivered at the Ordination of Rev. Joseph Hazard* (1797); *A Faithful Narrative of the Remarkable Revival of Religion...and Also an Account of the Revival of Religion in Bridgehampton and Easthampton in the Year 1800* (1808).

Biography: The son of a well-to-do farmer, Samuel Buell was born on Aug. 20, 1716. At first he planned to become a farmer, but about the age of 17, he decided to be a minister. While at Yale College, Buell fell under the influence of Jonathan Edwards (q.v.), with whom he resided during part of his college life. After college, Buell planned to study for the ministry with Edwards, but he found himself caught up in the religious ferment of the Great Awakening, and in response to the new demand for preachers, he became an itinerant minister. His great ability to draw a response from his audience and his skill as a preacher are remarked upon by his contemporaries from the very beginning of his career. However, in his travels, Buell often aroused the ire of some of the better established preachers whose congregations he charmed. In 1746, as the movement waned, Buell found a permanent position in East-Hampton, Long Island, where he remained for the next fifty-seven years of his life.

During the British occupation of East-Hampton during the Revolutionary War, Buell received recognition among his compatriots for his diplomacy, wit, and peacemaking skill. Throughout his life he was well known for the value of his opinions and advice and for his hospitality and geniality. In 1791 Buell received the degree of doctor of divinity from Dartmouth College, and he later contributed to the founding of Clinton Academy in East-Hampton. Buell married three times: to Jerusha Meachum of Coventry, Conn.; to Mary Mulford of East-Hampton; and to Mary Miller, also of East-Hampton. Of his ten children, only two outlived him.

During the course of the sermon preached upon the occasion of the death of his daughter Jerusha Buell Conklin, Buell claimed that he "buried his first comfort [his wife], six children, and one grandchild," along with eleven other members of his family. Jerusha Conklin had died at the age of 33, after having married twice and having borne four children. The last of the four, a baby girl, lived a few hours to die just before her mother. Jerusha and her infant daughter were buried together, the baby in its mother's arms.

In 1794 another sad occasion was the subject of a funeral sermon: the death of Buell's grandson Samuel Buell Woolworth, aged 3. The times seemed generally gloomy to the preacher, and he cataloged the threat of war with G.B. and an existing Indian War, as well as a "dangerous insurrection in the back parts of Pennsylvania," as causes for dismay. Two years later, however, he preached his church's and his own half-century sermon, wherein he claimed to have preached more than 10,000 times and to have baptized 1,600 people, a number that exceeded the entire population of East-Hampton at that time. Rev. Buell died in East Hampton, N.Y., on Jul. 19, 1798.

Critical Appraisal: It seems apparent that the sermons of Samuel Buell were influential and highly regarded by the people of his time, because the sermons were printed at the request of his parishioners. Two of the sermons were also published in Eng., further proof of his influence and recognition. Rev. Buell was also instrumental in a "Remarkable Revival of Religion" that occurred in his church and within surrounding churches. His parishioners came to him in sizable numbers, seeking his offices and counsel. There were nearly a thousand conversions as a result of this revival. In the course of his ministry, Buell preached ten ordination sermons, including that for Samson Occom (q.v.), who was being ordained to preach to his fellow Indians. Buell also preached funeral sermons for six members of his immediate family, among them that of his "first comfort" (his wife); his daughter Jerusha Conklin and her infant daughter; another grandchild, a boy, who died at the age of 3; and his 16-year-old son Samuel Buell, Jr.

For the most part, Buell's theology is predictable. In some of the sermons, philosophical ideas akin to those in the writings of Jonathan Edwards are developed. In *The Best New-Year's Gift*, a sermon preached in 1775, for example, Buell explained his ideas about the angel that the first Christians found in Jesus's grave upon the morning of the Resurrection. To find an angel in a grave was remarkable to Buell: spirits in the place where one finds dead bodies, immortality in the place of corruption. Buell in several places surprisingly associated God with evil: "As he is infinite in being, he is equally present with the blackest devils, as well as the brightest angels." But his "declarative presence" is special and "more" (greater?) in one place than another. This may be so, Buell claimed, because the ground for positing heaven is not spatial-temporal, but another mode: "Heaven may be more properly considered as a State or a moral Beauty, consisting in the Disposition and Affection of the Heart, than under the notion of place." Yet there are local heavens—within the mind of the individual who contemplates God—and Heaven is the Heaven of heavens.

To Buell, the bond between Christ and the believer is stronger than the bond between body and soul in an individual. At death the soul in this union with Christ becomes "perfect in Holiness." Christ's nature partakes of qualities of both man and God and performs necessary services to each. In Christ, human nature, as well as divine nature, is perfect. Faith in the salvation of Christ is an "evangelical mystery." As for the world, death is a necessity: "There is a Poverty, Emptiness and Insufficiency in [all created things]." "The World's all Title-Page; there is no contents." All hopes in earth and earthly things are false; deprivation of them should make them turn to their *true* hope, God. "One event of Providence resembles another," and "there is no stability in any part of the universe." "The joint tendency of all is to one common end." Buell likened the earth to the wheel of a conquering chariot and discussed the contingent nature of victory and defeat, of master and slave. He also likened it to the wheel of a clock or watch; the wheel (earth) is designed for motion and is in a state of constant flux. Yet "There is a perfect government of all things here below in a due accommodation between the material and the moral world." The wheel within a wheel that Ezekiel saw are both guided by one spirit to one end, God's glory. A denial of providence leaves all to chance and destroys the relationship between man and God. "Such high athiestical disparagement of God is implicitly...infinitely unworthy and absurd." Buell claimed that since the name "Jehovah" means "self-existence," God is essentially self-existence, and he claimed that eternity is a successive eternity "so instantaneous as to exclude all past and all future and to be but one point of duration: this would make that space of time to which millions of years are as nothing."

The impression that the reader gets overall by reading the sermons of Samuel Buell is that of a man—human, warm, reasonable, and restrained—who, although he suffered hardships, possessed a quiet dignity and a peaceful assurance about life. His sermons comforting the bereaved had to be assuagements of his own losses as well as those of his parishioners. He asserted his "remarkable conversions" with a cogency and reasonable tentativeness that remove any suspicion that the reader might have of a tendency toward "enthusiasm." Toward the end of his life, he expressed the "power of heartfelt, keen desertion" and said he was "fighting out the bitter lamentations." In 1797, one year before his own death, he preached what he called the "half-century sermon" of the church and also the "half-century sermon" of his own ministry. He wrote that he considered this sermon his valedictory to his parishioners after having served them for fifty-seven years. He recounted some of the accomplishments of his years and claimed that the "candle [had] burned down to the socket." He decried the gloom of the present: the war with Napoleon in Europe, the gloom about our "political affairs." It disturbed him that the exercise of religion was being replaced by "Pursuits of honor, gain, sensual pleasure, infidelity and security." He did not like the pernicious "errors and heresies" espoused by his countrymen, such as the "Deistical principles," the "Arian heresy," the beliefs of Arminians and Socinians, and especially the "delusive and destructive doctrine of universal salvation." He saw some hope in the increase of the congregation and in the propagation of the Gospel in Europe. He warned his successor: "You will need to be as wise as a serpent; and as harmless as a dove; as bold as a lion; and as meek as a lamb." He offered his church and congregation congratulations: They were engaged in a "most tremendous trial." He greeted his "fellow candidates for eternal Glory." They were blessed because they were already possessed of heaven. He grieved that the "preparation of God for sinners" had been rejected by them, and he exhorted them to repent.

Suggested Readings: CCMC; CCNE; Dexter (I, 664-669); Sibley-Shipton (I, 498, 578-579); Sprague (III, 102-113). *See also* Edwin Scott Gaustad, *The Great Awakening in New England* (1957), pp. 44 ff., 55, 70, 123, 128.

Virginia Levey
University of Central Arkansas

EDWARD BULKELEY (1614-1696)

Works: "A Threnodia upon Our Churches Second Dark Eclipse..." (1663) and "Upon the Death of...Mr. Jonathan Mitchell" (1668) in Nathaniel Morton, *New Englands Memoriall* (1669); a sermon upon a day of thanksgiving at Brookfield in Thomas Wheeler, *A Thankefull Remembrance* (1676).

Biography: The son of a famous father and the father of a prominent son, Edward Bulkeley was born in Eng. on June 12, 1614, and matriculated at St. Catherine's Hall, Cambridge, in 1629. Five years later he came to New Eng., where he briefly attended Harvard College. In 1642 he was ordained pastor of the church at Marshfield in Plymouth, remaining there until at least 1656. Following the death of his father, the pastor at Concord, Mass., Bulkeley was ordained minister there and served as pastor until his death on Jan. 2, 1696. Perhaps because of poor health, Bulkeley did not play a major role in any of the disputes affecting New Eng.'s ecclesiastical and political peace after 1660. He did, however, deliver the Artillery Election Sermon in 1679 and the General Election Sermon the following year; neither sermon was printed.

Critical Appraisal: Edward Bulkeley wrote his two published poems to eulogize two ministers, Samuel Stone (q.v.) of Hartford and Jonathan Mitchell (q.v.) of Cambridge. Neither work is an outstanding poem, suffering from uncertain rhythm and clumsy word choice and order. Nevertheless, both poems exemplify the Puritan tendency to use a person's name to describe his character. Among other things, Stone, for instance, is called a diamond, a whetstone, a lodestone, and a cornerstone.

Bulkeley preached his one published sermon to the survivors of the town of Brookfield, which had been besieged by Indians during King Philip's War. Puritan ministers often read great significance into historical events, and the attention paid to the battle of Brookfield was indicative of that tendency. Some saw the rescue of most of the settlers as a sign of God's providential intervention. Thomas Wheeler (q.v.), to whose account of the siege Bulkeley's sermon was appended, noted a number of occurrences that seemed to prove God's presence. Bulkeley believed that his task as preacher was to explain what was expected of the Brookfield residents in return for His assistance.

Employing the usual Puritan sermon organization of text, doctrine, reasons, and uses, Bulkeley called the settlers to reform their lives. He argued that God had done His people in New Eng. a number of favors but that the people had forgotten them. To remind them what they owed Him, God afflicted them with punishments and then rescued them. Cognizant of this divine mercy, the minister continued, those rescued from affliction had a special responsibility to abide by God's word. For Bulkeley the most important lesson to learn from the battle of Brookfield was that God expected the survivors to take their religious duties seriously, a promise Bulkeley imagined the settlers had made when they were in danger. Finally, the Concord pastor warned his listeners that the Lord would punish them in earnest if they refused to live up to their promise.

Bulkeley's thanksgiving sermon shows how common the jeremiad became for Puritan ministers after 1660. Even on days of thanksgiving, they sometimes emphasized the failure of the people to live up to their covenant with God and their need to reform their lives before God deserted them. In such sermons giving thanks and praise to God was subtly translated into an indictment of the colonists for their shortcomings. In fact, the only positive note in Bulkeley's sermon was the interpretation of the siege and rescue as signs that God had not yet totally abandoned New Eng.

From a literary perspective Bulkeley's sermon lacks stylistic polish, but it assumes significance because like the works of Mary Rowlandson (q.v.), Increase Mather (q.v.), and William Hubbard (q.v.), it is part of the body of contemporary historical literature which throws light on the events of King Philip's War and on the imaginative response of New Eng. to the crisis.

Suggested Readings: CCNE; FCNEV. See also Douglas E. Leach, *Flintlock and Tomahawk* (1958), pp. 78-84; Samuel E. Morison, *The Founding of Harvard College* (1935), p. 369; Richard Slotkin and James K. Folsom, eds., *So Dreadfull a Judgment* (1978), pp. 234-257 (for Wheeler's part of the tract).

Timothy J. Sehr
Indiana University Archives

GERSHOM BULKELEY (1636-1713)

Works: "An Voluntas Semper Sequater Ultimum Dictatem Intellectus Practici?" in *Quaestio In Philosophia Discutienda* (1658); *The People's Right to Election* (1689); *Will and Doom* (1689); *Some Objections Against the Pretended Government in Connecticut* (1692); *Some Seasonable Considerations for the Good People of Connecticut* (1693-1694).

Biography: Born in Cambridge, Mass., in Jan. 1636, Gershom Bulkeley was graduated from Harvard in 1655. He married Sarah Chauncy, the daughter of Harvard's first president. In 1660 he accepted a position as minister of New London, Conn., and in 1666 moved to Wethersfield, Conn., to assume a similar position. In addition to his ministerial duties, Bulkeley also practiced medicine and surgery and at times worked as surveyor and magistrate. A man of many skills, he was fluent in Latin, Greek, and Dutch and knowledgeable in chemistry and philosophy. To build his library, he sometimes copied out lengthy works by hand, to judge by a tome still surviving in the Connecticut Historical Society Library.

During King Philip's War, Bulkeley served as surgeon to the army, both in the Dec. "Fort Fight" of 1675, in which the Narragansett home base was burned and destroyed, and in the Major Treat expedition in the spring of 1676 against the Nipmuck stronghold at Mount Wachusett, near Princeton, Mass. Bulkeley is undoubtedly the "doctor" referred to by Benjamin Church (q.v.) in his account of the Fort Fight. Church said that he tried to stop the burning of the Indian village, in which scores of Indian women and children perished, on the grounds that the wigwams would provide shelter for the colonial army, but was opposed by the "doctor," who argued vociferously that Church's advice would kill more men than the enemy had, since the "stiffening" of wounded men would make them immovable. In fact, the army lost scores of men on the trek back that bitter Dec. night, and Bulkeley himself was wounded in the thigh during the Wachusett expedition.

After the war, in 1677, Bulkeley resigned his Wethersfield pastorate to Joseph Rowlandson (q.v.), husband of the celebrated hostage Mary Rowlandson (q.v.), and moved across the river to Glastonbury to practice medicine. He is probably the author of the preface to Mary Rowlandson's narrative of her captivity. Internal evidence shows the author to have been a man with ministerial concerns but also familiar with issues confronting the "Council of War" after the Fort Fight.

In his later years, Bulkeley was most notable for his opposition to the colonial rebellion against Sir Edmund Andros, the agent of the English crown. In a series of tracts, Bulkeley criticized the colonial usurpation, adopting what came to be known as the "Tory" position. That Bulkeley was an outspoken man, willing to oppose his neighbors, is suggested as early as 1664, when he demanded of his parishioners in New London the right to speak his mind in his sermons. Of Bulkeley's Toryism, John Palfrey said, "He was always a discontented and troublesome person. . . a bigoted partisan of Andros." Benjamin Trumbull (q.v.) said, "Bulkeley had few superiors in the colony, in natural ability, professional learning, or general scholarship. Overweening self-importance, obstinate adherence to his own opinions or prejudices, a litigious spirit, and the peculiarities of his political creed, detracted from his usefulness, and kept him almost constantly at strife with his parish, his neighbors, or the government of the colony."

In 1692 Bulkeley entered the witchcraft controversy by defending one Mary Disbrow (or Disborough) from the charge of witchcraft. Accused as a witch, Disbrow had lived with the Bulkeleys in New London. Bulkeley's letter in defence of Disbrow argued in some detail that the charges were misinformed and confused. Bulkeley died in Glastonbury on Dec. 2, 1713, aged 77.

Critical Appraisal: Gershom Bulkeley's major surviving works all argue an unpopular, and lost, cause. As a result they have been consigned to virtual oblivion. *Will and Doom* is representative of Bulkeley's Toryism. It attacks the "levelling, independent, democratical principle" he saw corrupting colonial society. Bulkeley argues that "Monachy is the best form. . .of civil government," and that the laws passed by the colonial government that usurped the power of Andros were more tyrannical than the laws of Eng. Though dogmatic, Bulkeley is a strong, lucid and logical writer—a formidable rhetorician. He often displays a gift for vigorous and concrete phrasing: "Let the saddle lay upon the right horse," he snorts regarding the who-is-more-tyrannical-than-whom issue. A man of stubborn and rugged honesty, his willingness to stand against the sway of popular opinion is an attractive feature. He perhaps shows at his best in the letter in defence of Disbrow, a strong and impassioned piece of writing less open to charges of wrong-headedness than most of his other works.

Bulkeley's only surviving poem, "An Voluntas Semper Sequater," provides a negative response, in fairly strong and well written lines, to the seventeenth-century Puritan debate concerning whether or not the human will always follows the dictates of the practical intellect. Harold Jantz notes that Bulkeley's poem is "the earliest preserved of the [Harvard] *Quaestiones* with verse."

Although Bulkeley's writings are now no more than historical curiosities, they reveal an author of considerable, if cantankerous, intelligence. He was a true New Englander.

Suggested Readings: CCNE; FCNEV; Sibley-Shipton (I, 389–402). *See also* Sherman Adams and Henry R. Stiles, *The History of Ancient Wethersfield, Connecticut* (1974); *The Andros Tracts* (1869); F. W. Chapman, *The Bulkeley Family* (1875). passim; Frances Manwaring Caulkins, *History of New London, Conn.* (1852), pp. 131-140; Donald Jacobus, *The Bulkeley Genealogy* (1933); Samuel Eliot Morison, *Harvard in the 17th Century* (1936), II, Appendix B, p. 595.

Robert K. Diebold
Husson College

PETER BULKELEY (1583-1659)

Works: *The Gospel-Covenant; Or, the Covenant of Grace Opened* (1646).

Biography: Peter Bulkeley was born in Bedfordshire, Eng., and attended St. John's College, Cambridge, where he took an M.A. in 1608. He returned home in 1620 to succeed his father in the parish of Odell and to inherit the family estate. Although he was even more extreme than his father in his dissenting opinions, he nonetheless preached undisturbed for fifteen years. In 1635, however, Laud suspended him, and Bulkeley with his family, servants, and followers emigrated to Mass. Stopping briefly in Newtown, later called Cambridge, they went west and founded Concord in 1636, there settling the twelfth church of the colony. Bulkeley served the church and town faithfully for over twenty years, notably involved in affairs beyond Concord only when he served with Thomas Hooker (q.v.) as moderator of the Hutchinsonian Synod in 1637. Although he occasionally expressed a longing to return to Eng. to die, he was still preaching in Concord at the time of his death in 1659.

Critical Appraisal: Peter Bulkeley, according to Cotton Mather (q.v.) in the *Magnalia*, wrote elegies for his most famous colleagues—Thomas Hooker, Thomas Shepard (q.v.), and John Cotton (q.v.)—as well as a few topical poems. His fame as a writer, however, rests on his only substantial publication, the lengthy sermon series *The Gospel-Covenant*, first published in 1646 and then enlarged and corrected by him for the 2nd edition of 1651. The sermons, probably delivered beginning in 1638 or 1639, were, according to Bulkeley, addressed to a time then "full of trouble in these American Churches." At every point in this series, Bulkeley clearly opposed the heresies of the Antinomian faction through a detailed analysis of the difference between the covenants of works and of grace. For the orthodox New Eng. preachers, federal theology—as the doctrine of the covenants was often termed—was an important device for teaching how God grants salvation to the elect and how the elect receive grace. Although several sermon series and numerous treatises on the covenant can be found in the first half-century of New Eng. religious literature, no work explicates the distinctions between the covenant of grace and of works more thoroughly nor indicates as fully the intricate defenses that the orthodox shaped against charges by the Antinomians than *The Gospel-Covenant*. Denying that the majority was "shut up under a Covenant of works," Bulkeley nonetheless stressed that the law dispensed under the covenant of works was "still of use, as a rule of life" under the covenant of grace.

The Gospel-Covenant methodically considers the following aspects of the covenant of grace: (1) its differences from the covenant of works; (2) the difference in its "administration" before and after the coming of Jesus Christ; (3) its benefits and blessings; (4) its condition—faith; and (5) its properties. Throughout the five sections, Bulkeley emphasized the omnipotence of God and the inability of humans to earn salvation through their own works. Yet because covenant theology clarified the individual's as well as God's role in this many-staged process, Bulkeley, essentially a preparationist, also stressed ways that individuals could ready themselves for entering into covenant with God. Like his fellow preachers, Thomas Hooker and Thomas Shepard, Bulkeley came to detail the mystery of salvation far more than Calvin, awed by God's inexplicability, had ever dared.

Stylistically, Bulkeley relied on many of the similitudes common to the preaching of the period, such as God the lover courting the soul. But unlike Hooker and Shepard, Bulkeley did not develop as ingeniously or extensively such imagery nor dramatize as fully with memorable soliloquies the struggling soul. What does lend literary power to *The Gospel-Covenant* is the passion with which Bulkeley stated his ideas: for example, his assurance that love is the very core of the covenant relationship. In his rigorous exegesis of the biblical theme of the covenant, Bulkeley won his congregation more by scriptural analogy than by abundant imagery. Salvation for each soul compares to the experience of scriptural heroes; the plight of the New Englanders resembles that of the people of Israel. Bulkeley developed here the double possibilities of federal theology; the covenant explained not only the intimacy between God and elected soul but also the special commitment of God to the community of the faithful, be they organized in a church or state. Thus part of the breadth and imaginative intensity of *The Gospel-Covenant* is its continual expansion from the individual in covenant with God to the church and state in league with him: "And for ourselves here, the people of *New England*, we should in a special manner labor to shine forth in holiness above other people...because we profess ourselves to be a people in Covenant with God."

Suggested Readings: CCNE; DAB; FCNEV; Sprague (I, 51-53); T$_1$. *See also* Elizabeth Lowell Everett, *Peter Bulkeley and His Times* (1935); Phyllis M. Jones and Nicholas R. Jones, eds., *Salvation in New England: Selections from the Sermons of the First Preachers* (includes a section of *The Gospel-Covenant* with commentary, pp. 25-41, and interpretive material relevant to Bulkeley throughout; 1977); Cotton Mather, *Magnalia Christi Americana* (1702); Norman Pettit, *The Heart Prepared: Grace and Conversion in Puritan Spiritual Life* (1966), pp. 114-122.

Phyllis M. Jones
Oberlin College

PETER BULKELEY II (1643-c. 1688)

Works: "Of the Trinity and the Unity of the Godhead," "Like to the Grasse Thats Green Tooday," "God so Loved the World," "The Dignity and Transcendant Excellency of Jesus Christ," "A Loving Conference Had with Christ and the Deceast Soule," "The Humanity of Christ," "O Death Where Is Thy Sting," "Use and Peruse This Book, with Greatest Care," Ms.a., Gershom Bulkeley Medical Mss. Collection, Hartford Medical Society.

Biography: The New Eng. records speak sparingly of Peter Bulkeley II, the youngest son of the Rev. Peter Bulkeley (q.v.), founder of the town of Concord, Mass. From *Sibley's Biographical Sketches of Graduates of Harvard University*, we learn that young Peter was born on the twelfth of either Jun. or Aug. 1643; he entered Harvard in 1656, graduated in 1660, returned later for another degree that was bestowed in 1663; and he was never ordained. He ultimately settled in Fairfield, Conn., as a physician and merchant. Harold Jantz, the first source of biographical information for the modern student, provides additional but con-flicting details. From Jantz, we learn that young Peter died in 1691 (not 1688 as Sibley avers); that he graduated from Harvard in 1662 (not 1660 as Sibley records). The Harvard graduation lists bear out Sibley's date, and the Peter Bulkeley who graduated in 1660 died in 1688. It would appear that Professor Jantz had access to information that has yet to be made generally available, or either he or Sibley has confused two Peter Bulkeleys, a very real possibility. At any rate, the available data serve best to confuse the historical person known to his contemporaries as a dour, melancholy, and extremely solemn poet, physi-cian, and businessman.

Critical Appraisal: "Verely, his sun did set in a cloud" observed a contemporary of Peter Bulkeley. Nearly 300 years later, this observation remains painfully accurate. Even Michael Wigglesworth (q.v.), at his gloomiest and most terrifying, can offer no more macabre a picture of human sin and mutability than Peter Bulkeley. The wages of sin are death, Bulkeley reiterated in poem after poem, but never did he adequately portray the life of the believer who repents and renounces his vain and evil actions and thoughts. This dark theme recurs through every poem, constantly reminding man of his evil nature, even in those poems in which Christ is the central figure. But there are other features of Bulkeley's poetry that warrant comment.

First, the figure of Christ is more prominent in Bulkeley's poetry than in that of any other American Puritan poet, including Edward Taylor (q.v.). Of his eight poems, one deals with the mystery of the trinity, five treat the figure of Christ exclusively, and one deals with the mystery of the Resurrection. As an example of the nonclerical Puritan's interpretation of the meaning of the figure of Christ, Bulkeley's stance may be invaluable to students of the period. Somewhat blithely and innocently, Bulkeley slid easily from Arian to Socinian to Arminian concep-tions of Christ as quickly as did John Milton, his English contemporary.

Bulkeley's poems, when viewed as a sequence, suggest a principle of organi-zation that is familiar to the student of seventeenth-century Protestant poetry: the Pauline pattern of salvation. The first seven poems in this sequence carry the reader, and probably Bulkeley himself, to the first step—calling—wherein the good Christian, having realized his evil nature, becomes aware that his nature has perceived a call to do God's will. The analysis, despair, grief, chaos, and gloom that characterize the precalling stage of conversion constitute the tone and the world view of the first seven poems. The figure of Christ, the redeemable nature of humanity, and the beauty of the world are untransformed and are subject to confusion and misinterpretation. The speaker reminds himself that his perceived needs are unattainable in his present natural, uncalled existence. As we move to poem eight, we see that progress has been made, that the speaker has moved to the starting point of discernible Christian behavior. This organization of the poems constitutes something unique in Puritan verse: an intense, sequential analysis of a pre-Christian state of mind, body, and soul, a look at sin as a state of mind, with the requisite Protestant bleakness that overwhelms the pre-Christian, he who has yet to step beyond the conversionary stage of calling.

Suggested Readings: CCNE; FCNEV; Sibley-Shipton (II, 68-73). *See also* John E. Trimpey, "The Poetry of Four American Puritans" (Ph.d. diss., Ohio Univ., 1969), pp. 40-84.

John E. Trimpey
University of Tennessee at Chattanooga

JOHN BULKLEY (1679-1731)

Works: *The Necessity of Religion in Societies* (1713); Preface, *Poetical Meditations* (by Roger Wolcott; 1725); *An Impartial Account* (1729); *The Usefulness of Reveal'd Religion* (1730); The Charge in *The Glorious Reward of Wise and Faithful Teachers* (by Solomon Williams; 1730), pp. 23-25.

Biography: John Bulkley, son of noted surgeon Gershom Bulkeley (q.v.) and Sarah (Chauncy) Bulkley, was born in Wethersfield, Conn., in 1679. He graduated from Harvard College with a B.A. in 1699 and completed an M.A. in 1702. On Dec. 20, 1703, he became the ordained minister of a small congregation in the relatively new frontier community of Colchester, where he had preached frequently during the preceding two years. He also served his fellow townsmen as a physician and lawyer, representing them in the latter capacity before Conn.'s General Assembly as well as on boundary commissions. As a theologian, he frequently served as a counselor to divided congregations and defended Presbyterian orthodoxy against challenges from splinter groups. For example, he debated questions of baptism and maintenance of ministers with Baptist elder Valentine Wightman at Lyme on Jun. 7, 1727. Years later, Charles Chauncy (q.v.) selected Bulkley as among the three greatest geniuses New Eng. had produced and especially praised him for "solidity of judgment and strength of argument." Bulkley died during his sleep on Jun. 9, 1731.

Critical Appraisal: In his earliest extant publication, the Conn. election sermon delivered at Hartford on May 14, 1713, John Bulkley demonstrated himself a prophet of rationalism. Titling the sermon *The Necessity of Religion in Societies*, he asserted that the usefulness of "true religion" to successful civil government is "a Principle which Nature furnishes men." In turn, good government contributes to the well being of religion. For example, as he wrote in *An Impartial Account*, natural law and common justice dictate that civil authorities have a moral duty to levy public taxes for ministerial support. Although he wrestled to demonstrate the reasonableness of the principle that Christian piety among the people preserves civil liberty, he admonished civil authorities to remember that their God-given power ought to be tempered by spiritually guided right reason. In his pointed condemnation of the "heathen" Tacitus's assertion that people have no right but "to obey the arbitrary Determination of Princes," Bulkley seemed to edge toward supporting popular government. He quickly disabused his readers of any such notion by turning to Machiavelli to support the condemnation of Levellers for their belief that the power of rulers was granted by the people rather than by God. On that score, he reflected the thinking of his father, who had expressed an abiding distrust of the will of popular majorities. At a time when religious authority had declined appreciably, Bulkley concluded that the decay of religion is a "sure sign" of a decaying state, and the pious few are best suited to rule, because they "will be most industrious" in doing everything within their power to encourage general piety, thereby arresting the process of decay.

The frontier clergyman further demonstrated the extent of his inclination toward rationalism in his sermon *The Usefulness of Reveal'd Religion*. Although he chastised Deists for their condemnation of Christians, whose revealed religion afforded the only true way to rescue natural piety from inevitable errors and corruptions, Bulkley poured abundant praise on nature's lessons; he asserted that any individual's spontaneous reasoning would lead to conclusions identical to the biblical record. Throughout natural religion, he found "an Intrinsick or Inherent Goodness" that goes beyond our idle curiosity to generate concern for our happiness and to excite our love for God. In this work, as well as his others, the most striking departure from contemporary thinking was not that rationalism led to religious and political conformity rather than freedom, but that it replaced the voluntarism of covenant theology as the generator of conformity.

Bulkley's preface to Roger Wolcott's (q.v.) *Poetical Meditations* offers an essay on the disparate topics of poetic style and property rights. Bulkley praised solid reason but distrusted wit because the latter risked being "misled by Similitude, and by affinity to take one thing from another." If wit made the "Accomplish'd Poet," it needed tempering with "exactness of Judgment, or Clearness of reason" to make the "Great Man." Because wit and judgment seemed so contrary, Bulkley found no surprise in the observation that few individuals become both accomplished poets and great men, but he hinted that Wolcott might be one such person.

Following his comments on poetry, Bulkley turned to the subject of property rights. Relying almost exclusively upon rational argument from natural law rather than the traditional ground of scriptural revelation (Genesis 1:28), he concluded that the English colonists' application of labor to unimproved land established property rights, even if the colonists had failed to purchase the land from the Indians; in fact, the Indians had no property rights in the land because they had not labored to improve it. He branded any other conclusion "a mere chimera of fiction" with criminal overtones. Finally, Bulkley rose above "the Multitude (who generally Speaking have too much rubbish in their Brain to think of anything with distinctness)" and demonstrated a clear, thorough understanding of John Locke's theory of property. In doing so, he established himself among the first in New Eng. to grasp the significance of "that man of deep tho'ts."

Suggested Readings: CCNE; LHUS; Sibley-Shipton (IV, 451-454). *See also* Perry Miller, *The New England Mind: From Colony to Province* (Beacon paperback ed.; 1961), pp. 382-383, 426-434. Bulkley's comments on poetic style from the preface to Wolcott's *Poetical Meditations* are reprinted partially in Perry Miller and Thomas H. Johnson, *The Puritans* (1938), pp. 681-684. Bulkley's comments on property rights from the preface to Wolcott's *Poetical Meditations* were reprinted under the title "An Inquiry into the Right of the Aboriginal Natives to the Lands in America," CMHS, 1st ser., 4 (1795), 159-181.

Rick W. Sturdevant
University of California, Santa Barbara

JOHN DALY BURK (c. 1772-1808)

Works: *The Trial of John Burk, of Trinity College, for Heresy and Blasphemy* (1794); *Bunker-Hill* (1797); *Female Patriotism, Or the Death of Joan D'Arc* (1798); *History of the Late War in Ireland* (1799); *An Oration* (c. 1803); *History of Virginia* (1804-1805); *Bethlem Gabor, Lord of Transylvania* (1807); *A Selection from the Ancient Music of Ireland* (1808; 1824).

Biography: Little is known about John Daly Burk's early life. He was born probably in County Cork, Ire., about 1772, christened John Burk, and brought up as a Protestant. He entered Trinity College, Dublin, in Jun. 1792, where in addition to the usual course of studies he became involved with Wolfe Tone's Society of United Irishmen and began writing for an antigovernment newspaper. After the College Board of Senior Fellows expelled him in 1794 for disseminating atheistic principles among the student body, he published a defense revealing that if not an atheist, he was certainly a Deist of the broadest stripe who was announcing plans to publish a history of "The Horrors of Bigotry and Superstition." Further involvement in secret republican revolutionary societies led to his denunciation to the authorities in 1796, and he was forced to flee to America. Family tradition claims he escaped arrest by boarding his ship while disguised as "Miss Daly," a young woman who had given him one of her costumes, and in a characteristically romantic act of gratitude, he added her name to his own.

Burk arrived in Boston by early Apr. 1796, apparently equipped with a draft of his play *Bunker-Hill*. By Oct. both Burk and Alexander Martin were publishing the *Polar Star and Boston Daily Advertiser*, Boston's first daily newspaper, but this enterprise lasted only through Feb. 2, 1797. Later in the same month, *Bunker-Hill* opened to popular acclaim and critical denigration. Before Burk left

Boston, his play was put on nine times, and it was performed several more times at the John Street theater in New York City after his arrival there. He followed his first dramatic success with *Female Patriotism*, a much better play but a failure with the public when it was produced in the New Theater on Apr. 13, 1798. In New York City, Burk succeeded Philip Freneau (q.v.) as editor of *The Time Piece*, a Republican triweekly, continued his association with the United Irishmen, and in Jul. was indicted under the common law for seditious libel, sharing with Benjamin Franklin Bache (q.v.) the dubious honor of being one of the only two editors so indicted before passage of the Alien and Sedition Laws. Aaron Burr was instrumental in persuading the district attorney to drop the case on the condition that Burk leave the U.S. He instead went into hiding in Va., leaving behind for publication a history of the Irish rebellion of 1798, until the election of 1800 removed the danger of prosecution. In Petersburg, Va., he became a lawyer and ardent Jeffersonian, continued to write plays that were produced there—only *Bethlem Gabor* survives—and produced three volumes of his *History of Virginia*. On Apr. 11, 1808, Burk was killed in a duel in Petersburg, and his *History* was completed by Skelton Jones, himself killed in a duel before he finished the work, and Louis Hue Girardin.

Critical Appraisal: Although the texts of only three of his plays survive, Burk was one of the major dramatists of his period in America. *Bunker-Hill* made his contemporary reputation; if William Dunlap (q.v.) called it "vile trash," the public flocked to see it, and the Boston run alone brought 2,000 dollars to the author. Burk made a real effort to portray human feeling and moral complexity in his somewhat sketchily drawn characters. Abercrombie, a British officer, is torn between a sense of honor that demands loyalty to his uniform and king and a realization of the justice of the American cause, made more poignant by his love for Elvira, a virtuous young patriot. Warren (q.v.), the American hero, embraces the Revolutionary cause as much from a desire for personal honor and fame as from patriotic commitment to liberty and national independence. Burk's attempt to give depth to his hero was rewarded in one instance when John Adams (q.v.), exiting the theater, told the manager, "Sir, my friend General Warren was a scholar and a gentleman, but your author has made him a bully and blackguard." What probably caught the public fancy, however, was the spectacular fifth act in which for nearly a quarter of an hour, American soldiers, firing from an artificial hill, beat off British troops, accompanied by a great deal of smoke, flame, musket fire, and off-stage sounds of cannon. Patriotic sentiment and a veritable indoor fireworks display were a winning combination, but this play's pioneering attempt at portraying physical action realistically on stage was also important.

Burk's best play, however, is *Female Patriotism, or The Death of Joan D'Arc*. The poetry and dramatic structure are superior to that of *Bunker-Hill*, and the characters, particularly that of Joan, are more fully and convincingly developed. His Pucella is an Enlightenment heroine who prays to a Deist God and is motivated not by divine voices, "a pious fraud / To raise the fainting courage of the land," but by a passion for liberty, "To make all free and equal, *all men kings*." At the same time, because of her growing love for Chastel and her consequent desire to revert to her purely feminine role, she is a genuinely tragic figure caught up in the toils of history and not merely a passive victim of tyranny and priestcraft. The play has plenty of vigorous, well-paced scenes, but it is the developing character of Joan that structures the dramatic action. It did not help the chances of *Female Patriotism* to open at the time of the XYZ Affair and a growing animosity toward Fr., and the quality of the acting was also apparently below the usual standard.

A number of other plays, none surviving, have been dubiously attributed to Burk; he certainly wrote two pantomimes to appear on the same bill with *Bunker-Hill*, and he may have completed scripts for "The Prince of Susa: A Tragedy" and "The Exiles: A Tragedy." His final surviving play, *Bethlem Gabor*, was written for the Thespian Society of Petersburg in which he took an active part. This Gothic melodrama, which borrows slightly from Godwin's novel *St. Leon* and perhaps Charles Brockden Brown's (q.v.) *Wieland*, features a harum-scarum plot full of ruined castles, dungeons, ventriloquism, mirrors, and miraculous reappearances of characters. Although not devoid of interest, it is inferior to the two earlier plays in point of structure and character.

Burk's work as a journalist and Republican propagandist was also significant, if less so than his contributions to the stage. His *History of Virginia* was the first account of the Old Dominion written after it became a state; its Jeffersonian bias guaranteed its favorable reception when first published, and Burk's documentation, partly from materials loaned by Thomas Jefferson (q.v.), ensured its importance after his death. He followed Jefferson in condemning slavery but then apologized for the Virginians' failure to abolish it, and his long account of the Indians in Va. reflected Jefferson's interests in Indian language and customs. Because he was interested in showing the growth of democracy in Va. as a paradigm for the history of the nation as a whole, he paid particular attention to Bacon's Rebellion and created the image of Nathaniel Bacon (q.v.) as a liberal hero, motivated by "the ardor and enthusiasm of liberty." Although Burk embraced the republican politics and society of his adopted homeland, he did not forget his Irish beginnings. His account of the *Late War in Ireland* was an effort at instant history, and its shortcomings are perhaps understandable in view of the scarcity of reliable information about these recent events. At his death, he was at work on a collection of American lyrics to be sung to Irish airs. When this work finally appeared in 1824 with music by John McCreery, it contained an essay on Irish music and fourteen poems by Burk, but by this time, Burk was most often remembered as the historian of Va. and as a former writer for the stage.

Suggested Readings: DAB; T₁. *See also* Walter J. Meserve, *An Emerging Entertainment: The Drama of the American People to 1828* (1977), pp. 119-125; Joseph I. Shulim, *John Daly Burk: Irish Revolutionist and American Patriot* (1964); idem, "John Daly Burk, Playwright of Libertarianism, from 1796 to 1807," BNYPL, 65 (1961), 451-463.

Frank Shuffelton
University of Rochester

THOMAS BURKE (c. 1744-1783)

Works: *The Poems of Governor Thomas Burke of North Carolina* (w. 1764-1782; pub. 1961); "On the Recovery of Some Ladies in Norfolk from the Smallpox" (pub. in *Virginia Gazette;* 1768).

Biography: Son of Ulick Burke of County Galway, Ire., and nephew of Sir Fielding Ould, Thomas Burke was born on the family estate of Tyaquin about 1744. After completion at age 16 of a university education (probably at Dublin), family adversities caused him to immigrate to America, and at Accomac County on the eastern shore of Va., he pursued the study of medicine. In 1769 he moved to Norfolk, turned to the practice of law, and shortly thereafter was married to Mary Freeman. In 1772 he settled on a plantation near Hillsborough, N.C., where the climate, he wrote, was "remarkably moderate and healthy," and soon was involved in the political turmoils of the time. During 1775-1776 he was a member of three successive N.C. Provisional Congresses and from then until 1781 represented his region at the Continental Congress in Philadelphia. In 1777 he rushed from the city to participate in the fighting at Brandywine. Patriotism and personal honor were his dearest possessions. His one-year term as governor of N.C. began in Jun. 1781. In Sept. he was captured in Hillsborough by the Tories and taken captive to Charleston, S.C. Although paroled, he continued to be harassed by the Tories and felt justified in making an escape. Returning to N.C., he resumed the governorship from Alexander Martin (q.v.). When even his friends considered the breaking of his parole a breach of honor, Burke's effervescence and high spirits drooped, and he died the following year at his home on Dec. 2, 1783.

Critical Appraisal: Thomas Burke was a doctor, lawyer, planter, soldier, and politician. He was also sentimental, as his romantic lyrics attest, and at other times a hot-headed, irascible Irishman who on four occasions challenged his opponents to duels and who, when the temper was upon him, flayed them in waspish quatrains and angry heroic couplets. His poetic lines bespoke his hatred of Eng. and his admiration of America. He was, it is reported, a ready raconteur, and he could hoist a merry song. Whether in a romantic or acrimonious mood, he composed rapidly and dispatched his effusions speedily on their way toward those for whom they were intended. Although secretly proud of his facile talent, Burke was reluctant to boast of it. Others, however, thought him an accomplished bard and were quick to say so. His blindness in one eye as a result of smallpox prompted the remark that "Burke's eye, in double sense, is single, / Enabling truth with wit to mingle." Another admirer spoke of his "flowing lines."

Most of Burke's occasional verses were circulated by hand. Of the twenty-three selections in *Poems* (1961), only three were published during his lifetime. A twenty-fourth has since been identified as Burke's and reprinted. Among the Burke papers are a number of other poems in shorthand that have not been deciphered.

Burke's early pastorals evince a familiarity with Greek and Roman mythology, with the works of Homer and Pindar, Horace and Juvenal. He confessed to the influence of Edmund Waller and James Thomson. Although his pastorals and love lyrics are derivative and although they rarely rise above the conventional, his poetic compliments to young ladies like Chloe and Delia are often attractive and impassioned.

More impressive are patriotic outbursts such as "Triumph America!" on the repeal of the Stamp Act in 1766. His bitingly satiric "Address to the Goddess Dullness," written when Burke was 20, is one of a number of poems from the *Virginia Gazette* during a period when political enemies were brutally attacking one another. Even more ruthless are invectives like those against the wealthy Va. aristocrat Landon Carter (q.v.) and the quarrelsome pamphleteer Thomas Paine (q.v.). Carter was "an Ass" whom "No God" could "e'er un-Ass." Paine's birth, so different from that of Minerva's springing from the head of Jupiter, was of a totally degrading sort. Burke wrote that "great *Common Sense* did surely come / From out the Crack in grizzly Pluto's Bum."

Suggested Readings: DAB. *See also* Richard Walser, Introduction and Notes, *The Poems of Governor Thomas Burke of North Carolina* (1961); John Watterson, "Thomas Burke," *Dictionary of North Carolina Biography*, ed. William S. Powell (1979), I, 280-281; John Watterson, ed., "Poetic Justice; Or, an Ill-fated Epic by Thomas Burke," NCHR, 55 (1978), 339-346 (reprints "On the Recovery...").

Richard Walser
North Carolina State University, Raleigh

WILLIAM BURNHAM (1684-1750)

Works: *God's Providence in Placing Men in Their Respective Stations & Conditions* (1722).

Biography: The son of William and Elizabeth (Loomis) Burnham, William Burnham was born at Wethersfield, Conn., on Jul. 17, 1684. Although little is known of his formative years, Burnham most likely prepared for college in his native state. The records of Harvard College, where he received an A.B. in 1702 and an A.M. the following year, show the erratic spending and debts of "an irresponsible youth." About 1707 Burnham began to preach to the settlers in the Great Swamp district of Farmington Township (now the towns of Berlin and New Britain), Conn. Supported by Timothy Woodbridge, Thomas Buckingham (q.v.), and Stephen Mix, three neighboring preachers, the settlers in the Great Swamp petitioned the Conn. General Assembly to permit the formation of a church "to prevent irreligion & heathenism growing up in the familys...in the wilderness." Without waiting for the Assembly's approval, the people asked Burnham to preside over their recently formed "religious Society," and on Jun. 5, 1709, he accepted, stipulating that, among other things, a house, land, and sufficient supply of firewood for the seasons serve as security for the arrangement.

Eventually, the Great Swamp Society was reorganized as the Second Parish of Farmington, and on Dec. 10, 1712, Burnham was ordained its minister by Woodbridge, Buckingham, Mix, and Samuel Whitman. During the next thirty-one years, Burnham served his congregation without interruption. As it happened, he accumulated a private fortune from successful farming ventures, which probably contributed to the harmonious relations between Burnham and his flock, since financial disputes between ministers and their congregations were otherwise quite common during that time. Burnham's early prosperity was shared by his congregation, for in 1721 the General Assembly renamed the parish Kensington and annexed portions of neighboring towns to it. On May 18, 1743, Burnham notified his church that failing health prevented the continuation of his ministry, and he urged members to seek another preacher. Edward Dorr (q.v.) was called to serve in 1745, but with his health recovered, Burnham interfered with the offer and resumed his position as pastor in 1746. He died on Sept. 23, 1750, during a general epidemic of dysentery. Married twice, first to Hannah Wolcott, who died in 1748, then to Ann Foster Buckingham, the widow of his friend Thomas Buckingham, Burnham was survived by Ann, four daughters, and a son, Josiah.

Critical Appraisal: A political and theological conservative, William Burnham enjoyed considerable popularity in his parish. His reputation, however, developed not on the basis of his literary or oratorical talent but on the basis of his practical contributions to the community, particularly his role in the development of the Kensington parish and township and his position as a defender of orthodoxy among Conn.'s clergy. Burnham was so well respected by his fellow ministers that they elected him moderator at the meeting of the association of ministers at Stratford in 1738.

One of the major events in Burnham's career occurred in 1722, when he was invited to preach the election sermon before the governor and other officials. *God's Providence*, Burnham's only printed work, was preached on May 10, 1722. His choice of Psalm 75:7 for his text (*"But GOD is the Judge: He putteth down one, and setteth up another"*) and his defense of Divine Providence as a political, social, and religious reality place him in the tradition of the leading election preachers of the late seventeenth and early eighteenth centuries. Although the sermon has been characterized as "a curious mix of old and new," Burnham's emphasis throughout was on the "old," and his aim was to preserve the old "New England Way." Defending the social and political status quo, he attacked supporters of change, saying,

> however atheistical wits may argue [for change] from the variety of mens Conditions, certain it is that the various Ranks and degrees of men are for the advantage and benefit of mankind. . . [for] without this variety. . . men would want some Motives and Encouragements to Vertue & Restraint from Vice, that now they have.

"Ranks and degrees of men" guarantee the need for law and strict order in government; government, in turn, under the guidance of Divine Providence, keeps the world from becoming "a heap of Confusion." It is God's good providence that "Exalteth those that are above others in wealth and Riches" and controls "Persons of a Lower Rank [that they] should not Envy those of a more Exalted Station." A practical political consequence of this arrangement is that all must obey civil and ecclesiastical rulers, for they act for God, and rulers must be "Humble & Condescending," for they have their authority from God. Speaking as mediator between God and the officials who derive their authority from Him, Burnham stated, "[The] Sins of Rulers Dishonour God more than the sins of others; & are more Hurtful to men: & Rulers discover more Ingratitude & baseness of Spirit by their Sins, than persons of a lower Rank." He concluded *God's Providence* by charging the newly installed officials to encourage new schools in Conn. and to defend the colony's chartered privileges. In the fashion of Jeremiah, he pleaded that "the sword of civil Justice be pointed against" the "Crying abominations of our Land," and in the fashion of a good theocrat, he saw no problem with "the promulgation & Execution of suitable Laws" against such "abominations."

Although preached in 1722, *God's Providence* establishes Burnham as a product of late seventeenth-century New Eng. Puritanism. The sermon is noteworthy among Conn. election sermons for both its clarity and its persuasiveness. Thus it is likely our misfortune that no other examples of Burnham's preaching survive in print.

Suggested Readings: CCNE; Sibley-Shipton (V, 137-141). *See also* Richard L. Bushman, *From Puritan to Yankee: Character and the Social Order in Connecticut, 1690-1765* (1967).

Ronald A. Bosco
State University of New York at Albany

AARON BURR (1716-1757)

Works: *A Sermon Preached at the Ordination of. . .David Bostwick* (1745); *The American Latin Grammar* (editor; c. 1750); *A Discourse Delivered at New-Ark* (1755); *The Watchman's Answer* (1756); *A Servant of God Dismissed* (1757); *The Supreme Deity* (1757).

Biography: Father of an infamous son and son-in-law of the celebrated Jonathan Edwards (q.v.), Aaron Burr achieved prominence in his own right as both minister and public man. Born in Fairfield, Conn., on Jan. 4, 1716, he was educated at Yale, where, after experiencing religious conversion, he turned to the ministry. Active first at Greenfield, Mass., and then at Hanover, N.J., he accepted a call in Dec. 1736 from the First Church of Newark. There, in addition to his ministerial duties, which helped to occasion the Great Awakening, his career as an educator began, as he founded a Latin school. Not long after, he began efforts to form the College of New Jersey (now Princeton), which with Governor Belcher's help became a reality in 1747 at Elizabethtown. After Jonathan Dickinson's death in Oct. of that year, Burr became the school's second president, the students moving to Newark. Thereafter, he was indefatigable in his efforts for the college and in his attempts to alert his fellow citizens to the spiritual, political, and physical dangers of their times. In 1752 the 36-year-old Burr took Esther Edwards [Burr] (q.v.), 21, as his wife. With her and seventy students, he moved the college in 1756 to the newly built Nassau Hall in Princeton. A year later, upon the death of Governor Belcher, an already ill Burr exhausted himself by traveling forty miles to deliver the funeral sermon. Within a month, he too died (Sept. 24, 1757) and was buried in the college cemetery.

Critical Appraisal: Aaron Burr's works reflect his principal functions as Puritan minister and civil leader. *A Sermon Preached at the Ordination of. . .David Bostwick* (1745), for example, exemplifies the standard three-part structure of the Puritan sermon—statement of text, doctrinal elaboration, and application of text to the audience. Filled with the religious commonplaces of the times, its interest lies principally in its description of the minister's duties and in its suggestion of the fearfulness with which he undertook his calling. *A Discourse Delivered at New-Ark* (1755), however, has a public theme. It makes plain the dangers the Americans face from the French, suggesting that the colonists' plight may be the result of God's anger. Burr called, therefore, for an acknowledgment of dependence upon God and for a radical change in behavior, but he also pleaded for a vigorous defense effort. The piece also suggests how closely the colonists identified themselves as Englishmen just twenty years before the Revolution. *The Watchman's Answer* (1756), preached before the Synod of New York City, depicts the Puritan minister's function of reading the hand of God in all visible things. Applying the enigmatic text of Isaiah 21:11-12 to both past and present church history, Burr saw God's anger in current problems such as the loss of Lake Oswego to the French and the trouble with the Indians. He urged his fellow ministers to prepare for dark times ahead by calling for a general moral reformation and a spirited effort in colonial defense. Unfortunately, in its tracing of church history, the sermon is tinged with a sense of sneering superiority.

The Supreme Deity. . .Maintained is an elaborate refutation, replete with seemingly impeccable logic and scriptural support, of Emlyn's *Inquiry*, which had challenged the divinity of Christ. As such, Burr's work represents a classic example of the kind of theological debate so prevalent in the eighteenth century, although Burr was quick to claim that he had not written the piece "for *Dispute* sake" but rather for the vindication of religious truth. Whatever the case, the work is principally interesting as a reflection of Puritan tenets and method. In describing his goals, Burr made clear one of the common assumptions of Puritan theology: "The main End of Speaking and Writing (especially when any Thing of a religious Nature and Importance is the Subject) should be, to be thoroughly understood." Consequently, he used "a manner plain and intelligible"—the so-called Puritan plain style.

A Servant of God Dismissed, the funeral sermon for Governor Belcher, is of note largely because of Belcher's importance and because of the circumstances surrounding its composition and effect. Written while Burr was at times delirious and delivered, after a forty-mile ride, by a man on the verge of collapse, the piece hastened Burr's own death. Because the manuscript was left in an unfinished state, Caleb Smith revised and published it at the request of the governor's widow. The text—"But go thy way till the End be; for thou shalt rest, and stand in thy Lot, at the End of the Days" (Daniel 12:13)—serves as an appropriate epitaph for Burr as well as for Belcher. Although the final part of the sermon deals primarily with Belcher's life as exemplum, it also reflects Burr's role as public man; in the "Improvement," Burr could not refrain from treating the problems the colonists were currently having with their enemies. His call, therefore, was not only for moral reformation but also for vigorous defense of his *"bleeding* Country."

Suggested Readings: CCMC; DAB; Dexter (I, 530-534); Sprague (III, 68-72). *See also* Varnum Lansing Collins, *Princeton* (1914); Matthew L. Davis, *Memoirs of Aaron Burr*, 2 vols. (1858), I, 17-25, passim; John Frelinghuysen Hageman, *History of Princeton and Its Institutions* (1879); Milton Lomask, *Aaron Burr: The Years from Princeton to Vice President, 1756-1805* (1979), pp. 3-9, 13-14, 16-18; William A. Packard, *The Princeton Book* (1879); Herbert S. Parmet and Marie B. Hecht, *Aaron Burr: Portrait of an Ambitious Man* (1967), pp. 1-5, 8-10; James Parton, *The Life and Times of Aaron Burr* (1858), pp. 31-47; Nathan Schachner, *Aaron Burr* (1937), pp. 3-17, passim; Joseph Shippen, Jr., to Joseph Shippen, 6 Jul. 1752, in NJHSP, 5 (1850-1851), 169-170; Caleb Smith, *Diligence in the Work of God, and Activity During Life: A Sermon Occasioned by the Much-Lamented Death of the Rev. Mr. Aaron Burr* (1758); Charles Burr Todd, *A General History of the Burr Family*, 2nd ed. (1891); Samuel H. Wandell and Meade Minnigerode, *Aaron Burr*, 2 vols. (1925), I, 3-19, passim.

Charles J. Nolan, Jr.
United States Naval Academy

ESTHER EDWARDS BURR (1732-1758)

Works: Ms. journal, 1754-1757, Beinecke Library, Yale University. Other papers are located at Andover-Newton Theological School and at Princeton University.

Biography: Esther Edwards was born in Feb. 1732 to the Rev. Jonathan Edwards (q.v.) and Sarah Pierpont of Northampton, Mass. She was educated by her parents, probably more with a view to her domestic accomplishments and her salvation than to her literacy. In 1751 she moved with her family to Stockbridge, Mass., after her father lost the Northampton pulpit. She remained in Stockbridge only a short time, however, because in Jun. 1752 she married the Rev. Aaron Burr (q.v.), pastor of the Presbyterian congregation in Newark, N.J., and president of the College of New Jersey (now Princeton). Their marriage produced two children: Sally in 1754 and Aaron in 1756.

Although Burr gave careful attention to matters of religious doctrine, she apparently found little time to continue her education. In 1755 she remarked in her journal that "Mr. Burr has had a mind that I should lern [French], but I have no time—The married woman has something else to care about besides lerning French tho' if I had time I should be very fond of lerning." If formal "lerning" wasn't Burr's preoccupation, her journal nevertheless detailed her habitual reading from the Bible and from the works of Elizabeth Singer Rowe, Isaac Watts, Edward Young, Samuel Richardson, and others.

When the College of New Jersey was moved from Newark to Princeton in 1756, the Burrs moved with it. Esther Burr found Princeton a more isolated community than Newark, one affording her fewer educated female companions. She took much pleasure, however, in a growing friendship with poet Annis Boudinot Stockton (q.v.). In Sept. 1757 Burr was widowed. She died soon after, in Apr. 1758, of complications arising from an inoculation against smallpox.

Critical Appraisal: Esther Burr's journal takes the form of letters addressed to her lifelong friend Sarah Prince of Boston. The abruptness with which the journal opens and the numbering system within it suggest that Prince and Burr had been exchanging journal-letters for some time, but the extant manuscript covers only the period from Oct. 1, 1754, to Sept. 2, 1757. Although the time is brief, the detail is not, and Burr's journal proves a rich source of materials on diverse topics such as the founding of Princeton College, religious revivalism, the French and Indian War, childrearing practices, women's roles, preaching practices and practitioners, and N.J. politics. These topics and others are discussed in terms of their effects on her community and family.

Burr's journal also contains information about her friendships, conversations, journeys to New York City and Stockbridge, guests (welcome and otherwise), gossip, almost constant illness, fear of Indian attack, concern for her soul—in short, most of her day-to-day thoughts, habits, and responsibilities. For example, Burr wrote almost solemnly of the extensive duties of the married woman, but she also wittily noted that people tend to marry in the winter because it is too cold to sleep alone. She recorded her pleasure in George Whitefield's (q.v.) "company & conversation as well as preaching" but remarked the difficulty her husband had in restraining Gilbert Tennent (q.v.), "for he is mighty forward to preach and pray, and would fain preach em to death if he could." She often lamented her limited communication skill yet did not shrink from "a smart combat with Mr. Ewing," a tutor at the college who had "mean thoughts of Women." Burr detailed her response to Ewing's suggestion that women "were hardly capable of anything so cool and rational as friendship": "My Tongue you know hangs pretty loose thoughts Crouded in so I sputtered away for dear life. . . .I retorted several severe things upon him before he had time to speak again, He blushed and seemed confused. . . .I talked him quite Silent."

The remarkable quality of Burr's journal derives from more than its variety, however: Burr's temperament adds a good deal to its force. Her sister Lucy had noted in a letter to Mary Dwight (undated) that Esther "never could bear pestering very well." Perhaps it is that lack of tolerance that led Burr to write so candidly. Directness was ever her habit. She assured Sarah Prince, for example, that she "make[s] conscience of telling in case I am in [the] least dissatisfied with a friend, Such things Should not lay *grumbling* within, untill they are forced to *belch* out all at once like a floud." Concrete diction and subject matter give Burr's prose a force rare in the diary literature of the period. "I am like working Liquor Bottled up [that] will . . . burst unless it has vent Soon," she wrote in Apr. 1756. If Burr's exchange of journal-letters with Sarah Prince was her "vent," it is for us an important record of life in eighteenth-century America.

Suggested Readings: James Axtell, *The School upon a Hill: Education and Society in Colonial New England* (1974), passim; Mary Sumner Benson, *Women in Eighteenth-Century America* (1935), passim; Josephine Fisher, "The Journal of Esther Burr," NEQ, 3 (1930), 297-315; Maureen Goldman, "Esther Edwards Burr," *American Women Writers*, ed. Lina Mainiero (1979), I, 277-278; Mary Beth Norton, *Liberty's Daughters: The Revolutionary Experience of American Women, 1750-1800* (1980), passim; Jeremiah Eames Rankin, *Esther Burr's Journal*, 3rd. ed. (a fictionalized "edition" of Burr's journal; 1903); Ola Elizabeth Winslow, *Jonathan Edwards* (1940), pp. 287-291.

Pattie Cowell
Colorado State University

STEPHEN BURROUGHS (1765-1840)

Works: *Memoirs of the Notorious Stephen Burroughs* (1798); *Stephen Burroughs's Sermon, Delivered in Rutland on a Hay Mow* (1798).

Biography: One of the most notorious colonial rogues, Stephen Burroughs was born in 1765 and spent most of his childhood in Hanover, N.H. While his father, the Rev. Eden Burroughs, was the town's pastor and one of the most respected men in the area, Stephen Burroughs was among the least respected individuals in the community. According to one source, his "volatile, impatient temper of mind" was unsuited to the harsh Puritanism of his family and community, and Burroughs quickly gained the reputation as "the worst boy in town."

Throughout his long life, Burroughs was unable to escape his reputation as a rascal and a rogue. At times he attempted to hide from it by posing under an assumed name as a preacher or a schoolteacher, but respectability was never long maintained. In 1785 he was arrested in Springfield, Mass., for passing counterfeit money and was sentenced to three years in jail. In spite of his eventual reform and marriage, he was again arrested late in 1790 on three charges of rape, charges later reduced to "open, gross, lewd, and lascivious conduct." While serving his sentence in the Worcester jail, he escaped and subsequently traveled to Long Island, where his reputation soon caught up with him. Leaving family, reputation, and New Eng. behind, he then journeyed south to Ga., where he briefly taught school and surveyed Indian land. In 1796 he returned north and settled on his father's farm in Hanover, where he prepared his *Memoirs* for publication. After quarreling with his father, Burroughs left New Eng. for Can., where he soon "commenced business" as a counterfeiter. Late in life, however, he sincerely repented and joined the Roman Catholic Church. He moved to the small Canadian town of Three Rivers, where he resumed his often interrupted career as a schoolteacher. He died a "peaceful death" in 1840, unknown as a real person but notorious as the character of his *Memoirs*.

Critical Appraisal: During his lifetime, Stephen Burroughs was something of an early American folk hero, and stories about his rogue exploits, both factual and fictional, published and unpublished, are still passed throughout New Eng. Often Burroughs experienced (or claimed to have experienced) the peculiar situation of hearing irreverent and distorted stories about himself from total strangers. He wrote his *Memoirs* hoping both to vindicate himself and to capitalize on his notoriety. Although the success of either attempt is questionable, the popularity of his book cannot be questioned. By 1900 *Memoirs of the Notorious Stephen Burroughs* was published in nearly thirty editions in fourteen cities.

Burroughs's narrative is part of an old but little discussed genre of early American writing—the rogue history. One of the most popular of all colonial narratives, the "rogue history" was ostensibly published to edify and terrify readers by illustrating God's stern justice, but it also served to titillate readers as much as to educate them. Burroughs's narrative makes little pretense of either moral instruction or justice and represents a merging of the more secular and sensational English "rogue history" with the more Puritanical American equivalent, the criminal life and "last confession." Although structurally weak and altogether too self-righteous, the narrative contains many of the best elements of picaresque literature. Supposedly responding to a friend's request for his life story, Burroughs attempted verisimilitude through a series of autobiographical, episodic letters, somewhat resembling earlier English writers of the picaresque, in which he described his adventures and misadventures as an impetuous, impatient, and ambitious youth. Although admitting his life "has been one continued course of tumult, revolution and vexation," he was hesitant to blame either himself or the will of God and was quick to name his oppressors. From a literary standpoint, the first section of the book is the best and is filled with stories of his jokes, pranks, and exploits, ranging from stealing beehives to stealing a handful of sermons from his father. Some of its more noteworthy episodes include his year and a half as a student at Dartmouth College, where his "thirst for amusement" was far greater than his thirst for knowledge, and his six-month tenure as a Presbyterian clergyman, in Pelham, Mass., where he preached the sermons stolen from his father.

The book's lively tone changes, however, when Burroughs describes his 1785 arrest and conviction for counterfeiting. His repeated escape attempts resulted in severe, often cruel, punishment, and he spent his entire three-year imprisonment under miserable conditions. After his release, he attempted to redeem himself (or so he would have both his neighbors and readers believe), and the rest of the book is filled with the various ups and downs that characterized his middle years. In these sections, Burroughs's confused intention about whether to vindicate, educate, or entertain is felt the most. Far too much attention is given to the petty intrigues that forced his removal from Long Island, and far too little attention is given to his southern journey and Georgian experiences.

In addition to its literary value, Burroughs's *Memoirs* is of great historical value, offering vivid insights into many areas of late colonial history. His descriptions of the unpredictable colonial justice system reveal a world where sin and crime were often confused and where punishment was whimsical. His graphic descriptions of the jails, jailers, and inmates provide a rich source of material for those interested in the colonial judicial system. His descriptions of Dartmouth College, then only twelve years old, offer a direct glimpse into colonial higher education. After his departure (the circumstances of which he and his first editor disagree on), Burroughs went to sea, where he was involved in the privateer war raging between Eng. and the newly independent colonies. His ship carried eighteen guns, although ten of them were wooden, and chased several English vessels, resulting in two battles on the high seas. His brief descriptions of his southern experiences provide bits and pieces of a valuable story. He encountered an emerging plantation society, a booming economy based on rampant land speculation, and several Indian tribes, including the highly advanced Creek nation. His dealings with Robert Morris, the ubiquitous Philadelphia merchant, are also informative. Overall, Burroughs was especially good at describing the atmosphere of small colonial communities, where a man's name was his most valuable possession.

Burroughs's only other publication, the *Hay Mow* sermon, reveals something of his mischievous nature and literary aspirations. While awaiting trial for counterfeiting, Burroughs wrote the "sermon" to amuse himself and his many visitors. Written in a biblical, sermonic style, the piece satirizes the outrage of the townspeople of Pelham and their pursuit of Burroughs after they discovered that their "Pastor Davis" was neither pastor nor Davis. The "Pelhamites" caught up with Burroughs in Rutland, Mass., and ineffectually chased him through streets, fields, and buildings until they finally trapped him in the hayloft of a barn. Armed with a pitchfork and an aroused sense of indignation, Burroughs stood off the "Pelhamites" until the situation was settled by the townspeople of Rutland. Burroughs later satirized the incident for the purpose of gaining revenge on the town of Pelham and enhancing his reputation as a clever rascal.

Suggested Readings: The best information concerning Burroughs can be found in the introductions, prefaces, sequels, and appendixes included in the different editions. See especially the "Sequel" in the 1811 Albany edition, the "Appendix" in the 1858 Amherst edition, and the "Preface," written by Robert Frost, in the 1924 Dial Press edition. *See also* Rev. William Cogswell, ed., NEHGR (1847), I, 88-89; (1855), IX, 174; James Grant Wilson and John Fisk, eds., *Appleton's Cyclopedia of American Biography* (1887), I, 470.

Daniel E. Williams
Absteilung Für Amerikanistik
University of Tübingen

JONATHAN BURT (c. 1632-1715)

Works: *A Lamentation Occasion'd by the Great Sickness & Lamented Deaths of Divers Eminent Persons in Springfield* (1720).

Biography: Born around 1632, probably in Eng., Jonathan Burt came to Springfield, Mass., in 1640. Despite the fact that most of his education must have taken place in Springfield, which did not even have an official schoolhouse until 1679, Burt's extensive civil and religious service to his community suggests that he was a man of considerable intelligence and knowledge. At an early age, he was appointed deacon, and in 1652 he received his first civil position, that of surveyor of highways. He later served as land measurer, appraiser of livestock, town clerk, commissioner, and, for fifteen years, selectman. In addition, he took the oath of attorney on Sept. 28, 1686. In all ways, "Deacon Jonathan," as he was fondly called, was an accomplished and well-respected member of his community. Since Springfield had no town government or religious organization when he arrived as a child, it is fair to say that Burt played a large role in creating the community of which he was a part.

Although Burt's public activities are well documented, we know little about his attitudes toward the great concerns of his day. Besides what can be assumed from his exemplary service as deacon and selectman and from his *Lamentation*, we know only his attitudes toward witchcraft and Indians. In 1651 Burt testified in the famous trial of Hugh Parsons, a Springfield sawyer, for witchcraft. In sharp contrast to most of the other witnesses, he limited his testimony to facts. As Henry Burt noted in his *Early Days in New England*, Burt seemed totally "unaffected by the prevalent delusion" about witchcraft. Indeed, Burt later purchased and lived in Parsons's house after he was acquitted and had moved away. However, Burt was not unaffected by the prevalent delusion that Indians were cannibals. As town clerk, Burt concluded an eye-witness account of the burning of Springfield by Indians by saying that "god did wonderfully preserve us or we had been a prey to there [sic] teeth."

Even less is known about Burt's personal life. He married Elizabeth Lobdell of Boston on Oct. 20, 1651, and fathered seven children by her, the last of whom died at birth. Elizabeth died on Nov. 11, 1684, and Burt married Deliverance Hanchet, a Suffield widow, on Dec. 14, 1686. They had no children. Burt died, of unknown causes, on Oct. 19, 1715.

Critical Appraisal: Jonathan Burt's only known work is a 128-line poem written in hymnal meter. A jeremiad, the poem records Burt's sorrow over the deaths of Johny Holyock, John Hitchcok, Japhet Chapin, and other leading citizens of Springfield, his hope that Christ will turn this misfortune into good, and his plea to his friends and family to work even more diligently at being good Christians.

Besides its own considerable literary merits, the poem is noteworthy as an interesting and instructive contrast to Cotton Mather's (q.v.) *Seasonable Thoughts upon Mortality, a Sermon Occasioned by the Raging of a Mortal Sickness, in the Colony of Connecticut; and the Many Deaths of Our Brethern There.* Although both Mather and Burt interpreted the mysterious disease that killed several hundred colonists in 1712 as evidence that, in Burt's words, "The Lord on us hath greatly frown'd," and although both men lamented the untimely deaths of so many fellow colonists and offered their readers advice for future behavior, Mather's approach and tone differed greatly from Burt's. Mather used the occasion to harangue and frighten his audience into goodness. Arguing that a considerable part of those that had died, and that would die, were "in some Degree Self-Murderers," Mather attacked their modes of death:

> By Intemperance men Shorten their Lives. The Lewd Livers themselves do call it, Living apace. The Intemperate and Immoderate are but Short-Lived; a Short-Age their Portion! In Excessive Eating, men Dig their own Graves with their Teeth. In Excessive Drinking, men Drown their Despised Lamp. Intoxications are Suffocations. By Unchast Excesses, men Extinguish their Brightness in a Premature Snuff of Rottenness.

Burt, too, would have liked to reform his readers, but instead of vituperating his readers for their vicious behavior, he stressed the positive values of virtuous living. Although his suffering was great—"The Lord is pleased with the Rod / to visit me when Old"—his faith supported him still—"But yet the Arms of Jacobs GOD / under me do uphold." Because his approach was more positive than Mather's, his tone was also more personal, direct, and sympathetic. Instead of addressing his audience as adversaries, as Mather did, he addressed them as "friends." Early in the poem, Burt interrupted his account of those who died, saying, "It is too hard for me to make / a Record of them all, / For it doth make my heart to ake / when I these things recall." The conclusion of the poem is also very personal, for Burt addressed his "dear Children that survive," advising them to "build upon the ROCK, / *Christ Jesus*" and ignore worldly things, because "it is a world of Sorrow." Burt's admonitions to his children were conventional, but they were made personal, even poignant, by his awareness that "my Time draws nigh." The poem ends, "It is from One in his Old Age, / that willeth you no hurt; / GOD take you for His Heritage, / your Father Jonathan Burt." As an example of the personal use of a poetic convention, Burt's *A Lamentation* is impressive. It makes one suspect that he honed his skill in numerous poems, none of which, unfortunately, has survived.

Suggested Readings: FCNEV. *See also* Henry Burt, *Early Days in New England. The Life and Times of Henry Burt of Springfield* (1893), pp. 115-160; Ola Winslow, *American Broadside Verse from Imprints of the 17th and 18th Centuries* (1930), pp. 176-177.

David Jauss
University of Arkansas at Little Rock

JAMES BUTLER (1755-1842)

Works: *Fortune's Football; Or, The Adventures of Mercutio* (1797-1798); *American Bravery Displayed* (1816).

Biography: James Butler was an Englishman who lived in Pa., earning his living as an itinerant schoolmaster. Nothing is known of Butler's early life, including the period when he published his novel *Fortune's Football*, but local records for the period from 1804 to 1842 place him in various parts of Mifflin and Indiana counties, with his longest stays in Milford and Mifflintown. A contemporary account describes how Butler "used to indulge himself in framing a kind of doggerel, mostly satirical, not withstanding which, they [sic] possessed some degree of merit." Some of this material was published, including a tragic piece on Gen. Arthur St. Clair's defeat, but none of it has survived. In 1816 Butler published *American Bravery Displayed*, a record of the ships captured by the American navy during the War of 1812. Until his death in Mifflintown in 1842, Butler served as an unofficial archivist, recording all births and deaths in the surrounding area.

Critical Appraisal: As literature, *Fortune's Football* is only important as an illustration of the emergence of the American novel. It illustrates the workings of providence by tracing the adventures of one Mercutio, with occasional interruptions while his friends tell stories. Although Butler made the conventional claim "for the authenticity of the narrative" and argued for the moral value of his work "to stimulate youth to the dispensations of providence," the novel is obviously fictional. Butler's moral sentiments ring more of convenience than of conviction, and his purpose in relating Mercutio's adventures was clearly to entertain.

The narrative is governed by "fortune, that fickle goddess," who propels Mercutio through three love affairs; several captures by Mohammedan pirates; innumerable storms and hurricanes; impressment by the British navy during the American Revolution; and travels through Spain, France, Italy, Persia, and Russia. The three love affairs illustrate the forced workings of Butler's frenetic narrative. The first with the virtuous Lucinda, whom Mercutio early rescues from drowning, is soon ended when Lucinda unexpectedly dies on the day the happy lovers were to have married. (Typically, even this brief episode is interrupted by an interpolated tale in which a would-be highwayman, George Wright, tells of his unhappy love.) The second, an illicit liaison with Leonora, the daughter of the doge of Venice, ends when Leonora and her infant son are killed during an assault by Turkish pirates. The third affair with the lovely Isabella, whom Mercutio marries early in the novel, is finally consummated at the novel's end in volume II when Mercutio remarries his beloved according to proper Protestant rites.

Love in *Fortune's Football* combines sensibility and melodrama. Fortunately, Butler's descriptions of the sensations of love are usually brief: "love, like the electrical fire, diffused itself through each avenue of our hero's heart." The impediments to love are taken from melodrama or romantic adventure—usually in the form of fathers who view their children's marriages as extensions of their own financial affairs. Through the workings of providence, these fathers are "educated," and love triumphs. An interesting undercurrent in Butler's treatment of love is the woman's role. For Butler, convention restricts women in ways that it does not restrict men in love relationships. Leonora's apologia for initiating her liaison with Mercutio forcefully voices women's predicament: "How peculiarly hard must that woman's situation, who possessing the most unadulterated passion. . .must, in obedience to an arbitrary custom, linger out her days in the most excruciating torture." Interestingly, Leonora and Isabella both defy custom to invite Mercutio's love. Later, Mercutio convinces the sophi of Persia that women also have rights in love relationships.

The most important theme in the novel is the workings of fortune, which is closely allied for Butler with "the invariable justice of Providence." Because fortune's favors and frowns are so transitory, Butler's characters must resign themselves to their situations. Mercutio's education consists of becoming "habituated to crosses and disappointments" so that he "in gratitude, returned thanks to the Supreme Disposer of every event, for the measure of contentment he still possessed." Although fortune is inevitably fickle, providence is always just; as the narrator observes, "it is an undeniable truth, confirmed by reason and revelation. . .that God is invariably the patron of virtue and punisher of vice." The tension between fickle fortune and providential justice is never explored: Butler never explained why Leonora can die, seemingly the result of her sexual indiscretion, while Mercutio survives.

In *American Bravery Displayed*, Butler simply listed all ships captured by Americans during the War of 1812. The usual entry records the name of the ship captured, its cargo, and the disposition of the ship and crew. This book also contains the official captains' records of all naval battles, including Isaac Hull's account of the *Constitution*'s capture of the *Guerriere*, and Stephen Decatur's account of the *United States*'s capture of the *Macedonia*. In explaining his purpose, Butler said his book would "exhibit to the view of astonished posterity the amazing, nay almost incredible exertions of their ancestors, in resisting the arrogant, and no less villainous depredations and murders of the most formidable naval power. . .that ever unfurled a sail or explored the Antipodal seas."

Except to the literary historian, Butler's works no longer hold much interest. In his most important work, *Fortune's Football*, Butler's florid style—especially in moments of love or crisis—inadequate characterizations, overcrowded narrative, and inability to interweave the different strands of his tale critically impair the art of the novel.

Suggested Readings: Herbert Ross Brown, *The Sentimental Novel in America: 1789-1860* (1940), passim; Franklin Ellis, *History of that Part of the Susquehanna and Juniata Valleys Embraced in the Counties of Mifflin, Juniata, Perry, Union, and Snyder* (1886), passim; Tremaine McDowell, "Sensibility in the Eighteenth-Century Novel," SP,

24 (1927), 383-402; Henri Petter, *The Early American Novel* (1971), pp. 287-289; Arthur Hobson Quinn, *American Fiction: An Historical and Critical Survey* (1936), p. 13.

David M. Craig
Clarkson College

MATHER BYLES (1707-1788)

Works: *A Poem on the Death of His Late Majesty* (1727); *Poem Presented to . . . William Burnet* (1728); *A Discourse on the Present Vileness* (1732); *To His Excellency Gov. Belcher* (1736); *On the Death of the Queen* (1738); *The Character of the Perfect and Upright Man* (1739); *Affection on Things Above* (1740); *The Glories of the Lord of Hosts* (1740); *The Flourish of the Annual Spring* (1741); *The Visit to Jesus by Night* (1741); *A Collection of Poems by Several Hands* (1744); *The Comet* (1744); *God Glorious in the Scenes of Winter* (1744); *Poems on Several Occasions* (1744); *The Glorious Rest of Heaven* (1745); *The Prayer and Plea of David* (1751); *God the Strength and Portion of His People* (1752); *Divine Power* (1755); *Poems. The Conflagration* (1755); *The Man of God* (1758); *The Christian Sabbath* (1759); *A Sermon Delivered March 6* (1760); *The Vanity of Man* (1761); *A Sermon on the Nature and Necessity of Conversion* (1769); *The Death of a Friend* (1772); *A Present for Children* (1782).

Biography: Mather Byles was born on Mar. 15, 1707, the son of Josiah Byles, a saddler, and Elizabeth (Mather Greenough) Byles, a widow and the daughter of Increase Mather (q.v.). When Josiah Byles died in 1708, Increase Mather and Cotton Mather (q.v.) took up the responsibility of Mather Byles's education, seeing that he received the proper training for a young man destined for the ministry. At the age of 14, Byles entered Harvard College, and by the time he received the A.B. in 1725, he had already begun to show his talents for writing and had begun to publish poems in the *Courant*. After graduation he briefly held an interest in the *New England Weekly Journal*, where he published poems and essays. Byles received the M.A. in 1728, and while awaiting a call to the ministry, he served as assistant in several churches. In 1732 he was called to the ministry of the newly formed Hollis Street Church, where he remained for forty-four years.

Even in his early years Byles was impressed with aristocratic tastes and English ways, and he preferred to make his acquaintance among those inhabitants of Boston who shared his feeling for the mother country and the established order. He cemented his relationship to this group through his marriage in 1733 to Anna Gale, the niece of Governor Jonathan Belcher. The couple had six children, only one of whom, Mather Byles, Jr., survived his father. Anna Byles died in 1744, and in 1747 Byles married again, this time to Rebecca Tailer, the daughter of a former lieutenant governor. With Rebecca, Byles had three children, a son who died in infancy and two daughters, who took care of their father in his old age and continued to live in Boston.

Throughout the years leading to the Revolution, Byles ministered to his congregation, delivering sermons known for their elegance of expression and warmth of feelings. Although Byles was an ardent supporter of the crown, he never brought his Loyalist sentiments into the pulpit and thus avoided open conflict with his congregation. When the British invaded Boston, however, Byles won the anger of many when he refused to flee the city and entertained the British officials, who used his church as barracks. When the British evacuated the city in 1776, members of the Hollis Street congregation brought charges against Byles and dismissed him from the ministry. The Boston Committee of Correspondence then held a hearing on Byles's unpatriotic actions and ordered that he be banished from the country. Due to his age and to his former position, however, Byles was allowed to remain in Boston under house arrest. Finally, after two years, the patriots abandoned even this precaution, and Byles remained in Boston, living quietly on the generosity of friends until his death in 1788. To the end, he remained loyal to the religion of his forebears, but his son and daughters embraced Anglicanism, and Mather Byles, Jr., eventually entered the Anglican ministry and settled in Nova Scotia.

Critical Appraisal: Although his Loyalism and his defiance of the Revolution sometimes overshadow his literary achievements, the poetry and prose of Mather Byles, who was one of the most ambitious writers in early America, reflect his appreciation of literary styles and conscious artistry.

Byles began writing and publishing poetry in the mid-1720s and continued his ardent interest in poetry until 1744, the year of his first wife's death and of the preparation for press of both of his published collections of poetry. *Poems on Several Occasions* (1744) contains thirty-one poems, many of which had been published earlier. *A Collection of Poems by Several Hands* (dated 1744 but actually published in 1745) contains another sixteen poems attributed to Byles as well as prefatory poems praising his poetry. Byles was eager to gain recognition for his poetry, and although he dismissed his poems as "Amusements of Looser Hours, while the Author belonged to the College," he also sent copies of his works to Alexander Pope and Sir Isaac Watts, whom he took as models and with whom he carried on correspondence. Pope, with his moral concerns and Classical translations, particularly appealed to Byles, himself well trained in the Classics. Byles, attempting to follow Pope's example, affected an air of Classical dignity and tried for polished and elegant poetry that would nonetheless find acceptance in New Eng. "The Comet" and "The Conflagration" are perhaps Byles's most successful attempts at refined, heroic poetry. Using heroic couplets, Classical images, and the clichés of neo-Classical language, Byles extolled the dangers and mysterious powers of the natural world. Although he referred in both poems to a "Judging God" and a "wayward people," a favorite theme in New Eng. literature, he emphasized the darker side of nature and thus reflected the preromantic concerns of his age. Byles's elegies on King George, Queen Caroline, and prominent contemporaries also adopt formal diction and neo-Classical devices such as frequent addresses to the muses. Although this style allowed Byles to present himself as an American poet laureate, it also deprived his poetry of genuine feeling or originality.

In the poem "To the Memory of a Young Commander," Byles's neo-Classical rhetoric prevented him from putting the American landscape or the particular historical events to any real purpose. His attempt at satire in "Commencement," written about the festivities of a Harvard commencement, likewise slighted its particular setting. Byles, in fact, appears to have believed that American circumstances are not conducive to poetry; in "To Pictorio" he described the land of his forefathers as a place where "Politeness, and the softer Arts (are) unknown" and where life is "inelegant and rigorously good." But as much as Byles wanted to be known as a writer of elegant and refined verse, he also asserted, "I never forget the Character of the Divine." Byles's religious poems, his hymn stanzas modeled on those of Watts, are accessible and lend themselves to singing. William Billings (q.v.) recognized the merits of hymns such as "Hymn at Sea" and "New England Hymn" and set them to music in his *New England Psalm-Singer* (1770).

During his lifetime, Byles was known as a fine preacher, and his published sermons support this reputation. In his sermons, as in his poetry, Byles was conscious of style and the effect he wanted to produce in his listeners. In *The Man of God*, the sermon he delivered at his son's ordination, Byles defined the good minister as one intimately acquainted with the Bible, as a good public speaker, and particularly as one with "a Good taste for Writing...learned without Pedantry, and truly Eloquent, without Stiffness and Affectation." He added that "The Style of the Pulpit should be Solemn and Manly...Rich and Polite." Byles followed this style in all of his sermons, and his sermons are both vivid and conversational. He did not, however, break with the theology of his forebears, and in *The Glories of the Lord of Hosts*, a sermon given to the Artillery Company, Byles wrote that in preparing the sermon, he had read through the records of the company to see the topics chosen by earlier ministers. Like his predecessors, Byles relied on typological arguments to explain his doctrines.

In other sermons, we find examples of eighteenth-century New Eng. taste for ornamental and artificial prose. "The Flourish of the Annual Spring," on a passage from Canticles, developed Byles's own aesthetic as he explained that the metaphors and allusions in this biblical book are "bold and grand, elevated and lofty, all Fire, all consecrated Rapture and Inspiration." He interpreted the book as a "Pastoral Opera" in which men are called by Christ to give up worldly pleasures and seek heavenly ones. This theme was frequent with Byles, and he often demonstrated the glories of God by celebrating the natural world.

In addition to leaving his written works attesting to the influence of English letters on American tastes, Byles also left us a legacy of his wit. Many of Byles's contemporaries wrote down his puns and jibes, and these anecdotes have provided us with an image of Byles as a jester. Among his most infamous puns is his request to a distiller to come and "still" his wife, Rebecca, often the victim of Byles's humor. On another occasion, Mrs. Byles, surprised during her housework by visitors, took refuge in a closet. When the guests asked Byles to see some of his curiosities, he opened the closet to expose his wife, "his greatest curiosity of all." Later, during his house arrest, Byles referred to his guard as his "Observe-a-Tory." When the guard was finally removed, Byles said that he had been "guarded, re-guarded, and dis-re-guarded."

In the career of Mather Byles, we see the changes in New Eng. and its traditions during the eighteenth century. We see both a time of literary experimentation and a revolution in tastes and manners. Most importantly, we see a change in the ministry itself when ministers began to concern themselves more with refinements than with religious doctrine.

Suggested Readings: CCNE; DAB; LHUS; Sibley-Shipton (VII, 464-493); Sprague (I, 376-382); T₁. *See also* C. Lennart Carlson, Introduction, *Poems on Several Occasions*, by Mather Byles (1940); E. A. Duyckinck, *Cyclopedia of American Literature* (1855), I, 116-120; Arthur Wentworth Hamilton Eaton, *The Famous Mather Byles* (1914); Benjamin Franklin V., Introduction, *Mather Byles's Works* (1978); Kenneth Silverman, *Colonial American Poetry* (1968), pp. 201-209, 235-242; Clifford K. Shipton, *New England Life In the 18th Century* (1963), pp. 227-253.

Cheryl Rivers
Manhattanville College

WILLIAM BYRD OF WESTOVER (1674-1744)

Works: Two notebooks containing miscellaneous *Letters & Literary Exercises* included with *Another Secret Diary* (w. 1696-1726; pub. 1942); *Correspondence* (1697-1742; coll. pub. 2 vols., 1977); "An Account of a Negro Boy That Is Dappl'd in Several Places on His Body with White Spots," *Royal Society Philosophical Transactions*, 19 (1698), 781-782; *Secret Diary* (w. 1709-1712; pub. 1941); *"London" Diary* (w. 1717-1721; pub. 1958); twelve poems "by Mr. Burrard" in *Tunbrigalia: Or, Tunbridge Miscellanies, for the Year 1719* (1719); *A Discourse Concerning the Plague, with Some Preservatives Against It*, "by a Lover of Mankind" (1721); "The Female Creed" (w.c. 1725; pub. 1942); *The Secret History of the Line* (w. 1731-1732; pub. 1929); *The History of the Dividing Line Betwixt Virginia and North Carolina, Run in the Year of Our Lord 1728, A Progress to the Mines in the Year 1732*, and *A Journey to the Land of Eden Anno 1733* (pub. in Edmund Ruffin, ed., *The Westover Manuscripts*; w. 1732-1737; pub. 1841); *Description of the Dismal Swamp and a Proposal to Drain the Swamp* (w. 1737; pub. 1789); *Neu-gefundenes Eden* ("von Wilhelm Vogel," 1737; ed. and trans. R.C. Beatty and W. J. Mulloy as *William Byrd's Natural History of Virginia*, 1940); *Another Secret Diary* (w. 1739-1741; pub. 1942).

Biography: Unquestionably the premier *litterateur* of the colonial South, William Byrd II was born at "Belvidere" plantation, within the present city of Richmond, Va., to a prosperous immigrant planter and Indian trader and his well-connected English wife. He was sent to school in Eng. and thence, at 16, to Rotterdam to study Dutch mercantile methods. After a year in Holland, he spent two years in London learning English business practice in a banking house and then studied law at The Middle Temple, where he was admitted to the bar in Apr. 1695. Through the influence of his patron Sir Robert Southwell, the president of the Royal Society, he was elected a member of that body in 1696 and served two terms, 1697-1701, with Lister, Newton, and Wren as a member of the society's Council. In 1696 Byrd returned briefly to Va., to be elected to the colonial legislature (House of Burgesses) and, in 1697, was sent back to London as agent for the colony to the Board of Trade.

At his father's death in 1704, Byrd returned to assume his patrimony at "Westover" plantation and, in 1706, to succeed his father as receiver-general of crown revenues in Va. In 1708 he was appointed for life to the Council of State, serving as its president (the second highest office in colonial Va.) during the last year of his life, 1743-1744. He was reappointed colonial agent in 1715, residing almost uninterruptedly for eleven years thereafter in London. In 1728 he was appointed one of the Va. commissioners to settle his colony's disputed boundary with N.C. and, placing himself at the head of the surveying expedition, he recorded the experiences that went into his twin Dividing Line histories, the chief works upon which his literary reputation rests.

In 1708 he married Lucy Parke, who died in 1716, and in 1724 he married Maria Taylor, of Kensington, who survived him. By these marriages he had eight children, five of whom survived him and one of whom, William III, left a numerous progeny. In 1730-1731 Byrd built the splendid Georgian house at Westover that still stands, decorating and furnishing it in high fashion and amassing there a library of more than 3,600 volumes—one of the three largest in the American colonies. One of the most powerful and influential of the Va. plantation oligarchy in the first half of the eighteenth century, Byrd was often "land poor" and in the thrall of London creditors during his lifetime, but at his death, he left debt-free 179,000 acres in N.C. and Va., part of which, in 1733, he laid out in lots to found the present cities of Petersburg and Richmond.

Critical Appraisal: Although Byrd's writings were mainly the by-products of his nonliterary endeavors and concerns—politics, business, scientific interests, or social occasions—he was an elegant stylist and a witty, often satirical raconteur whose works exhibit considerable versatility. His three laconic cipher diaries are his least "literary" writings. Lacking the introspective qualities of the colonial Puritan diaries, they are, nonetheless, of great historical interest as documents of the life-style and habits of an early southern planter-politician at home and abroad. They also afford an image, albeit incomplete, of the real scion of Westover with which to understand the various *personae* he assumed in many of his other works as, for instance, "Steddy" in *The Secret History of the Line*, "Mr. Burrard" the *Tunbrigalia* poet, and the unnamed woman who narrates "The

Female Creed." His two dozen poems, mostly *verses de société* written to amuse his London circle, are facile and conventional rather than inspired. The same might be said of the character sketches he wrote after the fashion of St. Evremonde except for one, "inamorato L'Oiseaux," containing a skillful self-portrait. Some of his best prose may be found in his nearly 350 extant letters. Living at the onset of a great age of English letter writing—the age that produced Chesterfield and Walpole, among others—some of Byrd's correspondence compares favorably in such company. His letters to "Sabina" (Mary Smith) and "Charmante" (Lady Elizabeth Lee?) in which he signed himself "Veramour" may be read almost as epistolary novellas.

The impulse to entertain with a good story as well as to chronicle, inform, and promote his own political interests may be discerned in the twin Dividing Line histories that, taken together, form a kind of protonovel. A close comparison of the same episodes in *The Secret History of the Line* reveals much about Byrd as a myth maker and belletrist as well as a historian. The chronicler is at his finest in his introduction to the *History* and in his even-handed account of the Indians and slightly satirical treatment of the N.C. squatters, but it is the ribald escapades of the surveyors and commissioners that are narrated most vividly and memorably by the uxorious "Steddy" in *The Secret History*. Byrd returned to the factual tone of his *History* in his two later, shorter travel accounts: *A Progress to the Mines*, recounting his visit to Alexander Spotswood's (q.v.) iron works near Fredericksburg, Va. (Sept.–Oct. 1732), and *A Journey to the Land of Eden*, one year later, recording his trip to survey his recently acquired tracts in N.C. on which he hoped to settle a colony of German Swiss. This latter project resulted in a promotional work, published in Berne, Switz., in 1737 as *Neu-gefundenes Eden* (by "Wilhelm Vogel") into which the translator, presumably, interpolated sections of John Lawson's (q.v.) *History of North Carolina*. The only other work by Byrd published in his lifetime is a pseudoscientific pamphlet, *A Discourse Concerning the Plague, with Some Preservatives Against It*, "By a Lover of Mankind," which is chiefly interesting for its advocacy of the use of the Chesapeake colonies' chief product, tobacco, as the best "preservative."

Suggested Readings: DAB; LHUS; T$_1$. *See also* R. C. Beatty and W. J. Mulloy, eds., *William Byrd's Natural History of Virginia, or The Newly Discovered Eden* (1940); R. M. Cutting, *John and William Bartram, William Byrd II and St. John de Crèvecoeur: A Reference Guide* (1976), pp. 73-105; E. G. Swem, ed., *Description of the Dismal Swamp with a Proposal to Drain the Swamp, by William Byrd of Westover* (1922); M. Tinling, ed., *The Correspondence of the Three William Byrds of Westover, Virginia, 1684-1776*, 2 vols. (1977); M. H. Woodfin and M. Tinling, eds., *Another Secret Diary of William Byrd of Westover, 1739-1741, with Letters & Literary Exercises, 1696-1726* (1942); L. B. Wright, ed., *The Prose Works of William Byrd of Westover* (1966); L. B. Wright and M. Tinling, eds., *The London Diary (1717-1721), and Other Writings, of William Byrd of Virginia* (1958); idem, *The Secret Diary of William Byrd of Westover, 1709-1712* (1941).

Carl Dolmetsch
College of William and Mary

C

ROBERT CALEF (c. 1647-1719)

Works: *More Wonders of the Invisible World* (1700).

Biography: Little is known about Robert Calef's life. Born in Eng., he came to America in or before 1688. Cotton Mather (q.v.) called him a weaver; he called himself a merchant, and since he was "styled Clothier" in 1709, the former may be closer to the truth. Although he is chiefly remembered as Mather's opponent in the arguments concerning witchcraft, he took no known interest in the subject during the Salem trials. About a year after they had ended, on Sept. 13 and 19, 1693, he visited Margaret Rule of Boston, who was being treated by Cotton and Increase Mather (q.v.) for bewitchment, and wrote an account which he circulated in manuscript. That was the beginning of *More Wonders*, a collection of accounts, letters, and documents he assembled between 1693 and 1697. Beginning in 1692, he held a number of minor civil offices, including constable, hayward and fenceviewer, overseer of the poor, assessor, and tithingman. In 1707 he bought a house in Roxbury and was a selectman of that town when he died in 1719.

Critical Appraisal: *More Wonders of the Invisible World* is a collection of materials relating to Mass. witchcraft, in five parts. Part I is Cotton Mather's account of his treatment of Margaret Rule for bewitchment in 1693, "Another Brand Plucked out of the Burning, or More Wonders of the Invisible World." Part II contains Calef's own account of Rule, an exchange of letters between himself and Mather over this account, and letters from Calef to various other persons. Neither Mather's nor Calef's account is to be taken at face value. Mather's is colored by his belief that devils and witches were the cause of his patient's behavior, and by the consequent excitement, which made him think he had observed some things which probably did not happen. He omitted a significant fact which he confided to his *Diary*: that among the "specters" appearing in his patient's hallucinations was his own image. In spite of these defects, his account is valuable for its careful and comprehensive description of his patient's hysterical symptoms: convulsions, hallucinations, loss of appetite, and psychosomatic skin lesions and blisters which healed "in two or three days at farthest."

The modern reader will be sympathetic to Calef if only because he is attacking many now-discarded ideas about witchcraft, but Calef's account is marred by his flagrant and intentional distortion of facts. Through ambiguous syntax, assigning statements to the wrong persons, and omissions, Calef created two false impressions about the Mathers: first, that one of their methods for treating their patient was rubbing her naked breast and belly, and second, that they had encouraged her to identify the persons appearing in her hallucinations (thus making them liable to prosecution). Cotton Mather's indignant refutation of these charges in his letter of Jan. 15, 1694, and Calef's evasive response of Jan. 18 deserve close reading; they reveal much about their authors' characters and intentions.

Part III of *More Wonders* is a collection of documents concerning the quarrels between the Rev. Samuel Parris of Salem Village and those of his parishioners who blamed him (apparently with good cause) for his part in the trials. Part IV consists of four letters between Calef and an unknown person, possibly a Scottish clergyman named Stuart, which are valuable chiefly for this person's exasperated characterization of Calef as an antagonist toward the end of his second letter.

Part V is an account of the Salem trials, partly composed of documents that vividly portray the sufferings of innocent persons who had been wrongly accused. One of them, Mary Easty's petition to the judges that no more innocent blood might be shed, survives in manuscript in the Essex County Archives; it differs only in minor details from Calef's printed version. This fact suggests that Calef was working from copies of the official records and also suggests that although his own prose is not to be trusted, he did not falsify documents. This account is followed by substantial excerpts from Cotton Mather's ill-advised, partisan, and overwrought attempt to justify the proceedings of the witchcraft court, *The Wonders of the Invisible World* (1693). It is Part V (with Parts I and II) which has made *More Wonders* a minor classic, in spite of its abundant defects. By contrasting the voices of the innocent with Mather's mistaken apology for the establishment, Calef was asking his readers, with devastating effect, which version of the trials was more deserving of sympathy and belief. The verdict of history has understandably been on Calef's side, so much so that his distortions of fact and his animus against the Mathers have been overlooked in the process.

Where Calef got the documents which are the backbone of his book is not known for certain. According to an eighteenth-century note of unknown source, they were supplied by two political and ecclesiastical enemies of the Mathers, Thomas Brattle (q.v.) and William Brattle (q.v.), and "other gentlemen." That, coupled with Calef's lengthy Postscript to *More Wonders*, which is an attack on Mather's *Life of Sir William Phips* (1697)—Phips was an ally of the Mathers who had been governor during the witchcraft trials—and with the series of minor offices Calef held, suggests that one motive for the composition and publication of *More Wonders* may have been political.

Suggested Readings: DAB; T_1. *See also* George Lincoln Burr, ed., *Narratives of the Witchcraft Cases* (1914), pp. 291-296; Samuel Gardner Drake, Preface, Genealogical

Table, and Memoir, *More Wonders of the Invisible World* in *The Witchcraft Delusion in New England* (1896), II, v-xxix; Chadwick Hansen, Introduction, *More Wonders of the Invisible World* (1972), pp. v-xvi; idem, *Witchcraft at Salem* (1969), chs. 11 and 12; Perry Miller, *The New England Mind: From Colony to Province* (1953), ch. 16, pp. 249-252; William F. Poole, "Witchcraft in Boston" in *The Memorial History of Boston*, ed. Justin Winsor (1881), II, 167-171.

Chadwick Hansen
University of Illinois at Chicago Circle

JOHN CALLENDER (1706-1748)

Works: *An Historical Discourse on the Civil and Religious Affairs of the Colony of Rhode-Island and Providence Plantations* (1739); *A Sermon Preached at the Ordination of Mr. Jeremiah Condy* (1739); *The Advantages of Early Religion* (1741); *A Discourse Occasioned by the Death of the Reverend Mr. Nathaniel Clap* (1746).

Biography: John Callender was born in Boston, Mass., in 1706. His family had long been influential among colonial Baptists, and from 1708 to 1726 his grandfather had been pastor of the First Baptist Church of Boston. At 13 Callender entered Harvard and after completing his B.A. degree in 1723, he joined his grandfather's church. In 1728, Callender was licensed to preach, and following a short tenure of ministry at the Baptist church in Swansea, the oldest Baptist church in Mass., he became pastor of the Baptist church at Newport, R. I., where he remained as pastor from his ordination in 1731 until his death on Jan. 26, 1748, at age 42.

From all accounts, Callender was well respected in Newport, both by members of his church and by the community at large. He participated in the local literary, philosophical, and cultural life of the community, and he belonged to the same literary club as Bishop George Berkeley (q.v.), the English philosopher and churchman who lived there for a period.

Critical Appraisal: While most of Callender's sermons and discourses are undistinguished, one work stands out as worth special attention. On Mar. 24, 1738, Callender delivered a sermon on the occasion of the centennial celebration of the settlement of R. I. Later known as the "Century Sermon" and dedicated to William Coddington, whose grandfather had come to Massachusetts Bay in 1630 and later left Boston to help establish the community of religious dissenters in R. I., this sermon reviews the first hundred years of R.I.'s history and is an important contribution to colonial historiography as well as an invaluable source of information about the history of Baptists in America.

Like most colonial histories, the sermon is structured around Callender's belief that divine providence destined R. I. for success. In recounting the general history of the settlement of the New World, Callender points out that so many previous attempts at settlement in North America had failed because providence had not yet intervened and blessed a colony for its efforts at religious reform. After reviewing the events which led to Roger Williams's (q.v.) banishment from Massachusetts Bay and commenting upon the issue of religious freedom and toleration among the colonials, Callender traces the events of the main towns, Providence and Newport, up through King Philip's War to his own day, driving home the point, on every appropriate occasion, that God was protecting and shaping the future of New Eng. In this respect, Callender's *Historical Discourse* provides insight into the workings of the historical imagination as it was filtered through the lens of early New Eng. piety.

In addition, Callender's *Discourse* is noteworthy for the light it throws on colonial attitudes toward the Indians. Very much conditioned by the general outlook of his day, Callender believed that destruction of Indians at the hands of white settlers was inevitable because it was the will of God. He regarded the Narragansetts, for example, as drunken and lazy, traits which in his mind led to the decrease in their numbers. At one point he even observed that "Their few miserable remainders are left, as monuments of the anger of a righteous God." As such, Callender's *Discourse*, like so many other seventeenth- and eighteenth-century historical documents, helped to popularize and perpetuate an attitude toward the Indians which eventually led to their total subjection.

Finally, Callender's sermon is particularly valuable for its perspective on such issues as religious freedom in early R. I., a freedom eventually confirmed by the Constitution. Callender was also an early advocate of the separation of church and state, contending quite earnestly that Americans should tolerate religious persuasions of all kinds and should take strict care to separate religious differences from civil affairs, thus anticipating the philosophy of the Founding Fathers by some fifty years.

Suggested Readings: CCNE; DAB; Sibley-Shipton (VII, 150-155); Sprague (VI, 34-37); T₁. *See also* Appendix, Century Sermon, RIHSC, 4 (1838), 177-270; Isaac Backus, *A History of New England, with Particular Reference to the Baptists* (1871; rep. 1969), I, 357; II, 29-34; Romeo Elton, "Memoir," RIHSC, 4 (1838), 9-25; Albert H. Newman, *A History of the Baptist Church in the U.S.* (1894), p. 117.

Reed Sanderlin
University of Tennessee at Chattanooga

JOHN CAMM (1718-1778)

Works: *A Single and Distinct View* (1763); *A Review of the Rector Detected* (1764); *Critical Remarks on a Letter Ascribed to Common Sense* (1765); *Sermon Preached. . .at the Funeral of Mr. Nelson* (1772).

Biography: Born in 1718, in Hornsea, Yorkshire, and educated in the school at nearby Beverley, John Camm was admitted to Trinity College, Cambridge, on Jun. 16, 1738, and took a B.A. in early 1742. In 1745 he became minister of Newport Parish, Isle of Wight County, Va., and from 1749 until 1771, he served on the faculty of the College of William and Mary as professor of divinity. During this period, he was also minister of York-Hampton Parish, York County. In 1771 Camm became president of the college, rector of Bruton Parish Church in Williamsburg, commissary of the bishop of London in Va., and a member of the Royal Council of Va.

Although Camm's fierce Tory advocacy of the prerogatives of the crown and of the established church embroiled him in controversy for thirty years, his impressive intellectual leadership abilities were attested to by friend and foe alike, and throughout his career in Va., his peers elected him to many positions of responsibility. A leader in organizing clerical opposition to the Va. legislature's Two-Penny Acts of 1755 and 1758, he was elected to carry the clergy's case to the Privy Council in Eng. in 1758. After successfully petitioning the king to disallow the acts, Camm returned to Va., where he was drawn into a heated pamphlet war with two members of the Va. legislature, Landon Carter (q.v.) and Richard Bland (q.v.). In addition to his opposition to the Two-Penny Acts, Camm defied the Board of Visitors of the college in their attempts to curb the authority of the president and faculty and was recognized during the 1770s as the leader of the church-and-college party in controversies such as the American episcopate debates. Despite his opposition to the popular will, however, Camm was never molested, even at the height of the Revolutionary fervor in Va. He died in 1778.

Critical Appraisal: John Camm's essays and pamphlets compare favorably in quality with any written in his generation in Va. His writings include three lengthy pamphlets, copious letters, contributions to addresses to the king, several dozen essays to the gazettes, and some scattered poetry. His pamphlets— *A Single and Distinct View* (1763), *A Review of the Rector Detected* (1764), *Critical Remarks Ascribed to Common Sense* (1765)—were thoroughly competent responses to the Two-Penny Acts pamphlets of Landon Carter and Richard Bland. Probably most significant among his essays to the gazettes are those he contributed to the 1766 debates over separating the offices of treasurer and speaker of the Va. House of Burgesses and those he published during the 1770-1772 American episcopate controversy.

Although he has not been appreciated as a literary figure, Camm's writings reveal a sharp, logical mind at work and an author with a high degree of literary consciousness, fully aware of his Classical and contemporary models. As a polemicist, he was thoroughly versed in suasive discourse, employing the elements of Classical rhetoric in the best tradition of the Classical and contemporary writers whom he imitated and quoted. His prose combined wit, irony, parody, burlesque, invective, and a host of other suasive and satirical devices to top his opponents in the eyes of a highly literate and well-read audience.

The first of Camm's Two-Penny pamphlets was *A Single and Distinct View*, published in 1763 in response to Landon Carter's *A Letter to the Bishop of*

London (1759) and Richard Bland's *A Letter to the Clergy of Virginia* (1760). The Va. colonels' pamphlets had attacked the group of clergy who had opposed the Two-Penny Acts—especially Camm—and had defended the colonial legislature's right to a certain degree of independence from the home government. Camm's pamphlet is a carefully reasoned point-by-point refutation of the colonels' arguments, in which he proved himself the equal of Carter and Bland in using statistics, employing the usual devices of rhetoric and satire, redefining and turning his opponents' words back on them, and carrying his opponents' arguments to their ridiculous conclusions.

Camm's *A Review of the Rector Detected* was written as a retort to Landon Carter's *The Rector Detected* (1764). Except for a few conceits, some metaphors, and a number of analogies, the pamphlet is an unembellished point-by-point refutation of Carter's assertions about Camm, who was the spokesman for a small group of English-bred and English-educated Tory clergymen who were unable to adjust to the lay control of the clergy by the vestries and the Council. As he looked in *A Review of the Rector Detected* at the acts of legislature, the treatment of the clergy in their lawsuits to recover damages from the 1758 Two-Penny Act, and the recent impassioned speech by Patrick Henry in the lawsuit of the Rev. James Maury (q v), Camm saw the seeds of treason and the destruction of all that he considered truly British.

The last and best of Camm's three pamphlets, *Critical Remarks*, has been largely ignored by students of the polemical essay of the 1760s. Most scholars of the southern colonial essay have focused upon the ideas, the political significance to the Revolution. In this context, *Critical Remarks*—as the last pamphlet in the paper war—is only a rather anticlimactic statement of Tory views on crown prerogatives. As literature, however, the pamphlet is in every way the equal of Richard Bland's *The Colonel Dismounted* (1764), in answer to which it was written and to which it has usually been unfavorably compared.

In the essay, Camm skillfully employed the devices of irony that are found in his models Jonathan Swift and John Dryden, and he effectively used the elements of Classical discourse to counter his opponents' arguments. A satiric persona, the Rector's Amanuensis, begins the essay with a mock dedication to the Rector and consistently sustains the mask through a mock advertisement at the end. An elaborate Madame Drowsiness-Goddess of Dullness conceit borrowed from Dryden's *Mac Flecknoe* and Pope's *Dunciad* is developed early and maintained throughout the pamphlet. Copious allusions and quotations from Classical authors, John Dryden, Sir Robert Filmer, Algernon Sidney, *Don Quixote*, histories, books on jurisprudence, and many other sources are used effectively in the author's arguments. Camm directed a significant amount of competent literary criticism at Bland's rhetorical devices, style, logic, and breaches of satiric mask and turned Bland's basic principles back on him in the form of personifications. The pamphlet also contains four pieces of doggerel verse, one over 200 lines long, that burlesque Carter, Bland, and Patrick Henry. All in all, *Critical Remarks* is a highly effective piece of satire in a tradition that included predecessors such as Swift, Steele, and Defoe.

John Camm was not the great constitutionalist that Richard Bland was, nor was he as accomplished a writer as his contemporaries William Stith (q.v.) and Thomas Jefferson (q.v.); he was, however, a thoroughly competent writer who made a valuable contribution to American Revolutionary literature by stating cogently the minority viewpoint of Va. Loyalists, and he represents at its best that portion of Va. society that looked at the same constitution and laws upon which Richard Bland and Landon Carter wrote and saw there the "rights of Englishmen" in a different light.

Suggested Readings: CCV; DAB. *See also* Edward Lewis Goodwin, *The Colonial Church in Virginia* (1927), pp. 329, 340-341, 358; Jack P. Greene, "A Mirror of Virtue for A Declining Land: John Camm's Funeral Sermon for William Nelson" in *Essays in Early American Literature Honoring Richard Beale Davis*, ed. J. A. Leo Lemay (1977), pp. 181-201; Homer D. Kemp, "The Pre-Revolutionary Virginia Polemical Essay: The Pistole Fee and the Two-Penny Acts Controversies" (Diss., Univ. of Tenn., 1972), for the annotated texts of the pamphlets of Camm, Carter, and Bland; idem, "The Reverend John Camm: 'To Raise A Flame and Live in It' " in *Essays in Early Virginia Literature Honoring Richard Beale Davis*, ed. J. A. Leo Lemay (1977), pp. 165-180; Richard L. Morton, *Colonial Virginia* (1960), II, 751-819, for a discussion of the Two-Penny Acts controversy; Lyon G. Tyler, "Descendents of John Camm, President of William and Mary College," WMQ, 1st ser., 4 (1895-1896), 61-62, 275-278.

Homer D. Kemp
Tennessee Technological University

ISAAC CAMPBELL (c. 1724-1784)

Works: *A Rational Enquiry into the Origin, Foundation, Nature and End of Civil Government, Shewing It to Be a Divine Institution, Legitimately Deriving Its Authority from the Law of Revelation Only, and Not from the Law of Nature* (c. 1787).

Biography: Nothing is known of Isaac Campbell's early years except that he was born in Scot. about 1724, ordained an Anglican minister in 1747, and soon thereafter departed for Va. From 1748 until his death, Campbell served as rector of Trinity Parish, Charles County, Md. He also operated a school at his residence for approximately thirty years and in 1774 became a founder and trustee of the publicly supported Charlotte Hall School. Unlike many of his Anglican colleagues, Campbell supported the American Revolution, as a member of a Charles County committee that enforced nonimportation and nonexportation against G.B., by signing an oath of allegiance to the Revolutionary state government and by writing *A Rational Enquiry*, his only known published work. Campbell's wife was Jane Brown, the daughter of Dr. Gustavus Brown of Charles County. At least ten children were born of the union. The dedicated rector owned land in Md. and Va. and, at his death on Jul. 30, 1784, left personal property valued at 747 pounds. Included was an extensive library devoted to the Classics, Scottish commonsense writers, and works in religion, philosophy, and pedagogy.

Critical Appraisal: Several powerful intellectual currents infused the ideology of the American Revolution. From Protestant convenant theology came a deeply religious perception of the struggle with G. B. and a millennial vision that Americans had the opportunity to establish the best government on the face of the earth. English radical Whig writings encouraged an acute distrust of power and the conviction that only a virtuous citizenry could forestall political corruption and social decay. Enlightenment rationalism inspired thinkers on both sides of the Atlantic to design political institutions based on natural law and right reason.

Few Americans of the eighteenth century embraced the strands of the rich Revolutionary ideology in equal measure. Rather, they subscribed to those ideas most in accord with their own convictions and experiences. The Rev. Isaac Campbell used Scripture and religious faith, not philosophical constructs of natural and rational law, to advocate representative government founded on popular sovereignty. Explicitly denying John Locke's views on the origin of civil government, Campbell nevertheless reached conclusions strikingly in accord with principal Enlightenment tenets on the subject.

Inspired by the Revolution itself, Campbell was engrossed in writing *A Rational Enquiry* from the beginning of the war until his death. He sought to prove that neither the law of nature nor reason could account for the institution of government, the purposes of which he described as protecting life, punishing vice, and fostering a virtuous citizenry. Finding the essence of government in the power to coerce, to punish "those proportionate to their crimes who are found guilty upon trial," Campbell argued that the institution was divinely ordained in Genesis IX: 2-3, 5-6. There God delegated to Noah and his progeny—and thus to the entire human race in their loins—dominion over the animal kingdom as well as the authority to punish all who would shed the blood and take the life of another. From this "capital power" mankind derived, by implication, every lesser power to punish abuses against life, liberty, and property. Maintenance of civil government was, for Campbell, a religious obligation.

From what he interpreted as the general grant of political authority in the Genesis passages, Campbell inferred biblical justification for both the Americans' revolt against Britain and the republican state governments they established following the Declaration of Independence. He argued that, because God had vested civil government in the entire human race, monarchy was usurpatious. From this situation flowed divine sanction of the right of revolution and the need for majority rule and a broadly representative legislature.

Campbell's obscure treatise serves as a reminder of the deeply religious overtones that some Americans imparted to what others saw as an entirely secular event. In addition, *A Rational Enquiry* stands apart from the more common jeremiads of Calvinistic New Eng., which interpreted the trials of the late colonial period and the sufferings of wartime as God's punishment for the sins of a chosen people. Yet if Campbell did not contend that Americans were chosen of God, he nevertheless believed that their republican order was.

The treatise surely had little impact upon the outpouring of political theory and experimentation that led finally to the Constitution of 1787. But in Md.—where the Revolution brought disestablishment of the Church of England and drove more than 50 percent of the Anglican clergy from the state—the convictions of the respected rector of Trinity Parish may have helped justify the Revolution to the many planters who had family ties and commercial connections in Eng., who emulated the ways of the English gentry, and who realized that their world could never be quite the same after 1776.

Campbell did not live to see his treatise in print. Following his death in 1784, his executors sporadically advertised for subscribers to help underwrite the cost of publication. Campbell, they stressed, had considered his work "as a legacy he was in duty bound as a christian, and lover of mankind, to give the world." Presumably, *A Rational Enquiry* appeared some time in 1787, shortly after the last notice inviting subscriptions. The publisher was Frederick Green of Annapolis, editor of the *Maryland Gazette*. The only known copy of the tract is in the Maryland Diocesan Archives at the Maryland Historical Society, Baltimore, and although the title page announced that the volume was the first of four, no others are known to have been published.

Suggested Readings: CCMDG. *See also* Bernard Bailyn, *The Ideological Origins of the American Revolution* (1967); William G. McLoughlin, "The Role of Religion in the Revolution: Liberty of Conscience and Cultural Cohesion in the New Nation" in *Essays on the American Revolution*, ed. Stephen G. Kurtz and James H. Hutson (1973); James F. Vivian and Jean H. Vivian, "The Reverend Isaac Campbell: An Anti-Lockean Whig," HMagPEC, 39 (1970), 71-89; Gordon S. Wood, *The Creation of the American Republic, 1776-1787* (1969).

Jean Butenhoff [Vivian] Lee
University of Virginia

JOSEPH CAPEN (1658-1725)

Works: "A Funeral Elegy upon the Much to Be Lamented Death and Most Deplorable Expiration of the Pious, Learned, Ingenious, and Eminently Usefull Servant of God Mr. John Foster, Who Expired and Breathed out His Soul Quietly into the Arms of His Blessed Redeemer, at Dorchester, Sept. 9th Anno Dom: 1681, Ætatis Anno 33" (lost broadside, 1681) rep., Thomas C. Simonds, *History of South Boston* (1857), pp. 38-39, and Samuel A. Green, *John Foster* (1909), pp. 36-37.

Biography: Born in Mass. on Dec. 20, 1658, and baptized on Jan. 2, 1659, Joseph Capen was the son of Capt. John Capen of Dorchester, Mass., by his second wife, Mary, who was the daughter of Samuel Bass of Braintree. Capen graduated from Harvard in 1677 and was admitted to the church at Dorchester on "4.10.81." In 1681 he declined a proposition to settle in New Haven, and on "ye first of ye 4 82," he was dismissed from the church at Dorchester in order to be ordained as pastor of the church at Topsfield, Mass., succeeding Jeremiah Hobart (H.C. 1650). Upon his ordination, a Topsfield town meeting voted to offer Rev. Capen use of the parsonage house and land, and either seventy-five pounds in country pay such as corn, pork, and beef or twenty pounds in silver and forty-five pounds in country pay; Capen chose the latter.

That Capen was either an unacceptable pastor or an outstanding one is not discernable from the extant records; he seems to have been discreet in matters of his personal life, and he was "faithful to the obligations of his spiritual calling." Although not a close friend, Capen was well enough acquainted with Samuel Sewall (q.v.) to have been mentioned on several occasions in Sewall's day book.

In 1684 Capen married Priscilla Appleton (1657-1743), daughter of John Appleton of Ipswich, Mass. Between 1685 and 1699, Capen and his wife had seven children—four girls and three boys. He continued in his ministry at Topsfield until his death on Jun. 30, 1725. Parson Capen's house, built in 1683 and still standing, is considered "perhaps the most perfect of New England houses."

Critical Appraisal Emerging as early as 1620, the basic form and content of the Puritan funeral elegy came from the funeral sermon, especially with regard to the sermon's attempt to apply doctrine, raised from spiritual texts, to everyday life. Although frequently laborious and sentimental, elegies such as Capen's make up a genre that, for the first 100 years of New Eng.'s history, was widely practiced by magistrates, ministers, housewives, merchants, schoolmasters and their students, and anyone else who wanted to memorialize a deceased friend or relative in verse.

Typical of the funeral elegies that flourished in Puritan New Eng., Capen's elegy to John Foster (q.v.) is built upon a personalized portraiture and an exhortation. The elegy consists of fifty-two iambic pentameter lines (including several purely mechanical metrical variations) rhymed *aa, bb, cc,* and so on. Also characteristic of the majority of New Eng. funeral elegies, Capen's poem is adroitly balanced between constraint and direct involvement; the closeness of the actual event prevented most minister elegists from bearing down "very hard upon any resistance their subjects might have had." Although the poem may seem heavy-handed and excessively pious to contemporary readers, it is essential to remember that the funeral elegy was a functional and thoughtful social gesture, for the most part not intended for artistic consideration and critical analysis. Capen's elegy was notable enough, however, to have been mentioned in William Brattle's (q.v.) *Ephemeris* (1682) and described as "suitable verses to the memory of John Foster." Curiously, the last five lines of the poem bear a striking similarity to Benjamin Franklin's (q.v.) epitaph on himself.

Suggested Readings: CCNE; FCNEV; Sibley-Shipton (II, 519-522). *See also* Evert A. Duyckinck and George L. Duyckinck, *Cyclopedia of American Literature* (1875), I, 105; Joseph B. Felt, *History of Ipswich, Essex, and Hamilton* (1834), p. 171; Emory

Elliott, "The Development of the Puritan Funeral Sermon and Elegy: 1660-1750," *EAL*, 15 (1980), 151-164; Samuel P. Fowler, "Biographical Sketch and Diary of Rev. Joseph Green, of Salem Village," *EIHC*, 8 (1866), 91-96, 165-168; Harrison T. Meserole, ed., *Seventeenth-Century American Poetry* (1968).

Bruce Weigl
Old Dominion University

BAMPFYLDE-MOORE CAREW (1693-c. 1758)

Works: *The Surprising Adventures of Bampfylde-Moore Carew, King of the Beggars* (1812).

Biography: Born in 1693, Bampfylde-Moore Carew was the son of the rector of Bickley in Devon, Eng. At the age of 12, he was sent to school at Tiverton but ran away after three years. He then joined a group of wandering gypsies and adopted their life-style, thus beginning a career of petty deceptions that lasted more than a half-century and spanned two continents. Carew wandered about begging in various disguises: an unfortunate farmer who had lost his livestock in a flood, a tin miner ill from the mines, a blacksmith whose shop had burned down, a shipwrecked sailor, mad Tom of Bedlam, a rat catcher, a dog merchant, a clergyman, a cripple, a magician, and even a helpless grandmother in petticoats with several small children. His clever deceptions earned him both money and recognition.

After a visit to Newfoundland, Carew was married and then elected king of the beggars to succeed Clause Patch. But Carew was soon arrested and banished to Md. as a vagrant. Once in Md., however, he escaped; was recaptured, punished, and made to wear a heavy iron collar; and escaped again. After a stay among friendly Indians, Carew practiced his profession throughout the colonies, visiting Philadelphia, New York City, and New London, where he reembarked for Eng. Continuing his travels and impostures, Carew again wandered about Eng., traveled to Scot., where he accompanied the pretender's army, and sailed to the Baltic aboard a man-of-war and again to America (the result of a second deportation), where he visited Providence and Boston. The last part of Carew's life was the same as the first, a series of cunning deceptions, frauds, and disguises. His death has been variously ascribed to either 1758 or 1770.

Critical Appraisal: Bampfylde-Moore Carew was both a king and a beggar during his life, one of the best known of all English rogues and one of the least recognizable. The only authority on him is a curious book that has been published as many times and in as many different forms as Carew had disguises, and attempting to trace its publishing history is as difficult as trying to count all of the king of beggars's deceptions. The first Carew book was published in 1745 and was supposedly related by Carew during his first voyage to America. No mention of his American adventures is made. But in 1749 Robert Goadby published a complete rewriting of the 1st edition (this one supposedly written by Goadby's wife under Carew's direction) and includes Carew's troubles and travels in America. This edition also draws upon other travel books and writers, such as Capt. John Smith (q.v.), for information concerning early America. Subsequent editions, nearly fifty not counting a "romantic melodrama" produced on stage, make use of both the first two editions.

As a rogue and antihero, Carew was extremely popular in Eng. during the last half of the eighteenth and first half of the nineteenth centuries, and if for no other reason than his popularity, he is worthy of being remembered today. The rogue history tradition is very old in Eng., dating back as far as Robin Hood and perhaps further, and Carew is one of the most popular characters in this tradition. Consequently, as an English rogue on American soil, his descriptions and observations have considerable effect on his readers. The accuracy of his descriptions is debatable. His list of wild animals in the Chesapeake region includes "rattlesnakes, horn-snakes, black-snakes, lions, leopards, bears, wolves, and wildcats"; there is even a "great white bear" that attacked him somewhere south of Philadelphia. His descriptions of Indians include two highly unusual and altogether nonhistorical tribes, "one of which are distinguished by a very flat forehead, who use cross-bows in fighting; the other of a very dwarf statute (sic), who are great enemies, and very cruel to whites."

His long, romantic description of the "friendly Indians" who saved him is important for similar distortions. Carew's narrative is a literary creation shaped by a succession of hands and imaginations. Running consistently throughout the editions is an attempt to exploit certain literary techniques first fashioned by writers like Swift, Defoe, and More; the use of the journey as a vehicle for satire and irony is unmistakable. Both the "friendly Indians" and Carew's own gypsy beggars in Eng. lead happy, ideal existences, entirely opposed to English and colonial society. The idealized descriptions of the former point out the shortcomings of the latter. The "friendly Indians" are too perfect. Physically, they are the "most perfect in the world" and "stronger than others." Not only are they physically healthy, but spiritually as well, being chaste, honest, loyal, loving, generous, and innocent. Indeed, Carew's descriptions of the "friendly Indians" reveal less about Native Americans than they do about early English conceptions of them.

Like most picaresque rogues, Carew was somewhat of a philosopher. His journeys provided him with an excellent opportunity for "knowing mankind." As a result of his experiences, he saw through all pretensions and was therefore justified in deceiving a society that itself practiced deception. As soon as he was no longer among the "simple honest Indians, neither polite, lettered, nor deceitful," but among "polished people, whose knowledge has taught them to forget the ways of nature, and to act everything in disguise," Carew again put on "a fresh disguise as often as it suits his convenience." The contrast and irony are obvious: because he openly practiced deception, Carew was the most honest.

There is good reason to doubt whether Carew actually existed, or if he did, what he actually did. But this is not important. Above all, Carew exists as a literary creation—a mixture of European picaresque and English rogue. Living in a world of unrest and changing values, he relied on his cleverness not only to live, but to maintain his own integrity and prosper. His deceptions became a mirror for society to see itself—without pretense, free of traditional assumptions. Verisimilitude was used to enhance this. The list of specific names of people and places is endless.

Carew's narrative was written and rewritten as popular reading to provide entertainment, and it is his impressive ability to deceive that becomes most entertaining. Carew continually fooled people who knew him and should have known better, including friends and relatives. Once he fooled the same man three times in one day with three disguises. No one was safe from the king of beggars, neither commoner nor aristocrat. While in America, Carew deceived everyone from an Irish inn keeper to Thomas Penn, Governor Thomas, and even the Rev. George Whitefield (q.v.). His clever abilities and popularity gave him a legendary status. He became an irresistible force, a social cathartic.

Structurally, the narrative is weak and at times tedious. It is both travel book and rogue history, and the mixture of descriptions explaining the salting and curing of cod in Newfoundland, or the number and appearance of houses in Philadelphia, with Carew's tricks is uneven. Certain editions (notably Goadby's) contain long passages attacking Fielding and *Tom Jones*, and most later editions include a "Dictionary of Cant Language." Even the adventures become tedious after a while. Carew is simply too successful too many times, and the sheer number of deceptions reduces both their importance and interest. Nevertheless, the narrative remains enjoyable and significant. It is one of the best examples of popular English rogue histories and one of the very few that contain American experiences.

Suggested Readings: DNB. *See also* Frank W. Chandler, *The Literature of Roguery* (1907), I, 166-168; Thomas D. Clark, *Travels in the Old South, The Southern Colonies, 1600-1750* (1956-1959), pp. 54-56; N&Q, 2nd ser., 3 (1957), 4; 4 (1957), 330-331, 401, 522.

Daniel E. Williams
Absteilung Für Amerikanistik
University of Tübingen

MATHEW CAREY (1760-1839)

Works: *The Pennsylvania Herald* (editor; 1785); *The Columbian Magazine* (editor; 1786); *Debates . . . of the General Assembly of Pennsylvania . . . on the Law Annulling the Charter of the Bank* (editor; 1786); *An Epistle to Mr. Eleazer Oswald* (1786); *The Plagi-Scurriliad* (1786); *The American Museum* (editor; 1787-1792); *A Short Account of the Malignant Fever*, 4 eds. (1793-1794); *The American Remembrancer* (editor; 1795-1796); *Miscellaneous Trifles in Prose*

(1796); *To the Public* (1796, 1799); *A Plumb Pudding for...Peter Porcupine* (1799); *The Porcupiniad: A Hudibrastic Poem* (1799); *The School for Wisdom: Or, American Monitor* (editor; 1800). For Carey's numerous miscellaneous publications after 1800, such as his much revised *Olive Branch* (1811); his Franklin almanacs; his family Bibles; his atlases; his history of Algiers; his comments on banking, slavery, the Missouri question; and so on, see R. R. Shaw and R. H. Shoemaker, *American Bibliography* (1958-1968), and *A Checklist of American Imprints* (1967-1972).

Biography: Edgar Allan Poe praised the printer Mathew Carey for "his energy, his high-mindedness and his indomitable perseverance," calling him that "noblest work of God, an honest man." These encomia in the *Southern Literary Messenger* for Mar. 1836 did not, of course, take note of Carey's more youthful inflammable temper, a quality that almost cost him his life in a duel with Col. Eleazer Oswald in 1786. As Carey explained in his Franklinesque *Autobiography* (a series of thirty-two letters published in the *New England Magazine*, 1833-1835, 1837), the duel resulted from a paper war carried on between him and Oswald (both editors of papers representing different political parties) that reached a climax in Carey's accusing Oswald of plagiarism ("The Plagi-Scurriliad"). Oddly, Carey's first publication was an essay against duelling, published in Ire. in *The Hibernian Journal* in 1777.

Born in Dublin, Ire., on Jan. 28, 1760, Carey was lamed for life during his first year when his nurse dropped him. Carey early ran counter to an oppressive establishment with his *To the Roman Catholics*, in which he appealed to the Catholics' sense of injustice and tyranny, visited upon them by the British Parliament. Exiled to Fr. as a result of his criticism, he worked for Benjamin Franklin (q.v.) in 1779 at Passy, reprinting dispatches from America and other papers and later working for the famous printer Didot *le jeune* in Paris. There he also met Lafayette, who then was investigating an invasion of Ire. and who later (1785 in Philadelphia) was to set him up financially in printing the *Pennsylvania Herald*. On his return to Ire. after his year in Fr., Carey edited the *Freeman's Journal* and the *Volunteers Journal*, in which he defended Irish political and commercial rights. Arrested and temporarily jailed by the British House of Commons, he fled to America rather than face further charges.

With five other partners, he started the *Columbian Magazine* in Oct. 1786, writing four articles for its first number. Giving up this venture in Dec., because of differences with the partners, he then founded his famous *American Museum*, an anthology of miscellaneous newspaper and other earlier items that embodied important governmental writings and, in fact, preserved the entire tradition of the Revolution. The *Museum* found favor with George Washington (q.v.), John Dickinson (q.v.), Benjamin Rush (q.v.), Francis Hopkinson (q.v.), and others. As a successful printer, publisher, and writer, Carey followed in the Franklin-B.F. Bache (q.v.) tradition. He was happily married to Bridget Flahavan, the daughter of a poor but respectful citizen who had lost his money supporting the Revolution. Six of the nine Carey children survived.

Critical Appraisal: As a writer and publisher, Mathew Carey produced a great variety of work, almost all of it for public benefit. His account of the yellow fever not only underwent four editions but was also translated into German. He wrote dramatic criticism for the Chestnut Street Theater. His printing of Bibles, one of his most extensive projects, contributed to his financial success after 1800. In satire, as one writer put it, "he took a joy in vituperation." Here he proved himself a master with works such as "The Plagi-Scurriliad," "The Porcupiniad," and "A Plumb Pudding" wherein he attacked his political opponents Oswald and the Englishman William Cobbett (q.v.). (Both Cobbett and J. W. Fenno (q.v.), another of his political enemies, felt the lash of his scorn in *To the Public* [1799], a reply to their own attacks.) His interests and publications ranged widely: the debates of the Pa. Assembly on the bank question; the Jay treaty; the medical writings of Benjamin Rush and Carey's observations on them; catalogs of books, pamphlets, maps, atlases of all kinds; the American Catholic question; spelling and reading books for children. One of these reading books, *The School of Wisdom: Or, American Monitor*, expressed in its preface his attempts at indoctrinating the minds of the young with "political sentiments." By recourse to short but complete passages from writers such as Shakespeare, Dryden, Milton, Pope, Addison, Swift, Fielding, Dr. Johnson, and Montesquieu—in short, "through the writings of the best men of all ages"—Carey endeavored to instill "the advantages of liberty, of peace, of good order—the dignity of human nature—to inspire an abhorrence of war—and to display its tremendous consequences." Although radically different in temperament, in one way at least Carey resembled Cotton Mather (q.v.): he was deeply involved in, and in the forefront of, the life of his day and equally concerned about the welfare of posterity.

The miscellaneous nature of his editing is perhaps most evident in the work he is best known for, *The American Museum: Or, Repository of Ancient and Modern Fugitive Pieces, etc. Prose and Poetical*. This monthly at first contained mainly reprints of political documents, but after 1790 it exhibited an increasing number of belletristic works. In his *Museum*, Carey reprinted the Constitution; an abridged version of Franklin's autobiography as well as other Franklin papers; Washington's account of the Battle of Trenton; Howe's account of the same; Daniel Boone's autobiography; "Hints for Married Women"; the proceedings of the Pennsylvania Society for the Abolition of Slavery and other antislavery tracts such as "A Slave's Muzzle" (dated Kingston, Jam., Apr. 11, 1789); temperance tracts; various essays on agriculture, manufactures, politics, manners; moral tales; poetry (both ancient and modern); sketches of national heroes; items concerning natural and civil history; biographies; legal information. Thus the *Museum* expanded into a rich storehouse for investigators interested in American life in the last quarter of the eighteenth century. In the fourth letter of his autobiography, Carey stated that he contributed no single article of his own to this comprehensive monthly, but he did write occasional prefaces for the various issues. In conclusion, the value of Carey's *Museum* lies in its expression of many-sided public opinion in the postwar period and in reminding its readers of important issues and documents of the Revolution itself, truly a significant contribution to our democratic tradition.

Suggested Readings: DAB; DNB; LHUS; T_2. *See also* Earl Bradsher, *Mathew Carey: Editor, Author, and Publisher* (AMS reprint [1966] of a Columbia Univ. dissertation; 1912); E. C. Carter, "Mathew Carey in Ireland, 1760-1784," CHR, 51 (1965), 503-527; William J. Free, *"The Columbian Magazine* and American Literary Nationalism" (Ph.D. diss., Univ. of N.C., 1962); J. F. Hindman, "The Irishman Who Developed American Culture," RACHSP, 71 (1960), 23-30; David Kaser, "The Retirement Income of Mathew Carey," PMHB, 80 (1956), 410-415; Kenneth Rowe, *Mathew Carey: A Study of American Economic Development* (AMS reprint of a Johns Hopkins dissertation; 1933); Eugene L. Schwaab, ed., *Mathew Carey's Autobiography* (1942); R. G. Silver, *The American Printer, 1787-1825* (1966), pp. 37-39, passim; idem, "The Cost of Mathew Carey's Printing Equipment," SB, 19 (1966), 85-122; idem, "Mathew Carey's Proofreaders," SB, 17 (1964), 123-133; Howard E. Sylvester, *"The American Museum,* A Study of Prevailing Ideas in Late Eighteenth-Century America" (Ph.D. diss., Univ. of Wash., 1954).

Richard E. Amacher
Auburn University

CHARLES CARROLL OF CARROLLTON (1737-1832)

Works: *Letters to His Father* (w. 1749-1782; pub. 1902); *First Citizen Letters* (1773); *Journal* (w. 1776; pub. 1876; rep., 1969); *Senator to the Public* (1780); *On Samuel Chase, Censor* (1781, 1782-1787); *On the Federal Constitution* (w. 1787-1788; pub., Pt. I, 1941; Pt. II, 1976).

Biography: Charles Carroll of Carrollton was born in Annapolis, Md., on Sept. 19, 1737, educated in Jesuit colleges in Fr., and died in Baltimore in 1832, the last surviving signer of the Declaration of Independence. At the Md. Convention, Carroll authored the Jun. 28, 1776, motion to declare independence and was named to the committee to draft the state's constitution. Until 1800 he served as senator from the Assembly's first session, and he was Md.'s senator at the first federal Congress. His service to the Continental Congress was also outstanding, including his achievements as a commissioner to Can., a member of the Board of War, and a delegate for Md. at several sessions. His distinguished family, long prominent in the affairs of Catholic Marylanders, and private career after leaving public office in 1800 left him a noteworthy figure for the period: a landed aristocrat who owned Doughoregan and Carrollton manors; an entrepreneur who managed the Baltimore Iron Works and the Baltimore and Ohio Railroad; and a philanthropist who helped found Georgetown and Washington Colleges. In addition to his manors, other sites associated with Carroll are now historic landmarks, among them the Annapolis and Baltimore mansions, where he was born and died, and Homewood on the campus of The Johns Hopkins University. Carroll died on Nov. 14, 1832.

Critical Appraisal: A Roman Catholic education abroad perhaps best accounts for the distinctive turn Charles Carroll's written works took under the stimulation of the American Revolutionary movement and in a family under civil and religious disabilities for its religion. English Jesuit masters in Fr. guided him through his literary formation at St. Omer and Rheims Colleges, concluding in a philosophical experience of the Enlightenment at the College of Louis the Great in Paris. Here Pascal's Calvinism was adversary, updated Scholasticism was the reigning metaphysics, and Francis de Sales's "sweet reasonableness" with *The Spiritual Exercises* of St. Ignatius of Loyola was the nurture of his faith-life. After the study of French civil law, Carroll went to London for about four years to study English law, and there he kept close contact with gentry life and observed parliamentary politics on the eve of the Stamp Act. Shortly thereafter, Carroll returned to Md., respected and articulate in the developing constitutional discourse in America. In Md., Carroll's wealth and Catholicism made him conspicuous, and a deferential political society afforded him an appreciative readership and access to Benjamin Franklin (q.v.) and others at the highest level of leadership.

His *First Citizen Letters* of 1773 flowed easily from such a background. Addressing the issue of taxation without representation, Carroll unfolded a distinctive and effective literary style, one marked by erudition, rhetoric, drama, and controversy. He used Montesquieu and Locke in his reasoning for a declaration of independence, and he had read Hume and understood the importance of political realism and common sense when adjusting constitutional principles and their force on policy. Perhaps his most mature political writings were *Senator to the Public*, written in 1780, and his response to Samuel Chase (q.v.) ("Censor") the following year in the pages of the *Maryland Gazette*. Arising from the situation of Tories threatened with confiscation, the first document defended civil liberties and the right to private property. The piece on Chase was a plea for statesmanship in opposition to a politics of parties and cronies.

An aristocratic republican in fact and theory, Carroll found no conflict between this philosophy and his role as a senator of the people, whose sovereignty he regarded as the *locus ultimus* of civil authority. His writings carry a passion for human liberty, especially with regard to religious freedom and freedom of speech and the press. In 1776 Carroll openly opposed the slave trade, and in the 1780s he proposed legislation for a progressive emancipation of slaves. From very early on, Carroll felt that the government of Md. should emerge in a federal form founded on the constitutional principles he espoused, and when formation of the state of Md. approached realization, he wrote in favor of its constitution's central concepts, concluding with a lyrical quality in a statement of early American nationalism.

Curiosity about such a man in his personal life and tastes is partially satisfied by Charles Carroll's *Journal*, which was written in 1776 in the companionship of Benjamin Franklin and John Carroll (q.v.) as they traveled between Philadelphia and Montreal on a congressional mission. Written for his father's amusement, its narration and descriptions of the N.Y. waterways and their environs give way to scientific observations full of hope that the young nation will grow strong once free. More unique was a lifelong correspondence with his father. It marked every period of absence, one from the other, beginning with the schoolboy's letter from Europe until the year after Yorktown. A more subtle and perhaps more significant emotional force affecting Carroll's attitudes during his most important period of writing and statesmanship was his sickly wife. Plagued for several years by addiction to laudanum, Mary Darnall Carroll died in 1782, only a few weeks after her father-in-law. Amid all of these experiences public and private, however, the continual reading of the best books helps explain the high quality of what Carroll wrote.

Suggested Readings: DAB. *See also* Thomas F. Field, ed., *Letters of Charles Carroll...and of His Father* (1902); Thomas O'Brien Hanley, *Charles Carroll of Carrollton: The Making of a Revolutionary Gentleman* (1970); idem, ed., *Charles Carroll Papers* (microfilm of mss., 1971); Ronald Hoffman, *A Spirit of Dissension* (1973); Peter S. Onuf, ed., *Maryland...and First Citizen* (1973); Kate M. Rowland, *The Life and Correspondence of Charles Carroll*, 2 vols. (1898); Ellen Hart Smith, *Charles Carroll of Carrollton* (1942).

Thomas O'Brien Hanley
Loyola College, Baltimore

JOHN CARROLL (1735-1815)

Works: *Journal of European Tour* (w. 1771-1772; pub. 1976); *Narrative of Suppression* (w. 1773-1774; pub. 1976); *Letters to Charles Plowden* (w. 1779-1815; pub. 1976); *Constitution of Clergy* (w. 1783; pub. 1976); *Address to the Roman Catholics of the United States* (1784); *Address on Wharton* (1784); *Sermon on Independence* (w. 1785; pub. 1976); *To Columbian Magazine* (1787); *Pacificus* (1789); *Establishment of the Catholic Religion in the U.S.* (w. 1790; pub. 1830, 1976); *Address to President Washington* (1790); *Pastoral Letter* (1792); *John, Bishop of Baltimore* (1797); *Pastoral Letter* (1799); *Eulogy of Washington* (1800).

Biography: John Carroll was born on Jan. 8, 1735, in Upper Marlboro, Md., the son of Daniel and Eleanor (Darnall) Carroll and the second cousin of Charles Carroll of Carrollton (q.v.). In 1748 Carroll traveled with his cousin Charles to St. Omer, French Flanders, for an extended education on the Continent. In 1753 he entered the Society of Jesus, was ordained to the priesthood in 1769, and was teaching at Bruges when its Jesuit college was closed in 1773 as part of the general suppression of the order. Beginning in 1774, Carroll took his place, with his brother Daniel of Rock Creek Manor (signers of the Federal Constitution), among the Md. gentry and rapidly rose to civil as well as church leadership, serving with Charles Carroll on the commission of the Congress to Canada in 1776, juridically organizing the clergy under a new form following independence, becoming bishop and archbishop of Baltimore in 1790 and 1808, respectively. Carroll's values and vision of the Catholic community and its place in early America are credited for its solid foundation. The first Catholic bishop in America, Carroll died on Dec. 13, 1815. Appropriately, Benjamin Latrobe designed the architectural landmark—Baltimore Cathedral—where Carroll's remains are buried in its crypt.

Critical Appraisal: John Carroll's family, education, and position in large measure explain his success as a writer, the quality of his works, and their considerably diverse character. His *Journal* of a European tour and the *Narrative* of his last days as a Jesuit struggling against the autocratic procedures of the French civil government at Bruges illustrate, for example, his capacity to write movingly about human freedom and dignity. Equally effective are his occasional letters to the press urging an enlargement of religious freedom and his positive declarations of admiration at the liberation of the human person achieved by American independence, which he saw as a providential deterrent to any inclination toward repression of Roman Catholic congregations.

In fact, Carroll's natural moderation as a man of reason in the spirit of the Christian Enlightenment marked his protests at any infringements of freedom he encountered and made him at home in a Federalist segment of American writers. His concern for his duties as bishop of the small Catholic community after 1790 and for order in the new Federal Republic was expressed with dignity and reverence. In particular, Carroll's public writings on George Washington (q.v.) epitomize his distinctive use of style to underscore his love of freedom. In these writings, Carroll freed himself from Jesuit rules that clerics should preach Christ crucified and not the self performing feats of rhetoric. His *Eulogy of Washington*, he said, was modeled on St. Ambrose's composition for a similar occasion and was consciously academic in tone. At the same time, an earlier sermon or homily he gave on the same subject reveals a middle form of expression, far more moving than the general style of his many sermons, which were primarily intent upon doctrinal instruction and moral suasion.

As Carroll grew older, the role of religion in civil life increasingly became the subject of his greatest public influence and literary attainment. Particularly related to this thrust of his writings were his *apologetic* pieces. But even in these writings, the response to an attack on a religious figure or faith was always placed in the larger civil setting to prevent misrepresentation of the Catholic faith and its believers and to protect the religious freedoms won by a War of Independence. Particularly noteworthy in this area was Carroll's extended pamphlet directed at Charles Wharton, a Jesuit who had joined the Anglican Church. In this document, Carroll's use of literary techniques like *reductio ad absurdum* and *a fortiori* elevated his rhetoric above the ordinary. Although *ad hominem* overtones to Wharton's marriage are out of Carroll's natural style, when Wharton responded, Carroll turned from the contest, and this gesture gave him the image of the prudent man, disinclined to disruptive interfaith bickering. As a result, his writings on this case and on similar issues usually had the effect he intended:

respect for the American Catholic community with roots in a liberal Anglo-Irish tradition of freedom rather than the Continental one as caricatured by English Protestant writers.

All of Carroll's published works reveal a disciplined writer, even the official documents, reports, and pastorals demanded by his office. When he enforced church discipline, for example, he drew on his literary skills. Somewhat akin to diplomatic correspondence in civil affairs are his letters settling differences among parties, appointments, and corrections of individuals. On one occasion, he even showed his ability to portray the historical context of his church.

In contrast to these works, Carroll's correspondence with friends and relatives holds the delights found in the exchanges of figures in literary history. Particularly, a lifelong correspondence with Charles Plowden of Eng. stands out and to a striking degree portrays the personal life of a man deeply experiencing the great movements of his times. Those closest to Carroll, it would seem, apparently saw him as Rembrandt Peale portrayed him: a thoughtful man at ease with God, himself, his neighbors, and the humane values he found in his times

Suggested Readings: CCMDG; DAB; DARB. *See also* Peter Guilday, *The Life and Times of John Carroll, Archbishop of Baltimore*, 2 vols. (1922; rep., 1954); Thomas O'Brien Hanley, ed., *The John Carroll Papers*, 3 vols. (1976), with volume introductions for general information and editorial notes for initiating research with complete texts.

Thomas O'Brien Hanley
Loyola College, Baltimore

LANDON CARTER (1710-1778)

Works: *A Letter from a Gentleman in Virginia* (1754); *A Letter to a Gentleman in London, from Virginia* (1759); *The Rector Detected* (1764); Jack P. Greene, ed., *The Diary of Colonel Landon Carter of Sabine Hall, 1752-1778*, 2 vols. (1965); Jack P. Greene, ed., " 'Not to be Governed or Taxed, but by . . . our Representatives': Four Essays in Opposition to the Stamp Act by Landon Carter" (w. 1765-1766; pub. in VMHB, 76 [1968], 259-300).

Biography: Landon Carter was born on Aug. 18, 1710, the fourth of five sons of Robert "King" Carter, one of the wealthiest and most influential men in early eighteenth-century Va. and the second-generation head of one of the truly great Va. dynasties. Possessing an estate of more than 330,000 acres of land, King Carter was able to leave even his fourth son eight operating plantations. Landon received an excellent education at the private school of Solomon Low in London and at William and Mary College. His native intelligence and abilities, his wealth, his excellent education, and the fact that he was related by blood or marriage to virtually every important leader in Va. ensured him a prominent place in Va. society. As a justice of the peace and county lieutenant and burgess, Carter was widely influential in Va. politics, and from 1752 until 1768, he was one of the most important members of the House of Burgesses. He was an influential participant in all of the major debates leading up to the Revolution in Va.: pistole fee, Two-Penny Acts, paper currency, Stamp Act. He also claimed the distinction of first raising the alarm against the Stamp Act in the House of Burgesses and of instigating petitions of protest six months before Patrick Henry's famous resolutions. At his death on Dec. 22, 1778, Carter left an estate of nearly 50,000 acres of land, perhaps as many as 500 slaves, and a list of public accomplishments impressive by any standard.

Critical Appraisal: As pamphleteer, essayist, satirist, diarist, and scientific writer, Landon Carter was perhaps the most prolific author in Va. during the two decades before the Revolution. He produced at least four major pamphlets and nearly fifty essays thus far identified as his in colonial gazettes and British newspapers. His diary is the longest one to survive from colonial Va. and is for the student of colonial culture one of the most important southern private journals. One of his essays on the weevil fly won for him election to the American Philosophical Society.

Perhaps his most significant literary achievement, Carter's *Diary* (1752-1778) provides invaluable insight into the minds of the pre-Revolutionary Va. gentry and into the society that produced those minds. At the center of everything of importance during the twenty years preceding the Revolution and able to crystalize the ideals of his society in a lifelong quest for distinction, Carter seemed compelled to write down almost everything he thought or experienced. An irascible, moody, introspective, self-conscious, brilliant, independent aristocrat who possessed a passion for knowledge, a profound distrust of human nature, a rigid code of behavior to which he insisted that others measure up, a deep commitment to moderation, an almost uncontrollable temper, an obsession for thoroughness, an unrelenting devotion to public duty, an uncompromising candidness with associates, and an insistence that all things be utilitarian, Carter was as introspective as any of the Puritan diarists, and his increasing tendency toward withdrawal caused him to confide more and more intimately in his journal.

One of the most important discoveries the reader makes indirectly in the *Diary* is Carter's reading, those books that helped form his mind and from which he took the ideas and copious quotations to be found in his many writings. References in the *Diary* and other evidence indicate that Carter's library may have included a thousand or more titles during his prime years of writing. About one-third of this library remains intact at the family seat of Sabine Hall, and the extensive marginalia in his handwriting attest to Carter's extensive use of the library. The copious citations throughout the *Diary* combined with a knowledge of the extant library provide a reasonably accurate picture of Carter's intellectual interests. Like most of the Va. gentry, Carter was first of all a hard-working farmer; indeed, the diary and library indicate that his holdings in agricultural volumes were one of the largest gatherings of his day on the subject. He also drew heavily upon the Classics, belles lettres, politics, philosophy, theology, history, law, and an extensive file of current periodicals.

The overriding theme of Landon Carter's *Diary* is that one must relentlessly pursue self-improvement in a quest for distinction. A perfectionist who demanded that others measure up to his rigid code of behavior and who was never reticent in making known his displeasure at their failings, Carter never mingled or formed intimate friendships, because he thought that he would endanger his disinterestedness and impartiality in his public duties. An empiricist in everything and especially in agriculture, he was an excellent experimental agriculturalist, constantly looking for new ways to improve crops, eradicate pests and diseases, and operate a plantation more efficiently. All in all, his extraordinary accomplishments made him much respected for his abilities; however, his uncompromising nature, aloofness, and rigid standard of behavior alienated even his closest acquaintances, resulting in his never being very popular and in his being intensely disliked by many. In his later years, the *Diary* reveals that he became increasingly bitter in his disappointments over not making his mark upon his generation and over being denied proper credit for his contributions toward independence. Especially galling was Patrick Henry's being given credit for the first protest against the Stamp Act.

During his forty-four years of active involvement in the political life of Va. (especially during the sixteen years of his service in the Burgesses), Landon Carter produced a body of political comment more voluminous than that of any other Virginian of his generation and, in the words of his editor, "probably reveals more fully than the writings of any other individual the framework of political assumptions and ideas within which his generation of Virginians operated." From the 1750s until the Revolution, Carter was one of the leading writers in a group that developed in print the ideology and established a tradition of expression adopted in the 1770s by such writers as Thomas Jefferson (q.v.). Carter appeared in print during the Pistole Fee dispute, the paper currency and Two-Penny Acts controversies, the 1760s debate with Britain over such policies as the Stamp Act, and the 1770s discussions of independence.

Above all, Carter's devotion to the constitution as the guardian of the general welfare of the community is at the heart of his many writings against governors, British merchants, the clergy in Va., and British Parliament. During the Pistole Fee dispute with Lieutenant-Governor Robert Dinwiddie, Carter wrote *A Letter from a Gentleman in Virginia, to the Merchants of Great Britain*, in which he appealed to the merchants' usually pernicious self-interest as a means of overturning Dinwiddie's fee on land patents. Here and in an essay to the *Maryland Gazette* of Oct. 24, 1754, Carter defended the colonial legislature's right to establish fees and argued that government officials should have the welfare of all the people as their guiding principle. Again during the paper currency controversy, Carter penned *A Letter to a Gentleman in London from Virginia* (1759), a pamphlet that attacked the British merchants for their greed in having colonial currency banned as legal tender during a time of economic depression. In this pamphlet, Carter revealed the same belief in the autocracy of the Va. legislature and the resentment of crown interference that he expressed in his Pistole Fee writings and was to express in his later essays.

Carter's concern that the home government should allow the colonial legislature to attend to the immediate welfare of the community is expressed in his Two-Penny Act pamphlets and Stamp Act essays. In *A Letter to the Bishop of London* (1759), Carter vehemently and systematically refuted the charges the bishop made against the Va. General Assembly in a letter to the Privy Council in securing the disallowance of the Va. Two-Penny Act. Again in *The Rector Detected* (1764), written in response to the Rev. John Camm's (q.v.) *A Single and Distinct View* (1763), Carter insisted that a prince should be more than willing to suspend his royal prerogative to favor his people in times of distress. His four Stamp Act essays continued the same opposition to British interference with the rights of a representative colonial legislature. All of these writings reveal Carter to be a master of the devices of satire and an accomplished craftsman with the elements of Classical rhetoric in effectively reasoned, felicitously phrased polemical prose.

Suggested Readings: Richard Beale Davis, *Intellectual Life in the Colonial South, 1585-1763*, 3 vols. (1978), passim; Jack P. Greene, "Landon Carter, Diarist, Essayist, and Correspondent," *Manuscripta*, 11 (1959), 35-37, 52; idem, *Landon Carter: An Inquiry into the Personal Values and Social Imperatives of the Eighteenth-Century Virginia Gentry* (1967), a revised separate printing of the introduction to the author's edition of Carter's *Diary*; idem, "Landon Carter and the Pistole Fee Dispute," WMQ, 3rd ser., 14 (1957), 66-69; Walter Ray Wineman, *The Landon Carter Papers in the University of Virginia Library: A Calendar and Biographical Sketch* (1962).

Homer D. Kemp
Tennessee Technological University

JONATHAN CARVER (1710-1780)

Works: *Travels Through the Interior Parts of North America* (1778); *Treatise on the Culture of the Tobacco Plant* (1779).

Biography: Carver's importance to literary history rests on one book, his *Travels*, published two years before he died in Eng. at the age of 69. What little is known of his life has had to be reconstructed from scanty records of marriages, wills, commissions, and the like.

According to existing records, Carver was born in Weymouth, Mass., in 1710 to what one biographer described as "a family that was stable, thrifty, respectable, and ambitious, with a regard for religion, education, and civic responsibility." In 1744 Carver married Abigail Robbins and moved to Montague, Mass., where in 1759 he served as a selectman, and from 1755 to 1763 he served in the colonial militia, achieving the rank of captain before his release. At 53 years of age, a father of seven (five girls, two boys), and without the rewards for service that regular officers enjoyed upon discharge, Carver began to look about for new ways to get back into the frontier drama of which the war had been a part. Robert

Rogers's (q.v.) new expedition to the interior Northwest gave Carver the chance to capitalize on his recent military experiences, skills as a mapper, and sense of imperial destiny. Regrettably, the Rogers-Carver association caused Carver some difficulties when Rogers fell out of favor, and it remained to haunt his reputation in the twentieth century when partisans of Rogers's worth blamed Carver for usurping the fame that should rightly have been Rogers's. Scholarship, however, absolves Carver of any reprehensible designs on his friend's fame.

The years 1766-1768 found Carver deep in the interior, beyond Rogers's Michilimackinac headquarters, in what is now Wisconsin and Minnesota. There he mapped; met, dealt, and wintered with Dakota (Sioux) and Chippewa; and gathered the facts and feeling and fictions that ten years later would find their way into his published *Travels*. The story of his "three years" in the interior is best told by Carver himself, in manuscript and print, supplemented by contemporary, parallel accounts.

A second story, that of his ten years struggle in Eng. to bring his manuscript "Travels" to press, has been told in part by Carver himself in his introduction and has been expanded and adjusted by modern scholars. He relinquished his manuscripts to the crown and then had to buy them back; he tried to mount new expeditions; he wrote and rewrote his "Travels"; he sought patrons (among them Sir Joseph Banks, John Fothergill, and Richard Whitworth); he eventually married a second wife, widow Mary Harris, although Abigail remained alive and undivorced in America; and he succeeded at last in publishing his work. In 1779 Carver issued a 2nd edition of the *Travels*, published a *Treatise on...Tobacco*, and apparently lent his name to *The New Universal Traveller*, described as a "catchall volume of travel literature." Nonetheless, he died broke the following year.

Critical Appraisal: No longer very well known, Jonathan Carver's *Travels* had, according to Henry Nash Smith, "a greater international reputation than any other book of American authorship in the eighteenth century," and this popular regard must be taken into account in any latter-day assessment of Carver's contribution to our times or his own. The meaning of such a work lies, perhaps, as much in what its readers make of it as in what the author meant to convey. The same sort of thing can always be said, of course, but some works are interesting almost without regard to their audience, and some public excitements matter more than the texts that triggered them. In Carver's case, a meeting of minds and a congruence of interests sprang up between the text by one Yankee and the context brought to the reading by countless late eighteenth- and early nineteenth-century readers, English and Continental as well as American, Romantic (Coleridge, Wordsworth, Chateaubriand, Schiller, Bryant) as well as practical.

Carver's maps, tales, and reports realized a myth better than many more self-consciously crafted narratives; more particularly, the *Travels* presents an especially American embodiment of the formula. Carver and his readers shared a belief in the paramount reality of nature. News of nature and its workings and its layout seemed to them as obviously good and useful as religious good news had to earlier ages. Nature reporters like Carver worked out a new genre, *nature reportage*, with its appropriate conventions and fit inventions. The persona is a palimpsest of Yankee on Crusoe on Gulliver on privateer on Everyman. The texture of the work swings from glossaries to tall tales to journal to ethnography to plant and animal lists. Maps and other graphics do not merely decorate; they too "report" on nature and convey their own somewhat distinct tenor to the reportage.

The congruence of American destiny and nature's arrangements is made plausible by the matter-of-fact details of Carver's reports on waterfalls, natives, watercourses, fruits, and useful creatures. The plausibility of going it pretty much alone is advanced by the first-person, picaresque adventures of Carver. Many of his most moving anecdotes feature him alone, in contact with nature: looking down through six fathoms of Lake Superior water at huge stones on the bottom, testing the depths of a remarkable cave (since called "Carver's Cave") on the Mississippi by tossing pebbles back in it and listening to the reverberations, eating moose-lip soup or sand cherries, breasting a thunderstorm to the amazement of the natives who wanted to hide under a tree. The usefulness of common sense leavened by some uncommon learning is underlined not only by the lightning incident but by his amusement at the tale of the Frenchman and his trained rattlesnake. Finally, tales of the "Shining Mountains" of the interior beyond and of the place where the four capital rivers rise and run out north, south, east, and west (Northwest Passage) cast America as a new Eden or Asylum at the same time as it is open to settlement.

Carver's creation touched the right chords at just the right time. So great was his fame in the nineteenth century that fraudulent real estate claims, through none of his own doings, continued to be pressed even into the twentieth century. It was in the face of his inflated reputation and notoriety that Edward Gaylord Bourne began debunking Carver in 1904, charging him with plagiarism. Bourne's charges have not stuck. Carver "borrowed," often without quotation marks, but that was not unusual then, especially in nature reportage. The best result of Bourne's charges was the lively research that followed, research that led to the discovery of the Carver manuscripts in the British Museum and to the work on those documents by subsequent scholars. Their steady if small stream of writings has restored Carver's reputation. The times have changed, and nature reportage now attracts only a relatively small audience. If he was a secular prophet in his own time and for a century thereafter, today Carver is important more as an informant from the midst of a nexus of values and meanings central to the development of American culture but no longer intact. His *Travels* is an instance of a sort of composition our criticism has not dealt with well: the back and forth between author and editor, author and audience, texts already out and ones going to press.

   Suggested Readings: DAB; DNB; LHUS; T$_2$; *See also* Theodore C. Blegen, *Minnesota: A History of the State* (1963), pp. 67-70, 509, 606-607; Edward Gaylord Bourne, "The Authenticity of Carver's 'Travels,'" Wisconsin State Historical Society, *Bulletin of Information*, no. 24 (1905), and, later, in AHR, 11 (1906), 287-302; William

Browning, "Early History of Jonathan Carver," WMH 3 (1920), 291-305; three articles on Carver, Rogers, and James Tute by Thomas C. Elliott: "The Strange Case of Jonathan Carver and the Name Oregon," "The Origin of the Name Oregon," and "Jonathan Carver's Source for the Name Oregon," OHSQ, 21 (1920), 341-368; 22 (1921), 91-115; 23 (1922), 53-67; Russell W. Fridley, "The Writings of Jonathan Carver," MiH, 24 (1954), 154-159; Louise Phelps Kellogg, "The Mission of Jonathan Carver," WMH, 12 (1928), 127-145; John Parker, *The Journals of Jonathan Carver and Related Documents, 1766-1770* (1976); Milo M. Quaife, "Jonathan Carver and the Carver Grant," MVHR, 7 (1920), 3-25; David Scofield Wilson, *In the Presence of Nature* (1978), pp. 47-87, 120-33, passim. Dr. John Coakley Lettsom's posthumous biography of his friend for the 1781 edition of the *Travels* is unreliable (listing 1732 as his birthdate, for example). The best source of biographical (and bibliographical) information is John Parker's "Introduction" to *The Journals*.

David Scofield Wilson
University of California, Davis

MARK CATESBY (1683-1749)

Works: *The Natural History of Carolina, Florida and the Bahama Islands* (1731-1747); "Of Birds of Passage," Royal Society of London *Philosophical Transactions* (1747); *Hortus Britanno-Americanus* (1763).

Biography: Little is known of Mark Catesby's early life. He was born in 1683, probably in Castle Hedingham, Essex, to John and Elizabeth (nee Jekyll) Catesby. The Jekylls appear to have introduced him to the virtuoso pursuits of natural history and antiquarian research and to the great John Ray—botanist— and Samuel Dale—physician, apothecary, and contributor to the Royal Society of London. The example and instruction of such persons prepared him better than any formal schooling could have for his eventual field work in America and his twenty years of labor on *Carolina*.

In 1712 he set out to visit his married sister Elizabeth in Va. He met and traveled the back country with William Byrd of Westover (q.v.). He made sketches of flora and fauna, collected specimens, and sent them back to Eng., but "chiefly," by his own account in *Carolina*, he "gratified [his] Inclination in observing and admiring the various Productions of those Countries." In Eng. (1719) his sketches and specimens won for him the patronage he needed to return to America and begin seriously on his major work. From 1722 to 1726, Catesby traveled through the southern colonies and the Bahamas learning, collecting, sketching. He sent packets to his several English patrons: William Sherard, Sir Hans Sloane, and others.

Catesby returned to the "Center of all Sciences" in 1726 and spent the next two decades writing, engraving, printing, and selling his magnun opus piece- meal, 20 plates (with accompanying French and English text) at a time. In all, *Carolina* eventually included 200 regular plates and 20 more in an appendix. The plates with their accompanying texts inform the "reader" about all manner of "productions" of Carolina: natural ones like snakes, eels, fish, turtles, acorns, plants, mammals, birds, and berries; civil ones like tar and chimneys and grains. His folio-sized plates also present compositions in which a bird on a branch, or, say, a snake on a vine, achieves an iconic presence unique in nature reportage. In many cases, the bits are assembled in ways that signify natural relationships, as when he placed woodpeckers on oak branches. In others, he combined items in "unnatural" relationships that nevertheless symbolize patterns of order and design he and his age appreciated in nature: see his Tumble Turds and Lilies plate or his Flamingo and *Keratophyton* plate, for example.

Critical Appraisal: *Carolina* is a landmark in nature reportage. It won high praise from English and Continental virtuosi, earned him a fellowship in the Royal Society of London (1733), and became the standard natural history of America, the one work that Carl Linnaeus, Thomas Jefferson (q.v.), Dr. Alexander Garden (q.v.), and similar serious naturalists always took as given and then tested and found wanting or not in some way.

Catesby has been called an "artist-naturalist" and "the colonial Audubon," two denominations that testify to his reputation as a graphic artist and his importance to ornithological history. However, given his considerable interest in plants, geology, useful products, and weather and his very competent prose in *Carolina* and other works, it is better to call Catesby a "nature reporter." He dispatched, at first, and then wrote and published in Eng., all news of nature he had been able to gather in America. Although as a fellow of the Royal Society he ventured into synthetic speculation in his piece on bird migration and pulled together his vegetable "cabinet" for *Hortus*, his genius lay in presenting anecdotes and icons of compelling interest to lay and professional naturalists for their delight and good use. *Gentleman's Magazine* noted his death Dec. 23, 1749, and called his *Carolina* "perhaps. . . the most elegant performance of its kind that has yet been published."

Catesby's prose in *Carolina* chiefly accompanied his graphic work, contextualizing, naming species, telling uses, and now and then relating anecdotes or citing the findings of others. Often plain in style, Catesby's prose occasionally displays his enjoyment of drama or his sense of the rhythms of language. His anecdote of the rattlesnake found in his bed, which he included in the text opposite his rattlesnake plate, is a good example of his talent at displaying such relationships. Most of his more felicitous prose accomplishments, however, occur in the lengthy forematter of *Carolina*, where he recounted the devastation he found after a hurricane or noted his observations of flying fish pursued by dolphins. In this latter case, he suited the sound to the sense by syntactically suspending the fish in air for three adjectival phrases before dropping them exhausted into the jaws of their pursuers. He drew his diction from the ancients and moderns and folk without prejudice, composing polynominal denominations for flora and fauna in Latin, at the one extreme, and passing on vernacular names, at the other: Tumble-Turd, Mock-Bird, Pole-Cat, and Licking hole Church, for example. His love of particulars comes through in his report on the outrage domestic animals seem to feel at the invasion of their space by a rattlesnake: "the Hogs, Dogs and Poultry united in their Hatred to him, shewing the greatest Consternation, by erecting their Bristles and Feathers." He said of a scarab that the "thorax of this is covered with a shield of crimson metallick lustre, . . . blended with green," and "From the crown of the head rises a shining black horn recurved backward."

Catesby was good with words and unusually effective at graphics. Certain of his most interesting achievements bridge the gap between line and word as medium, but the imagery of his verbal description of the beetle and the "wit" and "conceit" of his Globe Fish and *Cornus* plate and Tumble-Turd and Lilies piece make the distinction between prose and iconography problematic as far as nature reportage is concerned. To scholars interested more narrowly in letters, Catesby's usefulness will likely lie more in his prose-as-reportage and prose-as-instance of usage than in his prose-as-art.

Suggested Readings: BDAS; DAB; DNB; T$_1$. *See also* Elsa Guerdrum Allen, "The History of American Ornithology Before Audubon," TAPS, New Series, 41, pt. 3 (1951), 463-478, passim; William Darlington, ed., *Memorials of John Bartram and Humphrey Marshall* (1849; rep. 1967); Brooke Hindle, *The Pursuit of Science in Revolutionary America, 1735-1789* (1956); Joseph Kastner, *A Species of Eternity* (1977), pp. 16-19, passim; W. L. McAtee, "The North American Birds of Mark Catesby and Eleazer Albin," JSBNH, 3, pt. 4 (1957), 177-194; Richard Pulteney, *The Historical and Biographical Sketches of the Progress of Botany in England* (1790); Edmund and Dorothy Smith-Berkeley, *Dr. Alexander Garden of Charles Town* (1969); idem, *Dr. John Mitchell: The Man Who Made the Map of North America* 1974); Raymond Phineas Stearns, *Science in the British Colonies of America* (1970); David S. Wilson, "The Iconography of Mark Catesby," ECS, 4 (1971), 169-183; idem, *In the Presence of Nature* (1978), pp. 122-189, passim. The more complete bibliographies in Wilson, Frick and Stearns, Allen, and McAtee should be consulted by those pursuing interdisciplinary topics. Catesby's writing is widely available through microcard collections, e.g., *Travels in the Old South*, vol. 1, no. 55.

David Scofield Wilson
University of California, Davis

THOMAS CHALKLEY (1675-1741)

Works: *An Exhortation to Youth and Others* (1707); *A Loving Invitation unto Young and Old in Holland and Elsewhere* (1709); *Forcing a Maintenance Not Warrantable* (1714); *A Letter to a Friend in Ireland* (1720); *Youth Persuaded to Obedience* (1730); *Free Thoughts Communicated to Free Thinkers* (1735); "Thomas Chalkley's Last Letter to His Wife" (w. 1741; pub. in John and Isaac Comly, eds., *Friends Miscellany*; 1838); *A Journal or Historical Account* (1749). *A Collection of the Works* (1749) reprints everything except "Last Letter" and prints several previously unpublished tracts, meditations, and letters.

Biography: According to his *Journal*, Thomas Chalkley, a leading American Quaker minister of the early eighteenth century, was born on Mar. 3, 1675, in Southwark, Eng., to Rebecca and George Chalkley, a dealer in meal. After completing an apprenticeship to his father, Chalkley began a lifelong career of traveling as a merchant and public minister, combining the two vocations into one journey, a practice that he generally followed for the remainder of his life. In 1698 Chalkley visited America, where he traveled through most of the colonies. Returning to Eng., he married Martha Betterton, also a Quaker minister. Together they immigrated to Md. in 1700 and a short while later settled in Philadelphia. In 1714, two years after the death of his first wife, Chalkley married Martha Brown. Only one of the twelve children borne to him by his two wives survived.

In spite of his being, by his own admission, "corpulent and heavy" and often seasick, Chalkley persevered in his labors. His trading and preaching carried him through many of the British colonies, often to the W. Ind., and occasionally even back to Eng. Wherever Chalkley stopped, he preached, and he consequently became well known in his usual ports of call. Although his journeys are too numerous to be noted individually, two early ones deserve specific mention. In 1706 he visited the Seneca and Shawnee Indians of Pa. and was impressed with both their religious understanding and the participation of their women in tribal counsels. His single most extensive journey took place between 1707 and 1710, when he preached in the W. Ind., Ire., Scot., Wales, Eng., Hol., and Ger. During the final years of his life, Chalkley traveled less widely. Occasionally, however, he retraced the paths of earlier journeys, where he frequently rejoiced at the growth of the Quaker religion. On Nov. 4, 1741, while on the island of Tortola in the Virg. Is., Chalkley died of a fever he had contracted there.

Critical Appraisal: Thomas Chalkley is best known for his long autobiographical journal, which is more concerned with the temporal world than most Quaker journals. As a successful merchant and trader, Chalkley labored to show that business matters did not necessarily conflict with spiritual ones. Rather, he considered the material world the arena where the spiritual must prove itself. Thus Chalkley defended his combined trading and preaching trips, recording throughout his journal the many meetings he attended and the preaching he accomplished while on such trips. He noted, for example, his efforts to hire sailors of good reputation and the religious meetings he conducted on board ship, usually twice each week, and he emphasized the moments when God seemed to intervene in affairs aboard ship, whether saving the ship from being swept onto rocks during a hurricane or providing a dolphin when food supplies had dwindled and Chalkley himself had offered his body to the mutinous crew as food.

In addition, Chalkley recounted his sufferings in the name of his faith: the taunts he received as a child for his dress and religion, his refusal to fight after he was pressed into the navy, and the gunshot wound he received in Barbados for advocating better treatment of slaves (although the assailant was captured, Chalkley refused to prosecute).

As a Quaker journalist, Chalkley is particularly noteworthy for the temporal concerns of his journal, but from a literary point of view, those concerns create a more richly textured work than is often the case with such documents, at least in their published forms. He quoted, for example, letters written in his ministry, including one written to Quakers who had settled west of the mountains, in which he urged them to recognize the Indians' claim to the land. On occasion, he paraphrased his own preaching, and he even quoted a poem by Addison as well as some verse that his young son had memorized. Nonetheless, the unifying element of the journey stems from its concern that the minister can work in and through the temporal world and that God's presence is felt throughout the affairs of this life. Written for the most part in the understated and unadorned style typical of the best Quaker writings, Chalkley's narrative, although in conventional language, is both dramatic and pathetic, but the drama and the pathos have a didactic purpose, and neither is ever exploited merely for the sake of entertainment. He related, for instance, his narrow escapes directly and saw in them the hand of God; he related the moments of pathos equally directly, as when he eulogized his tenth child and namesake, stating that he took comfort in knowing that his dead children were free from the dangers and temptations of the world. Throughout the journal, drama and pathos are used to instruct the reader and to illustrate the workings of God, not to excite or to entice.

Chalkley's other writings generally defend Quaker beliefs, often against Calvinistic accusations. He wrote, for instance, against election and the paid ministry, and he defended the perfectability of man. Even his meditative writings, direct and unadorned, are assertive. In a meditation on the Sermon on the Mount, first published in the collected works, he argued that the Quaker beliefs despised by the world develop directly from this sermon and that the doctrine of the sermon might serve as a means of reconciling various portions of Christianity.

Chalkley's writings, particularly his journal, remained popular into the nineteenth century and were valued for their style and for the portrait of their author, whom John Greenleaf Whittier called the "gentlest of skippers, the rare seasaint." In addition, Chalkley's writings were of interest for their strong biblical emphasis. Although Quaker writers usually relied on the primacy of the inner light to the near exclusion of biblical authority, Chalkley's writings are rooted in the biblical tradition more typical of earlier writers.

Suggested Readings: DAB; LHUS. *See also* Howard H. Brinton, *Quaker Journals, Varieties of Religious Experience Among Friends* (1972); Daniel B. Shea, Jr., *Spiritual Autobiography in Early America* (1968), pp. 16-22; Luella M. Wright, *The Literary Life of the Early Friends, 1650-1725* (1932), pp. 155-197.

John Stratton
University of Arkansas at Little Rock

RICHARD CHAMBERLAIN (1632-c. 1698)

Works: *Lithobolia, or The Stone-Throwing Devil* (w. 1682; pub. 1698).

Biography: Born in London sometime in 1632 into a family with a pedigree that went back several generations, Richard Chamberlain (also spelled *Chamberlayn*) was heir of a "William Chamberlayn, Esq. of London." Educated at Trinity

College, Cambridge, and trained in law at Gray's Inn, Chamberlain was admitted and called to the bar on Nov. 11, 1659. Probably as a result of his connections and friendship with a Robert Mason, legal heir to vast tracts of land in N.H., Chamberlain was appointed secretary of the province of N.H. in 1680. In 1682 he lodged at the home of a prosperous Quaker, George Walton (1615-1696), on Great Island in Piscataqua; also residing in this household were Walton's wife, Elizabeth, and his daughter Abishag. In 1695 Abishag wedded a "Martin Lumley, Esq.," to whom *Lithobolia* is dedicated. Although he lost his secretaryship with the change of government in 1686, Chamberlain became clerk of courts until 1689, when the collapse of the Andros administration forced him to leave that position. At that time, Chamberlain seems to have returned to Eng. In 1798 he advertised, from a broadside published in Boston, "European and India Goods." Chamberlain died sometime around 1698.

Critical Appraisal: *Lithobolia* (Greek for "stone throwing") is a copiously annotated account of a series of supernatural phenomena (the inexplicable movement about the house of objects such as stones, bricks, and various household utensils) that allegedly occurred in the house of George Walton during a three-month period in 1682 while Richard Chamberlain boarded at the Walton house. The original work, printed and sold by E. Whitlook near Stationers-Hall in London in 1698, consists of a title page, a dedicatory poem ("To the Much Honoured R. F., Esq.") written in triplets, and a narrative description of the phenomena Chamberlain witnessed. Also included in the original work is a list of signatures of supposed eyewitnesses to the events, including "Samuel Jennings, Esq., Gov. of West-Jarsey," and "Walter Clark, Esq., Deputy Gov. of Rhode Island."

Although Chamberlain initially attributed the attacks to a Hannah Jones, a neighbor of the Waltons, she was never "formerly detected" in witchcraft. She was, however, the daughter of Jane Walford, who had been tried and found innocent of witchcraft in 1656. The curious events Chamberlain described began on Jun. 11, 1682, at 10:00 P.M., when Chamberlain and the Walton family heard the sound of stones hitting the top and sides of their house. The stone throwing continued with increasing intensity until the members of the household were forced to protect themselves from stones supposedly flying around inside the house. The flying stones continued for four hours and were interrupted only by candlesticks, pewter pots, and other household utensils mysteriously flung to the floor and through the air. Finally retiring for the evening, the residents of the house were shortly awoken by the sound of even larger stones, one weighing eight pounds, slamming against the walls inside and outside the house. The following morning, Chamberlain witnessed such supernatural phenomena as a spit moving from the floor to the fireplace and back again, a pressing-iron "convey'd invisibly into the yard," and other items inexplicably removed and returned to their usual places.

The strange occurrences continued, and on Wednesday Walton encountered new phenomena in a neighbor's woods, where he heard the sound of glass and metal falling through the trees, and in a boat, where the anchor allegedly flew overboard. Returning home, Walton encountered nothing unusual until Friday evening, when three or four stones (one of them red hot) flew out of the fire and across the room. The stone throwing and utensil throwing continued inside and outside the house, and at least three people, including two young children, were slightly injured. To the previous phenomena were added more inexplicable occurrences, including Indian corn "invisibly" pulled from the ground, the sounds of snorting in the air and loud humming, and the mysterious removal of a large gate torn from its hinges and thrown into a field. Such phenomena continued intermittently throughout Aug., at which time they gradually ceased, with the exception of one final incident when Walton was struck on the head and back while on his way to court for a hearing on the matter of the possession of his house. What judgments the courts may have made do not appear from the extant records.

Given the extreme seriousness with which matters such as the incidents at George Walton's house were regarded in Puritan New Eng., Chamberlain's account is remarkably restrained. In fact, with the exception of the undistinguished dedicatory poem and a brief conclusion in which Chamberlain suggested that whoever was responsible for the acts "must tererariously unhinge, or undermine the Fundamentals of the best Religion in the World," the entire narration is objective to the point of being a direct report on the alleged incidents as Chamberlain and at least fifteen other people witnessed them. That Chamberlain chose not to embellish his narrative with theological rhetoric and undue moralizing adds credibility to his account and is reminiscent of the point of view in Increase Mather's (q.v.) *An Essay for the Recording of Illustrious Providences* (1684), which also recorded events of possible supernatural origin in an objective, almost scientific manner, including an account of the happenings at the Walton house. Published shortly after the Salem witchcraft trials, *Lithobolia* shows that although public interest in such events was officially declining, a belief in witchcraft and supernatural phenomena was still very much alive in New Eng.

Suggested Readings: FCNEV. *See also* Nathaniel Bouton, ed., "Provincial Records and Court Papers," CNHamHS, 8 (1866), 99-100; George Lincoln Burr, ed., *Narratives of the Witchcraft Cases* (1914), pp. 53-76; James A. Levernier, Introduction, *An Essay for the Recording of Illustrious Providences*, by Increase Mather (1684; rep., 1977); Harrison T. Meserole, ed., *Seventeenth-Century American Poetry* (1968), p. 423; *New Hampshire Provincial Papers*, I, 590, 600; Charles W. Tuttle, "Papers on New Hampshire in 1689-1690," PMHS, 17 (1879), 218-228; "William Vaughan's Journal of Transactions During His Impisonment, Etc.," CNHamHS, 8 (1866), 182-196.

Bruce Weigl
Old Dominion University

THOMAS BRADBURY CHANDLER (1726-1790)

Works: *An Appeal to the Public* (1767); *The Appeal Defended* (1769); *An Address from the Clergy of New-York* (1771); *The Appeal Farther Defended* (1771); *A Sermon Preached Before the Corporation* (1771); *The American Que-*

rist: Or, Some Questions (1774); *An Appendix to the American Edition of the Life of Archbishop Secker* (1774); *A Free Examination* (1774); *A Friendly Address to All Reasonable Americans* (1774); *The Friendly Address to All Reasonable Americans...Carefully Abridged* (1774); *What Think Ye of the Congress Now* (1775).

Biography: Thomas Bradbury Chandler was born at Woodstock, Conn., on Apr. 26, 1726. After graduation from Yale College in 1745, he taught school in Woodstock and studied under Samuel Johnson (q.v.), first president of King's College (now Columbia Univ.). In 1747 St. John's Church in Elizabethtown, N.J., asked him to fill deceased Rev. Edward Vaughan's pulpit. Since Chandler was too young to be ordained, he served as catechist and lay reader until 1751. After traveling to London for ordination ceremonies, be became minister at St. John's and missionary to Woodbridge. Oxford awarded him an M.A. in 1753 and a doctorate in 1766. He received a second doctorate in divinity from King's College in 1767.

Chandler became a leader in efforts to secure an Anglican bishop for America. He also proved himself an unswerving Loyalist. In Apr. 1775 he sadly departed his homeland for Eng. where he remained until 1785. During his self-imposed exile, an unhealed sore from his 1760 bout with smallpox became cancerous. Deteriorating health forced him to decline appointment as bishop of Nova Scotia. He returned to America in 1785 and, at the request of St. John's vestry, resumed his post as rector. The ailing Chandler remained in that office until his death from cancer on Jun. 17, 1790.

Critical Appraisal: Thomas Bradbury Chandler's published works fall into two categories: those advocating an American bishopric, and those professing loyalty to British imperial rule. Regardless of category, his writings demonstrate tedious repetition of arguments and ponderous verbosity. Despite these stylistic handicaps, however, he managed to achieve a respectable clarity in most of his writing. He relied extensively upon historical evidence in defending both his ecclesiastical and political beliefs, and despite a tendency to exaggerate the hostility of his opponents and to descend to name calling, he avowedly preferred rational discourse to emotional bullying.

Chandler plunged into the controversy over appointment of an American bishop when Samuel Johnson, whose "tremor of hand" prevented clear penmanship, requested his former student to compose *An Appeal to the Public* (1767). He began the eleven-section treatise by tracing historically the "uninterrupted Succession" of ecclesiastical authority from Christ through the Apostles to bishops. After reviewing church order from the first to third century and citing English treatises in defense of episcopacy, he concluded that the "universal silence of History" established the inaccuracy of the Presbyterian-Congregationalist viewpoint and, by implication, confirmed the validity of the Episcopalian position.

According to Chandler, the primary reason for obtaining an American bishop was that the power of ordination vested in his office would permit stricter clerical discipline without markedly affecting religious freedom among the laity. He said the lengthy duration, hazards, and expense of a voyage to Eng. for ordination resulted in an insufficient number of qualified clergymen. Pressing that point, he asserted that the vast distance from Eng. resulted in ordination of some who later proved to be "such Wretches, as are not only a Scandal to the Church, but a disgrace to the human Species."

In his enumeration of other reasons for appointment of an American bishop, Chandler reminded his readers that serious plans for such action dated from 1672. He traced the history of those plans and concluded the time was ripe for their implementation: growing numbers of blacks as well as whites were becoming Anglicans; disaffection with the British government had abated after repeal of the Stamp Act; and propagation of the Gospel among Indians needed reorganization in the wake of Britain's recent providential victory over the French.

Devoting two sections to the problems associated with communicating "Light" to the "American Heathens," Chandler reviewed the history of missionary activities from Queen Elizabeth's reign and the explicit provisions of the earliest colonial charters. He buttressed his analysis by emphasizing the commercial and military advantages accruing from Christianization of the Indians. Blaming missionary failures upon the notion that conversion could precede civilization, he felt certain that schools, agriculture, and "mechanic Arts" were needed to encourage Indians to forsake their "wandering and idle life" for "a settled and industrious Way of living." In writing this document, Chandler drew support from Sir William Johnson, imperial superintendent of northern Indian affairs, who said a local bishop would give unified direction to currently disoriented missionary activities.

Since the civil prerogatives and the ecclesiastical courts associated with episcopacy in Eng. would be banned in America and funding for the bishopric would come from English rather than American coffers, the plan seemed "universally harmless" to Chandler. Nevertheless, *An Appeal to the Public* sparked a 200-page reply titled *The Appeal to the Public Answered* (1768) from Charles Chauncy (q.v.) of Boston. Chandler responded with *The Appeal Defended* (1769), in which he consumed 268 pages repeating the essential arguments of his original work. To refute specific objections from Chauncy, Jonathan Mayhew (q.v.), and others, he enriched historical details about episcopacy in Reformation Eng. and furnished additional citations from English advocates of episcopacy. In *The Appeal Defended*, Chandler took particular exception to Chauncy's claim that Indians, because they were physically and culturally weakened by proximity to the "English way of living," could be converted without being civilized. Denying Chauncy's assertion that Indian depopulation resulted from acquisition of English habits and education, Chandler ascribed their declining numbers to "the immediate hand of God" casting out idolators to "make room for the settlement of his chosen People." Although he echoed Edward Johnson (q.v.) and other early New Eng. divines on that score, the advocate of episcopacy accused contemporary New Eng. Presbyterians and Congregationalists of squandering missionary funds supplied by G.B., thereby allowing Indian people to waste away.

He specifically denied Chauncy's and Andrew Eliot's (q.v.) suspicions that the Church of England had defeated New Englanders' recent efforts to establish a missionary corporation to proselytize among the Mohawks.

The literary tit for tat continued with Chauncy's publication of *A Reply to Dr. Chandler's "Appeal Defended"* (1770) and Chandler's *The Appeal Farther Defended* (1771). Chandler provided systematic answers to each of Chauncy's "standing" objections to an American bishopric but added little new to the debate. The same was true for three other works: *Address from the Clergy of New York* (1771), which castigated Va.'s Burgesses for their general condemnation of the plan; *An Appendix to the American Edition of the Life of Archbishop Secker* (1774); and *A Free Examination* (1774).

Although Chandler professed the purely ecclesiastical orientation of his call for an American bishop, his political pamphlets offered progressively more intense expressions of a connection between American religious and political affairs. In *The American Querist*, which went through at least eleven editions in 1774, he posed an illuminating series of interrogatives. For example, the thirteenth question in the 10th edition read, "Whether some degree of respect be not always due from inferiors to superiors, and especially from children to parents?" A query whether lack of respect did not violate laws of society as well as religion and morality immediately followed. He upheld the English government's right to tax the colonies as well as legislate for them, and he suggested that undue leniency toward colonial democracy had encouraged "unprincipled mobs" erroneously to equate political "privileges" with "rights." He asked whether independence would not generate civil war and commercial exploitation by marauding foreign powers. The final query of the 10th edition indicated the author's strict adherence to the Pauline doctrine of political obedience: "Whether it be not a matter both of worldly wisdom, and of indispensable Christian duty, in every *American, to fear the Lord and the King, and to meddle not with them that are GIVEN TO CHANGE?*"

Chandler's *A Friendly Address to All Reasonable Americans* (1774) furnished a far more frantic condemnation of political and religious dissent. Asserting that it would be foolish, if not fatal, to rush to arms against Eng. which could control ten Americas, the pamphlet opposed a martial posture and rejected "the Association's" nonimportation campaign. The Continental Congress's adoption of the Suffolk Resolves, which he perceived as the work of "hairbrained fanaticks, as mad and distracted as the Anabaptists of Munster," outraged Chandler. Convinced that "New England and other Presbyterian Republicans" would attack all who were not strict Calvinists, he declared with complete horror, "*The Dogs of War* will be let loose to tear out your vitals.... all-pitying Heaven! Preserve me! Preserve my friends! Preserve my Country!"

What Think Ye of the Congress Now (1775) continued in an identical vein. He said the Continental Congress's advocacy of free press but failure to maintain it smacked of the bigotry that had "disgraced the dark ages preceding the Reformation." He repeated the charge that since Congress had exceeded its delegated authority by endorsing the Suffolk Resolves, individuals were not obliged to obey its dictates. Calling Congress "a mad, blind monster" unable to see the efficacy of compromise with the English government, he left America with the resounding assertion that colonists' liberties would be best protected under absolute parliamentary authority. Two centuries later, his political pamphlets remain among the outstanding Loyalist testimonials in Revolutionary America.

Suggested Readings: CCMC; DAB; Dexter (II, 23-28); Sprague (II, 616); T₂.

Rick W. Sturdevant
University of California, Santa Barbara

EBENEZER CHAPLIN (1733-1822)

Works: *The Civil State Compared to Rivers, All Under God's Controul, and What People Have to Do When Administration Is Grievous* (1773); *The Godly Fathers and a Defence to Their People* (1773); *A Treatise on Church Government, in Three Parts* (1773); *A Second Treatise on Church Government* (1773); *Congregationalism, as Contained in the Scriptures, Explained by the Cambridge Platform, and by Approved Authors* (1794); *A Treatise on the Nature and Importance of the Sacraments* (1802).

Biography: Ebenezer Chaplin, born in Conn. on Sept. 16, 1733, was baptized in Hampton parish on Jun. 2, 1734. Chaplin's grandfather, Deacon Benjamin Chaplin, Sr., from Mass., arrived in Pomfret, Conn., around 1720. Chaplin, nearby town, was named after Ebenezer's uncle who had funded the village church. Benjamin Chaplin, Ebenezer's son, later kept a diary of his father's and his own daily activities during 1792, the year his father was dismissed from his position as minister. Henry Shumway wrote about the problems surrounding his dismissal in *An Old Minister*, published in 1883.

Ebenezer Chaplin, Jr., studied divinity at Yale under the Rev. Dr. David Hall (H.U., 1724), pastor of Sutton's First Parish. After his graduation from Yale in 1763, Chaplin became minister in 1764 of the nearby Second Parish in a town later named Millbury. In 1791 Chaplin was accused of ill treatment toward his daughter because of his disapproval of her suitor, and he was subsequently dismissed by vote of the parish in 1792. His surviving sons became physicians.

Despite his earlier Boston publications and the special agreement initially made with the congregation, Chaplin brought his case to the Court of Common Pleas and then appealed to the Superior Court, which decided against him in Sept. 1797. Chaplin continued to reside in Sutton until 1803. He died on Dec. 13, 1822, in Hardwick, where his remaining daughter lived, wife of the Rev. Thomas Holt (Y.U., 1784). His will divided his estate equally among his children.

Critical Appraisal: Ebenezer Chaplin sympathized with the country during the American Revolution and defended the individual rights of the people within the governance of the church. A member of the convention that framed the 1779 state constitution, Chaplin eloquently compared "the Civil State to Rivers," quoting biblical passages from books such as Psalms, Proverbs, Amos, Jeremiah, and other Old Testament books. He disagreed with Zabdiel Adams (q.v.), asserting that the head of state must act consistently with Christian liberty. His basic sense of democratic principles advocated the minister's responsibility to the congregation and his belief that people could decide their fates better than the church councils. After his 1792 dismissal, he later reversed this position in his writings.

With imagination and humor, Chaplin explained in his sermons the basic rules of church government, enunciated the beliefs of Congregationalism, and described the proceedings of the Bolton church. In his writings about Bolton, he relied on Luke and Matthew instead of confining himself to the Old Testament. The sermons and treatises frequently employed biblical passages to defend church positions. The Loyalist Thomas Goss (H.U., 1737), was ousted from his church for intoxication in 1737, and Chaplin morally and philosophically supported this action in his "pamphlet war" against Zabdiel Adams, a cousin of John Adams (q.v.). Chaplin vigorously accused Adams of being a "foe to the liberties of the people." Goss was discharged without a meeting of the advisory council, which was radical action, but Chaplin urged this expediency to protect the people against the ministers and councils that supported Goss.

The case of *Goss* vs. *Bolton* has endured as an important landmark in church history. Unlike his colleague Nathan Webb (H.U., 1725), whom Chaplin called a "star" of "uniform lustre," Chaplin did not avoid controversy. His writings therefore became a crucial part of the proceedings, because the published sermons educated the public about developments in the controversy surrounding Goss and his successor John Walley (H.U., 1734), a minister who, along with Governor Belcher, believed in orthodox religious practices of fasts and secret prayers to repent for sins.

Chaplin was closely involved with his colleagues and church affairs. He published a sermon in memory of Nathan Webb and extended the "right hand of fellowship" during Rev. Walley's installation as recorded in the Sept. 6, 1773, issue of the *Massachusetts Gazette: The Boston Newsletter*. During this troublesome period, religious writings flourished as each minister exhorted his followers. James Wellman (H.U., 1744) appointed himself the founder of the Second Church, but the majority proceeded with a new set of bylaws accepting the Westminster Catechism. Ebenezer Chaplin was installed as Wellman's successor in Sutton.

Suggested Readings: CCNE; Dexter (III, 13-17). *See also* Harriette Merrifield Forbes, ed., *New England Diaries, 1602-1800: A Descriptive Catalogue of Diaries, Orderly Books and Sea Journals* (1923), p. 54; Nicholas R. Jones and Phyllis M. Jones, eds., *Salvation in New England: Selections from the Sermons of the First Preachers*, (1977), p. xi; Charles Lemuel Nichols, *Bibliography of Worcester: A List of Books, Pamphlets, Newspapers and Broadsides, Printed in the Town of Worcester, Massachusetts, from 1775 to 1848* (1899), p. 78; Alden T. Vaughan, ed., *The Puritan Tradition in*

America: 1620-1730 (1972), pp. 98-115; Williston Walker, *Creeds and Platforms of Congregationalism* (1893), pp. 203-207, 210-237.

Jo England-Norton
University of Houston

SAMUEL CHASE (1741-1811)

Works: *To the Publick* (broadside; 1766); contributions in *Maryland Gazette*: letters, Jan. 14, Mar. 18, 1773 (with William Paca); Sept. 9, 1773 (with Thomas Johnson and William Paca); "Rationalis," Jul. 17, 1777; "Censor," May 24, 31, Jun. 7, 21, Sept. 27, Oct. 11, 1781; Jan. 10, 17, 1782; Feb. 22, 1787; U.S. Supreme Court opinions, 2-4 Dallas (1796-1800).

Biography: The son of the Anglican clergyman Thomas Chase (q.v.), Samuel Chase was born on Apr. 17, 1741, in Somerset County, Md. He grew up in Baltimore Town, studied law in Annapolis, and lived in one or the other of those cities all of his adult life. Elected to the colonial Assembly in 1764, he gained prominence as a mobilizer of crowds in the Stamp Act crisis and became a leader of the country party. Controversy and apparent inconsistency marked Chase's political career. He was one of Md.'s earliest and most effective advocates of independence, serving in the First and Second Continental Congresses (1774-1778) and signing the Declaration of Independence. But Chase's radicalism was limited to the issue of independence; it did not extend to sweeping political and social change. He helped to write Md.'s conservative state constitution of 1776. Serving in the House of Delegates almost continuously from 1777 to 1788, he became the state's foremost legislative leader but damaged his reputation by speculating in trade, currency, and confiscated British property. Chase opposed ratification of the U.S. Constitution, charging that it would emasculate the states and establish an aristocracy. By 1794, though, the contagion of the French Revolution had transformed him into a staunch Federalist thundering against the evils of democracy. Appointed to the U.S. Supreme Court in 1796, he served on that body until his death in Baltimore on Jun. 19, 1811. Chase's Federalist partisanship on the bench, his zealous enforcement of the Sedition Act of 1798, and his allegedly unfair conduct as a judge in several trials resulted in his unsuccessful impeachment in 1804.

Critical Appraisal: Like many colonial figures, Samuel Chase was a politician, lawyer, jurist, and only incidentally a writer. Fiery and impulsive, he was an accomplished agitator more noted for his oratory than for his prose. Nevertheless, Chase's published works reveal many aspects of his complex personality. He could cite political theory, legal concepts, and precedents for a learned audience, appeal in plain language to common farmers and craftsmen, or launch a stinging personal assault against a political opponent. His prose style, like his personality, was vigorous and direct.

Except for his Supreme Court opinions, Chase's published writings were occasional pieces prompted by political controversies of the day. Between 1764 and 1766, Chase led an assault on the city government of Annapolis, which was controlled by Lord Baltimore's proprietary officials. The Stamp Act crisis added to the tensions thus aroused. In his 1766 broadside *To the Publick*, Chase responded to a personal and political attack upon him by the mayor and aldermen of Annapolis with an unrestrained personal assault on them. This broadside is the strongest example of Chase's *ad hominem* invective.

Another controversy resulted from the expiration in 1770 of the Md. law that regulated the fees of government officials and set the tax rates for the support of clergymen of the established Church of England. In 1773 Chase joined with William Paca to refute the Rev. Jonathan Boucher's (q.v.) claim that clergymen were now entitled to more money under an earlier law. Another newspaper article found Chase, Paca, and Thomas Johnson supporting the country party's claim that the governor's interim regulation of officers' fees by proclamation violated common-law principles and undermined political liberty.

During the War for Independence, Chase as "Rationalis" defended his proposed "test act," designed to suppress Loyalists, that included a loyalty oath to the state. This and other legislative battles, coupled with charges that he had used his public station for private gain, led Chase to explain his side of all the issues in dispute during 1781 and 1782. His 1787 newspaper article supported a bill for a state issue of paper currency to stimulate the economy and relieve debtors during a period of depression. Chase's exposition of his theory of political representation makes this article the most significant of his newspaper essays.

The trenchant legal and constitutional analysis contained in Chase's judicial opinions made him one of the most significant associate justices of the early Supreme Court. In *Ware* vs. *Hylton* (1796), Chase defended the supremacy of national treaties over state laws. In *Hylton* vs. *United States* (1796), he ruled on the constitutional meaning of "direct taxes" and implied that the Supreme Court could strike down an unconstitutional act of Congress. Chase's opinion in *Calder* vs. *Bull* (1798) contained a lasting definition of ex post facto laws, and in the circuit court case of *United States* vs. *Worrall* (1798), he contended that the U.S. had no common law.

Suggested Readings: DAB; T_2. *See also* Robin D. Coblentz, "The Judicial Career of Samuel Chase, 1796-1811" (M.A. thesis, Columbia Univ., 1966); Irving Dilliard, "Samuel Chase" in *The Justices of the United States Supreme Court, 1789-1969: Their Lives and Major Opinions*, ed. Leon Friedman and Fred L. Israel (1969), I, 185-197; James Haw, Francis F. Beirne, Rosamond R. Beirne, and R. Samuel Jett, *Stormy Patriot: The Life of Samuel Chase* (1980); *Report of the Trial of the Hon. Samuel Chase...Taken in Short Hand by Charles Evans* (1805); Neil Strawser, "The Early Life of Samuel Chase" (M.A. thesis, George Washington Univ., 1958); idem, "Samuel Chase and the Annapolis Paper War," MdHM, 57 (1962), 177-194; Anne Y. Zimmer, "The

'Paper War' in Maryland, 1772-73: The Paca-Chase Political Philosophy Tested," MdHM, 71 (1976), 177-193.

James Haw
Indiana University-Purdue University

THOMAS CHASE (c. 1703-c. 1780)

Works: "In Every Charm Some Glorious Goddess Place," *Maryland Gazette*, Feb. 11, 1746; "See lovely R———, Happy, Hapless Maid," *Maryland Gazette*, Feb. 11, 1746; "To Thyrsis," *American Magazine*, 1 (1758), 605-607.

Biography: Thomas Chase was born in Eng. sometime around 1703. The boy Thomas went to Eton from his native St. Giles. At St. John's College, Cambridge, where he was educated, Chase studied medicine, won several college honors, and tutored students in Latin and Hebrew. After graduation, personal pressures sent Chase to the W. Ind., but preferring a career in the ministry to the practice of medicine, Chase returned to Eng., where he was ordained a deacon in the Church of England (Jan. 7, 1738) and eventually a priest (Feb. 11, 1738).

In 1739 Chase and his wife, Matilda Walker, settled in Somerset County, Md., and upon the death of Benedict Bourdillon in 1745, he assumed the position of rector at St. Paul's in Baltimore. In 1740, just one year after her marriage, Matilda Chase died while giving birth to a son. In 1763 Chase married Ann Birch, and they had three sons and two daughters. He died in Md. sometime around 1780. His son Samuel Chase (q.v.) became one of the most distinguished patriot-preachers of the American Revolution.

On July 4, 1976, Mayor William Donald Schaefer assisted at the rededication ceremony of the gravestones of Thomas Chase and Samuel Chase and of William Barney in Old St. Paul's Cemetery, in Baltimore. The mayor read a portion of the Declaration of Independence. Surely the independent spirit was personified by Thomas Chase. The counterbalancing trait, the "spirit of subordination and obedience to government," in the words of George Washington's (q.v.) prayer used at the ceremony, was much more difficult for Chase to personify. He displayed through most of his life the opposite of that "pacific temper" prayed for by Washington. Rather, Chase was Hector St. Jean de Crèvecoeur's (q.v.) "litigious" type, though Chase never got "purse-proud" by his litigation. Still, at life's end, Thomas Chase performed one civil act of obedience: in Feb. 1778, he took the oath of allegiance to the new United States. He was, however, to use John Adams's (q.v.) words, "not so zealous a Whig as his son." Whether he chose a particular cross, of cure or candle, and how obedient he was to that calling, we may fairly say that Rev. Thomas Chase made a very deep and favorable impression in the classroom and in the sanctuary. His greatest contribution probably was not so much in what he wrote as in the republican values of patriotism and self-sacrifice which he preached and taught.

Critical Appraisal: Thomas Chase's publications were few and scattered. In the fragments of his poems as quoted by Dr. Alexander Hamilton (q.v.) in the *Maryland Gazette*, Chase put a deft hand to his heroic couplets and made good use of invention. In the Maryland Diocesan Archives, on deposit in the Maryland Historical Society, are approximately twenty sermons, nearly half of which are in fragmentary form, done in the traditional manner—the tripartite doctrine from text with applications—in octavo manuscripts bearing dates when, and churches where the sermons were given. J.A. Leo Lemay saw Chase as a possible author of "To Thyrsis," an eighty-three-line poem in the *American Magazine* (1: 605-607), but he found Thomas Cradock (q.v.) the likelier author. Lemay did, however, credit Chase with coauthoring "The Baltimore Belles," a scatological satire. Regrettably, Chase's most substantial work has yet to be edited for publication: a two-volume translation of "Silius Italicus' PUNICKS," which, with Chase's full annotations, converts into nearly 14,000 lines of heroic couplets, the epic hexameters of the original, numbering more than 12,000 lines. Chase tried to condense Silius without losing the pace and vividness which have made Silius, in recent years, relatively a critical success with scholars and translators. The manuscript for this work is housed in the collections of the Maryland Historical Society. Two additional volumes of working manuscript accompany the translation.

Nonetheless, Chase's greatness probably lies in the fact that he made others greater. It is well that his preaching, as James Haw said, was "well attended and much talked of in Baltimore," about 1773. But it is a better thing to know that he tried to shape the mind of his son Samuel Chase for the sacred service in the kingdom of believers and for an epic service to the American public, which would have thrilled the heart of that old patriot Silius Italicus.

Suggested Readings: CCMDG. *See also* Robert Barnes, "Somerset Parish Records," MdHM, 69 (1974), 418; Francis F. Beirne, *St. Paul's Parish Baltimore: A Chronicle of the Mother Church* (1967), pp. 15-24; Rosamund R. Beirne, "The Reverend Thomas Chase: Pugnacious Parson," MdHM, 59 (1964), 1-14; Richard Beale Davis, *Intellectual Life in the Colonial South*, 3 vols. (1978), II, 743, 749; III, 1385-1386, 1390; James Haw et al., *Stormy Patriot: The Life of Samuel Chase* (1980), pp. 3-7, 12, 20, 33, 102-103; F. W. Kates, *Bridge Across Four Centuries: The Clergy of St. Paul's* (1957), pp. 14-16; J. A. Leo Lemay, Appendix, *A Bibliographical Guide to the Study of Southern Literature*, ed. Louis D. Rubin (1969), p. 340; idem, *Men of Letters in Colonial Maryland* (1972), pp. 190-191, 193-194, 197, 200, 229-230, 325-329, 333; Nelson W. Rightmyer, *Maryland's Established Church* (1956), p. 169; Carol L. van Voorst, "The Anglican Clergy in Maryland: 1692-1776" (Ph.D. diss., Princeton Univ. (1978), p. 234.

Fred R. MacFadden
Coppin State College

CHARLES CHAUNCY (c. 1592-1672)

Works: *The Retraction* (1641); *The Doctrine of the Sacrament* (1642); *God's Mercy* (1655); [Hebrew for "The LORD is our righteousness"], *or The Plain Doctrine of the Justification* (1659); *Anti-Synodalia Americana* (1662).

Biography: Although some authorities, following Cotton Mather (q.v.), list 1589 as his year of birth, it is widely accepted that Charles Chauncy, son of George and Agnes (Welch) Chauncy, was born in 1592, for he was baptized on Nov. 5 of that year at Yardley-bury, Herts, Eng. Educated at Westminster School, London, and Trinity College, Cambridge (B.A., 1613-1614; M.A., 1617; Bachelor of Divinity, 1624), Chauncy was Greek lecturer at Trinity College from 1624-1626; vicar of St. Michael's Church, Cambridge, in 1626; of Ware, Herts, from 1627 to 1633; and of Marston, St. Laurence, Northants, from 1633 to 1637.

On several occasions, Chauncy was charged with breaches of church discipline and was even forced to recant various Puritan convictions. For his objections to "railing" the communion table, he was briefly suspended from office and imprisoned. Perhaps anticipating further trouble in Eng., Chauncy immigrated to Mass. early in 1638, settling in Plymouth as assistant minister of the Congregational Church. When Chauncy was at Plymouth, a controversy erupted over his views that baptism should be administered only by immersion, not by sprinkling, and that the Lord's Supper should be celebrated every Lord's Day evening. Controversy over his views continued at Scituate, Mass., where he was settled as Congregational minister from 1641 to 1654, and as a result he had difficulty supporting his large family on the small salary paid to him there.

In 1654, with the Puritans in power in Old Eng., Chauncy decided to accept an invitation to return there, to minister to his former congregation at Ware, but while he was waiting for passage at Boston, he was invited to become the second president of Harvard College, on the condition that he refrain from disseminating or publishing his distinctive views about baptism and the Lord's Supper. As president of Harvard, Chauncy followed the example of his predecessor, Henry Dunster (q.v.), in giving the Hebrew language, as a key to the Old Testament, an important place in the curriculum. He continued in this position until his death at Cambridge, Mass., on Feb. 19, 1672. Chauncy's wife was Catherine Eyre, whom he married in 1630. He was the father of six sons, including Nathaniel Chauncy (q.v.) and Israel Chauncy (q.v.).

Critical Appraisal: Until the end of his life, Charles Chauncy reproached himself for his recantation of his objections to altar rails; in his *Retraction*, he disavowed his recantation. Against those who regarded railing the communion table as a trivial matter, Chauncy maintained that it is a small sin leading to a greater one: "the Devill seldome assaults any Christian inlightened, with great sinns, such as waste the conscience and all the World cryes shame of at the first dash, but he begins insensibly with lesser sinnes, to make way for greater." Chauncy argued that rails unscripturally turn the communion table into a high altar and encourage a false worship at this earthly altar, in competition with the true worship of the Christ who is in heaven. He organized his *Retraction* around six categorical syllogisms (five of them third-order enthymemes, with the conclusions understood rather than stated), citing as proof texts from the Scriptures to establish the truth of his premises.

God's Mercy is a sermon preached the day after the first Harvard commencement of Chauncy's presidency. His main topic was the justification of colleges for the training of ministers and the inclusion of secular subjects in the curriculum. In an aside, he rebuked those Harvard students who appealed to the example of the Old Testament Nazirites as a precedent for wearing long hair; according to the New Testament, it is an abomination for males to follow this practice. A century later, Charles Chauncy (q.v.) the younger took his great-grandfather and others of the seventeenth century to task for making such a big issue of this sort of thing. " 'Tis strange, men of learning, real good sense, and solid judgement, should be able to expend so much zeal against a trifle...a thing absolutely indifferent." Getting worked up about points widely regarded as trifles was characteristic of President Chauncy.

Chauncy's *Plain Doctrine of the Justification* is a series of twenty-six sermons, based largely on Romans 3:21-26. Chauncy proclaimed a substitutionary or satisfaction theory of the atonement of Christ, disavowing as pernicious "the *Socinian* Doctrines, that make Christ's death onely for Imitation, and Exemplary." Chauncy's anti-Socinian stance is prophetic of the Unitarian controversy that was to disrupt American Congregationalism a century and a half later. Chauncy sought to make biblical teachings relevant to the American scene; where Old Testament prophets warned of God's judgment against Jerusalem for her sins (II Kings 21:13), Chauncy warned of a parallel judgment against New Eng.: "The Lord will stretch over *New-England* the Line of Samaria, and the Plummet of the house of *Ahab*, and will wipe *New-England* as a man wipes a dish, wiping and turning it upside down. You have more to answer for, than the Indians have." Babette Levy takes note of Chauncy's tendency to parade his learning by introducing Hebrew and Greek terms in his sermons; supporting her point, but curiously overlooked in her citations of *Plain Doctrine*, is Chauncy's choice of a Biblical quotation in Hebrew (Jeremiah 23:6 and 33:16) to serve as his book's primary title. Chauncy recognized pedantry as a flaw in others; he once advised a minister: "Neither use any *dark Latin Words.*"

Anti-Synodalia Americana is a minority report by those messengers of the Congregational Churches to the New Eng. Synod of 1662 who dissented from the Half-Way Covenant measures on baptism adopted by the majority; it was published in London as an appendix to the majority report, *Propositions Concerning the Subject of Baptism and Consociation of Churches.* The preface contains a "slippery slope" argument that the Synod has taken steps toward establishing episcopacy in New Eng. and imposing the Book of Common Prayer on its churches. Although *Anti-Synodalia* was published anonymously, with the preface signed by Philalethes (lover of truth), Cotton Mather identified Chauncy as its author. George Winship suggested that the pledge Chauncy was required to make on becoming president of Harvard kept him from claiming authorship.

While Chauncy was at Cambridge University, he wrote Latin and Greek verse for various state occasions. Three Latin elegies he wrote in America are known, including two that were formerly attributed to his friend Edward Taylor (q.v.). Leo Kaiser and Donald Stanford evaluated the quality of his Latin verse as good, reflecting his fine Classical education. Chauncy's one known English poem is an anti-Catholic satire, published anonymously in John Richardson's (q.v.) New Eng. *Almanack* for 1670.

Ezra Stiles (q.v.) somewhat extravagantly included President Chauncy on his short list (five names) of "the greatest Divines among the first Ministers of N. Engld, & equal to the first Characters in Theology in all Christendom & in all ages." By contrast, Thomas Wertenbaker is of the opinion that Chauncy, because of his peculiar views, "could not be ranked among the religious leaders of New England" and could not succeed as a Puritan minister, although he made a good college president. Chauncy did indeed find his most satisfying calling as president of Harvard, in an age when college presidents were expected to devote most of their time to teaching rather than to administration.

Suggested Readings: CCNE; DAB; FCNEV; Sprague (I, 110-114); T_1; T_2. See also Charles Chauncy, the younger, "Life of the Rev. President Chauncy," CMHS, 1st ser., 10 (1809), 171-180; Leo M. Kaiser and Donald E. Stanford, "The Latin Poems of 'Edward Taylor,' " YULG, 40 (1966), 75-81; Babette May Levy, *Preaching in the First Half Century of New England History* (1945), pp. 14-16, 26, 31, 33, 88-90, 95, 113-114, 122, 125, 133-134, 136-137, 150-151, 160, 173, 178; Cotton Mather, *Magnalia Christi Americana* (1702), pp. 133-141; Samuel Eliot Morison, *The Founding of Harvard College* (1935), pp. 89-91, 371; idem, *Harvard College in the Seventeenth Century* (1936), Pt. I, pp. 188, 200, 320-339; idem, *Three Centuries of Harvard* (1937), pp. 30, 37-40; Thomas Jefferson Wertenbaker, *The Puritan Oligarchy* (1947), p. 151; George Parker Winship, *The Cambridge Press, 1638-1692* (1945), pp. 136-139, 250-252. William Chauncy Fowler's account in *Memorials of the Chaunceys* (1858), pp. 1-37, includes the texts of Chauncy's early Greek and Latin poems, pp. 6-10. In an earlier version of this account, NEHGR, 10 (1856), 105-120, 251-262, Fowler included a translation of Chauncy's Greek nuptual poem, p. 113.

Richard Frothingham
University of Arkansas at Little Rock

CHARLES CHAUNCY (1705-1787)

Works: *Man's Life Considered* (1731); *Early Piety Recommended* (1732); *Nathanael's Character Display'd* (1733); *Character and Overthrow of Laish* (1734); *Prayer for Help* (1737); *The Only Compulsion* (1739); *Joy, the Duty of Survivors* (1741); *The New Creature* (1741); *An Unbridled Tongue* (1741); *Enthusiasm Described* (1742); *The Gifts of the Spirit* (1742); *A Letter from a*

Gentleman in Boston (1742); *The Out-Pouring of the Holy Ghost* (1742); *Seasonable Thoughts* (1743); *Ministers Cautioned* (1744); *Ministers Exhorted* (1744); *Cornelius's Character* (1745); *Marvellous Things* (1745); *The Counsel of Two Confederate Kings* (1746); *Civil Magistrates* (1747); *The Blessedness of the Dead* (1749); *The Idle-Poor* (1752); *The Horrid Nature* (1754); *Earthquakes* (1755); *A Letter to a Friend...[on]...the Ohio-Defeat* (1755); *A Second Letter to a Friend...[on]...the Defeat of the French Army at Lake-George* (1755); *The Earth Delivered* (1756); *Charity* (1757); *The Opinion of One* (1758); *All Nations* (1762); *The Validity of Presbyterian Ordination* (1762); *Twelve Sermons* (1765); *A Discourse on "the Good News from a Far Country"* (1766); *A Discourse Occasioned by the Death of...Mayhew* (1766); *The Duty of Ministers* (1766); *A Letter to a Friend* (1767); *A Sermon Preached May 6, 1767* (1767); *The Appeal to the Public Answered* (1768); *A Discourse Occasioned by the Death of...Joseph Sewall* (1769); *A Reply to Dr. Chandler's "Appeal Defended"* (1770); *Trust in God* (1770); *A Compleat View of Episcopacy* (1771); *Breaking of Bread* (1772); *Christian Love* (1773); *A Letter to a Friend* (1774); *The Accursed Thing* (1778); *Salvation for All Men* (1782); *Divine Glory Brought to View* (1783); *The Benevolence of the Deity* (1784); *The Mystery Hid from Ages* (1784); *Five Dissertations on the Scripture Account of the Fall* (1785); *A Sermon Delivered at the First Church...March 13* (1785).

Biography: Charles Chauncy was born in Boston, Mass., on Jan. 1, 1705, son of Charles and Sarah Chauncy and the great-grandson of Charles Chauncy (q.v.), the second president of Harvard College. He graduated from Harvard in 1721, received an M.A. three years later, and in 1727 became the colleague of Thomas Foxcroft (q.v.) at the First Church in Boston, to whose congregation he ministered until his death. A product of John Leverett's liberal presidency at Harvard, Chauncy rose to fame as the most prominent critic of the emotional excesses of New Light ministers during the Great Awakening, his own theological position becoming increasingly Arminian during these years. During the Awakening, he frequently exchanged intellectual punches with the likes of George Whitefield (q.v.) and, more prominently, Jonathan Edwards (q.v.), against whose defense of the revivals Chauncy issued his lengthy *Seasonable Thoughts on the State of Religion in New England*. By the end of the 1740s, Chauncy was generally acknowledged as New Eng.'s foremost liberal clergyman.

As early as the 1730s, Chauncy began to formulate his sharp opposition to the Church of England, which from the 1720s had been increasingly evident in New Eng., and by the end of the 1730s, he had completed a large manuscript attacking episcopacy, a work not published, however, until 1771, when deteriorating relations between New Eng. and Old Eng. made its arguments even more trenchant. By the 1750s, Chauncy, along with Jonathan Mayhew (q.v.), pastor of Boston's West Church, became one of the most vociferous defenders of the Whig position in colonial politics, and through the 1760s and 1770s, his influence as a spokesman for America's cause continued to increase in importance.

After the Revolution, Chauncy again turned his attention to theological argumentation in a series of writings that mark him as one of the heralds of the "liberal Christianity" of the early nineteenth century. Of particular importance was his *The Mystery Hid from Ages, or The Salvation of All Men*, published anonymously in London, a book that won him considerable fame in Eng. Although in such works Chauncy took considerable pains to dissociate himself from the Universalism of John Murray and others, his radical proposition that God did not doom men to eternal punishment lent support to a conception of a benevolent Deity that formed a cornerstone of the Unitarian faith in America. By 1786, as Chauncy's health began to fail, his scholarly and controversial career ended. He died in Boston on Feb. 10, 1787.

Critical Appraisal: Charles Chauncy's writings fall distinctively into three categories, the most well known comprised of those sermons and tracts that spoke to the religious controversies spawned by the Great Awakening. Often writing pointedly against Jonathan Edwards, the intellectual leader of the Awakening, Chauncy wrapped himself and other "Old Light" ministers in the mantle of reason and attacked the supporters of the revivals as men who foolishly believed that the Christian faith could be defined by the hysterical behavior initiated by Whitefield, James Davenport, and others. In works such as *Enthusiasm Described and Cautioned Against, Seasonable Thoughts*, and *Ministers Cautioned*, he loudly warned against the theological and ecclesiastical results toward which the revivals tended. Although at best these early works are not so much doctrinal as polemical, within them one discerns the seeds of Chauncy's later, more overtly systematic, formulations of a liberal and reasoned faith.

Another group of Chauncy's writings centers around his attack on episcopacy, but these books and sermons treat as well the escalating political crisis within the colonies. In particular, works such as *The Appeal to the Public Answered, A Reply to Dr. Chandler's "Appeal Defended,"* and *A Compleat View of Episcopacy* reveal Chauncy's gradually increasing political involvement as he developed his proposition that the incursions of the Church of England formed another part of Eng.'s extensive plot against the liberties of the colonies. Although not as disciplined a political theorist as his friend Jonathan Mayhew, in works written during the 1760s and 1770s, Chauncy parried still another thrust against the encroaching power of the crown, one all the more important for its allowing colonists to focus their suspicions of the Church of England so clearly.

Finally, Chauncy's later writings on the salvation of all men and the scriptural account of the fall display his attempts at more systematic theological formulation. Although admittedly dry and noticeably unadorned by the forceful rhetoric and vivid examples that made Edwards's theology so compelling, works such as *The Benevolence of the Deity, The Mystery Hid from Ages*, and *Five Dissertations on the Scripture Account of the Fall* display the intellectual fruition of Chauncy's Arminian thought. At a time when his fellow ministers still were loathe to accept the theological innovation of a John Murray or an Ethan Allen (q.v.), Chauncy was able to move New Eng. Congregationalism in an important new direction. Although not directly responsible for the Unitarianism that flowered in New Eng. in the 1820s, Chauncy, along with other liberals such as

Mayhew and Ebenezer Gay (q.v.), began to liberate American Protestantism from its strict Calvinistic heritage.

Suggested Readings: CCNE; DAB; DARB; Sibley-Shipton (VI, 439-467); Sprague (VII, 8-13); T_1; T_2. *See also* Samuel A. Eliot, *Heralds of a Liberal Faith*, 4 vols. (1910-1952), I, 20-34; Edwin S. Gaustad, *The Great Awakening in New England* (1957), passim; Edward M. Griffin, *Old Brick: Charles Chauncy of Boston* (1980); James M. Jones, "Charles Chauncy," *The Shattered Synthesis: New England Puritanism Before the Great Awakening* (1973), pp. 165-197; Conrad Wright, *The Beginnings of Unitarianism in America* (1955), passim.

Philip F. Gura
University of Colorado, Boulder

ISRAEL CHAUNCY (1644-1703)

Works: *An Almanack of the Coelestial Motions for the Year... 1663* (1663); *An Almanack of the Coelestial Motions for the Year ... 1664* (1664).

Biography: The youngest son of Harvard president Charles Chauncy (q.v.), Israel Chauncy was born in Scituate, Mass., in 1644. He graduated from Harvard with the class of 1661, and in 1664 he received an M.A. with honors. Chauncy was apparently teaching school in Stratford, Conn., when, in the spring of 1665, the town asked him to assist a Rev. Blackman in his ministry. For Chauncy, this offer marked the beginning of nearly two decades of Congregational controversy that mirrored the division between "Presbyterian and Episcopal elements" throughout New Eng.

Chauncy's call was officially issued following an approving vote of the Town Meeting held in Jun. 1666, and he was ordained, in a lay ceremony, sometime before the end of that year. Details of this infamous "leather mitten" ordination are unclear, but it is certain that dissension within the congregation was already in evidence. The General Court's decision to require both factions of the Stratford congregation to pay Chauncy's salary until an acceptable colleague be called was not popular, particularly after Jun. 1668, when Chauncy reinstated the Half-Way Covenant that had been set aside in 1665. In May 1669 the Court determined that the Rev. Zechariah Walker be permitted to preach in the meeting house once a day, a "full three hours between the church's two meetings," a compromise that endured until Walker's services overlapped the time allotted to Chauncy and his supporters, who were faced with the need to conduct their second meeting in private houses. Maj. Gould, a Fairfield magistrate arbitrating the dispute, advised allowing Walker's party an additional hour for services, a measure upheld by the General Assembly in Oct. 1669, which added a recommendation that the two sides present their arguments to the Council.

This compromise was enacted, but the strife did not decline. After the Chauncy faction altogether denied Walker and his followers admission to the meeting house, Walker's party first met regularly in private dwellings and then, in 1673, moved to settle in Pomperaug, near Woodbury. In 1675 the Court appointed Chauncy to act as chaplain and surgeon to Maj. Robert Treat's army in its offensive against the Indians. Later admitted to membership in the Council of War, Chauncy was eventually awarded two acres of land in gratitude for his service. A founder and early trustee of Yale College, Chauncy declined the offer in 1701 to become the new college's first president. He died in Stratford on Mar. 14, 1703, "highly esteemed as a patriot and a Christian," survived by three children and his second wife, Sarah Hodson Chauncy.

Critical Appraisal: Israel Chauncy's almanacs are representative of such seventeenth-century texts. In addition to making the required predictions, presented according to the astrological symbols identified with the various planets and stars, the almanac is used to impart both moral and arcane knowledge. Both volumes include epigraphs from Ovid pointedly remarking the fundamental mutability of all things, and both texts contain opening essays on the nature of eclipses. Chauncy's statement of 1663, an examination of thoughts by "approved Authors," for example, refers to the importance of the particular "asterism" or form the eclipse takes. If the outline is a man, he noted, then humans are to be especially affected; if the form is that of a four-footed creature, then heavier repercussions are to be expected in the animal world. Of similar importance is the "Triplicity" involved, as, for instance, "In the airy and humane Triplicity, it presageth Famine and pestilent Diseases, and commonly brings Tempestuous and stormy Winds." But the ultimate factor cited is "the Lord of the eclipses," the force responsible for more specific effects of the eclipse—Saturn's bearing on increased storminess, Jupiter's relevance to good health and tranquility, Mercury's influence on "dry Diseases, Coughs, and Consumptions." Here, as well as in the 1663 essays establishing the absurdity of believing planetary orbs to have solid form, an extended rehearsal of "if...then" postulates, Chauncy supported his argument with quotations from Greek and Latin worthies, implicitly inviting readers to recognize him as a learned man. The most curious feature of this almanac, perhaps, is the reference to Isaiah 40:26 positioned immediately after the lines from Ovid, for in exhorting readers to lift their eyes to the heavens and consider the Creator of all, Chauncy expeditiously pointed to the blend of pagan and Christian theory undergirding the almanac's directives.

Suggested Readings: CCNE; FCNEV; Sibley-Shipton (II, 82-87). *See also* Joseph B. Felt, *The Ecclesiastical History of New England* (1862), II, 409-411, 467-473.

Cheryl Z. Oreovicz
Purdue University

NATHANIEL CHAUNCY (1639-1685)

Works: *An Almanack* (1662).
Biography: Nathaniel Chauncy was one of a pair of twin sons born in 1639

to Charles Chauncy (q.v.) and Catherine (Eyre) Chauncy at Plymouth, Mass. Their father, a celebrated Hebrew scholar who later became the second president of Harvard College, gave his twin sons Old Testament names. In Hebrew, Nathaniel means "gift of God" and Elnathan means "God has given." Concerning their baptism at Scituate in Dec. 1641, John Winthrop (q.v.) reported that "Mr. Chauncey of Scituate persevered in his opinion of dipping in baptism and practiced accordingly, first upon two of his own, which being in very cold weather, one of them swooned away." Both twins, however, survived their baptism, growing up to graduate together from Harvard in 1661 and to receive the M.A. from Harvard in 1664.

From 1663 to 1666, Nathaniel Chauncy was a tutor and fellow at Harvard, and from 1667 to 1680, he served as a Congregational minister at Windsor, Conn. Perpetually engaged in controversy, Chauncy frequently used the pulpit to criticize other preachers. Eventually, the members of his congregation became divided in their feelings toward him, and a minority withdrew to form a second church at Windsor. On Nov. 12, 1673, Chauncy married Abigail Strong, at Northampton, Mass. They had four children, including Nathaniel (1681-1756), who was the only member of the first graduating class of Yale College (1702). From 1680 to 1685, Chauncy served as minister of the Congregational Church at Hatfield, Conn., where he died on Nov. 4, 1685. Chauncy's twin brother Elnathan became a physician, practicing in Boston. He died at Barbados around 1684, leaving a widow, Thomazin (or *Thomasine*), but no surviving children.

Critical Appraisal: While at Harvard, Nathaniel Chauncy prepared the 1662 edition of the annual New Eng. *Almanack* for publication at Cambridge. The almanacs in that series were largely astronomical and Chauncy contributed to his edition a pair of poems on astronomical themes.

In "Upon the Eclipse of the Moon" (twelve lines), Chauncy described "the Queen of Night" as putting on "a Mourning Veile and Sable Gown / To paint her Sorrow," because her husband, the fiery sun, "seems to frown" at her. Her tears cause the high spring tides to rise:

Now in a Melancholy fitt she throwes,
And brooks no Comfort of her darksome woes,
But one poor Vessell, Almost Dround in Tears;
Which Tells us Women Leak when shott with feares;
Heavens now conspire to wreak some Female Greife
Which till some Males return findes no Releife.

These awkward and stumbling lines are of little interest, except perhaps to demonstrate that young Chauncy held a stereotyped view of women as frail and weepy creatures, emotionally dependent on the men in their lives.

Of similar quality is "New Englands Zodiake," in which Chauncy baptized the Zodiac by associating its signs with various themes of Christian faith and life.

Thy RAM for clothing is the Lamb of God:
Thine OX, unmuzled that thy Corne out-trod:

Thy TWINS, the Loving Saints Communion is.
Thy CRABBS, thy turning back from whats amisse:
Thy LYON eke, thy fortitude and Faith:
Thy VIRGIN undefiled worship hath:
Thy BALLANCE Justice is, the wicked's terrour,
Thy SCORPION, is Truth's Antidote 'gainst errour:
Thine ARCHER to the last end's aiming right:
Thy HORNED GOATES, against the World to fight:
Thy WATERMAN Sobriety would breed:
Thy FISH with Temperance thy selfe should feed.

This preachy poem gets off to a weak start in the opening couplet, where Chauncy has to strain especially hard to christianize the Zodiac: Aries the Ram suggests aggression, not the meekness of the Christian Lamb of God; and Chauncy castrated Taurus the Bull to produce the biblical ox of Deuteronomy 25:4. Regrettably, this same tendency to force metaphors continues throughout the poem, which perhaps justifies the comment of Samuel Eliot Morison that "the Chauncy brothers were better at reading poetry than writing it."

On the same page in his *Almanack*, Chauncy prints a companion poem, "The Phaethontick . . ." (the full title includes Greek words for "out of fire"). This poem is signed "Incerti Authoris" (author uncertain). Does "New Englands Zodiake" presuppose that Puritan saints, who persevere in Christian holiness, will find the world an agreeable place where the signs of the Zodiac can serve as reminders of God's continuing favor? By contrast, "The Phaethontick" issues a stern warning that God may destroy the world with fire if men turn from his ways.

Now if soft clothing for LAMBS fleece thou take,
And Bashan BULLS into thy heard do break,
And Helena instead of TWINS appear,
If from thy first Love CRAB-like thou retire:
Thy LYON, turned is to hare or Fox:
Thy VIRGIN Harlot-Wife for stumbling blocks,
Thy BALLANCE false and from the right is turning:
Thy SCORPION with Poyson'd sting is burning:
Thine ARCHER Shoots at rovers, or selfe endes:
Thy GOAT doth push the Sheep and peircing rendes:
Thy WATERMAN when Spirits down is powring
Thy FISHES, as was Jonah's, are devouring,
  Then Phaeton hath left th' Ecliptick way
  To burn up the New World, expect ye may.

In this poem, Taurus the Bull is back in line 2; but Aries the Ram has completely disappeared from the confusing first line, where "for" may be a misprint for "from." Line 6 may allude to God's command to the prophet Hosea that he make the symbolic gesture of marrying a harlot (Hosea 1:2-3).

Since "The Phaethontick" is printed as a reply to "New Englands Zodiake," which it closely parallels, it is difficult to believe that Chauncy really did not know who the author was. Jantz reminds us that the author of a poem signed "Incerti Authoris" in John Richardson's (q.v.) New Eng. *Almanack* for 1670 has been identified as President Charles Chauncy. Is Jantz hinting that father and son may have collaborated on a pair of poems for the 1662 *Almanack*? There is no hard evidence of any such collaboration.

Did Nathaniel Chauncy himself write "The Phaethontick"? The other side of Morison's suggestion that "Nathaniel is possibly not to blame for it" is that possibly he is. Perhaps Nathaniel wrote all three almanac poems but out of modesty claimed only two.

Nathaniel Chauncy's twin, Elnathan, was the author of an elegy on Sylvanus Walderne, a Harvard student, and another on Henry Dunster (q.v.) first president of Harvard. Rough drafts of both poems, which Elnathan probably wrote as a Harvard student, survive in his commonplace book. Each elegy contains a medial acrostic, spelling out an anagram of the subject's name. For Henry Dunster the anagram is "he runnes tried."

Y^e fame of H-E nry Neer shall rust
although he i- S now turnd to dust
[N]o presiden - T in learning's bin
excelling Dunste - R Learned men
from earth to sk- I es he takes his rode
a way wher- E in few 'fore him trode
but he was try' D or ere he went
at last wth tryall he was spent.

Jantz calls Elnathan's elegies "the only noteworthy contributions" of the four verse-writing Chauncy brothers; but Elnathan, in spite of the taste for Spenser reflected in his commonplace book, is not really all that much better a poet than his brothers. Perhaps it is Elnathan's experimentation with anagrams and acrostics that Jantz finds noteworthy.

Suggested Readings: CCNE; FCNEV; Sibley-Shipton (II, 73-90). *See also* William Chauncey Flower, *Memorials of the Chaunceys* (1858), pp. 33, 89-93; John Winthrop, *History of New England* (1853), II, 86-87. On Harvard poets and the New Eng. almanacs, see Samuel Eliot Morison, *Harvard College in the Seventeenth Century* pt. I (1936), pp. 132-137, 216-219; George Parker Winship, *The Cambridge Press: 1638-1692* (1945), pp. 76-81. On Elnathan Chauncy's elegies, see George Lyman Kittredge, "A Harvard Salutatory Oration of 1662," TCSM, 28 (1935), 1-5.

Richard Frothingham
University of Arkansas at Little Rock

JOHN CHECKLEY (1680-1754)

Works: *Choice Dialogues* (1720); *A Discourse Concerning Episcopacy* (1723); *A Modest Proof* (1723); *Animadversions upon Two Pamphlets* (1724); *A Defence* *of a Book Lately Reprinted* (1724); *A Discourse Showing Who Is a True Pastor* (1724); *A Letter to Jonathan Dickinson* (1725); *The Speech of Mr. John Checkley upon His Tryal* (1730); *Dialogues Between a Minister and an Honest Country-man* (1741).

Biography: Born in Boston, Mass., in 1680, John Checkley was educated at Ezekiel Cheever's (q.v.) Boston Latin School and then at Oxford, where he joined the Church of England. After completing his studies, Checkley traveled through Europe, returning to Boston in 1710. A notoriously handsome man of forceful and independent opinions, sharp wit, and good humor, Checkley attracted similar friends, including Thomas Walter (q.v.), John Read, and Mather Byles (q.v.). Outspoken in his views on political and ecclesiastical matters, Checkley proved a thorn in the side of Boston's civil and religious establishment. His contributions to James Franklin's (q.v.) *New England Courant* and his religious tracts defending the Anglican Church provoked such wrath that Checkley was suspected of High-Flyer sympathies, was fined for refusing to take the oath of allegiance to the king, and was later tried for libel. Although the ill will he stirred up in Boston no doubt delayed the bishop of Exeter from ordaining him in the English church, Checkley was finally ordained in 1739. He spent the remainder of his life as a missionary to Providence, R.I., where he was well regarded for his character and ministry. He died in Providence on Feb. 15, 1754, at age 73.

Critical Appraisal: Along with several contemporaries, John Checkley helped to establish the polemical grounds on which New Eng. Anglicans and Puritans would, for nearly a half-century, dispute issues of theology and ecclesiology. In a word, he set the terms for a long, loud, and bitter debate between Puritans and Anglicans in New Eng. Although not an original thinker, Checkley read widely in the literature of the Church of England and in the writings of the church fathers. In fact, his citation and reprinting of this material in itself contributed significantly to the intellectual life of New Eng. But it is through his tracts and pamphlets, however, that Checkley made his most lasting effect on New Eng. Replete with learned citation, they forced his Puritan opponents to take seriously a body of systematic religious thought that they would have preferred to ignore.

Two central concerns dominate Checkley's thinking and writing: (1) to disprove, through reason and Scripture, the Calvinistic theory of predestination; and (2) to disprove, by the same means, the institutional legitimacy of New Eng. Congregationalism. In his *Choice Dialogues*, for example, Checkley argued against predestination, attributing Puritan views on the subject to the excesses of a feverishly overheated imagination. Other of Checkley's pro-Anglican tracts attempted to discredit New Eng. Congregational theory through a vigorous defense of episcopacy as the only divinely instituted form of church government and of Episcopal bishops in particular as the only church officials with the scriptural authority to ordain ministers.

An adept rhetorician skilled in using the rigorous logical and intellectual traditions common to seventeenth- and eighteenth-century religious polemics and legal briefs, Checkley maintained a stubborn but sheer clear-headedness and at times even an acerbic style and was capable, for instance, of berating an opponent for "the Scurrility of his Temper, the Nature of his Principles, and the Manner of his Education." In this respect, Checkley's prose resembles in vitality, color, and force the wit of the British neo-Classical satirists, and it makes us regret that New Eng. clerics like Checkley did not turn their literary skills to a broader range of topics.

Suggested Readings: CCNE; DAB. *See also* Edgar L. Pennington, *The Rev. John Checkley* (1935); Thomas C. Reeves, "John Checkley and the Emergence of the Episcopal Church in New England," HMagPEC; 34 (1965), 349-360; Edmund F. Slafter, "Memoir of John Checkley," *John Checkley* (1897), I, 1-139.

Alan M. Kantrow
Harvard University

SAMUEL CHECKLEY (1696-1769)

Works: *The Death of the Godly* (1727); *The Duty of a People* (1727); *Mercy with God* (1733); *Murder: A Great and Crying Sin* (1733); *Sinners Minded of Future Judgment* (1733); *Little Children* (1741); *Prayer: A Duty When God's People Go to War* (1745); *A Day of Darkness* (1755).

Biography: Samuel Checkley was born in Boston, Mass., on Feb. 11, 1696, the son of Col. Samuel Checkley, a deacon of the Old South Church. A rowdy student, fined for breaking windows, Checkley graduated from Harvard College in 1715, and after a brief interval in Cambridge, he returned to Boston, where in 1719 he was ordained pastor of the New South Church, a position he held for the remainder of his life. In addition to his pastoral duties, which he fulfilled conscientiously, Checkley's other positions of responsibility included those of overseer at Harvard and chaplain to the House of Representatives, whose members commended him for the brevity of his sermons. He also preached the General Election Sermon in 1755 and the Artillery Election Sermon in 1757.

A family man who so liked young people that he frequently lodged students in his home, Checkley was nearly broken by the premature deaths of all but one of his eleven children. Eventually, the strain of this loss affected his work, and in 1766 a younger minister, Penuel Bowen, was engaged to assist him in his routine ecclesiastical chores. On one occasion, Checkley's grief is said to have been so overwhelming that, blinded by tears, he had to be assisted from the pulpit where he preached. In Dec. 1769, eighteen months after the death of his wife, Samuel Checkley died. An obituary in the *Boston Newsletter* described him as a "Gentleman of Learning, one that without any difficulty could preach the truth of any Self Evident proposition."

Critical Appraisal: In some respects, the sermons of Samuel Checkley reflect the more liberal element among New Eng. divines of the eighteenth century, particularly with regard to rhetoric and style of preaching. While exhorting his congregation to recognize the hand of God in all circumstances and to behave in accordance with the civil and religious laws of New Eng., Checkley achieved his ends without the recriminatory techniques characteristic of the time. He rarely intimidated his audience with salutory glimpses of eternal damnation. Instead, he conveyed his views through logic and the plain and simple style characteristic of earlier generations of Puritan prose. In fact, according to the obituary in the *Boston Newsletter*, Checkley strongly distrusted the artiface of "literary" language and veritably "despised the business of studying to please and entertain a curious ear." Nonetheless, Checkley was able to alter his style to fit the occasion. In a funeral sermon like *The Death of the Godly* or an execution sermon like *Mercy with God*, Checkley's tone was sentontious and at times severe, but in a work like *Little Children Brought to Jesus*, intended for a much less mature audience, he was tender and at times even sentimental.

Like most eighteenth-century New Eng. ministers, Checkley took seriously his role as the moral conscience of the community, and his sermons demonstrate the significance he placed on all church-related matters and their importance in ensuring social stability. Preached in 1727 on the death of George I, *The Duty of a People* expresses the need for allegiance, on the part of New Eng., to the royal house of Hanover. His election sermon, *A Day of Darkness*, endorsed the Protestant ethic of honest labor and encouraged family unity within the larger context of an ordered and diligent society, and his Artillery Election Sermon, *Prayer: A Duty When God's People Go to War*, described the proper conduct of the Christian soldier during times of national crisis. As such, the sermons of Samuel Checkley, both in form and in content, provide insight into the various facets and dimensions of the early cultural and literary heritage of the U.S. as this heritage developed and manifested itself in the literature of eighteenth-century New Eng.

Suggested Readings: CCNE; Sibley-Shipton (VI, 74-78). *See also* Henry Winchester Cunningham, ed., *Diary of the Rev. Samuel Checkley, 1723-1768* (1909).

Juliet Ward
University of Houston

EZEKIEL CHEEVER (1615-1708)

Works: *Accidence: A Short Introduction to the Latin Tongue* (w. c. 1645; pub. 1709); *Scripture Prophecies Explained* (w. c. 1685; pub. 1757).

Biography: Ezekiel Cheever was born in London on Jan. 25, 1615. His father, William Cheever, was a linen draper, but beyond these facts, nothing is known concerning his background or early youth. In 1637, after studying the Classics at Christ's Hospital and at Emmanuel College, Cambridge, Cheever immigrated to Boston. Within a year, he moved to New Haven, where be began a remarkable seventy-year career in teaching, first as a master at New Haven's only school, where one of his early pupils was Michael Wigglesworth (q.v.), and in 1641 at a second, more advanced school.

In addition to teaching, Cheever was actively and sometimes contentiously involved in the religious and public affairs of Conn. and Mass. One of the original signers of the Plantation Covenant of 1639, he became deacon of the First Church in New Haven, where he occasionally preached, in 1644, and, two years later, served as deputy to the General Court. When in 1649 certain church elders were censured for "partiality and usurpation," Cheever refused to join in the vote clearing them, whereupon he was himself charged with that refusal and other "uncomely gestures and carriage before the church." Conceding neither accusation, Cheever declared, "I had rather suffer anything from man than make a shipwreck of a good conscience, or go against my present life."

Although he was cleared, Cheever left New Haven in 1650 to assume direction of the Free School in Ipswich, Mass., where he remained until 1661. After an additional nine years of teaching in Charlestown, Cheever was appointed master of the famous Boston Latin School, a post he held for thirty-eight years. His pupils there, as Governor Thomas Hutchinson (q.v.) later wrote, included "most of the principle gentlemen in Boston who were then upon the stage." When Cheever died on Aug. 21, 1708, one of the most illustrious of those pupils, Cotton Mather (q.v.), preached an eloquent and affectionate funeral sermon, in which he characterized Cheever as "An OLD NEW-ENGLISH CHRISTIAN,... as Venerable a Sight, as the World, since the days of *Primitive Christianity*, has ever look'd upon."

Critical Appraisal: Although Ezekiel Cheever has been erroneously credited with several Latin dissertations in prose and verse, his only known surviving works are *Scripture Prophecies Explained* (consisting of three essays on the millennium) and *Accidence: A Short Introduction to the Latin Tongue*, and it is primarily upon this latter work, an introduction to Latin, that Cheever's literary reputation rests. This brief work—little more than a pamphlet—was for longer than a century the primary handbook of Latin instruction throughout the colonies. Especially popular in New Eng., Cheever's *Accidence* underwent some twenty editions by 1785 and as late as 1838 was still being republished for classroom use. Largely an abridgement of earlier textbooks and derivative in format (and perhaps even in title) from John Brinsley's *The Posing of the Parts, or A Most Plain and Easy Way of Examining the Accidence and Grammar by Questions and Answers* (1630), Cheever's textbook was successful primarily for its simplicity and utility. In a triumph of concision, Cheever took the complex subject of Latin grammar and, without violating its complexity, lucidly reduced it to the basics appropriate to an introductory manual. Moreover, as might be expected from so experienced an instructor as Cheever, his *Accidence* is carefully organized and above all eminently designed for practical classroom instruction, thus reflecting the care and patience that, in later life, John Barnard (q.v.) recalled as typical of his old master's pedagogical techniques.

In his formal funeral tribute, Mather noted that "when *Scholars* came to be

Admitted into the *Colledge*, they who came from the *Cheeverian Education*"
were generally the most accomplished. Living at a time and place where a single
schoolmaster necessarily wielded an influence far greater than might be the case
in more settled cultures, Cheever—both directly through his professional career
and indirectly through his textbook—played a crucial role in establishing a
Classical tradition in pre-Revolutionary America.

Suggested Readings: DAB; FCNEV. *See also* Henry Barnard, *Memoirs of Teachers
and Educators* (1859); Elizabeth Gould, *Ezekiel Cheever, Schoolmaster* (1904); J. T.
Hassam, *The Cheever Family* (1896); Cotton Mather, *A Funeral Sermon upon Mr.
Ezekiel Cheever* (1708).

Richard I. Cook
Kent State University

SAMUEL CHEEVER (1639-1724)

Works: *An Almanack for . . . 1660* (1660); *An Almanack for . . . 1661* (1661));
Gods Sovereign Government (1712)

Biography: Samuel Cheever, a 1659 graduate of Harvard College and a
Congregational minister, was born on Sept. 22, 1639, in New Haven, Conn., the
oldest child of the celebrated New Eng. schoolmaster Ezekiel Cheever (q.v.).
After completing his undergraduate education, Cheever served as the compiler of
the Cambridge almanacs for 1660 and 1661. He began preaching in Marblehead,
Mass., in Nov. 1668 and on Aug. 13, 1684, became the first ordained minister of
its Congregationalist Church, where he served without interruption until his
retirement in 1719. On Jun. 28, 1671, Cheever married Ruth Angier, and the
couple subsequently had several children, among them a son named Ames, who
graduated from Harvard in 1707 and later became the minister at the Congregational church in Manchester, Mass.

Although Cheever signed an address to the Mass. General Court in 1679, was
a spectator at the witchcraft trial of the Rev. George Burroughs in 1692, and
delivered the General Election Sermon for 1712, he seems not to have sought the
political involvement that contemporaries like Increase Mather (q.v.) and Cotton
Mather (q.v.) sought and enjoyed. Cheever died in Marblehead on May 29,
1724. At the time of Cheever's death, John Barnard (q.v.), who delivered the
funeral sermon, described him as "a man of peace, of a catholick mind, and
extreme philosophy."

Critical Appraisal: Samuel Cheever's literary activities consist primarily
of his contributions in 1660 and 1661 to the Cambridge (or "Philomath"—lover
of math) almanacs. These almanacs, which began at Harvard around 1645,
advanced Copernican theory and Newtonian science at a time when the new
astronomy found little support from the clergy of other countries. Sponsored by
the clerical heads of Harvard, they were usually compiled by ministerial stu-

dents, who did not receive royalties for their work but who were allowed to add about eight lines of their own calendar verse to each page. As a compiler of the 1660 and 1661 almanacs, Cheever also added to the astronomical calculations of the almanacs a historical essay on timekeeping and a discourse on the rise and progress of astronomy. Typically, the verse in these almanacs dealt with mythological themes such as Apollo's wooing of the earth goddess Tellus. Following this tradition, Cheever's monthly verses, with only a few exceptions, form a poetic continuum on the Tellurean theme they developed. During Mar. 1660, for example, Tellus became enamored of Apollo when his rays set "her heart on fire," and in Apr. Sol returned the love of Tellus, who "frisking comes o' the spangled floore." But despite anachronistic cannon leveled at mythological figures and Hudibrastic rhymings such as "custome due" and "not a few," Cheever's verses are surprisingly effective, particularly in their witty epithets and startling imagery, and they no doubt helped to foster popular interest in the Classics and to encourage a Classical poetic tradition in New Eng.

Cheever's only other known literary contribution is an election sermon delivered in 1712 before Governor Joseph Dudley (q.v.). Typical of election sermons for this period, this work expounds the Puritan philosophy of God's supremacy over civil officials, acknowledges God as man's creator and preserver, urges devotion and the practice of piety, and ends with an admonition to the people to fear the Lord and turn toward him.

Suggested Readings: CCNE; FCNEV; Sibley-Shipton (II, 38-40; 168-185; 327-332). *See also* George Bancroft, *History of the Colonization of the United States* (1873), III, 78-99; John Barnard, *Elijah's Mantle* (1724), pp. 33-40; Samuel E. Morison, *Harvard College in the Seventeenth Century* (1936), I, 132-137, 216-217; Robb Sagendorph, *America and Her Almanacs: Wit, Wisdom, and Weather* (1970), pp. 32-34; Marion B. Stowell, *Early American Almanacs: The Colonial Weekday Bible* (1977), pp. 40-45; Louis B. Wright, *The Atlantic Frontier: Colonial American Civilization, 1607-1763* (1951), pp. 116-160.

June Milligan
University of Houston

STEPHEN CHESTER (1639-1705)

Works: *A Funeral Elegy upon the Death of That Excellent and Most Worthy Gentleman John Winthrop Esq. Late Governour of His Majestyes Colony of Connecticut. Who Deceased April, 1676* (1676).

Biography: Stephen Chester was born in Wethersfield, Conn., in 1639. He was the son of Leonard Chester, an early settler there. Nothing is known of his life except that he spent it in Wethersfield and died, unmarried, in Hartford in 1705.

Critical Appraisal: Puritans wrote, circulated, and preserved funeral elegies conscientiously, often apologizing for their artlessness even while insisting that the ends of poetry should be placed before the means, the spirit before the expression. This order of things can be observed in Stephen Chester's letter to Wait Winthrop accompanying the elegy on Wait's father. The elegy is "possibly unworthy" to be read, Chester admitted; yet he did not doubt that it would receive a "good construction" because it was sincere. So certain was he, in fact, that sincerity would outweigh all other considerations that he had the elegy printed as a broadside and sent other copies to the governor's eldest son, Fitz-John Winthrop, and to his successor, Governor Benjamin Leeds.

Chester's verses may indeed be artless, but they typify, in many respects, the practice of poetry in early New Eng. He began with an anagram but was unable or unwilling to make thematic use of it, as an elegist of an earlier generation familiar with metaphysical wit might have done. Nor did he find much use for the humanist's courtly tradition. Several Classical references are dropped in at the end, but the context is so foreign that they do not even serve the function of apposite decoration. The main influence operating in the poem is the Puritans' own "plain" elegiac tradition. Chester employed the pentameter couplets, caesuraless lines, enjambment, and feminine rhymes favored in this tradition, and he followed an established pattern of portraiture exhortation. He began with a statement of loss in which scriptural figures predominate; proceeded to detail John Winthrop's (q.v.) life and character, emphasizing his particular talents as a statesman and scientist while relating these talents to the conventional Christian virtues of zeal and charity; and concluded with an exhortation of the sort that became popular after 1660 and reached a peak in the mid-1670s with King Philip's War. In these verses, individual deaths were almost unfailingly viewed as signs that the New Eng. experiment was failing, and survivors of the deceased were admonished to take heed: "Oh may this dismal loss ne'r be forgot, / Per Plimouth, Boston, and Connecticot." In short, although Chester used the portrait-exhortation pattern without distinction, he nonetheless did so with an assurance born of the knowledge that the Puritan elegist's obligation was to truth, not art.

Suggested Readings: FCNEV. *See also* Robert Henson, "Form and Content of the Puritan Funeral Elegy," AL, 32 (1960-1961), 11-27; "Letters," CMHS, 6th ser., 5 (1892), 7-8; Ola Winslow, *American Broadside Verse* (1930), pp. 8-10.

Robert Henson
Upsala College

BENJAMIN CHURCH (1639-1718)

Work: *Entertaining Passages Relating to Philip's War* (1716).

Biography: Conqueror of King Philip and the most successful Indian fighter of his time, Benjamin Church was born in Plymouth, Mass., in 1639. Church's father, Richard, was a carpenter who had served as a sergeant in the Pequot War of 1637. Little is known of Church's youth except that he learned his father's trade and that he married Alice Southworth of Duxbury, Mass., where he served for a time as constable. In 1674 Church moved to what is now Little Compton, R.I., where he cleared and developed land purchased from Awashonks, squaw sachem of the Sakonnet Indians, a branch of the Wampanoags. About this occasion, Church said, "I was the first Englishman that built upon that neck, which was full of Indians." Characteristically, he added that he took "the uttermost caution" not to offend his Indian neighbors.

According to the Church narrative, he tried, with mixed results, to keep both Awashonks and Weetamoo, squaw sachem of the Pocassets, out of King Philip's War. But when the war began, Church undertook the command of a company of soldiers, and throughout the war, his tactics differed noticeably from those of his contemporaries: he was more willing to employ Indians; he was more willing to adopt Indian tactics; and he was more merciful to captives. Clearly, these differences made him a more effective fighter and eventuated in his most famous exploit—the conquest, through Indian allies, of King Philip.

In the years following King Philip's War, Church was an extraordinarily active man—clearing and developing lands, building mills, helping found new communities. He also led five more expeditions against Indians, mostly up and down the coast of Maine, during the wars of King William and Queen Anne, and eventually he rose in rank from captain to colonel. Later in life, Church retired to Little Compton, where he was killed in a fall from a horse on Jan. 17, 1718, aged 77.

Critical Appraisal: The Church work is an old soldier's memoirs, actually written by his son Thomas Church (q.v.), but from the "minutes" of Church himself. How closely father and son collaborated on the work is unknown, but its general accuracy suggests that the collaboration must have been close. In any event, Church's memoirs are good reading, for they are generally lively, vivid, and persuasive. They also possess permanent value for historians because of Church's personal knowledge of some of the Indian leaders in King Philip's War and because his viewpoint seems independent of political, social, and religious issues. Often critical of colonial authorities, Church never directly criticized colonial policies toward Indians, but he was sometimes clearly saddened by them, especially by the policies toward conquered Indians at the end of the war. Writing on King Philip's War, Church prided himself on his ability to win the trust and confidence of Indians and on his humane treatment of captives. Ironically, the leading Indian fighter of his time consistently communicated a preference for living in peace and friendship with his Indian neighbors.

In fact, Church's humanity makes some of his sketches not only lively and vivid, but deeply moving as well. Most impressive is his superb account of the capture of Annawon, one of Philip's lieutenants, and of Annawon's presentation to him of Philip's regalia. Sensitively rendered, it is one of the finest and most compelling sketches in the whole of colonial literature.

There are, however, few such memorable moments in Church's story of his last five "eastern" campaigns, which are generally less interesting and more apologetic than his anecdotes of the earlier war. In his account of his last expedition, he had to explain and defend the careless massacre of a French family in Maine: the old soldier had gone to the well once too often. In addition, the work became increasingly marred by his personal grievances against the government and by the bragging that the reader has to make allowances for all along. Despite its defects, however, Church's *Entertaining Passages* is, as its title implies, one of the most "entertaining" of the personal narratives written about King Philip's War and is an important document in colonial American literature.

Suggested Readings: DAB; T$_1$; T$_2$. *See also* George Bodge, *Soldiers in King Philip's War* (1906); Howard Chapin, *Our Rhode Island Ancestors* (n.d.); John A. Church, *Descendants of Richard Church of Plymouth* (1913), p. 16; Alan and Mary Simpson, eds., *Diary of King Philip's War* (1974). Alan and Mary Simpson's *Diary of King Philip's War* is a good modern edition of Church's work. It omits, however, the later campaigns. Earlier, and more complete, editions are those of Ezra Stiles (1772), Samuel Drake (1825 and 1827), and Henry Martyn Dexter (2 vols.; 1865 and 1867). Materials from Church's memoirs are commented on in virtually all modern histories of King Philip's War.

Robert K. Diebold
Husson College

BENJAMIN CHURCH (1734-1778)

Works: *The Choice: A Poem* (1757); *A Poem Occasioned by the Death of the Honourable Jonathan Law* (1761); *Liberty and Property Vindicated* (1765); *The Times: A Poem* (1765); *Elegy on the Death of the Rev. Jonathan Mayhew* (1766); *An Address to a Provincial Bashaw* (1769); *An Elegy to the Infamous Memory of Sr. Francis Bernard* (1769); *An Elegy to the Memory of... The Reverend George Whitefield* (1770); *An Oration Delivered March 5* (1773).

Biography: Born on Aug. 24, 1734, in Newport, R.I., Benjamin Church was an important political and literary figure in Revolutionary New Eng. Namesake of his famous great-grandfather, the Indian fighter in King Philip's War, Church graduated from Harvard College in 1754 and began a medical career that quickly established him as a prominent Boston citizen. Three years later, he enlarged that reputation by publishing *The Choice* and by contributing in 1761 to *Pietas et Gratulatio*, the acclaimed collection of poems written by Harvard alumni and undergraduates to celebrate the accession of George III to the British throne. During the 1760s, Church joined several influential Whig political committees and through his political satire became their most celebrated and effective spokesman. In 1775 he was appointed first surgeon general of the Continental Hospital in Cambridge. Despite these accomplishments, Church, obsessed with personal ambition, made one mistake: in the mid-1770s, at the height of his reputation as poet, orator, essayist, and physician, he sold information to the British and was subsequently convicted of treason. Vilified by Bostonians, Church was jailed and in 1778 deported to the W. Ind. A storm, however, reportedly sank the ship, and with it Church disappeared.

Critical Appraisal: Although Benjamin Church's exploits as traitor in the American Revolution are renowned, few of his contributions to American literature are as celebrated. Nonetheless, Church was one of the most important and influential literary figures of his day, and his essays, poems, and orations were popular throughout the colonies on the eve of the Revolution.

Church's best poem, *The Choice*, was modeled after John Pomfret's poem of the same name, published fifty years earlier in London. In his version, Church described the aristocratic dream of the eighteenth-century American: the education and cultivation of the new man of leisure. Although the poem provides a series of choices for this gentleman, it also suggests that the path of success for this new generation of Americans requires a moral and religious awareness. As such, *The Choice* is important not only for its portrait of the eighteenth-century American, but also for its emphasis on a national poetry based on the use of American subjects for poetry.

Despite the applause Church received for *The Choice*, his reputation developed chiefly from a series of satiric poems and orations he wrote for the Whigs. Three poems are especially notable: *The Times* attacks the Stamp Act and those responsible for its attempted passage; *An Address to a Provincial Bashaw* and *An Elegy to the Infamous Memory of Sr. Francis Bernard* vilify Francis Bernard, colonial governor of Mass. in the 1760s, for his ineptitude and dishonesty. In *An Elegy*, for instance, Church called Bernard a "base contaminated Soul / Far Worse than Brute in Nature or in Heart!" and charged that Americans had been "Misguided thus by Villainy and Lyes, / Those Seeds of Discord, Hatred and Revenge!" Church's mock elegy is a fitting conclusion to the reign of a man whose "sordid Lust that Concubine of Power" had caused him to "devour / The Life of Freedom, and in triumph ride." Appropriately, Church concluded his poem by banishing Bernard to some place where "Slave-born Mohametans do dwell, / Whose menial Souls in Servitude delight." All three poems are scathing satires characterized by this use of caricature, innuendo, and name calling. They demonstrate Church's facility with language and his ability to orchestrate the responses of his audience in such a manner as to create the greatest possible outcry.

Church also fanned the Revolutionary ardor of his listeners by employing the form of the Puritan elegy in two other poems written to memorialize two important ministers of the era: Jonathan Mayhew (q.v.) and George Whitefield (q.v.). In *An Elegy on the Death of the Reverend Jonathan Mayhew*, Church created an epic stature for Mayhew and called on his audience, as the minister he eulogized once called on his congregation, to emulate a man whose mission was to serve not only the church, but also the drive for independence. Likewise, in *An Elegy to the Memory of . . . George Whitefield*, Church exalted Whitefield as a hero to

Revolutionary Americans and asked Americans to follow his example in fighting for the betterment of mankind and the principles of liberty. Both poems exhibit Church's combination of evangelical zeal and the techniques of propaganda he had learned in his days as a Harvard student.

Of Church's orations, two reveal his power of persuasion. *Liberty and Property Vindicated and the St—pm-n Burnt* is a response to the Stamp Act, and *An Oration Delivered March 5, 1773* is the address he delivered on the third anniversary of the Boston Massacre of 1770. Both are written in the sermon form and address the tottering liberties of America, liberties in danger from the British and their American agents. Using many of the same techniques he had earlier utilized in his satires, Church's orations were highly popular and quickly helped establish him as the voice of the Whigs. In many ways, then, Church's role in the American Revolution was important. He rallied his countrymen to arms in a time of crisis, and as a man of letters, he was instrumental in establishing both the need and the desire for an American poetic tradition.

Suggested Readings: DAB; Sibley-Shipton (VIII, 380-397); T₂. *See also* Edwin T. Bowden, "Benjamin Church's *Choice* and American Colonial Poetry," NEQ, 32 (1959), 174-184; Allen French, *General Gage's Informers* (1932); Jeffrey Walker, "Benjamin Church's Commonplace Book of Verse: Exemplum for a Political Satirist," EAL, 15 (1980), 222-236; Idem, *The Life and Poetry of Benjamin Church, 1734-1778*, in *Dissertations in American Biography*, ed. Richard B. Morris (1981).

Jeffrey Walker
Oklahoma State University

THOMAS CHURCH (1673-1748)

Works: *Entertaining Passages Relating to Philip's War* (1716).

Biography: Born in Duxbury, Mass., in 1673, Thomas Church was the first of fourteen children born to Benjamin Church (q.v.), the celebrated Indian fighter in King Philip's War and founder of Bristol, R.I. His grandfather, Richard Church, emigrated from Eng. to Mass. with John Winthrop (q.v.) on board the *Arbella* in 1630. Few details exist of Thomas Church's early life. Like most men of his age, he probably attended Harvard. He settled in Little Compton and was married three times. Widowed twice, his last wife, Sarah, outlived him, and like his father, he had fourteen children. His most notable accomplishment was his publication of *Entertaining Passages Relating to Philip's War*, a narrative describing his father's expeditions and adventures in the Indian wars. Thomas Church died in 1748 in Little Compton.

Critical Appraisal: Thomas Church published but one work: *Entertaining Passages Relating to Philip's War*. Written from memoranda kept by his father, Benjamin Church, *Entertaining Passages* chronicles not only his father's adventures in King Philip's War, but also his "Expeditions More Lately Made

Against the Common Enemy, and Indian Rebels, in the Eastern Parts of New-England." Published in 1712, the book became an instant best-seller and stirred, according to contemporary accounts, the "very heart" of New Eng. Church's book appears to have been popular with all ages of readers.

As it recounts a soldier's experiences, *Entertaining Passages* contains tales of dangerous and exciting battles, and it establishes the courage and valor of a soldier who took continual risks. Bloodshed, hand-to-hand combat, and dangerous leaps over chasms are all part of the adventures recorded for the reader. One tale describes Colonel Church's beheading of an Indian brave and another of his command of a party of soldiers that succeeded in killing King Philip (the name given to Metacomet, chief of the Wampanoag Indians). The second half of the narrative recounts Benjamin Church's exploits in several expeditions in Maine against the eastern Indians.

Although *Entertaining Passages* is somewhat melodramatic in the tradition of the Indian narrative, it is, nonetheless, a vivid and exciting tale of a man who is portrayed in heroic proportions. Church's style is picturesque and dramatic, enlivened occasionally by humor. Yet the book is also authentic, for it reveals the seventeenth-century hysteria that resulted from the Indian wars. Indians are typically perceived as treacherous, villainous, and faithless, and Benjamin Church is characterized as a true descendant of New Eng. military prowess. As a result, Benjamin Church emerges from the "entertaining narrative" as a prototype of the American frontier hero later used as the source for Cooper's "Leatherstocking Tales" and other stories of the American frontier myth.

Suggested Readings: T₁. *See also* Francis Jennings, *The Invasion of America: Indians, Colonialism, and the Cant of Conquest* (1976); Richard Slotkin, *Regeneration Through Violence: The Mythology of the American Frontier, 1600-1860* (1973); Richard Slotkin and James K. Folsom, eds., *So Dreadfull a Judgment: Puritan Responses to King Philip's War* (1977), pp. 370-470.

Jeffrey Walker
Oklahoma State University

JOHN CHURCHMAN (1705-1775)

Works: *An Account of the Gospel Labours and Christian Experiences of a Faithful Minister of Christ* (1779).

Biography: Churchman was born in Nottingham, Pa., on Jun. 4, 1705, the son of John and Hannah Churchman. In his mid-20s, he became an approved minister in the Society of Friends, and he took an early interest in reforming the society. In 1730 he married Margaret Brown, and in 1733 he was chosen an elder.

Along with Anthony Benezet (q.v.) and John Woolman (q.v.), John Churchman was one of the leaders of the reform movement within the Quakers of the mideighteenth century that led to the quietism and the withdrawal of nineteenth-century Quakers. As a result of his concern for the purity of the society, Church-man traveled extensively in the ministry. In the 1740s, he traveled throughout New Eng. and N.Y. In 1748 he spoke to the Pa. legislature about war taxes and the military preparations then being discussed. In that same year, he declined a nomination for justice of the peace, fearing that it would only involve him in worldly concerns. Between 1750 and 1754, he traveled through G. B. and Holl.

In 1756, when the bodies of several settlers were paraded through the streets of Philadelphia in an attempt to arouse war fever, Churchman had a vision that the Indian wars were a punishment from God for the people's participation in slav-ery. After his vision, Churchman actively supported abolitionist efforts among Quakers. Until the end, Churchman persevered in his reform efforts. He died in Nottingham, on Jul. 24, 1775.

Critical Appraisal: John Churchman's sole literary product is his spiri-tual journal, which chronicles its author's efforts to follow his divine leadings from an early awareness of them at age 8 through his adult years as a reformer. In many ways, his journal is conventional: moving from his anguish over youthful frivolities to his hesitancy about his fitness to serve as an elder, and his anguish about speaking out at meetings until, secure in his understandings of the spirit, his uncertainty disappears from the journal, and it becomes a report of the incidents in his traveling and in his ongoing concern with the state of the Society of Friends. Little of the turmoil or the strife around the reforms he tried to effect is reported in the journal. Typically, Churchman merely said he had a leading to visit a certain person or two to perform a certain act, such as speaking to the legislature, and that he did so. Reactions are generally vague and conventionally reported, and the narrator seems more concerned with the full and honest dis-charge of his duty than with the response he received. In addition, personal matters, unless they directly affect Churchman's spiritual life, are omitted, and there is little mention of business or family beyond an occasional note that he returned home and found his family well.

What distinguishes Churchman's journal is his insistence on generalizing and moralizing from almost every incident he reported, whether it is advising nurses not to allow convalescent patients to have too much light, the result of his own illness, or to recommend a mighty period of self-inspection. Eighteenth-century Quaker journals were generally written as cautions or guides to children and future generations, and so moralizing was frequent, but Churchman carried the moralizing and preaching to an unusual degree. This moralizing about the ordi-nary things and experiences of life reflects the Quaker sacramental view of life. In that view, all of life is to be lived attentively and as if each moment is a sacrament. Thus in even the most minute and commonplace happenings, the Quaker looks for manifestations of the divine.

The moralizing impulse seems to diminish as the journal progresses, but the later portions of the journal contain less overt moralizing and greater use of incident and narrative to point to a moral or desired behavior. Many of these later incidents in particular are narrated with a simple and direct grace that characterizes the best of Quaker writing.

Suggested Readings: Richard Bauman, *For the Reputation of Truth: Politics, Religion, and Conflict Among the Pennsylvania Quakers, 1750-1800* (1971); Howard H. Brinton, *Quaker Journals, Varieties of Religious Experience Among Friends* (1972); Sydney V. James, *A People Among Peoples, Quaker Benevolence in Eighteenth-Century America* (1963); Daniel B. Shea, Jr., *Spiritual Autobiography in Early America*, (1968), pp. 10-15; Luella M. Wright, *The Literary Life of the Early Friends, 1650-1725* (1932), pp. 155-197.

John Stratton
University of Arkansas at Little Rock

THOMAS JOHN CLAGGETT (1743-1816)

Works: "Sermon on Love" (1768); "Sermon on Wealth" (1768); *Journal of the Proceedings of a Convention of the Protestant Episcopal Church* (1793); *Bishop Claggett's Convention Address* (1797); *A Pastoral Letter, Addressed to Members of the Protestant Episcopal Church* (1805); *A Pastoral Letter, Proceedings of the Convention of the Protestant Episcopal Church* (with James Kemp, suffragan bishop; 1816).

Biography: Born on Oct. 2, 1743, to an aristocratic Md. family, Thomas John Claggett seemed destined to follow his father in serving the Anglican Church. Educated at the College of New Jersey, later named Princeton, Claggett received a B.A. in Latin and Greek in 1764. Inspired by an evangelist, Claggett studied theology for the M.A., and in 1767 he left for Eng. to be ordained, returning to Md. and serving as rector of St. Paul's by 1769. That year he petitioned the Church of England to appoint an American bishop to oversee religious life in the colonies, but, as in political matters, the Church of England wanted control in the mother country, a problem eventually solved by the Revolutionary War. After the war, Claggett, whose thinly disguised loyalty to Eng. once caused him to be locked out of his church, served his Americanized church with such distinction that on Sept. 17, 1792, he was consecrated its first bishop and in 1797 was awarded a doctorate of divinity. As bishop, he addressed congregations and conventions in the hope of disciplining, rejuvenating, and financing his ailing church. Afflicted with severe arthritis during his later years, Claggett was assisted by James Kemp, who succeeded him after his death on Aug. 2, 1816.

Critical Appraisal: The Rt. Rev. Dr. Thomas J. Claggett offers the reader a good example of a Md. eighteenth-century gentleman whose writing sought to awaken his fellow clergy and their congregations to dangers within and without the Protestant Episcopal Church. Although Claggett distinguished himself more in church administration than with the pen, his published writings served the Episcopal Church as addresses to conventions or as pastoral letters to his fellow clergy. From the early 1790s through 1816, Claggett officiated at most of the major church conventions, and his personal correspondence, quoted by his biographers, contains attractive glimpses into eighteenth-century life and even a vivid account of a British raiding party during the War of 1812. Two early sermons of 1768, written probably when Claggett served at St. Paul's in Md., are on the subjects of love and wealth. Like his letters, these sermons are intriguing but not exceptional in merit. Still, Claggett was bright, energetic, highly educated, and devoted to his cause, and these qualities are reflected in his writing.

Claggett's early 1768 "Sermon on Wealth" is a jeremiad whose theme is the conflict between material and spiritual values, between Mammon and God. The sermon touches all of the bases of the genre—the biblical epigraph, the use of biblical parables, a John Bunyanlike allegory about righteousness under stress. Wealth for Claggett, since it separates man from man, can only be justified by its serving some altruistic purpose, the same theme of doing good evident in the thinking of Benjamin Franklin (q.v.) and Cotton Mather (q.v.). True to Claggett's rationalist and Classical background, there is more sweet reasonableness in his approach to his listener than fear and brimstone. He emphasized the "absurdity" of selfishness and hedonism, that wealth without community-mindedness is an affront to God—and to sound thinking and good manners. He saw this by "the pure light of nature and without recourse to revealed religion." Claggett closed off the sermon with a *memento mori* to dramatize the final victory of the spiritual over the material.

During his lifetime, Claggett was perhaps best known for his conventional addresses and pastoral letters, writings that interest church historians more than literary scholars. These documents reveal problems of the bishopric such as financing the clergy and the church, policing the ranks of the clergy for indiscretions and immorality, and stiffening the loyalties of parishioners against the temptations of Quakerism, Methodism, and Tom Paineism. The bishop's final Pastoral Letter of 1816, written with the aid of James Kemp, is a type, exhorting church members to keep the Sabbath, pray with their families, and do good "publick service."

Once a chaplain to the U.S. Senate, with an epitaph composed by his friend Francis Scott Key, Bishop Claggett is an interesting model of the learned southern gentleman serving his church.

Suggested Readings: CCMDG; P; Sprague (V, 251-255). *See also* James Kemp, *A Sermon on the Christian Warfare; Preached at the Funeral of Rt. Rev. Dr. Claggett* (1817); John N. Norton, *The Life of Bishop Claggett* (1859), pp. 104-111; George B. Utley, *The Life and Times of Thomas J. Claggett* (1913); William Wilmer, *Sermon on the Death of Right Rev. T. J. Claggett* (1817).

Leonard Abram
Philadelphia, Pennsylvania

ROGER CLAP (1609-1691)

Works: *Memoirs of Capt. Roger Clap* (1731).

Biography: Roger Clap was born on April 6, 1609, in Eng. at Salcom, Devonshire. Attracted by the preaching of John Warham, he joined that clergyman in the 1630 migration to Mass., settling in Dorchester, where he joined the local church. He married Johanna Ford and fathered fourteen children. For many years, Clap served as a deputy for Dorchester at the General Court and was a lieutenant in the local militia. In 1655 the Bay government appointed him captain of the castle that defended Boston Harbor, but he voluntarily resigned his commission in 1686, after the revocation of the Mass. Charter and the imposition of requirements that were "grievous to his pious soul." Upon retirement, Clap moved to Boston, where he resided until his death on Feb. 2, 1691. Clap's piety and patriotism were so well known that Governor Simon Bradstreet and the entire general court attended his funeral.

Critical Appraisal: A didactic work in the tradition of the great Puritan spiritual autobiographies of the seventeenth century, Roger Clap's posthumously published *Memoirs* tells how God's providence directed the lives of the author and his contemporaries in New Eng. Like other Puritan autobiographers, Clap hoped that his *Memoirs* would convey to his progeny their responsibilities to God as partakers in the Covenant of Grace. Appended to the narrative is even a specific set of instructions for the would-be saint, including directions on how to search the soul for signs of grace and ways to hold religious observances in the family.

Unlike the Puritan autobiographer, Clap structured his narrative in such a way that his own life is subsumed into the pattern of the New Eng. experiment. Although the narrative begins with a conventional account of Clap's early life in Eng. and its attendant doubts and trials, the primary focus of the *Memoirs* is clearly on the development of the Puritan community in Mass. and not the life of the author, and although he noted incidents as late as King Philip's War (1675-1676), the main emphasis of his narrative concerns the events of the 1630s, when God "manifest[ed] his Presence among us." The narrative thus became a paean for the Puritans of the first generation, who confronted starvation and heresy but nonetheless maintained their faith and survived through God's intervention, and a jeremiad for later generations of Puritans, whom Clap believed were lapsing into a dangerous spirit of declension. Accordingly, Clap closed his narrative with the hope that his descendants could affirmatively answer the question: "You have better *Food* and *Raiment*, than was in former Times; but have you better *Hearts* than your Fore-fathers had?" Although the prose is undistinguished, Clap's *Memoirs* reveals the intensity of Puritan conviction even as the framework for that conviction had begun to crumble.

Suggested Readings: FCNEV; T$_1$. *See also* Charles I. Hambrick-Stowe, "Reformed Spirituality: Dimensions of Puritan Devotional Practice," JPH, 58 (1980),

17-33; Daniel B. Shea, Jr., *Spiritual Autobiography in Early America* (1968), pp. 118-126.

Robert Brunkow
Santa Barbara, California

THOMAS STEPHEN CLAP (1703-1767)

Works: *The Greatness and Difficulty* (1732); *Conjectures on the Nature and Motion of Meteors* (1744); *A Letter. . .to a Friend in Boston* (1745); *A Letter to the Rev. Mr. Edwards* (1745); *The Religious Constitution of Colleges* (1754); *The Answer of the Friend in the West* (1755); *A Brief History and Vindication of the Doctrines Received and Established in the Churches of New England* (1755); *An Answer to an Anonymous Pamphlet* (1761); *An Essay on the Nature and Foundation of Moral Virtue* (1765); *The Annals, or History of Yale College* (1766).

Biography: Thomas Stephen Clap was born in Scituate, Mass., on Jun. 26, 1703. He was educated at Harvard College (A.B., 1722; A.M., 1725), ordained a Congregational minister in 1726, and served the First Church in Windham, Conn., from 1726 to 1739. In 1740 Clap was appointed rector of Yale College, and under the Charter of 1745, he became Yale's first president. His long career at Yale (1740-1766) was marked by considerable success. He strengthened the role of the president, revitalized and modernized the curriculum, enlarged the faculty and student body, and increased the size of the physical plant. Nonetheless, while achieving these successes, he was embroiled in constant controversy. A defender of the old Puritan religious system, he sought to make Yale a bastion of "orthodoxy." His effort resulted in encounters with New Lights, Arminians, Anglicans, and even his own students, who reacted violently to his stern code of discipline and rigid religious policies. Eventually, student violence grew to such heights that Clap was forced to resign, and on Jan. 7, 1767, just a few months after his resignation, broken in health and spirit, he died in New Haven, where he was buried.

Critical Appraisal: Thomas Stephen Clap's major writing was his *Annals, or History of Yale College*. Published in 1766, it was the first history of Yale and is now regarded as the principal source for that institution's early history. Clap's book embodies many characteristic features of Puritan historiography. It manifests a pronounced religious point of view and contains the standard dogma of the Puritan faith. It is structured in the form of annals. It presents numerous source documents, printed in their entirety. It is strong on fact and woefully weak in interpretation and critical analysis. There is nary a mention, for example, of the controversies that raged during Clap's tenure.

Notwithstanding these defects, the book is of singular importance, for it embodies significant facts and statistics on the early history of Yale. It also provides an insight into the curriculum of Yale College and is a veritable encyclopedia of early Yale and an indispensable source for the history of higher education in colonial America.

Clap's *Brief History and Vindication of the Doctrines* and *The Religious Constitution of Colleges* relate to his role as an apologist for Puritanism and defender of Yale College as a citadel of orthodoxy. They are polemical tracts of the first order.

Suggested Readings: BDAS; CCNE; DAB; Sibley-Shipton (VII, 27-50); Sprague (I, 343-351); T_1; T_2. *See also* Louis Leonard Tucker, "President Thomas Clap and the Rise of Yale College, 1740-1766," *Historian*, 19 (1956), 66-81; idem, *Puritan Protagonist: President Thomas Clap of Yale College* (1962).

Louis L. Tucker
Massachusetts Historical Society

GEORGE ROGERS CLARK (1752-1818)

Works: *Clark's Mason Letter* (w. 1779; pub. 1869); *Clark's Memoir* (w. 1790-1791; pub. 1897).

Biography: George Rogers Clark was born near Charlottesville, Va., on Nov. 19, 1752, but grew up on a small Caroline County plantation. While he had little formal schooling, he read extensively and learned surveying. Fascinated by the western country, Clark served in Dunmore's War. Later he moved to Ky., where he worked to maintain that region's ties with Va. After the Revolution began and the small stations of Ky. were threatened with extinction from Indian raids, Clark became convinced that the territory could be saved through war with the enemy north of the Ohio River. With minimal assistance from Va., his tiny army of 175 men captured the Ill. towns in 1778, and after a famous midwinter march under appalling conditions, he recaptured Vincennes from British Lieutenant-Governor Henry Hamilton. Although Clark never received enough support to capture Detroit, his limited success probably saved Ky. Clark also led raids in 1780, 1782, and 1786 that helped curb Indian incursions, but after resigning his Va. commission in 1783, he declined in reputation, and that he sought solace in drink only gave more ammunition to detractors such as James Wilkinson, who worked at besmirching Clark's reputation. Clark's willingness to lead a French expedition against La. in 1793 further damaged his image, and as his physical and mental health deteriorated, he became, in later years, a pitiful relic of the leader he once had been. He died at Locust Grove, near Louisville, on Feb. 13, 1818.

George Rogers Clark wrote only two works. Neither work was necessarily intended for publication, but it is on these endeavors that his reputation as a historian and writer rests.

Critical Appraisal: On Nov. 19, 1779, after returning to Ky. from his Northwest campaign, Clark sent a long letter to Col. George Mason (q.v.), a Va.

friend and supporter, in which he detailed his adventures during the campaign. Although a secretary apparently wrote the text, it was signed by Clark and was obviously his handiwork. Lost for several decades, the manuscript was discovered during the nineteenth century by the indefatigable Lyman C. Draper and was published in 1869 by Henry Pirtle, president of the Historical Society of Kentucky. The manuscript ultimately found a home at The Filson Club Historical Society in Louisville.

In Jul. 1789, Senator John Brown implored Clark to compile an account of his campaigns for James Madison (q.v.), who promised to edit and publish the results. Unable to locate his Mason letter, Clark depended largely upon memory and some available papers to write a 128-page manuscript about his adventures through 1779. Never completed and never sent to Brown or Madison, the "Memoir" passed through several owners before reaching Draper in the 1840s. Now in the Draper Collection at Madison, Wis., the "Memoir" had earlier been consulted by several authors. It was not published in full, however, until 1897.

Although far from identical, the "Letter to Mason" and the "Memoir" closely resemble each other and, when analyzed against other sources, are surprisingly accurate. Although numerous authors of both history and fiction, including Shirley Seifert, George Sentman, Bruce Lancaster, and Harold Sinclair, have depended largely upon Clark's works for their knowledge of the 1778-1779 campaign, neither manuscript was written for publication, and this fact should be kept in mind by anyone who reads Clark's works. Clark was not an accomplished writer. His spelling was erratic, and he used a stream-of-consciousness approach with a fine disregard for punctuation. But his narrative moves, and its crudeness adds, in some ways, to its appeal, especially in the vivid descriptions that Clark provides for some of the most interesting exploits of the American Revolution, specifically the defense of the first Ky. settlement, securing the recognition of Ky. from Va., the invasion of the Ill. country and the capture of Vincennes and Col. Hamilton, and the defense of Ky. against British and Indian attacks. In addition, Clark's narratives display his rare qualities of leadership and personal courage, as well as an exceptional understanding of psychology and the sound instinct for diplomacy that served him well in his dealings, over the years, with the French, Indians, and British. Like several other eighteenth-century American narratives, the works of George Rogers Clark display the vitality that even the relatively unlettered citizen of the period often brought to his writings, and they help to document the emergence of a distinctly American personality and folk tradition.

Suggested Readings: DAB; T_2. *See also* John Bakeless, *Background to Glory* (1957); Temple Bodley, *George Rogers Clark: His Life and Public Services* (1926); Lowell H. Harrison, *George Rogers Clark and the War in the West* (1976); James Alton James, ed., *George Rogers Clark Papers*, 2 vols. (1912-1926); James Alton James, *The Life of George Rogers Clark* (1928).

Lowell H. Harrison
Western Kentucky University

PETER CLARK (1694-1768)

Works: *The Service of God* (1728); *The Scripture-Grounds of the Baptism*
(1735); *A Sinners Prayer* (1735); *Christian Bravery* (1736); *The Rulers Highest
Dignity* (1739); *The Captain* (1741); *The Banner of Divine Love* (1744); *The
Witness of the Spirit* (1744); *The Advantages and Obligations* (1745); *A Defence
of the Divine Right of Infant-Baptism* (1752); *Religion to be Minded* (1755);
Remarks on a Late Pamphlet, Intitled "The Opinion" (1758); *The Scripture-
Doctrine of Original Sin* (1758); *Spiritual Fortitude* (1758); *A Defence of the
Principles* (1760); *Man's Dignity* (1763).

Biography: An active clergyman for more than fifty years, Peter Clark was
born in Watertown, Mass., in 1694. He earned the B.A. from Harvard in 1712.
Four years later, he received an invitation to serve the people of Salem, a
position he assumed in Jun. 1717 and that lasted until his death. He wed Deborah
Hobart on Nov. 6, 1719. Throughout his long career, Clark frequently preached
before neighboring congregations and occasionally before governmental bodies;
for instance, he delivered election, artillery election, and ministerial convention
sermons in 1736, 1739, and 1745, respectively.

Clark, however, is primarily remembered for his participation in several controversies. He engaged in two skirmishes involving the issue of infant versus
adult baptism (1735; 1752). Between 1758 and 1760, Clark actively engaged in
the New Eng. pamphlet war concerning the doctrine of original sin. In addition,
he may have played a minor role in the Northampton controversy that resulted in
the dismissal of Jonathan Edwards (q.v.). Although at times a controversial
figure, Clark was generally respected for his learning and for his oratorical
talent. Peter Clark died in Danvers, Mass., on Jun. 10, 1768, at age 76.

Critical Appraisal: Peter Clark's contemporaries were impressed by his
wide reading, especially of modern authors, by his ability to adapt his style to
suit his topic, and by his participation in the pamphlet war over the doctrine of
original sin. Clark, for instance, is a good source for learning what Puritans were
reading. His many footnotes refer primarily and probably not surprisingly to
religious prose such as Louis Ellies Dupin's *History of the Church*, Gilbert
Burnet's *Book of the Pastoral Care*, and Theophilus Gale's *Anatomy of Infideli*.
Yet in his *Scripture-Doctrine of Original Sin* (1758), Clark cited Edward Young's
Night Thoughts.

Clark's stylistic diversity is also noteworthy, for he could range from exerting
"the energy of Boanerges" to assuming "the pathos of a Barnabas." For instance,
Clark is appropriately humble when addressing the governor at the end of his
election sermon, *The Rulers Highest Dignity* (1739), and appropriately militant
when addressing soldiers in his *Religion to be Minded* (1755). Clark's style is
especially effective in his Artillery Election Sermon, *Christian Bravery* (1736),
which is reminiscent of Joshua Moodey's (q.v.) *Souldiery Spiritualized*. Like his
predecessor, Clark discussed the similarities between the soldier and the Chris-

tian. Armed with the militant graces of faith, hope, and love, "the whole spiritual *Armour*," the Christian soldier can successfully wage war against evil both on the battlefield and in private life.

Clark's ability as a stylist has been overshadowed by his participation in the often vitriolic New Eng. pamphlet war concerning the doctrine of original sin. Clark became involved by answering Samuel Webster's *A Winter Evening's Conversation* between a pastor and three laymen. In his *Scripture-Doctrine of Original Sin* (1758), he again revealed his ability as a writer: he constructed a dialogue between a minister and Webster's "first gentleman" who is confused about the earlier conversation. Clark was silent until Charles Chauncy (q.v.) criticized his views in *The Opinion of One* (1758). Clark's response, *Remarks on a Late Pamphlet* (1758), was followed by two more attacks on Webster in 1760.

Although his first pamphlet attempted to defend Calvinistic tenets, Clark did deny the doctrine of infant damnation, which became the focus of the later attacks by Webster and Chauncy. But his response to Chauncy suggests that he may not have been as staunchly Calvinistic as he has been labeled or, of course, that he was modifying his ideas: "a Man may be a Favourer of the Calvinistic Doctrine in general, and yet not espouse every Point of Calvinism." Even though he played a minor role, Peter Clark is significant since his pamphlets reflect the keen eighteenth-century interest in the question of human depravity.

Suggested Readings: CCNE; Sibley-Shipton (V, 616-623); Sprague (I, 291-293). *See also* Edward M. Griffin, *Old Brick: Charles Chauncy* (1980), p. 122; Cyde A. Holbrook, Editor's Introduction, *The Works of Jonathan Edwards* (1970), III, 1, 13-16; H. Shelton Smith, *Changing Conceptions of Original Sin* (1955), pp. 41-43.

Susan A. Leazer
Illinois State University

JOHN CLARKE (1609-1676)

Works: *Ill News from New England* (1652).

Biography: John Clarke—Baptist minister, physician, deputy-governor, and agent of R.I.—was born in Suffolk, Eng., on Oct. 8, 1609, the son of Thomas and Rose (Kerrick) Clarke. Although the details of Clarke's education are unknown, evidence suggests that he was educated at Cambridge (A.B., 1627; A.M., 1630). According to his own account, Clarke immigrated to New Eng. at age 28, landing in late 1637 in Boston where he took up practicing medicine. Apparently quite disturbed by the events of the Antinomian controversy, which was then at its height, Clarke sought a more tolerant milieu, settling first in Exeter, N.H., and moving shortly thereafter to Providence, where he was warmly received by Roger Williams (q.v.). With Williams's help, he and seventeen others colonized Aquidneck, later called R.I.

In 1644, Clarke was ordained pastor of the First Baptist Church of Newport.

His life was not, however, without its difficulties. In Jul. 1651, when he returned to Mass. to minister to William Witter of Lynn, Clarke and his two brethren, Obediah Holmes and John Crandall, were arrested and sentenced by the Bay authorities for spreading erroneous doctrine. Later that year, Clarke was freed, and he and Roger Williams returned to Eng. as agents for Providence Plantations.

In 1663, after the Restoration, Clarke, still in Eng., renegotiated R.I.'s charter, returning in 1644 to Newport, where he was elected to the General Assembly three times. From 1669 to 1672, he also served as deputy-governor for the colony. By his participation in formulating the charter of Providence Plantations and its Code of Laws, Clarke was instrumental in establishing full religious liberty under a political democracy. Clarke died in Newport on Apr. 20, 1676, at age 66. He had bequeathed to his friend, Richard Bayley, a concordance to the Bible written by him while in Eng. which is apparently no longer extant.

Critical Appraisal: John Clarke's only published work, *Ill News from New England*, appeared in London one year after its author's imprisonment and fine by the Puritan authorities of Mass. for acting on his religious convictions by preaching to fellow Baptists at Lynn. Intended for Oliver Cromwell's Parliament and Council of State as well as for colonial readers, Clarke's tract was written to expose the rigid and repressive nature of the Mass. theocracy, particularly its persecution of dissenters. According to Clarke, while "old England is becoming new, New England is become Old."

As a document that advocates noninterference by the civil authority—constable and magistrate—in the spiritual concerns of the members who comprise the civil polity (in effect separation of church and state), Clarke's tract is of great historic significance. Like Roger Williams, Clarke argued the cause of religious liberty against the Puritan establishment. While Williams pushed his principles beyond their easy, pragmatic application to the religious dilemmas of the time, Clarke illustrated his personal experiences at Governor Endecott's hands as an example to his brethren, also living under the yolk of Puritan tyranny, to follow. Dedicated to the cause of freedom of conscience, Clarke was zealous in espousing its untrammeled expression.

Divided into two parts, Clarke's *Ill News* is at once entertaining, informative, and persuasive. The first part of the tract is a "tragicall story" of the ill treatment he and Obediah Holmes and John Crandall received after their seizure and imprisonment, and the second part recapitulates the repressive Mass. laws governing doctrinal deviation and heresy.

Carefully written in the tradition of the religious polemics of the time, Clarke's story is told in vivid detail for the reader's "recreation" and is structured so as to elicit sympathy while it entertains, informs, and wins others to the dissenting cause. Beginning with a recapitulation of his arrival in New Eng. during the Antinomian controversy, Clarke recounted his meeting with Roger Williams, his settlement of R.I., and, finally, the events of his imprisonment. Sentenced on the grounds of practicing adult baptism by dipping (a crime amounting to murder in Governor Endecott's eyes) and of seducing others into his erroneous practices,

Clarke was denied the right to "dispute" his "Faith" with the Puritan ministers in open court. Fined thirty pounds and twenty pounds, respectively, Clarke and Crandall were subsequently released, but Holmes, already excommunicated from the church at Rehoboth and suspected of having baptized an adult woman, Goodwife Bowdish, in the nude, was publicly whipped with fifty stripes. Two onlookers, John Spur and John Hazell, who extended him sympathy were themselves arrested and fined for "contempt of Authority."

In response to Clarke's *Ill News*, Thomas Cobbet (q.v.), the Puritan minister who shared William Hubbard's (q.v.) pulpit at Ipswich, published *The Civil Magistrates Power in Matters of Religion Modestly Debated* (1653), in which he defended the general right of civil authority to use the sword to prevent "corruptions in Religion" from outwardly breaking forth and called into question Clarke's testimony concerning his imprisonment and treatment at the hands of the Mass. authorities. From Cobbet's account it is clear that the Puritan attitude toward religious dissent was rooted in a strong adherence to control by established authority and a fear of factious rebellion. According to Cobbet, Clarke's wish for public debate, which might deviate from the agreed "points to be disputed on," could only undermine the "Law of all orderly Disputes" and fly in the face of "common Prudence." In the eyes of the theocratic establishment, Clarke and his Baptist brethren posed an immediate threat to the civil and religious fabric of saintly society, but to the cultural and literary historian, his *Ill News* is an important document in the fight for the rights of religious toleration and freedom of speech in early America.

Suggested Readings: CCNE; DAB; DARB. Thomas W. Bicknell, *The Story of Dr. John Clarke* (1915), includes only a short biography of Clarke, a series of biographical sketches of the founders of the Bay Colony, and a history of the settlement of Rhode Island; Samuel Eliot Morison, *Builders of the Bay Colony* (1964), pp. 115-116, for the Bay attitude toward dissent; Henry Melville King, *A Summer Visit of Three Rhode Islanders to the Massachusetts Bay in 1651* (1896); George Bancroft, *John Clarke of Rhode Island and His Accusers* (1863), for Bancroft's defense of Clarke against a charge of "baseness"; John C. C. Clarke, "The Pioneer Baptist Statesman," BQ, 10 (1876), 180-281. John Clarke's *Ill News from New England* (1652) is reprinted in CMHS, 4th Ser., 2 (1854).

Betty Kushen
West Orange, New Jersey

JOHN CLARKE (1755-1798)

Works: *A Letter to Dr. Mather* (1782); *Salvation for All Men* (1782); *A Sermon Delivered at the Church in Brattle-Street* (1784); *A Discourse Delivered at the First Church in Boston, Feb. 15, 1787, at the Interment of the Rev. Charles Chauncy* (1787); *A Discourse Delivered Before the Humane Society*

(1793); *An Answer to the Question, Why Are You a Christian?* (1795); *A Discourse, Delivered at the First Church in Boston, 19th, April, A.D. 1795* (1796); *Letters to a Student* (1796); *Sermons (1799).*

Biography: John Clarke was born in Portsmouth, N.H., in 1755. In 1774 he graduated from Harvard, where he studied Classical literature and philosophy. Having "discovered in early life the signs of genius and industry," Clarke soon became a colleague of the Old Light Presbyterian minister Charles Chauncy (q.v.), and was ordained in 1778. Soon after the ordination, Chauncy died, and Clarke succeeded him as minister at the First Church of Boston. Noted for his rhetorical ability and understanding of theology, he conducted a successful ministry until Apr. 1, 1798, when he died of apoplexy in Boston.

Critical Appraisal: John Clarke's literary style—measured, elegant, logical, and quietly forceful—reflects his religious and political sympathies. An admirer of Bacon, Locke, and Newton, he joined Charles Chauncy in denouncing religious enthusiasm (although Clarke was much milder and more ecumenical than Chauncy in his attitude toward the New Light revivalists in the Presbyterian Church). Politically, Clarke was an unobtrusive "young liberal," using the pulpit to air Lockean principles and impress "Americans" with the "benevolent tendency" of Christianity. The strongest evidence of his rationalism comes in his most popular sermon *An Answer to the Question, Why Are You a Christian?* which went into three editions in Boston and four in Eng. Clarke's "answer" clearly establishes him as a spokesman for enlightened principles:

> Not because I was born in a Christian country;—Not because I find the illustrious BACON, BOYLE, LOCKE, CLARKE, and NEWTON, among the professors and defenders of Christianity;—nor merely because the system itself is so admirably calculated to mend and exalt human nature; but because the evidence accompanying the gospel, had convinced me of its truth.

Arguing from "effects and causes," Clarke went on to outline the "evidence" of Christianity's validity: its ability to measure itself against severe obstacles, to accomplish some of its prophecies, and to prove itself through miracles—miracles recounted by reliable witnesses who shunned both superstition and extravagance. Clarke's insistence on man's perfectibility through reason crowns his argument: "Christians are rational agents," he proclaimed, and Christ "addressed himself to the reason of mankind" to "lift them to make up their own judgment."

Clarke's humanistic principles are applied to more specific issues in sermons such as "The Clearness of Revelation" and "The Nature of Faith," preached during his ministry at the First Church in Boston and published posthumously. With a reproachful glance at the Evangelical movement and its roots in Calvinism, he argued in "The Clearness of Revelation" that the Bible should be read and judged like any other book rather than worshipped in its entirety as an infallible and extraordinary revelation—an idea popular with Deists in Eng. and Europe throughout the eighteenth century. His faith in the Bible as an inspired record of "ancient custom" as well as a source of spiritual illumination reflects his faith in human reason and "historick Evidence" and informs the conviction he voiced in "The Nature of Faith" that every Christian's "religious duty" is to "believe upon sufficient evidence" and "manifest his faith by works."

According to John Clarke's biographer, "his temper was mild and cheerful, his manners easy and polite; and the social virtues of an honest heart gave a glow to his language and enlivened every circle in which he was conversant." His "penetration, judgement, perspicuity, and elegance" are borne out in the single theme that dominates his letters and sermons: the need for objectivity and common sense in all human affairs. Unlike Chauncy, who published a long and vehement indictment of the Awakening in 1743, Clarke repeatedly stressed the need for religious tolerance. "Nothing can less consist with the Christian character, than a bitter, censorious spirit," he once wrote, for "we find excellent Christians among all denominations." His most "censorious" publication was his early *Letter to Dr. Mather*, in which he castigated Samuel Mather (q.v.) not for rejecting the concept of universal salvation that Clarke embraced in his 1782 *Salvation for All Men*, but for exercising "low arts" in his rejoinder to the pamphlet. Mather did not oppose the issue "in a *serious, rational* manner," Clarke wrote, heaping "unprovoked abuse" on his opponent with "bungling affectation of *wit*, and *sly insinuations*." Clarke was also esteemed as "a friend to the rights of conscience and a free enquiry" (his eulogy to another Boston minister) in the secular world. He was a trustee of the Humane Society in Boston, where he once championed "the experimental mode of inquiry" by arguing the value of dissection as a means of examining "the wise and benevolent design" of the human frame. In 1796 he published *Letters to a Student in the University of Cambridge, Massachusetts*, a survey of the student's curriculum charged with Clarke's philosophy that "reason is a most glorious endowment" and the enlightenment of the understanding the basic object of "a publick education."

Suggested Readings: Richard L. Bushman, ed., *The Great Awakening: Documents on the Revival of Religion, 1740-45* (1970).

Eliza Davis
University of Alabama in Huntsville

JOHN CLAYTON (1657-1725)

Works: *A Letter to Dr. Grew* (1687); *A Letter to the Royal Society* (1693); *Mr. Clayton's Second Letter* (1693); *A Continuation of Mr. Clayton's Account* (1693); *Letter to the Royal Society* (1693); *A Continuation of Mr. Clayton's Account* (1694); *The Reverend John Clayton. His Scientific Writings and Other Related Papers* (w. c. 1687-1694; pub. 1965).

Biography: John Clayton was born in 1657 into a family of some means and distinction on a large estate in Lancashire, Eng., near the village of Preston.

Clayton, a third son, was sent to Oxford, where he matriculated at St. Alban Hall in 1674. He later transferred to nearby Merton College, where he absorbed the scientific fervor that prevailed there during the latter part of the seventeenth century. Although Oxford records do not indicate that Clayton received a medical degree, they do indicate that he received a B.A. in 1678 and an M.A. in 1682. Clayton's writings indicate, however, that he received substantial training in medicine, which he later practiced.

Ordained an Anglican minister in 1682, Clayton accepted a position as rector of James City Parish in Va., where he remained from 1684 until 1686, making his home on a tobacco plantation near Jamestown. Whether or not Clayton planned to live permanently in Va. is unknown, but during his residence there he wrote extensive observations of its natural phenomena and assiduously collected its flora and fauna, including some 300 herbs, which he believed unknown in Europe. In addition, Clayton transcribed his conferences with local Indians, noting among other things native use of medicinal remedies. Five of Clayton's letters were subsequently published, in 1693 and 1694, in the *Philosophical Transactions* of the Royal Society. After communicating his Va. observations to a number of English scientists, including Robert Boyle, Clayton was elected to the Royal Society. Nonetheless, he was never particularly active in the society, was frequently absent from its meetings, and apparently experienced considerable disappointment over the ambiguous reception his accounts received from some of the society's members.

The experimental scientific work for which Clayton is best known and that scientists have deemed his most significant contribution is a study of natural coal gas at Wigan, in Lancashire, in which he determined that coal can be distilled with the formation of coal tars and the release of an inflammable gas capable of storage. Clayton's many scientific achievements gain in impressiveness when it is recalled that they were always his avocation, the ministry being his actual professional calling and means of livelihood. He continued his clerical career in Eng. and Ire. until his death in 1725. The date and place of his marriage are not established, but sometime around 1694 he married Juliana Edmundson of Lancashire, and a son was born the following year.

Critical Appraisal: When John Clayton arrived at his Va. parish in 1684, he possessed a sound scientific background and the intention of learning as much as possible about the region's flora and fauna. His training at Oxford had thoroughly indoctrinated him in the importance of detailed observation, and in light of the relative brevity of his stay in the New World, the sheer extent of his collections and the range of his observations are truly remarkable.

Although some of the information in Clayton's writings has been proven inaccurate, it should be noted that almost all of his written accounts were committed to paper several years after his return to Eng. and that many of his accounts derive from the oral descriptions of other observers, from whom he no doubt acquired misinformation that he good-intentionedly passed on in his writings. Clayton, however, was aware of these limitations and cautioned his audience about them. In spite of these reservations, his descriptions of Va. flora and fauna contain materials still of interest to scientists. Ornithologists have been impressed by the number of birds identified in Clayton's descriptions, and ethnologists and anthropologists have profited from his detailed descriptions of Indian customs and behavior. In his studies of native plants and Indian remedies, Clayton manifested his medical knowledge and concern for the practical application of his research by paying special attention to matters such as the medicinal uses to which the Indians put the various exotic herbs he cataloged.

Like Jonathan Carver (q.v.), John Bartram (q.v.), William Bartram (q.v.), Mark Catesby (q.v.), and other early American naturalists, Clayton possessed a talent for writing vividly descriptive prose, a fact that no doubt enhanced the effectiveness with which he communicated his observations during his own lifetime. His accounts of the Va. climate, air and water, and plants and animals frequently benefit from his gift for colorful, direct, often charming description, which nonetheless never sacrifices accuracy for effect. Finally, Clayton's descriptions and findings, enhanced as they were by his ability to command language, helped to establish a picture and myth of the New World in the minds of seventeenth- and eighteenth-century Europeans and are among the earliest writings in that genre of American literature now known as "nature reportage."

Suggested Readings: CCV; T₁. *See also* Edmund and Dorothy Berkeley, eds., *The Reverend John Clayton: A Parson with a Scientific Mind. His Scientific Writings and Other Related Papers* (1965); C. A. Browne, "Reverend Dr. John Clayton and His Early Map of Jamestown, Virginia," WMQ, 2nd scr., 19 (1939), 1-7; B. C. Hoffman, "John Clayton's 1687 Account of the Medicinal Practices of the Virginia Indians," *Ethnohistory*, 11 (1964), 1-40; W. T. Layton, *The Discoverer of Gas Lighting, Notes on the Life and Work of the Reverend John Clayton D.D., 1657-1725* (1926); Stanley Pargellis, "An Account of the Indians in Virginia," WMQ, 3rd ser., 16 (1959), 228-243; Conway Zirkle, "John Clayton and Our Colonial Botany," VMHB, 67 (1959), 284-294. Peter Force in his *Tracts* (1844; rep. 1963) reprints all five of Clayton's letters to the Royal Society.

Robert Colbert
Louisiana State University in Shreveport

JOHN CLAYTON (1694-1774)

Works: *Flora Virginica* (with John Frederick Gronovius; Pt. I, 1739; Pt. II, 1743), and 2nd edition (1762). Reprints of both editions by the Arnold Arboretum (1946).

Biography: Although born and educated in Eng., John Clayton spent most of his life in Va., where his father was attorney general of the colony from 1714 to 1739. By 1720 the younger Clayton was clerk of Gloucester County Court, a position that he retained until his death. Since neither his clerkly duties nor plantation responsibilities were too onerous, Clayton was able to indulge botanical interests that had been aroused by Mark Catesby's (q.v.) Va. sojourn. The two men corresponded when Catesby returned to Eng., and the latter introduced Clayton to the Leiden physician John Frederick Gronovius. In 1735 Clayton first sent collections of dried plants to the Dutchman, who at that time was closely associated with Linnaeus. Both Europeans studied the New World plants, and as a result, Clayton gratefully compiled "A Catalogue of Plants, Fruits, and Trees Native to Virginia" for Gronovius. Over the years, Clayton continued to send specimens not only to Gronovius but also to Catesby, Peter Collinson, and Linnaeus, who named the genus *Claytonia* in his honor. Another recognition of Clayton's expertise was his elections to the American Philosophical Society and the Swedish Royal Academy of Science and his tenure as president of the Virginia Society for the Advancement of Useful Knowledge. Many of Clayton's specimens constitute part of the Banks Collection in the British Museum, where they are still studied. The exact date of Clayton's death is unknown, but his will was probated in early Jan. 1774.

Critical Appraisal: It is important to avoid confusion between the botanist and his distant relation, the Rev. John Clayton (q.v.; 1657-1725), who was rector of the church at Jamestown from 1684 to 1686 and who, returning to Eng., wrote several reports of his observations on Va. *flora, fauna*, and other aspects of nature. Most of the Rev. Clayton's writings were published in the *Philosophical Transactions* of the Royal Society of London during the clergyman's lifetime, but several did not appear until 1739 and have sometimes been erroneously attributed to the latter-day botanist by the same name.

Gronovius was so impressed with Clayton's "Catalogue" that he carefully edited it, adding synonymy, and published it in two parts without seeking the author's permission. Pleased with the publication, Clayton sent additional specimens for a proposed third part. Included in his research were plant descriptions employing Linnaeus's form of classification as well as sometimes lengthy notes on a particular plant. When more than a decade had passed and Gronovius still had not published, Clayton completed a *flora* of his own that he sent to Peter Collinson of London for publication. Collinson and his friends welcomed it and planned to make a grand production of it, illustrated by the renowned George Ehret, but their plans were too grandiose, and before they could be carried out, Gronovius's son Laurens published his father's edition in 1762. Several English botanists who had seen Clayton's manuscript (which has since been lost) considered it more complete than that of Gronovius.

Best known for this 1762 edition, Clayton is not as well known to botanists today as he should be, for his writings have never been translated into English from Latin, the *lingua franca* of eighteenth-century science. Gronovius has often been given the major credit for the publication, but many contemporaries as well as nineteenth-century botanists considered that Clayton was primarily responsible. With Gronovius's collection of Clayton's specimens available in the British Museum, the *Flora* has been and is an important reference for botanists.

Although the *Flora* was a valuable addition to eighteenth-century culture, it is difficult to evaluate it in a literary sense. Botanic Latin of the period was fairly standard and left little scope for individual style. Nonetheless, Clayton's writings have their value as early American "nature reportage." He did include, for example, fascinating notes on the medicinal properties of various plants as well as ethnological data on the practical uses to which country people and Indians put various types of plants. In addition, he often gave the common names of plants such as "Fly-Orchis," "Soopwood," "Spanish Needle," "Pole-Cat-weed," and "Belly-ach-root," and at times his plant description was even poetic, as in the case of the pink *chelone*: "Chelone with the most beautiful flowers painted the color of a Damascene rose." Clayton's comments on plant habitat, association, propagation, and effect of weather demonstrate his strong interest in ecology, and the value of his work can be appreciated when it is noted that there has been no complete *flora* of Va. since his time.

Suggested Readings: BDAS; DAB; DNB. *See also* Edmund Berkeley and Dorothy Smith Berkeley, "John Clayton, Scientist," VC, 13, (1964), 36-41; Edmund Berkeley and Dorothy Smith Berkeley, *John Clayton, Pioneer of American Botany* (1963); Richard Beale Davis, *Intellectual Life in the Colonial South, 1585-1763* (1978), I, 183-195; Raymond Phineas Stearns, *Science in the British Colonies* (1970), pp. 183-195; Caroline Heath Tunstall, "A Virginian in Dutch Eyes: John Clayton of Virginia and Frederick Gronovius of Holland," VC, 28 (1979), 149-153.

Dorothy Smith Berkeley
Edmund Berkeley
Charlottesville, Virginia

BENJAMIN CLEAVELAND (1733-1811)

Works: *Hymns on Different Spiritual Subjects* (1786).

Biography: Born in 1733 in Windham, Conn., Benjamin Cleaveland grew up during a period of religious turmoil concerning established authority and freedom of conscience, in which Cleaveland's family was seriously involved. In 1744 Elisha Paine was arrested for preaching in the home of a Benjamin Cleaveland, probably the poet's father, and in 1746 Benjamin and Anne [Church] Cleaveland, the poet's parents, were among a group excommunicated for separating from the Congregational Church of Windham's Scotland Parish. Their son Benjamin, like many other Conn. Separates, eventually became a Baptist. The title page of his *Hymns* indicates that the texts are suitable for Baptist worship. In 1754 Cleaveland married Mary Elderkin of Norwich; they had twelve children. After the death of his first wife, Cleaveland married Sarah Hibbert and immigrated to Nova Scotia, where a major religious revival took place during the late 1770s and early 1780s. Eventually settling at Horton (now Wolfville) and joining the Horton Baptist Church, Cleaveland died in 1811 and was buried in Wolfville.

Critical Appraisal: Few original hymns were written in America before 1750, and although George Whitefield (q.v.) and the Wesleys had promoted the use of "psalms and hymns and spiritual songs," metrical psalms continued to hold the field for decades. During the latter part of the eighteenth century, the psalms and hymns of Isaac Watts gradually won almost universal acceptance, but not until the nineteenth century did native hymns become well known. In America, as in Eng., Baptists were less reluctant than other denominations to turn from psalmody to hymnody. Many of the hymns written in America before 1800 were written by Baptists, who used emotional, homiletic texts, sung to familiar tunes for both regular worship and for revivals; a few became popular among other denominations.

Among the most noteworthy of America's early hymn writers was Benjamin Cleaveland. From the start, Cleaveland's hymns were unusually popular. John Trumbull of Norwich, Conn., published Cleaveland's *Hymns on Different Spiritual Subjects* in four editions, the latest in 1792 or 1793. Six of the hymns (Nos. II, VIII, XVIII, XIX, XXIII, and XXV) appeared in *Divine Hymns*, or *Spiritual Songs*, collected by Joshua Smith and others, as early as 1791 (the "Third Exeter Edition"). *Divine Hymns* saw at least nine editions before 1800, and Cleaveland's most popular hymn (No. XXIII), "O Could I Find from Day to Day," was incorporated, with a few textual changes, in the *Hartford Selection* (1799), a compilation favored by evangelists. A four-stanza abridgment was included in Asahel Nettleton's *Village Hymns* (1824), whence it found its way into various nineteenth-century hymn books.

Much of Cleaveland's success as a hymn writer rested on his ability to use standard meters and rhyme schemes effectively. Of the twenty-six texts in his collection, sixteen are in common meter (8686), six in long meter (8888), and two in short meter (6686). Alliteration, assonance, and consonance occur occasionally: "By faith my foes shall all be slain / And I attain the crown," and emphasis is sometimes gained through repetition: in Hymn V, for example, a portrayal of God's final judgment of sinners, the word *depart* appears six times. Cleaveland did not reach for poetic effects. In the tradition of Watts, he used homely diction and familiar phrases and images. He compared life to a journey, a race, and a war; he likened troubles to storms, heaven to a peaceful haven; he believed God is man's judge and God's son his advocate. In short, Cleaveland spoke directly to the believer's experience.

In addition to their poetic value, Cleaveland's hymns are significant as manifestations of the "experimental" religion of the Great Awakening and of the theological debate that accompanied it. A conversion narrative, Hymn I praises God for having saved a "guilty soul" and describes the stages from vileness and "enmity" toward God to acceptance of divine pardon and a desire to praise God forever. Praise and exhortation were Cleaveland's dominant modes, and in the manner of a New Light preacher, he reassured sinners of redeeming grace. This doctrine is most effectively presented in Hymn XXII, "Christ at the Door": Jesus waits outside the prison-house of sin, offering redemption. Repeatedly urging men to receive that gift while they may, Cleaveland describes, sometimes graphically, Christ's crucifixion and the agonies of judgment and of hell. But his Calvinism is not austere:

Electing love, redeeming grace,
Spreads o'er the world impartially,
Inviting all the fallen race;
Nor is it willing one should die.

He calls God and his son the saints' "friends" and insists that rebellious man is himself responsible for the fate of his soul.

Yet Hymn XI addresses disagreements and discord among believers—a subject on which a Cleaveland could speak with authority. The poet's grandparents Aaron and Dorcas Cleaveland of Woburn, Mass., had been convicted during the 1670s for Baptist practices. In 1744 his cousins John (q.v.) and Ebenezer Cleaveland were expelled from Yale for hearing a lay exhorter. His parents were pronounced "disorderly walkers" and excommunicated from the congregation of the Rev. Ebenezer Devotion. His father signed a formal statement explaining the dissenters' reasons for dissatisfaction; among them were the church's reception of members who had not given evidence of the Spirit's working in their souls and its opposition to the Great Awakening. Wounded and grieved by dissensions among Christians, the speaker in Cleaveland's Hymn XI prays for strength and charity, lest he, too, injure God's cause. Worded as a prayer, the hymn speaks not only to God but also to contentious and intolerant "saints."

More energetic, though, are texts arguing the power and pervasiveness of sin. Hymn IX, "Wickedness abounding," is a metrical jeremiad illustrating the proposition that "all the land is fill'd with crimes": opposed to the faithful few are "the adult'rer in twilight" seeking "his absent neighbour's spouse," the fornicator, the blasphemer, the thief unmindful of God's "piercing eye," the liar, "the drunkard foaming out his filth." All should take warning from the destruction of Sodom and Gomorrah. Nonetheless, Cleaveland left neither sinners nor saints "wrapp'd in keen despair," for he consistently portrayed Christ as the lover of men's souls. Frequently graphic and sometimes lyrical, Cleaveland's hymns express the central concerns of eighteenth-century revivalism.

Suggested Readings: Henry S. Burrage, *Baptist Hymn Writers and Their Hymns* (1888), pp. 223-225, 641; Richard L. Bushman, *From Puritan to Yankee: Character and the Social Order in Connecticut, 1690-1765* (1967), pp. 164-232; Horace G. Cleveland, *A Genealogy of Benjamin Cleveland* (1879), p. 84; Henry W. Foote, *Three Centuries of American Hymnody* (1940; rep., 1968), pp. 4, 143-171; Christopher M. Jedrey, *The World of John Cleaveland: Family and Community in Eighteenth-Century New England* (1979), pp. 3-13, 37; John Julian, ed., *A Dictionary of Hymnology* (1907; rep., 1957), I, 239; II, 1556; Ellen D. Larned, *History of Windham County, Connecticut* (1874, 1880), I, 415, 459-464; II, 42, 56-57.

Mary De Jong
The Pennsylvania State University

JOHN CLEAVELAND (1722-1799)

Works: *A Plain Narrative of the Proceedings* (1747); *The Chebacco Narrative* (1748); *An Epicedium* (1753); *An Essay to Defend* (1763); *A Reply to Dr.*

Mayhew's Letter (1765); *A Short and Plain Narrative* (1767); various *Letters* of "Johannis in Eremo" (John Cleaveland) in *Essex Gazette* (Mass.) beginning in Oct. 1768 and continuing through 1775; *An Attempt to Nip* (1776); *Infant Baptism* (1784); *The Rev. Dr. N. Whitaker's Neighbor* (1784); *Gospel Ministers* (1785).

Biography: John Cleaveland was born on Apr. 11, 1722, in Canterbury, Conn., where his father, a substantial farmer, was one of the town's leading citizens. Entering Yale in 1741, young John was expelled in 1744 for attending a Separatist religious service. After preaching for one year to a Separate congregation in Boston, Cleaveland was ordained as pastor of the Separatist Church in Ipswich (formerly in Chebacco parish, now Essex), Mass. He married Mary Dodge in 1747; this marriage produced nine children, two dying in infancy. Under Cleaveland's dynamic leadership, the new church grew rapidly and in 1774 received the remaining members of the old church into its membership. Eventually granted his Yale degree in 1764, Cleaveland remained as pastor in Ipswich until his death on Apr. 22, 1799. He served with distinction as a chaplain in both the French and Indian War and in the Revolutionary War. His first wife dying of breast cancer in 1768, Cleaveland, with seven dependent children, remarried a widow, Mary Foster, the following year.

Critical Appraisal: From the outset of his career, John Cleaveland seemed destined for controversy, in both his community and church. The narrow religious guidelines that prevailed at the Yale of his day triumphed when he was expelled one year short of receiving his baccalaureate. In his career as a Calvinist New Light minister and in his later opposition to rule by G.B., John Cleaveland typifies a great many evangelical New Eng. ministers of his era. Typical, for example, is his rebuttal of the religious liberalism ("Arianism") of Jonathan Mayhew (q.v.). In 1763 the prominent Mayhew published *Two Sermons on the Nature, Extent and Perfection of the Divine Goodness*. Although there was little in this production Mayhew had not said previously, the title itself was viewed by Calvinists as a challenge. In his lengthy *Essay* of 1763, Cleaveland contended that Mayhew had depicted God in a way that appeared to make the atoning sacrifice of Christ unnecessary. Like that of Jonathan Edwards (q.v.), Cleaveland's theory of the atonement was Anselmic, and Mayhew was attacked because he was seen to be promulgating the Grotian or governmental theory. However, although Cleaveland had struck at a weakness in Mayhew's theology, he gained little support outside of New Light circles. His opponent's response was strikingly condescending, evincing considerable class prejudice against the "low," "presumptuous" evangelical. In his *Reply*, Cleaveland responded only to the theological issues raised, refusing to descend to the level of Mayhew's *ad hominem* attack.

At the time of the Peace of Paris, and roughly coincident with the new "awakening" of 1763 in which his congregation took a notable part, Cleaveland became in both his sermons and published writings a spokesman for colonial liberty. Beginning in late Oct. 1768 and continuing at intervals over the next seven years, Cleaveland published a series of staunchly patriotic letters in the newly instituted *Essex Gazette*. His first essay (like so many of the others published under the pen-name of Johannis in Eremo) took the form of a strong protest against the Townshend Acts. Beginning in Jan. 1771, Cleaveland began to publish in the *Gazette* a series of articles on the dangers of a plot to install an American bishop in New Eng. His ardent patriotism, manifested in further anti-British polemics over the next several years, brought over to his side individuals who had earlier been his antagonists in the religious conflicts of the sixties. In 1771 he mounted a strong attack against the newly appointed governor of Mass., calling this crown appointee "a meer [sic] tool" and characterizing his administration as one which was depriving the colonists of their most important rights. In 1774 the evangelical congregations of Chebacco parish, Cleaveland's among them, banded together in the interests of "patriotic Christian unity" against the common enemy of British "despotism," agreeing to "bury forever all former differences." In a time of great social ferment, Cleaveland and a considerable number of his fellow evangelicals strove to give their parishioners a clear knowledge of the issues of the day, and then employed the ultimate sanction of the Calvinist "moral law" on the side of the struggle for independence.

Suggested Readings: CCNE; Dexter (II, 29-35); Sprague (I, 458-461); T₁; T₂. *See also* Alice M. Baldwin, *The New England Clergy and the American Revolution* (1928), pp. 17, 61, passim; C. C. Goen, *Revivalism and Separatism in New England, 1740-1800* (1962), pp. 72, 98, passim; Alan Heimert, *Religion and the American Mind: From the Great Awakening to the Revolution* (1966), pp. 142, 242, passim; Christopher M. Jedrey, *The World of John Cleaveland: Family and Community in Eighteenth-Century New England* (1979).

Robert Colbert
Louisiana State University in Shreveport

WILLIAM CLIFFTON (1772-1799)

Works: *The Group* (1796); *Poems* (1800).

Biography: William Cliffton was born in Philadelphia, Pa., in 1772. The son of a wealthy blacksmith, he was raised a Quaker, but as he grew older, he gradually rejected Quaker ideals and adopted instead a devotion to literature and politics. Adept at music, shooting, and painting, Cliffton was forced by the onset of tuberculosis at age 19 to maintain a relatively sedentary life-style. Cliffton's talent for writing satire attracted the attention of Philadelphia's Anchor Club, a literate and secretive Federalist association whose membership included John Fenno (q.v.) and William Cobbett (q.v.). As a member of the Anchor Club, Cliffton wrote his most popular work, a pro-British prose and verse satire titled "Some Account of a Manuscript...[on] ...Talleyrand's Descent into Hell." Cliffton died in Dec. 1799 at age 27.

Critical Appraisal: An eighteenth-century Philadelphia poet worthy of reconsideration, William Cliffton wrote both crisp neo-Classical verse, which articulately expressed Federalist politics, and lyric poems, which suggest late eighteenth-century sentimentalism and pre-Romantic images and sentiments.

Early nineteenth-century American critics, perhaps anticipating Sydney Smith's attack on American letters, found Cliffton a poet of strength and grace, one worthy of comparison with the major English authors of the period. *The Monthly Recorder* of 1813 linked Cliffton with Dryden, and the editor of Cliffton's *Poems* (1800) associated their "purity" and "sweetness" with the works of Pope and Goldsmith. Certainly, Cliffton's satiric couplets and rhetorically crafted lines recall Pope: "The friendly smile, a bulkier work repays; / For fools will print, while greater fools will praise." In fact, many of Cliffton's lines echo English masters and reflect his extensive reading: Shakespeare, Milton, Dryden, and Pope all influenced his work and lent depth to his many occasional satires.

Most of Cliffton's canon consists primarily of political verses such as *The Group* (a satire of minor officials and popular Jacobism), a "Song on Lord Nelson's Victory," "The Chimeriad" (an unfinished satire on Platonic states), and the "Soul of Columbia" (a patriotic song). In these poems, Cliffton decried contemporary political morality and the control of the "changeling mob," and he voiced a firm belief in Federalist policies and a distaste for Jeffersonian democracy. Thus he found the excesses of the French Revolution ("bloody France," as he referred to it) particularly repugnant, and his poems constantly call for the prelapsarian grace and political stability of the "golden age."

This same yearning for peace and stability also characterizes many of Cliffton's lyrics, and his works have been said to anticipate the poetry and sentiments of the Romantics. He typically found refuge in the life of the imagination, and, like many Romantic poets, he was guided by Fancy.

> And now to the regions of Fancy we soar,
> Thro' scenes of enchantment we stray,
> We revel in transports untasted before,
> Or loiter with love on the way.
> ("Song")

Unlike Shelley's Platonic legislator, however, the poet seeks "no hermit's dreary cave" ("A Flight of Fancy"), but rather "the quiet of an humble home" ("Il Penseroso"). If we seek an English biographical parallel, we should perhaps look to Keats.

Like Keats, Cliffton's career was cut short by tuberculosis, and perhaps this illness may in part account for his striving for a well-ordered poetic world ruled by fancy. In addition, Cliffton is also associated with poets and writers such as Joseph Rodman Drake, Joseph Dennie (q.v.), and Philip Freneau (q.v.), although certainly Cliffton would wince at comparison with "that rascal."

Cliffton's poetry offers much to praise: his verse is witty, articulate, and often moving, and although he is not a major American poet, we can agree with one early critic that "the variety and extent of Mr. Cliffton's poetical talents" are more than sufficient "to excite the regret of every one who is anxious for the literary reputation of his country, that he did not live to accomplish some greater and more finished work."

Suggested Readings: DAB. *See also* Leo Bressler, "The Anchor Club: Defender of Federalism," PMHB, 80 (1956), 312-319; idem, "William Clifton, Philadelphia Poet, 1771-1799: A Critical and Biographical Essay and a Collection of His Writings" (Ph.D. diss., Univ. of Pa., 1952); Evert Duyckinck and George Duyckinck, *Cyclopaedia of American Literature* (1855), I, 604-609; G. C. Verplanck, "William Clifton," *Analectic Magazine*, Jun. 1814, pp. 478-488.

Timothy K. Conley
Bradley University

GEORGE CLINTON (1739-1812)

Works: "Letters of Cato," *New York Journal* (1787-1788); "A Proclamation" [Offering Rewards for the Capture of Daniel Shays, Luke Day, Adam Wheeler, and Eli Parsons] (1787); "Address" [on Opposition to the Bank Bill] (w. 1811; pub. 1832).

Biography: George Clinton was born at Little Britain in Ulster County, N.Y., on Jul. 26, 1739. After service in the French and Indian War, he studied law with William Smith (q.v.) in New York City. In 1768 the freemen of Ulster County elected him their representative in the Provincial Assembly, where he soon earned a reputation as a radical patriot. He sat in the Second Continental Congress and, simultaneously, served as a brigadier general in N.Y.'s militia. Much to the surprise of John Jay (q.v.) and other members of N.Y.'s ruling elite, who felt his family connections did not entitle him to high office, Clinton was elected both governor and lieutenant-governor of N.Y. in Jun. 1777. On Jul. 30, 1777, he entered upon a series of six consecutive terms as governor, declining to run for a seventh term in 1795. He did, however, return for a seventh term from 1801 to 1804.

During the 1780s, Clinton emerged as a consistent opponent of strong national government. In 1781 he spoke against turning over to the Confederation government import duties collected by N.Y. As president of the Poughkeepsie ratifying convention in Jun. 1788, he reluctantly acquiesced in approval of the new U.S. Constitution after losing most of his anti-Federalist supporters in a lengthy, bitter campaign. Clinton became vice-president of the U.S. in 1804 and was reelected to the position in 1808. In 1811 he cast a tie-breaking vote in the Senate, which defeated a bill to recharter the National Bank. He died in office on Apr. 20, 1812.

Critical Appraisal: George Clinton's literary reputation rests almost exclusively upon the series of seven anti-Federalist letters that he published, under the pseudonym "Cato," in the *New York Journal*. Several months before the initiation of the series, friends of the proposed U.S. Constitution had recognized the N.Y. governor's strong opposition. In the New York *Daily Advertiser* of Jul. 21, 1787, Alexander Hamilton (q.v.) had accused him of "greater attachment to his own power than to the public good" and, consequently, of prejudicing the country against the Constitution before the document was even completed.

The first "Cato" letter appeared on Sept. 27, 1787, the same day as the first printing of the Constitution in N.Y. It contained a dispassionate development of the assertion that people's political safety was the chief aim of American government. Although Clinton claimed a neutral perspective on the proposed Constitution, he suggested that the unamended document failed to provide future generations with "a fair political inheritance, untouched by the vultures of power." Within five days, the letter evoked a reply from Alexander Hamilton, who, using the pseudonym "Caesar" in the *Daily Advertiser*, labeled Clinton one of those "designing croakers" best known for overconfidence in popular democracy and paranoia over threats to liberty.

On Oct. 11, 1787, Clinton responded to "Caesar" with the second "Cato" letter, in which he asserted that "exercise of the prerogative of free examination is essentially necessary" when proposed principles of government seem dangerous to personal liberty and happiness. He added that "cool and deliberate discussion" would prevent sensible freemen from giving allegiance to a government "founded in usurpation." In his third letter on Oct. 25, "Cato" attempted to show precisely how the Constitution threatened liberty and happiness. Citing Montesquieu, he argued that republican government can exist effectively only within a relatively small territory, not in a land as geographically vast and culturally diverse as America. "Intuitive reason" informed him that power-hungry men would use the Constitution to forge a monarchical government so "intricate and perplexed" as to be incomprehensible to the average citizen.

In letters IV and V, "Cato" examined the executive and legislative provisions of the Constitution. Remembering that Montesquieu had warned against the perniciousness of extended administrative tenure in republics, Clinton challenged the Constitution's vagueness on reelection of the president and vice-president. He also advocated direct election of the president by popular majority. Similarly, he favored direct annual election of all members of Congress and proposed an increase in the number of representatives.

The sixth "Cato" letter on Dec. 16, 1787, addressed the perceived unjust apportionment of representation and direct taxes. Since women, children, and slaves traditionally did not aid communities in their deliberations or defense, Clinton maintained that they should not be counted for purposes of representation or taxation. He added, "A poll-tax is at all times oppressive to the poor, and their greatest misfortune will consist in having more prolific wives than the rich." In his seventh and final letter on Jan. 3, 1788, Clinton argued that the president and Senate were in certain respects "improperly connected" and, consequently, could not effectively check each other, and moved on to condemn congressional supervision of state regulations in national elections, because he feared that such oversight could undermine democratic procedures established by the states.

It may be true, as one biographer has observed, that Clinton's reliance upon Montesquieu, Hume, Locke, and Sidney was tedious and contributed to the dull, ponderous nature of the "Cato" letters. It is certainly true that the letters manifest intemperate dogmatism and exaggeration. Nevertheless, they remain one of the best examples of the anti-Federalist response to the Constitution, and their contemporary impact was significant enough to prompt Alexander Hamilton, James Madison (q.v.), and John Jay to compose the well-known *Federalist* papers. The letters also contributed to the movement that culminated in adoption of the Bill of Rights.

Suggested Readings: DAB; LHUS; T₂. *See also* Hugh Hastings and J. A. Holden, eds., *Public Papers of George Clinton*, 10 vols. (1899-1914); "Letters of Cato" rep. in Paul Leicester Ford, ed., *Essays on the Constitution of the United States, Published During Its Discussion by the People, 1787-1788* (1892), pp. 245-278; Ernest W. Spaulding, *His Excellency George Clinton*, 2nd ed. (1964); idem, *New York in the Critical Period* (1963).

Rick W. Sturdevant
University of California at Santa Barbara

THOMAS COBBET (1608-1685)

Works: *A Just Vindication of the Covenant* (1648); *The Civil Magistrates Power* with *A Brief Answer to a Scandalous Pamphlet* (1653); *A Practical Discourse of Prayer* (1654); *A Fruitfull and Usefull Discourse* (1656).

Biography: Thomas Cobbet was born in Newbury, Eng., in 1608. Despite the humble circumstances of his parents, he studied at Oxford and earned an A.B. (1628) and an A.M. (1632) before leaving to avoid an outbreak of the plague. He then entered the ministry and settled at Lincolnshire. When the persecution of nonconforming ministers grew intolerable, Cobbet immigrated to New Eng. with John Davenport (q.v.), arriving in 1637 at Lynn, Mass., where he served his old friend, the Rev. Samuel Whiting (q.v.), as a pastoral colleague for almost twenty years.

In 1656, his support at Lynn no longer adequate, Cobbet accepted an invitation to succeed the Rev. Nathaniel Rogers as pastor of the First Church of Ipswich. A respected minister and an important political speaker (he delivered the election sermons for 1649 and 1666), Cobbet remained at Ipswich until his death there on Nov. 5, 1685. Burdened in his later years by increasing deafness and ill-health, Cobbet nevertheless maintained a reputation for learning and piety and for eloquent and effective prayer that characterized Cotton Mather's (q.v.) famous epitaph for him: "Stop, traveller! a treasure lies there, Thomas Cobbet: whose effectual prayers and most exemplary life thou, if thou art a New Englander, must have known. Admire, if you revere piety: follow, if you long for Happiness!"

Critical Appraisal: Thomas Cobbet's major works were published during his last ten years at Lynn. They consist of an arcane, although closely argued, defense of infant baptism that earned the praise of Increase Mather (q.v.), a treatise on the familial obligation of parents and children, and two remarkable texts that demonstrate Cobbet's thorough integration of personal piety and public responsibility.

The first of them, *The Civil Magistrates Power in Matters of Religion*, is a scriptural constitution for a theocratic state that Cobbet dedicated to Cromwell that was published with Cobbet's *Brief Answer to . . . a Certain Slanderous Pamphlet Called Ill News from New-England*, written in response to John Clarke's (q.v.) bitter and sensational account of persecution in New Eng. Exploiting the extreme aspects of that persecution, Clarke's narrative seriously challenged the religious and political authority of the Mass. theocracy. *The Civil Magistrates Power* argues the case for Mass., and it predictably echoes John Winthrop's (q.v) famous speech to the General Court of 1645. But unlike Winthrop, who had simply urged obedience to the magistrates as the representatives of God's authority on earth, Cobbet defended the use of civil power to enforce ecclesiastical rules on the basis of the familiar epistemological distinction between the visible and invisible worlds. According to Cobbet, true cases of conscience could not be punished by civil authority, because no "humane testimony from without [can] be produced, how Conscience doth carry it in its internall acts." Any visible demonstration of one's conscience, however, fell under civil jurisdiction, because its visibility meant it partook of the corporal world and was thus subject to its authority. When Cobbet went on to argue that "Heresie and Schism" were "fruits of the flesh" and so part of this world as well, he effectively lifted all restraints on the church's use of civil authority to ensure religious conformity. *The Civil Magistrates Power* stands as one of the most extensive defenses of Puritan hegemony in New Eng., and when read in conjunction with the more circumstantial *Brief Answer*, it provides an excellent example of the Puritans' smooth integration of scriptural authority and political efficacy in their social theory.

Cobbet's other notable work, *A Practical Discourse of Prayer*, is much less polemical. Intended as a handbook on the proper time and method for prayer, its pages are devoted to fine theoretical distinctions among different motives, ends, and techniques used in prayer, and it deals with the application of such topics in the everyday life of the colonies. Thus Cobbet defended the practice of "Ejaculatory prayer" not only from scriptural precedent but also because one can pray this way even in the midst of daily business. Similarly, silent prayer can be conducted even in crowds, and "closet prayer" can "expedit our weightiest temporal affairs" as well as cure stammering and increase one's skill in public speaking. Although the argument of the *Discourse* is much more simple than that of the *Civil Magistrates Power*, the style of the *Discourse* involves repetitive syntax and accumulations of metaphors unlike the utilitarian simplicity of the sentences in the political tract. In the course of one paragraph, prayer "broaches" the heart, "beats" the spices, "cuts the offering," and prospects for metals, a practice of Classical *copia* that reflects Cobbet's familiarity with the fashions of seventeenth-century rhetoric as well as an ambitious piety. Nonetheless, despite this obviously cultured rhetorical facility, Cobbet closely aligned the *Discourse* with the most democratic of plain-style prescriptions, and sprinkled throughout his work are allusions to domestic images and events that balance the scriptural evidence with the immediate power of the commonest experience.

The last twenty years of Cobbet's life were devoted to his ministry and a number of public debates on issues ranging from infant baptism to the legal and ethical responsibilities of the colonies to the king. The only surviving texts from this period are letters to Increase Mather that show Cobbet's persevering in his conservative Puritanism, worrying about the sins of "Quakerisme and swearing" that surround him, and complaining about the laxness of his congregation in their prayers and fasting. The most important of these letters is *A Narrative of New England's Deliverances*, a catalog of Indian attacks and miraculous victories for the colonists that includes a touching account of the capture and eventual release of his son. This brief and informal narrative serves as an extended application of Cobbet's faith in the efficacy of prayer and as such is an intriguing combination of the modes of military history and the captivity narrative.

Suggested Readings: CCNE; Sprague (I, 102-104). *See also* Cotton Mather, *Magnalia Christi Americana* (1702; rep., 1855), III, 518-521; "The Mather Papers," CMHS, 4th ser., 8 (1868), 288-297.

Michael P. Clark
University of Michigan

WILLIAM COBBETT (1763-1835)

Works: *Observations on the Emigration of Dr. Joseph Priestley...at New York* (1794); *A Bone to Gnaw, for the Democrats* (Pts. I-II, 1795); *A Kick for a Bite* (1795); *A Little Plain English, Addressed to the People of the United States, on the Treaty* (1795); *Le Tuteur Anglais* (1795); *The Bloody Buoy, Thrown Out as Warning to the Political Pilots of America: Barbarity of the French Revolution* (1796-1797); *The Gros Mousqueton Diplomatique...Citizen Adet* (1796); *A Letter to the Infamous Tom Paine, in Answer to His Brutal Attack on...Washington* (1796); *The Life and Adventures of Peter Porcupine* (1796); *A New-Year's Gift to the Democrats...Mr. Randolph's Resignation* (1796); *The Scare-Crow* (1796); *Observations on the Debates of the American Congress* (1797); *The Democratic Judge: Or, The Equal Liberty of the Press...Prosecution of William Cobbett* (1798; also, in Eng., *The Republican Judge:...Partial Prosecution of William Cobbett*); *The Detection of Bache; Or, The French Diplomatic Skill Developed* (broadside; 1798); *French Arrogance...X.Y.Z. and the Lady* (1798); *Porcupine's Works*, 12 vols. (1801); *A Grammar of the English Language, in a Series of Letters* (1818); *A Year's Residence in the United States of America* (1818); *Advice to Young Men and (Incidentally) to Young Women* (1829); *Rural Rides* (1830); *Surplus Population* (a play that originally appeared in the Jun. 1831 edition of *Two-Penny Trash*).

Biography: William Cobbett was born on Mar. 9, 1763, at Farnham, Surrey, Eng. The third of four sons of George and Ann Vincent Cobbett, Cobbett spent his childhood laboring as a field hand. At age 19, he abandoned his agricultural implements to seek his fortune in London, where he became a solicitor's clerk. He soon tired of this occupation and joined the army. During a year at an army training facility, Cobbett taught himself writing and grammar. By 1791 he had been promoted to the rank of regimental sergeant major. Sensitive to the gross corruption within both his regiment and the service, Cobbett clamored for an investigation and demanded a court-martial of the guilty soldiers. Cobbett soon realized that the system would prevent a fair hearing of the merits of the case—regardless of the evidence. With his discharge in hand, Cobbett departed in Mar. 1792, first for Fr. and later, America. He entered the U.S. with his new wife, Ann Reid, with the apparent hope of obtaining government employment, but his letter of introduction from Short, the American ambassador in Paris, to Thomas Jefferson (q.v.) proved futile. Administrative or political appointments were scarce, and he was forced to support himself in Wilmington, Del., and, later, Philadelphia, Pa., by teaching English to French nationals who had abandoned Fr. following the fall of the Girondins.

Cobbett's relationship with the *émigrés* led to the publication of two books—the controversial *Observations on the Emigration of Joseph Priestley* (1794) and *Le Tuteur Anglais* (an English grammar written in French and finally published in 1795). In the former, Cobbett cast aside his republican principles and entered the political fray with "John Bull" vengeance. A spate of political pamphlets followed that berated the French Revolution and castigated anyone who dared support its tenets. With the publication of *A Kick for a Bite* (1795), Cobbett adopted the pseudonym "Peter Porcupine"—drawn from a reviewer's comparison of Cobbett's barbed attacks to procupine quills.

By Jul. 1796 Cobbett had opened his own bookseller's shop, cluttering the windows with the likenesses of "obnoxious personages" such as Lord Howe and George III. His scathing attack upon the French revolutionaries—the *Bloody Buoy* (1796)—and his wholly unfounded *Life of Thomas Paine* (1796) underscored his brutal, although often canny, excision of the body politic. On Mar. 4, 1797, Cobbett introduced *Porcupine's Gazette and Daily Advertiser*—a hodgepodge of antirepublican rhetoric, pro-English effusiveness, and strident calls for war against Fr. Despite a large circulation, he constantly experienced financial difficulties. Matters were aggravated when Dr. Benjamin Rush (q.v.) sued Cobbett for libel as the result of Cobbett's criticism of Rush's treatment of yellow-fever victims with a combination of copious blood-letting and "Rush's powders" ("mercurial purges"). The trial, which lingered for two years, was a mixture of political maneuvering and personal invective. In the end, Cobbett was fined 5,000 dollars, and his property was attached with disastrous results: an impression of *Porcupine's Works*—still lying in sheets—was sold as waste paper and destroyed. Cobbett returned to his new operations base in N.Y. where he decided to publish *The Rush-Light* (Feb. 15-Apr. 30, 1800) rather than to revive *Porcupine's Gazette*. In five issues of *The Rush-Light*, he dissected Rush, exposing both his treatment and political opinions. In addition, he conducted a postmortem of the trial, probing the conduct of Chief Justice Shippen and the malignant influence of Thomas McKean.

In mid-1800 "Peter Porcupine" returned to Eng. and began publication of a daily newspaper, *The Porcupine* (Oct. 30, 1800-Dec. 31, 1801). The paper promptly failed, but with the assistance of William Windham in 1802, Cobbett established the anti-Jacobin weekly *The Political Register*, which he edited and contributed to until his death in 1835.

By 1805 Cobbett had undergone a political transformation. Recognizing the misery of the laboring classes with which he had always identified, Cobbett embraced radicalism. His voice quickly became synonymous with that of the people. Yet four years later, Cobbett found himself editing the *Register* from Newgate Jail as the result of a successful prosecution for sedition. His denunciation of the flogging of mutinous troops at Ely under the supervision of German mercenaries cost Cobbett 1,000 pounds in fines and another 5,000 pounds for bail and sureties—in addition to the two-year jail term. Although he was able to retain the *Register*, he was forced to sell lucrative copyrights for the *State Trials*, the *Parliamentary History of England*, and the *Parliamentary Debates*.

Once released from prison in 1812, Cobbett emerged as a powerful advocate for parliamentary reform. His unstamped *Register* became the rallying point for laborers and journeymen in the midland and northern counties. With the suspension of the Habeas Corpus Act in 1817, Cobbett fled to the U.S., where he withdrew from the tumult of American politics, dedicating most of his time to farming in North Hempstead, Long Island, or preparing articles for his English *Register*. The *Register* suffered only slight circulation losses during Cobbett's absence. Reprints of earlier numbers moved briskly, especially *Paper Against Gold* and *Address to the Journeymen and Labourers*—the latter with sales in excess of 200,000 copies. Profits were applied to Cobbett's English debts. Despite his return to the U.S., Cobbett continued to oppose emigration to America. He cataloged American freedoms for his English readers in an effort to encourage British reform—not to extol the virtues of the former colonies.

With the publication of *A Year's Residence in the United States of America* (1818), Cobbett began his discursive pastoralism that would lead to the series *Rural Rides* (collected; 1822-1826). His *Grammar of the English Language* (1818) served notice to the British government of the impact of growing literacy upon the populace.

When Cobbett's American residence burned in 1819, he no longer saw any reason to remain in the U.S. He packed up his household—and the disinterred bones of Thomas Paine (q.v.)—and returned to Eng. There he embraced a multitude of causes, including the plight of Queen Caroline, the cultivation of maize ("Cobbett's corn"), and, later, support of the Reform Act. In 1832 he stood for election to Parliament and was elected MP for Oldham. For two and one-half years, he led a small group of vocal radicals, often opposed to the Reformed Parliament of 1832. In 1835 his health deteriorated under the strain of political duties, and he died from an apparent attack of influenza on Jun. 18, 1835. Without Cobbett's slashing pen and porcupine wit, the *Register* faltered, then failed.

Critical Appraisal: William Cobbett, perhaps more than any other member of the American partisan press of the eighteenth century, was a stranger in a strange land. His rites of passage proved difficult, from moderate democrat to avowed "John Bull," from contentious scribbler to an esteemed member of the British Parliament. Cobbett, as "Peter Porcupine," unleashed his literary quills without regard for faction or fashion. A man with little taste for polite literature, Cobbett usually based his critical judgments upon the extent to which such writings could be molded to fit political opinions. He belittled William Shakespeare as a smut-monger and wrote of John Milton's *Paradise Lost* in 1817, "if one of your relations were to write a letter in the same strain, you would send him to a madhouse and take his estate."

American letters, he believed, were no better. He ridiculed Benjamin Franklin (q.v.) as "old lightning-rod" and, before his change of heart, depicted Thomas Paine as "a block head and an ass." He did, however, apparently feel kinship for Joseph Dennie (q.v.), to whom he offered support for publication of *The Lay Preacher*—first in the U.S. (Cobbett fled before the agreement could be concluded), and then abroad (he tried unsuccessfully to persuade Dennie to accompany him to Eng.). Cobbett thrived on controversy, noting with apparent glee, "there were in Philadelphia, about ten thousand persons, all of whom would have rejoiced to see me murdered." He vacillated between saber rattling and pacifism. He denounced the French as bloodthirsty rabble deserving no quarter; yet he often leaped at the chance to become a popular peacemaker. He claimed his pamphlet *A Little Plain English* helped to ratify the Jay Treaty.

Cobbett experimented in various literary forms to drive home his often barbed points. In 1797 he chose poetry—"French Arrogance"—to satirize Fr.'s attempt to extort an exorbitant sum of money from the U.S. as a preliminary condition to negotiations for the settlement of maritime disputes. He expressed his hatred for Parson Malthus in both letter and scene: "I have, during my life, detested many men," Cobbett wrote, "but never any one so much as you." In his play "Surplus Population," which appeared in the Jun. 1831 edition of *Two-Penny Trash*, Cobbett argued that "labourers never can breed too fast because they create food and clothing and other necessaries in proportion to their numbers because, indeed, subsistence must precede the population."

Cobbett, paradoxically, was a fundamental opponent of innovation. The old order in Eng. needed preservation, if not restoration. The "Thing" —government, the enclosure of fields—needed caging. Reform needed to be controlled, civilized. His *Political Register* clearly advocated the use of the petition to Parliament to right social inequities rather than the ploy of rioting. His highly acclaimed *Grammar of the English Language* was an early step in that direction, intended for working-class consumption in an effort to fit them for the revitalized society. Yet Cobbett was willing to admit that "people in extreme poverty" would always exist. On the one hand, he labored long and hard for universal manhood suffrage, the secret ballot, and the disestablishment of the Church of England. On the other, he only thinly veiled his distrust—if not hatred—for blacks, Jews, Quakers, "foreigners," and, after mid-1823, "landlords." "When farmers become *gentlemen*," Cobbett wrote, "the labourers become slaves."

But his views were always in motion. Cobbett was a leader in efforts to circulate Hannah More's (1745-1833) writings in America during the 1790s. Yet he later regarded her admonitions to the poor as patronizing and supportive of a servile mentality. He remained fond of Edmund Burke's writings, importing his works, reprinting his anti-Revolutionary speeches, and filling *Porcupine's Gazette* with references to the statesman. Cobbett set himself up as the standard vehicle for the dissemination of anti Jacobin tracts and treatises in the U.S. As a member of the partisan press in America, he described himself as "the evening and day star, the moon and the sun and the aurora of the press." A strong advocate of press and personal freedoms, he was no person or party's toady. In his later years, he wrote that political parties were a "mere sham intended to keep the people quiet while each party plunders them alternatively." Perhaps G. K. Chesterton expressed Cobbett's political penchant best: "It is not true that he belonged successively to two parties; it is much truer to say that he never belonged to any." Cobbett found persecution and prosecution at the hands of both Tory and Whig governments. Similar treatment was accorded to him in democratic Philadelphia. At first he turned pro-French sentiments to his advantage, producing his popular *Le Tuteur Anglais* (reprinted for more than half a century in France as *Le Maître Anglais*) and translating popular tracts. Like Joseph Dennie, however, he soon perceived the "true" character of the population, which Cobbett described in 1794 as indicative of a "sly, roguish gang."

His *Observations on the Emigration of Joseph Priestley* consisted of a series of outbursts against the knavery of a man who had had the audacity to support the colonies during the American Revolution. As noted by G.D.H. Cole (in *The Life of William Cobbett*), although *Observations* succeeded in advancing Cobbett to the vanguard of political pamphleteers, it lacked "those extraordinary characteristic and personal digressions" that marked Cobbett's best work. With the establishment of *Porcupine's Gazette and Daily Advertiser* in Mar. 1797, "Peter Porcupine's" true style began to emerge. He engaged his critics with polemical hammer and tongs, striving unceasingly to stretch the limits of what the state constituted as libel. For his efforts, he was prosecuted unsuccessfully before the State Court of Pennsylvania for alleged libels upon the king of Spain and the

Spanish minister. His literary assault upon the court's chief justice, Thomas McKean, took the form of a pamphlet, *The Democratic Judge* (published as *The Republican Judge* in Eng.). Although he would lose a similar action in the case pressed by Dr. Benjamin Rush, Cobbett retained his sense of justice and love for in-fighting.

With Cobbett's return to the U.S. in 1817, a new Cobbett emerged. Since 1807 he had become less vindictive toward America, admitting that "better times are now come" and implying that American literature had a future. Nearly two years before his second American sojourn, Cobbett had written in the *Political Register* (Nov. 11, 1815),

> America, comparatively, is yet an *infant* State, and ...therefore, as to literary talent she is entitled to every consideration;...she cannot be judged of in this particular, by the same rules which determine the quantity and value of learning in this country; and...she ought not to be held destitute of literary genius, when the means necessary to develope that genius have never been brought into play.

This, despite the fact that from the appearance of his first pamphlet in Philadelphia in 1794 until the day of his death in 1835, a steady stream of anti-Cobbett publications in the U.S. charged him with inconsistency of purpose, philosophy, and political persuasion.

Whether Cobbett cared to admit it, both his political and social commentaries drafted in the U.S. were having a profound impact upon both his own literary development and the nature of reform in Eng. *A Year's Residence in the United States of America*, although far less appreciated than his later series, "Rural Rides," clearly was the forebear of his brilliant, if characteristically digressive, treatise on rural economics. *A Year's Residence* was also Cobbett's first true book, combining personal journalism with a more incisive disclosure of his gifts of observation. As noted by Cole, Cobbett's political penchant finally gave way to expose the reformer's love of the countryside. Cole has argued that the segment detailing Cobbett's journey from London to Liverpool (before his departure for America) is the author's first "Rural Ride." Contrast, pastoral beauty, and political digressions punctuated Cobbett's emerging style. British privilege and American independence served as point-counterpoint in his sharply written work. The amenities of life—the simple joys and beauty—remained sparse in Cobbett's American landscape. During his exile, his simple joy seemed to be the writing of books. In addition to *A Year's Residence*, he completed his *Grammar of the English Language* and *The American Gardener* and developed plans for several other works. *A Grammar of the English Language* may be Cobbett's most important contribution. Intended for the masses, the *Grammar* juxtaposed pithy maxims with grammatical examples. Despite the appearance of thirteen editions within sixteen years of its issuance (and claims of sales of more than 100,000 copies), the social changes advocated by Cobbett did not occur. Nor, according to John W. Osborne, was it likely that the *Grammar* had reached its intended audience. The working classes were beset with life, not literature. Even Cobbett had made the point in his *Political Register* that the workers were more in need of bacon to eat than Bacon to read.

With his return to Eng. in 1819, Cobbett's attention turned to politics and the economic scene of English pastoralism. Although *A Year's Residence* lacked the research of a true journalistic inquiry into rural problems and proposed solutions, the series entitled "Rural Rides" (1822-1826) in the *Political Register* possessed the trappings of highly personal investigative journalism. In his search for the idyllic, Cobbett strived to restore the rustic necessities of life and ignored the luxuries. Public morals and public peace, he noted, were dependent upon a laborer's "full belly." Innovation was perceived as an encroachment upon established customs. To understand the series properly, it must be viewed as a portrait of the exigencies of English rural life rather than as a compendium of isolated tableaux. As both Cole and William J. Keith have pointed out, the "irrelevant" passages of political invective often hold the key to Cobbett's observations—much less his personality. Neither his rides nor his walks were accidental. He sought clear-cut goals using symbols easily recognizable within a political or pastoral construct. Unfortunately, as Chesterton has emphasized, Cobbett too often has been recognized for his style, rather than the richness of his subject. Porcupine's quills masked a writer and reformer committed to the nostalgia of an irretrievable past.

Suggested Readings: DAB. *See also* Asa Briggs, *William Cobbett* (1967); E. I. Carlyle, *William Cobbett: A Study of His Life* (1904); G. K. Chesterton, *William Cobbett* (1926); Mary E. Clark, *Peter Porcupine in America: The Career of William Cobbett, 1792-1800* (1939); G.D.H. Cole, *The Life of William Cobbett* (1924); Gerald Duff, *William Cobbett and the Politics of Earth* (1972); Pierce W. Gaines, *William Cobbett and the United States, 1792-1835* (1971); William J. Keith, *The Rural Tradition: William Cobbett, Gilbert White, and Other Non-Fiction Prose Writers of the English Countryside* (1975); Lewis Melville, *The Life and Letters of William Cobbett in England and America* (1913); John W. Osborne, *William Cobbett* (1966); James Sambrook, *William Cobbett* (1973).

William F. Vartorella
Mary Baldwin College

GEORGE COCKINGS (fl. 1760-1802)

Works: *War, an Heroic Poem, from the Taking of Minorca by the French to the Reduction of the Havannah* (1760, 1765, 1785; rep. as *War: An Heroic Poem, from the Taking of Minorca by the French to the Raising of Quebec by General Murray;* 1762); *Arts, Manufacturers, and Commerce* (a poem; 1766, 1769); *The Conquest of Canada; Or, The Siege of Quebec* (historical tragedy in five acts; 1766, 1772, 1773); *Benevolence and Gratitude* (poem; 1772); *Poems on Several Subjects* (1772).

Biography: In David Baker's *Biographia Dramatica; Or, A Companion to the Playhouse* (1782; I, 92), one can read: "Of this writer we can learn no account. He is the author of several very contemptible performances, and among the rest one Play, called, *The Conquest of Canada; Or, The Siege of Quebec. An Historical Tragedy.* 8 vo. 1766." More than a quarter-century later, Thomas Gilliard, *The Dramatic Minor* (1808), could provide no more information. Whatever the particulars of his background, Cockings would not have agreed with this assessment of his art. In prefaces to his play and to *War*, he begged the public to look with favor "and not chill the ardour of my genius, by severe criticism." So much for ardent pleas!

Cockings was born in Devonshire, Eng., and went to Newfoundland as a young man, eventually serving in the French and Indian War campaigns against Louisburg and Quebec before settling in Boston. For a few years, he held a minor position in the British government in Boston and was inspired to write poetry and one play. On returning to Eng., he obtained the post of registrar of the Society of Arts, Manufacturers and Commerce in the Adelphi. He held this post for thirty years, presumably until his death in 1802. The date of the Siege of Quebec (1759) and the London publications of his works would indicate that he lived and wrote in Boston during the early 1760s and left for Eng. before 1766.

Critical Appraisal: Events in America deeply interested Cockings, particularly military events.

> When I first poetic ardour knew,
> And big with martial themes my bosom grew!
> From pregnant fancy (fixed by warlike worth)
> My rising thoughts prepar'd to sally forth
> In years a child, in litt'rature more young;
> With secret transport on the theme I hung.

In this manner, he began his poem on *War*, a brief work of twenty-eight pages including a short appended poem on the defeat of the French and another titled "Brittain's Call to Her Brave Troops and Hardy Tars." Throughout his poem on *War*, he praised the British generals with a fierce patriotism and displayed his learning with references to Greek epic figures and characters from the Bible. He compared, for example, Generals Amherst and Wolfe to Ulysses and Diomed. Evidently, readers enjoyed both his patriotic spirit and his youthful verse, for by 1765 *War* had been presented in four editions.

Clearly, however, Cockings was neither a great poet nor an exceptional dramatist, nor did he pretend to be. "Not being conversant with the stage" and "the rules of the drama," he admitted in his preface to *The Conquest of Canada*, "I may have greatly erred" in composing the play. There is no doubt, however, that he believed in celebrating glorious events in art. Powerful emotions moved his pen "like gunpowder when touch'd by the match." Nevertheless, critics find little to praise in his work. In spite of seeming to be a reasonably well-read man, he lacked a feeling for language. His prose-poetry was artificially sustained, and he resorted to elaborate and unnatural words and phrases as well as long, stiff speeches. He paid little attention to character development and had a faulty understanding of plot. Once he had planned to write a play of epic proportions and call it *The Matchless Era*, but even as he settled upon the Siege of Quebec for his theme, his plot remained episodic, held together primarily by his continuing interest in General Wolfe, whose life and death determined the focus of his "historical tragedy."

Although some scholars have found it difficult to imagine that Cockings wrote his play for the stage, it was given a spectacular production on Feb. 17, 19, and 22, 1773. By means that are not clear, a Philadelphia printer published an edition of the play in Dec. 1772, and David Douglass, the most successful of early theatre managers in America, was persuaded to produce it. Spectacle was clearly the major asset of the play, and for this production, the audience (*Pennsylvania Gazette*, Feb. 17, 1773) was asked to "dispense with a Farce; as the stage will be much crowded with the Artillery, Boats, and etc. necessary for the representation of the piece; and with the Men from Both Corps, whose assistance the Commanding Officers are glad enough to indulge us with." Relying on music, spectacle, and the patriotic effect of martial scenes, Douglass created what would appear to have been an effective evening's entertainment. Like other contemporary dramatists who tried to capitalize upon an actual event, Cockings wisely chose a famous hero in General Wolfe and imitated in concept and focus the popular heroic tragedy of his time.

In the history of American letters, Cockings's reputation rests primarily upon his play, although his poem on the same subject of the French and Indian War was widely read. The poem, however, remains of minor significance among many other such poetic attempts. *The Conquest of Canada; Or, The Siege of Quebec* is important as an early contribution to the thin fare of colonial dramatists, and its production on three occasions adds to that importance. It must also have been reasonably well read for a 2nd American edition appeared in Albany in 1773, an achievement Cockings, if unknowingly, shared with no other dramatist of this pre-Revolutionary period.

Suggested Readings: DNB. *See also* Summer Oral Coad and Edwin Mims, Jr., *The American Stage*, Vol. 14 of *The Pageant of Americas* (1929), p. 50; Charles Durang, *History of the Philadelphia Stages Between the Years 1749 and 1855* (1868), I, 17; Paul Leicester Ford, "The Beginnings of American Dramatic Literature," NEM, New Series, 9 (Feb. 1894), 673-687; Walter J. Meserve, *An Emerging Entertainment: The Drama of the American People to 1828* (1977), pp. 55-57; Thomas Clark Pollock, *The Philadelphia Theatre in the Eighteenth Century Together with His "Day Book" of the Same Period* (1933; rep., 1968), pp. 123-124; Hugh F. Rankin, *The Theatre in Colonial America* (1965), p. 174.

Walter J. Meserve
Indiana University

MASON FITCH COGSWELL (1761-1830)

Works: Grace McClure Dixon Root, ed., *Father and Daughter: A Collection of Cogswell Family Letters and Diaries, 1772-1830* (1924) prints Cogswell's diary, journal, and letters.

Biography: Mason Fitch Cogswell was born on Sept. 28, 1761, in Canterbury, Conn., the fourth child of the minister James Cogswell and his wife, Alice [Fitch] Cogswell. When he was only 11, Cogswell's mother died, and shortly thereafter his family moved to Windham, Conn., where his father married a widow, Martha Lathrop Devotion.

From 1776 to 1780, Mason attended Yale, graduating as valedictorian and the youngest member of his class. Before beginning the study of medicine with a brother in N.Y., Mason traveled in N.Y. and Conn., keeping a journal that years after the Civil War was returned to the Connecticut Historical Society by a southern minister. After he completed his studies in N.Y., Cogswell moved to Hartford, Conn., where he practiced medicine. He married Mary Ledyard; four children were born to them. Cogswell gained a wide reputation as a surgeon. His services were in demand throughout New Eng., and he is credited as the first doctor to operate for cataract of the eye, the first to tie a carotid artery, and the first to initiate a school for deaf-mutes in America. In 1818, Cogswell was awarded the honorary degree of M.D. by the Connecticut Medical Society and Yale College. In addition, Cogswell played a flute, led a church choir, and according to one account was an "active friend and supporter of the Retreat for the Insane in Hartford." According to an obituary published in a Hartford newspaper in 1830, "As a physician, he [Cogswell] ranked among the first; and as a surgeon, he was pre-eminent, both in his own State, and in this country....He contributed greatly to elevate its younger members with hope and enterprise, and to shed over all a most happy influence by his kind and conciliatory example." He died on Dec. 10, 1830.

Critical Appraisal: Although associated with the Connecticut Wits, whose members—John Trumbull (q.v.), Theodore Dwight (q.v.), Richard Alsop (q.v.), Lemuel Hopkins (q.v.), and Elihu Hubbard Smith (q.v.)—consciously cultivated the image of men of letters, Mason Fitch Cogswell is better known for what he did than for what he wrote. He was primarily a practical man, not a literary one. His literary productions consist primarily of a diary that he kept during Nov. and Dec. of 1788, a journal he compiled from Jan. 31, 1791, to Feb. 22, 1791, and several letters. Like many such documents, Cogswell's diary, journal, and letters are of value to the literary and social historian because they provide insight into the mind and activity of an individual who was in many respects representative of the times and who was involved in some of the most important events of his day. Cogswell was entertained in the homes of some of the most prominent people of the times, and as a member of the Wits, Cogswell attended their weekly meetings and knew well the group's other members, many

of whom wrote some of the most significant political lampoons and satire as well
as some of the best poetry, diaries, and travel journals of the era. Cogswell's
own description of a journey in and around Hartford and into N.Y. reveals a
leisurely cultivated life of gracious manners, lively conversation, and early retirement. Always interested in women, Cogswell described them and their conversations with approval, and from the journal we learn interesting things such as
the fact that his father, who was a practicing minister for sixty years, was at one
time almost dismissed by a congregation for drinking a cup of tea to assuage
himself of his grief over his daughter's death. Happily, though, he and his
parishioners were reconciled. Among other things, Cogswell's letters reveal his
negotiations to establish a school for deaf-mutes and a description of the life of
his daughter Alice, herself a deaf-mute.

Suggested Readings: Dexter (IV 141-143); LHUS. *See also* Benjamin Franklin
V, ed., *The Poetry of the Minor Connecticut Wits* (1970); idem, *The Prose of the Minor
Connecticut Wits* (3 vols.; 1974); Francis Parson, *The Friendly Club and Other Portraits*
(1922), pp. 23-60; idem, *The Hartford Wits* (1936), pp. 9-27; Grace McClure Dixon
Root, ed., *Father and Daughter; A Collection of Cogswell Family Letters and Diaries*
(1924); Herbert Thomas, *Doctors of Yale College, 1702-1815, and the Founding of the
Medical Institution* (1960), pp. 55-59; Stephen W. Williams, *American Medical Biography* (1967), pp. 100-109.

Virginia Levey
University of Central Arkansas

CADWALLADER COLDEN (1688-1776)

Works: *Papers Relating to an Act of the Assembly* (1724); *History of the
Five Nations Depending on the Province of New York* (1727; rev. ed. pub. as *The
Five Indian Nations of Canada*; 1747); *An Explication of the First Causes of
Action in Matter* (1745; rev. ed. pub. as *The Principles of Action in Matter*;
1751).

Biography: Born in Ire. on Feb. 7, 1688, of Scotch parents, Cadwallader
Colden had a remarkably diverse career which spanned five decades of N.Y.
history. His father, a minister at Duns, Berwickshire, Scot., expected his son to
enter the ministry, but Cadwallader chose medicine instead and received the
A.B. degree from the University of Edinburgh in 1705. Finding few opportunities in Eng., Colden made his way to Philadelphia in 1710. Eight years later,
Colden, now married, moved his family to N.Y. when that colony's governor,
Robert Hunter (q.v.), promised him a position as the next surveyor-general—
which Colden received in 1720. Within two years, Colden became deeply immersed in the colony's factional politics. Appointed to the Executive Council, he
aligned himself with the merchant bloc against the large landholders, especially
by his support of Governor William Burnet's fur trade policies and by his

insistence on a just policy for buying land from the Indians and an orderly procedure for accurate surveys and registration of land grants. Colden served N.Y. honestly, but he also used his political position to acquire wealth, social status, and an estate near present-day Newburgh, N.Y., which he named Coldengham. In 1739 Colden retired from public life to devote his attention to other aspirations, including natural history, history, cartography, mathematics, medicine, moral philosophy, physics, astronomy, botany and educational philosophy, but in 1750 he returned to politics and by 1761 was appointed lieutenant-governor, a position he held until his death. During the series of constitutional crises that led to the American Revolution, Colden did much to undermine royal authority in N.Y., especially during the Stamp Act debates in 1765, with his staunch support of the king's prerogative. Colden died on Sept. 20, 1776, at his Long Island estate "Spring Hill" (near Flushing) at the age of 88.

Critical Appraisal: Above all, Colden sought fame, and this passion for public recognition drove him to write on a wide range of subjects and to correspond with the major scientists and philosophers of the Atlantic community, including Linnaeus, Gronovius, John Bartram (q.v.), James Logan (q.v.), Samuel Johnson (q.v.), and Benjamin Franklin (q.v.). Although Colden was held in high esteem by his associates (Franklin admittedly deferred to Colden on scientific subjects), history has not been so kind to him. The sole biography on him has been described as an example of how not to write one. Suggestions that Colden deserves attention as one of America's first philosophers have gone unheeded, and scientific historians have tended to relegate Colden to an intellectual backwater for his unwillingness to use scientific experimentation to test his hypotheses. According to most evaluations, Colden's primary contribution lay less in his political or intellectual efforts than in a correspondence that tied together the fledgling scientific community of eighteenth-century America.

Much of Colden's writings tends to support this generally negative assessment, in particular Colden's most ambitious effort and his most abysmal failure: An Explication of the First Causes (1745). In this work, Colden claimed he had discovered what Isaac Newton could not—the cause of gravitation. First published in N.Y. and then in London (1746), Colden's work, as he saw it, was an extension of Newtonian principles. According to Colden, the "apparent Attraction or Gravitation, is truly and really performed by Pulsion, or more properly is the Effect of the joint Actions of the moving, resisting and elastic Powers." Unfortunately, his argument was as unintelligible as his hypothesis. Many of his friends admitted that they could not understand it, and others either sent Colden copies of scientific treatises that they believed might help clarify matters or kindly criticized specific points in the argument. Viewing Colden's work as an audacious attack on Newton, European scholars were even less kind, and they criticized Colden for misunderstanding Newton's theories and for internal inconsistencies in his writing. Although Colden attempted to answer his critics in The Principles of Action in Matter (1751), interest in Colden's theory died away when Leonhard Euler's damning appraisal was read before the Royal Society.

Colden always believed that he had not made his case clearly, but the fact was that he was unaware of the work of scientists such as Euler, Bernoullis, Leibnitz, and Huygens, and he either had not read or had not understood parts of Newton's *Principia*, drawing his ideas instead from Newton's more philosophical "Queries" (*Opticks*) and "General Scholium" (*Principia*), where Newton relaxed his own stern rules for scientific inquiry—an approach that was more amenable to Colden's speculative approach to science. Colden's other writings provide additional offerings of his weaknesses as a scientist. His ideas were often in error (he claimed, for example, that "Tar water" could cure flatulence, and he planned a printing process shown defective some twenty years earlier). Sometimes he was correct, but often for the wrong reasons. He argued, for instance, that yellow fever was caused by the "airs" emanating from stagnant water. Still Colden had some notable successes, principally in subjects where observation provided a methodological replacement for experimentation. In botany, for example, Colden so mastered the Linnaean classification system that Linnaeus published Colden's classification of the flora on his estate and even named a plant for him.

Colden's most notable success, his *History of the Five Nations* (1727), and the expanded version, from which most modern editions are derived, *The Five Indian Nations of Canada* (1747), also relied on observation. Although the narrative is based on sources such as French accounts by Le Roy de Bacqueville de La Potherie and Louis-Armand Lahontan, the minutes of the Albany Board of Indian Commissioners, and available minutes of treaty negotiations, Colden also brought his personal experience to bear on the subject, for during his early years as N.Y.'s surveyor-general, he had lived among, and perhaps been adopted by, the Mohawks. Although anthropologists have qualified some of Colden's ethnographic comments and although his admiration for the Iroquois led him to equate them with natural man in simplicity and virtue, proclaiming that they "had a perfect Republican Government," Colden's history is nevertheless a valuable source for seventeenth- and eighteenth-century Iroquois-N.Y. relations.

"Elaborate but readable," Colden's narrative was designed to deny French claims to North America to support the imperialistic view of Eng.'s future in North America and to counter British public opinion that the Iroquois were uncivilizable savages. The description of the Five Nations in the title as "dependent On the Province of New York" emphasizes Colden's main theme of the importance of the Iroquois to N.Y.'s expansion. Thus the first volume traces Iroquois-white diplomacy and warfare through the seventeenth century, and the second volume is a documentary history of the importance of the Iroquois. Colden's second goal emerges most forcefully in the 1747 edition's dedication to Gen. James Edward Oglethorpe (q.v.). Treated properly, the Iroquois would become, Colden asserted, "A People whose Friendship might add Honor to the British Nation."

Although Colden at times exaggerated Iroquois influence, his *History* is extremely valuable for the light it sheds on Iroquois diplomatic abilities, the process of treaty negotiations, and for its examples of the Indian treaty as literature.

It is unfortunate that Colden appears to have lost interest in the project. When he turned to the task of carrying his history into the eighteenth century, the result was an unpublished and uninspired chronology for the years 1707-1720.

On balance, however, Colden's reputation has suffered undeservedly from the presentistic biases of later generations. Colden's Loyalist sympathies blocked serious study of his career until the Anglo-American *rapprochement* at the turn of the twentieth century. His materialistic hedonism went beyond most Deistic arguments (Benjamin Franklin once chided Colden after reading his "First Principles of Morality" [1746] that "'Tis well we were not, as poor Galileo was, subject to the Inquisition for Philosophical heresy") and probably violated the moral sensibilities of the nineteenth century. Moreover, Colden's personal pettiness and political obstinacy have done little to endear him to later generations, and his speculative approach to knowledge seems alien to the modern scientific method. Colden, therefore, has yet to be studied for what he was, a product of his time; and until his career is studied in full and in the context of the eighteenth-century Atlantic community, his reputation will be clouded.

Suggested Readings: BDAS; DAB; DNB; LHUS; T_1. *See also* Patricia Bonomi, *A Factious People: Politics and Society in Colonial New York* (1971); Vincent Buranelli, "Colonial Philosophy," WMQ, 16 (1959), 342-362; Louis Leonard Gitin, "Cadwallader Colden as Scientist and Philosopher," NYH, 16 (1935), 169-177; Brooke Hindel, "Cadwallader Colden's Extension of the Newtonian Principles," WMQ, 13 (1956), 459-475; Alfred R. Hoermann, "A Savant in the Wilderness: Cadwallader Colden of New York," NYHSQ, 62 (1978), 270-288; Wilbur R. Jacobs, "Cadwallader Colden's Noble Iroquois Savages," in *The Colonial Legacy*: Vol. III: *Historians of Nature and Man's Nature*, 34-58; Vol. IV: *Early Nationalist Historians* (1973), passim; Stanley N. Katz, *New Castle's New York: Anglo-American Politics, 1732-1753* (1968), pp. 177-180; Alice M. Keys, *Cadwallader Colden: A Representative Eighteenth Century Official* (1906); Milton M. Klein, "Politics and Personality in Colonial New York," NYH, 47 (1966), 3-16; L. Woodbridge Riley, *American Philosophy, The Early Schools* (1907), pp. 329-372; Max Savelle, *Seeds of Liberty: The Genesis of the American Mind* (1948), pp. 44-46, 93-102, 121-127, 383-385; Carole Shammas, "Cadwallader Colden and the Role of the King's Prerogative," NYHSQ, 52 (1969), 103-126; Raymond P. Stearns, *Science in the British Colonies of America* (1970), pp. 493-497, 559-575. Colden's correspondence and many of his unpublished essays are to be found in *"The Colden Letter Books,"* CNYHS, 1 and 2 (1877-1878) and *"Letters and Papers of Cadwallader Colden,"* CNYHS, 1 to 7 (1917-1923); 8 to 10 (1934-1935).

Richard L. Haan
Hartwick College

NATHAN COLE (1711-1783)

Works: "The Spiritual Travels of Nathan Cole" (w. 1765; pub. in WMQ, 3rd ser., 33 [1976], 89-126); *Dialogue Between a Separate Minister . . . and Cole* (second title, *On the Change of the Sabbath*; 1779); "Memoirs of Nathan Cole of Berlin, Conn." (w. c. 1780; pub. in BSPNEA, 25 [1935], 136-140).

Biography: Farmer, carpenter, and lay religious leader of Kensington, today a part of Berlin, Conn., Nathan Cole organized the Separates in his vicinity and frequently defended their tenets publicly. Following his religious conversion during the Great Awakening, Cole objected to the lax membership practices of the Kensington church. He withdrew to the Separates at Wethersfield in 1747, and by 1750 a congregation of twenty to thirty Separates was holding meetings at Cole's home. Because it could not find a permanent minister, however, the group eventually broke up, and in 1764 Cole joined Ebenezer Frothingham's (q.v.) Separate congregation at Middletown. In the face of Cole's defiant stance in support of freewill offerings, the non-Separates at Kensington usually abated his church taxes. Eventually, Cole's search for a pure church led him to become a Baptist. His wife, Anne (c. 1724-1780), lost her sanity in 1763. Childless, Cole willed his estate to Gideon Williams (c. 1739-1821), an orphan he had raised.

Critical Appraisal: "When I try to exhort," Nathan Cole confessed, "I can only give out a few blundering hints, and jump from one thing to another." Nonetheless, a sense of moral obligation to use his talents in God's service overcame his diffidence to speak out in the cause of true religion. Similarly, his lack of formal education did not stop him from promoting his beliefs in writing. As his manuscripts at the Connecticut Historical Society reveal, Cole, untrained in spelling and punctuation, relied on an educated hand to transcribe and revise his works for the press.

Often reprinted since its first publication in 1897, the opening passage of "The Spiritual Travels of Nathan Cole" has become a classic in the literature of the eighteenth-century revivals. This account of Cole's frantic twelve-mile horse-back ride to hear George Whitefield (q.v.) preach at Middletown dramatically captures the anticipation and excitement that accompanied the New Eng. tour of the itinerant evangelist. Only within the last twenty years, however, have scholars recognized Cole's "Spiritual Travels" as "one of the more remarkable documents of the intellectual life of eighteenth-century America" and a "marvel of Puritan autobiography." Because Cole was an articulate among the inarticulate, his "Spiritual Travels" offers rare insights into the meaning of the Great Awakening for its lay participants. Writing to show others what they should expect if they are to follow Christ, Cole described his year of spiritual distress culminating in a powerfully emotional conversion, his subsequent swings between doubt and assurance, and his discovery of fellowship with the Separates.

Cole's strength as an autobiographer lies in his ability to make his internal spiritual experiences immediate and concrete through imagery, detail, dialogue, and even humor. A debate with Satan, for instance, dramatizes Cole's temptation to suicide. On several occasions, Satan meets Cole in his fields and argues the merits and suggests ways of ending his life, with Cole arguing back, bidding Satan to stay away, and leaving his pocketknife at home, where it could do no harm. Cole's sense of humor appears in the form of puns. The greedy establishment ministers, he wrote, continually demand more money, "sometimes a sheep's fleece, and sometimes a lamb's fleece; and so they are fleecing their flocks." In another place, Cole compared himself to "a poor old coal buryed up in the ashes." Sometimes, however, his humor was unintentional, as, for example, in the rhyme in this poem: "Oh he was once a lump of Sin / But now he's Just a entering in / And here he comes a lovely Soul / I say to you make room for Cole."

The King James version strongly influenced Cole's style, and scriptural allusions shaped many of his expressions. Well-versed in the standard religious literature of his culture, Cole referred to Richard Alleine, Richard Baxter, John Foxe, Thomas Hooker (q.v.), and Isaac Watts, and in several places he paraphrased, without attribution, John Bunyan's *Grace Abounding to the Chief of Sinners*. Although he was conscious of his audience throughout, Cole's "Spiritual Travels" is remarkably self-revealing of an intense, serious, self-righteous, and yet gentle and humble man.

Cole evidently intended several of his manuscripts for publication, but only his *Dialogue Between a Separate Minister and Some of His People and Cole* and his *Change of the Sabbath* were printed during his lifetime. Consisting of a Separate's objections and Cole's replies, the *Dialogue* explains in simple, straightforward prose why Cole turned Baptist in his old age. The Separate, who seldom has any rebuttal to Cole's answers, finally admitted, "You have blocked me so with the scriptures, that I cannot see how to contradict you, without contradicting the bible." Because Cole's victory was too easy, the *Dialogue* is unconvincing as polemic. The best sections are those in which Cole departed from literal biblical interpretation and made use of homely analogies. Arguing against infant baptism, he asked, "What good doth it do any way, if we put our ear-mark on our young lambs, it will not secure them from the fox or wolf." To be baptized, he said in favor of total immersion rather than sprinkling, is to be buried with Christ. "Now if we bury a man, and leave part of his body out of the earth, it is not proper to say that man is buried." In the second title of this pamphlet, *On the Change of the Sabbath*, Cole used Scripture and logic to explain why Sunday rather than Saturday should be observed as the Sabbath. Cole's remark that if Seventh-Day Baptists "peruse what I have written, I think they might be convinced" shows a balance between humility and self-confidence, as well as a profound belief in reasoned argument.

Cole is best at narration, to which he returned in his "Memoirs," where he related the misadventures of Gideon Williams, who lost his army pay to cunning officers and was later unable to hold onto a farm. Through it all, Cole discerned the hand of God preserving the young man so that Cole might have an adopted son to whom he could leave his own carefully husbanded estate. Once again, Cole's purpose was didactic: he wanted his readers to learn from Gideon's mistakes. This time, however, the lessons are as economic as they are religious. Like a pious Poor Richard, Cole taught that the old-fashioned virtues of frugality and diligence are religious duties. His writings reflect well the character of eighteenth-century rural New Eng. Both Puritan and Yankee, Nathan Cole was motivated by a clear conviction of duty and was dedicated to the improvement of humanity.

Suggested Readings: Michael J. Crawford, ed., "The Spiritual Travels of Nathan Cole," WMQ, 3rd ser., 33 (1976), 89-126; Alan Heimert and Perry Miller, eds., *The Great Awakening: Documents Illustrating the Crisis and Its Consequences* (1967), pp. 183-186; Roswell A. Moore, ed., "Memoirs of Nathan Cole of Berlin, Conn.," BSPNEA, 25 (1935), 136-140; Daniel B. Shea, Jr., *Spiritual Autobiography in Early America* (1968), pp. 208-221.

Michael J. Crawford
Naval Historical Center, Research Branch

ELIHU COLEMAN (1699-1789)

Works: *A Testimony Against the Antichristian Practice of Making Slaves of Men* (1733).

Biography: Elihu Coleman was born in 1699 on Nantucket, Mass., and lived his life there active in the affairs of the Religious Society of Friends (Quakers) as a public Friend (minister), a frequent participant in the monthly meeting (the business meeting of Quakers), and an advocate of improving the lot of enslaved blacks. Tradition has it that Coleman was a carpenter. Respected and articulate, he is remembered now for his antislavery activities that came to fruition in North America among his fellow Quakers two generations after he wrote his first antislavery tract and shortly thereafter throughout New Eng. Coleman died in 1789.

Critical Appraisal: Although Elihu Coleman's antislavery writing could not match that of later and more successful Quaker antislavery reformers like John Woolman (q.v.) and Anthony Benezet (q.v.), it served to set out for a wider audience the antislavery views of many Friends at a time when Quakers found it impossible to force emancipation on all members of their sect. Like most early Quaker antislavery proponents, Coleman did not live in a mercantile center where wealthy and presumably slaveholding Friends effectively blunted the anti-slavery efforts of their less prosperous coreligionists. Friends like Coleman were able to keep alive antislavery at a time when, outside Quakerdom, there were few antislavery voices, save Samuel Sewall's (q.v.) lonely efforts earlier in the century. For Coleman and other antislavery Quakers, the Bible, the doctrine of the seed of Christ within, and the testimony of pacifism made it possible to criticize slavery at the time of its greatest growth in North America.

Coleman's *Testimony* was moderate in approach. Rather than indulging in highly personal attacks on opponents, he turned to the Bible to show how one could not be a Christian and at the same time own another human being. Less forceful than John Woolman's *Some Considerations on the Keeping of Negroes*, the *Testimony* nonetheless used scriptural proofs rather than arguments inspired by direct revelation from God as did the more effective *Some Considerations*. Coleman set out the moral dilemma for slaveowners who professed to be Christians while leaving to Woolman and others the task of showing the debasing nature of the peculiar institution for the owner and slave alike.

Suggested Readings: Thomas E. Drake, *Quakers and Slavery in America* (1950); Sydney V. James, *A People Among Peoples: Quaker Benevolence in Eighteenth-Century America* (1963); Arthur J. Worrall, *Quakers in the Colonial Northeast* (1980).

Arthur Worrall
Colorado State University

BENJAMIN COLMAN (1673-1747)

Works: *Faith Victorious* (1702); *The Government & Improvement of Mirth* (1707); *Imprecation Against the Enemies of God, Lawful and a Duty* (1707); *A Poem on Elijah's Translation, Occasion'd by the Death of the Reverend and Learned, Mr. Samuel Willard* (1707); *Practical Discourses on the Parable of the Ten Virgins* (1707); *The Piety and Duty of Rulers* (1708); *A Sermon Preached Before His Excellency the Governour...Being the Day of the Proclamation of the Happy Union of the Two Kingdoms of England and Scotland* (1708); *The Duty and Honour of Aged Women* (1711); *The Hainous Nature of the Sin of Murder* (1713); *A Plain and Familiar Discourse of Seeking God Early* (1713); *A Devout Contemplation on the Meaning of Divine Providence, in the Early Death of Pious and Lovely Children* (1714); *A Humble Discourse of the Incomprehensibleness of God* (1714); *A Devout and Humble Enquiry into the Reasons of...the Death of Good Men* (1715); *The Divine Compassions Declar'd and Magnified...upon the Sorrowful Occasion of a Miserable Woman Present, Under Sentence of Death for the Murder of Her Spurious Infant* (1715); *A Holy and Useful Life* (1715); *A Gospel Ministry* (1715); *Some of the Honours that Religion Does unto the Fruitful Mothers in Israel* (1715); *A Brief Inquiry into...Penitential Confessions* (1716); *A Sermon Preach'd at Boston...Thanksgiving for the Suppression of the Late Vile and Traiterous Rebellion in Great Britain* (1716); *A Sermon Preached at the Ordination of Mr. William Cooper* (1716); *A Sermon for the Reformation of Manners* (1716); *The Warnings of God unto Young People Not to Consent When Enticed to Sin* (1716); *A Discourse of the Pleasure of Religious Worship* (1717); *A Funeral Sermon Preached upon the Death of...Grove Hirst* (1717); *The Rending of the Vail* (1717); *A Sermon at the Lecture in Boston, After the Funerals of Mr. William Brattle and Mr. Ebenezer Pemberton* (1717); *Sermons Preached at the Lecture in Boston from Luke 21, 22* (1717); *The Religious Regards We Owe to our Country* (the election sermon; 1718); *The Blessing of Zebulun & Issachar* (1719); *Some Reasons and Arguments...for the Setting up Markets in Boston* (1719); *Ossa Josephi* (1720); *Early Piety Again*

Inculcated (1721); *The Honour and Happiness of the Vertuous Woman* (1721); *The Hope of the Righteous in Their Death* (1721); *The Nature of Early Piety* (1721); *Some Observations on the New Method of Receiving the Small-Pox* (1721); *Jacob's Vow* (1722); *Moses a Witness to Our Lord* (1722); *A Blameless and Inoffensive Life* (1723); *The Death of God's Saints* (1723); *David's Dying Charge to the Rulers and People of Israel* (the election sermon; 1723); *The Duty of Parents to Pray for Their Children* (1723); *God Deals with Us as Rational Creatures* (1723); *The Prophet's Death Lamented and Improved* (1723); *Two Sermons Preached in Boston. . .to Ask the Effusion of the Spirit of Grace on Their Children* (1723); *The Master Taken Up from the Sons of the Prophets* (1724); *The Doctrine and Law of the Holy Sabbath* (1725); *It Is a Fearful Thing to Fall into the Hands of the Living God* (1726); *Fidelity to Christ and to the Protestant Succession* (1727); *The Judgments of Providence in the Hand of Christ* (1727); *Parents and Grown Children Should Be Together at the Lord's Table* (1727); *A Prayer to the Lord of the Harvest* (1727); *An Argument for. . .Family Worship* (1728); *Death and the Grave without Any Order* (1728); *The Duty of Young People to Give Their Hearts to God* (1728); *The Holy Walk and Glorious Translation of Blessed Enoch* (1728); *Some of the Glories of our Lord. . .in Twenty Sacramental Discourses* (1728); *The Character of His Excellency William Burnet* (1729); *The Credibility of the Christian Doctrine of the Resurrection* (1729); *The Faithful Ministers of Christ Mindful of Their Own Death* (1729); *Dying in Peace in a Good Old Age* (1730); *Government, the Pillar of the Earth* (1730); *The Friend of Christ and of His People* (1731); *Ministers and People Under Special Obligations to Sanctity, Humility & Gratitude* (1732); *God Is a Great King* (1733); *The Fast Which God Hath Chosen* (1734); *A Brief Dissertation on the Three First Chapters of Genesis* (1735); *Reliquiae Turellae et Lachrymae Paternae* (1735); *A Dissertation on the Image of God* (1736); *The Merchandise of a People* (1736); *Righteousness and Compassion the Duty and Character of Pious Rulers* (1736); *The Great Duty of Waiting on God* (1737); *It Is of the Lord's Mercies That We Are Not Consumed* (1737); *Christ Standing for an Ensign of the People* (1738); *Faithful Pastors, Angels of the Churches* (1739); *The Unspeakable Gift of God* (1739); *The Faithful Servant in the Joy of His Lord* (1740); *The Lord Shall Rejoice in His Works* (1741); *Souls Flying to Jesus Christ* (1741); *The Great God Has Magnified His Word* (1742); *Dr. Colman's Return in Compliance with Mr. Seargeant's Request* (1743); *The Glory of God in the Firmament of His Power* (1743); *The Case of Satan's Fiery Darts* (1744); *Jesus Weeping Over His Dead Friend* (1744); *A Letter from the Reverend Dr. Colman of Boston to the Reverend Mr. Williams of Lebanon* (1744); *The Withered Hand Stretched Forth* (1744); *One Chosen of God* (1746); *The Vanity of Man as Mortal* (1746).

Biography: Benjamin Colman was born in Boston, Mass., on Oct. 19, 1673, shortly after his parents arrived from Eng. A somewhat frail child, he enjoyed scholarly pursuits, eventually developing a loyalty to Harvard, which marked his activities for many years to come. Several years after receiving the

M.A. from Harvard in 1695, Colman wrote to Thomas Hollis praising the "free and *catholic* air we breath at our little Cambridge." Before receiving his advanced degree, Colman spent six months as stated preacher in the village of Medford, and three weeks after, with degree in hand, he set sail for Eng., supported in part by his older brother John, the same one who advocated the land bank scheme. Captured by the French, Colman encountered a different kind of adventure than he was expecting, but after his delayed arrival in London, he quickly became acquainted with the leading dissenters of the city, preached for short terms in both Cambridge and Ipswich and for two years in Bath, and even found time for a romantic interlude with the young and attractive poet, Elizabeth Singer, who published first under the name of "Philomela" and later under her married name of Elizabeth Rowe.

Although Colman was probably looking for a London pulpit, in 1699 he was called back to Boston, where he became the founding pastor of the Brattle Street Church, the fourth Congregational Church to be founded in that city. This appointment involved a fiery exchange with Increase Mather (q.v.) and Cotton Mather (q.v.), who considered the new church, with the liberal policy toward membership proclaimed in its *Manifesto*, a threat to the theological unity of the city. Shortly after assuming his pastorate, Colman married Jane Clark, the daughter of one of his wealthy parishioners, and the family was increased by the birth of two daughters. Jane (Turell) (q.v.), the eldest, was a dutiful and submissive daughter, who wrote poetry of considerable merit and who later married the Rev. Ebenezer Turell (q.v.) of Medford. Abigail, with a penchant for rebellion as well as a bent for poetry, eloped with a young man of questionable reputation named Albert Dennie, who spent most of her fortune and then deserted her. After the death of his first wife in 1731, Colman married Sarah Crisp Clark, and in his 70s, after the death of his second wife, he married Mary Pepperell Frost, sister of the famous Col. William Pepperell, who was then celebrating his victory over Louisburg.

During his forty-seven-year pastorate, Colman's interests stretched far beyond the pastoral. As an overseer and later as a trustee of Harvard, he worked indefatigably to obtain funds and books for the institution, strove to maintain its free character against attack, and in 1724 was offered the presidency of the college. He also corresponded extensively with acquaintances in Eng. and Scot., most of which correspondence is unfortunately lost. In addition, he proposed schools for the poor of Boston, and his concern for financial matters clearly emerges in an election sermon and in a pamphlet urging the establishment of a market in Boston. His sermons following the earthquake of 1727 and his dissertation supporting inoculation show Colman's deep interest in the scientific discoveries of his day, to which he even made contributions himself. His interest in spiritual revival led to the writing and publication of Jonathan Edwards's (q.v.) *A Faithful Narrative*. He was the first Boston pastor to invite George Whitefield (q.v.) to his pulpit, but his enthusiasm for the Great Awakening cooled considerably when he saw it leading toward divisions among the brethren. Colman died in Boston on Aug. 29, 1773, at age 73.

Critical Appraisal: As noted by his contemporaries in Ebenezer Turell's 1749 biography and later by W. B. Sprague and also by Josiah Quincy, Benjamin Colman brought a new style to the colonies. "From the moment he began to publish," wrote Perry Miller, "the prose of Increase Mather (q.v.), let alone that of Cotton, in fact of all the older generation, became antiquated." Although Colman maintained some of the formulas of the Puritan sermon and although his style is imbued with biblical rhythms, there is a new sense of grace and balance, of urbanity and polish, to his writings, which justifies Miller's remark.

In addition, Colman's personal style of self-presentation brought a fresh wind to colonial writing. His genial spirit, for example, placed him in a role of conciliation and helped banish the defensive stance of Puritan polemic. Characteristically, his first extended publication was a dissertation on mirth. There he praised the smile, for "a glad Countenance transforms a man...; the Eye has new Life, and the Mein is Superior." "*A Chearful Spirit*," he wrote, "*is a happy & lovely thing*." Mirth should also pervade worship, for "it gives a Lustre to Religion," whereas "Melancholy People commonly make drooping Christians, to the disadvantage of Religion."

The work for which Colman was most known in his own lifetime, the *Practical Discourses on the Parable of the Ten Virgins*, is a 344-page expository work on the first fifteen verses of Matthew 25. In it Colman commented incisively on the material, which he related to the concerns of his day, many of which are also concerns of our own. The work is marked by a strongly visual imagination that vividly pictures events and situations. *A Humble Discourse of the Incomprehensibleness of God* treats an old theme in a new way and exhibits much of Colman's interest in the scientific theories of Restoration and eighteenth-century Eng., as do the extant manuscript sermons he preached in Bath. *Some of the Glories of God...in Twenty Sacramental Discourses* exhibits less unity as a work of theology but offers a wide panorama of Colman's ideas regarding the church. An interesting analysis of the spiritual masochist is presented in *Satan's Fiery Darts*, in which Colman offered a cure for this malady, which was not uncommon to the Puritan spirit.

Colman's poetry also introduced a new style to the Puritan colonies, for he brought back from Eng. the smooth prosody of the heroic couplet. Turell's biography recorded two short poems in heroic couplets that achieve a consummate sense of grace and compliment addressed to two young ladies he met in Eng. In a pair of poems addressed to *Urania*, Colman used tetrameter couplets in a mood both tender and severe as he counsels a parishioner who had lost a child to cease mourning and accept grace. Colman also composed two interesting poems of praise: one to Philomela after death and another to Alexander Pope in praise of his poetry, urging him to complete a projected work. He also wrote somewhat less successful poems to his children and tried his hand at psalm paraphrases. His most extended poetical work, *A Poem on Elijah's Translation Occasion'd by the Death of the Reverend and Learned Mr. Samuel Willard*, ostensibly a retelling of the biblical story, is a deft poem of celebration expressing Colman's jubilation of heart that the presidency of Harvard fell to John Leverett, his former tutor and a man of his own free persuasion. The college had narrowly missed falling into the hands of the Mather party, which was ready to impose an oath on all who would belong to the trustees or teach in Colman's beloved institution. Always a man of conciliation, peace, and love, Colman had a style of life and a style of writing in both prose and verse that marked the end of one age and the introduction to another.

Suggested Readings: BDAS; CCNE; DAB; FCNEV; Sibley-Shipton (IV, 120-137); Sprague (I, 223-229); T₁. *See also* Howard C. Adams, "Two Sermons and a Poem by Benjamin Colman," SCN, 34 (1978), 91-93; William D. Andrews, "The Literature of the 1727 New England Earthquake," EAL, 7 (1973), 281-294; Clayton H. Chapman, "Benjamin Colman and His Daughters," NEQ, 32 (1953), 169-192; idem, "Benjamin Colman and Philomela," NEQ, 42 (Jun. 1969), 214-231; Edwin Scott Gaustad, *The Great Awakening in New England* (1957); Theodore Hornberger, "Benjamin Colman and the Enlightenment," NEQ, 12 (1939), 227-240; Samuel K. Lothrop, *A History of the Church in Brattle Street* (1851); Harrison T. Meserole, ed., *Seventeenth-Century American Poetry* (1968); Perry Miller, *The New England Mind: From Colony to Province* (1953); idem, *The New England Mind: The Seventeenth Century* (1939); Samuel E. Morison, *Harvard College in the Seventeenth Century* (1936); Josiah Quincy, *The History of Harvard University* (1860); Ebenezer Turell, *The Life and Character of the Reverend Benjamin Colman* (1749); Alden T. Vaughan, *The Puritan Tradition in America 1620-1730* (1972).

Howard C. Adams
Frostburg State College

EBENEZER COOKE (c. 1667-c. 1732)

Works: *The Sot-weed Factor* (1708;1731); *An ELOGY on . . . Thomas Bordley* (1726); "An Elegy on . . . Nicholas Lowe" (1728); *Sotweed Redivivus* (1730); "The History of Colonel Nathaniel Bacon's Rebellion in Virginia" (1731); "An Elegy on . . . William Lock" (1732); "In Memory of . . . Benedict Leonard Calvert" (1732).

Biography: The son of Andrew and Anne Bowyer Cooke, Ebenezer Cooke, the self-appointed poet laureate of Md., was born in London around 1667 and came to Lord Baltimore's province shortly before the end of the seventeenth century; the earliest extant reference to him places the poet in St. Mary's City in 1694. Other available evidence, admittedly slight, suggests that Cooke, like many other southerners of his day, divided his time between the Old and New Worlds, returning to London, for example, around 1700 and again in 1708, when his most famous poem, *The Sot-weed Factor*, was published; from internal evidence, it appears that the poem may have been written as early as 1702. Cooke returned to Md. sometime before 1717, sold his share of the family estate at Malden to a cousin, Edward Cooke, and thereafter seems to have barely managed to support himself as a lawyer and land agent connected with the wealthy and prominent Bordley, Lowe, and Calvert families. His last years are memorable for an "ELOGY" on Thomas Bordley, the first belletristic production of William Parks's (q.v.) Annapolis press (1726), and for an extreme and chronic poverty to which he referred repeatedly in his final verses. Cooke apparently died shortly after 1732, the date of his elegy on Benedict Leonard Calvert.

Critical Appraisal: All but ignored until the past decade or so, Ebenezer Cooke has recently begun to gain recognition as an important contributor to the tradition of southern and southwestern humor in particular and to American literature in general. Prompted in large part by John Barth's treatment of the theme of identity in his version of *The Sot-Weed Factor* (1959), critics have come to see that the same issue is indeed involved in Cooke's poem of that title and that Cooke's protagonist bears strong family resemblances to the dispossessed, ambiguously Adamic figure who looms so large in later American poetry and fiction. Early commentators like Bernard Steiner and Lawrence Wroth focused attention on textual problems or on the historical accuracy of Cooke's portrait of seventeenth-century Md., determined to solve the various riddles involved in Cooke's historical identity and to sort out the autobiographical elements in *The Sot-weed Factor* and, to a lesser degree, in the other poems as well. More recent writers have taken for granted a shifting relationship between character and creator from episode to episode of the poem and have discussed instead the persona of the sotweed factor himself, clearly a type of the long familiar disgruntled merchant adventurer, and on the images and motifs, especially the motif of the curse, woven into the language.

The fact that Cooke wrote largely in Hudibrastic verse and thus seems more imitative of Samuel Butler than original in his own way must undoubtedly be blamed for a good deal of the delay in recognizing the connections between his work and what we have come to call native American humor. In particular, his technique of refusing to endorse or adopt unequivocally either the point of view of the British merchant or that of the view of the seasoned Marylanders in *The Sot-weed Factor* adumbrates the comic irresponsibility that is one hallmark of much later southern and American humor, as if in celebration of the joke itself, the joke for its own sake and not for the sake of any potential that comedy may possess to correct or reform. Cooke's portraits of "planting rabble," drunken justices, and cozening Quakers are also very much in the tradition of American humor, as is also his ambivalent stance, registered through his fondness for the Hudibrastic, in regard to high culture. A central bibliographical muddle involving *The Sot-weed Factor* is the disappearance of a 2nd edition of the poem; since William Parks's edition of "The Sot-Weed Factor" in 1731 is referred to by the printer as the 3rd edition, we must surmise either that a mistake was made or that there is indeed a lost 2nd edition.

Cooke's "History of Bacon's Rebellion," the second most important of his works, handles a subject extensively treated by historians and writers both before and after Cooke's time. We encounter in it, once again, the familiar imbroglio of images and events and the gallery of rogues, cowards, and scoundrels that, at one level at least, seem to be part and parcel of Cooke's assessment of the American experience. In this poem, however, he is less successful than in *The Sot-weed Factor* at blending subject matter and point of view and at creating a narrative persona whose ambivalent stance genuinely complicates rather than simply confuses the political issues involved. His fondness for earthy axioms and, once again, his choice of Hudibrastic meter tend to undercut the political conservatism, which would have been better projected by a more elegant vocabulary and regular iambics, that lies at the heart of the poem.

Another long poem, *Sotweed Redivivus*, is chiefly interesting for its deployment of Horatian allusions and images and for its treatment of contemporary political and economic controversies. In this work, Cooke treats a variety of Md.'s economic ills, including the single crop system, absentee landlords, and the lack of circulating specie.

An emphasis on the local marks the four elegies attributed to Cooke, which are otherwise chiefly remarkable for their subtle blending of politics and public sorrow. Certain autobiographical clues to the exact nature of Cooke's connections with Bordley and the Calverts also seem to lurk in the verses, but to date the references have proved too opaque for historical research to penetrate beyond the level of surmise.

Suggested Readings: LHUS; T₁. *See also* Robert D. Arner, "The Blackness of Darkness: Satire, Romance, and Ebenezer Cooke's *The Sot-weed Factor*," TennSL, 21 (1976), 1-10; idem, "Clio's *Rhimes*: History and Satire in Ebenezer Cooke's 'History of Bacon's Rebellion,' " SLJ, 6 (1974), 91-106; idem, "Ebenezer Cooke: Satire in the Colonial South," SLJ, 8 (1975), 153-164; idem, "Ebenezer Cooke's *The Sot-Weed Factor*: The Structure of Satire," SLJ, 4 (1971), 33-47; idem, "Ebenezer Cooke's *Sotweed Redivivus*: Satire in the Horatian Mode," MQ, 28 (1975), 489-496; Donald V. Coers, "New Light on the Composition of Ebenezer Cooke's *Sot-weed Factor*," AL, 49 (1978), 604-605; Edward M. Cohen, *Ebenezer Cooke: The Sot-weed Canon* (1975); J. A. Leo Lemay, "Ebenezer Cooke," *Men of Letters in Colonial Maryland* (1972), pp. 77-110; James Talbot Poole, "Ebenezer Cooke and the Maryland Muse," AL, 3 (1931), 296-302; Bernard C. Steiner, *Early Maryland Poetry* (1900); Lawrence C. Wroth, "The Maryland Muse," PAAS, New Series, 44 (1934), 267-335.

Robert D. Arner
University of Cincinnati

SAMUEL COOKE (1687-1747)

Works: *Necessarius* (1731); *Divine Sovereignty* (1741).

Biography: Son of Thomas, Jr., and Sarah Cooke, Samuel Cooke was born on Nov. 22, 1687, in Guilford, Conn. The death of his father in 1701 necessitated the sale of a house and lot to finance his education at Yale College, where Cooke was graduated in 1705. Although he began preaching shortly after graduation, Cooke's first real post was that of rector of the Hopkins Grammar School in New Haven, where he remained from 1707 to 1716. In 1715 Cooke was called to the pastorate in Stratfield (now Bridgeport), Conn., where he served until his death on Dec. 2, 1747.

During the Great Awakening, Cooke was a zealous advocate of the New Light movement and suffered for it, particularly for his part in the founding of a church in New Haven for those who wanted to separate from the Old Light church. Thus, in 1745, after a tenure of thirteen years, pressure from the Old Light majority on the board forced Cooke to resign his post as trustee of Yale College, and in his last years, his own parishioners vexed him with tardiness in the payment of his salary, which at his death was some 3,000 pounds in arrears. Nevertheless, his personal appearance was legendarily impressive: a slightly antique figure clad in heavy curled wig, black gown, and shoes with silver buckles, who commanded the respect and even fear of his people. Cooke died in Stratfield, Conn., on Dec. 2, 1747.

Critical Appraisal: Even though by 1731 such rhetorical embroidery was already somewhat quaint, a strain of seventeenth century wit, which suggests the continuity of Calvinist orthodoxy in this supporter of the New Lights of the Great Awakening, can be found in the sermons of Samuel Cooke. Thus in his first publication, *Necessarius*, a funeral sermon for the Rev. Mr. John Davenport (q.v.) of Stamford, he compared ministers to ambassadors, vineyard dressers, rain clouds, watchmen, bulwarks and defenses, shepherds, physicians, lights and candles, stewards, fathers, nurses, mothers, and patterns or fair copies. What is more, in the sermon's "Application," Davenport is viewed through each of these images. Such rhetorical embroidery was already somewhat quaint by 1731.

Perhaps more current in several respects was *Divine Sovereignty in the Salvation of Sinners*, preached in 1741, the same year as Jonathan Edwards's (q.v.) famous *Sinners in the Hands of an Angry God* and in several respects reminiscent of it. The statement of doctrine identifies God's mercy with "his mere sovereign, arbitrary good Pleasure," in language almost identical to that of Edwards. However, the sermon as a whole stresses the positive side of the doctrine of God's sovereignty in a way that Edwards's awakening sermon does not. Cooke insists that "God never damns by Prerogative, but he always saves by Prerogative." There is little real overlap between the sermons, but many interesting parallels in image, phrase, and theology. On the whole, the small output of Samuel Cooke reflects the subtle rhetorical changes between seventeenth-and eighteenth-century American sermons while nonetheless underlining the theological continuities in New Eng. orthodoxy.

Suggested Readings: CCNE; Dexter (I, 29-33). *See also* Leonard Bacon, *Thirteen Historical Discourses* (1839), pp. 199, 220, 232.

Wilson H. Kimnach
University of Bridgeport

SAMUEL COOKE (1709-1783)

Works: *The Solemn Charge Preached at the Ordination of Cotton Brown* (1748); *Christ Holding the Stars Preached at the Ordination of Nathaniel Robbins* (1751); *The Charge of St. Paul Preached at the Ordination of William Symmes* (1759); *A Sermon Being the Anniversary for the Election of His Majesty's Council* (1770); *The Violent Destroyed* (1777).

Biography: Born on Jan. 10, 1709, in Hadley, Mass., Samuel Cooke was the son of Samuel and Anne (Marsh) Cooke. At the age of 22, Cooke began his education at Harvard College. While at Harvard, he won the Hopkins Prize for excellence, and a few months after graduating in 1735, he returned with a Hopkins fellowship. He was appointed the university's butler in 1736, librarian pro tem in 1737, and the Quaestio collector (in charge of questions debated at public exercises) in 1738. As Quaestio collector, Cooke made one of his earliest religious statements: he argued that everything necessary for salvation can be found in the Holy Scriptures. The Board of Overseers publicly admonished Cooke for supporting the heretical side of this and other issues.

After Cooke left Harvard, his years as preacher and parson were marked by a mixture of personal tragedy and ministerial honors. During the fall and winter of 1738 and 1739, Cooke preached at Westborough, Menotomy (now Arlington), Roxbury, and Marlborough. On Sept. 12, 1739, he was ordained minister of the Second Precinct at Cambridge, Mass. A year after his ordination, he married Sarah Porter, who died on Aug. 22, 1741, of throat distemper after the loss of their infant son. On Sept. 23, 1742, Cooke married Anna Cotton, daughter of John Cotton (q.v.), who bore eleven children, lost four, and died on Feb. 12, 1761, at the age of 38. His third wife, Lucy Hancock, daughter of John Hancock, suffered for six years from the gravel before her death on Sept. 21, 1768.

During these turbulent years, Cooke was honored with invitations to deliver *The Artillery Sermon* (1753), the *Harvard College Dudleian Lecture* (1767), and the *Election Sermon* before the General Court in the Cambridge meeting house (1770). At the onset of the American Revolution, he was forced to leave the parsonage because of nearby fighting, but he later returned to care for the sick when the parsonage was converted into a hospital. In the spring of 1775, Cooke was chosen chaplain of the General Court sitting at Watertown. This appointment was the last ministerial office he held before he died of dropsy on Jun. 4, 1783.

Critical Appraisal: Throughout his long ministerial career, Samuel Cooke wrote sermons and lectures that reveal the changing religious and political scene in New Eng. during the 1700s. Cooke's religious works embrace his own development from religious liberalism to conservatism; these works also reflect the varied religious thinking of the period. His political pieces exhibit America's hatred for British imperialism and the country's growing interest in a government free from British control.

Cooke's early works—before 1770—are doctrines of religious liberalism. As a young man, Cooke was a member of the Harvard group of liberal religious advocates. Influenced by this group's radical beliefs, he argued for the independence of the New Eng. churches in the choice of ministers and for a complete faith in the Holy Scriptures and in the ministers charged with spreading the Scriptures; he also expressed a strong belief in the intelligence and goodness of his parishioners. These beliefs are particularly evident in *Solemn Charge, Charge of St. Paul*, and the *Dudleian Lecture*. In *Solemn Charge*, he supported each church's right to select the minister and charged these ministers with preaching the doctrine of revelation. His religious open-mindedness is also reflected in *Charge of St. Paul*, where he again supported the independence of the New Eng. churches; he argued that the right of each church to choose its minister devolves from the natural rights of men. In addition, Cooke expressed his support for universal salvation. Fourteen years later in the Dudleian Lecture, he startled the conservative bastion by arguing that natural religion did not interfere with revealed religion; the former, he claimed, provided proof of the latter.

By 1770, however, Cooke's religious sermons gradually became more conservative. J. L. Sibley, in a biographical sketch, indicated that the personal tragedies in Cooke's life might account for his shift toward religious conservatism. This shift, however, could also be Cooke's response to a period of religious unrest in the colonies. By the later 1700s, Calvinism in its purest form had long since faded away; New Lightism had invaded the Old Light churches; and many itinerant ministers were preaching Anglicanism throughout the colonies. At this time, Cooke's sermons assumed a frenetic, sometimes violent quality. In a 1770 sermon printed in Benjamin Cutter's *History of the Town of Arlington*, Cooke revealed his shaken faith in the goodness of his parishioners, claiming that the morality of the people of New Eng. was no better "than the Indians in the darkest corner of the land." In his 1773 sermons, he argued that immersion was vain, and he encouraged his Second Precinct to tax the protesting Baptists for his support. In the years immediately preceding his death, Cooke's religious liberalism had completely faded. He opposed the concepts of universalism and unitarianism, and *The Salem Gazette* claimed after his death that he opposed salvation for all men—a doctrine he supported in his early years.

In addition to reflecting a turbulent religious period in the colonies, Cooke's work also reflected the political tensions of the time. In fact, his *Election Sermon* is considered one of the clearest political discourses of the late eighteenth century. In it he highlighted the differences between the nature of a healthy government and the one presently tied to the British Empire, arguing that a healthy government is one in which choice and determination come from mankind. Cooke also showed his (and America's) distrust of an autocratic government; the power of government, he claimed, should come from the whole community, not a single person. He concluded the sermon by charging all Americans with respectfully and decently securing their liberties.

In *The Violent Destroyed*, delivered in memory of the deaths of outnumbered

American soldiers at Lexington in 1775, Cooke gave another impassioned sermon on the state of affairs between Britain and America. This time, however, he called for a more violent American response. The entire sermon is an extended typological metaphor likening the plight of the Americans to that of the Israelites. The British atrocities against the Americans, for example, are compared to those of the Amalekites on the Israelite camp. He called the Amalekites—and by extension, the British—unjust, savage, and barbaric. As God destroyed the Amalekites, Cooke pointed out, God would also destroy the British oppressors. Cooke ended his sermon by listing some of the issues in the British-American conflict—regulation of American trade, Parliament's lawmaking control over America—and by calling for war as the only means of securing America's liberties.

Suggested Readings: CCNE; Sibley-Shipton (IX, 500-509). *See also Boston Evening-Post*, Jan. 7, 1745, p. 2, col. 1; Corporation Records (Harvard Univ. Archives), II, 431-432; Benjamin Cutter, *History of the Town of Arlington* (1880), pp. 35, 50-51; William R. Cutter, *A History of the Cutter Family of New England*, comp. Benjamin Cutter (1871), pp. 291-295; Executive Records of the Province Council (Watertown, Mass.), XIX, 12; Overseers' Records (Harvard Univ. Archives), I, 177-179, 287; *Salem Gazette*, Jun. 26, 1783, p. 2, col. 3; Sibley's Letters Received (contains extracts of Samuel Cooke's diary; Harvard Univ. Archives), XV, 83; John Wingate Thornton, *The Pulpit of the American Revolution* (1860), pp. 147-186.

Donna Casella Kern
Michigan State University

THOMAS COOMBE (1747-1822)

Works: *An Exercise, Containing a Dialogue and Two Odes* (1767); *St. Stephen's, Walbrook Sermon* (1772); *The Harmony Between the Old and New Testaments Respecting the Messiah* (1774); *Edwin: Or, The Emigrant. An Eclogue. To Which Are Added Three Other Poetical Sketches* (1775); *A Sermon Preached. . .July 20* (1775); *The Peasant of Auburn* (1783); *The Influence of Christianity on the Condition of the World* (1789).

Biography: Thomas Coombe was born in Philadelphia on Oct. 21, 1747. Coombe graduated from the College of Philadelphia in 1766, and during his matriculation, he began his literary career by translating into English some Latin poems by John Beveridge (q.v.), which were later published in the latter's *Epistolae Familiares* (1765). Shortly after graduation, Coombe also published his commencement exercise, *A Dialogue with Two Odes*, a poem written in imitation of Vergil. In 1768 Coombe studied theology in Eng., and, upon his ordination in 1771, became chaplain to the marquis of Rockingham. On Oct. 29, 1771, the bishop of London granted Coombe passage money to settle in America, a practice originated by Charles II to encourage the immigration of Anglican clergymen to the colonies. Coombe returned to Philadelphia and, on Nov. 30, 1772, became an assistant minister with the Rev. William White to the combined parishes of Christ Church and St. Peter's. Joining hundreds of fellow clergy throughout the colonies, Coombe preached a Fast Day Sermon on Jul. 20, 1775, in which he blamed America's current hostilities on the British. Yet when the Declaration of Independence was signed, Coombe disengaged himself from the revolutionists' position, claiming that his ordination oath bound him to the Loyalists' side. Consequently, in 1777 he was ordered deported to Staunton, Va., but pleading ill health, he escaped both deportation and a subsequent arrest order in Philadelphia.

In 1779 Coombe sailed for London, and from this date, he received a series of posts and honors in the Church of England: in addition to receiving a doctor of divinity degree from the University of Dublin in 1781, he served as chaplain to the earl of Carlisle, chaplain in ordinary of King George (1794), prebendary of Canterbury (1800), and rector of the combined parishes of St. Michael's Queenhithe and Trinity the Less, at which ministry he served until his death on Aug. 15, 1822. Before his departure from America, Coombe had corresponded with Oliver Goldsmith, whom he eulogized in the dedicatory remarks of *Edwin: Or The Emigrant*, published in 1775, and on his return to Eng., Coombe enjoyed the acquaintanceship of others in the circle of Samuel Johnson, including Sir Joshua Reynolds and even the famous lexicographer himself. Comfortable with distinguished friends and advantageous church livings, Coombe apparently never regretted his Loyalist's position during the American Revolution, and in *The Peasant of Auburn* (1783), he rebuked his countrymen for having allowed war to shatter the growth of learning and commerce in the New World.

Critical Appraisal: Thomas Coombe published both sermons and poems. The sermons show no peculiarities in doctrine or style to distinguish Coombe from other churchmen educated in Eng. and sent to the colonies. His prose is generally a pleasing blend of exegesis and eloquence. In the Fast Day Sermon for Jul. 20, 1775, which he dedicated to Benjamin Franklin (q.v.), he urged his parishioners to recognize the causal relationships between sin and political defeat on the one hand and virtue and victory on the other. Candid in an assessment of public piety, he asked that the Fast Day not become another excuse for national hypocrisy. In *The Harmony*, actually two sermons combined into one printed message, Coombe argued that Christianity is the only true religion, because the prophecies of the Old Testament are fulfilled in the New. Moving typologically from Eden through the messianic figures of the Hebrew stories to the birth and ministry of Jesus, he urged believers to manifest their faith in works of charity. By thus linking faith and charity, Coombe united the sermon for the Sunday on which collections are taken for the poor with the Christmas message of the birth of the long expected saviour.

The spirit of charity, heartfelt in the sermons and free of sentimentality, underlies much of Coombe's poetry. Working in popular modes such as the quasi-narrative monologue and reflective ode, Coombe imitated Goldsmith's

"The Deserted Village" in the Edwin poems (his major work) and drew on the styles of the Warton brothers, Young, Collins, and Gray for his shorter poems, occasionally matching but never surpassing his models. Like many pre-Romantic writers and indeed the young Wordsworth himself, Coombe assumed that the honest poor are inherently tragic. According to this sensibility, a man's suffering makes him heroic; for many readers, however, that man must have some complexity as well, else he is unable to carry the emotional and moral significance with which his author burdens him. Such a character engages the reader's pity, but he is no Job or Lear. Edwin, of *Edwin: Or, The Emigrant* and *The Peasant of Auburn*, exemplifies Coombe's reliance on pathos rather than on characterization. In the shorter and first published of these poems, Edwin loses everything: an oppressor takes his land, his sons and wife die en route to America, and his daughter is captured by Indians. In *The Peasant of Auburn*, Coombe expanded the explanations of Edwin's misery, but he did little to make him tragic. In one fine moment of irony, however, Edwin bewails his immigration to a land of the free, only to have his daughter enslaved by savages. In other changes, Coombe dropped the rather pleasingly melancholy refrain of *Edwin*, and he added a homily on the inevitability of suffering and death and gave Edwin hallucinations about revenge on the Indians who kidnapped his daughter. These revisions, however, do not lift the pall of melodrama, and both poems (heroic couplets) show little experimentation with or command of prosody.

From a purely aesthetic point of view, the nadir of Coombe's poetry is "The Highwayman's Soliloquy" (published with *The Peasant of Auburn*). Its thesis—that a man whose wife and seven babies are starving will reject charity for fear he will be thought a robber—is simplistic and maudlin. In comparison, "On Throwing By an Old Black Coat" (published with *Edwin: Or, The Emigrant*), although overserious and flawed with latent antisemitism, is a rather successful treatment of the theme of charity. The narrator, foregoing the sale of his worn-out garment to a Jewish street vendor, gives the coat to an old derelict. Unable to resist a moral even though it could be of little comfort to the poor man, Coombe ended with an aphorism on the transience of riches: "Men turn to dust, as Broadcloth turns to rags."

Coombe's metier is the lyric. Of the two works published with *Edwin*, "Night," in elegiac quatrains, shares with the odes of the graveyard school an evenness of tone and sweet pensiveness. "An Hymn to Resignation," in ballad stanzas, is half prayer, half apostrophe. Both poems, cast in the artificial diction that Wordsworth condemns in the 1800 preface to *Lyrical Ballads*, represent competently the taste for pseudo-Miltonic rumination in late eighteenth-century American literature.

Suggested Readings: CCMC; DAB; Sprague (V, 280-281); T₂. *See also Appleton's Cyclopedia of American Biography* (1892), I, 723; Gerald Fotheringill, *A List of Emigrant Ministers to America, 1690-1811* (1904), p. 21; *National Cyclopedia of American Biography* (1939; rep., 1967), VII, 343-344.

Roslyn L. Knutson
University of Arkansas at Little Rock

MYLES COOPER (1737-1785)

Works: *Poems on Several Occasions* (1761); contributions to *Whip for the Whig* (1768); *Causidicus Mastix* (1772); *Ethices Compendium* (1774); a series of papers signed "Popsicola" (c. 1774); "Stanzas Written on the Evening of the 10th of May, 1776" (pub. in *Gentleman's Magazine*, Jul. 1776, 326-327); *A Sermon: National Humiliation and Repentence Recommended* (1777); "epitaph" (pub. in *Edinburgh Evening Courant*, May 28, 1785); Dubia: *An Address from the* Clergy *of New York and New Jersey to the Episcopalians in Virginia* (n.d.); *An Address to the Episcopalians of Virginia* (1771); *A Friendly Address to All Reasonable Americans* (1774); *The American Querist* (1774); *The Patriots of North America* (1775); *What Think Ye of Congress Now?* (1775).

Biography: Born in Feb. 1737, at Wha House Estate in Cumberland County, Eng., Myles Cooper was educated and ordained at Oxford. In 1762, the Rev. Dr. Edward Bentham (Christ Church, Oxford), acting for Archbishop Secker, sent Cooper to N.Y. to be groomed for the presidency of King's College (later called Columbia Univ.), where Cooper joined the faculty as professor of moral philosophy. There, in 1763, upon the resignation of the president, the Rev. Dr. Samuel Johnson (q.v.), he assumed the leadership of the college. Cooper's effects on King's College were many: he tightened discipline, added a medical school and a public art collection, established a grammar school and hospital, increased the faculty, acquired a grant from the Oxford press for a copy of each book it produced, and amassed substantial New York City property. In addition, Cooper was also deeply involved in the pastoral, charitable, and administrative dimensions of the Anglican Church, and he worked ceaselessly for an American episcopacy.

During the years leading up to the War of Independence, Cooper became increasingly associated with Loyalist pamphlets and was consequently marked by zealous patriots as a threat to the colonial cause. On May 10, 1775, following several harrowing encounters with angry mobs, he escaped to Eng. with the help of several former students, one of whom was Alexander Hamilton (q.v.). Like many Anglican clergymen, Cooper found refuge in the mother church, who provided both academic and ecclesiastical livings for those displaced by Eng.'s defeat in the war, and did not return to America. After his flight from the Sons of Liberty Cooper spent most of his ten remaining years in Edinburgh, at Cowgate, near the university. Reputed to have a palate for fine wines and an appetite for rich food, Cooper lacked the stomach and constitution for such habits. On May 20, 1785, he died from a chronic intestinal ailment and was buried in a now unmarked grave in the exclusive cemetery for clergymen amid the ruins of old Restalrig Church, Edinburgh.

Critical Appraisal: In 1776 Myles Cooper was hated throughout the colonies as a writer of Loyalist pamphlets that undercut the logic of rebellion and that supported the rights of Eng. to treat the colonies as colonies. According to C. H. Vance, however, Cooper did not write these pamphlets himself; he was, rather, "the critic and reviser of practically all this literature." Undoubtedly, the pamphlets bore Cooper's approval and in many cases reflected his logic, rhetoric, and wit. Nevertheless, his talents as writer must not be assessed in terms of work not his own.

Cooper began his writing career as a poet, and the lyrics in *Poems on Several Occasions* (a commencement volume Cooper called "juvenile amusements") suggest that his literary gift was solid and versatile. The volume contains 135 poems, some of which (undesignated) belong to two of Cooper's student friends. In its generic variety of odes, epigrams, lyrics, and songs, the Cooper volume resembles an anthology of late seventeenth-century verse. The poems are both serious and droll, both schoolboy fluff and portents of genuine talent. Unhappily, if "Stanzas Written on the Evening of the 10th of May, 1776" is a fair measure (and it is his only published verse after the book of juvenilia, except for his epitaph), the wit and assurance that mark Cooper's early poems do not survive the political turmoils of the 1770s. On the night in question, Cooper fled a violent mob who were outraged over his support of Eng. The resulting poem, a combination prayer and narrative that chronicles his harrowing escape, was published in Jul. 1776, in the *Gentleman's Magazine* (it has since been collected in Winthrop Sargeant's *The Loyalist Poetry of the American Revolution* [1857]). Using a long ballad stanza (aabccb), Cooper wrote in a sentimental mode, and he relied on tedious diction ("and joy was wont to dwell"; "and winged my rapid way") rather than the personal and immediate terror of such an experience. Consequently, the merit of the stanzas lies not in the poet's skill but in the historicity of the poetic subject.

Of Cooper's numerous sermons and ecclesiastical writings, only one has survived in print: the sermon for an annual Fast Day, on Dec. 13, 1776. Delivered before former and newly restored colleagues at the University of Oxford, the sermon is primarily a political speech. Within the framework of the Psalms, Cooper explained how the present revolution in America had come about, and he called on Englishmen to regain God's favor through a public act of humiliation. Of interest to historians and political analysts are Cooper's theories on the Revolution's genesis. Essentially, he blamed the colonials for a republicanism that is exploited by rebel leaders. Eng., responding too leniently, encouraged those who promoted the "Baal of Independence." Bewailing the fate of Loyalists trapped by the rebellion, Cooper prophesied political chaos in a land where men "conceive the Governed to be superior to the Governors." Occasional flashes of lyricism, a display of learning, a considerable reliance on sentiment and indignation (but without loss of the appeal to reason), repeated verbal allusions to the *Book of Common Prayer*—these characteristics describe the graceful, measured prose style of the sermon. But the tone of the sermon is often described as biting and sarcastic, and its hauteur, elitism, and absolute certainty of right confirm the belief that when Cooper spoke of the ignorant and misled, he was indeed sneering and derisive. Of broader significance, this sermon confirms the progressive secularization of the pulpit from 1700 to 1800, both in the colonies and in Eng., for although the occasion of a national fast invited a political sermon, Cooper pushed eschatological concerns into the background and gave governmental and social issues his primary attention.

Suggested Readings: CCMC; DAB; LHUS; T_2. *See also Appleton's Cyclopedia of American Biography*, I, 730; Gerald Fotheringill, *A List of Emigrant Ministers to America, 1690-1811* (1904), p. 21; *National Cyclopedia of American Biography*, VI, 341-342; Clarence Hayden Vance, "Myles Cooper," CUQ, 22 (1930), 260-286.

Roslyn L. Knutson
University of Arkansas at Little Rock

SAMUEL COOPER (1725-1783)

Works: *A Sermon Preached to the Ancient and Honourable Artillery Company* (1751); *A Sermon Preached in Boston* (1753); *The Crisis* (1754); *A Sermon Preached in the Audience of His Honour Spencer Phips* (1756); *A Sermon Preached Before His Excellency Thomas Pownall* (1759); *A Sermon Preach'd April 9* (1760); *A Sermon upon...the Death of Our Late Sovereign* (1761); *A Discourse on the Man of Sin* (1774); *A Sermon Preached Before His Excellency John Hancock* (1780).

Biography: Samuel Cooper was born in Boston, Mass., on Mar. 28, 1725, a son of the Rev. William Cooper (q.v.) and Judith Sewall, daughter of Judge Samuel Sewall (q.v.). A 1743 graduate of Harvard, Cooper was elected the following year to the pastorate of the Brattle Street Church, where he succeeded his father. He was ordained in 1746, and in 1767 he was awarded a doctor of divinity degree by the University of Edinburgh. Married to Judith Bulfinch, he had two daughters.

From the early 1760s until his death, Cooper actively participated in the patriot cause. A constant contributor to newspapers and a tireless correspondent and speaker, he was often called upon by the Sons of Liberty to address their meetings. Cooper was also a close associate of James Otis (q.v.), John Hancock, John Adams (q.v.), and Samuel Adams (q.v.), and he corresponded throughout the Revolutionary War with Benjamin Franklin (q.v.), who acknowledged Cooper's arguments in his own writing. In Apr. 1775, when order was issued by the British for Cooper's arrest, he fled the city and did not return until after the evacuation. The London *Political Register* in 1780 noted that Cooper, "though a minister of peace and to all outward appearances a meek and heavenly man, yet was one of the chief instruments in stirring up the people to take arms." In May 1780 Cooper was chosen to preach the election sermon for Mass., and the result was considered so eloquent and of such importance that it was translated into several European languages and printed together with the state constitution. Cooper was the first vice-president of the Academy of Arts and Sciences, founded in 1780, and a member of the Harvard College Corporation from 1767 until his death in Boston on Dec. 23, 1783.

Critical Appraisal: Almost all of Samuel Cooper's published works were sermons, ranging in subject matter from an antipapal discourse on "The Man of Sin" to his 1780 oration praising Governor John Hancock and the new Mass. constitution. Although at times ornamented, the style of Cooper's sermons was clear, and on the appropriate occasion he could be both eloquent and inspirational. Though he was very active in the Revolutionary cause, only one of his published sermons directly relates to the events and issues that were foremost in the public's mind. His "Man of Sin" attack on the papacy however is congruent with his extreme sensitivity to arbitrary power. Cooper on occasion preached to an official audience such as the Artillery Company or the Massachusetts Council and Assembly. Typical is his 1756 sermon before Lieutenant Governor Spencer Phips, the Council and Assembly, in which Cooper, taking his text from Hebrews 9:24-26, cited Moses as an example of piety, fortitude, and self-denial in public service and exclaimed "how happy the people who are governed by men of the same disinterested and public spirit." In 1759, "upon the occasion of the success of his majesty's arms in the reduction of Quebec," he preached a sermon of thanksgiving and praise for the power and greatness of God in supporting and defending the church, the Protestant religion, and the British nation and in preserving and prospering the American dominions. In this sermon, he gave thanks for the British army's defense of the colonies against the French and especially praised General Wolfe and mourned his heroic death.

Cooper's democratic sentiments are perhaps best revealed in his 1761 sermon on the death of George II and his 1780 election sermon. Cooper wrote that the text of the former sermon—"Put not your trust in Princes, nor in the Son of Man—His breath goeth forth, he returneth to his Earth"—is not to be taken to weaken the obligations of the relationship between prince and subject, for princes "bear the faint Image of the Power and authority of the Lord of all." Nevertheless, according to Cooper, the ruler who recognizes that he "partakes of the same nature with [his subjects], and is alike encompassed with the natural and moral frailties of humanity" will be a righteous and good ruler and will resist the temptations to extend his power and authority beyond their proper bounds. In the tradition of Puritan typology, the 1780 sermon preached before Governor John Hancock and the Assembly on the occasion of the inauguration of the new constitution compares the colonists to the ancient Israelites emerged from bondage and demonstrates that "the Hebrew government, though a theocracy, was yet . . . a free republic, and that the sovereignty resided in the people." In addition to these democratic sentiments, Cooper urged the importance of education: "a people enlightened and civilized by the sciences and liberal arts have sentiments that support liberty and good laws: they may be guided by a silken thread." He jubilantly echoed the most popular theme of the late Revolutionary years—America's mission in the world: "We seem called by Heaven to make a large portion of this globe a seat of knowledge and liberty, of agriculture, commerce, and arts, and what is more important than all, of Christian piety and virtue." All in all, Cooper's writings represent some of the best examples of eighteenth-century

American sermons, and his life reflects the patriot spirit of many New Eng. clergy, men who used their pulpits to advance the cause of American patriotism.

Suggested Readings: CCNE; DAB; Sibley-Shipton (XI, 192-213); Sprague (I, 440-444); T₂. *See also* Alice M. Baldwin, *The New England Clergy and the American Revolution* (1928), passim; Philip M. Davidson, *Propaganda and the American Revolution* (1941), pp. 22, 236, 404.

Elaine K. Ginsberg
West Virginia University

THOMAS COOPER (1759-1839)

Works: *Letters on the Slave Trade* (1787); *Propositions Respecting the Foundation of Civil Government* (1787); *Supplement to Mr. Cooper's Letters on the Slave Trade* (1788); *Tracts, Ethical, Theological and Political* (1789); *Observations on the Art of Painting Among the Ancients* (1790); *Observations Respecting the History of Physiognomy* (1790); *To the Right Honourable Edmund Burke* (1790); *Reply to Mr. Burke's Invective Against Mr. Cooper and Mr. Watt* (1792); *Political Arithmetic* (1794); *Some Information Respecting America* (1794); *Political Essays* (1799); *An Account of the Trial of Thomas Cooper* (1800). See Dumas Malone's *The Public Life of Thomas Cooper, 1783-1839* (1926), for a full bibliography of Cooper's writings after 1800.

Biography: Thomas Cooper was born in Weymouth, Eng., on Oct. 22, 1759. His father sent him to Oxford, but he did not take a degree. He subsequently trained in law and medicine, and until immigrating to America in 1794, he pursued a varied career in law and calico printing. Before that, Cooper made a reputation for himself as a political radical, advocating parliamentary reform, the abolition of the slave trade, and the repeal of the test acts. He visited Paris in 1792 and opened a correspondence between the Manchester Constitutional Society and the Jacobins, which earned him the contempt of English opponents of the French Revolution, including Edmund Burke. Later, however, Cooper tempered his initial admiration of the Revolution.

After his arrival in America, Cooper settled in Northumberland County, Pa., where he farmed and practiced law and medicine. A publicist for the Jeffersonian Republican party, Cooper was fined and briefly imprisoned under the Sedition Act of 1798, but after the triumph of the Jeffersonians in 1800, he served as a county commissioner (1801-1804) and as a state judge in Pa. (1804-1811). In 1811, after the legislature had accused him of arbitrary conduct, Cooper was removed from office by Governor Simon Snyder, and he turned to scholarship, teaching chemistry at Dickinson College (1811-1815) and the University of Pennsylvania (1815-1819) and publishing voluminously on scientific subjects. He was elected a member of the American Philosophical Society, but an appointment as professor of chemistry at the University of Virginia, advocated by

Thomas Jefferson (q.v.), never materialized, and in 1820 he took a similar chair at South Carolina College, where he was thereafter chosen president. At South Carolina College, he also taught political science and was instrumental in the establishment of a school of medicine and an insane asylum. Although the clergy attacked him for his materialist philosophy, Cooper managed to maintain his prestige in S.C. by advocating states rights and defending slavery. After retiring from the College in 1834, Cooper continued to be active in politics and to publish until his death on Nov. 11, 1839.

Critical Appraisal: An extraordinarily prolific writer, Thomas Cooper published dozens of books, whose topics ranged from philosophy, religion, law, and politics to chemistry, medicine, and business. He was also an editor of considerable skill, publishing J. B. d'Aumont's *Narrative of Proceedings Relative to the Suspension of the King of France* (1792) and compiling *The Statutes at Large of South Carolina* (1836-1839).

Although most of Cooper's writings appeared after 1800, the pattern of his career was set before then. During the years between 1787 and 1794, he established himself as one of the most strident and prolific pamphleteers in Eng. In *Tracts, Ethical, Theological and Political*, he expounded a philosophy of materialism and demonstrated his hostility to the established church, and in *Propositions Respecting the Foundation of Civil Government*, he provided a comprehensive statement of his political philosophy, which emphasized the popular basis of government, the value of individual freedom, and the evils of tyranny. He also vehemently attacked the slave trade and, in his *Reply to Mr. Burke's Invective*, defended the French Revolution. His active work in the parliamentary reform movement, his friendship with influential religious rationalists like Joseph Priestley, and his highly publicized visit to Fr. in 1792 marked him as a leading member of the political opposition. His writings in this period reflected a direct and passionate involvement with the issues of the day and a willingness to attack any person or institution that seemed to frustrate the cause of liberty.

When Cooper returned to Eng. in 1794 from an exploratory trip to the U.S., he published *Some Information Respecting America*. Written in the form of letters to an English friend, this tract is a compilation of travel descriptions, documentary material relating to the American economy and government, and personal observations on the quality of life in the new nation. He praised the establishment of religious and civil liberty in the U.S., the vigor of the economy, the ingenuity of the people, and the absence of extreme poverty. "The almost general mediocrity of fortune that prevails in America" and the opportunities for useful employment have allowed America to escape the idleness and vice so characteristic of Europe. Cooper is not entirely uncritical of the U.S. (he advised immigrants not to settle in slaveholding areas), but his pamphlet is a good statement of the reasons why many English intellectuals, disillusioned by the failure of the radical cause during the period of reaction against the French Revolution, immigrated to the New World.

Cooper's major contribution to the Jeffersonian cause was *Political Essays*, a compilation of materials he had published in the *Northumberland Gazette* while serving as its temporary editor. Like *Some Information Respecting America*, this book is a patchwork of original pieces and documentary material. Cooper, like other Republicans, believed that the Federalist administration was attempting to establish arbitrary government. He urged the citizenry to be vigilant: "I am jealous in a free government, of any gradual assumption on the part of persons high in office, of powers not given to them by the law of the land." He was especially alarmed by the Sedition Act, which posed a profound danger to free speech, and as always, Cooper placed the highest value on freedom of expression: "Who can prove an opinion to be true? Where is the infallible criterion of speculative truth? How are we to get at truth, how has it ever been attained, but by free discussion?" He defended popular government, castigated the commercial biases of the Federalists, argued that America should remain an agricultural country, and called for unlimited freedom of discussion and inquiry. Cooper was one of the many writers and editors whose work contributed to Thomas Jefferson's victory in the presidential election of 1800. His "description of the parties and issues," according to Harry M. Tinkcom, "was by far the best Republican statement to appear" in Pa. during 1799.

Cooper was a tireless advocate of political and intellectual causes. As Dumas Malone has written, he was "preeminently a controversialist and, in the larger sense, an educator." Despite his continuing concern with contemporary (and often fleeting) controversies, Cooper was not simply an occasional writer. His *Tracts* and his *Propositions* are coherent statements of the religious and political thought that dominated his writings to his death. Even if they do not represent the highest level of philosophical inquiry, they are vigorous and reasoned expositions of a type of political and intellectual radicalism that left a mark in both Eng. and America, and although Cooper in old age retreated from one of his most passionate early interests—antislavery—he nonetheless continued to advocate materialism and rationalism, oppose established religion, and defend the right of free inquiry and free speech.

Suggested Readings: BDAS; DAB; DNB; LHUS; *See also* Dumas Malone, *The Public Life of Thomas Cooper, 1783-1839* (1926); Herbert W. Schneider, *A History of American Philosophy*, 2nd ed. (1963), pp. 70, 91; Donald H. Stewart, *The Opposition Press of the Federalist Period* (1969), especially pp. 458, 477-478, 480-481, 541, 581, 639; Harry M. Tinkcom, *The Republicans and Federalists in Pennsylvania, 1790-1801* (1950), pp. 235-237.

Douglas M. Arnold
Yale University

WILLIAM COOPER (1694-1743)

Works: *How and Why Young People Should Cleanse Their Way* (1716); *Jabez's Character and Prayer* (1716); *Mr. Cooper's Confession of Faith* (1716,

1806); *A Sermon Concerning the Laying of the Deaths of Others to Heart* (1720); *A Letter to a Friend in the Country Attempting a Solution of the Objections . . . Against the New Way of Receiving the Small-Pox* (1721) [erroneously ascribed to Cotton Mather]; 3rd ed. titled *A Reply to the Objections* (1730); another ed. titled *A Reply to the Religious Scruples* (1791); *Objections to Early Piety Answered* (1721); *God's Concern for a Godly Seed [And, The Duty of Parents to Pray]* (1723, 1730); *The Service of God Recommended to the Choice of Young People* (1726); *The Blessedness of the Tried Saint* (1727); *The Danger of People's Losing the Good Impression Made by the Late Awful Earthquake* (1727); *Early Piety (1728); A Reply to the Objections Made Against Taking the Small Pox* (1730); *Divine Teaching* (1732); *Man Humbled* (1732); *Serious Exhortations Addres'd to Young Men* (1732); *Three Discourses Concerning the Reality, the Extremity, and the Absolute Eternity of Hell Punishments* (1732); *The Beatifick Vision* (1734); *The Greatness of Sin* (1734); *Life of Mr. Thomas Beard* (1735); *The Work of the Ministers* (1736); *Concio Hyemalis, A Winter Sermon* (1737); *Compendium Evangelicum* (1739); *The Doctrine of Predestination* (1740); *The Honours of Christ Demanded of the Magistrate* (1740); *One Shall Be Taken* (1741); *The Sin and Danger* (1741).

Biography: William Cooper was born on Mar. 20, 1694, to prominent Bostonian parents. His father, one of the Brattle Church founders, died suddenly in 1705 when his son was 11. From that time on Cooper became gravely preoccupied with religious matters. Yet even at the age of 7, he had come under the influence of the Rev. Benjamin Colman (q.v.), who became his mentor and later his colleague. Graduating from Harvard College in 1712, Cooper performed brilliantly as orator in the commencement exercises. His second public speaking engagement in the pulpit of Old South Church was even more successful, and thenceforth his preaching was in great demand. In 1715 he was called to share the pulpit of the Brattle Church with the Rev. Colman, but he was not ordained until the following year. In 1720 Colman officiated at the marriage of Cooper to Judith Sewall, daughter of Judge Samuel Sewall (q.v.), with whom Cooper was on intimate terms. Along with Cotton Mather (q.v.) and Increase Mather (q.v.), with whom Cooper also got along well, he participated in the smallpox controversy by advocating inoculation. In 1737 Cooper was elected president of the Harvard Overseers, but he declined the honor. Best known for his preaching, Cooper's vividness of sensatory detail and emphasis on divine judgment anticipated the sermons of Jonathan Edwards (q.v.). Together with Colman, Cooper invited George Whitefield (q.v.) to New Eng., and he became an ardent supporter of the revival. In addition, Cooper wrote prefaces for various works by Jonathan Edwards, Thomas Foxcroft, (q.v.), and others. He died in Boston on Dec. 13, 1743, at the ebb of the Great Awakening.

Critical Appraisal: In one sense, William Cooper may be said to be one of the earliest Calvinists in New Eng., only because that term perhaps first had its official use among his circle in the introduction to his *Doctrine of Predestination*. Cooper rejected any Arminian rationalization of this doctrine that would

make God's foreknowledge of sanctification the cause instead of the consequence of election: "God's fore-knowing his people means nothing less than his
eternal purpose to make them his friends and favourites." The number of the
elect became an issue for Cooper because of the Unitarian challenge that made
predestination contradictory to the nature of a benevolent God. Cooper argued
that the actual number is unknowable save to God alone, but "is such a great
number, an innumerable multitude," including the worst sinners, that it is "no
such discouraging doctrine as some would represent it." Preaching, he believed,
was truly an effective means to call in the saints. Thus his *Three Discourses
Concerning...Hell Punishments* was honed to piercing sharpness to awaken
complacent sinners. Rehearsing all exquisite torments invented by man, Cooper
maintained that the sufferings of hell held no comparison but combined "a
punishment of loss" with "a punishment of sense," which encompassed mind,
will, and conscience. The "very hell of hell," moreover, was eternity itself. Yet
the afflictions of life were to be understood as the chastisements of a loving God.
For all of Cooper's emphasis on divine judgment, the spiritual sensibility of
divine love was ever present. "God loves to try his children" is the message of his
Blessedness of the Tried Saint; but not for his own knowledge is God engaged in
sending afflictions to his people, only so "he make them known unto *themselves*."

In the *Beatifick Vision*, affliction is further enobled as an imitation of Christ
and an anticipation of heaven: "Being like him [Christ] in sufferings, they [the
saints] shall be like him in joys and glories." However, in *The Sin and Danger of
Quenching the Spirit*, disobedience to "the inward motions of...grace" is presented as a "dreadful sin" for which the punishment of hell awaits. Cooper's very
emphasis on predestination and divine judgment is an explication of love—its
presence and its absence. The cosmic drama had an intimate reality for him
undoubtedly because of his own youthful crisis, and it was the very soul of his
revivalist preaching style. Although he could never match the creativity and
intellectual depth of his younger friend and colleague, Jonathan Edwards, Cooper certainly contributed to the vitality of orthodox Calvinism in New Eng.
during the 1730s.

Suggested Readings: CCNE; Sibley-Shipton (V, 624-634); Sprague (I, 288-291).
See also Perry Miller, *The New England Mind; From Colony to Province* (1962), pp. 184,
273, 341, 347, 365-366, 395, 408, 414, 445-446, 451-452, 460, 471, 482; Williston
Walker, *A History of the Congregational Churches in the United States* (1894), p. 264.

Barbara Ritter Dailey
Boston University

JOHN COTTON (1584-1652)

Works: *God's Promise to his Plantation* (1630); *A Brief Exposition...of
Ecclesiastes* (del. before 1632; pub. 1654); *A Brief Exposition of the Whole Book*

of Canticles (del. before 1632; pub. 1642); *Christ the Fountain of Life* (del. before 1632; pub. 1651); *God's Mercy Mixed with His Justice* (del. before 1632; pub. 1641; rep. as *The Saint's Support and Comfort*, 1658); *A Practical Commentary...upon the First Epistle General of John* (del. before 1632; pub. 1656); *Some Treasure Fetched Out of Rubbish* (w. before 1632; pub. 1660); *A Treatise of Mr. Cotton's, Clearing Certain Doubts Concerning Predestination* (w. before 1632; pub. 1646); *The Way of Life* (del. before 1632; pub. 1641); *A Treatise* (w. 1634; pub. 1713); *The Controversy Concerning Liberty of Conscience in Matters of Religion* (w. c. 1634-5; first pub. in Roger Williams, *The Bloody Tenent of Persecution*, 1644; later pub. 1646); *The True Constitution of a Particular Visible Church* (w. c. 1634-5; pub. 1642; rep. as *The Doctrine of the Church*, 1643); *An Abstract or the Laws of New England*, often known as "Moses His Judicials" (1636; pub. 1641; rep. as *An Abstract of Laws and Government*, 1655); "Copy of a Letter from Mr. Cotton to Lord Say and Seal in the Year 1636" (pub. in Lawrence S. Mayo, ed., *The History of Massachusetts Bay*, 1936); *A Letter of Mr. John Cotton's...to Mr. Williams* (w. c. 1635-6; pub. 1643); *A Treatise of the Covenant of Grace* (del. 1636; first pub., incomplete, as *The New Covenant*, 1654; rep. as *The Covenant of Grace*, 1655; later pub. 1659); *A Conference Mr. John Cotton Held at Boston* (w. 1637; pub. 1646; rep. as *Gospel Conversion*, 1646); *A Copy of a Letter of Mr. Cotton of Boston* (w. 1637; pub. 1641); *A Discourse about Civil Government in a New Plantation Whose Design Is Religion* (w. c. 1637; pub. 1663); *Sixteen Questions of Serious and Necessary Consequence* (w. c. 1636-7; pub. 1644; rep. as *Several Questions*, 1647); *An Exposition upon the Thirteenth Chapter of the Revelation* (del. c. 1640; pub. 1655); Preface, *The Whole Book of Psalms* (1640); *A Brief Exposition with Practical Observations upon the Whole Book of Canticles* (del. 1641; pub. 1655); *The Way of the Churches of Christ in New England* (w. 1641; pub. 1645); *The Church's Resurrection* (1642); *The Pouring Out of the Seven Vials* (1642); *The Grounds and Ends of the Baptism of the Children of the Faithful* (w. 1643; pub. 1647); *The Keys of the Kingdom of Heaven* (1644); *The Covenant of God's Free Grace* (1645); *Milk for Babes* (1646; rep. as *Spiritual Milk for Boston Babes*, 1656); *The Bloody Tenent, Washed and Made White in the Blood of the Lamb* (1647); *A Reply to Mr. Williams His Examination* (1647); *Singing of Psalms a Gospel Ordinance* (1647); *The Way of Congregational Churches Cleared* (1648); *Of the Holiness of Church Members* (1650); *A Defense of Mr. John Cotton from the Imputation of Self-Contradiction* (w. 1651; pub. 1658); *Certain Queries Tending to Accomodation and Communion of Presbyterian and Congregational Churches* (1654); *A Sermon...Delivered at Salem, 1636* (1713).

Biography: Born in Derby, Eng., on Dec. 4, 1584, the son of prosperous parents, John Cotton took the B.A. at Trinity College, Cambridge, in 1603, and advanced to a fellowship at Puritan Emmanuel College, where he took the M.A. in 1606 and the doctor of divinity in 1613. Cotton was widely known at Cambridge as scholar, linguist, and especially preacher, at first adhering to the popular Anglican style of elegant and witty oratory. In 1609 a crisis of faith led

Cotton to experience a conversion; as a result, he began preaching in the Puritan plain style. Ordained to the Church of England in 1610, Cotton was two years later called to St. Botolph's in Boston, Lincolnshire. For twenty-one years, he managed to balance outward conformity to Anglican ceremonies with substantial Puritan reformation of the liturgy and parish government. In 1613 Cotton married Elizabeth Horrocks, who died childless in 1631. In 1632 Cotton remarried; his second wife, Sarah Hawkridge Story, a widow with one daughter, survived him and eventually married Richard Mather (q.v.). They had six children: Seaborn (1633), Sarah (1635), Elizabeth (1637), John (1640), Mariah (1642), and Rowland (1643). Mariah married Increase Mather (q.v.) and was the mother of Cotton Mather (q.v.).

In 1630 Cotton delivered the farewell sermon to a group of prominent Puritans, including John Winthrop (q.v.), leaving for New Eng. Three years later, in the face of increasing persecution of nonconforming ministers, Cotton himself emigrated. In New Eng. Cotton was swiftly appointed joint minister, with John Wilson (q.v.), of the church at Boston, a post he occupied until his death in 1652. His frequent sermons were widely attended and highly respected for their power of conversion. He was active in the political and religious life of New Eng. He took a central role in the Antinomian controversy of 1636-1638, acceding finally in the excommunication and banishment of Anne Hutchinson; he entered into lengthy debates with Roger Williams (q.v.), the founder of R.I.; and he participated in numerous conferences and synods responsible for defining the doctrines and laws of church and state. In the New World, Cotton continued to spend long hours over his scholarly endeavors, leaving not only a number of published sermons but also extensive writings on Congregationalism and colonial government. He died in Boston on Dec. 23, 1652.

Critical Appraisal: Although no one work of Cotton's impresses us for literary merit alone, his writings are an important window on the intricate and interwoven scenes of the first two decades of the Mass. colony. The writings cannot be separated from the writer and his times. The contemporary importance of Cotton's preaching accounts both for the wide publication of his sermons and for the inadequacy of these published versions: they are almost all based on shorthand notes taken by members of his congregations, often expanded and printed without the knowledge of the author. At their best, the sermons are clear, authoritative, and rich in learning and insight, but they appear pale next to the lively styles of some of Cotton's fellow preachers, notably Thomas Shepard (q.v.) and Thomas Hooker (q.v.). In oral delivery, Cotton's personality made his sermons powerful instruments of conversion, but that personality does not always appear in the printed versions.

Cotton shared with other Puritan preachers a central belief that the preaching of God's word was a primary tool in God's calling of the elect to their salvation. Cotton himself traced his conversion at Cambridge to the hearing of a sermon by Richard Sibbes, and he found that his own first sermon in plain style had a similar converting effect on a noted scholar, John Preston. In Cotton's sermons,

God's abundant grace to the chosen is described repeatedly as the basic force of conversion. Detailing the effects of grace is the central concern of Cotton's preaching of salvation: his frequent descriptions of the stages of grace are intended to help his listeners examine their souls for evidence of their election. *The Way of Life*, a sermon-series delivered during Cotton's English ministry, is a major example of Cotton's preaching of salvation. Its subtitles and structure demonstrate a familiar pattern of Puritan spiritual biography: "The Pouring Out of the Spirit" (God's call to the Christian); "Sin's Deadly Wound" (the increasing awareness of the state of sin and the possibility of grace); "The Christian's Charge" (the process of regeneration); and "The Life of Faith" (the new state of Christian holiness in the church, home and community).

Following the practice of Puritan preaching, the sermons in *The Way of Life* are strictly plain—that is, not lacking in literary grace, but composed without the self-conscious wit of contemporary Anglican preaching and aimed primarily at the conversion of the souls of the listeners. The sermons are, accordingly, explicitly shaped in Puritan four-part structure. A biblical *text* serves as the source and reference for the entire sermon. From that text, Cotton draws one or more *doctrines* and proceeds to show *reasons* for those doctrines; logical analysis and scholarship here combine to teach and inform the listener. The fourth division of the sermons, the *uses*, applies these doctrines to the congregation; these varied, extended sections of application with their qualities of exhortation are often the most immediate and appealing of Cotton's prose. In them we can still sense the urgency and power of Cotton's preaching.

In *The Way of Life*, Cotton addressed a church that still belonged to the Anglican establishment, but at the core of his audience was a group of intense Puritans, his particular followers. He preached, therefore, a mixed doctrine. At times, he asserted the Calvinist doctrine of the utter sufficiency of God's grace and the corresponding inability of the human soul to prepare for or advance the coming of the spirit. Yet at other times he preached preparation, urging "every ungodly soul, to stir up himself for the obtaining of the spirit of grace." Cotton's sermons demonstrate an idealism tempered by practicality. Although the purity of Calvinist predestination always attracted him in theory, the sermons in practice reflected the various, immediate needs of their audiences. Despite Cotton's often intricate logic and strict theology, the sermons frequently addressed the demands of a nonsanctified world, describing sainthood by showing how the saint coexists with the sinner. For Cotton, as finally for most of the orthodox New Eng. ministers, the saint must treasure sanctification, yet also live "a most busy life in this world": "by faith it is that we live comfortably in this present world."

One of the most eloquent of Cotton's published works is the sermon-series published as *A Treatise of the Covenant of Grace*. God's free gift of grace to the elect is here the subject of an excited and joyfully rhetorical prose, full of repetitions and parallelisms, imagined colloquies, exclamations, and apostrophes. The doctrinal emphasis of these sermons marks a significant difference between Cotton and other New Eng. preachers. For most Puritan preachers (e.g., Shepard, Hooker, and Peter Bulkeley [q.v.]), the action of salvation depended not only on God's actions but also on human preparation through repentance and faith. For Cotton, however, such a doctrine, with its emphasis on unregenerate human will, derogated God's all-powerful role in salvation. In A *Treatise of the Covenant of Grace*, preached in 1635-6 when these differences were first aired in New Eng., Cotton preached that God's grace is given unconditionally; yet with his characteristic sense of balance and compromise, Cotton allowed that Christians, although unable to act in preparation for God's work, might passively anticipate the divine action.

The latent debate between Cotton and the other ministers surfaced in the ensuing controversy about Anne Hutchinson. The preachers, founding a colony on theocratic principles, necessarily linked the inner process of individual salvation with the outward evidence of salvation: in practice, morality was held to be an inevitable sign of conversion, and the health of the state was seen to be tied to the health of the individual soul. Cotton's doctrine that human actions were meaningless in salvation, applied strictly by Hutchinson, threatened the colony with a radical individualism: the vast separation between God's work in the soul (grace) and human action in the world (works) meant for Hutchinson and her many supporters that the disciplinary and governing power of the ministers was a power of worldliness only, since morality and salvation were totally unconnected. Hooker, Shepard, and Bulkeley now found their theology disparaged as a "Covenant of Works," the Puritan term for the despised Roman Catholic emphasis on human action. In a number of writings, Cotton revealed his adaptation to the exigencies of the Antinomian crisis, as Hutchinson's dispute came to be called. Still maintaining that God's grace is utterly unconditional, he nonetheless joined ranks with the other ministers in repudiating the errors of his pupil Hutchinson.

Cotton's writings record the leading part he played in codifying and developing the New Eng. system of church government that he was to name Congregationalism. Although Cotton came to New Eng. considering himself a member of the Church of England, he quickly adapted to New Eng. Separatism. His 1636 sermon at Salem acknowledges his adoption of the de facto Congregationalism present in New Eng. when he arrived and is the first of a long series of descriptions, defenses, and modifications of that system in his published work. Behind all of Cotton's writings on church polity is the notion of the covenanting congregation, a church composed only of professing believers. The power of church government, for Cotton, resided primarily with the congregation of the faithful, not with the assemblage of all citizens. In Cotton's writings on Congregationalism, there is a wide-ranging vision: a hope that the congregation of believers might embody the spiritual core of the colony; that from that center would emerge the rulers of the state; and that the pure church and the larger, mixed, and impure state might cooperate to govern an organic community of diverse people. Written and published in large part to influence the debates in Eng. between the Presbyterian and Independent wings of the Puritan party, Cotton's important

Congregationalist treatises (*The Keys of the Kingdom* and *The Way Cleared*, in particular, along with his contributions to the published platform of the Cambridge Synod of 1648) did much to steer New Eng. along its path of moral strictness and spiritual separation from Eng. As the home country turned more toward toleration and secularism, Cotton's theocratic demands for a high standard of holiness in admission to church membership contributed strongly to the differences between Eng. and its colonies. Cotton's attitude in his writing, as in his life, is almost always conciliatory, diplomatic, and peacemaking. Yet his positions grew increasingly inflexible, and in controversies like his public debate with Roger Williams, Cotton seemed the proponent of rigid and intolerant orthodoxy.

Cotton's miscellaneous writings may be described briefly. *An Abstract*, also known as "Moses His Judicials," is the earliest compendium of the political practice of the New Eng. colony. Cotton's scholarly sermons on Revelations and Canticles are encyclopedic monuments of Renaissance learning, discursively applying Scripture to natural science, ethics, politics, and especially the history of Christianity (Cotton's fervent anti-Catholicism is here amply developed); they are perhaps most valuable for their insistence on God's continuing guidance of human history. Of importance mainly because of the book to which it is attached is Cotton's preface to *The Whole Book of Psalms* (The Bay Psalm Book); Cotton also wrote, with Shepard, a short treatise on the use of music in Puritan liturgy, *The Singing of Psalms*. Some few poems of little literary merit have survived, including a brief autobiographical piece ("A Thankful Acknowledgement of God's Providence").

Cotton's writings, lacking the vividness of imagery and warmth of expression in the work of many other New Eng. Puritans, can be disappointing. They are often inconsistent, cautious, and occasionally muddled by a scholarly limitation of vision. But they remain a major record of the forces that shaped New Eng.: in particular, they embody the depth of Puritan religious thought and its influence on all elements of New Eng. life.

Suggested Readings: CCNE; DAB; DARB; DNB; FCNEV; LHUS; Sprague (I, 25-30); T_1. *See also* John Cotton, *Gods Mercie Mixed with His Justice*, ed. Everett H. Emerson (1958); Everett H. Emerson, *John Cotton* (1965); Edward J. Gallagher and Thomas Werge, eds., *Early Puritan Writers: A Reference Guide* (1976); David D. Hall, ed., *The Antinomian Controversy, 1636-1638: A Documentary History* (1968); Phyllis M. Jones and Nicholas R. Jones, eds., *Salvation in New England: Selections from the Sermons of the First Preachers* (1977); Irwin H. Polishook, *Roger Williams, John Cotton and Religious Freedom: A Controversy in New and Old England* (1967); Julius H. Tuttle, "Writings of Rev. John Cotton" in *Bibliographical Essays: A Tribute to Wilberforce Eames* (1924); Larzer Ziff, *The Career of John Cotton: Puritanism and the American Experience* (1962); idem, ed., *John Cotton on the Churches of New England* (1968).

Nicholas R. Jones
Oberlin College

JOHN COTTON (1640-1699)

Works: *Verses upon the Death of Noah Newman* (1678); *Indian Translation of the Bible*, rev. ed. (by John Eliot, 1685); *Upon the Death of John Alden* (1687).

Biography: John Cotton, son of the more famous John Cotton (q.v.) and uncle of Cotton Mather (q.v.), was born in Boston, Mass., on Mar. 15, 1640. After receiving a degree at Harvard in 1657, he resided in Conn. from 1658 until about 1663, at which time he returned to Boston and commenced preaching to various congregations in the vicinity. The next year, in 1664, he was temporarily excommunicated from his father's church in Boston, apparently for adulterous behavior. The same charge was also brought against him at least twice more in his life, the last time being in 1697, when he was dismissed at Plymouth from a church he had served for more than thirty years.

Although he engaged in a brief exchange with Roger Williams (q.v.) about the controversy his father had had with the R.I. preacher, for the most part he was outside the major controversies of his day. His primary interest seems to have been working with the Indians around Plymouth. After hiring an Indian to teach him the language, he spent two years assisting Experience Mayhew (q.v.) in preaching to the Narragansetts, and he continued through the years to compile listings of Indian words and their English equivalents. In 1685 John Eliot (q.v.) requested his assistance in editing an earlier translation of the Bible for the Indians.

Following his expulsion from the Plymouth church in 1697, he accepted a pastorate in Charleston, S.C., and moved there in Dec. 1698. On Sept. 18, 1699, Cotton died in a yellow fever epidemic that struck that coastal city, and was buried there.

Critical Appraisal: Except for two broadsides written and published on the deaths of two of his acquaintances, there are no known strictly literary works by Cotton. According to his son, he "was a man of universal acquaintance and correspondence, so that he had and wrote (perhaps) twice as many letters as any man in the country." Some of the more interesting letters are those to members of his family, particularly those to Increase Mather (q.v.), his half-brother, and Cotton Mather, his nephew. His prose style is readable, similar in tone and manner to the "simple" style advocated by others of his period.

Perhaps his greatest contribution to American letters was his work on editing and revising John Eliot's translation of the Bible into the language of the various tribes of Indians who lived near the coast of Mass. Sometimes known collectively as the Massachusetts, the tribes belonged to the language family called the Algonquin. These tribes, whose populations were considerably diminished after the smallpox epidemic of 1617 and ranged from a few hundred to three or four thousand, included the Wampanoags, Niantics, and Montauks, as well as the Massachusetts.

Believing it their duty to convert the Indians, the early Puritan and Separatist settlers such as Experience Mayhew, John Eliot, Roger Williams, and John Cotton worked diligently to learn the language of the local tribes. They made lists of Indian words and tried to work out the principles of the languages so they could preach directly to the tribes and translate the Scriptures into the Indians' native tongue. Testimony by his son indicated that John Cotton had an excellent memory that made learning the Indian language fairly easy for him. His knowledge of the language and his extensive work with the Indians led John Eliot to ask him to revise the 1685 edition of Eliot's early Bible translation.

Suggested Readings: CCNE; FCNEV; Sibley-Shipton (I, 496-508); T$_1$. *See also* John Russell Bartlett, ed., *The Complete Writings of Roger Williams*: *The Letters of Roger Williams*, vol. VI (1963), pp. 351-357; Cotton's miscellaneous letters, CMHS, 3rd-5th ser. (1812-1841); Kenneth L. Miner, "John Eliot of Mass. and the Beginnings of American Linguistics," HL, 1 (1973), 169-183; John R. Swanton, *The Indian Tribes of North America* (rep., 1979), pp. 19-27.

Reed Sanderlin
University of Tennessee at Chattanooga

JOHN COTTON OF QUEEN'S CREEK (c. 1640-after 1678)

Works: "The History of Bacon's and Ingram's Rebellion" (w. 1677; pub. 1814).

Biography: Almost nothing is known about the man on whose shoulders uneasily rests the credit for the most eccentric of seventeenth-century southern narratives. By tracing the piece back to him through a suspect shorter version ostensibly written by his wife, literary detectives have concluded (although not unanimously) that the author of "The History of Bacon's and Ingram's Rebellion" was John Cotton, a planter with holdings along Queen's Creek in York County, Va. Sometime in the early 1640s, he was born to the Rev. William and Ann [Graves] Cotton in Hungars Parish, Northampton County. By the time he moved across the Chesapeake, he had fathered two children by his wife, Hannah (the name appearing on the briefer history mentioned above is "An. Cotton"). If this John Cotton actually did compose the narrative ascribed to him, it was apparently the one remarkable achievement of his life, for he is scarcely mentioned in surviving records of the time. Although he may in fact have lived into the eighteenth century, he disappeared from view soon after the conclusion of the rebellion, whose events he so curiously related.

Critical Appraisal: In style and tone, Cotton's history (sometimes referred to as the "Burwell Papers" after the earliest known possessor of the manuscript) is one of the most remarkably idiosyncratic of colonial times. Although its author's immediate subject is Nathaniel Bacon's (q.v.) revolt against Governor Sir William Berkeley (q.v.) of Va., he seems equally occupied with the display of his own whimsical wit. At times, indeed, his report becomes all but submerged beneath a flood of puns, mythological and historical allusions, references to various folktales and beast-fables, and citations of witty volumes such as *Scoggan's Jests* and Owen Felltham's *Resolves*. The dominant rhetorical element in Cotton's prose is balance and antithesis, a fact that, in conjunction with his fondness for alliteration and quaint lore, has led some to regard him as an imitator of euphuism. However this may be, his relish for balancing off opposites against one another extended even to his presentation of the rebellion itself, where he aimed roughly the same number of shafts at each of the parties and supported neither with much consistency. In the same fashion, the two poems incorporated into the history—perhaps the finest examples of early Va. verse—conform exactly to its antithetical pattern. The first, a hyperbolic elegy on Bacon somewhat in the metaphysical mold, credited Bacon with superhuman military and oratorical powers and blamed his early demise (which resulted from the "bloody flux"—severe dysentery) on black magic worked by "Verginias foes." The second poem is a direct rebuttal, insisting with equal vehemence that any means, fair or foul, are proper in subduing a traitor and lifting the colony out of chaos. Almost beyond doubt, the author of the prose account was also responsible for the poetic debate.

As does Nathaniel Ward's (q.v.) *Simple Cobbler of Aggawam*, the book to which the Burwell chronicle is most often compared, Cotton's work provides a startling corrective to the notion that colonial American writing is without humor or the impress of distinctive personalities. It is, moreover, not simply history but *literature*, if that slippery term is applicable to any narrative as notable for how it goes about telling its story as for the story itself. An unknown number of pages are missing from the beginning and end of the manuscript—apparently an eighteenth-century copy—and other clues indicate that even in its perfect state this transcription did not contain all that Cotton had originally set down. Despite its present condition, however, "The History of Bacon's and Ingram's Rebellion" is a queer national treasure and an essential document in the subsequent development of Bacon's insurrection as an American literary theme.

Suggested Readings: Charles M. Andrews, *Narratives of the Insurrections, 1675-1690* (1915), pp. 45-98 (includes the most recent edition of Cotton's history); Jay B. Hubbell, *South and Southwest* (1965), pp. 205-227; Howard Mumford Jones, *The Literature of Virginia in the Seventeenth Century*, 2nd ed. (1968), pp. 108-117; W. H. Ward, "To Caesar Friend or Foe? The Burwell Papers and Bacon's Rebellion" in *Essays in Early Virginia Literature Honoring Richard Beale Davis*, ed. J. A. Leo Lemay (1977), pp. 73-90.

W. H. Ward
Appalachian State College

DANIEL COXE (1673-1739)

Works: *A Description of Carolana* (1722).
Biography: Daniel Coxe was born in Aug. 1673, the oldest son of Daniel and Rebecca Coxe of London. A member of the Royal Society, his father was a

physician to Charles II and to Queen Anne. Daniel came to America in 1702 with Lord Cornbury, who appointed him commander of the forces in West Jersey, but his presence in America may also have been spurred by his interest in Dr. Coxe's assignment to Sir Robert Heath's patent for Carolana, a vast territory that included Norfolk County, Va., and the Mississippi Valley from the Great Lakes to the Gulf of Mexico.

In 1706 Coxe was given a seat in the governor's council in N.J. and made an associate judge of the Supreme Court of the province, but after clashing with the succeeding governor, Robert Hunter (q.v.), he was stripped of his seat and expelled. In 1707 he married Sarah Eckley, daughter of a Philadelphia Quaker, and after returning to London in 1715, he became involved, along with his father and a brother, in a campaign to prevent the renewal of Hunter's commission. In 1722, still in London, he published *A Description of Carolana* in the hopes of persuading the crown to turn its attention once more to Carolana, which Coxe believed rightfully belonged to England. Returning to America in 1725, Coxe resumed his political career as a candidate for the Assembly from Burlington. In 1730 he was appointed the first grand master of Masons in America, and in 1734 he served as third judge in the Supreme Court. He died on Apr. 25, 1739.

Critical Appraisal: *A Description of Carolana* is noteworthy first and foremost for the proposal in its preface that the colonies unite under one governing figure with representatives serving individual colonies. Not until Benjamin Franklin's (q.v.) similar suggestion thirty-two years later would anyone again publicly argue for such a degree of economic and political independence for the American colonies. Although the work belongs to the genre of promotional literature dating back to Richard Hakluyt's *Principall Navigations* (1589), in which copious and often inaccurate descriptions of the geography, agriculture, mineralogy, and the inhabitants constituted the bulk and format of the work, Coxe's motives, as explained in the preface, lie less in promoting colonization than in acquiring and defending lands properly and legally belonging to Eng. and restructuring the governing process so that already settled lands in the Northeast and Southeast would not fall into the hands of the French and their Indian allies.

The especially long title, *A Description of the English Province of Carolana, by the Spaniards Called Florida, and by the French La Louisiane; as also the Great and Famous River, Meschacebe or Mississippi, the Vast Navigable Lakes of Fresh-Water, and the Parts Adjacent; Together with an Account of the Commodities, of the Growth and Production of the Said Province; and a Preface Containing Some Considerations on the Consequence of the French Making Settlements There*, promises to provide information pertinent to navigation—with defense and efficient travel routes for trading purposes in mind—to enumerate the native commodities, and, finally, to expose the dangers of allowing the French to gain a monopolizing foothold in the western territories. Coxe offered a solution for the better governing and defense of the colonies and the subtly conflicting arguments of advocating, on the one hand, economic independence and self-defense for existent and future colonies and promoting, on the other hand, the establishment of colonies in Carolana as though they were nothing more than some collective commodity itself. Otherwise, *A Description of Carolana* is primarily a compilation of documents collected by his father from explorers and traders with hardly a trace of an aesthetic appreciation of a vast tract of wilderness like that which we see in William Byrd of Westover (q.v.), *Histories of the Dividing Line Betwixt Virginia and North Carolina*, and William Bartram (q.v.), *Travels*. In fact, Coxe's descriptions are little more than lists serving the explicit purpose of convincing the crown to protect its rights or else suffer the consequences. What those consequences were was clear to Coxe; once Fr. established settlements near N.Y., Pa., and N.J. and controlled the Great Lakes, the successful invasion and usurpation of the English provinces by the French were inevitable.

Suggested Readings: DAB; T$_2$.

L. A. Norman
University of Cincinnati

TENCH COXE (1755-1824)

Works: *An Examination of the Constitution* (1788); *A View of the United States of America* (1794); *An Essay on the Manufacturing Interest of the United States* (1804); *Thoughts on the Subject of Naval Power* (1807); *A Memoir . . . upon the subject of Cotton Wool Cultivation* (1817); "Considerations Respecting the Helots of the United States" (1820-1821); "Reflections Occasioned by the Allocution of the *Roman Catholic Pontiff*" (1822). For a complete list of works by Tench Coxe, see Jacob E. Cooke's, *Tench Coxe and the Early Republic* (1978), pp. 528-535.

Biography: Tench Coxe was born on May 22, 1755, into the family of William and Mary Coxe, both of whom were of prominent Philadelphia stock. For a short time, Coxe attended the College of Philadelphia and then studied law, but in 1776 what was to become a lifelong fascination with economic matters led him away from that career and into the firm of Coxe, Furman, and Coxe. During the American Revolution, he adopted the precarious stance of "neutral Loyalism," and at the outbreak of the war, he was forced to relocate in N.Y. In 1777, however, he accompanied the British troops under Gen. Howe back to Philadelphia. There he married Catherine McCall, who died shortly thereafter. After Howe's withdrawal, Coxe was arrested, but after managing to secure a release, he joined the patriot side. In 1782 he remarried, this time to his cousin Rebecca. Their union produced eleven children.

During the Confederation period, Coxe supported the centralist program, gaining patrons and influence sufficient to counterbalance his Revolutionary record. He attended the Annapolis Convention of 1786, served in the Confederation Congress in 1788, and launched his literary career with several articles supporting the Bank of North America. He did not attend the Constitutional

Convention, but he approved of its work and worked hard for ratification, producing (by his own count) "near thirty lengthy publications" in defense of the new system. These pamphlets, four of which were published in 1788 under the title *An Examination of the Constitution*, established him in Federalist circles. Under President George Washington (q.v.), Coxe served as assistant secretary of the Treasury and then as commissioner of revenue. After President John Adams (q.v.) removed him from that position in 1797 (apparently fearful of Coxe's political machinations), he established ties with the Republican opposition. In 1803 President Thomas Jefferson (q.v.) rewarded him with the position of purveyor of public supplies—an important appointment, but, as with his earlier posts, one not quite commensurate with his obvious abilities. A competent administrator, Coxe never, it seems, was thoroughly trusted.

Despite the change in party affiliation, Coxe remained a consistent champion of economic nationalism. Throughout his adult life, he published works promoting economic diversification and protection of American goods and trade, supplementing his writings with an active participation in societies dedicated to those goals and in projects designed to demonstrate the feasibility of attaining them. Ever mindful of the economic and psychological importance of agriculture, he became a particularly effective propagandist for the expansion of the southern cotton industry. He died in 1824, at age 69.

Critical Appraisal: A central position in the political and economic life of his time, combined with an almost compulsive urge to investigate and comment upon virtually every subject that came his way, led Coxe to produce a list of publications numbering in the hundreds. The sheer volume of his literary output rivals that of any of his contemporaries, and it is impossible to provide an adequate measure of its variety in the space of a brief essay. A good point of entry into his major preoccupation, however, is his collection of essays, *A View of the United States of America* (1794). In these essays, all but a handful of which were previously published, Coxe concentrated upon promoting the growth of the U.S. through a vigorous program of economic nationalism. His deep faith in progress, his vision of America as both unique and blessed, and his conviction that both laissez-faire and physiocratic ideas were antiquated notions positively detrimental to the development of the country are all introduced and reiterated here—often, it should be noted, with a predilection for data over theory that is at times more than mildly soporific. The essays also reveal the author's sensitivity to the problem of introducing manufacturing—essential, in his view, to an economy capable of surviving and competing in the modern world—into a society with an agricultural tradition so strong that agrarianism and republicanism were virtually synonymous. Coxe was no less an advocate of the "mixed" economy than was Alexander Hamilton (q.v.) (he had played a major collaborative role in the preparation of the latter's *Report on Manufactures*), but his expression of the mercantile vision was always carefully tempered with soothing reassurances that the economic redirection he supported would reinforce the pastoral tradition, not eliminate it.

Coxe often returned to these subjects in later essays, such as *An Essay on the Manufacturing Interest of the United States* (1804), *Thoughts on the Subject of Naval Power* (1807), and *A Memoir . . . upon the subject of Cotton Wool Cultivation* (1817). These works expressed few new ideas, Coxe being content as usual to express his convictions through an indefatigable marshaling of statistics. He turned also to many other subjects. In a series of articles titled "Considerations Respecting the Helots of the United States" (1820-1821), the tension between his abolitionist sentiments and his racist convictions produced what his major biographer has judged "an apologia for slaveholders . . . that not even southern hard liners on the subject could have bettered." Toward the end of his life, he concentrated upon religion, applauding its benign impact upon morality, stressing the importance of a separation between church and state, and, in "Reflections Occasioned by the Allocution of the *Roman Catholic Pontiff*" (1822), counselling American Catholics to renounce their allegiance to Rome. On no subject does Coxe emerge as an original, creative thinker. Still, his encyclopedic mind, his energy, and his tenacity made him an effective propagandist for those ideas he chose to espouse.

Suggested Readings: DAB; LHUS. *See also* Jacob E. Cook, *Tench Coxe and the Early Republic* (1978); Joseph Dorfman, *The Economic Mind in American Civilization*, vol. I (1946); Alexander DuBin, *Coxe Family* (1936); Harold Hutcheson, *Tench Coxe: A Study in American Economic Development* (1938); Leo Marx, *The Machine in the Garden* (1964).

David Sloan
University of Arkansas at Fayetteville

THOMAS CRADOCK (1718-1770)

Works: *Two Sermons, with a Preface* (1747); "A Poem Sacred to the Memory," *Maryland Gazette*, Mar. 15, 1753; "Sermon on the Governance of Maryland's Established Church" (w. 1753; pub. in WMQ, 3rd ser., 27 [1970], 629-653); *A Poetical Translation of the Psalms* (1754); *A New Version of the Psalms* (1756); "To Thyrsis," *American Magazine*, 1 (1757-1758), 605-607; David Curtis Skaggs, ed., *The Poetic Writings of Thomas Cradock, 1718-1770* (1982). Manuscript sermons and poetry are in the Cradock Papers and Maryland Diocesan Archives, Maryland Historical Society.

Biography: Born in Staffordshire, Eng., in 1718, Thomas Cradock matured on the Trentham estate of the first Earl Gower, where his father rented land and served as a tailor. Educated at the Trentham Free School, Cradock matriculated at but did not graduate from Magdalen Hall, Oxford. In 1741 he received ordination to the diaconate and two years later to the priesthood. In 1744 he immigrated to Md. and the next year became the first rector of St. Thomas Parish in western Baltimore County. During the following quarter century, Cradock achieved considerable reputation as a preacher, pastor, schoolmaster, and poet, and his extraparochial speaking engagements took him before audiences from Philadelphia to Annapolis.

After marriage into a local gentry family, Cradock established a plantation named "Trentham" near his parish church. He died there on May 7, 1770, after demonstrating, said a eulogistic broadside, all of those characteristics "so essentially necessary in the Christian, the Scholar, and the Gentleman."

Critical Appraisal: Most of Thomas Cradock's sermons and much of his poetry remain in manuscript collections housed in the Maryland Historical Society, Baltimore. What little fame he achieved before the mid-1970s concerned a sermon on the immorality of some of his fellow clerics of the Md. establishment preached before the governor and the General Assembly in 1753. This sermon was cited several times before its publication in 1970. It attacked the lack of faith and morals among many Anglican clergy and prescribed the creation of an American bishopric to remedy the situation. Although many Marylanders agreed with his diagnosis, neither the proprietor nor the General Assembly accepted his prescription. Nevertheless, this sermon has been acclaimed as perhaps the most courageous Anglican homily of the colonial era.

Titled "Innocent Mirth Not Inconsistent with Religion," one of Cradock's *Two Sermons* (1747) critiques the excessive sobriety of Puritanism. This Baltimore Town address and others—"On Education" delivered in Philadelphia and "On Patriotism" preached during an itinerary along the south-central Pa. frontier—constitute his major extraparochial discourses. The parochial sermons deal mostly with faith, morals, and anti-Deism. Written in the plain style developed by Archbishop John Tillotson, Cradock's homilies exemplify the expansion of English rhetorical traditions to the Chesapeake region. Although willing to publicly criticize its weaknesses, Cradock stoutly defended the Church of England and its traditional interpretation of faith and morals. He personified the normative and the orthodox. He typified the Anglican middle way and sought the continuity of British society and institutions on the Md. frontier. His moderate Christian rationalism exemplified an Episcopal tradition that kept that denomination from disintegrating into the Unitarianism of many New Eng. Calvinist churches.

Cradock's religious poetry consists primarily of two slightly different versions of the Psalms printed in London and Annapolis. Written in iambic pentameter, they lack imaginative imagery. His "To Thyrsis," a few hymns printed in 1854, and other religious poems express conventional theology in uninspired verse.

Far more important is the ambitious "Maryland Eclogues," nine pastoral satires imitating Vergil's *Bucolics*. Still in manuscript, these Md. idylls criticize the licentiousness, greed, blasphemy, pretention, infidelity, and drunkenness of the colonists. From servants and slaves to planters and parsons, no social group escapes the poet's wrath. Travesties on Vergil though they may be, they contain many stock characterizations of subsequent literature. Cradock romanticized the noble savage, exhibited disdain for the Scotch-Irish frontiersmen, and depicted Negroes as docile, happy, and singing although aware of their social disadvantages. In the tradition of American folk humor from Ebenezer Cooke (q.v.) to Uncle Remus, his country bumpkins and slaves cleverly survive in a hostile environment. There is little to indicate Cradock accepted the *translatio studii* motif—the westward migration of civilization—that characterized the writings of many British emigrants to the colonial Chesapeake, for America as a land of promise apparently did not intrigue this transplanted Englishman.

The least known of Cradock's poetic endeavors is his five-act, blank-verse tragedy on the trial and execution of Socrates. Small portions of the first and last acts are missing from the surviving manuscript, but it is clear the author imitated the literary style and moral intent of Joseph Addison's *Cato*, so popular with eighteenth-century audiences. "The Death of Socrates" represents an important discovery in early American intellectual history. No previously known colonial play exhibits as much sophistication of characterization and dramatic unity. Although not great theater, it clearly indicates the degree to which the neo-Classic drama of Augustan London penetrated Chesapeake culture.

Through his sermons and poetry, Cradock propagated the traditional values of his church and nation. He idealized standards of conduct of the good Christian—sincere piety, personal morality, generous benevolence, sensible conviviality, honest work in a God-given social hierarchy, prudent use of each talent, and fair treatment of all human beings regardless of the social status. Cradock's writings make him an exemplary figure of the Anglican mind of the mid-eighteenth-century South and serve to illuminate the literary situation of the Chesapeake region and its dependence upon the traditions of contemporary British literature.

Suggested Readings: CCMC; CCMDG; Sprague (V, 111-117). *See also* Ethan Allen, "Thomas Cradock," AGR, 7 (1854), 302-312; Charles A. Barker, *The Background of the Revolution in Maryland* (1940), pp. 276-277; Richard Beale Davis, "The Intellectual Golden Age in the Colonial Chesapeake Bay Country," VMHB, 78 (1970), 131-143; idem, *Intellectual Life in the Colonial South*, 3 vols. (1978), pp. 749-752, 1392-1395, passim; J. A. Leo Lemay, *Men of Letters in Colonial Maryland* (1972), pp. 190-197, passim; Henry F. May, *The Enlightenment in America* (1976), pp. 66-72; David Curtis Skaggs, "The Chain of Being in Eighteenth Century Maryland: The Paradox of Thomas Cradock," HMagPEC, 45 (1976), 155-164; idem, "Thomas Cradock and the Chesapeake Golden Age," WMQ, 30 (1973), 93-116; Carol Lee Van Voorst, "The Anglican Clergy in Maryland, 1692-1776" (Ph.D. diss., Princeton Univ., 1978), pp. 276-285, passim.

David Curtis Skaggs
Bowling Green State University

CHARLES CRAWFORD (1752-c. 1815)

Works: *A Dissertation on the Phaedon of Plato* (1773); *Sophronia and Hilario* (1774); *Richmond Hill: A Poem* (1777); *The Christian: A Poem* (1781); *Liberty: A Pindaric Ode* (1783); *A Poem on the Death of Montgomery* (1783); *A Poetical Paraphrase of Our Saviour's Sermon on the Mount* (1783); *Observa-*

tions on Negro Slavery (1784); *Observations on the Downfall of Papal Power* (1788); *George Foxe's Looking Glass* (1790); *Observations on the Revolution in France* (1793); *The Progress of Liberty* (1796); *The Dying Prostitute* (1797); *An Essay on the Propagation of the Gospel* (1799); *An Essay on the Eleventh Chapter of the Revelation of St. John* (1800); *Poems on Several Occasions* (1803); *The Poetical Works of Charles, Earl of Crawford and Lindsay, Viscount Garnock* (1814).

Biography: Born in 1752 in Antigua in the W. Ind., the son of a wealthy landowner, Charles Crawford was sent in his teens to London for education. There he proved to be a headstrong and recalcitrant young man, expelled from Queens College, Cambridge, in 1773 because of an assault upon another student. Religion and good intentions then took over, for he published at least five books in verse and prose, none of which was well received. By 1783 he was in Philadelphia, publishing and republishing tracts upholding every good measure of reform and decrying atheism especially, Quakerism, and Negro slavery. After some seven years, he seems to have returned to Eng., spending the remainder of his life in attempting to secure what he thought to be his rightful title of earl of Crawford and Lindsay, Viscount Garnock. Crawford is presumed to have died during the second decade of the nineteenth century, remembered in Eng. as an increasingly strange old gentleman who "distinguished himself by his liberal subscriptions to charities" and who "published several poems, for the most part...very indifferent."

Critical Appraisal: Charles Crawford seems to have been a dedicated eccentric, ready to rise to any challenge for what he considered Christian decencies. His importance is that he was there, in Philadelphia, immediately after the Revolution, a mirror of better men's moods, contentiously battling for every decent reform.

A man of intense pride of birth, an aristocrat as loyal to British institutions as to Christian morality, Crawford insisted that he was "no Democrat, no contender for the wilder and mischievous doctrine that all men are equal." Although he thought the "republican delusion" to be the "most mischievous that ever afflicted society" and to be manifestly "a perversion of scripture by ignorant and designing men" like Thomas Paine (q.v.) and the arch-infidel Voltaire, he nevertheless championed the downtrodden. He spoke not only of the horrendous evils of slavery, but he pointed to the achievement of Phillis Wheatley (q.v.) as evidence that blacks were in no way inferior. He spoke for "unlimited toleration of the Jews." He expressed sympathy for the prostitute. He would "tame and incorporate the Indian." He congratulated Americans for their fearless disavowal of the established church, and he urged them further to expand their tolerance and benevolence. But he felt more intensely than he thought. A troubled man writing in troubled times, his is finally a small contribution, as a reflector rather than as a creator. Eccentric, opinionated, and quick with words, he had little original to say and little talent for saying it memorably well. But he was there, and he spoke with apparent intense dedication that should ensure him a small but not completely unimportant place, if not in the history of literature, in the history of literature as an instrument for the alleviation of evils, real or imaginary.

Suggested Readings: A.W.C.L. Crawford, *Lives of the Lindsays* (1849); Lewis Leary, "Charles Crawford: A Forgotten Poet of Early Philadelphia" in *Soundings: Some Early American Writers* (1975), pp. 97-111.

Lewis Leary
University of North Carolina at Chapel Hill

MICHEL GUILLAŬME JEAN DE CRÈVECOEUR (1735-1813)

Works: *Letters from an American Farmer* (1782); *Lettres d'un Cultivateur Américain*, 2 vols. (1784), 3 vols. rev. ed. (1787); *Voyage dans la Haute Pennsylvanie et dans l'état de New York* (1801), Clarissa S. Bostelmann, trans., *Journey into Northern Pennsylvania and the State of New York* [1964]; *Sketches of Eighteenth-Century America* (w. 1776-1779; pub. 1925); H. L. Bourdin and S. T. Williams, eds., "Crèvecoeur on the Susquehanna, 1774-1776" (w. 1778; pub. in YR, 14 [1925], 552-584); idem, eds., "The Grotto: An Unpublished Letter from The American Farmer" (w. 1777; pub. in *Nation*, 121 [1925], 328-330); idem, eds., "Hospitals During the Revolution: An Unpublished Essay by J. Hector St. John de Crèvecoeur" (w. 1777; pub. in PQ, 5 [1926], 157-165); idem, eds., "Sketch of a Contrast between the Spanish and English Colonies" (w. 1773; pub. in UCC, 28 [1926], 152-163). Crèvecoeur's agricultural and botanical writings, as well as an account of the complete publishing history of his works, may be found in Howard C. Rice's *Le Cultivateur Américain* (1933), pp. 231-238. Except for purposes of comparison, Crèvecoeur scholarship has been based on the English editions, which reproduce the American manuscript the most accurately.

Biography: Michel Guillaŭme Jean de Crèvecoeur, the "American farmer," as he was called after the publication of his *Letters from an American Farmer*, was born in 1735 in Caen, in the province of Normandy, Fr. Endowed by petty-noble parents with a solid Jesuit education, only moderate means, and therefore a limited horizon, he left it all at the age of 19, going first to Eng. and then to Can., where Gen. Montcalm employed him as a cartographer. After the fall of Québec, Crèvecoeur left the army under a cloud his biographers may never penetrate and went south, arriving in New York City late in 1759. In the next decade, he traveled extensively in the Northeast, transforming himself from French nobleman into self-made American, surveyor, Indian trader, and farmer. In 1765 he became a citizen of N.Y. and four years later married Mehe[i]table Tippet, daughter of substantial landowners. The "American farmer" was now fully fledged, for in the same year he bought 120 acres in Orange County, N.Y. The agrarian idyll portrayed in the early "letters" represents the happiness of this period when Crèvecoeur, who also used the pseudonym *J. Hector St. John*, was absorbed in cultivating his farm, Pine Hill, raising his three children, and writing sketches and essays that celebrated America as a rustic paradise.

But his paradise was lost when the Revolution, demanding he take sides, rendered him a regretful Loyalist, alienated him from his neighbors, and finally separated him from his family. When in 1778 he applied for permission to visit Fr., probably to restore his rights in case of need, both sides suspected him of spying. Harassed by the Americans on the way to the port of N.Y. and there imprisoned by the British, he suffered a physical and mental breakdown and set sail in 1780 disillusioned and bereft.

In his trunk, however, was the manuscript, *Letters*, which he left with an English publisher, who brought it out in 1782. He was then back in Fr., where the book's immediate success spurred his reconciliation with the patriot cause. Known now as a friend of the Americans, indeed as "the American farmer," he was appointed consul to N.Y. in 1783. But he arrived to find his wife dead, his children missing, and his farm devastated, and although he was ultimately reunited with the children, he never tried to resume his American life. As a French agent, he was remarkably effective in establishing trade and communication, but he who had proclaimed the birth of a "new man" in the New World retired to the Old in 1790. His *Voyage dans la Haute Pennsylvanie et dans l'état de New York*, published in 1801, had not nearly the success of the *Letters*. He lived quietly until 1813, the peace and stability of his last years long sought, for he was never an adventurer. As he traversed oceans and revolutions, his constant ideal was the calm settled state of the farmer.

Critical Appraisal: If his life story comments ironically on his ideal of a quiet life, his best-known work, the *Letters from an American Farmer*, is its classic statement, an early but already fully elaborated exposition of the liberal agrarian philosophy that was a dominant strand of American thinking through the nineteenth century. In that respect, the *Letters*, consisting of twelve essays characterizing American life as represented by the regional societies of Pa., Nantucket, and Charles Town, is an essential text for the study of American culture. In fact, it is constantly cited, alike in textbooks and sophisticated cultural histories. Dubbed an eighteenth-century Thoreau, Crèvecoeur is typically placed alongside Thomas Jefferson (q.v.) and Benjamin Franklin (q.v.)—D. H. Lawrence wrote that "Franklin is the real *practical* prototype of the American. Crèvecoeur is the emotional"—or sometimes as their predecessor, as Albert E. Stone has seen him, the first literary "voice of our national consciousness."

The national consciousness defined in the first three letters springs from the national soil. The American, "this new man," is an independent and hardworking master of sufficient acres, on which he lives in regenerative harmony with a nature he improves by his labor. Crèvecoeur's vocabulary evokes a new mythology: neither "Russian boor" nor "Hungarian peasant," the American farmer is a "humble planter," a "tiller" of the soil, a "cultivator of the earth." Written ostensibly to a wealthy and learned Englishman, the *Letters* projects an American individualist whose simple style of life is yet wholesomely abundant and whose homeliness precludes neither sense nor sensibility—for in a pre-Romantic mode, he is inspired by the "salubrious effluvia" of his "odoriferous furrows." The book's extensive reputation refers mostly to these first rapturous letters. Despite some periods of eclipse, Crèvecoeur has been a foremost interpreter of America to Europe mainly through the image of Farmer James, with his plow and his beehives the agrarian counterpart to the young Franklin, two sturdy fellows making it in America.

But the *Letters*, like the contemporary essays and fragments published for the first time in 1925 as *Sketches of Eighteenth-Century America*, actually end in ignominious defeat, with James and the best among his neighbors driven from their farms. The villain is the Revolution and the social chaos it breeds, removing the protection that the monarchy had provided all of its subjects equally and allowing the unprincipled strong to prey on the vulnerable and the pacific. Crèvecoeur's Loyalism has been generally played down or recast as an untenable neutrality, perhaps because it seems incongruous in the democratic enthusiast of the early letters. The anguish of the last of these letters, titled "Distresses of a Frontier Man," may become more explicable, however, if like his earlier optimism, it is seen in the context of a life that spanned two worlds, both geographically and historically. He lived in an era of revolutionary changes and in revolutionary countries. Not himself a creator of new ideas—those ideas developed in his writings are mostly derivative of established Enlightenment doctrines—Crèvecoeur was particularly sensitive to the implications and complications of the ideas he adopted. He embraced whole-heartedly the "American dream" of individual autonomy but also saw the other side, how the marketplace could become an individualist jungle. In fact, the remarkable resonance of his writing, which was far more seminal than its own level of achievement explains, may indeed stem precisely from this dualism and the broader understanding it engendered.

At any rate, it has become clear that the *Letters* is not as naive a work as it first appeared. While earlier critics praised its "accuracy" and one called its author a "homespun Lockian," more recently the critical focus has been on the literary aspects of Crèvecoeur's writings. The naiveté of Farmer James, the tall tales he tells, and his wife's sensible diction tend now to be taken as instances of a self-conscious "complex artistry" comparable, for instance, to the art of Washington Irving.

Although neither of Crèvecoeur's other two published works, the *Sketches* and the more ambitious and somewhat metaphysical *Voyage* (written in Fr. in French but based on his earliest American experiences), has acquired a reputation comparable to that of the *Letters*, they have increased critical and historical interest in him generally. His other writings, on agriculture and botany, notably on the culture of potatoes, never received any attention after his time.

Withal, Crèvecoeur cannot be said to have been ignored, certainly, or even slighted, but he may have been simplified. Lawrence thought he was an idealist of "Nature-sweet-and-pure" and also a liar because he knew better and wore embroidered waistcoats in Fr. But one of the most fruitful recent approaches to

Crèvecoeur has been the close examination of his writing to see how it consciously mediates between belief and experience, the ideal of the New World and history's enduring realities.

Suggested Readings: DAB; LHUS; T$_2$. *See also* Percy G. Adams, Introduction, *Crèvecoeur's Eighteenth-Century Travels in Pennsylvania and New York* (1961); Robert de Crèvecoeur, *Saint John de Crèvecoeur: Sa Vie et Ses Ouvrages* (1883); D. H. Lawrence, *Studies in Classic American Literature* (1953), pp. 31-43; Julia Post Mitchell, *St. Jean de Crèvecoeur* (1916); Thomas Philbrick, *St. John de Crèvecoeur* (1970); Howard C. Rice, *Le Cultivateur Américain* (1933); Albert E. Stone, Jr., "Crèvecoeur's *Letters* and the Beginnings of an American Literature," EUQ, 18 (1962), 197-213.

Myra Jehlen
State University of New York at Purchase

SAMUEL CURWEN (1715-1802)

Works: *Journal and Letters of the Late Samuel Curwen* (w. 1738-1800; pub. 1842).

Biography: Samuel Curwen was born in Salem, Mass., on Dec. 17, 1715, the descendant of a wealthy and influential Salem family dating from 1638. After graduating from Harvard in 1735 and traveling briefly to Eng., he became a prosperous merchant in Salem. In 1744 he served as a captain in the expedition against Louisburg. In 1750 he married Abigail Russell, and in 1759 he received as a government favor the position of impost officer for Essex County. Following this appointment, he became a judge of admiralty, a post he held until the outbreak of the Revolution. In 1774 Curwen angered many fellow citizens by joining the Loyalist addressers who publicly commended Governor Thomas Hutchinson (q.v.), and in 1775 he fled Salem, going first to Philadelphia and then to Eng. His wife, however, refused to leave Salem with him. From 1775 to 1784, Curwen remained in Eng., traveling throughout the country, residing at various times in London and Bristol, and recording all in his journal and letters. He returned to America in Sept. 1784, only to find that he could no longer bear his wife's company and that a miscreant nephew had squandered much of his estate. To escape this unhappiness, he departed again for London in Jun. 1785. Upon the death of his wife in Mar. 1793, he sailed at once for America, and he remained in Salem until his death on Apr. 9, 1802.

Critical Appraisal: Samuel Curwen's place in American literature exists alongside those of Thomas Hutchinson, Katherine Amory, Benjamin Pickman, and other diarists on whom we rely for accounts of the life of American refugees in Eng. during the American Revolution. Within the genre, Curwen is agreeably thorough and readable.

The Curwen who emerges from his journal was a worried, sometimes irritable man, as much inclined to resent Englishmen who spoke of "*our colonies* and *our plantations* as if our property and persons were absolutely theirs" as he was to condemn Americans for the "unjustifiableness, imprudence, impolicy, ruinous consequences, and even madness" of their actions. Despite his own ambivalence and anxiety, though, Curwen provided vivid, delightful descriptions of an exile's life in Eng. He attended a packed performance of Handel's *Messiah* in Covent Garden and described the event as "most noble, grand, full, sonorous, and even awfully majestic." He witnessed firsthand the difficulties of a British recruiting officer in an unpopular war: "The fellows finding him out of their reach threw mud and sticks at the Coach to manifest their resentment at him and his business." He attended church often and described several services conducted by influential clergymen such as Josiah Tucker and John Wesley. He stood appalled and "thoroughly tired with the noise, huzzas and bustle" of London elections, and he kept his critical faculties at work in the presence of the mighty: "He [George III] is tall, square over shoulders, large, ugly, talks a great deal and shows his teeth too much." Most of all, perhaps, scholars value his writing for its clear expressions of the anxiety that grew among the American exiles as the war dragged on: "If this campaign [General Howe's campaign of 1777] proves disastrous, I shall look on our case as irretrievable and myself doomed to pass the few remaining days of a life I am heartily tired of in a land of aliens."

Curwen's *Journal and Letters* first appeared in 1842 in a single volume compiled by his great-grandnephew, George Atkinson Ward. This edition, reprinted with few changes in 1844, 1845, and 1864, was for more than 100 years a primary source of information about Loyalist refugees in Eng. In 1972, however, Andrew Oliver published a two-volume edition of *The Journal of Samuel Curwen, Loyalist*, in which he showed that Ward had corrupted Curwen's text significantly. Ward's version of the journal is seldom used today, but his volume still provides the only large, accessible sampling of Curwen's letters.

Although Charles Dickens devoted several pages of his *Household Words* to an unsigned review of the *Journal and Letters* in 1853, scholars of the nineteenth and early twentieth centuries gave relatively little attention to Loyalist writings. Given Andrew Oliver's excellent edition of the *Journal* and the growing interest in Loyalist writers, Curwen's work seems likely to receive the increased scholarly attention it deserves.

Suggested Readings: DAB; Sibley-Shipton (IX, 511-529); T_2. *See also* Charles E. Modlin, "The Loyalists' Reply" in *American Literature, 1764-1789*, ed. Everett Emerson (1977), pp. 59-71; Andrew Oliver, ed., *The Journal of Samuel Curwen, Loyalist*, 2 vols. (1972); "Seventy-Eight Years Ago," *Household Words* (1853), VII, 1-6, 157-163; George Atkinson Ward, ed., *Journal and Letters of the Late Samuel Curwen* (1842).

James C. Gaston
United States Air Force Academy

ROBERT CUSHMAN (c. 1579-1625)

Works: *A Sermon Preached at Plimmoth* (1622); "Reasons and Considerations" (pub. in *Mourt's Relation;* 1622).

Biography: A wool-carder born in Canterbury, Eng., sometime around 1579, Robert Cushman left for Holland in 1609 to join the Pilgrims at Leyden. After the death of his first wife, Sarah, he married Mary Chingleton (also spelled *Singleton*) in 1617. In Aug. of that year, the Pilgrims sent him and John Carver to London as agents to negotiate with the Virginia Company for financial backing for their planned emigration and to petition the king for permission to practice their religion in the New World. Cushman returned to Leyden in May 1618, and a year later, the Pilgrims sent him back to London with William Brewster to conclude the negotiations and to solicit more support from friends and merchants. When factious quarreling delayed the company's decision, Cushman visited Kent for two or three weeks. In Jun. 1619, shortly after he returned to London, the patent was granted. The man to whom the patent was formally granted decided not to accompany the Pilgrims, however, so after some brief negotiations with the Dutch the group at Leyden accepted the financial support of Thomas Weston and some other London merchants. They drew up an *Articles of Agreement*, which Weston approved. Carver and Cushman were then sent to Eng. in Apr. 1620 to get the promised money and to secure the provisions and ships for the voyage, but Weston then insisted on altering two of the articles. Fearing that the entire venture was in danger, Cushman himself finally agreed to make two changes: half of the Pilgrims' lands and houses were to go to the merchants, and the Pilgrims would no longer have the two days per week for their private business as originally agreed. Cushman's decision outraged William Bradford (q.v.) and the others at Leyden, but Cushman retorted to "entreat our friends not to be too busy in answering matters, before they know them. If I do such things as I cannot give reasons for, it is like you have set a fool about your business: and so turn the reproof to yourselves, and send another; and let me come again to my combs."

Despite his repeated threats to remain in Eng. and John Robinson's complaint that "we have had nothing from him but terms and presumptions," Cushman sailed from Southampton with the rest of the Pilgrims on the *Speedwell* on Aug. 5, 1620. But when the *Speedwell* had to give up the voyage and return to Eng. on Sept. 6, Cushman returned with it, although Bradford claimed that Cushman's "heart and courage was gone from him before." During the next year, Cushman continued to act as the Pilgrims' agent and procured the *Fortune* for the second emigration. In Jul. 1621 he and his son Thomas left for America on that ship, arriving on Nov. 21 of that year. Leaving his son with William Bradford, he sailed back for Eng. on Dec. 13, but during the return voyage, the *Fortune* was captured by the French pirate Fontenau de Pennart and did not arrive in Eng. until Feb. 14. Cushman never returned to New Eng., but he continued to oversee the Pilgrims' interests in Eng. and Holland in conjunction with the agent in New Eng., his brother-in-law Isaac Allerton. As a result of these efforts, Cushman and Edward Winslow (q.v.) received a grant from Lord Sheffield for territory in Cape Ann, where a new band of Puritans made the first permanent settlement within the limits of the Massachusetts Bay Colony. Cushman died in Eng. in 1625. A large granite monument is dedicated to him and his family in Plymouth, Mass.

Critical Appraisal: Robert Cushman's place in the literary history of America is ensured as the author of two firsts: his self-proclaimed first effort to defend the immigration, *Reasons and Considerations Touching the Lawfulnesse of Removing Out of England*, and the first sermon preached in America, *A Sermon Preached at Plimmoth*, afterward reprinted as *The Sin and Danger of Self-Love*. These texts are more than historical curiosities, however, for although Cushman's letters show him to be a stubborn and contentious man, his formal writings witness a more subtle mind capable of serious and effective argument.

Much of Cushman's justification of the immigration follows the usual arguments of such tracts: America is "spatious and void, and there are few and doe but run over the grasse, as doe also the Foxes and wilde beasts: they are not industrious, neither have art." Furthermore, since it is "our duty to convert them," and "to us they cannot come, our land is full: to them we may goe, their land is emptie." The image of America as a land populated only by subhuman savages, crying out for the civilizing and saving presence of Europeans, had been commonplace since the early letters of Columbus and Vespucci, and in using it as a justification for colonization, Cushman was simply following tradition. Unlike the arguments supporting the second emigration that appeared in the thirties, however, Cushman discounted the strictly typological justification for the colonial movement. God used to call up his people to wander in the desert, Cushman said, but not any more. There is no land "typicall" of heaven or Canaan now. Instead, we have a duty—not a divine obligation—to go live where we can do others the most good. Since New Eng. might provide a means for others to escape persecution as well as a forum for converting the savages, the colonists have a moral right to settle their new community.

Cushman's emphasis on the social and moral obligations of the Pilgrims is the basis for his sermon. The danger of self-love is one of the most common motifs in Puritan jeremiads, but Cushman is as interested in the economic consequences of the sin as in its scriptural interdiction. Even if it is legally acceptable to carry out an action for our own good, Cushman warned, when by this means we seek ourselves and have no regard for others, then the means are "unexpedient, unprofitable, yea unlawful." A mixture of economic and theological argument is typical of many Puritan sermons, of course, but Cushman repeatedly emphasized the more pragmatic aspects of selfish behavior until the scriptural allusions became support for the economic argument in a reversal of the usual rhetorical focus: he chastized those who expected others to work for them and claimed that "such idle Drones are intollerable in a settled Commonwealth, much more in a commonwealth which is but as it were in the bud; of what earth I pray thee art thou made, of any better than the other of the son of Adam? And canst thou see other of the brethren toil their hearts out, and thou sit idle at home, or takest thy pleasure abroad?" Similarly, he invoked monastic isolation not as a feature of a delusive religion but as an antisocial act and argued that Va. is having trouble not because of the secular motives of its founders but because the number of selfish people who have gone there keep the colony working against itself.

It is surprising that Cushman was chosen to deliver the first sermon to the Pilgrims and that he undertook a public justification of the enterprise since not only was he vilified by the other Pilgrims but had himself written a year earlier that "if ever we make a Plantation, GOD works a miracle...I see not, in reason how we shall escape." It is likely that much of the ill will between Cushman and the others was the product of the confusion and distress of the first voyage; once the colony was settled, the anger dissipated. Nevertheless, Cushman never spent much time in the community for which he worked so hard; the exhortations to communal unity and support that pervade his public works undoubtedly speak to his personal anguish as well as the social complexities that threatened to destroy the early settlement.

Suggested Readings: DAB; T₁. *See also* Edward Arber, *The Story of the Pilgrim Fathers* (1897), pp. 307-318, passim; William Bradford, *History of Plymouth Plantation* (1856; rep., 1912), II, 111-119, passim; *Proceedings at the Cushman Celebration* (1855); Charles M. Segal and David C. Stineback, *Puritans, Indians, and Manifest Destiny* (1977), pp. 55-56, Alexander Young, ed., *Chronicles of the Pilgrim Fathers* (1841), pp. 255-256.

Michael P. Clark
University of Michigan

_D

NATHAN DABOLL (1750-1818)

Works: *The Connecticut Almanack* for 1773 (1772); *Freebetter's New-England Almanack* for 1773, 1776, 1777 (1772, 1775, 1776); *Freebetter's Connecticut Almanack* for 1774 (1773); *Daboll's New-England Almanack* for 1775 (1774); *The New-England Almanack* for 1777 through 1801, except 1783 (pub. annually from 1776 through 1800, except 1782, under "Freebetter" (pseudonym) through 1792 and under "Daboll" thereafter); *A Register for the State of Connecticut* for 1785 (1784); *Green's Register* for 1786, 1789-1795 (1785, 1788-1794); *Sheet Almanack* for 1791, 1792, 1795-1801 (1790, 1791, 1794-1800); *An Almanack* for 1793 (1792); *Daboll's Schoolmaster's Assistant* (1800); *Daboll's Practical Navigator* (1820).

Biography: Born in Groton, Conn., on Apr. 24, 1750, the son of Nathan and Anna (Lynn) Daboll, Nathan Daboll was an almanac maker, teacher, and textbook author. He was tutored by Rev. Jonathan Barber, the village parson, and also attended the local school. He early exhibited remarkable talent for mathematics. Indeed, he was interested in little else, although he worked as a cooper for his living while he taught himself higher mathematics. He was first married to Elizabeth Daboll, a cousin, and, after her death, to Mrs. Elizabeth Brown.

Daboll began calculating *The New-England Almanack* for the printer Timothy Green III in 1772 (for 1773), usually under the name of Edmund Freebetter, a pseudonym already in use by Clark Ellicott, who had previously calculated this almanac for Green. After 1793 Daboll's own name appeared regularly on the title page. Expert in general mathematics, navigation, and nautical astronomy, he taught in the Plainfield (Conn.) Academy from 1783 to 1788, when he returned to Groton, where professional seamen were often his pupils. During these years, he devised his own text, published in 1800. He also prepared another textbook for his own courses, *Daboll's Practical Navigator*, published posthumously in 1820.

Critical Appraisal: *Daboll's Schoolmaster's Assistant; Being a Plain, Practical System of Arithmetic* was apparently widely used, as it was reprinted nearly every year for more than thirty years and was still published as late as 1837 in Ithaca, N.Y., by Mack, Andrus, and Woodruff. When it was first issued in 1799, recommendations and endorsements were inserted from eminent persons such as Noah Webster (q.v.) and Asa Messer, president of Rhode-Island College. The book was organized into chapters with examples of problems and their solutions. The subject matter, including assorted tables, covered all types of basic arithmetic with emphasis on what we now call "business math." Later, another section called *The Practical Accountant* was added, perhaps by Samuel Green, the printer and son of Timothy Green III. Green also published *Daboll's Practical Navigator: Being a Concise, Easy, and Comprehensive System of Navigation, Calculated for the Daily Use of Seamen, and Also for an Assistant to the Teacher...Also a New, Scientific and Very Short Method of Correcting the Dead Reckoning...in Which May Be Seen All the Varieties Which Can Possibly Happen in a Ship's Reckoning* (1820). Daboll's teachings were of particular value in a sailing community and whaling center. His reputation as a teacher resulted in an invitation by Commodore Rodgers to teach a class on board the frigate *President*.

Daboll's almanacs, published regularly during the Revolution, sometimes completely ignored the war. There were no stirring original propagandistic essays and verse. Occasionally, however, appeared humorous and satirical cartoons, equally effective as propaganda; for example, the 1774 title page of *Freebetter's Connecticut Almanack* for 1774 featured "a curious cut of his M———y's WIG" (George III), and the famous "Boston Cannonaded" cartoon was printed in *Daboll's New-England Almanack* for 1775. *The New-England Almanack* for 1777 (New London: Timothy Green) contained one of the most entertaining pieces of satirical Revolutionary propaganda ever printed in an American almanac. "The Politicians," a dialog between two Britishers, detailed an absurd fail-safe plan to conquer America: close the ports, dig a ditch around the area to keep the people from escaping, set the air afire, and "let the clouds down upon their heads." Dick, "a Country Man," is then told by Peter, "the newsmonger and Politician," that Eng. has another even "grander scheme": a plan to send horse regiments to the moon; board a comet there; land on Mars and the other stars and planets; take them by force, bring them to Eng., and "make them pay taxes."

This kind of humor helped to make Daboll's almanacs attractive. There were occasional factual accounts of war activities, a five-page biography of George Washington (q.v.) in 1782, and the complete text of the Treaty between G.B. and the U.S. in *A Register for the State of Connecticut* for 1785.

Daboll's almanacs were of outstanding quality and were varied in format: standard, sheet, and register. There was no emphasis on astrology, and the Man of Signs was rarely used. Since Daboll was a professional teacher of nautical astronomy, the calculations were first rate. The almanac contents were well balanced with the usual calendar information (with weather predictions); tables of interest, currency values, and travel distances; dates of courts and other meetings; calendar verse; homiletic sayings; household hints; occasional cures for disease; and some poems, songs, and anecdotes. We cannot be sure that Daboll controlled or contributed to the miscellaneous content; he may have simply prepared the astronomical calculations.

Nathan Daboll's almanacs were continued by the Daboll family for more then 100 years, and until 1971 the *Old Farmer's Almanac* (printed in Dublin, N.H., in the old Robert Bailey Thomas [q.v.] format) included the Daboll almanac.

Suggested Readings: BDAS; DAB. *See also* Robb Sagendorph, *America and Her Almanacs* (1970), pp. 108-112; Marion Barber Stowell, *Early American Almanacs* (1977), pp. 92-95; Isaiah Thomas, *The History of Printing in America* (c. 1810; rep., 1970), pp. 298, 307.

Marion Barber Stowell
Milledgeville, Georgia

THOMAS DALE (1700-1750)

Works: *Dissertatio medico-botanica inauguralis de Pareira Brava at Sorapia officinarum* (1723); "Epilog, *The Recruiting Officer*," *Gentleman's Magazine*, 6 (May 1736), 288; "The Case of Miss Mary Roche," *The South Carolina Gazette*, Nov. 2, 1738; "The Puff, or A Proper Reply to Skimmington's last Crudities," *The South Carolina Gazette*, Jan. 25, 1739; Translations: *Emmenologia* (by John Freind; 1729); *Methods of Extracting Stone Out of the Bladder* (by Henry Francis Le Dran; 1731); *Nine Commentaries upon Fevers: And Two Epistles Concerning the Small Pox* (by John Freind; 1731); *Philosophical Conversations* (by Noel Regnault, S.J.; 1731); *A Treatise of Continual Fevers* (by Joost van Lom; 1732).

Biography: Born in Hoxton, Eng., in 1700, Thomas Dale received a medical degree from Leyden on Sept. 23, 1723. After graduation, Dale returned to London and for the next eight to ten years practiced medicine and translated several medical treatises into English. A series of eleven letters to the Rev. Dr. Thomas Birch reveals that Dale sailed for America in Mar. 1732, leaving behind debts and broken relations with his family, the latter perhaps due to Dale's choice of a bride, who accompanied him to Charleston, S.C., and died shortly thereafter. Another source, it should be noted, made no mention of the London years, 1723-1732, and placed Dale in Charleston in 1725. On Mar. 28, 1733, Dale married the heiress Mary Brewton, thus cementing his place among the Charleston aristocracy and securing a residence that Col. Miles Brewton gave in dowry to his now "daughter Dale," Mary. On the southwest corner of Church and Tradd Streets, "Daughterdale" was the doctor's home until his death. There his first son, Thomas, died in 1736, followed by a daughter (Mary), who in 1737 was buried in the same coffin with her mother. In Jan. 1738 Dale married Anne Smith, and when she died (without issue) in 1743, he married Hannah Simons.

Except for the controversy over the treatment of smallpox victim Mary Roche, which Dale provoked with Dr. James Killpatrick (or *Kirkpatrick*) (q.v.) (the attending physician), Dale was less known for his medical career than for his activities as social and political leader. In 1733 he was appointed assistant justice by Governor Johnson, and in 1734 he was elected steward of Saint George's Club. Starting in 1735, he contributed to the success of the Charleston theater, both by financial support and by writing at least one epilog for the presentation of George Farquhar's *The Recruiting Officer*. Probably, he contributed other such pieces as well. In 1737 he became a justice of the peace, deciding issues such as the impoundment of livestock and the execution of slaves for burglary, and in 1739 he was appointed to the Court of General Sessions. He served two terms on a three-person board administering a slave detention workhouse and market, and he was a member of the Upper House of the S.C. Assembly. On Sept. 16, 1750, Dale died, leaving substantial personal effects, including "several very valuable negroes," to be sold for the benefit of his wife, Hannah, and their three children, Thomas Seinons, Jane, and Francis.

Critical Appraisal: As a young man, Thomas Dale demonstrated both intellect and industry in his translations of several medical treatises, which are still noted for their easy and readable style. When writing in his own name about a medical case he had witnessed, Dale also showed talent for vitriol and satire. The two responses he wrote to Dr. James Killpatrick concerning the Mary Roche case have been lost, but much of their nature can be inferred from Killpatrick's "A Full and Clear Reply," which has been preserved. Dale's first pamphlet, "The Case of Miss Mary Roche, More Fairly Related" (in response to Killpatrick's "The Case of Miss Mary Roche. . .Fairly Related" [*The South Carolina Gazette*, Sept. 14, 1738]), was not an objection to the practice of inoculation but rather a condemnation of Killpatrick's specific treatment of the 10-month-old child. According to Dale, the girl should not have been moved from her sickbed, and she should have been blistered with cantharides at an early stage in the fever (*The South Carolina Gazette*, Nov. 2, 1738). On Jan. 25, 1739, Killpatrick responded with a defense of his practice and a vehement dismissal of Dale as a medical authority. Dale's satire, "The Puff," also published in the *Gazette* on Jan. 25, continued the debate in the manner of Swift and Pope. On May 19, 1739, Killpatrick reiterated his medical position and accused Dale of plagiarism and indecorum; Killpatrick called Dale's satire "dirty Ribaldry" and Dale himself a "paltry Scribler." Alluding to Swift's mock-controversy between Isaac Bickerstaff and Partridge, Killpatrick humorlessly took Dale's ironies at face value. "The Puff" may indeed have seemed in bad taste (after all, the child inoculated did die), but Killpatrick's outrage in itself suggests that Dale's was effective satire.

In the epilog to *The Recruiting Officer*, Dale demonstrated literary skill in a genre other than satire. The epilog is conventional in verse form, subject matter, and tone. Written in heroic couplets, the typical poetic medium for such pieces in restoration and eighteenth-century drama, and spoken by Silvia, a character in the drama, the epilog called for the audience's indulgence and applause. The opening lines recalled the wordplay on female characters and male disguises that

Shakespeare made popular in Rosalind's epilog to *As You Like It* and that the following century warmly embraced. Dale's verse similarly joked with the audience about the sexual ambiguity of Silvia and the difficulties of love affairs created thereby. The Dale poem also contains a mildly ribald double-entendre in the reference to "ladies" and their "fears of a *first-night*." Although no doubt a small sample of Dale's work, the epilog shows the doctor to have affected the witty, risqué style that was fashionable for a gentleman of his class and culture.

Suggested Readings: Miller Christy, "Samuel Dale (c. 1659-1739), of Braintree, Botanist, and the Dale Family; Some Genealogy and Some Portraits," EN, 19 (1918-1921), 49-69; Francisco Guerra, *American Medical Bibliography 1639-1783* (1962), pp. 91, 92, 94, 658, 659-660; Robert Adger Law, "A Diversion of Colonial Gentlemen," TR, 51 (1916), 79-88; idem, "Early American Prologues and Epilogues," *Nation*, 98 (1914), 463-464; idem, "Thomas Dale, An Eighteenth Century Gentleman," *Nation*, 101 (1915), 773-774; Robert E. Seibels, "Thomas Dale, M.D., of Charleston, S.C.," AMH, 3 (1931), 50-57; Joseph I. Waring, "James Killpatrick and Smallpox Inoculation in Charleston," AMH, 10 (1938), 301-308.

Roslyn L. Knutson
University of Arkansas at Little Rock

JAMES DANA (1735-1812)

Works: *The Character and Reward of the Good and Faithful Servant* (1764); *Illustrations on Human Frailty* (1765); *Two Discourses Delivered at Cambridge* (1767); *A Century Discourse* (1770); *An Examination of the Late Rev. President Edwards's Enquiry on Freedom of Will* (1770); *The Examination of...Edwards's Enquiry...Continued* (1773); *A Discourse Delivered at Kensington* (1775); *A Sermon Preached Before the General Assembly* (1779); *Men's Sins* (1783); *The Reflection and Prospect of a Christian Minister* (1787); *Installation Sermon* (1789); *The Nativity of Christ* (1789); *The Intent of Capital Punishment* (1790); *The African Slave Trade* (1791); *The Doctrine and Mission of Jesus Christ* (1792); *The Pastoral Care* (1793); *A Sermon Preached...at the Ordination of the Rev. Elijah Waterman* (1794); *The Folly of Practical Atheism* (1795); *The Heavenly Mansions* (1795); *Christianity the Wisdom of God* (1799); *Two Discourses* (1801); *There Is No Reason to Be Ashamed of the Gospel* (1802); *A Sermon on the Much Lamented Death of Mr. Ebenezer Grant Marsh* (1803); *The Character of Scoffers* (1805); *The Wisdom of Observing the Footsteps of Providence* (1805); *Observations upon Baptism* (1806); *Sermons to Young People* (1806).

Biography: James Dana, Congregational clergyman and third-generation descendant of Richard Dana who came to America from Eng. in 1640, was born in Cambridge, Mass., to Caleb and Phoebe (Chandler) Dana on May 11, 1735. Graduating from Harvard at age 18, Dana was called in 1758 to the church in

Wallingford, Conn., an appointment that precipitated one of the most notorious incidents in the religious history of New Eng. Called the "Wallingford Controversy," this incident involved a hotly debated clash between New Light followers of the Great Awakening and the more conservative Old Light faction of the New Eng. Church. An Old Light preacher suspected of Arminian tendencies, Dana was hotly opposed by New Light ministers who refused to accept his appointment at Wallingford. Eventually, Dana formed an independent association of the ministers and churches that installed him. Although the controversy abated, it never disappeared. As late as 1770, for example, Dana published *An Examination of the Late Rev. Edwards's Enquiry on Freedom of Will*, which he continued in a 1773 pamphlet titled simply *The Examination*, and throughout his career, Dana defended the Old Light views of leaders such as Ezra Stiles (q.v.), whom Dana supported for the presidency of Yale, against the New Light opinions of leaders such as Joseph Bellamy (q.v.), Samuel Hopkins (q.v.), Stephen West, Samuel Austin, and Jonathan Edwards, Jr. (q.v.).

Although Dana's ministry was never very successful, he was known for his learning, judgment, and personal warmth. Moreover, his image of unorthodoxy was lessened in 1768 when the University of Edinburgh conferred upon him a D.D., and his popularity further increased as a result of the strong support he gave the patriots during the Revolutionary War. After his forced retirement in 1805, Dana lived out his remaining years in relative peace. Married three times, he died in New Haven, Conn., on Aug. 11, 1812. His son, Samuel Wittlesey Dana, became a U.S. senator.

Critical Appraisal: The works of James Dana reflect his lifelong crusade for human rights and his interest in social concerns and problems. Particularly notable, for example, is his criticism of slavery, which displays to advantage the painstaking scholarship and careful rhetoric evident in his writings. Beginning with an unpromising caution that liberty must be consistent with law, and that one must render unto Caesar, Dana presented a detailed historical analysis of the institution of slavery, complete with current statistics on the subject. While carefully locating the major blame for New World slavery on Old World practices, especially those of monarchists and papists, Dana nonetheless decried in no uncertain terms the evils of contemporary slavery and its inconsistency with Christianity. Refusing the common argument that Africans "must have been sinners above all men, because they suffer such things," he concluded that "All men are the offspring of God."

Although the Wallingford Controversy now appears a minor ecclesiastical squabble, at the time it was seen as a major battle in a holy war, and Dana's challenge to Jonathan Edwards's (q.v.) *Freedom of the Will* is easily his most significant work, a fact acknowledged even by Paul Ramsey, Edwards's editor, who called it "by far the best" of any of the works leveled against Edwards. The great merit of Dana's work lies in his ability to comprehend Edwards's position without being distracted from his own defense of what Ramsey called "a type of self-determination that was not so easily refuted by Edwards' reduction of the position to infinite regress." While Edwards conceded and in fact even argued that freedom resided only in freedom of action and in the exercise of a predetermined choice, Dana accused Edwards of avoiding the real issue: "Because a man cannot take the second step without the first; therefore he cannot take the first without a previous one." Using Hume, Spinoza, Leibniz, and other "ancient and modern Fatalists" to reduce Edwards's scheme to the hypothesis that God "is the cause of sin," Dana primarily concerned himself with the practical effect of such subtle reasoning on human behavior, rather than with Edwards's more subtle metaphysical reasoning, which he dismissed as "unintelligible, and void of distinct, consistent meaning." Although Dana frequently maintained that Edwards's motives are good, *ad hominem* attacks mar portions of his argument. Dana's practical concern with men's behavior is, however, a consistent theme of his later career, which he spent as an outspoken critic of infidelity, Deism, and "scoffers."

Suggested Readings: CCNE; DAB; Sprague (I, 565-571); T$_2$. *See also* John J. Dana, *Memoranda of Some of the Descendants of Richard Dana* (1865); C.H.S. Davis, *History of Wallingford, Conn.* (1870); *The National Cyclopaedia of American Biography*, vol. 23 (1933), 309-310; Richard J. Purcell, *Connecticut in Transition, 1775-1818* (1918; rep., 1963); Paul Ramsey, "Editor's Introduction," *Works of Jonathan Edwards: Vol. 1: Freedom of the Will* (1957); Benjamin Turnbull, *A Complete History of Connecticut* (1818); *Vital Records of Cambridge, Mass., to the Year 1850*, vol. I (1914).

Mark A. Johnson
Central Missouri State University

JASPER DANCKAERTS (1639-c. 1703)

Works: *Journal of a Voyage to New York* (w. 1679-1680; pub. 1867).

Biography: Born at Flushing, Zeeland, to Pieter and Janneke (Schilders) Danckaerts, Jasper Danckaerts became a cooper and was employed by the Dutch West India Company at Middelburg. By 1676 he and his wife (d. 1676) had joined the Labadist Church. With Peter Sluyter he traveled in N.Y., N.J., Del., Md., and Mass. in 1679-1680, seeking a location for a Labadist commune. They chose a tract at the head of the Chesapeake Bay. Danckaerts also directed a company of Labadists immigrating to Dutch Guiana (now Surinam) and made a second voyage to America. In 1684 he was naturalized in Md., but he apparently returned to his native land, residing mainly in Wieuwerd, Friesland, home of the mother church. He died at Middelburg sometime between 1702 and 1704.

Critical Appraisal: Jasper Danckaerts visited the New World as a secret agent of the Labadist sect founded by Jean de Labadie (1610-1674). The Labadists accepted the cardinal doctrines of the Dutch Reformed Church but formed a separate society of the truly elect, divinely inspired to lives of piety, zeal, and communion in all things spiritual and temporal. Surrounded by hostile magistrates in Europe, they sought religious toleration in America.

Danckaerts's *Journal* is imbued with the doctrine of election. He distanced himself from the "godless" and "miserable" individuals he had encountered aboard ship and in the New World. Esteeming only "good Christians who live like Christians," he constantly found fault with the conduct of others and with most of the preachers and congregations he observed. He was particularly critical of the Quakers: their meetings are monotonous; they set themselves above others, yet are "miserably self-minded" and "worldly"; they are hated by the Indians, he alleged, "on account of their deceit and covetousness." Occasionally, he made a point of exposing a Quaker's hypocrisy or incompetence. Danckaerts and Sluyter once hired a Friend as a guide; the three men soon became lost and made their way out of the wilderness only by chance. Danckaerts remarked, "Not to leave him like an empty calabash, we gave him an English shilling for leading us astray, and other things"—"other things" apparently meaning warmed-over beans and maize bread, served in the Quaker's "hut." Evidently, it was important to Danckaerts to differentiate Labadist from Quaker, for members of his sect in the Neth. had been ridiculed as Quakers. The groups' views and practices were not dissimilar; both, for example, relied on the inner light. Robert Barclay and George Keith (q.v.) had called on Labadie in Amsterdam and asked him to join the Friends; William Penn (q.v.) visited the Labadist sect at Herford and Wieuwerd and remarked that in certain ways they "came near to Friends."

Nor was Danckaerts favorably impressed by the Congregationalists. After staying in Boston for five days, one in a prayer meeting led by three ministers, he concluded that in Boston there was "even less [devotion] than at New York; no respect, no reverence; in a word, nothing but the name of Independents." A month later, in his entry for Jul. 23, 1680, he summarized his impression of New Eng.'s trade and government; he said of the Puritans' religion that it "all . . . consists in observing Sunday." (The Labadists did not consider the Sabbath a special day, all days being holy.) The magistrates might, if they wished, impose penalties for profanity and debauchery, but New Eng. displayed little concern for "truth and true godliness."

From time to time, however, he found evidence that God had sown "the seed of the elect" in America. Sometimes the two Dutchmen cultivated that seed. They offered one of their hosts "what was necessary, whether by instruction, admonition or reproof"; this man "promis[ed] himself as well as all his family to reform, which was quite necessary." Traveling under assumed names, telling almost no one the purpose of their tour, the Labadists were periodically suspected of being papists, Quakers, Mennonists, and French or Dutch spies. An acquaintance in Boston told them that he could not let them enter his house since they were rumored to be Jesuits—because, explained the scornful Danckaerts, he and Sluyter were unlike most Bostonians: "quiet and modest" and able to speak several languages.

Danckaerts also detailed his business transactions, meticulously noting prices, as well as his observations about the climate, terrain, soil, roads and waterways, and the flora and fauna of each colony. In a tirade against "that vile tobacco" he spoke of the hardships of slaves and indentured servants, calling Md. and Va. planters avaricious and "godless." (Tobacco, though forbidden to the Labadists in Friesland, was grown in their colony in Md.; Danckaerts's companion Sluyter, who directed America's first commune, acquired a reputation for cruel exploitation of slaves.) Danckaerts was also shocked and disgusted by the white man's mistreatment of Indians—in particular, calling a woman converted to Christianity a "sow" and overcharging the savages for the rum that was destroying them.

Sometimes displaying considerable narrative skill, he related what he learned of the Indians' ideas of God; described his visit to Harvard College (unimpressed, he considered 300 words sufficient); told the story of Theunis Idenszen, a New Yorker tormented by the devil; recorded his interpretation of a dispute between Edmund Andros and Philip Carteret, governors of N.Y. and N.J.; and recounted his meetings with the Rev. John Eliot (q.v.), who gave him an Old Testament in an Indian language, and Simon Bradstreet, governor of Mass. Having assessed the New World, Danckaerts offered his opinion of Eng.'s Whitehall and Westminster "and all within them": "not worth going to see." The journal is punctuated with caustic generalizations evidently intended to prepare fellow Labadists for life in America: Swedes and Finns overcharge strangers; Englishmen are liars and cheaters, their wives poor housekeepers; New Yorkers from the colony's interior are more unruly than Indians. The Dutch, however, are "the right kind of people, with whom we could at least obtain what was right."

Biased, occasionally tedious, but often entertaining, Danckaerts's *Journal* contains a wealth of detail about social, religious, economic, and topographical conditions in seventeenth-century America. The work will also interest students of communism and the Labadist sect, whose colony in Md. lasted from 1683 to 1727.

Suggested Readings: CCMDG; LHUS. Henry C. Murphy's translation and edition (1867) is the basis for two twentieth-century printings: Bartlett B. James and J. Franklin Jameson, eds., *Journal of Jasper Danckaerts, 1679-1680* (1913; rep., 1959), and *Journal of a Voyage to New York and a Tour in Several of the American Colonies in 1679-80* (1867; rep., 1966). Parts of the manuscript, held by the Long Island Historical Society, have been omitted from these editions. Excerpts are included in JNH, 2 (1917), 186-187; Perry Miller and Thomas H. Johnson, eds., *The Puritans* (1938; rep., 1963), II, 403-411; and Richard M. Dorson, ed., *America Begins: Early American Writing* (1971), pp. 116-118, 290-292, 334-335. *See also* Bartlett B. James, *The Labadist Colony in Maryland* (1899).

Mary De Jong
The Pennsylvania State University

JOHN DANE (c. 1612-1684)

Works: *A Declaration of the Remarkabell Prouedenses in the Corse of My Lyfe* (w. 1682; pub. 1854).

Biography: According to a statement in his *Declaration of Remarkable Providences* that he was 70 years old in 1682, John Dane was probably born in 1612 in Eng., perhaps in Berkhampstead. When Dane was still a child, his family moved to Stortford. There Dane learned the work of his father's tailor shop, a trade to be his livelihood while he lived in Eng. At 18, Dane quarreled with his father over the value of dancing school and moved to Hertford until several years later when he reconciled with his family. After marrying, Dane moved to Wood Roe and then to Hatfield but soon emigrated because of social and professional animosities. In New Eng., after a brief stay in Roxbury, he settled in Ipswich, where he became a farmer, remarried, and sired four daughters and two sons of whom the elder, John, was the grandfather of Nathan Dane, founder of the Dane law professorship at Harvard. John Dane died at Ipswich on Sept. 29, 1684. The manuscript of *Declaration of Remarkable Providences*, preserved by the Warner line, was given to the New England Historical and Genealogical Society by John J. Babson of Gloucester and subsequently published in 1854.

Critical Appraisal: Written in the tradition of Puritan spiritual autobiography, John Dane's *A Declaration of Remarkable Providences* is a compilation of a series of personal incidents that, in its author's opinion, demonstrate the protective spirit of providence and the mercy of God in preserving the author's fortunes. Brief and anecdotal, the *Declaration* is especially significant because unlike the spiritual autobiographies of its more celebrated contemporaries, it is the product of an amateur writer who has taken up the pen to urge his descendants to be aware of God's attentiveness to their lives. Dane betrayed little formal schooling in the literary arts, but the unpretentious style of his autobiography is itself a charming feature, and in its emphasis on Dane's growth from poor immigrant to successful farmer, it anticipates the archetype of the American Dream commonly present in later American autobiographical literature such as Benjamin Franklin's (q.v.) *Autobiography*, Michel Guillaume Jean de Crèvecoeur's (q.v.) *Letters from an American Farmer*, and even Herman Melville's *Redburn*.

Almost three-fourths of the narrative concerns episodes from Dane's early life in Eng. During these critical years, Dane painstakingly revealed that providence destined the economic survival of his family and his own struggle to obey his father's will. A failure in the latter leads Dane to the most significant episode in the narrative: Dane's father objects to the local dancing school, and rather than bow to his father's opinion, he leaves home, as he tells his mother, "to seke my fortin." In the break with family, Dane began his rite of passage, haunted for the rest of his life by his mother's parting prophecy: "goe whare you will, god he will find you out." Indeed, the maternal warning acted as a complementary theme to the protective mercy of God, for throughout the narrative, Dane recounted episodes that illustrate either his being discovered in some undesirable activity or his being spared injury or ruin.

In the midst of those adventures that take the author from runaway boy to married man and immigrant, Dane also provided an occasional digression on the social milieu in which he lived. Two particularly noteworthy episodes involve Dane and a buxom woman whom he found in his rooms at the inn. By the goodness of God's restraint, Dane said, he avoided this obvious temptation. Likewise, Dane mentioned meeting Indians on the path to Ipswich, and he observed the progress toward civilization in his adopted country by noting that a place where he contemplated suicide "is now a Rode, then it was a place that was not mutch walkt in."

Although Dane's narrative is not without its structural problems (he was, for example, too willing to telescope many troubles "two teadus to menshon" into one reference and he often failed to prepare the reader for the spiritual and emotional trials he underwent), his narrative is powerful not because his experiences are unique, although Dane perceived them as such, but because they are simply and ingenuously presented and most of all because they are universal. The names, towns, and circumstances differ from one early American spiritual autobiography to another, but the narrators agree that in each detail of their lives may be seen the unmistakably firm grasp of God's providential hand.

Suggested Readings: FCNEV. *See also* John Dane's *A Declaration of Remarkabell Prouedenses in the Corse of My Lyfe*, with a preface by John Ward Dean and a genealogy of the Dane family, NEHGR, 8 (1854), 147-156, printed separately in Boston (1854); Daniel B. Shea, Jr., *Spiritual Autobiography in Early America* (1968), pp. 126-138.

Roslyn L. Knutson
University of Arkansas at Little Rock

JOHN DANFORTH (1660-1730)

Works: *An Almanack...for...1679* (1679); *Kneeling to God* (1697); "A Poem to the Blessed Memory of the Venerable John Eliot" (1697); *A Funeral Elegy...of...Thomas Danforth* (1699); *The Right Christian Temper* (1702); *The Vile Prophanations of Prosperity* (1704); *A Pindarick Elegy upon...Samuel Willard* (1707); *The Blackness of Sin Against Light* (1710); *King Hezekiah's Bitterness and Relief* (1710); *Profit and Loss: An Elegy upon...Mrs. Mary Gerrish* (1710); *Honour and Vertue Elegized* (1713); *A Poem upon the Much Honoured...Maria Mather* (1714); *Judgment Begun at the House of God* (1716); *Greatness and Goodness...Hannah Sewall* (1717); *The Mercies of the Year Commemorated: A Song for Little Children in New England* (1720); *A Poem on the Death of Peter Thacher and Samuel Danforth* (c. 1727); "Two Vast Enjoyments Commemorated, and Two Great Bereavements Lamented" (1727); *A Sermon Occasioned by the Late Great Earthquake* (1728); *The Divine Name Humbly Celebrated* (n.d.).

Biography: Born in Roxbury, Mass., on Nov. 8, 1660, into the family of Samuel and Mary Danforth, John Danforth was the fifth of ten children and part of an illustrious New Eng. literary family whose American beginnings were established by his maternal grandfather, Rev. John Wilson (q.v.). John's younger brother, Samuel Danforth II (q.v.), in addition to undertaking the professions of minister, lawyer, and physician, prepared an Indian dictionary that exists today only in manuscript.

John graduated from Harvard in 1677. Like his brother and father, he published an almanac (1679) that contains some curious and interesting poetry, including some of his own verses. In 1682 he succeeded Josiah Flynt as minister at Dorcester Church, where he remained until his death on May 26, 1730.

Danforth published his poems infrequently and, with the exception of the year 1712, never more than one per year. At his death, no mention was made of any of his poetic activities, including thirty-six poems of varying "kinds" and lengths. Eighteen of these poems are elegies and epitaphs, some demonstrating extraordinary facility with these forms. All of the funeral poems extol piety, concern for the colony's continuance, and service to the community that included, for Danforth, four terms as an elected fellow of Harvard College.

Critical Appraisal: John Danforth is most frequently described as a "faithful, pedestrian versifier; who could produce poetry when the occasion demanded," but he is also sufficiently significant to elicit the observation that his work should be reprinted and studied. Indeed it should, for two reasons: first, he provides additional testimony to the variety of poetry that characterizes this period of American literature; second, he serves, through his poetry, to mark a transitional position in the development of American verse that shows clearly the newly emerging techniques and expertise of the Enlightenment.

Danforth's poetry contains two rare forms in the canon of Puritan verse: the pindaric and the dramatic monologue. Although Danforth handled these forms somewhat amateurishly, his treatment of them, nevertheless reveals a cosmopolitan reading penchant and a continuous concern for form. In "On My Lord Bacon," an unsophisticated dramatic monologue, one responds immediately to the absence of didacticism and philosophizing. This poem, a curiosity, is written as a Pindaric stanza. This combination of forms may well be seen as an example of Danforth's apparent need to extend the boundaries of verse forms available to him. But the great mass of his thirty-six poems are elegies, none of which calls attention to itself. In these poems, Danforth gave forth the typical tribal laments and apprehensions concerning the church and its members, as they did or did not find favor with God. Occasionally, a personal sadness emerged, but usually the formality of the occasions overrode the poet's sensitivity.

Danforth has been reprinted and studied in articles, theses, and dissertations. Currently, opinion of his work oscillates between its historical importance and its lack of lyric expression. It seems somewhat unfair, however, to hold Danforth to a concept of personal utterance that was purposefully alien to men of his persuasion. He does add significant dimensions to the body of Puritan verse, and his work, hopefully, will be given that respect due one who expands the limits of verse form and structure.

Suggested Readings: CCNE; FCNEV; Sibley-Shipton (II, 507-514). *See also*

Harrison T. Meserole, ed., *Seventeenth-Century American Poetry* (1968), pp. 309-321; John E. Trimpey, "The Poetry of Four American Puritan Poets" (Ph.D. diss., Ohio Univ., 1969).

John E. Trimpey
The University of Tennessee at Chattanooga

SAMUEL DANFORTH (1626-1674)

Works: *An Almanack for the Year of Our Lord 1646* (1646); *An Almanack for the Year of Our Lord 1647* (1647); *An Almanack for the Year of Our Lord 1648* (1648); *An Almanack for the Year of Our Lord 1649* (1649); *An Astronomical Description of the Late Comet or Blazing Star* (1665); *A Brief Recognition of New-Englands Errand into the Wilderness* (1671); *The Cry of Sodom Inquired Into* (1674).

Biography: Samuel Danforth was born in Framingham, Suffolk, Eng., Sept. 1626, into a prominent family of considerable property. In 1629 his mother, Elizabeth Danforth, died; and in 1634 his father, Nicholas Danforth, moved his family to Cambridge, Mass., where he quickly became active in civil and religious affairs and was several times elected to public office.

In 1643 Samuel Danforth graduated from Harvard College, where he later served first as a tutor and then as a fellow. On Sept. 24, 1650, he was ordained in Roxbury, Mass., where he began a long association with John Eliot (q.v.), the Puritans' leading "Apostle to the Indians." Danforth assisted Eliot both in his evangelical work among the Indians and especially in his ministry to the settlers of Roxbury. On Nov. 5, 1651, Danforth married Mary Wilson, "the virtuous daughter," wrote Cotton Mather (q.v.), of the Rev. Mr. John Wilson (q.v.) of Boston. To this marriage, twelve children were born, including John Danforth (q.v.) in 1660 and Samuel Danforth (q.v.) in 1666, both of whom later graduated from Harvard and went on to become writers. During his lifetime, Danforth was known both for the pious and elaborate sermons he preached and for the care and concern he gave his congregation. In 1670 he was chosen to deliver the "election sermon," and on Nov. 19, 1674, he died in Roxbury, passing, Mather said, "from *Natural Health*, to *Eternal Peace*."

Critical Appraisal: As a beginning student at Harvard, Samuel Danforth was so pious that he insisted on correcting the blasphemies of "the Heathen Poets" he was studying, despite the admonitions of his tutor that in translation, orthodoxy mattered less than accuracy. Later Danforth's intense piety earned him the praise of Cotton Mather, and in modified form it lasted him a lifetime. In *The Cry of Sodom Inquired Into* (1674), which was published in the year of his death, Danforth decried the "Prodigious Villainy" of New Eng.'s adults and beseeched her children to abandon their "Youthful Lusts." But Danforth soon moved beyond the unusual squeamishness of his early youth, and in 1646, at age

19, produced New Eng.'s earliest extant almanac verse by imitating "the Heathen Poets" he had been reading.

Like much Puritan verse that followed it, Danforth's shows clearly the influence of Classical writers such as Horace and Vergil and English writers such as Bacon and Campion. In it, Classical and mythological allusions mingle with biblical allusions and homespun images. In keeping with Danforth's piety, his poetry remained rigorously orthodox both in doctrine and in purpose. It instructed overtly. In addition, it displayed Danforth's concern for the well-being of his wilderness community. In the almanac of 1647, he played allegorically with current events; in the almanac of 1648, he celebrated New Eng. by likening it to a flourishing tree with Justice as its roots, Liberty as its top, and Peace, Unity, Truth, and Plenty as its fruit. Toward the end of his life, Danforth's capacity for image making again merged with his concern for the fate of New Eng., enabling him to write the finest of his published works, *A Brief Recognition of New-Englands Errand into the Wilderness* (1671), where he first decried the "Declension" that he saw around him, and then began "to review, and consider in earnest" the sacred charge that brought devout men and women "into this Wilderness" to make a new start.

Danforth's almanacs also show an early interest in astronomy. Having persisted for several years, that interest culminated in *An Astronomical Description* of the comets of 1664, the significance of which derives primarily from its efforts to reconcile old views with new. In discussing comets as divine portents of disaster, Danforth allied himself with an ancient, honored, yet dying, tradition. In discussing them as stellar phenomena governed by natural laws, he showed awareness of a new, emerging, reorienting perspective. Since Danforth knew Copernicus's work only through popularizations such as Vincent Wing's *Astronomia Instaurata* (1656), however, and since his own work was not based on independent telescopic observation, his treatise broke no new ground and remains of interest now primarily as a sign of a crucial transition in the imaginative and intellectual history of New Eng.

Suggested Readings: CCNE; FCNEV; Sibley-Shipton (I,88-92). *See also* Harrison T. Meserole, ed., *Seventeenth-Century American Poetry* (1968), pp. 414-419; Perry Miller and Thomas H. Johnson, eds., *The Puritans: A Sourcebook of Their Writings* (1963), II, 731-733, 738-739; Samuel Eliot Morison, *Harvard College in the Seventeenth Century* (1936), pp. 124-134, 214-219; Kenneth Silverman, ed., *Colonial American Poetry* (1968), pp. 31-45.

David Minter
Emory University

SAMUEL DANFORTH (1666-1727)

Works: *The New-England Almanack for the Year of Our Lord, 1686* (1685); *Account of an Indian Visitation, A.D. 1698* (with Grindal Rawson; 1698; rep.,

CMHS, 1st ser., 10 [1808], 129-134); *Piety Encouraged* (1705); *The Duty of Believers to Oppose the Growth of the Kingdom of Sin* (1708); *The Woful Effects of Drunkenness* (1710); *An Elegy in Memory of the Worshipful Major Thomas Leonard Esq.* (1713); *An Exhortation to All* (1714); "The Building Up of Sion" (pub. in *Bridgewater's Monitor: Two Sermons Preached unto a New Assembly of Christians at Bridgwater*; 1717); *An Essay by Several Ministers of the Gospel...Concerning the Singing of Psalms in the Publick Worship of God* (with Peter Thacher and John Danforth; 1723).

Biography: Samuel Danforth was born in Roxbury, Mass., on Dec. 10, 1666. Like his father, Samuel Danforth (1626-1674) (q.v.), and his brother, John Danforth (q.v.), Samuel Danforth the younger rose to prominence as a minister and writer. More than either his father or his brother, however, he was also a man of diverse affairs.

A ranging and inquisitive student, Samuel Danforth was twice chosen scholar of the house at Harvard, from which he was graduated in 1683. Four years later, he was called to the church in Taunton, Mass., where he was ordained on Sept. 21, 1687. Danforth exercised great influence over his congregation and community, in part because he was a learned and devoted minister but also because he ran the local grist mill and served as the town's teacher, lawyer, and doctor.

Throughout his life, Danforth retained an interest in American Indians that derived from his father's long association with John Eliot (q.v.). Danforth taught Indian boys in Taunton, where he also instituted an Indian Lecture Day. Following a visit to several Indian plantations in Mass. in 1698, he wrote a report for the Commissioners for the Propagation of the Gospel among the Indians. He also translated several works "into the native Indian language" and prepared an Indian dictionary, one part of which survives in manuscript in the library of the Massachusetts Historical Society.

On Oct. 4, 1688, Samuel Danforth married Hannah Allen, daughter of the Rev. James Allen (q.v.) of Boston. Of the fourteen children born to this marriage, ten outlived their father, who died in Taunton on Nov. 14, 1727.

Critical Appraisal: Samuel Danforth's first published work, *The New-England Almanack for...1686*, contains "Ad Librum," one of his two surviving poems. In this early poem, in which biblical and Classical allusions mingle with echoes of Chaucer's *Troilus and Criseyde* and Spenser's *The Shepheardes Calender*, Danforth abandoned Ptolemaic cosmology for Copernican theories. Yet despite this break with tradition, Danforth continued to put his learning to familiar, orthodox ends. "Goe little Book, and once a week shake hands / With thy *Good Reader*," he wrote, to remind himself that God controls the stars and tides and that his own time is swift. Written nearly thirty years later, Danforth's second surviving poem, "An Elegy in Memory of Maj. Thomas Leonard," belongs to the tradition of funerary verse that was much in vogue among Danforth's contemporaries and was soon to be satirized by Benjamin Franklin (q.v.) in "Receipt to Make a New-England Funeral Elegy" (1722). Such elegies were in fact more acts of loyalty than exercises in poetry, as Danforth clearly understood:

"Tho' I pretend no skill in Poetry, / Yet will adventure once to Mourn in Verse / Rather than such a Worthy, dead should ly / Without a due Encomium on his Herse."

On Danforth's other works, the strongest, and weakest, *Piety Encouraged, Exhortation to All,* and *The Duty of Believers,* belong to the tradition of the jeremiad. Like many New Eng. writings of the late seventeenth and early eighteenth centuries, Danforth's bespeak deep division. On one side, he saw declension that cried out for reform that was not forthcoming: he articulated communal norms that exposed failures and communal expectations that implied divine judgment. Still, although he saw the signs of change and failure clearly, and lamented them, he could not give up the habit of celebration. Voicing ambiguities and ambivalences that he could not master, he not only clung to the hope of New Eng.'s survival, he continued to proclaim her preeminence and promise.

Suggested Readings: CCNE; FCNEV; Sibley-Shipton (III, 243-249). *See also* Harrison T. Meserole, ed., *Seventeenth-Century American Poetry* (1968), pp. 414-419; Samuel E. Morison, *Harvard College in the Seventeenth Century* (1936), pp. 214-219.

David Minter
Emory University

JOHN DAVENPORT (1597-1670)

Works: *A Royal Edict for Military Exercises* (1629); *An Apologetical Reply* (1636); *A Profession of Faith* (1641); *An Answer of the Elders of the Several Churches in New England* (1643); *The Power of Congregational Churches* (w. 1646-1652; pub. 1672); *The Knowledge of Christ* (1653); *A Catechism of Christian Religion* (1659); *The Saint's Anchor-Hold* (1661); *Another Essay for Investigation of the Truth* (1663); *God's Call to His People to Turn unto Him* (1669); *A Sermon Preached at the Election of the Governor* (1670).

Biography: Born in Coventry, Eng., on Apr. 9, 1597, John Davenport attended Oxford but did not receive the bachelor of divinity degree until 1625, having interrupted his study to serve as a private chaplain and then as vicar of St. Stephen's in London. Sometime during the 1620s, he appears to have become familiar with Puritan practices, but he consistently denied any nonconformist leanings. In 1632 it was John Cotton (q.v.), in London on his flight to America, who persuaded Davenport to take off the surplice. Davenport went first to Holland but, disagreeing with the practice of baptism of the English church there, resolved to immigrate to Mass. On his arrival there, he stayed in Boston about nine months, trying to help the colony resolve the upheaval over the Antinomian controversy. In 1638 he became pastor of the new colony of New Haven in Conn., and in 1661 he hid the regicide judges in his house. In that same decade, he vigorously opposed the Half-Way Covenant, a more moderate policy on church membership. Called in 1667 to fill the pastorate of the First Church in

Boston, following the death of John Wilson (q.v.), Davenport implied that the New Haven congregation was more willing to let him leave than it was. That strategy occasioned the split of the First Church and probably hastened his death in Boston on Mar.15, 1670.

Critical Appraisal: Like the other first-generation preachers, John Davenport was published as pamphleteer and polemicist for theological and ecclesiastical Puritan directions taken in Eng., Holland, and New Eng. His argumentation ranged over a variety of topics: his defense of his differing stance on baptism from his Dutch copastor John Paget, his interpretation to the British Puritans of New Eng. Congregationalism, and his denunciation of the Half-Way Covenant designed by the Synod of 1662. Davenport's sermons make him especially noteworthy as a writer, for in preaching he was a peer of his distinguished contemporaries John Cotton, Thomas Hooker (q.v.), and Thomas Shepard (q.v.).

The election sermon of 1669, reprinted in the *Publications of the Colonial Society of Massachusetts*, vol. 10, (1904-1906), exemplifies the traditional sermonic form as practiced by John Davenport and the early Puritan preachers. It demonstrates the typical progression of text, doctrine, reasons, and uses; the further subdivisions into legalistic forms of argumentation such as motives and objections and answers; the peroration to remain faithful to "the first beginning of this Colony." In his concluding regret for the deaths of "many eminent Lights," the other founding preachers, and in his stress on past success and present uncertainty—"Would you yet see good days, and enjoy good things as in times past?"—John Davenport foreshadows the jeremiads of the second-generation (1660-1700) New Eng. preachers.

The Saint's Anchor-Hold, a sermon-series like *The Knowledge of Christ*, well illustrates Davenport's emphases and literary strengths. The five sermons of *The Saint's Anchor-Hold*, based on the text "The Lord is my portion, saith my soul; therefore will I hope in him" (Jeremiah 3:24) emerge from two contemporary troubles: the disintegration of the Puritan Commonwealth in Eng. and extensive sickness in New Haven in the years 1658 to 1660. The sermons deal with the auditors' afflictions as an occasion more for consolation and hope than for blame. Treating distinct phrases from the text, they establish a foundation and a method for that hope. For example, the first asserts the intellectual foundation of consolation. The middle sermon treats the single word *therefore* as a transition from the faculty of understanding to the will. As he went on to add will to intellect, Davenport completed the psychology of consolation. All knowledge is useless unless it moves the soul toward God; therefore, the last sermon fills more than half the volume with a threefold practical instruction: understanding hope, testing hope, and exercising hope.

The emphasis in *The Saint's Anchor-Hold* on logic and reason characterizes Davenport in particular and Puritan preaching of the first generation in general. Davenport presented rational enlightenment as a real and blessed gift of the spirit and developed extensively the image of "the full and powerful light" of the spirit. His language illustrates the fundamental intent of the plain style: all of his rhetoric acts to persuade and move his listeners to recognize the action of the spirit in themselves. Like most Puritan preaching, these sermons placed the final test of their efficacy on the listeners themselves and their examination of their spiritual life.

Suggested Readings: CCNE; DAB; DARB; DNB; T_1. *See also* Isabel MacBeath Calder, ed., *The Letters of John Davenport, Puritan Divine* (1937); Franklin B. Dexter, "Sketch of the Life and Writings of John Davenport," PNHCHS, 2 (1877), 205-233 (extensive primary bibliography, pp. 234-238); Phyllis M. Jones and Nicholas R. Jones, eds., *Salvation in New England: Selections from the Sermons of the First Preachers* (includes a section of *The Saint's Anchor-Hold* with commentary, pp. 143-152, and interpretive material relevant to Davenport throughout; 1977); Norman Pettit, *The Heart Prepared: Grace and Conversion in Puritan Spiritual Life* (1966), pp. 168-177, 198-200.

Phyllis M. Jones
Oberlin College

SAMUEL DAVIES (1723-1761)

Works: *Collected Poems* (w. 1723-1761; pub. 1968); *An Appendix Proving the Right of the Synod* (1748); *The Impartial Trial Impartially Tried* (1748); *A Sermon on Man's Primitive State* (1748); *The State of Religion* (1751); *An Account of the Remarkable Work of Grace* (1752); *Miscellaneous Poems* (1752); *A Sermon Preached at Henrico* (1754); *The Rev. Samuel Davies Abroad: The Diary of a Journey to England and Scotland* (w. 1753-1755; pub. 1967); *A Sermon Preached Before the Reverend Presbytery at New-Castle* (1753); *The Duties, Difficulties and Rewards of the Faithful Minister* (1754); *A General Account of the Rise and State of the College* (with Gilbert Tennent; 1754); *The Good Soldier* (1756); *Religion and Patriotism* (1756); *Virginia's Danger and Remedy* (1756); *The Crisis* (1757); *The Duty of Christians* (1757); *Letters from the Rev. Samuel Davies* (1757); *The Curse of Cowardice* (1758); *Little Children Invited to Jesus* (1758); *The Vessels of Mercy* (1758); *A Catalogue of Books in the Library of the College of New-Jersey* (1760); *An Ode on the Prospect of Peace* (1760); *Viro Praeclarissimo Ingenius Artibus* (1760); *Letters from the Rev. Samuel Davies* (1761); *Religion and Public Spirit* (1761); *A Sermon Delivered at Nassau Hall* (1761); *The Military Glory of Great Britain* (1762); *Sermons on the Most Useful and Important Subjects* (1766-1771); *The Method of Salvation* (1793); *Sermons and Tracts* (1793); *Pregeth ar yr Adgyfodiad Cyffredinol* (1798); *A System of Family Duty* (with Philip Doddridge; 1814); "Letters of Samuel Davies," VELM, 2 (1819), 537-543; "Old Documents," VELM, 4 (1821), 538-552; "Copy of an Original Letter from the Rev. S. Davies to the Rev. Joseph Bellamy," VELM, 6 (1823), 567-569; "A Recovered Tract of President Davies: Now First Published," BRPR, 9 (1837), 349-364; "Remarks on the Philosophical Works of Lord Bolingbroke," BRPR, 9 (1837), 349-364; "Letter to Joseph

Bellamy, July 4, 1751," PM, 4 (1854), 513; "Three Letters from Samuel Davies, D.D. President of Princeton College," NJHSP, ser. 1, 1 (1845), 77-78; Louis Fitzgerald, ed., "The Hymns of President Davies," JPHS, 2 (1903), 343-373; Thomas Clinton Pears, ed., "Charity and Truth United or the Way of the Multitude Exposed in Six Letters to the Rev. Mr. William Stith, A.M.," JPHS, 1 (1940-1941), 193-323; *Christ Precious to All True Believers* (n.d.).

Biography: Born in the Welsh Tract in New Castle County, Del., on Nov. 3, 1723, Samuel Davies grew up in a pious household. At the age of 15, he commenced his formal education at the Rev. Samuel Blair's (q.v.), dissenting academy, or "Log College," located in Fagg's Manor, Pa. A noted New Light preacher, Blair directed most of his Classically educated students into the Presbyterian ministry. Davies was formally ordained on Feb. 19, 1747, in Hanover County, Va., where he soon settled and became prominent for the dramatic preaching style and oratorical skills he turned to the cause of dissenter's rights in the Anglican colony.

In 1753 Davies was selected by the trustees of the College of New Jersey (now Princeton) to undertake a fund raising mission to G.B. Accompanied on this campaign by Gilbert Tennent (q.v.), he used the occasion to help secure legal rights for Va. dissenters. Successful in both efforts, he returned to Va. in 1755 to become that colony's most effective recruiter of militia during the French and Indian War. In 1758 he was chosen to succeed the Rev. Jonathan Edwards (q.v.) as president of the College of New Jersey. He died in that position on Feb. 4, 1761, after a tenure of less than three years.

Critical Appraisal: The literary manifestation of the Great Awakening is usually associated with the famous preachers of New Eng. and, to a lesser extent, the middle colonies. Samuel Davies, however, was clearly associated with Va., where he became famous for his unique style of pulpit oratory and his publications of sermons, hymns, poetry, and essays, with some of the latter not attributed to him until the 1970s.

Davies's historical and literary reputation rests primarily upon his sermons, many of which were individually published during his lifetime and later collected and reprinted in several more-or-less complete editions before the Civil War. Although Davies's sermons have not attracted the attention devoted to the sermons of his fellow New Light Jonathan Edwards, they probably were much more influential than Edwards's work, at least during the late eighteenth and early nineteenth centuries, for during that period, they helped develop an emotional style of religious and political oratory now associated with "revival preaching" and demagogic politicians. The best examples of Davies's contributions to this genre are *The Crisis* and *The Curse of Cowardice*, in which he used the pulpit to recruit soldiers for the French and Indian War. Davies's sermons are also valuable for their explication of moderate New Light attitudes toward the Great Awakening. Through his sermons, Davies popularized the ideas of great revivalists such as George Whitefield (q.v.), Edwards, and the Wesleys, making their thoughts relevant to contemporary events.

Davies's poems, published in the *Virginia Gazette*, although highly sentimental, are significant as some of the first poems published in Va. His hymns, which were designed to be sung with music, predate those of the Bostonian Samson Occom (q.v.) and are among the first composed in North America. At least one of the latter, "Lord I am Thine, Entirely Thine," remained in Methodist and Baptist hymnals until the middle of the twentieth century.

One scholar recently identified a series of some twenty political essays, originally published pseudonymously in the *Virginia Gazette* and signed "The Centinel," as having been authored by Davies. Addressed to contemporary political issues, especially the failure of the colony's leaders during the French and Indian War, these may be the author's most important writings, for they began the articulation of what would eventually become the philosophy of the American Revolution in Va.

Suggested Readings: CCMC; CCV; DAB; DARB; Sprague (III, 140-146); T₁.
See also J. A. Leo LeMay, "The Reverend Samuel Davies' Essay Series: The Virginia Centinel, 1756-1757" in *Essays in Early Virginia Literature*, ed. J. A. Leo LeMay (1977), pp. 121-164; George William Pilcher, *Samuel Davies; Apostle of Dissent in Colonial Virginia* (1971).

George W. Pilcher
Ball State University

WILLIAM DAWSON (1704-1752)

Works: *Poems on Several Occasions* (1736).

Biography: Born in Cumberland County in Eng. in 1704, William Dawson entered Queen's College, Oxford, at age 15 and earned an M.A. in 1728 before immigrating to Va. in 1729. In that year, he was appointed professor of moral philosophy at William and Mary. Eventually, he was to become the second president of the college (1743-1752), succeeding James Blair (q.v.). He received the doctor of divinity degree from Oxford in 1747. In America he was married to Mary Randolph Stith, sister to William Stith (q.v.) and niece to Sir John Randolph. In addition to publishing his *Poems on Several Occasions*, Dawson published anonymously or under pseudonyms a number of poems in the *Virginia Gazette* and *London Magazine*. He died in 1752. Dawson's papers are in the Library of Congress.

Critical Appraisal: William Dawson's volume, a thirty-page collection of poems on a variety of topics written in various styles, has the distinction of being the first known volume of poetry to be published in Va. Since Dawson himself described the poems as "the casual Productions of Youth," they were most likely written in Eng., probably during the nine years he spent at Queen's College, Oxford, from 1719 to 1728. Interspersed with references to student life at Oxford, "Our Oxford Quirps and Quiddities," the poems also stress Dawson's appreciation of Latin and Greek literature. Although his poetry is often imitative and lacks a strongly individual style of purpose, Dawson evinced talent in a variety of poetic forms. Above all, Dawson's poems attest to his wide knowledge of contemporary and Classical poetry. The influence of Milton, James Thomson, Herrick, Waller, and Pope is evident, along with frequent reference to Classical models such as Horace and Anacreon, and several poems addressed to "Sylvia" follow the carpe diem theme of Cavalier poetry. In addition, a strain of aristocratic restraint and withdrawal from the follies of society runs through the entire volume, which ends with the satiric poem "On the Corruptions of the Stage." The pastoral element in Dawson's poetry is indebted to British neo-Classical models, especially to works such as Pope's "Windsor Forest," to which Dawson refers in "To Mr. ———at London," and not, regrettably, to the poet's experience in America, which he never mentions in the volume. Nonetheless, he is significant as one of the colonial South's earliest published poets.

Suggested Readings: LHUS. *See also* Richard Beale Davis, *Intellectual Life in the Colonial South, 1585-1763* (1978), III, 1474-1476, passim; Harold Lester Dean, "An Identification of the 'Gentleman of Virginia,' " PBSA, 31, pt. 2 (1937), 10-20; Jay Broadus Hubbell, *The South in American Literature, 1607-1900* (1954), pp. 33-35; Howard Mumford Jones, *O Strange New World* (1964), pp. 355-356; Ralph L. Rusk, "Bibliographical Note," *Poems on Several Occasions by a Gentleman of Virginia* (1736; rep. 1930), pp. v-vii.

Jeffrey J. Folks
Tennessee Wesleyan College

THOMAS M. DAY (1777-1855)

Works: *The Suicide* (1797); *An Oration* (1798); *A Colloquy* (1799); *Reports of Cases* (1806-1853); *To the Gentlemen of the Bar* (1810); *A Concise Historical Account* (1817); *Supreme Court of Errors* (1817-1819); *A Historical Discourse* (1844); *A Digest of the Reported Cases* (1846); *Memoirs of the Class of 1797* (1848).

Biography: Thomas Day was born on Jul. 6, 1777, in New Preston, Conn., the son of the Rev. Jeremiah Day and the younger brother of the Jeremiah Day who in 1817 followed Timothy Dwight (q.v.) as president of Yale. After attending a New Milford academy, Day enrolled at Yale, where he graduated in 1797. After two years at Hartford studying law, Day was admitted to the bar in 1799. For the remainder of his life, Day lived and practiced law in Hartford.

During his remarkably active and productive life, Day received innumerable appointments and honors: 1809—appointed to act as secretary of state (Conn.); 1810-1835—reelected by popular vote for twenty-five consecutive years as secretary of state; 1814-1853—appointed the first official State Supreme Court reporter; 1815-1825—appointed associate judge of the Hartford County Court;

1818-1831—appointed one of the judges of the (Hartford) City Court; 1825-1833—chief judge; 1847—awarded honorary degree of doctor of law by Yale. His many official legal endeavors notwithstanding, Day was especially instrumental in perpetuating and promoting various multicharitable or economic institutions such as the Hartford Retreat for the Insane and the Hartford Savings Society (the largest savings bank in the state); he was also a founder and first president of the Connecticut Historical Society.

In 1813 Day married Sarah Coit, who bore him eight children and outlived him by ten years. He died of a heart attack in Hartford on Mar. 1, 1855.

Critical Appraisal: Thomas M. Day was a prolific chronicler. With the exception of three works (*The Suicide, An Oration*, and *Memoirs of the Class of 1797*), the majority of his writings were focused exclusively upon the law. His ecclesiastical upbringing and natural propensity for scholarship aided him as a lawyer, voluntary court reporter, and, later, judge in the city and state court systems. He was renowned for an exactitude in his recordings and writings that was rarely surpassed. His *Reports of Cases, Argued and Determined in the Supreme Court of Errors, of the State of Connecticut* (two series with 26 volumes published between 1806 and 1853), considered to be his greatest lifetime endeavor, and the numerous books he edited during the same period confirm his superior achievements. His political affiliations via the court systems seem to have sustained his activities. Day's juridically literate writings followed one after the other. He continuously studied, compared, edited, and published his observations on American jurisprudence—its application and implications.

To the literary historian, however, Day is best remembered as the author of *The Suicide*, a short play or "dialog," as Day termed it, performed on Sept. 13, 1797, at Day's Yale commencement. Day himself played the part of Bellamy at the performance. Heavily didactic and characteristic of much of the college drama popular during the 1790s in America, *The Suicide* is, in the words of Arthur Hobson Quinn, "a moral argument against suicide." In the play the protagonist, an outcast son named Alphonso Bellamy, attempts suicide after his father disowns him but is brought back to sanity by the compassion and understanding of a friend. According to Walter J. Meserve, the "subject matter of the play and the dramatized moral stance against suicide suggest a distinct gap between real and fictionalized life at this early period when suicide was a popular resolution in both romantic fiction and drama whether the hero or heroine was culpable or a victim of fate." Nonetheless, as Quinn explains, college dramas such as *The Suicide* remain important today as "another indication of the unquenchable interest in the dramatic form" which existed in America during the last decades of the eighteenth century.

Day's literary accomplishments, involvement in a number of community enterprises, commitment to excellence, and persistent devotion to civic duty during the formative years of Conn. statehood and American independence are undeniable cultural contributions. In his *An Oration on Party Spirit*, which he delivered before the Connecticut Society of Cincinnatus in Hartford on Jul. 4, 1798, by special request of its president, he ended with the following words: "Unite, then, and prepare for the defense of all that is sacred—all that is dear. Let it never be told, in future, that the SONS OF FREEMEN were DASTARDS." Throughout his life, Thomas Day committed himself to these high principles espoused at the age of 21 in his speech on American Independence Day.

Suggested Readings: Dexter (V, 273-276). *See also* Walter J. Meserve, *An Emerging Entertainment: The Drama of the American People to 1828* (1977), p. 129; Arthur Hobson Quinn, *A History of the American Drama from the Beginning to the Civil War* (1923), p. 134.

J. J. Steinway-Stillman
University of Houston

SILAS DEANE (1737-1789)

Works: *To the Free and Virtuous Citizens of America* (1778); *Paris Papers* (1782); *An Address to the Free and Independent Citizens of the United States* (1784).

Biography: Silas Deane was born in Groton, Conn., on Dec. 24, 1737, to a family that included five brothers and a sister. Although Deane's father was a blacksmith, he sent his son to Yale, where Deane graduated in 1758. While still studying law, Dean began teaching school, and he was admitted to the bar in 1761. In 1763 he married Mehitabel Webb, widow of Joseph Webb. Taking over her business, Deane quickly became one of the leading merchants in Conn., trading extensively with the W. Ind. In 1768, after Mehitabel's death, Deane married Elizabeth Saltonstall and in the same year was elected to the Colonial Assembly of Conn. In 1773, Deane became first secretary of the Connecticut Committee of Correspondence, and he was elected to the first two Continental Congresses in 1774 and 1775, when Congress selected Deane to serve as an agent for purchasing supplies.

Arriving in Fr. in 1776, Deane began shipping war supplies back to the U.S. with the tacit consent of the French government. Deane, Benjamin Franklin (q.v.), and Arthur Lee (q.v.) were the American commissioners who signed the Defensive and Commerical Treaties with Fr. in Feb. 1778. After Congress recalled him for exceeding his instructions, Deane returned to Philadelphia to appear before Congress. Receiving no satisfaction from Congress, he published *To the Free and Virtuous Citizens of the United States*, a broadside that bitterly attacked Arthur Lee and his three brothers. Controversy surrounding this publication became one of the most divisive political conflicts of the American Revolution. After returning to Paris in 1780, Deane discovered that he could no longer play a role in French-American relations, and he moved to Ghent.

Obsessed by rebukes from both the Americans and the French, he wrote a series of letters to American leaders, pleading for a return to the old ties with

G.B. before independence and castigating Fr. for trying to dominate the U.S. Most of the letters were intercepted by the British and later printed in the Loyalist and rebel press in late 1781 and 1782. Moving to London after the peace treaty, Deane published *To the Free and Independent Citizens of the United States*. This work recapitulated his defense of his role as a commissioner to Fr. and attempted to justify his letters of 1781. In his last years in London, Deane lived in abject poverty and suffered from debilitating illnesses. In 1789, after receiving contributions from friends in London, he secured passage to return to Conn., but he died the first day at sea.

Critical Appraisal: A figure thrown up by the events of the Revolution, Silas Deane was for a brief period one of the leading men of the American Revolution. He then faded quickly into obscurity. Deane's writings consist of a defense of his own conduct and an intimate picture of American leaders during the Revolution. In 1778 Deane revealed for the first time the bitter divisions among the Americans in Paris, Fr.'s clandestine role in aiding the U.S. before the treaty, and the deep sectional rivalries in Congress. Later his growing suspicion of Fr. caused him to reverse his position, and he wrote the letters, which were in reality essays on the role of Fr. and G.B. in the future of American commerce and independence. When Deane's letters were published just after the victory at Yorktown, he was denounced by his former friends and enemies alike as a traitor of the same character as another Conn. merchant, Benedict Arnold (q.v.).

Deane's other writings, published long after his death, were general memorials to the French Court advocating more aid to the U.S. In these and other writings, he revealed a deep understanding of the role of commerce in the Atlantic world of the eighteenth century. In fact, Deane's authority on the subject was so widely acknowledged that he was accused of writing Lord Sheffield's bitter anti-American pamphlet *Observations on the Commerce of the American States* (1784). Deane knew Sheffield but did not write for him. The strong forces of nationalism after the Revolution denied Deane his place as a prominent Revolutionary figure, but his writings should be remembered for their contribution to the tradition of pamphlet debate among Americans during the Revolution.

Suggested Readings: DAB; Dexter (I, 521-527); T₂. *See also* Albert Bates, *The Deane Papers, 1771-1795*, CHSC, 22 (1930); Julian Boyd, "Silas Deane: Death by a Kindly Teacher of Treason?" WMQ, 3rd ser., 16 (1959), 165-187, 319-342, 515-550; Charles Isham, ed., *The Deane Papers, 1774-1790*, CNYHS, 19-23 (1887-1890); Coy H. James, *Silas Deane: Patriot or Traitor?* (1975); Edmund S. Morgan, "The Puritan Ethic and the American Revolution," WMQ, 3rd ser., 24 (1967), 3-43; Brian Morton, ed., *Beaumarchais Correspondance*, 3 vols. (1969-1972); William Stinchcombe, *The American Revolution and the French Alliance* (1969); idem, "A Note on Silas Deane's Death," WMQ, 3rd ser., 32 (1975), 619-624.

William Stinchcombe
Syracuse University

JOSEPH DENNIE (1768-1812)

Works: *The Lay Preacher; Or, Short Sermons, for Idle Readers* (1796); *The Spirit of the Farmer's Museum and Lay Preacher's Gazette. Being a Judicious Selection of the Fugitive and Valuable Productions, Which Have Occasionally Appeared in That Paper* . . . *Consisting of a Part of the Essays of the Lay Preacher, Colon and Spondee* . . . (1801); *The Plays of William Shakespeare*, vol. 2 (editor; 1805); *The Lay Preacher* (collected and arranged by John E. Hall; 1817); *New and Original Essays by Joseph Dennie* (1818).

Biography: Joseph Dennie was born in Boston, Mass., on Aug. 30, 1768—the only child of Joseph and Mary (Green) Dennie. His early interest in literature may have been fostered by his mother, whose family had been associated with the printing of the Boston *News Letter*. During the siege of 1775, the family moved to Lexington, where Dennie was enrolled in school. Under the tutelage of the Rev. Samuel West at Needham, Dennie prepared for matriculation at Harvard. Although he entered Harvard as a sophomore, his term there was not pleasant. Plagued with illness and a six-month suspension over tutorial differences, Dennie nevertheless succeeded in graduating with his class in 1790. His later writings, however, were laced with an undisguised bitterness toward that institution. In a Mar. 9, 1795, diatribe, Dennie characterized his learned colleagues' efforts as "dull discourses upon dull departed brethren" and "embarrassed essays on philosophy and exploded logic." Following admission to the Charlestown, N.H., bar in Mar. 1794, Dennie briefly embarked upon a legal career, but he abandoned his practice to pursue literary goals.

An opportunity to fill the pulpit of the Charlestown Episcopal Church as a "lay preacher" led to the publication of his first "lay sermons" in local newspapers. He had already published a medley of light essays, "The Farrago," which appeared in numerous newspapers including the *Morning Ray* (Windsor, Vt.), *The Eagle: Or, Dartmouth Centinel* (Hanover, N.H.), and the Boston *Centinel*. With his friend, Royall Tyler (q.v.), Dennie produced a spate of essays under the firm name of "Colon & Spondee." As "Colon," Dennie sought to merge the literary skills of Joseph Addison and Oliver Goldsmith into his own distinctive style. By 1795 Dennie was persuaded to undertake in Boston a "Miscellaneous Paper, devoted to the Belles Lettres" titled *The Tablet* (May 19-Aug. 11, 1795). Dennie's "Farrago" and J.S.J. Gardiner's criticism of the English poet Charles Churchill were the mainstay of the volume. The experiment was discontinued by the publisher, William Spotswood, following the issuance of the thirteenth number.

Between 1792 and 1802, Dennie wrote twenty-nine numbers of "The Farrago" for numerous publications. Within three months of the collapse of *The Tablet*, Dennie had returned to N.H., where he hobnobbed with a coterie of ardent and affable Federalists. During the autumn of 1795, Dennie transferred his legal practice to Walpole. On Oct. 12, 1795, the first of a new series of essays, "The

Lay Preacher," appeared in the *New Hampshire Journal; Or, Farmer's Weekly Museum*, published by Isaiah Thomas (q.v.) and David Carlisle, Jr. Almost immediately, Dennie began conducting the political and literary departments of the *Farmer's Weekly Museum*. In Apr. 1796 he was appointed editor of the weekly. His "Lay Preacher" essays emerged irregularly until the end of vol. IV in Apr. 1797. The *Museum* cast aside its nonpartisan tradition and became regarded as a staunch Federalist organ, offering literary wares such as "Colon & Spondee's" political satires on the anti-Federalists—"The Runner: Or, Indian Talk." Despite the popularity of the journal, it began experiencing financial difficulties during the late 1790s. Thomas rejoined the paper with the Feb. 20, 1798, issue, and Dennie, with a reduced salary, continued as editor.

Times seemed to portend a move for Dennie into the political sphere—with disastrous results. He was persuaded to stand for election to Congress—and promptly lost. His Federalist loyalty managed to earn him an appointment in 1799 as private secretary to Timothy Pickering, secretary of state. He declined an invitation from Boston bookseller James White to edit the *Independent Chronicle* as a nonpartisan sheet. Instead, he was persuaded by John Fenno (q.v.) to join the staff of his *Gazette of the United States* in Philadelphia. There Dennie confronted editor William Duane (q.v.) of the *Aurora* and his stable of democratic scribblers. In addition, Dennie proposed a small weekly pamphlet, *The Lay Preacher's Magazine*, which was to contain examples of "elegant literature." It, as in the case of many of Dennie's projects, never materialized, nor did William Cobbett's (q.v.) scheme for an edition of the *Lay Preacher*. Cobbett even went so far as to suggest that Dennie accompany him to Eng., where they would seek some European publisher. One month before Cobbett sailed for Eng. (Jun. 1800), President John Adams (q.v.) removed Pickering and replaced him with John Marshall as secretary of state. Dennie's connection with government was severed, and by May Caleb Parry Wayne had purchased the *Gazette of the United States*.

By Dec. Dennie was free of the *Gazette* and eager for a new challenge. On Jan. 3, 1801, Dennie and Asbury Dickens established the *Port Folio*—a weekly dedicated to politics and literature. This Philadelphia magazine attracted the attention of the city's literati and became the focus of the Tuesday Club, an elite group comprised chiefly of the city's finest legal minds and most gifted writers. The year 1801 also marked the publication of *The Spirit of the Farmer's Museum and Lay Preacher's Gazette*. From 1802 to 1805, the *Port Folio* basked in the intellectual limelight as the largest of any American magazines ever attempted. The magazine carried the "American Lounger" series whose contributors included Dennie, John E. Hall, John Davis, and a host of pseudonymous authors. In addition, the *Port Folio* carried essays and poems culled from English and European journals. Within five years, the weekly quarto became a popular monthly octavo. Dennie, as "Oliver Oldschool, Esq.," attracted able writers, including Charles Brockden Brown (q.v.) and John Quincy Adams (q.v.), whose "Letters from Silesia" first appeared in the *Port Folio*.

Despite his apparent success, Dennie experienced constant financial difficulty. By 1808 the *Port Folio* had become staid. Dennie lost financial control of the journal by late 1808, although he retained his editorship. At the beginning of 1809, the journal became a nonpartisan "Monthly Miscellany" under the guidance of Dennie and his "Confederacy of Men of Letters." The first number for 1810 carried Dennie's name in place of the traditional "Oliver Oldschool." In the end, the health of the *Port Folio* proved stronger than that of Dennie. He died in Philadelphia on Jan. 7, 1812. The *Port Folio*, in several forms, survived until 1827.

Critical Appraisal: When the Charlestown, N.H., Episcopal Church hired Joseph Dennie as "Lay Preacher" and liturgist for four months "at the rate of 24s per Sunday," little did the congregation realize it had retained what even his contemporary critics would regard as the most influential literary editor of the Federalist period. His "Lay Sermons," which differed radically from the staid Poole's commentaries, adopted a pastor's style of direct address unblemished by mere moralizing. Jacobin misadventures and the hint of scandal proved Dennie's favorite satirical targets. He scandalized his more provincial audiences with his plainly partisan jabs at the democrats, sedition, revolution, and the failure of the republican form of government. His critics accused him of deriding the pulpit and undermining the rock of established religion with his sharp banter. Yet as he explained in the introduction to his 1796 volume, Dennie never intended his scribbling to be mistaken for a "volume of sermons." Rather, he was experimenting stylistically, modeling his assault upon convention after the "designs of Addison" and the "harmless and playful levity of Oliver Goldsmith." "The citadel of christianity," Dennie wrote, "is well guarded by the lynx-eyed vigilance of Bishop Porteus, Watson, and Horseley."

His "Farrago" series had been cut from the same literary cloth. As he confided in a letter to his mother on Jan. 4, 1794, his "miscellaneous" essays were construed in the tradition of Goldsmith's "vivacity of thought" and Addison's "sweetness in expression." His contempt for American letters and democratic principles emerged in even his earliest works. The public, he wrote, merely "saw or fancied, some merit" in his essays, which was not surprising, since most American essays were "hitherto unmarked, except for flimsy expression and jejune ideas." In the "Farrago," Dennie was obsessed with dandies, prodigals, and idlers whose lives were merely shams in a world turned upside down. It is perhaps ironic that Dennie, the writer, would sacrifice his art in exchange for the overblown, vindictive phraseology of an editor who disparaged all things American and would be forced to compile incomprehensible Classical sentimentality from foreign journals.

Yet his "Farrago" series did establish Dennie as a journalist with uncommon literate, if forced, qualities. The series quickly became the literary underpinning for the *Tablet*, whose thirteen-week run (May 19-Aug. 11, 1795) intrigued the Boston bluebloods. Royall Tyler joined forces with Dennie "from the shop of Colon and Spondee" to contribute poetry for the *Tablet* and, later, both the

Farmer's Museum and the *Port Folio*. The barbed paragraphs from the "Shop" were favorites among the Federalists, who reprinted them widely in their press. Also popular were the "Vigil" essays that succeeded the "Farrago" papers in the *Eagle* during the fall of 1794. Although several contributors were responsible for the series, Dennie's style is unmistakable in essays V-VII. Apparently, Tyler and Dennie ceased writing for the *Eagle* in early 1795.

The scheme for the *Tablet* marked a departure from the misshapen tradition of American magazine publishing. Advertisements and "tiresome news" were to be omitted. The journal would remain placidly nonsectarian and nonpartisan. What followed was something less than an original effort. Seven of the twelve "Farrago" essays were reprinted from the *Morning Ray* or the *Eagle*, as were the *Eagle* versions of several "Colon & Spondee" offerings. When the *Tablet* failed, Dennie blamed the "waywardness of the times" and the "dulness of the Bostonians" for his journal's demise.

By late 1795, the *New Hampshire Journal: Or, Farmer's Weekly Museum* had captured his fancy. The *Museum*, under the direction of David Carlisle, Jr., had distinguished itself with essays culled from English and American journals as well as contributions drafted by the Rev. Thomas Fessenden, Philip Freneau (q.v.), and—not surprisingly—Joseph Dennie. From 1793 to 1795, the *Museum* had reprinted several "Farrago" essays, examples of the "Vigil," and the initial number of the "Saunterer." With the Oct. 12, 1795, number, "The Lay Preacher" surfaced to exhibit truths "in a plain dress to the common people." A secondary venture, "Country Critic," introduced Dennie, as critic, to his growing readership. Within the year, Dennie's editorial adeptness had transformed the *Museum* into the most popular paper dedicated to literature and politics in New Eng. Yet the "Lay Preacher" essays were perhaps most responsible for sparking reader interest. Although H. M. Ellis has successfully isolated the influence of Laurence Sterne's *Sermons of Yorick* upon the essays, Dennie's adventures in the pulpit cannot be discounted. In the *Farmer's Museum*, Dennie succeeded in stimulating serious literary debate amidst the political lampoons of "Simon Spunkey," or F.T.G. Fessenden. Dennie juxtaposed bagatelles with the biographical notes of such American luminaries as Joel Barlow (q.v.) and John Trumbull (q.v.). These items, combined with the biographies of statesmen, summaries of foreign affairs, and the excerpts from the works of English authors, satisfied more than 2,000 patrons "in Georgia and on the banks of the Ohio."

Dennie, who wrote quickly if not always lucidly from his "stock of ideas," abandoned the semblance of the journal's political neutrality in 1800, when it became unabashedly Federalist. Despite the periodical's popularity, Dennie disdained any hopes for pecuniary success. His growing contempt for the common man—Burke's "miserable sheep of society"—set him astride the most pedantic of hobby-horses. To Dennie, the vulgar voice of the people was not the voice of an urbane Deity.

By 1797 the *Farmer's Museum* had reached the pinnacle of its influence, with members of the Walpole Literary Club, late writers of the *Tablet*, and "Colon &

Spondee" contributing essays, verse, and criticism. Again and again, Dennie demonstrated his knack for surrounding himself with a circle of bright, doting literati, whether in Boston, Walpole, or, later, Philadelphia. Such a following and the levee atmosphere it fostered may have had a profound impact upon his burgeoning obsession that democratic roguery had deprived him of the recognition he so justly deserved in upper class society. His ultimate entry into the ranks of Federalist scribblers through Fenno's *Gazette of the United States* further bolstered such self-aggrandizement. Dennie was perceived by many Federalists as a man of "genius and literary talents" who was "correct in his morals and notions of Government" (according to Timothy Pickering's Apr. 29, 1801, letter to Alexander Hamilton [q.v.]). Dennie's "leaders" written for Fenno delighted the besieged Federalists and rankled the irascible Jeffersonians. With such notoriety, Dennie and Asbury Dickens founded the *Port Folio* in Philadelphia, loosely modeled after the defunct *Tablet*.

In his "Prospectus of the *Port Folio*" (1801), Joseph Dennie outlined his desire "to combine literature with politics, and attempt something of a more honorable destiny, than a meagre journal." What he achieved during his editorial reign (1801-1812) were the accolades of Federalist intelligentsia and diatribes from the Jacobinical Jeffersonians who derided his journal as the "Portable Foolery." Dennie, known by then as the "American Addison," composed his screeds and critical essays under the guise of "Oliver Oldschool, Esq." His penchant for literary perfection led him to countenance American literature in only the most condescending of terms. Dennie could not refrain from lauding Charles Brockden Brown as writing "uncommonly well for an American." The American multitudes no longer were merely benign oafs mucking about in a pastoral tableau, but had become "republican boors" who "have convened with a resolution to destroy culture." Dennie deplored the American Revolution and, in the tradition of the *Farmer's Museum* and the *Gazette of the United States*, strived to prohibit Jacobinical propaganda from infiltrating his journal's columns. The "Fairy Tales of France" in which "all men are kings and emperors . . . and statesmen" found no sanctuary within the *Port Folio*. He never forgave the "chimney sweepers" responsible for the execution of Marie Antoinette. Neither did he approve of the late Benjamin Franklin's "hackneyed deism." Dennie depicted Franklin as "the first to lay his head in the lap of French harlotry; and prostrate the Christianity and honour of his country to the deism and democracies of Paris." "Whoring" became a favorite topic in the *Port Folio* between 1802 and 1804, with Dennie publishing fourteen anonymous poems that insinuated an unsavory liaison existed between Thomas Jefferson (q.v.) and a slave, Sally. Worse, the editor queried whether President Jefferson could construct "one sentence of correct and classical English."

Although Dennie has been assaulted as an ineffectual critic of Romantic and democratic poets (he did, on occasion, praise Freneau's work), he was influential in bringing English belles-lettres to the attention of a growing cosmopolitan audience in America. His publication of the earliest known notice in America of

Wordsworth's poetry led members of his Tuesday Club to imitate Wordsworth's style during the period 1801-1803. In addition, he published Coleridge's work, despite the poet's "inflamation" with "French liberty." Unfortunately, he occasionally confused Coleridge's poetry with that of Wordsworth—and vice-versa—a habit he acquired during his brief tenure as literary editor of the *Gazette of the United States*. Later, Dennie denigrated Wordsworth's art for its depiction of undignified humble characters. He befriended Leigh Hunt and published several poems, none of which was a first printing. He continued his tradition of published literary biographies—Goldsmith, Defoe, Racine—and argued for the encouragement of the literary efforts of women. "The influence of women over the fate and fortune of this paper," he wrote, "is much greater than that of statesmen." In 1806 he offered his services to the literary community as a supporter of a confederacy of letters to serve as arbiter of literary taste. The confederacy's purpose, he proclaimed, would be to "absolutely eradicate every bad book in the country." Such an unrealistic goal was doomed to failure.

Dennie had succeeded where others failed in the establishment of a literary magazine with a national circulation and intellectual patronage. Yet his espousal of Classical literary standards and his penchant for English writers may have dampened the enthusiasm for American literature and language then emerging through the vehicle of the American press. Instances of his direct influence upon fledgling writers are lacking. His style discouraged imitation, as much from his excessive use of obscure quotations as from his overblown literary narcissism. His reputation as a witty conversationist certainly is evident in his writing. However, his brash, rambling style betrays a lack of attention to the drudgery of polished writing. It is such contempt for sustained effort that ties him most clearly to his antidemocratic views. In his constant assault upon the "revolutionary jargon so much in vogue," he lost sensitivity to the refined elegance that he had so often advocated. Dennie refused to consider American literature in isolation, rather debating the merits of literature writ large. Within the strictures of such heated contests, he often sacrificed his art for rhetoric as vacuous as that of his detractors.

Suggested Readings: DAB; LHUS. *See also* William W. Clapp, Jr., *Sketches of Joseph Dennie* (1880); Harold M. Ellis, *Joseph Dennie and His Circle* (1915); Milton Ellis, *The Lay Preacher* (1796; rep., 1943); Thomas P. Govan, "The Death of Joseph Dennie: A Memoir by Nicholas Biddle," PMHB, 75 (1951), 36-46; Lewis Leary, "Joseph Dennie on Benjamin Franklin: A Note on Early American Literary Criticism," PMHB, 72 (1948), 240-246; John T. Queenan, "The *Port Folio*: A Study of the History and Significance of an Early American Magazine" (Ph.D. diss., Univ. of Pa., 1955); Randolph C. Randall, "Joseph Dennie's Literary Attitudes in the *Port Folio*, 1801-1812," in James Woodress, ed., *Essays Mostly on Periodical Publishing in America: A Collection in Honor of Clarence Gohdes* (1973), pp. 57-91; Donald W. Rhinesmith, *Joseph Dennie: Critic of Jeffersonian Democracy* (1961); Guy Woodall, "The Relationship of Robert Walsh, Jr., to the *Port Folio* and the Dennie Circle: 1803-1812," PMHB, 92 (1968), 195-219.

William F. Vartorella
Mary Baldwin College

DANIEL DENTON (fl. 1656-1696)

Works: *A Brief Description of New York* (1670).

Biography: The early details of Daniel Denton's life are unknown. The eldest son of a Presbyterian clergyman, Denton joined an increasingly predominant English colony near New Amsterdam in 1656, where he was among the original grantees of Rust-Dorp, or Quiet Village, later renamed Jamaica by the English. In Jamaica he became a gentleman farmer and elected official, serving in time as clerk, magistrate, overseer of the poor, and purchaser of land from local Indians. In 1670, while in London on business, he was encouraged "through the Instigation of divers Persons in England, and elsewhere," to write "a Brief but true Relation" of N.Y., for "the encouragement of many that have a desire to remove themselves." The resulting tract was apparently the first description of N.Y. printed in English. On his return to N.Y., Denton discovered that his wife had been unfaithful. He was granted a divorce and left Jamaica in disgrace. Some years later, he remarried and was allowed by the town to return to his farm, where he once again became a planter and an elected official. He died in Jamaica, apparently in 1696.

Critical Appraisal: In the introduction to his *Description*, Daniel Denton pointed out that he has "writ nothing, but what I have been an eyewitness to all or the greater part of it." The detailed description of the geography, flora, and fauna of N.Y., as well as of the customs of its native and immigrant inhabitants, does indeed suggest that Denton described only what he had meticulously observed. Moses Coit Tyler noted that Denton's tract is "uncommonly graphic and animated" and admired Denton for keeping "closely to the facts that had come under his own eyes." Victor Hugo Paltsits similarly made mention of Denton's accurate description.

Nevertheless, the tract, designed to encourage immigration to the colony, presents an idyllic discussion of life in N.Y.; no mention is made of hardships incurred by the colonists. The *Description* thus establishes Denton as one of a long line of colonial promotionalists—including Samuel Purchas (q.v.), Capt. John Smith (q.v.), and George Alsop (q.v.)—who portrayed America as a terrestrial paradise, a "land that flowes with milk and honey." Loosely organized and written in the style of a personal narrative, the tract recounts, in glowing terms, the geography, trade, agriculture, and natural bounty of N.Y., which is so great, said Denton, that a man need only arrive with his clothes. His long catalog of the natural bounty of the land includes furs, skins, tobacco, and strawberries in "such abundance in June, that the fields and Woods are died red." Nature has also provided the colony with "all sorts of Wilde Beasts and Fowle," which every man "may hunt at his pleasure." The greatest wonder to Denton, however, was the abundant land available to even the poorest settler:

> If there be any terrestrial happiness to be had by people of all ranks, especially of an inferior rank, it must certainly be here. Here anyone may furnish himself with land, and live rent-free; yea, with such a quantity of

land that he may weary himself with walking over his fields of corn and all sorts of grain.

Interjected in the catalog of blessings bestowed on the American settler is an encouraging description of the Indians and their relationship with the settlers. Denton clearly had close dealings with local Indians and had closely observed their customs, for he described in vivid detail their food (fish, fowl, polecats, and skunks), clothing (loincloths and snakeskins), games (football and cards), and their penchant for drunkenness ("They are great lovers of strong drink, yet do not care for drinking unless they have enough to make themselves drunk"). The Indians that are left, said Denton, are friendly; but to his amazement, if not to ours, the Indians had miraculously decreased in numbers with the coming of the English: "It is admired, how strangely they have decreast by the Hand of God, since the English first settling of those parts.... Where the English come to settle, a Divine Hand makes way for them by removing or cutting off the Indians, either by Wars one with the other, or by some raging mortal Disease." It has been noted, however, that Denton's portrayal of trouble-free Indian relations might not be inaccurate, for it was not until a few years after the publication of the tract that King Philip's War began.

Denton's *Description of New York* is valuable both as a rare first-hand and unusually descriptive portrayal of colonial N.Y., and as a testament to the early American belief that North American colonists were blessed in their settlement of the New World, "blessed in their country, blessed in their fields . . . , in a word blessed in whatever they take in hand, or go about."

Suggested Readings: LHUS; T$_1$. *See also* Gerald F. Rooney, "Daniel Denton, Publicist of Colonial New York," NYHSQ, 55 (1971), 272-276. Denton's *Description* is available in a publication by the Facsimile Text Society (1973), with a bibliographic note by Victor Hugo Paltsits.

Linda Palmer Young
University of California, Davis

JOHN DICKINSON (1732-1808)

Works: *Last Tuesday Morning* (1764); *Eine Rede, Gehalten* (1764); *A Reply to a Piece Called the Speech* (1764); *A Speech Delivered . . . May 24th* (1764); *Friends and Countrymen* (1765); *The Late Regulations Respecting the British Colonies* (1765); *Letters from a Farmer in Pennsylvania* (1768); *The Liberty Song* (1768); *A New Song* (1768); *To the Publick* (1768); *A Letter from the Country to a Gentleman in Philadelphia* (1773); *An Essay on the Constitutional Power of Great-Britain* (1774); *A Fragment* (1796); *The Letters of Fabius* (1797); *A Caution* (1798); *The Political Writings of John Dickinson*, 2 vols. (1801).

Biography: John Dickinson, son of Samuel and Mary [Cadwalader] Dickinson, was born on a family estate on the eastern shore of Md. on Nov. 8, 1732. In 1740 the family moved to Kent County, near Dover, Del., and Dickinson was educated by a tutor until in 1750 he began studying in the law office of John Moland of Philadelphia. From 1753 to 1757, Dickinson also studied law at the Middle Temple in London, eventually returning to Philadelphia to practice. In 1760 Dickinson was elected to the Del. Assembly and became its speaker, and in 1762 he was elected to represent Philadelphia in the Pa. Assembly, where he and Benjamin Franklin (q.v.) argued opposite sides on questions such as the Quaker proprietary government, taxation, and representation.

Although a conservative, Dickinson was chief draftsman of the 1765 "Declaration of Rights and Grievances" of the Stamp Act Congress held in N.Y. In Dec. 1767 he began publishing anonymously in the *Pennsylvania Chronicle* a series of "letters" concerning the Sugar and Stamp Acts, which were later widely reprinted in pamphlet form and in other newspapers as *Letters from a Farmer in Pennsylvania*. Dickinson chaired the Philadelphia Committee of Correspondence and was a member of the First and Second Continental Congress. Although he was chief draftsman of the "Declaration of the Causes and Necessity of Taking Up Arms" (Jul. 6, 1775), he opposed the Declaration of Independence and refused to sign it. In 1781 Dickinson was elected president of the Supreme Executive Council of Del. Returning to Philadelphia the following year, he was elected to the same position in Pa. As a delegate from Del., he actively participated in the drafting of the federal Constitution, urging its ratification in a series of letters signed "Fabius."

Dickinson married Mary Norris, daughter of Speaker Isaac Norris of the Pa. Assembly, in 1770. He died on Feb. 14, 1808.

Critical Appraisal: As a member of the Pa. Assembly, the Continental Congress, and later the Constitutional Convention, John Dickinson displayed a talent for writing that was often called upon for the drafting of official messages, resolutions, and letters. His initial publication in the American cause was a pamphlet entitled *The Late Regulations Respecting the British Colonies* (1765). Using the epistolary form as a convention, this pamphlet purported to be "from a Gentleman in Philadelphia to his Friend in London," and it argued that London, as well as the colonies, would suffer from the enforcement of the Sugar Act. Dickinson pointed out the disastrous economic effects of not only this act but of the proposed Stamp Act as well. He warned prophetically: "we can never be made an independent people, except it be by *Great-Britain* herself; and the only way for her to do it, is to make us frugal, ingenious, united and discontented." His *An Address to the Committee of Correspondence in Barbados* replied to the British accusation that it is rebellion for the colonies to resist the Stamp Act. His tone was ironic and his attack vigorous as he accused the committee of ignorance of the source of human rights and chastised them for censuring those (the North Americans) who merited "their highest esteem, —their warmest praise." He defended the resistance to the Stamp Act with eloquent analogies:

If my father, deceived and urged on by bad or weak men, should offer me a draught of poison, and tell me it would be of service to me, should I be undutiful, if, knowing what it is I refuse to drink it? or if inflamed by passion, he should aim a dagger at my heart, should I be undutiful, if I refuse to bare my breast for the blow?

Dickinson's most well-known writings are the *Letters from a Farmer in Pennsylvania*. First printed as a series in the *Pennsylvania Chronicle* beginning Dec. 2, 1767, they were reprinted many times and quoted everywhere. The persona of the letters is a gentleman farmer, an idealized American who represents the traditional qualities of industry, frugality, and integrity but who is also an educated, rational man. He spends a "good deal" of time in his library and has acquired "a greater knowledge in history, and the laws and constitution" of his country than most people. Dickinson's farmer is, above all, a peaceful man, who only reluctantly enters the public fray. Thus the credibility of the *Letters* is enhanced by their attribution to a man who is not personally involved in the conflict. The *Letters*, despite their original serial publication, appear to be a carefully planned composition following the pattern of a Classical oration in five divisions: proem (Letter I), narrative (Letters II, III, IV), argument (Letters V, VI, VII, VIII), remarks (Letters IX, X, XI), and peroration (Letter XII). The first letter presents the farmer and warns his countrymen of imminent danger. The next three examine the relationship between the colonies and the mother country. Letters five through eight present the grievances of the colonies and nine through eleven offer further reflections on the subject. The twelfth letter reiterates the warning and urges the necessity of colonial vigilance and unity. Throughout the letters, there are rhythmic variations of tone, effective rhetorical devices, and a judicious use of quotation.

Dickinson composed his "American Liberty Song" about the same time he was writing the *Farmer's Letters*. The ten stanzas reflect the themes common to most contemporary rhetoric: slavery or freedom, the sufferings of the first settlers in defense of liberty, the penalties of submission, the necessity for union, and the rewards of victory. The song was widely reprinted and soon became one of the most popular of the time. A very different kind of work is Dickinson's *An Essay on the Constitutional Power of Great Britain* (1774), in which he argued, with ponderous documentation, the legalistic position that "the sovereignty over the colonies must be limited," that a line must be drawn setting off Parliament's powers from those of the colonial legislatures, and that this line would give to Parliament the right to regulate commerce and foreign affairs and to the colonial assemblies "exclusive right of internal legislature," including taxation.

Dickinson wrote two series of letters signed "Fabius." The first, in 1788, advocated the adoption of the federal Constitution; the second, in 1797, defended the profederal position of the Democrats. In them he dropped his pose of gentleman farmer and adopted the tone of elder statesman and philosopher. The nine 1788 letters answer the various objections to the proposed Constitution, contending that "the power of the people pervading the proposed system. . .together with the strong confederation of the states, forms an adequate security against every danger that has been apprehended." The ideas expressed in these letters parallel many of the ideas in Thomas Paine's (q.v.) *Rights of Man*, a fact made obvious by the many footnotes to Paine's work added to the letters when they were collected in book form. In 1797 "Fabius" published fifteen letters defending Fr. and her recent actions. He reminded Americans that in 1783 Congress expressed the hope that our Revolution would set an example to the world; that "example has been followed by the greatest people upon earth." Dickinson called upon his extensive knowledge of the Classics and of history to draw parallels between ancient and modern nations and finally urged Americans to adhere "to the good old precepts of common sense, and to the sound dispositions of human nature" in remaining loyal to the French, "who first acknowledged our independence, and set the blessed example to others."

Dickinson published his collected political writings in two volumes in 1801. Taken together, the writings trace the extraordinarily productive career of one of the foremost statesmen and propagandists of the Revolutionary and early national periods.

Suggested Readings: DAB; LHUS; T₂. *See also* A. Owen Aldridge, "Paine and Dickinson," EAL, 11 (1976), 125-138; H. Trevor Colbourn, "The Historical Perspective of John Dickinson," *Early Dickinsoniana* (1961); David L. Jacobson, *John Dickinson and the Revolution in Pennsylvania, 1764-1776* (1965); Pierre Marambaud, "Dickinson's *Letters From a Farmer in Pennsylvania* as Political Discourse," EAL, 12 (1977), 63-72; Charles J. Stillé, *The Life and Times of John Dickinson* (1891).

Elaine K. Ginsberg
West Virginia University

JONATHAN DICKINSON (1663-1722)

Works: *God's Protecting Providence Man's Surest Help and Defence in the Times of Greatest Difficulty and Most Imminent Danger* (1699).

Biography: Born in 1663 to a prosperous landholding family in Jamaica, Jonathan Dickinson spent his entire life as a merchant trader. Although a pious Quaker, he engaged actively in the slave trade and objected strongly to Negro import duties. His literary fame is based entirely on the publication of his *Journal* concerning a voyage from Jamaica to Philadelphia in 1696, which was interrupted by a storm and shipwreck off the coast of Fla. Taking up temporary residence in Philadelphia, he eventually decided to remain there permanently, while making one or two annual trips back to Jamaica for a number of years. In Philadelphia he continued as trader and merchant and acquired a counting house, a wharf, a shipyard, and large holdings of real estate. In addition, he held a number of public offices, including clerk, member, and speaker of the Provincial

Assembly; alderman and mayor of the city of Philadelphia (a post he considered "drudgery"); and justice of the peace and judge of the Provincial Court. He also performed various financial and administrative services for his fellow Quakers. Dickinson died in Philadelphia in 1722.

Critical Appraisal: Although Jonathan Dickinson's *Journal* has been published as a religious tract, it is more correctly described as straightforward narration and description in the overlapping literary genres of Indian captivity and disasters at sea. Dickinson was cast ashore off the coast of Fla. in Sept. 1696 in company with his wife and infant child, the ship's captain, eight mariners, two other passengers including a Quaker missionary Robert Barrow, and ten slaves belonging to Dickinson. The original edition contained an anonymous preface commenting on the miraculous salvation of the voyagers and describing the death in Philadelphia of Barrow, six days after reaching his destination. The title page of the 1699 edition has no reference to Barrow but adds to the material given above "Evidenced in the Remarkable Deliverance of Divers Persons, from the Devouring Waves of the Sea, amongst which they Suffered Shipwreck, and also from the more cruelly devouring Jawes of the Inhumane Canibals of Florida." The work became a best-seller, with at least eight printings in America and seven in Eng. before 1830; there were also two separate translations in German and one in Dutch, the latter with a sixty-line poem as prolog. In most later editions, the phrase "Deliverance of Divers Persons" was changed to "Deliverance of Robert Barrow," probably because the latter's death provided a type of anticlimax or ironic denouement. In our times, the plight of Dickinson's wife with an un-weaned child would be more likely to engage reader interest.

Dickinson's journal is composed in a vigorous, straightforward narrative style with surprisingly little pious reflection. It concentrates on simple matters such as food and clothing or the want of them and the commonplace events in the four-month trip by canoe and land from the place of shipwreck to Philadelphia. Since Dickinson and his group were passed from one group of Indians to another, his description of native behavior has become the focus of attention. Although the anonymous preface speaks of the "man-eaters' fury" and the title pages of the "inhumane Canibals," the text of the journal itself does not suggest that the Fla. Indians ate human flesh. Their inhuman treatment consisted primarily of strip-ping their captives naked and keeping them without clothing even in cold weather, of depriving them of food, and of appropriating all of their possessions. One Indian, however, seemed to express a homoerotic feeling for one of the mariners. Although most of the Indians had previously had little or no contact with the English, referring to them disparagingly as *Nickaleer*, one of them had learned to say "English Son of a Bitch." Details such as this provide an atmosphere of verisimilitude. Doubts have, nevertheless, been expressed concerning the au-thenticity of the narrative, primarily because Dickinson could not possibly have kept a daily record between Aug. 23, and Nov. 15, when he was presumably naked most of the time and suffering from cold and acute hunger every night. Presumably, Dickinson reconstructed the events of this part of the journey and wrote them down in St. Augustine, where he was humanely received by the Spanish governor.

The preface to the 1st edition declares that Dickinson is a man of good credit and reputation and that his testimony is supported by that of his wife and of the master of the shipwrecked vessel. There is also corroborating evidence in the form of a letter from Barrow to his wife written from S.C. before the shipwrecked party reached Philadelphia and a second written by a resident of Philadelphia referring to their arrival, dated more than a year before the printing of the journal. Barrow, who had lived nearly all of his life in Eng., complained of the scorching heat of the sun during the day, but Dickinson, who had been born in Jamaica, referred constantly to the unaccustomed hail, ice, and frost. By and large, his narrative is equally as entertaining as that of *Robinson Crusoe* and despite its title contains less moralizing.

Suggested Readings: T₁. *See also* a complete scholarly edition with biography and detailed history of all reprints by Evangeline Walker Andrews and Charles McLean Andrews, *Jonathan Dickinson's Journal, or God's Protecting Providence* (1945). A biographical sketch accompanies Harold E. Gillingham, "The Estate of Jonathan Dickinson," PMHB, 59 (1935), 420-429.

A. Owen Aldridge
University of Illinois at Urbana-Champaign

MOSES DICKINSON (1695-1778)

Works: *A Sermon Preached at the Ordination of the Rev. Mr. Elisha Kent* (1732); *A Discourse Shewing That the Consideration of God's Sovereignty* (1742); *A Second Vindication of God's Sovereign Free Grace* (1748); *An Inquiry into the Consequences Both of Calvinistic and Arminian Principles* (1750); *A Sermon Preached Before the General Assembly* (1755); *An Answer to a Letter from an Aged Layman* (1761); *An Answer in the Form of a Familiar Letter to Two Important Questions* (1770); *A Sermon Delivered at the Funeral of the Honorable Thomas Fitch, Esq.* (1774).

Biography: Moses Dickinson was born in Springfield, Mass., to Hezekiah and Abigail Dickinson on Dec. 12, 1695. He graduated from Yale College in 1717 and later that year became pastor of the Presbyterian churches at Hopewell and Maidenhead, N.J., posts he accepted to be near his oldest brother, Jonathan Dickinson, who later became president of the College of New Jersey (now Princeton Univ.). On Nov. 1, 1727, Dickinson left N.J. to become pastor of the Presbyterian Church at Norwalk, Conn., where he remained for the rest of his life. Franklin Bowditch Dexter's *Yale Biographies* (1885) states that he had four sons and three daughters; William B. Sprague's *Annals of the American Pulpit* (1866) says that he had eight children, "the first of whom was born in 1721, the last in 1734." On Jul. 28, 1757, Dickinson married his second wife,

Hannah, by whom he had no children. He died in Norwalk on May 1, 1778, at the age of 82.

Critical Appraisal: A zealous Calvinist, Moses Dickinson would have been more at home in John Cotton's (q.v.) congregation than he was in his own. Preaching his narrow, hell-fire message during the French and Indian War and just before the Revolution, he was in many respects an anachronism. Whether preaching at the ordination of a fellow Calvinist or delivering an election sermon to the Assembly, Dickinson's main concern was to smite Arminianism and to prove the total depravity of the nonelect. Wherever he looked, he found "arminian, arian, socinian, antinomian, and pelagian errors" flooding into the country and saw himself as one of the last champions of orthodox Calvinism, striving mightily to repair its broken dikes against the ungodly tide of modernism.

In his attempts to stem the Arminian tide, Moses Dickinson enthusiastically engaged in several controversies, the most notorious of which involved his refusal to ordain James Dana (q.v.) at Wallingford when Dana "refused to let the church know what his principles are." Dana and his supporters at Wallingford apparently refused to draw up a declaration attesting to their belief in "the Trinity, the atonement of Christ, God's eternal decrees, original sin, free will, effectual calling, justification, and perseverance of the Saints." There was, in fact, strong reason to suspect Dana of believing that man could work toward his own salvation and that good deeds could sway God's judgments. Moses Dickinson's brother had engaged in similar controversy with John Beach (q.v.), a Presbyterian minister who had gone over to the Episcopalians. Jonathan Dickinson died while writing an anti-Beach treatise, and Moses Dickinson took up his brother's cause, berating Beach for his supposed denial of original sin and his refusal to believe that God's decrees concerning sinners are eternal and unalterable.

Dickinson's vast theological knowledge and his skill at logic chopping are manifest in all his sermons, and his arguments demonstrating that free will and predestination are compatible rather than contradictory are truly masterful. As a writer, however, Dickinson ultimately lacked the fire and eloquence that Jonathan Edwards (q.v.) brought to these same ideas. In fact, Dickinson's best passages are often borrowed directly from Edwards: "Poor mortals that hang as it were over that lake that burns with fire and brimstone, upon nothing but a brittle thread, that grows weaker and weaker, every hour, and may break before the next minute."

Dickinson's theology offers no comfort to those in doubt about their spiritual state. For Dickinson, sanctification must precede justification. "The repentance of the non-Elect, no matter how sincere, is an abomination. Their good deeds are no better than sins. . . . Our very tears need to be washed in the blood of Christ." Replete with Calvinistic zeal, his sermons are masterpieces of hair-splitting logic that repeat and emphasize the same theme: Presbyterianism is the only way to heaven. According to Dickinson, all other religions, although they must be tolerated by civil law, are in error and lead only to damnation. In Dickinson's opinion, Arminianism threatened to surge through the colonies like a deluge, and Dickinson and his followers were the sturdy dam stemming the hellish tide.

Suggested Readings: CCMC; CCNE; Dexter (I, 165-168); Sprague (I, 310-312).

Zohara Boyd
Appalachian State University

THOMAS ATWOOD DIGGES (1741-1821)

Works: *The Adventures of Alonso* (1775).

Biography: Thomas Atwood Digges was born in Warburton, Md., in 1741, the second of Ann Atwood's and William Digges's six sons. Educated in Eng. —at Oxford according to family tradition—Digges spent much of his adult life abroad. After a stay in Portugal, he wrote *The Adventures of Alonso*, printed in London, in 1775.

During the Revolutionary War, Digges was a confidential agent for various people—shipping locks and muskets to the colonies, providing Benjamin Franklin (q.v.) with political and military information, and aiding American prisoners of war. In 1778 he also served as intermediary between pacifist M.P. David Hartley and Franklin in Hartley's proposal for negotiating a truce in the hostilities. However, Digges's methods, his mysterious imprisonment, and his embezzlement of money intended to aid American prisoners raised doubts for Franklin and the London merchant William Hodgson about his loyalty to the colonial cause. Franklin, for example, once called Digges "the greatest villain I have ever met with." Digges later regained his reputation, partially through the assistance of George Washington (q.v.), an acquaintance of Digges's family who wrote on his behalf: "I have no hesitation in declaring that the conduct of Mr. Thomas Digges...has not been only friendly, but I might add zealous."

After the war, Digges remained abroad trying, despite English government opposition, to persuade English and Irish artisans to immigrate to America. His activities during this period remain mysterious, for he seems to have been involved in Irish nationalist activities working with the Irish patriot Theobald Wolfe Tone. In 1799 he returned to his estate, Warburton Manor, in Md., where he became involved in a series of disputes over the construction of Fort Washington on Digges land. After a long illness, he died in Washington in Dec. 1821.

Critical Appraisal: Thomas Atwood Digges's literary reputation rests solely on his novel *The Adventures of Alonso*. Although sometimes described as the first American novel, *Alonso* would more properly be described as the first novel by an American because its Portuguese protagonists; European, African, and South and Central American settings; and picaresque plot make the label "American" inappropriate.

The novel tells of its hero Alonso's falling in love and then eloping with

Donna Eugenia, the young bride of an elderly Portuguese gentleman, and the results of this indiscretion. After traveling in Sp. and Fr., Alonso is forced by financial difficulties to seek his fortune in Braz., while Donna Eugenia enters a convent to await his return. After a series of adventures—being imprisoned in Braz. for smuggling a diamond, smuggling with a British captain in the Spanish colonies, and being captured and sold into slavery by Algerines—Alonso returns to Lisbon to obtain his father's forgiveness and to discover that Donna Eugenia, who had become a nun, has died.

The novel includes elements of sentimental, picaresque, and travel fiction. The love between Alonso and Donna Eugenia is the result of matched sensibilities: "a silent tear would now and then steal down his cheeks, claiming the sympathy of Eugenia: she again catching the sorrowful state of his mind, would be so sunk in dejection and grief, as to require all his tenderness and love to alleviate." Such descriptions invite the reader to sympathize with the protagonists' illicit romantic love, a love that challenges social and moral conventions. But this aspect of their relationship is never explored; instead Alonso suffers his "adventures" for having indulged his passion.

The adventure sections have the episodic organization of the picaresque novel, and Alonso's motivations often are governed by the amoral common sense of the picaro and perhaps even of Digges's own questionable ethical attitudes. Alonso betrays his Brazilian patron's trust by smuggling a diamond, later bribes his way out of prison, and finally persuades an English captain to trade in contraband goods. He has the enthusiasm of the picaro for his adventures; only the homosexual advances of a lecherous Moor seem to discomfort him. During the novel's journeys, Digges makes use of the convention in the travel narrative of discussing contemporary affairs, especially Pombal's Portuguese government. In these discussions, Alonso frequently contrasts English and Iberian character, crediting English rationality with better administrative ability than Latin emotion.

Digges avoided the stylistic excesses of much sentimental fiction and exercised control over the pace of his narrative more effectively than many early adventure novelists. However, the conventional plot, the thin characterization, and the outdated discussions of colonial affairs limit interest in *The Adventures of Alonso* to the literary historian.

Suggested Readings: William Bell Clark, "In Defense of Thomas Digges," PMHB, 77 (1953), 381-438; Robert H. Elias, "The First American Novel," AL, 12 (1940-1941), 419-434; Katharine A. Kellock, *Colonial Piscataway in Maryland* (1965); Lynn Hudson Parsons, "The Mysterious Mr. Digges," WMQ, 22 (1965), 486-492; Henri Petter, *The Early American Novel* (1971), pp. 285-287.

David M. Craig
Clarkson College

CHRISTOPHER DOCK (c. 1698-1771)

Works: *Schulordnung* (School Management) with two hymns (w. 1750; pub. 1770); four entries in C. Sauer's *Geistliches Magazien* (Spiritual Magazine): one letter to his pupils, 1, no. 33 (c. 1764); "A Hundred Necessary Rules of Conduct for Children," 1, no. 40 (c. 1766); "A Hundred Christian Rules of Life for Children," 1, no. 41 (c. 1768); and two hymns, 2, no. 15 (c. 1770). Additional published hymns, poems, and fraktur-schritten (illuminated writings) have been ascribed to Dock, but all are unsigned; positive identification remains in doubt.

Biography: Very little can be stated with certainty about Christopher Dock's background. He was probably born in S. Ger., possibly into a Mennonite home, but the exact location, date, and his family origin remain undetermined. After teaching school in Europe for four years, he immigrated to America in 1718 and settled in what is now Montgomery County in eastern Pa. Immediately upon arriving, he resumed his teaching career, his first love and Christian calling, in the Mennonite community of Salford. After ten years, for reasons that are somewhat puzzling, Dock turned his back on teaching and began farming. Except for four summers when he taught for brief periods after harvest, he farmed for ten years. However, his heart was in the classroom, and in 1738 he returned to teaching full time—three days a week at Salford and three days at Skippack—until his death in 1771. Dock died quietly in his school while in a kneeling position, presumably in prayer, after he had dismissed his pupils at the end of the day. His wife had died earlier. They had two daughters.

Critical Appraisal: Christopher Dock was known variously as the "Colonial Schoolmaster," "Father of American Pedagogy," and "Schoolmaster on the Skippack" and is generally regarded as the most innovative, effective, and influential educator in colonial Pa. Unlike many typical schoolteachers of his time, Dock had a wholesome attitude toward children. Although he felt compelled to use the rod at times, he much preferred to discipline by giving rewards for achievement and good behavior. He believed that all children, including the poor, had a right to an education, subsidized by the church rather than by the state. The primary purpose of education, in his opinion, was the shaping of character, not the accumulation of knowledge.

Dock was an exceptionally skillful fraktur artist. His beautiful calligraphy served as a model of handwriting to be copied by his pupils. He frequently presented small decorative pieces of fraktur as "rewards of merit" for good work and exemplary behavior.

In his *School Management*, written at the request of the publisher Christopher Sauer I (q.v.) but with great reluctance and with the stipulation that it not be published in his lifetime, Dock described in considerable detail his philosophy on education, his methods of teaching, his handling of children, and his approach to involving parents in the educational activities of their young. As a model of pedagogy, this work is still widely held as a classic by both Christian and secular educators. A former governor of Pa. called Dock "the first true American Educator" and officially declared Oct. 1971 "Christopher Dock Bicentennial Month" on the 200th anniversary of Dock's death.

Dock's deep spiritual wisdom and genuine concern for youth were rooted in the mystical-pietistic teachings of religious practitioners such as Philipp Spener and August Hermann Francke. In his treatise on education, the influence of the Moravian educator Comenius also is evident.

Despite characteristic reticence of the Mennonite Church and although Dock himself was excessively modest, renouncing all personal glory, some Mennonites, especially those who are conscious of their heritage, have ironically come close to bestowing sainthood on Dock. In recent years, Mennonites have named a school after him and have written and performed a play, a pageant, and a cantata in three parts. They have produced a film depicting his life as a teacher and have commissioned the painting of his portrait. Numerous essays, articles, theses, books, and other accounts have been written about him. Dock would have considered himself unworthy of such honors and would have discouraged them. Although he was a good and gifted man, he was genuinely humble and in all things was careful to give God the praise.

Suggested Readings: Harold S. Bender, "Christopher Dock," AGR, 9, no. 3 (Feb. 1945), 4-7, 36; Martin G. Brumbaugh, *The Life and Works of Christopher Dock* (1908); Gerald C. Studer, *Christopher Dock: Colonial Schoolmaster* (1967). Part II of Studer's book consists of all of Dock's published works in translation.

Willard Martin
The Pennsylvania State University

JOHN DODGE (1751-1800)

Works: *A Narrative of the Capture and Treatment of John Dodge* (1779).

Biography: John Dodge was born in Conn. on Jul. 12, 1751. His parents were John and Lydia (Rogers) Dodge. A Baptist minister, Dodge's father was also a blacksmith. At the time of the Revolutionary War, the younger Dodge was working as an Indian trader at Sandusky, Oh., where he had settled at age 19. Through his work with the various Indian tribes along the Great Lakes, Dodge had become proficient in several Indian dialects and had gained the respect and trust of many of the Indians in the region. Because he was an outspoken advocate of maintaining Indian neutrality during the Revolutionary War, Dodge was closely watched by the British soldiers in the region, who feared that his influence over the Indians might affect their efforts to win Indian support of British military activities along the frontier. In Jan. of 1776, Henry Hamilton, the British official in charge of Detroit, ordered Dodge's arrest. Captured by a band of British soldiers and Indians, Dodge was brought to the British prison at Detroit where he remained under intolerable circumstances for several months.

Acquitted of any wrongdoing, Dodge was eventually released and in 1777 he resumed his activities as a trader, this time in Detroit itself. As the war continued to escalate Dodge became, in the eyes of the British, increasingly dangerous, and he was once again arrested and this time sent to a prison in Quebec. After his escape from prison in 1778, Dodge took his story of ill-treatment at the hands of the British to Boston and then to Philadelphia, where his *Narrative* was first published. After the war Dodge was appointed Indian agent for Kaskaskia (now Ill.). He is believed to have died somewhere in Mo. sometime in 1800.

Critical Appraisal: With the outbreak of the Revolutionary War, Indian captivity narratives became vehicles for anti-British propaganda as previously they had served a like purpose against the French during the French and Indian Wars. *A Narrative of the Capture and Treatment of John Dodge* (1779) not only reports its author's own difficulties as a prisoner of the British but also tells how the British governor of Detroit, Henry Hamilton, gave Indians a bounty for American scalps, ordering both Indians and British soldiers alike "not to spare man, woman or child." "To this cruel mandate," reports Dodge, "even some of the Savages made an objection, . . . but they were told the children would make soldiers and the women would keep up the flock." Because the British "offered no reward for Prisoners, but they gave the Indians twenty dollars a scalp," states Dodge, "they induced the Savages to make the poor inhabitants, who they had torn from their peaceable homes, carry their baggage till within a short distance of the fort, where, in cold blood, they murdered them, and delivered their green scalps in a few hours after to those British barbarians, who, on the first yell of the Savages, flew to meet and hug them to their breasts reeking with the blood of innocence." According to Dodge, the Indians around Detroit were in "no ways interested in the unhappy dispute between Great-Britain and America" until the British aroused them by telling them that the Americans intended "to murder them and take their lands." In addition, Dodge relates the pathetic story of an American captive whom he saved from torture by the Indians only to see him die from mistreatment in a British military jail.

Lively, dramatic, and direct, Dodge's *Narrative* about the injustices he witnessed did much to stimulate American patriotism and to promote the American cause in Britain where it was published in John Almon's periodical, *The Remembrancer* (1779). It also brought Dodge to the attention of General George Washington (q.v.), who was so impressed by what Dodge had to say and the way that he said it that Dodge was sent to report to Congress on the events that he had seen. Reprinted in Danvers in 1780 for the purpose of satisfying "the curiosity of every one throughout the United States," Dodge's account of British atrocities was also instrumental in the eventual conviction of Hamilton and his subordinates for war crimes.

Suggested Readings: T₂. *See also* Phillips D. Carleton, "The Indian Captivity," *AL*, 15 (1943), 169-180; James A. Levernier and Hennig Cohen, eds., *The Indians and Their Captives* (1977), pp. xxi, 50-54; Roy Harvey Pearce, "The Significances of the Captivity Narrative," *AL*, 42 (1971), 544-546; R. W. G. Vail, *The Voice of the Old Frontier* (1949), pp. 15, 307, 308-309; Richard VanDerBeets, ed., *Held Captive by Indians* (1973); idem., "The Indian Captivity Narrative as Ritual," *AL*, 43 (1972), 548-562; idem, "A Surfeit of Style: The Indian Captivity Narrative as Penny Dreadful," *RS*, 39

(1971), 297-306; " 'A Thirst for Empire': The Indian Captivity Narrative as Propaganda," RS, 40 (1972), 207-215.

James A. Levernier
University of Arkansas at Little Rock

BENJAMIN DOOLITTLE (1695-1749)

Works: *An Enquiry into Enthusiasm* (1743); *A Short Narrative of Mischief Done by the French and Indian Enemy* (1750).

Biography: Benjamin Doolittle was born in Wallingford, Conn., on Jul. 10, 1695, the son of John Doolittle and his first wife, Mary Peck. He was the grandson of Abraham Doolittle, one of the first settlers of Wallingford. Doolittle studied theology at Yale College, receiving an M.A. in 1716. On Oct. 14, 1717, he married Lydia Todd, the eldest child of Samuel and Susanna Todd of North Haven, Conn., and began preaching in Northfield, then a frontier settlement in northwestern Mass., on Nov. 10 of that year. On Aug. 2, 1718, he was invited to settle there, and his ordination as a Congregational minister probably took place on Sept. 2.

Doolittle was both pastor and doctor to his community: his tombstone inscription tells us that "well schooled in two important arts, / Nobly he filled the double station / both of a preacher and physician." About 1737 objections regarding the extent of his medical practice arose in his congregation. He was also accused of Arminianism, a religious heresy counter to the Calvinistic teaching of predestination. The majority of his congregation supported him, however, and he was retained. His published *Enquiry into Enthusiasm* shows that he opposed the Great Awakening of the 1740s.

Doolittle remained pastor at Northfield until his death of a heart attack on Jan. 9, 1749. The *Boston Gazette* of Jan. 24, 1749, reported his demise: "We are informed that on the 9th instant, the Rev. Mr. Doolittle, pastor of the Church in Northfield, was suddenly seized with a pain in his breast, as he was mending a fence in his yard, and died in a few minutes' time, to the inexpressible grief of the town in general, as well as his own family in particular."

His funeral sermon was preached by the Rev. Jonathan Ashley (q.v.) of nearby Deerfield, a friend of long standing. The tone of Ashley's remarks suggests a fondness for his colleague, who had delivered the charge published with Ashley's 1741 ordination sermon. In addition, the eulogy offers a portrait of Doolittle's sense of decorum and his wit.

> As to his Powers and Abilities (it is well known) they were much above the common Sort; and some of good Judgment have thought, had he been situated under the Advantages of Men and Books, he would have shone as a Star of the first Magnitude....He was naturally facetious, but if at any Time he might seem to exceed the Bounds of Decency, so as to give

Offence to Persons of a more melancholy Temper, I can assure them he bewailed it as his Infirmity.

Although Benjamin Doolittle had twelve children, five sons and seven daughters, he was survived by only two sons and four daughters. His widow, who remarried twice, died Jun. 16, 1790.

Critical Appraisal: Benjamin Doolittle's primary literary contribution was his *Short Narrative of the Mischief Done by the French and Indian Enemy*. This twenty-four-page pamphlet was posthumously published in octavo from manuscripts found among Doolittle's papers. It is unpolished but contains a wealth of specific details of the events in and around the frontier outposts of Northfield, Deerfield, and Fort Massachusetts during the years of King George's War (1744-1749). Samuel Gardner Drake's more celebrated history of the war is much indebted to Doolittle's work; he found Doolittle's study "one of the most important and valuable records of [the war], so far as his plan extended, that can be found of any similar period in our history. His location gave him the best means of ascertaining the truth of the transactions, all of which he appears to have narrated with singular impartiality."

Doolittle's purpose in writing his *Narrative* was "only to relate Facts, as near as I am capable, from the best information I could get." He seems to have followed this plan, inserting very little in the way of commentary. Although the narrative is written in the form of a journal, individual entries are not strictly confined to describing events of the record date. A plain style, as well as a direct and concise tone, is evident throughout the work: "The Enemy doubtless lost many; they went off without Shouting, and when some Captives saw them about a Week after, they looked very sorrowful." The title page, however, notes that the volume, "at the Desire of some, is now published, with some small additions, to render it more perfect." Although it is not precisely known which part of the text is Doolittle's manuscript and which the additions, the additions appear to be mainly editorial remarks—criticizing the poor management of the war in the hands of the colonial government and attempting to arouse sympathy for the frontier townspeople in anticipation of the renewal of the conflict—and can be identified from variations in style and typography. The final portion of the text, for example, seems entirely the work of the editor and is headed: "The following remarks are easy and natural from the preceeding History."

That Doolittle was also capable of a more polished rhetoric than that found in the *Short Narrative* is evidenced by his *Enquiry into Enthusiasm*, a carefully stylized treatise decrying the extravagant emotionalism of the Great Awakening. Drawing upon biblical and historical references, he disparaged the "enthusiasm" of New Light preachers who profess "some great and wonderful communication from God." Their pride is the same fault that led Eve to eat the apple in the Garden of Eden. Although he used strong language against those who set themselves above established revelation, the same tolerance that characterized the *Short Narrative* emerges in his closing statement:

Godly men (some more than others) are many times filled with considerable Degrees of Enthusiasm: and for a Man to determine precisely what
degree of it is inconsistent with true Piety, I think is very difficult; and how
far the kind Author of our Beings, who knows our Darkness, Infirmities,
and Mistakes, may pardon and overlook them, in and through Christ,
where he sees an honest, sincere, and upright heart, I think is too much
Boldness to determine.

Carefully written, Doolittle's *Enquiry* provides an insightful view into the more
conservative aspects of the controversial religious currents of the time.

Suggested Readings: CCNE; Dexter (I, 151-154). *See also* O. P. Allen, *Abraham Doolittle and Some of His Descendants* (1893), pp. 6-12; Jonathan Ashley, *Ministers
and People* (1749); idem, *The United Endeavors* (1742); William Frederick Doolittle, *The
Doolittle Family in America* (1901), pp. 62-64, 79-96; Samuel G. Drake, "Doolittle
Genealogy," NEHGR 6 (1852), 293-295; idem, *A Particular History of the Five Years
French and Indian War* (1870; rep., 1970) passim; James Savage, *A Genealogical Dictionary of the First Settlers of New England* (1860-1862; rep., 1965), II, 60; Josiah Temple
and George Sheldon, *A History of the Town of Northfield, Massachusetts* (1875), passim.

Alice H. Brink
University of Houston

EDWARD DORR (1722–1772)

Works: *The Duty of Civil Rulers* (1763); *A Discourse Occasioned by the
Death of the Hon. Daniel Edwards, Esq.* (1765).

Biography: Edward Dorr was born in Lyme, Conn., on Nov. 2, 1722, to
Edmund and Mary [Griswold] Dorr. A graduate of Yale College, he received
both the B.A. and M.A. in 1742. Licensed to preach by the New Haven Association on May 29, 1744, Dorr preached between 1744 and 1746 at Kensington
Society (now Berlin), Conn., but left after "difficulties about the salary." In
1747 he temporarily assumed the pulpit of the First Church in Hartford to relieve
its ailing minister, the Rev. Daniel Wadsworth. After Wadsworth's death, Dorr
was ordained minister of that church on Apr. 27, 1748. He married Helen
Talcott, Wadsworth's sister-in-law, and remained pastor of the First Church in
Hartford until his death on Oct. 20, 1772, at the age of 50.

Critical Appraisal: Edward Dorr's published works consist of a funeral
oration for Daniel Edwards, a Conn. magistrate, and an election sermon. Both
works reveal a warm-hearted, gentle individual more concerned with good works
and public welfare than with Calvinistic doctrine and scholastic hair splitting.
Conventional in form and sentiment, Dorr's funeral oration is dedicated to Sarah
Edwards, Daniel Edwards's widow, who had recently suffered several
bereavements—the losses of her only surviving adult daughter, the daughter's

husband, two grandchildren, a sister, and a brother—all in the nine months preceding her husband's death. In this sermon, Dorr assured the widow that there is sincere mourning for a truly good man. Using the parable of the talents as his text, Dorr told the listeners they must improve the gifts God has given them. The servant who buries five talents sins five times as grievously as the servant who has been given only one. All must do their duty according to their place in life. Those individuals in a lowly position have their responsibilities to God and should strive to excel at their humble duties. Those who have been set high in life must strive even harder, however, because their sphere of influence is greater. He lauded Daniel Edwards as one who was set high, had that great sphere of influence, and labored hard for the public good. He was a judge and magistrate; well educated, honest, and faithful in his public charge; kind, devout, and friendly in his private life. He was one who received many talents and improved all of them. Addressing the widow directly, Dorr tells her, "Mourn you may, but not for him, not like they that mourn without hope. You may mourn for yourself, mourn for the church, and mourn for the world, who are deprived of his Prayers, Counsel, and Assistance." Edwards himself does not need their tears. He is now with God, "happier than any here on earth." While all this may be conventional funeral piety, there is a simplicity, directness, and sweetness in Dorr's tone that bespeaks warmth and sincerity.

Simple and direct, Dorr's election sermon, preached on May 9, 1765, provides practical advice on how the leaders of New Eng. can materially and temporally further the cause of religion in Conn. Searching out "secret vices" is not the duty of the state; punishing public lawbreakers is. Supporting the church by their own godly example is good; raising some money for the maintenance of churches and ministers is better; and levying a tax for this purpose is highly laudable. In addition, Dorr assured his listeners that "the rights of conscience are sacred" and that each man "should be left at liberty to worship God according to the dictates of his own conscience," but that a "generous, catholic" religion with no quibbles about "little differences of opinion...mere modes and ceremonies, or nice, speculative points of controversy, that don't greatly affect practical godliness or virtue" could be supported with public funds to the detriment of none and for the general good of all. Governmental support of religion is a valid civic function, because religion "makes men quiet and peaceable and full of good will." Gospel virtues of benevolence, temperance, charity, and chastity promote civil virtue, too.

Most particularly, Dorr urged the governor to promote peace with the Indians. According to Dorr, every effort should be made to educate and convert them and to persuade them that the British are their friends. The French used these means to gain influence over the Indians: "Why mayn't we learn wisdom from their experience?" He urged all citizens to "cast their mite into the treasury" to support this endeavor. If every citizen, from the highest to the lowest, does his share, "Religion may spread from one man, from one family and neighbor to another, till at length it run through the town, through the colony, through the land and nation; and may at last cover the earth, as the waters do the seas." Thus although Dorr's sermons are not particularly erudite, they do reveal a man of sincerity, warmth, eloquence, and generous, practical piety.

Suggested Readings: CCNE; Dexter (II, 704–705).

Zohara Boyd
Applachian State University

WILLIAM DOUGLASS (c. 1691-1752)

Works: *Abuses and Scandals* (1722); *Inoculation of the Small Pox* (1722); *Postscript to Abuses* (1722); *Some Historical Remarks on the City of St. Andrews* (1728); *Dissertation Concerning Inoculation of the Small Pox* (1730); *Practical Essay Concerning the Small Pox* (1730); *Practical History of a New Epidemical Eruptive Miliary Fever* (1736); *Essay Concerning Silver and Paper Currencies* (1738); *Discourse Concerning the Currencies of the British Plantations in America* (1740); *Postscript to a Discourse* (1740); *Letter to...Merchant in London* (1741); *Mercurius Nov-Anglicanus or Almanack, Anno Domini* (1743); *A Summary, Historical and Political*, I (1749), II (1751). For "Letters from Dr. Wm. Douglass to Cadwallader Colden of New York, 1721-1736," see CMHS, 4th ser., 2 (1854), 164-189.

Biography: Physician, naturalist, and historian—William Douglass was born sometime around 1691 in Gifford, Haddington County, Scotland. His father, George Douglass, was "factor" for the marquis of Tweeddale and "portioner" of Gifford. Proficient in Latin, Greek, Dutch, French, and English, Douglass studied in Edinburgh, Leyden, and Paris, receiving a degree in medicine from the University of Utrecht in 1712. During his training in Europe, Douglass came under the influence of the leading scientific authorities of his day, including Herman Boerhaave, Thomas Sydenham, and Archibald Pitcairne, whose theories about the causes of disease and their treatments were to have a lasting effect on his career.

In 1718, after a sojourn in the West Indies, Douglass immigrated to Boston, Mass., where he began practicing medicine. The only physician in Boston with an earned medical degree, Douglass held himself and his training in high esteem and was quick to criticize his colleagues. For the first few years Douglass seems to have gotten along well enough, but in 1721, when an epidemic of smallpox broke out in Boston, he vociferously opposed the efforts of Zabdiel Boylston (q.v.), Increase Mather (q.v.), and Cotton Mather (q.v.) to introduce inoculation into the colonies. Tempers flared, and although Douglass managed to keep the professional respect of his adversaries, he lost their friendship and was never again to remain completely at ease in Boston intellectual circles.

A man with a curious mind and vast intellectual capacities, Douglass made numerous contributions to the scientific community of his day. In addition to his research on inoculation, he was the first to provide a clinically sound account of scarlet fever. He collected some 1,100 plant species from the area around Boston, and he was among the first to use mercuric substances in the treatment of disease. Just before he died, Douglass published a two-volume account of the history of the British colonies in North America, and for many years he exchanged information on a variety of scientific topics with Cadwallader Colden (q.v.). Indefatigable in his efforts to communicate and share scientific knowledge, Douglass founded a medical society in Boston, and although he was never known as a particularly tolerant or patient individual, he was for a considerable time president of the Scottish Charitable Society in Boston. Douglass also calculated an almanac, performed meteorological experiments, and wrote a highly acclaimed investigation into the problems of the North American monetary system. Douglass never married. At the time of his death on Oct. 21, 1752, he was at work on a map which he hoped would for the first time provide accurate latitudinal and longitudinal data for New Eng.

Critical Appraisal: Among literary historians William Douglass is best remembered for his spirited participation in the inoculation controversy of the 1720s. When, at the urgings of the Mathers, the Boston physician Zabdiel Boylston began using inoculation as a way to combat the spread of a smallpox epidemic which ravaged Boston during the summer of 1721, Douglass orchestrated popular resistance to the practice. In principle, Douglass was not necessarily opposed to inoculation. Ironically, it was Douglass who had first brought Cotton Mather's attention to the use of inoculation in foreign lands, and later in life Douglass not only endorsed inoculation against smallpox but practiced inoculation himself. What Douglass objected to in 1721 was what he considered the dangerous experimentation on the part of Boylston with a practice that few people knew much about. Of particular concern to Douglass was Boylston's refusal to isolate inoculated individuals from those who remained uninoculated. Douglass had good cause to worry, for there was strong scientific evidence to suggest that healthy individuals could easily be infected by an inoculated patient. There was also evidence to suggest that an inoculated individual who might otherwise not have contracted smallpox could easily die from an unsuccessful attempt at inoculation. Jonathan Edwards (q.v.), for example, was later to die in this way.

These were the facts that Douglass brought to the attention of a worried public in his pamphlets on *The Abuses and Scandals. . .of Inoculation* and on *Inoculation of the Small Pox as Practiced in Boston*, as well as in a series of essays in James Franklin's (q.v.) *New-England Courant*. Unable to refrain from *ad hominem* attacks on the opposition, Douglass called his opponents "vain self-conceited Men" who knew little more about medicine than "*Greek old Women, Madmen, and Fools.*" For Cotton Mather, Douglass showed particular contempt, singling him out as "a Degener a Patre, the hero in this Farce of Calumny." Within a matter of weeks, nearly all of Boston was engaged in the controversy. Set upon by Douglass, the Mathers quickly accused him of being "*impious* & Satanic," a teller of "impudent and malicious Lies," and one of "the known Children of the Wicked one." To the Mathers' defense rallied many of New Eng.'s leading ministers, including Benjamin Colman (q.v.), William Cooper (q.v.), Thomas Prince (q.v.), and John Webb (q.v.). Only the aging John Williams (q.v.) supported Douglass. The ordinary citizen, however, resisted inoculation with a vehemence, and on Nov.14, 1721, a lighted bomb was thrown into a window at Cotton Mather's house. Eventually, both the epidemic and the controversy subsided, but not until after a considerable amount of ink had been spilt both supporting and opposing further inoculations.

Even in retrospect, the entire controversy is difficult to assess. Douglass has been accused of stubbornly supporting a practice which has subsequently become commonplace, and professional jealousy toward Boylston and the Mathers for beginning inoculations before he had a chance to do so is one of the many devious motives attributed to his actions. The Mathers, on the other hand, have been accused of meddling in scientific matters which should have been none of their concern and of using inoculation as a way of bolstering their rapidly sagging political influence. In fact, however, each side had its point. Douglass was correct in fearing that inoculation had not been sufficiently tested for it to be safe when practiced too widely, and the Mathers had long been recognized for the high quality of their scientific investigations. Moreover, religion and medicine had, for many years, been traditionally linked in New Eng., where the minister was often the only highly educated member of the community and by virtue of his scientific training naturally took over responsibility for the physical as well as the spiritual welfare of his congregation.

Too frequently overlooked, however, are the significance of Douglass's other writings and the credit they reflect upon their author. Based soundly on his observations of the disease, Douglass's *Practical History of a New Epidemical Eruptive Miliary Fever* is a model of eighteenth-century scientific writing at its best and has been acclaimed in scientific circles as "the first adequate clinical description of scarlet fever in English and probably in any language." His *Discourse Concerning the Currencies of the British Plantations in America* has been compared to Pelatiah Webster's (q.v.) *Political Essays* and is considered "one of the very best of the eighteenth-century discussions of the money question." Arguing for the maintenance of a "universal commercial medium," Douglass blamed inflation on the desire of colonials to live beyond their means by forcing government to print paper money without adequate economic backing in silver and without proper concern for balancing the flow of money to and from the colonies. According to Douglass, it was the responsibility of the people to make money for themselves through their industry, not for the government to make it for them.

Finally, Douglass's two-volume *Summary, Historical and Political, of the First Planting, Progress and Progressive Improvements and Present State of the British Settlements in North America*, while flawed by errors in accuracy, is nonetheless important both for the wealth of information it contains on the botany and science of eighteenth-century America and for the glimpses it provides into the personalities and issues of Douglass's day. Written primarily for "the Writer's private Amusement" and consisting for the most part of notes "loosely put together, but in an historical Manner," Douglass's *Summary* lacks the concentrated tightness of purpose normally associated with effective historical writing, but what the *Summary* may lack in structure and design, it gains in wit and charm. About his early experiences, for example, with the physicians of New Eng., Douglass comments, "When I first arrived in New England, I asked . . . a noted, facetious practitioner, what was their general method of practice. He told me their practice was very uniform: bleeding, vomiting, blistering, purging, anodyne, and so forth; if the illness continued, there was 'repetendi'; and finally 'murderandi.'" The product of a highly educated individual with a quick wit and a subtle mind, the writings of William Douglass have much to recommend them. In the words of one biographer, they constitute "a real addition to the literature of the world."

Suggested Readings: BDAS; DAB; T$_1$. *See also* John B. Blake, "The Inoculation Controversy in Boston, 1721-1722," NEQ, 25 (1952), 489-506; Charles J. Bullock, ed., "A Discourse Concerning the Currencies of the British Plantations," ES, 2 (1897), 265-375; David Freeman Hawke, "William Douglass's *Summary*" in *The Colonial Legacy: Some Eighteenth-Century Commentators*, ed. Lawrence H. Leder (1971), pp. 43-74; Arnold C. Klebs, "The Historic Evolution of Variolation," BJHH, 24 (1913), 69-83; Raymond P. Stearns, *Science in the British Colonies of America* (1974), pp. 477-491; George H. Weaver, "Life and Writings of William Douglas, M.D. (1691-1752)," BSMHC, 2 (1921), 229-259.

James A. Levernier
University of Arkansas at Little Rock

FRANCIS DRAKE (c. 1650-c. 1668)

Works: *To the Memory of the Learned and Reverend, Mr. Jonathan Mitchell, Late Minister of Cambridge in N.E. Inhumed July 10, 1668* (1668; rep. in Nathaniel Morton, *New Englands Memoriall* [1669], pp. 193-196, signed "F.D."; and in Cotton Mather, with fourteen lines omitted, *Ecclesiastes* [1697], pp. 109-111, and in *Magnalia Christi Americana* [1703], II, 94-96, signed "F. Drake").

Biography: Francis Drake's dates and parentage are obscure. He was perhaps the son of Captain Francis Drake of Portsmouth, N. H. The family appears to have moved to Piscataway, N. J., in 1666-7. In the following year, Drake was a boarder in the home of Jonathan Mitchell (q.v.), Cambridge Mass.'s esteemed minister who died in Jul. It is not clear whether Drake planned to enter Harvard College in the fall of 1668; if he had such plans they were not carried out. A final glimpse of him occurs in Daniel Gookin's (q.v.) *Historical Collections of the*

Indians in New England, where he is seen accompanying a Harvard-educated Indian to Eng.

Critical Appraisal: "To the Memory of Jonathan Mitchell" belongs to a category of Puritan funeral elegy that might be called, in common with sermons of the same sort, the jeremiad. In them, warnings and upbraidings overshadow and sometimes replace other elements altogether. Between 1640 and 1660, the formal element of exhortation in elegies had been for the most part restrained and proportional. Following a statement of loss, the elegist "memorialized" personal details of the character and conduct of the deceased. The exhortation that accompanied this portraiture simply admonished the living to remember and imitate a sanctified life.

With their disposition to read lessons into every event, however, the Puritans—especially after 1660—could hardly escape finding in the death of a saint more than just a normal process of nature. The bitter dispute over the Half-Way Covenant in the 60s, the Indian uprisings in the 70s, the Andros regime in the 80s—every decade offered proof that the times were declining. In elegies, as in sermons, the passing away of any eminent person, particularly a pillar of orthodoxy like Mitchell, came to argue, in Drake's phrase, "present Woe and future Miserie" for New Eng. Mitchell's life as an example and comfort interested Drake less than the "sad presage" of his death. "Feverish Heat"—"Cold Sweat" —"Convulsions"—"a Mourning Cloud / Replete with Vengeance for succeeding Times"—"These are my Muses; These inspire the Sails / Of Fancy with Their Sighs in stead of Gales."

As a jeremiad, "Jonathan Mitchell" succumbs to the almost inevitable problem of diminishing returns. In an effort to convey his sense that "Stars falling speak a Storm," Drake often crossed the line from funeral to funereal and fell into bombast. He was more successful when he was concentrating on Mitchell as a minister whose teachings and daily life "clear'd Men" of error. Then he was capable of sounding the note of loss with dignity and restraint: "His System of Religion half unheard, / Full double in his Preaching Life appear'd. / Happy that place where Rulers Deeds appear / I'th'Front o'th'Battel, and their Words i'th'Rear." Drake's elegy was evidently appreciated in its own time, for both Nathaniel Morton (q.v.) and Cotton Mather (q.v.) reprinted it in works of their own on Mitchell.

Suggested Readings: FCNEV. *See also* Daniel Gookin, "Historical Collections of the Indians in New England," CMHS, 1st ser.,1 (1806), 173; Robert Henson, "Form and Content in the Puritan Funeral Elegy," AL, 32 (1960-1961), 11-27; Cotton Mather, *Magnalia Christi Americana* (1703), II, 94-96.

Robert Henson
Upsala College

WILLIAM HENRY DRAYTON (1742-1779)

Works: *The Letters of Freeman* (1771); *Answer to Considerations on Certain Political Transactions of the Province of South Carolina* (1774); *A Letter* *from Freeman of South-Carolina* (1774); *South Carolina* (1775); *A Charge on the Rise of the American Empire* (1776); *To Their Excellencies Richard Viscount Howe, Admiral; and William Howe, Esq., General, of His Brittanick Majesty's Forces in America* (1776); *Georgia* (1777); *The Genuine Spirit of Tyranny* (1778); *The Speech of the Hon. William Henry Drayton, Esq., . . . upon the Articles of the Confederation of the United States of America* (1778); *Memoirs of the American Revolution, from Its Commencement to the Year 1776, Inclusive*, ed. John Drayton, 2 vols. (1821).

Biography: William Henry Drayton was born in Sept. 1742 to a well-to-do patrician planter family in S.C. As a boy, he was sent to Eng., where he received a Classical education at Westminster School and Oxford, and in 1763 returned to his home on the very eve of the pre-Revolution ferment. A conservative with both family ties and personal interest inclining him to support the established order, Drayton sided with the king and Parliament. When South Carolinians, in company with other colonials, resorted to nonimportation of British goods to compel Parliament to rescind the hated Townshend Duties, he wrote a series of letters to the *South Carolina Gazette* strongly opposing such pressure and supporting the royal prerogative. For taking this unpopular position, not only was he subjected to vilification by his fellow Carolinians but was also himself boycotted and unable to sell his goods. Thus injured both psychologically and economically, Drayton sailed for Eng. to stay until the clamor had subsided. By early 1772, the anti-British hysteria had ebbed, and he returned.

For his fidelity to Eng., Drayton was rewarded by appointment to the powerful colonial Council, and in 1772 he took his seat. He had not, however, received either of two positions of profit and prestige that he had tried for, a postmastership and a judgeship. Instead, he was passed over in favor of influential Britishers, "placemen" as the Carolinians contemptuously called them. This disappointment was one of several factors that led him to shift his position from staunch Loyalist to radical Whig. By 1774 he was an ardent patriot, and early in 1776 he was one of the first South Carolinians to advocate publicly complete independence from G.B. From then until his death, Drayton was an enthusiastic, sometimes headstrong leader of the southern radical Whigs. As politician, judge, member of the Continental Congress, and especially as a polemical essayist, he supported American independence, sometimes with more zeal than discretion.

When it came to establishing a government to replace the ousted British, Drayton was an extreme states' rightist. When the states were debating acceptance of the first American Constitution, the Articles of Confederation, and many people were decrying the document as the handiwork of the state sovereignty faction, William Henry Drayton criticized it from the other extreme as far too much concession to the American nationalists and centralists. He did not live to see the achievement of independence or establishment of a government. While serving as a member of the Continental Congress in 1779, Drayton died, still in his 30s.

Critical Appraisal: William Henry Drayton was a superb polemicist. His letters to the newspaper and his tracts and pamphlets were sharp, hard hitting, uncompromising, and effective. They reveal a proud, self-assured, Classically educated student of English Whig political thought.

The first of his pamphlets was printed in London in 1771. Drayton, at the time a staunch supporter of royal and parliamentary authority in America, had written several letters to the *South Carolina Gazette* under the pseudonym "Freeman," defending his Loyalism and castigating those who ostracized him for his stand. In London he published these letters and those of the critics who answered him, titling the pamphlet *The Letters of Freeman &c*. Interestingly, he chose to omit one letter by his antagonists. He had struck out at the S.C. working people who had taken it upon themselves to criticize their betters. Several middle-class artisans wrote a reply to the newspaper, suggesting that Drayton should be lodged in the madhouse and remarking that had he not been born to the purple and married a rich wife, the best he could have done was eke out a living by driving a cart through the streets of Charleston. This letter of criticism by the "meaner sort of people" was the one in the exchange of correspondence that "Freeman" did not include.

Three years later, however, and back home in S.C., Drayton had reversed his position and not only was a supporter of the cause of American rights against Parliament's and the king's usurpation but had taken a leadership role at the radical edge of the movement. His rhetoric was sharper: his 1769-1771 letters had assumed the stance of reason and scholarly moderation, but in a series of tracts in 1774 directed against Loyalists, he wrote with vitriol. For example, he attacked Sir Egerton Leigh, a Tory and fellow councillor, as a man of "weak Head and a wicked Heart." A British publication scored Drayton for this vengeful language "from a most coarse and virulent antagonist, who defeats whatever advantages argument might afford him by the gross illiberality of his language."

It was in 1774 that Drayton wrote what was probably the most important of his pamphlets, *A Letter from Freeman of South-Carolina*, addressed to the delegates to the First Continental Congress. The meeting of this Congress in the autumn of 1774 to consider what the American response should be to Parliament's Intolerable Acts elicited several notable papers, notably that of James Wilson (q.v.) and Thomas Jefferson's (q.v.) *Summary View of the Rights of British America*. None of the others took so extreme a position as that of Drayton, who called for defiance in response to Parliament's outrages. "Freeman" stressed the parallels between 1774 and 1688, when the English overthrew their tyrannical monarch James II in the Glorious Revolution. The Americans' complaint in 1774 was, he wrote, "infinitely more serious" than the English complaint in the late seventeenth century. Drayton clearly implied the right and propriety of revolution.

Some time later, but still several months before the Congress proclaimed American independence from G.B., Drayton went a step further. By this time a judge, he took the occasion of a charge to the grand jury to support the separation of the Americans from the British king and Parliament. He anticipated the format of the Declaration of Independence by presenting a catalog of indictments against the British authority. He then proceeded to drive home the analogy to 1688, the similarities between the behavior of the despotic James II and George III, and followed with the statement that "George the third, king of Great Britain, has abdicated the government, and...the throne is thereby vacant; that is, HE HAS NO AUTHORITY OVER US, and WE OWE NO OBEDIENCE TO HIM."

After the Declaration of Independence, the members of the Continental Congress addressed the task of framing a constitution. Their efforts brought forth the Articles of Confederation, which were then submitted to the states and finally ratified and adopted. This first Constitution of the U.S. is commonly considered, and rightly so, to be a victory for the antinationalist, states' rights faction of the American people. During the debates in the states over acceptance or rejection, centralists vehemently criticized the document for vesting so little authority in the central government. In view of this, it comes as something of a surprise to read William Henry Drayton's address to the S.C. legislature, scoring the Articles from the other extreme, for the inadequacy of protection to the states and insufficiency of state powers. In this speech, also, Drayton showed an awareness of the South as a conscious minority in the American Republic.

During the last three years of his life, Drayton worked on his memoirs, which he intended to be a history of the Revolution in the South. He declared that his intention was to show future generations that S.C. played a decisive part in the Revolution and that "our Star shall be as brilliant as any in *the new constellation*." His death cut short his production, but many years later, his manuscript was edited and published by his son John as *Memoirs of the American Revolution*. Although it is poorly arranged, this is probably the most valuable single source for the Revolution in S.C.

Drayton was about the same age as Thomas Jefferson, who lived almost fifty years longer than he did. Whether he would have modified his extreme positions and used his writing skills in a constructive way in the building of the American Republic cannot be said, but in his short life he was one of the most capable propagandists in the country.

Suggested Readings: DAB. *See also* William M. Dabney and Marion Dargan, *William Henry Drayton and the American Revolution* (1962); R. W. Gibbes, ed., *Documentary History of the American Revolution...Chiefly in South Carolina*, 3 vols. (1853-1857); Edward McCrady, *The History of South Carolina in the Revolution* (1899), pp. 1-349; idem, *The History of South Carolina under the Royal Government* (1901), pp. 400-798; M. Eugene Sirmans, *Colonial South Carolina: A Political History, 1663-1763* (1966); Robert M. Weir, " 'The Harmony We Were Famous for': An Interpretation of Pre-Revolutionary South Carolina Politics," WMQ, 26 (1969), 473-501.

William M. Dabney
University of New Mexico

ELIZABETH SANDWITH DRINKER (1734-1807)

Works: Elizabeth Drinker's diary is excerpted in Cecil Drinker, *Not So Long Ago* (1937); Henry Drinker, ed., *Extracts from the Journal of Elizabeth*

Drinker (1889); *Pennsylvania Magazine of History and Biography*, 13 (1889), 298-308; 15 (1891), 246.

Biography: Born in Philadelphia, Pa., in 1734, Elizabeth Sandwith Drinker was a birthright Quaker, the daughter of William and Sarah Sandwith. Having studied under the Quaker teacher and antislavery leader Anthony Benezet (q.v.), she married Henry Drinker, like her father of the Philadelphia mercantile elite, in 1761. A leading Friend, Drinker occasionally stepped into the larger world as when she petitioned George Washington (q.v.) for the release of her husband imprisoned in Va. for refusing to pledge allegiance to the new government. For the most part, however, Drinker's activities were circumscribed by her family and religious preoccupations, substantial enough compared to women not Quakers, but far from the activity noted for nineteenth-century Quaker women such as Lucretia Mott.

Critical Appraisal: Elizabeth Drinker's diary is an invaluable source for the cultural historian interested in social history, the history of women, wartime Philadelphia, and views of leading mercantile Friends. Written between 1758 and her death in 1807, it is particularly detailed for the years of the War for Independence and for the period following the 1793 Philadelphia yellow fever epidemic.

Elizabeth Drinker wrote frankly about the problems faced by women in Pa. during the eighteenth century. She was especially candid, for example, about her attitude toward matters such as childbirth: to her the good years for women followed the fertile period. She also made frank statements on contraception: late eighteenth-century Quaker women used prolonged nursing of children to reduce family size. She demonstrated catholic tastes in reading: although Henry St. John Bolingbroke's deistical religious views offended her, Mary Wollstonecraft's *Vindication of the Rights of Women* was acceptable, indicating the support of at least one wealthy Quaker woman for its progressive views. In addition, the diary contains useful descriptions of the difficulties of wartime Philadelphia, of the fright caused by the yellow fever epidemic, of the great fear among women of childbirth, and, for those few able to afford one, the eagerness of women to employ a male physician with obstetrical training to help during chidbirth.

As the diary did not appear in print until over a century after she began to write it, its influence on contemporaries was nil. But as an account of a perceptive and articulate woman, it is an essential source for the historian.

Suggested Readings: Pattie Cowell, *Women Poets in Pre-Revolutionary America, 1650-1775: An Anthology* (1981); Linda Kerber, *Women of the Republic: Intellect and Ideology in Revolutionary America* (1980); Mary Beth Norton, *Liberty's Daughters: The Revolutionary Experience of American Women, 1750-1800* (1980).

Arthur Worrall
Colorado State University

WILLIAM DUANE (1760-1835)

Works: *Letter to George Washington President of the United States: Containing Strictures...By Jasper Dwight* (1796); *The Aurora* (editor; 1798-1822,

1834-1835); *A Caution: Or, Reflections on the Present Contest Between France and Great Britain* (1798); *A History of the French Revolution* (1798); *A Report of the Extraordinary Transactions* (1799). Works published by William Duane after 1800 are listed in *The National Union Catalog Pre-1956 Imprints* (Vol. 149).

Biography: William Duane was born near Lake Champlain, N.Y., of Irish parents on May 17, 1760. When his father died in 1765, Duane was taken to Ire., where he eventually learned the printer's trade. Disinherited by his Catholic mother for marrying a Protestant, Catharine Corcoran, Duane shipped for Calcutta in 1787, where he began to publish the *Indian World*. Arrested and deported for criticizing the East India Company and for defending the grievances of army officers, his property confiscated, he returned to Eng. There he worked as a parliamentary reporter for the *General Advertiser* while trying unsuccessfully to recover his lost property in Ind. Finally, he immigrated to Philadelphia, became Benjamin Franklin Bache's (q.v.) associate on the *Aurora* and, when Bache died in 1798, succeeded him as editor. Duane's first wife died in 1798, a few months before Bache's death. Two years later, he married Bache's widow, Margaret. He had five children by his second wife.

As spokesman for Thomas Jefferson (q.v.), Duane attacked John Adams (q.v.) and Theophilus Pickering (q.v.), who tried to deport him under the Alien Law. Arrested in 1799 for his efforts to repeal this law, he won acquittal in the state court. He supported the French cause against the English and at one time was assaulted by a group of armed henchmen of the Hamiltonian faction. Indicted under the Sedition Law in 1799, he managed to gain postponements of his trial until Jefferson became president and the charges were dismissed. Jefferson once described Duane as honest, "sincerely republican," passionate, but "very intolerant."

After 1800 Duane unsuccessfully resisted the National Bank in the revived *Aurora*, printed separately a series of seven letters by Camillus (pseud.) (*The Mississippi Question*, 1803), and wrote four books on military science. When the capital was removed to Washington, D.C., Duane's career ran downhill. He lost the support of Albert Gallatin (q.v.), James Madison (q.v.), and James Monroe; but Jefferson helped him out of financial trouble. During the War of 1812, Duane was adjutant general. After his retirement from the *Aurora* in 1822, he visited South America and wrote *A Visit to Columbia in the Years 1822 and 1823*. He served as a prothonotary on the supreme court in Pa. until his death in 1835.

Critical Appraisal: William Duane's *History of the French Revolution* is a full-dress work, covering four volumes—respectively: the Revolution (including the involvement of Louis XVI), the Legislative Assembly (1789-1792), the National Convention (1792-1795), and the Republic (including the rise of Bonaparte during 1795-1796). After a somewhat stereotyped character description of the French people (following the lead of Mrs. Wollstonecraft), Duane analyzed the numerous causes of the Revolution, especially stressing the igniting event, the dismissal and exile of the popular favorite Jacques Necker on Jul. 11, 1789. Paris was filled with consternation, he wrote, for Necker was considered as a sacrifice to the patriotic sentiments he had avowed; the people regarded his exile as the first step to the subversion of their freedom; the exchange was shut; the public spectacles were suspended; and the crowds that assembled tumultuously in the street, proclaimed by their countenances their grief and indignation. Their fury at last blazed out in open violence; the bells were sounded on every side as signals for the citizens to arm; the rabble during the night had pillaged several houses. . . . The city. . . had been divided into sixty districts and the electors, on the first alarm. . . were classed into different regiments, they assumed a cockade of various colours, which was dignified with the title of National; while the court, whose versatility had provoked the insurrection, seemed lost in astonishment at its progress.

After describing the capture of 30,000 rifles at the Hotel des Invalides, Duane went on to depict with great vividness the fall of the Bastille and the immediate execution of its governor, the Marquis de Launay. Since "human events are greatly influenced by the actions of individuals," Duane gave considerable attention to analyzing the character and career of Necker, whose two-volume history of the French Revolution served as one of his major sources.

As a historical writer, Duane made quick work of Marie Antoinette: "She reached the place of execution about noon; and when she turned her eyes towards the gardens and the palace, she became visibly agitated. She ascended the scaffold with precipitation, and her head was in a moment held up to the people by the executioner." His treatment of George-Jacques Danton is more extended and more sympathetic, for he elaborated both the trial and Danton's gallows humor with the crowd on the day of his execution, closing with this passage: "on the way to the scaffold he continued his jocularity; his head, which was bare, struck many persons with a resemblance to Socrates." Duane's history is well written, clear, interesting; many parts of it give the impression of an eye-witness account.

As a writer of controversy, Duane is probably best remembered for his admirable work in connection with resistance to and repeal of the Alien and Sedition Laws. His *Report of the Extraordinary Transactions* at Philadelphia in Feb. 1799 concerns an attempt at repeal of the Alien Bill. With some fellow Irish, he had put up a memorial (urging repeal) on the walls of St. Mary's Church. A scuffle ensued, and Duane and three others were accused of conspiring to cause a riot. The *Report* is a seven-page record of the trial and his acquittal.

But another work usually attributed to him shows far greater polemical power: *The Letter to George Washington. . .by Jasper Dwight of Vermont*. In this letter, the author suggested tht George Washington (q.v.) should have stopped at the end of the sixth page (or introduction) of his famous farewell address. Mainly, it criticized the president for his stand on the French Revolution and for not making public the papers on the Jay Treaty. The author of the letter not only viewed Washington's speech as "the loathings of a sick mind" but also defended Thomas Paine (q.v.), "that great assertor of Freedom," from Washington's invidious attack on Paine. Considering Paine's services to Washington and America, the author wrote, Washington's attack was "particular[ly] ungracious." The author wished Washington had retired four years earlier and said that posterity would search in vain "for the monuments of wisdom" in his administration.

According to one biographer, Duane's "genius in controversy and management, his courage and audacity, the sincerity and intensity of his convictions, and his virile style of writing made him the most effective printer of his time." "No single person," he added, "did more to discredit the projected war with France over the XYZ incident, to make the Alien and Sedition Laws abhorrent, to arouse and munition the masses, and make the triumph of Jefferson in 1800 inevitable."

Suggested Readings: DAB. *See also* "The Letters of William Duane," PMHS, 2nd ser., 20 (1906-1907), 257-394; John C. Miller, *Crisis in Freedom: The Alien and Sedition Acts* (1951), pp. 195-202.

Richard E. Amacher
Auburn University

JACOB DUCHÉ (1738-1798)

Works: *Pennsylvania: A Poem* (1756); *The Life and Death of the Righteous* (1763); *Human Life a Pilgrimage* (1771); *Observations on a Variety of Subjects* (1774); *The American Vine* (1775); *The Duty of Standing Fast* (1775); *Copy of a Letter...to Gen. Washington* (1777); *Discourses on Various Subjects* (1779).

Biography: Jacob Duché was born in Philadelphia, Pa., on Jan. 31, 1738, of a well-established and prosperous family. He graduated with the first class of the College of Philadelphia (later the Univ. of Pa.) in 1757 and then attended Cambridge for one year. Returning to America, he taught at the college and served as assistant rector of two combined Anglican parishes (Christ Church and St. Peter's) in Philadelphia. After marrying the sister of his friend and former classmate Francis Hopkinson (q.v.) in 1759, Duché returned to Eng. for ordination and then took up the rectorship of his church. A popular preacher and member of Philadelphia society, Duché was elected chaplain of the Continental Congress. His views on the relationship between America and Eng. changed, however, and in 1777 he wrote a letter to George Washington (q.v.) calling on Congress to end the rebellion and recall the Declaration of Independence. When the letter was made public, Duché was denounced as a traitor and forced to abandon Philadelphia and exile himself to Eng. Only in 1792 was he allowed, after direct appeals to Washington and others, to return to his homeland. Physically crippled and emotionally exhausted by his experience, Duché died in his native Philadelphia on Jan. 3, 1798.

Critical Appraisal: Jacob Duché was a gentlemanly writer of verse and essays who ended up on the losing side of a war; there is no evidence, however, that his involvement in politics distracted him from higher literary achievement. He simply did not conceive of himself as a dedicated writer.

Duché's occasionally reprinted poem *Pennsylvania* (1756) is thoroughly competent, especially for an eighteen-year-old college student. It sings praises of the natural beauty of his native state, expresses admiration and gratitude for British efforts in the French and Indian War, and looks for a future of cultural achievement in the colonies that would reflect well on—*not* against—the mother country.

His published sermons are eloquent and artful, evidence of his skills as a preacher. *Discourses on Various Subjects* (1779), published in London during his exile, collects several sermons delivered in Philadelphia during his tenure at Christ Church. They are, as befits an eighteenth-century Anglican gentleman, more moral than theological, a fact to which he drew attention in the preface.

Not surprisingly, Duché's most comfortable and successful literary form is the epistolary essay; and his best-known work is a collection of them: *Observations on a Variety of Subjects, Literary, Moral, and Religious* (1774), later republished (and better known) as *Caspipina's Letters*. The essays are purportedly the occasional letters of one Tamoc Caspipina to his friends, mostly Englishmen. (The pieces appeared as letters signed with that name in *The Pennsylvania Packet* beginning in the spring of 1772.) The pseudonym is thus uncoded: The Assistant Minister of Christ Church and Saint Peter's in Philadelphia in North America.

The observations lack the insight and seriousness of later commentators— Michel Guillaŭme Jean Crèvecoeur (q.v.) is a notable example—who worked in a similar form but with greater imagination. Duché failed to capture distinctive customs, speech, or beliefs as later writers in the same vein did. It was, of course, not his intention to do so; he wrote at a higher level of generalization, looking for moral messages and aiming at self-consciously lofty expression. He was aware, though, of the promise of America that many of his contemporaries and friends celebrated in verse and prose. In Letter VII, for example, he observed:

> My attachment to America, I am apt to think, in a great measure proceeds from the prospect of its growing greatness, to which every day seems more or less to contribute. In Europe, the several arts and sciences are almost arrived at their meridian of perfection; at least, new discoveries are less frequent now than heretofore.—Architecture, gardening, agriculture, mechanics, are at a stand.

Written in the style of the London coffeehouse, this comment nonetheless indicates Duché's sense of the future of his native land.

Duché's status as a minor writer of belles-lettres derives mostly from his lack of an informing vision and centralizing theme. His native land, which provided that vision and theme for others, did not excite Duché, in part because of his social and political loyalties, but in part also because he saw America through British eyes and wrote of it in a British voice.

Suggested Readings: CCMC; DAB; Sprague (V, 180-185); T$_2$. *See also* Ellis P. Oberholtzer, *The Literary History of Phildelphia* (1906).

William D. Andrews
Philadelphia College of Textiles and Science

JOSEPH DUDLEY (1647-1720)

Works: *An Almanack of the Coelestial Motions for the Year . . .1668* (1668); *The Speech of the Honourable Joseph Dudley. . .May 17, 1686* (1686); *Speech of Governor Dudley to the Council and House of Representatives. . .June 16th, 1702* (1702); *The Speech of the Honourable Joseph Dudley. . .March 19, 1702* (1702); *A Declaration Against the Penicooke and Eastern Indians* (1703); *A Declaration Against Prophaneness and Immoralities* (1704); *A Modest Enquiry into the Grounds and Occasions of a Late Pamphlet Intituled, A Memorial of the Present Deplorable State of New-England* (1707); *The Case of the Governour and Council of the Province. . .Truly Stated* (with others; 1715).

Biography: Joseph Dudley, son of Governor Thomas Dudley (q.v.), was born in Roxbury, Mass., on Sept. 22, 1647. Upon graduating from Harvard in 1665, he studied briefly with Increase Mather (q.v.) before embarking on a long and stormy career in politics. Between 1673 and 1682, Dudley served ably in the General Court, in the Court of Assistants, and as a commissioner for the United Colonies. The crucial point in his career came in 1682, when he agreed to represent Mass. in the all but hopeless negotiations to save the colonial charter. When that charter was annulled in 1684, Dudley returned home where he was publically denounced by Increase Mather as an enemy to his country. He was thereafter, as a biographer stated, "the most hated man in the colonies."

Unpopularity, however, never proved a bar to his ambition. Edward Randolph, a prime mover in the revocation of the charter, managed to get Dudley appointed by the crown to head the reorganized government. When, a short while later, Sir Edmund Andros took control of the Dominion of New Eng., Dudley continued in service, thereby rendering himself still more odious to the popular faction. Indeed, when Andros was overthrown in 1689, Dudley was conducted by a mob to jail, where he remained for nearly a year. In 1691, as a result of the efforts of friends in Eng., he secured the post of chief justice of N.Y. and served just long enough to sentence to death the popular insurrectionist Jacob Leisler. After a self-imposed exile of ten years in Eng., during which he gained important and powerful friends, he was chosen to succeed the earl of Bellomont as provincial governor of Mass. As governor from 1702 to 1715, he conducted the defense of much of New Eng. during Queen Anne's War, captured Nova Scotia for the English, feuded with the Mathers, and represented the interests of Eng. in the province. He left office a wealthy man and died in 1720.

Critical Appraisal: During his lifetime, Joseph Dudley enjoyed a modest reputation as a writer on political and philosophical subjects, largely for works that circulated in manuscript among friends. His published writings, although dignified and lucid, are unremarkable. His importance to literary history consists primarily in his relationship to Increase and Cotton Mather (q.v.).

When Lord Bellomont died, the Mathers strongly urged Dudley's appointment as successor on the grounds that he was, at least, a New Eng. man, and one whom they might perhaps control. Despite Increase Mather's conciliatory election sermon of 1701 in which he sought to soothe feelings that had been rankling since 1684, it quickly became evident that Dudley, a political realist, had no need of the Mathers's support, and he broke with them in a quarrel soon after arriving in Boston. Having spent nearly ten years as deputy governor of the Isle of Wight under the patronage of Lord John Cutts, Dudley had lost much of his provincialism and saw more clearly than ever that his interests lay with the English court against those "Turbulent Spirits," like the Mathers, "that can't endure Conformity in Church or *State*." He made it known early in his administration that he would favor not only King's Chapel, the Anglican church in Boston, but also the progressive faction of John Leverett, Thomas Brattle (q.v.), William Brattle (q.v.), and Benjamin Colman (q.v.), the party allied against the Mathers.

The conflict came to a head in 1707 when Cotton Mather published in London *A Memorial of the Present Deplorable State of New-England*, charging Dudley and his son Paul Dudley (q.v.), who served as attorney-general, with bribery, nepotism, and corruption generally. This pamphlet, apparently written in haste and certainly in anger, laid out a host of charges in the emotional style of the jeremiad but lacked the detailed evidence necessary to make it effective with Dudley's superiors. The governor's cool and closely reasoned reply, *A Modest Enquiry*, simply made the Mathers appear ridiculous. Before this rejoinder made its way to Boston, however, Cotton Mather fired off another attack, equally wild, entitled *The Deplorable State of New-England* (1708), which added further charges relating to the failed expedition against Port Royal and including a caustic reference to the imminent appointment of "a *Tory* Judge, one *Leveret*," to the presidency of Harvard, a post that Cotton Mather had long desired for himself. Smarting under this succession of defeats at Dudley's hands, the Mathers followed up these anonymous pamphlets with personal letters to the governor on Jan. 20, 1708, containing substantially the same charges as before. As Perry Miller has written, "the two letters and the three pamphlets are memorable not only because they display a few of the more opprobrious habits that had accrued to the New Eng. language, but also because indirectly they show that the frame of the jeremiad was broken by the obstinacy of Joseph Dudley."

Suggested Readings: DAB; FCNEV; Sibley-Shipton (II, 166-188); T_1; T_2. *See also* Benjamin Colman, *Ossa Josephi, or The Bones of Joseph* (1720); "Dudley Records," PMHS, 2nd ser., xiii (1899), 222-286; "The Governor and Council, 1714-1715," PMHS,

2nd ser., 15 (1901), 327-362; Everett Kimball, *The Public Life of Joseph Dudley* (1911); the Mathers's letters with Dudley's reply, CMHS, 1st ser., 3 (1794), 126-138; Rep. of pamphlets by Mather and Dudley, CMHS, 5th ser., 6 (1879), 29-131.

Albert J. von Frank
Harvard University

PAUL DUDLEY (1675-1751)

Works: *Objections to the Bank of Credit* (1714); contributions to the Royal Society of London *Philosophical Transactions*: on making maple sugar (1720); on "the Moose-Deer," the "Poyson Wood Tree," a method to discover bee hives and get their honey (1721); on Niagara Falls, a new sort of molasses from apples, and "Degenerating of Smelts" (1722); on rattlesnakes (1723); on "Indian Hot-Houses" and a "Cure by Sweating," on New Eng. plants (1724); on the natural history of whales (1725); on a stone taken from a horse (1727); and on earthquakes in New Eng. (1735); *An Essay on the Merchandize of Slaves and Souls of Men...with an Application Thereof to the Church of Rome* (1731).

Biography: Grandson of Thomas Dudley (q.v.), son of Joseph Dudley (q.v.), and himself a chief justice and attorney general of Mass., Paul Dudley is well known to New Eng. historians. His education (at Harvard and the Inns of Court) and his character, as well as family, well-suited him to his position of influence in early eighteenth-century public life. What has been called "his unbending mannerisms, aristocratic background, wealth, and religious bigotry" made it easy to attack him when feelings were high and issues serious. His and his father's politics brought the Dudleys into conflict with the Mather dynasty. His contentious side showed itself in religious matters as well; he joined Samuel Sewall (q.v.) and Cotton Mather (q.v.) in attacking religious decay and "gross immoralities" at Harvard. He composed *An Essay on the Merchandize of Slaves* and left an endowment to Harvard for an annual series of Dudleian lectures, every fourth of which was to expose the idolatry, tyranny, heresies, and the like of the "Romish Church," a condition "it has not been deemed expedient by the college authorities to honor" for many years past, according to one biographer.

Dudley's piety and politics will interest students of early American culture; his nature reportage speaks to certain modern issues and values as well: his reports on making maple sugar and finding honey trees address interests many modern back-to-nature pilgrims share; his sensitive and informed treatment of whales should speak to modern conservationists; his work on rattlesnakes and moose fit easily into the backwoods lore loved by naturalists. His reports have lasted well, but they were timely and to the point when they were written. Dudley, like his father and like John Winthrop (q.v.) and John Winthrop, Jr. (q.v.), as well as Cotton Mather and Increase Mather (q.v.) before him, sent his observations off to the Royal Society of London—the "Center of all Science" as Mark Catesby (q.v.) called it—and was elected a fellow in 1721, an honor he well deserved in light of the quality of his submissions. Some remain in manuscript; the ones published in the *Philosophical Transactions* are listed above. These nature reports make him one of the more interesting minor writers of the colonial period. He died in 1751.

Critical Appraisal: Dudley's nature reportage is characterized by good method and good sense. He observed closely, collected informed lore and experience from others, inferred wisely, and put observations in context. Beyond method and good sense, Dudley wrote engaging, sometimes anecdotal, clear, and arresting prose. His moose, for example, "does not spring, or rise in going, as an ordinary Deer, but shoves along side-ways, throwing out the Feet, much like a Horse in a rocking pace." The image is precise and economical, and the vernacular tone of "shoves along side-ways" lends the report just the right touch of color to enhance his authority in backwoods matters. As a rule, Dudley made his points by juxtaposing homely diction and imagery with the exotic subject matter of his reports, so that the *"sonus sui generis"* of an earthquake at first made him think someone was trundling a bed upstairs. He described a rattlesnake's tail by invoking the familiar lobster's tail and described a particularly big one as "big as the Calf of a Man's Leg," a chillingly apt figure given the usual height of snakebites.

Dudley's short essay on bees and ways to "line" their hives is remarkable in part for its presentation of a theme that in varied forms would reappear over and again in American frontier humor and outdoor lore: the tale of a canny Yankee showing off his science to the amazement of local boobs as he catches bees, releases them at points separate from each other, eyes their two courses, and by triangulation and trigonometry traces them to their very tree and, although none of the natives believe he has found the right tree, cuts it down and secures the honey. Circumstantial evidence has led one scholar to credit Dudley's father with authorship of this essay, but the case is moot.

Dudley's description of whales is at once informative and affecting, as when he described their mating: "she throws herself upon her Back, sinking her Tail, and so the Bull slides up, and, when the Bull is slid up, she clasps him with her fins." On family feeling: if a calf is harpooned the cow "grows so violent, that there is no managing her." Worst is his description of the horror of a killer whale attack on other whales: "They go in Company by Dozens, and set upon a young Whale, . . . and bite and thresh him, till the poor Creature . . . lolls out his Tongue, and then some . . . catch hold of his Lips, and if possible of his Tongue." This particular savagery in nature is no more vividly rendered by Melville or Capt. Scammon. What separates this moving reportage from later natural history literature is Dudley's equivalent, unsentimental interest in the matter-of-fact uses of whale oil, ambergris, and so on. So he talks of the oil that killers yield as well as of their killings and of cutting in at the base of the genitals to get ambergris from sperm whales as well as of their dalliance in the deep. In his best reportage,

Dudley simultaneously pleases and informs. As one scholar of science has said, he may well rate as one of New Eng.'s best students of natural history before the end of the colonial era.

His essay on "merchandize of slaves," on the other hand, is a cranky, legalistic, symbol-stuffed brief against popery and of such a "massy style" as almost to burlesque Cotton Mather's production, although circumstantial evidence suggests he was entirely serious in his crusades against heresy and religious folly.

Suggested Readings: BDAS; DAB; Sibley Shipton (IV, 42-54); T₁. *See also* James Britten and George S. Boulger, *A Biographical Index of Deceased British and Irish Botanists* (1931), p. 94; Brooke Hindle, *The Pursuit of Science in Revolutionary America, 1735-1789* (1956), pp. 4-5, 17, 30, 60, 94; E. Alfred Jones, *American Members of the Inns of Court* (1924), pp. xvii, xxviii, 65-67, 160; Joseph Wood Krutch, *Forgotten Peninsula* (1961), pp. 176-177; Perry Miller and Thomas Johnson, *The Puritans* (rev. 1963); Raymond Phineas Sterns, *Science in the British Colonies of America* (1970), pp. 438, 444, 455-472, passim; David S. Wilson, *In the Presence of Nature* (1978), pp. 27-29, 36-43, passim.

David Scofield Wilson
University of California, Davis

THOMAS DUDLEY (1576-1653)

Works: *Letter to the Countess of Lincoln* (w. 1631; pub. 1696).

Biography: Born in Eng. at Northampton in 1576, Thomas Dudley spent his youth in what one biographer calls "the midst of wealth, luxury, and splendor." In the midst, but not in command—Dudley was a professional aide to gentlemen. As page to Lord Compton, he poured the wine and laid the tables for gaming, in which he was probably allowed to partake. At 21 he left the Compton household and joined the war against Sp., eventually finding his way to the battlefield at Amiens. After clerking for a justice of the Court of Common Pleas, Dudley returned to a gentleman's service, this time as steward to the earl of Lincoln, a position he held well into middle age. Here he met both laymen and clerics of Puritan temperament—John Dod, John Cotton (q.v.), and the earl himself, who was hot against Charles's forced taxation. At one point the steward even had to dissuade his zealous master from rushing off to aid the Elector Palatine. Dudley became Lincoln's indispensable advisor, steering the family through financial trouble, and even finding his employer a suitable wife—the future countess to whom Dudley years later was to write a famous letter from the wastes of New Eng. His most thorough biographer tempts us to embellish the story of the match: "It is by no means certain whether it was the earl or the steward who first discovered the perfections of [the] lady."

Certainty, indeed, is scarce in our knowledge of Dudley's motivation. Emigrating with John Winthrop (q.v.) in 1630, he was chosen deputy governor at the

last moment when John Humphry decided against embarking. Almost immediately, disputes arose between the governor and his deputy; the first quarrel was
over the capital and, consequently, the governor's house. Dudley preferred Cambridge (then called Newtown) to Winthrop's choice of Boston. But the contention ran further than geographical preferences or a military man's taste for inland
security versus the vulnerable site on the sea. Cambridge and Boston "parties"
began to emerge, a division that later cut deep during the Antinomian crisis.
Things were not improved by Winthrop's accusation in 1632 that Dudley was
profiting on loans to the poor or by Dudley's public complaints about Winthrop's
leniency and personal power. For nearly two decades, the two men performed a
see-saw exchange of their offices. One senses that beneath the struggle was a
fight for the future of the colony, a contest in which Dudley seems to have
attracted more support from the well-to-do property owners of Cambridge and
those actively speculating in land.

Dudley served the colony until his death on Jul. 31, 1653, helping to blunt
new threats from home, as Eng. turned Presbyterian and tolerant. One may
postulate, with due caution, a greater hunger for personal authority than for
religious satisfaction in his original decision to sail. It is perhaps worth noting
that the man who refused in a huff to sign a document bearing the phrase
"Reverend Bishops" a few years later failed to recognize an agent sent under
cover by Archbishop Laud. But whatever the depth of Dudley's religious conviction, he was a founder who made the colony work. He left as well a legacy of
notable children—a daughter, Anne Bradstreet (q.v.), wife of Simon Bradstreet,
who became America's first poet, and a son, the future Governor Joseph Dudley
(q.v.), who rose high on the enemy list of Increase Mather (q.v.) and Cotton
Mather (q.v.). Examining Dudley's life is a caution against speaking too readily
of collective purpose in Mass. Bay and a reminder of the early appearance in
America of faction: one of the plagues from which the Puritans had hoped to
escape.

Critical Appraisal: Apart from a few verses that Cotton Mather reported
were "found after his death, in his Pocket" and papers pertinent to the early
political history of Mass., Thomas Dudley's surviving utterance is his letter to
the countess of Lincoln, written in Mar. 1631. Anne Bradstreet may have found
vocational encouragement in the fact that her father was moved to versify, but his
couplets are hardly more than a rhymed confirmation of what Thomas Hutchinson (q.v.) wrote of him, that "he was zealous, beyond measure, against all sorts
of hereticks." Dudley, perhaps thinking back on Anne Hutchinson and Roger
Williams (q.v.) and Samuel Gorton (q.v.), put it this way: "I DY'D NO
LIBERTINE."

The letter to the countess confirms the sternness. It is an anthology of early
Puritan attitudes: self-denigration, for example, that has a touch of bitterness.
"Having yet no table, nor other room to write in, than by the fire-side upon my
knee," Dudley both basks and seems embarrassed in the role of pioneer. There is
a hint of jealousy toward the forerunners at Plymouth, who landed "about the

moenth of December, by the favour of a calm winter, such as was never seene here since." There is retrospective regret over the settlers' decision "to plant dispersedly" and a shrill good riddance to those who sailed back to Eng.: "glad were wee so to bee ridd of them." But relatively free of craft, the letter is also touching in its undercurrent of nostalgia for a place of milder winters and better ale. One hears the special Dudley frankness as he upbraids those who have written "too large commendacons of the Country," a complaint that almost suggests he felt duped in having come.

Most significantly, Dudley's letter affords a glimpse of an Englishman being transformed into a colonial. There are vestiges of the obsequious tone in which Dudley had been variously practiced, a certain fluffy elegance. Mrs. Skelton of Salem, for example, "lived desired and dyed lamented." The habit of deference, built-in of course to the epistolary form, is heightened by the writer's new circumstance.

> If any taxe mee for wastinge paper with recordinge theis small matters, such may consider that little mothers bring fourth little children, small commonwealths;—matters of small moment, the reading whereof yett is not to be despised by the judicious, because small things in the beginning of naturall or politique bodyes are as remarkable as greater in bodyos, full growne.

"All our affairs," wrote Benjamin Franklin (q.v.) about a century later, "are *petit*. They have a miniature resemblance only, of the grand things of Europe." Thomas Dudley, settled in New Eng. for barely half a year, was already an American writer.

Suggested Readings: DAB; FCNEV; LHUS; T₁. *See also* Everett Emerson, ed., *Letters from New England* (1976), pp. 68-83; Thomas Hutchinson, *The History of the Colony and Province of Massachusetts Bay* (1764), ed. Lawrence Mayo (1936), pp. 13-18, 23, 156; Augustine Jones, *The Life and Work of Thomas Dudley* (1899); Cotton Mather, *Magnalia Christi Americana*, ed. Kenneth B. Murdock (1702; rep., 1978), pp. 229-234 (Mather's fuller account of Dudley's life is in PMHS, 11 [1870], 207-222); John Winthrop, *The History of New England* (1630-1649), 2 vols., ed. James Savage (1853), passim; Alexander Young, ed., *Chronicles of the First Planters of the Colony of Massachusetts Bay* (1846), pp. 303-340. For Dudley's role in the Antinomian crisis, see David Hall, ed., *The Antinomian Controversy, 1636-1638* (1968), pp. 311-348. Dudley's *Letter* was first published in Joshua Scottow (attributed ed.), *Massachusetts* (1696), pp. 7-27. It is reprinted in Edmund S. Morgan, ed., *The Founding of Massachusetts* (1964), pp. 157-173.

Andrew Delbanco
Harvard University

WILLIAM DUER (1747-1799)

Works: *Address to the Inhabitants of Alexandria and Other Sea-Ports in the United States of America, from a Proprietor of Lands on the Scioto* (1790).

Biography: Born in Eng. in 1747, William Duer came to N.Y. in 1768 to arrange for a supply of timber for his family's W. Ind. plantations. He settled in the upper Hudson Valley and attached himself to the American cause during the Revolution, serving in the N.Y. Convention and Assembly and the Continental Congress. In 1778 he left the Congress and presently became an army contractor in the Hudson Valley. In 1783 he moved to New York City and speculated on a large scale in Continental securities, serving also as secretary to the Board of Treasury of the Congress from 1785 to 1789. He used his position to float the Scioto Land Company speculation by hiding it inside the Ohio Company venture of Manasseh Cutler. His *Address to the Inhabitants* was written to protect the Scioto's plan to settle French emigrants on the Ohio River. From Sept. 1789 to Mar. 1790, Duer was assistant to the secretary of the Treasury. After leaving the Treasury, he increased his speculations to the point that, when he failed in Mar. 1792, the economy of New York City was shaken. He died in debtors' prison in 1799. Throughout his career, he devoted the utmost attention to using his public offices for his private profit.

Critical Appraisal: William Duer's one published work is a fifteen-page pamphlet printed under a pseudonym. This slim accomplishment hides his aspirations as a political analyst, aspirations of which he left some evidence. But his first printed work was a series of letters signed "Plain Truth" that were part of the tangled Deane-Lee controversy of 1778-1780, letters filled with sarcasm and pointed ridicule of the critics of Silas Deane (q.v.), the Congress's agent in Fr. and Duer's business partner. His next set of letters was very different. Appearing in New York City newspapers during the contest over the ratification of the federal Constitution, they supported *The Federalist* of James Madison (q.v.), Alexander Hamilton (q.v.), and John Jay (q.v.). Since they used the pseudonym "Publius," Duer signed himself "Philo-Publius." His essays were quiet and sensible, copying the patiently reasonable tone of the parent work. It was probably about this time that he took notes from Emmerich deVattel's *The Law of Nations* and applied them, in parallel columns, to the controversy over the Constitution, possibly as a preparation for a more important book he never wrote.

Duer's *Address to the Inhabitants* was also written in answer to a specific need. Some citizens of Alexandria, Va., had pointed out to the emigrants, correctly, the disadvantages of settling on the Ohio, especially the fact that the Indians might take umbrage. Their pertinent comments were put down by Duer with the flat assertion that the Congress had bought the land and then deeded it to "several of the most respectable individuals in America," from whom the French settlers had purchased, as if that settled the Indian question. The remaining pages presented the economic benefits of emigration and argued that, spurred by its Revolution, large-scale emigration from Fr. would soon begin and that while the French were heading for the Ohio, those who followed would help to fill the interior from the frontier to the eastern seaboard with consequent benefits to the port cities. Thus, according to Duer, Alexandrians would be well advised to follow the example of New York City and Perth Amboy, N.J., in welcoming emigrants seriously. With the exception of an unfortunate reference to the Alexandrians' accusations of Congress committing actions "below the dignity of a Jew pedlar [sic] to commit," the tone is otherwise that of a gentleman patiently setting straight mistaken assumptions by those less informed than he.

Suggested Readings: J. S. Davis, *Essays in the Earlier History of American Corporations*: I: "William Duer, Entrepreneur" (1917), pp. 111-338; R. F. Jones, "William Duer and the Business of Government in the Era of the American Revolution," WMQ, 3rd ser., 32 (1975), 393-416; R. W. G. Vail, ed., *The Voice of the Old Frontier* (1949) for the attribution of *An Address* to Duer.

Robert F. Jones
Fordham University

GEORGE DUFFIELD (1732-1790)

Works: *A Sermon Preached in the Third Presbyterian Church* (1784).

Biography: Born in Pequea, Lancaster County, Pa., on Oct. 2, 1732, George Duffield was the son of a Huguenot farmer. After graduating from the College of New Jersey (Princeton) in 1752, he returned to his birthplace to study theology with Robert Smith, a local minister. He then served for two years as a tutor at Princeton. An evangelical Presbyterian, Duffield aroused the suspicions of the traditionalists. Both his ordination as a minister in 1761 and his appointment as pastor of the Third Presbyterian Church of Philadelphia in 1772 provoked controversy. Before removing to Philadelphia, Duffield served as minister of several congregations in Cumberland County, Pa., and in 1766 he joined the Rev. Charles Beatty (q.v.) on a missionary tour to the frontier.

Duffield enthusiastically supported the American cause during the Revolution, earning the praise of John Adams (q.v.) and other patriot leaders. On several occasions, he preached to the troops, and he also served as chaplain of the Continental Congress. A manager of the Philadelphia Academy, a member of the American Philosophical Society, and a trustee of the College of New Jersey (1777-1790), he also played a part in the reorganization of the Presbyterian Church after the Revolutionary War. When he died on Feb. 2, 1790, he was still an active minister.

Critical Appraisal: George Duffield's single publication, *A Sermon Preached in the Third Presbyterian Church*, was one of the most famous pulpit orations of the Revolution and, despite a rambling construction, is still impressive in its vigor and eloquence.

Preached on the occasion of the peace with G.B., the sermon is unabashedly political. Like the Puritan leaders of seventeenth-century Mass. and the evangelical preachers of the Great Awakening, Duffield believed that America had a special mission in the world. But although earlier ministers stressed its religious role, Duffield placed an equal emphasis on politics: "Here has our God erected a banner of civil and religious liberty." According to Duffield, freedom is essential to the nurturing and expansion of true Christianity, for liberty places "religion on its own proper basis; as supported by its own evidence and the almighty care of its divine Author; without the aid of the feeble, angry arm of civil power."

Much of Duffield's sermon is indistinguishable from the writings of the secular patriots. He cataloged the grievances of the Americans, castigated the British for their corruption and tyranny, praised the French allies, and celebrated the military and political heroes of the Revolution. But his theology is integral to his message. The surprising victory of the Americans against enormous odds is evidence of the hand of God. The Lord has chosen America to be the bastion of religious liberty, political equality, social justice, and human brotherhood. The vast improvements in American society will make the U.S. the leader of world redemption: "the light of divine revelation [shall] diffuse it's beneficent rays, till the gospel of Jesus [has] accomplished it's day, from east to west, around our world."

In the writings of Duffield and other ministers of the Revolutionary generation can be seen the beginnings of that combination of evangelism, patriotism, religious toleration, and social reformism that became characteristic of the great Protestant preachers of the nineteenth century.

Suggested Readings: CCMC; DAB; Sprague (III, 186-192); P; T$_2$. *See also* Sidney E. Ahlstrom, *A Religious History of the American People* (1972), pp. 379-384; Nathan O. Hatch, *The Sacred Cause of Liberty* (1977), pp. 1-96; Alan Heimert, *Religion and the American Mind from the Great Awakening to the Revolution* (1966), pp. 410, 493-494; Edward Frank Humphrey, *Nationalism and Religion in America* (1924), pp. 96-98, 268 ff.; Perry Miller, "From the Covenant to the Revival" in *The Shaping of American Religion*, ed. James Ward Smith and A. Leland Jamison (1961), pp. 348-349; [Frank Moore], *Patriot Preachers of the American Revolution* (1860), pp. 344-368.

Douglas M. Arnold
Yale University

DANIEL DULANY, THE ELDER (1685-1753)

Works: *The Right of the Inhabitants of Maryland to the Benefits of the English Laws* (1728); A Letter. . .to the Rev. Mr. Jacob Henderson (1732).

Biography: Daniel Dulany was born in 1685 in Queen's County, Ire., of an ancient and numerous family. Educated at Queen's College, Dublin, he immigrated in 1703 to Md., where he served an apprenticeship as clerk to a prominent provincial lawyer. By 1710 he was practicing in the county courts of southern Md. His marriage to the heiress of an affluent local family brought him into the ruling squirearchy. Within ten years, he had established himself as a leading attorney and acquired further property by a second marriage (c. 1715) to Rebecca

Smith, daughter of an influential planter. Thereafter his career is the paradigm of the American success story. In 1720 Dulany moved to Annapolis, the provincial capital, where he held lesser offices and became a leader of the "country party" in the House of Delegates. In 1733 Dulany accepted appointment to three major offices from the lord proprietor, in whose service he spent the last twenty years of his life. As attorney general and judge of vice-admiralty, he became a bulwark of the "court party" and a personage of consequence, eventually a councillor. Through shrewd investment in iron works and extensive landholdings, Dulany grew wealthy, but in his last years, he laid the basis for truly immense fortunc by speculation in western lands. He died on Dec. 5, 1753.

Critical Appraisal: Daniel Dulany's thirty-one page pamphlet, *The Right of the Inhabitants*, narrowly escaped oblivion. It is preserved in a unique copy deposited in the Calvert Papers, archives of the lords Baltimore, the ruling family of proprietary Md., who recognized it as the most eloquent statement of the provincial viewpoint in their long struggle with the "country party" of their American palatinate. When the pamphlet appeared, Dulany had been a leader and principal spokesman for almost a decade in the battle against the "court party," adherents of the lords proprietors in the Md. Assembly, and his practiced hand had already drafted a series of polemics and manifestos stating the case for local rights. In his pamphlet, Dulany focused these diverse statements on an overarching issue: whether the people of Md. "are to be governed by *Laws*, which their *Mother-Country* has experimentally found, to be beneficial to Society" or whether they are to be "governed by . . . the *Caprice*, and *Arbitrary Pleasure*" of the lords Baltimore and a knot of adherents.

Dulany's argument took the form of a lawyer's brief. With relentless logic, he moved to the conclusion that the common law and supplemental statute law were parts of a single garment, the palladium of British liberty, and the security of all honest men against oppression and threats to their "Lives, Liberties, and Properties." The framework and expressions smacked of the lawyer's study, but the humane, liberal doctrine quickened the rigid prose into life. The notion of fundamental law that he announced later became a staple element in American Revolutionary thought.

Both literally and figuratively, Dulany was a man of letters. The scant handful of his personal letters that have survived show a fine epistolary style, later to become the mode of Enlightenment prose. His public writings, scattered through legislative and judicial proceedings, look backward toward the prolix meanderings of seventeenth-century style, exemplified by Roger Williams (q.v.) and Cotton Mather (q.v.). Dulany stands squarely in the literary tradition of colonial America, which offers little that is belletristic but abounds in "practical letters" such as pamphlets, sermons, personal letters, and essays. Like other educated men of his day, Dulany put his pen to public service in the heyday of the pamphlet.

Suggested Readings: DAB. *See also* Aubrey C. Land, *The Dulanys of Maryland* (1955, 1968); St. George d. Sioussat, *Economics and Politics in Maryland, 1720-1750, and the Public Services of Daniel Dulany, the Elder* (1903); idem, *The English Statutes in Maryland* (1903).

Aubrey C. Land
University of Georgia

DANIEL DULANY, THE YOUNGER (1722-1797)

Works: *Considerations on the Propriety of Imposing Taxes in the British Colonies, for the Purpose of Raising a Revenue, by Act of Parliament* (1765); *The Right to the Tonnage* (1766); *Antilon* (1773).

Biography: Daniel Dulany, surnamed "the younger" to distinguish him from his father, Daniel Dulany, the elder (q.v.), was born in Annapolis, Md., on Jun. 28, 1722. Sent to Eng. for his education, first at Eton, then in 1739 at Clare College, Cambridge, and finally in 1742 at the Inns of Court, Dulany returned to Annapolis in 1749 to practice law and to carry on his aging father's interests in land speculation, iron manufacturing, and money lending. Shortly after his return, Dulany married Rebecca Tasker, daughter of the rich and influential Councillor Benjamin Tasker. As a result of his marriage, Dulany was able to move easily among the elite of wealth and power: as councillor and chief judge of the Testamentary Court after 1755 and after 1760 as secretary of the province, the most rewarding post in income and patronage open to a provincial. Dulany's pamphlet *Considerations* carried his name throughout the colonies and Eng. as a critic of British imperial policy and a spokesman for American rights. He was also known as an incomparable orator and an "oracle of the law." His support of the lord proprietor in a pamphlet, *The Right to the Tonnage*, and in the *Antilon* letters cost him some popularity. In the final crisis of empire that led to the War for American Independence, Dulany became a neutral, with each of his two sons on opposing sides. After 1776 he withdrew from public office to live two decades as a wealthy retired patriarch. He died on Mar. 17, 1797.

Critical Appraisal: In both letters and public life, Daniel Dulany proved a worthy successor to his talented father. With a superior British education that no doubt gave him immense advantages over his Md. contemporaries, he early displayed his literary skill during the Stamp Act crisis with the publication of his *Considerations*, a work that went through numerous American and English editions. In this work, Dulany demolished the British premise that Parliament could tax the colonies because they were "virtually represented" in that body. As a countermeasure, he recommended economic boycott of the mother country as the response most likely to bring repeal of the detested Stamp Act. The elegant logic and witty, aphoristic style of the *Considerations* put Dulany's writing in the mainstream of Enlightenment prose and contributed to its popular success.

In *Right to the Tonnage*, Dulany took a more conservative position, arguing that the lord proprietor possessed the legal authority to collect an unpopular duty on ships trading to Md. Wholly lacking in the bright rhetoric of his earlier pamphlet, *The Right to the Tonnage* displays Dulany's virtuosity in handling the legal syllogism, an ability that stood him in good stead as a politician and writer.

The least successful of the published writings, Dulany's *Antilon* letters (1773) were his contribution to a newspaper war with a personal and political enemy, Charles Carroll of Carrollton (q.v.), who wrote under the pseudonym "First Citizen." In these documents, Dulany once again took a conservative, law-and-order position against his revolutionary-minded opponent, but the exchanges quickly descended from the high plane of political philosophy to invective and epithet in the worst tradition of Grub Street. Although Dulany may not be a major writer of early America, he deserves recognition as a significant and sometimes even eloquent voice in the exchange of pamphlets that prepared the way for the American Revolution.

Suggested Readings: DAB; LHUS; T₂. *See also* Charles A. Barker, *Background of the Revolution in Maryland* (1940); Aubrey C. Land, *The Dulanys of Maryland* (1955, 1968); Peter S. Onuff, *Maryland and the Empire, 1773: The Antilon First Citizen Letters* (1976).

Aubrey C. Land
University of Georgia

JOSEPH DUMBLETON (fl. 1740-1750)

Works: "*Solomon's* Pursuit after *Content*" (c. 1740); "The Paper Mill" (1744); "ODE for St. PATRIC's Day" (1749); "A RHAPSODY on RUM" (1749); "The NORTHERN MIRACLE" (1750).

Biography: Joseph Dumbleton, creator of newspaper verse in Va. and S.C., is a vague and mysterious figure in colonial literary history. Although he may have been a native of Gloucestershire, few details of his life are available. Perhaps he moved to Va., where he seems to have lived until 1749. He contributed verses to the *Virginia Gazette* after 1740 and apparently was a close associate of its editor, William Parks (q.v.). His signature to a poem, "A RHAPSODY on RUM," first published in the *South Carolina Gazette* and reprinted in the *Gentleman's Magazine*, among other journals, suggests that he was residing in S.C. by 1749. He appears to have been a significant contributor of verse to the *South Carolina Gazette* from early 1749 until early 1750, when contributions bearing his characteristic signature, "J. Dumbleton," ceased. Incidentally, Dumbleton's full name is known only because he abandoned the usual "J." for "Joseph" in acknowledging one of his efforts. Despite limited biographical information, the various poems that Dumbleton produced for the Va. and S.C. papers, with epigraphs from Vergil and Ovid and allusions to Greek and Roman deities, suggest that he had a substantial educational background.

Critical Appraisal: It is impossible to determine the extent of Joseph Dumbleton's poetic output since files of the *Virginia Gazette* and the *South*

Carolina Gazette are incomplete. But at least five poems with his signature may be traced to these journals, and they reflect a striking range of subject matter and tone. Furthermore, the fact that several of these works were reprinted in newspapers and magazines throughout the colonies and even in London indicates that Dumbleton attracted the attention of editors and readers beyond his immediate locales. His earliest known poem is a serious philosophical analysis titled "*Solomon's* Pursuit after *Content*." This work, 114 lines arranged in iambic tetrameter couplets, depicts Solomon as he considers his lot in life. Things such as power, wealth, love, wine, and music, he decides, have failed to bring him "divine CONTENT." But then he realizes that in seeking to find contentment through such means he has actually been trying to mask the advent of old age. In lines that stress Dumbleton's obvious didactic purpose, the analysis closes with Solomon voicing the absurdity of his effort: "'Tis hence Content dissolves to Air, / This gives a Body to Despair; / These sacred Truths, I Solomon, / With Pains have fought, and sadly known."

Several of Dumbleton's poems are occasional. "ODE for St. PATRIC's Day" is an obvious example. In a note preceding the text, first published in the *South Carolina Gazette*, Dumbleton dedicated his remarks "to the President and Members of the Irish Society." The poem consists of eight rhyming stanzas, each containing eight iambic tetrameter lines. A noteworthy achievement, it skillfully blends pagan and Christian elements: "The Muse an Ode select prepares, / With splendid Bowls the Board is crown'd / Thine Harp awakes in solemn Airs, / O Saint! while thy great Name goes round; / As Victims on thy festal Day / Our choicest Firstlings we resign, / And for a glad Libation, pay / Our finest Wheat, and purest Wine." Another occasional piece is "The Paper Mill," which first appeared in the *Virginia Gazette* and which was prompted by the opening of a paper mill near Williamsburg by William Parks, editor of the *Gazette*. Using thirty-two iambic tetrameter couplets, the poet encouraged the citizenry of Williamsburg to supply Parks with linen rags, but he also displays a whimsical sense of humor, sometimes employing double entendres: "Nice *Delia's* Smock, which, neat and whole, / No Man durst finger for his Soul; / Turn'd to *Gazette*, now all the Town, / May take it up, or smooth it down. / Whilst *Delia* may with it dispence, / And no Affront to Innocence."

If one may judge by the number of times it was reprinted, Dumbleton's most popular work was "A RHAPSODY on RUM." First appearing in the *South Carolina Gazette*, the poem consisted of twenty-eight lines of heroic couplets. Later it was revised and expanded to fifty-three lines (one triplet appears in this version) and apparently first printed in this form in the *Virginia Gazette*. Both versions were later carried in newspapers and magazines in Philadelphia, Annapolis, Boston, Cincinnati, and London. In both versions, the tone is somber and the theme serious: excessive indulgence in rum destroys the drinker's self-respect, his initiative, and, perhaps most important, his health. These lines illustrate both the poet's intent and method: "We owe, great DRAM! the trembling Hand to thee, / The headstrong Purpose; and the feeble Knee; / The Loss of

Honour; and the Cause of Wrong; / The Brain enchanted; and the fault'ring Tongue; / Whilst Fancy flies before Thee unconfin'd, / Thou leav'st disabl'd Prudence far behind." That "A RHAPSODY on RUM" is another exercise in didacticism is more than evident.

The last poem that may be attributed to Dumbleton differs from any of his other works. It is "The NORTHERN MIRACLE," a narrative of 127 lines, primarily in iambic tetrameter couplets. In this work, one sees a broad Rabelaisian brand of humor that exceeds the more subtle humor of the earlier "The Paper Mill." The story concerns two Northumberland friars and their experiences with two peasant women. The first friar stops overnight in the house of one woman who chances to see him undress for bed and notices that he lacks appropriate underclothing, having only a coarse hair shirt under his habit. Next morning the woman, touched by the friar's apparent poverty, offers to weave him a linen shirt. But he declines, saying that he wears haircloth by choice, and he suggests that she weave an altar cloth in honor of the Virgin instead of a garment for him. She sets about the task and weaves a prodigious amount of cloth in a single day—enough "That all the Country might have clad." Seeing this woman's good fortune, an avaricious neighbor coaxes another friar to pass a night in her home, offers the next morning to weave a shirt for him, and accepts his suggestion that instead she weave an altar cloth as a charitable act. Upon the friar's departure, she prepares to weave, fully expecting great reward for her work:

"WELL, now!" she crys,
"for Cloth an Heap,
Shall make for ever Linnen cheap,
But hold!—I ween a lucky Thought
Informs me of my Morning's Draught,
Lest that should interrupt the Matter,
I'll stop and make a little Water."
So said, so done, when—slap! she feels
Herself entangl'd Neck and Heels;
Nor might she, (strictly hamper'd so)
Or fall, or rise, or stand, or go.

The woman prays to the Virgin for immediate aid, but to no avail. She remains shackled until "Night the Magic Noose unties, / And lets the crippl'd Suff'rer rise." Then

For twenty Miles the lowland Ground
Lay under Water all around. —
'Twas long before the Silence broke.
But thus, at length, 'tis said, she spoke.
"To drown the World in Times of Old
Its Flood-gates, Ocean did unfold;
But then those Gates ('twas ne'er denied)
Were vastly deep, and wond'rous wide;

But could one ever dream, a Lake
Its mighty way thro' me should take?
While Men, (ambitious of Dominion)
Have call'd the weaker Vessel, Woman;
They'll grant, (to view these Floods audacious)
The weaker Vessel's most capacious."

The poem ends with a less-than-serious moral to the effect that the church will gain from this woman's predicament.

Although certainly not a poet of major stature, Joseph Dumbleton clearly possessed literary ability, and his poems deserve a place among the more respected eighteenth-century colonial verses. His development of theme, sureness of diction, and mastery of meter and rhyme are noteworthy. To be sure, his work sometimes seems derivative of contemporary English poetry, but then the productions of few early American poets can be exempt from this charge. Drawing on a large body of interests and an apparently sound educational background, Dumbleton managed to employ a modest poetic gift to produce verses that are sometimes serious, sometimes humorous, but always worthwhile for the light they shed on the cultural development of colonial America.

Suggested Readings: Robert Bolick, "Joseph Dumbleton" in *Southern Writers—A Biographical Dictionary*, ed. Robert Bain, Joseph M. Flora, and Louis D. Rubin, Jr. (1979), p. 136; Hennig Cohen, "The Poems of Joseph Dumbleton, 1740-1750," BB, 20 (1952), 220; idem, *The South Carolina Gazette, 1732-1775* (1953), pp. 198-199, 203-204, 211-213; Richard Beale Davis, *Intellectual Life in the Colonial South, 1585-1763*, 3 vols. (1978), II, 614, 985; III, 1396-1397, 1496, 1498, 1712; Richard Beale Davis, C. Hugh Holman, and Louis D. Rubin, Jr., eds., *Southern Writing, 1585-1920* (1970), pp. 190-193; J. A. Leo Lemay, *A Calendar of American Poetry* (1972), pp. 91-92, 108, 133, 135, 136; "The Paper Mill," VMHB, 7 (1899-1900), 442-444; Kenneth Silverman, ed., *Colonial American Poetry* (1968), pp. 326-328, 448.

William H. Castles, Jr.
University of South Carolina

JEREMIAH DUMMER (1681-1739)

Works: *Tres Miscellaneae Dissertationes* (1702-03), includes *Disputatio Theologica de Christi ad Inferos Descensu* (1702), *Disputatio Philosophica Inauguralis* (1703), *Dissertatio Theologico Philologica* (1703), and *De Jure Judaeorum Sabbati* (1703); *A Discourse on the Holiness of the Sabbath-Day* (1704); Manuscript diary (1709-11); *A Letter from a Dissenter* (1710); *A Letter to a Noble Lord Concerning the Late Expedition to Canada* (1712); "The Case of the Province of Massachusetts Bay" (1715), in Abel Boyer, ed., *Political State of Great Britain*, X, 175-179; *A Defence of the New-England Charters* (w. 1715; pub. 1721); Letter to Sir Hans Sloane, in Cotton Mather, *An Account of the Method* *and Success of Inoculating the Small-Pox* (1723); *A Letter from Jer. Dummer, Esq.* (1729?); "Reasons for Exempting the Fishermen of N.E. from Paying the Sixpenny Duty" (w. 1731-32; pub. in *Essex Gazette*, Sept. 13-20, 1768); "Plaistow," *Gentleman's Magazine*, 3 (1733), 490-91, 546. *A Letter to a Friend in the Country* (1712), sometimes attributed to Dummer, is probably not his work.

Biography: Born in Boston, Mass., early in 1681, Jeremiah (or Jeremy) Dummer was the son of Jeremiah and Ann (or Hannah) Atwater Dummer. Jeremiah Sr. was by trade a silversmith and engraver, and seemingly an occasional painter of portraits. A first cousin of Samuel Sewall (q.v.), the elder Dummer was a prominent Boston citizen and public servant. Thus his brilliant son Jeremiah had the opportunity and the means to prepare himself for a leading role in Mass. society. Having studied at Ezekiel Cheever's (q.v.) Latin school and at Harvard College, where he graduated in 1699, Dummer decided to continue his education in Holland. There he studied at Leyden and at Utrecht, receiving the Ph.D. in 1703. Dummer's return to Boston the following year should have been profoundly rewarding; instead, it was profoundly disappointing. His European credentials were perhaps envied and certainly distrusted. Edward Taylor (q.v.), for example, termed Dummer's thesis on the Jewish sabbath "atheistical poison." Though he preached in a number of churches and published a sermon, Dummer was blocked in his attempts alternatively to obtain a pulpit or a Harvard professorship. He entered his father's business and in 1708 sailed for England, never to return to America.

In London Dummer found a stage large enough to accommodate his ambitions and talents. Having arrived armed with a commission to represent Mass.'s claim to Martha's Vineyard, Dummer rapidly expanded his commercial, political, and social contacts and confirmed his ability to defend New Eng. interests. In 1710 he was appointed colonial agent for Mass., serving in that position until 1721. Additional appointments followed, as colonial agent for Conn. (1712-30) and as temporary agent for N.H. (1717-20). Not without some spiritual agonies, which he faithfully recorded in a diary, Dummer turned his back on a religious and scholarly vocation and achieved success as an agent, businessman, lawyer, and man-about-town. Samuel Sewall, who had once advised his young kinsman to be modest about his European degrees if he hoped to teach at Harvard, was by 1716 defending Dummer against charges that he consorted with London prostitutes.

Dummer's undoubted abilities and wide circle of friends among London's elite enabled him to perform many valuable services for his native land. He was probably the most effective colonial agent prior to Benjamin Franklin (q.v.). Thoroughly familiar with the personalities and politics of England, Dummer followed transatlantic developments through a voluminous correspondence with New Eng. leaders such as Cotton Mather (q.v.). He published eloquent explanations and defenses of New Eng.'s interests and lobbied against British policies and royal appointments that he deemed unwise. In addition, he helped assure the survival of the Collegiate School at Saybrook by gaining the patronage of Elihu Yale, and he gathered an important gift of nearly 1,000 books for the college library. These books had incalculable effects upon the intellectual development of Yale graduates of the period, notably Jonathan Edwards (q.v.) and Samuel Johnson (q.v.). Dummer never married, and when the last of his appointments was lost he retired to the life of a country gentleman. Dummer died at Plaistow, Eng., on May 19, 1739.

Critical Appraisal: Jeremiah Dummer possessed an active and acute intellect that led him into trouble in his earliest writings. While in Holland he published several Latin theses and disputations, including *De Jure Judaeorum Sabbati*, his doctoral dissertation. There he speculated too freely on the nature of the sabbath for conservative New Eng. tastes, opening himself to the charge that he had acquired Arminian tendencies. By emphasizing the role of man's will in the process of regeneration and downplaying the primacy of God's sovereign will, this heretical doctrine was believed to pervert the sabbath. In essence Dummer was accused of being too liberal and insufficiently Calvinist. Thus when Dummer was invited to preach at Boston's First Church on Oct. 29, 1704, he chose the sabbath as his subject, and when he published the resulting sermon he obtained the formidable assistance of Increase Mather (q.v.). Mather contributed a six-page preface arguing that the young scholar had written his dissertation "for Arguments sake" and thus "not so cautiously" as a minister should write. *A Discourse on the Holiness of the Sabbath-Day* was clearly intended to prove both Dummer's orthodoxy and the true relevance of his academic accomplishments. He learnedly argued that the sabbath's observance is ruled not by a "moral precept" (i.e. one discoverable by man), but by a "positive precept" that "cannot be known without the *Assistance of Revelation*." Dummer ably defended himself in his single published sermon, but this did not gain him a call to the ministry.

Dummer's later works were published in London, but his important writings were quickly reprinted in Boston. In these pamphlets, we see Dummer defending American interests as a colonial agent. *A Letter to a Noble Lord*, for example, answered recriminations attendant upon the defeat of Sir Hovenden Walker's 1711 expedition against the French in Quebec. The English leaders of this expedition claimed that New Eng. had not adequately supported them. Dummer answered by enumerating colonial contributions and by defending Boston's merchants against accusations that they continued to trade with the French. But his most telling argument was a vivid portrayal of the threat to New Eng.'s very survival posed by the French and Indians, thus showing that the colonists had a compelling reason to support the English attack. By explaining the colonies' basic interests to those who might be ignorant of them, Dummer shrewdly hoped to suggest that any violation of those interests—such as less than wholehearted support of the Walker expedition—would be unimaginable: "I have often heard it said, *That Men may lie, but Interest will not*."

Of far greater significance, however, were Dummer's efforts to defeat English proposals to recall the colonial charters and reorganize the colonies by fiat. To meet this threat, Dummer wrote *A Defence of the New-England Charters* in 1715; when a recall was again proposed in 1721, he published his argument. In *A*

Defence Dummer returned to the concept of self-interest, but his problem was more complex than in *A Letter*. Charter governments, he claimed, *"will grow great and formidable"*; non-charter governments might decline because they could be despotic. Thus retaining the charters was in the colonial interest, but more to the point retention was in Eng.'s interest, as the strength of the homeland arose from that of her colonies: "It were no difficult Task to prove that *London* has risen out of the Plantations, and not out of *England*." In a conflict of English power versus colonial rights, however, the colonists' case rested upon more than pragmatic considerations. The settlers had gained possession of their land from the Indians and earned its fruits through their own exertions: "For to speak the Truth, those Parts were but *bare Creation* to the first Planters, and their Labour *like the Beginning of the World*." This claim gave Dummer's argument moral force. But if the colonists were new men making a new world, they were also Englishmen, claiming "the Privilege of *Magna Charta*." Thus Dummer buttressed the moral claim of the colonists to their charters with a legal claim. As Englishmen they had a right to the protection of English law, under which they could assert that their charter rights were of "a higher nature" than that of the privileges granted by the crown's "mere grace and favor" to English corporations. The crucial distinction was that English corporations "were granted upon improvements already made," while Englishmen in the New World received charters as a reward "for services to be performed." These "services" were being performed; the colonies thrived and Eng. grew more powerful as a result. Since the value of the charters was created not by the crown's issuance of them but by the exertions of the holders of the charters, the colonists' own "improvements" of the New World had confirmed their moral *and* legal right to retain the charters. Lacking evidence that the charter governments had forfeited their rights by "misbehaviour," the king could not arbitrarily rescind the charters and take for himself control of lands that would have been valueless but for the issuance of the charters in the first place. By successfully settling and improving the New World, the colonists had earned the right to control the destiny of that world within the terms of their charters.

Dummer's analysis of charter rights withstood the challenges of time. *A Defense* was republished in 1745 and again in 1765; John Adams (q.v.) and other makers of the American Revolution valued it highly. But ironically, while Dummer spent his life serving his native land, his last published work was a poem celebrating the pastoral beauties of Plaistow. He clearly preferred the English way of life to that of America. Yet throughout his life Dummer identified himself as an American; in his work, in his sympathies, and in his sense of himself he retained a strong connection to the land that had disappointed his own youthful hopes. Writing his will, he suggested that the motto *"Nulla retro via"*—no way back—might be worthy of "a good deal of reflection" for "all such New England gentlemen who shall be in London at the time of my decease." Certainly he had given some thought to the complexities of the American identity, and his life and writings may interest those who will continue to examine that problem.

Suggested Readings: DAB; Sibley-Shipton (IV, 454-468); T₁. *See also* Sheldon
S. Cohen, "The Diary of Jeremiah Dummer," WMQ, 24 (1967), 397-422; Anne Stokely
Pratt, "The Books Sent from England by Jeremiah Dummer to Yale College," in *Papers
in Honor of Andrew Keogh* (1938), pp. 7-44; Charles L. Sanford, "The Days of Jeremy
Dummer, Colonial Agent" (Ph.D. diss., Harvard Univ., 1952); Calhoun Winton, "Jeremiah
Dummer: The 'First American'?", WMQ, 26 (1969), 105-108.

Douglas R. Wilmes
The Pennsylvania State University

SAMUEL DUNBAR (1704-1783)

Works: *True Faith* (1748); *Brotherly Love* (1749); *Man, Like Grass* (1749);
Righteousness by the Law (1751); *The Duty of Ministers to Preach* (1753); *The
Duty of Ministers to Testify* (1754); *The Presence of God* (1760); *The Ministers
of Christ* (1763); *The Duty of Christ's Ministers* (1775).

Biography: Born in Boston, Mass., on Oct. 2, 1704, Samuel Dunbar was
the only son of John and Margaret [Holmes] Dunbar. After the elder Dunbar's
death in 1708, Cotton Mather (q.v.), in spite of his own rather formidable family
and community commitments, became Samuel's unofficial patron, enrolling him
in the Boston Latin School in 1711 and, although Dunbar lacked Mather's
academic genius, partially supporting him through the completion of an undergraduate degree at Harvard College in 1723. After teaching school for a year in
Boston, Dunbar returned to Harvard with financial aid granted by various benefactors of the college and completed an M.A. in Jul. 1726. In 1727 he accepted a
post as pastor of the First Church of Stoughton, Mass., where he was ordained
on Nov. 15 of the same year and where he spent the next fifty-six years of his
life. He married three times—in 1729, 1747, and 1751—to Hannah Danforth,
Experience (Fisher) Woodward, and Mary Pierce—and although most of his
children died young, his son Elijah became an influential minister. Dunbar died
in Stoughton on Jun. 15, 1783, at the age of 79.

Among Dunbar's admirers was Jason Haven (q.v.) who, in his eulogy to
Dunbar, said that Dunbar "knew the great design of preaching too well; and
pursued it with too much fidelity, to give into the practice...of entertaining
people with the subtilities of metaphysicks....He used great plainness of speech.
A more courageous and faithful reprover of vice, both in public, and private,
perhaps hath never been known among us....He was, on proper occasions, a
Son of Thunder."

Critical Appraisal: Until the Great Awakening of 1734, Samuel Dunbar
and Jonathan Edwards (q.v.) shared more than the same printer. They initially
shared the tenets of a fairly orthodox brand of Calvinism based upon the immen-
sity of original sin, the necessity for infused religious awakening, and the ultimate salvation of the elect. But although Edwards eventually departed from

religious concepts such as the belief in the existence of a covenantal relationship between a man and his God, Dunbar upheld them in their most literal sense throughout his long career.

Dunbar, like Cotton Mather and Mather's maternal grandfather John Cotton (q.v.), staunchly supported the Congregationalist doctrine that individual adherence to ecclesiastical law within the confines of Christianity but outside the confines of a church was unjustifiable in the eyes of God. Inasmuch as he believed there was one, and only one, redeeming way to worship God, he preached outspokenly against Jewish dogma, Catholic grace, Antinomian morality, Arminian ecumenical salvation, and Deistic rationalism. In general, he preached against any organization that upheld free will and ignored or downplayed the concepts of original sin and the doctrine of the elect.

Although he was well known for his cogent, exhortative sermons, Dunbar supported Charles Chauncy's (q.v.) disapproval of the revivalist approach of the New Light proponents of the Great Awakening. Dunbar's basic dislike for the revivalists, whose manner of preaching—it should be noted—very much resembled his own, stemmed from a belief that only diligent, well-prepared men should approach the pulpit to preach. In *The Duty of Christ's Ministers*, for example, Dunbar asserted that well-studied ministers are the best servants of God and that ministers should not "indulge themselves in extempore [*sic*] preaching...nor should they turn their people off with their own sermons."

Dunbar reportedly wrote more than 8,000 sermons during his long and active lifetime, but only 9 were published. According to the custom of the time, he often addressed or mentioned contemporary events such as the British victory over the French at Louisborg, Wolfe's victory over Montcalm at Montreal, and the Boston fires of 1711 and 1760. As such, his sermons are of considerable historical and cultural value for the information they shed on the role of the ministry in shaping the politics and the course of eighteenth-century America.

As Dunbar grew older, he became increasingly more severe in his view of the human condition. In his later works, he characteristically equated mankind with visceral objects such as "dung" "dross," and "rags." In *Righteousness by the Law*, for instance, Dunbar stated that humans are "no better than filthy rags, nor more valuable than dross and dun," and in *The Duty of Ministers to Preach*, he asserted that "our own moral virtue...has no real value in it, is no better than rags, and will not cover the shame of our nakedness."

In his extant sermons, many of which were expanded for printing, Dunbar usually introduced his subject in a short passage, encapsulated it in one or two sentences, and posed two rhetorical propositions that, when discussed at length, supported his initial summary. He often addressed his sermons to specific groups such as the young or the old, and in *The Presence of God*, an election sermon, he explicitly admonished Governor Thomas Pownall and the House of Representatives to consider the duties of their offices and how they might best be used to serve God. Actively involved in the politics of his day, Dunbar willingly served on numerous church and community committees, zealously defended G.B. during the French and Indian War, and later became an ardent supporter of the Revolutionary cause. According to one tradition, he is even said to have read the Declaration of Independence from his pulpit.

Suggested Readings: CCNE; Sibley-Shipton (VII, 166-174). *See also* Richard Frothingham, *Life and Times of Joseph Warren* (1865), p. 342; Edwin Gaustad, *The Great Awakening in New England* (1957), p. 114; Jason Haven, *A Sermon Preached at Stoughton* (1783), pp. 16-17; Daniel Huntoon, *History of the Town of Canton* (1893), p. 178, passim.

Bryan R. Brown
University of Houston

WILLIAM DUNLAP (1766-1839)

Works: *Diary of William Dunlap* (w. 1786-1834; pub. 1930); *Darby's Return* (1789); *The Father; or American Shandy-ism* (1789); *The Archers* (1796); *Tell Truth and Shame the Devil* (1797); *André* (1798); *False Shams and Thirty Years* (w. 1799, 1828; pub. 1940); *Pizarro in Peru* (1800); *The Virgin of the Sun* (1800); *The Wild-Goose Chase* (1800); *Abaellino, the Great Bandit* (1802); *Ribbemont* (1803); *The Voice of Nature* (1803); *The Wife of Two Husbands* (1804); *The Dramatic Works of William Dunlap* (1806-1816); *Fountainville Abbey* (1807); *Leicester* (1807); *The Man of Fortitude; Or, The Knight's Adventure* (1807); *Fraternal Discord* (1809); *The Italian Father* (1810); *The Yankee Chronology* (1812); *Memoirs of the Life of George Frederick Cooke* (1813); *A Record, Literary and Political, of Five Months in the Year 1813* (1813); *The Good Neighbor* (1814); *The Life of the Most Noble Arthur, Marquis and Earl of Wellington* (with Francis L. Clarke; 1814); *Lovers Vows* (1814); *A Narrative of the Events Which Followed Bonaparte's Campaign in Russia to the Period of His Dethronement* (1814); *Peter the Great* (1814); *Life of Charles Brockden Brown* (1815); *The Glory of Columbia; Her Yeomanry* (1817); *A Trip to Niagara* (1830); *Address to the Students of the National Academy of Design* (1831); *A History of the American Theatre* (1832); *History of the Rise and Progress of the Arts of Design in the United States* (1834); *Thirty Years Ago; Or, The Memoirs of a Water Drinker* (1836); *A History of New York, for Schools* (1837); *History of the New Netherlands, Province of New York, and State of New York, to the Adoption of the Federal Constitution* (1839-1840).

Biography: William Dunlap was born on Feb. 11, 1766, in Perth Amboy, N.J., the only child of an Irish merchant and retired army officer. As a youth, Dunlap read extensively, learned to play the flute and to draw, and witnessed military theatrical productions in British-occupied N.Y. For three years in Eng. ostensibly studying painting under Benjamin West, Dunlap became deeply attached to the theater, and aside from brief periods in his father's business and as assistant paymaster of the N.Y. militia, he spent his career advancing the arts in

America. His career was marked with various achievements, and among other things, he managed theaters, painted portraits, exhibited large historical canvases, and helped found the National Academy of Design, where he served as vice-president and lectured on historical painting. In addition, he published a journal, and he encouraged writers such as Elihu Hubbard Smith (q.v.), Charles Brockden Brown (q.v.), Washington Irving, James Fenimore Cooper, and his brother-in-law Timothy Dwight (q.v.). Dunlap died on Sept. 28, 1839, in Perth Amboy.

Critical Appraisal: A prolific and diverse writer, William Dunlap wrote, adapted, or translated about fifty plays, compiled historics of the theater and visual arts in America and the state of N.Y., published biographies of Charles Brockden Brown and British actor George Frederick Cooke, contributed to periodicals, and wrote poems and even a novel, *Thirty Years Ago*, which sums up his lifelong condemnation of drunkenness.

"To combine rather than to invent is the lot of modern dramatists," Dunlap contended in the preface to his collected plays. Consequently, the labels "original," "adaptation," and "translation" blur when applied to his work. His original plays, for example, are often derivative, and his adaptations and translations freely alter their sources. Dunlap applied similar principles when revising his own plays. *The Glory of Columbia*, for instance, is constructed around material from *André*. Since he wrote most of his plays while managing a theatrical company, the combinations were often dictated by the whims of audiences, competition among actors, and the need to turn a profit.

Convinced that "the stage is a vehicle" of "moral instruction," Dunlap often allowed unrestrained sentimentality to dominate both comedy and tragedy. Even *The Father*, one of his better comedies, opens with bright, witty dialog, moves to a hilarious scene mispairing three couples in a dark room, and then dissolves into a saccharine resolution. A series of supposed but nonexistent murders robs *Ribbemont* of its tragic impact by substituting instead a pious admonition against excessive pride. In writing tragedy, Dunlap slowed dramatic development by forcing significant action offstage. Even the real murder in *Ribbemont* occurs behind the boards. In comedy his experiments with lavish sets, music, and elaborate action sequences, such as the battle in *The Glory of Columbia*, sometimes deliver patriotic spectacles rather than fully realized dramas.

But the flaws in Dunlap's dramatic vision do not always prevail. His best play, *André*, extracts a compelling historical tragedy from the Benedict Arnold (q.v.) conspiracy. Emotional action and philosophical themes turn lack of movement into an integral part of the tragedy. More important, the major antagonists, André and the General (George Washington), are motivated by values higher than mere sentimentality. The general may shed a tear when Honoria pleads for her lover's life, but he orders the execution nonetheless. Dunlap's last play, *A Trip to Niagara*, parades an effective farce in front of a panorama of American landscapes, where an Englishman's bias against America is overturned by Cooper's Leatherstocking and by another Englishman's impersonation of other national critics. The dialog is clever, the situations well-conceived, and the resolution palatable.

Dunlap's histories and biographies are repositories of historical documents, many unavailable elsewhere. His *History of the Theatre* records the rosters of important acting companies each year between 1752 and 1830, and his *History of the Arts* reprints scores of letters from Dunlap's acquaintances as well as published discussions of artists. The biographical sections of the *Life of Brown* frame samples of the novelist's work. Interest in such books stems, however, from their subjects rather than their original treatment of those subjects. As biography, the *Life of Cooke* is more engaging than the *Life of Brown*, simply because the actor led a more fascinating life. In fact, Dunlap often treated history as collected biography. The *History of the Arts* is a series of biographical sketches of artists who practiced in America before 1830. The *History of the Theatre* follows a similar pattern by filling in the personal background of each new actor who enters the narrative. Unfortunately, Dunlap's concern with character and morality sometimes forces critical comment to the background.

Dunlap's nonfiction also draws heavily on the author's memory. For more than forty years, he was professionally involved with the N.Y. theater, and as a painter, he met the leading artists of his day. Brown had been a close friend, and Dunlap escorted Cooke on the actor's American tour in 1810 and 1811. Dunlap's intimacy with his subjects affects the histories in two important ways. Some of the books are disproportionately autobiographical. The period during which Dunlap managed the N.Y. company plays an inflated role in the *History of the Theatre*, and his own sketch in the *History of the Arts* is a few pages longer than the sketch of Benjamin West, the book's hero. But Dunlap's contact with artists and his practitioner's eye produce critical insights that are still valuable. His proposal for a state-supported theater suggests modern methods for subsidizing the arts, and his judgment about paintings often agrees with modern criticism.

Spreading his talents over too many fields may have restricted Dunlap's accomplishment in each of those fields. Aside from *André*, none of his works achieves greatness. Still, working at the center of the nation's first generation of artists, Dunlap produced a body of work matched by few of his contemporaries. His career and his understanding of art's place in the new nation illustrate both the problems and the promise of his age.

Suggested Readings: DAB; LHUS. *See also* William P. Campbell, Introduction, *History of . . . the Arts of Design in the United States* (1965), I, vii-xxxii; Robert H. Canary, *William Dunlap* (1970); Oral Sumner Coad, *William Dunlap* (1917).

Kennedy Williams, Jr.
Bentley College

DAVID DUNSTER (1645-c. 1696)

Works: "Gospelmanna" (autograph manuscript written in 1683 and housed in the Rare Books collection of The Pennsylvania State University Library).

Selections from "Gospelmanna" are printed by Harrison T. Meserole in "New Voices," an essay in *Discoveries and Considerations*, ed. Calvin Israel (1976), pp. 24-45.

Biography: Virtually all that is known about the life and works of the colonial poet and sometime reprobate, David Dunster, is given us by Harrison T. Meserole, who edited and interpreted selections from Dunster's poetry in an essay written for a *festschrift* honoring Harold Jantz. Born in Mass. on May 16, 1645, David Dunster was the oldest child of Henry Dunster (q.v.), the controversial first president of Harvard College. Had the elder Dunster, known for his abilities as an instructor of youth, lived long enough, he no doubt would have been disappointed with his son; in 1662 the records of the General Court of Massachusetts Bay indicate that Henry Dunster was convicted of fathering the illegitimate offspring of a local maidservant by the name of Jane Bowen, whose punishment it was to be "severely whipt." As punishment for his part in the crime, Dunster was required to pay a substantial fine of 70 pounds to be used to defer court fees and to pay for the expenses of the child.

Although the title page of Dunster's "Gospelmanna" describes the author as a "sometime student of Harvard College in New England," no records exist to verify the truth of such a statement. Nor have any records been discovered to validate that Dunster ever received the M.A. degree with which he also credits himself on the title page of his manuscript. It is known, however, that shortly after his troubles with the General Court, Dunster left for England, possibly at the insistence of his embarrassed mother. Whether or not Dunster later returned to New Eng. is uncertain, and even his subsequent activities in Europe are unclear. After serving for a time as Prebendary of Kilpeacon in Limerick, Dunster disappears from public view. He died in England sometime around 1696. The exact date and circumstances of his death are unknown.

Critical Appraisal: David Dunster's reputation as a seventeenth-century American poet rests on his only surviving work, a 150-page manuscript titled "Gospelmanna," described on the title page as "Written by the Author in the Year. 1683," at about the time when Dunster was forced to leave Mass. for Eng. Subtitled "conveniant Food for them of riper age, who by reason of use have their senses exercised to discerne both good & evill," the manuscript consists of a rather pedestrian dialog between a "Catechumen" and a "Catechist" on the various theological ramifications of the sacrament of the Eucharist and a series of highly acclaimed devotional poems on a variety of religious topics and themes. It is primarily on this latter group of poems, consisting for the most part of "Meditations, Prayrs, . . . Hymnes, Psalmes, & Anthemnes," that Dunster's excellence as a colonial poet remains to be determined.

Among these poems is an elaborate and highly imaginative "Accrostick" on the phrase "None but Christ," a "metaphrase" of the *Song of Songs*, a poem on "On Advent," a series of poems on "Christ" and the "Church," and two poems on Christ's nativity which Professor Meserole has determined "are the earliest we have record of in American literature, . . . their composition antedating by some years Richard Steere's [q.v.] 'Upon the Cælestial Embassy Perform'd by Angels.' " In addition, a long poem on the martyrdom of St. Stephen is, according to Meserole, "the only one on that subject extant from the era," and in its form (two heroic couplets followed by an alexandrine), "unique . . . in early American verse."

Like many seventeenth-century American poets, Dunster suffered from occasional lapses into triteness of phrasing and poorly rhymed and metered lines. Nonetheless, as Professor Meserole has indicated, despite these flaws, "there rings through the best of Dunster's work the clear sound of a true poetic voice," and his willingness to experiment in "a variety of forms, from the simple quatrain in iambic or trochaic foot, in varying tetrameter and trimeter lines, to an elaborate four-part acrostic," as well as the "sheer amount of his work," makes Dunster a poet ranking "well up the scale in the canon of early American literature" and worthy of comparison with such poets as Anne Bradstreet (q.v.), Edward Taylor (q.v.), Michael Wigglesworth (q.v.), Samuel Sewall (q.v.), Richard Steere, John Saffin (q.v.), and Cotton Mather (q.v.).

Suggested Readings: Jeremiah Chaplin, *Life of Henry Dunster* (1872); Harrison T. Meserole, "New Voices" in *Discoveries and Considerations: Essays on Early American Literature & Aesthetics Presented to Harold Jantz*, ed. Calvin Israel (1976), pp. 24-45; Samuel Eliot Morison, *Builders of the Bay Colony* (1930), pp. 183-216.

James A. Levernier
University of Arkansas at Little Rock

HENRY DUNSTER (1609-1659)

Works: *The Psalms Hymns and Spiritual Songs of the Old and New Testament, Faithfully Translated into English Metre*, 3rd ed. (1651).

Biography: Henry Dunster, baptized Nov. 26, 1609, was born in the parish of Bury, Lancashire, Eng. The son of a moderately prosperous farmer, he was sent to Magdalen College, Cambridge, where he received a B.A. in 1630/31 and an M.A. in 1634. In the summer of 1640, after a brief term as curate of Bury, he sailed for Mass. Within weeks of his arrival, he was asked to assume the presidency of Harvard College, a school first envisioned only four years before and still struggling to be born. Dunster supervised the building and fitting out of the Old College, instituted the curriculum of 1642, taught all the classes, managed the shaky finances of the school, secured the charter of 1650, and won for Harvard the recognition of the English universities. An accomplished scholar and linguist, Dunster served as president for fourteen years, resigning in 1654 under attack for his conscientious opposition to infant baptism. A short while later, having been convicted in a Cambridge court of interfering in the ordinance of baptism and no longer allowed to teach or preach in Mass., he removed to the more tolerant environment of Scituate, in Plymouth Colony, where he died on Feb. 27, 1659. As his will directed, he was buried in Cambridge near Harvard.

Critical Appraisal: As Harvard's first president, Henry Dunster transformed a plot of ground and a single unfinished building into an internationally recognized college where literature and the sciences as well as theology were taught. In designing the college and its curriculum, keeping to a scale the colony could support, he drew not only on his memories of Cambridge but also on the educational theories of Petrus Ramus, as is shown by the report of the college contained in *New Englands First Fruits* (1643). As at Cambridge in Eng., Harvard students were given a generally Classical education in subjects such as logic, ethics, geometry, and languages. Apart from the tutors' instruction in divinity, much of the students' religious training came through their study of Greek and the "oriental" languages—Hebrew, Chaldee (Aramaic), and Syriac— which were Dunster's favorite subjects. The course of study that he instituted, relying heavily on declamation, recitation, and the copying out of scarce texts read aloud, remained in place for the rest of the century. Dunster is also to be remembered for his missionary work with the Indians and his contention that they should be taught in their own language.

Ill-paid and overworked but never complaining, Dunster was too preoccupied with his duties to write and publish very much on his own. The only volume with which his name is associated is the revised 3rd edition of the work informally known as the *Bay Psalm Book*. The first two editions, 1640 and 1647, were compiled under the direction of John Cotton (q.v.), who, in his preface, sought to excuse the roughness of the literally translated verses by saying that "Gods Altars need not our polishings." But others, including especially Thomas Shepard (q.v.) of Dunster's church in Cambridge, thought that "a little more of art was to be employed," as Cotton Mather (q.v.) later said, and the task of improvement fell to Dunster. The precise division of labor between Dunster and his assistant, a Harvard tutor named Richard Lyon (q.v.), is uncertain, although it would seem that Dunster was primarily responsible for the translations, Lyon for the versifying. Their edition was a marked improvement, and it remained popular on both sides of the Atlantic for nearly a century. Of Dunster's other writings several letters, an "autobiographical memorandum," and a will survive, together with an interesting "Confession of Faith and Christian Experience" submitted by Dunster at the time of his joining with Shepard's church in 1640.

His last years as president of Harvard were clouded by the doctrinal dispute over infant baptism, which was the immediate cause of his removal, but there were other problems as well. His plan to lengthen the course of study from three to four years encountered serious resistance, though it was finally adopted. A plea to the General Court for money to repair the buildings was answered by a demand for a full accounting of the college's finances. Meanwhile, Dunster was sued by his stepson, and the protracted litigation that followed was a source of annoyance and embarrassment to the magistrates. The strain of these events shows in Dunster's letter of resignation and in the almost punitive terms under which his resignation was accepted.

In the end, as Josiah Quincy wrote in his history of Harvard, the hardworking and devoted Dunster met with "the common fate of the literary man of this country at that day,—thankless labor, unrequited service, arrearages unpaid, posthumous applause, a doggrel dirge, and a Latin epitaph."

Suggested Readings: CCNE; DAB; DARB; DNB; FCNEV; Sprague (I, 125-126); T_1. *See also* Jeremiah Chaplin, *Life of Henry Dunster* (1872); "The Dunster Papers," CMHS, 4th ser., 2 (1854), 190-198; Robert W. Lovett, ed., "Documents from the Harvard University Archives, 1638-1750," PCSM, 49 (1975); G. Andrews Moriarity, Jr., "Genealogical Research in England: Dunster," NEHGR, 80 (1926), 86-95; Samuel Eliot Morison, *Builders of the Bay Colony* (1930), pp. 183-216; idem, *The Founding of Harvard College* (1935); idem, *Harvard College in the Seventeenth Century* (1936), passim; "President Dunster's Quadrennium Memoir, 1654," PCSM, *Collections*, 31 (1935), 279-289.

Albert J. von Frank
Harvard University

JOHN DUNTON (1659-1732)

Works: *A Friendly Dialogue Between Two London-Apprentices* (1681); *A Detection of the Court & State of England* (1696); *Athenae Redivivae* (1704); *The Life and Errors of John Dunton* (1705); *The Pulpit-Fool* (1707); *The Phoenix* (1707-1708); *Athenian News: Or, Dunton's Oracle* (1710); *Neck or Nothing* (1719); *An Essay on Death-Bed Charity* (1728). Dunton has more than 450 titles attributed to him.

Biography: Born into a family of English clergymen on May 4, 1659, John Dunton displayed little interest in that profession and therefore was apprenticed to Thomas Parkhurst, a leading London bookseller, in 1674. In 1681, having served his apprenticeship, he set up as a printer, publisher, and bookseller in London. Marriage to Iris Annesley brought to him not only useful connections within the city but also a capable manager for his shop, and his success over the next few years in great part reflected his wife's stabilizing efforts. However, the political problems associated with the succession of James II in 1685, along with the decreased interest in Protestant religious literature in a city dominated by a Roman Catholic king, encouraged Dunton to transport his books to Boston, Mass., where he hoped to sell his excess stock and to collect a debt owed to him in the colonies. From Jan. through Jun. of 1686, he resided first in Boston and then in Salem, selling his books to the Americans and enjoying—as he always did—a new scene and new people. Returning to London later in the summer, he spent much of the next two years avoiding his creditors.

The invasion of William of Orange marked the beginning of Dunton's most prosperous years; from 1688 through 1697, he published and printed widely and was a respected member of his profession associated with the Protestant and with the Whiggish cause. The death of his wife in 1697, increased competition from a rapidly expanding printing and publishing trade, and his own—now unchecked— tendency to speculate on risky ventures, all undermined his business; and from 1699 until his death in 1732, he rarely enjoyed more than momentary financial stability. Throughout the reign of Queen Anne, Dunton printed and sold a wide variety of literature, including periodicals, political and religious tracts, and pornography; but his constant search for instant success exhausted his credit and infuriated his friends. Imprisoned on several occasions for debts, he spent his last decades a figure of mirth and scorn in a London he once had thought to entertain and instruct through his pen and his press.

Critical Appraisal: John Dunton is best remembered for his candid and intricate examination of the London printing and publishing establishment in his *Life and Errors*, published in 1705. In that remarkable work, he examined not only his own career but also that of the more prominent men who dominated the exploding London industry of pamphlet and newspaper publication. Despite Dunton's known reputation for invective and prefabrication, his study remains the best introduction to the turbulent world of writers and printers activated by the party politics of the reign of Queen Anne. Dunton's constant adherence to the Protestant cause and to the Hanoverian succession—although earning him a medal from George I—did not distinguish him significantly from others in the period who did the same with more constancy and even greater success.

Overall, Dunton's greatest contribution, other than the *Life and Errors*, was his ability to ascertain and to cater to the demand for pamphlets and periodicals that would entertain and instruct the increasingly literate reading public. To his credit are numerous periodical firsts, and without doubt his inventiveness and his ability to turn an idea into a reality amazed and awed the age. His downfall, however, came from his inability to adhere to a single purpose; he jumped from one good idea to another, and since more of his ideas failed than succeeded, he destroyed his slender fortune and, ultimately, his credibility.

John Dunton's experiences in Boston and Salem resulted in the publication of one sermon by Increase Mather (q.v.) and in the later publication of Dunton's own *Letters Written from New England, A.D. 1686*. Here, as in his *Life and Errors*, Dunton wrote of his experiences and his friends in the New World, but in the end, neither did he play a great part in the printing development of New Eng., nor did New Eng. greatly influence his own subsequent development in London.

Suggested Readings: DNB; FCNEV; T₁. *See also* John Dunton, *The Life and Errors of John Dunton* (Rep., 1974); W. R. and V. B. McLeod, *Graphical Directory of English Newspapers and Periodicals, 1702-1714* (1981); Stephen Parks, *John Dunton and the English Book Trade* (1976); W. H. Whitmore, ed., *Letters Written from New England, A.D. 1686* (1867).

W. R. McLeod
West Virginia University

THEODORE DWIGHT (1764-1846)

Works: *The Anarchiad* (1786-1787); *The Echo* (1791-1805); *An Oration Spoken Before the Society of Cincinnati* (1792); *An Oration Spoken Before "The Connecticut Society"* (1794); *An Oration Spoken at Hartford* (1798); *The Political Greenhouse* (1799).

Biography: Theodore Dwight was born in 1764 in North Hampton, Mass. His father was a merchant and landowner; his mother was a daughter of Jonathan Edwards (q.v.). After his father's death, Dwight was reared on a farm by his mother but was injured and obliged therefore to leave farming. He studied law with his uncle Pierpont Edwards in New Haven. Admitted to the bar in 1787, Dwight began his practice in New Haven. In 1791 he left Haddam for Hartford, where he practiced until 1815. Dwight married Abigail Alsop, sister of Richard Alsop (q.v.), the poet, in 1792. His brother was Timothy Dwight (q.v.). Together with Alsop, Timothy Dwight, Joel Barlow (q.v.), Lemuel Hopkins (q.v.), and David Humphreys (q.v.), Theodore Dwight labored in a group of Federalists variously known as the Hartford or Connecticut Wits. In 1806-1807 he served as a member of Congress, completing the term of John Cotton Smith, who had resigned. In 1815 he moved to Albany, N.Y., where he founded a newspaper, *The Daily Advertiser*. Two years later, he moved to New York City and founded the *New York Advertiser*, which he managed until 1836, when he returned to Hartford to spend his remaining years. He died in N.Y. in 1846 while on a visit there.

Critical Appraisal: As a member of the Hartford Wits, Theodore Dwight was associated with John Trumbull (q.v.), Joel Barlow, Lemuel Hopkins, Timothy Dwight, David Humphreys, and Richard Alsop—mostly intellectual children of Yale. His work and training as a lawyer doubtless contributed to his reputation as an able writer and eloquent speaker. A 1794 antislavery speech before the Connecticut Society for the Promotion of Freedom anticipates both in language and force the arguments of a later century. Although he wrote much verse, it is of "antiquarian rather than literary interest." His addresses on the occasion of the New Year published in the *Connecticut Courant* and *Connecticut Mirror* are clever imitations of Hudibras.

Suggested Readings: DAB; LHUS; T_1. *See also* Benjamin Franklin, V, "Theodore Dwight and the Problem of Attributing Authorship," CHSB, 43 (1978), 120-128; idem, "Theodore Dwight's 'African Distress': An Early Anti-Slavery Poem," YULG, 54 (1979), 26-36; Leon Howard, *The Connecticut Wits* (1943); Vernon L. Parrington, *The Connecticut Wits* (1926).

L. Lynn Hogue
Georgia State University at Atanta

TIMOTHY DWIGHT (1752-1817)

Works: *America: Or, A Poem on the Settlement of the British Colonies* (w. c. 1771; pub. 1780); *A Dissertation on the History, Eloquence, and Poetry of the*

Bible (1772); *Proposals for Printing by Subscription* (1775); *A Valedictory Address* (1776); *A Sermon, Preached at Stamford. . .Upon the General Thanksgiving* (1778); *A Sermon, Preached at Northampton. . .Occasioned by the Capture of the British Army* (1781); *The Conquest of Canaan* (1785); *The Triumph of Infidelity: A Poem* (1788); *Virtuous Rulers* (1791); *Greenfield Hill: A Poem in Seven Parts* (w. 1787, pub. 1794); *Columbia: An Ode* (c. 1794); *A Discourse on the Genuineness and Authenticity of The New Testament* (1794); *The True Means of Establishing Public Happiness* (1795); *A Discourse Preached at the Funeral of the Rev. Elizar Goodrich* (1797); *The Duty of Americans* (1798); *The Nature, and Danger, of Infidel Philosophy* (1798); *A Discourse . . .on the Character of George Washington, Esq.* (1800); *A Discourse on Some Events of the Last Century* (1801); *A Sermon on the Death of Mr. Ebenezer Grant Marsh* (1804); *The Folly, Guilt, and Mischiefs of Duelling* (1805); *A Sermon Preached at the Opening of the Theological Institution in Andover* (1808); *A Discourse, Occasioned by the Death of . . .Jonathan Trumbull* (1809); *The Charitable Blessed: A Sermon* (1810); *A Statistical Account of the City of New-Haven* (1811); *The Dignity and Excellence of the Gospel. . .Delivered at the Ordination of the Rev. Nathaniel W. Taylor* (1812); *A Discourse. . .on the National Fast* (1812); *A Sermon Delivered in Boston* (1813); *Remarks on the Review of Inchiquin's Letters* (1815); *An Address, to the Emigrants from Connecticut* (with others; 1817); *Theology, Explained and Defended*, 5 vols. (1818-1819); *Travels in New-England and New York*, 4 vols. (1821-1822).

Biography: Timothy Dwight, a grandson of Jonathan Edwards (q.v.), was born in Northampton, Mass., on May 4, 1752. At the age of 13, he entered Yale College where, after receiving an M.A., he and John Trumbull (q.v.), as tutors, popularized the study of modern English poetry. Their combined interest in belles-lettres and American independence attracted the attention of Joel Barlow (q.v.) and David Humphreys (q.v.), among others, and thus the loosely associated group later known as the Connecticut Wits began to form.

In Mar. 1771 Dwight, still a tutor, married Mary Woolsey; in Jun. he was licensed to preach, and by Aug. he had joined the Continental Army at Peekskill, N.Y., as a chaplain. After the death of his father in 1778, he returned to Northampton, where for five years he labored to support his mother's family and his own. Toward the end of this period, he was twice elected to the state House of Representatives and might have had an illustrious career in politics had he not determined to follow his religious vocation. When in 1783 he was called to minister to the congregation at Greenfield, a parish of Fairfield, Conn., he accepted. There he lived quietly but productively for twelve years, publishing his three major poetical works, *The Conquest of Canaan, The Triumph of Infidelity*, and *Greenfield Hill*, while augmenting his already considerable reputation as an eloquent minister of the New Divinity.

Dwight's accession to the presidency of Yale following the death of Ezra Stiles (q.v.) in 1795 made him the most prominent Congregational minister in New Eng. and an influence so powerful in the affairs of Conn. that his enemies were soon calling him "old Pope Dwight." His typically energetic battle against

Deism or "Infidel Philosophy" among the undergraduates was so successful that he shortly found himself in the midst of a spreading collegiate revival, a part of the second Great Awakening. His term as president and professor of divinity ended with his death on Jan. 11, 1817.

Critical Appraisal: Although only a small fraction of Timothy Dwight's voluminous writings may be said to possess lasting literary merit, he remains, nevertheless, an important and interesting figure. A formidable defender of the values of New Eng.'s past, he was finally more than a mere reactionary: he was a writer who, for all his intolerance of human diversity, had a vision of the just and happy society that belongs genuinely to the conservative mythology of America.

Dwight's earliest visions of an ideal society, conveyed in works such as the *Valedictory Address, America*, the *Sermon Preached at Northampton*, and the brief, frequently anthologized patriotic song "Columbia," owe much to the old Puritan conviction that New Eng. might claim a special, providential destiny. Each of these works predicts for America as a "Land of light and joy" not only an imminent flowering of science, philosophy, and the arts, but a future of cultural and political imperialism that, in completing the historic movement of civilization westward, would culminate in Asia, where history began. In Dwight's millennial view, the American Revolution was truly a matter of world significance. That it was foreshadowed in the Bible and sanctioned by God was the burden of the sermon at Stamford, and *The Conquest of Canaan*, begun before the Revolution, implicitly connects the American cause with the Israelites' fight for the promised land.

Granted these expectations, it was inevitable that after the war, Dwight's attention would increasingly focus on America's failure to realize its special destiny and that he would wave in response the tattered ensign of the Puritan theocracy. His career as a writer was thereafter largely shaped by tensions between utopian visions of society and perceived threats, mainly of a liberal or radical character. *The Triumph of Infidelity*, for example, attacked the Boston minister Charles Chauncy (q.v.) for promulgating the Universalist heresy that all men might be saved. In the poem, Dwight imagined Satan gloating over this novel departure from Calvin's creed and supposed that "Each villain started at the pleasing sound" of Chauncy's sermons, "Hugg'd his old crimes," and "new mischiefs 'gan devise." Here as elsewhere Dwight was less interested in the villain's soul than in the smooth operation of the social machinery, for the sake of which religious orthodoxy must be preserved. "The same principles," he said in a note, "which support or destroy christianity, alike support or destroy political order and government."

The Triumph of Infidelity is an intemperate, angry poem in which one cannot always distinguish Dwight's voice from that of Satan, the ostensible narrator. In *Greenfield Hill*, however, Dwight achieved a more effective balance between the utopian background and the unpleasant foreground detail. Working in the tradition of John Denham's *Cooper's Hill* and Alexander Pope's *Windsor Forest*, Dwight surveyed the landscape around his own home in Conn.:

How bless'd the sight of such a numerous train
In such small limits, tasting every good
Of competence, of independence, peace,
And liberty unmingled; every house
On its own ground, and every happy swain
Beholding no superior, but the laws,
And such as virtue, knowledge, useful life,
And zeal, exerted for the public good,
Have rais'd above the throng.   (I, 42-50)

Although Dwight was wholly committed to this picture of village felicity (a sort of Federalist agrarian image), he never entirely forgot that he was speaking as a Calvinist of "this sin-ruin'd, this apostate world." The immediate past of the poem is the nightmare vision of Fairfield burning in the Revolution; behind that, on the same ground, one confronts the dying Pequots. Dwight portrayed a society given now to the arts of peace, a society without landlords in which property is evenly divided but that nevertheless—and unhappily—supports a system of slavery. The schools are not very rigorous, Dwight declared, but they promote good morals and all New Eng. towns have them. Fashion and luxury are temptations to be resisted, but Conn. is fortunate in being neither poor nor wealthy; in fact, guided by their own common sense and the uncommon wisdom of their ministers, the people shun all extremes in favor of a golden mean of "Competence" and so occupy an actual rather than an imaginary or theoretical utopia. Not all the wealth of decadent Europe can match the "pure pleasures of parochial life."

Dwight's verse is always hortatory or illustrative. In the introduction to *Greenfield Hill*, he spoke of poetry as "an instrument of making useful impressions" and defended it with the same arguments that Cotton Mather (q.v.) had used nearly a century before. Like most writers of his age, he believed that poetry was essentially a rhetorical rather than a strictly truth-telling medium, and he could therefore indulge, as he often did, in excessive praise or downright bombast without much damage to his otherwise scrupulous conscience: "Poetical representations are usually esteemed flattering," he said in another of his interesting footnotes; "possibly this is as little so, as most of them." Dwight's attitude toward his own poetry became increasingly casual and distant after the hostile reception accorded *The Conquest of Canaan*, and by the end of the century, almost all of his writing was in prose. Perhaps only in *The Conquest*, an epic retelling of the story of Joshua, had he consciously sought fame as a poet.

Two of Dwight's prose works retained an audience well into the nineteenth century, long after his poetry had fallen into neglect. His *Theology Explained and Defended*, which went through thirteen editions in less than forty years, is a course of 173 sermons originally delivered at Yale in his capacity, after 1805, as professor of divinity. It set out a theological system derived from Jonathan Edwards but—the irony has often been observed—skewed in the direction of

Charles Chauncy's liberalism. Dwight held that although man is depraved, he might be made good through the incentives of wordly success and comfort. Influenced in religion as in poetry and politics by the Scottish common sense philosphers, Dwight easily substituted ethics for piety and moralism for metaphysics. The *Theology*, then, is an important link between Edwards and nineteenth-century figures such as Lyman Beecher and Nathaniel William Taylor, both of whom studied with Dwight at Yale.

The other significant prose work is, of course, the *Travels in New-England and New York*, a massive compendium of useful and entertaining facts concerning the history and present appearance of the American Northeast, set forth in a series of letters to a gentleman in Eng. The materials for this work were gathered during excursions that Dwight regularly took for his health and represent, in all, some 18,000 miles of travel and observation. The book has little form or structure but is nevertheless the most ample working out, in the midst of all the statistics, of Dwight's view of the moral state of man in a healthy climate where religion is established, land is held in fee simple, and industry is rewarded. The *Travels*, like the earlier *Remarks on the Review of Inchiquin's Letters*, is notable for its running debate with malignant British commentary on America and for its statement of a theory of frontier settlement that anticipates by seventy years that of Frederick Jackson Turner.

Suggested Readings: CCNE; DAB; Dexter (III, 321-333); LHUS; Sprague (II, 152-165); T_2. *See also* Stephen E. Berk, *Calvinism Versus Democracy: Timothy Dwight and the Origins of American Evangelical Orthodoxy* (1974); Charles E. Cuningham, *Timothy Dwight* (1942); Leon Howard, *The Connecticut Wits* (1943); Vernon L. Parrington, *The Connecticut Wits* (1926); Kenneth Silverman, *Timothy Dwight* (1969); *The Major Poems of Timothy Dwight* (1969) includes facsimile reproductions of *America* and the *Dissertation on . . . the Bible* in addition to Dwight's three major poems. The *Travels* has been edited (1969) by Barbara Miller Solomon.

Albert J. von Frank
Harvard University

E

JOHN EASTON (c. 1624-1705)

Works: *A Relacion of the Indyan Warre* (1675).

Biography: One of the early governors of R.I., John Easton was a member of one of the first Quaker families to settle that state. His family came to America from Wales in 1634 and to R.I. in 1638. They were part of the group, led by William Coddington, that seceded from Portsmouth and founded Newport in 1639. According to tradition, John Easton sailed with his father, Nicholas, and brother, Peter, from Pocasset in an exploratory trip that resulted in their building the first house in Newport. Easton was in his early teens at the time; he saw in its virginal state a place that was to become perhaps the most famous summer resort in the country.

Easton began a career of public service in 1653 as attorney general for Portsmouth and Newport. In 1674 he became deputy governor of R.I., a position he held throughout King Philip's War. He served as governor of R.I. from 1690 to 1695.

Twice married, Easton was the father of five children. Aside from his account of the beginnings of King Philip's War, Easton is notable mainly as a man who roused the wrath of Roger Williams (q.v.). Easton had evidently charged that the purchase of Qunnunnagut Island was made possible by taking advantage of Indian drunkenness, a charge Williams vigorously rebutted in a pamphlet notable for its contemptuous view of Indians. This exchange occurred around 1658 and was occasioned by the continuing conflict between Portsmouth and Newport. Williams was especially angry that Easton had sent his charges to authorities in Mass.

Easton died on Dec. 12, 1705, and was laid to rest in "Coddington's burial-place" in Newport.

Critical Appraisal: John Easton's *Relacion* is one of the more remarkable documents to come out of King Philip's War. Written in 1675, in the early stages of the conflict, the *Relacion* undertakes to contradict the view of the war put forth by authorities in Plymouth and Boston. The *Relacion* charges that the official Puritan view of the murder of Sassamon, a murder for which the Puritans blamed the enmity of King Philip, was not credible; that the Mass. and Plymouth authorities were so eager to prosecute the war that they rejected all peaceful solutions, including one proposed by Easton; that the Indians had many just grievances; that Indian leaders, notably Weetamoo, were driven reluctantly into the conflict by mistreatment at colonial hands; that the English had conducted themselves more barbarously than the Indians; and that the authorities had begun the war "without proclamation."

The *Relacion* undoubtedly reflects both Easton's Quaker pacifism and R.I.'s unhappiness with the way in which the Mass. and Plymouth authorities were stirring up powerful Indian tribes—such as the Narragansetts, whose territory bordered R.I.—without first consulting R.I. Nevertheless, when all due allowance is made for the political background, the *Relacion*'s arguments still accord well with the known facts. All available evidence quite clearly suggests that Puritan authorities were indeed eager to prosecute the war and that they did indeed prosecute it in a manner that lent little credit to their claim of superior civilization. At the very least, the *Relacion* presents a good counterbalance to the views of Puritan historians like Increase Mather (q.v.) and William Hubbard (q.v.): although a Quaker and R.I. point of view, it is as close to the Indian point of view as is available. The *Relacion* is semiliterate; its grammar and spelling are dismaying. But its views deserve serious consideration from all serious students of the era.

Suggested Readings: DAB. *See also* Samuel Greene Arnold, *History of the State of Rhode Island*, vol. I (1959); Howard Chapin, *Our Rhode Island Ancestors* (n.d.); Welcome Greene, *The Providence Plantations* (1886), p. 402. The Easton pamphlet is referred to in most modern histories of King Philip's War.

Robert K. Diebold
Husson College

WILLIAM EDDIS (1738-1825)

Works: *Letters from America* (1792).

Biography: William Eddis was born on Feb. 6, 1738, at Northleach in the Cotswold hills of Eng. At age 26 he married and moved to London, where he supported his family on the salary of a petty clerk and consorted with the younger actors and writers of the metropolis. In 1769 Eddis came to Md. as a protégé of Governor Robert Eden, who gave him the post of Surveyor and Searcher of his Majesty's Customs in the port of Annapolis at 60 pounds a year plus fees. Sponsored by the governor, Eddis mingled with the social elite, who found his manners ingratiating and his avidity for the theatre, race track, and club life equal to their own. He wrote unremarkable bits of verse and prose for the *Maryland Gazette* and, as secretary, kept the minutes of the exclusive Homony Club. But his important writing, a series of charming letters to friends back home, took fifteen years to find its way into print. Early in the War for Independence, Eddis wound up his Md. affairs and returned to Eng., where he received a pension of 180 pounds for his loyalty to the crown during the American crisis. Eddis lived in obscurity until his death on Dec. 14, 1825, a few weeks before his 88th birthday.

Critical Appraisal: Occasional essays and verse, which William Eddis published in the *Maryland Gazette*, have the defects of the worst eighteenth-century style, trivial matter and stilted manner, in a word unmemorable. By contrast, his personal letters home, fresh and charming, reveal the keen observer and the born storyteller. They cover the full period of his stay in Md., 1769 to 1777. In 1792 Eddis selected forty-two and published them under the title, *Letters from America*, for some 800 subscribers. Obviously intended to picture the Md. scene for his friends back home, the letters read like short informal essays, spiced with wit and sallies. In turn Eddis described and passed judgment on slavery and indentured servitude (Letter VI), sketched economic arrangements with special attention to the novel land system (Letter X), gave an account of the burgeoning West Country (Letter XI), and spoke in some detail of the geography and climate (Letters III, IX). But one subject above all attracted Eddis, and he returned to it again and again—the elite—their pleasures and accomplishments, their balls, the races, the theatre, their fortunes (Letters III, V, VII, VIII, IX).

In May of 1774 the tone and subject matter of the letters changed with the news of parliamentary punishment visited on Mass. Bay for the Boston Tea Party. Bewildered by the violent American reaction to these "coercive acts," Eddis thereafter confined his letters to a single subject—the unfolding revolutionary movement (Letters XVII to XL). These later letters, abounding in shrewd observations, are valuable as a commentary of a sympathetic Briton witnessing American travail that eventually led to independence. The war ended many of Eddis's provincial friendships and terminated his past. When he sailed for England in Sept. of 1777 the colonies lost an able and balanced observer and commentator.

Suggested Readings: DAB; T$_2$. *See also* Aubrey C. Land, ed., *Letters from America* (1969), pp. xi-xxxiv (biographical introduction) and 5-232 (the letters); idem, *Colonial Maryland: A History* (1981), pp. 179-326; Charles A. Barker, *Background of the Revolution in Maryland* (1940), pp. 257-377.

Aubrey C. Land
University of Georgia

JONATHAN EDWARDS (1703-1758)

Works: *God Glorified* (1731); *A Divine and Supernatural Light* (1734); *Part of a Large Letter* (pub. in William Williams, *The Duty and Interest*; 1736); *A Faithful Narrative* (1737, 1738); *A Letter to the Author of the Pamphlet* (1737);

Discourses on Various Important Subjects (1738); *The Distinguishing Marks* (1741); *The Resort and Remedy* (1741); *Sinners in the Hands of an Angry God* (1741); *Some Thoughts Concerning the Present Revival* (1742); *The Great Concern* (1743); "From Seven Rev. Pastors in the County of Hampshire," *The Christian Monthly History*, no. 5 (1744), 32-34; *The True Excellency* (1744); *Copies of the Two Letters* (1745); *An Expostulatory Letter* (1745); "Extract of a Part of the Reverend Mr. Jonathan Edwards's Letter," *The Christian Monthly History*, no. 9 (1745), 259-263; "Letter from Mr. Edwards," *The Christian Monthly History*, no. 5 (1745), 127-130; "Mr. Edwards's Letter to His Scots Correspondent," *The Christian Monthly History*, no. 8 (1745), 234-254; *The Church's Marriage* (1746); *A Treatise Concerning Religious Affections* (1746); *True Saints* (1747); *An Humble Attempt to Promote Explicit Agreement* (1748); *A Strong Rod Broken* (1748); *An Account of the Life of David Brainerd* (1749); *An Humble Inquiry into the Rules* (1749); *Christ the Great Example* (1750); Preface, *True Religion Delineated* (by Joseph Bellamy; 1750); *A Farewel-Sermon* (1751); *Misrepresentations Corrected* (1752); *True Grace Distinguished* (1753); *A Careful and Strict Enquiry into Freedom of Will* (1754); *The Great Christian Doctrine of Original Sin* (1758); *Remarks on the Essays by Lord Kames* (1758); *Personal Narrative* (pub. in Samuel Hopkins, *The Life and Character of Jonathan Edwards*; 1765, 1785); *Two Dissertations*: I. *Concerning the End for Which God Created the World*, II. *The Nature of True Virtue* (1765); *A History of the Work of Redemption* (1774); Jonathan Edwards, Jr., ed., *Sermons on the Following Subjects* (1780); *Practical Sermons Never Before Published* (1788); John Erskine, ed., *Miscellaneous Observations on Important Theological Subjects* (1793); *Remarks on Important Theological Controversies* (1796); *Select Sermons of President Edwards* (1799); E. Williams and E. Parsons, eds., *Works*, 8 vols. (1806-1811); supplement, 2 vols. (1847); *Advice to Young Converts* (1807); Samuel Austin, ed., *Works*, 8 vols. (1808-1809, 1844, 1847); "A Letter from Rev. Jonathan Edwards," CMHS, 10 (1809), 142-153; *The Theological Questions* (1822); Sereno E. Dwight, ed., *Works*, 10 vols. (1829-1830); "A Letter," *The Spirit of the Pilgrim*, 6 (1833), 545-546; E. Hickman, ed., *Works*, 2 vols. (1833, 1834); "Original Letter of President Edwards," *Bibliotheca*, 1 (1844), 579-591; "The Rev. Mr. Edwards of Stockbridge to the Rev. Mr. Erskine" (pub. in John Gillies, ed., *Historical Collections Relating to Remarkable Periods of the Success of the Gospel*, pp. 522-523; 1845); "A Letter," *The Biblical Review and Congregational Magazine*, 1 (1846), 223-224; Tryon Edwards, ed., *Charity and Its Fruits* (1852); Alexander B. Grosart, ed., *Selections from the Unpublished Writings of Jonathan Edwards* (1865); "Jonathan Edwards' Last Will, and the Inventory of his Estate," *Bibliotheca*, 33 (1876), 438-443; Egbert C. Smyth, ed., *Observations Concerning the Scripture Oeconomy of the Trinity and Covenant of Redemption by Jonathan Edwards* (1880); "A Letter," PMHS, 2nd ser., 10 (1896), 429; "Some Early Writings of Jonathan Edwards, A.D. 1714-1726," PAAS, New Series, 10 (by Egbert C. Smyth; 1896), 212-247; Franklin B. Dexter, ed., "Letters and Extracts from Letters Quoted in the Manuscripts of

Jonathan Edwards," PMHS, 2nd ser., 15 (1902), 2-16; George P. Fisher, ed., *An Unpublished Essay of Edwards on the Trinity* (1903); H. Norman Gardiner, ed., *Selected Sermons of Jonathan Edwards* (1904); Stanley T. Williams, ed., "Six Letters of Jonathan Edwards to Joseph Bellamy," NEQ, 1 (1928), 226-242; Perry Miller, ed., *Images or Shadows of Divine Things* (1948); idem, ed., "Jonathan Edwards on the Sense of the Heart," HTR, 41 (1948), 123-145; idem, ed., "Jonathan Edwards' Sociology of the Great Awakening," NEQ, 21 (1948), 50-77; Vergilius Ferm, ed., *Puritan Sage: Collected Writings of Jonathan Edwards* (1953); "Jonathan Edwards at Princeton," PULC, 15 (by Howard C. Rice, Jr.; 1954), 69-89; Harvey G. Townsend, ed., *The Philosophy of Jonathan Edwards from His Private Notebooks* (1955); George Pierce Clark, ed., "An Unpublished Letter by Jonathan Edwards," NEQ, 29 (1956), 228-233; Perry Miller and John E. Smith, general eds., *Works*, 6 vols. to present (1957-present); Leon Howard, ed., *"The Mind" of Jonathan Edwards: A Reconstructed Text* (1963); Henry Abelove, ed., "Jonathan Edwards's Letter of Invitation to George Whitefield," WMQ, 3rd ser., 29 (1972), 487-489.

Biography: Jonathan Edwards was born on Oct. 5, 1703, in East Windsor, Conn., the only son among the eleven children of Timothy and Esther [Stoddard] Edwards. A religiously sensitive youth, Edwards received his early education at home. In 1716 he entered Yale College and in 1720 was awarded the B.A. For the next two years, he studied theology in New Haven in preparation for the ministry. In 1722-1723 Edwards served for eight months as a supply at a small Presbyterian Church in New York City. In the latter year, he also received an M.A. from Yale. In 1724 Edwards returned to Yale, where he held the position of tutor at the college until 1726, when he was invited to become the associate minister with his grandfather Solomon Stoddard (q.v.) in Northampton, Mass. There in 1727 he was ordained into the Congregational ministry. Later the same year, he married Sarah Pierrepont of New Haven.

In 1729, after the death of Stoddard, Edwards became the sole minister at Northampton. In 1734-1735 the town experienced a religious revival under his leadership that subsequently spread throughout the Connecticut River Valley. Edwards's description of the events moved him into the public eye in both America and G.B. In the early 1740s, when the colonies were swept by the Great Awakening, Edwards became the most prominent American advocate of the cause. During the 1740s, he published a series of sermons and treatises defining evangelical religion and defending it against attacks from without and excesses from within. In 1750 he himself became a victim of the revivals. After an extended controversy, Edwards was dismissed by the congregation at Northampton for his insistence upon strict regulations governing admission to communion.

In 1751 Edwards accepted a pastorate at a frontier outpost in Stockbridge, Mass., where he ministered to a small congregation, which included Housatonic Indians. For Edwards, the 1750s were especially productive years. During this period, he worked on various theological and philosophical projects. In 1757 he was invited to become the president of the College of New Jersey, a post he accepted with some reluctance. After less than three months of service, he died at Princeton on Mar. 22, 1758, a victim of a smallpox inoculation. He left behind numerous unfinished projects and a vast body of manuscript writings.

Critical Appraisal: Jonathan Edwards is probably America's foremost theologian-philosopher. During his lifetime, he emerged as the leading colonial spokesman for the evangelical party and the architect of its defense of the revivals. In the nineteenth century, he exercised theological authority through his voluminous writings, which were printed and reprinted in multiple editions cited even by those who differed with him. In the twentieth century, Edwards attracts attention from diverse groups, including evangelicals who share a common religious perspective, conservatives who reject the assumptions of nineteenth-century liberalism, intellectuals who find his system of thought attractive for its own sake, and historians who point to him as a pivotal figure in the development of American culture.

Edwards's *Religious Affections, Freedom of the Will, Original Sin*, and *True Virtue* are his most significant theological and philosophical writings. Several of his more occasional pieces, however, including the *Faithful Narrative*, the *History of Redemption*, and the *Life of Brainerd*, have been among his most popular writings. It has been estimated that the American Tract Society distributed a million copies of selected writings by Edwards during the nineteenth century. Some of his publications have been translated into other languages. A modern edition of his complete works is being published by Yale University Press, making newly available his published texts with critical introductions and formerly unavailable manuscript materials, including the celebrated "Miscellanies" and many of the more than 1,300 extant sermons. This edition promises to provide fresh grounds for a reappraisal of Edwards.

Among the manifold writings of Edwards that are instructive for understanding his life and thought are several personal writings: a fragmentary diary begun in 1722; a set of youthful resolutions; an "apostrophe" on Sarah, his future wife; and a retrospective account of his religious struggles and conversion as a young man. Together with letters from various periods of his life, these documents reveal the rigorous demands Edwards made upon himself, the nature of his quest for holiness, and the measure of assurance he obtained. Edwards struggled religiously even after he experienced conversion. His inability to achieve a classic resolution of personal anxieties gave him occasion to point to the experiences of others—his wife, Sarah; the young child Phebe Bartlett; and the missionary David Brainerd (q.v.)—as examples of true religion. For Edwards, the religious ideal was symbolized by the lowly spring flower drinking in the sun's ray—a type of the Christian receiving the grace of God.

Edwards's own anxieties were writ large in his career as a minister in Northampton. Pastoral obligations shaped his life and writing. In particular, he attempted to help the people of his congregation discern the difference between true and false religion. In his account of the early revival in Northampton, he described in detail the awakening in his community. When the floodtide of the

Great Awakening spread across New Eng., he struggled in his sermons to distinguish the works of the spirit from false and imagined works of grace. He defended the divine character of the revivals against the criticism of the Arminians who adopted a liberal perspective on human nature and a negative attitude toward the awakening and also against the enthusiasts who carried the evangelical position to extremes. The treatise *Religious Affections* is his most mature pastoral statement in which he defined true religion as consisting in gracious affections and love to God, which is manifestly different from false religion. Edwards's pastoral work in Northampton ended in anguish with his dismissal. For him the business of religion required a public commitment from the saints.

Despite the occasional character of some of his writing, Edwards's works form a coherent theological and philosophical system of thought. According to Edwards, the fall of Adam into sin upset the design of God in which the ultimate end of creation was glorification of the creator. Originally, mankind, created in the image of God, was to reflect the knowledge and love of God and thereby obtain happiness. With the fall into sin, however, the supernatural principle of benevolence was withdrawn from the creature, leaving mankind under the domination of self-love. Universal depravity resulted from this original sin, because an identity exists between fallen Adam and all persons. The pure love of God was impossible for sinners, because self-love determined their every action. Therefore human beings have no capacity for assisting in their salvation.

Regeneration, according to Edwards, is a product of the sovereign grace of God, unconditioned by any quality in mankind. From eternity God elected some to be saved and others not. The excellency of Christ's death became the efficacious means of implementing the mercy of God. The infusion of God's spirit in conversion marks the beginning of the Christian life—an act that is entirely God's doing, although the Spirit uses means of grace such as prayer, the ordinances, the Bible, and preaching. The regenerate person has a new sense of the heart implanted by God, and Christ lives in the converted person. Genuine religion thus consists of love to God and holy affections. True virtue is the opposite of self-centered action. The saints engage in the business of religion as an evidence of their conversion, conforming their lives to biblical principles. The large number of conversions during the revivals persuaded Edwards that the end times were near. During the millennial reign of the saints, the world will be filled with the knowledge and love of God. All creatures will reflect God's glory, consistent with the ultimate end of creation.

Edwards was a philosophical idealist who affirmed at an early age the importance of the mind in all knowledge, including religious knowledge. He used his understanding of human psychology in defense of evangelical religion. In his view, both the intellect and the will were transformed in conversion, reversing the situation existing before regeneration. Drawing upon the ideas of John Locke and others, Edwards formulated a sensationalist perspective in which the ideas God communicates to humans become the grounds for conversion. When the person is converted, he experiences a new sensation, a supernatural infusion of

God's spirit. In conversion, the intellect perceives, and the will inclines, the individual to act. True religion consists necessarily in the movement of both of these faculties toward God and not merely one or the other. The choice of good by the spiritual person who is under the influence of grace is similar to the choice of evil by the natural or graceless person; namely, the will is always determined by the strongest apparent motive. The love of God or the greatest good is therefore possible only for those who possess a new heart. The new sense of the heart affects the whole being of an individual. Conversion is a transforming experience that also alters the way in which a person perceives the world. In fact, according to Edwards, God uses the things of the world to accomplish his objectives. Therefore both preaching and writing are means of grace that affect the lives of individuals and elicit religious experiences. Edwards's most moving sermon, *Sinners in the Hands of an Angry God*, although not fully representative of his preaching, is consistent with his aesthetic and with his attitude toward the nature and character of conversion.

The passage of years since the death of Edwards has witnessed an expanding judgment concerning his contribution to American religion, thought, and culture. In earlier centuries, he was proclaimed a significant theologian, an astute scientific observer, a rigorous philosopher, and a founder of the evangelical tradition. More recently he has been declared an innovative thinker, a literary figure of distinction, and a major contributor to the development of American democratic and cultural ideals. Most likely, the future will yield yet other dimensions to the multifaceted understanding of Edwards's place in American life and letters.

Suggested Readings: CCMC; CCNE; DAB; DARB; Dexter (I, 218-226); LHUS; Sprague (I, 329-335); T$_1$. *See also* Sacvan Bercovitch, *The American Jeremiad* (1978); Conrad Cherry, *The Theology of Jonathan Edwards: A Reappraisal* (1966); Sereno E. Dwight, *The Life of President Edwards* (1829); Douglas J. Elwood, *The Philosophical Theology of Jonathan Edwards* (1960); Terrence Erdt, *Jonathan Edwards: Art and the Sense of the Heart* (1980); Clarence H. Faust and Thomas H. Johnson, *Jonathan Edwards: Representative Selections* (1962); Philip Greven, *The Protestant Temperament* (1977); Alan Heimert, *Religion and the American Mind from the Great Awakening to the Revolution* (1966); Thomas H. Johnson, *The Printed Writings of Jonathan Edwards 1703-1758: A Bibliography* (1940); Wilson H. Kimnach, "The Literary Techniques of Jonathan Edwards" (Ph.D. diss., Univ. of Pa., 1971); David Leverenz, *The Language of Puritan Feeling* (1980); Davin Levin, ed., *Jonathan Edwards: A Profile* (1969); Mason I. Lowance, Jr., *The Language of Canaan: Metaphor and Symbol in New England* (1980); Perry Miller, *Jonathan Edwards* (1949); Thomas A. Schafer, "The Role of Jonathan Edwards in American Religious History," *Encounter*, 30 (1969), 212-222; William J. Scheick, ed., *Critical Essays on Jonathan Edwards* (1980); idem, *The Writings of Jonathan Edwards: Theme, Motif, and Style* (1975); Stephen J. Stein, "The Quest for the Spiritual Sense: The Biblical Hermeneutics of Jonathan Edwards," HTR, 70 (1977), 99-113; Patricia J. Tracy, *Jonathan Edwards, Pastor* (1979); Ola Elizabeth Winslow, *Jonathan Edwards, 1703-1758* (1940). See also the significant monographic essays preceding each text in the Yale edition of *The Works of Jonathan Edwards* (1957-present).

Stephen J. Stein
Indiana University

JONATHAN EDWARDS, JR. (1745-1801)

Works: *The Faithful Manifestation of Truth* (1783); *Brief Observations on the Doctrine of Universal Salvation* (1784); *Three Sermons on the Necessity of the Atonement* (1785); *Observations on the Language of the Muhhekaneew Indians* (1788); *The Salvation of All Men Strictly Examined* (1790); *The Injustice and Impolicy of the Slave Trade* (1791); *All Divine Truth Profitable* (1792); *Faith and Good Conscience* (1792); *The Marriage of a Wife's Sister Considered* (1792); *A Sermon Delivered at the Funeral...of Roger Sherman* (1793); *The Belief of Christianity Necessary to Political Prosperity* (1794); *A Dissertation Concerning Liberty and Necessity* (1794); *The Duty of Ministers* (1795); *The Soul's Immortality and Future Retribution* (1797); *A Farewell Sermon* (1799). Numerous essays were published in *The Theological Magazine*.

Biography: The ninth child and namesake of colonial New Eng.'s most brilliant theologian, Jonathan Edwards, Jr., was born in Northampton, Mass., on May 26, 1745. He graduated from Princeton, where his father had briefly served as president, in 1765. He spent the next year studying theology with his father's leading New Divinity disciples, Samuel Hopkins (q.v.) of Great Barrington, Mass., and Joseph Bellamy (q.v.) of Bethlehem, Conn. Licensed to preach in 1766, Edwards returned to Princeton to serve as a tutor for a year. He then accepted a call from the White Haven Church in New Haven, Conn., and was ordained in 1769.

Edwards followed the clerical role model his father and his father's New Divinity followers provided for him. He published theological treatises and essays dealing with the doctrinal and ecclesiastical problems that preoccupied the Congregational ministers of his day. He was actively engaged in reform efforts, particularly missionary work. He also instructed candidates for the ministry in his parsonage.

Edwards remained in New Haven until 1795, when a series of disputes over theological and ecclesiastical issues led to his dismissal from the White Haven Church. Within several months, he was installed in a new pastorate in Colebrook, Conn. From this small western Conn. town, he was summoned to the presidency of Union College in Schenectady, N.Y., in 1799. His death two years later on Aug. 1, 1801, recalled his father's tragic, untimely death at Princeton in 1758.

Critical Appraisal: In preparing for the ministry, Jonathan Edwards, Jr., spent countless hours studying his father's published and unpublished works, and as an ordained minister, he devoted considerable time and energy, often to the neglect of pastoral duties, in defending, explaining, and modifying his father's thought. He published two lengthy theological treatises and more than a dozen sermons; in addition, he contributed numerous essays to *The Theological Magazine*, an influential religious periodical. All of these works were published in the 1780s and 1790s, when, after a decade-long interruption caused by the American Revolution, New Eng. ministers resumed their theological "pamphlet warfare."

Edwards's contributions to these intellectual hostilities reveal a skilled polemicist, with a critical, penetrating mind, rather than a creative religious thinker.

Like other New Divinity theologians, Edwards responded in print to rationalistic and humanistic critics of the high Calvinism that his father had done so much to revitalize. In his replies to such critics, Edwards seemed to be searching for some middle ground between his father's thought and the more humanistic and democratic intellectual currents of late eighteenth-century America.

The polemical and mediating characteristics of Edwards's thought are illustrated in two of his major works, *The Salvation of All Men Strictly Examined* (1790) and *Three Sermons on the Necessity of the Atonement* (1785). In the former volume, Edwards responded to the idea that God was too benevolent to inflict eternal damnation on sinners. Advocates of universal salvation argued that punishment after death was merely temporary. God used such punishment to produce a moral reformation in sinners, all of whom would ultimately be reconciled with him. Endeavoring to refute these ideas in the *Salvation of All Men Strictly Examined*, Edwards maintained that eternal damnation was an essential part of a providential scheme of government that encouraged moral order in the world. Eternal damnation upheld a divine system of rewards and punishments, deterred sinners, and thus promoted the moral good of the world. Edwards's arguments reveal an important shift away from his father's thought—a shift influenced in part by the Revolutionary attack on absolute political authority. Where the father had portrayed God as an absolute sovereign for whom the good of the universe was subservient to divine glory, the son depicted God as a Moral Governor of the world bound to promote the good of his creatures.

Edwards's democratization of his father's God is even more evident in *Three Sermons on the Necessity of the Atonement*. Constructed with tight logic and written in the classic Puritan plain style, these sermons were delivered before the Conn. General Assembly in 1785. Christ's death demonstrated that sin will be punished, Edwards argued. Hence, the atonement upheld God's plan for moral order in the world and contributed to the general good of his creatures. Again, Edwards described God as a Moral Governor of the universe who seeks the good of his subjects. Clearly, like the work of other New Divinity ministers, Edwards's writings display elements of the humanism and rationalism of his post-Calvinist age.

In addition to being involved in his theological efforts, Edwards was involved in reform activities. He was an early supporter of the antislavery movement in New Eng. He published an important antislavery tract, *The Injustice and Impolicy of the Slave Trade and Slavery* (1791), in which he argued that slavery was a sin against "the law of nature and...the law of God." He warned Christians that they were "obligated" to free their slaves "immediately." Edwards was also committed to missionary work. Indeed, he was the individual chiefly responsible for the famous Plan of Union (1801)—a cooperative missionary effort between New Eng. Congregationalists and Mid. Atl. Presbyterians that was designed to bring Protestant Christianity to the rapidly developing western frontier.

All in all, Edwards was one of the more active Congregational ministers of his generation. The literary side of his clerical career is important primarily because Edwards's theological writings disclose significant aspects of the New Eng. Calvinist mind in transition.

Suggested Readings: CCMC; CCNE; DAB; DARB; P; Sprague (I, 653-660). *See also* Tyron Edwards, "Memoir of His Life and Character" in *The Works of Jonathan Edwards, D.D.*, 2 vols. (1842), I, ix-xl; Robert L. Ferm, *Jonathan Edwards the Younger, 1745-1801* (1976); Joseph Haroutunian, *Piety Versus Moralism: The Passing of the New England Theology* (1932).

Joseph Conforti
Rhode Island College

NATHANIEL EELLS (1677-1750)

Works: *The Ministers of God's Word* (1725); *The Ministers of the Gospel* (1729); *The Evangelical Bishop* (1734); *The Pastor's Introduction* (1739); *Religion Is the Life of God's People* (1743); *Letter Against Whitefield* (1745); *The Wise Ruler* (1748).

Biography: Nathaniel Eells was born on Nov. 26, 1677, the son of Maj. Samuel and Ann (Lenthal) Eells of Milford, Conn. Following his graduation from Harvard College in 1699, Eells served for one year as a schoolmaster at Braintree, Mass. To encourage him to remain at their church, the proprietors of Pamet voted Eells seventeen acres of land and the privilege of firewood, timber, and fencing. A committee from the Second Church of Scituate in Norwell convinced him, however, to accept the pastorship of its church, where he was ordained on Jun. 14, 1704.

A liberal, Eells helped to lead the group of churches opposed to George Whitefield (q.v.). In 1704 Eells married Hannah North, who was nine years his junior. Two of their nine children, Nathaniel and Edward, graduated from college and entered the ministry. Rev. Eells preached the ordination sermons for Nathaniel in 1734 and for Edward in 1739. Noted for the "patriarchal sway" he held over his parishioners, Eells apparently earned their respect and affection during the nearly fifty years he served at Norwell. When Eells died on Aug. 25, 1750, the parish voted money for his funeral expenses and a gravestone.

Critical Appraisal: The theological views of Nathaniel Eells, especially with regards the nature of preaching, were well in advance of their age. Although written many years before the Great Awakening, his early sermons anticipate the controversies that the Awakening was later to provoke. *Ministers of God's Word* (1725), for example, criticizes, at great length, itinerants whose manner of preaching "tickles the Ear, or . . . works upon the Fancy," an opinion Eells would repeat, in even sharper terms, as the Awakening approached. In the sermon preached at the ordination of his son Edward, Eells even attacked the notion that the itinerants had the authority to move about in their preaching. According to Eells, "Men are made overseers of the Flock they have been set over," and the "minister is...not an officer of every particular church—only that particular church which is committed to his charge."

During the Great Awakening, Eells intensified his crusade against the itinerants, whom he characterized as "wandering stars" who do nothing to illuminate the lives of the congregation, and against George Whitefield in particular, whose itinerant and emotional manner of preaching Eells condemned as "a Blemish, Reproach and Scandal to the Ministry." A leader with moderate inclinations and the courage to defend them, Nathaniel Eells held his congregation close to him and to the church by his strong concern for their well-being. For the most part, the style of his life and his sermons is perhaps best characterized by his own words: "The ministers of God's word are to preach fervently and frequently, clearly and plainly, impartially and boldly, cheerfully and willingly, carefully and skillfully."

Suggested Readings: CCNE; Sibley-Shipton (IV, 468-471). *See also* Joseph J. Ellis, *The New England Mind in Transition* (1973); Edwin Scott Gaustad, *The Great Awakening in New England* (1957); Alan Heimert, *Religion and the American Mind* (1966); Perry Miller, *The American Puritans* (1951); idem, *Jonathan Edwards* (1949); idem, *The New England Mind* (1967).

George Craig
Edinboro State College

ANDREW ELIOT (1718-1778)

Works: *The Faithful Steward* (1742); *An Inordinate Love* (1744); *A Burning and Shining Light* (1750); *An Evil and Adulterous Generation* (1753); *A Sermon Preached at the Ordination of...Joseph Roberts* (1754); *A Sermon Preached October 25, 1759* (1759); "Right Hand of Fellowship" (w. 1763; pub. 1822); *A Sermon Preached Before His Excellency Francis Bernard* (1765); "Letters from Andrew Eliot to Thomas Hollis" (w. 1766-1771; pub. 1858); *A Sermon Preached Sept. 17, 1766* (1766); Preface, *Sermons on Important Subjects. By John Huntington* (with Ebenezer Pemberton; 1767); "Remarks on the Bishop of Oxford's Sermon" (w. 1767; pub. 1814); Appendix, *A Discourse* (by Charles Chauncy on the death of Joseph Sewall; 1769); *A Discourse on Natural Religion* (1771); "The Right Hand of Fellowship" (pub. in Nathaniel Robbins, *A Sermon Preached at the Ordination of...Peter Thacher*, pp. 37-40; 1771); "The Right Hand of Fellowship" (pub. in John Hunt, *A Sermon Preached September 25, 1771*, pp. 33-36; 1772); *Christ's Promise* (1773); *A Sermon Preached at the Ordination of...Joseph Willard* (1773); *A Sermon Preached at the Ordination of Andrew Eliot* (1774); *Twenty Sermons* (1774).

Biography: Born in Boston on Dec. 21, 1718, Andrew Eliot attended South

Grammar School under the tutelage of Nathaniel Williams and John Lovell. In 1737 he received a bachelor's degree from Harvard, where he also earned an M.A. in 1740. At Harvard's commencement exercises for 1740, Master Eliot defended the proposition that absolute, arbitrary monarchy contradicts reason. A "vast assembly" heard Eliot deliver his own ordination sermon at Boston's New North Church on Apr. 14, 1742, where he and John Webb (q.v.) served as joint pastors until the latter's death in Apr. 1750. Under Eliot's exclusive charge, New North experienced a steady liberalization, which included a decrease in public confession of sin, selection of two nonchurch members to represent the congregation in meetings of the Standing Committee, inclusion of Bible reading as part of the service, substitution of Tate and Brady for the New Eng. psalm book, relaxation of the rules for baptism, and abolition of public testimony of one's conversion experience as a requirement for church membership.

An enthusiastic supporter of efforts to Christianize Indians, Eliot actively worked with the London Society for Promoting the Gospel and served as a commissioner of the Edinburgh Society for Propagating Christian Knowledge Among the Indians. His respect for Eng. began to wane when Anglicans blocked approval of the charter for the Massachusetts Society for Propagating Christian Knowledge Among the Indians of North America.

Between 1765 and 1775, Rev. Eliot gained a reputation for political moderation without willingness to compromise his faith. The appointment of a Roman Catholic bishop for Can. and efforts to install an Anglican bishop in America earned his unequivocal condemnation. When the political order that supported Congregationalism seemed threatened by parliamentary initiatives, he foreswore his opposition to revolutionary mob action and accepted the inevitability of violent measures to preserve liberty among "the people." By the time he died on Sept. 13, 1778, Eliot had committed himself to the vision of an independent America—"a quiet habitation—a land of liberty—a land of knowledge."

Critical Appraisal: One of several recurring themes in Andrew Eliot's sermons is the urgent need to renew religious commitment in the face of worldly corruption. First voicing this concern in *An Inordinate Love*, the minister of New North identified at least nine examples of how individuals can place love of the world above love for God. The fact that each of the examples existed in such profusion among his contemporaries as to constitute an "habitual Frame and Temper of the Mind" caused him to fear God's reprisal upon the entire community. In a very traditional jeremiad entitled *An Evil and Adulterous Generation*, originally preached during a public fast on Apr. 19, 1753, he praised the "men of exalted Goodness" who had founded New Eng., but he declared that most of his own generation had "degenerated from their excellent Ancestors." Indeed, like the Jews of old, "Sins were general, so that publick and national Guilt was contracted by them." Especially upset by the rudeness and ungovernableness of young people in his society, the minister urged heads of families to "endeavor to amend what is amiss at home," for he believed any successful public reformation had to begin within private homes. In the twelfth and thirteenth of his *Twenty*

Sermons, which he published near the end of his life, he continued to emphasize parental religious instruction as the key to prevention of pervasive social corruption.

Eliot, who devoted much thought to the character of worthy ministers, consistently stressed the importance of an educated clergy. While believing that truth lay in the Scriptures alone, he encouraged ministers to apply themselves diligently to "Polite literature, an acquaintance with the works of nature, and of providence, especially the knowledge of mankind" in order to prepare themselves better for "dispensing" knowledge to their charges. In *A Sermon Preached at the Ordination of. . .Joseph Willard*, he stated, "Men of weak minds, or who have not improved their powers by study and application, cannot be able to teach others," and he built a strong case for careful public examination of potential clergymen by ordained ministers, whom he viewed as "the wise and sober part of the community."

Stylistically, Eliot favored plainness, clarity, and decency in both preaching and writing. As he indicated in the preface to *Twenty Sermons*, he had always avoided "abstruse Speculations" and, as far as possible, "Subjects of Controversy," because the pulpit was not a forum for disputation. *A Sermon Preached at the Ordination of Andrew Eliot* (his son) contains the warning that ministers do not convert men to Christianity by "artful addresses" to their passions; such performances might convert people "to metaphysical jargon, to enthusiasm, to folly, to madness, but not to the truth." During *A Sermon Preached at the Ordination of. . .Joseph Roberts*, Eliot suggested that his colleagues confine themselves to "scripture language," if they desired "scripture truth," because decency dictated avoidance of low, groveling language as well as uncouth or affected pronunciation. His published works indicate that Eliot did, indeed, practice what he preached.

A Discourse on Natural Religion, preached at Harvard's annual Dudleian Lecture in 1771, indicated Eliot's unwillingness to join many of his contemporaries in unbounded celebration of the power of reason. As early as his 1754 sermon at Joseph Roberts's ordination, the minister of New North reminded his audience that reasoned truths of natural religion are important but only secondary to the revealed truths of the holy scriptures. Reiterating that position in the Dudleian Lecture, he cited John Locke's observation that our imperfect reason does not allow us to reconcile the truth of God's omnipotence and omniscience with the truth of our freedom. Praising Locke, Eliot added, "If some of our modern reasoners, who have not a tenth part of his understanding, had a little more of his humility, the world would be free from those angry disputes about fate and free-will, liberty and necessity, which puzzle the heads, but seldom mend the hearts, of those who engage in them." He left little doubt that unbridled reason, prone as it is to being "blinded by a thousand passions," would lead his generation ever further from the city on a hill envisioned by their Puritan ancestors.

Eliot clearly believed the epochal feature of modern history was the redemption of God's church from the twin tyrannies of popery and political despotism. In *A Sermon Preached October 25th, 1759*, he portrayed the unexpected British victory at Quebec as the result of Divine Providence—the latest in a series of propitious interventions that began with the English Reformation. By 1765, when he delivered *A Sermon Preached Before His Excellency Francis Bernard*, Eliot feared loss of the civil and religious privileges so painstakingly established over the course of two centuries. Delivering that election sermon during the height of the Stamp Act crisis, he asserted "all power has it's [sic] foundation in compact and mutual consent, or else it proceeds from fraud or violence." He quoted Grotius, Burlamaqui, and Montesquieu to show that rulers who ignore the constitution deserve punishment as "public disturbers and the enemies of mankind." Refusing to believe that the English government had embarked upon a willful "design" to enslave the colonists, he called upon the king and Parliament to rectify the "mistake" they had made in adopting the stamp tax. While trusting that the authorities would confirm the colonists' longstanding civil and religious liberties, he defended the right of God-fearing subjects to resist rulers who fail to promote "public happiness." By Jan. 5, 1768, he presciently told his English correspondent Thomas Hollis, "I may be mistaken, but I am persuaded the dispute between Great Britain and her Colonies will never be *amicably* settled." Although he feared revolution as a breeder of anarchy and demagoguery, Eliot harbored even greater fear of unresisted imperial designs against his community's free pursuit of religious and civil truths.

Suggested Readings: CCNE; Sibley-Shipton (X, 128-161); Sprague (I, 417-421); T_2. *See also* Bernard Bailyn, "Religion and Revolution: Three Biographical Studies," PAH, 4 (1970), 87-110; "Letters from Andrew Eliot to Thomas Hollis," CMHS, 4th ser., 4 (1858), 398-461; "Remarks on the Bishop of Oxford's Sermon Preached Before the Incorporated Society for the Propagation of the Gospel in Foreign Parts," printed in CMHS, 2nd ser., 2 (1814), 190-216.

Rick W. Sturdevant
University of California, Santa Barbara

JARED ELIOT (1685-1763)

Works: *The Two Witnesses* (1736); *Give Caesar His Due* (1738); *The Blessings Bestow'd* (1739); *God's Marvellous Kindness* (1745); *Essays on Field Husbandry in New England* (1748-1759); *Repeated Bereavements* (1748); *The Blessedness of Those Who Die in the Lord* (1757); *An Essay on the Invention* (1762).

Biography: Jared Eliot—Congregational minister, physician, and agricultural scientist—was born on Nov. 7, 1685, in Guilford, Conn. The grandson of the missionary "Apostle to the Indians" John Eliot (q.v.), Jared Eliot was the son of Joseph Eliot, a 1658 graduate of Harvard, ordained minister at Guilford, and a physician. After studying for a year at Harvard in 1699, Eliot spent several months learning medicine on Long Island with Rev. Joshua Hobart. He then continued his formal education this time at Yale College (then known as the "Collegiate School" at Saybrook). Eliot served as Guilford town schoolmaster until he was called to preach at Killingsworth, Conn., where he was ordained in 1709 and settled until his death. As an academic courtesy, Harvard awarded Eliot the M.A. at its 1709 commencement. Eliot was well loved by his Congregational Church members, even after he declared for Episcopal ordination in 1722, following New Eng.'s growing interest in the English church.

From 1730 to 1763, Eliot served as a trustee of Yale College, making many important contributions to its early development, including his influence in obtaining substantial donations to the college from the Irish Dean George Berkeley (q.v.). In addition to assuming his clerical duties and those of a trustee, Eliot became the best-known physician of his day in Conn., and between 1713 and 1746, he personally trained more than 50 medical students under the apprenticeship system of medical training.

In 1723 Eliot built "Mulberry Farm" at the edge of Killingsworth, where he carried out his many agricultural experiments, including silkworm culture. From the wide observation he gained in riding the countryside as a physician, Eliot became interested in methods of improving farming. Out of this interest, coupled with his concern for the welfare and economy of the colonies, grew his *Essays on Field Husbandry*, (1748-1759), the first important treatise on American agriculture. As a scientist, Eliot was also interested in obtaining iron ore to promote the colony's economy, and for his *Essay on the Invention*, in which he described the removal of iron from black sand, he was awarded a gold medal by the Society for the Encouragement of the Arts, Manufactures, and Commerce of London. Eliot died in Killingsworth on Apr. 22, 1763, recognized as a leader in the colony's religion, medicine, agriculture, and science.

Critical Appraisal: Between 1736 and 1757, Eliot published six sermons, all of which reveal his skill at argumentation and his wide familiarity with Scripture, the Classics, and history. In perhaps his finest sermon, *The Two Witnesses*, (1736), he established logical evidence for the articles of faith, deriding both the "enthusiasm" of emotional appeals for conviction and the atheism of the seemingly rational disbelievers. His much-praised annual sermon delivered at Hartford in 1738, *Give Caesar His Due*, led to rumors of Eliot's even becoming Conn.'s next governor. All of Eliot's published sermons adhere closely to the traditional Puritan sermon in both form and style. In fact, as a staunch Old Light, he appeals primarily to the rational side of his audience, providing logical demonstrations of doctrine as opposed to the emotional appeals of the Great Awakening evangelists then preaching throughout Conn.

Yet Eliot is primarily remembered for his *Essays on Field Husbandry*. Published in six parts between 1748 and 1759, these essays were the first agricultural treatises printed in America. In the *Essays*, Eliot noted the importance of building on and recording past advances in agriculture and urged experimentation as the only way to make further progress in the science. According to Eliot's stated purposes, the *Essays* were written to increase knowledge by giving faithful accounts of experiments and to communicate new discoveries to American farmers. Much of Eliot's knowledge was gathered either from observation during his travels as a physician or from his own experiments. Each essay is preceded by an inspirational introduction and followed by a quote from the Bible. After discussing one subject at length, Eliot broke into brief paragraphs on a variety of subjects, reporting in a personal and direct style bits of information gathered from conversation, observation, or correspondence. In the first essay, Eliot, now known as the "Father of Soil Conservation," discussed redemption of worn-out lands and reclamation of swamps. In the following essays, Eliot covered possible ways to increase food production, diversification of crops, and ordering of crops. The fifth essay reported on problems of tillage, describing the theories of the British scientist Jethro Tull on the subject and giving Eliot's modification of those theories. Specifics are here given for Eliot's famous drill plow. In the sixth and final essay, Eliot encouraged the growth of the silk-making industry, which he proposed as a promising way to develop Conn.'s trade. Out of his interest in extracting iron from black sea sand grew Eliot's *Essay on the Invention* (1762), including interesting accounts of his own and his son's experiments with iron, a resource then much in demand in the colonies.

Jared Eliot is now recognized as the first great American agricultural investigator and writer. A pioneer of the modern scientific method, Eliot collected knowledge from experiments in the field and from treatises of European agronomists, bringing both together to urge the American farmer to consider agriculture in the light of science.

Suggested Readings: CCNE; DAB; Dexter (I, 52-56); Sibley-Shipton (V, 191-204); Sprague (I, 270-272); T₁. *See also* Harry J. Carman and R. G. Tugwell, eds., *Essays upon Field Husbandry in New England* (1934); Brooke Hindle, *The Pursuit of Science in Revolutionary America, 1735-1789* (1956), pp. 33, 95, 108, 113, 195-196, 207; Walter R. Steiner, M.D., "Jared Eliot," in *Founders and Leaders of Connecticut, 1633-1783*, ed. Charles E. Perry (1934), pp. 158-161; Herbert Thomas, *Jared Eliot, Minister, Doctor, Scientist, and His Connecticut* (1967).

Linda Neal Bates
University of California, Davis

JOHN ELIOT (1604-1690)

Works: *Tears of Repentance* (with Thomas Mayhew; 1653); *A Primer or Catechism in the Massachusetts Indian Language* (in Algonquian; no known copy; 1654); *A Late and Further Manifestation of the Progress of the Gospel* (1655); *The Christian Commonwealth* (1659); *Christiane OOnoowae Sampoowaonk, A Christian Covenanting Confession* (in Algonquian; 1660); *A Further Account of the Progress of the Gospel* (1660); *Communion of Churches* (1665); *The Indian Grammar* (1666); *The Indian Primer* (in Algonquian; 1669); *A Brief*

Narration of the Progress of the Gospel (1671); *Indian Dialogues* (1671); *The Logic Primer* (in Algonquian; 1672); *The Harmony of the Gospels* (1678); *A Brief Answer* (1679); *The Dying Speeches of Several Indians* (c. 1685).

Translations of Others' Works into Algonquian: *Genesis* (no known copy; c. 1655); *The Gospel of Matthew* (no known copy; 1655); *A Few Psalms in Meter* (no known copy; 1658); *The New Testament* (1661); *The Assembly's Shorter Catechism* (no known copy; 1663); *The Holy Bible (Mamusse Wunnutupanatamwe Up-Biblum God)* (1663; rev., 1685); *The Psalms of David* (1663); *The Psalter* (1663); Richard Baxter, *Call to the Unconverted* (1664); *Godly Living* (abridgment of Lewis Bayly, *Practice of Piety*; 1665); Thomas Shepard, *Sincere Convert and Sound Believer* (1689).

Biography: John Eliot was born in Widford, Hertfordsire, Eng., where he was baptized on Aug. 5, 1604, the son of a substantial Essex landowner. After receiving the B.A. from Cambridge in 1622, he taught grammar school at Little Barrow, where Thomas Hooker (q.v.) inspired his commitment to Puritanism. The future "Apostle to the Indians" joined the Great Migration to New Eng. in 1631 and the following year began his lifelong ministry to the church at Roxbury, Mass. By 1646 he had begun preaching to the Indians of Mass. who had submitted to the Bay Colony, soon learning to preach in the Algonquian tongue, and translating several works, including the Bible, into that language.

At first, Eliot's work among the Indians prospered. He established his first mission town, Natick, Mass., in 1650, and by 1674 thirteen more, populated by about 1,100 Praying Indians. King Philip's War, however, nearly destroyed Eliot's accomplishments. At this time, the newer Praying Towns joined the Indian uprising, and the English settlers forced the Christian Indians who remained loyal to the colony to winter, under nearly impossible conditions, on islands in Boston Harbor.

During the war, Eliot did what he could to protect the loyal Indians from white men's cruelty, but his success was limited. When the war ended, the Praying Indians, their number halved, regathered in four towns, but Eliot had small success reviving the mission enterprise, and no one replaced his leadership when he died in Roxbury on May 21, 1690. John Eliot, Jr., who had been preaching to the Indians in their language and would have been his father's logical successor, had died in 1668.

Traditionally, Eliot has been portrayed as a self-sacrificing Christian, deeply concerned for the spiritual welfare of his red neighbors, but some historians see him rather as the witting agent of the English invaders of North America, primarily interested in the pacification of the natives.

Critical Appraisal: John Eliot's works include promotional literature for his missions, educational books for the Indians, inquiries into government of church and state, religious tracts for his Puritan audience, and translations into the Indian tongue. They reveal an active, inquisitive, but not profoundly original mind. Intense biblicism and fervent anticipation of Christ's reign on earth inform the corpus.

The Eliot Tracts, eleven pamphlets promoting Christian missions to New Eng.'s Indians, were published in London between 1643 and 1671. Most contain letters from Eliot about his work, and at least four can be considered his own compositions: *Tears of Repentance* (with Thomas Mayhew [q.v.], missionary on Martha's Vineyard), *A Late and Further Manifestation, A Further Account*, and *A Brief Narration*. Together, the Eliot Tracts recount the story of the establishment of Praying Towns and the founding of Indian Churches. Occasional in nature, they are replete with detail but lacking in overviews. For instance, although Eliot insisted that the Indians adopt a European life-style, nowhere did he discuss the broad ramifications of relations between redman and white.

Eliot composed the *Indian Grammar*, which he called "some Bones and Ribs preparatory at least for such a work," for the use of English missionaries who wanted to learn the Mass. dialect of Algonquian. Because so few Puritan ministers added their labors to his, Eliot relied primarily on Indian converts as evangelists. For their use, he prepared in Algonquian *The Indian Primer*, a compilation of catechistic exercises in Christian doctrine and morality, and *The Logic Primer*, a guide to the formation of syllogisms to help the Indians deduce lessons from Scripture. To provide Indian teachers with examples of how to bring fellow redmen to Christianity, he wrote *Indian Dialogues*. This work holds our attention because the Indians are eloquent, both Christian and non-Christian speak intelligently, and the story line, which holds the speeches together, discloses native manners, such as a tradition of gracious hospitality. In these vignettes, Praying Indians try to convince other Indians that their traditional way of life is sinful and deserving of God's wrath. The resistance of the non-Christians is stiff, and their objections sensible:

> "May we not rather think that English men have invented these Stories [of heaven and hell] to amaze and scare us out of our old Customes, and bring us to stand in awe of them, that they might wipe us of our Lands, and drive us into Corners, to seek new wayes of living, and new places too? and be beholding to them for that which is our own, and was ours before we knew them?"

The *Dialogues* supplied answers to these and other questions Indian missionaries met in their work.

Puritans believed that the Bible contains all knowledge essential to salvation and that it gives God's instructions for the structure of church government. Eliot found yet more in Scripture: the Lord's platform for civil government. The thesis of his *Christian Commonwealth* is that Christ would reign on earth when all laws, both civil and ecclesiastical, were taken from God's word alone. He sent the manuscript to Eng. as a plan of government to replace the monarchy shortly after the execution of Charles I. The plan is based on Exodus 18, where the Israelites are told to choose rulers of tens, fifties, hundreds, and thousands. Eliot showed how this structure could be expanded to govern the whole world. He described a system of courts consisting of these rulers, in which all judgments are drawn from Scripture, the same form of government that Eliot established in the Christian Indian towns. After the Restoration, Mass. condemned the book and forced Eliot to retract his strictures against monarchy. The *Communion of Churches* is Eliot's ecclesiastical counterpart to the *Christian Commonwealth*. It describes a plan for a hierarchy of church councils: twelve churches form a local council; twelve locals, a province; twelve provincial councils, a national; twelve nationals, an ecumenical council. In both works on civil and church government, Eliot made a fetish of numbers and order: "Order is one of the *Beauties of Heaven," "Order* is better than any of our lives." *The Harmony of the Gospels* is an aid to a better appreciation of the Lord's Supper as a memorial of Christ's suffering and death. In *A Brief Answer*, a defense of infant baptism, Eliot refuted John Norcott's *Baptism Discovered Plainly* (London, 1672).

A Hebraist adept at linguistics, Eliot was one of three Mass. ministers appointed to direct the translation of the Psalms into English meter for *The Bay Psalm Book* of 1640. His rendering of the Bible into Algonquian with the help of Indian interpreters was the first Bible published in America north of the Rio Grande and has been judged by posterity to be as good as any first translation into a previously unwritten language.

Suggested Readings: CCNE; DAB; DARB; DNB; FCNEV; LHUS; Sprague (I, 18-23); T_1. *See also* Peter S. Duponceau, "Notes and Observations on Eliot's Indian Grammar," CMHS, 2nd ser., 9 (1832), after 313; Francis Jennings, *The Invasion of America: Indians, Colonialism, and the Cant of Conquest* (1975), pp. 228-253; Samuel Eliot Morison, *Builders of the Bay Colony* (1930), pp. 289-319; James C. Pilling, *Bibliography of the Algonquian Language* (1891), pp. 127-185; Neal Salisbury, "Red Puritans: The 'Praying Indians' of Massachusetts Bay and John Eliot," WMQ, 31 (1974), 27-54; J. Hammond Trumbull, "The Indian Tongue and Its Literature as Fashioned by Eliot and Others" in *Memorial History of Boston*, by Justin Winsor (1881), I, 465-480; Alden T. Vaughan, *New England Frontier: Puritans and Indians, 1620-1675* (1965), pp. 235-338; Ola Elizabeth Winslow, *John Eliot: "Apostle to the Indians"* (1968).

Michael J. Crawford
Naval Historical Center
Research Branch

JAMES ELLIOT (1775-1839)

Works: *The Poetical and Miscellaneous Works of James Elliot* (1798).

Biography: James Elliot was born in 1775 in Gloucester, Mass., the son of a seafaring father who enlisted in the cause of the Revolution and died at sea of smallpox during the war. Elliot's mother then moved the family to New Salem, Mass., where she supported her three boys as a seamstress and versed the young James in *The Pilgrim's Progress, Dilworth's Speller*, and the *Catechism*. At the age of 7, Elliot was put to work as a farmhand and errand boy for a beneficent employer who taught him grammar and led him to *Josephus* and Rollin's *Ancient*

History, books that fired the boy's zeal to become a soldier and to further his self-education. Elliot's enthusiasm, however, did not always meet with success; twice he tried unsuccessfully to teach himself Latin. In 1790 Elliot moved to Guilford, Vt., where he became acquainted with the dramatist Royall Tyler (q.v.), who was eighteen years his senior. At age 18, out of a sense of patriotism and a desire to see the West, Elliot left Guilford and enlisted as a noncommissioned officer in the United States Sub-Legion and during his three-year tour of duty saw service in the Whiskey Rebellion in western Pa. and the Indian warfare in the Northwest Territory.

Two years after being mustered out of the military, and before settling into a lifetime career as a public servant, Elliot published his sole literary work, *The Poetical and Miscellaneous Works of James Elliot*. In an appendix to the book, the 23-year-old author said that he "never shall write for the press again," a prediction that was not quite accurate since later in life he edited for a short time the *Freeman's Journal* in Philadelphia. In 1803 Elliot moved from Guilford to Brattleboro, and in that same year, he was admitted to the bar and elected to the U.S. Congress, where he served three consecutive terms in the House of Representatives. After his congressional service, Elliot reentered the army, this time as a captain, to serve in the War of 1812. Returning to Brattleboro after the war, Elliot devoted the remainder of his life to a succession of public offices, among them state legislator and, for twenty-one years, justice of the peace. He died in 1839 at the age of 64.

Critical Appraisal: As a young man of meager education, James Elliot collected his political and moral essays, his poetry—some of which had appeared previously in the *Greenfield Gazette*—and his western journal and had printed these collected works in an edition of 300 copies, 225 of which were secured by subscribers in and around Guilford, Vt., where Elliot then lived. The youthfully— and conventionally—romantic Elliot thought of himself as possessing "a soul of exquisite sensibility" and "several of the eccentricities, and a few of the useful qualities, of genius," and *The Poetical and Miscellaneous Works of James Elliot* was intended to be the author's sole bid for the attention, perhaps even the adulation, of the wider world. The inscription to the volume is a passage from Pope that ends, "O grant me honest fame or grant me none," and the quest for fame is a leitmotif that runs through the poetry. Elliot, however, did not believe that fame would be his lot. Speaking in the third person about his work, he ruefully predicted about a vague but distant future: "Some passages in his writings are yet read with pleasure; the rest have sunk into oblivion as they did not deserve a better fate." The prophesy is accurate and just.

Elliot's poetry is of historical interest because it exemplifies a problem common among writers of the post-Revolutionary period, that is, how to find distinctively American themes and subjects and how to treat them in distinctively American ways. One of Elliot's American subjects is the new Republic, which he celebrated in verse that in its vigor is reminiscent of the Connecticut Wits, contemporaries of Elliot's whom he had probably read. Elliot did find other

American subjects for his poetry—some of the poems deal with Indian warfare and the Northwest wilderness—but he was unable to break away from a conventionally romantic (and Old World) treatment of his subjects, and the wilderness of the Ohio River Valley is described largely in imported European diction that sounds more appropriate for pastoral Greece or Eng. Although some of Elliot's versifying is competent—an achievement, given his youthfulness and lack of formal education—it is of interest chiefly because Elliot disclosed himself as a man of his times, a soldier in the struggle for America's literary independence.

Elliot's essays, and especially his western journal, are of more importance than his poetry. Some of the essays—those reprinted from a periodical titled *The Rural Moralist*, which Elliot explained that he wrote and edited in company with his brother Samuel and a J. N. Palmer—are didactic and, often, fastidiously moralistic and excessively discursive; a few of the more successful essays promote education for women and champion the writings of Mary Wollstonecraft and Ann Radcliffe. In his political essays, Elliot revealed himself as a fierce patriot, exuberant democrat, and suspicious Anglophobe. Because of his military experience, Elliot felt entitled to warn his readers against standing armies as destructive of both liberty and morality, and he feared that his country would soon drift into destructive entanglements with Britain.

In the journal that he kept while a soldier in the Northwest Territory, Elliot portrayed some of the wonder—and the fear and isolation—that travelers often felt in the western wilderness. Although at times he feared for his life at the hands of the Indians, Elliot judiciously considered them as "not inferior, and perhaps generally superior, to more civilized nations," and he believed they lacked only education to become a great nation. In a despairing moment, Elliot described the pain of being isolated in the wilderness from the brother he loved and of how precious their letters were to him. At other times, Elliot was taken by the splendors of the untouched Northwest. Once, for instance, climbing toward a mountain ridge, he marveled at "a little world of mountains" that suddenly appeared to the north, south, and west of him when he reached the crest. Like Michel Guillaŭme Jean de Crèvecoeur (q.v.) and others before and after him, Elliot regarded the West as "the Garden of North America" and saw it in both aesthetic and economic terms. Of those people who were then streaming into the Northwest, Elliot predicted that "should their industry be commensurate with the fertility of their soil, the world will exhibit no parallel to them."

Suggested Readings: DAB. *See also* M. R. Cabot, ed., *Annals of Brattleboro* (2 vols., 1921-1922), passim; W. G. Eliot, *A Sketch of the Eliot Family* (1887).

Paul Lehmberg
Northern Michigan University

JOSEPH EMERSON (1700-1767)

Works: *Heart-Purity Encourag'd* (1727); *The Important Duty* (1727); *An Offering of Memorial* (1732); *Meat Out of the Eater* (1735); *Early Piety* (1738);

A Word to Those That Are Afflicted (1738); *Mr. Emerson's Exhortation to His People* (1742); *Wisdom Is Justified* (1742); *Advice of a Father* (1747).

Biography: Born at Chelmsford, Mass., on Apr. 20, 1700, the son of Rebecca (Waldo) and Edward Emerson, later justice of the peace and merchant at Charlestown (1704-1707) and deacon of the Fourth Church at Newbury (1707-1752), Joseph Emerson descended on his mother's side from the important Puritan writers Peter Bulkeley (q.v.) and Edward Bulkeley and on his father's side from Joseph Emerson, the first settled minister of Mendon. Preaching sermons at the age of 8, Emerson entered Harvard at 13, from which he was graduated ninth in a class of seventeen and "out of which," his son recorded, "he came with an unspotted character."

After two years of teaching and occasionally preaching at York, Maine, Emerson resided at his Uncle Waldo's in Boston and declined a unanimous call to be pastor at Wenham before accepting the pastorate of Malden, Mass., in 1721, a post he maintained until his death on Jul. 13, 1767. Famous for having had Michael Wigglesworth (q.v.) as an earlier pastor, Malden at the time of Emerson's arrival was torn by "bitter strife" caused in large part by the previous pastor. In guiding his community through factionalism, dissension, epidemics of "throat distemper," and revivalism known as the "great earthquake" of 1727, Joseph became "the pattern of a New England pastor" and was affable, benevolent, earnest, and—as his tombstone reads—"learned, pious, and faithful." His congregation's respect was shown by replacing within a year the manse that burned in 1724. Emerson married Mary Moody on Dec. 27, 1721, and they had thirteen children, ten of whom lived to adulthood; of the three who became ministers, two died (including William Emerson, Ralph Waldo Emerson's grandfather), while chaplains in the American Revolution.

Critical Appraisal: When Joseph Emerson took his wife, Mary, to visit her father, the eccentric Samuel Moody of York, who was known for his rambling sermons, Emerson delivered a sermon that so impressed Moody's congregation that Moody was persuaded to try Emerson's coherent, logical, carefully crafted style, but soon gave up, saying from the pulpit, "Emerson must be Emerson, and Moody must be moody." Although Cotton Mather (q.v.) wrote the introduction to one of Emerson's tracts, praising him for being a "pattern of early piety," Emerson shunned Mather's convoluted style and, in his address at his son's ordination, called for a style that was both "skillful" and "pungent," skillful in that it was clear and orderly to the audience's understanding, pungent in that it struck to the audience's heart and drew lessons so vivid that they "gall and trouble their Consciences." As he called for simplicity of style, so he insisted upon simplicity as opposed to vain materialism in life.

Four other recurrent themes in his writings include the assurance, despite epidemics, that God is a god of order not confusion; the three forms of worship— sabbath, family, and closet (meditative) religion—practiced by a complete Puritan; that man is naturally corrupt, or, as Emerson said in one tract citing Revelations 3:17, "wretched, miserable, poor, blind, and naked"; and that the minister is as sinful as any in his flock, referring in *An Offering* to the "lustful glances, immodest touches, self-pollution, fornication, and other breaches of the Seventh Commandment that we have any of us been guilty of in the days of our youth." Two further themes are worth special mention: Emerson's linking of Christianity with Judaism, defining children of God at one point as "believing Jews and Gentiles" (*Heart-Purity*); and his view of Jesus as a "God-Man with Transcendent Excellency" (*The Important Duty*), anticipating the Unitarian-Puritan controversy over whether Jesus was a man who became divine or a god who assumed human form.

Nevertheless, Emerson was essentially a conservative, albeit a tolerant one. During the Great Awakening, for example, he crafted this ambiguous position on revivalism and enthusiasm: "We seem to be pretty confident (and I cannot help thinking we have sufficient Reason for it) that *some Particular Ministers* have gone *too far*; but does it not behoove *us* to examine whether we have gone *far enough*" for enthusiasm and even madness "may lead to *right Reform*" (*Wisdom Is Justified*).

Joseph Emerson's journal, which Ralph Waldo Emerson loaned to A. W. McClure in 1849, is lost, perhaps having burned in the Emerson house fire of 1872. *Prince's Chronology* of 1852 includes Joseph among 800 or so early American writers who "may be justly regarded as the principal Literati of New England."

Suggested Readings: CCNE; Sibley-Shipton (VI, 170-175). *See also* D. P. Corey, *The History of Malden, Mass., 1633-1785* (1898), pp. 477-485, passim; A. W. McClure, *The Bicentennial Book of Malden* (1850), pp. 161-166, genealogical table, p. 244.

Henry L. Golemba
Wayne State University

JOSEPH EMERSON (1724-1775)

Works: *Diary of a Naval Chaplain at the Siege of Louisburg, Mar. 15-Aug. 14, 1745* (pub. in PMHS, 44 [1910], 72-84); *Diary of an American Minister, . Aug. 1, 1745-April 9, 1740,* (pub. in PMHS, 44 [1910], 263-282, and in JAH, 3 [1909], 120-127); *The Fear of God* (1758); *A Thanksgiving Sermon Preached at Pepperrell, Jan. 3d, 1760* (1760); *A Thanksgiving Sermon Preached at Pepperrell, July 24, 1766* (1766); *An Extract from a Late Sermon on the Death of the Rev. Mr. Joseph Emerson* (1767).

Biography: Joseph Emerson was born in Malden, Mass., on Aug. 25, 1724, the son of the Rev. Joseph Emerson (q.v.) and Mary (Moody) Emerson. He was a grandson, in fourth descent, of the distinguished Rev. Peter Bulkeley (q.v.), a well-to-do immigrant to America in 1635 and first minister of Concord, Mass. His mother was a daughter of the Rev. Samuel Moody of York, Maine, and his brother William was the grandfather of Ralph Waldo Emerson. Joseph

Emerson graduated from Harvard with his class of 1743. In the spring and summer of 1745, he served as a chaplain aboard the frigate *Molineux* during the siege of Louisburg. On Feb. 25, 1747, he was ordained pastor of the church in Pepperrell, Mass., a position he held until his death on Oct. 29, 1755. Emerson took an active part in public affairs, often playing a prominent role in the settlement of local questions. In his later years he became identified with the patriot cause.

Critical Appraisal: Joseph Emerson's two diary fragments have more historical than literary value. Obviously not intended for publication, the entries contain many fragments and awkward and / or ungrammatical constructions. Nor do they have many of the other virtues of the better American diaries: incisive character sketches, descriptive details, and facts colored by the sensibility of the author. Emerson seemed content to report merely the facts and events of his life without revealing the effects they had on him or their relationship to any larger context. His *Louisburg Diary* covers the period of Mar. 15 to Aug. 14, 1745, during which time Emerson was a chaplain on the *Molineux*. Most of the entries deal with things such as the weather, the ships they saw, and the rumors they heard about the progress of the battle. The diary is, however, unified around a single event, the siege of Louisburg, and has one virtue of the better war diaries: it conveys a sense of immediacy. We relive the confusion and isolation of a participant whose perspective is limited to the events and rumors immediately surrounding him and who has little knowledge of the larger context of which he is a part.

Emerson's *Diary of an American Minister* covers the period from Aug. 1, 1748, to Apr. 9, 1749, when he was a young minister at the Second Church of Christ in Groton (later named Pepperrell). Like the *Louisburg Diary*, it is mainly limited to an objective reporting of facts, and it too has the stylistic shortcomings of the former. The author reported on the families he visited, the miles he traveled, his sermon topics, things such as the fact that he studied all day or went to Boston on business, all of which amount to little more than standardized entries that, when subtracted from the whole, leave little space for the development of character, descriptive details, and the like. One series of entries does, however, rise above the level of factual reporting: his unsuccessful courtship of Esther Edwards, daughter of Jonathan Edwards (q.v.) of Northhampton. Emerson's agony over Esther's rejection of him, an agony so great that he could barely perform his ministerial duties, reveals a man of strong sensibilities. Probably the diary's greatest value, though, lies in the detailed account it provides of the varied duties performed by an eighteenth-century New Eng. clergyman. As such, it is a valuable historical record.

Joseph Emerson's literary reputation rests mainly on four sermons published during his lifetime. *The Fear of God* (1758) is an exhortation to Capt. Thomas Lawrence and his company, upon going against the French in King George's War, to fight courageously; *A Thanksgiving Sermon* (1760) details the mercies that God has bestowed on the people of Pepperrell, with emphasis on the subsiding of the fever and the success of the soldiers in the war; *A Thanksgiving Sermon* (1766) celebrates the repeal of the Stamp Act, an act the effect of which was to make "every true lover of Zion...tremble for the Ark of God"; and *An Extract from a Late Sermon* (1767) is a eulogy delivered upon the death of his father, the Rev. Joseph Emerson of Malden. All of these sermons are topical, relating in some way a contemporary occurrence to God's divine plan for the American colonists. For example, in *The Fear of God* Emerson reminded the troops of their unworthiness to receive God's mercy and admonished them to conduct themselves as "Christian Soldiers" in their campaign against the French. As such, they will pray, read the Bible, avoid profanity, and fear God, not man. They are to understand that they are serving "the Cause of God, the Cause of Religion, the Cause of Liberty," and that should they not defeat their "Popish Enemies," there will be "no Peace for the pure Profession of the Religion of Jesus." Emerson is in the tradition of a long line of New Eng. ministers who merged their theology with politics and their politics with the advancement of the kingdom of God.

As literary performances, Emerson's sermons are probably better than the average of similar works of his day. Although occasionally displaying the rhetorical excesses typical of New Eng. ministers attempting to persuade through fear of eternal damnation, his sermons are tightly structured, and their content reflects credit on both the author's scholarship and his sensitivity to the intellectual limitations of his audience. His sentences embody considerable parallelism, antithesis, and balance, giving them a Classical grace that enhances their value as literary works.

Suggested Readings: CCNE; Sibley-Shipton (XI, 217-220). *See also* Dr. Samuel Abbott Green, "Joseph Emerson's Diary, 1748-1749" and "Emerson's Louisburg Journal," PMHS, 44 (1910), 65-71, 262-263; Edith March Howe, "Experiences of an American Minister from His Manuscript in 1748," JAH, 3 (1909), 119.

Don Mortland
Eastern Kentucky University

WILLIAM EMERSON (1769-1811)

Works: *A Discourse Delivered in Harvard* (1794); "On Regeneration," "On Living Under the Eye of God," and "A View of the Divine Perfections" (pub. in *Sermons...* [by] *Members of the Northern Association* [1799]); *Piety and Arms* (1799); *A Discourse...Before the Roxbury Charitable Society* (1800); *A Sermon...Ordination of Robinson Smiley* (1801); *An Oration Pronounced July5* (1802); *A Sermon...Decease of the Rev. Peter Thacher* (1803); *A Sermon...Interment of Madam Elizabeth Bowdoin* (1803); *A Sermon...Ordination of the Rev. Thomas Beede* (1803); *A Discourse...Boston Female Asylum* (1805); *A Sermon...Death of Mr. Charles Austin* (1806); *A Discourse...the Massachusetts Humane Society* (1807); *A Selection of Psalms and Hymns...* (compiler;

1808); *A Sermon...Ordination of Rev. Samuel Clark* (1810); *History of the First Church in Boston* (includes two sermons dated Jul. 17, 1808, and Jul. 21, 1808, on the change of the First Church to a new building; 1812); *A Sermon...Boston* (1812); *Sketch of the Late Rev. Dr. Clarke* (1812).

Biography: William Emerson was born in Concord, Mass., on May 21, 1769, the son of the minister of the Concord church. His father, also William, was regimental chaplain to the troops at Ticonderoga, stayed with them during their exposure to weather and hardships, and died of "bilious fever" in 1776, when his son was only 7. The elder William built the Old Manse in 1767, and from out those famous windows, his namesake witnessed the battle of Concord when he was only 6. The younger Emerson's mother, Phebe, was the daughter of the Rev. Daniel Bliss; shortly after the death of William's father, she married Ezra Ripley, who became for William the head of the house, family, and church.

Emerson attended Harvard, where he established a "singular reputation for composition, rhetoric, and classical studies." He graduated in 1789, taught school for two years, studied divinity at Cambridge, and was eventually ordained minister of the Unitarian church at Harvard, Mass. Descriptions of Emerson attest that he was blond, handsome, graceful, and "benignant"; that he was both simple and scholarly; and that he had a melodious voice. On Oct. 25, 1796, he married Ruth Haskins of Boston, and in 1799 he accepted his call to the First Church of Boston, where he remained until his death on May 12, 1811.

William was reputed to be the most liberal minister of his time ever employed at Boston and to be devoted to those aspects of religion universal and ethical. He was especially compassionate in human proceedings concerned with, and successfully avoiding, the residues of contention for which the First Church was so well known as a result of the early examinations and expulsion of Anne Hutchinson. He strove to break down barriers between the church and the town, and while at Harvard he planned a church in Washington based on Congregational principles requiring no confession of faith and providing open communion for anyone who wished it. Entering freely into Boston society, he did both his church and civic duties well. He was an overseer of Harvard College, was active in the Massachusetts Historical Society, edited the *Monthly Anthology*, and founded the Anthology Club, whose books eventually became the core of the Boston Athenaeum Library. In fact, his widespread social involvements caused his sister, Mary Moody Emerson, to chastize him for his "tributes to fashion and parade" and for his valuing "the present world" too highly. In addition to his church history, Emerson published several sermons and orations, edited a volume of psalms and hymns, and generally gained the respect of persons in the literary, educational, civic, and church institutions.

William Emerson's reputation was far eclipsed by Ralph Waldo, the fourth of his eight children. One biographer has written that William "was, probably, what Ralph Waldo Emerson would have been, had he remained in the church." Unfortunately, the elder Emerson died when only 42, depriving the world of the potentially revealing interchanges between the father, a mainstay of Unitarian liberalism, and the son, the foremost American advocate of Transcendentalism.

Critical Appraisal: Although William Emerson's reputation as a literary figure is relatively undistinguished, he was important to the times and culture in which he lived, and his life and writings are embodiments of civilized, educated, and liberal attitudes at the beginning of the nineteenth century. His surviving sermons, for which he was well known during his day, are of two types. Most are ordinary and are adapted to the specific occasion for which they were preached. In this category are celebrations of America's independence and national goals (usually given for July 4th gatherings), ordination sermons outlining the requirements and tribulations of ministership, funeral sermons that use the individual's passing as a reminder of certain death and needs for good living, and artillery sermons preached to commemorate the elections of military officers. Several other orations and sermons exist, however, that stand as waymarks of the new religious liberalism of Unitarianism and clearly distinguish the then-current theological beliefs and attitudes from the early Puritan and reawakening points of view. Especially in his early sermons, Emerson felt at ease quoting from Classical authors, as well as from Milton and Shakespeare. He kept abreast of the new science and infused his works with metaphors drawn from physiology and experiment.

Emerson's Unitarian philosophy permeates his work—he continually downplayed religious differences, choosing rather to emphasize the common elements of religion. He asserted, for example, in his introduction to his psalms and hymns, that he selected them "to reject what savours of party spirit and sectarian notions." His philosophic inquiries, although they point the path his famous son was to take, proceeded but a few steps in that direction, mainly because he lacked his son's supreme sense of ego. Although he believed that moral attributes of God were "communicable" and that the "perfect and manifold wisdom of God is wonderfully displayed in his works of creation," he warned that attempts to understand the Almighty required a "due sense of weakness" regarding man's abilities to know.

William Emerson's longest and best-known work is his *History* of the First Church. The greatest portion of this work examines that church's early troubles with Anne Hutchinson. Obvious from the *History* are Emerson's sympathies for both parties, reflecting, perhaps, his own appreciation of the sometimes contradictory duties of church officer and compassionate human being. Even though the event happened decades before, Emerson vacillates, first finding fault with one party and then the other. About the Hutchinson case, he wrote that "we can hardly help dropping a tear of compassion over the intolerance of the age, and the hardships attending the case." At the same time he labeled Hutchinson a "female fanatick" with an "unquiet, bold and turbulent spirit. . .full of enthusiasm" and maintained that "the governor and majority of the clergy. . .could hardly have been more lenient." Typical of his attitude is his summation that "the whole controversy originated in too strict an attachment to the words of scriptures, without regarding their connexion and spirit."

Suggested Readings: DAB; Sprague (VIII, 241-246). *See also* J. E. Cabot, *A Memoir of Ralph Waldo Emerson* (1887); *The Christian Monitor*, no. 4 (discourses one, two, three, and seven are unsigned but attributed to William Emerson in the list of his works appended to his *History*); B. K. Emerson, *The Ipswich Emersons* (1900); E. W. Emerson, *Emerson in Concord* (1889); Moncure Daniel Conway, *Emerson at Home and Abroad* (1883; rep., 1968), pp. 21-31; H. S. Nourse, *History of the Town of Harvard, Massachusetts, 1732-1893* (1894).

Dean G. Hall
Wayne State University

NATHANIEL EMMONS (1745-1840)

Works: *A Discourse Concerning the Process of General Judgement* (1783); *Christ the Standard of Preaching* (1786); *The Office of the Ministry* (1786); *The Dignity of Man* (1787); *A Discourse Delivered November 7* (1790); *A Dissertation on the Scriptural Qualifications for Admission and Access to the Christian Sacraments* (1793); *A Candid Reply to the Rev. Doctor Hemmenway's Remarks* (1795); *Sprinkling the Proper Mode and Infants the Proper Subjects of Christian Baptism* (1795); *National Peace* (1797); *A Discourse Delivered May 9* (1798); *A Collection of Sermons*, 6 vols. (1800, 1812-1813, 1815, 1823, 1825-1826; vol. 7, 1850); *A Sermon on the Death of Gen. George Washington* (1800); *A Sermon Delivered Before the Massachusetts Missionary Society* (1800); *Sermons on Some of the First Principles and Doctrines of True Religion* (1800); *A Discourse Delivered on the Annual Fast in Massachusetts, April 9th* (1801); *The Danger of Embracing That Notion of Moral Virtue Which Is Subversive of All Moral, Religious, and Political Obligation Illustrated* (1804); *The Giver More Blessed Than the Receiver* (1809); *A Sermon on the Doctrine of the Trinity* (1811); Jacob Ide, ed., *A System of Divinity*, 2 vols. (1842).

Biography: Born on May 1, 1745, at Millington in East Haddam, Conn., Nathaniel (also spelled "Nathanael") Emmons was an important Congregational minister and theologian. A 1767 graduate of Yale College, Emmons later studied theology at Coventry, Conn., with Nathan Strong, the elder, and at Berlin, Conn., with John Smalley (q.v.). On Oct. 3, 1769, Emmons received his license to preach, and he spent four years as an itinerant in N.Y. and N.H. On Apr. 21, 1773, Emmons became pastor at Wrentham (later Franklin), Mass., where he remained until his retirement on May 28, 1827, at age 82.

Well known for his sermons and theological controversies, Emmons was sought out as teacher by numerous theological and ministerial students, many of whom reached national prominence. He received an M.A. in 1786 and a doctor of divinity in 1798 from Dartmouth College. A founder of the Massachusetts Missionary Society, he served as its first president for twelve years. From May 1803 until May 1808, Emmons edited and contributed to *The Massachusetts Missionary Magazine*. He also contributed extensively to numerous other periodicals, including the *Connecticut Evangelical Magazine*.

A strong Federalist, Emmons opposed Thomas Jefferson's (q.v.) election, expressing his views in a fast-day sermon on Apr. 9, 1801, shortly after Jefferson's inauguration. In the sermon, he compared Jefferson to Jeroboam, the king of Israel who set up centers for prayer and worship in various areas of the kingdom as well as the images of the golden calf, thus making Jefferson proverbial for one who leads the chosen people into sin. Emmons was also an opponent of slavery and freemasonry, and he argued against fusion of the Congregationalists with the Presbyterians. Married to Deliverance French (d. 1778) and to Martha Williams (d. 1829), Emmons was survived by his third wife, Abigail (Moore Mills) Emmons, whom he had married on Sept. 28, 1831. He died in Franklin on Sept. 23, 1840.

Critical Analysis: Discussions of Nathaniel Emmons's works and theological positions have been prejudiciously colored by the author's own beliefs and attitudes. Emmons was in the line of theological thought that linked the New Eng. orthodoxy of Jonathan Edwards (q.v.), John Smalley, Samuel Hopkins (q.v.), and Timothy Dwight (q.v.). But as he himself commented, his thinking was evolved from Hopkins and not simply an extension of Hopkins's ideas. There have been those who cast Emmons as not being influential and as not having founded a "system," but neither view is accurate. Although they are derivable from his other works, eight tenets defining his thought appear in his 1800 *Sermon* on first principles. As formulated by E. A. Park in an entry in the Schaaf-Herzog *Encyclopedia of Religious Knowledge* (1882-1884) and repeated by F. A. Foster in the *New Schaaf-Herzog Encyclopedia* (1909; IV, 121), they are (1) "Holiness and sin consist in free voluntary exercise"; (2) "Men act freely under the divine agency"; (3) "The least transgression of the divine law deserves eternal punishment"; (4) "Right and wrong are founded in the nature of things"; (5) "God exercises mere grace in pardoning or justifying penitent believers through the atonement of Christ, and mere goodness in rewarding them for their good works"; (6) "Notwithstanding the total depravity of sinners, God has a right to require them to turn from sin to holiness"; (7) "Preachers of the gospel ought to exhort sinners to love God, repent of sin, and believe in Christ immediately"; (8) "Men are active, not passive, in regeneration." According to Emmons, the soul and man's mental life are a series of "exercises" resulting from divine action (agency) and creating a constant, renewed regeneration, for man has freedom of choice (although the choices be limited) and moral responsibility. Any act of will must be preceded by exercise of freedom of choice, which choosing limits that freedom. Although absolute freedom does not exist, God produces volition within man, who acts freely because he acts voluntarily. All moral characteristics consist in such "exercises." The agency of divinity that Emmons stressed places him in a supralapsarian position, which had long plagued orthodox Calvinism.

While accepting original sin, total depravity, election, and eternal punishment, Emmons nonetheless emphasized man's internalizing of morality, under the benevolence of God, leading to sanctification. Morality is not religion, as he accused Moses Hemmenway (q.v.) of believing. Although such saints, through "exercises," renew their sanctification, "Good evidence of sanctification," Emmons argued, was reserved to true saints only; those who lapse are not true saints. "Religion" in Emmons's eyes did not always exact morality, and those who were not true saints were too often involved in "religion." Such inner morality should be made public by confession of faith, a practice that was frequently ignored. Emmons's antagonism to Arminianism, which was growing steadily and making Separatist inroads into the New Eng. Church, is clear. His influence in stemming some of this tide for certain Congregational groups came from his published works and, to a great extent, from the various clergymen who had been his students.

Although no formulated system of theology was produced by Emmons, his son-in-law Jacob Ide put together a two-volume cento of his ideas, defining a neo-orthodox position. An important part of that system depended on Emmons's understanding of the Atonement. Since "The goodness, the justice, and the mercy of God are founded in the nature of things," the Atonement, which "was necessary entirely on God's account," does not obligate God to reward or not reward the sinner. The sufferings of Christ show that grace is consistent with justice. Furthermore, Emmons believed in infant baptism—Baptists were becoming stronger outside Boston at this time—as his *A Candid Reply* (1795), reacting to Hemmenway's *Remarks on the Reverend Mr. Emmons's Dissertation* (1794), and his *Sprinkling the Proper Mode* (1795) show. Opposed to the latter work was Abraham Cummings's *Believers Proved to Be the Only Proper Subject of Baptism* (1798). To that Emmons would have answered that since "belief" is "faith," believers are "*in* Christ, and the child may be as easily a believer in Christ as an adult. In opposition to the growing Unitarian church, Emmons was an anti-Universalist who construed the Trinity as three *persons* in one *being* (not "one person"), thus emphasizing the distinctness of Father, Son, and Holy Spirit and the unity of God. An area in which Emmons's belief was strongly felt was the concept of the Congregational Church as a federated institution. For Emmons, the organization of the church was dependent upon the mutual duties of its members; it thus became essential to admit only those whose actions would fit in with the mutualities of the existing members and would be maintained. Opposed views led to sectarian and Separatist institutions, but the Congregational Church remained fairly well intact.

Emmons's prose shows an intellectual and metaphysical ability at argument and ideas that are closely reasoned, sincere, analytic, but it is not a strong literary or creative ability. His favorite form of statement involves the paradox and crypsis; yet a tone of *sermo* (that conversational, dialog style common to the sermon) overrides and makes his work seem less theoretic than it is.

Suggested Readings: CCNE; DAB; DARB; Dexter (III, 216-230); Sprague (I, 693-706); T₂. *See also* Frank Hugh Foster, *A Genetic History of the New England Theology* (1907), pp. 210-211, 241-242, 330-331, 340-357, 463-464; Joseph Haroutunian, *Piety Versus Moralism: The Passing of the New England Theology*, 2nd ed. (1964) [*Studies in Religion and Culture*, 1st ed. (1932)], pp. 123-130, 146-148, 165-166, 247-248;

Jacob Ide [Emmons's son-in-law], ed., *The Works of Nathaniel Emmons...with a Memoir of His Life*, 6 vols. (1842-1850); Edwards Amasa Park, *Memoir of Nathaniel Emmons; with Sketches of His Friends and Pupils* (1861), rep. as the first volume of the 2nd ed. of *The Works of Nathaniel Emmons* (1861-1863), with additions; Thomas Williams, *The Official Character of Reverend Nathaniel Emmons, D.D.* (1840).

John T. Shawcross
University of Kentucky

OLAUDAH EQUIANO (c. 1745-1797)

Works: *The Interesting Narrative of...Olaudah Equiano or Gustavus Vassa, the African* (1789).

Biography: Olaudah Equiano (also known as "Gustavus Vassa") was born in or about the year 1745 in Benin, Africa, in what is now known as the eastern interior of Nig.; his language was apparently Ibo. He was the youngest of six brothers and one sister. At the age of 11, he and his sister were abducted by slavers, but the two were soon separated before embarking on the infamous middle passage to the New World. The young boy was taken first to Barbados and then to Va., where a Lt. Michael H. Pascal of the royal British navy bought him. During his time with Pascal, Equiano saw service in the Seven Years' War in Can. with Gen. Wolfe and in the Mediterranean with Adm. Boscawen. Pascal, now a captain, sold Equiano to James Doran, captain of the *Sally*; he served Doran for only a short time and was sold to Robert King, a Quaker merchant and sea captain from Philadelphia.

At this time, the black youth was about 18 years of age. King promised to see that Equiano received training in arithmetic and to improve his knowledge of navigation and reading; in addition, the merchant seaman pledged eventually to give the black youth his freedom. King made good his promise to educate Equiano but reneged on his commitment to free him. The reason King refused to free his slave was, of course, because he was making a good yearly sum—over 100 pounds—from the efforts of his bright and talented charge. Nevertheless, after some three years, Equiano finally managed to accumulate 40 pounds toward the purchase of his freedom and then shamed his master into freeing him.

During his servitude to King, Equiano observed closely the cruel bondage practiced among those slaveholders of the Caribbean, the Carolinas, and Ga. But it was also during this time that the young man heard the Great Awakener, George Whitefield (q.v.), preach in Philadelphia. Within a year of his liberation, Equiano left the cruelties of America behind (so he thought) and set out to find a more liberal place, Eng. Although he thought never to return to "the cruel Whip" of the Americas, his curiosity "once more to try my fortune in the West Indies" moved him to ship as steward in 1771 on a journey to Madeira, Barbados, and Jamaica.

Equiano nevertheless found London fascinating. There he learned to be a hairdresser and to play the French horn with some facility; he also attended night school, always concerned to improve his reading skills, and became an assistant to Dr. Charles Irving, with whom he later went on an expedition into the Arctic. Constantly looking for a land that would permit him more freedom, he subsequently traveled to Tur., where he found the Turks treated him "always with great civility," to other parts of the Mediterranean including Genoa, to Sp. and Port., to the Mosquito regions of Hond. and Nic., and even to Philadelphia again in 1785.

In the meantime, Equiano participated in numerous attempts to better the conditions of his black brethren, including making plans for an African diaspora, becoming the close friend of noted abolitionists such as Granville Sharp and Thomas Clarkson, and petitioning the queen, consort of George III, in their behalf, signing his name "The Oppressed Ethopean [sic]." He married Susanna Cullen of Ely in 1792 and died on Apr. 31, 1797, "well known as the champion and advocate for procuring the suppression of the slave trade."

Critical Appraisal: Seeing eight editions in its first five years, Olaudah Equiano's *Narrative* rivaled the popularity of Phillis Wheatley's (q.v.) 1773 *Poems on Various Subjects, Religious and Moral*. A recent critic has called the *Narrative* "the first truly notable book in the genre now known as slave narratives," and the book continues to be popular to this day. To be sure, the work is significant because of the information its Gulliver-like narrator reveals about slave conditions in the Caribbean and other places, but its importance as a literary text extends beyond its anthropological value. Equiano tells his lamentable odyssey in vivid, direct, and sometimes haunting language, and his control of the narrative conjures up a spontaneity and immediacy that are expertly realized.

For example, Equiano, ever curious and imaginative (a true teacher's dream of a student), related an incident when he longed "to talk to the books" as he had seen his first New World master, Lt. Pascal, do on numerous occasions. Equiano was about 12 at this time and had as yet learned but little English; nevertheless, he tried to duplicate his master's behavior. So he often took up a book, "talked to it, and then put my ears to it, when alone, in hopes it would answer me." But, alas, he became "very much concerned when I found it remained silent." Here Equiano conveyed much more than the retelling of simple events; he communicated the attitude and wonder of the human urge to want to know and not to be satisfied with inadequate and naive ignorance.

Indeed, how can anyone remain naive when he has endured the unspeakable tortures of slavery? Certainly, young Equiano was not ignorant of cruelty when he became Pascal's property. Perhaps the true wonder here is that, after the horror of the middle passage, the young black's intellect still remained alive. The chapter in which Equiano related the manner, and ensuing consequences, of his abduction is a minor masterpiece of point of view. His introductory remarks to Chapter II are those of a man who has lived much and who has acquired much wisdom: "whether the love of one's country [his native Africa] be real or imaginary, or a lesson of reason, or an instinct of nature, I still look back with pleasure on the first scenes of my life, though that pleasure has been...mingled with sorrow." From this point, Equiano plunged directly into the story of his first eleven years.

He dropped the adult perspective of one experienced in more than his share of life's vicissitudes and adopted that of a child, bewildered by the incredible viciousness of his white captors. Upon his reluctant arrival on the deck of the slaver, Equiano asked other blacks who could understand his dialect "if we were not to be eaten by those white men with horrible looks, red faces, and *loose hair* [my emphasis]." He thought that the ship moved and stopped because of some sort of white magic. At another point, he observed that the slavers unmercifully flogged a black man whom they had retrieved from the ocean "for thus attempting to prefer death to slavery." But it is the unfortunate experience of the adult that forced him to conclude that the only motive for the terrifying cruelties of the middle passage perpetrated on the blacks must be "the improvident avarice...of their purchasers." He closed this chapter with a statement explaining why memories of his native Africa were "mingled with sorrow." Commenting on the New World practice of separating family members for purposes of sales (Equiano had himself been cruelly separated from his sister in the African baracoons), the committed abolitionist asserted, "Surely this is a new refinement in cruelty, which... aggravates distress and adds fresh horrors even to the wretchedness of slavery."

The real purpose of Equiano's literary effort here becomes unmistakable. As he put it in his prefatory remarks to the *Narrative*, which are addressed to "the Lords Spiritual and Temporal, and the Commons of the Parliament of Great Britain," his avowed intention was to realize "the hope of becoming an instrument towards the relief of his suffering countrymen." As is the case with others of the slave-narrative genre, this narrative begins by acquainting the reader with the atrocities of his degrading oppression. In subsequent chapters, Equiano, as did others, inevitably revealed how he struggled steadily to achieve his own freedom.

Although he had heard the inspirational Rev. George Whitefield, the Great Awakener, in Philadelphia before he obtained his freedom, it was not until after he won the struggle and relocated in Eng. that Equiano experienced religious conversion. He composed a series of twenty-eight quatrains of iambic tetrameters to celebrate the occasion. These "Miscellaneous Verses" he included in the tenth chapter of the *Narrative*. Although they do not constitute great poetry, they do demonstrate that Equiano was proficient in composing verse, just as he was even better in writing prose. The quatrains tell the story of his spiritual search for truth that began in Africa at the point when he discovered himself "taken from my native land, / By an unjust and cruel hand." These lines recall those from a poem by Phillis Wheatley: "I, young in life, by seeming cruel fate / Was snatch'd from Afric's fancy'd happy seat." At the point of his conversion, he recorded, "Thus light came in, and I believ'd; / Myself forgot, and help receiv'd!"

Although the quality of these lines is not particularly exceptional, the quality of the sentiment is. Equiano's devotion to the quest to liberate all of his black brothers and sisters certainly attests how he could and did forget himself. In vigorous and carefully plotted prose, Equiano constructed one of most effective of the slave narratives. Along with the earlier slave narratives of Briton Hammon (q.v.) and John Marrant (q.v.), his *Narrative* established the tenets of the genre, but it was Equiano's spontaneity, his rich and fascinating details, his narration of adventures in exotic places, and at the same time his constant coloring of all events with the human struggle for liberation that set the standards of quality for the genre.

Suggested Readings: Arna Bontemps, "The Slave Narrative: An American Genre" in *Great Slave Narratives* (reprints Equiano's *Narrative* entire; 1969), pp. xiv-xv, 1-3; Benjamin Brawley, *The Negro Genius* (1937), pp. 28-30; Paul Edwards, Introduction, *The Life of Olaudah Equiano*, 2 vols. (1789; rep., 1969), pp. v-lxxi (Edwards's Introduction is the most extensive discussion); Sidney Kaplan, *The Black Presence in the Era of the American Revolution: 1770-1800* (1973), pp. 193-206; Theresa Rush et al., *Black American Writers Past and Present* (1975), p. 278; Roger Whitlow, *Black American Literature: A Critical History* (1973), pp. 24-25.

John C. Shields

Illinois State University

ISRAEL EVANS (1747-1807)

Works: *A Discourse, Delivered, on the 18th Day of Dec. 1777* (1778); *A Discourse Delivered at Easton* (1779); *An Oration Delivered at Hackinsack* (1781); *A Discourse Delivered Near York in Virginia* (1782); *A Discourse Delivered in New-York* (1784); *A Sermon Delivered at Concord Before the Hon. General Court, of the State of Newhampshire* (1791).

Biography: Israel Evans was born in Pa. in 1747, the son and grandson of ministers. Educated at Princeton (A.B., 1772) and later at Dartmouth (A.M., 1792), he was ordained a Presbyterian minister in Philadelphia in 1776 but instead of seeking a parish enlisted as a chaplain in the Continental Army, serving in that capacity from 1777 until the close of the Revolutionary War in 1783. Assigned to the N.H. brigade commanded by Gen. Enoch Poor, he accompanied the brigade on its campaign against Joseph Brant's Iroquois Indians in 1779 and in the siege of Yorktown in 1781. During the war, Evans preached and published numerous patriotic sermons, including one after Yorktown to the combined American and French troops under the command of the Marquis de Lafayette. When Lafayette visited America in 1825 and was shown a portrait of Evans, he immediately exclaimed, "It is our worthy chaplain."

After the war, Evans moved to Concord, N.H., where he served as minister from 1789 to 1797. As pastor he combined a taste for good living with a preaching style so animated that it once provoked the comment that Evans's preaching was "more *spirited* than spiritual." For several terms, Evans served as a chaplain to the N.H. legislature, and in 1791 he preached the annual N.H. election sermon. Although there had been no controversy between himself and his parishioners, Evans abruptly asked to be relieved of his ministry in 1797. Released from his office, he remained in Concord until his death on March 9, 1807. During his wartime service, Evans had developed a reverence for George Washington (q.v.), and it was reported that on his deathbed, when a fellow minister prayed that Evans would soon sit down in the kingdom of heaven with Abraham, Isaac, and Jacob, Evans responded, "and with Washington too."

Critical Appraisal: Israel Evans's reputation as an enthusiastic preacher rested on the five published sermons based on his Revolutionary War service—a 1777 sermon following the Battle of Saratoga, a 1779 sermon at the conclusion of the expedition against the Iroquois, a 1781 oration at the interment of Gen. Poor, a 1781 sermon after the victory at Yorktown, and a 1783 sermon honoring the thanksgiving proclaimed by Congress to mark the end of the war. In all of these discourses, Evans consistently stressed the themes of God's active providence in the world and the need for soldiers and civilians alike to recognize that providence. In 1777, for instance, Evans began his discourse by observing that "there is one most wise and omnipotent being, who governs the whole universe, and superintends the actions of all his creatures. To deny this, would be to deny and contradict our reason." Two years later, he similarly commented that "GOD influences the minds of men in the important affairs of national defence." "Those nations and commanders" in the past, he stressed in 1781, "who placed the greatest confidence in Almighty God, have been most victorious and most flourishing."

The American Revolution, Evans insisted, demonstrated the interposing hand of divine providence at almost every instance. In 1777, for example, he exclaimed that "it is the Lord our God who has fought for us, in every successful battle, and has hitherto supported our righteous cause," and he proceeded in that same discourse to trace the campaign that ended at Saratoga, ascribing to God all mistakes made by the British and the successes achieved by the American commanders. In his discourse celebrating the surrender of Cornwallis at Yorktown, he went to even greater lengths in describing the providential support shown the American cause and concluded by telling the citizens of America that "The Lord helps you and invites you by every national blessing...to press on and gain a complete conquest over the tyranny of your enemies!"

Like many of his fellow ministers at the time of the American Revolution, Evans foresaw a glorious future for the U.S., a future that would be the fulfillment of God's divine plan for the world. In 1781 he urged his listeners to "consider the numerous inhabitants of Europe. Do they not all wish you to be free and independent? They will date their days of unmolested freedom from the Aera of your independence!" Later he was even more certain that in America "the oppressed shall find a secure retreat, from all the poverty and misery of merciless tyranny." Evans's most consistent theme was summed up in his 1783 thanksgiving sermon: "We praise that GOD who has triumphed gloriously."

Evans's sermons did not contribute original themes; the notion that providence was directing the events of the American Revolution was shared by hundreds of ministers and laymen throughout the new nation. But as much as anyone else, Evans gave powerful expression to those providential images that contributed to the fashioning of American nationalism in the years after 1776.

Suggested Readings: CCMC; P; Sprague (II, 138); T_2. *See also* Nathaniel Bouton, *The History of Concord* (1856), pp. 567-569.

John F. Berens
Northern Michigan University

LEWIS EVANS (c. 1700-1756)

Works: *A Brief Account of Pennsylvania* (1753); *Geographical, Historical, Political, Philosophical, and Mechanical Essays. The First Containing an Analysis of a General Map of the Middle British Colonies in America* (1755); *Geographical, Historical, Political, Philosophical, and Mechanical Essays. Number II* (1756).

Biography: Lewis Evans was born in Carnavonshire, Wales, in approximately 1700. Little is known of his life before his arrival in Pa. in 1736. During the following twenty years, he resided in Philadelphia and traveled extensively within the middle colonies. A surveyor and draftsman by trade, Evans's travels resulted in a series of maps published between 1749 and 1755. It is for these maps, particularly "A General Map of the Middle British Colonies in America," that Evans is chiefly known today.

Yet, as the titles of Evans's *Essays* indicate, his interests extended far beyond cartography. These interests, and Evans's own active and engaging character, led him to form friendships with a number of important contemporaries, including Benjamin Franklin (q.v.), the botanist John Bartram (q.v.), the Swedish scientist Peter Kalm, Governor Thomas Pownall, and Cadwallader Colden (q.v.), a historian and naturalist who served as surveyor general of N.Y. Evans shared Franklin's interest in science and technology, lecturing on electricity and perhaps helping to develop the Franklin stove. Evans accompanied Bartram and Conrad Weiser on their trip in 1743 to Onondaga, described in Bartram's *Observations* (1751). Kalm respected Evans's knowledge of natural history and referred to him as "that ingenious engineer" in the *Travels in North America*.

Because of the political and military import of cartography in a period when the colonies, Eng., and Fr. were attempting to establish their ownership of imperfectly mapped lands, particularly to the west of the Alleghenies, Evans's activities often led him into controversy. In addition, Evans held political views and expressed them strongly, allying himself to the Pownall faction in opposition to William Shirley (q.v.) and a N.Y. group that included William Livingston (q.v.) and William Smith, Jr. (q.v.). Thus there exist conflicting views about his character and abilities. Franklin referred to Evans as "a gentleman of great American knowledge," but Smith countered Evans's opinions about French territorial claims with an *ad hominem* attack on Evans's "violent passions, great vanity, and rude manners." *A Review of the Military Operations in North America* (1757), sometimes ascribed to Livingston, attacks Evans in similar terms. As these attacks suggest, Lewis Evans was a man to be reckoned with; he was, perhaps, one of the more fascinating men of his age. He was deeply involved with the issues of the time and keenly interested in the advancement of scientific and geographical knowledge. He died in N.Y. while awaiting trial for slander against Governor Robert Hunter Morris.

Critical Appraisal: Literary analysis of Lewis Evans's writings begins with the English reviews of the *Essays*, notably Samuel Johnson's review in the *Literary Magazine and Universal Review*. To Johnson, Evans's work suggested that "literature apparently gains ground" in America. After praising the quality of the "General Map," Johnson remarked that the *Essays* were "written with such elegance as the subject admits tho' not without some mixture of the American dialect." In America, commentary was more polemical than critical, although a writer in the *Monthly Review* suggested that the *Essays* (*Number II*), in which Evans defended himself against an attack published in the *New York Mercury*, had "the appearance of much solidity of argument."

Indeed, the quality of Evans's published work makes it regrettable that many of the projects that he apparently planned were never completed. His extant prose consists only of a few letters, an extract from the 1743 journal of the Bartram-Weiser expedition published in Pownall's *Topographical Description* (1776), the manuscript "Brief Account of Pennsylvania," and the two volumes of *Essays*. The *Essays* are effectively written, giving a coherent account of the western lands, including their physical properties and political importance. To see these lands, Evans noted, was to look out upon "an Ocean of Woods, swell'd and deprest here and there by little Inequalities not to be distinguished, one Part from another, any more than the Waves of the real Ocean."

Evans's maps and narratives represent a new direction in American "travel" writing, in which adventure gives way to scientific, economic, and geopolitical content. Evans recognized the importance of his subject; the western lands that were "as great a prize, as has ever yet been contended for, between two Nations." His maps were useful in the military struggle with Fr. and in later settlement of the area. Evans's cogent analyses, delivered in skillful rhetoric, aided in the western expansion of the eighteenth century. His work is of both historical and literary interest and importance.

Suggested Readings: DAB; LHUS; T$_1$. *See also* Hazel Shields Garrison, "Cartography of Pennsylvania Before 1800," PMHB, 59 (1935), 269-274; Lawrence Henry Gipson, *Lewis Evans* (prints "A Brief Account of Pennsylvania" and fascimilies of the *Essays* and maps; 1939); William Smith, Jr., *The History of the Province of New York*, 2 vols., ed. Michael Kammen (1972), I, 152-153; II, 196; Henry N. Stevens, *Lewis Evans: His Map of the Middle Colonies in America* (1905; rev. 1920); idem, *Lewis Evans: His Map of 1752 Recently Brought to Light* (1924); Lawrence C. Wroth, *An American Bookshelf, 1755* (1934), pp. 32-35, 48-56, 102, 148-166.

Douglas R. Wilmes
The Pennsylvania State University

NATHANIEL EVANS (1742-1767)

Works: *Ode on the Late Glorious Successes* (1762); *A Dialogue on Peace* (1763); *The Love of the World* (1766); *Poems on Several Occasions* (1772).

Biography: Nathaniel Evans was born in Philadelphia on Jun. 8, 1742, the son of a merchant who desired the same career for him. He attended the Academy of Philadelphia for six years, worked briefly in business, then returned to receive (despite his lack of an A.B.) an M.A. from the Academy and College of Philadelphia (later the Univ. of Pa.). This school, founded by a group inspired by Benjamin Franklin's (q.v.) ideas of practical education for American youth, and led in Evans's time by its energetic provost William Smith (q.v.), played a central role in the intellectual and artistic life of many young Philadelphians in the mideighteenth century. Encouraged by Smith, Evans went to London and was ordained in the Church of England. He returned as a missionary priest to Gloucester County, N.J., across the Delaware River from Philadelphia. He died in N.J. of tuberculosis at the age of 25 and was buried at Christ Church, Philadelphia. William Smith assembled and published Evans's *Poems on Several Occasions* as a memorial, sold by subscription, in 1772.

Critical Appraisal: The 160 pages of verse in Nathaniel Evans's *Poems on Several Occasions* include songs, pastorals, odes, and elegies, most conventional in style, form, and theme and replete with expected Classical allusions and other exhibitions of Evans's self-conscious learning. These light pieces are his least successful and appealing poems. This stanza from "The Morning Invitation, to Two Young Ladies at the Gloucester Spring" is typical:

Now Celia with thy Cloe rise
Ye fair unlock those radiant eyes,
  Nor more the pillow press;
Now rise and taste of vernal bliss,
Romantic dreams and sleep dismiss, '
  New joys your sense shall bless.

Evans's importance as an early American poet comes chiefly from his verse on the prospect of the new land and its promise as a site of art, science, and culture. In "Daphnis and Menalcas, A Pastoral Eclogue" (1758), he anticipated a reign of artistic accomplishment in his native land: "O Pennsylvania! shall no son of thine

/ Glow with the raptures of the sacred nine?" In such works as "Ode on the Prospect of Peace" (1761) and "An Exercise" (1763), presented at the Commencement of the College of Philadelphia, Evans elaborated the theme that America was destined by its western location to be the eventual home of the ancient muses, a special spot chosen by God for the acting out of secular history.

This "rising glory of America" theme, common in the verse of the second half of the eighteenth century, probably became a central motif in Evans's work through the influence of William Smith, who wrote both poems and sermons around it. It is well illustrated in Evans's "Verses, Addressed to the Trustees of the College and Academy of Philadelphia" (1765), written on the occasion of his receiving an honorary M.A.: "O haste, blest days! till ign'rance flee the ball, / And the bright rays of knowledge lighten all, / Till in you wild new seats of Science rise, / And such as you the arts shall patronize!"

Evans was at his best as a poet—and his most important as a cultural figure—in works that link the Georgian theme of the young poet seeking an acceptable voice with the notion of American specialness implicit in the rising glory theme. He achieved on such occasions a clarity of image, crispness of language, and dramatic force characteristic of the best American writing of his day and after.

Suggested Readings: CCMC; DAB; LHUS; T_2. *See also* M. Katherine Jackson, *Outlines of the Literary History of Colonial Pennsylvania* (1906); Andrew B. Myers, *George Washington's Copy of Poems on Several Occasions by Nathaniel Evans* (1976); Edgar L. Pennington, *Nathaniel Evans, A Poet of Colonial America* (1935).

William D. Andrews
Philadelphia College of Textiles and Science

DAVID EVERETT (1770-1813)

Works: *Common Sense in Dishabille; Or, The Farmer's Monitor* (1799); *Daranzel; Or, The Persian Patriot* (1800); *An Address on the Principles of Masonry* (1801); *An Oration in Vindication of Free Masonry* (1803); *An Oration...Pronounced at Amherst, New Hampshire* (1804); *From the Carrier of the Farmer's Cabinet: A New Year's Address Attempted in Rhyme* (1805); *An Essay on the Rights and Duties of Nations* (1807); *Appendix to a Late Essay* (1808); *Demonstration of the Divinity of the Scriptures* (1811); *Slaves in Barbary* (1817).

Biography: David Everett was born in Princeton, Mass., on Mar. 29, 1770, the eldest son of David Everett and Susannah (Rolfe) Everett. His father was killed early in the War of American Independence, and the family's straitened financial circumstances during the war resulted in his being sent to the home of his grandmother Mary Gerould, who raised him to maturity. He began his formal education at the local academy in Ipswich, N.H., and then continued on to Dartmouth College, where he graduated as valedictorian in 1795. After teaching school for a brief period, he turned to the study of law, practicing first in Boston and then, from 1802 to 1807, in Amherst, N.H. His legal reputation is anchored less in his own achievements than in his sponsorship of the future chief justice of the state of Mass., Lemuel Shaw, who first studied under Everett in Boston and later accompanied him to Amherst. In 1799 Everett married Dorothy Appleton, whose family was very prominent in mercantile circles. Their union produced no children.

By this time, Everett had already begun dividing his energies between law, politics, and literature. In 1797 he wrote the series of essays collected and published under the title *Common Sense in Dishabille*, and in the following year, his play *Daranzel; Or, The Persian Patriot* opened for a single performance in Boston. An active supporter of the Democratic-Republican party, Everett often contributed essays and orations in defense of its philosophy, interests, and actions, and in 1809 he founded his first newspaper, the *Boston Patriot*, to continue the work. For this support, the party leaders rewarded him from time to time with minor patronage positions. By 1812, when he assumed the editorship of the short-lived periodical *The Pilot*, Everett's tubercular condition had beome extreme enough to dictate a move to the supposedly more healthful climate of Marietta, Ohio. There he started another "public journal," *The American Friend*, but he died on Dec. 21, 1813, less than a year after its founding.

Critical Appraisal: Unlike most of the minor participants in the formative period of the American literary tradition, David Everett managed to avoid the plunge into complete historical obscurity. Generations of New Eng. schoolboys kept a tiny portion of his work alive in dutiful recitations of the poem beginning, "You'd scarce expect one of my age / To speak in public on the stage." Everett would undoubtedly have considered that a whimsical winnowing, and justifiably so, for in a short career, and in an age when literature could rarely be a vocation, he produced a wide variety of works.

Everett first came to the attention of the reading public in the above-mentioned *Common Sense in Dishabille*, a pleasant series of homiletic essays introducing themes and attitudes that would continue to characterize his work. A devout man, Everett cautioned the reader against mistaking the title to be a commendation of Thomas Paine (q.v.) and his "deistical colleagues" ("I had rather see spiders' webs hanging on the shelves of thy library") and endorsed Christianity, patriotism, moderation, family stability, strict discipline, and a regular attendance at "Nature's University." Students of social attitudes in the New Eng. of Everett's day would be particularly interested in his projection of the chaotic reaction of "Sambos" to contemporary French notions of reason, liberty, and equality, as the essay assumes the existence of deeply racist attitudes within the audience of readers.

Everett's forays into the field of imaginative literature resulted in numerous poems and three plays. The most ambitious of the latter, *Daranzel; Or, The Persian Patriot*, is a somewhat tedious vehicle for the celebration of patriotism, honor, and duty, but it displays workmanlike blank verse and an adequate sense of dramatic structure. Everett was more effective when concentrating his legal training and literary talent upon political and religious subjects. A good example of this merger is *An Essay on the Rights and Duties of Nations*, a long, closely reasoned analysis of the British-American confrontation of 1807 known in history as the Chesapeake affair. Drawing upon his impressive knowledge of international precedent and British law, Everett developed a sound case against the British action (boarding an American vessel to remove suspected deserters) and an equally firm defense of the response of the Thomas Jefferson (q.v.) administration. Shortly thereafter he displayed his versatility in *Appendix to a Late Essay*—a marvelously convoluted satiric response to critics of the earlier essay. A more intriguing use of his logic and erudition is his *Demonstration of the Divinity of the Scriptures*. Here Everett returned to two themes—Christianity and nationalism—that had first surfaced in *Common Sense in Dishabille*, and he interwove the two in an attempt to demonstrate that the prophetic accuracy of the Scriptures not only proved their divine origin, but also that the U.S. was the "New Israel" and thus the peculiar beneficiary of divine favor. The essay deserves attention as a remarkable illustration of the effort to integrate a providential element into the nationalistic self-definition under formation at the time.

Suggested Readings: DAB. *See also* F. E. Blake, *David Everett* (n.d.); G. T. Chapman, *Sketches of the Alumni of Dartmouth College* (1867); E. F. Everett, *Descendants of Richard Everett of Dedham, Massachusetts* (1902); I. A. Jewett, *Memorial of Samuel Appleton* (1850); J. S. Loring, *The Hundred Boston Orators* (1852), pp. 337-344; Walter J. Meserve, *An Emerging Entertainment* (1977), pp. 57, 156-157, 272; Arthur Hobson Quinn, *A History of American Drama From the Beginning to the Civil War* (1923), p. 120.

David Sloan
University of Arkansas at Fayetteville

F

MARGARETTA V. BLEECKER FAUGERES (1771-1801)

Works: *The Posthumous Works of Ann Eliza Bleecker* (1793); *Belisarius: A Tragedy* (1795); *The Ghost of John Young the Homicide* (1797); "Ode" [for the 4th of Jul.] (pub. in George Clinton, *An Oration Delivered on the Fourth of July 1798*, pp. 15-16; 1798).

Biography: Margaretta V. Faugeres, born in N.Y. in 1771, was the daughter of John J. Bleecker of New Rochelle and Ann Eliza (Schuyler) Bleecker (q.v.), an accomplished poetess in her own right. From infancy, Faugeres lived in the village of Tomhanick, a frontier settlement about eighteen miles north of Albany. At age 4, while her father was in Albany, she fled with her mother and sister before the advance of Burgoyne and the marauding Indians accompanying his army. The shock of the flight was made even harder by the sudden deaths of young Margaretta's sister and Mrs. Bleecker's mother and only surviving half-sister. Because of Tomhanick's nearness to the Canadian border, there were other incursions, and these vicissitudes took their toll on the young Margaretta's sensitive nature.

When her mother died in 1783, Margaretta, then 13, moved with her father to N.Y., where, because of her liberal fortune and social connections, her home was thronged with suitors. In 1791, however, she married Peter Faugeres, an "infidel" physician, a French "adventurer," and a profligate who rapidly reduced Margaretta to poverty after the death of her father in 1795. Following the death by yellow fever of her husband in 1798, Faugeres tried to support herself and her daughter as a teacher in New York City and Brooklyn until, broken-hearted and worn with toil, she died in N.Y. on Jan. 9, 1801, age 29.

Faugeres published most of her poetry after her marriage. Her major effort was editing the posthumous works in prose and verse of her mother (1793), to which she added thirty-eight of her own poems and four short essays. As she noted in the preface, her poetry had first appeared in the *New York Magazine*, under the signature "Ella."

Critical Appraisal: Most of Margaretta Faugeres's poems in the *Posthumous Works* and those separately published—a patriotic ode, the tragedy

Belisarius, and a "gallows" poem—derive form and substance from English neo-Classicism. In length, *Belisarius* is her major work. Submitted unsuccessfully to the John St. Theatre in N.Y., the blank-verse drama, vaguely reminiscent of *King Lear*, departs from history in adopting the legend that the noble conqueror of Carthage in the late Roman Empire was "a blind, abandoned, beggared old man." Like Lear, the old general has a lovely and devoted daughter, but unlike Lear, Belisarius knows her worth. "The Ghost of John Young" cannot be dismissed as a sensational gallows poem, for it abjures death's-door repentence and gruesome descriptions to concentrate on the murderer's motive— "rage" and "fury" rather than premeditation—on the inhuman treatment of the defendant—the judge forcing him to stand four hours unrelieved at his trial—and on the waste of capital punishment as a deterrent of crime.

Much of the poetry in *Posthumous Works*, being the "lamp" of Faugeres's experiences, is revealingly autobiographical. One finds in the more confessional ones fascinating insights into her troubled life, that of a freedom-seeking female unable to revolt successfully against a repressive environment, and one reconstructs the persona of a disillusioned and world-weary romantic rebel. In a verse paraphrase of part of Job 7, she longs for rest with the "quiet dead": "Forgot— Abandoned—Destitute—Alone." One surmises an allusion to her husband's betrayal in her address to personified "Friendship," whose name she hates, and in "Elegy to Miss Anna Dundas," her mother, on her deathbed, anxiously wonders who will care for her daughter when she is gone. In "Evening," amid "mouldering ruins" near the Hudson, she asks for "resignation" to cope with the loss of her brother, her father, mother, and another "loved one," until Death shall wake her from the dream of life.

Faugeres's rebellion extended to politics and religious enthusiasm. Two of her poems extol the French Revolution, for example, "See the Bastille's iron walls thrown down. . . crushed by the giant arm of Liberty!" Her "To the Reverend J— N—" (1792) panegyrizes the Englishman John Newton ("fair Olney's aged bard"), whom she knew primarily through the *Olney Hymns* (1779), probably the most important collection in the Evangelical movement.

Throughout, Faugeres's poetry is encumbered with eighteenth-century poetic diction, figures, and genres. Typical of her contemporaries, she wrote in the didactic mode odes, pastoral elegies, epistles, occasional verse, and descriptions of the seasons. However, her anguished feelings and vivid imaginings resulted in verse anticipating Poe, as in "Night" (suggestive of "Dream-Land") and "To Arribert," in which the poet spoke from the grave to loved ones (as "To Annie"). Charitably, these poems anticipate Poe; more correctly, they continue the tradition of English graveyard poetry, inaugurated by Parnell, Blair, and Young.

The one neo-Classic form that allowed her didactic urge and love of nature full range was the topographic genre. Sir John Denham's *Cooper's Hill* (1642) originated the type, and in America, as in England, poets described, meditated upon, and embellished with historical data specific geographical features, such as hills, streams, towns, and estates. Faugeres published three works in this genre. "Silence" (published under the pseudonym "Ella" in the *New York Magazine* in 1792) offers reflections on loneliness in a specific setting—a prospect of the Delaware near Philadelphia. In "To Miss Mason" the separation of the poetess and her friend is made doubly poignant by her separation from "Beauteous Rochelle. . . , / Where yon gay locusts shade the green, / And gently whisper to the breeze; / Where chirps the wren their boughs between, / And flowers and shrubs conspire to please."

Much eighteenth-century magazine verse developed similar topics. A nationalistic urge and an emerging cult of nature worship elicited numerous mediocre responses like hers. "The Hudson" stands out, however, for no one before her had described a major American river from its source to the sea, in travelog detail, noting its towns, scenery, and history. Not that the river poem lacked conventions, which she used, that would give her feelings form, such as sublime and picturesque descriptions, panegyrics to commerce, the appearance of river nymphs, a formal invocation to the "Genius of old Hudson's stream," and a concluding prophecy of the future glory of America.

The strength of the poem is its concrete imagery. From its source near "where rough Ontario's restless waters roar" to "fair Nassau's isle," vistas presage the Hudson River school of painters. Flowers are cataloged (e.g., water lilies, blue crocus, scarlet larkspur, columbine, wild-rose, and honeysuckle), and historical reminiscences are added: the capture of Ticonderoga, the murder of Jane McCrea by Indians near Ft. Edwards, Gen. Horatio Gates's victory at Saratoga, Benedict Arnold's (q.v.) treason at West Point, the storming of Stony Point, among other incidents on or near the river. The poet's pride in "Eboracia's stately towers" elicits genre sketches of city activities—the fish market, the busy docks, and carpenters hard at work. For the grand scenery along the river, the poet attempted the sublime, as at the Palisades. Below the Highlands,

> Tall mural rocks shoot proud into the air;
> In shapes fantastic lift their turrets high,
> Fit for the shadowy forms who revel there;
> The hardy pines that on the steep sides grow,. . .
> Appear like shrubs to the strained eyes below.
> The wandering goat adventures to the brink,
> And peeps across the fretted edge with care;
> Then from the awful precipice she shrinks,
> As though relentless Ruin hovered there.

Suggested Readings: NAW. *See also* Rufus W. Griswold, ed., *The Female Poets of America* (1849), pp. 35-37; Eugene L. Huddleston, "Topographical Poetry of the Early National Period," AL, 38 (1966), 303-322; Emily Stipes Watts, "The Magazine Poets," *The Poetry of American Women from 1632 to 1945* (1977), pp. 51-56.

Eugene L. Huddleston
Michigan State University

JENNY FENNO (fl. 1791)

Works: *Original Compositions in Prose and Verse. On Subjects Moral and Religious* (1791).

Biography: Details of family connection and birth are not available for Jenny Fenno. We know only that she was living in Boston, Mass., in 1791, when she composed the preface to her *Original Compositions*. The dateline of the preface and one of the poems, "On the Dreadful Conflagration in Boston, in 1787," suggest that her residence there extended at least from the late 1780s; probably it was even longer. Her elegy "On the Death of the Rev. Mr. THOMAS GAIR," pastor of the Second Baptist Church in Boston, may indicate that Fenno herself was Baptist. Additionally, her *Original Compositions* reveals a woman of considerable education, well acquainted with the imagery and poetic diction common to neo-Classical poetry. Her references to John Milton, Isaac Watts, and Elizabeth Singer Rowe emphasize the literary direction of her education. These conjectures about Fenno's residence, religion, and education are all that remain to provide a biographical context for her work.

Critical Appraisal: The subject matter and forms of Jenny Fenno's *Original Compositions* reflect the conventional literary concerns of late eighteenth-century America; her preface reflects her unconventional position in an environment unsympathetic to women writers. She began her *Original Compositions* on the defensive. Like so many women writers, she felt the need to justify publication, to answer "*the important question, what has induced me to make public my private thoughts and reflections?*" She disclaimed any desire "*for honor and applause*," of course, citing instead her duty to God and the pressure of friends. But Fenno had no illusions about her audience: "*I expect to meet the censures of many*; but none of these things move me. *The like things have happened to others that have gone before me.*"

Most of Fenno's *Original Compositions* treat "Subjects Moral and Religious," as her subtitle suggests. Her poems and essays are works of praise, of "the joys of religion . . . lasting and true." The agonies of confession and personal examination are not for her, but rather "the happiness of feeling [her] dependence on GOD." An illness that had brought Fenno near death combines with her theology to focus her attention on themes of human mortality: "Death with his scythe is come to cut you down, / Now like the tender grass you must be mown."

But Fenno's theology goes beyond this preoccupation with death and eternity to a concern for the affairs of this world as well: her essays repeatedly emphasize that "the more we love God, the more we feel concern for our fellow creatures." Her poems and essays develop secular topics such as the limits of language, feelings of national pride, praise for President George Washington (q.v.), and observation of nature and include neo-Classical set-pieces such as "On Contentment" or "On Friendship." In addition, Fenno's verses occasionally explore pre-Romantic themes of the imminence of God in nature: "In ev'ry object, sure a GOD is seen."

Fenno's verse illustrates, for the most part, the influence of British neo-Classical poetry. She frequently makes use of poetic diction (e.g., "finny tribe," "radiant globe") and of conventional imagery. Most of her verse is in heroic couplets. These materials are combined in a variety of contemporary poetic forms: elegies, odes, an acrostic, biblical paraphrases, a verse patterned on the doxology, prose dialogs. Although Fenno's essays read more like exercises in praise than explorations of ideas and although her poems seem more faithful to the rules of verse than to the spirit of poetry, students of American religion and of pre-Romanticism will find ample material in Fenno's *Original Compositions* to repay their attention.

Suggested Readings: Jacqueline Hornstein, "Jenny Fenno," *American Women Writers*, ed. Lina Mainiero (1980), II, 23-24; idem, "Literary History of New England Women Writers: 1630-1800" (Ph.D. diss., N.Y. Univ., 1978), pp. 230-231, 283-293.

Pattie Cowell
Colorado State University

JOHN FENNO (1751-1798)

Works: *The Gazette of the United States; a National Paper Published at the Seat of Government: Containing a History of the Proceedings of the Legislature of the United States under the New Constitution...A Series of Original Essays, upon the Most Interesting Subjects of Life, Manners and Politics* (1789-1790). Established as a semiweekly on Apr. 15, 1789, and published in N.Y. until Oct. 13, 1790 (vol. 2, no. 53), when it was removed to Philadelphia. Continued with the issue of Nov. 3, 1790 (vol. 2, no. 54), but suspended on Sept. 18, 1793, because of yellow fever epidemic and faltering financial support. Resumed as a daily on Dec. 11, 1793, as *The Gazette of the United States & Evening Advertiser*. Title varied thereafter: Jan. 7, 1794, *The Gazette of the United States and Daily Evening Advertiser*; Jul. 1, 1795, *The Gazette of the United States*; Jul. 1, 1796, *The Gazette of the United States, & Philadelphia Daily Advertiser*. Additional title changes followed John Fenno's death on Sept. 14, 1798.

Biography: Reputedly the son of an ale-house keeper and leather dresser—Ephraim Fenno—and Mary Chapman, John Fenno was born in Boston, Mass., on Aug. 12, 1751(o.s.). For a brief time, he was employed as an "usher"—an assistant teacher—in Samuel Holbrook's Writing School. While residing in Boston, Fenno contributed several articles to the local press. During the Revolutionary War, Fenno served with distinction as the secretary to Gen. Artemas Ward. On May 8, 1777, Fenno married Mary Curtiss. His dabbling as an importer led to a row with creditors, and in 1789 he journeyed to N.Y. with a letter of introduction from Christopher Gore of Boston to Rufus King, a prominent Federalist. Fenno had cut his journalistic teeth on Benjamin Russell's *Massachusetts Centinel* and came prepared with a scheme for a political organ dedicated "for the purpose of demonstrating favorable sentiments of the federal constitution and its administration." Gore considered Fenno's literary achievements as "handsome" and lauded the journalist's "unquestionable" honor and integrity.

In mid-Apr. 1789, Fenno issued his first number of the *Gazette of the United States*, in time to announce the preparations for George Washington's (q.v.) inauguration. In his prospectus, Fenno promised to make the newspaper "a National, Impartial, and Independent Conveyancer to all parts of the Union, of News, Politics, and Miscellanies." He perceived himself as a true editor, rather than a mere printer or distant publisher. Fenno assured readers he would publish an unadulterated description of congressional debates in addition to the proceedings of Congress. Essays upon "great subjects of Government," "living manners," and "the interests of the United States as connected with their literary institutions" were high on his list of priorities. His proposal to include commentary on "the state of national funds" later led to the introduction of anonymous diatribes against the Jeffersonians drafted by Secretary of the Treasury Alexander Hamilton (q.v.). Fenno sought nothing less than to provide the new government and the nation with a permanent record of public events—complete with an index and a supply of back numbers for subscribers. Oddly enough, Fenno initially hoped to attract common readers—"the mechanics"—as well as the aristocratic Federalists. Early in the tenure of his semiweekly venture, Fenno, along with Francis Childs (publisher of the *Daily Advertiser*) and Thomas Lloyd (editor of the *Congressional Register*), was accused in Congress of inaccurate reporting.

At first, Fenno refused to solicit advertising to support his newspaper. However, by late 1789, Fenno had opened his columns to advertisements that would "convey intelligence of an interesting nature." In addition, he carried occasional republican articles drafted by the Federalists' political enemies. By the end of his first six months in New York City, Fenno had succeeded in raising his circulation to nearly 650 copies, although his expenses exceeded his revenues.

The impact of Fenno's journalistic agitation upon political developments did not escape the scrutiny of Secretary of State Thomas Jefferson (q.v.). Virtually all journals in the U.S. were replete with British accounts of foreign affairs, a situation that did not assuage the predicament of pro-French republicans. Philip Freneau (q.v.), an editor of the New York *Daily Advertiser*, published a Philadelphia account that alleged the public prints were carrying "mere echoes" of G.B. unsuitable for the "genius of our government." Jefferson characterized the monthly influx of such "lies" as throwing the democratic elements "into a very disagreeable suspense." Instead of requesting the assistance of Freneau and others, Jefferson turned to Fenno's *Gazette of the United States*, which was then publishing John Adams's (q.v.) anonymous "Discourses on Davila." Shrewdly, Jefferson arranged for Fenno to publish translations of articles appearing in the *Gazette de Leide*. As noted in the *Papers of Thomas Jefferson, Volume 16*, such a move succeeded in countering the spate of reprinted English foreign dispatches and in providing Jefferson a forum for lashing out obliquely at John Adams. In return, Fenno's newspaper was selected to print the federal statutes. The alliance was short-lived, in part because of the lack of timeliness of *Gazette de Leide* articles. Truer to the mark, however, was the less-than-subtle change in Fenno's declared editorial impartiality. The threat of democracy to the Federalist political order and the shifting tide of public passions apparently convinced Fenno to accept material financial backing from Jefferson's opponents. Jefferson turned his allegiance in 1791 to Benjamin Franklin Bache's (q.v.) *General Advertiser*. Yet Jefferson retained his dedication to the utility of the *Gazette de Leide*, arranging later to have it supplied to Philip Freneau for inclusion in the *National Gazette*.

By 1790 Fenno's vituperative organ still teetered upon the brink of financial insolvency. Less than one-half of the expense of publication was supported through receipts. With the removal of the national government to Philadelphia, Fenno packed up his *Gazette of the United States* and became a political camp follower. The prospect of ceremony and the assumption of the duties of a "court journal" in a dignified setting apparently appealed to the editor. Monetary problems pursued him to Philadelphia. Of the 1,400 copies circulated by 1791, only 1,000 issues of his journal reached legitimate subscribers. Pleas for payment of delinquent accounts failed to move tardy subscribers. By 1793 Fenno would be forced to beseech Alexander Hamilton and others to relieve him of a $2,500 debt. His problems were compounded with the emergence of Philip Freneau's *National Gazette* on Oct. 31, 1791.

Freneau had met with Jefferson in N.Y. while the former was writing for the *Daily Advertiser*. One of Freneau's journalistic cohorts, John Pintard, had been working as a translating clerk in the Department of State. When Pintard declined to move to Philadelphia with the new government, the position became available for Freneau. At the urging of James Madison (q.v.) and Henry Lee (q.v.), Jefferson ultimately induced Freneau to sojourn to Philadelphia where the former "Poet of the Revolution" established his unofficial republican newspaper. Freneau's stable of scribblers proved more formidable than that of Fenno. For Freneau, an able writer in his own right, was assured contributions from James Madison and Hugh Henry Brackenridge (q.v.). Hamilton, the colossus of Fenno's *Gazette of the United States*, soon found himself beset by incisive essays deploring his handling of the national treasury. Hamilton, writing as "T.L." and "An American" in the *Gazette of the United States*, accused Jefferson of wire pulling at the *National Gazette* as well as authoring several of the more pungent of the character assassinations. Hamilton's allegations served to fragment further the factional split within President George Washington's cabinet. Washington pleaded for reconciliation between Hamilton and Jefferson, a position neither was willing to take. In a now famous letter to Washington, Thomas Jefferson wrote, "He [Freneau] & Fenno are rivals for the public favor. The one courts them by flattery, the other by censure, & I believe it will be admitted that one has been as servile, as the other severe. . . . No government ought to be without censors: & where the press is free, no one ever will."

On Oct. 26, 1793, the *National Gazette* ceased publication, apparently, as Jefferson himself admitted, for "want of money." Fenno's *Gazette of the United*

States, despite a brief suspension that fall as a result of a yellow fever epidemic and financial instability, regained much of its vitality and became a daily. Fenno's power, however, declined with the erosion of Federalism. John Fenno died during one of the recurrent yellow fever outbreaks on Sept. 14, 1798. His death was announced in the Sept. 17, 1798, edition of the *Gazette of the United States* with a single line on the front page. His son, John Ward Fenno, assumed publication that day with vol. XIV, no. 1872. He retained control until he sold the venture to Caleb P. Wayne, who began publishing the paper on May 28, 1800.

Critical Appraisal: With the establishment of the *Gazette of the United States* in 1789, the Federalists succeeded in entrenching the first avowed organ of American political government and in breaking from the tradition of mercantile newspapers only incidentally interested in the political arena. As John Fenno stated on Apr. 27, 1791, American citizens would benefit from the *Gazette*'s impartial rendition of the course of daily events. He wrote,

> To hold up the people's own government, in a favorable point of light— and to impress just ideas of its administration by exhibiting FACTS, comprise the outline of the plan of this paper—and so long as the principles of the Constitution are held sacred, and the rights and liberties of the people are preserved inviolate, by "the powers that be," it is the office of patriotism, by every exertion, to endear the GENERAL GOVERNMENT TO THE PEOPLE.

Unfortunately for the Federalists, Fenno's effusiveness toward the administration of President George Washington and his capricious treatment of the "mechanics" soon undermined his influence with the growing literate populace. The Federalists found themselves in a quandary. They considered journalistic scribbling as a disreputable profession beneath their contempt. Politics, many Federalists firmly believed, should be left to the oratory of the elite, rather than to the pens of societal misfits. Fenno, who had not served an apprenticeship as a printer, was a radical compromise for the "old school" committed to the genteel rule of a silent multitude. Fenno strove to overcome the Federalist prejudice against the impropriety of public discussion of political affairs. At best, his efforts to bolster the staid old order proved an admixture of pathos and panegyric, for to risk the reduction of constitutional questions to the tastes of mass panderers meant almost certain dilution of elitist Federalist tenets. Equality was to be feared, the Federalists contended, because it fostered mediocrity in public affairs and literature.

By 1791 a dozen newspapers were published in Philadelphia, with the *Gazette of the United States* enjoying the largest national circulation of any newspaper of the period. Fenno's "court journal" was filled with accounts of levees, titles, and what Thomas Jefferson later characterized as the "doctrine of monarchy, aristocracy, and the exclusion of the people." Clearly, the polarization that had seized American life by the 1790s left little middle ground for general debate. Press diatribes replaced discussion. Issues of separation and balance within the constitutional arena quickly spilled over into the news and views columns. Republican newspapers, including John Dunlap's *Daily American Advertiser* and Benjamin Franklin Bache's (q.v.) Pa. *Daily Advertiser*, castigated Federalist policies but proved incapable of waging prolonged literary warfare. Fenno succeeded in fostering the support of ardent and articulate Federalists such as Alexander Hamilton and John Adams. Within months of its appearance, the *Gazette of the United States* became common journalistic currency among the intelligentsia of Europe, Can. and the W.Ind.—as well as the U.S. Fenno blanketed the administration's political servants with copies of the newspaper—often provided gratis. Some 120 postmasters and printers received free copies of the organ by 1791.

Fenno's philosophy, like that of the Federalists before 1800, emerged unvarnished with any semblance of paternalism toward the public. The often inconsequential movements of President Washington flooded the news columns. Fenno quickly adopted a peerage mentality, referring to the president as "His Excellency," although preferring pretentious titles such as "Your Magistracy" or "Your Supremacy." Congressional acts were lauded as works of enlightened political genius. The Constitution was held inviolable. The mere suggestion of amendment was received as heresy. Change, reform, or innovation were depicted in Fenno's columns as insidious evils. Public disapproval of administrative acts were blights upon the honor of the nation. Allegations of "stretches of power and acts of oppression" were leveled against state and local governments. As noted in Douglas Southall Freeman's biography of George Washington, Fenno attempted to rationalize his blatant partisanship by denouncing the concept that "reserve and silence" evince public approval. Such a belief, Fenno wrote, "was strongly tinctured with the Turkish policy of employing mutes!"

Federalist editors were quick to follow Fenno's lead, even while the editor stung the opposition from his temporary base in N.Y. With roughly two-thirds of the newspapers leaning heavily Federalist, it was not unexpected that the trend of reprinting articles from the *Gazette of the United States* and of emulating Fenno's aristocratic style should alarm the Jeffersonians. Hamilton's fiscal programs had garnered considerable support by the spring of 1790, with newspapers such as the *Massachusetts Centinel, Massachusetts Spy, Virginia Herald*, and Charleston *State Gazette* parroting the Federalist line. Despite opposition from vocal organs such as Thomas Greenleaf's *Journal* and Benjamin Edes's *Gazette*, Fenno's *Gazette of the United States* reigned supreme in its youth, discarding fairness for faction. Republicans were eager to act, but lacked a contentious popular editor. "We have been trying," Thomas Jefferson wrote to his son-in-law, "to get another weekly set up [in Philadelphia], but failed."

On Oct. 31, 1791, the complexion of the partisan press in America changed. Philip Freneau established the *National Gazette* and immediately engaged Fenno in literary combat. Within months, Freneau discarded any semblance of impartiality, publishing excerpts from Thomas Paine's (q.v.) *The Rights of Man* and stinging letters from bitter republicans. Fenno mistakenly struck out at these "mad dogs," implying that many administration critics were merely immigrants who knew not "how to enjoy liberty." Worse, Fenno denigrated the "abusers of government" as pretending to exercise "a right given them by the constitution." As noted by Lewis G. Leary, Fenno's action isolated him from the new capital's Scotch, Irish, German, and French populace who had suffered under aristocratic rule.

Fenno's sniping, coupled with the falcated pen strokes of Freneau's *National Gazette*, did not augur well for the Federalists battling for congressional control. Alexander Hamilton was stung by Freneau's barbed attacks upon his administrative ability—but, worse, suffered from the adulation heaped upon that "Colossus of Liberty," Thomas Jefferson. When Hamilton discovered that Freneau had received an appointment in Jefferson's department as a translator, the secretary of the Treasury immediately inferred that he was being singled out for character assassination. Fenno's *Gazette of the United States* served as the battleground for Hamilton's salvos against Thomas Jefferson—whom he believed responsible for the campaign against his reputation. Writing as "T.L." and "An American" during Jul. and Aug. 1792, Hamilton advanced a series of arguments implying the duplicity of Freneau and Jefferson. Unlike Fenno's effusive rhetoric, Hamilton's letters cut to the quick. Hamilton wrote on Jul. 28, 1792,

> I have often heard that authors in England . . . when they find their books do not sell . . . hire some garretteer to write against them—then publish a reply to his own lucubrations—and so go on . . . until the attention of the public is drawn towards the book, and thus it is brought into demand. If there were as many pieces in the *National Gazette* in favor of government and public characters, as there are against them, I should be apt to conclude that Congress and their officers were playing us the same trick, in hopes of keeping their seats and places for life; but when all the publications are against them, and none in their favor—when this "free newspaper" is always
>
> Free to defame, but never free to praise,
>
> it does not appear easy to account for this branch of national expence.

Freneau, according to Hamilton on Aug. 4, 1792, "is not then, as he would have supposed, the Independent Editor of a News Paper, who through receiving a salary from Government has firmness enough to expose its maladministration." Hamilton ignored Freneau's affidavit of innocence, later writing that at the very least a "particular friend" of Jefferson had opened negotiations with Freneau for the establishment of a paper. In addition, Hamilton implied that Jefferson was the true author of unnamed *National Gazette* articles. Naturally, Fenno fell under suspicion as a logical candidate for the true identity of "T.L." On Jul. 28, 1792, Fenno responded to correspondent "A.Z." that "T.L." was "neither the editor, publisher or printer of any newspaper whatever, nor directly or indirectly concerned in any." Despite the apparent realization by Freneau of "T.L.'s" identity, Fenno continued to suffer at the hands of critics who reminded the public of

Fenno's lucrative printing arrangements with the U.S. Senate, Treasury Department, and the Bank of the U.S. Fenno's countercharge was equally as effective:
the N.Y. firm of Childs and Swaine, from whose Philadelphia office the *National Gazette* was published, had cornered patronage from the House of Representatives, the Department of State, and some additional business from the
Treasury Department.

President Washington attempted to reconcile the differences between Jefferson
and Hamilton—with little success. Hamilton continued battering Jefferson through
the columns of the *Gazette of the United States*. Only the demise of the *National
Gazette* brought a brief armistice to the internecine conflict that had rent Washington's cabinet.

In spite of coverage of the trivialities of Washington's administration, Fenno's
journal did serve as a useful barometer for measuring the political pressures
inherent within the democratic and Federalist factions. He touched upon the most
sensitive of political nerves when he reprinted letters of John Adams and the
important "Discourses on Davila." Adams posed a critical question in the "Discourses" when he queried "whether equal laws, the result only of a balanced
government, can ever be obtained and preferred without some signs or other of
distinction and degree." Federalists readily equated the pernicious notion of
equality with mediocrity and the threat of demagoguery. Fenno countered such
democratic principles—the secret influence of public opinion—with stinging
diatribes aimed against the dread French example. News of the execution of
Louis XVI evoked sentimental eulogies to the late king from Fenno's newspaper.
Fenno reprinted a foreign report describing Marat at the French Hall of the
convention, which characterized the Revolutionary as "deprived by nature of all
those qualities which render man beloved and respectable in society." The *Gazette of the United States* held "Citizen" Genet in equal disrepute.

Fenno's newspaper did, regardless, supply a polarized public with a smatter-
ing of foreign news from Br., Fr., Sp., the United Neth., and Prus. Essays
touching upon a variety of subjects found their niche in Fenno's journal. Slavery,
religious toleration, American manufacture, debates on the Sedition Bill, and the
intrigues of warring nations received careful attention. Fenno—and later his
son—culled essays from the *Columbian Magazine* and *The Farmer's Weekly
Museum* (including fourteen numbers of Joseph Dennie's "The Lay Preacher") to
delight an elite audience. Verse written or reprinted by Fenno proved more
effusive than evocative. In "To the President of the United States," a poet wrote,

> For in the annals of mankind,
> Who ever saw a compact bind
>   An empire's utmost bound,
> Who ever saw ambition stand,
> Whithout [sic] the power to raise her hand,
>   While ONE the people crown'd.

Clearly, Fenno was more interested in levees than literature. An exception was

the work of Joseph Dennie, whose *The Lay Preacher* (1796) had led to fond
correspondence between the two Federalists. With the death of Fenno, his son—
John Ward Fenno—immediately implored Dennie to join his efforts to continue
the *Gazette of the United States*. J. W. Fenno reprinted articles Dennie drafted
for *The Farmer's Weekly Museum* and gave them prominent play (see Sept. 20,
1798, issue for "And sad visions appeared unto them with heavy countenance").

Until the end of his life, John Fenno probably believed he had fulfilled his
promise "To Correspondents" on May 16, 1789:

> The *Gazette of the United States* is devoted to the cause of Truth and the
> Public Good; and Speculations wrote [*sic*] with *propriety, candor*, and
> *decency*, which have that object, and the general Welfare for their basis,
> will always meet with a ready insertion.

The yellow fever epidemic of 1798 silenced such rhetoric in the press, carrying
with it Fenno, Bache, and sixty other Philadelphians affiliated with public prints.
Fenno, like his Federalist colleagues, had embraced an elitism whose millennial
promise failed to materialize. Yet Fenno's antidemocratic tenets served as the
underpinning for a final Federalist attempt to turn the masses away from republicanism at the turn of the century. John Ward Fenno perhaps best summarized the
Federalists' desperation when he wrote in 1799,

> The American newspapers are the most base, false, servile and venal
> publications, that ever polluted the fountains of society—their editors the
> most ignorant, mercenary, and vulgar automatons that ever were moved by
> the continually rusting wires of sordid mercantile avarice....
>
> The newspapers of America are admirably calculated to keep the country
> in a continued state of insurrection and revolution.

Suggested Readings: DAB. *See also* Seth Ames, ed., *Works of Fisher Ames:
With a Selection from His Speeches and Correspondence, Volume I*, 2nd ed. (1854);
Willard G. Bleyer, *Main Currents in the History of American Journalism* (1927); Julian
P. Boyd, ed., *The Papers of Thomas Jefferson*, Vol. 16 (1961); 18 (1971); Clarence S.
Brigham, *History and Bibliography of American Newspapers, 1690-1820* (1947); David
H. Fischer, *The Revolution of American Conservatism: The Federalist Party in the Era of
Jeffersonian Democracy* (1965); S. E. Forman, "The Political Activities of Philip Fre-
neau," JHS, 20th ser., nos. 9-10 (Sept.-Oct. 1902), 465-570; John R. Howe, Jr., "Repub-
lican Thought and the Political Violence of the 1790s," AQ, 19 (1967), 147-165; C. R.
King, *Life and Correspondence of Rufus King, Vol. I* (1894); Lewis G. Leary, *That
Rascal Freneau: A Study in Literary Failure* (1964); Philip Marsh, "The Griswold Story
of Freneau and Jefferson," AHR, 51 (1945), 68-73; John C. Miller, *The Federalist Era,
1789-1801* (1960); Frank Luther Mott, *American Journalism* (1931; rev. ed. 1962);
George H. Payne, *History of Journalism in the United States* (1931); James E. Pollard,
The Presidents and the Press (1947); Lewis P. Simpson, "Federalism and the Crisis of
Literary Order," AL, 32 (1960), 253-266; Donald H. Stewart, "Jeffersonian Journalism:
Newspaper Propaganda and the Development of the Democratic-Republican Party, 1789-
1801" (Ph.D. diss., Columbia Univ., 1950); Harold C. Syrett, ed., *The Papers of Alexander
Hamilton*, Vol. 12 (1967); 14 (1969); 15 (1969);19 (1973); 21 (1974); 24 (1976). For a

glimpse of Fenno's earlier exploits, see the "General and Division Orders" of Gen. Artemas Ward, Mass. militia, 1 vol., Apr. 20, to Sept. 6, 1775, in the Massachusetts Historical Society. Fenno served as Ward's secretary.

William F. Vartorella
Mary Baldwin College

ELIZABETH GRAEME FERGUSSON (1737-1801)

Works: "A Hymn to the Beauties of Creation" (w. 1766; pub. 1791); *Paraphrases of the Psalms of David* (w. 1766-1767); *Telemachus* (w. 1766-1769); epistolary correspondence with Nathaniel Evans, "Answer by Laura," and "On the Death of the Reverend Nathaniel Evans" (pub. in Nathaniel Evans, *Poems on Several Occasions, with Some Other Compositions*; 1772); "Ode to Summer" (w. 1775; pub. 1791); "Lines Written on a Blank-leaf of Dr. Young's *Night Thoughts*" (w. 1779; pub. 1791); "On the Death of Leopold, Prince of Brunswick" (1786); "On the Re-perusal of the Foregoing Lines by 'Sylvia' " (w. 1786; pub. 1791); "Lines on Herschel's Comet" (w. 1787; pub. 1809); "On a Beautiful Damask Rose" (1789); "Friendship Preferable to Love" (1790), "On the Importance of Time" (1790); "Lines on Five Modern Evangelical Characters" (1790); "On Reading the Sorrows of Werter" (1790); "The Rose-bush an Emblem of Life" (1790); "Addressed to Mrs. F—r on the Death of Her Son" (1791); "A Paraphrase on Augur's Prayer" (1791); "The Rose and Lilly a Tale" (1791); "The Woodlands" (1809). Transcriptions of Fergusson's complete poems appear in Chester T. Hallenbeck, "The Life and Collected Poems of Elizabeth Graeme Fergusson" (Master's thesis, Columbia Univ., 1929).

Biography: Elizabeth Graeme was born in Philadelphia, Pa., on Feb. 3, 1737, to the prominent Dr. Thomas Graeme and Ann Diggs Graeme, stepdaughter of Sir William Keith, the first provincial governor of Pa. She was engaged to marry Benjamin Franklin's (q.v.) son William in 1757, but the relationship was broken off. On a trip to Eng. in 1764-1765, she had an audience with George III, became friends with Dr. John Fothergill, and met Laurence Sterne. Later she befriended Nathaniel Evans (q.v.) and Francis Hopkinson (q.v.), wrote and circulated her own poetry, and presided over one of America's first literary salons. In 1772 she married Henry Hugh Fergusson, but during the Revolution, her marriage created difficulties, for her husband supported the British and in 1777 became a commissioner of prisoners under Gen. Howe. During the war, Elizabeth tried to remain neutral, but her marriage and prominent connections drew her into intrigues that cast suspicion on her patriotism and caused her to live under the threat of forced exile and the loss of Graeme Park, her family's estate. Able, finally, to avoid both of these misfortunes, she lived the remainder of her life separated from her husband and in constant financial difficulty. She died, having found it necessary to sell Graeme Park, at a local farmhouse on Feb. 23, 1801.

Critical Appraisal: Elizabeth Graeme Fergusson is primarily important as one who both participated in and encouraged America's early national literary culture. She came into direct contact with the literary life of Eng. and, as a prominent hostess of pre-Revolutionary Philadelphia, helped spread the English literary-salon spirit in America, thereby encouraging better known poets such as Nathaniel Evans and Francis Hopkinson. She may have been the first to translate François Fénelon's *Télémaque* into English verse and was almost certainly the first American woman to undertake such a major translation.

Her published poetry, most of which appeared under the name "Laura," includes a flirtatious poetical correspondence with Nathaniel Evans and a variety of magazine verse, the latter of which appeared in *The Columbian Magazine; Or, Monthly Miscellany* from 1786 to 1789, *The Universal Asylum, and Columbian Magazine* in 1790-1791, and *The Port Folio* in 1809. In her later years, she tried but failed to have her *Telemachus* published. Besides *Telemachus* and *Paraphrases of the Psalms of David*, her two longest and most serious works, her unpublished poems include *Il Penseroso, or The Deserted Wife*, which refers to obscure circumstances in which her husband was accused of fathering an illegitimate child, and *Cadavera's Ghost, or A Visit to Tomboso*, a humorous sequel to a satire by Francis Hopkinson in which a medical student falls in love with a corpse.

Chester T. Hallenbeck, who edited Fergusson's poems, is also her most scholarly biographer and critic. He provided the following comment on her literary ability: "Unfortunately Miss Graeme was a slave to the literary conventions of her age. With a few minor exceptions everything she wrote was cast in either the four-stress or the heroic couplet. The influence of Dryden and Pope was strong upon her; so strong, in fact, that whatever originality she might have possessed was lost in imitating her masters." Hallenbeck complained of her "inappropriate diction and forced rhyme" but commended "a certain smoothness of rhythm and occasional felicitous lines."

Though her poetry is sometimes entertaining and witty and is generally competent, for the most part it is rather flat and conventional. When her entire career is surveyed, her work shows a typical eighteenth-century movement from Augustan conventions to those of the later graveyard school and poets of sensibility. Fergusson is best remembered as a literary salon hostess and minor poet who participated in the earliest stirrings of national literature in America.

Suggested Readings: DAB; NAW; T_2. *See also* Rufus W. Griswold, *The Female Poets of America* (1873), pp. 24-27; Chester T. Hallenbeck, "The Life and Collected Poems of Elizabeth Graeme Fergusson" (Master's thesis, Columbia Univ., 1929).

Judy F. Parham
College of St. Benedict

DAVID FERRIS (1707-1779)

Works: *Memoirs of the Life of David Ferris* (w. 1779; pub. 1825). An 1855 edition of the *Memoirs* contains several previously unpublished letters by Ferris on slavery and other subjects.

Biography: David Ferris was born on Mar. 10, 1707, in Stratford, Conn., the third of eight children born to Zachariah and Sarah Ferris. In his journal, Ferris reported visions and guiding dreams that began at age 12. As a result of his continuing concern for such revelations, Ferris was openly accused of heresy, both before and after entering Yale. Although Ferris was cleared each time, he refused to graduate from Yale, believing that education alone could not make a person a fit minister and "that all right understanding in spiritual concerns must proceed from the immediate revelation of the Holy Spirit." Such beliefs led Charles Chauncy (q.v.) to accuse Ferris of always having been a Quaker, but Ferris was reared a Presbyterian and apparently knew nothing of Quakers until his final year at Yale, when he read the writings of Robert Barclay. After leaving Yale, Ferris visited Quakers on Long Island and then moved to Philadelphia, where he joined the Society of Friends and established a school.

In 1735, following the advice of his divine guide, Ferris married Mary Massey, daughter of Samuel and Sarah Massey. Two years later, he moved to Wilmington, Del., where he set up shopkeeping and lived the rest of his life. During the next twenty years, Ferris occasionally spoke in meetings and traveled in the ministry, but in spite of dreams and counsel—both divine and human—that he was not fulfilling his proper role in the church, he avoided making the commitment to the ministry that he believed he was supposed to make. In 1755 Ferris finally made his commitment. For the next twenty years, he traveled extensively in the ministry and was active in the efforts to abolish slavery among Friends. He died on Dec. 5, 1779, after a three-year illness.

Critical Appraisal: David Ferris's *Memoirs*, conventional in most ways, is surprising for the spiritual discontent that it contains. This discontent results from Ferris's belief that he was not living up to the requirements of the inner light— which he usually refers to as his divine guide or divine leader—particularly in fulfilling his place in the church. Such spiritual discontent and insecurity are much more typical of Puritan than Quaker journals.

This tension gives a measure of cohesiveness to the journal that many Quaker journals do not have, and as a result of this tension, the Quaker doctrine of the inner light receives much more attention than is customary for Quaker journals. Usually, Quaker journalists report such tensions only until they come to accept the light, and having decided to follow the light—whether it is manifested as voices and dreams, as it often is for Ferris, or simply as leadings—the journalists typically display great spiritual contentment after deciding to follow the light.

Ferris's discontent, sometimes a result of his feeling unworthy for his allotted place but at other times a result of his feeling dissatisfied with it, is well illustrated by a dream he reported. While he was struggling with committing himself to the ministry, having grown increasingly reluctant to speak at meetings, he wrote of a dream in which he was shown a large, unfinished building. The builder showed Ferris how he was needed as one of the support pillars, and the builder showed Ferris that he fit the place exactly. When Ferris questioned his ability to fill the place and was unwilling to occupy it, the builder said, "If thou wilt not be a pillar, thou shalt be a plank for the floor." The builder showed Ferris how he "might be flatted and prepared for that purpose." But Ferris refused this place "on the ground that it looked too diminutive to be a plank to be trod upon by all who came into the house."

Yet Ferris followed his guide in many things including replenishing his stock, and he did, after initially being put off by her limp, marry the woman picked out for him. He also reported times when he failed to consult his inner guide—agreeing to sell spirits and joining in a shipping venture—but even this sorrow merely reconfirmed his belief in the divinity of the unconsulted guide.

Ferris's *Memoirs* is, however, in many ways typical of Quaker journals: in its language used, concern that business not intrude into one's spiritual life, and lack of mention of matters not directly relating to his spiritual life. There are, for instance, only a few minor mentions of his family (even though several children died during the years covered by the journal), no direct mention of the Revolutionary War (although his journal extends through 1776), and no mention of his own efforts to persuade Friends to give up their slaves.

The letters appended to the 1855 edition, most dealing with slavery, develop the arguments that Friends were using at the time, showing equal concern for the spiritual salvation of the slave and the slaveholder. He also set out, again as was becoming typical among Quaker abolitionists in the 1750s, the slaveholder's obligations to the slaves beyond simply freeing them, including paying them for past labor, making certain that young slaves had learned a trade or were well apprenticed, and that slaves too old to work were pensioned off or cared for. Other letters directly and simply urge friends and relatives to put aside vanities and come to know the love and unity of salvation even to the extent of being thought "fools for Christ's sake."

Suggested Readings: Howard H. Brinton, *Quaker Journals, Varieties of Religious Experience Among Friends* (1972); Charles Chauncy, *Seasonable Thoughts on the State of Religion in New England* (1743), pp. 208-213; Daniel B. Shea, Jr., *Spiritual Autobiography in Early America* (1968), pp. 22-29; Luella M. Wright, *The Literary Life of the Early Friends, 1650-1725* (1932), pp. 155-197.

John Stratton
University of Arkansas at Little Rock

JOHN FILSON (c. 1747-1788)

Works: *Kentucke and the Adventures of Col. Daniel Boone* (1784).

Biography: John Filson was born in the township of East Fallowfield, Pa., a descendant of English immigrant stock. The exact date of his birth is unknown, but the conjecture of R. T. Durrett, his first biographer, of 1747 seems reasonable, even though other dates as late as 1753 have been assigned. Practically nothing is known of Filson's early life in Pa. other than the intriguing fact that he was tutored there by the Rev. Samuel Finley (q.v.), who later became president of the College of New Jersey (now Princeton Univ.), a point of more than passing interest in that it may explain Filson's obviously superior education.

After the American Revolution, Filson appeared in Ky., where he used Va. military warrants good for land to obtain several thousand acres. The inference that he had served in the Revolutionary War, though tempting, is not inevitable; land warrants were often acquired by speculators from veterans of the Continental armies who, in the belief that they were worthless, wanted to dispose of them for whatever they would bring. In Ky. Filson became a land speculator and part-time surveyor, and he wrote *Kentucke* (1784) as an attempt to "boom" the new territory. Ironically, Filson was killed by an Indian while on a surveying expedition in Oct. of 1788.

Critical Appraisal: The importance of John Filson to cultural and literary historians depends almost entirely upon his book *Kentucke*, which, with the exception of two minor prospectuses that appeared in the last year of his life, is apparently the only work he wrote. It would be difficult to imagine, however, a book of equivalent size (the original edition of 1784 is under 120 pages) that was of equal importance to the new West of the U.S. *Kentucke* contained the first account of Ky., the first map of the area, and—among other miscellany—the first report of the "Adventures of Col. Daniel Boon[e]."

This last account, although often distorted and factually in error, may be regarded as the single most important document in establishing Daniel Boone's reputation as an American folk hero. The frequently quoted remark that Filson "lifted Boone from relative obscurity to heroic levels of international spread" is, though hyperbolic, no more than the simple truth. The relationship of Filson to Boone has long been the subject of often heated debate. Although the "Adventures" are written in the first person and signed by Boone himself, they are clearly not Boone's own (Boone was nearly illiterate), but there is no good reason to doubt that Filson is the author, presumably working from material related to him directly by Boone. From a modern perspective, the most interesting aspect of the "Adventures" is their blatant attempt to "sell" Ky. as a desirable goal for immigration. "I now live in peace and safety," concluded Boone, "enjoying the sweets of liberty, and the bounties of Providence, . . . in this delightful country, . . . delighting in the prospect of its being, in a short time, one of the most opulent and powerful states on the continent of North-America."

This purported statement of Boone's illustrates as well as anything the purpose behind *Kentucke*: to present Ky. as a desirable place for settlement. Speaking in his own person elsewhere in the book, Filson urged the same point. Of "good soil, air, water and trade," the "four natural qualities necessary to. . .the happiness of a country" Ky. already possessed the first three, and the fourth would come in time, given the growth of that western market that would inevitably follow the immigrants Filson hoped to attract. It should also be mentioned that one of the great aids in attracting these immigrants was the map Filson included in *Kentucke*. This map was immensely popular, going through at least six different issues.

Containing as it does a compendium of contemporary knowledge about the region, *Kentucke* is still intriguing reading today. An engaging mixture of sophisticated insights with gullible remarks, Filson's commentary is always interesting, if not completely reliable. Thus Filson attributed an Asiatic origin to the Native Americans, shrewdly conjecturing that Asia was once connected to North America by a land bridge, while at the same time holding to that strange bit of early American folklore that some Indians are descendants of Welsh King Madoc, who disappeared in 1170 A.D. with ten ships "and was never more heard of." Filson heard of Madoc through the testimony of one Capt. Abraham Chaplain of Ky., "a gentleman, whose veracity may be entirely depended upon." While on garrison duty at Kaskaskia, Chaplain was allegedly approached by "some Indians" who, "speaking in the Welsh dialect, were perfectly understood and conversed with by two Welshmen in his company."

It is easy to laugh, but few of us could do better, and Filson must be given real credit—especially considering the obvious propaganda purpose of his volume—for attempting to sort out fact from fiction. *Kentucke* has always had a small but secure reputation among scholars and western history buffs; it deserves to be better known.

Suggested Readings: DAB; LHUS. *See also* R.T. Durrett, *John Filson, the First Historian of Kentucky* (1884); John Filson, *Kentucke, and the Adventures of Col. Daniel Boone*, ed. Willard R. Jillson (1929), a facsimile edition of the 1784 text; imprint varies. The 1929 edition contains an extensive introduction with a good capsule biography of Filson.

James K. Folsom
University of Colorado at Boulder

SAMUEL FINLEY (1715-1766)

Works: *Christ Triumphing and Satan Raging, A Sermon on Matth. XII. 28* (1741); *A Letter to a Friend* (1741); *Clear Light Put Out in Obscure Darkness* (1743); *Satan Stripp'd of His Angelic Robe* (1743); *A Charitable Plea for the Speechless* (1746); *A Vindication of the Charitable Plea for the Speechless* (1748); *The Approved Ministers of God* (1749); *Faithful Ministers* (1752); *The Madness of Mankind* (1754); *The Power of Gospel Ministers* (1755); *The Curse of Meroz* (1757); *The Disinterested and Devout Christian* (1761); *The Successful Minister* (1764); *The American Latin Grammar* (by Robert Ross; revisor; 1780-1794).

Biography: Samuel Finley was born in the province of Ulster, Ire., in 1715, and he immigrated to Philadelphia in 1734. One of seven sons, "all esteemed pious," Finley followed the example of his brother James, a Presbyterian minister and evangelist: he probably attended William Tennent's Log College and was licensed to preach under the aegis of the New Brunswick Presbytery in 1740. After two years following George Whitefield (q.v.) and Gilbert Tennent (q.v.) as an itinerant evangelist in West Jersey, Finley was ordained and became one of the more controversial participants in the Great Awakening: in 1743 he was arrested on his way to preach to a Separatist congregation in New Haven, Conn., and was later expelled as a vagrant for his unorthodox views. But in 1744 Finley was called to a church in Nottingham, Pa., where he remained for seventeen years. There he became renowned as an accomplished Classical scholar and teacher, and there he instituted an academy to prepare young evangelists for the ministry. In May of 1761, Finley was unanimously elected president of the College of New Jersey (formerly the Log College); two years later, he became the first Presbyterian minister in America to receive an honorary doctorate of divinity from the University of Glasgow. In 1766 Finley succumbed to a liver disease, brought on, according to one of his biographers, by "too great assiduity in his studies, and too constant occupation in the public duties of his office." He died in Philadelphia on Jul. 17, 1766, and was buried beside Gilbert Tennent in the Second Presbyterian Church.

Critical Appraisal: According to Samuel Finley's earliest biographer, "his sermons were rather solid than brilliant; not hasty productions, but composed with care...pleasing to the cultivated mind [yet] intelligible by the illiterate." In the tradition of Jonathan Edwards (q.v.), Finley did, indeed, pursue logical method in organizing his sermons, emphasizing "right reason" as the basis of his thinking. But his enthusiastic, homely, unabashedly didactic rhetoric belies his "solid" framework and places him squarely in the mainstream of the Great Colonial Awakenings instigated in the Middle Colonies by the sons of William Tennent. One of Finley's earliest and most popular sermons, the 1741 *Christ Triumphing, and Satan Raging, A Sermon on Matth. XII. 28*, was even "recommended" by George Whitefield, who inscribed it to "a worthy friend of mine abroad" when it was reprinted in Edinburgh. The endorsement was fitting. Whitefield consistently strengthened the influence of Log College men with the general public, encouraging the revival that led to schism in the Presbyterian Church in 1745. Finley's allegiance to the "New Side Synods," or the "New Lights," as well as to Whitefield, is clear: in *Christ Triumphing* he drew an analogy between Christ and his disciples and the "new" order in Presbyterianism, zealously insisting that "only the POWER OF GOD'S WORD on the Heart and Lives of Mankind can provide the conviction necessary for regeneration." In *A Letter to a Friend*, also published in 1741, Finley openly defended Whitefield, elaborating on the unique "Conviction" that makes "Mr. Whitefield...very sure of God's eternal Love." For Finley, the thrust of this "conviction" is "being Powerfully convinced by God's spirit" of one's "miserable State," a concept very Puritan in character, since it emphasizes human depravity and the need for a cataclysmic conversion experience before one can enjoy either faith or grace.

The growth of this "Conviction," its roots in the "Law" and "the Scripture-Method of Salvation," and its application to the more profane aspects of human existence preoccupied Finley for the rest of his life and established him as a single-minded champion of the New Light revival forces. In a 1743 sermon titled *Clear Light Put Out in Obscure Darkness*, he defended Gilbert Tennent's tract *Remarks on the Protestation*, urging "the Necessity of preparatory Convictions" before accepting Christ and denouncing the "Antinomian" views of the Moravians. In 1743 Finley contended with still another Protestant faction, publicly arguing for two days with the Anabaptist Abel Morgan over infant baptism. In 1746 he published *A Charitable Plea for the Speechless; Or, The Right of Believers' Infants to Baptism Vindicated*; Morgan offered a rejoinder, and in 1748 Finley responded with *A Vindication of the Charitable Plea for the Speechless*. Again he attacked Antinomianism, maintaining that God's covenant with Abraham extended to Christ and therefore to all Christians "and their seed." In his 1754 tract *The Madness of Mankind*, Finley targeted all denominations that denied the need for divine revelation, discovering "Saving Grace" in "moral honesty" or "the Observation of invented Forms." Impatient with Latitudinarians, he defined *madness* as "impiety, superficiality, and irreligiousness," including in his argument a graphic description of hell and its tortures. In 1757 Finley subtly denounced Quakers for their pacifism during the French and Indian War in *The Curse of Meroz; Or, The Danger of Neutrality, in the Cause of GOD, and Our Country*.

As Richard Bushman observed, Finley perceived himself as a warrior against "the natural hatred of ungodly men for the work of God"; but he was not merely "a firebrand." As his school at Nottingham flourished, he successfully pursued his Classical studies, revising and correcting Robert Ross's *American Latin Grammar*. He also gradually tempered his religious enthusiasm. On the death of the Rev. Samuel Davies (q.v.), whom he succeeded as president of the College of New Jersey in Princeton, he preached an "instructive discourse" in which he praised Davies for his ecumenical spirit and asserted that "Right reason itself peremptorily denies that the dictates of our own minds are our supreme rule of conduct." The style as well as the form of the published sermon, *The Disinterested and Devoted Christian*, suggests that the mature Finley, although still convinced of man's weakness and humility in the face of omnipotent divinity, found "Conviction" to be a product not only of the heart and an extraordinary revelation but of the understanding as well. Using the language of the constructive Deists of his century, he argued the value of "self-evident principles," asserting that "the evangelical duty of self-denial is founded on the everlasting reason of things."

Suggested Readings: CCMC; DAB; Sprague (III, 96-101). *See also* Archibald Alexander, *Biographical Sketches of the Founder and Principal Alumni of the Log College* (1845); Richard L. Bushman, ed., *The Great Awakening: Documents on the Revival of Religion, 1740-1745* (1970); William W. Sweet, *Religion on the American Frontier, 1783-1840: The Presbyterians: A Collection of Source Materials*, vol. II.

Eliza Davis
University of Alabama in Huntsville

GILES FIRMIN (c. 1614-1697)

Works: *A Serious Question Stated* (1651); *Separation Examined* (1652); *A Sober Reply to the Sober Answer of Reverend Mr. Cawdrey* (1653); *Stablishing Against Shaking* (1656); "Notes" to *The Power of the Civil Magistrate in Matters of Religion Vindicated* (by Stephen Marshall, 1657); *Of Schism* (1658); *Tythes Vindicated* (1659); *Presbyterial Ordination Vindicated* (1660); *The Liturgical Considerator Considered* (1661); *The Real Christian* (1670); *Meditations upon Mr. Baxter's Review* (1672); *The Questions Between the Conformist and Nonconformist* (1681); *The Plea of the Children of Believing Parents* (1683); *Scripture-Warrant Sufficient Proof for Infant Baptism* (1688); *An Answer to Mr. Grantham's Vain Question* (1689); *Weighty Questions Discussed* (1692); *Παvουργία: A Brief Review of Mr. Davis's Vindication* (1693).

Biography: Giles Firmin was born sometime around 1614 in Ipswich, in the county of Suffolk, Eng., the son of Deacon Giles Firmin, who settled at Boston, Mass., in 1632. Converted as a youth by John Rogers, he enrolled in 1629 at Emmanuel College, Cambridge. Firmin probably came to New Eng. with his father in 1632, but he may have returned to Eng. the following year to study medicine at Cambridge. By 1637 Firmin was back in Mass., where he was a member of the church at Boston during the Antinomian crisis there. In Jan. 1639 Firmin received a grant of land in Ipswich, Mass., where he married the daughter of Nathaniel Ward (q.v.) and practiced physic.

Disillusioned with the theology and church polity of New Eng., Firmin finally sailed for Eng., probably in the fall of 1644. Having survived shipwreck off the coast of Sp., Firmin was eventually ordained by Presbyterians in Eng., and until he was ejected in 1662, he served as minister at Shalford, Essex. Engaged almost continually in published theological controversies, he practiced physic following his ejection, tending both the gentry and the poor. For many years he carried on a friendly debate with Richard Baxter that occasionally surfaced in print. In 1672 Firmin became minister to Presbyterians at Ridgewell. He served there until his death on Apr. 1, 1697.

Critical Appraisal: Giles Firmin gave up on New Eng., but his extensive writings, in addition to dealing with contemporary English theological battles, are also a half-century's reflection and commentary on his experiences on this side of the Atlantic.

Firmin approved of the excommunication of Anne Hutchinson, whose trial he attended (*Separation Examined*); he wrote also in opposition to the Quakers (*Stablishing Against Shaking*); and in *A Serious Question Stated*, he attacked several contemporary "Errors, Heresies and Schisms," including Arminianism, to clear himself of the charge that he was an Independent. In the process, he explained the reasons for his disaffection with Congregationalism. Agreeing that an individual church "might execute all the power of the Keyes within it selfe," he insisted that this fact is no warrant for abandoning mutual dependency among churches. Moreover, he faulted the rigidity of Congregational churches, particularly the requirement of confession before the whole church, on the grounds that it terrified some souls: "in this way, many lambs of Christ must be beaten off."

Firmin's opinions concerning the sacraments suggest that although he owed much to the Reformed tradition, he had worked out a highly personal stance combining evangelical fervor and pragmatism. In *A Serious Question Stated*, for example, he wrote that sacraments are, in a sense, "externall things" but that to dismiss them as such is to ignore the "*Divine Authority*" for certain rites. He also held that baptism could be denied children of scandalous parents as a means of keeping control and standards in church affairs. In *A Sober Reply*, Firmin further diminished the spiritual importance of baptism, declaring that it is not a "means of Regeneration, as is the Preaching of the Word." Again, in *The Liturgical Considerator Considered*, he downplayed the significance of the liturgy, which he believed is often an appropriate expedient but never a necessity.

Firmin's greatest work, and his most incisive critique of the New Eng. way, is *The Real Christian* (1670), which was published in Boston as late as 1742 and reprinted in 1745. At great length, Firmin accused Thomas Hooker (q.v.) and Thomas Shepard (q.v.) of causing "Trouble" with their Preparationist theology. Their stages of preparation for salvation were so arduous and their promises of assurance so slight that they cast "Blocks" in the way of many souls, creating terrible despair. Firmin was particularly disturbed by Hooker's belief that one should be willing to be damned and by Shepard's insistence on determining the precise moment of conversion: "This is a meer vanity and devils delusion," Firmin declared, "to trouble thy self about the time." According to Firmin, individuals are "justified not by our Wisdom, Understanding, Piety, or Works which we have wrought in Purity and Holiness of Heart but by *Faith*, by which the Almighty God hath justified all from the Beginning."

The "work of God," Firmin maintained, should lead not to agony but to cheerfulness. To his thinking, the rigid steps prescribed as the order of salvation failed to account for the variety of human responses to the steps by which the spirit works regeneration: "no matter how many of them, or how few, if the Spirit useth any of them, they shall do the work he intends." In his view, although "legal fears, terrors and sorrows" may chasten us, they have no power to keep us from sin. Instead, all self-examination should lead to assurance, or else it is "a vain thing."

By insisting on the paramount importance of assurance, Firmin spurned the difficulties posed by Hooker and Shepard, but he did not, as a result, embrace the simplistic vision of Antinomianism. In *The Real Christian*, he described regeneration as an "illumination" of the understanding and the faculties that enable the "new Creature" to see God and sin in ways impossible before conversion. Christianity, he said, is both "*Rational*" and "*Scriptural*." Unlike the Hutchinsonians, he emphatically denied that the faculties are destroyed in conversion: "Christianity doth not at all destroy Reason, the faculties of man, as to their essence, are the same after Christ, union with him; which they were before he knew Christ." His major pastoral complaint against New Eng. Puritanism was that it burdened the "many plain-hearted Christians" with complex meditation strategies, sermon heads, and so on. Above all, he urged "much prudence," lest Christians be discouraged.

From Firmin's easing of the strenuous demands of Reformed theology may be traced, according to Norman Pettit, "the beginnings of an era in which Puritanism finally degenerated into moralism and sentimentalism." Yet to the end, Firmin was a staunchly original controversialist, combining what he believed to be the best elements of episcopacy, Presbyterianism, and Congregationalism. Although he had long since abandoned the New Eng. way, Firmin asserted an independent position in *The Questions*, attacking the Church of England for letting in papal influences; criticizing formalism and the power of bishops; and calling for the spreading of power within congregations.

Finally, in *Παvουργία*, as vigorous as any of his tracts, the aging Firmin recalled meeting Anne Hutchinson some sixty years earlier and defended legal preachers against the attacks of Mr. Davis, whom he likened to John Wheelwright (q.v.) and the English Antinomian Tobias Crisp. Being subject to the law, Firmin asserted, makes one appreciate the need for the Gospel. Speaking of the conjugal metaphor for conversion, he declared: "Dr. *Crisp* makes it a *Ravishment*, not a *Marriage*, a Dishonour to Christ." In conversion, he went on, the faculties are not forced "but they do all move according to their Nature." In lambasting the disruptive influence of Davis, he invoked as a symbol of order the spirit of Thomas Hooker. Never settled for long in any theological camp, Firmin had in a sense come full circle from his disillusionment with New Eng.

Suggested Readings: CCNE; DNB; FCNEV. *See also* John Ward Dean, "A Brief Memoir of Rev. Giles Firmin," NEHGR, 20 (1866), 47-58; David D. Hall, *The Faithful Shepherd: A History of the New England Ministry in the Seventeenth Century* (1972), pp. 70, 119, 165-167, 170, 173; Norman Pettit, *The Heart Prepared: Grace and Conversion in Puritan Spiritual Life* (1966), pp. 183-193, 200, 206, 214, 217, 221-222; idem, "Hooker's Doctrine of Assurance: A Critical Phase in New England Spiritual Thought," NEQ, 47 (1974), 530-534.

Wesley T. Mott
University of Wisconsin at Madison

JOHN FISKE (1608-1677)

Works: "Upon the Decease of Tho. Hooker" (w. 1647; pub. 1943); "Upon the Departure of. . . Sa: Sharp" (w. c. 1652; pub. 1943); "Ezechiel Rogersius" (w. c. 1652; pub. 1943); "To His Very Good Friend Mr. Snelling Phisitian" (w. c. 1652; pub. 1943); "Ad Matronam Pientissimam Spectatissimam Ipsius. . . John Cotton" (w. c. 1652; pub. 1943); "Upon the Much-to-Be Lamented Desease

of...John Cotton" (w. 1652; pub. 1943); "In Obitum Reverendissimi Viri...
Domini Joannis Cottoni" (w. c. 1652; pub. 1943); "Thomas Parkerus" (w. c.
1652; pub. 1943); "Reverendo viro Domino Joanni Wilsono" (w. 1653; pub.
1943); "Upon the Decease of Mris. Anne Griffin" (w. 1655; pub. 1943); "Upon
the Decease of...Nathaniel Rogers" (w. 1655; pub. 1943); "In Obitum Viri
Tum Pietatis Tum Integritatis Probate...Domini Samuelis Sharpij...Carmen
Funebrae" (w. c.1655; pub. 1943); *The Watering of the Olive Plant* (1657).

Biography: In his *Magnalia*, Cotton Mather (q.v.) called John Fiske "Luke,
the Beloved Physician." This appellation is indeed appropriate, for Fiske was a
licensed physician as well as an ordained man of the cloth. Although he was
himself renowned for his piety and devotion to his Chelmsford, Mass., congregation, his immediate ancestry also claimed an esteemed reputation for commitment to preserving the faith. During the reign of Mary Tudor, whose relentless
persecution of English Protestants earned her the title of Bloody Mary, his
grandfather and a greatuncle endured bitter persecution.

The young John Fiske was born in Suffolk, Eng., in 1608. He was sent to the
local grammar school, where he prepared for a university education. After taking
a B.A. from Cambridge in 1628, he attempted to minister the Puritan Gospel but
found himself increasingly harassed by the silencers (or Anglican Church officers charged with ferreting out dissenters) to the extent that he eventually gave up
the ministry (although only temporarily) and took up the study of "physick." In
addition to his persecution, Fiske, the eldest of four children, became upon his
father's death the head of the household; doubtlessly feeling the onus of supporting his mother, two sisters, and a brother, he took up a new vocation probably as
much for economic reasons as for a temporary solution to his persecution. At any
rate, Fiske relocated his mother, sisters, brother, and new wife (who had given
up a large portion of her inheritance from her father for marrying a nonconformist and leaving the country) to New Eng., where his Congregationalist noncon-
formity would be encouraged. The journey of 1637 was, however, not felicitous,
for he lost his mother shortly after setting sail and his first child soon after
landing.

Eventually, after tenures of service as minister and tutor in Salem and in
Wenham, Fiske became pastor at the new town of Chelmsford, where he remained, ministering to the spiritual and medical needs of his congregation, until
he died on Jan. 14, 1677. His first wife, having become blind for the last several
years of her life, had died in 1672. But shortly after, Fiske married again, this
time to a woman named Elizabeth. When he died, Fiske left behind his new wife
and four children, one of whom was named Moses, a 1662 Harvard graduate.

Critical Appraisal: Although it is now known from the recent discovery
of his poems in manuscript that he was a poet, John Fiske published only one
work during his lifetime, *The Watering of the Olive Plant in Christ's Garden.
Or, A Short Catechism for the First Entrance of Our Chelmsford Children*
(1657). As one can tell from this title, Fiske was indeed solicitous of the spiritual
needs of his people. Actually, only the first quarter of the book addresses training

in the catechism per se. The remaining three-quarters the author devoted to a treatment of three theological problems; each of these problems he took up in a separate appendix. To be sure, these discussions represent extensions of the instruction begun in the catechism but more properly expanded upon in the manner Fiske has selected. The first appendix explicates the Lord's Prayer and its importance as instruction in how and for what we should pray, and the second touches the nature and use of Puritanism's two sacraments (those of baptism and holy communion). The third and final section argues the necessity of obeying God's law.

As suggested from the title, the emphasis throughout this treatise is upon the metaphor set down in Psalms 128:3: "Thy children shall be like Olive plants round about thy Table." Although this work can hardly be construed to be great literature, its purpose was not to attain such status. Its purpose was avowedly practical—that is, to instruct the young in matters of New Eng. Congregational-ism. But even as such, *The Watering of the Olive Plant* attests the importance to the early Puritans of growth into a new life removed from the restrictions of the old country. This growth motif predicted, and doubtless helped to promote, the American idea of growth through experiment and renewal of goals and aspira-tions. Indeed, the line drawn between the vigor and hope of Fiske's *Olive Plant* and Walt Whitman's vital and energic *Leaves of Grass* is straight and uninterrupted.

As one may expect, Fiske employed his growth metaphor in several of his poems, all of which are anagrams. Like his illustrious contemporary, John Wil-son (q.v.), Fiske first selected an *anagram*, a phrase made by transposing the letters of a person's name, that appropriately described his subject and then developed the anagram contrapuntally as a theme throughout the poem. Unlike Wilson, however, whose poems often seem intriguing mental exercises in which the author's counterpoint is literally a pattern of letters that speak the name of his subject in a single line or collection of lines, Fiske developed his pattern of counterpoint thematically—that is, he used the words of the anagram to develop or expand upon the idea or ideas that the anagram called up, usually within a quatrain of rhyming iambic pentameters.

His elegy, "Upon the Departure of...Mr. Sa: Sharp" (Samuel Sharp), pro-vides an excellent example of Fiske's poetic techniques. Fiske selected the anagram "Us! Ample-share" and then explored from stanza to stanza the imagi-nation's capacity to derive variations on the theme (as Harold Jantz has rightly suggested, somewhat after the manner of the contrapuntal compositions of Fiske's European musical counterparts, Buxtehude and Bach). Throughout the elegy, the reader is reminded that the loss is to the "us" of the anagram—which is of course those of Sharp's congregation. This "us" of the poem remains constant; it is the "Ample-share" motif that moves in counterpoint with the theme of "Our Losse!" First Sharp is described as having exchanged the vicissitudes of this world for his deserved "ample-share of Blisse," nonetheless having left those still confined to this world with deplorable "losse."

In succeeding stanzas, the poet spoke of Sharp's ample share of life on earth and how he managed, because of his good works, to store an ample share of just reward in heaven. In the penultimate stanza, Fiske recommended Sharp's example to those who suffered his loss. The final two lines articulate succinctly the theme of harvesting one's own "Ample-share," despite the tragedy of loss: "so much the more Ample a share thou [the poem's listeners] shalt / of blessing reape, even thou when hence thou goe." Implicit in the clause "when hence thou goe" is the phrase "from us," following and hence completing the thought. Since the first word of the poem is *Us*, the poet has ended the poem where he began it, thus effectually resolving his counterpoint. By henceforth following Sharp's example, Fiske seemed to be saying that those left behind may "grow" toward God and accumulate their "Ample-share."

In another elegy, Fiske developed a different counterpoint, this one between wind and ship. In "Upon the Decease of . . . Anne Griffin," the poet adopted the anagram "In Fanne: Rig," deriving the effects of a fan and ship's rigging. The interplay of these two motifs in one stanza is particularly arresting. Beyond the restricted world of time, Mistress Griffin has discovered "the sweetest Rest, the sweet Anchorage," a realm "where Rockes endanger not nor Billowes Rage." In death the aged Mistress Griffin (96 years), one of the community's most prominent anchors, has moved, finally, beyond the danger of earth's destructive winds.

Both of these poems and most of his others are largely concerned not with merely playing upon the letters in a subject's name, but with attempting to discover how the particular anagram derived from the subject's name is a direct indication of the nature of the deceased's soul and how discovery of that nature ensures his or her promised union with God. Although the practice of anagrammatizing is now a lost skill, examination of Fiske's mastery of the anagram demonstrates that in the right hands, even the writing of anagrams can be an art, the appreciation of which is essential to gaining an adequate perspective of the Puritan aesthetic. Fiske's convoluted but energetic style, sometimes called baroque, aligns him with many baroque painters, sculptors, architects, and musicians of the seventeenth century. Hence Fiske's importance is certainly that he is representative of the times. But he is more than that; his use of the metaphor of growth suggests the logical process by which it became gradually appropriated as an accurate description of the uniquely American adventure.

Suggested Readings: CCNE; FCNEV; LHUS; Sprague (I, 106-107). *See also* James Bray, "John Fiske: Puritan Precurser of Edward Taylor," EAL, 9 (1974), 27-28; Cecelia L. Halbert, "Tree of Life Imagery in the Poetry of Edward Taylor," AL, 38 (1966), 22-34, esp. pp. 24-25; Harold S. Jantz, "American Baroque: Three Representative Poets" in *Discoveries and Considerations*, ed. Calvin Israel (1976), pp. 3-23, esp. pp. 9-10, 15-18, 21; idem, *The First Century of New England Verse* (1944), pp. 30-33, 118-131 (for the first printing of Fiske's twelve manuscript poems), 207-218; Cotton Mather, *Magnalia Christi Americana* (1701, rep. in 1852), I, 476-480; Harrison T. Meserole, *Seventeenth-Century American Poetry* (1968), pp. 185-191, 381; Astrid Schmitt-v. Muhlenfels, "John Fiske's Funeral Elegy on John Cotton," EAL, 12 (1977), 49-62; Roy H. Pearce, *The Continuity of American Poetry* (1961), pp. 36-39, 42, 55; Roger B.

Stein, "Seascape and the American Imagination: The Puritan Seventeenth Century," EAL, 7 (1972), 17-37, esp. pp. 27-28.

John C. Shields
Illinois State University

NATHAN FISKE (1733-1799)

Works: *The Importance of Righteousness* (1774); *Remarkable Providences* (1776); *A Sermon Preached at Brookfield* (1778); *The Character and Blessedness of a Diligent and Faithful Servant* (1779); *An Oration. . .in Celebration of the Capture of Lord Cornwallis* (1781); *The Sovereignty of God* (1784); *An Historical Account of the Settlement of Brookfield* (1792); *Twenty-Two Sermons on Various and Important Subjects* (1794); *A Sermon Preached at the Dudleian Lecture* (1796); *The Moral Monitor; Or, A Collection of Essays on Various Subjects*, 2 vols. (1801).

Biography: Born at Weston, Mass., on Sept. 9, 1733, the son of Nathan and Anna (Warren) Fiske, Nathan Fiske early evinced a fondness for reading and at age 17 entered Harvard College to study for the ministry. In 1758, after graduation from Harvard, Fiske was called to the third ministry at the First Congregational Church of Brookfield, Mass., where he remained for the rest of his life, guiding his parishioners with a benevolent, sympathetic, and charitable hand. As a mark of his open acceptance of others, he welcomed Arminian and Baptist preachers to share his pulpit, a gesture most uncommon among Calvinist ministers. Throughout his career, Fiske was universally admired. His life was defined by an even temper and unassuming manner, and his published sermons and other writings were suffused with an eloquent style and sound judgment. In 1792, as an acknowledgement of its respect for his contribution to the furtherance of Christian love and tolerance in New Eng., Harvard awarded Fiske an honorary doctorate of divinity. On Nov. 24, 1799, Fiske preached a sermon on "The path of the just. . .as the shining light, which shineth more and more unto the perfect day." That night, at age 66, he died peacefully in his sleep.

Critical Appraisal: The sermons of Nathan Fiske are generally regarded as some of the best of his time. They serve as the valuable legacy of a learned, sophisticated country minister whose quiet piety and refined sensibilities provided models of Christian behavior for his people. To preach of the fire-and-brimstone Calvinist hell, to scare his charge into heaven, was not his method. Rather, he shaped his works into a certain uniformity by arguing for tolerance, benevolence, and candor among men. As one of Fiske's contemporaries put it: "The object of them all was to establish men in the faith of Christianity, and to enlighten their minds, with the knowledge of the works and ways of God; to strengthen their habits of piety, and to encourage in them on religious principles, the practice of all Christian virtues." To instill in his congregation the notion that natural phenomena are portents of impending woe was not Fiske's method either. In one of the sermons collected in his 1794 volume, for example, he tried to ease the minds of his congregation about comets:

> Even in these later times of discovery and knowledge, there are many who consider comets in this light [as omens] only; and expect that they will soon be followed by the ravage of war, the arrows of pestilence, the gripings of famine, or by some other formidable judgement. But that this is the design and business of their appearing, to spread consternation, and then destruction amongst mankind, we have no reason to conclude, since they are found to be subject to the same laws as the planets; and, like them, have stated courses and revolutions.

Perhaps more important for our understanding of American literary history and culture, however, are the numerous periodical essays he wrote during the last twelve years of his life. These essays began in 1787, when a group of young men under Fiske's guidance joined together with the expressed purpose of improving their speaking and writing abilities. Before long, though, their enthusiastic scheme to publish essays on diverse useful topics dulled. Fiske carried their idea forward, publishing his essays, 151 in all, as "The Worcester Speculator" and "The Neighbor" in the Worcester *Spy* and as "The Philanthropist" in the *Massachusetts Magazine*. Shortly after his death, the essays were collected in two volumes as *The Moral Monitor* and for a time used extensively as texts for schoolchildren. His "desultory essays"—modeled after Daniel Defoe's *Review* (1704-1713) and Joseph Addison's and Richard Steele's *The Tatler, The Spectator*, and *The Guardian* (1709-1714)—suited well the literary tastes of late eighteenth-century America. In fact, the public's eager acceptance of all such periodical publications caused Fiske to observe in an early number of "The Worcester Speculator":

> Every magazine, and almost every newspaper, teems with periodical essays. . . . [Each] must have its literary mark of distinction, the feather, or cockade of the periodical essay. . . every vehicle of intelligence must be enriched with a dish of essays in succession, under some expressive signature or title; some, like solid beef, affording substantial nourishment; others, like sillabubs and nicknacks, tickling the palate, or only tasting sweet in the mouth.

The "solid beef" essays were on predictable subjects such as religious toleration, agriculture, and music; and the "sillabubs and nicknacks" on unlikely topics such as watermelon stealers, female indelicacy, and open debauchery. Although they may seem in retrospect to be superficial and vaporous, these periodical essays furnish an important contemporaneous history of their time and provide a substantial record of our literary and cultural heritage. According to one biographer of Fiske, they "are the fullest spectrum of one man's ideas to survive from his generation."

Suggested Readings: CCNE; Sibley-Shipton (XIII, 400-406); Sprague (I, 571-573); T₂. *See also* Bruce I. Granger, *American Essay Serials from Franklin to Irving* (1978), pp. 11-12, 238-239.

Jayne K. Kribbs
Temple University

SARAH SYMMES FISKE (1652-1692)

Works: *A Confession of Faith; Or, A Summary of Divinity* (w. 1677; pub. 1704).

Biography: The facts surrounding the life of Sarah Symmes Fiske are relatively scant. Born in Charlestown, Mass., in 1652, she was the daughter of William Symmes and his first wife, whose name has been lost. If the inventory of her father's estate taken at his death is any indication, Fiske was apparently raised on a farm. Sometime around 1671, she married the Rev. Moses Fiske, who served from 1672 until his death in 1708 as minister for the Congregational Church at Braintree (now Quincy), Mass. In 1677 Sarah Fiske was admitted to full communion with the church at Braintree, for which occasion she prepared her only extant work, *A Confession of Faith; Or, A Summary of Divinity*. She bore fourteen children, six of whom died during infancy.

Although these dates and details of family connection are all that remain for reconstructing Fiske's life, they imply a good deal, for much of a woman's role and status in seventeenth-century New Eng. was determined by her male relations. It is, for example, probably safe to conclude that Fiske, as a minister's wife, was accorded a social status and economic security enjoyed by few of her contemporaries. Her house and its six acres of land were maintained by the Braintree congregation. Her husband's annual salary (apparently paid regularly) was sixty pounds in 1672 and by 1704 had been raised to ninety pounds. Additionally, the diction, allusions, and complex organization of Fiske's *Confession* indicate that she possessed an extensive education for a woman of her time, perhaps received from her grandfather Zechariah Symmes, who had graduated from Emmanuel College in Cambridge, Eng., or from her husband, a 1662 Harvard graduate. Fiske died in 1692. The details surrounding her death are unknown.

Critical Appraisal: Sarah Fiske's *A Confession of Faith; Or, A Summary of Divinity* is a spiritual autobiography, but unlike the usual seventeenth-century spiritual autobiography, which concerned questions of individual grace, Fiske's six-page narrative sketches a comprehensive summary of Puritan historiography. Instead of recounting a personal conversion experience, Fiske distanced herself, offering instead a series of creedal statements more suitable for teaching the uninitiated than for baring her soul. Avoiding introspection, Fiske's "summary of divinity" reveals nothing of the spiritual struggles and doubts or of the occasional moments of religious ecstasy typically developed in spiritual autobiography.

But if Fiske submitted no account of her personal salvation, she did provide a list of conventional Puritan theological propositions, each of them prefaced by a simple declarative acknowledgment: "I believe." The very organization of the *Confession* reinforces the impersonal nature of its contents. Opening with a detailed discussion of the creation and its consequences, Fiske outlined Puritan historiography in a point-by-point movement toward God's judgment. She developed the logical relationship of topics such as the nature of sin, the role of the church, the covenanting process, the sacraments, the problem of guilt, and the plan of providence. Causes and effects, definitions and divisions, analysis, and yet more definitions carry a properly Puritan sense of inevitability: "The principal (blameable) cause [of the Fall] was their abusing their Free-will: The helping cause was the Devil.... The Consequences whereof, were *Guilt, Filth*, and *Punishment*."

Despite its conventional theology, Fiske's *Confession* is something of an anomaly: it was, after all, written by a woman. Publisher Benjamin Eliot's preface reminds us by its care to defuse objections to publication that the readers of early American women writers were often skeptical of the intellectual capabilities of women. Describing the author as "a Deceased Gentle-Woman" (Sarah Fiske is not identified by name but rather as Moses Fiske's "Consort"), Eliot assured readers that her *Confession* was "drawn up by her, altogether without [her husband's] Assistance." For those who considered writing and publishing unfeminine, Eliot noted that "Tis not with a design to blazon the Fame and Reputation of any Person, that this is now presented to the Publick View:... the design of it is purely to do Good." Further emphasizing the *Confession*'s didactic function, Eliot defined Fiske's audience as "the Children in this Land." Although what Fiske's *Confession* has to teach modern readers is vastly different from what it was designed to teach contemporaries, it will interest anyone who wants to learn more about religion, literature, and women in early America.

Suggested Readings: Alice Morse Earle, *Customs and Fashions in Old New England* (1894), p. 628; Jacqueline Hornstein, "Literary History of New England Women Writers: 1630-1800" (Ph.D. diss., N.Y. Univ., 1978), pp. 52, 180-182; idem, "Sarah Symmes Fiske," *American Women Writers*, ed. Lina Mainiero (1979-1981), II, 38-39; Frederick Clifton Pierce, *Fiske and Fisk Family* (1896), pp. 66-68; John Adams Vinton, *The Symmes Memorial* (1873), pp. 18-24, 28-30.

Pattie Cowell
Colorado State University

ELIJAH FITCH (1746-1788)

Works: *A Discourse* (1776); *The Beauties of Religion* (1789); "The Choice" (1789).

Biography: Elijah Fitch was born on Jan. 8, 1746, in Windham, Conn. His parents, Capt. John Fitch and Alice (Fitch) Fitch, had two older sons, John and James. After receiving an A.B. from Yale in 1765, Fitch requested admittance to Harvard College, where he received an A.M. in 1769. In Apr. 1766 Fitch married Hannah Fuller of Ipswich and one year later applied for licensure to preach. Denied permission because he had been baptized by a lay preacher, Fitch accepted a temporary ministerial appointment at Wrentham (now Franklin), Mass., where baptism by an ordained minister was not required for a preacher. When invited to remain in Wrentham permanently, Fitch declined the invitation because of a division in the church, eventually accepting the post of colleague pastor to the Rev. Samuel Barrett of the First Congregational Church in Hopkinton. Ordained on Jan. 15, 1772, Fitch became full pastor of the church when the Rev. Barrett died one year later. Admired by his neighbors and celebrated for his interest in literature and the sciences, Fitch fell ill in 1786, and two years later, on Dec. 16, 1788, he died at age 43, survived by his wife, Hannah, who lived to be 80, and by three daughters and two sons, one of whom, Elijah, was educated at Brown and became a minister.

Critical Appraisal: On Mar. 24, 1776, the first Sunday following the British evacuation of Boston and a few months before the colonies declared their independence from G.B., Elijah Fitch addressed his congregation in Hopkinton. The evacuation of Gen. Howe's troops from Boston was an occasion for celebration, a joyous event that Fitch aptly eulogized in his Sunday sermon. His congregation was so moved by his harsh denouncement of G.B. and his uplifting encouragement of their cause that they requested publication of the topical address. The *Discourse* is thus the sole work published during the author's lifetime.

The Puritan plainstyle of preaching and writing is clearly evident in Fitch's *Discourse*. He first outlined his purpose, proceeded to the "Application," and concluded with words of direction and encouragement. He described the conflict between good and evil, the wicked versus the righteous, and the just versus the unjust. Common scriptural themes, however, are given greater emphasis with images reflecting the political upheaval of the times, whereby the modern reader is provided emotional insight with historical fact. The wickedness of G.B., for example, is contrasted with the righteousness of the colonists by the use of dark and light imagery. The British are seen as children of the devil, working underground in collusion with the Prince of Darkness, and the colonists are characterized as children of light; the deceitful designs of the wicked are dark designs, well hidden from the righteous but capable of being brought to light by God. Fitch's God is the God of Armies and the Governor of the World, and Christ is the great Captain of Salvation, protecting the faithful. The successes of the British are thus explained with a conception of a human God who allows the wicked to raise high their expectations, only to destroy their hopes. In addition, Fitch used animal imagery to contrast the brutishness of G.B. and the innocence of America. The metaphor of a roaring lion, for example, illustrates the power of G.B. and the fear of the colonists. The lion has mouth open and teeth bared and is a beast with "cruel jaws wreaking in the gore of human flesh," ready to swallow the colonists in one bite.

Themes of war, politics, and religion are also prevalent in Fitch's poetry, which was published posthumously in 1789 and which shows the influence of his reading and interests. His long poem of 3,559 lines, *The Beauties of Religion*, is separated into five books and written in blank verse. Each book begins with a quotation from Edward Young, the English author of *Night Thoughts* (1742-1744), whose poetry, in a frontispiece, introduces the poem's recurring metaphor: the Goddess of Religion's charming allurements and promises of happiness. Like Young, Fitch portrayed religion with the attractiveness of a female as he wrote in Book I, "To paint her beauteous form, I go in quest / Of her to guide my pencil; and to learn / Her heavenly charms from her sweet lips inspired." He wrote of the "ardent prayer" that "opens Heaven and courts her [Religion] from the skies." Fitch captured the attention of youth by using as examples political figures of the day and alluding to familiar literary and legendary characters. Books I and II include narrative sections about Alexander the Great, Socrates, Diogenes, Raphael, and Leander. Book III praises contemporary heroes and espouses their virtues as religious qualities to emulate. Gens. Washington, Warren, and Montgomery are praised as true and god-fearing patriots.

Written in rhyming iambic pentameter couplets and imitative of John Pomfret's *The Choice* (1700), Fitch's short poem, "The Choice," contrasts the noise and sophistication of the city with the serenity and innocence of a rural setting, clearly indicating the rural as the more desirable.

Suggested Readings: CCNE; Dexter (III, 119-120); Sibley-Shipton (XVI, 156-158). *See also* Perry Miller, ed., *The American Puritans* (1956); Kenneth Silverman, *A Cultural History of the American Revolution* (1976).

Katherine K. Harris
University of Houston

JAMES FITCH (1622-1702)

Works: *Peace the End of the Perfect and Upright* (1672); *An Holy Connexion* (1674); *The First Principles of the Doctrine of Christ* (1679); *An Explanation of the Solemn Advice, The Covenant Solemnly Renewed, A Brief Discourse Proving That the First Day of the Week Is the Christian Sabbath* (1683).

Biography: James Fitch was born in Bocking, Essex, Eng., in 1622. At 16 he immigrated to New Eng., where he soon began seven years of study under Thomas Hooker (q.v.) and Samuel Stone (q.v.) in Hartford. After launching his ordained ministry in Saybrook in 1646, he went off with Maj. John Mason (q.v.) and most of his congregation to become the first minister of Norwich, Conn. In this station, which Increase Mather (q.v.) called "one of the obscurest places" in the New English wilderness, he spent the remainder of his active ministry.

Sometime after 1670, while maintaining his regular pastorship, Fitch began preaching to the Mohegan Indians in their own tongue. With Abraham Pierson (q.v.), he deserves notice as the nearest counterpart in Conn. to John Eliot's (q.v.) example of missionary zeal. For several reasons, including land disputes and resistance from the great chief Uncas, his efforts produced few lasting results. But in a 1674 letter to Daniel Gookin (q.v.) recounting his labors, he claimed "above thirty grown persons" as converts.

For his service as a civic leader and government agent, Fitch also gained renown in the colony, with his activities commonly on record at the General Court. He initiated and defended covenant renewal proceedings associated with King Philip's War, preached in Hartford and Boston, and wrote in refutation of John Rogers's (q.v.) Sabbatarian heresy. In 1674 his daughter married the Rev. Edward Taylor (q.v.) of Westfield; in 1679 he published his *First Principles*. Retiring to Lebanon, Conn., at the close of his ministry, he died there in his 80th year. He is memorialized in Cotton Mather's (q.v.) *Magnalia* as "the Holy and Acute."

Critical Appraisal: As a writer James Fitch is best remembered for his catechetical treatise *The First Principles*. Cited in its own day, the work has received modern praise from Perry Miller as "the best succinct summary of the creed and philosophy of the New England variety of Calvinism." It is not so expansive a *summa* of the faith as was printed later in Samuel Willard's (q.v.) *Complete Body of Divinity*; and its more direct, question-and-answer format distinguishes it from Book I of William Ames's earlier *Marrow of Sacred Divinity*, with which it otherwise shares a great deal. Starting like Ames with the doctrine of "living unto God," Fitch went on to explain the nature of God, faith, and providence; man's condition and fall; and the subsequent application of Christ's redemption through church and covenant. The intended audience is twofold: Fitch gave a clear exposition of fundamentals for those who need training in "first principles"; he also offered abstruse distinctions in a matter like "extraordinary" vs. "ordinary" rule of the visible church as "Stronger meat for them that are skil'd in the Word of righteousness." Stylistically, the work is dominated by bare statement and adherence to the pairing strategy of Ramistic logic. But now and then Fitch admitted a turn of affective poeticism, as when he wrote of Christ's shameful death "hanged up between the heaven and the earth, as if the heaven at present rejected him, and as if the earth would not bear him."

Among other writings, Fitch's funeral sermon (*Peace the End*) is worth reading for its stress on the value of gathering supernatural hints by observing outward details of a person's death. This tradition would seem to have later relevance to several of Emily Dickinson's death poems. David Stannard singles out *Peace the End* as the oldest extant funeral sermon from New Eng.

Fitch's election sermon on *An Holy Connexion* and his *Explanation of the Solemn Advice* are classic exercises in the jeremiad genre, containing the usual litany of "abominations" and exhortations to renewal. *An Holy Connexion* is at once a forbidding and a forcefully reasoned, encouraging plea against a holy people's decline from glory. If this hard-pressed community will only uphold the Lord as the glory in their midst, argued Fitch, the Lord will remain "a wall of fire round about" them and halt their gradual dissolution. Bewailing the "vile Examples" given by white settlers, Fitch took special pains in the *Explanation* to absolve his native "heathen" from intentional blame in New Eng.'s calamities.

Fitch has another claim to attention in American letters by virtue of his association with, and possible influence upon, our finest colonial poet. Not only did Edward Taylor marry Fitch's daughter, but he is said to have studied with Fitch for a time in Norwich. One evidence of Fitch's influence is the Taylor "Extracts" manuscript in Boston, which shows the poet to have copied out a portion of *The First Principles* for his own use.

Suggested Readings: CCNE. *See also* Frances M. Caulkins, *History of Norwich, Connecticut: From Its Possession by the Indians, to the Year 1866* (1866), esp. pp. 148-155; Emory Elliott, *Power and the Pulpit in Puritan New England* (1975), pp. 106-107; Perry Miller, *The Puritans: A Sourcebook of Their Writings*, 2 vols. (1963), pp. xlviii, 34-35, 38n., 391; David E. Stannard, *The Puritan Way of Death* (1977), pp. 88, 93, 116, 129. Fitch's letter to Daniel Gookin may be found in CMHS, 1 (1792), pp. 208-209.

John J. Gatta, Jr.
University of Connecticut

THOMAS FITCH (1700-1774)

Works: *Reasons Why the British Colonies in America Should Not Be Charged with Internal Taxes* (1764); *An Explanation of Say-Brook Platform* (1765); *Some Reasons That Influenced the Governor* (1766).

Biography: Thomas Fitch—lawyer, judge, and governor of the colony of Conn.—was born in Norwalk, Conn., in 1700. His father, Thomas Fitch, Jr., had immigrated to Conn. in 1639, establishing a family that became one of the wealthiest and most prominent in the colony for three generations. The future governor graduated from Yale College in 1721 and married Hannah Hall three years later. In the spring of 1726, the year he entered the General Assembly, he also served occasionally in the pulpit of his church in Norwalk. He later served in the upper house as assistant in 1734-1735 and again five years later until 1750. Upon the death of Governor Jonathan Law, Fitch was chosen deputy governor and reelected to the post for three consecutive years. In 1754 he became governor, an office he held until 1796, when he was defeated in the furor that followed his taking the oath to uphold the stamp tax. Fitch had opposed the act in *Reasons Why* and attempted to defend his capitulation after passage in *Some Reasons*.

A lawyer by profession, Fitch revised the laws of the colony, a task he completed before becoming deputy governor. Expressed in a "plain and intelligible manner," the revised code was judged by his contemporaries the best code of plantation laws ever published. During his term as deputy governor, Fitch filled, as was customary, the post of chief justice of the Superior Court. According to his minister, the Rev. Moses Dickinson (q.v.), Fitch was noted for his "justice" and "impartiality." In this capacity, he displayed a facility in "summing up evidence" and explaining the law to the jury so that they as laymen might understand the juridical issue and reach a right verdict.

After his defeat in the election of 1766, Fitch lived a retired life, bearing his dismissal with resignation and employing his time in reading. Even in bad health, he was assiduous in attending church. Fitch confided to Dickinson that he felt "better and more relieved" at public worship than if he had remained at home. He died on Jul. 18, 1774, after a brief illness, at the age of 74.

Critical Appraisal: During the last years of his final term as governor of Conn., Thomas Fitch wrote two pamphlets dealing with the Stamp Act. The first, a remonstrance against the impending legislation, *Reasons Why the British Colonies in America Should Not Be Charged with Internal Taxes*, was printed by Benjamin Franklin's (q.v.) nephew, Benjamin Mecom, in New Haven in 1764. The second, a defense of Fitch's taking the oath once the act had passed, *Some Reasons That Influenced the Governor*, was published in Hartford in 1766. The only other pamphlet attributed to Fitch, *An Explanation of Say-Brook Platform*, was published in 1765, the year of the Stamp Act, and attempted to interpret the Presbyterian form of church government adopted in Conn.

Reasons Why was probably not wholly Fitch's work, for it was prepared under the auspices of a committee, with Fitch at its head, appointed expressly for this purpose by the Conn. General Assembly. Nonetheless, according to another prominent constitutional lawyer and member of Fitch's committee, Jared Ingersoll, Fitch was the primary author. Ingersoll credited his colleague with being "the principal compiler and Draughtsman" of the piece.

Reasons Why presents a conservative and conciliatory view of the constitutional relationship between the colony of Conn. and the mother country. The pamphlet never questions the right of the "British Parliament" as the "supreme director over all His Majesty's dominions." As Fitch reiterated in a letter to Ingersoll, written in Dec. 1764, the remonstrance made no objection to the power and authority of Parliament to tax the colonies; it only endeavored to show that the exercise of such power would take away part of their ancient privileges.

As free British subjects, no law could or should be made or abrogated without the consent of the colonists or their representatives in Parliament. Since no colonials sat in the British legislature, no law such as a stamp tax could be passed and imposed. According to Fitch, the case against taxation without representation rests on the rights of colonials as free British subjects. Parliament could, nonetheless, charge external taxes designed to regulate the commerce of the empire. *Reasons Why* develops the argument against the legislative imposition of internal taxes deductively, building point upon point to a final cogent summary of the Conn. position.

The primary argument presented to strengthen the legal ground of colonial freedom is based on historical precedent as established under Conn.'s charter. This Charter of Incorporation was granted by Charles II. Thus the colonists' "privileges and immunities" are claimed not only as subjects under the British Constitution but more specifically and immediately under the charter. These rights have thereby been in their possession and exercise for a "long time." Fitch made the equally forceful and pragmatic case against the imposition of an internal tax on the basis of property rights. To impose a stamp tax is tantamount to nullifying the privilege of colonials to own and retain property and thereby to turn them into mere tenants at the will of the superior legislature. Thus by threatening property rights, Parliament could create an atmosphere of instability and mistrust adverse to industry in the colonies and ultimately harmful to the larger economy of G. B. Fitch proposed to avoid these consequences by an external tax on slaves and furs, if any tax be necessary.

The pamphlet concludes with a recapitulation of Conn.'s generosity in aid to her colonial neighbors and to G. B. during the French and Indian War, citing specific figures for money and men contributed. In this voluntary way, by the old system of requisitions, the colony has met its obligations, and the system that has worked so well in the past need not be changed.

When in fact the Stamp Act passed, in 1765, and Jared Ingersoll accepted the post of stamp master or collector for Conn., feeling in the colony ran high among its more radical and restless inhabitants. Governor Fitch postponed taking his oath to uphold the tax until Oct. 29, 1765, the ultimate moment. He was finally sworn by four of the braver and more conservative assistants. After he had pledged to uphold the hated tax, he lost political support. According to the Rev. Moses Dickinson, although "every one" knew Fitch had had no choice but to do so, the people were in "a ruffle," the majority of freemen voting against him in the next election for governor. In 1766, in a final effort to regain favor before the vote, Fitch published, anonymously, *Some Reasons That Influenced the Governor*.

The defense of his action in taking the oath comprised fourteen pages of explicit and careful argument in support of the "Governor in taking, and of the Councillors in administering the Oath enjoined by the . . . Stamp-Act." Fitch based his argument on the precedent established by three previous acts that provided that should the oath be ignored, charter rights probably would be lost and the governor fined 1,000 pounds and removed from office. The people should be deprived of the "Privilege of electing . . . Officers; and then the whole Charter would be at once struck up."

Fitch concluded his plea for a consensus supporting his act on purely personal grounds by appealing to the sympathy of his constituents to make his "Case" theirs. He found the fine too heavy for a governor of the colony to bear and his removal from office too great a blot on his reputation, rendering him "Infamous" and leaving him with no further use in life. Thus governor and councillors "acted the Part of faithful Officers to the Crown, and that of true Patriots to their Country." They merited the support of all loyal citizens.

The final tract attributed to Fitch, *An Explanation of Say-Brook Platform*, in legal, deductive style, affirmed the right of each church or congregation in Conn. to determine its own ecclesiastical affairs, doctrinal and disciplinary, independent of the authority imposed by a higher church council. It was in this sense antijuridical. The congregation's right was held to derive from divine authority and not the authority of any merely human, clerical synod.

Fitch's *Explanation* was answered in the Rev. Noah Hobart's (q.v.) *An Attempt to Illustrate*. Hobart saw only democratic chaos if Fitch's interpretation of the nature of consociation stood. Such a polity was "big with anarchy," leading to the rebellion of whole congregations whose members could censure and dismiss their pastors with impunity.

Suggested Readings: DAB; Dexter (I, 247-257); T$_2$. *See also* Moses Dickinson, *A Sermon Delivered at the Funeral...of Thomas Fitch* (1774); Lorenzo Sabine, *Biographical Sketches of Loyalists of the American Revolution* (1864), I, 425. *Reasons Why* is included in *Pamphlets of the American Revolution*, ed. Bernard Bailyn (1965), I, 378-407.

Betty Kushen
West Orange, New Jersey

PHILIP VICKERS FITHIAN (1747-1776)

Works: Hunter Dickinson Farish, ed., *Journal and Letters of Philip Vickers Fithian, 1773-1774* (1968); Robert Albion and Leonidas Dodson, eds., *Journal, 1775-1776* (1934).

Biography: When Philip Vickers Fithian was born in Greenwich, N.J., on Dec. 29, 1747, his family had already lived in America for more than a century. His early education was directed by Presbyterian ministers, and after two years at Princeton (1770-1772), he had begun formal study for the ministry. However, in 1773 Fithian was advised by Dr. John Witherspoon (q.v.), president of the college at Princeton, and others to delay his entrance into the ministry and to accept a "very profitable" offer from Robert Carter, the owner of a large Va. estate. On Oct. 20, 1773, Fithian rode from N.J. toward the "Nomini Hall" plantation in Va., where he would tutor the Carter children.

All during this period, Fithian maintained an extensive diary and was an active correspondent, especially with Miss Elizabeth Beatty, the woman he would later marry. Fithian stayed in Va. for a year and then returned to N.J., where he began a career as a clergyman. Beginning in May 1775, Fithian served as a missionary and itinerant minister in the Susquehanna and Shenandoah valleys of Pa. and Va. By the summer of 1776, Fithian became the chaplain for a regiment in the N.J. militia. While in the service, he contracted dysentery and died on Oct. 8, 1776.

Critical Appraisal: Philip Vickers Fithian's importance as a writer is almost solely dependent on that portion of his diary written in Va. This material is essentially a travel diary, for even though he lived almost a year in one place, Fithian seems always to have maintained the role of spectator of, rather than participant in, the life of the region. Part of the sense of separateness that Fithian expressed in his account is attributable to the social and economic differences between Fithian's middle-class background and that of the aristocratic world of the Carters, by whom he was employed. However, this attitude can also be ascribed to the disparity between the cultures of the regions. Although Fithian's N.J. home was only 260 miles from the Carter plantation, there was a difference between the two societies that went far beyond surface appearances.

The thematic direction of the diary stems from a tension between two visions of colonial Va. In some entries, Fithian described what seems, at least on the surface, to be an ideal life-style, one that Hunter Dickinson Farish termed the "Golden Age" of colonial Va. In these entries, genteel and elegantly attired ladies and gentlemen glide easily through a world of majestic estates, lavish balls, and foxhunts. Evenings are filled with harpsicord music, and sunny days are spent sailing on the river. Yet, beneath the surface of this "seeming" utopia is slavery. Although his acute recognition of the problems may have such roots, Fithian's concerns cannot be dismissed as the product of his northern upbringing or his Presbyterian religious training. Fithian presented evidence that slavery was not the benign institution its practitioners claimed it to be but rather was a force that corrupted the slaveholder as it degraded the slave. The diary shows that the slaveholders were guilty of actions ranging from minor hypocrisy to harsh physical torture and that they suffered from their own constant fears about slave revolts and unsuccessful attempts to suppress an awareness of miscegenation. Fithian did not refrain from voicing his own opinion of such a situation, but he avoided extensive preaching, preferring to let the lights and shadows of his picture portray the moral position for him.

The later sections of Fithian's diary describe his travels as a minister and services as a military chaplain and are very different from that written on the Va. plantation. The entries still contain much of interest, but their focus and subjects shift constantly. Fithian did create a good picture of life on the frontier and of his own growing patriotic response to the Revolution. It is this patriotism that sometime during a five-month hiatus in diary production (from mid-Feb. to mid-Jul. 1776) led to Fithian's enlistment. He described some military actions, but as with many Revolutionary War journals, he gave greater attention to the hardships and behavior of the men. A recurrent subject is prevalence of disease in the army, and it was such a sickness that ended Fithian's journal and his life.

Suggested Readings: CCV; P. *See also* Steven E. Kagle, *American Diary Literature* (1979), pp. 67-71; Louis Morton, *Robert Carter of Nomini Hall: A Virginia Tobacco Planter of the Eighteenth Century* (1941).

Steven E. Kagle
Illinois State University

WILLIAM FITZHUGH (1651-1701)

Works: Richard Beale Davis, ed., *William Fitzhugh and His Chesapeake World, 1676-1701: The Fitzhugh Letters and Other Documents* (1963); idem, "William Fitzhugh and the Northern Neck Proprietary: A Letter [Dec. 14, 1695]," VMHB 89 (1981), 39-43.

Biography: The youngest child of Henry Fitzhugh, a wealthy woolen-draper, William Fitzhugh was born in Bedford, Eng., and baptized on Jan. 10, 1651. Already a lawyer when he arrived in Va. about 1670, he either purchased lands in the Northern Neck or received them on Aug. 26, 1674, as a partial dowry for Sarah Tucker. Within two years, Fitzhugh was a prosperous grower and exporter of tobacco and the Stafford county representative to the House of Burgesses. He came to legal prominence through his defense of Robert Beverley (q.v.) against the crown (1682-1685), was a known authority on colonial law, and became lieutenant colonel of the militia and justice of the peace (1684). A supporter of the Stuarts, Fitzhugh was ordered to take the oath of allegiance and complied on May 26, 1693. He completed a brief history of Va. as a preface to his edition of its laws (1693–never published; not extant) and projected a longer history to encourage settlement (1697). Fitzhugh died on Oct. 21, 1701, after returning from a trip to Eng.

Critical Appraisal: William Fitzhugh's importance derives from his 213 letters, some speeches, 2 letters to the Commission of the Peace, his will, and a few miscellaneous documents that together yield a wealth of information on seventeenth-century Va. His letters may surpass those of William Byrd I, the only other significant epistolary collection of that time and place, in giving a detailed picture of day-to-day plantation life and in reflecting Fitzhugh's interlocked occupations of lawyer, businessman, and gentleman farmer. His legal expertise is apparent from his career as a lawyer's lawyer and his service in the House of Burgesses. He was the first to introduce large-scale slave labor in Stafford County, to seek to establish a central trading town in hopes of profiting from the exchange of American tobacco for English goods, and as one of the two resident agents for the Northern Neck Proprietors, to help set the pattern of land grants and patenting for future American land speculation and development. His tobacco farming made him a voracious acquirer of land who left 54,054 acres to his descendants even though he failed in his bid to buy his entire parish and a tract of 100,000 acres.

Fitzhugh's love of the good life matched his desire for the wealth with which to support it. He gave the best physical description of a seventeenth-century plantation and of his "own Dwelling house, furnished with all accommodations for comfortable & gentile living." The 1686-1687 travel account of a Frenchman named Durand attests to Fitzhugh's hospitality. Two days before Christmas, Durand and his friends

> rode twenty strong to Colonel Fichous', but he has such a large establish-
> ment that he did not mind. We were all of us provided with beds, one for

two men. He treated us royally, there was good wine & all kinds of beverages, so there was a great deal of carousing. He had sent for three fiddlers, a jester, a tight-rope dancer, an acrobat who tumbled around, & they gave us all the entertainment one could wish for. It was very cold, yet no one never thinks of going near the fire, for they never put less than a cartload of wood in the fireplace & the whole room is kept warm.

Such lordly festivals are neither denied nor recorded in Fitzhugh's correspondence, which portrays a busy, practical man. His numerous requests for silver stemmed more from sound investment than from love of craftsmanship. Purchase orders given to the English merchants who received his tobacco underscore his refusal to spend beyond his means with stipulations such as "but let me not be a farthing in Debt."

These business communications consistently provide personal insight. Trial shipments of ore and black walnut timber to Eng. and an attempt to grow olives in Va. are speculative ventures that may hint at dissatisfaction with his dependence upon tobacco. Combine these attempts with his negative refrain concerning uncertain tobacco prices, vagaries of shipping, and dealings with unreliable merchants and one may discern one of the reasons behind his emphasis upon personal control and his pursuit of the *via media* as the most suitable philosophy for a man whose fortunes are never completely secure. Enforced overproduction and consequent lack of demand for tobacco, quickly exhausted lands, Indian uprisings, and political upheaval were matters over which he could exert little influence. Instead, he ordered his life by a stress upon moderation that permeated the letters and led as well to some of his more literary comments. Examine the reasons for his resilient constitution:

I never much frequented Bacchus Orgyes, & always avoided Adoration to Ceres shrine, & never was one of Venus Votarys: To speak plainly to you, I never courted unlawfull pleasures with women, avoided hard drinking as much as lay in my power, & always avoided feasting & consequently the surfeits occasioned thereby.

The same method makes for a peaceful mind. He praised his uncle's
contented Condition, which in my opinion far exceeds the other, for its the mark that all drive at from the Monarch on the Throne, to the lowest Tradesman, without which the Riches of Croesus are not satisfactory, & with it the lowest Degree passes his time away here pleasantly. Sr. My Condition here is in a very equal temper, I neither abound nor want.

Even his metaphors evince support of the middle way. With the choice between conciseness and perfect clarity through repetition, he elected the latter, despite the perception of his correspondent's taxed patience, and explained, "I am more afraid of falling upon Scylla to avoid Charybdis."

Typical of his day, Fitzhugh regarded the letter as a literary form of which, at his best, he was an able practitioner. Although he once said, "I must confess I want abilitys, to polish & adorn my expressions," he underestimated his effectiveness:

Necessity as 'tis the Mother of Invention, so it is the Nurse of Industry... with the same Content & satisfaction as wearyed travellers take up their Inn, or weather beaten Voyagers their desired Port, after a long tedious & stormy Voyage, so did I the most welcome joyfull, & glad news of your health, welfare, & prosperity...you are not Yorkshire enough, to set the Course of your advice by the Compass of your Interest...what a hard Game we have to play the contrary party that is our Opposers, having the best Cards & the Trumps to boot especially the Honor[.] Yet would my Lord Fairfax there, take his turn in Shuffling & Dealing the Cards & his Lordship with the rest see that we were not cheated in our game, I question not but we should gain the Sett, tho' the game is so far plaid.

Such is the literary quality of the letters. Although his achievement as an author will not eclipse the history the correspondence contains, it does provide an indispensable framework for the correct evaluation of the life and mind of William Fitzhugh. To appreciate the gentle art of his letters is indeed to understand more fully both the age and the man.

Suggested Readings: DAB; LHUS. *See also* Philip A. Bruce, *Institutional History of Virginia in the Seventeenth Century*, 2 vols. (1910), passim; Gilbert Chinard, ed., *A Huguenot Exile in Virginia* (1934), p. 158; Richard Beale Davis, "Chesapeake Pattern and Pole-Star: William Fitzhugh in His Plantation World, 1676-1701," PAPS, 105 (1961), 525-529; idem, *Intellectual Life in the Colonial South, 1585-1763*, 3 vols. (1978), passim; idem, *Literature and Society in Early Virginia, 1608-1840* (1973); idem, ed., *William Fitzhugh and His Chesapeake World, 1676-1701* (1963); Howard Mumford Jones, *The Literature of Virginia in the 17th Century* (1968), pp. 79-85; Bishop Meade, *Old Churches, Ministers and Families of Virginia*, 2 vols. (1857); Louis B. Wright, *The First Gentlemen of Virginia* (1940), 155-186.

Michael A. Lofaro
University of Tennessee, Knoxville

BRIDGET RICHARDSON FLETCHER (1726-1770)

Works: *Hymns and Spiritual Songs* (1773).

Biography: Despite the posthumous publication of a substantial volume of Bridget Fletcher's *Hymns and Spiritual Songs*, little information is available to reconstruct her life. Her second hymn, "On the Authors Proceeding on This Work," indicates that Fletcher considered her family background to be humble: "I no proph'tess am, / Of prophets line I ne'er did spring, / Only of an herdsman." The title page notes that she married Timothy Fletcher of "Wesford" (probably Westford, Mass.). Beyond these cryptic details, the volume reveals little of its author.

Critical Appraisal: The paucity of information that her anonymous editor provided about Fletcher's temporal existence was probably deliberate, for it serves to underscore the spiritual message of her songs. In a brief preface, the editor explained that the author had undergone a noticeable change in her relationship with her God: "She had formerly been exercised with a melancholy, and under great desertion of God's spirit. . . and sometimes about tempted to despair; but for several years before her death, she was in a great measure relieved therefrom." If we may safely assume that the order of the published hymns approximates their order of composition, the editor's perception of Fletcher's growing confidence in her salvation is accurate. The eighty-three extant hymns in the volume (only one copy survives and several of its pages are missing) move from themes of abstract melancholy to gratitude for God's specifically enumerated mercies. The contrast, for example, between the simple thanks of "Hymn LXXVII. God's Protecting Hand Shewn in Deliverance, When in Danger of Fire" and the self-pity of the apparently earlier "Hymn XXXIII. No Darkness to Be Compared with Spiritual Darkness, No Sorrow Like Soul Sorrow" illustrates Fletcher's spiritual movement. Although themes of redemption, God's glory, and human sin predominate, many of Fletcher's songs adopt a lighter tone as they consider more temporal subjects. Her "Hymn LXX. The Duty of Man and Wife," for example, cautions "every head that is married" to attend her advice: "If any hiss, I say at this, / Then let him be expel'd." Men are urged to value their wives, and women are reminded of their duty to submit to their husbands "As reason there, shall say is fair, / And as it shall seem fit."

Unfortunately for modern readers, the spiritual growth traceable in Fletcher's songs was not accompanied by a corresponding development in poetic skill. Her uniform ballad stanzas adapt the poems for singing, but rough rhythms, conventional imagery, and a general lack of variety make them less interesting as poetry. Never intending her work for publication, Fletcher "was deprived of an opportunity of revising, or so much as giving titles to many of [her hymns]," by her death in 1770. Perhaps with that circumstance in mind, her editor asked her readers "to make allowances for the many inaccuracies of a female pen." Because the volume was offered as a memorial for friends, the editor urged that no one "be so disingenuous as to criticise, upon the poetry or composition, which may be serviceable and instructive to some, but injurious to none." Perhaps the editor was right: the hymns have more value today as history than as poetry.

Suggested Readings: Pattie Cowell, *Women Poets in Pre-Revolutionary America* (prints selections from the verse; 1981), pp. 247-252.

Pattie Cowell
Colorado State University

PETER FOLGER (1617-1690)

Works: *A Looking-Glass for the Times* (w. 1676; pub. 1725).
Biography: Born near Norwich, Eng., in 1617, Peter Folger came to Mass.

with his father in 1635. In 1642 he went to Martha's Vineyard, where he worked as a schoolmaster and surveyor and assisted the Rev. Thomas Mayhew, Jr. (q.v.), in his work with the Indians. After a brief stay in R.I., Folger took his family to Nantucket in 1663, following an offer of a half-share of land; he had already been involved in missionary work and surveying on that island. One of the first settlers, Folger served in several public offices but later became involved in political controversies, even spending a brief term in jail when the half-shareholders attempted to take control from the original proprietors. His daughter Abiah Folger was the mother of Benjamin Franklin (q.v.). Praised by Cotton Mather (q.v.) in the *Magnalia* as "an able Godly Englishman," Folger died on Nantucket in 1690.

Critical Appraisal: Benjamin Franklin praised *A Looking-Glass for the Times* as "written with a good deal of Decent Plainness and manly Freedom" in "the homespun Verse of that Time." Folger himself had no pretensions to being a poet and apologized to his readers for the "uncomely Dress" of his production. Certainly, the chief interest of *A Looking-Glass* is in its political and religious ideas and not in the quality of its verse.

Written mostly in rough ballad stanzas, the poem is a plea for religious freedom. Folger spoke, as his grandson said, for "the Baptists, Quakers, and other Sectaries" who had been persecuted by the clergy (the "College Men") and banished by the government of Mass. From his perspective as a Baptist and his experience as a worker with the Indians, Folger contended that the Indian wars and other evils that had recently befallen New Eng. were God's punishment for the intolerance of the leaders of the Bay Colony—"The Sin of Persecution." He called for benevolence toward the "natives," who had acted merely as God's instruments, and religious freedom for the dissenters: "I count it worse in Magistrates / to use the Iron Sword / To do the Work which Christ alone / will do by his own Word."

Folger's spirited call for peace and toleration illustrates the vigor of seventeenth-century New Eng. dissent. But it must be recognized that the author put himself in little personal danger. The poem remained unpublished until after his death, and Folger was out of the jurisdiction of Mass. when he wrote it. Nantucket, a refuge for dissenters, was under the administration of N.Y. in 1676.

Suggested Readings: CCNE; DAB; FCNEV; T$_1$. *See also* Leonard W. Labaree et al., eds., *The Autobiography of Benjamin Franklin* (1964), pp. 51-52; Babette May Levy, "The Life and Work of Peter Folger" (M.A. thesis, Columbia Univ., 1939); Florence Bennett Anderson, *A Grandfather for Benjamin Franklin* (1940); Clifford K. Shipton, "Report of the Librarian," PAAS, 63 (1954), 323-324.

Douglas M. Arnold
Yale University

THOMAS FORREST (1747-1825)

Works: *The Disappointment: Or, The Force of Credulity* (1767).
Biography: Although there has been some question concerning who wrote

The Disappointment, critics generally accept Thomas Forrest as the author. Born of Quaker parents in Philadelphia, Pa., on July 12, 1747, Forrest attended David James Dove's school, where he met John Reily, later the model for the character "Parchment" in his play. In 1770, at the age of 23, Forrest married Anne Whitepain. In 1776 he was commissioned a captain in the Pa. Artillery. During the Revolution, Forrest fought in several major battles and was wounded at Brandywine. When he resigned in 1781, Forrest was a lieutenant colonel. Records show, however, that at one point, Forrest was court-martialed, but the offense for which he was convicted was probably minor, for he received only a light sentence. In 1785, 1786, and again in 1789, Forrest returned to the military, and he served as a captain during the Whiskey Insurrection of 1794. Following the war, Forrest became a trustee of the Germantown Academy and in 1799 was elected president of the Board. Besides working in business and education, he served in the Pa. Assembly and in Congress. He died in Germantown (now a part of Philadelphia) on March 20, 1825.

Critical Appraisal: Written under the pseudonym "Andrew Barton," *The Disappointment* is Thomas Forrest's only known work. Today, it is practically forgotten, at least partially because of its "production" history. In Apr. 1767 the American Company of Comedians advertised a performance of the play at the Southwark Theater near Philadelphia. Two days before opening night, a local newspaper reported that the play, "as it contains personal reflections, is unfit for the stage." Because it dealt with a practical joke recently pulled on several prominent Philadelphians, the butts of the joke apparently objected enough to prevent the play from being performed. As a result, *The Disappointment* lost the distinction of being the first play written by an American to be performed professionally on an American stage. Several days later, the honor went instead to Thomas Godfrey's (q.v.) *The Prince of Parthia*. Forrest's play is, however, generally accepted as America's first ballad opera.

In writing *The Disappointment*, Forrest was clearly aware of British theater, for he adopted stock techniques in Restoration and eighteenth-century comedy, farce, and opera, and he borrowed two ballads from John Gay's *The Beggar's Opera*. Much of the play's farcical nature results from the interplay of its ethnic characters, whose broad actions are sometimes bawdy but always amusing. Although there are problems with unnecessary repetition of details and with the incorporation of subplots into the main plot, the play moves fairly well as it recounts how "four humorous gentlemen" tricked the "principal dupes" into believing in the existence of buried treasure. As "Andrew Barton" said in his preface,

> The moral shows the folly of an over-credulity and desire of money and how apt men are—especially old men—to be unwarily drawn into schemes where there is but the least shadow of gain and concludes with these observations; that mankind ought to be contented with their respective stations, to follow their vocations with honesty and industry—the only sure way to gain riches.

When Forrest published a revised version in 1796, he added characters and scenes that emphasized dialect, offered more satire, and clarified some of the original action, but the play attracted little attention. Instead it had to wait until 1976, when it was produced as part of America's Bicentennial celebration.

Suggested Readings: T$_2$. *See also* Andrew Barton, *The Disappointment*, ed. David Mays (contains the most complete discussion of Forrest and the play; 1976); W. A. Newman Dorland, "The Second Troop Philadelphia City Cavalry," PMHB, 47 (1923), 371; John MacPherson, "Letter to William Patterson, May 30, 1767," PMHB, 23 (1899), 52-53; Walter J. Meserve, *An Emerging Entertainment: The Drama of the American People to 1828* (1977), pp. 51-52, passim; *Official Master Register of Bicentennial Activities*, 4th ed. (1975), pp. 5-100; George O. Scilhamer, *History of the American Theatre* (1888), I, 176-184; John F. Watson, *Annals of Philadelphia and Pennsylvania in the Olden Time* (1823), I, 73-74.

Paul Sorrentino
Virginia Polytechnic Institute and State University

HANNAH WEBSTER FOSTER (1759-1840)

Works: *The Coquette: Or, The History of Eliza Wharton* (1797); *The Boarding School; Or, Lessons of a Preceptress to her Pupils* (1798).

Biography: Hannah Webster Foster was born on Sept. 10, 1759, in Salisbury, Mass. Although details of her early life are inaccessible to biographers and literary historians, it is known that in 1785 she married Rev. John Foster of Brighton, Mass., and that they had five children. After the death of her husband, Foster went to Montreal to live with two of her daughters. She died there on Apr. 17, 1840, at the age of 81. In her two novels, Foster managed successfully to adapt the form of the British novel to the moral and religious needs of the new Republic, which tended to distrust fiction as a vehicle for Satanic thought.

Critical Appraisal: Hannah Webster Foster's best known work, *The Coquette: Or, The History of Eliza Wharton* (1797), was published under the pseudonym, "A Lady of Massachusetts." An epistolary novel after the style of Samuel Richardson's *Clarissa Harlowe, The Coquette* claims to be "Founded on Fact" and is in actuality based on the life of Elizabeth Whitman, of Hartford, Conn., a distant cousin of Foster's husband, who was reported to have been seduced by Jonathan Edwards's (q.v.) son Pierrepont and to have died in childbirth. Although purporting to have a moral purpose, the novel actually defends female liberty. Eliza Wharton insists on her right to function as a free agent: "But I despise those contracted ideas which confine virtue to a cell. I have no notion of becoming a recluse." The novel depicts in elaborate detail the courtship of Eliza by Maj. Peter Sanford, who is described as a "second Lovelace." Eliza rejects a marriage proposal from Rev. Boyer, who promises her a secure and virtuous life, in order to pursue romance with Sanford who is a self-acknowledged cad, "If she will play with the lion, let her beware the paw, I say."

The Coquette rivaled the bestselling *Charlotte, A Tale of Truth* (1791) by Susanna (Haswell) Rowson (q.v.), but because it was unseemly for women to seek public attention or fame, Foster identified herself only as "A Lady of Massachusetts." With the 2nd edition of Foster's novel in 1802, the publisher emphasized its moral content: "The rapid sale of the first edition, is a proof of its estimation by the moral, instructive and entertaining reader." A 3rd edition of the novel appeared in 1811 followed by eight reprintings between the years 1824 and 1828.

Although *The Coquette* disdained sensationalism, readers were fascinated by its terrifying yet thrilling plot of seduction and betrayal. The novel consists of seventy-two letters artfully constructed to provide multiple points of view and to sustain the suspense of the plot. Herbert Ross Brown observed, "The seventy two letters which comprise the novel reflect the varying moods of their authors, and, at the need of the plot, shift from the easy circumstantiality of familiar correspondence to moments of agonizing self-betrayal." In this correspondence, Eliza Wharton confides in her cousin Lucy Freeman while Maj. Peter Sanford boasts of his progress in his seduction attempts to Charles Deighton. Although Eliza Wharton is attracted to Peter Sanford because he offers her the promise of freedom from a sedate and predictable life, he is motivated by revenge as well as lust: "I must own myself a little revengeful too in this affair, I wish to punish her friends, as she calls them, for their malice towards me; for their cold and negligent treatment of me whenever I go to the house." Unaware of Sanford's malice, Wharton rejects Boyer's proposal—a decision that gives her the illusion of being in charge of her life. Because she lacks the wisdom to make a constructive choice of a mate, her rebellion results in personal disaster and a tragic conclusion to her life.

The Coquette was extremely successful and appeared in thirteen editions in forty years. Foster's second novel, *The Boarding School; Or, Lessons of a Preceptress to her Pupils* (1798), was less popular with readers. The conventional plot of the novel narrates the efforts of Mrs. Williams to train young ladies in proper deportment suitable to their roles as future wives and mothers. Disputing the maxim that "reformed rakes make the best husbands," this novel insists that licentious men are the Devil's agents.

Both of Foster's novels attempt to inculcate moral training. In the Dedication of *The Boarding School*, Foster made her didactic purpose clear: she wanted "to instil such principles of piety, morality, benevolence, prudence and economy, as might be useful through life." Self-improvement is emphasized and idleness is scorned: "We ought never to be idle. No moment should be unoccupied. Some employment, salutary, either to the body or mind, or both, should be constantly pursued; and the needle is always at hand to supply the want of other avocations."

Foster warned against the evils of romantic novels that "pervert the judgment, mislead the affections, and blind the understanding." In a series of contrasting portraits of female virtue and vice, the author made it clear that prudence, piety, and practicality are the traits to which American women should aspire. The Puritan habit of self-scrutiny is adapted to the secular lives of eighteenth-century women who are advised to eschew dissipation and pleasure: "Make it an invariable practice to re-trace the actions and occurrences of the day, when you retire to rest; to account with your own hearts for the use and improvement of the past hours; and rectify whatever you find amiss, by greater vigilance and caution in the future."

The Boarding School lacks the sensational plot elements of *The Coquette* and has been criticized for being dull, if proper. The novel consists of a series of lectures by Mrs. Williams to her seven pupils, all of whom come from affluent families. Her self-defined role is to "polish the mental part, to call forth the dormant virtues, to unite and arrange the charms of person and mind, to inspire a due sense of decorum and propriety." Mrs. Williams instructs her pupils in the domestic arts such as needlework, which is the antidote to idleness. She repeatedly warns her pupils against imaginative excess and the dangers of romanticism and urges the reading of history and the Bible instead of novels. Insisting that romantic attraction is a snare, Mrs. Williams outlines a hierarchy of love in which filial piety ranks highest followed by fraternal love, friendship, and conjugal love.

Reason, not romance, is to guide these young women, and when a sensible match has been arranged, they are advised to be patient, loving, and kind: "Let prudence, therefore, be your pole-star, when you enter the married state. Watch with the greatest circumspection over yourself; and always exercise the tenderest affection, the most unwearied patience, and the most cheerful acquiescence in the treatment of your companion." In this novel, sense has replaced sensationalism.

Suggested Readings: DAB; LHUS; NAW. *See also* Charles Knowles Bolton, *The Elizabeth Whitman Mystery at the Old Bell Tavern in Danvers* (1912); Herbert Ross Brown, *The Sentimental Novel in America, 1789-1860* (1940); Charles H. Dall, *The Romance of the Association* (1875); Henri Petter, *The Early American Novel* (1971); R. L. Shurter, "Mrs. Hannah Webster Foster and the Early American Novel," AL, 4 (1932), 306-308.

Wendy Martin
Queens College of the City University of New York

JOHN FOSTER (1648-1681)

Works: *Foster's Almanac(s) of Celestial Motions for the Year(s) 1675-1681* (1675-1681).

Biography: Born in Dorchester, Mass., John Foster was baptized on Dec. 10, 1648, by Richard Mather (q.v.). Two years after graduation from Harvard in 1667, he began to teach grammar school in Dorchester, an occupation he continued through 1674. In addition, Foster is known for his work as the earliest engraver in North America, an occupation he took up as early as 1671. Among the engravings attributed to Foster are "A Map of New England" in William Hubbard's (q.v.) *Narrative of the Troubles with the Indians* (1677) and the famous portrait of Richard Mather that appears in Increase Mather's (q.v.) biography of his father. In 1675 Foster became Boston's first printer, publishing fifteen pieces by Increase Mather and various works by writers such as John Eliot (q.v.), Samuel Willard (q.v.), Roger Williams (q.v.), and Anne Bradstreet (q.v.), as well as the almanacs he annually compiled from 1675 until his early death from tuberculosis on Sept. 9, 1681, at age 32.

Critical Appraisal: Although John Foster compiled almanacs for much of his adult life and was active in the publishing trade at Boston, he wrote only two short pieces: "Of Comets, Their Motion, Distance, and Magnitude" and "Observations of a Comet Seen This Last Winter." Published in his *Almanac* for 1681, these works reveal a writer of considerable scientific and philosophical precision. "Of Comets," Foster's first work, is a logical disquisition on the nature of comets and is characterized by emotional restraint as the author strived for a consensus of opinion on a phenomenon that had long puzzled the scientists and theologians of New Eng. He insisted, for example, that he would concern himself only "with such things as come under a mathematical Demonstration," and he stressed his objectivity with phrases such as "it is commonly thought. . ." and "it was judged. . ." His long, balanced sentences create a smooth and elegant style that persisted as he shifted from the sermon logic of his first piece to the appended, more personal "Observations of a Comet," where he continued his accurate, detailed description but in the context of words such as *terrible* and *prodigious spectacle*, indicative of a more emotional and philosophical appraisal of the event. Surmising some evil in this comet, Foster concluded with a standard seventeenth-century Puritan inference about the relationship between natural phenomena and providence: "Sure it is that these things are not sent for nothing, though man cannot say particularly for what."

At a time before America's first newspaper (1704) or magazine (1740), Foster's almanacs offered contemporary readers original astrological calculations and spare, entertaining filler. To the standard almanac format, Foster added illustrations and meteorological advice for the farmer while increasing to two pages the entry for each month. In 1678, he introduced the illustration of "The Man of Signs," a convention in American almanacs from this point on. This addition of commercial astrology, accompanied by twelve humorous lines, was a significant departure from the earlier almanacs compiled and published in Cambridge by Harvard astronomers and philomaths. In 1679, Foster gave his almanac a distinctive character by concentrating on the tides; in 1680, he focused on planets, and in 1681, on comets. This last almanac also includes his illustration of the Copernican system. With later innovations by John Tulley (q.v.) and Daniel Leeds (q.v.), Foster's imaginative and scholarly additions adumbrated eighteenth-century almanacs.

Foster's almanacs appeared before proverbs and predictions became common features, and the writer does not include these in his work, but almanac verse began as early as Samuel Danforth's (q.v.) almanac, the second extant in America, and Foster is conventional in his inclusion of rhymed couplets in groups of four and six lines. The motifs which unify the poetry in his almanacs for 1676 and 1679 are also not unusual; the poems before each month in the first almanac trace the frail course of "Man, a little World, entering Life's Stage," while the 1679 almanac offers images of assault and battle as "Sol's burning Chariot hurries on." Foster's most charming verse is probably the poem under "The Man of Signs" in his 1678 almanac; here he advises "When Seelings crack, and fowles do cry amain / Soon after look for tempest or for rain." The couplet in his almanac for 1679 under Dec. 19, 1675, further reveals his occasional forcefulness and humor. Noting the death in Canada of eighty English soldiers and three hundred Indian men "beside squaws and children," Foster adds, "Tis fear'd a thousand Natives young and old / Went to a place in their opinion cold."

Although finally more significant as a printer and an engraver than as a writer, Foster seems worthy of attention for two reasons. Like many seventeenth-century Americans, he was creative in a variety of areas despite a lack of specific training. Although generally excessively laudatory, Foster's biography is probably correct that "in certain lines of learning John Foster was a man of some attainments." Furthermore, his careful separation of objective and essentially subjective material in his two original pieces suggests the Puritans' distinction between the relative importance of reason and emotion and the psychology that, stemming from this distinction, has colored much of early America's literature.

Suggested Readings: DAB; FCNEV; Sibley-Shipton (II, 222, 228). *See also* Samuel Abbott Green, *John Foster: The Earliest American Engraver and the First Boston Printer* (1909); *The National Cyclopedia of American Biography* (1932), XXII, 345; Robb Sagendorph, *America and Her Almanacs* (1970).

Caroline Zilboorg
Lake Erie College

SAMUEL FOTHERGILL (1715-1772)

Works: *A Few Hints Addressed to the Inhabitants of Warrington* (1756); *To Friends of the Island of Tortola* (c. 1760); *Remarks on an Address to the People Called Quakers* (1761); *An Epistle from the Friends Who Visited the Quarterly and Monthly Meetings of the Kingdom of Ireland* (1762); *A Reply to a Pamphlet* (1763); *Two Discourses and a Prayer* (c. 1767); *The Prayer of Agur* (1768); *The Grace of Our Lord Jesus Christ* (1771); *The Substance of a Few Expressions* (1772); *A Sermon Preached at Horsly-Down* (1773); *Repent and Be Converted* (1778); *The Necessity and Divine Excellency* (1780); *Sermons Preached by Samuel Fothergill* (1783); *Discourses Delivered at Several Meeting Houses* (1790);

Discourses Delivered Extempore (1800); *Letters* (1803); *Some Discourses, Epistles, and Letters* (1803); *Ten Discourses* (1808); *Eleven Discourses Delivered Extempore* (1817); *A Discourse Delivered at the Friends' Meeting House in Leeds* (1823); "Original Letter" (w. 1756, containing an account of his travels in America; pub. in *Friends' Magazine*, 1, no. 3 [Jan. 1830]); *Memoirs of the Life and Gospel Labours* (1843). See also Joseph Smith's *Descriptive Catalogue of Friends' Books* (3 vols., 1867), for several sources of Fothergill's letters.

Biography: Samuel Fothergill was born the sixth son of John and Margaret Fothergill and the younger brother of physician and botanist Dr. John Fothergill, in Nov. 1715 in Eng., at Carr End, Wensleydale, Yorkshire. His father was a respected Quaker itinerant minister; his mother died when he was 3. After his early education at Sedbergh and later at Sutton, Cheshire, Fothergill was apprenticed at 17 to a Stockport shopkeeper, and although he rebelled at first against his father's strict manner of life, he at length embraced the Quaker faith. A tea dealer and American merchant, he also set aside time to travel in the ministry: to Wales (1739); Ire. (1744, 1762); the American colonies (1754-1756); and Scot. (1764). In the colonies, he traveled 8,765 miles, visiting the meetings of Friends from Maine to Ga. and becoming one of the best known "publick Friends" of his day. In 1738 Fothergill married Susannah Croudson, also a Quaker minister. Never a robust man, he suffered from chronic gout and other ailments no doubt aggravated by his extensive travels and labors. He died at Warrington, Eng., in Jun. 1772.

Critical Appraisal: During his lifetime and well into the nineteenth century, Samuel Fothergill was a preacher of repute on both sides of the Atlantic. Like all Quaker preachers of his day, Fothergill spoke *extempore*, and it is remarkable that any of his sermons or, for that matter, any Quaker sermons from the period are extant. Those few Quaker sermons that have survived were usually copied in shorthand by auditors and are a testimony to the popularity and importance of their authors. In Fothergill's case, non-Quaker admirers handed his sermons to posterity, thus allowing his reputation to increase in notoriety after his death.

Fothergill's surviving sermons, particularly *The Grace of Our Lord Jesus Christ*, reveal why he was so popular, even among non-Quakers. Adept at interpreting Scripture, Fothergill was skilled in the use of metaphor, particularly from the Old Testament, and he was able to build his sermons in such a way as to emphasize a well-placed and eloquent peroration. In addition, Fothergill's sermons provide insight into the form of Quaker preaching during the eighteenth century. Beginning with a quotation from Scripture, Fothergill structured his exhortation around an interpretation of that quotation.

Fothergill's *Memoirs*, largely compiled from letters and a personal journal (most of which he reportedly burned before his death), is significant for what it reveals about both the American colonies and the Society of Friends during a particularly turbulent political period in both their histories. Visiting places where the Great Awakening had sprung up some fifteen years earlier, Fothergill was surprised to find a ready hearing in large meetings of non-Quakers. Regarding Friends' meetings, however, his *Memoirs* and letters reveal a general disappointment with most everyone except the youth. In addition, the *Memoirs* shows Fothergill growing in a conviction to discipline and order American Quakerism through "queries" designed to provoke self-examination and hopefully to winnow out the uncommitted. Finally, the *Memoirs* reveals the iron-clad testimony against war that led Fothergill to advise Pa. Quakers to withdraw from public life rather than to compromise their antiwar teachings through support of the struggle against the French and the Indians.

In addition to the information they provide about history and preaching, Fothergill's writings, particularly his *Memoirs*, are an important record of the personal philosophy, outlook, and style of a man who in many ways was representative of the best in his culture. Historians and critics may argue over the merits of Fothergill's positions and methods, but his place among the outstanding Quakers of the eighteenth century is secure, his influence on the course of events in Pa. well-established, and his abilities as an orator apparent in his works.

Suggested Readings: DNB. *See also* Richard Bauman, *For the Reputation of Truth: Politics, Religion, and Conflict Among the Pennsylvania Quakers, 1750-1800* (1971), pp. 40-46; Lucia K. Beamish, *Quaker Ministry, 1691 to 1834* (1967), pp. 93-100; Davis H. Forsythe, "The Fothergills" in *Quaker Biographies* (1910), IV, 27-66; R. Hingston Fox, *Dr. John Fothergill and His Friends* (1919), pp. 239-262; Rufus Jones, *The Later Periods of Quakerism* (1921), I, 12-16; idem, *Quakers in the American Colonies* (1910), pp. 127-130; Joseph Smith, *A Descriptive Catalogue of Friends' Books* (1867), I, 635-642; *Supplement*, p. 133; Luella M. Wright, *The Literary Life of the Early Friends, 1650-1725* (1932).

Michael P. Graves
George Fox College

JOHN FOX (c. 1686-c. 1725)

Works: *Motto's of the Wanderers* (1718); *The Publick Spirit; A Poem* (1718); *The Wanderer* (1718); *To My Friend, the Author of a Letter, Under the Title of Patricius to Manlius* (1720).

Biography: John Fox was born in Va. sometime around 1686. His father, Henry Fox, was a vestryman of St. John's Parish in King and Queen County, a justice, and eventually a representative in the House of Burgesses. His mother, Anne Fox, was a descendant of Capt. John West and a sister of Nathaniel West. An attorney, John Fox may have been trained, as was Ebenezer Cooke (q.v.), by Thomas Bordley, Md.'s attorney general. As this evidence suggests, Fox was a well-born man of standing in Va.

However, by 1715 Fox was no longer either living in Va. or living as a man of standing. Indeed, he was in fact in a London prison for "a Debt Due to ye Crown for the Customs of Tobaco." The justices of the Courts of King William and New Kent Counties petitioned the House to the king, but the House rejected the petition. While in jail, Fox wrote *The Wanderer*, a periodical containing essays on moral and topical subjects. He began this project in part, it seems, to change his reputation as a man of questionable character (Fox referred, in the Preface to *Motto's of the Wanderers* to "The frequent Misrepresentation of me") and in part to earn enough money to gain release from prison. *The Wanderer* appeared weekly from Jan. 9 to Aug. 7, 1717. Of the twenty-six issues, twenty-four were written by Fox and two by Daniel Hanchet. Despite his efforts, Fox was still in prison when the last issue of *The Wanderer* appeared.

In what was most likely an attempt to win the aid of William Byrd II (q.v.), Fox wrote an effusive dedication to him in *Motto's of the Wanderers*, published in 1718. A draft of Byrd's scathing response, which may or may not have been sent to Fox, appears on a flyleaf of his copy of the book. In it, Byrd said "that next to appearing on the Title page of no extraordinary Performance, a man makes the unhappyest figure in the Dedication." He concluded, "My servant will bring you a Guinea, which I would intreat you by no means to look upon as an acknowledgment for the favour you have done me, but as a bribe to do it no more."

Fox's attempts to win influence were not, however, limited to Byrd. The collected edition of *The Wanderer* contains a paragraph eulogizing Governor Alexander Spotswood (q.v.) of Va. Since Spotswood and Byrd were political rivals, Fox was careful not to flatter both individuals in the same work. Hence Fox's dedication of the *Motto's of the Wanderers* to Byrd does not appear in the collected edition of *The Wanderer*, which includes the text of the *Motto's*. Fox also sought the favor of former Va. Governor Francis Nicholson by writing *The Publick Spirit*, a poem that praises him as "the godlike Man, / From whom Virginia's golden Days began."

Although it is highly unlikely that Byrd, Spotswood, or Nicholson came to Fox's aid, someone must have, for by 1720 he was freed from jail, and by May 1723 he was back in Va., petitioning a title to lands in King William County. In Jun. 1720 he received the title. Apparently Fox lived a quiet life in Va., no longer composing essays or verses, from that time until his death sometime after 1725.

Critical Appraisal: *The Wanderer*, "one of the many ephemeral English literary periodicals of the early eighteenth century," was written in obvious imitation of the essay style of the period. As one writer pointed out, it was similar in form—if not excellence—to the productions of Joseph Addison. Fox intended to avoid party issues and "to make the Economy of Private Life" his subject. Indeed, his chief topics are religion and morals, contemporary manners, and especially affairs of the heart. *The Wanderer* combined mild satire with a flowery and conventionalized literary style. According to one writer, the periodical had become, by its conclusion, "almost entirely made up of invented letters— sentimental, frothy stuff in the guise of admonition."

Fox's poem *The Publick Spirit* is obviously self-serving in its intent. Written in heroic couplets, the work is filled with conventional Classical allusions and rhetorical devices. Fox praised the people and society of Va.: "The Men, tho' bless'd with Peace, are train'd to War, / Fair are the Women, yet more chaste than Fair." He went on to heap praises upon former Governor Francis Nicholson, who had returned to Eng. in 1705 and whom Fox might well have seen as a sponsor. The governor, Fox told us, was mild, but not meek; wise; just; and active—in short, a perfect administrator who had improved the lot of the colony in many ways: "Peace was his Pleasure, War his last Recourse, / And nothing was oppos'd with Force, but Force. / To glorious Heights his gen'rous Soul aspires, / And civil Virtues blend with martial Fires. / Expos'd his Person for the Country's Good, / And for her Peace with Pleasure risqu'd his Blood."

John Fox's trivial essays and stereotyped versifying have little merit as great literature, but they do show something about politicals in Va., current English literary and cultural conventions, and the way these conventions influenced an American imitator. In the light of Fox's cessation of literary activity after his return to Va., it is fair to agree with those commentators who feel that he wrote mostly for self-interested reasons while in London.

Suggested Readings: John G. Ames, Jr., *The English Literary Periodical of Morals and Manners* (1904), pp. 94-95; Richard Beale Davis, *Intellectual Life in the Colonial South* (1978), III, 1357, 1370, 1489, 1604; W. Graham, *English Literary Periodicals* (1930), p. 99; George S. Marr, *The Periodical Essayists of the Eighteenth Century* (1924), pp. 71-72; Kenneth Ballard Murdock, "William Byrd and the Virginia Author of *The Wanderer*," *Harvard Studies and Notes in Philology and Literature* (1924), pp. 129-136.

David Jauss
University of Arkansas at Little Rock

THOMAS FOXCROFT (1697-1769)

Works: *A Practical Discourse Relating to the Gospel-Ministry* (1718); *Cleansing Our Way in Youth Press'd* (1719); *A Discourse Concerning Kindness* (1720); *A Discourse . . . Occasioned by the Death of Elder John Loring* (1720); *Exhortations & Directions to Young People* (pub. in Cotton Mather, *A Course of Sermons on Early Piety*; 1721); *A Sermon Preach'd . . . After the Funeral of Mrs. Elizabeth Foxcroft* (1721); *The Day of a Godly Man's Death* (1722); *A Funeral Sermon Occasion'd by Several Mournful Deaths* (1722); *The Character of Anna* (1723); *The Hope and Strength of a Nation Whose Wars Are of God* (w. 1723; pub. 1885); *God's Face Set Against an Incorrigible People* (1724); *The Ruling and Ordaining Power of Congregational Bishops* (1724); *A Vindication of the Appendix to the Sober Remarks [of Edward Wigglesworth]* (1725); *Death the Destroyer* (1726); *Ministers, Spiritual Parents* (1726); *A Serious Address to*

Those Who Unnecessarily Frequent the Tavern (1726); *A Brief Display* (1727); *A Discourse Preparatory to the Choice of a Minister* (1727); *Divine Providence Ador'd* (1727); *God the Judge* (1727); *The Voice of the Lord from the Deep Places of the Earth* (1727); *The Importance of Ministers* (1728); *Eli the Priest* (1729); *Observations Historical and Practical on the Rise and Primitive State of New England* (1730); *The Pleas of Gospel-Impenitents* (1730); *The Divine Right of Deacons* (1731); *Eusebius Inermatus* (1733); *Lessons of Caution to Young Sinners* (1733); *Elisha Lamenting* (1737); *Some Seasonable Thoughts on Evangelic Preaching* (1740); *The Blessings of a Soul in Health* (1742); *An Apology in Behalf of the Revd, Mr. Whitefield* (1745); *A Seasonable Memento for New Year's Day* (1747); *Humilis Confessio* (1750); *The Earthquake a Divine Visitation* (1756); *Like Precious Faith* (1756); *Grateful Reflexions* (1760).

Biography: Thomas Foxcroft—pastor of the prestigious First Church of Boston, overseer of Harvard College, trustee of the Hopkins Charity, and spirited defender of old New Eng. orthodoxy—was born in Boston, Mass., on Feb. 26, 1697. His parents were Col. Francis Foxcroft, warden of King's Chapel, Boston, and Elizabeth (Danforth) Foxcroft. As residents of Boston and by the turn of the century of the Danforth mansion in Cambridge, the Foxcrofts were prominent members of the Church of England, and despite the animosity that such religious allegiances would likely have attracted from Congregationals at the time, Col. Foxcroft expected that his son would eventually take Anglican orders. During his early years at Harvard College, from which he obtained an A.B. in 1714 and an A.M. two years later, Foxcroft continued his connection with the Church of England, but on Nov. 30, 1712, following his parents' course, he was taken into full communion in the Cambridge church. After completing an A.B., Foxcroft kept school in Roxbury, Mass., where, under the influence of the Rev. Nehemiah Walter (q.v.), he formally espoused the Congregational way in church discipline and politics. About 1716 he began preaching in Congregational meetinghouses, and in the early months of 1717, he was invited to preach as a candidate for a vacancy at the First Church. On Mar. 6, 1717, Foxcroft was called to serve there as the colleague of the Rev. Benjamin Wadsworth (q.v.), and on Nov. 20, 1717, he was ordained at the First Church in an impressive ceremony organized by Increase Mather (q.v.), Cotton Mather (q.v.), Benjamin Colman (q.v.), Joseph Sewall (q.v.), and Wadsworth.

The choice of Foxcroft to serve at the First Church was a tribute to the young minister's orthodox stand, for according to one account, the First Church congregation was "reckoned the most narrow [in New Eng.] in their Principles, and to approach nearest the Brownists." A favorite of the conservative Mather faction in Boston religious and political circles, Foxcroft quickly became a sought-after preacher. In 1721 he provided a sermon for Cotton Mather's course of lectures on early piety, and in 1723 he gave the Artillery Election Sermon. When Wadsworth became president of Harvard College in 1725, Foxcroft assumed control of the First Church, serving alone until 1727, when Charles Chauncy (q.v.) was called to serve as his colleague. The relation between Foxcroft and Chauncy is curious, for from the start, as much as the orthodox Foxcroft would defend the old Calvinist bias, the Arminian Chauncy would sound for the opposing view. Nevertheless, theirs was an honorable partnership that lasted for more than forty years, largely because of their trust in and fairmindedness toward one another. By the 1730s Foxcroft was well on his way toward taking the leading role in Boston's Congregational affairs. Along with Sewall, Thomas Prince (q.v.), and John Webb (q.v.), he tried to share control of the intellectual and pastoral dynasty left unattended at the Mathers's deaths in the 1720s. He campaigned for stricter theology in the schools and churches, supported limited lay participation in church matters, and with an impressive publication record for the time prepared sermons and tracts to explain his own and his conservative colleagues' position.

Foxcroft's career was in fine form until 1736, when he suffered a debilitating stroke. At first he was given up for dead, but he survived, living on-and-off as an invalid for the next thirty-three years. Almost immediately after his stroke, he was forced to relinquish many of his pastoral responsibilities to Chauncy, a move that significantly diminished his influence over the congregation they shared. At the height of the Great Awakening, some of his strength seemed to return. Foxcroft and Chauncy were, of course, on opposing sides, with the former as vocal a supporter of the New Light movement as the latter is famed for being of the Old Light bias. Foxcroft was prominent among the Boston clergymen who welcomed George Whitefield (q.v.) to Boston in 1740, and due to his poor health, Foxcroft invited Whitefield to preach privately for him. Even when by 1745 the excesses of Whitefield and the revivalists were well-known and the failure of the Awakening was apparent, Foxcroft again invited Whitefield to come to Boston, and in his behalf he wrote *An Apology...[for] Whitefield*, a pamphlet that went through two editions.

During the 1750s and 1760s, after most of the diehard defense of the Awakening had quieted down, Foxcroft continued to champion the old New Eng. way both in print and in the pulpit. However, during that time he probably realized that he was out of step with the intellectual and social ranks of an increasingly cosmopolitan Boston, including the ranks of his own lately liberalized congregation. Despite his title of senior pastor, Foxcroft had lost control of the First Church to Chauncy. As a tribute to his tenacity and to his yet-eloquent defense of the past, Foxcroft was invited to give the Dudleian Lecture in 1761. He died of a massive stroke in Boston on Jun. 18, 1769. Married on Mar. 9, 1719, to Anna Coney, who died in 1749, Foxcroft was survived by a son Samuel and a daughter Anna. It is sadly ironic that at the time of his death, this once-famous minister of power and promise was all but forgotten by most of Boston society. Shortly after Foxcroft's death, Chauncy upbraided the congregation of the First Church for its failure to respect Foxcroft's "Christian candor" and to appreciate "the benefit [that it yet enjoyed] of his former more vigorous labors." The concluding remarks in an obituary notice of Foxcroft in the *Boston Gazette* for Jun. 26, 1769, fairly well express the character of his life and career:

He was in sentiment a strict *Calvinist*; tho' catholic in his disposition towards others who did not think just as he did. And, what might too be mentioned to his honor, he was no Trimmer, but steadily and uniformly adhered to the Calvinian principles, which he took to be the true Scripture ones; making them the chief subjects of his pulpit discourses, as he thought he should thereby "please God," if he did not always "please men."

Critical Appraisal: In *A Discourse Occasioned by the Death of...Thomas Foxcroft*, the funeral sermon that Chauncy preached for his colleague in 1769, Foxcroft was celebrated as one "Not...[often] exceeded in quickness of apprehension, clearness of perception, copiousness of invention, liveliness of imagination, strength of memory, soundness of judgment, and the faculty of reasoning." Foxcroft was, according to Chauncy, "a stranger to all the arts of intrigue and dissimulation, and he detested them in others. His conversation was serious, but not affected; pleasant and affable, but not light and vain. He had a turn for satyr...but was always cautious that he did not needlessly give offence." Chauncy's appraisal of Foxcroft's talent and personality is supported by a review of Foxcroft's printed works, which range from sermons for practically every occasion that a Puritan would have considered appropriate for a sermon, to tracts touching on matters of faith, morals, and church discipline, to letters and editorials on topics of public interest and debate. Although most of these materials were printed while Foxcroft enjoyed good health, several—including a debate carried on in Boston newspapers during Apr. 1742 with Andrew Croswell on the subject of religious toleration, a defense of Whitefield and the Awakening, and a half-dozen sermons on various subjects—were printed after his health had become impaired. In all we find a command of language and pulpit oratory noteworthy for its time as Foxcroft spoke at one time as a spiritual father praying for the enlightenment of his flock and at another time as a latter-day Jeremiah warning God's people that God's patience with them is at an end and that the time for them to mend their ways has come. We also find a commitment to New Eng.'s past that is hardly equalled in print in the early eighteenth century. Finally, and perhaps most important, we find displayed an energetic and resourceful mind, one worthy to carry on the pastoral charge so well established by three generations of Mathers and one equal to the task of defending that charge against all challengers in the early and mideighteenth century.

Although a case might be made for Foxcroft's *A Discourse Preparatory to the Choice of a Minister* (1727), *Observations Historical and Practical on the Rise and Primitive State of New England* (1730), *Lessons of Caution to Young Sinners* (1733), or *Humilis Confessio* (1750) as a particularly noteworthy piece, no one Foxcroft work is, in the final analysis, the best or most typical of his writings. Indeed, it is more fair to Foxcroft's literary talent and to his gifted and complex mind to collect evidence of his views and pulpit manners from various sources. For instance, although *Observations Historical and Practical* is probably Foxcroft's fullest expression of belief in the old New Eng. way, that subject informed practically all of the fast, humiliation, funeral, and ordination sermons that he preached during his career. Foxcroft, as these sermons show, was well entrenched in the psychology and language of declension and argued, as his persuasive models the Mathers had done before him, that New Englanders had to humble themselves before God and reform. Apparently, the new science of the eighteenth century meant little to Foxcroft, for in these same sermons, he relied on the metaphysics and cosmology of seventeenth-century Puritan New Eng. to demonstrate that God yet spoke to New Eng. through events. At the time of the 1727 earthquake, for example, he used his commitment to and confidence in the old ways of thought to apprise New Englanders of their peril. In *The Voice of the Lord from the Deep Places of the Earth* (1727), he wrote, "When we heard the Lord of Hosts roring out of the Deep, and felt Him shaking the Earth and our Habitations upon it; was the Lord displeased with the Sea? Was his Anger against the Land? Was his Wrath against our Houses, when they saw Him, and trembled?" "No," Foxcroft responded, God's "roring" and anger were directed "against the guilty Inhabitants." As he explained in *Divine Providence Ador'd*, his funeral sermon for William Waldron that was also preached in 1727, negative events such as natural disasters and the death of godly men are not "a mere necessity of Nature"; they are an intervention of the Divine Will in the affairs of man first for warning and then for judgment and punishment. Interestingly, when nearly a generation later Foxcroft preached *Humilis Confessio* at a lecture and *The Earthquake, a Divine Visitation* on a day of public humiliation, neither his language nor his point of view had substantially changed.

An intriguing aspect of Foxcroft's sermons is his use of language. On many occasions, he eschewed revivalist or evangelical methods of preaching and winning converts, especially the use of either highly emotive or inflated language. When he preached *A Discourse* at the First Church in 1727 on the occasion of the congregation's selection of his colleague, Foxcroft warned the audience against being impressed with any who employed such tactics. "A liberty of prophesying," he then said, is "but an unlawful Licence. . . . The Lord is a God of Order, and not the Author of Confusion, but of Peace. . . . We are not now-a-days to look for extraordinary Calls." Yet this statement is not precisely in keeping with Foxcroft's own practices, for as *The Voice of the Lord from the Deep Places*, which was preached in the same year as *A Discourse* and cited above, shows, Foxcroft could and did rise to an occasional use of inflated, indeed inflammatory, language. Actually, ten years before that sermon was preached, in *A Practical Discourse Relating to the Gospel-Ministry*, which he preached at his own ordination, Foxcroft allowed that it was appropriate for preachers to use language to shock people to a proper awareness of their spiritual state, and he said that he was willing to "breath heavenly *fire* to melt and enliven. . . dead affections." As it happens, in most sermons that can be classified as jeremiads and in some that do not fit into that classification, Foxcroft breathed "heavenly *fire*." In *Lessons of Caution to Young Sinners* (1733), an execution sermon, Foxcroft bewailed the sins of the time, and in a litany of "Bewares" developed for the edification of the young people in his audience, he surpassed the finest fire-breathing jeremiad performances of his models. On the other hand, in *The Blessings of a Soul in Health*, a sermon preached in the calm and pleasant surroundings of a family meeting in 1742, Foxcroft tried to intimidate the audience to seek holiness by treating them to descriptions of sin and the sinner such as this: "O what an odious horrid Spectacle is the Sinner, with a rotten Heart and unclean Hands, with the Image of Death and the Smell of Hell-Fire upon him!"

Finally, one special feature of Foxcroft's ministry should not go unnoticed, particularly for the impact it had on his published works: Foxcroft's commitment to the religious education of New Eng.'s rising generations. Like many members of his own generation, Foxcroft believed that the salvation of the rising genera-tion was New Eng.'s last hope to stay the tide of backsliding and godlessness throughout the land. To that end, he began his career with several major works developed for the edification of the young and never missed an opportunity in the application sections of his sermons to relate the text or doctrine to the use of the young. In *Cleansing Our Way in Youth Press'd* (1719), a work based upon several earlier preached sermons, Foxcroft explained his interest in New Eng.'s young people thus:

> The Abounding of Iniquity in a Christian Land is just matter of Lamenta-tion, and is a daily Grief to such as have at heart the Concerns of Gods Glory. [It] is the unquestionable Duty of All...to promote an happy Ref-ormation,—And if the Rising Generation among us might be induced to Cleanse their Way, This wou'd be one glorious step and afford a most hopeful prospect of the desir'd Blessing.

Works such as *Exhortations & Directions to Young People* (1721) and, again, *Lessons of Caution to Young Sinners* indicate that Foxcroft strove to complete that "hopeful prospect" throughout his career.

Despite his bodily infirmity after 1736, Foxcroft remained an important figure in New Eng.'s social, political, and religious affairs at least until the mideighteenth century as witnessed by his position during the Great Awakening and by his continued publication. Certainly, before his untimely illness, Foxcroft was a leading figure in Boston, and his decline in later years should not be taken to diminish his influence during the 1720s and 1730s. For his lively and inventive mind, his position as an inheritor of the Mather pastoral dynasty, and his role as a defender of old New Eng. orthodoxy, Foxcroft deserves more attention and critical consideration than scholars have thus far given him.

Suggested Readings: CCNE; Sibley-Shipton (VI, 47-58); Sprague (I, 308-310). *See also* Charles Chauncy, *A Discourse Occasioned by the Death of the Rev. Thomas Foxcroft* (1769).

Ronald A. Bosco
State University of New York at Albany

RICHARD FRAME (fl. 1692)

Works: *A Short Description of Pennsilvania* (1692).

Biography: Facts about Richard Frame's life are not available. The writer of the *Description* was evidently an Englishman with first-hand knowledge of William Penn's (q.v.) colony, settled in 1681. The work was printed in Philadelphia by Quaker William Bradford (q.v.); Frame himself may have been a Quaker.

Critical Appraisal: Addressed "to all our Friends" in Eng. who want to learn about Pa., Richard Frame's *Description* attempts to explain why men living in a wilderness regard it as a "good Exchange" for their native country. Frame described in verse "what things are known, enjoyed, and like to be discovered" in Pa., enumerating works of God that "those that live at home do never see." Like other writers of promotional literature, he catalogued wild and domestic animals (lingering over the female opossum, "much admired with her double Belly"), native plants and trees, and crops; he spoke of valuable metals, "Treasures in the Earth." So bountiful is this country that "each Day our Substance doth increase."

In the manner obligatory with this genre, Frame described the Indians and offered theories of their origin; he discounted the possibility that they were, as James Adair (q.v.) was later to propose, descendants of "the scattered Jews." As if to allay his readers' fears about these "Infidels," Frame briefly portrayed them as simple folk who live "without much Care" and concluded of them "so far so good."

The second half of the poem described improvements made by the settlers. Clearing the land of its "Trees so thick and strong" is treated as a heroic enterprise: "with Might and Strength...We laid them all along" and either "confounded" them to ashes or built houses of them. (Now, he noted, better houses are made of brick and stone.) Frame mentioned some of the towns of eastern Pa., calling Philadelphia "our choicest Habitation" and citing Germantown's linen and paper industry as an example of the commonwealth's ability to sustain trade. In closing, he stated for the fifth time in a poem of 190 lines that he was telling the truth and indicated that he might some day "tell [the reader] more of [his] Mind."

Frame's *Description* is far less detailed than Pa. promotional tracts by Penn, Gabriel Thomas (q.v.), and Thomas Budd (q.v.), but it conveys a stronger sense of colonization as an adventure. More successful as a promoter than as a poet, Frame has provided a readable description of late seventeenth-century Pa. as a land of opportunity.

Suggested Readings: T₁. *See also* M. Katherine Jackson, *Outlines of the Literary History of Colonial Pennsylvania* (1907; rep., 1966), p. 10; Albert Cook Myers, ed., *Narratives of Early Pennsylvania, West New Jersey, and Delaware, 1630-1707* (1912), pp. 297-305.

Mary De Jong
The Pennsylvania State University

BENJAMIN FRANKLIN (1706-1790)

Works: *The Pennsylvania Gazette* (1729-1766); *Poor Richard's Almanac* (1733-1758); *The General Magazine* (1741); *Autobiography* (1790, 1868). Paul Leicester Ford's *Franklin Bibliography* (1889) has been superseded by the voluminous and definitive information on individual items in *The Papers of Benjamin Franklin*, ed. Leonard W. Labaree, Whitfield J. Bell, Jr., et al. (1959-continuing).

Biography: "Beyond question he was one of the best known and most admired men in the world during the latter half of the eighteenth century." This statement by Theodore Hornberger is no exaggeration. Principally, Benjamin Franklin's fame was due to his researches in the new science of electricity, which he dramatized by means of his kite experiment, and to his espousal of the American cause of independence. But in a broader sense, his life and public career made him a commanding representative of the American Enlightenment that emanated from his Philadelphia print shop.

Franklin was born in Milk Street in Boston, Mass., on Jan. 17, 1706. His father, Josiah, had emigrated in 1683 from Banbury (Oxfordshire) in Eng., where he had worked as a silk dyer. In Boston he became a tallow chandler. Benjamin was the child of Josiah's second wife, Abiah Folger. In his autobiography (the main source for most of our knowledge about his early life), Franklin explained that he was the youngest son of the youngest son for five generations. Franklin's father was a Congregationalist, and since Benjamin was his tenth son, he had thought of dedicating him to the ministry as a tithe. But Franklin had a mind of his own, and since he liked books, his father apprenticed him (at age 12) to his brother James Franklin (q.v.) as a printer. So far as we know, Franklin had no formal schooling beyond the age of 10. When his brother was jailed in 1722 and prohibited from publishing the *New England Courant*—for criticism of the British government's failure to defend the American coast from pirates—Franklin became temporary publisher. This state of affairs eventually resulted in a quarrel with his brother and a broken apprenticeship. Consequently, at age 17 he ran away to Philadelphia to start a new life. The following year, he shipped to London, where he worked in Watts's and Palmer's printing shops. Returning to Philadelphia with type he had purchased in London, he succeeded in 1728 in setting up a partnership with Hugh Meredith, whose interest he bought out in 1730. On Sept. 1 of this year, he took to wife Deborah Read; their common-law marriage lasted until Dec. 19, 1774, the date of her death.

William Franklin was born out of wedlock sometime during the winter of 1730-1731; his mother has never been identified. By Deborah Read, Franklin had two other children—Francis Folger, who died at age 4 of smallpox, and Sarah, who married Richard Bache.

As a successful printer, Franklin had managed in 1729 to buy from Samuel Keimer (q.v.), and later to improve, *The Pennsylvania Gazette*. His annual *Poor Richard's Almanac* (1732-1757) contributed greatly to his wealth; it sometimes appeared in issues as large as 10,000 copies. Government printing—paper currency, and so on—facilitated not only his economic rise but also his entrance into politics, for he did public printing for several colonies: Pa., N.J., Del., and Md. Two of his ventures, however, failed: his German newspaper collapsed early in 1732, and his monthly, *The General Magazine*, lasted only six months in 1741. Nevertheless, Franklin was able to retire at age 42 and devote himself to scientific pursuits. For eighteen years after this retirement (1748-1766), he continued as a partner of David Hall. He also had partnerships and contracts with printers in N.Y., the Carolinas, and the W.Ind.

Franklin's scientific investigations brought him to the attention of the Royal Society, which conferred the Copley medal on him in 1753 and elected him a fellow in 1756 in recognition of his *Experiments and Observations on Electricity* (1753, 1754). Harvard, Yale, and William and Mary gave him honorary M.A. degrees; Oxford and St. Andrews, honorary doctorates. After 1759 he was usually addressed as "Dr. Franklin." He was elected to the Royal Society of Sciences at Göttingen (1766), the very exclusive Royal Academy of Sciences of Paris (1772), and numerous other European scientific societies.

In public life, Franklin had an enviable record as an initiator of projects for the public good: his Junto (started in 1727), as a self-improvement club; the Library Company (1731), where he said he studied languages and read an hour or two every day; a paid city police force; a volunteer Union Fire Company (1736); the American Philosophical Society (1743); the Pennsylvania Defense Association (1747); the Pennsylvania Hospital and the Pennsylvania Academy (both in 1751). In addition, Franklin helped raise funds for churches and joined the St. John's Masonic Lodge, supposedly the first of its kind in America.

In politics, of course, Franklin's rise was prolonged but always upward—from his career as clerk, regular member, and speaker of the Pa. Assembly (1736-1764) to his post as commissioner and minister to Fr. (1776-1785). In-between stations included his quartermaster job for the disastrous Braddock expedition that nearly spelled his financial ruin; his jobs as postmaster of Philadelphia (1737-1753) and later as one of two deputy postmasters general (1753-1774); his diplomatic missions as agent for the Pa. Assembly against the Penn family, who wanted tax-exempt status (1757-1762), and later for Ga. (1768), N.J. (1769), and Mass. (1770) in similar disputes. He was also the delegate to the Second Continental Congress in 1775 and the first postmaster general under the Articles of Confederation. On his return from Fr. after the war, he found himself one of the world's most honored men, and he was elected president of the Pa. Executive Council. In 1787 he served as delegate to the Constitutional Convention from his state and also as president of the Pennsylvania Society for the Abolition of Slavery.

As a man, Franklin has been described as "a revolutionist with a sense of humor." His eminent common sense, his good judgment, and his simplicity have endeared him to all Americans. He died in Philadelphia on April 17, 1790, and was buried at Christ's Church.

Critical Appraisal: Critics generally agree that the first part of Benjamin Franklin's *Memoirs* or autobiography is the best. In the form of a letter (dated Twyford, 1771) to his son William (royal governor of N.J. since 1763), it explains why he wrote the book: to acquaint his son with his English ancestors; to tell him parts of his father's life with which he was yet unacquainted; to acquaint future descendants of Franklin's family with the means of his success, for which he thanked "Divine Providence"; and finally (with characteristic objectivity and humor), to relive the past and to gratify his own vanity. Accordingly, he detailed the family background from the year 1555 to the time of his parents, giving short sketches of several persons. In general, this part then proceeds to deal with Franklin's growth from poor apprentice to master printer with his own shop, his trips to Boston and London, his marriage to Deborah Read, and the start of his public projects such as the Junto and the Library Company. The second part (dated Passy, 1784) considers mainly the causes for his success in later life—his bourgeois virtues of industry and frugality, religious principles, and "bold and arduous project" in which he attempted (but failed) to achieve moral perfection. Part three (at home, August 1788) continues with the application of this experiment ("The Art of Virtue") from an individual to a worldwide basis (by means of a projected Society for the Free and Easy). Mainly, however, this part provides a record of his public projects, including his role in the disastrous Braddock expedition. This part relates to the preceding one by the implied premise that the attainment of individual virtue is inseparable from projects designed for one's fellow man. Part four (presumably written during the winter of 1789-1790—by evidence of his shaky handwriting) provides continuity by treating one large project—the dispute with the proprietaries and its settlement through the mediations of Lord Mansfield.

Franklin's autobiography has a few factual inaccuracies and exaggerations. His editors stated that Franklin "frequently misremembered public and private details, and occasionally even distorted versions of important events." Others have pointed out, too, that the image of Franklin projected in the book does not always reflect the real man. Critics from Theodore Parker to Leslie Stephen to Charles Francis Adams to D. H. Lawrence have found fault with Franklin—for Babbittry, for considering honesty as mere policy rather than as sound moral principle, for a narrow sense of freedom and life. But the fact remains that the book is withal extremely readable. Its style—"*smooth, clear,* and *short,*" Franklin's own recipe for the good style—makes it an outstanding example of his best expository writing. Furthermore, the influence of this book has been tremendous, for as Clinton Rossiter said, it has been "translated and retranslated into a dozen languages, printed and reprinted in hundreds of editions, read and reread by millions of people, especially by young and impressionable Americans. The influence of these few hundred pages has been matched by no other American book."

Franklin's versatility as a writer extended far beyond his autobiography. In proverbs, satires, essays, letters, and philosophical writings (such as his playful but highly logical *Dissertation upon Liberty and Necessity*, a Deistic work of 1725), he exhibited amazing versatility. His Poor Richard sayings that appeared in the almanacs and were partially collected in *The Way to Wealth* (1758) incorporate the wisdom of the ages. Drawn as they were by Franklin from various sourcebooks of proverbs collected by earlier writers such as George Herbert, James Howell, Thomas Fuller, George Savile, Samuel Richardson, and others, they were then abbreviated or otherwise rewritten and improved for readability by Franklin for the audience of his own day. The ingenious revisions he made in these sayings—only rarely did he fail to improve them—helped greatly to promote the success of *Poor Richard's Almanac*. These sayings have influenced the minds and lives of his contemporary and later readers and played a powerful role in shaping popular culture in America.

In the realm of political satire, Franklin also excelled. Possibly more than any other American writer in the eighteenth century, he followed the influence of Jonathan Swift in satire. Two satires that are often singled out as among his best, *Rules by Which a Great Empire May Be Reduced to a Small One* (1773) and *An Edict of the King of Prussia* (1773), embody a summary justification of the American Revolution and present the list of grievances (violations of natural rights) und objections to British trade regulations that Thomas Paine (q.v.) later made use of in *Common Sense* and Thomas Jefferson (q.v.) transcribed in the Declaration of Independence. The *Rules* and the *Edict* were only two of numerous satires and other articles that Franklin fed into his propaganda mill—the London newspapers—during the period 1764-1775. Most of them were anonymous or written under a variety of pseudonyms, to give the effect of large numbers of sympathizers with the American cause. Perhaps the most Swiftian of all of his satire, although of later date (1777), is *The Sale of the Hessians*, a blistering, earthy attack on the British use of mercenaries. As late as 1790, Franklin satirized racial prejudice in *On the Slave Trade*, an ironical parody of an actual speech by one Mr. Jackson from Ga. that defended slavery.

The personal essay was one of the most popular genres of the time, and Franklin wrote three large series of them—the Dogood letters (Apr. 2 to Oct. 8, 1722), the Busy-Body papers (Feb. 4 to Mar. 27, 1729), and the Bagatelles (1776-1785). In the fourteen Dogood letters, Franklin, aged 16, pretended to be a young widow, Silence Dogood, who satirized in a somewhat didactic vein every two weeks in the *Courant* matters such as pride in clothing, pretentious learning at Harvard, sentimentality in literature, religious hypocrisy in governmental office, censorship of the press, alcoholism, gossip, and night strolling in Boston. These letters, written for fun, imitated the *Spectator* of Addison and Steele. In the third letter, Franklin invited correspondence from the female sex, saying he would look on such correspondence as favors and acknowledge them "accordingly." The Busy-Body papers, on the other hand, had a well-defined purpose; they attacked a rival printer, Samuel Keimer, who had heard of Franklin's plan to start a newspaper and had beat him to it. Eventually, because Franklin was a cleverer writer than Keimer, the latter went into bankruptcy and had to sell to Franklin what ultimately became the *Pennsylvania Gazette*. Of the eight Busy-Body papers, Franklin wrote only the first four, part of the fifth, and part of the eighth. Turning from these utilitarian essays with their air of the print shop about them, we come, finally, to Franklin's most charming and most belletristic essays—the Bagatelles. They were a series of letters written purely for the entertainment of his friends at Passy—Mme. Brillon, Mme. Helvétius, Abbé Morellet, Abbé de la Roche, and others. They were beautifully printed on a private press that Franklin had set up there for the printing of government dispatches, passports, and other official documents. Nearly twenty of them, the Bagatelles include little masterpieces such as *The Ephemera, The Whistle, The Elysian Fields*, and the *Dialogue Between Franklin and the Gout*. Some the them, like *The Handsome and the Deformed Leg*, are marred by Franklin's penchant for moralizing. *The Letter to the Royal Academy*, intended for his English friend Dr. Richard Price and the scientist Joseph Priestley, employs earthy humor. But most of the Bagatelles reveal Franklin's charm and skill in the niceties of style.

Franklin had always been popular with the ladies, and he carried on lengthy correspondences with some of them—his sister Jane Mecom, for example, with whom he exchanged letters during most of his life. With Catherine Ray (Mrs. William Greene), he corresponded for over thirty-five years. Polly Stevenson (later Mrs. William Hewson) was another of his special favorites, one whom he had known for nearly thirty years and to whom he frequently wrote. She attended him during the last four years of his life when she was in Philadelphia. Many of these letters rival the Bagatelles in their playful wit, charm, and gracious style.

Suggested Readings: BDAS; DAB; LHUS; T₁; T₂. *See also* A. O. Aldridge, *Benjamin Franklin; Philosopher and Man* (1965); idem, *Franklin and His French Contemporaries* (1957); Richard E. Amacher, *Benjamin Franklin* (1962); idem, *Franklin's Wit and Folly: The Bagatelles* (1953); Melvin H. Burnbaum, *Benjamin Franklin and the Zealous Presbyterians*, (1975); Paul W. Conner, *Poor Richard's Politics: Benjamin Franklin and His New American Order* (1965); Verner W. Crane, *Benjamin Franklin's Letters to the Press, 1758-1775* (1950); Bruce I. Granger, *Benjamin Franklin: An American Man of Letters* (1964); W. S. Hanna, *Benjamin Franklin and Pennsylvania Politics* (1964); Theodore Hornberger, *Encyclopedia Britannica* (1972), IX, 802-807; Claude-Anne Lopez, *Mon Cher Papa: Franklin and the Ladies of Paris* (1966); Benjamin W. Newcomb, *Franklin and Galloway: A Political Partnership* (1972); William Roelker, ed., *Benjamin Franklin and Catherine Ray Greene: Their Correspondence, 1755-1790* (1949); Carl Van Doren, *Benjamin Franklin* (1938); idem, ed., *Benjamin Franklin's Autobiographical Writings* (1945); idem, *The Letters of Benjamin Franklin and Jane Mecom* (1950).

Richard E. Amacher
Auburn University

JAMES FRANKLIN (1697-1735)

Works: *New England Courant* (1721-1726); *The Life and Death of Old Father Janus* (1726); *Rhode-Island Almanacs* (1728-1741); *Rhode-Island Gazette* (1732-1733).

Biography: James Franklin was born in Boston, Mass., on Feb. 4, 1696/7. After learning his trade in London, Franklin returned to Boston, where in 1717 he set up a printing shop of his own, taking his young brother Benjamin Franklin (q.v.) as apprentice a year later. In 1721 Franklin founded the *New-England Courant*, the third newspaper in Boston. From the first, it raised a campaign of protest against the attempt, by Cotton Mather (q.v.) and others, to introduce smallpox inoculation into Boston during an epidemic there. In addition, Franklin opened the pages of his journal to essays of satire and light humor, including the skillful pieces by his brother. James was first warned by the authorities, then imprisoned, and finally forbidden to conduct a newspaper without prior censorship, whereupon he circumvented the authorities by making his apprentice the new proprietor. But Benjamin took advantage of him and ran off to Philadelphia; the smallpox crisis subsided; and slowly the *Courant* died out.

In 1726 Franklin moved to Newport where he established the first printing business in R.I. He eventually gained all government printing work in that colony. He also turned out a series of "Poor Robin's" *Rhode-Island Almanacs*. James Franklin died in R.I. in Feb. 1735, leaving a wife, three daughters, and a young son, who was eventually apprenticed to his more prosperous uncle Benjamin.

Critical Appraisal: Benjamin Franklin remembered his brother as a stern master, who bullied and beat him. But as Perry Miller remarked, the pages of the *Courant* reveal another side of James Franklin: the shrewd and daring adversary of Puritan authoritarianism. As such, Franklin was an early and effective example of a recurring type in American literature—the imaginative journalist or editor who pits himself against the established powers and narrow tastes in his community. In addition, Franklin's journalism won a real victory for his views, for it brought an end to the experiments with inoculation.

James Franklin also managed to transplant to this continent a new kind of humorous writing. Trained in London around the time of Joseph Addison and Richard Steele, he imported to the colonies a clear grasp of what had made their *Spectator* papers effective and entertaining. He not only copied many of their features in his writings; he worked to create in New Eng. some of the same cultural and literary circumstances out of which the sketches and essays of writers like Joseph Addison and Richard Steele had developed. He gathered and encouraged a circle of wits, who contributed occasional amusements to his papers. (A file of 111 issues, probably kept by Benjamin Franklin, is now at the British Museum; it includes ascriptions to John Checkley (q.v.), William Douglass (q.v.), a Captain Taylor, Matthew Adams, John Eyre, Thomas Fleet, and George Stewart.) He accepted and printed anonymous observations on trivial customs and manners. He looked around at Puritan Boston with an amused sense of distance; and he even strained to attract additional female readers for his publications. Benjamin Franklin's *Dogood Papers*, published in the *Courant*, are very polished imitations of the *Spectator*, and they would not have existed without the framework his brother created for them. Together these two brothers baffled and vexed Cotton and Increase Mather (q.v.) at the same time that they entertained their fellows with an amused urbanity of a kind provincial New Eng. had never known.

Although it cannot be known for certain whether James's "Poor Robin" influenced "Poor Richard" as an almanac maker, there is a striking family resemblance in these productions. Unlike his predecessors and contemporaries, James printed his essential calendar information on a portion of the page and filled the blank spaces with verses and witticisms, including proverbs, both original and adapted.

James Franklin's second attempt at a newspaper, the *Rhode-Island Gazette,* is less literary than the *Courant* and is memorable chiefly as the first New Eng. paper published outside of Mass. After James's death in 1735, another bookish career developed within his household. Upon his demise, the Franklin press fell to his wife, Ann Franklin, who proved an extraordinarily capable entrepreneur. Eventually surviving both her husband and her son, she was more sensible and reliable than the latter, involving even her daughters in the practical work of setting type and running the business.

Suggested Readings: DAB; LHUS; T$_1$. *See also* Clarence S. Brigham, "James Franklin and the Beginnings of Printing in Rhode Island," PMHS, 65 (1936), 536-544; Worthington C. Ford, "Franklin's New England Courant," PMHS, 57 (1924), 336-353; Albert Furtwangler, "Franklin's Apprenticeship and the *Spectator,*" NEQ, 52 (1979), 377-396; Susan Henry, "Ann Franklin: Rhode Island's Woman Printer," *Newsletters to Newspapers: Eighteenth-Century Journalism,* ed. Donovan H. Bond (1977), pp. 129-143; Leonard W. Labaree, ed., *The Papers of Benjamin Franklin,* vol. I (1959); Perry Miller, *The New England Mind: From Colony to Province* (1953), pp. 324-344.

Albert Furtwangler
Mount Allison University

THEODORUS JACOBUS FRELINGHUYSEN (1691-c. 1748)

Works: *Drie Predicatien* (1721); *Een Trouwhertig Vertoog* (1729); *A Clear Demonstration of a Righteous and Ungodly Man* (1731); *Een bundelken Leer-Redenen* (1736); *A Summons to Repentance* (1738); *Versamelinge* (1747).

Biography: The influential Dutch Reformed minister Theodorus Frelinghuysen was born at Lingen, Ger., on Nov. 9, 1691, the third son of Johannes Frielinghausen, the Reformed pastor in the community, and Anna Bruggemann, a pastor's daughter. Educated first at Hamm and then at the University of Lingen, Frelinghuysen began his education in philosophy but while at Lingen switched to theology. After receiving a license to preach from the Classis of Emden in 1717, Frelinghuysen spent a brief, harrowing period as chaplain in the small, flood-devastated town of Logumer Voorwerk in East Friesland. Shortly after moving to Enkhzuien in the Neth., he accepted a call to the Dutch congregations in the colony of N.J. At the time, Frelinghuysen apparently thought that he had accepted a pastorate in Flanders, but he did not hesitate when he found that his true destination was the American wilderness.

In N.J. Frelinghuysen quickly established a reputation as a powerful, pietistically oriented, severe preacher. Under his guidance many new congregations were established, and the Dutch Reformed faith became a dominant force in the region. However, his methods, questions concerning his orthodoxy, and perhaps a measure of professional jealousy aroused intense animosity in some quarters. The long and bitter battle that ensued, led by the contentious N.Y. pastor Henrieus Boel, was highlighted by the publication of a *Klagte* of 146 pages against Frelinghuysen in 1725, and although Frelinghuysen successfully defended himself against these charges, the hostility continued for a decade. Meanwhile Frelinghuysen had married twelve-year-old Eva Terhune; the couple had five sons, each of whom entered the ministry, and two daughters, both of whom married ministers.

Working closely with William Tennent II (q.v.), Gilbert Tennent (q.v.), George Whitefield (q.v.), and other major figures in the movement, Frelinghuysen helped lay the foundation for the Great Awakening in America. Particularly close to the Tennents, he strongly supported their much-maligned "Log College" centers of religious instruction and was himself actively involved in training young men for the ministry. Late in his career, Frelinghuysen championed another controversial cause, the creation of an independently governed Dutch Reformed Church in America, and he challenged the authority of the Amsterdam Classis by participating in the 1741 ordination of John Henry Goetschius. Frelinghuysen died in Raritan, N.J., sometime around 1748.

Critical Appraisal: Frelinghuysen's influence grew predominantly from his preaching and pastoral activities. Although twenty-two of his sermons were published, only five were translated into English during his lifetime. All have since been translated, but no additional manuscript sermons have been recovered. Out of the small portion of his published work emerges a picture of a pietism quite foreign to the standard view of that part of the Christian tradition. Appreciating the importance of emotional commitment, Frelinghuysen valued the essential mystery of the process of Christian rebirth, but he did not extend this concept into the nonintellectualism or even antiintellectualism generally, and perhaps wrongly, associated with pietism. His sermons, particularly those that appeared early in his career, display a rigorous concern for theology soundly interpreted, for church discipline, and for a policy of exclusivity on the part of the "watchers on the walls of Zion." In addition, they reinforce the view, gathered from the observations of his contemporaries, that Frelinghuysen's concept of the pastoral role was firmly of the "I speak, you listen" school more characteristic, according to Perry Miller, of the seventeenth than the eighteenth century. Frelinghuysen's type was a strong-minded, even disputatious sort of Christianity. His first published work, the *Drie Predicatien*, concentrated upon the subject of proper theology, and his second, translated by his close friend Hendrick Visscher under the title *A Mirrour that flatereth not*, was in the nature of a polemic in answer to the aforementioned *Klagte* published against him four years earlier.

Frelinghuysen's later work, however, seems to reflect his growing sense of fellowship with Gilbert Tennent, William Tennent II, and others outside his own sect with whom he shared a common zeal in promoting the Great Awakening. These sermons, especially the two published in 1738 under the title *A Summons to Repentance*, are aimed, as the title suggests, directly at the unrepentant and are more concerned with inspiring in the listener a vivid sense of the magnitude of the crisis confronting him than with convincing him of the propriety of Frelinghuysen's particular variety of Christianity. This fact is not to suggest, however, that Frelinghuysen's earlier concerns were no longer important to him in later life; rather a combination of personal maturation (he was, after all, a very young man and hardly a seasoned pastor when he arrived in the colonies and was plunged into the doctrinal squabbles that resulted in the *Klagte*), an ebbing of the tide of hostility that had threatened to engulf him, and a growing understanding of the value of the contribution to be made by others gradually seems to have moved Frelinghuysen toward the denominationalist spirit that would characterize American Protestant Christianity of the nineteenth century. Both his life and his published work offer valuable insights into the evolution of that tradition.

Suggested Readings: CCMC; DAB; DARB; Sprague (IX, 8-15). *See also* E.T. Corwin, *A Manual of the Reformed Church in America...1628-1902* (1902); P.H.B. Frelinghuysen, *Theodorus Jacobus Frelinghuysen* (1938); T. J. Frelinghuysen, *Sermons...Translated from the Dutch and Prefaced by a Sketch of the Author's Life, by Rev. William Demarest* (1856); C. H. Maxson, *The Great Awakening in the Middle Colonies* (1920; rep., 1958); J. R. Tanis, *Dutch Calvinistic Pietism in the Middle Colonies, A Study in the Life and Theology of Theodorus Jacobus Frelinghuysen* (1967).

David Sloan
University of Arkansas at Fayetteville

DAVID FRENCH (1700-1742)

Works: Two verse translations of Ovid's elegies and four verse translations of Anacreon's odes (pub. in John Parke, *The Lyric Works of Horace*; 1786).

Biography: David French was born in New Castle, Del., in 1700, the son of Mary Sandelands and Robert French. Although his father's will stipulated that French study either medicine or theology at the University of Glasgow, he decided instead to study law. On Jul. 25, 1726, French was commissioned attorney general for the Lower Counties on the Del., and in 1728 he succeeded his cousin as "Clerk of the Peace and Prothonotary of the Court of Common Pleas" for the county of New Castle, a position he held until his death. In addition, French was elected a member and later speaker of the Assembly of the Lower Counties. In 1740 he served on a commission to settle the boundary dispute between Pa. and Md. French died unmarried in August of 1742. According to an obituary in *The Pennsylvania Gazette*, he was "a young Gentleman of uncommon Parts, Learning and Probity, join'd with the most consummate Good-Nature; and therefore universally beloved and regretted."

Critical Appraisal: That any of David French's work survives is due entirely to the care and scholarship of John Parke (q.v.), in whose translation of

Horace French's verse appears. French's six translations, said Parke, "had been consigned to oblivion through the obliterating medium of rats and moths, under the sequestered canopy of an antiquated trunk." Parke rescued the verses and subsequently included them in his *Lyric Works of Horace* (1786).

As one early commentator pointed out, several of French's translations date from 1718 and are therefore "amongst the earliest, as they are of the best colonial poetry we are likely to discover," and although earlier and better American poetry has since been discovered, French's verses still remain among the earliest attempts at Latin translations in the middle colonies. Praised for their "elegant and fluent" style and for their "learning and taste," French's translations, although at times metrically unbalanced, are usually appropriate: "Ye heroes now a long farewell! / A softer theme best suits my shell, / Love's passion it will only tell." At best, they combine the classic simplicity of Latin verse with a finely tuned ear for English cadences: "This truth I know, infallibly, / 'Tis time to live, if death be nigh." Thus although the verses by French that have survived are limited in scope and number, they make his early death seem regrettable.

Suggested Readings: Evert Duyckinck and George Duyckinck, *Cyclopaedia of American Literature* (1855), p. 116; Gregory B. Keen, "Descendants of Joran Kyn, The Founder of Upland," PMHB, 3 (1887), 218-223.

Timothy K. Conley
Bradley University

PHILIP FRENEAU (1752-1832)

Works: *The American Village* (1771); *A Poem on the Rising Glory of America* (with Hugh Henry Brackenridge; 1771); *American Liberty* (1775); *General Gage's Confession* (1775); *The Last Words, Dying Speech, and Confession of J—s R—s—n* (1775); *A Voyage to Boston* (1775); *The Travels of the Imagination* (1778); *Description of the Sufferings of Those on Board the Jersey* (c. 1780); *The British Prison Ship* (1781); *New Year's Verses* (1783-1786); *The Poems of Philip Freneau* (1786); *A Journey from Philadelphia to New York* (1787); *The Miscellaneous Works of Mr. Philip Freneau* (1788); *The Village Merchant* (1794); *The Monmouth Almanac* (1795); *Poems Written Between the Years 1768 & 1794* (1795); *Megara and Altova* (1797); *Letters on Various Interesting and Important Subjects* (1799); *Poems Written and Published During the American Revolutionary War* (1809); *A Collection of Poems on American Affairs* (1815); Lewis Leary, ed., *The Last Poems of Philip Freneau* (1945); Michael Davitt Bell, ed., *Father Bombo's Pilgrimage to Mecca, 1770* (with Hugh Henry Brackenridge; 1975); Judith R. Hiltner, ed., *The Final Poems of Philip Freneau* (1979).

Biography: Born in New York City on Jan. 2, 1752, Philip Freneau was moved as a boy to Monmouth County, N.J., where he prepared for Princeton, graduating there in 1771. He taught school briefly on Long Island, preparing meanwhile in a desultory fashion for the ministry. In 1775 Freneau was in N.Y.

writing verse diatribes against the British invaders of New Eng. Then, war approaching, he spent two years in the W.Ind., perhaps as a clerk on a sugar plantation, perhaps engaged in privateering. In 1788 he returned, joined the N.J. militia, almost certainly engaged in patriotic privateering, was captured at sea by the British, and spent some months in a prison ship in N.Y. harbor. On release, Freneau went to Philadelphia, where he spent the rest of the war years, perhaps as editor, certainly as a principal contributor in verse and prose to the patriotic *Freeman's Journal*. The war over, he went again to sea as master of coastal vessels plying between N.Y. and Charleston, writing meanwhile light verses that were dropped off for newspaper publication when he reached either port.

In 1790 Freneau left the sea, married, and became briefly the editor of the *Daily Advertiser* in N.Y. When the national government moved to Philadelphia, he moved with it, becoming a clerk in the Post Office Department, then in the office of the secretary of State, meanwhile editing from 1791 to 1793 the outspokenly Jeffersonian *National Gazette*. Tiring of partisan politics, he then retired to his Monmouth County homestead, where he edited the *Jersey Chronicle* from 1795 to 1796. In 1797 Freneau came to N.Y. to edit the *Time-Piece and Literary Companion*, which he hoped could be nonpartisan. But it was not, so he retired again, although not completely, for he wrote actively in support of the presidential candidacy of Thomas Jefferson (q.v.). But much of his time until 1804 was spent again at sea as master of merchant vessels. He then returned to Monmouth County, living quietly there, contributing occasional verse to periodicals, and seeing to the publication of two more volumes of his collected writings. Freneau died on Dec. 18, 1832, almost forgotten by most of his later literary contemporaries.

Critical Appraisal: Philip Freneau's reputation has suffered because even during his lifetime he was often celebrated exclusively as "the Poet of the American Revolution." But he was greatly more than that. He was a recorder in verse and prose of many homely aspects of American life: the country inn, the virtue of tobacco, eccentric Dutch husbandmen, the strange blue laws of New Eng., and curious Indian customs. Even more, he was a poet who, although he sometimes reached for more than he could grasp, produced a few brief lyrics that in almost any other country or situation would have certified him as superior. He wrote perhaps too much, and he wrote it too fast and sometimes perhaps for the wrong reasons, but a solid residue remains in which he did capture in words the fragile substance of his poetic vision.

Caught between the beckoning of his fancy and the fervor of his patriotic fire, Freneau produced a few poems that invite continuing critical attention. What is needed is a sensitively selected new edition of his better writings—many of them early, like "The Power of Fancy," "The House of Night" (as he first wrote, before it became soiled through revision), "The Vanity of Existence," "The Dying Indian," and a handful more, including, of course, his most often anthologized "The Wild Honeysuckle"—and added to them some of the inconsequential gems of his later years—like "The Brook in the Valley" and "To a Caty-Did." Freneau always did need an editor in his prose writings also, much of which is undistinguished, and the whole of which has never been satisfactorily studied or collected, but which also contains segments that identify him as a man of wit and discrimination. But Freneau founded no school. He had no literary descendants. Poets who came after him looked to other models, most often from abroad, so that it can be doubted whether the direction of literature in the U.S. would have been in any important respect different without him. But he was there, isolated by politics and his own limitations, not even really a transitional poet, only a person with a vision that the distractions of his time, and his own personal shortcomings also, sometimes distorted. "To write," he said, "was my sad destiny, The worst of trades, we all agree." Writing was a trade in the early U.S. It was required to be useful, and Freneau was a useful writer. As the voice of his time, he shares the fate of time, except that in a few poems, he confronted mysteries and spoke of them in words that outlive him. It need not be embarrassing to remember Freneau as among America's first respectworthy poets.

Suggested Readings: DAB; LHUS; P; T_1; T_2. *See also* Nelson F. Adkins, *Philip Freneau and the Cosmic Enigma* (1949); Jacob Axelrad, *Philip Freneau: Champion of Democracy* (1967); Mary Weatherspoon Bowden, *Philip Freneau* (1976); Lewis Leary, "Philip Freneau: A Reassessment" in *Soundings: Some Early American Writers* (1975) pp. 131-160; idem, *That Rascal Freneau: A Study in Literary Failure* (1941); Richard C. Vitzthum, *Land and Sea: The Lyric Poetry of Philip Freneau* (1978).

Lewis Leary
University of North Carolina at Chapel Hill

EBENEZER FROTHINGHAM (c. 1717-1798)

Works: *The Articles of Faith and Practice* (1750); *A Key to Unlock the Door* (1767); *A Letter Treating upon the Subject and Mode of Baptism* (c. 1768).

Biography: Ebenezer Frothingham was baptized on Jun. 9, 1717, at Charlestown, Mass., where the Frothingham family had lived since 1630. His father, Samuel Frothingham, a housewright, was captain of the Charlestown Military Company and a deacon of the First Congregational Church; his mother was Hannah (Hunting) Frothingham. The record of Frothingham's admission to the First Congregational Church of Charlestown as a full communing member on Jun. 6, 1734, demonstrates that he was reared in Charlestown. It is not known when Frothingham left Mass., but evidence suggests that he became a Separate while living at Wethersfield, Conn., sometime around 1741. When a Separate Church was organized at Wethersfield on Jan. 7, 1747, Frothingham was ordained as its first pastor. Like most Separate ministers, Frothingham lacked a college degree.

Because they threatened the Congregational framework of New Eng. society, the Separates at Wethersfield were severely persecuted, and Frothingham, as their minister, was no exception. For preaching without the permission of the parish minister of Wethersfield, he was imprisoned at Hartford three times, once for almost five months; he was also imprisoned twice for refusing to pay taxes to support the establishment of religion. To escape persecution, some of the Wethersfield Separates moved to N.Y.; others settled at Middletown, Conn. When the Separate Church of Wethersfield was moved to Middletown in 1754, Frothingham was reinstalled as pastor there. That same year he was chosen to carry a petition for religious liberty to King George II in Eng., but he cancelled the trip after the death of his fellow commissioner Solomon Paine (q.v.). Frothingham continued to serve as pastor at Middletown until 1788, when he was dismissed, probably because of age. He had two sons, Ebenezer and Samuel; the names of his wife and daughters are unknown. Frothingham died at Middletown on Nov. 30, 1798.

Critical Appraisal: Ebenezer Frothingham is most important as an apologist for the Separates. The Strict Congregationalists, whose movement grew out of the revivals of the Great Awakening, came to be called Separates or Separatists from their insistence on separation from the government establishment of Congregationalism in New Eng. Whereas the Regular or Standing Congregational churches were supported by government revenues, the Separates believed that churches should rely entirely on voluntary contributions. At the beginning of his *Articles*, Frothingham provided the earliest known text of a significant summary of Separate principles, which he presented in fifteen Articles of Faith and eighteen Articles of Practice. Significantly, Frothingham devoted a great deal of space to a vindication of Article of Faith 15, in which membership in the true Church of Jesus Christ is restricted to real believers, and it is affirmed that "whoever presumes either to administer or to partake of the ordinance of Baptism, or the Lord's Supper, without saving Grace, are in Danger of sealing their own Damnation." In line with Article 15, Frothingham opposed Half-Way Covenant measures concerning baptism; he also opposed the Stoddardean view of the Lord's Supper as a "converting ordinance." In a scathing criticism of false teachers, he wrote that they

> may be known by their preaching always round about Religion, and never can get into the Heart and Life of Religion.... And behold he comes almost up to the Point, and off he turns, and is like the miscarrying Womb, for there is no living child there; and the poor Sheep and Lambs are worried almost to Death, and do not know that they are a trying to get Milk out of dry Breasts.

There is a strong element of premillenarianism in the *Articles*, and Alan Heimert held that Frothingham resorted to this sort of thinking in the absence of any program to bring about the redemption of society for which he longed.

In his short *Letter upon Baptism* (written in 1760), Frothingham argued that its administration both to believers in Christ and also to their seed is in conformity with God's will, although not enjoined in the bare letter of God's word. Frothingham acknowledged that he himself once so strongly doubted the validity of his own baptism in infancy that he would have had himself rebaptized if he had encountered a Baptist elder, but he changed his mind, after considering I Peter 3:21. Isaac Backus (q.v.), who had gone from the Strict Congregationalists to the Baptists, responded to Frothingham's *Letter* in an appendix to the 2nd edition of his *Short Description* (1770). Frothingham's "Reply to Elder Backus's Answer" (1772) is unpublished; the manuscript is owned by the American Baptist Historical Society, Rochester, N.Y.

Called "a classic of American popular thought and a neglected milestone in American intellectual history" and "a key document within the American pietistic tradition," Frothingham's *Key to Unlock the Door* called for the disestablishment of the Standing Congregational churches of Conn. in the interest of liberty of conscience. In this work, Frothingham criticized the absurdity of a law that permits all townspeople of a specified economic status, whether or not they are church members, to vote at town meetings on the calling of ministers. He argued that the religion commanded by God "wants no civil power under heaven to support it; but false religion, or that which men's wisdom has planned, cannot well subsist without civil power, to be its prop." He also urged Separates to persist in their refusal to pay taxes for the support of ministers, and he scolded those who had weakened and paid their taxes. Noting that the state establishment of religion promotes worldliness in ministers instead of encouraging them to concentrate on pastoral oversight, Frothingham wrote, "may a merciful God pity such carnal ministers that put on a sabbath day countenance in the pulpit, as tho' they would teach fools the way to heaven, when in the week time, their carnal conversation and practice tends to lead poor souls down to hell!"

M. Louise Greene called Frothingham's *Key* "another powerful and closely argued tract. . . probably the strongest work put forth from the dissenter's standpoint," and she noted that "within three years it was followed by a legislative act granting a measure of toleration" in Conn. But full disestablishment of the Congregational churches of New Eng. did not come about until much later (1807 in Vt.; 1818 in Conn.; 1819 in N. H.; and 1833 in Mass.), after others besides the Separates had taken up this cause. The failure of the Separates to survive as a denomination—many Separates returned to the ranks of the Regular Congregationalists or became Baptists—may account for why Frothingham is not better remembered as their major apologist. Despite the fact that he sometimes lapsed into grammatical errors, Frothingham wrote in a vigorous style that holds our interest. C. C. Goen held that an appreciation that Ezra Stiles (q.v.) originally wrote about three other Separate writers can also be applied to Frothingham: "He has written some things very sensibly; This. . . might be shewn as a specimen of the Abilities of the Illiterate Men of New England even in Writing as well as in the Things of Religion. These productions would be considerable even for University Men."

Suggested Readings: CCNE. *See also* Isaac Backus, *A History of New England* (1871), II, 78-80; "Record Book of the First Church of Charlestown," NEHGR, 31 (1877), 215; 33 (1879), 205; S. Leroy Blake, *The Separates* (1902), pp. 122-123, 179-181;

Emerson Davis, *Biographical Sketches of the Congregational Pastors of New England*, typescript, from a nineteenth-century ms., deposited in the Congregational Library, Boston, III, 291-292; Edwin Scott Gaustad, *The Great Awakening in New England* (1957), p. 116; C. C. Goen, *Revivalism and Separatism in New England, 1740-1800* (1962), pp. 126-136, 152-156; M. Louise Greene, *The Development of Religious Liberty in Connecticut* (1905), pp. 283-297; Alan Heimert, *Religion and the American Mind* (1966), pp. 6-7, 128-129, 558; Alan Heimert and Perry Miller, eds., *The Great Awakening* (1967), pp. 441-464; William G. McLoughlin, *New England Dissent, 1630-1833*, 2 vols. (1971), I, 399-416; William J. Scheick, ed., *Critical Essays on Jonathan Edwards* (1980), pp. 67-69; Anson Phelps Stokes, *Church and State in the United States* (1950), I, 219-220; Thomas Bellows Wyman, *The Frothingham Genealogy* (1916), pp. 32, 33, 58, 136, 159.

Richard Frothingham
University of Arkansas at Little Rock